Lecture Notes in Computer Science 14200

The series Lecture Notes in Computer Science (LNCS), including its subseries Lecture Notes in Artificial Intelligence (LNAI) and Lecture Notes in Bioinformatics (LNBI), has established itself as a medium for the publication of new developments in computer science and information technology research, teaching, and education.

LNCS enjoys close cooperation with the computer science R & D community, the series counts many renowned academics among its volume editors and paper authors, and collaborates with prestigious societies. Its mission is to serve this international community by providing an invaluable service, mainly focused on the publication of conference and workshop proceedings and postproceedings. LNCS commenced publication in 1973.

Olga Viberg · Ioana Jivet ·
Pedro J. Muñoz-Merino · Maria Perifanou ·
Tina Papathoma
Editors

Responsive and Sustainable Educational Futures

18th European Conference
on Technology Enhanced Learning, EC-TEL 2023
Aveiro, Portugal, September 4–8, 2023
Proceedings

Springer

Editors
Olga Viberg
KTH Royal Institute of Technology
Stockholm, Sweden

Ioana Jivet
Goethe University Frankfurt
Frankfurt am Main, Germany

Pedro J. Muñoz-Merino
Universidad Carlos III de Madrid
Madrid, Spain

Maria Perifanou
University of Macedonia
Thessaloniki, Greece

Tina Papathoma
CODE University of Applied Sciences
Berlin, Germany

ISSN 0302-9743 ISSN 1611-3349 (electronic)
Lecture Notes in Computer Science
ISBN 978-3-031-42681-0 ISBN 978-3-031-42682-7 (eBook)
https://doi.org/10.1007/978-3-031-42682-7

This Springer imprint is published by the registered company Springer Nature Switzerland AG
The registered company address is: Gewerbestrasse 11, 6330 Cham, Switzerland

Paper in this product is recyclable.

Preface

Welcome to the proceedings of the *18th European Conference on Technology Enhanced Learning* (ECTEL 2023) – the largest event of the European Association of Technology Enhanced Learning (EATEL). This year, the University of Aveiro in Portugal hosted ECTEL 2023 from September 4–8, 2023.

The theme of this year's conference was *Responsive and Sustainable Educational Futures,* building upon the theme of the previous year's conference. The theme focused on sustainable teaching and learning practices in the post-pandemic educational ecosystem. During the COVID-19 pandemic educational institutions were compelled to adopt various educational technologies to continue serving their students. For many of these institutions, it was a new practice, and they had to quickly adapt by implementing different strategies, tools, services and digital platforms to provide learning opportunities for a wide range of students.

As we are adjusting to the "new normal", educational institutions can take one of three trajectories in responding to the needs of learners and teachers in the post-pandemic world: returning to the pre-pandemic status quo, focusing on short-term remediation of learning loss, or making an organized effort to reinvent education to be more *human-centered*, *responsive* to current needs of both teachers and students in a rapidly changing world, and *responsible* in providing education to all while protecting students' privacy when using tracking technologies. We dedicated this year's conference to exploring the third proposition and thus called for contributions that enhanced our understanding of how such an organized effort can be designed and implemented sustainably to improve teaching and learning.

For ECTEL 2023, we received 126 research papers. All submissions went through a double-blind review process, with at least three members of the TEL community reviewing each paper. The review process was followed by discussions and a meta-review provided by a senior member of the program committee. As a result, 34 papers were accepted for presentation at the conference, resulting in a 27% acceptance rate. Additionally, 24 posters and 16 demonstration papers were presented at the conference to encourage discussions among the attending TEL researchers and practitioners. All the research, poster and demo papers are included in this volume. Furthermore, the conference featured ten workshops and a doctoral consortium as pre-conference activities held on September 4–5, 2023.

Finally, we would like to express our gratitude to all colleagues involved in organizing, writing and reviewing the contributions to this year's conference. Special thanks go to all the members of the Program Committee who performed reviews on submitted contributions, engaged in discussions and facilitated decision-making on their acceptance. We would particularly like to thank the keynote speakers, Paul Prinsloo and António Dias de Figueiredo, and the expert panelists, Rebecca Ferguson and Marco Kalz, as well as the moderator of the panel discussion, Marcus Specht, for their valuable contributions to the conference program. Additionally, we extend a big thank you to the workshop chairs,

Kairit Tammets and Tomohiro Nagashima, the poster/demo chairs, the communication chairs, Mikhail Fominykh, Guanliang Chen and Manuel Caeiro Rodríguez, the doctoral consortium chairs, Daniele Di Mitri, Oleksandra Poquet and Alejandro Ortega-Arranz, and the steering committee representatives, Marcus Specht and Tobias Ley, for their efforts, ideas and time dedicated to assembling the conference program. We would like to acknowledge the outstanding and continuous work of Luis Pedro and Carlos Santos, the local chairs, without whom ECTEL 2023 would not have been possible. Thank you!

We dedicate these conference proceedings to the extraordinary legacy of Ralf Klamma, whose unwavering commitment to scientific advancement and profound impact on the EATEL community will forever be remembered and celebrated.

July 2023

Olga Viberg
Ioana Jivet
Pedro J. Muñoz-Merino
Maria Perifanou
Tina Papathoma

Organization

General Chair

Pedro J. Muñoz-Merino	Universidad Carlos III de Madrid, Spain

Program Committee Chairs

Olga Viberg	KTH Royal Institute of Technology, Sweden
Ioana Jivet	Goethe University Frankfurt & DIPF, Germany

Poster/Demo Chairs

Maria Perifanou	University of Macedonia & Aristotle University of Thessaloniki, Greece
Tina Papathoma	CODE University of Applied Sciences, Germany

Workshop Chairs

Kairit Tammets	Tallinn University, Estonia
Tomohiro Nagashima	Saarland University, Germany

Doctoral Consortium Chairs

Daniele Di Mitri	DIPF, Germany
Oleksandra Poquet	Technical University of Munich, Germany
Alejandro Ortega-Arranz	Universidad de Valladolid, Spain

Communication Chairs

Mikhail Fominykh	Norwegian University of Science and Technology, Norway
Guanliang Chen	Monash University, Australia
Manuel Caeiro Rodríguez	University of Vigo, Spain

Local Organization Chairs

Luis Pedro	University of Aveiro, Portugal
Carlos Santos	University of Aveiro, Portugal

Steering Committee Representatives

Marcus Specht	Delft University of Technology, The Netherlands
Tobias Ley	University for Continuing Education Krems, Austria

Senior Program Committee

Vincent Aleven	Carnegie Mellon University, USA
Manuel Caeiro Rodríguez	University of Vigo, Spain
Manuel Castro	UNED, Spain
Mohamed Amine Chatti	University of Duisburg-Essen, Germany
Mutlu Cukurova	University College London, UK
Tinne De Laet	Katholieke Universiteit Leuven, Belgium
Carrie Demmans Epp	University of Alberta, Canada
Yannis Dimitriadis	University of Valladolid, Spain
Monica Divitini	Norwegian University of Science and Technology, Norway
Hendrik Drachsler	DIPF|Leibniz Institute for Research and Information in Education & Goethe University Frankfurt, Germany
Anastasios Economides	University of Macedonia, Greece
Rafael Ferreira Mello	Cesar School, Brazil
Dragan Gasevic	Monash University, Australia
Michail Giannakos	Norwegian University of Science and Technology, Norway
Wolfgang Greller	Vienna University of Education, Austria
Åke Grönlund	Örebro University, Sweden
Ángel Hernández-García	Universidad Politécnica de Madrid, Spain
Davinia Hernandez-Leo	Universitat Pompeu Fabra, Spain
Isabel Hilliger	Pontificia Universidad Católica de Chile, Chile
Jelena Jovanovic	University of Belgrade, Serbia
David Joyner	Georgia Institute of Technology, USA
Marco Kalz	Heidelberg University of Education, Germany
Roland Klemke	Open University, The Netherlands

Vitomir Kovanovic	University of South Australia, Australia
Tobias Ley	University for Continuing Education Krems, Austria
Alejandra Martínez-Monés	Universidad de Valladolid, Spain
Agathe Merceron	Berliner Hochschule für Technik, Germany
Alexander Mikroyannidis	Open University, UK
Tanja Mitrovic	University of Canterbury, New Zealand
Abelardo Pardo	University of South Australia, Australia
Luis Pedro	University of Aveiro, Portugal
Oleksandra Poquet	Technical University of Munich, Germany
Luis P. Prieto	Universidad de Valladolid, Spain
Marc Rittberger	DIPF|Leibniz Institute for Research and Information in Education, Germany
José A. Ruipérez Valiente	University of Murcia, Spain
Nikol Rummel	Ruhr-Universität Bochum, Germany
Demetrios Sampson	Curtin University, Australia
Carlos Santos	University of Aveiro, Portugal
Olga C. Santos	UNED, Spain
Patricia Santos	Universitat Pompeu Fabra, Spain
Sergey Sosnovsky	Utrecht University, The Netherlands
Slavi Stoyanov	Open University, The Netherlands
Barbara Wasson	University of Bergen, Norway
Jacqueline Wong	Utrecht University, The Netherlands

Program Committee

Marie-Hélène Abel	Heudiasyc, Université de Technologie de Compiègne, France
Andrea Adamoli	Swiss Federal Institute of Technology (ETH), Switzerland
Ademar Aguiar	University of Porto, Portugal
Atezaz Ahmad	DIPF|Leibniz Institute for Research and Information in Education, Germany
Kamil Akhuseyinoglu	University of Pittsburgh, USA
Mohammad Al-Smadi	Jordan University of Science and Technology, Jordan
Carlos Alario-Hoyos	Universidad Carlos III de Madrid, Spain
Laia Albó	Universitat Pompeu Fabra, Spain
Sarah Alcock	Open University, UK
Giora Alexandron	Weizmann Institute of Science, Israel
Ainhoa Alvarez	University of the Basque Country, UPV/EHU, Spain

Nardie Fanchamps	Open University, The Netherlands
Alejandro Fernández	Universidad Nacional de La Plata, Argentina
Carmen Fernández-Panadero	Universidad Carlos III de Madrid, Spain
Angela Fessl	Know-Center, Austria
Olga Firssova	Open University, The Netherlands
Mikhail Fominykh	Norwegian University of Science and Technology, Norway
Rolf Fricke	Condat AG, Germany
Francisco José García Peñalvo	University of Salamanca, Spain
Sébastien George	Le Mans Université, France
Sebastian Gombert	DIPF|Leibniz Institute for Research and Information in Education, Germany
Eduardo Gómez-Sánchez	Universidad de Valladolid, Spain
Samuel González-López	Technological University of Nogales, Sonora, Mexico
Monique Grandbastien	Université de Lorraine, France
Geraldine Gray	Technological University Dublin, Ireland
Julio Guerra	Universidad Austral de Chile, Chile
Nathalie Guin	LIRIS, Université Lyon 1, France
Joerg Haake	FernUniversität in Hagen, Germany
Carolin Hahnel	DIPF|Leibniz Institute for Research and Information in Education, Germany
Areum Han	University of Luxembourg, Luxembourg
Bastiaan Heeren	Open University, The Netherlands
Birte Heinemann	RWTH Aachen University, Germany
Maartje Henderikx	Open University, The Netherlands
Tore Hoel	Oslo Metropolitan University, Norway
Adrian Holzer	University of Neuchâtel, Switzerland
Andrea Horbach	FernUniversität Hagen, Germany
Stefan Hrastinski	KTH Royal Institute of Technology, Sweden
Francisco Iniesto	Open University, UK
Alessandro Iop	KTH Royal Institute of Technology, Sweden
Ioana Jivet	Goethe University Frankfurt & DIPF, Germany
Elis Kakoulli Constantinou	Cyprus University of Technology, Cyprus
Rogers Kaliisa	University of Oslo, Norway
Reet Kasepalu	Tallinn University, Estonia
Tanja Käser	EPFL, Switzerland
Md. Saifuddin Khalid	Technical University of Denmark, Denmark
Mohammad Khalil	University of Bergen, Norway
Styliani Kleanthous	CYENS CoE and Open University of Cyprus, Cyprus
Tomaž Klobučar	Jožef Stefan Institute, Slovenia

Vasileios Mezaris	Centre for Research and Technology Hellas, Greece
Christine Michel	Université de Poitiers, France
Konstantinos Michos	University of Zurich, Switzerland
Miguel Morales	Universidad Galileo, Guatemala
Pedro Manuel Moreno-Marcos	Universidad Carlos III de Madrid, Spain
Juan A. Muñoz-Cristóbal	Universidad de Valladolid, Spain
Jorge Munoz-Gama	Pontificia Universidad Católica de Chile, Chile
Pedro J. Muñoz-Merino	Universidad Carlos III de Madrid, Spain
Stylianos Mystakidis	University of Patras, Greece
Rob Nadolski	Open University, The Netherlands
Tanya Nazaretsky	Weizmann Institute of Science, Israel
Anna Nikolaou	Cyprus University of Technology, Cyprus
Stavros Nikou	University of Strathclyde, UK
Efi Nisiforou	University of Nicosia, Cyprus
Nicolae Nistor	Ludwig Maximilian University of Munich, Germany
Alexander Nussbaumer	Graz University of Technology, Austria
Alejandro Ortega-Arranz	Universidad de Valladolid, Spain
Nikos Palavitsinis	Eummena Foundation, Belgium
Viktoria Pammer-Schindler	Graz University of Technology, Austria
Zacharoula Papamitsiou	SINTEF, Norway
Tina Papathoma	CODE University of Applied Sciences, Germany
Sofia Papavlasopoulou	Norwegian University of Science and Technology, Norway
Antigoni Parmaxi	Cyprus University of Technology, Cyprus
Ronald Pérez-Álvarez	Universidad de Costa Rica, Costa Rica
Maria Perifanou	University of Macedonia and Aristotle University of Thessaloniki, Greece
Yvan Peter	Université de Lille, France
Nicolaescu Petru	Mercedes-Benz AG, Germany
Andriani Piki	University of Central Lancashire Cyprus, Cyprus
Niels Pinkwart	Humboldt-Universität zu Berlin, Germany
Gerti Pishtari	University for Continuing Education Krems, Austria
Beck Pitt	Open University, UK
Hans Põldoja	Tallinn University, Estonia
Elvira Popescu	University of Craiova, Romania
Francesca Pozzi	Istituto Tecnologie Didattiche - CNR, Italy
Sambit Praharaj	CAIS & Ruhr University Bochum, Germany
Eyal Rabin	Open University of Israel, Israel
Slavisa Radovic	FernUniversität in Hagen, Germany

Juliana Elisa Raffaghelli	University of Padua, Italy
Mladen Rakovic	Monash University, Australia
René Röpke	RWTH Aachen University, Germany
Mohsen Saadatmand	University of Helsinki, Finland
Merike Saar	Tallinn University, Estonia
John Saint	Regent's University London, UK
Teresa Sancho-Vinuesa	Universitat Oberta de Catalunya, Spain
Eileen Scanlon	Open University, UK
Daniel Schiffner	DIPF|Leibniz Institute for Research and Information in Education, Germany
Andreas Schmidt	Karlsruhe University of Applied Sciences, Germany
Marcel Schmitz	Zuyd Hogeschool, The Netherlands
Jan Schneider	DIPF|Leibniz Institute for Research and Information in Education, Germany
Ulrik Schroeder	RWTH Aachen University, Germany
Clara Schumacher	Humboldt Universität zu Berlin, Germany
Yann Secq	Université de Lille, France
Karim Sehaba	LIRIS, CNRS, France
Niels Seidel	FernUniversität in Hagen, Germany
Audrey Serna	LIRIS, INSA Lyon, France
Sergio Serrano-Iglesias	Universidad de Valladolid, Spain
Shashi Kant Shankar	Amrita Vishwa Vidyapeetham, India
Andrzej M. J. Skulimowski	AGH University of Science and Technology, Poland
Alan Smeaton	Dublin City University, Ireland
Maria Victoria Soule	Cyprus University of Technology, Cyprus
Sebastian Strauß	Ruhr University Bochum, Germany
Alexander Streicher	Fraunhofer IOSB, Germany
Bernardo Tabuenca	Universidad Politécnica de Madrid, Spain
Kairit Tammets	Tallinn University, Estonia
Stefano Tardini	Università della Svizzera italiana, Switzerland
Marco Temperini	Sapienza University of Rome, Italy
Alexander Tillmann	Goethe University Frankfurt, Germany
Paraskevi Topali	Universidad de Valladolid, Spain
Richard Tortorella	University of Turku, Finland
Yi-Shan Tsai	Monash University, Australia
Thrasyvoulos Tsiatsos	Aristotle University of Thessaloniki, Greece
Katerina Tzafilkou	University of Macedonia, Greece
Corrie Urlings	Open University, The Netherlands
Manuel Valle Torre	Delft University of Technology, The Netherlands

Vivian van der Werf	Leiden University & Delft University of Technology, The Netherlands
Gitte van Helden	Delft University of Technology, The Netherlands
J. Ángel Velázquez-Iturbide	Universidad Rey Juan Carlos, Spain
Olga Viberg	KTH Royal Institute of Technology, Sweden
Markel Vigo	University of Manchester, UK
Esteban Villalobos	Université Toulouse III Paul Sabatier, IRIT, France
Joshua Weidlich	DIPF|Leibniz Institute for Research and Information in Education, Germany
Fridolin Wild	Open University, UK
Sebastian Wollny	DIPF|Leibniz Institute for Research and Information in Education, Germany
Lixiang Yan	Monash University, Australia
Jane Yau	DIPF|Leibniz Institute for Research and Information in Education, Germany
Fabian Zehner	DIPF|Leibniz Institute for Research and Information in Education, Germany
Torsten Zesch	FernUniversität Hagen, Germany
Xiaoling Zhang	Delft University of Technology, The Netherlands

Contents

An Agile Concept Inventory Methodology to Detect Large Sets of Student Misconceptions in Programming Language Courses

Andrea Adamoli(✉)

Department of Computer Science, Swiss Federal Institute of Technology (ETH), Zürich, Switzerland
andrea.adamoli@inf.ethz.ch

Abstract. While learning new subjects, students often develop misconceptions that affect their results and even their academic success. Concept inventories (CIs) – collections of multiple-choice questions – are widely used instruments for spotting misconceptions and allowing instructors to correct them promptly. While the main advantage of CIs is responsiveness in analyzing answers, their measurement speed (the number of misconceptions that can be tested in a time frame) is poor. In this paper, we introduce an improved CI methodology that allows for accurate detections of broader sets of misconceptions in classes and, thus, to obtain detailed pictures of the student difficulties. Our methodology is based on observing the answers to the individual options of the multiple-choice questions, rather than to the question as a whole. We are therefore able to get more information from an item and thus improve the measurement speed. We integrated our methodology in a CS1 Java Programming Language course, and we tested 89 distinct misconceptions in 15 sessions of 30 min. Our methodology showed a 4x speed up in the measurement speed compared to state-of-the-art CIs, while preserving satisfactory accuracy. Thanks to this extensive coverage of misconceptions, we built a new metric, the "knowledge fitness", to objectively measure student difficulties.

Keywords: programming · programming languages · pedagogy · misconceptions · concept inventories · learning analytics · learning metrics

1 Introduction

Teaching is much more than providing knowledge of the subject content. To be effective, educators must understand student difficulties and find appropriate ways to help them, even individually [13]: identifying and objectively assessing in real time the misconceptions developed by students is therefore a key task of pedagogy [10]. Misconceptions are in fact comparable to latent knowledge bugs capable of threatening student learning and, potentially, their academic

O. Viberg et al. (Eds.): EC-TEL 2023, LNCS 14200, pp. 1–15, 2023.
https://doi.org/10.1007/978-3-031-42682-7_1

success [17]. The computer education community, and especially the area of programming languages (PLs), has produced a large body of research in this field. However, publications are primarily focusing on defining and classifying misconceptions and rarely provide exhaustive estimates of their severity and diffusion [2,3,12,19]. Moreover, despite the importance of this task, the application of the findings in the real world remains very limited [15], mainly due to the high costs in terms of time and resources.

Thanks to qualities such as scalability and responsiveness, the most practical methodologies to investigate misconceptions are based on concept inventories (CIs), that is, collections of validated multiple-choice questions. CIs are widely used in education and psychometrics to assess abilities and attitudes called *latent traits*. Considering that those traits cannot be directly measured, the underlying idea is that there is a direct relationship between the performance on a test item and the ability necessary to answer it correctly. In the area of STEM[1] disciplines, the best known CI is the Force Concept Inventory [9] by Hestenes, which addresses misconceptions related to Newton's laws. In computer science, CIs were introduced for example in digital logic [8], algorithms [4], data structures [11], and programming languages [2] courses. Although CIs provide good responsiveness (analysis of the results), their measurement speed (i.e., the number of traits we can accurately measure in a time frame) remains problematic: with sessions of 30 min per week, it would not be possible to test more than 15 misconceptions in one semester [1], and this is insufficient to have an exhaustive picture of student difficulties. A further critical point is the validation of the CIs. While there are many mathematical tools such as Item Response Theory (IRT) [6], only a few studies "have undergone rigorous validation" [18]. To be effective, a CI must be accurate in measuring the latent trait, which means that a CI should also provide an objective quantification of its accuracy.

In this paper, we introduce an efficient methodology to measure misconceptions in PL courses with concept inventories, which takes into account important qualities such as accuracy, speed, responsiveness, and comprehensiveness. Our methodology is based on the observation of the individual option selections, rather than looking at the multiple-choice question as a whole. This finer granularity in the observation allows us to investigate multiple misconceptions (traits) with a single question and, thus, improve the measurement speed. We further propose a 2-phase validation approach of the CI, which delivers a 4-factor quantification of its accuracy. In our study, we thus aim to answer the research question:

RQ: Is it possible to design Concept Inventories to measure programming language misconceptions while ensuring accuracy, speed, responsiveness, and comprehensiveness?

To answer this RQ, we rely on *progmiscon.org*, a recently published catalog of PL misconceptions presented by Chiodini et al. [3]. *progmiscon.org* exhaustively describes 198 misconceptions observed through various methodologies and, thus, provides valuable support for our study. In *progmiscon.org* each misconception

[1] Science, technology, engineering, and mathematics.

is identified with a compound name (or tag) written in camel case style: for example, *AddMemberAtRuntime*[2] identifies the misconception that occurs when a student (wrongly) thinks that the "set of class members can change at runtime". The name actually describes its underlying misunderstanding.

We integrated our methodology, which we called Agile Misconception Concept Inventory (AMiCI), into a CS1 Java programming course with about 50 students, and we tested 89 distinct misconceptions in 15 sessions of 30 min each. Thanks to this extensive coverage of misconceptions, we built a new metric, the "knowledge fitness", to objectively quantify class and individual understanding, and then help students via open discussions and focused activities.

The rest of this paper is organized as follows: Sect. 2 introduces the AMiCI methodology, presenting its process and discussing its differences with the state of the art; Sect. 3 explains our experiment to verify the measurement speed and accuracy of AMiCI; finally, Sect. 4 presents our conclusions and future work.

2 The (A)gile (Mi)sconception (C)oncept (I)nventory: AMiCI

2.1 Structure of Multiple-Choice Questions and Terminology

Institutions, communities, and researchers dealing with measurements in education provide a glossary of terms related to multiple-choice questions, while describing their structure. Designating an authority in this field is a challenging task, in our short survey we however found a certain consensus.

A *multiple-choice question* is composed of a *stem* that describes a problem (and, thus, "question" is often used also to designate the stem only) and of some plausible answers, called *options*. The options are distinguished between correct options, called *key (answers)* or *(correct) answers* and wrong options, called *distractors* or *distracters*.

The *(test) item*, often confused with the question, is the *unit of observation*, that is, the element in our instrument, the outcome of which allows us to measure the researched trait. In state-of-the-art CIs, there is no difference between items and questions, but this distinction is crucial in our methodology, where the observed units are the options (Sect. 2.3).

2.2 Motivation for an Improved Methodology

After thoroughly analyzing previous researches on multiple-choice questions, in [1] authors state that CIs should:

(S1) "focus on common student misconceptions",
(S2) "require at most 30 min to complete",
(S3) "include 3 to 5 items (i.e., questions) addressing each potential misconception".

[2] https://progmiscon.org/misconceptions/Java/AddMemberAtRuntime/.

We ran a pilot experiment, consisting of 6 quiz sessions and an average population of 23 students (29 distinct[3]), in a CS1 Java course for undergraduates at the Faculty of Informatics of the Università della Svizzera Italiana (Switzerland). In each session, we administered 2 questions of 5 options each, addressing the same misconception. Each of the 6 misconceptions was therefore tested only 2 times (2 items). In a very relaxed environment and considering also all contextual operations, students took on average 17.8 min to complete a session on paper. In particular, we noticed how questions involving the interpretation of code snippets took a long time. By allocating a single slot of 30 min per week, in a semester we could therefore barely investigate 15 misconceptions, that is, only the 7.6% of the *progmiscon.org* catalog. Even if we could manage to shorten the sessions by 5 min, it would not have made a significant impact on our capability to cover a substantial portion of the catalog.

Considering statement (S1), testing 15 misconceptions could be enough, but we actually disagree with it. How can we be sure that the set of the "common" misconceptions is the same in every course and in every year, considering that their origins are still undetermined? (and if not, why don't we just fix them?) If we already know that a misconception is "common" (how?), why should we deploy an instrument to measure it again?

In our view, an instrument should be independent of beliefs and preconceptions (i.e., observer bias) and, thus, it should cover as many misconceptions as possible, to deliver an objective picture of the understanding of the class. Statements (S2) and (S3) and the rejection of statement (S1) demonstrate a need to improve the efficiency of CIs and, in particular, improve their measurement speed, without compromising other qualities such as accuracy.

2.3 Improving Measurement Speed with a Unit Testing Approach

Our search for an improved methodology for CIs begins with the observation that much information is contained in distractors: a particular selection of (plausible) distractors could indicate the occurrence of a misconception, different from the one explicitly addressed by the multiple-choice question.

If we consider the whole question as an item of our CI, this information is unfortunately wasted. On the contrary, if we increase the granularity of the observation up to options, then we could take advantage of this side information, too. Thus, with one "question", we could cover multiple misconceptions and consequently increase the speed of our instrument.

In this new format, the stem would serve as a common reference for the assertions related to the options, each addressing distinct misconceptions. Students would have to read and understand the stem just one time, and then evaluate the correctness of the options (Fig. 1). However, we are aware that by using true-false items we are introducing a crucial threat to measurement accuracy: for example, random selections would average 50% of the total score.

[3] The participation was not mandatory, some students attended fewer sessions.

The proposed idea shows an important similarity to software unit testing. Unit tests aim to verify the functionality of small pieces of code (usually procedures or methods) through assertions that check if certain inputs match the desired outputs: if the assertion is not satisfied, the test ends with a failure, indicating a bug. Likewise, with the AMiCI multiple-choice questions, we aim to identify bugs in students' knowledge (i.e., misconceptions) through true-false items (options). Figure 1 makes this similarity explicit: selecting a distractor (red background) or not selecting a correct answer (green background) is interpreted as an indication of the addressed misconception (tag).

The elements of our multiple-choice questions remain the same, but their function is updated. The primary task of the *stem* is to define a common context for all the options. In the analogy with unit testing, it corresponds to the *setUp method*. The *options* are, instead, the *call to the unit* (i.e., misconception) we wish to test for the given inputs. The actual question (the *assertion* with the desired output) is inserted in a new element that we called *claim*: students, without misconceptions, should only select options that satisfy the claim.

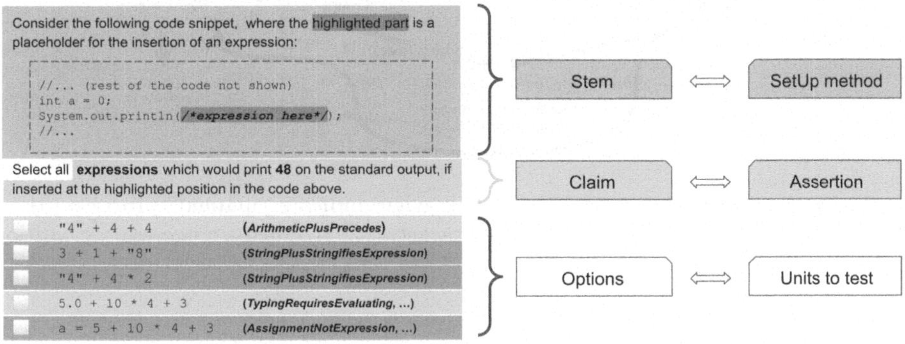

Fig. 1. Multiple-choice questions of AMiCI as unit tests: the options are the test items, addressing different misconceptions within the same question.

2.4 The AMiCI Process

Figure 2 introduces the AMiCI process, which implements an updated version of the five activities originally proposed by Richardson [16], divided into two phases: (1) **Development phase** (analyze misconceptions, investigate their "compatibility" and build a draft of the CI); (2) **Validation phase** (review questions, administer quizzes in validation mode, review the CI based on student feedback).

Development Phase. The process begins with the analysis of the *progmiscon.org* catalog. The goal is to identify misconceptions that could be inserted into the same question, based on their proximity in terms of course timing (*temporal proximity*) and topic similarity (*spatial proximity*). For example, a misconception regarding constructors in Java could be associated with a misconception regarding the initialization of fields, while it should not be associated

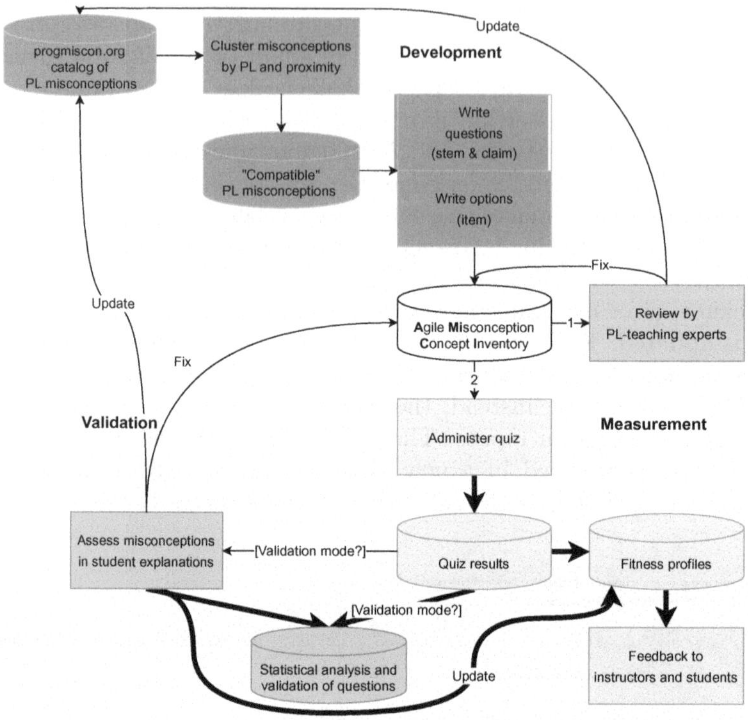

Fig. 2. Development process of AMiCI. Thin edges indicate "manual" processes, thick edges "automated" processes. The square brackets ([...]) indicate a necessary condition (?) to traverse the edge.

with a misconception regarding primitive types or recursion. To ensure a certain portability of the CI, it is necessary to rely on a general taxonomy. In our investigation, we mainly focused on Java and, therefore, we have evaluated several papers and textbooks presenting the topics for this language. We identified the commonalities, and we built a 5-levels taxonomy, which we used to cluster the misconceptions.

The second part of the development phase consists in writing the stem, the claim, and the options for the selected misconceptions. This task is crucial, finding a *concise* stem (in the form of code, text, or images) is not straightforward, as well as to distill the options to point out as few misconceptions as possible.

Validation Phase. With the initial draft of AMiCI, the first stage of the validation phase is enabled. Experienced PL instructors review questions and suggest improvements. This stage incorporates the collaborative idea originally presented by Porter [14]. The review is organized exactly like in conferences: the author submits the question, describing stem, claim, options and misconceptions, while the experts evaluate its qualities. Besides accuracy, the goal of this stage is to find a consensus among instructors coming from different contexts, and therefore also to ensure the *portability* of the CI.

The second stage of the validation phase involves the administration of a "beta version" of the questions (grouped in quiz sessions) to classes. At this stage, we *instrument*[4] the options with an additional text field for students to fill in. We, thus, distinguish between 2 administration modes: the *measurement mode* and the (instrumented) *validation mode*. In the measurement mode, students are only asked to select the options that satisfy the claim. In the validation mode, we add one more input field, where students have to clearly explain why they assess the claim for the option correct or wrong. This idea is inspired by our previous research [7], in which we showed how with active recall (i.e., a written summary of the assimilated knowledge) is possible to detect misconceptions of students: the explanation is, in fact, a sort of active recall triggered by the option and therefore focused on the addressed misconception.

The validation phase ends with the evaluation by PL experts of the student explanations to find out whether the misconceptions (addressed by the options) do occur or not. Given that it would be difficult to provide a simple binary assessment, we have decided to provide 5+1 rating degrees (Fig. 3): student "clearly has" the misconception (quantified as fitness[5] = 0%), "seems to have" (25%), shows "contradicting hints" (50%), "doesn't seem to have" (75%), "clearly has not" (100%). The additional degree ("No hints") leaves the expert the possibility of not deciding, as the student explanations do not always involve the addressed misconception.

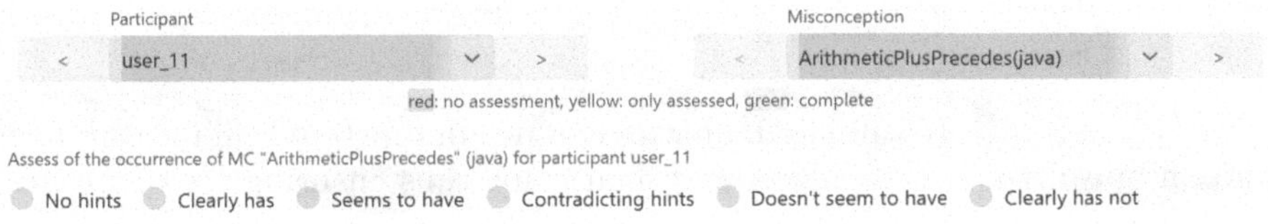

Fig. 3. Validation interface for PL experts assessing misconceptions in students.

The evaluations of the experts are then aggregated and statistically analyzed with the results provided by the multiple-choice questions. For each option and for each addressed misconception (a *validation case*), the validation is based on 4 factors:

(1) **Magnitude**. This parameter just indicates if the option is able to measure the occurrence of the addressed misconception in the class. To answer this question, we display the average of the measurement (red-to-green bar in Fig. 4) and the average of the experts' assessment (blue line). If the measured value lies within the 95%-confidence interval of the assessment (light-blue bar, t-student distribution), we can accept the option as a general indicator.

[4] Similarly to software instrumentation.

[5] Sect. 2.5.

(2) **Significance**. The number of participants (students) and expert consensus is important in determining the significance of the validation. Experiments suggest that, already with 40 participants, the confidence interval is appreciably narrowed. However, valid information is also obtained with samples of 20 students only.
(3) **Accuracy**. To determine the accuracy of the option, we correlate (Pearson) the measurement with the experts' assessment. According to Frost [5], "studies that assess relationships involving human behavior tend to have correlation coefficients weaker than +/- 0.6", we thus consider *acceptable* a correlation ≥ 0.6. To stress the importance of significance, we also indicate the lower and upper limits of the 95%-confidence interval for this parameter.
(4) **Precision**. The Spearman's correlation is a Pearson's correlation based on the rank of the measurements. This last parameter is therefore an indication of precision, understood as the ability to order the (knowledge) fitness of the participants.

Misconception	Validated Fitness vs. Detected by Options	Validated Fitness (# Participants)	Pearson's Correlation	Spearman's Correlation
ArithmeticPlusPrecedes (java)	A.O1	78.26 ± 17.34 (23/28)	0.71 < **0.87** < 0.94	0.56 < **0.81** < 0.93

Fig. 4. Successful validation of misconception *ArithmeticPlusPrecedes* for option 1 (O1) of the first quiz question (A) as depicted in Fig. 1: magnitude (column 2), significance (c. 3), and correlations with a 95%-confidence interval (c. 4-5).

Once collaboratively validated, quizzes can be administered (in measurement mode) and results can be analyzed automatically, thus ensuring *responsiveness*, *reliability*, and *scalability*. Collaboration between instructors is the key to lowering validation costs and producing an accurate instrument for the community.

2.5 A Metric for Misconceptions: The Knowledge Fitness

To quantify the measurement of misconceptions, we define a new metric: the *knowledge fitness*. This value is an indication of how healthy knowledge is, that is, "free of misconceptions". The metric can be applied to different entities (students, classes) and with different granularity (general fitness, single misconception fitness) (Figs. 5, 6 and 7).

Fitness can be computed on the basis of a single question/option or, more reliably, as the result of multiple quizzes. The fitness related to a single misconception is simply the average of the correctly selected options over the total number of options addressing that misconception. For example, if a student correctly selects 3 options over a total of 5 occurrences for a misconception, the related fitness is $3/5 = 60\%$.

However, it is not always possible to precisely address only one misconception with an option. As in medical science, one symptom (option) could be the effect of several distinct diseases (misconceptions). For example, if a student believes the (Java) expression `new String(''Hello'').substring(1)` to be incorrect, this could be due to misconceptions such as *ObjectsMustBeNamed*, *CannotChainMemberToConstructor*, or *RightToLeftChaining*[6]. For this reason, we have introduced an additional measure called *weighted fitness* (w-fitness), where the weight of a single option in the computation of the average is $\frac{1}{\#\ addressed\ misconceptions}$. In weighted fitness, therefore, "pure" options (indicators of a single misconception) have a greater weight. In the example described above, the weight of the option would be 1/3 for each of the misconceptions.

Finally, we also consider the *validated fitness* (v-fitness), that is, the fitness derived from the experts' assessment, which is the reference to compute the accuracy of the CI.

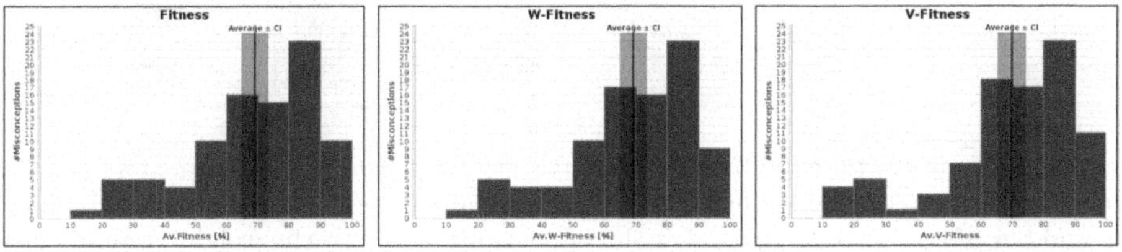

Fig. 5. Example of *general fitness*, *general weighted fitness*, and *general validated fitness* profiles of a class after 15 quiz sessions. The blue histograms show the number of misconceptions (y-axis) that have a certain fitness range (x-axis). The gray histogram represents the average and its confidence interval (width).

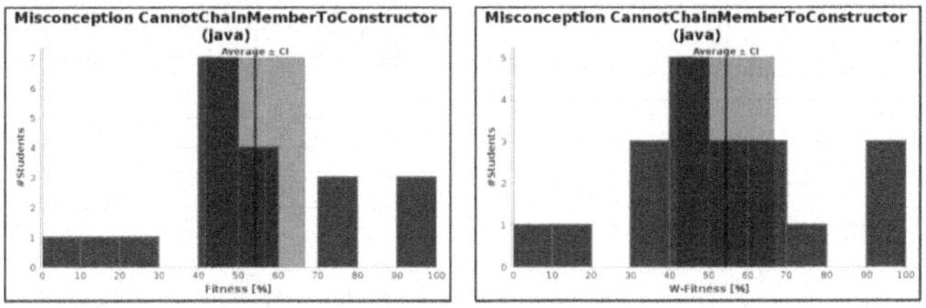

Fig. 6. Example of *misconception fitness* and *misconception weighted fitness* profiles of a class after a single quiz session. The blue histograms show the number of students (y-axis) that have a certain fitness range (x-axis) for misconception *CannotChainMemberToConstructor*. The gray histogram represents the average and its confidence interval (width).

---

[6] https://progmiscon.org/misconceptions/Java/ObjectsMustBeNamed/, https://progmiscon.org/misconceptions/Java/CannotChainMemberToConstructor/, https://progmiscon.org/misconceptions/Java/RightToLeftChaining/.

In our investigation, we set 3 *zones* to visually render the priority with which a misconception should be fixed. The range of these zones was established based on personal experience, but further studies should better motivate them (Fig. 7):

- **Red zone (0%-60%).** The misconception is diffused and should be possibly fixed as soon as possible.
- **Yellow zone (60%-75%).** The misconception is present, but not so crucial.
- **Green zone (75%-100%).** The misconception could be ignored.

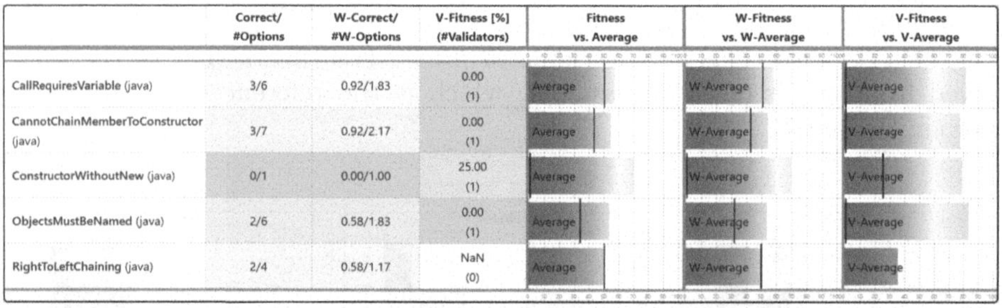

Fig. 7. Example of *student's fitness*, *student's weighted fitness*, and *student's validated fitness* profiles after a single quiz session. For each misconception (column 1), we report the number of correct selections over the opportunities (c. 2), the weighted number (c. 3), the expert assessment (c. 4), and the resulting fitness (c. 5-7, blue line: student's fitness, red-to-green bar: class average).

3 Experiment: Accuracy and Speed of AMiCI

The main goal of our experiment is verifying the efficiency of AMiCI, with a focus on accuracy and measurement speed. We thus administered the quizzes in *validation* mode.

3.1 Experimental Setup

We ran our experiment in a CS1 Java course for undergraduates, consisting of 6-lecturing hours per week. Lessons were held at the Faculty of Informatics of the Università della Svizzera italiana (Switzerland), in a successive instance of the course in which we ran the pilot experiment. We, thus, tried to preserve the same conditions to have the possibility to compare the results. The course was held in English. Although part of the teaching team, we have had no influence on its contents, nor on the evaluation of the students.

An almost weekly slot of about 30 min was allocated for the quiz sessions (S2), which were composed of 2 questions, each consisting of 5 options addressing 1 or more misconceptions. The number of correct answers was unknown to students and varied from question to question: students were informed that there might even be no correct options or only correct options.

The class consisted of around 50 students, who however were not required to participate in the quizzes. Before each session, students were clearly informed that the results of the quiz would not have affected the final grade of the course in any way, but "a significant[7] participation would have been accounted for the course participation grade" (equal to 20% of the final grade). We especially pointed out that there was no point in cheating. Students' natural language was mostly different from English (Italian, German, French, Slavic languages, Farsi, etc.).

The expert pool consisted of ourselves (as authors of the questions), and 3 PL professors coming from 3 different universities (Canada, Portugal, and Switzerland).

3.2 Results

Within the experiment, we had **15 quiz sessions** and 30 questions, covering **89 misconceptions**. The average population for each session was 29 students, while the whole experiment counted 45 distinct participants.

On average, it took students **25.5 ± 3.3 min** to complete a quiz session. Having tested a total of 89 misconceptions (**45%** of the **progmiscon.org catalog**), each quiz (consisting of 2 questions and 10 options) addressed on average 5.9 distinct misconceptions. The **rate of measurement** for a misconception is therefore $\frac{5.9}{25.5} = \mathbf{0.23}$ **[mcs/min]**. In our pilot experiment with state-of-the-art questions, we got instead $\frac{1}{17.8} = \mathbf{0.06}$ **[mcs/min]**. For each **unit of observation** (option), we tested **0.6 misconceptions**, while with the state-of-the-art CI we tested **0.5 misconceptions** (question).

We performed **5359 assessments of the explanations**, of which only **297** (5.5%) did not allow us to determine the occurrence of a misconception ("**No hints**").

We had a total of **185 validation cases** (option vs. misconception), of which 112 for options addressing 1 single misconception (i.e., weight = 1), 36 for options addressing 2 misconceptions[8] (weight = 0.5) and 37 for options addressing 3 or more misconceptions at the same time (weight < 0.5). We excluded, from these counts, 15 cases (too easy or too hard options) that had constant answers (or validations), for which the correlation is indeterminable. The **average accuracy** (i.e., the mean of the absolute values of Pearson's correlations) for all cases was **0.62 ± 0.04**, while the precision (Spearman's correlations) **0.60 ± 0.04**. Table 1 summarizes the correlation values for the distinct cases:

[7] That is, at the best of one's abilities: the submission is complete and with "reasonable" explanations.

[8] Therefore, 2 cases for each option.

Table 1. Average accuracy (Pearson's correlation) and precision (Spearman's correlation) for the validation cases.

	Av. Pearson's Correlation	**Av. Spearman's Correlation**
All cases (185)	0.62 ± 0.04	0.60 ± 0.04
- Cases weight = 1 (112)	0.71 ± 0.04	0.68 ± 0.04
- Cases weight = 0.5 (36)	0.53 ± 0.10	0.53 ± 0.09
- Cases weight < 0.5 (37)	0.42 ± 0.07	0.42 ± 0.07

3.3 Discussion

With an average coverage of 0.6 misconceptions per unit of observation (vs. 0.5 in the pilot experiment), it is possible to compare the results of AMiCI with those of state-of-the-art CIs: each misconception was in fact tested about 2 times in both cases. The **measurement speed** of AMiCI turns out to be **4 times higher** than that of the state-of-the-art CI and, this, despite the quizzes being administered in validation mode, in which the explanation takes most of the time.

Although the **overall accuracy** is barely ***acceptable*** (0.6), it must be evaluated in the respective cases. As easily understandable, the options with weight = 1 show greater accuracy than the less focused ones (weight ≤ 0.5): in this regard, the introduction of weighted fitness in AMiCI is justified.

Each validation case was analyzed in detail. Excluding some "complicated" or "badly formulated" questions for novice students, the major source of inaccuracy (i.e., *false negatives* and *false positives*) turned out to be the so-called *response bias* (up to 15% of the participants). In particular, students showed some incoherence between actual selections and related explanations. During the validation, however, we discovered an important gap between instructors' expectations of a question and the student's real understanding of the described problem. It is therefore essential to have a field validation of the CI.

Having a **written explanation** about selections proved to be a **valid approach** for obtaining a realistic and synchronized picture of student knowledge fitness: in fact, only in less than 6% of all explanations we were unable to assess the occurrence of a certain misconception. Furthermore, the (relatively few) interviews with students interested in finding out more about the quizzes always confirmed the assessment we made.

Unfortunately, IRT is not applicable to AMiCI, because some of its assumptions (unidimensionality and local independence) do not hold. However, we believe that our approach objectively validates the CI.

3.4 Additional Observation on Accuracy

During the validation of our CI, we noticed a significant difference in the accuracy of questions based on code (interpretation of the execution) and those based on textual descriptions. The 55 validation cases for code questions have an average Pearson's correlation of 0.50, while for other types of questions the correlation is ≥ 0.67. In general, we noticed a certain diffidence of students in considering unusual code (meant to test their understanding) as valid, and this has negatively impacted the accuracy of the related questions.

3.5 Limitations

Apart from the limited population and context, which do not allow us to easily generalize our findings, in our experiment we cannot ignore the *observer effect*, due to the insertion of the explanation field: some students have indeed admitted that the writing of the explanation made them to think more deeply about the question and change the initial selection. This behavior is also demonstrated by the fact that sometimes the selections differ from the content of the explanations, indicating that the student has probably changed his mind, forgetting to also update the selection. Quantifying the impact of the observer effect on the general fitness and accuracy is however difficult.

4 Conclusions and Future Work

In this paper, we have presented an improved methodology to build (programming language) Concept Inventories: the Agile Misconception Concept Inventory (AMiCI). **AMiCI proved to be more efficient** than state-of-the-art CIs, assuring, even in the "validation mode", a 4x speed up in the measurement process, while preserving an acceptable accuracy. We, thus, positively answered our RQ. We also introduced a metric, called **knowledge fitness**, to **quantify the severity and the diffusion of misconceptions** and, thus, objectively measure student difficulties.

We further discussed how accuracy is not only a quality of the content of the question, but also of its form and type, showing how these attributes can impact it. **Response bias**, in particular, has proved to be an issue for the validation of questions. We have already addressed this problem in a new Web application, the **AMiCI - Platform**[9], developed to manage (AMi)CIs, administer quizzes, (automatically) analyze and validate the outcomes. The platform is still in the experimental phase, but initial observations suggest that it is a valuable support for the AMiCI process, providing immediate results and speeding up the collaborative experts' validation activity, as well as reducing cases of response bias.

Our CI currently counts 75 questions, covering 153 misconceptions from 3 different languages (Java, Python, JavaScript). However, these numbers are growing rapidly, also thanks to modularization and the consequent flexibility allowed by the usage of options as test items. In existing questions, we can always add new options or delete others, while limiting the efforts for their validation. This

[9] Some of the presented figures are screenshots taken from the AMiCI - Platform.

feature makes our methodology "agile", ready to meet new needs related to the natural evolution (of the specifications) of programming languages and of students.

Our investigations have already allowed us to understand the origin of some misconceptions and determine their cruciality for 3 different PL courses, thanks to the fitness profiles. As future work, we are now looking forward to involving other programming language instructors, to further expand our CI and provide a more significant evaluation of its qualities. Our ultimate goal is to build an instrument that can objectively measure the diffusion of misconceptions in different contexts, and possibly also evaluate the efficacy of courses.

Acknowledgments. We are grateful to the Faculty of Informatics at the Università della Svizzera italiana (Switzerland) for having provided us with the valuable resources for the development and the testing of the AMiCI methodology. We especially thank Dr. Edgar Eduardo Rosales Rosero for the support.

References

1. Almstrum, V.L., et al.: Concept inventories in computer science for the topic discrete mathematics. SIGCSE Bull. **38**(4), 132–145 (2006). https://doi.org/10.1145/1189136.1189182
2. Caceffo, R., Frank-Bolton, P., Souza, R., Azevedo, R.: Identifying and validating java misconceptions toward a CS1 concept inventory. In: Proceedings of the 2019 ACM Conference on Innovation and Technology in Computer Science Education, pp. 23–29. ITiCSE 2019, Association for Computing Machinery, New York (2019). https://doi.org/10.1145/3304221.3319771
3. Chiodini, L., Moreno Santos, I., Gallidabino, A., Tafliovich, A., Santos, A.L., Hauswirth, M.: A curated inventory of programming language misconceptions. In: Proceedings of the 26th ACM Conference on Innovation and Technology in Computer Science Education, vol. 1, pp. 380–386. ITiCSE 2021, Association for Computing Machinery, New York (2021). https://doi.org/10.1145/3430665.3456343
4. Farghally, M.F., Koh, K.H., Ernst, J.V., Shaffer, C.A.: Towards a concept inventory for algorithm analysis topics. In: Proceedings of the 2017 ACM SIGCSE Technical Symposium on Computer Science Education (SIGCSE 2017), pp. 207–212. ACM, New York (2017). https://doi.org/10.1145/3017680.3017756
5. Frost, J.: Interpreting correaltion coefficients (2022). https://statisticsbyjim.com/basics/correlations/. Accessed 10 Apr 2022
6. Hambleton, R., Swaminathan, H.: Item Response Theory: Principles and Applications. Evaluation in education and human services, Springer, Netherlands (1985). https://books.google.ch/books?id=jKFMUFI-e1UC https://doi.org/10.1007/978-94-017-1988-9
7. Hauswirth, M., Adamoli, A.: Identifying misconceptions with active recall in a blended learning system. In: Lavoué, É., Drachsler, H., Verbert, K., Broisin, J., Pérez-Sanagustín, M. (eds.) Data Driven Approaches in Digital Education, pp. 416–421. Springer International Publishing, Cham (2017)
8. Herman, G.L., Loui, M.C., Zilles, C.: Creating the digital logic concept inventory. In: Proceedings of the 41st ACM Technical Symposium on Computer Science Education (SIGCSE 2010), pp. 102–106. ACM, New York (2010). https://doi.org/10.1145/1734263.1734298

9. Hestenes, D., Wells, M., Swackhamer, G.: Force concept inventory. Phys. Teach. **30**(3), 141–158 (1992). https://doi.org/10.1119/1.2343497
10. Kaczmarczyk, L.C., Petrick, E.R., East, J.P., Herman, G.L.: Identifying student misconceptions of programming. In: Proceedings of the 41st ACM Technical Symposium on Computer Science Education - SIGCSE 2010, p. 107. ACM Press, Milwaukee, Wisconsin (2010). https://doi.org/10.1145/1734263.1734299, http://portal.acm.org/citation.cfm?doid=1734263.1734299
11. Karpierz, K., Wolfman, S.A.: Misconceptions and concept inventory questions for binary search trees and hash tables. In: Proceedings of the 45th ACM Technical Symposium on Computer Science Education (SIGCSE 2014), pp. 109–114. ACM, New York (2014). https://doi.org/10.1145/2538862.2538902
12. Kurvinen, E., Hellgren, N., Kaila, E., Laakso, M.J., Salakoski, T.: Programming misconceptions in an introductory level programming course exam. In: Proceedings of the 2016 ACM Conference on Innovation and Technology in Computer Science Education, pp. 308–313. ITiCSE 2016, Association for Computing Machinery, New York (2016). https://doi.org/10.1145/2899415.2899447
13. Loughran, J., Berry, A., Mulhall, P.: Pedagogical content knowledge. In: Understanding and Developing Science Teachers' Pedagogical Content Knowledge, pp. 7–14. SensePublishers, Rotterdam (2012). https://doi.org/10.1007/978-94-6091-821-6_2
14. Porter, L., Taylor, C., Webb, K.C.: Leveraging open source principles for flexible concept inventory development. In: Proceedings of the 2014 Conference on Innovation and Technology in Computer Science Education (ITiCSE 2014), pp. 243–248. ACM, New York (2014). https://doi.org/10.1145/2591708.2591722
15. Qian, Y., Lehman, J.: Students' misconceptions and other difficulties in introductory programming: a literature review. ACM Trans. Comput. Educ. **18**(1), 1–24 (2017). https://doi.org/10.1145/3077618
16. Richardson, J.: Concept Inventories: Tools for uncovering STEM students' misconceptions. Invention and Impact: Building Excellence in Undergraduate Science. Technology, Engineering and Mathematics (STEM) Education (2004). https://www.aaas.org/sites/default/files/02_AER_Richardson.pdf
17. Sadler, P.M., Sonnert, G.: Understanding misconceptions: teaching and learning in middle school physical science. Am. Educ. **40**(1), 26–32 (2016)
18. Sherman, A.T., et al.: Experiences and lessons learned creating and validating concept inventories for cybersecurity. In: Choo, K.K.R., Morris, T., Peterson, G.L., Imsand, E. (eds.) National Cyber Summit (NCS) Research Track 2020, pp. 3–34. Springer International Publishing, Cham (2021). https://doi.org/10.1007/978-3-030-58703-1_1
19. Sorva, J.: Visual program simulation in introductory programming education, Ph.D. thesis, Aalto University, Espoo (2012), 00114

A Transformer-Based Approach for the Automatic Generation of Concept-Wise Exercises to Provide Personalized Learning Support to Students

Muhammad Afzaal[1(✉)], Jalal Nouri[1], and Aayesha Aayesha[2]

[1] Department of Computer and Systems Sciences, Stockholm University, Stockholm, Sweden
{muhammad.afzaal,jalal}@dsv.su.se
[2] TU Wien Informatics, Vienna, Austria
aayesha.aayesha@tuwien.ac.at

Abstract. Providing personalized support to students during courses is essential to facilitate them in their desired learning goals and reduce the dropout rate. Although teachers can play an effective role in providing personalized support, achieving individual-level assistance for massive courses becomes challenging. To overcome this challenge, this paper proposes a transformer-based approach that first models students' knowledge of various course concepts based on their performance in various assessed tasks. Afterwards, the students' concept-wise knowledge level derived from the models is combined with the available course material, leading to the generation of personalized concept-wise exercises by employing fine-tuned Text-to-Text Transfer Transformer (T5) architecture. These generated exercises help students to improve their knowledge about different course concepts. The proposed approach has been evaluated with various university courses to determine its quality, utility and effects on students' academic performance. The evaluation results revealed that teachers and students were satisfied with the quality of the generated exercises, and these were found to be helpful for students to improve their concept-wise understanding. Furthermore, the generated exercises positively impacted students' academic performance.

Keywords: Automatic Exercises Generation · Personalized Learning · Transformer-Based Approach · Generation of Concept-Wise Exercises

1 Introduction

In higher education, students take classes that include a list of learning concepts, which are centred on the main topics of the course [1]. The students vary in their understanding level of different course concepts [2]. Some students are

O. Viberg et al. (Eds.): EC-TEL 2023, LNCS 14200, pp. 16–31, 2023.
https://doi.org/10.1007/978-3-031-42682-7_2

excellent at comprehending a set of concepts, but others are less skilled. So, students need individual-level study support from teachers [3]. However, in the case of massive courses where many students are enrolled, it is not easy for a teacher to identify the knowledge level of each student regarding each concept and provide them with the respective support [4]. The students are unable to receive personalized support from the teachers, which leads to some failures or dropouts at the end of the course [5]. In prior work, several approaches have been proposed to address these challenges by generating course-related questions for students that could help them to improve their academic performance. For example, rule-based approaches create questions for students utilizing the grammatical transformation of text sentences [6,7]. Similarly, template-based approaches use a fixed question structure and change the variables to generate multiple questions for students [8–10].

However, these approaches are not able to generate automatic concept-based exercises using course materials where each question is tagged with a specific concept. Moreover, the questions created by these approaches cannot reflect students' knowledge level, which plays a vital role in improving students' performance during the course. Hence, providing individual or personalized support to students based on their learning needs becomes challenging.

To address these challenges, we aim to employ natural language processing (NLP) techniques for modelling student knowledge regarding each course concept and identifying the ones for which students need to improve their understanding. Furthermore, by using NLP, we generate automatic concept-wise exercises for students at the individual level to provide personalized support in their learning. In order to achieve this aim, we seek to answer three leading research questions.

- **Question 1:** How can we employ NLP techniques to generate automatic concept-based exercises to support personalized learning?
- **Question 2:** What are the quality and utility of the automatically generated concept-based exercises?
- **Question 3:** What are the effects of the generated exercises on students' academic performance in the course?

To tackle the above-discussed research questions, we propose a transformer-based approach that takes students' quiz data and course material (e.g. lecture PDFs and videos) as the input and delivers automatically generated concept-wise exercises for each student at an individual level. The proposed approach consists of two main phases. The first involves knowledge modelling, in which students' understanding of different course concepts is extracted from their quiz data to develop their knowledge models. The second phase includes the automatic generation of concept-wise exercises that use course material along with students' knowledge models and employ fine-tuned Text-to-Text Transfer Transformer (T5) architecture to generate exercises intended to improve knowledge of the concepts with which students are struggling.

The evaluation of the proposed approach was conducted in two different settings. (1) The first was the teachers' evaluation, where generated exercises were delivered to the teachers, and their feedback was obtained by conducting interviews. The purpose of this evaluation was to measure the quality and utility of the generated exercises. (2) The second was a real-world educational evaluation, where generated exercises were given to the students based on their current knowledge during the course. The purpose of this assessment was to measure the effects of the generated exercises on students' academic performance.

The evaluation results show that generated exercises using the proposed approach were beneficial from three main perspectives. First, the teachers established that generated question-answer pairs in exercises were accurate at a satisfying level, suitable for a basic understanding of concepts, and an efficient choice for teachers to create a variety of assessments for students with varying concept-wise levels of understanding. However, more clarity and depth could be added to the question-answer pairs. Second, it was found that generated exercises positively affected students' academic performance and helped them to improve their concept-wise knowledge for exam preparation. Third, the impact of the automated exercises was found to be helpful in terms of adding valuable resources to course material by generating question pools and bringing efficiency to the laborious and time-consuming task of creating exercises manually.

2 Literature Review

This section discusses the related work on the artificial intelligence in education, educational data mining and learning analytics research streams of the education field, which have proposed generating exercises from course content to improve students' knowledge. The objective of this section is to analyse recently proposed approaches and to identify their limitations and drawbacks.

In the existing work, an important aspect for automatic question generation is called context selection, where meaningful parts of the given text are selected to generate questions. Huang et al. [6] proposed a statistics-based approach in which sentence dependence, structural completeness, and key parts selection were employed with the aim of appropriate text selection for language learners. However, this was limited to short, less complicated, and intermediate texts with a lack of optimal key parts selection from the sentences and was unable to deal with the sentence interdependence. Similarly, Kumar et al. [11] ranked the sentences in order of importance by using topic distributions, keeping the assumption that a few topically meaningful coherent sentences will result in the generation of good questions. Yet, no evaluation of the approach was provided, and the authors' assumption will not always hold. A non-central sentence may provide additional information that is essential for the student's understanding. Finally, classifier-based methods classify a sentence or a part of a sentence as question-worthy by applying typical pattern-matching algorithms like logistic regression or neural networks [12,13]. Alongside good performance, their main weakness is that the classifier learns whether a sentence constitutes valuable information implicitly from the training dataset. It is unclear why a particular sentence is question-worthy according to the classifier.

The literature distinguishes three main approaches for generating questions from textual inputs. The first and most important one includes rule-based approaches that utilize grammatical transformations to develop questions from specific sentences (e.g. [6]). These approaches develop an accurate question from a simple sentence; however, with complex sentences and arbitrary texts, such approaches often fall short [7]. On the other hand, template-based approaches have fixed templates for question generation, but a few variables in these temples can be changed to create different questions. (e.g. [8]). Templates-based approaches perform better in a few domains if there are enough to cover the language phenomena in a given text. Reaching high coverage on arbitrary textbooks is challenging because of the different writing styles and vocabulary in various domains [8]. Moreover, creating each template is time-consuming and tends to sound repetitive. Neural and semantics-based approaches are the third kind of method that emphasizes the semantic analysis of texts, although they typically also use some syntactic analysis. For instance, Huang and He [9] proposed a lexical functional grammar representation-based question generation system that uses both syntactic and semantic layers. Similarly, neural question generators use statistical language models to transpose declarative inputs into questions (e.g. [14]).

In the educational sector, rule-based and template-based systems are the most widespread [15]. Outside the academic world, neural and semantics-based question generators outperform their template-based and rule-based competitors [7] in the intrinsic evaluation of the generated questions' grammaticality, expressiveness and naturalness. In distractor generation (DG), various strategies are involved, such as the identification by experts of common reasoning errors, as well as thinking and solving problems associated with a particular area [16]. In the end, this is not always effective in formulating such distractors. In this sense, when generating distractors for multiple-choice questions (MCQs), different factors, such as grammar correspondence with the context and consistency between distractors and the correct answer, must be considered [17]. Traditional automatic DG implementations revolve around similarity calculations between the distractor, the proper response and/or the context, using approaches based on embeddings [18], lexical databases such as WordNet [19], ontologies, and thesauruses, among others, which subsequently lead to a selection of candidate elements based on a ranking strategy [17].

3 Methodology

This section presents a transformer-based approach that automatically generates concept-wise exercises for each of the learning concepts of the course to provide personalized support for students. It consists of three main phases: (1) knowledge modelling that models students' concept-wise knowledge from their assessment data, (2) the generation of concept-wise exercises that utilize the students' knowledge models and course material to generate exercises for each concept, and (3) the evaluation of the generated exercises to examine the quality and impact of the generated exercises on students' academic performance. In the following sections, the phases of the proposed approach are discussed in detail.

3.1 Knowledge Modelling

In the first phase of the proposed approach, the students' knowledge was modelled for the concepts studied during the course. It consisted of two sub-phases that are detailed in the following paragraph.

The first sub-phase collected data about the attempted quizzes during the course. Each question of the quiz gives information about the question context and the student's score for the question. In the collected students' quiz data, all questions incorrectly answered by the students or in which they received zero scores were filtered out for further processing. The second sub-phase dealt with concept extraction from the filtered questions. The incorrectly answered questions were given to the concept extractor, which determined the key concepts discussed in the text of the questions. In this work, the Spotlight concept extractor [20] was employed to extract concepts from the text of the questions. Table 1 shows examples of question texts and extracted concepts. The concept extractor produced a list of concepts for each student that actually refers to the ones that need to be improved on by the students. These lists of concepts provided information about the concept-wise knowledge models developed with the students.

Table 1. Examples of extracted concepts from question texts

Question Text	Concepts
Which Hadoop module was introduced in Hadoop 2.0 to allow for specialized applications to exist in the Hadoop ecosystem?	Hadoop
In the Sort and Shuffle stage of MapReduce, each node must only contain key-value pairs with one and the same key	MapReduce
In which order of preference are MapReduce jobs scheduled to run on HDFS?	MapReduce, HDFS
Imputation is a reasonable way to deal with which type of missing values?	Imputation, missing values
Which type of graph analytics is most suitable for determining the robustness of a network?	graph analytics

3.2 Automatic Concept-Wise Exercise Generation

After obtaining each student's conceptual knowledge and group information, the next phase of the proposed approach was to generate automatic concept-wise exercises that could help students to improve their knowledge of different concepts. This phase consists of four sub-phases, and the output of this phase delivers concept-wise exercises to the students.

Course Material Pre-processing: In this sub-phase, data derived from the course material were pre-processed to make them more structured and organized for further processing. The study material consisted of lecture PDFs and videos. The text was extracted and processed to remove grammatical mistakes and eliminate vagueness in the sentence-level text. In the case of the transcribed text of videos, the following steps needed to be performed. (1) Insert stop words such as full stops, commas and semicolons to split the text into well-defined sentences. (2) Address the textual mistakes regarding spellings as some terms have the same sound but refer to different words, e.g. except and accept. (3) Replace incorrectly transcribed words with correct ones as sometimes a slight change of pronunciation leads to incorrect word identification. (4) Decide the paragraph boundaries by splitting the whole transcribed text into paragraphs. (5) Assign labels to the text paragraphs where each paragraph should represent one or multiple concepts derived from the course content.

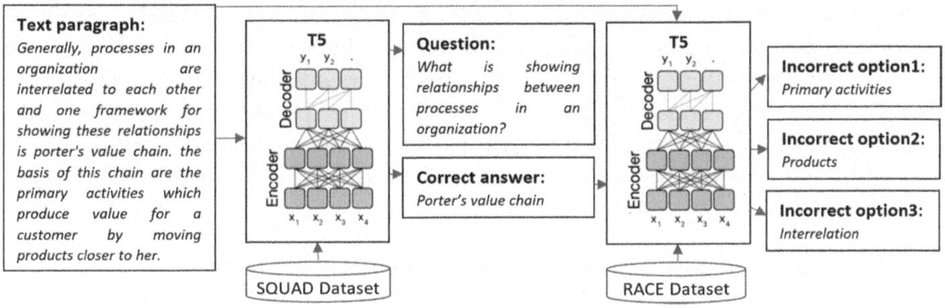

Fig. 1. Architecture for question-answer pairs and corresponding option generation

Generation of Question-Answer Pairs: This sub-phase dealt with the generation of questions and their respective correct answers using the text paragraphs, as shown in Fig. 1. For generating questions and answers, we used a T5 [21] that performs an answer-aware question generation strategy. According to this strategy, key terms or phrases from the given text are chosen as answers and then questions referring to already chosen answers are generated. In this study, the T5 was fine-tuned on an extensive Stanford Question-Answering Dataset (SQuAD) [22]. The fine-tuned T5 model was used to generate questions and answers from the pre-processed study content. This model took labelled paragraphs (the output of the content pre-processing subphase) as the input and output a list of questions along with their answers. The labels of paragraphs were used to tag the questions, where tags represented the concepts discussed in the question.

Fine-Tuning of T5 on SQuAD: T5 is an encoder-decoder model pre-trained on multiple tasks (unsupervised and supervised) where each task is converted into a text-to-text format. This study used the T5 small model for the question-answering task. It was fine-tuned on SQuAD 1.1, which is a reading comprehension dataset and consists of more than 100k question-answer pairs that were posed by the crowd workers on text paragraphs extracted from more than 500 Wikipedia articles. To fine-tune the T5 model, the input data representation, which encodes text as tokens, consisted of a maximum 512 tokens that contained the embedding of words in the given text paragraphs. The hyper-parameters setting for effective fine-tuning comprised an Adam optimization scheme with a learning rate of 0.0001. The model was trained on 10 epochs with batch size of 32. The maximum target length was reported to be 32 tokens that were produced in terms of generated questions.

Generation of Multiple Options: After generating the questions and their correct answers, the next sub-phase creates multiple options for the given questions. For the generation of multiple options, another pre-trained T5 was used that applies a distraction strategy. In this strategy, the text of the paragraph and the answer to the given question are taken as the input and multiple distractors based on the surrounding textual context and the actual answer are provided as the output. These distractors reflect the various options in the generation of MCQs. Before using T5 for this task, it was fine-tuned on a large-scale Reading Comprehension dataset from Examinations (RACE) dataset [23]. The fine-tuned model took labelled paragraphs and answers to the questions as the input obtained by the above sub-phases and produced a list of tagged MCQs.

Fine-Tuning of T5 on the RACE Dataset: In this subphase, the T5 model was fine-tuned on the RACE dataset, which consists of more than 28,000 passages and nearly 100,000 questions. Each question was associated with four candidate options, one of which was the correct answer. To fine-tune the T5 model on this dataset, the input data representation, which encodes text as tokens, included a maximum of 512 tokens (27 tokens with answers and 484 tokens of given paragraph text) containing the embedding of words in the answer and text paragraphs. The hyper-parameters setting for effective fine-tuning consisted of an Adam optimization scheme with a learning rate of 0.0001. The model was trained on 20 epochs with a batch size of 24. The maximum target length was reported to be 64 tokens that were created in terms of the generation of multiple options

Generation of Concept-Wise Exercises: The last sub-phase generated concept-wise exercises for the students to improve their knowledge of different concepts in a personalized way. To generate personalized exercises for a student, student knowledge model information was gathered, consisting of a list of concepts with which the student was struggling. Then, question-answer pairs and corresponding options were extracted from the questions list based on these concepts. Lastly, exercises were generated for each concept (containing 10 to 15 questions) and delivered to the student along with the current knowledge model. The knowledge model updates after every exercise attempt that students make during the course.

3.3 Evaluation

This section presents the evaluation of the proposed approach in two different settings. Both evaluations aimed to examine the quality of the generated exercises and their impact on student performance.

Teachers' Evaluation. For this evaluation, three teachers from different courses were interviewed to measure the quality of the exercises and point out the features that could be useful to improve exercise automation. In course selection, one bachelor-level course (Java programming) and two master-level courses (Big Data with NoSQL and Enterprise Computing and ERP Systems) were selected, and their course material was used to generate exercises for different course concepts. Overall, 52 exercises were generated, of which 21 exercises belonged to the Java programming course, 17 to the Big Data course, and 14 to ERP Systems.

After generating the exercises, 10 exercises were randomly selected from each course and delivered to each course teacher. Each was asked to carefully evaluate the generated questions, answers and options. Then, in-person semi-structured interviews were conducted to determine the quality of the exercises. The interviews were recorded, and the key points were noted down by the interviewer. Later, recordings of all the interviews and the key points were put together and used for a thematic analysis of the interview discussions.

Real-World Educational Evaluation. For this evaluation, generated exercises were evaluated in a real course to measure the impact of those exercises on students' performance. The Big Data with NoSQL course was selected for this evaluation because it includes technical and theoretical concepts, and 146 students were enrolled on the course. Half of the students (N=73) were randomly selected to deliver the exercises based on the student's needs, and the remainder (N=73) were not allowed to interact with the exercises. Moreover, notifications (emails and direct messages on the learning management system) were regularly sent to each student about their current knowledge model, and consent was taken prior to the study.

At the end of the course, data collection and analysis were performed in two steps. (i) Data on students' performance and their attempts at the exercises, including each student's score in the final exam and the number of exercise attempts students made during the course, were collected. Then, statistical tests were performed to measure the impact of the exercises on students' performance. (ii) A survey was conducted to which all 73 students responded to measure the exercises' utility and limitations. Then, a thematic analysis was performed to categorize the students' responses, including coding, categorization and thematizing. Accordingly, the identified themes were later classified into different feedback categories based on each theme.

4 Results

This section presents the evaluation results to examine the quality, utility and effects of the generated exercises in regard to students' academic performance.

4.1 Results of the Teachers' Evaluation

In order to examine the exercises' quality and utility, the teachers' interview discussion and written keynotes were thematized, and four main discussion themes emerged: (1) exercise quality, (2) exercise correctness, (3) exercise difficulty level, and (4) the utility of automation. The responses of each teacher in relation to the themes are reported in Table 2. These four main themes were further categorized into 15 sub-themes, and the teachers' responses regarding each sub-theme are presented as a heatmap in Fig. 2 to provide a clear picture of this evaluation.

Table 2. Teachers Evaluation Results

Main Themes	Teacher 1 (Big Data with NoSQL)	Teacher 2 (Java programming)	Teacher 3 (ERP Systems)
Exercise quality	Positive	Negative	Positive
Exercise correctness	Positive	Positive	Negative
Exercise difficulty-level	Positive	Positive	Negative
utility of automation	Positive	Positive	Positive

Regarding the exercise quality, the teachers' feedback was mixed. One of the teachers complained about the questions' vagueness, while others wanted more clarity in the available options. One teacher claimed that the available options were too close to each other, but others said in some questions that the given options were highly distracting in relation to each other. Almost all the teachers agreed that a human should first read questions before delivering them to the students. The teachers' feedback for the different courses was found to be different in the question correctness case. Two teachers described the automatically generated questions as very accurate and suggested that these could be used as a question pool for the teachers to create exercises for the students. On the other hand, one teacher raised a question about the correctness of the available options and answers because the provided options did not align with the asked questions.

From the difficulty-level perspective, one of the teachers found that the generated exercises were beginner-level and could be helpful for students who want basic knowledge about the course concepts. In contrast, two teachers appreciated that the concept-wise question generation had an acceptable difficulty level, and they found the difficulty level suitable for the course students and applicable to assessments. With respect to the utility and impact of the exercises, all the teachers agreed that the automation in concept-wise exercises is beneficial, not only for students, but also for teachers, as it inspires them to quickly create a variety of questions without adding any manual effort. One teacher suggested that these exercises could be helpful for the students before taking the final exam, to briefly review all essential knowledge about the course. Another added that these exercises could be used to measure the basic understanding level of students in relation to various learning concepts.

4.2 Results of the Real-World Educational Evaluation

Impact of the Generated Exercises on Student Performance: In order to examine the exercises' effects on student performance, two statistical analyses were performed. (1) An independent samples t-test was conducted to measure the difference in students' academic performance between those who attempted the exercises and those who did not. In this test, students were divided into two groups: Group 1 consisted of those students who attempted the exercises during the course, while Group 2 contained those who did not. (2) Pearson and Spearman's correlations were conducted to find the correlation between exercise attempts and students' academic performance.

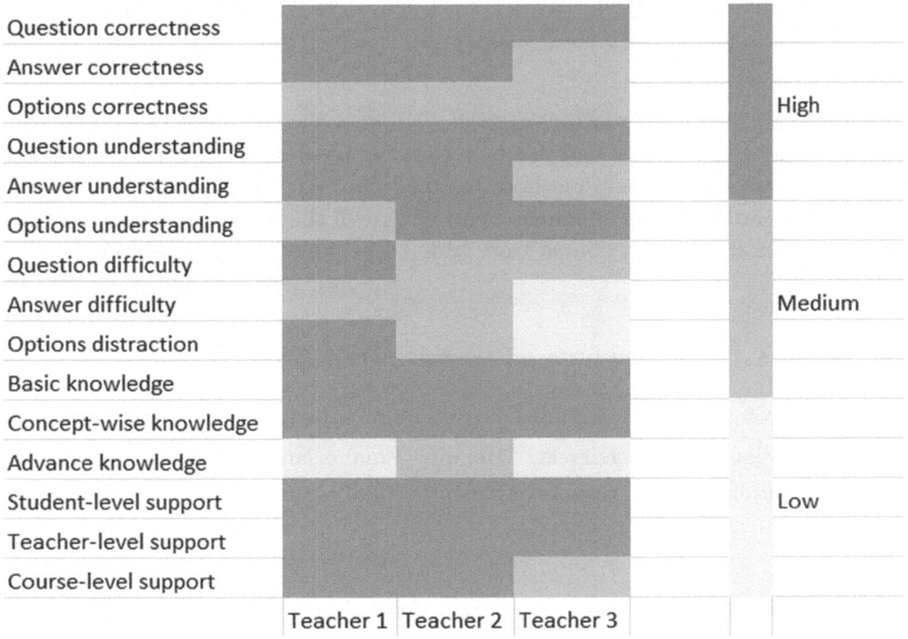

Fig. 2. Heatmap View of Thematic Analysis of Teachers Evaluation

Table 3. Statistics on groups of students

Group	N (users/students)	Mean	Std.deviation	Std.error mean
Group 1 (Exercise users)	73	40.08	4.23	0.49
Group 2 (Non-Exercise users)	73	33.12	10.42	1.22

The results obtained from the t-test for the t- and p-values (Table 4) showed a significant statistical difference (t=5.28, p<0.001) between the groups. A comparative analysis of the means for both groups was conducted to determine whether this difference positively or negatively affected the students' performance. The results indicated (Table 3) that the mean for Group 1 (m=40.08) was higher than for Group 2 (m=33.12). The higher mean for Group 1 shows that students who attempted the exercises achieved better final exam scores than those who did not. In the final exam, 50 was the maximum score, and 21 was the minimum score needed to pass the final exam.

Table 4. Results of the independent samples t-test

-	-	F	Sig.	t	df	Sig.(Two-Sided p)
Final exam score	Equal variances assumed	18.99	< .001	5.28	144	< 0.001
	Equal variances not assumed			5.28	95.13	< 0.001

The results of the correlation analysis (Table 5) showed a positive correlation between exercise attempts and student performance. As shown in Table 5, the correlation with the Pearson method was 0.63, and 0.62 with the Spearman one. Based on this analysis, the conclusion can be drawn that students who attempted more exercises during the course were able to achieve better scores in the final exam.

Table 5. Correlations between exercise attempts and Final exam score.

Correlation technique	N	Variable	by Variable	r	Sig.(2-tailed)
Pearson Correlation	73	Exercise Attempts	Final exam score	0.63	< 0.001
Spearman Correlation	73	Exercise Attempts	Final exam score	0.62	< 0.001

Quality and Utility of the Generated Exercises: The quality and utility of the generated exercises were also examined from the students' side through a survey. The students' survey responses were analysed based on the coding scheme described in Sect. 3.3.2. Three main themes emerged from the responses: (1) Questions' difficulty level, (2) Questions' quality, and (3) Concept-level understanding, as shown in Table 6. In the following paragraphs, each theme is discussed in detail.

In terms of the difficulty level of the questions, students' responses were categorized into four main types (very easy, easy, normal, and difficult). A percentage of 8.22% agreed that the questions in the exercises were "very easy", and the same rate (8.22%) noted that the questions were "difficult". However, according to 21.92%, the questions were "easy", while 61.64% argued that the questions were "normal" or of an average difficulty level. Concerning the quality of the questions, overall, 75.34% provided positive feedback, while the remaining 24.66% provided negative feedback. Several respondents summarized the positive experience as follows: "Really liked the way the questions in exercises were decided as they were based on your own experience".

Third, regarding enhancing concept-level understanding, the exercises either improved the students' understanding of different concepts or did not. This analysis showed the positive responses of approximately 84.93% of students who commented in varying ways. A couple of students responded, "The exercises were super helpful to improve my knowledge and I want to have more exercises to do and practise". The remaining 15.07% were not satisfied. One student noted, "I already have enough understanding of the question concepts, but more practical questions could be useful for the course".

Table 6. Real-world Educational Evaluation Results (N=73)

Survey Themes	Feedback	# of Responses	Percentage (%)
Questions' difficulty level	Very Easy	6	08.22
	Easy	16	21.92
	Normal	45	61.64
	Difficult	6	08.22
Questions' quality	Positive	55	75.34
	Negative	18	24.66
Concept-level understanding	Positive	62	84.93
	Negative	11	15.07

5 Discussion

This paper has described an automatic concept-wise exercise generation approach to providing personalized learning support to students during their courses.

5.1 Findings and Implications

We started with the first research question: how can we employ NLP techniques to generate automatic concept-based exercises to support personalized learning? As described in Sects. 3.1 and 3.2, we proposed a transformer-based approach that can automatically construct question-answer pairs and corresponding multiple options using the course material. Moreover, the proposed approach can model student knowledge to identify concepts with which a student is struggling and use constructed question-answer pairs to generate and deliver concept-based exercises to provide personalized support during a course.

These findings led us to the second research question: "What is the quality and utility of the automatically generated concept-based exercises?" To answer this question, the generated exercises were evaluated by the teachers and students. In the teachers' evaluation, the teachers admitted the importance of using automation in exercise generation and found that the constructed question-answer pairs and multiple options were accurate, but wanted more clarity in the available options. Moreover, they added that such advanced features could improve students' knowledge about different course concepts; however, these exercises provide basic knowledge instead of in-depth information about course concepts. In the students' evaluation, which was conducted in a real-world educational setting, it was found that the constructed question-answer pairs were at a normal level, which means the pairs were not too difficult and not overly simple. Furthermore, the exercises were highly helpful in improving their understanding and knowledge of concepts with which they were struggling during the course.

Finally, we measured the effects of the generated exercises on students' academic performance. For this purpose, we performed two statistical analyses on final exam scores and students' exercise attempts. The results in Sect. 4.2 raised two important findings. First, the exercises generated through the proposed approach positively impacted students' academic performance because students who were allowed to attempt exercises during the course achieved higher final exam scores than those who were not. Second, a positive correlation was found between the number of exercise attempts that students made during the course and their final exam scores. Based on these findings, the answer to the third question is that the generated exercises positively affected students' academic performance, and students who attempted more exercises had a higher tendency to achieve better scores in the final exams of the course than those who attempted fewer ones.

The findings of this work are interesting from three main perspectives. From the students' perspective, these provide personalized support to the students and improve their concept-wise knowledge level. They help students to practise course content to achieve high grades in final exams. In the case of the teachers' perspective, automation assists teachers in generating a bank including various types of questions of mixed difficulty. The teachers can use this question bank to construct exercises of different levels (beginner and advanced levels) to measure students' abilities during the course. From a course perspective, automatic exercise generation can add a pool of questions for the given course content where each question is targeted to one or multiple learning concepts. It can be used to create pre-course tests, quizzes, and other course assessments to assess students' knowledge.

5.2 Limitations and Future Directions

Regarding limitations, this paper provides automatic question answering only when the course content is theoretical. However, for coding exercises in the case of programming courses, the proposed approach limits automation and the need to manually make templates for programming code exercises. This limitation reduces the generalizability of the proposed approach, where the input is always the text of properly structured sentences that are either transcribed from videos or taken from PDFs. Another limitation of this work is the lack of advanced-level question generation, as reported in the teachers' evaluation. Since the proposed T5-based architecture takes text in the form of paragraphs labelled with concepts that are discussed in them, in question generation, it targets single-paragraph concepts. It cannot generate questions about the dependency and relationships of concepts discussed in different paragraphs. Although labelled paragraphs are helpful in concept-wise question generation, at the same time they produce less detailed or comparatively basic-level questions.

In future, we will improve the proposed approach, which could be able to generate more advanced-level questions to provide deep knowledge of all learning concepts in the course. Our emphasis will be to encourage dependency, relationship, similarity, and contrasts among all concepts discussed within a topic. Moreover, we will target the automatic generation of programming exercises for coding practice where the model will be trained on all basic programming constructs, and then utilized to generate coding exercises including questions with different templates and parameters.

6 Conclusion

This study proposed a transformer-based approach that provides personalized concept-wise learning support to students about courses by automatically generating exercises. According to this approach, students' knowledge about various learning concepts was first modelled. Second, knowledge models and available course content were used to generate concept-wise exercises at the individual level. Lastly, the automatically generated exercises were evaluated by the teachers and students. The teachers' evaluation was performed by interviewing the course teachers at the beginning of the course to examine the quality and utility of the generated exercises. In contrast, the students' evaluation was performed in a real-world educational setting to examine the exercises' effects on students' academic performance. The evaluation results show that the quality of exercises was at a satisfying level, and the exercises positively impacted student academic performance in the course. Moreover, the proposed approach can be useful in assisting teachers in assessment preparation and course resource improvement through the generation of a question pool.

References

1. Barria-Pineda, J., Brusilovsky, P.: Explaining educational recommendations through a concept-level knowledge visualization. In: Proceedings of the 24th International Conference on Intelligent User Interfaces: Companion, pp. 103–104 (2019)
2. Rivers, M.L., Dunlosky, J., Joynes, R.: The contribution of classroom exams to formative evaluation of concept-level knowledge. Contemp. Educ. Psychol. **59**, 101806 (2019)
3. Andrade, H., Brookhart, S.M.: The role of classroom assessment in supporting self-regulated learning. In: Laveault, D., Allal, L. (eds.) Assessment for Learning: Meeting the Challenge of Implementation. TEPA, vol. 4, pp. 293–309. Springer, Cham (2016). https://doi.org/10.1007/978-3-319-39211-0_17
4. Winstone, N., Carless, D.: Designing Effective Feedback Processes in Higher Education: A Learning-focused Approach. Routledge (2019)
5. Kizilcec, R.F., Pérez-Sanagustín, M., Maldonado, J.J.: Recommending self-regulated learning strategies does not improve performance in a MOOC. In: Proceedings of the Third (2016) ACM Conference on Learning@ Scale, pp. 101–104 (2016)
6. Huang, Y., He, L.: Automatic generation of short answer questions for reading comprehension assessment. Nat. Lang. Eng. **22**(3), 457–489 (2016)
7. Du, X., Shao, J., Cardie, C.: Learning to ask: neural question generation for reading comprehension. arXiv preprint arXiv:1705.00106 (2017)
8. Mazidi, K., Tarau, P.: Infusing NLU into automatic question generation. In: Proceedings of the 9th International Natural Language Generation Conference, pp. 51–60 (2016)
9. Huang, Y., He, L.: Automatic generation of short answer questions for reading comprehension assessment. Nat. Lang. Eng. **22**(3), 457–489 (2016)
10. Matsumoto, Y., Prasad R.: In: Proceedings of COLING 2016, the 26th International Conference on Computational Linguistics: Technical Papers (2016)
11. Kumar, G., Banchs, R.E., Fernando D'Haro, L.: Revup: automatic gap-fill question generation from educational texts. In: Proceedings of the Tenth Workshop on Innovative Use of NLP for Building Educational Applications, pp. 154–161 (2015)
12. Du, X., Cardie, C.: Identifying where to focus in reading comprehension for neural question generation. In: Proceedings of the 2017 Conference on Empirical Methods in Natural Language Processing, pp. 2067–2073 (2017)
13. Wang, Z., Lan, A.S., Nie, W., Waters, A.E., Grimaldi, P.J., Baraniuk, R.G.: QG-net: a data-driven question generation model for educational content. In: Proceedings of the Fifth Annual ACM Conference on Learning at Scale, pp. 1–10 (2018)
14. Wang, Z., Lan, A.S., Nie, W., Waters, A.E., Grimaldi, P.J., Baraniuk, R.G.: QG-net: a data-driven question generation model for educational content. In: Proceedings of the Fifth Annual ACM Conference on Learning at Scale, pp. 1–10 (2018)
15. Kurdi, G., Leo, J., Parsia, B., Sattler, U., Al-Emari, S.: A systematic review of automatic question generation for educational purposes. Int. J. Artif. Intell. Educ. **30**(1), 121–204 (2020)
16. Haladyna, T.M., Rodriguez, M.C.: Developing and Validating Test Items. Routledge (2013)
17. Liang, C., Yang, X., Dave, N., Wham, D., Pursel, B., Giles, C.L.: Distractor generation for multiple choice questions using learning to rank. In: Proceedings of the Thirteenth Workshop on Innovative Use of NLP for Building Educational Applications, pp. 284–290 (2018)

18. Jiang, S., Lee, J.S.Y.: Distractor generation for Chinese fill-in-the-blank items. In: Proceedings of the 12th Workshop on Innovative Use of NLP for Building Educational Applications, pp. 143–148 (2017)
19. Miller, G.A.: Wordnet: a lexical database for English. Commun. ACM **38**(11), 39–41 (1995)
20. Mendes, P.N., Jakob, M., García-Silva, A., Bizer, C.: DBpedia spotlight: shedding light on the web of documents. In: Proceedings of the 7th International Conference on Semantic Systems, pp. 1–8 (2011)
21. Xue, L., et al.: mT5: a massively multilingual pre-trained text-to-text transformer. arXiv preprint arXiv:2010.11934 (2020)
22. Rondeau, M.-A., Hazen, T.J.: Systematic error analysis of the stanford question answering dataset. In: Proceedings of the Workshop on Machine Reading for Question Answering, pp. 12–20 (2018)
23. Lai, G., Xie, Q., Liu, H., Yang, Y., Hovy, E.: Race: large-scale reading comprehension dataset from examinations. arXiv preprint arXiv:1704.04683 (2017)

Generative Pre-trained Transformers for Coding Text Data? An Analysis with Classroom Orchestration Data

Ishari Amarasinghe(✉), Francielle Marques, Ariel Ortiz-Beltrán, and Davinia Hernández-Leo

ICT Department, Universitat Pompeu Fabra, Barcelona, Spain
{ishari.amarasinghe,francielle.marques,ariel.ortiz, davinia.hernandez-leo}@upf.edu, ishari.amarasinghe@donders.ru.nl

Abstract. Video content analysis is of importance for researchers in technology-enhanced learning. A common starting point typically involves transcribing video into textual transcripts that enable the application of a coding scheme to group the text into key themes. However, manual coding is demanding and requires time and effort of human annotators. Therefore, this study explores the possibility of using Generative Pre-trained Transformer 3 (GPT-3) models for automating the text data coding compared to baseline classical machine learning approaches using a dataset manually coded for the orchestration actions of six teachers in classroom collaborative learning sessions. The findings of our study showed that a fine-tuned GPT-3 (curie) model outperformed classical approaches (F1 score of 0.87) and reached a 0.77 Cohen's kappa, which indicated a moderate agreement between manual and machine coding. The study also brings out the limitations of our text transcripts and highlights the importance of multimodal observations that capture the context of orchestration actions.

Keywords: Collaborative learning · Automatic coding · Machine Learning · Generative AI · Classroom orchestration

1 Introduction

Increased digitisation of education has allowed educational institutes to collect data on everyday classroom teaching and learning situations. The interactions between teachers, students and educational technologies are now being captured using different modalities such as audio, video, images, text, and physiological sensors. By combining quantitative and qualitative data through mixed methods, researchers can triangulate and contextualise study findings to derive meaningful insights [1, 2]. Video content analysis is often used in qualitative research and a common starting point typically involves transcribing video into textual transcripts. Researchers can then segment text into meaningful units

I. Amarasinghe—Is now with the National Education Lab AI, Radboud University, the Netherlands.

O. Viberg et al. (Eds.): EC-TEL 2023, LNCS 14200, pp. 32–43, 2023.
https://doi.org/10.1007/978-3-031-42682-7_3

and start coding the text [3]. Codes can be thought of as descriptive labels for condensed meaning units [3]. Related codes can be later grouped together, formulating categories [3]. Agreement between coders on how the same data should be coded can be measured using statistical tests, e.g., Cohen's kappa, Krippendorff's alpha, Scott's pi and Fleiss' K [3].

On the one hand, data coding is known as a labour-intensive complex task which is time-consuming and can even become biased and impractical when the data to be coded is large [4]. Moreover, to minimise any inconsistencies and conflicts during the coding process and to establish acceptable agreement levels between the coders, it is essential to discuss conflicting interpretations and carry out multiple iterations of coding [3]. On the other hand, the importance of qualitative content analysis is well recognised for its usefulness in producing robust research findings [1], therefore despite the difficulties, researchers often employ content analysis and therefore engage in data coding.

The present study lies within the context of computer-supported collaborative learning (CSCL) in which students enacted scripted CSCL activities using a tool called PyramidApp [5]. PyramidApp provides a teacher-facing dashboard for the teacher to orchestrate or, in other words, to effectively regulate students' collaboration in real-time. The orchestration actions of the teachers while enacting CSCL sessions have been captured using video recordings. Following the work of [4] discourse includes both oral and chat-based communication between two or more individuals. In this sense, in the present study, the video recordings that depicted classroom discourse captured not only the orchestration actions of the teachers alone (using the teacher-facing dashboard of the PyramidApp) but also their interactions with the students at different social levels, e.g., individual students, groups and the whole class. The video recordings that captured classroom discourse were later transcribed to text and manually coded following a coding scheme proposed in our previous work [5]. As described before, manual data coding is a challenging task that motivated our research in which we have explored the use of Machine Learning (ML) models, specifically Generative Pre-trained Transformer 3 (GPT-3) to automate the coding of text transcripts from video recordings that captured classroom discourse. More specifically, the study aimed to answer the following research question: *How well a fine-tuned GPT-3 model codes text data when compared to other baseline classical machine learning models?*

Recently, advances in deep learning and specifically Natural Language Processing (NLP) techniques received the attention given the ability of those technologies to automate textual content analysis. For instance, in the context of NLP, Large Language Models (LLMs) such as GPT-3 have been reported as being useful for a variety of tasks including but not limited to text classification, translation, summarisation [6]. Among those, text classification is of interest for the present study, given it involves classifying text into a predefined set of labels. In this sense, coding of text data can also be described as a text classification task given the objective is to automatically assign a related predefined code or label to a text excerpt in a given transcript. Automatic assignment of labels into text excerpts derived from transcripts can assist in video content analysis and mitigate the time spent during manual data coding.

The following sections of the paper are organised as follows: First, we provide related background, and then the details of data collection and manual coding of the video transcripts. Next, we describe the proposed technical approach, which involves fine-tuning GPT-3 models for automatic coding compared to other baseline classical ML models. Using test datasets and baseline models (i.e., Multinomial Naive Bayes (MNB) and k-nearest neighbors (k-NN)) we report the agreement between manual and machine coding as well as the study limitations. The paper concludes with several implications for research and outlines future research directions.

2 Background

Over the last few years, researchers have explored different techniques to automate text data coding. Early efforts in this line of work have explored the use of keywords or phrases based approaches. However, those approaches have been criticised due to their lack of contextual understanding, ultimately resulting in a frequency count of texts that matches a certain keyword(s) and phrases [7]. In addressing the limitations of keyword-based approaches [8] proposed the use of discourse markers based semi-automatic approach to code dialogue acts. Although the findings of their study indicated that the automatic coding of dialogue acts was correlated with the results of manual coding, manually generating coding rules was seen as a limitation. [9] addressed the problem of automated content analysis of students' online discussion transcripts. They have applied a combination of lexical features, e.g., N-grams, part-of-speech tags, word dependency, as well as features related to the context of cognitive presence constructs (i.e., entity count, stage of the discussion) and reported that the use of trigrams improved accuracy of automatic coding and it helped to reach a fair to good agreement between manual and machine coding. nCoder [10] is another tool that can assist researchers to discover and code key concepts in text data with minimum human judgement. Using nCoder researchers can first define their coding scheme and a list of regular expressions that can detect a language pattern to code the text data automatically. nCoder reports the agreement between machine coding and manual coding using several statistics. In case of disagreements, the tool enables researchers to refine the regular expressions iteratively and to achieve a higher agreement between manual and machine coding.

In the context of collaborative learning, [11] used supervised ML models, i.e., MNB and k-NN, to automatically classify chat messages students posted into collaborative problem-solving skills. The study findings have indicated that the k-NN classifier reached a strong agreement between automatic and human annotations even with a relatively small amount of training data. In another study [12] have examined the affordances of deep learning techniques to automatically code discourse data collected during collaborative problem solving tasks into three main categories, i.e., metacognition, cognition, and social interactions, and have claimed that to the best of their knowledge, it is one of the first studies to introduce artificial intelligence techniques into dialogue analysis in the context of collaborative learning.

Recent studies have also focused on the use Bidirectional Encoder Representations from Transformers (BERT) to automate the analysis of classroom discourse. For instance, in [13] BERT models have been used to classify teachers' interactions with simulated students with the objective of assessing teachers' performance levels. In [14] supervised classifiers and BERT models have been used to predict the presence or absence of specific discourse variables (e.g., use of questions, elaborated evaluations) in teachers' utterances. The study findings have brought attention to the tradeoff between data quantity and accuracy, where deep models exhibit an advantage when working with larger datasets. The potential of transformers to predict the label associated with student-teacher discourse in mathematics classrooms have also been explored in [15]. Several studies have also proposed that employing LLMs such as GPT models could yield higher performance. Our study takes the advantage of recent developments in GPT-based LLMs to automate the coding of text transcripts derived from video recording collected during classroom CSCL situations.

GPT-3 is a LLM consisting of 175 billion parameters that improve the generalisation ability for different types of NLP tasks without the need to develop specific task-dependent architectures. As mentioned before GPT-3 models can perform challenging tasks, such as classification, reading comprehension, question answering, and explaining concepts, including detailing the reasoning behind a decision in their process [16].

GPT-3 models from OpenAI are currently available for fine-tuning [6]. Although recently more powerful models have been released, such as GPT- 3.5, and GPT- 4, we will detail the base models from GPT-3 that we considered in the present work. GPT-3 contains four base models *davinci, curie, ada,* and *babbage.* The main difference among the base models is the number of parameters of each model, which indicates its powerfulness and capabilities [16]. However, at the time of preparing this manuscript the parameters of the models are not explicitly available. According to [17], *davinci* is the model that can perform a number of tasks, mostly with fewer instructions, and can identify problems of cause and effect. The *curie* model is indicated for tasks linked to classification, and summarization. *Ada* is another model that is faster and can perform text classification but is not capable of identifying nuances in the text. Finally, *babbage* model can be used to perform tasks such as simple text classifications, semantic search, or search queries. In the present study we explored the usefulness of several of the aforementioned models to automate text data coding and compared the results with baseline classical ML models.

3 Methods

3.1 Data Collection and Manual Coding

As mentioned in the Introduction section we collected textual transcripts from video recordings that captured teachers' orchestration actions in classroom based CSCL scenarios. Additional details about CSCL sessions were described in our previous publication [5]. In summary, orchestration actions of six higher-education teachers (three females) from a public university in Spain were video recorded.

The teachers' orchestration actions were manually coded following a coding scheme defined in [5]. The original coding scheme defined in our previous work consisted of six codes. However, in the current study, we only considered four codes that captured teachers' orchestration actions as the remaining two were aimed at detecting teachers' use of a teacher-facing dashboard and those actions were complemented with the log data (and could not be captured only using video recordings). Therefore, the input dataset used in the study only consisted of the excerpts that were related to the four codes considered. Table 1 provides the coding scheme considered in the current study.

Table 1. Coding Scheme.

Code	Definition and examples
Teacher Individual Interactions	This code captures interactions between teachers and individual students, e.g., questions about how to use the CSCL tool
Teacher Class Interactions	This code captures interactions between teachers and the whole class (e.g., Teacher requesting activity progress from the class, final answer debriefing, guidance to the class about CSCL activity)
Announcements To Class	This code captures announcements teachers make to the class (e.g., announcements about time remaining and phase transitions of the script)
Teacher Perception	This code captures the following two behaviors: (a) Teacher is looking at individual student devices (e.g., mobile or desktop monitors) (b) Teacher is looking at the task description on screen projector display

Two researchers were involved in manual coding. The dataset consisted of 328 excerpts. There was high agreement between the coders and relatively few disagreements were resolved through discussion. Table 2 shows the distribution of different orchestration actions in the input dataset used in this study. As it can be seen in Table 2 a majority of orchestration actions of the teachers (55.79%) were labeled as *Teacher Class Interactions* and the least presence is observed for the *Teacher Perception*.

Table 2. Amount of data manually coded.

Code	No. of excerpts	No. of excerpts (%)
Teacher Individual Interactions	40	12.19%
Teacher Class Interactions	183	55.79%
Announcements To Class	81	24.70%
Teacher Perception	24	7.31%

3.2 Machine (Automatic) Coding

As mentioned before, the goal of this study is to automate the time-consuming manual data labelling process. To this end, we explored the possibility of using GPT-3 models, as well as classical ML models, i.e., MNB, and k-NN (which were proved to be effective and accurate classifiers in previous similar research [11]).

At the time of writing, OpenAI has released four pre-trained language models based on the GPT-3 architecture and named *Ada, Babbage, Curie* and *Davinci* [6]. These models vary in terms of size and capability, with *Ada* being the smallest and fastest, and *Davinci* being the largest and most capable. To evaluate the suitability of these models for different NLP tasks, tests have been conducted on the fastest model (*Ada*), the most capable model (*Davinci*), and an intermediate option (*Curie*), which offers a balance between speed and capability. These tests provide insights into the performance of the models on various tasks and can assist in selecting the most appropriate model for a given NLP application.

We fine-tuned the aforementioned models for text data coding. We split randomly 80% of the manually coded data to train the models ($N_{training} = 209$ and, $N_{validation} = 53$). Then the remaining data ($N_{test} = 66$) was used to evaluate the performance of the models, and to report accuracy, precision, recall, F1-score, and to indicate the agreement level with an experienced human coder using Cohen's kappa measure.

The same datasets created for training and testing, were also used to train two classical ML models as baseline references (i.e., MNB and k-NN Classifier). For this case, the automatic coding of the data was treated as a multiclass classification problem, in which we attempted to predict the class that best described the teachers' orchestration actions. For that, text data was tokenized, and features were extracted by the words' total frequency (tf-idf). In addition, for the k-NN, we also experimented with a number of nearest neighbors ($n = 3, 5, 7$), which is a well known parameter that could influence the classification results of the model. Moreover, previous research has also shown that the removal of the stopwords can be slightly beneficial or in some cases, it can even become disadvantageous for text classification [11, 18]. In order to measure the impact of the stopwords for our classification task, we created two different pipelines for the models to assess the scenarios.

We used scikit-learn [19], an open-source ML library, to implement the MNB and k-NN algorithms, while GPT-3 models were implemented using the OpenAI API [6]. To tailor the pre-trained models for our specific task of interest, we performed fine-tuning, which involved incorporating our data. The analysis also involved examining the impact of the 'temperature' parameter of the best performing model (varying from 0 to 2 in the latest version of the API). This parameter affects the model's randomness, where lower temperature corresponds to less randomness, and vice versa. OpenAI API is a paid interface that charges for the usage and pre-processing of training data in their specific format. Once the fine-tuning was completed, the model could be saved for future use in making predictions. However, processing the testing dataset also requires calling the OpenAI API again, which produces additional costs.

4 Results

In the following, we report the performance of the ML models using four metrics: precision, recall, F1-score and Cohen's kappa. F1-score is a measure that consists of a weighted harmonic mean of the precision and recall. We applied our experiments to the weighted average due to the imbalanced dataset. The weighted average considers the proportion of each class's support, in this sense, taking into account the frequency of each target in the metric.

Regarding the kappa measure as described in [10] we considered human annotations '1's as 'human positives' and '0's as 'human negatives'. Similarly, regarding machine coding '1' indicated 'machine positives' and '0' as 'machine negatives'. Considering manual coding as ground truth we considered '1–1' by tp (true positive), '1–0' by fn (false negative), '0–1' by fp (false positive), and '0–0' by tn (true negative) [10]. In Eq. 1, *po* represents the total agreement between the human and machine annotations, and the chance agreement between the human and machine annotations is represented by *pc*.

$$k = \frac{po - pc}{1 - pc} \tag{1}$$

Table 3 presents the performance of the classical ML models and GPT-3 models for automatic coding of the dataset using the aforementioned metrics. Based on the results presented in Table 3, GPT -3 models outperformed baseline classical ML approaches in predicting class labels.

Specifically, GPT-3 (curie) model reached an F1-score of 0.84 and Cohen's kappa value of 0.72. As indicated in [20] Cohen's kappa at the 0.60–0.79 range can be considered as a moderate agreement. Figure 1 below shows how changing the temperature parameter influences the best performing model's decision, i.e., GPT-3 (curie).

Table 3. Performance of MNB, k-NN and GPT-3 models.

Model	Precision	Recall	F1 Score	Cohen's kappa
MNB (with stopwords)	0.94	0.56	0.69	0.02
MNB (without stopwords)	0.94	0.56	0.69	0.02
kNN (with stopwords, n = 3)	0.74	0.74	0.74	0.56
kNN (without stopwords, n = 3)	0.74	0.74	0.74	0.56
kNN (with stopwords, n = 5)	0.73	0.73	0.73	0.53
kNN (without stopwords, n = 5)	0.73	0.73	0.73	0.53
GPT-3 (ada)	0.78	0.72	0.73	0.57
GPT-3 (curie)	0.86	0.83	0.84	0.72
GPT-3 (davinci)	0.77	0.68	0.69	0.50

As it can be seen in Fig. 1, setting up the temperature value to 0.5 reached the maximum agreement between manual and machine coding which was 0.77, which is at the upper limit of moderate agreement (range 0.60–0.79). An agreement above 0.80 is considered strong but is not yet feasible with the GPT-3 (curie) model. This model reached a precision value of 0.88, recall value of 0.86 and F1-score of 0.87.

In addition to the results presented above regarding the performances of the machine learning models when compared to baseline classical approaches, in the following, we

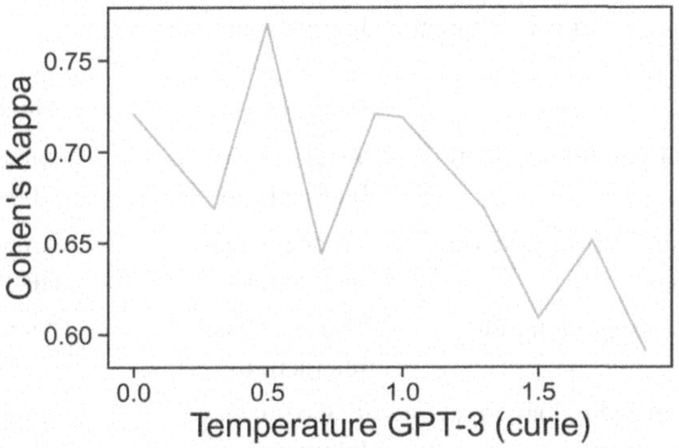

Fig. 1. Temperature GPT-3 (curie) model vs. agreement between manual and machine coding.

report in detail the classification results obtained from the best model, i.e., GPT-3 (curie) with a temperature value of 0.5. Specifically, we looked at automatic coding that disagreed with manual coding in order to understand the reason behind the disagreements. It was found that out of a total of 66 excerpts from the test data only 9 excerpts (13.6%) reached disagreements between human and machine annotations. Table 4 below outlines those excerpts and the related labels. As it can be seen 6 excerpts that were manually labelled as *Teacher Class Interactions* were labelled as either *Announcements to Class* (5 excerpts) or as *Teacher Individual Interactions* (1 excerpt) by machine. One excerpt that was manually labelled as *Announcements to Class* was labelled as *Teacher Class Interactions* by machine. Another excerpt that was manually labelled as *Teacher Perception* was labelled as *Announcements to Class* by machine. Finally, another excerpt that was manually labelled as *Teacher Individual Interactions* was labelled as *Teacher Class Interactions* by machine.

The disagreements between manual and machine coding can be interpreted as follows. 5 excerpts that were manually labelled as *Teacher Class Interactions* may have been labelled as *Announcements to Class* by machine due to multiple reasons. For instance, 3 excerpts, i.e., E2, E3, E5, were labelled by human annotators as *Teacher Class Interactions* given they are indicating a guidance to the class. However, those excerpts also include details about activity duration which can also be interpreted as *Announcements to class* as coded by the machine. E6 excerpt was automatically labelled as *Teacher Individual Interactions* as the transcript misses details about the context of teachers' actions, e.g., teacher was talking to the whole class. Finally, E1 and E4 excerpts indicate a clear disagreement.

E7 was coded as *Announcements To Class* by the human annotators while automatic code assigned was *Teacher Class Interactions*. The video recording indicated that teacher noticed many students have not finished the CSCL activity within the allocated duration of a certain script phase (i.e., evaluating/rating answers from group members). However, the teacher wanted to motivate those students to finish the task before the script moves to the next phase. Therefore, humans have labelled E7 excerpt as *Announcements To Class* given that it is related to the phase transition of the CSCL script. However, the label *Teacher Class Interactions* is also possible as the excerpt can be interpreted as general

Table 4. Human coding vs. machine coding.

No	Excerpt	Human Code	Machine Code
E1	Ok many of you have already submit it	Teacher Class Interactions	Announcements To Class
E2	So you have the time here one minute to go	Teacher Class Interactions	Announcements To Class
E3	I gave you one more minute	Teacher Class Interactions	Announcements To Class
E4	Now it is not individual answers but group answers	Teacher Class Interactions	Announcements To Class
E5	I can give you one extra minute but not more	Teacher Class Interactions	Announcements To Class
E6	Yes!	Teacher Class Interactions	Teacher Individual Interactions
E7	Remember to click the rating button so rating is submitted	Announcements To Class	Teacher Class Interactions
E8	Ok now we have the winning answers	Teacher Perception	Announcements To Class
E9	Yes?	Teacher Individual Interactions	Teacher Class Interactions

guidance to the class about the CSCL activity and the text transcript does not capture teacher's action in detail.

E8 was coded as *Teacher Perception* by the human annotators as the video recording indicated that teacher observed the status of the activity by looking into a student's mobile device. However, such information was missing in our text transcript and may have created a difficult classification task for the machine.

Finally, as indicated in the video recording excerpt E9, "Yes?" was a conversation between a teacher and an individual student to confirm that the student understood the CSCL activity. However, again whether this action was directed to an individual or to the whole class is missing in the textual description, which led to misclassification.

5 Discussion

Considering our research question *How well a fine-tuned GPT-3 model codes text data when compared to other baseline classical machine learning models?* the findings of the study indicated that GPT-3 models outperformed the baseline classical ML approaches, but the limitations of the transcripts have also led to misclassifications. The findings of the study should be taken with caution as it is a first exploration with an input dataset only consisting of 328 excerpts that was also imbalanced considering the four codes. Class imbalance and relatively small sample size influences the accuracy of classification models.

In particular, the GPT-3 (curie) model with a temperature value of 0.5 reached the upper limit of moderate agreement (range 0.60–0.79). Although GPT-3 (davinci) model was considered more robust and with higher quality, this model did not reach the best agreement for our task. A possible explanation for the higher performance of the GPT-3 (curie) model might be due to the nature of the classification task. For instance, as mentioned in [17] GPT-3 (curie) model is suitable for text classification. Although a deep analysis using explainability and/or a deep understanding of the architecture of the pre-trained model is required to understand the differences in the performance of the models, unfortunately, it is not possible at present due to the lack of transparency of the models. We also found that fine-tuning the parameters played an important role in improving classification accuracy. The process of fine-tuning helped to achieve better performance as we used a pre-trained model and updated the model weights by training it for a specific task using a supervised learning approach. Other approaches may be applicable, such as Zero-shot learning that leverages the model's prior knowledge of the problem domain and the descriptions provided for the unknown categories without needing to depend on labelled datasets.

Moreover, based on the disagreements between human and machine coding (as presented in Table 4), it is evident that the focus of teachers' actions e.g., whether they are focusing on individual students or addressing the whole class, are not explicitly indicated in the textual transcripts. On the one hand, it outlines a limitation of the textual transcripts that we used, which did not capture in detail teachers' orchestration actions. On the other hand, it indicates the importance of including such contextual information in the transcripts and multimodal observations to improve the accuracy of automatic data coding.

Finally, it should also be noted that fine-tuning GPT-3 models involved a payment and as 'black box' models it is not possible to explain the model's decisions. Currently, the API function used to extract the *logprobs* of the predictions from GPT API is not available (always returns null values), this prevents further tests from assessing the confidence of the results.

6 Conclusions and Future Work

This study explored the use of ML techniques to automatically code textual transcripts that depicted teachers' orchestration actions in classroom CSCL situations. The main contributions of the study are twofold. First, we developed ML classifiers for coding teachers' orchestration actions that reached a moderate agreement between manual and machine coding even with relatively less amount of training data. Second, we have shown that GPT-3 models (also tested with different values for *temperature* parameter) can outperform baseline classical ML models for text data coding. We think that the technical details provided in this study regarding fine-tuning the relatively new GPT-3 models may inform future research related to automatic coding of textual transcripts. Moreover, the lessons learnt during this exploratory study regarding the limitations associated with the textual transcripts that miss contextual information could inform future research dealing with qualitative research that involves observing classroom discourse.

In the future, we are planning to use other advanced models such as GPT-4 and other LLMs e.g., Bard, in order to compare the performances of those models to GPT-3 [21, 22]. Moreover, how changing the values of other hyperparameters (e.g., *Top p* that controls diversity via nucleous sampling, frequency penalty, presence penalty [6]) influence the performance of the models can be tested apart from *temperature* parameter, as well, adding more data for the training step in order to achieve a higher level of agreement. Finally, prompt engineering has received a lot of attention with the recent advances of LLMs. Prompt engineering involves understanding how different prompts can impact the quality of the results [23] and how some current techniques such as *few shots prompting* or *chain of thought prompting* can improve the final outputs. We anticipate that prompt engineering is of importance in the context of this study and in educational research in general given the limited size of manually labelled datasets available to train ML classifiers. In such situations prompt engineering may facilitate to obtain improved results using zero-shot learning.

Acknowledgments. This work has been partially funded by AEI/10.13039/501100011033 (PID2020-112584RB-C33) and (PLAWB00322) and the Department of Research and Universities of the Government of Catalonia (SGR 00930). DHL (Serra Hunter) also acknowledges the support by ICREA under the ICREA Academia programme. IA acknowledges the support by National Education Lab AI, Radboud University.

References

1. Creswell, J.W., Creswell, J.D.: Research Design: Qualitative, Quantitative, and Mixed Methods Approaches, 4th edn. Sage Publications, Thousand Oaks (2017)
2. Johnson, R.B., Onwuegbuzie, A.J.: Mixed methods research: a research paradigm whose time has come. Educ. Res. **33**(7), 14–26 (2004)
3. O'Connor, C., Joffe, H.: Intercoder reliability in qualitative research: debates and practical guidelines. Int. J. Qual. Methods **19**, 1609406919899220 (2020)
4. Dowell, N., Kovanović, V.: Modeling educational discourse with natural language processing. In: Handbook of Learning Analytics, 2nd edn. (2022)
5. Amarasinghe, I., Hernández-Leo, D., Ulrich Hoppe, H.: Deconstructing orchestration load: comparing teacher support through mirroring and guiding. Int. J. Comput. Support. Collab. Learn. **16**(3), 307–338 (2021)
6. OpenAI. GPT3. https://platform.openai.com/docs/models/overview. Accessed 12 Apr 2023
7. Rose, C., et al.: Analyzing collaborative learning processes automatically: exploiting the advances of computational linguistics in computer-supported collaborative learning. Int. J. Comput. Support. Collab. Learn. **3**, 237–271 (2008)
8. Erkens, G., Janssen, J.: Automatic coding of dialogue acts in collaboration protocols. Int. J. Comput. Support. Collab. Learn. **3**, 447–470 (2008)
9. Kovanović, V., et al.: Towards automated content analysis of discussion transcripts: a cognitive presence case. In: Proceedings of the Sixth International Conference on Learning Analytics & Knowledge, pp. 15–24 (2016)
10. Cai, Z., Siebert-Evenstone, A., Eagan, B., Shaffer, D.W., Hu, X., Graesser, A.C.: nCoder+: a semantic tool for improving recall of nCoder coding. In: Advances in Quantitative Ethnography: First International Conference, ICQE 2019, pp. 41–54 (2019)

11. Flor, M., Andrews-Todd, J.: Towards automatic annotation of collaborative problem-solving skills in technology-enhanced environments. J. Comput. Assist. Learn. **38**(5), 1434–1447 (2022)
12. Li, Z., Xie, H., Wang, M., Wu, B., Hu, Y.: Automatic coding of collective creativity dialogues in collaborative problem solving based on deep learning models. In: 15th International Conference on Blended Learning: Engaging Students in the New Normal Era, pp. 123–134 (2022)
13. Nazaretsky, T., Mikeska, J.N., Beigman Klebanov, B.: Empowering teacher learning with AI: automated evaluation of teacher attention to student ideas during argumentation-focused discussion. In: Proceedings of the 13th International Conference on Learning Analytics & Knowledge, pp. 122–132 (2023)
14. Jensen, E., Pugh, S.L., D'Mello, S.K.: A deep transfer learning approach to modeling teacher discourse in the classroom. In: Proceedings of the 11th International Conference on Learning Analytics & Knowledge, pp. 302–312 (2021)
15. Suresh, A., et al.: Using transformers to provide teachers with personalized feedback on their classroom discourse: the TalkMoves application. arXiv preprint arXiv:2105.07949 (2021)
16. Brown, T., et al.: Language models are few-shot learners. In: 34th Conference on Neural Information Processing Systems (NeurIPS 2020), pp. 1877–1901 (2020)
17. Microsoft Azure. OpenAI documentation. https://learn.microsoft.com/en-us/azure/cognitive-services/openai/. Accessed 12 Apr 2023
18. Saif, H., Fernandez, M., He, Y., Alani, H.: On stopwords, filtering and data sparsity for sentiment analysis of twitter. In: 9th International Conference on Language Resources and Evaluation (LREC 2014), pp. 810–817 (2014)
19. Pedregosa, F., et al.: Scikit-learn: machine learning in Python. J. Mach. Learn. Res. **12**, 2825–2830 (2011)
20. McHugh, M.L.: Interrater reliability: the kappa statistic. Biochemia Medica **22**(3), 276–282 (2012)
21. GPT4. https://openai.com/research/gpt-4. Accessed 12 Apr 2023
22. Bard Experiment. https://bard.google.com. Accessed 12 Apr 2023
23. Learn prompting. https://learnprompting.org/docs/intro/. Accessed 12 Apr 2023

What Makes Problem-Solving Practice Effective? Comparing Paper and AI Tutoring

Conrad Borchers(✉), Paulo F. Carvalho, Meng Xia, Pinyang Liu, Kenneth R. Koedinger, and Vincent Aleven

Carnegie Mellon University, Pittsburgh, PA 15213, USA
{cborcher,pcarvalh,aleven}@cs.cmu.edu, {mengxia, pinyangl}@andrew.cmu.edu, koedinger@cmu.edu

Abstract. In numerous studies, intelligent tutoring systems (ITSs) have proven effective in helping students learn mathematics. Prior work posits that their effectiveness derives from efficiently providing eventually-correct practice opportunities. Yet, there is little empirical evidence on how learning processes with ITSs compare to other forms of instruction. The current study compares problem-solving with an ITS versus solving the same problems on paper. We analyze the learning process and pre-post gain data from N = 97 middle school students practicing linear graphs in three curricular units. We find that (i) working with the ITS, students had more than twice the number of eventually-correct practice opportunities than when working on paper and (ii) omission errors on paper were associated with lower learning gains. Yet, contrary to our hypothesis, tutor practice did not yield greater learning gains, with tutor and paper comparing differently across curricular units. These findings align with tutoring allowing students to grapple with challenging steps through tutor assistance but not with eventually-correct opportunities driving learning gains. Gaming-the-system, lack of transfer to an unfamiliar test format, potentially ineffective tutor design, and learning affordances of paper can help explain this gap. This study provides first-of-its-kind quantitative evidence that ITSs yield more learning *opportunities* than equivalent paper-and-pencil practice and reveals that the relation between opportunities and learning gains emerges only when the instruction is effective.

Keywords: intelligent tutoring systems · learning curve analysis · mathematics education

1 Introduction

While the COVID-19 pandemic has been a driving force for increased technology use in education, it is an open question to what degree post-pandemic education will be characterized by a "return to normal" or by a reform of past practices with greater technology use [1]. Therefore, it is worthwhile to better understand when technology is most useful, for example, in helping students learn. To address this need, we conducted a classroom study comparing a key TEL system against a representative non-TEL alternative: an intelligent tutoring system (ITS) versus paper.

The original version of the chapter has been revised. A correction to this chapter can be found at https://doi.org/10.1007/978-3-031-42682-7_75

O. Viberg et al. (Eds.): EC-TEL 2023, LNCS 14200, pp. 44–59, 2023.
https://doi.org/10.1007/978-3-031-42682-7_4

Intelligent tutoring systems [2], one form of TEL, are increasingly used in educational practice (MATHia, ALEKS, ASSISTments, iReady) [3–6]. These systems support the deliberate practice of challenging cognitive skills. Many scientific studies confirm the overall effectiveness of ITSs and curricula with ITSs, relative to other TEL and non-TEL environments [7–9]. Scientific studies have also revealed why ITSs are effective, particularly through (a) step-level feedback and hints within problems that respond to individual learners' strategies and errors [9–11] and (b) individualized mastery learning based on the assessment of individual knowledge growth [12]. Yet, ITSs have not always been found to be effective [13–15].

As pen-and-paper practice continues to be prominent in K-12, it is worthwhile to compare tutor practice to paper practice to better understand factors affecting learning in ITSs and math problem-solving practice. Yet, there is a dearth of studies that elucidate practice differences between ITS and paper. Instead, comparisons of ITSs against non-TEL controls have often focused on comparing curricula with varying math content and instructional activities [16] or only compared learning gain or grade outcome differences [17, 18]. What is lacking is a comparison that measures learning process differences next to outcomes. Such a process-level comparison might yield insight into the differential learning affordances of paper and ITS practice. More broadly, it may inform when, how, and for what instructional content the affordances of an ITS, versus those of paper, might be most helpful for learners. Problem-solving on paper represents a lower level of instructional assistance [19] compared to ITSs' assistance (step-level tutoring, individualized mastery learning). The lower level of paper assistance may make it harder for students to complete steps successfully and may slow them down. Further, working on paper, students could skip steps (i.e., make omission errors), reducing the number of successful practice opportunities. Then again, paper practice might have unexpected affordances for learning, for example, freedom in strategy choice. Conversely, high assistance (as in an ITS) may have certain costs. For example, it might open the door to students' gaming-the-system, that is, systematic attempts to get problem steps right by exploiting features in the software that aim to support learning [20].

Process-level data is likely to help understand these differences better. A key theoretical assumption that has emerged from past ITS research is that *eventually-correct steps* are instrumental in student learning from deliberate practice [12, 21, 36]. Following past research, we consider a competency to be learned as comprising multiple Knowledge Components (KCs) [22]. We then consider a "practice opportunity" to be attempts to complete a step in a practice problem that "exercises" one or more KCs, including any feedback or instruction toward completing that step. Such opportunities help students learn and refine the KC(s) needed to perform that step [23]. A practice opportunity is considered successful if the student eventually gets it right, with or without help (e.g., hints or feedback). To the best of our knowledge, no study has rigorously compared eventually-correct steps learning gain differences between ITS and paper practice (or other forms of non-TEL learning) for matched content. We do so using a representative ITS, Mathtutor [24] as a platform. Specifically, the current study tests the following research hypotheses:

- H1: Problem-solving practice with an ITS yields greater learning gains than doing the same problems on paper due to the higher assistance in an ITS.

- H2: Working on paper, students have fewer eventually-correct KC opportunities, compared to working in an ITS, due to its high assistance.
- H3: The number of eventually-correct steps relates positively to learning gains in both conditions.

2 Method

2.1 Sample and Experimental Design

We conducted a classroom experiment at a suburban school in the United States, with 97 ninth-grade students across seven classes and three teachers participating. The study took place during students' regular mathematics class periods. It employed a within-subject design with tutor and paper practice alternating in a crossover fashion such that each student experienced both conditions [25] (see Fig. 1). For each math content unit, classes were assigned to conditions such that approximately half the students solved problems using the tutoring software first, and the other half used paper first. The sequence of problem units was held constant. We opted for this design to minimize the effects of individual differences on the outcome, avoid unfairness from unequal conditions, and increase statistical power.

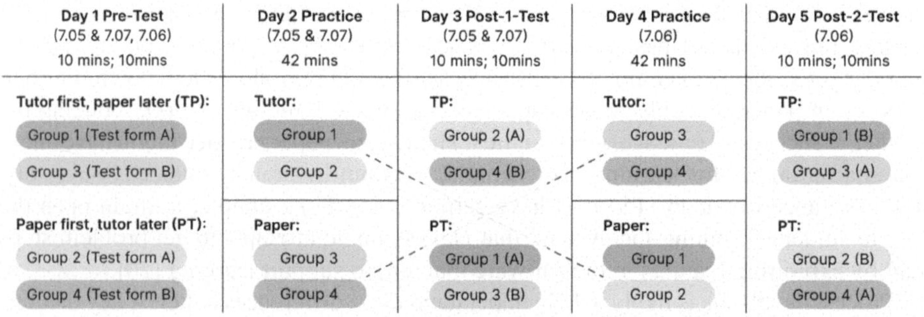

Fig. 1. Schematic representation of the experimental setup with three linear graph practice units 7.05, 7.06, and 7.07 across test item counterbalancing conditions A and B.

2.2 Procedure

In all, the study lasted five days. On the first day, two research team members gave each class a 10-min introduction to the tutoring software (described in Sect. 2.3, see Fig. 2). On days one, three, and five, the students took a 20-min pre-test, post-1-test, and post-2-test (see Fig. 1). Every student took each of the three tests in two different formats. Students worked on one test format (tutor or paper, as described below) for 10 min, then switched to the other for the remaining 10 min. During the practice session on days two and four, students solved math either with the tutor or on paper for the entire 42-min period. The post-test afterward (i.e., post-1-test on day three and post-2-test on day five) had items for just that content.

We asked the teachers to follow their usual instructional practices as closely as possible during the practice and test sessions. Based on our informal observations, teachers actively moved around the classroom in some classrooms and provided guidance and motivation. In other classrooms, teachers remained seated at their desks, offering guidance whenever students sought help. In the tutor condition, we (informally) noticed that students asked more questions and received more teachers' assistance. This was primarily due to students' unfamiliarity with the tutor or technical issues. Students were allowed to use calculators in all sessions. On paper, students could work in any order or omit any problems (though omitted steps were considered incorrect on the test). In the tutor, the system determined problem order; students needed to complete one problem before advancing to the next. During practice, correctness on all steps was mandatory for proceeding to the next problem.

2.3 Materials: Tests, Tutoring Software, and Paper Practice

Over the two practice days, students practiced problems on linear graphs. From the ITS employed in the study, Mathtutor, we selected three problem sets: 7.05 Graph Interpretation I & 7.07 Graph Interpretation II, and 7.06 Problem Solving, Equations, and Graphs I. The 7.05 problem set focused on quantitative interpretation of graphs by translating given lines to numerical x-y points in a table. Problem set 7.07 consisted of qualitative graph interpretation of relationships between multiple linear graphs. Problem set 7.06 focused on linear graph plotting, deriving the symbolic formula, and using the line to infer an x-value for a given y-value. We devoted one practice period to 7.05 and 7.07 together and one to 7.06, a problem set representing more work. During practice, the tutor (see Fig. 2, left) offered step-by-step guidance through hints, correctness feedback, and feedback messages on errors. Furthermore, the tutor displayed a skill bar panel to students representing their mastery of individual KCs. During the computer-based tests, the guidance from the tutoring software was disabled; what was left was the problem-solving interface without hints, feedback, or skill bars. Each test included two problems per practice unit (7.05, 7.06, and 7.07) and was of the same type as practice problems.

We developed an analogous exercise on paper for each tutored problem. We consulted with the participating teachers regarding different exercise designs to simulate the students' default seatwork without feedback (i.e., working independently at desks) as closely as possible while generating equivalent problem-solving steps across tutor and paper for a fair comparison. An example problem from one of the tutor problem sets and its adaptation to paper are shown in Fig. 2.

We created two test forms, A and B, with isomorphic problems (i.e., same problem type as the practice problems), so students would not see the same test items twice. We counterbalanced the test forms across the pre-test, post-1-test, and post-2-test (i.e., we randomly assigned periods to either the A-B-B or B-A-A sequence of forms on these respective tests; note that the two post-tests together covered the same range of math content as the pre-test). In addition, each test was done partly on paper and partly in the tutor to control for the effects of matching practice and test environment. The test format order was also counterbalanced.

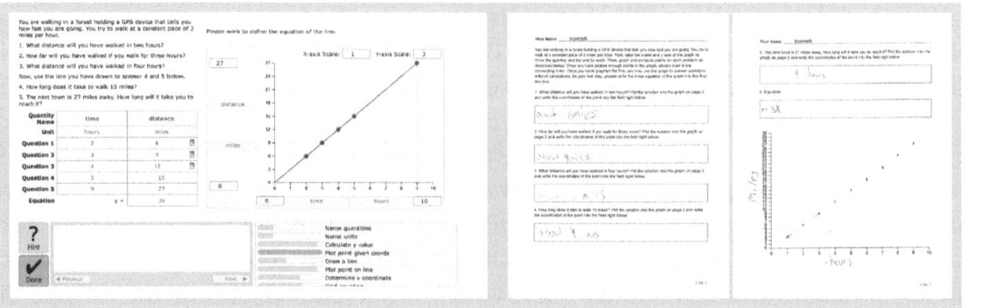

Fig. 2. Tutor version (left) and paper (right) with example student responses of a tutor problem from problem set 7.06 Problem Solving, Equations, and Graph 1.

2.4 Data Preprocessing

We analyzed the work on the exercises on paper through a novel approach of entering the paper solutions into the tutoring software; doing so generates log data comparable to that used to analyze the student's work with the tutoring software [26]. Importantly, the tutoring system evaluates the correctness of the student's steps. This way, we can analyze process data in both conditions using log data.

Two research assistants entered the students' paper responses to both test and practice items into the corresponding problem screens in the tutoring software. The order of multiple attempts at a step on paper cannot always be determined from paper responses, so coders were instructed only to enter the attempt in the tutor that they perceived to be the student's final attempt (i.e., only one attempt per step) into the tutor. In this way, to not bias the experiment in favor of the tutor, the student would get credit for self-correcting on paper. The agreement between the two coders was 93.4% based on the coding of the paper test data. Given this high agreement, we present results based on the inputs of one of the two coders in this study.

2.5 Analysis Methods

We analyze tutor log data, data from paper practice, and test data, collected partly in computer-based format and partly on paper, in terms of problem steps, which, following standard practice in the field of Educational Data Mining [23], we define as actions in the tutor interface. These include, for example, entering unit labels in a designated text field, plotting points in a graph, or selecting answers to multiple-choice questions or explanations from a menu. The tutoring system maps steps to KCs as part of its normal operation [27]. Thus, each step is considered an opportunity to apply a particular KC.

To analyze our test data results and H1 (learning gain differences across conditions), we restrict our sample to the students present during both the pre- and post-test of the respective practice section ($N = 81$ for 7.05 & 7.07; $N = 82$ for 7.06). On tests, only the last step attempts were evaluated, and steps without responses were evaluated as errors, including steps of problems that had not been started. This procedure yielded a $2 \times 3 \times 2$ design of Practice Condition (paper vs. tutor practice), Unit (7.05 vs. 7.06 vs. 7.07), and Test Format (interface alignment vs. interface transfer). We conducted an Anova with

Condition and Unit as between-subject factors and Test Format as a within-subjects factor. Learning gain functioned as the dependent variable, which we operationalized as the difference in pre-to-post step correctness averages. Two-sided t-tests were employed for post-hoc comparisons, dividing the critical threshold ($\alpha = .05$) by the number of comparisons.

To test H2 (fewer eventually-correct practice opportunities during paper practice), we included all students present on day two ($N = 90$) or day four ($N = 93$). For each tutor and paper practice unit, we compute, per student, the number of attempted steps, eventually-correct steps based on last step attempts, and the percentage of correct first attempts. To capture hypothesized interface differences between ITS and paper, we aggregated the average step frequency of gaming-the-system behaviors in the tutor (i.e., dividing the number of steps where gaming-the-system was detected by the total number of steps). We employed a detector validated on data from Cognitive Tutor Algebra. The detector takes into account rapid attempts and hint use in the tutor, among others, and is further described in [28]. Furthermore, we aggregated the average number of omission errors on paper per unit. We further analyzed students' knowledge growth on each KC during practice using the AFM model, a logistic regression model commonly used to analyze log data from tutoring systems [29]. This model provides parameter estimates for the initial ease and the learning rate per KC by estimating the log odds of correct steps (i.e., on first attempts) as a function of the opportunity count for the KC being used at the step. Using the tutoring system's KC model, we fit and compare AFM for each of the three problem sets (i.e., 7.05, 7.06, and 7.07). We fit the model separately for paper and tutor logs to estimate learning rates and intercepts averaged by unit and practice condition. Omission errors on paper were treated as learning opportunities.

For H3 (associations between eventually-correct steps and gains), we use the same sample as for H1. We test our hypothesis that eventually-correct steps relate to learning gain via correlation tests. We conduct automated feature selection via stepwise regression to further explore the associations between learning process measures aggregated on the student-level and gain. *AIC*-based backward search was employed to select factors of our experiment (i.e., Condition, Unit, and Test Format), omission errors, and gaming-the-system. The condition factor controls for the absence of gaming-the-system on paper and step omissions in the tutor (coded as 0).

3 Results

3.1 Learning Gain Differences Between Tutor and Paper (H1)

We start by investigating the test scores across measurement points, conditions, and units (Table 1). The learning gains students exhibited in both the tutor and the paper conditions were statistically significant (see Table 2): tutor, $t(281) = 2.76$, $p < .001$, paper, $t(287) = 7.94$, $p < .001$. The gains were also statistically significant for each of the units separately: 7.05, $t(189) = 4.22$, $p < .001$, 7.06, $t(189) = 4.84$, $p < .001$, and 7.07, $t(189) = 9.75$, $p < .001$.

To test whether problem-solving practice with an ITS yields greater learning gains than problem-solving practice on paper (H1), we looked at the main effect of Condition on learning gain (see Table 2). Contrary to H1, this main effect was not significant, $F(1,$

Table 1. Test scores across measurement points and units broken out by condition.

Unit	Paper/Pre	Paper/Post	Tutor/Pre	Tutor/Post
7.05	24.06%	34.52%	25.46%	33.91%
7.06	12.87%	18.9%	11.62%	24.96%
7.07	3.00%	29.53%	3.87%	21.13%

Table 2. Anova table of learning gains across Conditions (paper vs. tutor practice) x Unit (7.05 vs. 7.06 vs. 7.07) x Test Format (interface alignment vs. transfer).

Effect	F	p	η2
Intercept	174.14	<.001	0.18
Condition	5.30	0.023	0.01
Unit	15.61	<.001	0.04
Test Format (Alignment/Transfer)	8.71	0.003	0.02
Condition: Unit	5.28	0.006	0.01
Condition: Test Format	0.61	0.435	0.00
Unit: Test Format	1.65	0.194	0.01
Condition: Unit: Test Format	0.41	0.665	0.00

222) = 0.40, $p = .526$. Overall, learning gains of students practicing with the tutor ($M = 0.13$, $SD = 0.30$) were similar to those of students practicing on paper ($M = 0.15$, $SD = 0.31$). However, there was a significant interaction between Condition and Unit, $F(2, 222) = 5.28$, $p = .006$. As shown in Fig. 3, this Condition by Unit interaction reflects gains favoring the tutor in 7.06 but favoring paper in 7.07. Our follow-up *t*-tests of the simple main effects indicate no statistically significant condition differences in learning gains for 7.06 or 7.05 ($p's > .069$) but a significant difference in favor of paper for 7.07 ($p = .039$). Nevertheless, given the reliable interaction, it is worth trying to explain, as we do in the discussion, why the tutor is relatively better for 7.06 while paper is relatively better for 7.07.

We note the two other statistically reliable effects in the Anova in Table 2. There was a significant main effect of Test Format, indicating that learning gains were higher when the test format (computer vs. paper) *matched* the practice environment (computer vs. paper) versus when there was no such match and students had to transfer knowledge across formats, $t(567.96) = -3.28$, $p = .001$. Learning gains were nearly twice as high when the test matched the practice format ($M = 0.18$, $SD = 0.30$) than when there was no format match ($M = 0.10$, $SD = 0.30$). All other interactions were not statistically reliable. Thus, there is no evidence, in any Unit, that either tutor or paper produces better transfer to the alternate format than the others.

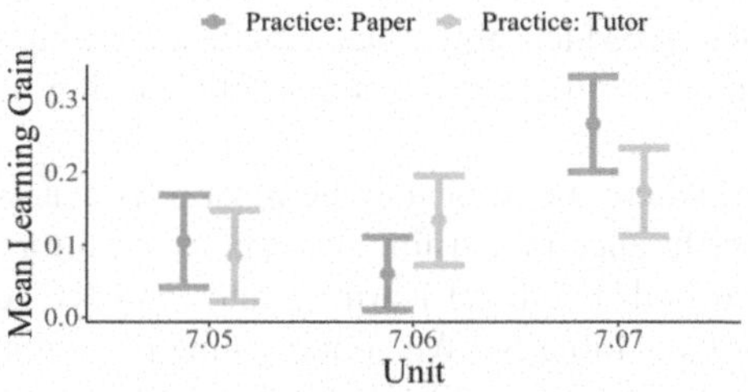

Fig. 3. Relatively greater learning from tutor practice in 7.06 versus from paper practice in 7.07 is illustrated by average learning gains (post minus pre) across Condition and Unit, including 95% confidence intervals.

3.2 Fewer Eventually-Correct Steps on Paper (H2)

We now test the hypothesis that students engaging in problem-solving practice with paper have fewer eventually-correct KC opportunities in the same amount of time than students practicing with the tutor (H2). A process-level measure breakdown during practice is in Table 3.

Table 3. Per-condition process measures averaged across students and units.

Condition	N Steps Attempted	%Corrects on First Attempts	Eventually Correct Steps	%Eventually Correct Steps
Paper	91.55	48.86	44.75	48.89
Tutor	98.56	71.20	97.79	99.22

Consistent with H2, students practicing in the tutor experienced 2.19 (97.79/44.75) times more eventually-correct steps than students practicing on paper, $t(119.76) = 7.57, p < .001$. This ratio ranged from 2.35 for 7.06 to 1.48 for 7.05. Further, students practicing with the tutor reached a correct answer on almost all steps they attempted (99.2% = 97.79/98.56), whereas students practicing with paper reached a correct answer on less than half of the steps they attempted (48.9% = 44.75/91.55). Steps in the tutor on which students did not reach correctness can be explained by students starting but not finishing their last problem. Notably, students working with the tutoring system had a significantly higher accuracy on first attempts, $t(171.62) = 7.62$, $p < .001$.

To better understand potential interface differences during practice, we also report unit-level differences in omission errors on paper, gaming-the-system in the tutors), and learning rates across practice conditions (see Table 4). We found significantly more frequent tutor gaming-the-system behavior per step in 7.07 than in 7.05, $t(68.55) = 8.22$, $p < .001$, and in 7.06, $t(96.54) = 6.60, p < .001$. Furthermore, working on paper, students omitted steps significantly more frequently in 7.06 compared to 7.05, $t(139.57) = 4.67$, $p < .001$, and 7.07, $t(156.92) = 3.76, p < .001$. We also found unit-level differences in the analysis of learning rates across practice conditions (see Table 4). In line with the test results, students exhibited the largest advantage from tutoring (compared to paper) on the 7.06 units according to AFM learning rates. Notably, learning rates were low in both conditions in 7.07. Meanwhile, there was comparable learning between the conditions in 7.05.

To better understand where the tutor may be most effective, we focus on unit 7.06, which had the greatest difference in learning gains between tutor and paper (in favor of the tutor). We compared both KC-level learning rates and KC-level pre-post learning gains across conditions (see Table 5). We found, generally, greater KC-level learning rates ($\Delta\beta$) and KC-level test gains (ΔLG) due to tutor practice compared to paper practice. Students showed the largest test improvements due to tutor practice (i.e., ΔLG in Table 5) on the KCs representing point plotting (15% more learning gain), calculating y coordinates given x coordinates (ΔLG = 13%), and line drawing (ΔLG = 12%). For the line-drawing and point-plotting KCs, these test advantages corresponded to within-practice learning rate advantages (denoted $\Delta\beta$) compared to paper ($\Delta\beta = 0.94$ and $\Delta\beta = 0.70$, respectively). The one substantial exception is the KC for calculating y coordinates given x coordinates, where the tutor produced larger learning gains as measured on the tests, but no learning was observed in the learning rate. This KC definition (i.e., the mapping of this KC to problem steps) may be flawed, or the associated items on the tests require other KCs than those on paper.

Table 4. Mean KC-level AFM tutor learning rates and intercepts, tutor gaming-the-system step frequency, and paper step omissions, broken out by units.

Unit	Learning Rate		Learning Intercept		Gaming-the-system	Omissions
	Tutor	Paper	Tutor	Paper	Tutor	Paper
7.05	0.44	0.49	1.78	−0.08	0.00	21.3
7.06	0.19	−0.20	0.51	0.14	0.08	51.1
7.07	0.04	0.06	0.90	−2.16	0.27	26.72

3.3 Association Between Eventually-Correct Steps and and Learning Gains (H3)

There was no general correlation between the number of eventually-correct steps and learning across the factors of our experiment, $r(568) = 0.00$, $CI = [-0.08, 0.09]$, $p = .902$. Nor was there such a correlation when separating tutor practice ($r(280) = 0.05$, $CI = [-0.06, 0.17]$, $p = .327$) and paper practice ($r(286) = -0.08$, $CI = [-0.19, 0.04]$, $p = .181$). Focusing on the results of the computer test (rather than the combined computer and paper test results), there was a significant positive correlation between the number of eventually-correct steps in practicing with the tutor and gains, $r(139) = 0.20$, $CI = [0.04, 0.36]$, $p = .001$. We further break out our correlation analysis by unit (see Table 6) and find that more eventually-correct steps in the tutor were associated with larger gains in 7.05, $r(90) = 0.19$, $CI = [-0.01, 0.38]$, $p = .067$ and, when evaluated on the tutor test, also in 7.06, $r(47) = 0.42$, $CI = [0.16, 0.63]$, $p = .003$. Conversely, more eventually-correct steps during paper practice related to larger gains in 7.07 when evaluated on paper tests, $r(47) = 0.29$, $CI = [0.01, 0.53]$, $p = .043$.

Table 5. KC-level overview of learning slopes and condition-specific learning gains for each condition (including slope differences $\Delta\beta$ and learning gain differences ΔLG) for 7.06.

Knowledge Component (7.06)	Learning Rate			Pre-Post Learning Gain		
	Tutor	Paper	$\Delta\beta$	Tutor	Paper	ΔLG
Plot Points given Coordinates	0.17	−0.53	0.70	16.33%	1.06%	15.26%
Calculate Y given X	−0.07	−0.05	−0.01	20.07%	7.45%	12.62%
Draw a Line	0.55	−0.39	0.94	19.39%	7.45%	11.94%
Name Quantities	0.09	−0.64	0.73	5.26%	1.52%	3.74%
Find Equation	0.51	0.07	0.44	15.31%	12.77%	2.54%
Name Units	0.12	0.20	−0.08	6.68%	5.89%	0.79%
Determine X off Point	0.00	−0.04	0.04	14.29%	15.96%	-1.67%

Table 6. Correlation tests between the number of eventually-correct steps and learning gain broken out by unit and transfer condition, including significance levels.

Unit	Tutor Practice			Paper Practice		
	Tutor Test Gain	Paper Test Gain	Overall Gain	Tutor Test Gain	Paper Test Gain	Overall Gain
7.05	0.34*	0.09	0.19	0.21	0.14	0.15
7.06	0.42**	−0.23	0.04	−0.28	0.02	−0.10
7.07	−0.10	0.20	0.04	−0.18	0.29*	0.05

$p < 0.1$, * $p < .05$, ** $p < .01$, *** $p < .001$..

To better understand what process data features predict pre-to-post learning gains, we performed an automatic feature selection process described in Sect. 2.5. Of the non-process features (those in Table 2), the Unit and Test Format features were selected as significant control variables. Adjusting for these controls, the selected models indicated that gaming-the-system (in the tutor practice) and omission errors (in the paper practice) were significantly negatively associated with learning gain, $\beta = -0.14$, $p = .006$ and $\beta = -0.13$, $p = .012$, respectively. Students experienced approximately 0.13 *SD* lower learning gains per additional standard deviation in omission errors or per-step gaming-the-system frequency.

4 Discussion

We present a novel investigation of the relative benefits and limitations of deliberate practice with a computer-based intelligent tutoring system versus on paper. We measured learning gains with pre- and post-tests on both paper and computer. Our experimental method involved identical practice and test problems on paper and tutor with process-level analyses of practice opportunities across interfaces. To our knowledge, this comparison is a first of a kind.

4.1 Why Was Tutoring not Generally Better Than Paper?

The hypothesis that a tutoring system, with its step-level feedback and other guidance, would yield better learning than paper practice (H1) was not confirmed. We saw an increase in performance in all practice conditions, whether done on paper or in the tutor, but not an overall significant effect of condition. We did, interestingly, find a significant interaction between tutor unit and condition such that students learned more from the tutor in the 7.06 unit on graphing linear equations, (significantly) more from paper in the 7.07 unit on qualitative graph interpretation, the same in the 7.05 unit on quantitative graph interpretation. Why did we not find a general tutor advantage? We discuss three possible explanations.

Before doing so, it is worth emphasizing that had our study been done only on unit 7.06, we would see results in both outcome and process analyses consistent with the tutoring benefit posed by H1. In this unit, the tutor condition had marginally significant greater learning gains as well as a higher learning rate and more eventually-correct steps during training. Moreover, students on paper showed the largest omission error frequency on 7.06. In contrast, students working in the tutor appeared to receive enough tutor assistance to grapple with challenging steps, reach correctness on problems, and learn from that assistance.

A first possible explanation for the lack of a general tutor advantage is that the selected tutor units may have design flaws that may hide the tutor benefits of immediate feedback, adaptive hints, and problem selection. These units had not previously benefited from data-driven redesign. It is possible that out-of-the-box tutor design with little data-driven redesign may not give students straightforward practice advantages, despite immediate feedback and assistance [35].

A second possible explanation is that students did not have adequate time to get acquainted with the tutoring software. According to our observation notes, the relatively short time frame for students and teachers to get acquainted with the software in this study (which sparked ample teacher-help behavior during tutor practice) might have diminished learning gain returns on intelligent tutoring. This explanation aligns with prior studies highlighting the importance of integrating a tutor's pedagogy into classroom practices [30].

A third possible explanation for the lack of a general tutor advantage is that paper practice may have distinct benefits for specific mathematical or learning contexts, particularly ones that leverage free-form writing and drawing that paper affords [31]. Or conversely, the tutor may have specific disaffordances. We have not identified why qualitative graph interpretation (unit 7.07) might benefit more from paper affordances than graph production (unit 7.06). Indeed, it would seem that graph production would benefit from free-form entry (e.g., in the plotting of points and drawing lines) more so than graph interpretation, but we found just the opposite -- paper benefited graph interpretation (7.07) more so than graph production (7.06).

Perhaps the converse is true: a tutor may have disaffordances in some contexts. Our process analysis provides some support for this explanation. We found that students exhibited significantly more gaming-the-system behavior during tutor practice in the 7.07 unit than in other units. Such behavior, which is known to be associated with worse learning outcomes [32], might have been invoked by menu-based interface elements in 7.07 not found in the other two units. Such menus have been observed to evoke more gaming-the-system [32] as students are tempted to systematically try multiple options and use the tutor's immediate feedback to get a step correct rather than reasoning towards correctness. Consistent with this explanation, students showed the lowest learning rates in the tutor on 7.07. To be sure, the suggestion here is *not* that menu-based input or multiple-choice questions are bad. Afterall, plenty of tutors with menu-based interactions (e.g., where students explain their steps) have demonstrated enhanced student learning (e.g., [33, 34]). Further, students in the paper condition were also given choices to select from. They could have also taken the easy way out by guessing. The availability of feedback in the tutor is thus a crucial part of this explanation. When immediate feedback allows many fast inputs, students are tempted to turn off their thinking. Yet, as indicated in the studies referenced above, menus with immediate feedback are not generally enough to harm learning. We suspect a third factor is needed: the material is particularly hard. This factor was present in 7.07, where the mean pre-test score was only 3.4% and learning rates were low. In sum, menus *and* immediate feedback *and* insufficient prior preparation may evoke a learning disaffordance from tutoring.

4.2 Does Paper Practice Produce Fewer Eventually-Correct Steps?

We found strong evidence for hypothesis H2, in particular, that students are much less likely to produce eventually-correct steps on paper than in the tutor. Indeed, on paper, students achieved less than half the number of eventually-correct steps, in the same amount of time, as students practicing in the tutor. This finding is an important confirmation that feedback and adaptive instruction impact student performance. Tutored students achieved more eventually-correct steps not because they attempted more steps (they did not) but because on the steps they could not solve independently, the tutor aided them through feedback, instructional hints, or a worked example. In contrast, on paper, students had no recourse when they reached steps they could not solve on their own but to omit the step or make a guess. However, students could only partially translate these practice advantages into learning gain advantages. In the next section, we discuss potential reasons why.

4.3 Conditional Association Between Eventually-Correct Steps and Learning

Similar to hypothesis H1, we found that hypothesis H3 was not generally supported but was supported in particular and sensible contexts. Following prior theory [12, 36], H3 predicts that the number of eventually-correct steps a student experiences is associated with their learning gains. We did not find this relationship generally across all tutors, units, and test formats. We did, however, find support for a more specific version of this hypothesis that suggests that in a tutor without a gaming-the-system disaffordance (i.e., not unit 7.07), the number of eventually-correct steps a student experiences is associated with their learning gains in a near-transfer context. This hypothesis is supported by the fact that this correlation was significant in the tutor conditions for units 7.05

and 7.06 when the gains were measured on the matched or near-transfer test (i.e., the computer-based test). Interestingly, the other significant correlation was found for the paper condition in 7.07 on the matched test. In other words, it was found in the Unit where paper affordances for learning were better than the tutor affordances, but again, only on the matched or near-transfer test.

This pattern of findings supports the idea that comparing the strength of associations between learning process and outcome data can help predict and explain when an instructional approach, whether paper-based or ITS-based, is working better. In particular, we propose a general conjecture that for a given instructional approach, the number of eventually-correct steps will be predictive of learning gain if and only if that approach is effective in supporting learning.

To support this conjecture, we delineate potential characteristics of suboptimal instruction in our sample. Next to gaming-the-system the system behavior which was previously found to be associated with worse learning outcomes [32], we found omission errors on paper were negatively related to learning gains. What do these errors represent? Perhaps students with higher prior knowledge may be able to generate their own feedback while practicing on paper, but students with lower prior knowledge may not, disengage on paper, and learn less. Furthermore, students can (and do) skip steps on paper, presumably the steps they do not know how to do, which might be the ones they most need practice on. Indeed we found that students with more omission errors on paper learn less from paper. If these errors indicate where students require assistance most, redesigning tutoring systems based on diagnosed needs at paper assessment could guide deliberate practice. For example, skipped steps may guide focused practice on difficult steps or motivational support.

Why do we not see correlations on mismatched tests assessing cross-format transfer? Perhaps students who pursue more successful practice (i.e., eventually correct steps) opportunities reach better near-transfer learning because of the benefits of deliberate practice. But, to the extent that they hurry to complete repeated practice, they may not be doing sufficient reflection to produce more general learning needed for farther transfer. Further research is needed to see if such explanations work out.

4.4 Why Does This Research Matter for TEL?

The current study compares two ecological conditions of paper and tutor practice to do research relevant to classroom practice. Although students could reach correctness on more than twice as many steps during tutor practice, our data indicate that the relation between eventually-correct steps and learning gains was conditional on the tutor design. As such, our study gathers novel insights into how and when tutoring systems, a popular form of TEL, might be most effective. These insights emerged through a methodology contribution for comparing process-level learning differences between pen-and-paper practice and tutor practice via generating log data for paper responses on matched content. A lesson learned from this study is that comparing TEL against paper on a process level might be more useful than thought (e.g., comparing how interfaces invoke gaming-the-system), suggesting that data-driven tutor redesign is perhaps more urgent than previously thought.

We see three future directions for refining and applying our contribution of entering paper problem-solving responses into analogous ITS interfaces. First, future work may improve our operationalization of learning opportunities, particularly on paper, via additional data streams (e.g., gaze data, think-aloud data), our counting the number of completed steps achieved through gaming-the-system. Second, future work may reduce the cost of paper entry, for example, through computer vision automation. Two coders worked 6–7 weeks full-time to generate log data for this study. Third, future work may investigate how the affordances of TEL and paper practice may be merged. Free-form input on paper could be leveraged for TEL environments to augment the range of inputs and problem-solving strategies. Conversely, mixed reality may bring personalized instruction and reactive feedback to paper practice.

References

1. Kerres, M., Buchner, J.: Education after the pandemic: what we have (not) learned about learning. Educ. Sci. **12**(5), 315 (2022)
2. VanLehn, K.: The behavior of tutoring systems. Int. J. Artif. Intell. Educ. **16**, 227–265 (2006)
3. Ritter, S., Fancsali, S.: MATHia X: the next generation cognitive tutor. In: EDM, pp. 624–625. ERIC (2016)
4. Fang, Y., Ren, Z., Hu, X., Graesser, A.C.: A meta-analysis of the effectiveness of ALEKS on learning. Educ. Psychol. **39**, 1278–1292 (2019)
5. Heffernan, N.T., Heffernan, C.L.: The ASSISTments ecosystem: building a platform that brings scientists and teachers together for minimally invasive research on human learning and teaching. Int. J. Artif. Intell. Educ. **24**, 470–497 (2014)
6. Silva, T.B.: The effects of the i-Ready computer assisted instruction program on the reading and fluency achievement of first graders (2016)
7. du Boulay, B.: Recent meta-reviews and meta–analyses of AIED systems. Int. J. Artif. Intell. Educ. **26**, 536–537 (2016)
8. Kulik, J.A., Fletcher, J.D.: Effectiveness of intelligent tutoring systems: a meta-analytic review. Rev. Educ. Res. **86**, 42–78 (2016)
9. VanLehn, K.: The relative effectiveness of human tutoring, intelligent tutoring systems, and other tutoring systems. Educ. Psychol. **46**, 197–221 (2011)
10. Aleven, V., McLaughlin, E.A., Glenn, R.A., Koedinger, K.R.: Instruction based on adaptive learning technologies. In: Handbook of Research on Learning and Instruction, vol. 2, pp. 522–560 (2016)
11. Corbett, A.T., Anderson, J.R.: Locus of feedback control in computer-based tutoring: impact on learning rate, achievement and attitudes. In: Proceedings of the SIGCHI Conference on Human Factors in Computing Systems, pp. 245–252 (2001)
12. Anderson, J.R., Corbett, A.T., Koedinger, K.R., Pelletier, R.: Cognitive tutors: lessons learned. J. Learn. Sci. **4**, 167–207 (1995)
13. Cabalo, J.V., Ma, B., Jaciw, A.: Comparative Effectiveness of Carnegie Learning's "Cognitive Tutor Bridge to Algebra" Curriculum: A Report of a Randomized Experiment in the Maui School District. Research Report. Empirical Education Inc. (2007)
14. Ritter, S., Kulikowich, J., Lei, P., McGuire, C.L., Morgan, P.: What evidence matters? A randomized field trial of Cognitive Tutor Algebra I. In: Hirashima, T., Hoppe, U., Young, U.U. (eds.) Supporting Learning Flow Through Integrative Technologies, vol. 162, pp. 13–20. IOS Press, Amsterdam (2007)
15. Steenbergen-Hu, S., Cooper, H.: A meta-analysis of the effectiveness of intelligent tutoring systems on K–12 students' mathematical learning. J. Educ. Psychol. **105**(4), 970 (2013)

16. Koedinger, K.R., Anderson, J.R., Hadley, W.H., Mark, M.A.: Intelligent tutoring goes to school in the big city. Int. J. Artif. Intell. Educ. **8**(1), 30–43 (1997)
17. Mendicino, M., Razzaq, L., Heffernan, N.T.: A comparison of traditional homework to computer-supported homework. J. Res. Technol. Educ. **41**(3), 331–359 (2009)
18. Magalhães, P., Ferreira, D., Cunha, J., Rosário, P.: Online vs traditional homework: a systematic review on the benefits to students' performance. Comput. Educ. **152**, 103869 (2020)
19. Koedinger, K.R., Aleven, V.: Exploring the assistance dilemma in experiments with cognitive tutors. Educ. Psychol. Rev. **19**, 239–264 (2007)
20. Baker, R.S., Corbett, A.T., Koedinger, K.R.: Detecting student misuse of intelligent tutoring systems. In: Lester, J.C., Vicari, R.M., Paraguaçu, F. (eds.) ITS 2004. LNCS, vol. 3220, pp. 531–540. Springer, Heidelberg (2004). https://doi.org/10.1007/978-3-540-30139-4_50
21. Anderson, J.R., Conrad, F.G., Corbett, A.T.: Skill acquisition and the LISP tutor. Cogn. Sci. **13**, 467–505 (1989)
22. Koedinger, K.R., Corbett, A.T., Perfetti, C.: The knowledge-learning-instruction framework: bridging the science-practice chasm to enhance robust student learning. Cogn. Sci. **36**, 757–798 (2012)
23. Koedinger, K.R., Baker, R.Sj., Cunningham, K., Skogsholm, A., Leber, B., Stamper, J.: A data repository for the EDM community: the PSLC DataShop. In: Handbook of Educational Data Mining, vol. 43, pp. 43–56 (2010)
24. Aleven, V., McLaren, B.M., Sewall, J.: Scaling up programming by demonstration for intelligent tutoring systems development: an open-access web site for middle school mathematics learning. IEEE Trans. Learn. Technol. **2**, 64–78 (2009)
25. Sibbald, B., Roberts, C.: Understanding controlled trials crossover trials. Bmj **316**, 1719–1720 (1998)
26. Koedinger, K.R., Stamper, J.C., Leber, B., Skogsholm, A.: LearnLab's DataShop: a data repository and analytics tool set for cognitive science. Top. Cogn. Sci. **5**, 668–669 (2013)
27. Koedinger, K.R., Anderson, J.R.: Illustrating principled design: the early evolution of a cognitive tutor for algebra symbolization. Interact. Learn. Environ. **5**, 161–179 (1998)
28. Paquette, L., de Carvahlo, A., Baker, R., Ocumpaugh, J.: Reengineering the feature distillation process: a case study in detection of gaming the system. In: Educational Data Mining 2014 (2014)
29. Cen, H., Koedinger, K., Junker, B.: Learning factors analysis – a general method for cognitive model evaluation and improvement. In: Ikeda, M., Ashley, K.D., Chan, TW. (eds.) ITS 2006. LNCS, vol. 4053, pp. 164–175. Springer, Heidelberg (2006). https://doi.org/10.1007/11774303_17
30. Pane, J.F., McCaffrey, D.F., Slaughter, M.E., Steele, J.L., Ikemoto, G.S.: An experiment to evaluate the efficacy of cognitive tutor geometry. J. Res. Educ. Effect. **3**(3), 254–281 (2010)
31. Anthony, L., Yang, J., Koedinger, K.R.: Towards the application of a handwriting interface for mathematics learning. In: 2006 IEEE International Conference on Multimedia and Expo, pp. 2077–2080 (2006)
32. Huang, Y., et al.: Item response theory-based gaming detection. Int. Educ. Data Min. Soc. (2022)
33. Aleven, V.A., Koedinger, K.R.: An effective metacognitive strategy: learning by doing and explaining with a computer-based cognitive tutor. Cogn. Sci. **26**(2), 147–179 (2002)
34. Atkinson, R.K., Renkl, A., Merrill, M.M.: Transitioning from studying examples to solving problems: effects of self-explanation prompts and fading worked-out steps. J. Educ. Psychol. **95**(4), 774 (2003)
35. Huang, Y., et al.: A general multi-method approach to data-driven redesign of tutoring systems. In: LAK21: 11th International Learning Analytics and Knowledge Conference, pp. 161–172 (2021)

36. Koedinger, K.R., McLaughlin, E.A., Jia, J.Z., Bier, N.L.: Is the doer effect a causal relationship? How can we tell and why it's important. In: Proceedings of the Sixth International Conference on Learning Analytics & Knowledge, pp. 388–397 (2016)

Exploring Indicators for Collaboration Quality and Its Dimensions in Classroom Settings Using Multimodal Learning Analytics

Pankaj Chejara[1(✉)], Luis P. Prieto[2], María Jesús Rodríguez-Triana[1], Adolfo Ruiz-Calleja[1], Reet Kasepalu[1], Irene-Angelica Chounta[3], and Bertrand Schneider[4]

[1] Tallinn University, Tallinn, Estonia
{pankajch,mjrt,adolfo,reetkase}@tlu.ee
[2] Universidad de Valladolid, Valladolid, Spain
luispablo.prieto@uva.es
[3] University of Duisburg-Essen, Duisburg, Germany
irene-angelica.chounta@uni-due.de
[4] Harvard University, Cambridge, MA, USA
bertrand_schneider@g.harvard.edu

Abstract. Multimodal Learning Analytics researchers have explored relationships between collaboration quality and multimodal data. However, the current state-of-art research works have scarcely investigated authentic settings and seldom used video data that can offer rich behavioral information. In this paper, we present our findings on potential indicators for collaboration quality and its underlying dimensions such as argumentation, and mutual understanding. We collected multimodal data (namely, video and logs) from 4 Estonian classrooms during authentic computer-supported collaborative learning activities. Our results show that vertical head movement (looking up and down) and mouth region features could be used as potential indicators for collaboration quality and its aforementioned dimensions. Also, our results from clustering provide indications of the potential of video data for identifying different levels of collaboration quality (e.g., high, low, medium). The findings have implications for building collaboration quality monitoring and guiding systems for authentic classroom settings.

Keywords: Multimodal Learning Analytics · MMLA · Computer-Supported Collaborative Learning · CSCL · Collaboration Quality · Correlation Analysis · Machine Learning · Clustering · Facial Action Units

1 Introduction

Teachers are often expected to orchestrate Computer-Supported Collaborative Learning (CSCL) activities, monitor groups, identify groups who need help, and

O. Viberg et al. (Eds.): EC-TEL 2023, LNCS 14200, pp. 60–74, 2023.
https://doi.org/10.1007/978-3-031-42682-7_5

then offer support. These tasks are difficult for teachers to carry out efficiently in the classroom given their limited time [32], and especially when the number of groups increases [5]. Moreover, the COVID-19 pandemic pushed teachers to design and enact online group activities, which further complicated the aforementioned tasks of orchestrating and monitoring [20]. Since then, the organization of CSCL activities in hybrid settings has become mainstream, raising the need for supporting teachers during those activities.

To reach that goal, researchers have analyzed digital log data from the group's activities to gain insight into collaboration behavior and to develop monitoring systems [5]. However, this log-based analysis offers only a partial understanding of CSCL in classroom settings involving physical and digital spaces of interaction. The need for a more holistic understanding of collaborative learning (& learning in general) has led to the use of additional data sources [10,24]. This field of research is known as Multimodal Learning Analytics (MMLA) [1,17].

To better understand collaboration behavior, MMLA Researchers have used different types of data such as audio, video, eye-gaze, skin-conductance, and body-pose [18,24]. These data have been used with various analysis methods ranging from statistical analysis [2], to unsupervised [13], and supervised machine learning [30,33]. With these methods, MMLA researchers have identified several data features as potential indicators for collaboration behavior [18,24], and shown the feasibility of building automated models for collaboration estimation [3,19,33]. For example, speaking time distribution [18] and physiological synchrony (Directional Agreement) were found as potential indicators for overall collaboration quality [23].

The current state of MMLA research has enabled the development of mirroring systems [29] which provides visualization of the group's activities and their overall quality of collaboration [16]. However, such systems are limited in actionability (i.e., lack of suggestions on potential intervention strategies). Furthermore, such systems do not offer any information on the resultant estimation of collaboration quality which often leaves teachers clueless about what could be done to improve the current situation. Consequently, there is a need to develop guiding systems that can offer actionable feedback to teachers which would require knowledge about underlying dimensions of collaboration quality (refer for more details, Collaboration Intervention Model from [15]).

Certain research studies have explored collaboration quality dimensions using log [5] and audio [19] data. However, these studies along with a majority of current research studies are conducted in controlled settings [24] which allows higher quality data. On the other hand, there are inherent data noise issues when working within *authentic* classroom settings [28]. For example, the use of audio data in such settings is most likely to result in lower-quality data due to background noise. Consequently, there is a need to explore alternate data sources which could be employed in authentic settings for understanding and estimating collaboration quality dimensions.

To address the aforementioned gaps of the lack of research on the exploration of the relationship between *multimodal data and collaboration quality dimensions* in *authentic classroom settings*, we set up the following research questions:

(RQ1) What is the relationship between video-log data and collaboration quality (and its dimensions as per Rummel et al., 2011 [22]) of small groups in authentic classroom settings? **(RQ2)**; To what extent can video-log data features reveal differences in terms of collaboration quality and its dimensions in authentic classroom settings? This paper is structured as follows. Section 2 provides the state-of-the-art MMLA research in CSCL. We then explain the study context, the data collection tool used, the procedure followed to conduct the study, and data features extracted from the data in Sect. 3. Section 4 presents our methods for annotation and analysis, followed by the results and their implications in Sects. 5 and 6, respectively. Finally, we conclude in Sect. 7 with future research work directions.

2 Related Work

The use of MMLA for understanding and modeling collaboration settings has grown significantly in the past decade [6,18,24]. Researchers have shown the potential of multimodal data such as audio, video, eye gaze, and heart rate, towards unraveling the complexity of collaboration [3,19,23,30]. These data have been used in current state-of-the-art research for extracting features, ranging from speaking time [33], turn-taking [3], speech features (e.g., coh-matrix) [21] to facial action units [2,26], emotions [12], distance between hands [30]. Using these features, researchers have explored the relationship between multimodal data and collaboration measures (e.g., collaboration quality [13] or collaborative experience [26]). Several data features have been identified as potential indicators for collaboration, e.g., equal speaking time distribution [18], number of words spoken [21], the distance between participants [30].

There are a few research studies that have even delved deeper and explored collaboration dimensions [4,19]. For example, Pugh et al., [19] showed the potential of language models to detect aspects of collaborative problem solving, i.e., knowledge exchange, and coordination. Similarly, Cai et al., [2] explored the relationship between facial action units and different states of learning as per the ICAP framework during a group-work activity. Hayashi et al., [12] explored relationship between emotions and collaboration quality dimensions. These research studies provide preliminary evidence of the potential of multimodal data to identify underlying dimensions of collaboration.

We identify two research gaps in current MMLA research on understanding collaboration behavior. The first gap is that researchers have seldom investigated authentic classroom settings for understanding collaboration or exploring the relationship between multimodal data and collaboration [6,24]. Consequently, the applicability of knowledge gained (or automated models developed) from research studies conducted in laboratory settings to authentic classroom settings is still in question. The second gap is that the current research focused primarily on high-level collaboration measures (e.g., collaboration quality [33], artifact quality [30]), and despite the rich behavioral and interaction data captured through video, current state-of-art has scarcely used it. Thus, there is a

Table 1. Dataset characteristics

Class	Language	Subject	Groups	Students	Data instances (30s windows)
10th	Estonian	Office work	3	10	193
10th	English	Biology	7	25	88
9th	Estonian	Homeroom teacher lesson	7	24	273
12th	English	Biology	3	10	227

lack of knowledge about the relationship between video data and dimensions of collaboration quality.

3 Study Setup

This section describes the study context, data collection setup & procedure, and data features.

3.1 Context

The study was conducted in Estonian upper secondary school classrooms with four different teachers during biology, office work, and homeroom teacher lessons. The students were mainly of Estonian background. The languages of communication were Estonian and English. There were a total of 69 students in 20 groups. We had to discard the data from 7 groups due to missing video recordings from those groups. Table 1 provides details about the study contexts.

3.2 Activity Tasks

While the specific topic of the activities varied depending on the subject, each lesson had the same structure. This required students to discuss a certain topic face-to-face and write their outcomes in a collaborative text editor (e.g., Etherpad). In the homeroom teacher's lesson, the students were given the task of

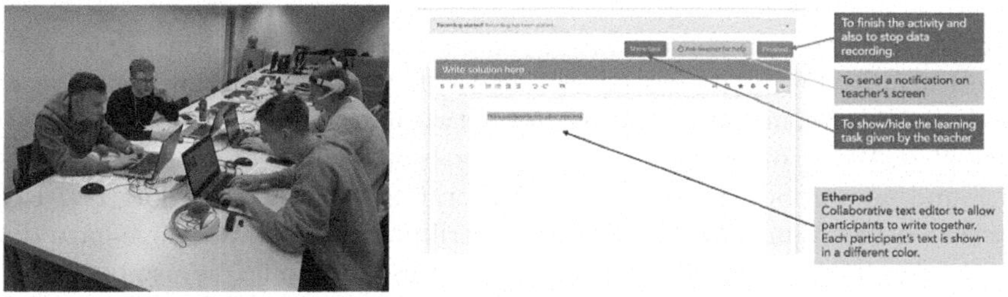

(a) (b)

Fig. 1. (a) Students working on the collaborative activity in the classroom (b) Collaborative activity space in CoTrack planning a class trip involving collaboratively selecting a destination, allocating a budget (travel, meals, accommodation), and creating a schedule for the entire trip. In the office work session, the task involved discussing and synthesizing the process of archiving (e.g., the preparation of the description and the necessity for this, and who the end-user of an archive's description is). In the biology session, the groups were given worksheets that had questions on DNA sequencing and mutation (e.g., on the effect of GTA $\rightarrow$ GTT mutation) to be answered in the collaborative text editor. Figure 1 shows an example of the student arrangement and the collaborative editor used in the activities.

3.3 Data Collection Tool

To carry out the study we used CoTrack[1] [3]. This web-based application offers a collaborative text editor (Etherpad[2]) for students to work on a given task (Fig. 1b). In addition, CoTrack records audio/video using computer's microphone/camera along with log data and process these data in real-time to extract data features (e.g., the number of characters added by a student in the group). These data features are used to generate a dashboard to help teachers monitor the groups' work.

3.4 Procedure

Prior to the research study, a researcher from education science (also a co-author of this paper) co-designed the lesson with the teacher who was to instruct the collaborative activity. The consent was taken from the students in advance of the study (parents' consent was taken in the case of students younger than 18 years). On the day of enactment, the same researcher was also present in the classroom and gave a brief introduction about the research to the students. Following that, the teacher assigned groups to the students who then used CoTrack to work on the given activity collaboratively. The average duration of the activity was approximately 30 minutes.

3.5 Features

We extracted features based on the current state-of-the-art in MMLA for collaborative learning. From the video, we decided to use facial action units because of preliminary evidence of a relationship between action units and collaboration quality [2,7]. We also decided to use head pose as a proxy of eye gaze which has been found as a good indicator for collaboration quality behavior [18]. Previous research has found that head pose contributes 68% towards eye-gaze direction [31]. In addition, we also extracted features that could be used as a proxy for speaking, a widely used feature in MMLA [33]. Due to the limitations of captured video (i.e., recording mainly above shoulder area), we decided not to

[1] https://www.cotrack.website.
[2] https://www.etherpad.org.

extract features, e.g., body posture, hand-movement, and interaction with artefact. We did not use audio due to background noise affecting the audio quality, a frequently reported issue with MMLA research in the classroom [8]. Instead, we used video-based features for the speaking activity. Such vision-based speaking activity features could be useful in authentic classroom settings where audio data is often of a lower quality due to background audio noise. We used mouth region as a proxy for speaking based on computer vision research work focusing on speaking activity detection using image processing [27]. In their research work, the mouth area region (the grey area inside a bounding box around the mouth of the speaker) has been used to distinguish speaking activity from non-speaking activity.

From logs, we extracted simple features, namely the number of characters written or deleted. Our decision was based on research that highlighted individual participation as one of the quantitative key features for collaborative learning [34]. Furthermore, we also found in our previous studies that models based on these log features in addition to aforementioned audio features (i.e., turn-taking, speaking time) performed well on collaboration quality estimation tasks [3,4].

4 Methods

4.1 Annotation

We used Rummel et al., 2011 rating scheme to annotate the collaboration quality [22]. This rating scheme specifies seven dimensions of collaboration quality: argumentation, sustaining mutual understanding, cooperative orientation, knowledge exchange, collaboration flow, individual task orientation, as well as structuring problem solving and time management. We annotated these seven

Table 2. Correlation between multimodal features and collaboration quality (STR: structuring problem solving process and time management, ITO: individual task orientation, CF: collaboration flow, SMU: sustaining mutual understanding, ARG: argumentation, CO: cooperative orientation, KE: knowledge exchange, CQ: collaboration quality, avg: average, sd: standard deviation).

Feature	**Aggregation**		**STR**	**ITO**	**CF**	**SMU**	**ARG**	**CO**	**KE**	**CQ**
	window	group								
AU01	count	avg	−.38	–	–	–	–	–	–	–
AU01	count	sd	−.35	–	–	–	–	–	–	–
Head rotate x−axis	std	avg	–	–	.30	.30	–	–	–	.31
Head rotate y−axis	std	avg	–	.32	–	–	–	–	–	–
Mouth_area	avg	avg	–	.34	.30	–	.31	–	–	.30
Chars add	sum	avg	–	.31	–	–	–	–	–	–
Chars del	sum	avg	–	.31	–	–	–	–	–	–

dimensions for every 30 s time window, as recommended in prior works [3]. Each dimension was assigned a score on a 5-Likert scale [-2 to +2] and added together to compute the overall collaboration quality score. The rating scheme was adapted to the set of activities conducted in this study. The first 10 min of video of a group was coded independently by two researchers and conflict among their scores was discussed. The rating scheme was used to train four MA students who went through two rounds of annotation (one in a group, another independent). After the training, all video recordings were assigned to them for annotation. The inter-rater reliability (Cohen's Kappa = .61) was above a substantial level for all the dimensions.

4.2 Analysis

We performed a Spearman correlation analysis to identify the relationship between multimodal data and collaboration quality dimensions. We used this non-parametric test because the underlying data was not following normal distribution as found in the normality test (Shapiro-Wilk). Next, we used the K-means clustering technique to investigate whether the used features could reveal differences among collaboration quality scores. For clustering, we used the correlated features. To identify the most important features in clustering, we followed the approach proposed in [14]: first, we considered cluster membership as class labels and then trained a random forest model using our features and labels; next, we identified the most important features using the trained random forest model. We used the identified features to interpret the resultant clusters. Finally, we checked the differences in resultant clusters' collaboration quality scores for statistical significance and for that, we used the Kruskal-Wallis test.

5 Results

Relationship Between Video-Log Features and Collaboration Quality (and Its Dimensions). Table 2 reports statistically significant (p-value<.001) correlation measures between video-log features and collaboration quality (and its dimensions) scores. We found that the average frequency of facial Action Unit 1 (AU01), the inner brow raiser, was negatively correlated ($\rho = -.38$) with the structuring problem solving and time management (STR) dimension. We also observed a similar relationship when the standard deviation of AU01 was taken at the group level. That means that as the variation of group members' frequency of inner brow raiser goes higher, a lower rating of STR was observed. In addition to this, we found that variation in vertical head movement[3] was positively correlated with collaboration quality ($\rho = .31$), collaboration flow ($\rho = .30$), and sustaining mutual understanding ($\rho = .30$). We can also notice from the table that variation in horizontal head movement[4] was found to be positively

[3] Head rotation along the x-axis (i.e., moving the head up and down).
[4] Head rotation along the y-axis (i.e., moving the head left and right).

correlated with individual task orientation ($\rho = .32$). The average mouth region area at the group level was found to be positively correlated with argumentation ($\rho = .31$), individual task orientation ($\rho = .34$), collaboration flow ($\rho = .30$), and collaboration quality ($\rho = .30$). We found a positive correlation ($\rho = .31$) between individual task orientation and Etherpad activities (i.e., the number of characters added or deleted).

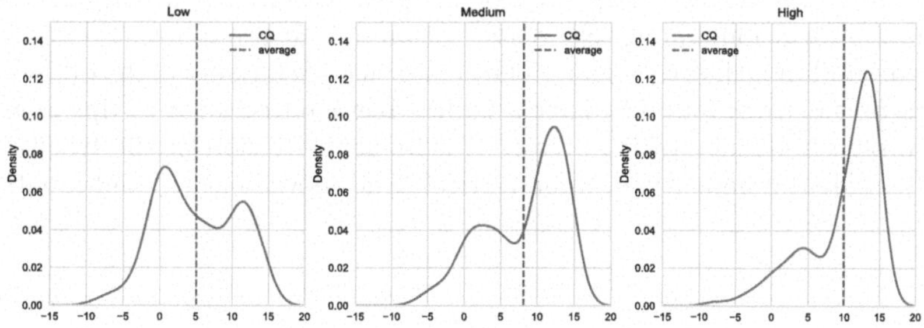

Fig. 2. K-means clusters and distribution of collaboration quality scores of those clusters

Unsupervised Machine Learning Revealing Differences Amongst Students' Group Collaboration Quality Using Multimodal Data. Our results from K-means clustering showed that the resulting clusters had differences in their collaboration quality scores. Figure 2 shows the distribution of collaboration quality scores for each cluster. When comparing with the other two clusters, the first cluster had lower scores for collaboration quality (average CQ score = 5). Therefore, we interpreted the cluster as having low collaboration quality. The third cluster had the highest scores for collaboration quality

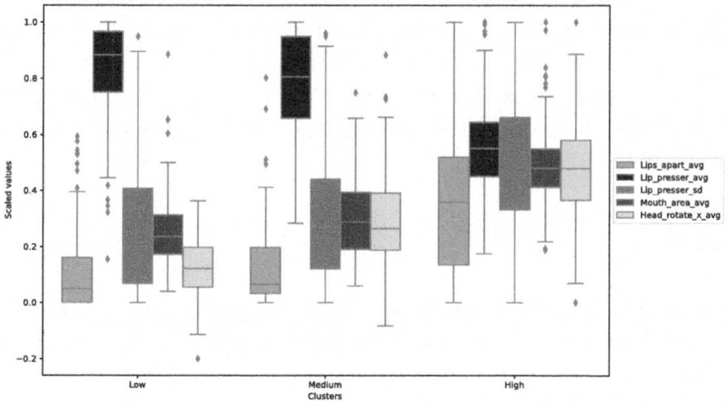

Fig. 3. Cluster-wise distribution of top five important features

(average CQ score = 9.9) among the three, thus, interpreted as having high collaboration quality. The second cluster had intermediate collaboration quality scores (average CQ score = 8.1), therefore we considered it as having medium collaboration quality. We also analyzed clusters obtained from k-means with respect to the scores of collaboration quality dimensions and observed a similar pattern of high, medium, and low collaboration quality. Figure 3 shows the distribution of the top five most important features for resultants clusters. These features were the average frequency of lip presser (AU24), lips apart (AU25) action units, variation among lip presser action unit at group level, vertical head movement, and mouth area region. The cluster with relatively high collaboration quality scores (↑) was found to have a higher average frequency of lips apart (↑), lower average frequency of lip presser (↓), higher variation in the frequency of lip presser (↑), and higher values for vertical head movement (↑) and mouth area region (↑).

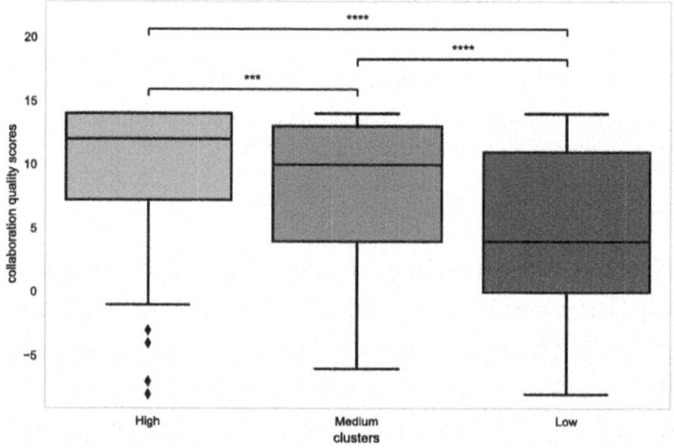

Fig. 4. Post-hoc analysis results (***: p-value ≤ 1.00e-03; ****: p-value ≤ 1.00e-04)

Statistical Significance of Differences in Collaboration Quality Scores of Resultant Clusters. Our results from Kruskal-Wallis test showed that the differences between the three clusters in terms of collaboration quality and its dimensions were of statistical significance (P-value < .001). The posthoc results from Dunn's test also revealed that the pair-wise differences among clusters were statistically significant (Fig. 4).

6 Discussion

6.1 What Is the Relationship Between Multimodal Data Collected and Collaboration Quality (and Its Dimensions) of Small Groups in Authentic Classroom Settings? (RQ1)

Finding 1: *Inner brow raiser (AU01) is negatively correlated with structuring problem solving and time management dimension of collaboration quality.*

The structuring problem-solving dimension involves deciding the strategy for solving the given problem in the group. This might trigger negative emotions (e.g., frustration or confusion) in the group if there are group participants who disagree with the decision. These negative emotions could also be due to the pressure of completing the activity within the given time. Prior research suggested a relationship between inner brow raiser (AU01) and frustration [7]. This might indicate that frustration may appear when groups cannot structure their collaborative activity. This interpretation aligns with previous research on the investigation of the relationship between emotions and dimensions of collaboration quality [12].

Finding 2: *Vertical head movement is positively correlated with collaboration quality, collaboration flow, and sustaining mutual understanding.*
The relationship between higher vertical head movement (i.e., looking up and down) in the group and collaboration quality dimensions could be either due to participants looking at the screen or looking at other group members while discussing. The latter may be an indication of participation. The same feature also correlated with collaboration flow and sustaining mutual understanding. A vertical head movement could also be due to head nods which are found as non-verbal cues for understanding [11]. However, the collaborative activities described in this paper involved the use of Etherpad (a collaborative text editor) which may have caused participants to look at the screen frequently.

Finding 3: *Horizontal head movement is positively correlated with individual task orientation.*
The horizontal head movement (i.e., looking left and right) positively correlated with the individual task orientation dimension. This dimension refers to participants' motivation, externalized as active participation in the activity, and consequently can be measured in terms of participants' contribution towards the problem solution. As the participants were interacting with Etherpad, this might have resulted in looking at the screen. While doing that their head movement in horizontal direction can be explained by looking across the screen and also at others' contributions in Etherpad. Another explanation could be that horizontal head movement may have been caused by participants looking at their group members sitting on their left or right side, depending on their sitting arrangement.

Finding 4: *Mouth area region positively correlates with collaboration quality, argumentation, collaboration flow, and individual task orientation.*
We used this feature (mouth area region) as a proxy for speaking because the increased average value of mouth region pixels can be used as a visual cue for speaking activity [27]. Previous research pointed to speaking time as an indicator of collaboration [21]. Our results confirm that speaking is positively associated with collaboration quality and its underlying dimensions.

Finding 5: *The number of characters written and deleted is positively correlated with individual task orientation dimensions.*
The individual task orientation dimension looks upon individual participation in solving the given problem. This participation could be partially measured by the number of writing actions (e.g., writing or deleting text). This may explain the positive relationship between individual task orientation and quantitative log features.

6.2 To What Extent, Video-Log Data Features Can Reveal Differences in Terms of Collaboration Quality and Its Dimensions in Authentic Classroom Settings? (RQ2)

Finding 6: *K-means clusters of video-log data match three different levels of collaboration quality (high, medium, and low).*
The emerging clusters demonstrated a different distribution of scores of collaboration quality and could be characterized as of high, medium, and low collaboration quality. The high collaboration quality cluster had comparatively higher values for mouth region area, vertical head movement, lips apart action unit, variation in the lip presser action unit, and lower values for lip presser action unit. For low collaboration quality clusters, these values were inverted. The higher value of lips apart and the lower value of lip presser action units in the high collaboration quality cluster could be explained by both negative and positive emotions occurring during group activity [12,26]. Lip presser is often related to the expression of anger [25]. Thus, a higher occurrence of lip presser at the group level may indicate a higher level of anger. However, the higher variation in lip presser action units was observed to have higher collaboration quality scores. This could be explained by the conflicts which usually arise in the group during the activity and which are likely to trigger anger. This situation is unlikely to be resolved if all participants experience the same level of anger. To be resolved, some participants – possibly the ones in a relaxed state – need to mediate the situation. This could explain higher variation in lip presser in the cluster of high collaboration quality scores. The high value of the lips apart action unit could be explained by prior research [2] suggesting that AU25 was observed more frequently in the constructive state than the interactive and passive state (as per ICAP framework). Vertical head movement could be due to students' focusing on Etherpad and their peers causing the up-down head movement. Moreover, the head nods used for acknowledgment and agreement might also cause the up-down head movement. The high value on the mouth area region could indicate more speaking activity in the group. Speaking has previously been found as a potential indicator for collaboration quality [18].

Finding 7: *The scores of the underlying dimension of collaboration quality in resultant K-means clusters also have statistically significant differences.*
Our findings suggest that there were statistically significant differences among clusters in terms of their scores of collaboration quality dimensions. These results

suggest that video data along with log data could be used in authentic classroom settings for collaboration quality (and its dimensions) estimation tasks. For example, vertical head movement during CSCL activities in authentic classroom settings is found to contribute towards differentiating three different levels of collaboration quality scores. Prior research has shown the potential of log data [5] and audio data [4,19] for classifying collaboration quality dimensions. With our findings, we extend those research works and present preliminary evidence over the potential use of video data along with logs for estimating collaboration quality and its dimensions.

6.3 Limitations

The presented study has three main limitations. The first limitation is related to the seating arrangement of students. Due to the nature of the activities and the availability of resources in the school, one session was conducted in a computer lab where participants were sitting side by side. The head movements along the y-axis (looking left and right) may have been caused by participants looking at their group members sitting on their left and right sides. Thus, the found relationship between a head movement along the y-axis and individual task orientation dimension needs further validation. The second limitation is the limited scope of the findings' generalizability. As the participants in the study were upper secondary students mostly of Estonian background, it restricts us from making any claim over the applicability of the research findings on students from a different age or cultural background which may condition their communication and collaboration style. The third limitation is that this paper mainly analyzed all the multimodal features independently and did not utilize interaction between those features in the exploration.

7 Conclusion and Future Work

This paper addresses the current gap in our understanding of the relationship between multimodal (video and log) data and collaboration quality dimensions in authentic classroom settings. We collected data from Estonian classroom CSCL activities and performed correlation analysis to identify relationships between features extracted from data and collaboration quality dimensions. Our results showed that simple features from the video and log data, more concretely inner brow raiser (AU01), mouth region area, vertical head movement (i.e., up-down head movement), and number of characters written could be used in authentic settings as indicators of collaboration quality dimensions (namely structuring problem solving and time management, collaboration flow, argumentation and sustaining mutual understanding). Among these indicators, the features capturing vertical head movement and mouth region area could potentially be used as an overall indicator of collaboration quality in authentic classroom settings. We also provided preliminary evidence on the potential of video data along with the logs in estimating collaboration quality (and its dimensions) using unsupervised machine learning. Future research should verify whether these findings apply to other contexts and can be generalized.

The current MMLA research in CSCL often employs supervised machine learning techniques which require a large amount of data to work with. However, given the need for human resources for data annotation, the final datasets are often of a smaller size. The use of unsupervised learning can help in dealing with the issue of the lack of a large amount of annotated data. With the use of unsupervised machine learning, we foresee a hybrid use of supervised and unsupervised learning techniques to model collaboration behavior with multimodal data also suggested in the prior work [35]. In our future work, we plan to assess the potential of video data for the prediction of collaboration quality and its dimensions utilizing both supervised and unsupervised learning techniques. We will also analyze multiple features together to understand the found relationship better following prior work [9]. We plan to look at the differences in the relationship between multimodal data and collaboration dimensions across a wider range of learning activities, student groups, and education levels.

Acknowledgements. The presented work has been partially funded by the Estonian Research Council's Personal Research Grant (PRG) under grant number PRG1634. It also has been supported by grant RYC2021-032273-I, financed by MCIN/ AEI/ 10.13039/501100011033 and the European Union's "NextGenerationEU/PRTR".

References

1. Blikstein, P., Worsley, M.: Multimodal learning analytics and education data mining: using computational technologies to measure complex learning tasks. J. Learn. Analyt. **3**(2), 220–238 (2016)
2. Cai, Y., Shimojo, S., Hayashi, Y.: Observing facial muscles to estimate the learning state during collaborative learning: a focus on the ICAP framework. In: ICCE 2020–28th International Conference on Computers in Education, Proceedings, vol. 1, pp. 119–126 (2020)
3. Chejara, P., Prieto, L.P., Rodriguez-Triana, M.J., Kasepalu, R., Ruiz-Calleja, A., Shankar, S.K.: How to build more generalizable models for collaboration quality? lessons learned from exploring multi-context audio-log datasets using multimodal learning analytics. In: LAK23: 13th International Learning Analytics and Knowledge Conference, pp. 111–121. LAK2023, ACM, NY, USA (2023)
4. Chejara, P., Prieto, L.P., Ruiz-Calleja, A., Rodríguez-Triana, M.J., Shankar, S.K., Kasepalu, R.: EFAR-MMLA: an evaluation framework to assess and report generalizability of machine learning models in MMLA. Sensors **21**(8), 2863 (2021)
5. Chounta, I., Avouris, N.M.: Towards a time series approach for the classification and evaluation of collaborative activities. Comput. Informatics **34**(3), 588–614 (2015)
6. Chua, Y.H.V., Dauwels, J., Tan, S.C.: Technologies for automated analysis of co-located, real-life, physical learning spaces: where are we now? In: LAK19: 9th International Conference on Learning Analytics & Knowledge, pp. 11–20. LAK19, ACM, NY, USA (2019)
7. Craig, S.D., D'Mello, S., Witherspoon, A., Graesser, A.: Emote aloud during learning with AutoTutor: applying the facial action coding system to cognitive - affective states during learning. Cogn. Emot. **22**(5), 777–788 (2008)

8. Crescenzi-Lanna, L.: Multimodal learning analytics research with young children: a systematic review. Br. J. Edu. Technol. **51**(5), 1485–1504 (2020)
9. Cukurova, M., Luckin, R., Milln, E., Mavrikis, M.: The NISPI framework. Comput. Educ. **116**(C), 93–109 (2018). https://doi.org/10.1016/j.compedu.2017.08.007
10. Di Mitri, D., Schneider, J., Specht, M., Drachsler, H.: From signals to knowledge: a conceptual model for multimodal learning analytics. J. Comput. Assist. Learn. **34**(4), 338–349 (2018)
11. Duncan, S.: Some signals and rules for taking speaking turns in conversations. J. Pers. Soc. Psychol. **23**(2), 283 (1972)
12. Hayashi, Y.: Detecting collaborative learning through emotions: an investigation using facial expression recognition. In: Coy, A., Hayashi, Y., Chang, M. (eds.) ITS 2019. LNCS, vol. 11528, pp. 89–98. Springer, Cham (2019). https://doi.org/10.1007/978-3-030-22244-4_12
13. Huang, K., Bryant, T., Schneider, B.: Identifying collaborative learning states using unsupervised machine learning on eye-tracking, physiological and motion sensor data. In: EDM 2019 - Proceedings of the 12th International Conference on Educational Data Mining, pp. 318–323. EDM (2019)
14. Ismaili, O.A., Lemaire, V., Cornuéjols, A.: A supervised methodology to measure the variables contribution to a clustering. In: Loo, C.K., Yap, K.S., Wong, K.W., Teoh, A., Huang, K. (eds.) ICONIP 2014. LNCS, vol. 8834, pp. 159–166. Springer, Cham (2014). https://doi.org/10.1007/978-3-319-12637-1_20
15. Kasepalu, R., Prieto, L.P., Ley, T., Chejara, P.: Teacher artificial intelligence-supported pedagogical actions in collaborative learning coregulation: a wizard-of-Oz study. Front. Educ. **7**, 736194 (2022)
16. Martinez-Maldonado, R., Clayphan, A., Yacef, K., Kay, J.: MTFeedback: providing notifications to enhance teacher awareness of small group work in the classroom. IEEE Trans. Learn. Technol. **8**(2), 187–200 (2014)
17. Ochoa, X., Worsley, M.: Augmenting learning analytics with multimodal sensory data. J. Learn. Analyt. **3**(2), 213–219 (2016)
18. Praharaj, S., Scheffel, M., Drachsler, H., Specht, M.: Literature review on co-located collaboration modeling using multimodal learning analytics-can we go the whole nine yards? IEEE Trans. Learn. Technol. **14**(3), 367–385 (2021)
19. Pugh, S.L., Rao, A., Stewart, A.E., D'Mello, S.K.: Do speech-based collaboration analytics generalize across task contexts? In: LAK22: 12th International Learning Analytics and Knowledge Conference, pp. 208–218. ACM, Online, USA (2022)
20. Rannastu-Avalos, M., Siiman, L.A.: Challenges for distance learning and online collaboration in the time of COVID-19: interviews with science teachers. In: Nolte, A., Alvarez, C., Hishiyama, R., Chounta, I.-A., Rodríguez-Triana, M.J., Inoue, T. (eds.) CollabTech 2020. LNCS, vol. 12324, pp. 128–142. Springer, Cham (2020). https://doi.org/10.1007/978-3-030-58157-2_9
21. Reilly, J.M., Schneider, B.: Predicting the quality of collaborative problem solving through linguistic analysis of discourse. In: Desmarais, M.C., Lynch, C.F., Merceron, A., Nkambou, R. (eds.) Proceedings of the 12th International Conference on Educational Data Mining, EDM 2019, pp. 149–157. International Educational Data Mining Society (IEDMS), Montréal, Canada (2019)
22. Rummel, N., Deiglmayr, A., Spada, H., Kahrimanis, G., Avouris, N.: Analyzing collaborative interactions across domains and settings: an adaptable rating scheme. In: Puntambekar, S., Erkens, G., Hmelo-Silver, C. (eds.) Analyzing Interactions in CSCL. Computer-Supported Collaborative Learning Series, vol. 12, pp. 367–390. Springer, Boston (2011). https://doi.org/10.1007/978-1-4419-7710-6_17

23. Schneider, B., Dich, Y., Radu, I.: Unpacking the relationship between existing and new measures of physiological synchrony and collaborative learning: a mixed methods study. Int. J. Comput.-Support. Collab. Learn. **15**, 89–113 (2020)
24. Schneider, B., Sung, G., Chng, E., Yang, S.: How can high-frequency sensors capture collaboration? a review of the empirical links between multimodal metrics and collaborative constructs. Sensors **21**, 8185 (2021)
25. Sell, A., Cosmides, L., Tooby, J.: The human anger face evolved to enhance cues of strength. Evol. Hum. Behav. **35**(5), 425–429 (2014)
26. Sharma, K., Papavlasopoulou, S., Giannakos, M.: Joint emotional state of children and perceived collaborative experience in coding activities. In: Proceedings of the 18th ACM International Conference on Interaction Design and Children, IDC 2019, pp. 133–145 (2019). https://doi.org/10.1145/3311927.3323145
27. Siatras, S., Nikolaidis, N., Krinidis, M., Pitas, I.: Visual lip activity detection and speaker detection using mouth region intensities. IEEE Trans. Circuits Syst. Video Technol. **19**(1), 133–137 (2008)
28. Smith, J., et al.: Spoken interaction modeling for automatic assessment of collaborative learning. In: Proceedings of the Speech Prosody 2016, pp. 277–281 (2016)
29. Soller, A., Martínez, A., Jermann, P., Muehlenbrock, M.: From mirroring to guiding: a review of state of the art technology for supporting collaborative learning. Int. J. Artif. Intell. Educ. **15**(4), 261–290 (2005)
30. Spikol, D., Ruffaldi, E., Dabisias, G., Cukurova, M.: Supervised machine learning in multimodal learning analytics for estimating success in project-based learning. J. Comput. Assist. Learn. **34**(4), 366–377 (2018)
31. Stiefelhagen, R., Zhu, J.: Head orientation and gaze direction in meetings. In: CHI 2002 Extended Abstracts on Human Factors in Computing Systems, pp. 858–859. No. 1 in CHI EA 2002, ACM, New York, NY, USA (2002)
32. Van Leeuwen, A., Rummel, N., Van Gog, T.: What information should CSCL teacher dashboards provide to help teachers interpret CSCL situations? Int. J. Comput.-Support. Collab. Learn. **14**(3), 261–289 (2019)
33. Viswanathan, S.A., VanLehn, K.: Using the tablet gestures and speech of pairs of students to classify their collaboration. IEEE Trans. Learn. Technol. **11**(2), 230–242 (2018)
34. Weinberger, A., Fischer, F.: A framework to analyze argumentative knowledge construction in computer-supported collaborative learning. Comput. Educ. **46**(1), 71–95 (2006)
35. Worsley, M.: (dis)engagement matters: identifying efficacious learning practices with multimodal learning analytics. In: LAK18: 8th International Conference on Learning Analytics and Knowledge, pp. 365–369. LAK 2018, ACM, NY, USA (2018)

The Promise of Physiological Data in Collaborative Learning: A Systematic Literature Review

Wicaksono Febriantoro(✉), Andrea Gauthier, and Mutlu Cukurova

UCL Knowledge Lab, Institute of Education, University College London (UCL), London, UK
Wicaksono.febriantoro.21@ucl.ac.uk

Abstract. Collaborative learning is an important approach in education. Researchers are increasingly interested in using physiological data, such as Electrodermal Activity (EDA), as an objective tool to measure bodily reactions during collaborative activities. However, it remains unclear how physiological data can contribute to our understanding, monitoring and support of the collaborative learning process. To address this gap, a Systematic Literature Review (SLR) was conducted, focusing on the contribution of physiological data to collaborative learning, the features of physiological data that correlate with effective outcomes, and interventions designed to support collaboration based on physiological data. The review identified 13 relevant publications that revealed physiological data can indeed be useful for detecting certain aspects of collaboration including students' cognitive, behavioral, and affective (emotion and motivation) states. Physiological arousal in the form of EDA peaks and physiological synchrony (interdependence or associated activity between individuals' physiological signals) were the most commonly used features. Surprisingly, only one publication presented a prototype of a learning analytics dashboard that used physiological data to guide student reflections. Furthermore, the review highlights the potential for integrating physiological measures with other data sources, such as speech, eye gaze, and facial expression, to uncover psychophysiological reactions and accompanying social and contextual processes related to collaborative learning. Future research should consider embedding methods for the physiological detection and modeling of learning constructs within explicit, feedback-driven interventions for collaborative learning.

Keywords: physiological data · collaborative learning

1 Introduction

Collaboration and collaborative problem-solving (CPS) are increasingly recognized as crucial skills for employment and success in modern society [1]. While, Collaboration involves two or more individuals working together to learn or study a subject [2], CPS refers to the coordinated attempt between two or more people to share their skills and knowledge for the purpose of constructing and maintaining a unified solution to a problem [3]. CPS is thus, at its core, a joint activity that requires the cooperative exchange

O. Viberg et al. (Eds.): EC-TEL 2023, LNCS 14200, pp. 75–88, 2023.
https://doi.org/10.1007/978-3-031-42682-7_6

of information to successfully transform a problem state into a desired goal state. These processes hinges on how well individuals can establish common ground concerning the nature of the problem, develop a solution plan, monitor progress along the way, and accommodate multiple perspectives while respectfully managing disagreements. This requires the ability to understand task goals and constraints and consider others' perspectives and knowledge, along with the ability to communicate this understanding through negotiation, mutual regulation, and shared responsibilities [1]. Hadwin highlights the importance of iteratively fine-tuning cognitive, behavioral, motivational, and emotional states in achieving success within a group, as discussed in socially shared regulation during group interactions [4]. In addition, psychological factors such as cognitive load, attention, and emotion are crucial in the learning process of students, according to Gasevic [5].

Behavioral data captured through log and video recording are commonly utilized in computer-supported collaborative learning. In addition to this objective data, researchers often employ subjective measures such as questionnaires or surveys to gather information about learning constructs that are not directly observable. These measures are commonly used in educational technology research due to their ease and cost-effectiveness [6, 7] and to study constructs related to student engagement and learning, including cognitive, non-cognitive, and meta-cognitive constructs [8–10]. However, subjective measures have two primary limitations. First, they are susceptible to cognitive biases and internal validity issues as the accuracy of responses cannot be easily verified [11]. Second, unlike logs, subjective measures cannot provide continuous and real-time information about users.

The examination of neurophysiological data from individuals, known as neuro measurements, is a different approach for assessing concepts in educational technology and broader information systems. This method has become more prevalent in information systems and has led to the development of a new interdisciplinary field of study called Neuro-Information-Systems (NeuroIS). NeuroIS utilizes neuro measurement tools to collect and analyze neurophysiological data related to the Central Nervous System (CNS) and the Autonomic Nervous System (ANS) of participants, combining knowledge from disciplines such as neurobiology, behavior, and engineering. Riedl et al. conducted an extensive review of research on NeuroIS, published between 2008 and 2016, and found that most papers focused on either cognitive or emotional processes [12], which were classified based on Dimoka's approach (cognitive, emotional, social and decision making processes) [13].

More recently, Schneider and his team conducted a study to investigate how various physiological measures, including EEG (brain), heart rate, and electrodermal activity (EDA), are associated with collaborative outcomes. According to their findings, although physiological data, particularly EDA, are frequently used in research, they are not consistently linked to successful outcomes such as cognitive, affective, and performance outcomes (e.g. completion time, success of task, quality of task, correctness). They suggested that EDA and the connection to collaborative outcomes could be developed into a collaborative diagnostic system that identifies which outcomes were lacking and which metrics were used to identify them [14].

In another study, Darvishi *et al.* [15] reviewed the literature on physiological measurements in higher education, classified them into ANS (facial expressions, eye movements, heart rate, skin conductance, and blood pressure) and CNS (EEG, fMRI, NIRS, and fNIRS), and mapped them with different types of learning constructs, such as cognitive, non-cognitive, and meta-cognitive. Their findings showed that EEG (CNS) was mainly used to study cognitive constructs, while ANS-related measurements were used to investigate non-cognitive constructs. Recent research has focused on measuring ANS activity because it is less invasive than CNS measures such as EEG. Additionally, advances in ANS measurement instruments have made them more reliable, portable, and affordable.

NeuroIS research suggests that while the relationship between neuro measurements and constructs is intricate, it is possible to capture psychological constructs with neuro measurements. This has the potential to overcome the two limitations of subjective measures. Specifically, it can (1) quantify constructs that cannot be measured accurately with self-reporting techniques and (2) provide nearly real-time and continuous information about a user's psychological constructs [12]. Cognitive outcomes and affective states are notable examples of constructs that can be effectively captured through physiological measures [15].

For instance, collaboration often involves synchrony, an important group feature [16]. While some synchrony behaviors, such as joint attention, are directly observable, others are detected through the physiological responses of group participants. Some research has indicated a positive correlation between physiological synchrony and collaborative learning features, including willingness to collaborate, score of the collaborative report delivered by students, and sum of the individual learning gains [17]. Furthermore, physiological synchrony has been linked to stress [18, 19] and emotional changes [20]. However, as already mentioned, Schneider pointed out that physiological data, including synchrony, has not been consistently associated with cognitive and affective constructs [14]. This raises the question of what physiological data features and metrics researchers can use as a proxy for learning constructs. Additionally, researchers are interested in integrating physiological measures with other types of data to gain a more comprehensive understanding of collaborative learning, known as multimodal analysis.

After detecting and modeling learning constructs, interventions such as feedback and adaptive systems can be developed [15]. High-quality actionable feedback has been shown to positively impact student reflection, performance, and achievement [21]. One potential usage of physiological data is to measure arousal, which indicates excitement and stress levels during learning. Students can utilize this data for reflection purposes, both individually and collaboratively as a group [18]. However, previous research has identified several limitations of current Learning Analytics (LA) to provide effective feedback, including difficulty for non-data experts to understand, ineffective communication of insights, provision of meaningless information, and lack of meaningful impact on education [22]. These challenges might be even more obvious when physiological data is used due to its high frequency, noisy, and difficult-to-interpret nature.

In this paper, our goal is to conduct a systematic review of literature, focusing on three primary areas: (1) investigating how physiological data can help identify learning constructs related to cognition, behavior, and emotion; (2) identifying physiological data metrics and features that serve as indicators for these constructs; and (3) examining the phase where physiological data can be utilized as one of the metrics to support learning interventions.

2 Methods

This systematic literature review (SLR) follows the guidelines of the PRISMA statement [23]. All articles that used physiological data to research collaborative learning were initially within the scope of this review. We restricted our search to a timeframe from 2012 to 2022, knowing that more studies were adopting physiological data collection technologies over the past ten years. Additionally, we concentrate our studies on the ANS (Autonomic Nervous System) rather than the CNS (Central Nervous System).

As already mentioned, our focus in investigating physiological data in collaborative learning will be framed in to three research questions (RQ):

1. What is the contribution of physiological data to our understanding of collaborative learning?
2. What physiological data features correlate with effective collaborative learning outcomes?
3. What interventions are designed to support student learning based on insights from physiological data?

2.1 Search Method

During the identification step, records are identified by database searching utilizing search terms. We conducted our search in the SCOPUS and Web of Sciences (WoS) databases due to their extensive coverage of peer-reviewed academic publications pertinent to the topic of our study as well as their usability as SLR search engines.

The search terms were formulated based on the review's scope and research questions (Table 1). Duplicate items were deleted before the screening step and then title/abstract screening was conducted. In the eligibility step, full-text articles were examined using inclusion–exclusion criteria. The scope of the review determined which papers were included.

A set of search terms was developed based on themes derived from the three research questions above, which are outlined in Table 1.

As such, our query was designed to find papers on physiological data in collaborative learning and the interventions used to enhance collaboration quality or learning outcomes. Upon reflection on initial limited results, we deemed that we should modify our search strategy. After further discussion, we decided to conduct a 2nd search by limiting the search terms to only two themes, namely physiological data and collaborative learning. We also indicated to the database our categories in educational research/education scientific disciplines/psychology education/education special. For full search strings both of 1st and 2nd round search, please refer to our supplementary materials document (link provided before the references).

Below, we outline the data items (metrics) that were extracted from each study, structured based on the general characteristics of studies and our three research questions. An overview of our research questions and corresponding metrics is given in Table 2.

We divided *learning environment* into three categories: online, face-to-face/co-located learning, and blended learning. *Learning domain* is the domain subject being taught/discussed. *Collaboration type* in this paper divided into three: verbal interaction, hands-on activity, and virtual experimentation. With regards to *collaboration scenario*,

Table 1. Search Term Structure

Research Question Theme	Search Terms
Physiological data	• "physiological data" OR • "skin temperature" OR • "heart rate" OR • "electrodermal activity" OR • "EDA" OR • "body temperature" OR • "blood volume pulse" OR • "blood pressure" OR • "skin conductance" OR • "multimodal" OR • "multimodal data" OR • "multi channel data" AND
Collaborative Learning	• "learn" OR • "educate" OR • "collaborate" OR • "collaboration learning" OR • "regulated learning" OR • "computer-supported collaborative learning*" OR • CSCL OR • "Socially shared regulation" AND
Learning Outcome	• "learning outcome" OR "educational outcome" OR "learning output" OR • "educational output" OR • "learning objective" OR "educational objective" OR "learning performance" OR • "academic achievement" AND
Intervention	• "intervention" OR • "supporting" OR • "feedback" OR • "understand" OR • "improvement" • OR "enhancement"

we used the 13 collaboration scenarios proposed by Praharaj [2]. *Group counts* refers to the total number of groups used as the experimental sample, while *group size* refers to the number of group members.

2.2 Data Analysis for RQ1

To better understand the contribution of physiological data in collaborative learning, we are using Darvishi classification that categorized psychological constructs into three high level groups of cognitive, non-cognitive and meta-cognitive constructs [15]. The

Table 2. Overview of Research Questions and Metrics

Question	Label
General Characteristic	1. Learning Environment 2. Learning domain 3. Collaboration Types 4. Collaboration Scenario 5. Group Counts 6. Group Size
What is the contribution of physiological data to our understanding of collaborative learning?	1. Psychological Construct 2. Construct Label 3. Sub Construct 4. Independent Variables 5. Dependent Variables 6. Contribution of Collaborative Learning
What physiological data features correlate with effective collaborating learning outcomes?	1. Construct to investigate 2. Physiological data analysis 3. Indices correlate with effective collaborative learning outcome 4. Multimodal data 5. Physiological Indices
What interventions are designed to support student learning based on insights from physiological data?	Type of Intervention/Support

cognitive construct includes attention, cognitive load, and skill; the non-cognitive construct includes attitudes and beliefs, social and emotional factors, habits and processes, and personality traits, based on the work by Lipnevich et al. [24] and the meta-cognitive construct includes knowledge about cognition and self-regulation of cognition.

For further clarification, we have categorized an exploratory independent and dependent variable, which can be found in Table 1 of our supplementary material. Additionally, we have described the contribution of collaborative learning, which is the finding of each paper.

2.3 Data Analysis for RQ2

To facilitate effective collaboration, it is essential for team members to engage in joint attention, transactive interaction (i.e., building on each other's ideas), and behavioral synchronicity [25, 26]. The purpose of this inquiry is to provide an overview of the construct being studied (cognitive, behavioral, affective), the physiological data being analyzed (arousal and synchrony), and the indices that correlate with effective collaboration and learning outcomes (exploratory). In addition, we created a data table (Table 2 in supplementary material) that combines subjective, objective, and physiological data to better understand collaborative learning through the lens of multimodal data.

2.4 Data Analysis for RQ3

High quality actionable feedback can have a strong positive effect on student reflection, performance, and achievement [21]. Therefore, we are interested in identifying what kind of feedback have been developed based on insight from physiological data.

2.5 SLR Procedure

A visual representation of the study selection process under PRISMA statement can be found in Fig. 1.

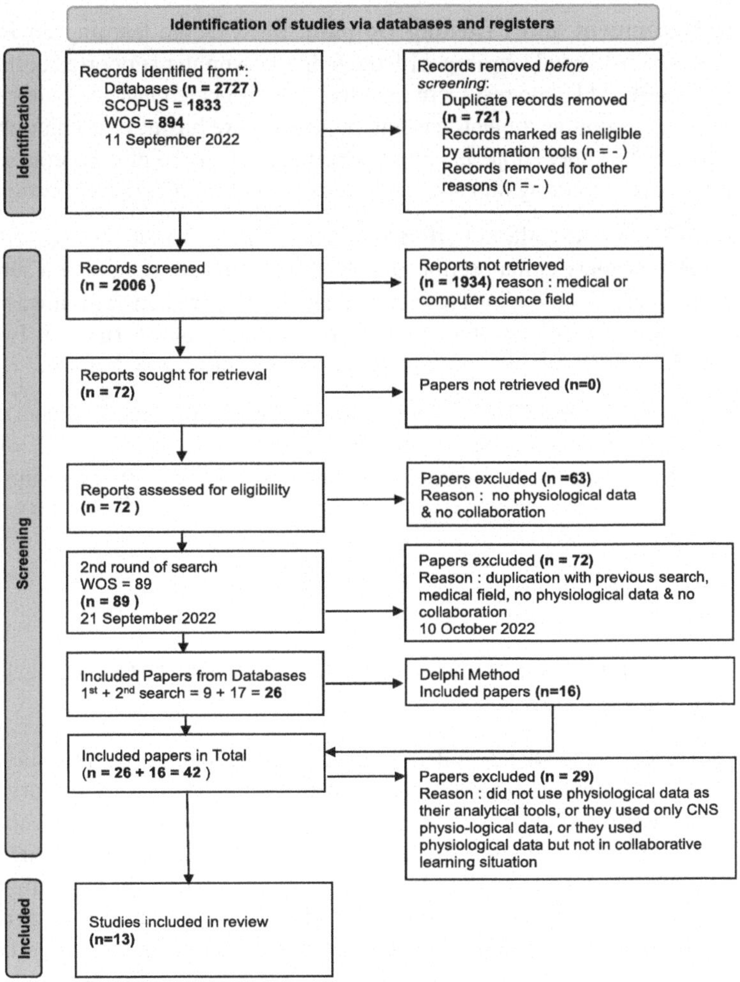

Fig. 1. PRISMA diagram showing SLR Procedure

2.6 Excluded and Included Studies

A search was conducted on WoS and Scopus, resulting in 894 and 1833 papers respectively. After eliminating 721 duplicates and conducting a preliminary screening, 72 articles were left. After a second search on WoS and parallel exclusion verification with a second researcher, 42 papers were selected for full-text review. Of these, 29 papers did not use physiological data as their analytical tools, used only CNS physiological data, or did not involve physiological data in a collaborative learning situation. The remaining 13 papers were included in the study.

2.7 General Characteristics of Studies

Learning Environment and Learning Domain. Most of the learning environments were face-to-face/co-located learning with the help of computer supported collaborative learning (CSCL) (n = 11), the rest were face-to-face/co-located learning without CSCL (n = 2). The most common subject/learning contexts were business simulation (n = 3) and nutrition (n = 3). Other subjects included nursing, advanced physics course, impact of social media, programming and strategic management of information system.

Collaboration Type and Collaboration Scenario. The papers identified verbal communication as the primary collaboration type (n = 9), followed by hands-on activities (n = 4). Among collaboration scenarios, learning and knowledge acquisition was the most frequently used (n = 7), followed by collaborative problem solving (n = 3). Two papers focused on healthcare simulation and one on programming as collaborative scenarios.

Group Counts and Group Size. Dyadic and Triadic (2–3 group members) collaboration was the most common grouping of the research conducted (n = 10), while only two studies looked at groups of 4–5 members and one study examined groups of up to 6 members.

3 Results

3.1 RQ 1. What is the Contribution of Physiological Data to Our Understanding of Collaborative Learning

To answer the research question, we first explore and categorize the synthesis of studies on collaborative learning into psychological constructs as categorized by Darvishi [15], and further detailed into their respective sub-constructs. Our analysis reveals that the *emotional* sub-construct, including stress, emotional state, challenge, and engagement, has been the most extensively studied (n = 5), followed by the *cognitive* sub-construct of learning gain (n = 4) and the *meta-cognitive* sub-construct of monitoring (n = 4).

We then delve deeper into the contribution of physiological data to collaborative learning by breaking it down into independent and dependent variables and mapping it to the learning constructs of cognitive, affective, and behavior. Most of the reviewed papers utilize Electrodermal Activity (EDA) as an objective measure to detect affective constructs such as stress [18, 19], emotion [20, 27], and mental effort [28]. Other contributions include the detection of cognitive aspects such as learning outcomes [17], learning gain, and collaboration quality [29]. Several papers also focus on metacognitive monitoring using physiological data [30–32].

3.2 RQ 2. What Physiological Data Features Correlate with Effective Collaboration Learning Outcomes?

Regarding physiological data, all papers reviewed utilized physiological arousal and synchrony as the primary proxies to detect learning constructs. In cognitive constructs, EDA Peak [31, 33], Directional Agreement (DA) [17, 29], and Single Session Index (SSI) [31, 32] are the most commonly used indices (2 papers each), followed by Instantaneous Derivative Matching (IDM) [17], Pearson Correlation (PC) [29], Shared Physiological Arousal Events (SPAE) [34], and Hidden Markov Model (HMM) [30] (1 paper each). All indices, except for SPAE and HMM, showed a positive relationship with measuring cognitive constructs.

In affective constructs, EDA Peak is used in three papers [18, 19, 31], while SSI [31, 32] and Multidimensional Recurrence Quantification Analysis (MdRQA) [27, 28] are used in 2 papers each, IDM [20] and SPAE [34] are used in 1 paper each. All the metrics showed positive correlation with affective or emotional constructs, for instance EDA Peak to detect stress-related incidents, IDM as a gauge for emotional changes, and MdRQA change refer to the groups' collective mental effort.

In terms of behavior constructs, one paper [31] utilized EDA Peak and SSI. The results indicated a correlation between EDA Peak and behavior in monitoring situation (awareness of learning progress against learning goals in socially shared regulation phase) but there was no straightforward connection between monitoring events and SSI.

Multimodality refers to the use of multiple sources of data to gain a more complete understanding of a particular phenomenon. In the context of research papers, 10 studies have utilized video data in combination with EDA (Electrodermal Activity) data to collect observational activities such as dialogue (voice/speech) [17, 18, 27, 29–35], facial expressions [33, 35], and gaze recognition [20]. Four of these studies collected objective data in the form of pre and posttests [17, 18, 29, 32], while four papers used subjective data in the form of self-report questionnaires [17, 28, 32, 33].

In general, cognitive, affective, and behavioral constructs exhibited a positive correlation with physiological data indices, including EDA Peak, SSI, and IDM. It is important to note most of these studies were conducted in a laboratory setting (classroom-like research space) and the majority of them focused on small-sized groups consisting of 2–3 members per group.

3.3 RQ 3. What Interventions Are Designed to Support Student Learning Based on Insights from Physiological Data?

Only one study by Fernandez-Nieto et al. [18] was discovered that examines interventions designed to support student learning through the utilization of insights derived from physiological data. This paper aims to provide actionable feedback to students during clinical training by utilizing multimodal data, including EDA, observation logs, and video, through the means of data stories and learning analytics. The feedback is designed to support students directly in their learning process. The role of physiological data is to leverage changes in physiological arousal to detect stress-related incidents and present this information visually to students. During reflection sessions, students found the use of data stories to be beneficial. The data stories helped guide the students' reflections on the evidence by simplifying the representation of complex data, which reduced the likelihood of incorrect interpretation. Moreover, the students recognized and valued the advantages of enhancing the timeline of action with explanatory annotations and visual elements. These annotations and visual elements clarified the errors they made and the extent of their arousal during the reflection process. As a result, students used these stories to reflect on their arousal status and understand the reasons behind their feelings of excitement or stress during specific periods of time. The intention behind using these tools was to enhance the provision of feedback by utilizing concrete evidence rather than solely relying on the teacher's memory during debriefing sessions. The ultimate aim was to improve student's clinical practice.

4 Discussion

In previous research on collaborative learning, physiological data has mainly been used to measure affective (e.g., stress, emotions) and cognitive (e.g., mental effort, learning outcomes, learning gain, collaboration quality) aspects of learning. This is in line with a previous literature review by Riedl, which found that out that, out of 103 empirical papers in NeuroIS research from 2008–2016, 50% focused on cognitive processes and 32% on emotional processes [12]. Another recent literature review from 2014–2018 on the use of neuro measurement, specifically skin conductance, showed that 5 articles studied non-cognitive constructs such as social and emotional processes, while 2 articles researched cognitive constructs such as attention and cognitive load [15].

Regarding physiological data features that are associated with successful collaborative learning outcomes, physiological arousal and synchrony were the main factors identified through various indices including EDA peak, DA, SSI, IDM, SPAE, HMM, PC, and MdRQA. Many of these indices were created by researchers themselves, and most of them have been evidenced to be useful predictors of specific learning constructs. However, these findings appear to contradict the results of a previous systematic literature review by Schneider [14], who examined 74 papers published between 2010 and 2020. According to Schneider's review, physiological data is commonly used in research to identify the link between metrics and outcomes, such as the relationship between EDA and affective or cognitive engagement. However, the review found that metrics were more often unsuccessful in establishing such associations [14]. The observed differences may be attributed to researchers currently using more stable indices compared to previous studies. Another point to note is that, currently, there are no studies that can align physiological data features or characteristics with a collaboration quality framework. A few noteworthy examples are the rating scheme in computer-supported collaboration processes quality [36] and the more recent studies by Chen Sun et al., who developed a generalized competency model of collaborative problem solving [1]. Both of these studies utilized primarily verbal (utterance/dialogue) and non-verbal behavioral data, captured through video and audio recordings, which served as indicators of collaboration quality. It would be intriguing to explore in the future whether physiological data features can be incorporated as additional indicators within a collaboration quality framework.

In addition, ten studies were identified that leveraged both video and EDA data to observe various activities such as dialogue, facial expressions, and gaze recognition. These studies were made possible by the development of machine learning algorithms that enable automatic detection of these behaviors. Video data is easy to be collected, is unobtrusive, and is frequently combined with speech/voice recognition for the analysis of the dialogue that occurred during collaborative learning. The increasing use of multimodal data is a positive sign that researchers are using different sources of data to gain a more comprehensive understanding of collaborative learning [37, 38].

However, only one study was found that used physiological data to provide feedback to students on their learning [18]. This study used a combination of multimodal data, including EDA, observation logs, and video, to provide students with actionable feedback on their learning process. Our results suggest that more research is necessary to investigate how to effectively incorporate physiological data into feedback interventions for students, to complement existing learning analytics.

4.1 Limitation and Further Research

This review has a few limitations that are worth acknowledging. Firstly, we only searched for papers in WoS and Scopus databases, which means we may have missed some papers that were published elsewhere. Secondly, we used a specific framework to classify the learning construct based on physiological data, and other frameworks may have different classifications. Despite its limitations, this review has provided significant insights into the role of physiological data, particularly EDA, in collaborative learning.

Future research should explore how physiological data, such as EDA, can be used to create feedback mechanisms that help students reflect on their learning and make adjustments to their collaborative behavior. This could lead to more effective and efficient learning, as well as improved collaboration skills among students.

5 Conclusion

This systematic literature review highlights the growing interest in utilizing physiological data, particularly Electrodermal Activity (EDA), in the study of cognitive and emotional processes related to collaborative learning. The use of EDA has been shown to measure stress, emotions, mental effort, learning outcomes, learning gain, and collaboration quality. Physiological arousal and synchrony were identified as the main factors associated with successful collaborative learning outcomes, as measured by various EDA indices. However, the effectiveness of these metrics in establishing associations between EDA and learning outcomes has been debated, with some studies showing limited success in this area. While there is limited research on using physiological data to provide feedback to students on their learning, there is a clear need for further exploration of this area to complement existing learning analytics.

Supplementary Material: Supplementary Material (The Promise of Physiological Data in Collaborative Learning).pdf

Acknowledgements. This research was partially funded by The Indonesia Endowment Fund for Education (LPDP) and the European Union's Horizon 2020 research and innovation programme under grant agreement No. 101004676.

References

1. Sun, C., Shute, V.J., Stewart, A., Yonehiro, J., Duran, N., D'Mello, S.: Towards a generalized competency model of collaborative problem solving. Comput. Educ. **143**, 103672 (2020)
2. Praharaj, S.: Measuring the Unmeasurable? Towards automatic co-located collaboration analytics (2022)
3. OECD: PISA 2015 Results (Volume V): Collaborative Problem Solving. Organisation for Economic Co-operation and Development, Paris (2017)
4. Hadwin, A., Järvelä, S., Miller, M.: Self-regulation, co-regulation, and shared regulation in collaborative learning environments. In: Schunk, D.H., Greene, J.A. (eds.) Handbook of Self-Regulation of Learning and Performance, pp. 83–106. Routledge (2017)
5. Gašević, D., Dawson, S., Siemens, G.: Let's not forget: learning analytics are about learning. TechTrends **59**, 64–71 (2015)
6. Beg, M.M.S.: A subjective measure of web search quality. Inf. Sci. **169**, 365–381 (2005). https://doi.org/10.1016/j.ins.2004.07.003
7. Saw, A.E., Main, L.C., Gastin, P.B.: Monitoring the athlete training response: subjective self-reported measures trump commonly used objective measures: a systematic review. Br. J. Sports Med. **50**, 281–291 (2016)
8. Greene, B.A.: Measuring cognitive engagement with self-report scales: reflections from over 20 years of research. Educ. Psychol. **50**, 14–30 (2015)
9. Henrie, C.R., Halverson, L.R., Graham, C.R.: Measuring student engagement in technology-mediated learning: a review. Comput. Educ. **90**, 36–53 (2015)
10. Sinatra, G.M., Heddy, B.C., Lombardi, D.: The challenges of defining and measuring student engagement in science. Educ. Psychol. **50**, 1–13 (2015)
11. Jahedi, S., Méndez, F.: On the advantages and disadvantages of subjective measures. J. Econ. Behav. Organ. **98**, 97–114 (2014)
12. Riedl, R., Fischer, T., Léger, P.-M.: A decade of NeuroIS research: status quo, challenges, and future directions, 29 (2017)
13. Dimoka, A., Pavlou, P.A., Davis, F.D.: Research commentary —NeuroIS: the potential of cognitive neuroscience for information systems research. Inf. Syst. Res. **22**, 687–702 (2011)
14. Schneider, B., Sung, G., Chng, E., Yang, S.: How can high-frequency sensors capture collaboration? A review of the empirical links between multimodal metrics and collaborative constructs. Sensors **21**, 8185 (2021)
15. Darvishi, A., Khosravi, H., Sadiq, S., Weber, B.: Neurophysiological measurements in higher education: a systematic literature review. Int. J. Artif. Intell. Educ. **32**, 413–453 (2022)
16. Cukurova, M., Luckin, R., Baines, E.: The significance of context for the emergence and implementation of research evidence: the case of collaborative problem-solving. Oxf. Rev. Educ. **44**, 322–337 (2018)
17. Pijeira-Diaz, H.J., Drachsler, H., Jarvela, S., Kirschner, P.A.: Investigating collaborative learning success with physiological coupling indices based on electrodermal activity. In: Lak 2016 Conference Proceedings: The Sixth International Learning Analytics & Knowledge Conference, pp. 64–73 (2016). https://doi.org/10.1145/2883851.2883897
18. Fernandez-Nieto, G.M., et al.: Storytelling with learner data: guiding student reflection on multimodal team data. IEEE Trans. Learn. Technol. **14**, 695–708 (2021)

19. Ronda-Carracao, M.A., Santos, O.C., Fernandez-Nieto, G., Martinez-Maldonado, R.: Towards exploring stress reactions in teamwork using multimodal physiological data. In: CEUR Workshop Proceedings, vol. 2902, pp. 49–60 (2021)
20. Aoyama Lawrence, L., Weinberger, A.: Being in-sync: a multimodal framework on the emotional and cognitive synchronization of collaborative learners. Front. Educ. 7 (2022)
21. Hattie, J., Timperley, H.: The power of feedback. Rev. Educ. Res. **77**, 81–112 (2007)
22. Matcha, W., Uzir, N.A., Gašević, D., Pardo, A.: A systematic review of empirical studies on learning analytics dashboards: a self-regulated learning perspective. IEEE Trans. Learn. Technol. **13**, 226–245 (2020)
23. Page, M.J., et al.: The PRISMA 2020 statement: an updated guideline for reporting systematic reviews. Syst. Rev. **10**, 89 (2021)
24. Lipnevich, A.A., MacCann, C., Roberts, R.D.: Assessing non-cognitive constructs in education: a review of traditional and innovative approaches. In: The Oxford Handbook of Child Psychological Assessment, pp. 750–772. Oxford University Press, New York (2013)
25. Cukurova, M., Luckin, R., Millán, E., Mavrikis, M.: The NISPI framework: analysing collaborative problem-solving from students' physical interactions. Comput. Educ. **116**, 93–109 (2018). https://doi.org/10.1016/j.compedu.2017.08.007
26. Noroozi, O., Weinberger, A., Biemans, H.J.A., Mulder, M., Chizari, M.: Facilitating argumentative knowledge construction through a transactive discussion script in CSCL. Comput. Educ. **61**, 59–76 (2013)
27. Haataja, E., Malmberg, J., Dindar, M., Jarvela, S.: The pivotal role of monitoring for collaborative problem solving seen in interaction, performance, and interpersonal physiology. Metacognition Learn. **17**, 241–268 (2022)
28. Dindar, M., Jarvela, S., Haataja, E.: What does physiological synchrony reveal about metacognitive experiences and group performance? Br. J. Educ. Technol. **51**, 1577–1596 (2020)
29. Schneider, B., Dich, Y., Radu, I.: Unpacking the relationship between existing and new measures of physiological synchrony and collaborative learning: a mixed methods study. Int. J. Comput. Support. Collab. Learn. **15**, 89–113 (2020)
30. Malmberg, J., Fincham, O., Pijeira-Diaz, H.J., Jarvela, S., Gasevic, D.: Revealing the hidden structure of physiological states during metacognitive monitoring in collaborative learning. J. Comput. Assist. Learn. **37**, 861–874 (2021)
31. Malmberg, J., Haataja, E., Seppanen, T., Jarvela, S.: Are we together or not? The temporal interplay of monitoring, physiological arousal and physiological synchrony during a collaborative exam. Int. J. Comput. Support. Collab. Learn. **14**, 467–490 (2019)
32. Haataja, E., Malmberg, J., Järvelä, S.: Monitoring in collaborative learning: co-occurrence of observed behavior and physiological synchrony explored. Comput. Hum. Behav. **87**, 337–347 (2018)
33. Malmberg, J., Järvelä, S., Holappa, J., Haataja, E., Huang, X., Siipo, A.: Going beyond what is visible: what multichannel data can reveal about interaction in the context of collaborative learning? Comput. Hum. Behav. **96**, 235–245 (2019)
34. Dindar, M., Jarvela, S., Nguyen, A., Haataja, E., Cini, A.: Detecting shared physiological arousal events in collaborative problem solving. Contemp. Educ. Psychol. **69** (2022)
35. Dafoulas, G.A., Maia, C.C., Clarke, J.S., Ali, A., Augusto, J.: Investigating the role of biometrics in education – the use of sensor data in collaborative learning. In: MCCSIS 2018 - Multi Conference on Computer Science and Information Systems, Proceedings of the International Conference on e-Learning, vol. 2018, pp. 115–123 (2018)
36. Meier, A., Spada, H., Rummel, N.: A rating scheme for assessing the quality of computer-supported collaboration processes. Int. J. Comput. Support. Collab. Learn. **2**, 63–86 (2007)

37. Ouyang, F., Xu, W., Cukurova, M.: An artificial intelligence-driven learning analytics method to examine the collaborative problem-solving process from the complex adaptive systems perspective. Int. J. Comput. Support. Collab. Learn. **18**, 39–66 (2023)
38. Ouyang, F., Wu, M., Zhang, L., Xu, W., Zheng, L., Cukurova, M.: Making strides towards AI-supported regulation of learning in collaborative knowledge construction. Comput. Hum. Behav. **142** (2023)

A Learning Design to Support Transfer of Training in Continuing Education

Jaanika Hirv-Biene[1(✉)], Gerti Pishtari[2], Marlene Wagner[2], Edna Milena Sarmiento-Márquez[1], and Tobias Ley[2]

[1] Tallinn University, Tallinn, Estonia
hirvja@tlu.ee
[2] University for Continuing Education Krems, Krems an der Donau, Austria

Abstract. Transfer of training refers to the application of what has been learned in formal educational settings to the workplace. While technologies for workplace learning have gained ground in recent years, there is less of a focus on learning designs that bridge formal and workplace learning contexts and effectively support transfer. We present a design-based research intervention in which we developed a learning design guiding learners through several stages of planning, transfer attempt, and reflection. We demonstrate implementation of the learning design with a cohort of students in two continuing education courses and an evaluation with the teaching staff. Data collected during implementation suggests that students had strong transfer intentions and were successful in attempting transfer, but that reflection needs stronger scaffolding and social support. We propose adaptations to the learning design including conversational guidance and automated analysis of free texts collected from students in the transfer process.

Keywords: continuing education · transfer of training · technology-enhanced learning · reflection · learning design · learning analytics

1 Introduction

The idea of transfer is central to education: what is learnt in education is expected to be applicable in a broad range of other contexts [4]. This expectation is especially relevant in the case of continuing education programs. There, the participants tend to be older, have more diverse backgrounds and more working experience than the students in initial education, and thus, tend to have higher expectations towards the applicability of the knowledge gained in their professional lives. However, transfer between workplace and educational settings is far from straightforward [9].

Therefore, technology-enhanced learning (TEL) in continuing education needs to focus especially on helping students transfer what has been learned to workplace settings. Educational technologies have traditionally been more targeted at formal education, and less at workplace settings. However, as transfer describes an interface between formal education and workplace settings, then this process should be supported across these settings. Transfer process starts already before the formal course begins (when transfer

O. Viberg et al. (Eds.): EC-TEL 2023, LNCS 14200, pp. 89–103, 2023.
https://doi.org/10.1007/978-3-031-42682-7_7

intentions are formed) and ends much later than the course itself ends (when transfer has been attempted). TEL solutions should then cross these contexts and draw on research both in education as well as at workplace.

In the recent years, workplace learning has been increasingly studied by TEL researchers [17]. Several tools and environments have been designed and developed to support different learning processes at work, such as self-regulated learning [28], sensemaking [7], and reflection [31]. However, what has not been investigated is how to combine the lessons learnt from TEL research in education on the one hand, and workplace learning on the other to create learning designs to support transfer of learning across contexts.

In this paper, we report a design-based research intervention and propose a learning design and several applications of learning technologies to support the transfer of training by guiding learners through stages of planning transfer, transfer attempt, and reflection. We seek to answer the following question: *Which learning design elements and learning technologies in the proposed design support continuing education students in transferring learning to their work context?*

Following recent ideas on learning design, we model the learning situation, implement it in two courses, and apply several data analysis methods to gain an understanding of the efficacy of the design and to support its redesign. We close by discussing design and theoretical insights we gained on TEL support for transfer of training.

2 Technologies for Transfer of Training in Continuing Education

2.1 Transfer of Training in Continuing Education

The more difference there is between the initial situation and the new situation, the more difficult the transfer. This kind of transfer requires more effort and mindful abstraction of general principles underlying the situation [26]. The transfer between education and workplace usually falls into this category, due to significant differences in context, culture, and modes of learning [9].

Learning how to transfer is an important skill that should be taught in any formal schooling system. Research into transfer has established several mechanisms that increase the likelihood of successful transfer, such as diverse practice, explicit abstraction, active self-monitoring, generating mindfulness, and using metaphors and analogies [22]. Several of these mechanisms, such as self-monitoring, are also part of the process of self-directed learning.

Professional continuing education is a learning setting in which adult learners who already work in a profession are involved in formal education (e.g., a degree course) to upgrade their skills. Participants in continuing education usually have practical work experience that may be closely related to the course topic, and they have usually been away from formal education for a longer time. Very often, professional continuing education programs are organized so that they can be completed alongside regular employment.

Participants of these programs usually start their studies with a very high intention to apply what they learn in their regular work, or in a new job opportunity. For these reasons, learning transfer is of special relevance in continuing education programs.

Specifically, the term "transfer of training" is often used to denote the extent to which trainees effectively apply the knowledge, skills and attitudes gained in a training context to their work [2] and there is a long research tradition that has examined the conditions for transferring knowledge from the training to the work context.

With some variation, the models of transfer (e.g., [3]) describe following processes in the transfer of training:

- Forming transfer intentions
- Setting transfer goals
- Transfer attempt
- Evaluation and reflection

Transfer between education and workplace often requires substantial additional learning later at the workplace to make the knowledge acquired usable for a particular work [9]. However, learning is not the main activity at most workplaces and occurs usually in a relatively unstructured manner, during the daily work tasks and interactions with colleagues, clients, superiors etc., and without an instructor. Thus, the learners themselves often assume an important role in directing their learning—setting their goals, monitoring progress towards those goals, and evaluating the results.

One of the essential processes in self-directed learning is reflection. Reflection is a key in linking training outcomes and transfer [5]. Reflection is also a link between individual and collective/organizational learning [15]. Reflection in this sense can be conceptualized as an inquiry into experiences that can be both done individually or collectively.

Reflection is triggered by a discrepancy between expectations and experiences that is usually accompanied by affective reactions (surprise, confusion). Reflection then has the function to revisit and re-evaluate the experience.

At the same time, research into workplace learning reveals that there seems to be a general lack of reflection for learning, either because of a lack of opportunity or a focus on reflecting work tasks rather than learning [18].

2.2 Learning Design and Technologies for Supporting Transfer of Training

Transfer of training or some of its subprocesses have been supported by different TEL approaches. Especially, due to the interrelationship between transfer and *self-directed learning* (SDL), transfer of training research could benefit from the technologies created for supporting self-directed learning (including self-regulated learning) processes. For example, [28] designed and developed a learning environment to support processes of planning, enactment (application) and evaluation in workplace learning. Their Learn-B environment provided different technological scaffolds (interventions) which were mapped on SRL processes (e.g., system-recommended learning paths for supporting task analysis) and researchers used trace data to establish impact of interventions on learners' behavior.

Another key process in the transfer of training as well as SDL is *reflection,* which has been an active topic of research in the TEL community. Examples include the use of electronic learning journals [19], dedicated apps [10, 25], and conversational agents [31]. [25] created an application to support collaborative reflection at the workplace, which allowed the users to compile, share and discuss their reflections on their experiences at work. Their study provided interesting insights about the socio-technical embedding of such tools, for example about process integration, influence of workplace characteristics, and role of dominant users.

[10] developed a reflection guidance concept and three applications to support reflection at workplace. The researchers evaluated the apps in four field trials and although they observed limited depth in reflections, the applications were used, accepted, and found to be supportive of learning. Recent work in that direction has gone a step further and proposed more interactive formats. [31] developed a conversational agent for supporting the development of reflective competence in vocational school students. In a field trial with apprentices, the researchers established an increase in apprentices' reflective competence and general appreciation of the application among the users.

Besides technological applications that support particular subprocesses, more extensive *learning designs* have also been suggested that aim to enhance transfer from training to the work context. These need to clearly focus on planning for transfer, allow trainees to practice learned skills in a controlled but realistic setting, and support reflective learning to link training and work context. An example is the Teacher Innovation Laboratory for in-service schoolteachers [16]. This program includes several phases of application of what has been learned during training in the teachers' classroom setting: implementing new teaching methods developed in the training, a systematic collection of data on student learning, and a joint reflection of the results in the training group. For the same setting of schoolteachers training and workplace learning, [30] have recently proposed a learning analytics ecosystem that supports these inquiry cycles. By enabling data collection along the experiential learning cycle, learning technology becomes a source of data to support inquiry and professional learning.

Data collection during transfer can also enable new forms of research on transfer of training. Most commonly, self-report instruments (delivered either on paper or online) with one point of measurement have been used in transfer of training research for data collection [27]. Thus, several authors have highlighted the need for using more diverse data sources and longitudinal designs [3, 14], for which the tools and methods of technology-enhanced learning provide ample opportunities.

3 A Design-Based Research Study

While workplace learning technology has started to make an impact in the TEL domain, a systematic approach that specifically focuses on supporting the transfer from continuing education to the work context has yet to be found. Thus, the current work is embedded into a longer design-based research (DBR) initiative that intends to find out what impact different learning design elements and learning technologies have on students' progress through key phases of transfer process, and to identify main barriers to their transfer attempts and possible ways to overcome these barriers. Here, we report one DBR cycle focusing particularly on the development of a learning design for transfer. The design was implemented on the course level and evaluated with researchers and teaching staff. The current iteration was aligned with two courses, which took place in parallel and with the same cohort of students. In line with the purposes of DBR, we intended to advance both design knowledge (suggesting and validating a learning design and prototypical supportive technologies), and as well as theoretical knowledge (on important challenges in transfer of training).

3.1 Research Context and DBR Team

The current research is embedded into several study programs of the University for Continuing Education Krems. These courses cater to continuing education students (professional learners) who seek to obtain an MA degree and advance their career in their area of specialization. All of them are working full-time while studying and it is expected that the courses contribute more or less directly to their job demands. We have worked with teaching staff of the following courses for this research:

- Learning Analytics (3 ECTS, MA e-education): The course introduces different ways of how learning analytics (LA) can be used in practice. Students learn about a structured implementation process to introduce LA in an organization. They propose how to employ LA in their own organization and prepare an implementation plan.
- Trends in Technology-enhanced Learning (3 ECTS, MA e-education): The course introduces current technological trends in teaching and learning (such as Artificial Intelligence, Augmented or Virtual Reality). Students select one of these technologies, create a case for their own organization and prepare an implementation plan.

Structure of the Courses. The typical setup of these courses is that they are structured according to the following three phases:

- *Pre-phase* (8 weeks): This phase consists of individual and collaborative tasks that introduce the topic, give students some theoretical and practical material to read and study, and help them to prepare them for the on-site seminar. The students learn according to their own schedule, and teaching staff provides support in distance learning mode. Communication with other students and teaching staff takes place asynchronously (through a learning management system and forum communication).
- *On-site Phase* (one full day): The on-site phase is usually organized on a weekend with several onsite courses blocked into one weekend. Students receive some input from the teaching staff, but there are also individual and collaborative working sessions. An emphasis is placed on tasks where students create solutions, receive feedback from teaching staff and peers. The tasks are designed in such a way that they should prepare students for the post-phase tasks.
- *Post-phase* (14 weeks): The post phase is dedicated to applying what was learned to students' own context. Tasks are aimed at applying the concepts they learned, and a final project is prepared that shows accomplishment of this transfer. This phase is also supported by the teaching staff from a distance and in an asynchronous mode.

The course is roughly modelled according to ideas of the Teacher Innovation Laboratory [16], although the time available is much shorter and students are taking several similar courses in parallel. Also, due to time constraints, it is usually not possible to implement a particular solution in the post-phase.

DBR Team. The design team consisted of the authors. It included both researchers on transfer of training (two PhD researchers and the head of the research team) as well as the teaching staff responsible for the two courses (two postdoc researchers).

3.2 DBR Cycle and Research Methods

The design iterations followed a typical DBR process that consisted of a *phase of designing artefacts* (learning designs and technology) that should be introduced into practice, an *implementation phase* in which the artefacts were introduced in the two courses mentioned above, and an *evaluation phase* in which results of the implementation were evaluated by the DBR team and conclusions for further DBR iterations were drawn.

Design. In the design cycle, the main artefact that was created and iteratively improved was a *learning design for transfer* that consisted of several activities across all three phases of the course. It was supported by several smaller applications implemented either in the Moodle course environment or as links to free-text or structured forms implemented as Google forms. The teachers of the two courses discussed the general principles and components that would support transfer. These were documented in a joint design document specifying the learning goals, activities, and the supporting tools. The main principle of the learning design was centered around motivating students to think of an individual *transfer project* that could be implemented in their own work context. In the case of the "Trends in Technology-enhanced Learning" (TEL) course, this would be an implementation of an innovative learning technology for teaching or learning (e.g., AI, VR, AR etc.), in the case of the "Learning Analytics" (LA) course, an implementation of a learning analytics application.

Table 1 presents an overview of the resulting learning design. In the pre-phase, students were exposed to different innovative TEL and learning analytics applications using the latest educational technology reports (e.g., EDUCAUSE Horizon Report). Students were asked to define key terms (e.g., gamified learning, learning analytics) and they were prompted to describe their *transfer intentions and goals.* Specifically, they had to describe an example of a possible use scenario in their professional context by filling out a Google form. In the TEL course, the students chose one trend that they were particularly interested in and that was most relevant for their professional context. In the LA course, a data analytics approach to the same technological implementation or one that was already running in their organization was chosen.

In the on-site phase, results of the exercises of the pre-phase were discussed. To guide *implementation of the transfer project*, two frameworks were introduced that guided students through phases of developing an implementation plan of their project. In the case of the TEL course, students were introduced to the "Educational Technology Analysis Toolkit", which aims to structure the process of implementing educational technologies in five steps: 1) analyzing functions of the tool, 2) looking for scientific evidence 3) analyzing institutional context (based on the 5 + 3 framework by [23], 4) decision regarding the use, 5) first implementation plan. In the case of the LA course, students were introduced to the Orchestrating Learning Analytics (OrLA) framework by [24].

In the post-phase, students had to present the implementation plan for their transfer project at work, interview one colleague, and finalize the implementation plan based

Table 1. Learning design, technologies, and data analysis for transfer.

	Pre-phase	On-site Phase	Post-phase
Course setting	Online, 8 weeks	Face-to-face, 1 day	Online, 14 weeks
Course contents	Terms, approaches and technologies of TEL and LA. Implementation methodologies	Trade-offs, risks and opportunities of TEL and LA solutions. Develop transfer project for own context	Understand contextual constraints, barriers, costs, and benefits for implementing TEL and LA
Learning goal	Form transfer intention and set first goal	Validate goal and plan transfer attempt	Undertake and evaluate transfer attempt
Learning activities for transfer	Activate prior knowledge of TEL and LA Describe own context Describe transfer intention and goal	Discuss transfer goal and project with peers. Specify transfer project using implementation frameworks	Discuss transfer project with stakeholders. Specify transfer project using frameworks (graded). Identify and reflect on barriers and own learning
Learning Technology	Textual prompts and free-text form	Project implementation guideline and template in LMS	Submission, grading and feedback of transfer project Textual prompts and free-text form for reflection

on the feedback from their peers. Both courses ended with a *transfer evaluation and reflection* task, in which students had to reflect on their major learnings in the course as well as opportunities and barriers discovered during the attempted transfer, i.e., while implementing the chosen technologies in their organization. The general prompts for this task were modeled according to a previous diary study on transfer of training [5].

Students then selected one barrier, described it, and reflected about the experiences with this barrier using the following questions adapted from the model of [8]:

1. What happened and what did you do or try to do?
2. What were the reasons that it did not work?
3. What have you learned from this?

The prompts had a dual purpose, namely (a) to support reflection by prompting key processes of metacognitive thinking, and (b) to allow later analysis of these processes by inspecting the produced texts.

Implementation. Implementation of the learning design was done in the two courses (TEL and LA) described above during the fall semester 2022/23, with the pre-phase starting in June 2022, the on-site phase during two days at the end of August, and the post-phase ending in November. Participants were the same students in both courses (N

= 11). The students had a variety of professional backgrounds, including teachers in secondary and higher education or in other educational institutions (e.g., with a focus on health care management) and human resource development professionals in the private sector. Only the report on the transfer project submitted at the end of the post-phase was graded, the other activities were not graded. Participants were informed about the research taking place during the implementation of the courses. They were informed of the possibility to decline participation in the research, but not in the course. All students signed informed consent sheets.

Evaluation. Evaluation took place after completion of the course. Data collected in each phase was analyzed and sent to the teachers of the course for inspection and interpretation. This analysis was mainly in the form of frequency tables giving an overview of the type and frequency of students' statements in the free text forms collected within the course activities. These activities focused on key processes in the transfer process, such as transfer intentions, goals, transfer attempts and reflections. An overview of data sources is provided in Table 2.

Table 2. Data sources for evaluation.

Phase of transfer	Forming transfer intentions	Setting transfer goals	Transfer attempt	Evaluation and reflection
Data sources	Students' descriptions of transfer ideas (free-form text) (N = 18)	Students' transfer projects (N = 18)	Students' transfer projects/reflections (free-form text) (N = 18)	Students' reflections (free-form text) (N = 19)
Type of analysis	Categorization of statements on transfer intentions	Analysis of teacher feedback and grading of projects	Analysis of teacher feedback and grading of projects/ content analysis of reflections	Content analysis on dimensions of reflection

Two evaluation sessions were then designed with the teachers to discuss the results of the data collection in their courses along the following guiding questions:

1. Is there evidence for transfer of training (students formed transfer intentions, attempted transfer, and evaluated/reflected on transfer attempts)?
2. What elements in the course design supported transfer?
3. What barriers did the students face when attempting to transfer?
4. How can barriers be addressed in the learning design (including TEL and LA solutions)?

4 Results

We report results for each of the phases of transfer.

4.1 Forming Transfer Intentions

We analyzed student answers to textual prompts submitted in pre-phase, where they described an idea for transferring learning from the course into their own context, and how they would implement this idea. We collected 18 ideas across both courses which we manually categorized. Students showed in general high intention to transfer. In 14 of 18 descriptions, intention to transfer was clearly visible and described in detail. In almost all texts, there was a clear link to both the course topics (15 of 18) as well as the own context of the students (17 of 18). Examples of those ideas were the use of VR/AR for vocational training and onboarding, installing hybrid learning equipment to classrooms (TEL), improving planning of training courses with a competence-based analysis, and visualization of individual learning paths in secondary school (LA). When checking how concretely the idea was described, half of the ideas were judged to be of sufficient detail. The implementation plan, however, was only fully developed in 4 of the 18 cases.

Teachers concluded from these results that their course design had succeeded in helping students to form and evidence intention to transfer. They noted high levels of student motivation and concrete plans which had allowed them to adapt the course towards contents that were perceived relevant. In terms of possible improvements in the course design, the teaching team noted the importance of helping students to turn their intentions into effective plans. This would mean making students aware of all aspects that need to be considered in the implementation phase and offering concrete tools to guide implementation.

4.2 Setting Transfer Goals

For setting a transfer goal, students had to make a connection between the theoretical models and frameworks taught in the course and their workplace context. We therefore analyzed students' transfer projects, in which they described an application of some of the course contents in their own setting using the frameworks introduced in the course. The projects had been started during the on-site phase and finalized in the post-phase.

Out of 11 students, 9 had submitted their transfer projects in each of the two courses, giving a total of 18 project descriptions. In the case of the Trends course, implementation plans were analyzed and graded based on the criteria as follows: students were quite successful in analyzing the functionalities of their chosen tool (91%), their institutional context (89%), formulating their decision (91%) and their concrete implementation plan (90%). Students mostly had problems with finding scientific evidence (74%) related to both the pedagogical approach as well as the specific tool, and with the interview with stakeholders (76%). Reasons for the deduction of points were that students did not discuss in detail what they had learned from the interviews with their colleagues and what consequently needs to be changed in their implementation plan.

In the case of the LA course, implementation plans were analyzed and graded based on the criteria as follows: students were quite successful in describing their projects (89%) and summarizing the interviews with stakeholders (98%). However, students mostly had problems with applying the introduced frameworks (Greller & Drachsler [12]) (79%) and OrLa (78%) to their organizational context. Reasons for the deduction of points were that students' plans remained generic (e.g., not clear how data will be analyzed) and some aspects of the models (e.g., future implementation) were missing or not discussed in detail.

Teachers concluded from these results that the course design succeeded in supporting students in setting transfer goals. Students developed concrete implementation plans for introducing new educational technologies and LA solutions in their professional context and discussed their plans with co-workers. Regarding possible improvements in the course design, the teaching team realized that more support and additional feedback in the post-phase would help students to specify their transfer goals and select the most relevant aspects when applying theoretical frameworks.

4.3 Attempting Transfer

Students' transfer attempts became mainly visible in their transfer projects and in the reflections submitted in the post phase. For each combination of student and course, we classified the content included in their transfer project together with the related reflection into three categories:

- *Plan*: when the student's transfer attempt did not go further than an idea, or a plan for a future implementation.
- *Discussion:* when the student discussed his/her ideas with a third party, such as a colleague and used that feedback to improve their initial plan.
- *Implementation:* when there was evidence of a pilot that a student conducted in real settings (e.g., tried to implement an LA solution).

Out of 18 plans and their corresponding reflections, 6 were classified as *plan,* 6 as *discussion,* and 6 as *implementation.* This means that in third of the cases, students went beyond what was expected from them in the courses and took concrete implementation steps. Given that time was quite short for actual implementation (with a course duration of less than 6 months), and students had other commitments (fulltime work and several other courses in parallel), the teachers concluded that the degree of transfer was rather high. The main barriers that the students described in their reflections were related to the insufficient digital competences of the target group or the student him- or herself; problems with technical infrastructure; little institutional support or users' low interest in new technology; communication barriers; and lack of time, personnel, or technical expertise.

4.4 Evaluation and Reflection

We assessed students' reflections on their transfer attempt submitted in the post-phase, where they reflected on one of the barriers they had experienced. 19 reflections were submitted. Two of the authors performed a content analysis by categorizing the students' answers. Disagreements were discussed until they reached agreement. The codes for the analysis were based on the dimensions of reflective writing proposed by [1]. Following the framework, we coded the reflections for:

- Three metacognitive levels of reflection (awareness, evaluation, regulation)

- Short-term dimension of the reflection (behavioral, emotional, affective)
- Long-term dimension of the reflection (professional development, academic development, personal development, organizational development)

Table 3 shows that students' short-term reflections focused mostly on the behavioral level (11 out of 19). Students' long-term reflections addressed mostly the level of organizational development (10 out of 19), while nobody reflected on their academic development. This may have been because the reflection was focused on the application in a work context. As for the metacognitive levels, the reflections, for both short-term and long-term dimensions, commonly evidenced evaluation.

Table 3. Dimensions of reflection. Percentages based on the total number of reflections (19).

Metacognitive levels	Short-term dimension of reflection			Long-term dimension of reflection		
	Cognitive	Behavioral	Affective	Professional	Personal	Organizational
Awareness	6 (31.7%)	8 (42.1%)	5 (26.3%)	0	0	2 (10.5%)
Evaluation	7 (36.8%)	11 (57.9%)	6 (31.7%)	2 (10.5%)	1 (5.3%)	7 (36.8%)
Regulation	0	6 (31.6%)	2 (10.5%)	0	0	3 (15.8%)

We also investigated if the students who had reached further in their transfer attempts, (i.e., implementing their transfer project) also show higher levels of reflection. We found that students whose attempts had remained at the *plan* level (7 students) showed evidence for evaluation (13 reflections), especially in short-term reflections, but their reflections did not show evidence for regulation. Students who went a step further and engaged in *discussion* with their colleagues (6 students) about their projects evidenced more the level of awareness, especially in short-term reflections (11). This group also evidenced some regulation regarding organizational development (2 reflections). Finally, the students who went further from discussion and engaged in further *implementation* of their project (6 students) often evidenced evaluation (15 reflections) for both short- and long-term reflections. These reflections also displayed the level of regulation more often (7). These findings might indicate that students who progressed farther in their transfer attempts were using more effectively their experience to regulate their future actions.

The teachers concluded that for the students, the reflection task served as a useful tool for evaluating their transfer attempts and for the teachers, as a good source of feedback about the students' progress. However, as the highest level of reflection (regulation) was not often achieved, the task could be re-designed. Instead of textual prompts, a dialogue-format should be used, such as employing conversational agents (e.g. [31]), or by letting the students interview each other. At the same time, it may still be helpful to use short textual reflection prompts throughout the course to help both the teachers and the students monitor their transfer process. To trigger more regulation, prompts should also ask more explicitly about future changes in behavior.

5 Discussion

Taking the results together, the learning design used in the two courses can be considered conducive to transfer, given that a third of the projects (6 out of 18) went farther in their transfer attempts, beyond the level of application required for the course. This conclusion is also supported by the students' estimations on the likelihood of their transfer project being implemented further in their organization: in Trends course, 36% of students rated the likelihood of further implementation with 4 points on the 5-point scale and in LA course, 33.3% rated the likelihood equally with 3 or 4 points on a 5-point-scale. Further informal feedback we gathered confirmed that the students appreciated the cohesion across the three phases, with their individual transfer project being the common theme across the course. This opportunity to choose a task from their own work context probably increases the perceived utility or value of the training, which is known to have a strong influence transfer [6].

Students' submissions demonstrated that the learning activities helped to guide them through the key phases of transfer (forming intentions, setting goals, attempting transfer, evaluating transfer attempt) and, at the same time, gave the teachers an overview of students' progress and difficulties. As these processes resemble processes of self-directed [29] and self-regulated learning, it can be assumed that the tasks directed students to monitor and reflect on their progress. Short textual prompts with free-text form used during the course to gather data on students' transfer intentions and reflections turned out to be a useful data source as well as learning design element to support transfer and self-directed learning. Using a familiar tool such as Google Forms meant ease in implementation for the teaching staff and students, but it also required manual, time-consuming data analysis for gaining insights.

Students faced certain challenges in transferring their learning which seemed to be characteristic for the particular transfer phase. When forming intentions and setting goals, students seemed to struggle especially with relating the course contents to their own setting. The transfer literature has long highlighted abstraction of general principles [26], and provision of concrete examples [4] as learning design elements that support transfer. Our work also illustrates the conclusions of these earlier studies that finding the right balance requires teachers to have a very good understanding of their learners and their context. In our case, a research-oriented LA framework was introduced to the students, and they were guided in extracting the principles that they could apply in their own contexts. However, some of them struggled in making the right connections, maybe because the framework emphasized factors that were not so relevant in students' contexts. The teachers concluded that more practical examples of implementation are needed and that a different framework should be provided, which the students could more easily apply to their own contexts.

When attempting transfer, the most difficult part for the students in both courses seemed to be the online post-phase. Several factors were probably at play. Firstly, when students took first steps in implementing their transfer projects, they naturally came across various barriers, which caused negative emotions and lowered motivation. These barriers were representative of what the transfer of training literature usually summarizes under "work environment" [6] and factors such as transfer climate, supervisory and peer support, and opportunity to perform [13]. Secondly, the post-phase was in distance learning mode with the teaching staff providing support asynchronously, which meant that motivational factors could be less readily addressed. Motivation to learn and to transfer have been found to have considerable influence on transfer, even if mechanisms and interrelationships with other transfer factors is unclear [11]. Although the students in our study were adult learners who came to the course with high motivation and clear intentions, the learning design would benefit from (LA) elements for tracking and boosting motivation throughout the course.

Finally, the main challenge in the evaluation and reflection phase of transfer seemed to be in the depth of reflective thought that was triggered by the current learning design elements.

6 Conclusions and Future Work

This iteration of the DBR process resulted in a validated learning design for transfer in continuing education. We received confirmation that students engaged in some of the key processes of transfer and reflection. In this first iteration, the learning technologies employed were rather simplistic, but these initial applications have given rise to ideas on enhancing the learning design in the future. Our sample was small, but still provided several insights. We believe reflection needs to be more conversational and we have taken first steps to employ conversational agents as well as technologies for collaborative reflection in our next iteration. At the same time, planning of and reflecting on transfer also needs stronger scaffolding, especially in the post phase of the course. In the future, we will organize online consultations sessions to discuss typical barriers faced by students and to come up with ideas to overcome them.

Learning analytics technology will also play a more prominent role in future implementations. Currently, we are using the categorized dataset of this first iteration to train machine learning models, so that in the future those could be used to dynamically adapt the prompts that a conversational agent uses to trigger reflection. Also, these models could more efficiently provide an overview to the teaching staff of how far students are in their transfer attempts and what barriers they face to allow better scaffolding in the online post phase of the course.

References

1. Alt, D., et al.: Higher education students' reflective journal writing and lifelong learning skills: insights from an exploratory sequential study. Front. Psychol. **12**, 707168 (2022). https://doi.org/10.3389/fpsyg.2021.707168
2. Baldwin, T.T., Ford, J.K.: Transfer of training: a review and directions for future research. Pers. Psychol. **41**(1), 63–105 (1988). https://doi.org/10.1111/j.1744-6570.1988.tb00632.x
3. Blume, B.D., et al.: A dynamic model of training transfer. Hum. Resour. Manag. Rev. **29**(2), 270–283 (2019). https://doi.org/10.1016/j.hrmr.2017.11.004
4. Bransford, J.D., Schwartz, D.L.: Rethinking transfer: a simple proposal with multiple implications. Rev. Res. Educ. **24**, 61–100 (1999). https://doi.org/10.2307/1167267
5. Brown, T., et al.: 'Don't forget to write': how reflective learning journals can help to facilitate, assess and evaluate training transfer. Hum. Resour. Dev. Int. **14**(4), 465–481 (2011). https://doi.org/10.1080/13678868.2011.601595

6. Burke, L.A., Hutchins, H.M.: Training transfer: an integrative literature review. Hum. Resour. Dev. Rev. **6**(3), 263–296 (2007). https://doi.org/10.1177/1534484307303035
7. Dennerlein, S. et al.: Making sense of bits and pieces: a sensemaking tool for informal workplace learning. In: Rensing, C., de Freitas, S., Ley, T., Muñoz-Merino, P.J. (eds.) EC-TEL 2014. LNCS, vol. 8719, pp. 391–397. Springer, Cham (2014). https://doi.org/10.1007/978-3-319-11200-8_31
8. Driscoll, J., Teh, B.: The potential of reflective practice to develop individual orthopaedic nurse practitioners and their practice. J. Orthop. Nurs. **5**(2), 95–103 (2001). https://doi.org/10.1054/joon.2001.0150
9. Eraut, M.: Transfer of knowledge between education and workplace settings. In: Daniels, H., Lauder, H., Porter, J. (eds.) Knowledge, Values and Educational Policy, pp. 75–94. Routledge, London (2009)
10. Fessl, A., et al.: In-app reflection guidance: lessons learned across four field trials at the workplace. IEEE Trans. Learn. Technol. **10**(4), 488–501 (2017). https://doi.org/10.1109/TLT.2017.2708097
11. Ford, J.K., et al.: Transfer of training: the known and the unknown. Annu. Rev. Organ. Psychol. Organ. Behav. **5**(1), 201–225 (2018). https://doi.org/10.1146/annurev-orgpsych-032117-104443
12. Greller, W., Drachsler, H.: Translating learning into numbers: a generic framework for learning analytics. Educ. Technol. Soc. **15**, 42–57 (2012)
13. Grossman, R., Salas, E.: The transfer of training: what really matters: the transfer of training. Int. J. Train. Dev. **15**(2), 103–120 (2011). https://doi.org/10.1111/j.1468-2419.2011.00373.x
14. Huang, J.L., et al.: Ignored no more: Within-Person variability enables better understanding of training transfer. Pers. Psychol. **70**(3), 557–596 (2017). https://doi.org/10.1111/peps.12155
15. Knipfer, K., et al.: Reflection as a catalyst for organisational learning. Stud. Contin. Educ. **35**(1), 30–48 (2013). https://doi.org/10.1080/0158037X.2012.683780
16. Ley, T., et al.: Adopting technology in schools: modelling, measuring and supporting knowledge appropriation. Eur. J. Teach. Educ. **45**(4), 548–571 (2022). https://doi.org/10.1080/02619768.2021.1937113
17. Ley, T.: Knowledge structures for integrating working and learning: a reflection on a decade of learning technology research for workplace learning. Br. J. Educ. Technol. **51**(2), 331–346 (2020). https://doi.org/10.1111/bjet.12835
18. Margaryan, A., et al.: Self-regulated learning in the workplace: strategies and factors in the attainment of learning goals: self-regulated learning in the workplace. Int. J. Train. Dev. **17**(4), 245–259 (2013). https://doi.org/10.1111/ijtd.12013
19. Mejia-Domenzain, P., et al.: Evolutionary clustering of apprentices' self- regulated learning behavior in learning journals. IEEE Trans. Learn. Technol., 1–14 (2022). https://doi.org/10.1109/TLT.2022.3195881
20. Meyer, E., et al.: Opportunities and barriers to successful learning transfer: impact of critical care skills training. J. Adv. Nurs. **60**(3), 308–316 (2007). https://doi.org/10.1111/j.1365-2648.2007.04422.x
21. Perez-Soltero, A., et al.: Knowledge transfer in training processes: towards an integrative evaluation model. IUP J. Knowl. Manag. **17**(1) (2019)
22. Perkins, D.N., Salomon, G.: Transfer of learning. In: Husén, T., Postlethwaite, T.N. (eds.) International Encyclopedia of Education. Pergamon Press, Oxford (1992)
23. Prieto, L.P., et al.: Orchestration in learning technology research: evaluation of a conceptual framework. Res. Learn. Technol. **23** (2015). https://doi.org/10.3402/rlt.v23.28019
24. Prieto, L.P., et al.: Orchestrating learning analytics (OrLA): supporting inter-stakeholder communication about adoption of learning analytics at the classroom level. AJET **35**(4) (2019). https://doi.org/10.14742/ajet.4314

25. Renner, B., et al.: Effects of prompting in reflective learning tools: findings from experimental field, lab, and online studies. Front. Psychol. **7** (2016). https://doi.org/10.3389/fpsyg.2016.00820
26. Salomon, G., Perkins, D.N.: Transfer of cognitive skills from programming: when and how? J. Educ. Comput. Res. **3**(2), 149–169 (1987)
27. Schoeb, G., et al.: Measuring transfer of training: review and implications for future research. Can. J. Adm. Sci. **38**(1), 17–28 (2021). https://doi.org/10.1002/cjas.1577
28. Siadaty, M., et al.: Measuring the impact of technological scaffolding interventions on micro-level processes of self-regulated workplace learning. Comput. Hum. Behav. **59**, 469–482 (2016). https://doi.org/10.1016/j.chb.2016.02.025
29. Simons, P.R.J.: Towards a constructivistic theory of self-directed learning. In: Self-Learning. Waxman, New York (2000)
30. Tammets, K., et al.: A digital learning ecosystem to scaffold teachers' learning. IEEE Trans. Learn. Technol. **15**(5), 620–633 (2022). https://doi.org/10.1109/TLT.2022.3198739
31. Wolfbauer, I., et al.: A script for conversational reflection guidance: a field study on developing reflection competence with apprentices. IEEE Trans. Learn. Technol., 1–14 (2022). https://doi.org/10.1109/TLT.2022.3207226

Implementing a Desktop VR Tool in a European University: Priorities and Challenges

Kateryna Holubinka[1](✉), Corrie Urlings[1], Slavi Stoyanov[1], Rocío del Pilar Sosa-Fernández[2], Roi Méndez-Fernández[2], Enrique Castelló-Mayo[2], Roland Klemke[1], and Renate de Groot[1]

[1] Open University, Valkenburgerweg 177, 6419 AT Heerlen, The Netherlands
kateryna.holubinka@ou.nl

[2] The University of Santiago de Compostela, Avda de Castelao, s/n, 15782 Santiago de Compostela, Spain

Abstract. Virtual reality technologies in educational settings have demonstrated their potential to improve understanding, engagement, motivation and learning outcomes. However, there are multiple technical, pedagogical, and institutional challenges on the way of technology adoption in the education sector. In this group-concept-mapping study within the CloudClass project we aim at identifying the requirements for implementing a desktop VR tool (CloudClass) for education in the university context. Teachers, multimedia experts and managers from a Spanish and a Dutch university (a face-to-face and a distance learning one) were asked to complete the focus prompt "*To use/implement CloudClass in education it is required/ needed that....*". The generated statements were classified thematically and rated for importance and feasibility. 95 unique statements were generated and sorted statistically into 5 clusters: *Evaluation, Institutional Requirements, Maintenance and Training, Student Requirements, Affordances and infrastructure.* A strong correlation was identified between the importance and feasibility of the identified clusters. To ensure a sustainable implementation of a desktop VR tool like CloudClass in a university setting a holistic approach considering all identified clusters is needed. Clusters *Maintenance and Training* and *Institutional requirements* are the low-hanging fruits to invest in, as both clusters scored highest on importance and feasibility.

Keywords: Virtual Reality · Group Concept Mapping · Higher Education

1 Introduction

Virtual reality (VR) technologies have become a powerful and promising tool in education because of their potential to enrich learning experiences with high immersion and presence experienced by learners [2–4]. VR can be described as a mosaic of technologies that support the creation of synthetic, highly interactive three-dimensional (3D) spatial environments that represent real or non-real situations [5]. High-immersive VR environments (iVR) generally involve a head-mounted display (HMD), while low-immersive or desktop VR (DVR) is based on traditional widely accessible devices like mouse and keyboard [6, 7].

O. Viberg et al. (Eds.): EC-TEL 2023, LNCS 14200, pp. 104–117, 2023.
https://doi.org/10.1007/978-3-031-42682-7_8

Implementing VR in educational settings has been reported highly motivating, increasing student engagement, their presence and supporting the learning process by providing high-quality visualisations [e.g., 8, 9, 6]. Presence is considered as "the subjective experience of being in one place or environment, even when one is physically situated in another" [10]. Immersion, on the other hand, can be classified into *physical immersion*, a technological attribute that can be assessed objectively [11], and *mental immersion*, considered as a subjective, individual belief, i.e., a psychological phenomenon [10]. Several meta-analyses have reported positive educational outcomes when using VR, sometimes exceeding those associated with traditional classroom instruction [4, 5, 12–14]. The field of higher education has experienced a growing interest in the use of VR technologies showing positive effect sizes in effectiveness of VR interventions in basic science, social science, and engineering [15]. At the same time, using VR technologies in education should be a balanced decision that considers a multitude of factors including its positive and restrictive attributes [3, 16]. The drawbacks associated with utilizing VR technologies are mainly related to the time and costs required for the development of hardware and software [17]. Additionally, there may be potential health and safety concerns with iVR, as well as discomfort associated with wearing head-mounted displays (HMDs). The use of iVR environments may also lead to user distraction and overload, resulting in lower levels of learning comparing to less immersive VR environments [18]. There is also a reported lack in integrating VR into learning scenarios [2, 16].

In most domains, VR is still experimental, and its usage is not systematic or based on best practices [2]. The technologically-heavy development of the software and steep learning curves in the use of VR puts constraints on teachers effectively and flexibly deploying these technologies in their practice and makes educators dependent on solution providers [17]. Therefore CloudClass technology has been developed as a DVR visualisation and presentation tool aiming to overcome the previously identified problems and to foster teachers in creating and customizing the virtual environment that they can use at rather low cost. Having been developed for the broadcasting industry, CloudClass evolved as a low-cost cloud-based solution that can be used in the classroom without big hardware investments and integrated in existing video-conferencing systems. This has potential to enhance the learning experience in the virtual classroom by a possibility to work with virtual spaces (e.g. a room), 3D models (e.g. solar system) and pre-sets of virtual camera positions, importing and blending pre-recorded video material, images and 3D models with streamed video and other digital objects without the need of using HMDs. What is more, CloudClass is being developed as a low-threshold desktop tool that teachers can flexibly use in their practice without having to go through specialized graphic design or programming training, or being dependent on technology developers.

As previous studies identified numerous challenges and barriers for wider institutional implementation of VR tools in educational context [4, 12, 5, 14], this paper aims at identifying the requirements for implementing a DVR tool (CloudClass) for education in the university context to foster efficient, effective and enjoyable learning. Therefore the two research questions are addressed:

1. What are the requirements for implementing and using a DVR tool like CloudClass in university education? (RQ1)

2. What is the feasibility and the importance of the identified implementation requirements for the use of a DVR tool like CloudClass in higher education? (RQ2)

We applied the Group Concept Mapping (GCM) research methodology [19, 20] to collect, objectively aggregate and analyze the opinions of core stakeholder groups – teachers, educational media experts and managers – to depict their shared vision on the potential of implementation of a tool like CloudClass in higher education in the long term.

2 Method

2.1 Group Concept Mapping

Group Concept Mapping (GCM) is a participatory mixed-methods research methodology that identifies a shared understanding of a particular issue or topic that a group of individuals have [19, 20]. It differs from traditional data collection methods by placing the power of idea generation and organization in the hands of the participants, rather than researchers. GCM involves several stages, including brainstorming, sorting, and rating, and uses advanced statistical techniques such as Multidimensional Scaling (MDS) and Hierarchical Cluster Analysis (HCA) to detect patterns and connections within the data, which offer valuable insights into the factors affecting the topic under investigation. Results are presented visually through a concept map, pattern matches and go-zone charts, among others, making them easy to understand and apply [19, 20]. By utilizing the GCM methodology, educational research can gain valuable insights into the factors that impact technology adoption and educational policies.

2.2 Procedure

Employees across two European universities were approached – a distance learning university in the Netherlands – the Open Universiteit (OU) and a traditional Spanish face-to-face-learning university – the University of Santiago de Compostela (USC). The study was reviewed and approved by the Research Ethics Committee of the OU (under the reference number U202200751). Data collection and main statistical analyses were performed in GroupWisdom™ software. Participants were invited to take part in the GCM institution-wide with a post on the intranet, via email, as well as during faculty and department meeting presentations and ongoing events. The information letter outlining the aim of the research and procedure was included in the email or distribution materials together with a link to a 6-min infomercial describing the functionality and affordances of the tool CloudClass. Participants had to give their informed consent in GroupWisdom before starting each stage of the GCM. Anonymous demographic questions about the role in the institution and faculty of affiliation were mandatory to answer for each stage.

Brainstorming. The purpose of this phase was to generate and collect ideas of the three stakeholder groups across the two universities – OU and USC. Having watched a video introducing the affordances of CloudClass, participants were asked to complete the following focus prompt: "*To use/implement CloudClass in education it is required/*

needed that...". For the USC, the GroupWisdom environment was set to Spanish as the interface language, and the focus prompt was translated as: "Para utilizar/implementar CloudClass en la educación se requiere/se necesita…". Participants were encouraged to add as many ideas as they wished, while keeping each statement limited to one thought and formulating it as if they were completing the focus prompt. Each participant was working independently from others, but could see all the previous contributions under the input field. Participants from the USC were asked to complete the focus prompt in Spanish, while in OU instructions were given in English, but participants could respond in English or Dutch. There was no time limit for completing the brainstorming activity and participants could leave GroupWisdom and return at a later point.

Idea Synthesis. Upon the completion of the brainstorming phase the generated statements from both universities were combined and edited with the purpose of unifying the format of the data set to be used in the following stages of GCM process. Idea synthesis was an iterative group process that involved researchers from both OU and USC. Because of the different languages, some sentences had to be back-translated from Spanish and Dutch into English for analysis and editing.

While editing, the following criteria were used: each statement represents one idea, so entries having several ideas were split; each statement is unique, so ideas close in meaning were combined without the loss of meaning; each statement is relevant to the focus prompt, so grammatical formulations were adjusted to fit the focus prompt if needed, and ideas out of the scope were weeded out. The value, popularity or priority of ideas was not considered. After the idea synthesis was complete, the unique statements were fed back into the GroupWisdom so that participants could sort them into meaningful groups and rate for feasibility and importance.

Sorting and Rating. Participants from OU representing three stakeholder groups were contacted again via email, faculty and department meetings and other ongoing events and invited to participate in sorting and rating. During the sorting activity participants were asked to categorize statements into piles according to their view of the meaning and give each pile a name that describes its theme or contents. A statement could be put alone in its own category, and participants were discouraged to create piles according to priority or value. Although there was no time limit for the activity and participants could leave and get back to GroupWisdom if they wanted, it took on average between 30 and 50 min to complete.

After the sorting activity, participants were asked to rate the same set of statements for importance and feasibility on a 5-point scale, from 1 as least important to 5 as most important, and from 1 as least feasible to 5 as most feasible respectively. Participants were encouraged to spread out their ratings using all 5 given options. With higher values in importance scale participants articulated their values, while feasibility displayed the understanding of opportunities and challenges in practical implementation of the CloudClass tool.

2.3 Analysis

The rating activity collected the data that can be analysed with multidimensional scaling and hierarchical cluster analysis of the aggregated coding data.

Multidimensional Scaling (MDS). Participant grouping of statements was analyzed with MDS to identify the position of each idea relative to others in a 2-dimensional space resulting in a point map. The points that are closer together on a point map indicate a closer relationship in meaning, reflecting the way participants had grouped them together during the sorting activity. This mathematical model was evaluated for accuracy with a routinely-generated stress value index, which for GCM studies typically ranges between 0.20 and 0.35 [21].

The output of the MDS analysis provided information on the anchoring and bridging values of each statement. Statements with low bridging values have been grouped together with statements in close proximity, while those with higher bridging values have been grouped together with some statements further apart from either side. These values are valuable in understanding the point map [19]. By knowing which ideas serve as anchors or bridges, the researchers were able to make more informed judgments about the content. This knowledge also guided their decisions regarding cluster formation before the cluster map was fully completed. Once the cluster array had been decided upon, the average anchoring and bridging values for each cluster were calculated.

Hierarchical Cluster Analysis (HCA). To organize content into meaningful clusters of statements that aggregate to reflect similar concepts, HCA was applied [22, 23]. Based on the established GCM research and practice [19, 24], the 15-to-4 heuristics was applied, where HCA started with a 15-cluster solution and at each step proposed merging two of the clusters until the 4-cluster solution was reached. A group of four researchers considered the generated cluster solutions individually and discussed the suitability of each cluster solution keeping in mind the purposes of the project.

3 Results

3.1 Participants

Brainstorming. During the brainstorming phase participants of the OU and USC were approached, reaching out to all the university faculties and service media departments of both institutions (see the Annex [1], figures 1–4). Three stakeholder groups were included in this study – teachers/lecturers, educational media experts and university managers (deans of faculties and management board), which was reflected in demographic questions that participants had to complete before each activity. Out of 121 participants who opened GroupWisdom environment at OU, 59 participants across all the six faculties answered the demographic questions and were able to start the brainstorming. In USC out of 50 participants 22 answered the questions, representing 8 out of 28 faculties.

Brainstorming phase was conducted in both universities, and idea synthesis resulted in a single list of final statements. Responses about participants' role in their university are summarized in Table 1 below.

Sorting and rating phases involved participants from OU across all the faculties. USC participants were not included in the sorting and rating due to organizational factors. The demographic data for each GCM activity collected through participant questions in GroupWisdom is given in Table 2 below.

Table 1. Participant numbers for GCM activities.

Activity	University	Teachers		Media experts		Managers		Total, 100%
		N	%	N	%	N	%	N
Brainstorming	OU	35	59	9	15	15	25	59
	USC	13	59	3	14	6	27	22
Sorting	OU	49	89	6	11	0	0	55
Rating	OU	66	83	9	11	5	6	80

Table 2. Participation in sorting and rating activities by faculty.

Faculty/division	Sorting		Rating	
	N	%	N	%
Science	1	1.8	10	12.5
Humanities	1	1.8	1	1.3
Management Sciences	1	1.8	3	3.8
Educational Sciences	40	72.7	42	52.5
Psychology	4	7.3	7	8.8
Law	0	0.0	3	3.8
Expertise Centre Education	8	14.6	14	17.5
Total	**55**	**100**	**80**	**100**

3.2 CloudClass Implementation Requirements

As the result of the brainstorming activity 236 ideas were collected (57 at USC and 179 at OU) in response to a focus prompt: *To use/implement CloudClass in education it is required/ needed that....* After the idea synthesis this number was reduced to a list of 95 single unique statements that complete the focus prompt (see the Annex [1], Table 1).

Sorting activity and MDS resulted in a graphical representation of a point map (see the Annex, figure 5) with all the 95 statements. The stress value index for this study is 0.27 indicating that the map quite accurately reflects the participants' original sorting. Bridging values for each statement are also displayed on the point map (figure 5 in the Annex [1]).

Based on the results of the HCA, the group of researchers chose upon the 5-cluster solution as the one reflecting the core themes of the project. The following themes were identified, which are reflected in the cluster names: *Evaluation, Institutional Requirements, Maintenance and Training, Student Requirements, Affordances and Infrastructure.* These are displayed in the cluster map in Fig. 1 together with the average bridging values for each cluster. The description of each cluster summarizing main themes is given below and the statements within each cluster are presented in the Annex [1].

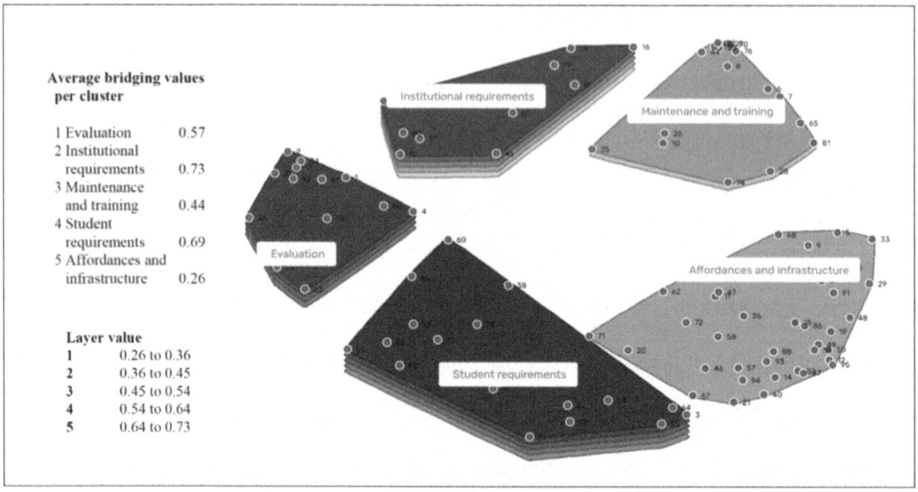

Fig. 1. 5-cluster solution with average bridging values for each cluster.

Affordances and Infrastructure. Within this cluster with the lowest bridging value of 0.26 participants seem to agree on the coherence of this theme, having grouped the statements with the ones close to them on the point map. The theme connects the expectations of the CloudClass system affordances with the requirements for the infrastructure and hardware, both for students and teachers.

Maintenance and Training. This cluster features two closely related sub-themes. The first embraces teacher training in various formats – from self-study resources like instruction manuals and videos, to in-person training sessions, workshops (e.g. script-writing, using a green screen, lighting), and availability of support by an expert. The second sub-theme reflects the need of awareness of how CloudClass should be used in specific contexts, which pedagogical scenarios are suitable and how they can be translated in technical design.

Evaluation. This cluster embraces statements around the evaluation of CloudClass in various forms. The array of coherent sub-themes includes the need for structured research and evaluation approaches to explore efficiency and effectiveness of the tool in multiple contexts with different target groups (e.g. learners with disabilities); investigating short- and long-term effects on learning, as well as comparison with other similar tools; involvement of all the stakeholder groups in implementation and evaluation processes; and finally, the expediency (reasonableness) of the tool use in relation to its cost.

Student Requirements. This cluster covers sub-themes ranging from technical affordances available to students (e.g. manipulating 3D objects, collaboration, usability), their privacy (e.g. data processing, anonymity), agency in shaping the usage of the software (participative design) to the skills' requirements of students themselves and the effect of using the software on learning (e.g. increase student engagement).

Institutional Requirements. This cluster has the highest average bridging value of 0.73, meaning least agreement among the participants on the groupings of the statements which were often sorted with statements that were not in their vicinity. Within this cluster there is also a range of sub-themes that participants attribute to the institutional organization. These include the strategic vision of the reason for using CloudClass, accompanied by a clear plan and communication of these widely within the organization. There is a need to define the institutional support in the use of the tool, both in the form of extra working hours, and teaching/academic recognition for educators. Finally, instructional objectives for the use of CloudClass should be clear, transparent, and should be reflected in the recommended instructional design.

3.3 Importance and Feasibility Ratings of the Identified Requirements

Rating data brings another dimension to the analysis making not only numerical, but also visual comparisons possible in the form of pattern matches and go-zones.

Average cluster ratings that were calculated based on individual statement ratings for importance and feasibility were quite high, spanning from 3.69 to 4.17 for importance and from 3.38 to 3.66 for feasibility on a 5-point Likert scale.

The absolute pattern match presented in Fig. 2 illustrates the average rating comparison of importance and feasibility for each cluster with a correlation of $r = 0.66$ between the two ratings. Here the higher ratings for importance for all the thematic clusters are apparent.

T-tests were produced for each cluster rating. A statistically significant difference was found between the importance and feasibility rating for the following clusters: *Evaluation* (T-Value = 4.28, $p < 0.001$) and *Maintenance and Training* (T-Value = 4.99, $p < 0.001$); moderately significant difference is seen in clusters *Institutional Requirements* (T-Value = 2.45, $p < 0.05$) and *Affordances and Infrastructure* (T-Value = 2.03, $p < 0.05$); and no significant difference was identified in the cluster *Student Requirements* (T-Value = 1.68, $p > 0.05$). More detail on the T-tests is given in the Annex [1].

Go-Zones. To take a closer look at the rating differences within each cluster, go-zones were produced for each cluster. Each go-zone shows the entire content of a particular cluster allocating each statement on the two-dimensional x/y scale according to its rated importance (horizontal axis) and feasibility (vertical axis). All the charts are provided in the digital Annex [1] (in figures 6–10 and tables 2–6), and an example of two go-zones for cluster *Evaluation* and *Maintenance and Training* is given in Fig. 3 below.

Based on the means of rating values, go-zone charts divide the scatter plot into quadrants that can be analyzed further. In the context of the CloudClass project, statements located in the upper right quadrant represent immediate or first-priority action points based on participants' shared vision of highest importance and feasibility. Ideas in the yellow quadrant with high importance rating but lower feasibility (if located at the top of the quadrant) are seen as strategic goals for the project. Finally, statements in the right part of the orange quadrant can be considered as further steps in the workflow of technology implementation, or sub-actions within the major tasks.

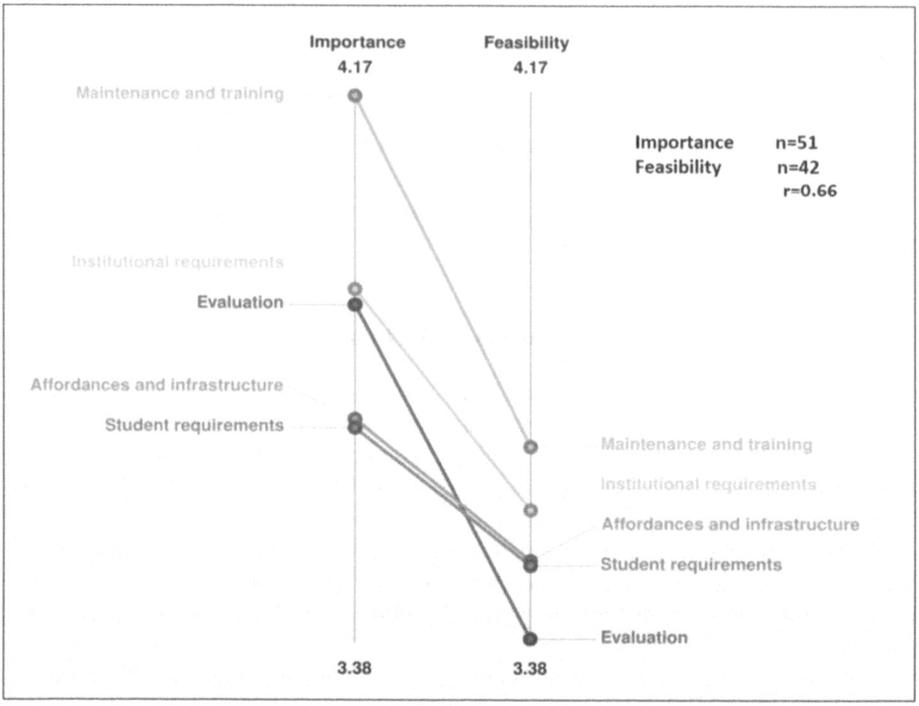

Fig. 2. Absolute pattern match for Importance versus. Feasibility.

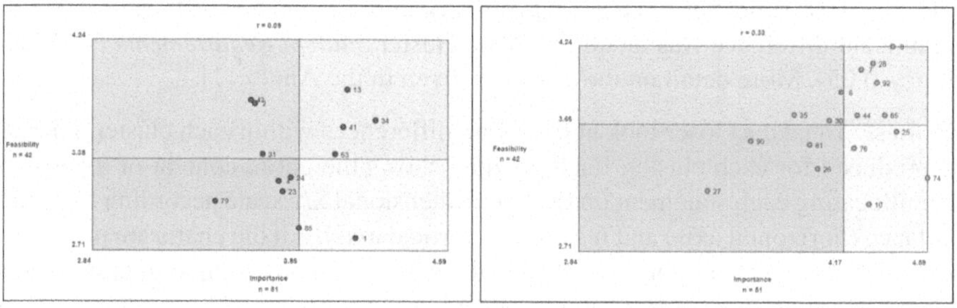

Fig. 3. Examples of go-zones for clusters *Evaluation* (left) and *Maintenance and Training* (right).

4 Discussion

The present study aimed at identifying the requirements for implementing a DVR tool like CloudClass for education in the university context to foster efficient, effective and enjoyable learning. Therefore the two research questions were addressed.

RQ1: What are the requirements for implementing and using a DVR tool like CloudClass in university education?

The list of 95 unique individual statements with requirements was produced based on the input from the participants across two universities. The requirements were statistically sorted in five core thematic clusters representing the major requirements that need to be considered for the implementation of CloudClass within an institution: *Maintenance and Training, Institutional Requirements, Evaluation, Affordances and Infrastructure, Student Requirements.*

RQ2: What is the feasibility and the importance of the identified implementation requirements for the use of a DVR tool like CloudClass in higher education?

Feasibility and importance ratings of each individual requirement, as well as thematic cluster were identified and presented in different graphical and statistical ways to inform the implementation process – in the cluster map (Fig. 1), pattern match (Fig. 2), and go-zones (see figures 6–10 and tables 2–6 in the Annex [1]).

Using the GCM methodology, the present study collected and statistically aggregated the views of three stakeholder groups (teachers, educational media experts and managers) within two European universities from different countries – a distance learning university and a face-to-face one, thus depicting the diversity of contexts in the ideas generated within the brainstorming phase. The numbers of participants involved in sorting and rating activities were sufficient to draw robust conclusions for the further analyses.

The requirements for implementation and use of VR technology in education identified in this study go in line with the factors reported in the literature. Financial cost [12, 17], complexity and accessibility of software and hardware [16, 17], the need for evidence-based didactic frameworks [13, 16, 25, 26] and teaching practices that can support teacher training [2, 12], have been mentioned as factors affecting technology adoption as well as effective and widespread implementation of VR tools outside specialized domains like engineering and computer science [2].

This study also took a systematic approach to prioritize the identified implementation requirements according to their importance and feasibility ratings within an institution. The importance cluster ratings on a scale from 1 to 5, ranging from 3.69 (*Student Requirements*) to 4.17 (*Maintenance and Training*), and feasibility ratings from 3.38 (*Evaluation*) to 3.66 (*Maintenance and Training*) highlighted that all the major factors identified through clustering are of significant importance and high feasibility with a strong correlation between the two. It is worth noting that the order of priority for all the clusters except for *Evaluation* is the same, emphasizing that all the indicated factors need to be considered early on in the project development. Although it is quite typical to have higher importance ratings in GCM projects as a way for participants to voice their values, the statistically significant difference between importance and feasibility ratings for the clusters *Maintenance and Training* and *Evaluation* emphasizes their first-line importance that should be part of technology implementation policy. The former cluster also scored highest on average ratings, bringing about the importance of the identified themes that can be taken as action points in the implementation process. Although cluster *Evaluation* scored lowest on feasibility, the significantly high importance rating values underscore the urgency to address the research needs early on within the project.

One of the major findings of this study is the result obtained by means of generating go-zones which list the action points for each thematic cluster with a specific level of priority. This way, the present study is addressing an identified absence of systematic approach in the field of VR use for educational purposes [2]. Based on go-zone charts, the statements in the three quadrants of interest were further analyzed qualitatively to inform the CloudClass project. The outcomes of each thematic category are summarized for each cluster in order of average importance and feasibility ratings.

Maintenance and Training. Statements in this cluster prioritise the ease of meaningful use by teachers and smooth operation for students. Teacher training should include knowledge on why when and how to use CloudClass, in other words, which didactic strategies should be used in specific learning situations. For this purpose instructional materials need to be developed, including hands-on workshops and lectures. In further stages of the project teachers can be supported by previously developed pedagogical scenarios and best practice examples that are readily available. A helpdesk or a CloudClass expert is required to assist teachers with the use of the tool, and after the end of the project continuous maintenance is required.

Institutional Requirements. Within this cluster the need is voiced to have clear goals for the use of CloudClass that teachers will know about. More specifically, instructional objectives for the use of CloudClass should be defined in specific contexts and supported institutionally by developing teaching practices and suitable instructional design. As a further step, information about CloudClass should be disseminated widely throughout the university.

Evaluation. Research should be conducted on the effectiveness of CloudClass including short- and long-term effects, comparison with other tools and effects on different target groups (students with disabilities). Further steps suggest forming a working group to evaluate and discuss the added value of CloudClass. It should be mentioned that participants found important that added value of CloudClass would outweigh its costs, but this item scored low on feasibility (2.80 out of 5.00, cluster mean 3.38).

Affordances and Infrastructure. Within this cluster, interaction support between students and teachers is of primary importance, as well as the possibility of operation with a large group of students. User-friendliness and a short learning curve for using the technology are seen as core features, together with the flexibility of use on the available equipment that students and teachers have, including sufficient connection speed. Apart from that, making CloudClass templates for the use of 3D objects is seen as immediate action point, later including libraries of 3D models available for teachers' use. Strategic goals include integration of CloudClass in the university eco-system on all levels: hardware and software facilities, as well as appropriate design of learning materials (both instructional and media design).

Student Requirements. Based on the go-zone analysis of this cluster, participants see the need for CloudClass environment to be easy to use and engaging/appealing as opposed to distracting. Knowing how to balance effectiveness, efficiency and enjoyability within the environment for students is a strategic goal, as well as students being able to opt for a plain background. Technology acceptance and learners' data protection need to be considered as goals of primary importance.

The present study has some limitations with respect to generalization of the findings. Because participants involved in the sorting and rating phases represented one institution

(OU), the results drawn from the analyses can reliably inform the workflow of the specific project set in the Netherlands in a distance-learning university. It would be interesting to compare these findings with those of other institutions, countries and/or developed for other tools. What is more, the majority of participants for the sorting and rating phases were represented by teachers (89% and 83% respectively), whereas it would be interesting to compare this data with other stakeholder groups, potentially including students and representatives of companies developing the tools.

Another limitation derives from the fact that the study was based on evaluating the possible application of DVR tools based on an example of CloudClass. Despite the fact that participants' responses were triggered by the technical affordances of one tool, we consider the generated output informative and transferable to a range of similar DVR tools that have relatively low technical threshold and do not require extensive training in graphic design or programming.

The results of this GCM study make a solid starting point in addressing technology implementation and integration projects within universities in a holistic and systematic way to ensure effective, efficient and sustainable use and further development of these technologies. Such approach gives voice to the core stakeholder groups and end users and can foster the development of the DVR tool by informing the involved partners of the factors that need to be considered for the successful implementation of similar projects.

5 Conclusions

The present study focused on identifying the requirements for implementing a DVR tool like CloudClass in a university setting. The results of the study provide valuable insights into the priorities and challenges associated with the wide-scale adoption of VR technology in educational institutions.

The findings of this GCM study revealed that the requirements identified across the two European universities (OU, USC) can be grouped into five thematic clusters: *Evaluation, Institutional Requirements, Maintenance and Training, Student Requirements*, and *Affordances and Infrastructure*. Go-zones generated from the importance and feasibility ratings for each cluster provide an informative overview of steps to ensure the holistic implementation of a DVR tool like CloudClass. It considers a balance of pedagogical needs and technological affordances of the given tool.

The findings of this study offer insights to the scientific community, addressing the pressing issue of integrating DVR tools into mainstream education beyond experimental endeavours. By shedding light on the perspectives and challenges faced by the core stakeholders, the study not only facilitates a better understanding of their needs but also empowers them to articulate their struggles. Moreover, it strives to bridge the gap between technology developers and educators/practitioners, fostering collaboration, and provides guidance to other similar implementation projects by acknowledging the current experimental phase of DVR tool adoption in educational institutions.

In conclusion, the findings of this study emphasise the importance of considering the identified requirements when implementing DVR tools like CloudClass in educational institutions and offer valuable insights into the priorities and challenges associated with DVR adoption in universities.

References

1. Annex. https://tinyurl.com/GCM4AA
2. Radianti, J., Majchrzak, T.A., Fromm, J., Wohlgenannt, I.: A systematic review of immersive virtual reality applications for higher education: design elements, lessons learned, and research agenda. Comput. Educ. **147**, 103778 (2020). https://doi.org/10.1016/j.compedu.2019.103778
3. Fowler, C.: Virtual reality and learning: Where is the pedagogy?: Learning activities in 3-D virtual worlds. Br. J. Educ. Technol. **46**, 412–422 (2015). https://doi.org/10.1111/bjet.12135
4. Villena-Taranilla, R., Tirado-Olivares, S., Cózar-Gutiérrez, R., González-Calero, J.A.: Effects of virtual reality on learning outcomes in K-6 education: a meta-analysis. Educ. Res. Rev. **35**, 100434 (2022). https://doi.org/10.1016/j.edurev.2022.100434
5. Mikropoulos, T.A., Natsis, A.: Educational virtual environments: a ten-year review of empirical research (1999–2009). Comput. Educ. **56**, 769–780 (2011). https://doi.org/10.1016/j.compedu.2010.10.020
6. Lee, E.A.-L., Wong, K.W.: Learning with desktop virtual reality: low spatial ability learners are more positively affected. Comput. Educ. **79**, 49–58 (2014). https://doi.org/10.1016/j.compedu.2014.07.010
7. Limniou, M., Roberts, D., Papadopoulos, N.: Full immersive virtual environment CAVETM in chemistry education. Comput. Educ. **51**, 584–593 (2008). https://doi.org/10.1016/j.compedu.2007.06.014
8. Allcoat, D., von Mühlenen, A.: Learning in virtual reality: effects on performance, emotion and engagement. Res. Learn. Technol. **26** (2018). https://doi.org/10.25304/rlt.v26.2140
9. Levin, M.F., Weiss, P.L., Keshner, E.A.: Emergence of virtual reality as a tool for upper limb rehabilitation: incorporation of motor control and motor learning principles. Phys. Ther. **95**, 415–425 (2015). https://doi.org/10.2522/ptj.20130579
10. Witmer, B.G., Singer, M.J.: Measuring presence in virtual environments: a presence questionnaire. Presence **7**, 225–240 (1998). https://doi.org/10.1162/105474698565686
11. Slater, M., Wilbur, S.: A framework for immersive virtual environments (FIVE): speculations on the role of presence in virtual environments. Presence Teleoper. Virtual Environ. **6**, 603–616 (1997). https://doi.org/10.1162/pres.1997.6.6.603
12. Merchant, Z., Goetz, E.T., Cifuentes, L., Keeney-Kennicutt, W., Davis, T.J.: Effectiveness of virtual reality-based instruction on students' learning outcomes in K-12 and higher education: a meta-analysis. Comput. Educ. **70**, 29–40 (2014). https://doi.org/10.1016/j.compedu.2013.07.033
13. Smetana, L.K., Bell, R.L.: Computer simulations to support science instruction and learning: a critical review of the literature. Int. J. Sci. Educ. **34**, 1337–1370 (2012). https://doi.org/10.1080/09500693.2011.605182
14. Vogel, J.J., Vogel, D.S., Cannon-Bowers, J., Bowers, C.A., Muse, K., Wright, M.: Computer gaming and interactive simulations for learning: a meta-analysis. J. Educ. Comput. Res. **34**, 229–243 (2006). https://doi.org/10.2190/FLHV-K4WA-WPVQ-H0YM
15. Luo, H., Li, G., Feng, Q., Yang, Y., Zuo, M.: Virtual reality in K-12 and higher education: a systematic review of the literature from 2000 to 2019. J. Comput. Assist. Learn. **37**(3), 887–901 (2021)
16. Mulders, M., Buchner, J., Kerres, M.: A framework for the use of immersive virtual reality in learning environments. Int. J. Emerg. Technol. Learn. **15**, 208 (2020). https://doi.org/10.3991/ijet.v15i24.16615
17. Mujuru, T., Lopez, C.: Creating virtual reality teaching modules for low-cost headsets. In: Volume 2: 41st Computers and Information in Engineering Conference (CIE), p. V002T02A083. American Society of Mechanical Engineers, Virtual (2021). https://doi.org/10.1115/DETC2021-72084

18. Makransky, G., Terkildsen, T.S., Mayer, R.E.: Adding immersive virtual reality to a science lab simulation causes more presence but less learning. Learn. Instr. **60**, 225–236 (2019). https://doi.org/10.1016/j.learninstruc.2017.12.007
19. Kane, M., Rosas, S.: Conversations About Group Concept Mapping: Applications, Examples and Enhancements. SAGE, Los Angeles (2018)
20. Trochim, W.M., McLinden, D.: Introduction to a special issue on concept mapping. Eval. Program Plann. **60**, 166–175 (2017). https://doi.org/10.1016/j.evalprogplan.2016.10.006
21. Rosas, S.R., Kane, M.: Quality and rigor of the concept mapping methodology: a pooled study analysis. Eval. Program Plann. **35**, 236–245 (2012). https://doi.org/10.1016/j.evalprogplan.2011.10.003
22. Anderberg, M.R.: Cluster Analysis For Applications. Academic Press, New York (1973)
23. Everitt, B.: Cluster analysis. Qual. Quant. **14**, 75–100 (1980). https://doi.org/10.1007/BF00154794
24. Kane, M., Trochim, W.: Concept Mapping for Planning and Evaluation. SAGE Publications, Inc., Thousand Oaks (2007). https://doi.org/10.4135/9781412983730
25. Makransky, G., Petersen, G.B.: The cognitive affective model of immersive learning (CAMIL): a theoretical research-based model of learning in immersive virtual reality. Educ. Psychol. Rev. **33**, 937–958 (2021). https://doi.org/10.1007/s10648-020-09586-2
26. Dalgarno, B., Lee, M.J.W.: What are the learning affordances of 3-D virtual environments? Br. J. Edu. Technol. **41**, 10–32 (2010). https://doi.org/10.1111/j.1467-8535.2009.01038.x

Student Perception of Social Comparison in Technology Enhanced Learning

Aditya Joshi(✉), Bente Molenkamp, and Sergey Sosnovsky

Utrecht University, Utrecht, The Netherlands
{a.joshi,s.sosnovsky}@uu.nl, b.l.molenkamp@students.uu.nl

Abstract. People often compare themselves to their peers in various contexts, including education. Usage of this general tendency becomes an effective strategy to enhance students' motivation. Several successful implementations of social comparison in educational applications have demonstrated positive outcomes. Yet, they largely disregard the fact that people differ in how they react to social comparison, and how they process and interact with social information. In this study, we have built and evaluated a set of interface prototypes visualising different types of social comparison based on the directions and distance of comparison, as well as its privacy policy and social space. We found that not all students have similar social comparison preferences. On some questions, students in a low-performance scenario have provided significantly different answers compared to students at the top of the class. We also discovered that students with different achievement goal orientations can differ in their perception of social comparison. These results provide us with insights on how the effect of social comparison can vary depending on individual differences between students. This line of research can potentially lead to creating adaptive social comparison interfaces that support and motivate students in an individually-optimized manner.

Keywords: education psychology · social comparison · online learning · leaderboard

1 Introduction

Fostering motivation is important for successful learning in any context [38, 39]. Increased motivation has been associated with several important learning outcomes such as persistence [37], retention [25], achievement [10], and course satisfaction [13]. It can influence what, when and how one learns, and has proven to be a significant predictor of performance [33,34]. Moreover, research shows that motivated learners are more likely to take on challenging activities, stay engaged, be creative, enjoy the learning process, and adopt a deep learning approach [32]. In most online learning scenarios, motivation gains even greater significance, as in such setting students are often left to their own devices and need to learn in self-regulated manner lacking guidance, feedback and stimuli usually administered by teachers [28].

O. Viberg et al. (Eds.): EC-TEL 2023, LNCS 14200, pp. 118–132, 2023.
https://doi.org/10.1007/978-3-031-42682-7_9

Students' motivation can be enhanced through various factors (e.g. interest in the subject) and techniques (e.g. gamification). Several investigations have shown that social comparison (SC) can be beneficial in educational settings as a powerful driver of motivation and an effective source of instructional feedback [9,15,36,40]. Moreover, many experiments have demonstrated that SC can have different effects on different categories of students. Olson & Evans [30] found that students who were high in neuroticism reported a greater increase in positive affect after comparing to under-achieving peers, while students high in openness preferred to compare with those who performed better. Leung [26] highlighted the need of individualising information given by SC. In a study on how the position on different types of leaderboards affects learning performance, [3] compared absolute and relative leaderboards and found that students' motivation and preference differed based on where they stand on a leaderboard.

Yet, most of the existing online learning support environments that leverage SC, while successful in general, disregard individual differences of students. To escape this one-size-fits-all design, we need to achieve a deeper understanding of the interplay between student motivation and SC. We need to explore the ways, in which personal, social and contextual factors may influence students' attitude towards SC and their perception of educational interfaces based on this technology. Such an approach would allow to organise online learning environments in a way that uses SC to facilitate student motivation as optimally as possible.

The goal of this study is to make one of the first steps in this direction and investigate students' perception of different implementations of a SC-enabled educational interface in different scenarios. Consequently, the general research question of this study is:

"What is the student perception of SC implementations in online learning environments?"

This question is narrowed down by focusing on the effects of students' performance and achievement motivation profile, on their perception of SC. The three main research subsections are:

RQ 1: What is the general student perception of different SC implementations?
RQ 2: What is the relation (if any) between student performance and their perception of SC?
RQ 3: What is the relation (if any) between a students' achievement motivation and their perception of SC?

2 Related Work

SC is a well-explored phenomenon. In his classical work, Festinger [11] stated that there is an inherent desire in people to evaluate their abilities, opinions, and beliefs. He states that this desire is satisfied through SC. Wood [41] extended this definition and concluded that in addition to self-appraisal, people may engage in SC also to self-improve and self-enhance. SC is spontaneous, effortless, unintentional and happens relatively automatically, especially when there is lack of other information. In educational scenarios, when students receive infrequent and constrained feedback from their teachers, they end up engaging in SC with their peers to reduce uncertainty, evaluate their performance, build their self-concept and direct their efforts. It is a major feature of the classroom environment [27] as comparing one's performance to others results in higher engagement and motivation, as it allows individuals to determine their effort and performance expectations.

In technology-enhanced learning, leaderboards or ranking charts have been widely used as SC tools improving student motivation and engagement [3,12,23]. A critical examination of existing Learning Analytics dashboards [24] highlighted that the dashboards use SC to help the students understand the behavior of their peers and use it a feedback on how they could improve. However it was also noticed that some designs may shift the focus on competition between the learners rather than mastering the subject. SC visualizations like Comtella [5] and Knowledge Sea II [1] allowed students to compare their performance with their peers. Such comparative information can also be provided through widgets on a Learning Analytics Dashboard that has been shown [8] to improve course completion rates in Massively Open Online Courses (MOOCs).

There are more advanced interfaces that use ideas from Open Student Models [7] like Progressor [20–22], QuizMap [6], Reading Circle [17], and Reading Mirror [4] that combine personalized and social learning to motivate and engage students by nudging them to learn or read more. Mastery Grids [16,29] is a social Educational Progress Visualization that shows a students' expertise across various topics and shows how they compare with the class average. This form of visualization was shown to improve the motivation and engagement of the students. Recent variations [2] have implemented learner-controlled SC by studying a novel fine-grained peer group selection interface.

Despite the positive effects, SC has been said to have mixed effects, as it leads to competition and makes individuals aware of their lack of skill, status or position relative to others [14]. It has also been noticed that in some cases, such SC can diminish intrinsic motivation and overall performance [18].

This leads to the question about the factors that decide when SC leads to positive outcomes and when it does not. It is found that mastery-oriented individuals preferred to compare with someone who outperformed them because they wanted to self-improve [31]. On the contrary, performance-oriented individuals were more self-enhance, which in turn led them to prefer less competent peers to compare themselves with. If implemented incorrectly, SC may have detrimental effects [19] on motivation and engagement. It was also found [35] that students' SC own preferences do not necessarily align with their best interests.

3 Methodology

The aim of this research is to explore how different students perceive different types of SC. The *perception* is approached to understand how the students' attitude and performance are affected. We are especially interested in exploring the perceived preference, informativeness, comfort, and motivation. We are also interested in finding out if there are differences in the perceptions of students depending on their academic performances. We have constructed prototypes that provide SC information to students to analyse and provide their opinions using a structured questionnaire. This section describes the methodology of this research in details.

3.1 Questionnaire Design

The goal of the questionnaire is to identify possible relations between students' motivational profiles and their perceptions of different types of SC implementations. Consequently, the questionnaire has been divided into two parts. The first part contains questions about the basic demographics of the participants and a scale to measure participants' motivation profile. The second part focused on showing to the participants different SC implementations using predefined prototypes and asking them questions about different implementations.

2 x 2 Goal Achievement Framework. The part of the questionnaire used to measure the participant's motivation profile is the 2×2 Goal Achievement Framework by Elliot & McGregor (2001). The texts of the questions have been slightly modified to fit the scenario better. This framework consisted of 12 items using five-point Likert scale. It is divided into four parts, each measuring one of the four goal orientations: performance-approach, performance-avoidance, mastery-approach, and mastery-avoidance.

When students have performance-approach goals, they are focused on demonstration of competence relative to others. In contrast, students having performance-approach goals are concerned with avoiding failing in front of others. Students who have mastery-approach goals are committed to learning and self-improvement. They are not necessarily motivated by the design to show their competence to others. Students who have mastery-avoidance goals are concerned about their inability to master the subject. They might worry that they may not learn all that they possibly could in the class. The students having different types of goals use different strategies to achieve their goals. This emphasises the need of having personalized support in TEL, and thus is a necessary element that should be addressed.

High vs. Low Performance. For the second part of the questionnaire, a between-subject design was employed in order to compare the perceptions of high performing students and low performing students, and determine whether there are any significant differences between the two groups. We refrained from within-subject design to prevent the questionnaire from being too long and avoid potential interaction between the scenarios. Participants were asked to imagine that they took part in a course for which the midterm exam results had just been posted online. We randomly assigned them to either the 'high-performance' or 'low-performance' group. Depending on the group, they either passed with an

8.5/10.0 and ranked in top ten of the class, or failed the exam with 5.4/10.0 and placed at the bottom ten of the class. The effects of the students responding to hypothetical situation were validated and are discussed later in Sect. 5.1. To aid the participants in visualising themselves as a student in the scenario, and to give them more of an idea of what each SC implementation entails, prototypes were used as visual support.

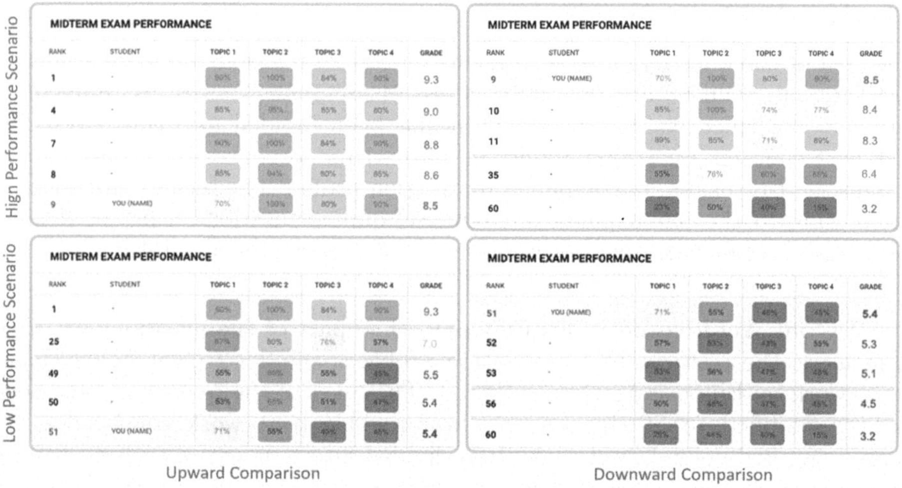

Fig. 1. Upward and Downward Comparison prototypes for High and Low Performance Scenarios.

Prototypes. The prototypes showed the scoreboard of the midterm exam which displayed the class rankings, grades and performance per exam topic in percentages of five students including the participant. The performance per exam topic is shown in percentages and is colour coded in five colours ranging from dark red for a score below 50% to dark green (above 90%) with yellow representing 70%-80%.

We created four pairs of prototypes for low-performing and high-performing scenarios each, thus resulting in a total of sixteen prototypes. The four pairs represent:

- Anonymous SC versus Public implementation
- Close/adjacent comparison versus far/non-adjacent comparison
- Upwards comparison versus Downwards comparison
- Results of only friends versus results of friends and other students

The prototypes in each pair were labelled with Design A and Design B and were accompanied with short descriptions of what each prototype represented. The four prototype pairs based on the students' performance group were shown to all the students in the order presented above. A deliberate decision was made to ask the participants about their perception of public vs. anonymous comparison first and keep all the other prototypes anonymous (with the exception of the prototypes that show the names of friends) so as not to let the issue of privacy interfere with their opinion regarding other implementations. Figure 1 shows the prototypes related to Upward vs. Downward comparison for both high and low performance scenarios. We chose the positions moderately near the top and the bottom of the class to make them look realistic and relatable. Based on the student's scenario, a corresponding pair would be shown.

The other three pairs are displayed in Fig. 2, but only for the high-performance scenario. We do not include their low-performance counterparts to save space.

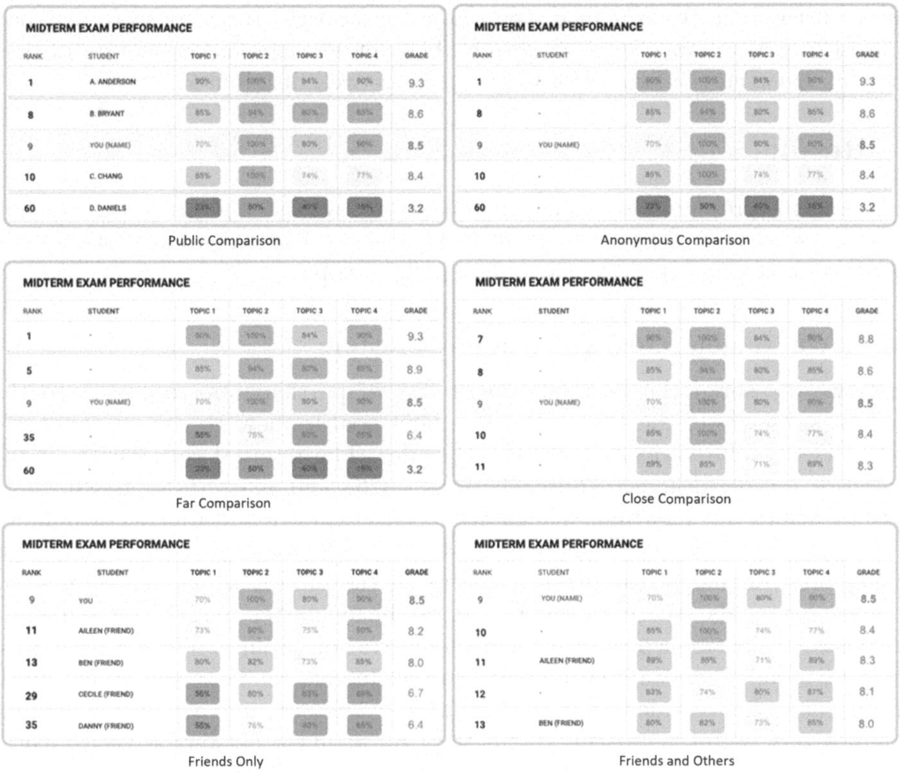

Fig. 2. Remaining three prototype pairs for the High Performance Scenario.

Questions About Student Perception. For each pair of prototypes, four questions were asked to find out participants' perception about the SC implementation represented by these prototypes. These questions asked the users to choose which of two versions they prefer from (1) strongly prefer prototype A, to (2) somewhat prefer prototype A, to (3) consider both prototypes equal, to (4) somewhat prefer prototype B, to (5) strongly prefer prototype B. Students had to rate these prototypes based on their perception in terms of general preference, how comfortable they would be with using such a prototype, in terms of the prototype informativeness, and in terms of the prototype capacity to motivate. Each of these questions was followed by an optional open-ended question that asked the participant to explain their answer.

3.2 Participants

A total of 56 participants were gathered over a two-week span. 51.8% of participants were male and 48.2% female, with the age of participants ranging from 18 to 29 and a mean age of 23. The majority of participants (69.6%) were Bachelor students, after which Master students were the largest group (25.0%), followed by a small group of high school students (5.4%). 27 participants ended up being placed in the high-performance scenario group and the other 29 were assigned to the low performance scenario group. The gender, age and education of participants between the two scenario groups were well distributed.

4 Results

This section, presents the results of our study by first analyzing the clusters based on students' response to identify typical motivation profiles followed by details on how users perceive the different SC setups.

4.1 Achievement Goal Orientation Clusters

First, we measured the internal consistency of participants' responses to the the four subscales of the 12-item achievement goal framework using Cronbach's alpha. The results varied across the subscales. The internal consistency of the responses for performance-approach (α = .926) and mastery-approach (α = .806) subscales was very high. The internal consistency of performance-avoidance (α = .508) and mastery-avoidance (α = .698) subscales was rather low. Thus we explored further possibilities of analyzing the groups while considering the achievement goals. We performed a hierarchical cluster analysis of students' responses to identify typical achievement motivation profiles. Three strong clusters were found. Cross-tabulation between the clusters and the achievement motivation subscales revealed that performance-avoidance and mastery-avoidance were not very useful in creating distinctions between the clusters as their answer distributions were scattered across the three groups. These observations were in agreement with the results of the internal consistency analysis of the "avoidance" subscales. Therefore motivational profiles were created for each cluster based only on the levels of performance-approach and mastery-approach.

The obtained clusters are summarized below:

- Cluster 1: 12 participants, scored low in performance-approach (score $\leq$ 2.33) and low to moderate scores in mastery-approach (score $\leq$ 3.33)
- Cluster 2: 23 participants, scored high in mastery-approach (score $\geq$ 3)
- Cluster 3: 21 participants, scored high in performance-approach (score > 3)

4.2 General Consensus About the SC Implementations

The four pairs of SC implementations described in Sect. 3.1 reveal students' perceptions and preferences across the four chosen dimensions that represent the design considerations during development of an SC interface.

Table 1. Descriptive Statistics of participants response to four prototype pairs

		Preference	Comfort	Informativeness	Motivation
Public (1) vs Anonymous (5)Results	Median	5	4	3	3
	Mode	5	5	3	3
	Std. Deviation	1.180	.903	.952	.815
	Skewness	**−1.143**	**−1.174**	.366	.083
Close (1) vs. Far (5) Comparison	Median	3	3	3	3
	Mode	3	3	3	3
	Std. Deviation	1.309	1.003	1.289	1.135
	Skewness	.040	−.025	−.085	−.031
Upward (1) vs Downward (5) Comparison	Median	2	2	3	2
	Mode	2	3	3	2
	Std. Deviation	1.098	.864	.844	.930
	Skewness	.415	−.558	−.436	.056
Friends (1) vs. Friends and Others (5)	Median	3	3	3	3
	Mode	4	3	3	3
	Std. Deviation	1.182	1.009	1.274	.921
	Skewness	−.321	−.040	−.053	−.142

Public vs. Anonymous Results. When the participants were presented with these two prototypes, more than half of the participants (51.8%) strongly preferred the anonymous prototype and 21.4% more somewhat preferred it. Open questions revealed that this preference mostly stems from participants being uncomfortable with other people knowing their grades and position on the leaderboard. When asked which prototype design the participants felt more comfortable with, 22.6% strongly felt 'more comfortable' with the anonymous prototype, followed by 35.7% being 'somewhat more comfortable' with the anonymous prototype.

In terms of informativeness, when shown the two prototypes, both were considered to be equally informative by most students. Both the designs were found to be almost equally motivating. More details are presented in the table 1.

Close vs. Far Comparison. The close comparison and far comparison prototypes show very different view of SC. However the descriptive statistics show that for the questions regarding the preference, comfort, informativeness, and motivation the median lies around 3, which means that most students were neutral about both of the prototypes. However, the result become significantly different, when we split students into two groups based on "their performance". This is discussed in Sect. 4.3.

Upward vs. Downward Comparison. The response on upward and downward comparison shows that there students in general have a slight preference towards upward comparison design. More than a half of participants (55.5%) strongly preferred or somewhat preferred the upwards comparison compared to only 16% preferring the downward option. Almost a half of participants (48.2%) considered upward SC more motivating compared to only 5% considering downward SC more motivating. When answering questions about which of the two designs was more comfortable and informative, participants considered both the implementations to be almost equal.

Showing only Friends vs. Showing Friends and Others. The general consensus based on the central tendency of the questions was that both prototype designs were equally preferred, comfortable, informative, and motivating in the eyes of the participants.

4.3 Between-Group Analysis: High Performance vs. Low Performance

To check for any significant difference in SC perception between the high performance and low performance scenario samples, Mann-Whitney U tests were performed on student's answers to the 16 questions evaluating 4 preferences over 4 prototypes comparisons. The results of the tests came out significant only for two questions comparing close SC vs. far SC implementations. Students form the high performance group preferred the close SC more than students from the low-performance group. At the same time, students from low-performance group regarded the prototype implementing far SC more informative than students from the high-performance group. For all other questions, no significant differences were found.

High-performance group strongly preferred the SC prototype that showed the results of peers directly adjacent to the target student on the leaderboard (Mean = 2.4; Median = 2.0; SD = 1.28) compared to the low-performance group (Mean = 3.3; Median = 3.0; SD = 1.22); U = 195.5 (p-value = 0.042). The reoccurring reason in the answer explanations given by the "high performing students" was that they were not interested in seeing people far away from them, especially far down in ranking. Seeing and comparing the results of people that have a "similar score" or are 'more equal' to them felt more interesting to them. Students in the low-performance group, were more equally distributed in their opinion regarding the two SC implementations. While some of them felt similarly to the high-performing counterparts and preferred to focus on the results of their "neighbours", others valued a wider overview of the leaderbaord for enabling them to better understand how the class at large is doing.

In a similar fashion, low-performance students considered far SC significantly more informative (Mean = 3.7; Median = 3.0; SD = 1.09) compared to the high-performance students (Mean = 2.9; Median = 3.0; SD = 1.29); U = 183.5 (p-value = 0.023). On this questions, the high-performing students did not express a strong unified preference; while the low-performance students definitely saw the interface that allows them to compare with the results of a wider range of peers as more informative.

Regarding the feeling of comfortableness, the majority of both groups felt equally comfortable with both prototypes. However, a noticeable number of students in the high performance group felt much more comfortable with the close comparison prototype. Participants elaborated on this by mentioning that they found that the far comparison prototype gave too much attention to the 'best and worst performers' or 'outliers'.

It is worth mentioning that the results on the two remaining questions comparing these two prototypes were similar. High-performance students felt more comfortable with a close SC, while low-performance students did not have a strong tendency either way. At the same time, low-performance students felt that the far SC prototype motivates them better, while high-performance students regarded the prototypes equally motivating. However, these differences were not significant.

4.4 Achievement Motivation and SC Perception

After identifying three clusters based on the achievement motivation scale in Sect. 4.1, a Kruskal-Wallis test was performed to find out if there was any relation between a participant's achievement motivation profile and their SC perception. Two pairwise comparisons turned out significant. When comparing students' opinion regarding the informativeness of anonymous vs. public SC implementations, there was a significant difference in answer distributions between cluster 3 "high in performance-approach" (Mean = 2.11; Median = 2; SD = 0.809) and cluster 1 "low in performance-approach and low in mastery-approach" (Mean = 3.18; Median = 3; SD = 0.751); H = 18.27 (p-value = 0.001). Students in cluster-1 found public comparison to be more informative than the other students.

For the upward vs. downward comparison implementations, there was a significant difference between the answer distributions for the question regarding how comfortable the two implementations are. Students in Cluster 3 "high in performance-approach" (Mean = 3.21; Median = 3; SD = 0.787) are significantly more comfortable with downward comparison implementation than students in Cluster 2 "high in mastery-approach" (Mean = 2.59; Median = 3; SD = 0.825); H = 10.54 (p-value = 0.016). They are also significantly more comfortable with downward comparison implementation than students in Cluster 1 "low in mastery-approach and low in performance approach" (Mean = 2.55; Median = 3; SD = 0.688); H = 11.88 (p-value = 0.024).

5 Discussion

This study of students' perception of different SC design choices can provide interesting insights for the developers of effective educational interfaces using SC.

It is quite clear that most students are much more comfortable with anonymous leaderboards compared to public. A reoccurring explanation from students was that though they are interesting in finding out where they stand, they don't care about who they are outperforming. They also feel uncomfortable by the prospect of being judged by their peers should their performance be publicly observable and identifiable. These results are similar (both quantitatively and qualitatively) to the outcomes of another recent study that focused on this issue [3].

When we looked at Close vs Far comparison, there was no strong general trend. However the between-group tests show that high performing students have a significantly stronger preference of the prototype that shows the results of students who are similar to them. These results are in agreement with the general trend characterising another aspect of SC - upward vs. downward comparison. Answers to the questions about Upward vs Downward comparison show a slightly higher general preference in favour of upward comparison as more preferred and motivating. Hence, when looking at these two aspects together, an argument can be made, that a higher preference in favour of far SC among low-performance students is directly linked to the fact that they prefer upward comparison, as for them, comparing far mean comparing upward. At the same time, for high-performance students, upward comparison means comparing near. However, one important exception here comes from the analysis of students' achievement orientation. It shows that people high in performance approach orientation found downward SC to be more informative.

Student behavior is complex, and there are indeed, major individual differences that explain how they perceive, and how they get motivated by the design of SC interfaces. This study highlights the need of developing interfaces that adapt to the needs of each individual.

5.1 Limitations and Mitigation

This research is based on a sample size of 56 participants. Future work will address this and we will conduct similar studies in real courses with much larger number of participants.

Another major limitation of this research was that the students were presented a hypothetical scenario. This means that participants might have answered the questions based on a scenario that does not adequately reflect their real-life situation. e.g., a top-performing student must answer questions while imagining themselves to be at the bottom of a class.

To mitigate potentially erroneous conclusion, we conducted an additional study to understand how different the hypothetical low and high performing students are compared to actual performance and expectations of the students. The participants were asked what is a general satisfactory result of a course for them in terms of a course grade. With these answers, another round of analysis was conducted by only selecting the data of participants that were matched with a hypothetical scenario that matches their actual performance or expectations. Thus we limited the data to actual high performing students (or at least striving to be) that were also present in the high performance scenario, and under performing students (or students who are satisfied with their grade as long as they pass the course) that were present in the low performance scenario. This resulted in two groups that both consisted of 12 participants. We examined the answers of these two groups. It turns out, the answers from true low and high performance students were similar to the answers given by students in the hypothetical groups. This led us to conclude that students in fact were quite effective in placing themselves in the required hypothetical scenarios and providing truthful and reliable answers. As a result, perhaps, this limitation of using scenarios to measure the effect of performance might not be as severe as it seems at first.

5.2 Future Work

The future work should focus on uncovering the actual students' behavior and actual use of SC implementations by executing a longitudinal experiments in the framework of a real course. Such experiments can lead to clearer and more conclusive results when the analysed sample size is larger. Another idea that could be investigated is the temporal changes in the preferences or behavior of the students during a course. It could also be interesting to analyse whether the perception changes after receiving a good or a poor grade for an assignment. Design of SC interfaces is another interesting area that should be explored. It might be valuable to explore what type of SC visualisation is preferred by students or is most effective in eliciting positive learning behaviour.

Another primary direction of future work is to find how personal factors and individual characteristics such as personality type, confidence level etc. affect a student's SC and behavior. It would be interesting to see what factors make a student more willing and open to engage in SC than others.

6 Conclusion

SC is a powerful motivator. But because of individual differences among the students, everyone responds differently to what and how the SC information is displayed. In this study, we examined the preferences of students with regards to different SC implementations. The four SC implementations were represented through prototype designs of a hypothetical midterm exam scoreboard of an online course and were presented in an online survey. Each prototype represented a choice for a certain SC implementation: keeping the results anonymous or public, showing only upward or downward comparison information, showing people in proximity with their ranking or farther away, and showing only the results of their friends or of friends and other students. We learnt which type of SC interfaces the high performing students and the low performing students prefer, find comfortable, informative, and motivating. We also found that there is an interplay between achievement orientation and the preferences towards the design of SC.

We investigated the validity of using hypothetical scenarios and compared them with participants who actually match the scenarios they were provided. We discovered that the differences in imagined scenarios and responses with students who are actually in high performance or low performance groups might not be as severe as it might seem. We acknowledge that there is a need of uncovering actual behavior of the students in a real course. Identifying students' perception of SC, provides us with insights that can lead to effective design decisions that help the students improve their motivation, comfort and engagement with learning systems regardless of their individual differences.

References

1. Ahn, J.W., Farzan, R., Brusilovsky, P.: A two-level adaptive visualization for information access to open-corpus educational resources. In: Proceedings of Workshop on the Social Navigation and Community-Based Adaptation Technologies at the 4th International Conference on Adaptive Hypermedia and Adaptive Web-Based Systems, pp. 497–505 (2006)
2. Akhuseyinoglu, K., Milicevic, A.K., Brusilovsky, P.: Who are my peers? Learner-controlled social comparison in a programming course. In: Hilliger, I., Munoz-Merino, P.J., De Laet, T., Ortega-Arranz, A., Farrell, T. (eds.) Educating for a New Future: Making Sense of Technology-Enhanced Learning Adoption. EC-TEL 2022. LNCS, vol. 13450, pp. 1–15. Springer, Cham (2022). https://doi.org/10.1007/978-3-031-16290-9_1
3. Bai, S., Hew, K.F., Sailer, M., Jia, C.: From top to bottom: how positions on different types of leaderboard may affect fully online student learning performance, intrinsic motivation, and course engagement. Comput. Educ. **173**, 104297 (2021)
4. Barria-Pineda, J., Brusilovsky, P., He, D.: Reading mirror: social navigation and social comparison for electronic textbooks. In: iTextbooks@AIED (2019)
5. Bretzke, H., Vassileva, J.: Motivating cooperation on peer to peer networks. In: Brusilovsky, P., Corbett, A., de Rosis, F. (eds.) UM 2003. LNCS (LNAI), vol. 2702, pp. 218–227. Springer, Heidelberg (2003). https://doi.org/10.1007/3-540-44963-9_30
6. Brusilovsky, P., Hsiao, I.-H., Folajimi, Y.: QuizMap: open social student modeling and adaptive navigation support with TreeMaps. In: Kloos, C.D., Gillet, D., Crespo García, R.M., Wild, F., Wolpers, M. (eds.) EC-TEL 2011. LNCS, vol. 6964, pp. 71–82. Springer, Heidelberg (2011). https://doi.org/10.1007/978-3-642-23985-4_7
7. Bull, S.: See yourself write: a simple student model to make students think. In: Jameson, A., Paris, C., Tasso, C. (eds.) User Modeling. ICMS, vol. 383, pp. 315–326. Springer, Vienna (1997). https://doi.org/10.1007/978-3-7091-2670-7_32
8. Davis, D., Jivet, I., Kizilcec, R.F., Chen, G., Hauff, C., Houben, G.J.: Follow the successful crowd: raising MOOC completion rates through social comparison at scale. In: Proceedings of the Seventh International Learning Analytics & Knowledge Conference, pp. 454–463. LAK 2017, Association for Computing Machinery, New York, NY, USA (2017). https://doi.org/10.1145/3027385.3027411
9. Dijkstra, P., Kuyper, H., Van der Werf, G., Buunk, A.P., van der Zee, Y.G.: Social comparison in the classroom: a review. Rev. Educ. Res. **78**(4), 828–879 (2008)
10. Eccles, J.S.: Understanding women's educational and occupational choices: applying the Eccles et al. model of achievement-related choices. Psychol. Women Quart. **18**(4), 585–609 (1994)

11. Festinger, L.: A theory of social comparison processes. Hum. Relat. **7**(2), 117–140 (1954). https://doi.org/10.1177/001872675400700202
12. Fotaris, P., Mastoras, T., Leinfellner, R., Rosunally, Y.: Climbing up the leaderboard: an empirical study of applying gamification techniques to a computer programming class. Electr. J. e-learn. **14**(2), 94–110 (2016)
13. Fujita-Starck, P.J.: The effects of motivation and classroom environment on the satisfaction of noncredit continuing education students. University of Hawai'i at Manoa (1994)
14. Garcia, S.M., Tor, A., Gonzalez, R.: Ranks and rivals: a theory of competition. Pers. Soc. Psychol. Bull. **32**(7), 970–982 (2006)
15. Gibbons, F.X., Buunk, B.P.: Individual differences in social comparison: development of a scale of social comparison orientation. J. Pers. Soc. Psychol. **76**(1), 129–142 (1999)
16. Guerra, J., Hosseini, R., Somyurek, S., Brusilovsky, P.: An intelligent interface for learning content: Combining an open learner model and social comparison to support self-regulated learning and engagement. In: Proceedings of the 21st International Conference on Intelligent User Interfaces, pp. 152–163 (2016)
17. Guerra, J., Parra, D., Brusilovsky, P.: Encouraging online student reading with social visualization, vol. 1009 (2013)
18. Hanus, M.D., Fox, J.: Assessing the effects of gamification in the classroom: a longitudinal study on intrinsic motivation, social comparison, satisfaction, effort, and academic performance. Comput. Educ. **80**, 152–161 (2015)
19. Herodotou, C., Boroowa, A., Hlosta, M., Rienties, B.: What do distance learning students seek from student analytics? (2020)
20. Hsiao, I.H., Bakalov, F., Brusilovsky, P., König-Ries, B.: Progressor: Social navigation support through open social student modeling. New Rev. Hypermedia Multimedia **19**, 112–131 (2013). https://doi.org/10.1080/13614568.2013.806960
21. Hsiao, I.-H., Brusilovsky, P.: Motivational social visualizations for personalized e-learning. In: Ravenscroft, A., Lindstaedt, S., Kloos, C.D., Hernández-Leo, D. (eds.) EC-TEL 2012. LNCS, vol. 7563, pp. 153–165. Springer, Heidelberg (2012). https://doi.org/10.1007/978-3-642-33263-0_13
22. Hsiao, I.H., Guerra, J., Parra, D., Bakalov, F., König-Ries, B., Brusilovsky, P.: Comparative social visualization for personalized e-learning. In: Proceedings of the International Conference on Advanced Visual Interfaces, pp. 303–307 (2012)
23. Huang, B., Hew, K.F.: Do points, badges and leaderboard increase learning and activity: a quasi-experiment on the effects of gamification. In: Proceedings of the 23rd International Conference on Computers in Education, pp. 275–280. Society for Computer in Education Hangzhou, China (2015)
24. Jivet, I., Scheffel, M., Drachsler, H., Specht, M.: Awareness is not enough: pitfalls of learning analytics dashboards in the educational practice. In: Lavoué, É., Drachsler, H., Verbert, K., Broisin, J., Pérez-Sanagustín, M. (eds.) EC-TEL 2017. LNCS, vol. 10474, pp. 82–96. Springer, Cham (2017). https://doi.org/10.1007/978-3-319-66610-5_7
25. Lepper, M.R., Cordova, D.I.: A desire to be taught: instructional consequences of intrinsic motivation. Motiv. Emot. **16**(3), 187–208 (1992)
26. Leung, W.: How do one's peers on a leaderboard affect oneself? In: Proceedings of the 2019 CHI Conference on Human Factors in Computing Systems, pp. 1–11. CHI 2019, Association for Computing Machinery, New York, NY, USA (2019). https://doi.org/10.1145/3290605.3300397
27. Levine, J.M.: Social comparison and education (1983)

28. Lim, D.H.: Cross cultural differences in online learning motivation. Educ. Media Int. **41**(2), 163–175 (2004)
29. Loboda, T.D., Guerra, J., Hosseini, R., Brusilovsky, P.: Mastery grids: An open-source social educational progress visualization. In: Proceedings of the 2014 Conference on Innovation & Technology in Computer Science Education, p. 357 (2014)
30. Olson, B.D., Evans, D.L.: The role of the big five personality dimensions in the direction and affective consequences of everyday social comparisons. Pers. Soc. Psychol. Bull. **25**, 1498–1508 (1999)
31. Park, Y., Park, S.W.: Goal orientations and social comparison: the role of different motivations in affiliation preferences. Motiv. Emot. **41**(5), 617–627 (2017)
32. Ryan, R., Deci, E.: Self-determination theory and the facilitation of intrinsic motivation, social development, and well-being. Am. Psychol. **55**(1), 68 (2000)
33. Schunk, D.H.: Self-efficacy and education and instruction. In: Maddux, J.E. (ed.) Self-Efficacy, Adaptation, and Adjustment. The Plenum Series in Social/Clinical Psychology. Springer, Boston (1995). https://doi.org/10.1007/978-1-4419-6868-5_10
34. Schunk, D.H., Usher, E.L.: Social cognitive theory and motivation. Oxford Handbook Hum. Motiv. **2**, 11–26 (2012)
35. Sosnovsky, S., Fang, Q., de Vries, B., Luehof, S., Wiegant, F.: Towards adaptive social comparison for education. In: Alario-Hoyos, C., Rodríguez-Triana, M.J., Scheffel, M., Arnedillo-Sánchez, I., Dennerlein, S.M. (eds.) EC-TEL 2020. LNCS, vol. 12315, pp. 421–426. Springer, Cham (2020). https://doi.org/10.1007/978-3-030-57717-9_38
36. Suls, J., Martin, R., Wheeler, L.: Social comparison: Why, with whom, and with what effect? Curr. Dir. Psychol. Sci. **11**(5), 159–163 (2002). https://doi.org/10.1111/1467-8721.00191
37. Vallerand, R., Blssonnette, R.: Intrinsic, extrinsic, and amotivational styles as predictors of behavior: a prospective study. J. of personality **60**(3), 599–620 (1992)
38. Vallerand, R., Pelletier, L., Blais, M., Briere, N., Senecal, C., Vallieres, E.: The academic motivation scale: a measure of intrinsic, extrinsic, and amotivation in education. Educ. Psychol. Measur. **52**(4), 1003–1017 (1992)
39. Vallerand, R.J., Reid, G.: On the causal effects of perceived competence on intrinsic motivation: a test of cognitive evaluation theory. J. Sport Exerc. Psychol. **6**(1), 94–102 (1984)
40. Veroff, J.: Social comparison and the development of achievement motivation. Achievement-Related Motives in Children, pp. 46–101 (1969)
41. Wood, J.: Theory and research concerning social comparisons of personal attributes. Psychol. Bull. **106**(2), 231–248 (1989)

Relation Between Student Characteristics, Git Usage and Success in Programming Courses

Aleksandar Karakaš[1(✉)] and Denis Helic[2]

[1] Graz University of Technology, Rechbauerstr. 12, 8010 Graz, Austria
aleksandar.karakas@tugraz.at

[2] Modul University Vienna GmbH, Am Kahlenberg 1, 1190 Vienna, Austria
denis.helic@modul.ac.at

Abstract. Students' prior knowledge and self-regulated learning are important predictors of academic success. A growing body of literature studies these predictors with respect to introductory programming courses. Especially in the first semester, cohorts exhibit a wide range of backgrounds with many students having no previous programming experience at all. Furthermore, many first semester students lack self-regulated learning capabilities. In the light of high drop-out rates in introductory programming courses, it is crucial to consider student characteristics, such as previously acquired programming skills or self-regulated learning capabilities. In this work, we collected data on such student characteristics via surveys and investigated the relation between survey data and students' use of a version control system during a first semester programming course at a European university. We also related the survey data to the number of test cases students pass in their assignments. Using random forests, we investigated, how version control data can be used to predict student performance in an assignment and to what extent additional survey data can improve such predictions. Our results show that especially in an early phase of an assignment, data on prior knowledge and self-regulated learning can help predict student success.

Keywords: Computer science education · Self-regulated learning · Version control · Git · Learning analytics

1 Introduction

Self-regulation can be defined as a self-directed "process by which learners transform their mental abilities into academic skills." [26] Self-regulated learning (SRL) processes are executed in three cyclical phases. In the *forethought phase*, students analyze the task at hand, set goals, and plan their learning activities to reach their goals. These processes, together with motivational beliefs, set the foundation for the subsequent *performance phase* in which selected strategies are applied. In this phase, attention focusing plays a crucial role. Another set

O. Viberg et al. (Eds.): EC-TEL 2023, LNCS 14200, pp. 133–148, 2023.
https://doi.org/10.1007/978-3-031-42682-7_10

of processes during this phase concerns self-observation. The following phase of *self-reflection* is based on these self-observations and the achieved performance. In this third phase, the reached performance is causally attributed to one's self-observed actions, abilities, and circumstances. Students compare their performance to a benchmark, which affects motivational beliefs and thus the following SRL cycles. [26]

As "[s]elf-regulated students are [...] more likely to succeed academically" [26], many researchers have attempted to measure students' self-regulated learning capabilities. As a result, many questionnaires were devised, the most popular appearing to be the *Motivated Strategies for Learning Questionnaire* (MSLQ) [22] which was devised by [18] and consists of 81 items. A recent alternative questionnaire targeted at online courses is the *Self-Regulation for Learning Online questionnaire* (SRL-O) [6] which comprises 44 questions on ten scales to measure various dimensions of SRL.

Past research also investigated students' prior knowledge (PK) alongside SRL. It was found that experts use different learning strategies than novices [26].

The last two decades have seen the formation of new research fields which do not rely on survey data, but rather on students' digital traces to gain insights into student behavior and how it is related to learning outcomes. In these research fields, namely learning analytics (LA) and educational data mining (EDM), traces are predominantly taken from learning management systems (LMS) and the universities' student information systems (SIS) [10].

In computer science education and especially in programming courses, LMS and SIS are superseded by version control systems (VCS) as the most important data sources. Students use version control systems to save snapshots of their solutions to assignments, thus allowing instructors and researchers to track students' progress. These snapshots are called *commits* and are usually created locally on the students' computers and then pushed to an online version control platform to perform a submission.

In many programming courses, students are given an incentive to push commits regularly, as this allows them to obtain feedback on the pushed snapshot. This feedback commonly comes in the form of an automatically generated test report. A test report is usually produced by testing a student's code in various predefined scenarios, called *test cases*. The test report may, for instance, show the comparison of the output produced by a student's program with the expected output for each test case, thus hinting at potential errors in the committed code.

The use of version control systems and test cases are two major trends [11,13] and have been "identified as the two most popular tools in computing education" [1]. Although learning a programming language and how to use a VCS at the same time places an additional cognitive load on students [1], more and more universities are introducing VCS even in first-semester courses.

Studies have shown that commit behavior, including the timing of commits, can be indicative of student struggles [1,2]. In this paper, we investigate the associations between the PK, SRL, commit behavior and number of passed test cases. We do not restrict our study to commits and test cases at the end of an assignment, but analyze these variables over time. We formulate the following research questions (RQs):

1. Does PK have a significant effect on students' use of a VCS and student performance over the course of an assignment?
2. Which SRL dimensions have a significant effect on students' use of a VCS and student performance over the course of an assignment?
3. To what extent does the knowledge about students' levels regarding PK and SRL dimensions help to predict student performance in an assignment?
4. How do data about PK and SRL affect predictions of student performance in an assignment?

To answer the RQ 1 and 2, we use a non-parametric statistical test by Brunner and Langer [7] and focus on the number of commits (number of passed test cases) to measure VCS usage (student performance) throughout an assignment. To address RQ 3, we employ random forests and measure the improvement of the model's predictions when adding features related to PK and SRL to VCS data. RQ 4 is addressed by analyzing the impact of a random forests' features on the prediction of student performance. To this end, we use SHAP values [14]. These values show whether a feature influences the prediction of a student's performance and if so, whether high feature values lead to predictions of higher or lower student performance.

In our RQs, SRL dimensions are measured using the scales of the SRL-O questionnaire. To the best of our knowledge, this is the first analysis of student commit behavior based on the SRL-O questionnaire. Furthermore, we are not aware of any studies leveraging Brunner-Langer models and SHAP values in the context of students' commit behavior.

2 Related Work

2.1 SRL and PK in Computer Science Education

A vast body of literature investigates the relation between PK, SRL, and student success in programming courses. Using four questionnaires, [4] analyzed which variables best predict student success. One of their questionnaires covered the students' backgrounds, while another one was a shortened version of the MSLQ, covering 8 of the original 15 scales. Among the variables they analyzed, math skills, the time a student spends playing games, and self-esteem/self-efficacy were the most predictive ones. [4] presented an extensive list of other studies which predict student success in programming courses using a wide range of variables. In several of these studies, math skills were found to be good predictors. In courses where most students have never been exposed to programming before, math skills may be a useful substitute for PK in programming. As nowadays more and more students learn programming at school, survey items focusing on PK can be useful.

In [25], students were surveyed about their PK and their ability to memorize a program (program recall) was tested. Furthermore, data about self-efficacy was collected - once at the beginning and once at the end of the course. In their study, program recall had the strongest (positive) correlation with the course grade. Post-self-efficacy and previous programming experience were positively correlated with student success as well.

[3] analyzed whether PK and the six motivation-related scales of the MSLQ are associated with student success. They found that students' understanding of programming concepts as well as their perceived ability to design programs without help are positively correlated with student success. Regarding the analyzed MSLQ dimensions, self-efficacy, intrinsic motivation, and task value showed the highest positive correlations with programming performance. This underlines the importance of motivational beliefs which play a crucial role in the SRL cycle's forethought phase. However, the study's authors did not find a significant correlation between extrinsic motivation and performance. Also in [5], intrinsic motivation and task value were found to be associated with performance, while several motivation-related dimensions, such as self-efficacy and extrinsic motivation were not analyzed. Furthermore, this study showed that metacognitive and resource management strategies were positively correlated with performance.

[9] investigated which SRL processes students use and identified strategies specific to computer science education, such as the use of diagrams to describe a program's design.

Recent studies use VCS, as commits are artefacts of students' learning processes. [2] identified struggling students based on their pushed commits. In their study, students were asked which SRL processes they were having problems with. The authors found cases of struggles in each of the three phases of the SRL cycle.

Some of the studies mentioned above only analyze the association between features and student performance. In this paper, we also investigate the relation between features and VCS usage. Many studies that analyze VCS usage either do not consider students' PK or SRL characteristics or have a course setting which encourages fine-grained commit histories. In Sect. 5 we discuss how the course setting of this study might have lead to less fine-grained commit histories and how information on PK and SRL can be useful in such situations.

2.2 Methodology

Brunner-Langer Models. Brunner-Langer models are well-suited for analyzing longitudinal data. [15] define longitudinal data as "measurements collected from the same experimental units, usually referred to as subjects or individuals, over time." As such, Brunner-Langer models are widely used in many fields including medicine, dentistry, and biology.

Longitudinal data also arise in the educational context where students work on several successive assignments throughout a semester. However, there have only been few studies in the educational context leveraging Brunner-Langer models. For instance, [19,20] tested alternatives to the traditional textbooks for dental students and 12-year old children learning mathematics, respectively. To the best of our knowledge, Brunner-Langer models have not been used yet in studies concerning programming education.

When using Brunner-Langer models, individuals "are divided into several groups" [7]. Hence, this approach allows to compare groups of students defined by their level of PK or certain SRL dimensions regarding their use use of VCS or performance over time.

SHAP Values. Many studies in LA and EDM use easily interpretable machine learning models, such as logistic regression, where the model parameters express how the change in one feature affects predictions. For instance, [24] used logistic regression to predict student success and justified their choice with the model's explainability. The authors also use random forests, as they are "considered one of the most powerful classification techniques available nowadays" [24].

For a long time, a major drawback of random forests has been their lack of interpretability, with interpretability meaning "that we can understand how the model uses input features to make predictions" [14]. Recent approaches aim at improving the interpretability of black box models, such as random forests and neural networks. One of these approaches uses SHAP values to attribute to each feature its effect on a prediction [14]. This approach which originated in game theory is now being increasingly applied in LA and EDM. For instance, [8] predicted student performance with deep learning and used SHAP values to explain their model. [17] used SHAP values in connection with random forests to predict student persistence in an introductory programming course. In their course setting, each assignment only lasted for one day and students did not use a VCS. [23] compared various tree-based models for predicting student success. They also used SHAP values to evaluate the features' effects on predictions.

3 Setting

The course analyzed in this work is an introductory programming course offered in the winter semester 2022/23 at a European university of technology. 750 students were registered, most of whom were in their first semester. The course was offered as a flipped classroom where students prepare for the live lecture units by going through video materials.

The programming language taught is C and despite the introductory character of this course it comprises more advanced concepts as well, such as pointers, dynamic memory management, and structs. Furthermore, the students learn the basics of the VCS Git: how to clone their assignment repositories, add files to the staging area, create commits and push them to a version control platform.

As a result, many students were facing difficulties. According to the course evaluation, 44.7% and 30.9% of students perceived this course as having a high or very high difficulty, respectively. Many programming courses have high dropout rates [2,4] and the course investigated in this study is no exception with only around 300 students obtaining a positive grade. (Students who do not submit assignment 1 (approximately 190 students) are not graded.) Hence, it is important to investigate which factors govern student behavior and contribute to student success.

To gain insights into the students' characteristics, perceptions, and workloads we administered five questionnaires – we call them $Q_0, \ldots, Q_4$ – throughout the semester. Among other topics, these questionnaires covered all SRL-O items. The SRL-O was chosen over many alternatives, as it is targeted at undergraduate online courses. It aims to measure a wide range of SRL dimensions, while containing considerably fewer items than, for instance, the popular MSLQ.

Table 1 shows the number of participants in each questionnaire as well as a subset of each questionnaire's topics. 236 students participated in each of the five questionnaires, 164 of whom were in their first semester. As each questionnaire had more than 270 participants, this means that a considerable number of students skipped at least one questionnaire. In this study we focus on first-semester students and exclude those students who were found to have used code by their peers or websites without citing their sources, as this was considered cheating. Thus, 159 students have completed all questionnaires in this study.

All survey participants voluntarily gave their consent that their questionnaire data may be merged with data about their Git commits for research purposes. As an incentive to participate in the survey, bonus points are awarded to students who filled out all questionnaires – less than 3% of the achievable points. However, only students with enough points to pass the course can gain bonus points.

The questionnaires were spread over the whole semester. Q_0 was available before assignment 1 and all following questionnaires Q_i were administered after assignment i. This approach allowed each of the questionnaires $Q_1, \ldots, Q_4$ to also cover the students' experiences with the preceding assignment.

To submit their solution to an assignment, students had to commit and push their code before the assignment's deadline. Prior to the deadline, students were free to choose, when and how often to commit their code using Git. This freedom is also reflected in Fig. 1, were the x-position of each point denotes a student's first commit time for an assignment, with the assignment being indicated by the point's color. The y-position of each point specifies the ratio of test cases a student's last commit before the deadline passes. In line with previous work (e.g., [2]), we can see that earlier first commits are associated with a higher amount of passed test cases at the end of an assignment.

We can see some overlap between assignments, as the task descriptions of assignment 2 and 3 were published early. Assignment 4 had a soft and a hard deadline. Submissions after the soft deadline were subject to point deductions, hence only few students committed for the first time after 15 January.

Table 1. The five questionnaires used in the course.

questionnaire	participants	content
Q_0	488	Prior knowledge and semester at university
Q_1	389	SRL-O scales self-efficacy, intrinsic motivation, and extrinsic motivation
Q_2	336	SRL-O scales negative achievement emotion, planning and time management, and effort regulation
Q_3	297	SRL-O scales social support and task strategies
Q_4	271	SRL-O scales metacognition and study environment

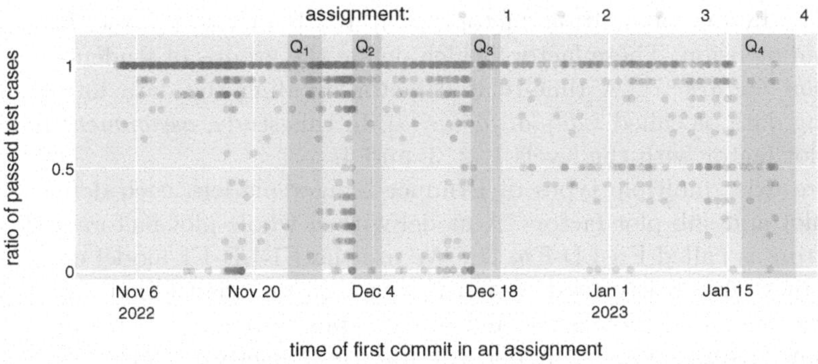

Fig. 1. Students' first commit times (x-axis) and ratio of the submission's passed test cases (y-axis) per assignment (color). Earlier first commits are positively correlated with passed test cases. Shaded areas indicate when questionnaires were available.

Students were provided with a test system allowing them to run several test cases locally. Upon running the test cases, an HTML test report is generated automatically. This report shows comparisons of expected and obtained program outputs and return values. Furthermore, these reports contain links to detailed descriptions of any memory problems per test case. By pushing a commit to the course's version control platform, students were able to initiate server-side tests of their code which resulted in the same detailed test report that students could generate locally. However, the online test report contains additional information on which further (private) test cases are passed (without further details). This additional information serves as incentive for students to push regularly (and to think about possible edge cases), however, as Fig. 1 shows many students did not create commits until close to the deadline.

Besides the assignment-related information, Fig. 1 also shows when questionnaires were administered (shaded areas labeled Q_1, Q_2, Q_3, and Q_4).

4 Methods and Results

4.1 Statistical Inference (Addressing RQs 1 and 2)

Brunner-Langer Models. In our setting, longitudinal data naturally arise. We take *repeated measurements* of commits (frequency and associated number of passed test cases) *from the same experimental units* (students). These measurements happen *over time*, as there are four assignments spread over the course of a semester. Hence, our data fits the definition of longitudinal data [15] and thus, Brunner-Langer models are suited for statistical inference.

Due to their non-parametric, rank-based nature, Brunner-Langer models do not impose any distribution characteristics on the data. Parametric methods would require certain characteristics of the data (e.g., normality).

Brunner-Langer models allow for detecting significant differences between the commit behaviors of different groups of students over time. These groups can be defined by one or multiple factors, such as PK or the score with respect to an SRL dimension. These factors which define the groups of students are called *whole-plot factors* [7]. A time-related factor dividing the data into rounds of collecting data, is called *sub-plot factor* [7]. In this study, *assignment* represents a sub-plot factor with the levels 1, 2, 3, and 4.

There exist multiple types of Brunner-Langer models, each defined by the whole-plot and sub-plot factors. A model with n whole-plot factors and m sub-plot factors is called Fn-LD-Fm [7]. We use the F1-LD-F1 model design which "is the most frequently used design in the area of longitudinal data" [7] and considers one whole-plot factor and one sub-plot factor. To perform statistical tests using Brunner-Langer models, we use the R-package *nparld* [15].

For each of the two response variables (i.e., number of commits and number of passed test cases) we conduct multiple tests using the F1-LD-F1 design with *assignment* as the sub-plot factor. The tests differ by whole-plot which represents either the levels of PK (0, ..., 4) or an SRL dimension. We do not use the raw SRL data with values ranging from 1 to 7. Instead, for each SRL dimension we partition the students into three groups with *low*, *medium*, and *high* levels on the corresponding SRL dimension.

We do not restrict our tests to the assignment deadlines, but conduct separate tests for three different assignment stages. For the assignments 1, 2, and 3, we define the levels of the factor *assignment stage* as 10, 5, and 0 days before deadline. Assignment 4 spanned a longer time frame. Thus, for this assignment, we double each stage's number of days before the deadline compared to the first three assignments. The stages were defined in such a way that they roughly translate to (i) *one third into the assignment*, (ii) *two thirds into the assignment*, and (iii) *assignment deadline*. Hence, we call these three stages $^1/_3$, $^2/_3$, and $^3/_3$.

Since the F1-LD-F1 model does not differentiate between assignment stages, we provide it with data related to only one assignment stage per statistical test, e.g., the deadline of the assignment. To test whether a whole-plot factor has an effect at different stages in an assignment, we conduct one test per stage.

In each test, the null-hypothesis states that for each group of students (defined by the whole-plot factor), the distribution of the response variable is the same for any given assignment. Hence, using the F1-LD-F1 model, we can test if the effect of the whole-plot factor is significant. We define significance by a p-value of < 0.05.

Results. As described in Sect. 3, we used multiple questionnaires to measure the students' levels of PK and SRL. Table 1 indicates, which questionnaire covered which whole-plot factor (i.e., PK or SRL dimension). Table 2 shows all possible whole-plot factors in its first column. Columns 2-4 show the p-values of the corresponding whole-plot factor for the response variable *number of commits* (NC) at different assignment stages. The results for each whole-plot factor are based on those students who participated in the corresponding questionnaire and the questionnaires preceding it.

Table 2. p-values in Brunner-Langer F1-LD-F1 models for *commit counts* using various whole-plot factors and varying stages within an assignment.

	p-values for NC considering students with					
	all questionnaires up to the corresponding questionnaire			all questionnaires		
stage of assignment / whole-plot factor	1/3	2/3	3/3	1/3	2/3	3/3
Prior knowledge	**3.6e–7**	**4.9e–8**	**2.5e–9**	**1.9e–4**	**8.8e–4**	**0.026**
Self-efficacy	**8.5e–6**	**4.5e–5**	**6.7e–4**	**1.6e–5**	**3.1e–4**	0.21
Intrinsic motivation	**0.0045**	0.060	0.32	**0.0040**	**0.031**	0.32
Extrinsic motivation	**0.031**	0.50	0.68	0.076	0.73	0.92
Negative achievement emotion	**7.6e–6**	**2.8e–8**	**2.8e–7**	**0.0079**	**0.0043**	0.31
Planning & time management	0.81	0.41	0.75	0.75	0.58	0.78
Effort regulation	0.41	0.69	0.32	0.44	0.70	0.30
Social support	0.11	0.23	0.41	0.22	**0.049**	0.061
Task strategies	0.076	0.23	0.67	0.084	0.22	0.57
Metacognition	**0.0028**	**0.0097**	0.055	same values as on the left		
Study environment	0.14	0.092	0.14	same values as on the left		

Table 2 shows, for instance, that PK is highly significant for NC at all three assignment stages with p-values of 3.6e–7, 4.9e–8, and 2.5e–9, respectively. The motivation-related SRL dimensions self-efficacy and negative achievement emotion are highly significant at all stages as well. The other two motivation-related dimensions intrinsic & extrinsic motivation are significant at stage 1/3 with the former almost reaching significance for 2/3. Apart from PK and motivational beliefs, only metacognition appears to have a significant effect regarding NC - especially before an assignment deadline.

Different questionnaires were completed by different students. To increase comparability of results, we can consider the subset of students who filled out all questionnaires. The corresponding p-values are shown in the three rightmost columns of Table 2. Within this subset of students, we can see two additional significant effects: now, intrinsic motivation and social support are significant at stage 2/3. However, the three most significant effects now have much larger p-values. Self-efficacy and negative achievement emotion are not even significant at stage 3/3. This phenomenon is discussed in Sect. 5. Furthermore, extrinsic motivation is not significant in any of the three rightmost columns.

Analogous results for the response variable *number of test cases* (NT) instead of NC are listed in Table 3. The table's columns 2-4 show that again PK, self-efficacy, and negative achievement emotion are highly significant at all stages. As with NC, intrinsic motivation and metacognition have a significant effect early in an assignment. Extrinsic motivation shows p-values above 0.05 at all stages. Social support and study environment are more important for NT than it was the case when modeling NC.

As before, considering only the subset of students who filled out all questionnaires, leads to much larger p-values for the three most significant effects.

Table 3. p-values in Brunner-Langer F1-LD-F1 models for *passed test cases* using various whole-plot factors and varying stages within an assignment.

	p-values for NT considering students with					
	all questionnaires up to the corresponding questionnaire			all questionnaires		
stage of assignment / whole-plot factor	1/3	2/3	3/3	1/3	2/3	3/3
Prior knowledge	**4.2e–6**	**2.7e–7**	**9.5e–10**	**1.0e–3**	**0.0039**	0.077
Self-efficacy	**7,5e–6**	**1.1e–5**	**1.1e–5**	**7.9e–6**	**1.5e–5**	**0.034**
Intrinsic motivation	**0.019**	0.30	0.87	**0.0087**	0.064	0.55
Extrinsic motivation	0.091	0.82	0.80	0.12	0.88	0.91
Negative achievement emotion	**8.0e–6**	**4.3e–8**	**1.1e–7**	**0.0012**	**3.8e–4**	**0.0052**
Planning & time management	0.50	0.53	0.42	0.41	0.60	0.081
Effort regulation	0.39	0.85	0.22	0.46	0.92	0.14
Social support	**0.037**	0.059	**0.0068**	**0.041**	**0.016**	**0.038**
Task strategies	0.095	0.52	0.85	0.12	0.53	0.88
Metacognition	**0.027**	0.099	0.51	same values as on the left		
Study environment	0.15	**0.029**	0.096	same values as on the left		

4.2 Random Forests (Addressing RQ 3)

To investigate how commit data, PK, and SRL can be used to predict student performance we focus on assignment 4, as SRL capabilities are especially challenged during long-term projects [26]. Furthermore, we focus on those students who filled out all questionnaires. Analogous to [1,2], we model whether or not a student passes all test cases at the assignment's deadline, as failure to pass all test cases has been shown to indicate student struggles [2].

For our prediction analyses we use the random forest implementation of *scikit-learn* [16]. For each day during the assignment, we train three random forests, each using a different set of features to predict which students will pass all test cases at the end of the assignment. The feature sets are (i) commit data (i.e., the number of commits and passed test cases until the day under investigation), (ii) commit data and PK, and (iii) commit data, PK, and SRL. We use 10-fold stratified cross-validation and measure the model's accuracy on each fold. The average of the ten accuracy values forms the overall model accuracy.

Figure 2 shows the accuracy of random forests using each of the three feature sets. When provided with the commit data at the deadline, all models use the number of passed test cases to correctly predict the same variable. Close to the deadline, the three different feature sets barely lead to differences in accuracy.

However, in the early stages of the assignment the differences are considerable, with the model provided with SRL data outperforming the other two models.

4.3 SHAP Values (Addressing RQ 4)

To see how the random forests use the additional data about PK and SRL early in an assignment, we calculate SHAP values [14] of the random forest that is fit with data 20 days before the deadline. For obtaining the SHAP values, we use the whole sample without splitting it into a training and validation set. This approach is chosen, as we aim at understanding the model's decisions rather than predicting a response variable.

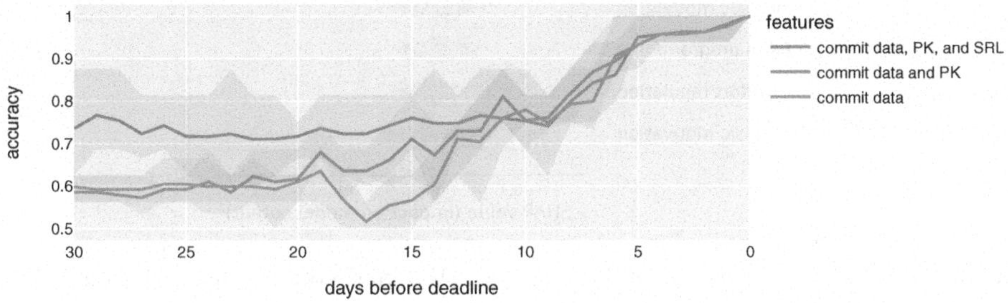

Fig. 2. Accuracy of various random forests over the course of assignment 4. Lines indicate means of accuracy values over ten cross-validation folds and shaded areas indicate the corresponding 60 % confidence intervals.

Figure 3 summarizes the results. Among the five features with the highest impact, we find two SRL dimensions related to motivational beliefs: negative achievement emotion and self-efficacy. High values of the former (latter) lead to a lower (higher) probability of predicting that all test cases will be passed at the deadline. High levels of the SRL dimensions study environment and metacognition lead to more optimistic predictions about a student. High levels in the planning and time management dimension are associated with more pessimistic predictions. More commits and passed test cases are related to optimistic predictions, however, they are not the predictors with the most impact. At an early stage, the number of commits affects the model output more than test cases.

The random forests that used PK were provided with information about PK in programming in general and, additionally, in the C programming language. The SHAP values indicate that the model values PK – especially PK in C.

We have repeated the calculation of SHAP values for other stages within the assignment and observe an increasing impact of test cases towards the assignments deadline.

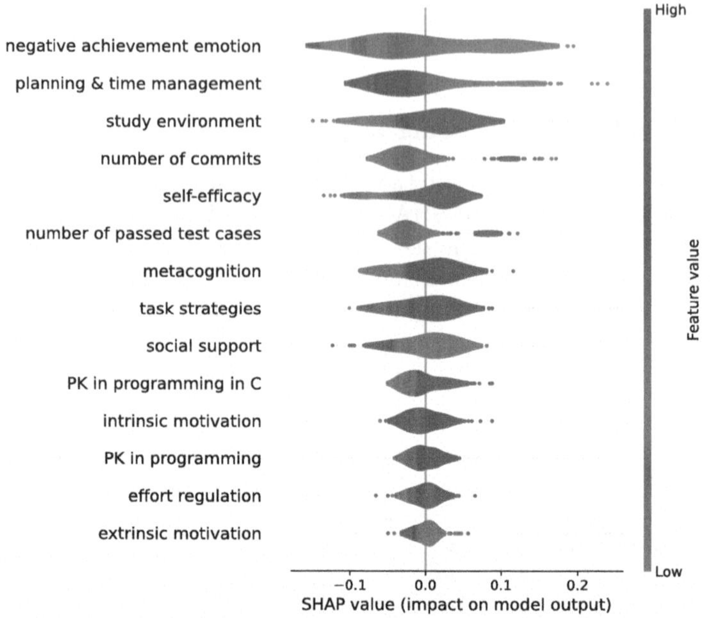

Fig. 3. SHAP values for the model using PK, SRL, and commit data 20 days before the assignment deadline.

5 Discussion and Limitations

Using Brunner-Langer models we identified that throughout an assignment PK, self-efficacy, and negative achievement emotion are the most significant factors with regards to commit behavior and the number of passed test cases. As Tables 2 and 3 show, the p-values of these effects increase when considering the smaller sample of students who finished all questionnaires. We attribute this phenomenon to selection bias. Students who fill out the last questionnaire did not drop out before the last assignment and thus they tend to create commits and perform well in the earlier assignments. Hence, there are fewer differences when only taking students with all questionnaires into account – especially at an assignment's deadline.

The three most significant effects are correlated (PK/self-efficacy: $\rho = 0.494$, PK/negative achievement emotion: $\rho = -0.337$, self-efficacy/negative achievement emotion: $\rho = -0.539$). Nonetheless, SHAP values indicate that both, self-efficacy and negative achievement emotion, are crucial performance predictors.

Besides these two motivation-related SRL dimensions, several other aspects of SRL have a high impact on the model output. Somewhat unexpectedly, high self-reported levels of planning and time management are associated with negative SHAP values. This result might be caused by interactions between planning and time management and other features, such as the number of commits. We consider a deeper analysis of this result as future work.

As is the case with planning and time management, high levels of social support coincide with negative SHAP values. Several questionnaire items covering this dimension measure a student's tendency to seek help. It might be the case that well-performing students report to seek less help, because they are capable of solving more challenges on their own.

Our random forest results showed that performance prediction is difficult when only using commit data. Especially at an early stage of an assignment this data is hardly available. The low accuracy when restricting the features to commit data seems to contradict the results from past research. [1] used version control data to identify struggling students within a few days with a high accuracy. They argue that this is possible, since version-control data is fine-grained. However, students in [1] have already completed an introductory programming course, hence they probably tend to use VCS more frequently. Furthermore, test reports in [1] are only available upon pushing one's code, which is a strong incentive to commit often. In our study, many students were new to programming and version control. Furthermore, the incentive to push code was limited, as students were able to generate a test report locally as well. This resulted in less fine-grained data, rendering predictions based solely on commits more difficult. To ensure that students' traces in a VCS are fine-grained some instructors (e.g., [21]) try to automate the process of committing and pushing code. Our results underline that the usefulness of VCS data for prediction purposes depends on the context in which the VCS is employed.

Interestingly, adding data on PK to commit data does not improve accuracy in the early assignment stage. However, this result is in line with the statistical tests we performed. As Table 3 shows, PK does not have a significant effect on the number of test cases at the deadline of an assignment. Our results are also in line with [12] were students with PK outperformed students without PK in the early stages of the semester. However, the significance of this effect vanished at the final exam which - as our assignment 4 - took place late in the semester. Furthermore, our random forest analysis focuses on students who have reached the last assignment, hence again introducing a selection effect. As shown in Subsect. 4.1, this selection effect can affect results considerably.

Further limitations concern the nature of surveys and their dependence on the participants and their subjective perceptions. Besides the questionnaires, this work is based on commit data generated by students. Most students immediately pushed their code after committing it, in order to save their work on the university's server or to obtain a more complete test report. However, not every commit was directly followed by a push. In this study, commits are analyzed irrespective of when they were actually pushed. In future, we intend to further investigate potential repercussions arising from the discrepancy between times of commit creation and push of a commit.

The course setting analyzed in this study represents a limitation, as other courses may differ, for instance, in taught content, VCS usage, or availability of test cases. As limitation on a methodological level we note that this work highlights associations between PK, SRL, student's commit behavior and performance. However, no causality-related claims are raised.

6 Conclusion

In this work, we analyze the relation between prior knowledge (PK), self-regulated learning (SRL) and version control data in the context of an introductory programming course. We show that at various stages of an assignment PK and SRL are significantly associated to the use of version control as well as the number of passed test cases.

Furthermore, we show that data on PK and SRL can improve random forest predictions about student performance considerably – especially at an early stage of an assignment. Information on PK and SRL can be particularly important in course settings where commit data is not fine-grained. Using SHAP values, we explain to what extent and in which direction each feature influences model predictions of student performance.

References

1. Arakawa, K., Hao, Q., Deneke, W., Cowan, I., Wolfman, S., Peterson, A.: Early identification of student struggles at the topic level using context-agnostic features. In: Proceedings of the 53rd ACM Technical Symposium on Computer Science Education, vol. 1, pp. 147–153 (2022). https://doi.org/10.1145/3478431.3499298
2. Arakawa, K., Hao, Q., Greer, T., Ding, L., Hundhausen, C.D., Peterson, A.: In situ identification of student self-regulated learning struggles in programming assignments. In: Proceedings of the 52nd ACM Technical Symposium on Computer Science Education, pp. 467–473 (2021). https://doi.org/10.1145/3408877.3432357
3. Bergin, S., Reilly, R.: The influence of motivation and comfort-level on learning to program (2005)
4. Bergin, S., Reilly, R.: Predicting introductory programming performance: a multi-institutional multivariate study. Comput. Sci. Educ. **16**(4), 303–323 (2006). https://doi.org/10.1080/08993400600997096
5. Bergin, S., Reilly, R., Traynor, D.: Examining the role of self-regulated learning on introductory programming performance. In: Proceedings of the First International Workshop on Computing Education Research, pp. 81–86 (2005). https://doi.org/10.1145/1089786.1089794
6. Broadbent, J., Panadero, E., Lodge, J., Fuller-Tyszkiewicz, M.: The self-regulation for learning online (srl-o) questionnaire. Metacognition and Learning, pp. 1–29 (2022). https://doi.org/10.1007/s11409-022-09319-6
7. Brunner, E., Domhof, S., Langer, F.: Nonparametric analysis of longitudinal data in factorial experiments, vol. 373. Wiley-Interscience (2002)
8. Clavié, B., Gal, K.: Deep embeddings of contextual assessment data for improving performance prediction. In: International Educational Data Mining Society (2020)
9. Falkner, K., Vivian, R., Falkner, N.J.: Identifying computer science self-regulated learning strategies. In: Proceedings of the 2014 Conference on Innovation & Technology in Computer Science Education, pp. 291–296 (2014). https://doi.org/10.1145/2591708.2591715

10. Gašević, D., Dawson, S., Rogers, T., Gasevic, D.: Learning analytics should not promote one size fits all: the effects of instructional conditions in predicting academic success. Internet High. Educ. **28**, 68–84 (2016). https://doi.org/10.1016/j.iheduc.2015.10.002
11. Glassey, R.: Adopting git/github within teaching: a survey of tool support. In: Proceedings of the ACM Conference on Global Computing Education, pp. 143–149 (2019). https://doi.org/10.1145/3300115.3309518
12. Hagan, D., Markham, S.: Does it help to have some programming experience before beginning a computing degree program? In: Proceedings of the 5th Annual SIGCSE/SIGCUE ITiCSE Conference on Innovation and Technology in Computer Science Education, pp. 25–28 (2000). https://doi.org/10.1145/343048.343063
13. Krusche, S., Seitz, A.: ArTEMiS: an automatic assessment management system for interactive learning. In: Proceedings of the 49th ACM Technical Symposium on Computer Science Education, pp. 284–289 (2018). https://doi.org/10.1145/3159450.3159602
14. Lundberg, S.M., et al.: From local explanations to global understanding with explainable AI for trees. Nature Mach. Intell. **2**(1), 56–67 (2020). https://doi.org/10.1038/s42256-019-0138-9
15. Noguchi, K., Gel, Y.R., Brunner, E., Konietschke, F.: nparLD: an R software package for the nonparametric analysis of longitudinal data in factorial experiments (2012)
16. Pedregosa, F., et al.: Scikit-learn: machine learning in Python. J. Mach. Learn. Res. **12**, 2825–2830 (2011)
17. Pinto, J.D., Zhang, Y., Paquette, L., Fan, A.X.: Investigating elements of student persistence in an introductory computer science course. In: 5th Educational Data Mining in Computer Science Education (CSEDM) Workshop (2021)
18. Pintrich, P.R., Smith, D.A., García, T., McKeachie, W.J.: A manual for the use of the motivated strategies for learning questionnaire (mslq) (1991)
19. Radović, S., Radojičić, M., Veljković, K., Marić, M.: Examining the effects of Geogebra applets on mathematics learning using interactive mathematics textbook. Interact. Learn. Environ. **28**(1), 32–49 (2020). https://doi.org/10.1080/10494820.2018.1512001
20. Ramseier, C.A., Ivanovic, A., Woermann, U., Mattheos, N.: Evaluation of a web-based application versus conventional instruction in the undergraduate curriculum of fixed prosthodontics. Eur. J. Dent. Educ. **16**(4), 224–231 (2012). https://doi.org/10.1111/j.1600-0579.2012.00748.x
21. Rodriguez-Rivera, G., et al.: Tracking large class projects in real-time using fine-grained source control. In: Proceedings of the 53rd ACM Technical Symposium on Computer Science Education, vol. 1, pp. 565–570 (2022). https://doi.org/10.1145/3478431.3499389
22. Roth, A., Ogrin, S., Schmitz, B.: Assessing self-regulated learning in higher education: a systematic literature review of self-report instruments. Educ. Assess. Eval. Account. **28**, 225–250 (2016). https://doi.org/10.1007/s11092-015-9229-2
23. Sahlaoui, H., Nayyar, A., Agoujil, S., Jaber, M.M., et al.: Predicting and interpreting student performance using ensemble models and shapley additive explanations. IEEE Access **9**, 152688–152703 (2021). https://doi.org/10.1109/ACCESS.2021.3124270
24. Van Goidsenhoven, S., Bogdanova, D., Deeva, G., vanden Broucke, S.K.L.M., De Weerdt, J., Snoeck, M.: Predicting student success in a blended learning environment. In: Proceedings of the Tenth International Conference on Learning Analytics & Knowledge, pp. 17–25 (2020). https://doi.org/10.1145/3375462.3375494

25. Wiedenbeck, S.: Factors affecting the success of non-majors in learning to program. In: Proceedings of the First International Workshop on Computing Education Research, pp. 13–24 (2005). https://doi.org/10.1145/1089786.1089788
26. Zimmerman, B.J.: Becoming a self-regulated learner: an overview. Theory Pract. **41**(2), 64–70 (2002). https://doi.org/10.1207/s15430421tip4102_2

The "How" Matters: Evaluating Different Video Types for Cybersecurity MOOCs

Daniel Köhler(✉), Wenzel Pünter, and Christoph Meinel

Hasso-Plattner-Institute, University Potsdam, Potsdam, Germany
{daniel.koehler,wenzel.puenter}@hpi.de

Abstract. Teachers and educators are usually required to transfer knowledge to groups of learners simultaneously. However, not all students necessarily learn in the same way. In cybersecurity education, severe differences between understanding and applying knowledge are observed. In our study, we performed Randomized Controlled Trials with more than 1,500 participants to compare different educational videos: a presentation with slides, an interview, and a short animation. We evaluate learning success for the three dimensions of cybersecurity: Perception, Protection, and Behavior and observe that traditional presentations with slides perform best for achieving fundamental understanding (Perception), tested in recall exercises. Animation videos achieve the best learning success in transfer tasks, such as for assessing protective measures. While statistically insignificant, we observe a slight tendency of animation video learners to apply the learned behavior best, while learners of the interview videos performed worst.

Keywords: Video Styles · Online Education · Cybersecurity Awareness · Field Study

1 Introduction

Massive Open Online Courses (MOOCs) have found application worldwide in the last ten years. Enabling teachers and learners to come together, online education technologies have seen a surge in usage during the Covid19-Pandemic. The availability of MOOCs allows every learner to find a course on almost any topic. With the ongoing digitization of the world, internet-connected devices are used in evergrowing areas of our lives. Unfortunately, all these connected devices pose a range of attack surfaces to cyber criminals. With the increasing penetration of day-to-day computer use, laypersons and smaller companies are also becoming victims of cybercrime [3,8]. Cybersecurity awareness can hence be considered one of the most essential skills to develop in the upcoming years. Online education programs often target knowledge recall with videos and multiple choice quizzes [24]. In the field of cybersecurity awareness, however, different types of skills are required. Awareness requires an inherent sensitization for a topic in addition to the technical understanding and knowledge about protective

O. Viberg et al. (Eds.): EC-TEL 2023, LNCS 14200, pp. 149–163, 2023.
https://doi.org/10.1007/978-3-031-42682-7_11

measures. MOOCs are often mainly based on traditional video formats such as the *Talking Head with Slides* [27]. However, past research has already shown (c.f. Sect. 2.1) that educators can generate some impact on learner's perceptions by providing them with different types of educational videos [7,16,28,31]. We, therefore, pose the following research question:

Research Question: Which impact on learning outcomes can teachers provide by varying the video type employed in online cybersecurity education?

We provide an overview of past work on different video styles in Sect. 2.1, followed by an introduction to cybersecurity awareness in Sect. 2.2. In our real-world field study, we derive honest results by sending the unknowing users phishing emails to assess them for their behavior towards the threat of phishing. Our experiment employs randomization to assign learners to different video types, described in Sect. 3. Section 4 presents the results of our study and the employed tests for the different dimensions of cybersecurity. We discuss our findings, methodology, and threats to validity in Sect. 5. We thereby contribute to the body of research on different video types in online education:

Contribution: We provide a real-world study with more than 1,500 participants covering the impact of different video types on learning success for different task types. We identify that the video type does play a significant role in learning success for *Recall* and *Transfer* tasks (c.f. Sects. 4.2 and 4.3). Noticeable, but statistically insignificant is the observation that learners who watched *Animation* videos were best in appropriately reacting to phishing emails (c.f. Sect. 4.4). E.g., approximately 3% fewer participants who watched the *Animation* submitted personal information to malicious websites in our field study (*Animation*: 7.4%, *Interview*: 9.3%, *Slides*: 10.7%).

2 Background and Related Work

In most studies, the impact of different video styles is evaluated by success in recall tasks. However, learning can take different levels, e.g., recall and understanding or applying the knowledge in transfer tasks. Various models have been developed to conceptualize the levels of learning, such as, e.g., Bloom's Taxonomy [2], Anderson and Krathwohl's model [20], or Metzger's framework [23]. Our education context of cybersecurity superimposes even different challenges. Concretely, learners must constantly be aware of threats and dangers, even when simply checking their emails. Such unconscious awareness might require additional training compared to other areas of knowledge. In Sect. 2.2, we present a model to evaluate dimensions of security awareness. Further, we briefly introduce the threat of phishing in Sect. 2.3.

2.1 Related Work on Video-Styles

In their 2016 literature review, *Santos-Espino et al.* qualitatively analyzed the used video styles of 115 MOOCs [27]. The authors build on several pieces of literature trying to define available video styles, e.g., [10,21]. *Santos-Espino et al.* derived seven video styles, such as *Talking Head*, *Live Lectures*, or *Slides*. They further quantitatively analyzed the usage of different styles throughout the MOOCs. The authors report five style combinations, of which *Talking Head with Slides* was the most used in the analyzed courses. In 2014, *Guo et al.* analyzed 6.9 million video-watching sessions, deriving the impact of different video styles on learner success [11]. The authors identified that e.g., shorter videos are much more engaging to learners and that videos of the combination *Talking Head with Slides* are more engaging than *Slides* alone.

Besides categorizing video types, some researchers have already studied the impact of different video types on the learning success of different task types, such as *Recall* and *Transfer*. Studies from as early as 2014 [7,16] or 2017 [31], however were largely inconclusive. While *Kizilcec et al.* [16] observe no difference for recall tasks and motivate to research transfer tasks, *Wang and Antonenko* [31] observe differences only for easy recall tasks, but explicitly not for transfer tasks.

Building on the previous work, in 2022, *Steinbeck et al.* evaluated a field experiment conducted in a German-speaking MOOC with approximately 3000 participants on the impact of video styles on learner perception and learning success [28]. The authors prepared modern *Explainer* videos as seen on platforms such as YouTube to compare against traditional *Talking Head with Slides* videos. The authors observed a different perception of the speaker's focus as well as better scores on *Recall* posttests in their study. Still, they did not identify an impact on scores in *Transfer* tasks.

2.2 Dimensions of Security Awareness

To adequately cover the context of cybersecurity in education technologies, particularly cybersecurity awareness, we build on a definition for security awareness by *Jaeger* [13]: *Security Awareness is a state of mind, derived by education and experience in which persons are capable of understanding and protecting themselves against security threats.* Such cybersecurity awareness is not only related to companies and professional activities of people anymore. Instead, it is similarly required in one's private life.

In 2014, *Hänsch and Benenson* performed a literature review on the scope and dimensions of *Security Awareness* [12]. The authors analyzed more than 25 publications from previous years. They derived three major dimensions towards security awareness: *Perception* covers the awareness and knowledge required to (theoretically) understand that dangers in cyberspace exist. *Protection* covers knowledge on possible security measures users can employ to enhance their security hygiene and increase their protection against cybersecurity threats. However, *Protection* only covers the knowledge about those security measures; e.g., most people know they should use complex passwords. However, the least people do it [9,25]. Hence, the dimension of *Behavior* assesses whether people are applying their knowledge to a reasonable behavior (change). Conceptionally, the dimensions of security awareness can be compared to levels of learning from educational models such as Bloom's Taxonomy [2].

2.3 Phishing Attacks

Phishing describes the malicious practice of tricking individuals into illicit actions such as revealing (confidential) information or performing unintended actions [32]. In security incidents like data breaches, phishing is one of the most prominent vectors for initial access [6].

Usually, attackers send, e.g., a fake email to their targets, presenting an issue that the recipient must react to. One typical example is a supposed full email postbox. Recipients would be asked to click on a link and log in to their postbox to remediate the issue. Prevalent research in phishing susceptibility and cybersecurity awareness shows that while technical measures to increase security exist, there is no absolute protection [14,15,19]. Hence, users — laypersons and professionals alike — need to be educated about the possible dangers. In professional contexts, employees are often offered dedicated training programs. In private contexts, one form of training can be participation in an online course such as our MOOC on cybersecurity. Generally, embedded training programs in which employees are sent fake phishing emails and educated after falling for the bait are reported as most impactful towards increased sensitization among trainees [15].

3 Methodology and Experiment Setting

Our study evaluates different levels of learning success for cybersecurity awareness generated by three different video types presented to learners. We embedded the experiment into a German-speaking Massive Open Online Course on cybersecurity aimed at beginners. The course spanned six weeks (Oct. - Dec. 2022), with the study being performed during week 4 of the course, alongside the respective thematic context of threats from the internet. The first stage of our study features a Randomized Controlled Trial [29], covered in more depth in Sect. 3.1 for the three types of learning content and the cybersecurity awareness dimensions of *Perception* and *Protection*. In the second phase, all learners who consented to participate in a phishing study were sent three iterations of phishing emails described in Sect. 3.3. The phishing study was approved by the Institutional Review Board of the University of Potsdam.

Fundamentally, our study uses a *True Experimental Design* according to principles outlined by Campbell and Stanley [4]. The experiment features both randomization to distribute participants equally and a pre-test to ensure that the distribution is not accidentally biased by other influences.

3.1 Experiment Setup

The fourth week of our online cybersecurity course covered threats from the internet. Twelve videos present various threats and protective measures, respectively.

$$O_P \quad R \quad \begin{pmatrix} X_1 \\ X_2 \\ X_3 \end{pmatrix} \quad R^* \quad \begin{pmatrix} O_1 \\ O_2 \end{pmatrix} \quad O_M$$

The semi-formal description of our study shows that all learners take a pre-test for knowledge (O_P). After that, they are randomly (round-robin) assigned (R) to either of the three treatments in the form of three different types of learning videos, covered in more detail in Sect. 3.2:

X_1: Traditional video with one presenter and slides; *(Talking Head with) Slides*
X_2: Interview with two presenters, without slides; *Interview*
X_3: Short animation video; *Animation*

Some users skip the videos and directly go to the following self-tests. We do not take that group of users into account for our analysis of differences between the three treatment groups. To evaluate learning success towards the levels of *Perception* as well as *Protection* of cybersecurity awareness (c.f. Sect. 2.2), we conducted two different self-tests (O_1, O_2) after learners consumed their respective video. Again, learners were randomly (round-robin) assigned (R^*)to either test group. One self-test covered the theoretical understanding of phishing threats (O_1) as a recall exercise. The other covered assessing exemplary emails to identify possible phishing emails (O_2) as a transfer exercise. Finally, all learners who participated in the phishing study (c.f. Sect. 3.3) received multiple phishing emails over three months (O_M).

3.2 Video Types

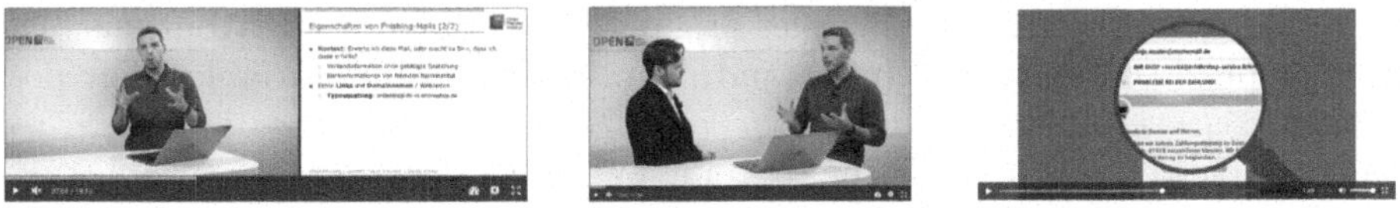

X_1: *Slides*: Traditional video with a presenter and slides

X_2: *Interview:* Two speakers, no slides

X_3: *Animation*: Short, animated video[1]

Fig. 1. Screenshots of the three video types used in the MOOC

We presented the randomized groups of learners with one of three video types[1]. Figure 1 shows screenshots from all three video types. The treatment X_1, *(Talking Head with) Slides*, is our control group for the default video type employed in most of our online courses. To perform a reliable study, we aimed

[1] For the German-speaking participants of the MOOC, we embedded an animation video provided by the *Federal Office for Information Security*, available at: https://multimedia.gsb.bund.de/BSI/Video/Sicher_im_Internet/Phishing.mp4.

to ensure that all videos cover the same content. As we included an external animation video, which's content we could not define, we used that as a base for developing the content for the *Slides* and *Interview* videos. Obviously, with the formats of a non-scripted *Slide* presentation and an *Interview*, in both variants, the speakers took longer to present the content. The traditional video with slides and the interview with two presenters were approximately 14 min long, and the animation video was 3.5 minutes.

3.3 Phishing Study for Security Awareness

As previously highlighted, the learning goals of security awareness cover three dimensions: *Perception*, *Protection* and *Behavior* (c.f. Sect. 2.2). Phishing studies in which (unknowing) participants are sent phishing emails are one of the most prominent assessment measures for *Behavior* in security awareness [15,17]. During our study, participants were sent multiple phishing emails throughout three months [18]. Each month, we sent one email to participants. To account for missing difficulty between the three emails, we evaluate accumulated responses throughout the emails. Learners would have been able to identify all of the phishing emails because of their missing or wrong context. Notably, the missing context has been one of the main criteria highlighted throughout all three learning videos to identify phishing emails.

3.4 Statistical Analysis

During our analysis, we employ *Kruskal-Wallis* as well as *chi-squared* tests to verify the statistical validity of our results. The Kruskal-Wallis test [22] is a statistical method to analyze non-parametric datasets. It indicates whether the compared samples could originate from the same distribution. A significance in test results confirms that the samples originate from different distributions. The test is applied to categorical input and quantitative output variables. For post hoc analysis, we employ *Dunn Bonferroni Tests*. On the other hand, we use Pearson's chi-squared test [5,26] to compare categorical output variables. By performing chi-squared (χ^2) tests of independence, one verifies that occurrences of variables in different groups are independent of one another. Throughout our analysis, we employ $\alpha = 0.05$ as a quasi-standard in significance tests. We use Cohen's d [30] to calculate standardized effect sizes.

4 Study Results

4,490 participants engaged in our MOOC during the course start, from which 1,867 were still active in course week four, which contained the content on phishing and our study. Table 1 presents the amounts of participants in each of the respective sections of our study. Our study employed randomization between X_1, X_2, X_3 and between the self-tests O_1, O_2. Learners who chose not to watch any of the education videos are neither listed nor considered for further analysis. Participants who provided consent to receive emails were enrolled into O_M.

Table 1. Number of learners participating in the study, divided for the different types of learning content and the form of learning assessment.

		Participants			
	Learning Content	O_P	O_1	O_2	O_M
X_1	Slides	513	217	198	172
X_2	Interview	517	204	225	189
X_3	Animation	472	219	213	179
	Total	1,502	1,276		540

The following sections discuss the different stages of the experiment in detail. Section 4.1 presents our analysis of the pretest O_P employed to compare the three groups of participants before any treatment. Section 4.2 presents the results for the level of *Perception* (O_1), verifying knowledge retention directly after the learning videos. We present the email assessment task results (O_2) in Sect. 4.3. Finally, we conclude by analyzing the actual behavior of our participants with the phishing study (O_M) in Sect. 4.4.

4.1 Pretest Analysis

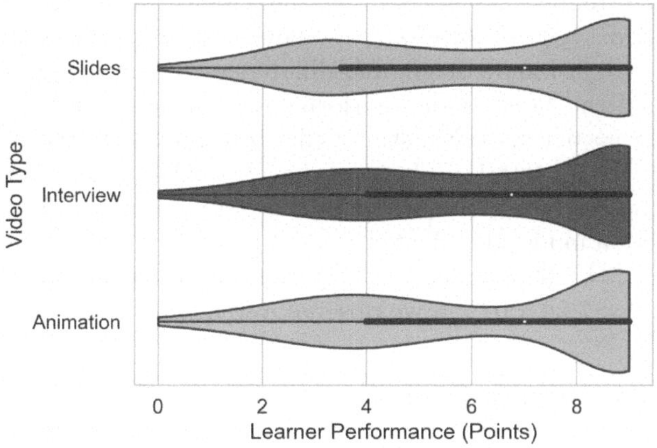

Fig. 2. Overview of learner performance in the pretest (O_P). N = 1,502

In the pretest, learners achieved a mean score of 6.07 points (*Standard Deviation*, $\sigma = 2.73$) out of 9 points available. Figure 2 presents an overview of the results divided by the later consumed treatment. All three groups show very similar performances, with medians almost identical at 6.5 points for *Slides* and *Interview* and 7.0 points for participants in the *Animation* group. A Kruskal-Wallis test rejects the hypothesis of statistically significant differences between the groups ($p = 0.86; p > 0.05$), thus proving no significant difference between them.

4.2 Perception: Results From O_1

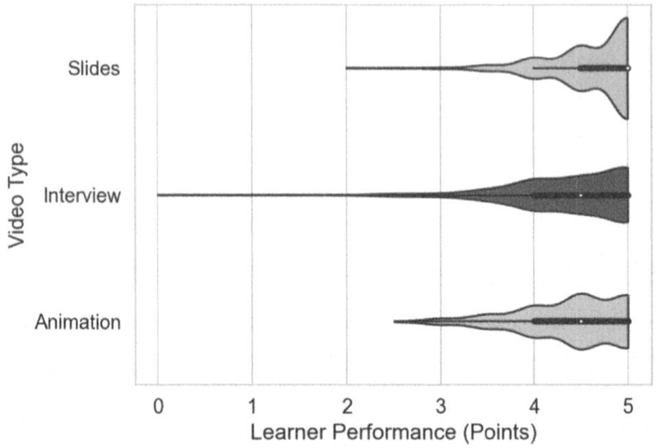

Fig. 3. Learner performance in the self-test for *Perception* (O_1). N=640

The overall score for learners completing the knowledge retention quiz averaged 4.5 ($\sigma = 0.59$) out of 5 points (90%). Figure 3 presents violin plots of learners' performance categorized by the video type they previously consumed. The video types of *Interview* (mean: 4.42, $\sigma = 0.68$) and *Animation* (mean: 4.40, $\sigma = 0.56$) show negligible differences. However, learners who previously consumed the *Slides* video performed significantly better, with a mean result of 4.68 ($\sigma = 0.47$). A Kruskal-Wallis test proves statistical significance ($p = 2.64 * 10^{-8}; p < 0.001$). The post hoc test (Dunn Bonferroni) revealed significant differences between learners of the *Slide* group and both other video types. We observe a moderate effect size ($d_{S;A} = 0.54$) between the groups *Slides* and *Animation* ($z = 5.68, p = 4.03 * 10^{-8}$). Between learners of *Slides* and *Interview* ($z = 4.21, p = 7.54 * 10^{-5}$), we observe a weak effect ($d_{S;I} = 0.41$).

4.3 Protection: Results From O_2

For the second dimension of cybersecurity awareness — *Protection* — we asked learners to evaluate which of the four given emails should be considered phishing. The mean result for the self-test was 3.65 ($\sigma = 0.59$) out of 4 available points. Figure 4 presents the distribution of points as violin plots for the three respective video types.

Learners having watched the *Slides* video performed weakest with a mean score of 3.58 ($\sigma = 0.61$). This is followed by learners having watched the *Interview* (mean: 3.65, $\sigma = 0.64$). Learners performing best had previously watched the *Animation* video (mean: 3.72, $\sigma = 0.51$). The slight difference between the performance of the three groups shows to be significant, as verified with

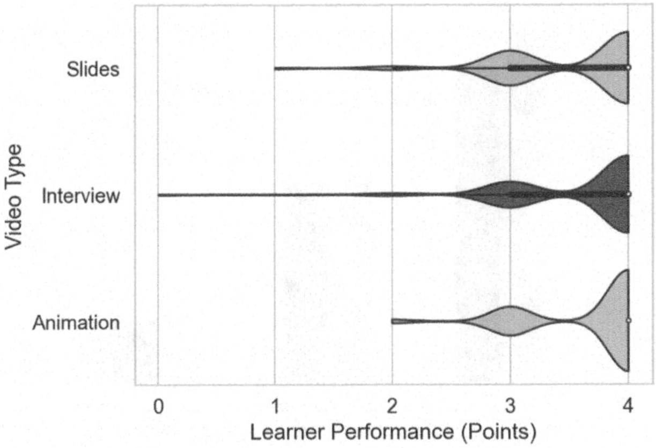

Fig. 4. Learner results of self-test for *Protection* (O_2). N=636

a Kruskal-Wallis test for significance ($p = 0.03, p < 0.05$). The post hoc test shows a significant but weak ($d_{S;A} = 0.25$) effect only between the groups *Slides* and *Interview* ($z = 2.55, p = 0.03$). For *Slides* and *Interview* ($z = 1.83, p = 0.20$) as well as *Interview* and *Animation* ($z = 0.76, p = 1.00$), the null hypothesis of significant differences in-between the data sets is rejected in the post hoc test.

4.4 Behavior: Results from O_M

The third level of security awareness — *Behavior* — describes how a user behaves in real situations. Our study featured a real-world study with laypersons, the learners from our education platform, as participants. Throughout three months after the course ended, all participants received multiple emails. The emails covered different topics and features to assess different contexts. To account for those differing topics and varying difficulties of the emails, we evaluate if and how a learner has reacted to at least one of the three emails. Reactions can range from *opening* the mail, *clicking* on a link, to *submitting* personal information.

Figure 5 provides an overview of the reactions performed by learners who had previously consumed different learning videos. With phishing emails, however, ideally, a recipient does not react at all. Hence, the lower the share of reactions, the better the respective group performed. Generally, we observe that learners who consumed the *Animation* video performed best throughout all stages of reactions to a phishing mail, while learners of the *Slides* Video performed worst. When testing for statistical significance of the differences in reactions, only the response *Mail Open* showed significance. A chi-squared (χ^2) test [5] showed a significant relationship between the consumed video type and opening at least one phishing email ($\chi^2 = 6.76, p = 0.034, p < 0.05$). Only 34% of learners who watched the *Animation* opened any mail, while we observed more than 7% higher open rates among learners consuming the *Interview* (41%) and the *Slides* Video (47%). The indicated trend of enhanced awareness among learners

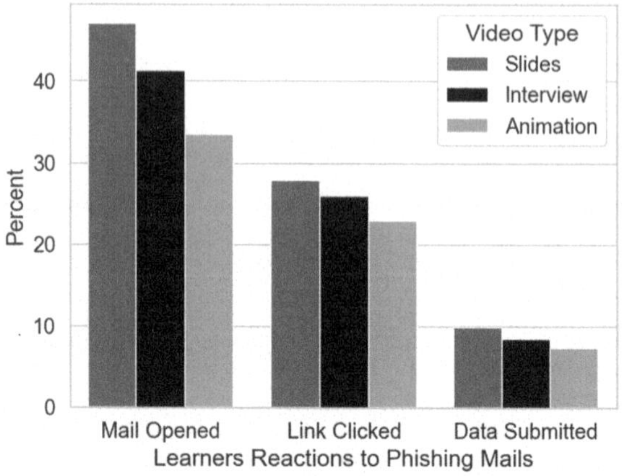

Fig. 5. Reactions of learners to the sent phishing emails (O_M), N=540

of the *Animation* group appears to continue in Fig. 5. However, we could not prove statistical significance for either of the two reactions *Link Click* ($\chi^2 = 1.17, p = 0.556$) or *Data Submission* ($\chi^2 = 0.77, p = 0.68$).

5 Discussion

In the previous analysis of the pretest as well as the three different tests for the three dimensions of cybersecurity awareness we introduced in Sect. 2.2, we observed the following results:

R1 Learners having watched the *Slides* perform best for *Knowledge*
R2 Learners having watched the *Animation* perform best when actively asked to assess emails. Thus they are best educated for the dimension of *Protection*
R3 Learners having watched the *Animation* show the best *Behavior* in real-life phishing scenarios

The observed results indicate that different education methods can help to focus the learner's experience on various levels of understanding. Concretely, in our case of cybersecurity awareness, the dimensions *Perception*, *Protection*, and *Behavior*. This finding, however, deviates from findings of previous research, such as [16,28,31] (c.f. Sect. 2.1). We therefore refrain from drawing generalizations and challenge our results and methodology in the following paragraphs.

We discuss potential alternative explanations (Sect. 5.1) for our observed results as well as threats to validity of our study (Sect. 5.2). We further discuss and list limitations to the results presented in this work, which in itself could be subject to further exploration in future research (Sect. 5.3).

5.1 Alternative Explanations

Our observations on the impact of the different types of educational videos derive from learners exposed to different types of videos. However, there are potential alternative explanations for the results.

Different Content in the Videos. *Hypothesis: Different learning results could derive from different content being presented in the different videos.*

In principle, all three videos covered the same pieces of information on the topic of phishing. Such were cues to identify phishing emails or the motivation of cybercriminals. To do so, all videos followed a content script developed based on the animation video. While all videos covered that same information, some types of videos inherently contained more dialogue accompanying that information. One example is the *Interview*, in which the speakers covered more accompanying information than initially planned, and hence the content structure was less strict than in the other two videos. This might have led to additional content being covered, e.g., in the *Interview* in comparison to the *Slides* or *Animation*. Still, the learners of *Animation* videos performed best. Further, this insecurity on the actual content is inherent with the format (e.g. *Interview*) and should therefore be considered when selecting how content is prepared.

Knowledge Levels for Protection and Behavior. *Hypothesis: The difference in the tests for the dimensions of Protection and Behavior is caused by learners having had a different skill level in advance.*

While we employed a pretest for knowledge (c.f. Section 4.1), which showed no significant difference between results for the three groups of learners, we did not employ a similar pretest for the other two dimensions. We used randomization to distribute learners equally into the three groups and hence expect that previous knowledge for all three dimensions is distributed equally among the learners. Still, we cannot claim with certainty that all groups have been equal before the treatment. In a follow-up study, we would pursue pretests for all three levels of learning and understanding.

The Factor "New". *Hypothesis: Learners are not used to animations or interviews and hence pay closer attention to the content of those.*

Our learners are used to videos in the style of *Talking Head with Slides*, as we employed in treatment X_1. A difference in learning video style could hence have caused additional interest and increased attentiveness during the videos and might have therefore helped to achieve higher learning success. Unfortunately, with our study setup, we cannot counteract this bias.

5.2 Threats to Validity

Discussing the (threats to) validity of any study helps to reflect on potential limitations for interpretation of the results and possible room for improvement in future studies. While experimental study methodologies as employed in our study are generally more robust against threats to validity [4], we want to highlight:

Threats to Internal Validity. The interaction in-between criteria of internal validity is a challenge for any study. As we cross-compare learners of different types of treatments for different dimensions of cybersecurity awareness, we are relatively confident that we properly faced potential influences in-between the threats to validity such as *Maturity*, *Mortality*, or *Selection* of learners. To ensure further robustness, we compared the results of learners who did not consume any of the videos to those of the other three groups. Throughout all three tests (O_1, O_2, O_M), learners who had not watched any learning video performed worse than participants in any of the other three groups. We are hence confident that our observations are caused by the treatments X_1 through X_3.

Threats to External Validity. Singular studies cannot achieve external validity interpreted as generalizability of study results. Aaronson and Ellsworth state that generalizability can only be inferred through repeated testing and verification of hypotheses across different studies in various contexts [1]. We performed our analysis in the niche of cybersecurity education, evaluating our learners' sensitization to cybersecurity threats. External validity, as generalizability, can only be achieved through repetition of the study in different contexts, such as, e.g., misinformation on social media. The particular limitations of our study in terms of unobserved or unaccounted variables are presented in Sect. 5.3

5.3 Limitations and Study Group

We previously discussed potential alternative explanations to our study result as well as threats to the validity of our study results. Still, we refrain from drawing any generalizable conclusions from our study, as there are too many variables that we did not assess in our first take on the impact of video types on learning outcomes, as presented in this work. This section provides an overview of the variables not challenged in the current study and hence subject to future research. We also provide an overview of the general conditions in which the analysis was performed, such as participant demographics.

The cybersecurity course we performed this study alongside is aimed at beginners. Still, participants were rather technical, as self-supplied during a post-study survey (distribution of IT-Experience: 7.8% *Beginner*, 52.5% *Advanced*, 39.5% *Expert*). From the study population who provided their demographics in the optional post-study survey, 75,9% were male, and 23.9% self-identified as female. The shares (S) of participants who self-supplied their ages is distributed as follows: $S_{<20\ Years} = 2.0\%$; $S_{20-29} = 4.4\%$; $S_{30-39} = 7.9\%$; $S_{40-49} = 15.4\%$; $S_{50-59} = 15.4\%$; $S_{60-69} = 25.7\%$; $S_{>70\ Years} = 14.2\%$. As observable from the screenshots in Fig. 1, we recorded the videos used for our study in the same professional studio as the remainder of the course. The presenters, were different from the presenter or the remainder of the MOOC. Still, all presenters were known to the participants, as they had been introduced as part of the teaching team and had presented few other previous videos. For this study and analysis, we did not investigate learning analytics information of the video, such as playback speeds, jumps between content, or quitting the video earlier, as we could not get that information for the external video. The learning success towards learners' sensitization, as observed in O_M, was measured through the user's reactions to three phishing emails. We designed the study to account for variations in difficulty between the three emails by accumulating results between all three. Therefore, however, we cannot observe changes in performance regarding time passed since the learning activity. A dedicated study would have to be performed as a follow-up.

6 Conclusion

This manuscript contributes to the body of research on the impact of different learning video styles. Previous research showed inconclusive about the effects of video styles on different types of challenges and exercises that learners are presented with. We, therefore, studied the impact of video styles on cybersecurity awareness with a cohort of more than 1,500 learners in the context of a German-speaking MOOC.

While we identified that learners of traditional *Talking Head with Slides* videos performed significantly better for recall tasks, learners exposed to *Animation* videos best applied the knowledge in different transfer tasks, such as identifying phishing emails, however, we refrained from drawing generalizable conclusions, as we are biased by the fact that both *Animation* and *Interview* videos are relatively uncommon in our MOOCs and therefore potentially particularly interesting for the learners.

We contribute more arguments and aspects to the discussion on the impact of video types, with, to the best of our knowledge, the first identification of differences in learning success for *Transfer* tasks. We aim to motivate fellow researchers to imitate our study or to perform similar ones in their contexts. For our context of cybersecurity, we welcome the fact that the shorter animation videos provide better measures towards the learners' security awareness, as they are easier to disperse, e.g., means of social media.

References

1. Aronson, E., Ellsworth, P.C.: Methods of Research in Social Psychology. Social Sciences & World Languages, McGraw-Hill Humanities (1990)
2. Bloom, B.S.: Taxonomy of Educational Objectives: The Classification of Educational Goals. Longmans, Green (1956)
3. Bundeskriminalamt: Bundeslagebild Cybercrime 2021. Bundelagebild Cybercrime, Germany (2022). https://www.bka.de/DE/Presse/Listenseite_Pressemitteilungen/2022/Presse2022/220509_PM_CybercrimeBLB.html
4. Campbell, D.T., Stanley, J.C.: Experimental and Quasi-Experimental Designs for Research. Wadsworth, Belomt, CA (2011)
5. Chernoff, H., Lehmann, E.L.: The use of maximum likelihood estimates in χ^2 tests for goodness of fit. Ann. Math. Stat. **25**(3), 579–586 (1954). https://doi.org/10.1214/aoms/1177728726

6. Cisco: cybersecurity threat trends: phishing, crypto top the list (2021). https://umbrella.cisco.com/info/2021-cyber-security-threat-trends-phishing-crypto-top-the-list
7. Cross, A., et al.: Online learning versus blended learning: an exploratory study. In: Proceedings of the first ACM conference on Learning@Scale. ACM, Atlanta Georgia USA (2014). https://doi.org/10.1145/2556325.2567869
8. European union agency for cybersecurity.: ENISA threat landscape 2022: 2021 July to 2022 July. Publications Office, LU (2022). https://data.europa.eu/doi/10.2824/764318
9. Furnell, S.: Assessing website password practices-unchanged after fifteen years? Comput. Secur. **120**, 102790 (2022). iSBN: 0167-4048 Publisher: Elsevier
10. Goodyear, P., Steeples, C.: Creating shareable representations of practice. ALT-J **6**(3), 16–23 (1998). iSBN: 0968-7769 Publisher: Taylor & Francis
11. Guo, P.J., Kim, J., Rubin, R.: How video production affects student engagement: an empirical study of MOOC videos. In: Proceedings of the First ACM Conference on Learning @ Scale Conference, pp. 41–50. ACM, Atlanta Georgia USA (2014). https://doi.org/10.1145/2556325.2566239
12. Hänsch, N., Benenson, Z.: Specifying IT security awareness. In: 2014 25th International Workshop on Database and Expert Systems Applications, pp. 326–330 (2014). https://doi.org/10.1109/DEXA.2014.71. iSSN: 2378-3915
13. Jaeger, L.: Information security awareness: literature review and integrative framework. In: Proceedings of the Annual Hawaii International Conference on System Sciences. IEEE Computer Society, Waikoloa Village, HA USA (2018). http://hdl.handle.net/10125/50482
14. Jaeger, L., Eckhardt, A.: Eyes wide open: the role of situational information security awareness for security-related behaviour. Inf. Syst. J. **31**(3), 429–472 (2021). https://doi.org/10.1111/isj.12317. https://onlinelibrary.wiley.com/doi/pdf/10.1111/isj.12317
15. Jampen, D., Gür, G., Sutter, T., Tellenbach, B.: Don't click: towards an effective anti-phishing training. HCIS **10**(1), 33 (2020). https://doi.org/10.1186/s13673-020-00237-7
16. Kizilcec, R.F., Papadopoulos, K., Sritanyaratana, L.: Showing face in video instruction: effects on information retention, visual attention, and affect. In: Proceedings of the SIGCHI Conference on Human Factors in Computing Systems, pp. 2095–2102. ACM, Toronto Ontario Canada (2014). https://doi.org/10.1145/2556288.2557207
17. Köhler, D., Meinel, C.: The right tool for the job: overview, comparison and assessment of methods for cybersecurity awareness education and verification. Preprint (2023). https://doi.org/10.13140/RG.2.2.11102.51528
18. Köhler, D., Pünter, W., Meinel, C.: Quantitatively exploring phishing susceptibility in private contexts. Preprint, In Review (2023). https://doi.org/10.13140/RG.2.2.21865.47201
19. Lain, D., Kostiainen, K., Čapkun, S.: Phishing in organizations: findings from a large-scale and long-term study. In: 2022 IEEE Symposium on Security and Privacy (SP), pp. 842–859 (2022). https://doi.org/10.1109/SP46214.2022.9833766. iSSN: 2375-1207
20. Anderson, L.W., et al.: A taxonomy for learning, teaching, and assessing: a revision of bloom's taxonomy of educational objectives. Longman (2001)
21. Majid, S., Khine, W.K.K., Oo, M.Z.C., Lwin, Z.M.: An analysis of YouTube videos for teaching information literacy skills. In: Thaung, K. (ed.) Advanced Information

Technology in Education. Advances in Intelligent and Soft Computing, vol. 126. Springer, Heidelberg (2012). https://doi.org/10.1007/978-3-642-25908-1_20
22. McKight, P.E., Najab, J.: Kruskal-Wallis test. In: The Corsini Encyclopedia of Psychology. Wiley, Ltd. (2010). https://doi.org/10.1002/9780470479216.corpsy0491
23. Metzger, C., Waibel, R., Henning, C., Hodel, M., Luzi, R.: Anspruchsniveau von Lernzielen und Prüfungen im kognitiven Bereich. Universität St, Gallen (1993)
24. Moore, R.L., Blackmon, S.J.: From the learner's perspective: a systematic review of MOOC learner experiences (2008–2021). Comput. Educ. **190**, 104596 (2022). https://doi.org/10.1016/j.compedu.2022.104596
25. Pearman, S., Zhang, S.A., Bauer, L., Christin, N., Cranor, L.F.: Why people (don't) use password managers effectively. In: Fifteenth Symposium on Usable Privacy and Security (SOUPS 2019). USENIX Association, Santa Clara, CA (2019)
26. Pearson, K.: X. On the criterion that a given system of deviations from the probable in the case of a correlated system of variables is such that it can be reasonably supposed to have arisen from random sampling (1900). https://doi.org/10.1080/14786440009463897
27. Santos-Espino, J.M., Afonso-Suárez, M.D., Guerra-Artal, C.: Speakers and boards: a survey of instructional video styles in MOOCs. Tech. Commun. **63**(2), 101–115 (2016). iSBN: 0049-3155 Publisher: Society for Technical Communication
28. Steinbeck, H., Zobel, T., Meinel, C.: Using the YouTube Video style in a MOOC: (Re-)testing the effect of visual experience in a field-experiment. In: Proceedings of the Ninth ACM Conference on Learning @ Scale, pp. 142–150. L@S 2022, Association for Computing Machinery, New York, NY, USA (2022). https://doi.org/10.1145/3491140.3528268
29. Stolberg, H.O., Norman, G., Trop, I.: Randomized controlled trials. Am. J. Roentgenol. **183**, 01831539 (2004)
30. Vogt, W.P., Johnson, R.B.: The SAGE dictionary of statistics & methodology: a nontechnical guide for the social sciences. SAGE Publications (2015)
31. Wang, J., Antonenko, P.D.: Instructor presence in instructional video: effects on visual attention, recall, and perceived learning. Comput. Hum. Behav. **71**, 79–89 (2017). https://doi.org/10.1016/j.chb.2017.01.049
32. Winther, P.: MITRE ATT&CK technique t1566: Phishing (2022). https://attack.mitre.org/techniques/T1566/

Role of Multimodal Learning Systems in Technology-Enhanced Learning (TEL): A Scoping Review

Yoon Lee[1(✉)], Bibeg Limbu[2], Zoltan Rusak[3], and Marcus Specht[1]

[1] Faculty of Electrical Engineering, Mathematics and Computer Science, Delft University of Technology, Mekelweg 4, 2628 CD Delft, The Netherlands
y.lee@tudelft.nl

[2] Faculty of Engineering, University of Duisburg-Essen, Forsthausweg 2, 47057 Duisburg, Germany

[3] Faculty of Industrial Design Engineering, Landbergstraat 15, 2628 CE Delft, Netherlands

Abstract. Technology-enhanced learning systems, specifically multimodal learning technologies, use sensors to collect data from multiple modalities to provide personalized learning support beyond traditional learning settings. However, many studies surrounding such multimodal learning systems mostly focus on technical aspects concerning data collection and exploitation and therefore overlook theoretical and instructional design aspects such as feedback design in multimodal settings. This paper explores multimodal learning systems as a critical part of technology-enhanced learning used for capturing and analyzing the learning process to exploit the collected multimodal data to generate feedback in multimodal settings. By investigating various studies, we aim to reveal the roles of multimodality in technology-enhanced learning across various learning domains. Our scoping review outlines the conceptual landscape of multimodal learning systems, identifies potential gaps, and provides new perspectives on adaptive multimodal system design: intertwining learning data for meaningful insights into learning, designing effective feedback, and implementing them in diverse learning domains.

Keywords: Multimodal Learning Analytics (MMLA) · Sensor-based Technology · Learning Domains

1 Introduction

With the increasing application of Technology-Enhanced Learning (TEL), the educational roles of teachers and students are constantly changing [39]. The seismic shift was observed during the pandemic in the last few years, which forced the educational focus from traditional classroom learning to online and hybrid environments [39]. Owing to the proliferation of digital platforms and devices designed for educational purposes [25], TEL technologies have resulted

O. Viberg et al. (Eds.): EC-TEL 2023, LNCS 14200, pp. 164–182, 2023.
https://doi.org/10.1007/978-3-031-42682-7_12

in the availability of copious amounts of data on both the learner and their learning process. As a direct consequence, TEL technologies are being further enhanced with sophisticated Artificial Intelligence (AI), particularly Machine Learning (ML) techniques and Learning Analytics (LA).

Such technological advancements have reinforced the role of TEL, not only as a LA tool but also as a form of feedback agent in learning. For instance, the advent of ChatGPT[1] appears to bring transformative development in the field, as it has the potential to change the foundations of learning and education [27]. Although such interactions are currently limited only to text modality, information acquisition will become even more accessible via multiple sensory modalities, with the convergence of diverse speech-based conversational agents [31] and sensor technologies, in the form of multimodal interactions (e.g., Generative AI combined with VR agents) [27]. In this context, the importance of multimodality is not only confined to TEL as data input from the digital world [13], but also as outputs in both the physical and the virtual world, which can trigger cognitive, behavioral, and emotional changes in learners.

Multimodal learning systems, a subgroup of TEL, frequently employ multiple sensors and AI techniques to gather contextual learning data from diverse modalities to provide a comprehensive understanding of learning processes. This understanding can assist us, as practitioners and researchers, to reflect on the efficacy of the design of multimodal learning systems: how to digitize learning and learner information as data [25], how to process and intertwine multimodal data to best contextualize learning [21,25,44], and how to design and implement feedback and LA, also called multimodal learning analytics (MMLA) in learning systems to address students necessities [25,40].

The field of MMLA combines different types of data from multiple modalities and sources to gain contextual insights into the learning process. Di Mitri et al. [13], in their conceptual framework called "Multimodal Learning Analytics Model (MLeAM)", portrayed multimodality in learning systems as a series of steps involving sensor capturing, annotation, predictions, and feedback implementation, in a loop. Although their conceptual framework has precisely aligned the multimodal data stream in input space, the framework has yet to be extended to the dimensions of feedback design and its implications for learning domains. In order to get insights into the design of feedback and MMLA, a critical component of TEL, we examine through a review how previous studies utilize multimodality in their learning systems from data collection to feedback implementation, which has yet to be collectively understood in previous research. Therefore, we investigate multimodal learning systems in three primary stages: 1) data collection and integration, 2) design decisions for the design of multimodal feedback, and 3) implications for system implementation in diverse learning domains. The following three research questions will be tackled by reviewing and analyzing studies in the field.

- RQ1. How is multimodal data collected and processed to get insights about learning in MMLA?

[1] https://openai.com/.

- RQ2. How is learner feedback designed in the context of multimodal learning systems?
- RQ3. What are the considerations for implementing multimodal learning systems in various learning domains?

2 Methodology

The literature search was conducted with the PRISMA (Preferred Reporting Items for Systematic Reviews and Meta-Analyses) approach. The review itself was later adapted to a *scoping review* due to the erratic landscape of the multimodal learning systems we observed based on our preliminary searches, as our focus was on investigating the emerging topic, multimodality, as a critical component of TEL. Therefore, we adopted the five-stage approach of a scoping review of Arksey and O'Malley [3]: 1) identifying the research questions, 2) identifying relevant literature based on inclusion and exclusion criteria, 3) selecting studies, 4) analyzing and synthesizing the data, 5) and summarizing and reporting the results.

Through various search engines, such as Scopus and Web of Science, 1,794 search results were found based on keyword search (i.e. (multimodal OR multisensory) AND feedback AND (learning OR education)). Only results that included a description of learning systems designed for human users were selected, resulting in 274 papers. The results included papers from various subject areas, such as computer science, engineering, social sciences, psychology, and art and humanities. Six researchers further coded and filtered the remaining 274 papers in the eligibility check process with inclusion and exclusion criteria, such as having multimodal components as both the input and output of the system implementation. Using Cohen's Kappa coefficient by comparing observed and random probabilities, the inter-rater reliability among six coders' scores has been evaluated (Cohen's Kappa: good, $0.9 > 0.81 \geq 0.8$). The primary author solely proceeded with the rest of the overall review, and 27 papers were chosen for the final review. To compensate limitation of the PRISMA methodology caused by its strict application of inclusion and exclusion criteria, we applied the snowball method to extend the discussion with other relevant research in the field for a further scoping review, which resulted in 30 papers ranging from 2010 to 2023.

3 Results

The search conducted with the methodology described above resulted in 30 papers published between 2010 and 2023. Most of the systems in the resulting studies were based on a sensor-based approach and built for on-site learning than online learning. Similarly, they were often geared towards individual learning scenarios instead of collaborative learning. The majority of the selected studies' primary intervention was in the form of real-time feedback rather than post-hoc feedback, and most targeted learners more than teachers. A significant proportion of studies were conducted in K-12 education and higher education. Table 1 provides an overview of all the selected studies and their learning domains, data inputs, and feedback modalities.

4 Discussion

4.1 RQ1. How Is Multimodal Data Collected and Processed to Get Insights About Learning in MMLA?

Multimodal data collection in MMLA is performed using a host of sensors that correspond to the five primary modalities used by humans (i.e., visual, auditory, tactile, taste, and smell [11]), with various information layers, such as data types, frequencies, and resolutions. Our literature search yielded no studies that addressed the modalities of taste and smell, indicating a dearth of technology capable of capturing them. Of the 30 papers, six studies (20.0%) collected visual and auditory data, two studies (6.7%) collected visual and tactile data, two studies (6.7%) collected auditory and tactile data, and two studies (6.7%) collected all three of them. Tactile data has been most frequently used as the major data stream in eleven studies (36.7%), while visual and auditory data have been used in five (16.7%) and two studies (6.7%), respectively.

Sensor-Based Data Collection *Visual and auditory sensors* are frequently used to collect audio and video data. Visual data is collected using different types of cameras (e.g., webcam [30], infrared camera [31], motion capture camera [52]), which consist of various information layers such as RGB [9], shapes, sizes, and textures. Visual data is further processed, often with AI and ML techniques, for various purposes such as image recognition [41], facial expression analysis [10], gaze and posture analysis [15,37], and trajectory tracking of the body [7,24] and objects.

Auditory data is captured through the microphone, having volume and frequency as essential features. The human voice is commonly captured as an auditory modality that is used for corpus analysis [1], speech analysis, voice trait analysis [15,47], and musical trait analysis [34,52].

Tactile sensors, such as Inertial Motion Units (IMUs), are used to capture learners' physical movement and orientation detection [20,47] while force trajectory is tracked via force sensors [7]. Additionally, *environmental sensors* collect information about the physical learning environments, such as temperature, humidity, noise level, and air quality [49]. More sophisticated *physiological sensors* technologies (e.g., eye tracker [31,32], electroencephalogram (EEG)) are also applied for more accurate and deeper insights into the physiological state of the learner. Such sensors collect physiological information such as heart rate and skin conductance, which are further interpreted as clues of learners' stress levels, arousal, and emotional states [12]. For example, one dominant tendency in MMLA is the inclusion of physiological sensors to evaluate learners' affective

Table 1. List of papers included in the scoping review.

Lit.	Learning Domains	Data Input	Feedback Modalities
[1]	**Language Learning (Foreign)**: Personalized foreign language training	**Auditory**: Vocal traits and sentence formulation from microphone	**Visual/Auditory** : Dashboard (analytic dashboards), Text (paraphrasing), Voice (model voice, dialogue simulation)
[4]	**Medical Education** : Gamified palpation training	**Tactile** : Pressure sensitivity and timing from wearable glove (ParsGlove)	**Visual/Auditory** : Graphics (gamified task), Sound Effects (rewarding purpose for successful task completion)
[5]	**Medical Education** : Palpation analytics for training	**Tactile** : Orientation, position, and pressure of hand from wearable glove (ParsGlove)	**Visual** : Dashboard (real-time monitoring panel, feedback panel, post-hoc examogram with tables, graphs, and scores)
[6]	**Conceptual Learning** : Teaching properties of graphs and diagrams for visually impaired students	**Tactile** : Stylus orientation from Phantom Omni	**Auditory/Tactile** : Voice (task guidance), Physical Movements (Phantom Omni)
[7]	**Language Learning (First)** : Teaching handwriting for children	**Tactile** : Characters written on touch screen	**Visual/Tactile** : Graphics (cartoon face, color trajectory for guidance), Text (message alerts), Vibrations (error), Physical Movements (haptic rendering of correct trajectory)
[9]	**Conceptual Learning** : Gamified interface for better knowledge gain in collaborative learning	**Visual / Auditory** : Learner poses from a camera, Group corpus from microphone	**Visual** : Graphics (virtual farmland getting mature with better participation in the class)
[10]	**Clear Communication** : Practicing public speaking	**Visual/Auditory** : Behavior (gaze, facial expressions) from webcam and speech, voice activity from a microphone (Multisense)	**Visual** : Graphics (interactive virtual audiences), Dashboard (after-action report with analysis, containing text and graphs, and video recording)
[15]	**Clear Communication** : Presentation training	**Visual/Auditory** : Speech rate and filled pauses from six microphones, Gaze detection from six cameras (HAAR Cascade), posture skeleton (Kinect)	**Visual** : Graphics (symbolic icons-thumbs up and down with color coding, video capture of presentation), Text (evaluation summary with statistics)

(continued)

Table 1. (*continued*)

Lit.	Learning Domains	Data Input	Feedback Modalities
[16]	**Conceptual Learning** : Immersive organic chemistry education with gamified VR	**Tactile** : Finger tracking via haptic glove	**Visual/Tactile** : Graphics (3D-gamified molecule graphic with color changes via VR headset), Vibrations (for approval or disapproval for task performance)
[19]	**Language Learning (First)** : Teaching reading to children with dyslexia	**Tactile** : Letters and spatial arrangements recognized by pogo pins	**Visual/Auditory** : 3D Physical Prototype alphabets with colored LED, Graphics (colored text graphics), Voice (associated sound for letters)
[20]	**Sports Education** : Dancing supports from expert performances	**Auditory/Tactile** : Movement features (timing, intensity) from a 3D accelerometer, electromyography sensor, and vocalization from a microphone	**Auditory** : Voice (Pre-recorded experts' vocalization mapped and synthesized with learner's movement)
[23]	**Conceptual Learning** : Haptic rendering for elementary science education	**Visual** : Images that student took using mobile phone cameras	**Tactile** : Vibrations (haptic rendering which represents the texture of photos taken)
[24]	**Sports Education** : Motion analysis for golf swing	**Visual** : Visual marker recognition from motion capture cameras	**Visual/Auditory** : Graphics (comparing color-coded trajectory traces with reference), Sound Effects (putting sound with different pitch, indicating performance levels)
[29]	**Medical Education** : Injection simulator for veterinary education	**Visual / Tactile** : Visual marker from AR tracking camera and orientation from gyro sensor on syringe simulator	**Visual/Auditory/Tactile** : Graphic (AR/VR graphic with simulator and vein with evaluative color coding), Sound Effects (bell chimes and dog barks as evaluation), Physical Movements (force from syringe simulator)
[30]	**Conceptual Learning** : Companion robot for e-reading in higher education	**Visual** : Webcam-based video recording on learners' behaviors	**Visual/Auditory** : Robot Gestures (facial expressions), Robot LED (approval, disapproval), Robot Speech (dialogue)
[32]	**Language Learning (First)** : Calligraphy trainer based on expert's handwriting	**Tactile** : Touch from tablet and muscle activities, gesture embedded accelerometer and gyroscope on Myo sensor, and eye tracker glasses from SMI	**Visual/Tactile** : Graphics (characters with colored trajectory guidance), Dashboard (summative evaluation with graphs, video recording), Physical Movements (pressure feedback with saturation)

(*continued*)

Table 1. (*continued*)

Lit.	Learning Domains	Data Input	Feedback Modalities
[34]	**Musical Education** : Musical ensemble between human and machine	**Visual/Auditory** : Motion of cueing data from the camera, evaluating tempo from the microphone	**Visual/Auditory** : Graphics (projection of shadow-like pianist, Music (violin, viola, cello, double bass play in coordination)
[35]	**Sports Education** : Indoor rowing training with VR	**Visual/Tactile** : Hand movements from cameras and ergometer on handles	**Visual/Tactile** : Graphics (VR simulation for hand movement trajectories and gauge bar with color coding), Physical Prototype (feedback for hand position based on haptic markers)
[37]	**Clear Communication** : Automatic feedback for oral presentation skills	**Visual/Auditory** : Head gaze, posture detection from the camera, usage of filled pauses and volume from the microphone, pitches from text, and image size/density recognition from presentation slides	**Visual/Auditory**: Dashboard (post-hoc report with statistical scores and advice for weaknesses), Graphics (video, image recording), Audio (audio recording)
[38]	**Medical Education** : VR Epidural Administration	**Tactile** : Interaction with 3D-syringe with Novint Falcon, Leap Motion, and Touch 3D	**Visual/Auditory** : Graphics (virtual patient in a mixed-reality environment with Oculus Rift DK2, Dashboard (score, time completion, and number of attempts performed), Sound Effects (needle injection)
[41]	**Conceptual Learning** : Mathematics education for children with visual impairments	**Visual** : Image recognition based on markers (TopCodes)	**Auditory/Tactile** : Sound Effects (drum and piano), Voice (number reading, verbal rewards), Tangible user interface with braille (iCETA)
[42]	**Language Learning (First)** : Teaching handwriting for blind children	**Auditory/Tactile** : Audio pan and pitch represents from microphone and stylus gestures from Phantom Omni	**Auditory/Tactile** : Sound Effects (Pitch differences for drawing in the appropriate trajectory), Physical Movements (force feedback to minimize the distance with trajectory and playback feedback from Phantom Omni)
[45]	**Sports Education** : Virtual training for rowing skills	**Tactile** : Velocity of rowing tracking from accelerators	**Visual/Auditory/Tactile** : Graphic (Immersive virtual reality for immersion and optimal trajectory guidance), Sound Effects (errors), Vibrations (errors)

(*continued*)

Table 1. (*continued*)

Lit.	Learning Domains	Data Input	Feedback Modalities
[46]	**Clear Communication** : Presentation trainer for public speaking	**Visual/Auditory** : Body posture, hand gesture analysis based on a visual marker recognition from Kinect, voice volume, buffer, and pauses from the Kinect microphone	**Visual/Tactile** : Dashboard (mirrored video of the users), Graphics (symbolic icons for approval/disapproval), Text (evaluation and guidance), Vibrations (correction alert. through wristband)
[48]	**Language Learning (Foreign)** : Mobile tutoring system for English pronunciation	**Auditory** : Phoneme recognition from the microphone on mobile device	**Visual** : Graphics (flash card, emoji-based mouth shape animation), Dashboard (list of mispronounced words), Text (word-to-text with color-coded highlights)
[50]	**Medical Education** : Ultrasonography training	**Visual** : Position recognition of simulator from Kinect	**Visual** : Graphics (3D organ models and simulations, suggestive trajectory in guided mode)
[51]	**Clear Communication** : Presentation trainer	**Visual/Auditory/Tactile** : Body posture and movements from Kinect and voice volume, voice modulation, and phasing of speaking from microphone	**Visual** : Dashboard (posture analysis with skeleton, color-coded symbolic icons, suggestive text)
[52]	**Musical Education** : Violin play training	**Visual/Auditory/Tactile** : Video with visual markers from motion capture camera and Kinect, ambient audio from the microphone, and physiological (EMG) data from Myo sensors	**Visual/Auditory** : Dashboard (audio, video, and motion-capture recording with data visualization as post-hoc feedback)
[53]	**Medical Education** : Gross anatomy education for undergraduate medical students	**Tactile** : Stylus orientation from Phantom Omni haptic stylus	**Visual/Tactile** : Graphics (3D human anatomical structures), Physical Movements (rotation, touch feedback from Phantom Omni haptic stylus)
[54]	**Conceptual Learning** : Geometrical concept teaching for children with virtual 3D space	**Tactile** : Stylus orientation from Phantom Omni haptic stylus	**Visual/Auditory/Tactile** : Graphics (3D graphics with gamification), Sound Effects (immersive object moving sound), Physical Movements from Phantom Omni haptic stylus

states (e.g., cognitive load from pupil dilation and blinks based on eye tracking data [30,32]). However, such applications are often criticized for their obstructiveness. To compensate for such limitations, remote detection technologies that are developed and implemented in affective computing can be utilized: assessing learners' bio-data based on vision-based detection (e.g., heart rate [55]) and behavior recognition algorithms [30], without having to have intrusive biosensors implemented, which allows more stealth monitoring of learner activities.

With the current advancement of deep learning technologies, a subset of ML, and increased computational capabilities, high-resolution sensor data, with an unstructured data form, has become the resource of deep neural network developments. Deep neural networks can be used to make a sophisticated prediction about the learners' performance in LA, such as their attention prediction during e-reading [30], and provide personalized support. Before the emergence of deep learning technologies, only structured data with statistical explainability, such as log data from learning management systems, had been the target resources of traditional ML and LA [36]. However, dynamic data with uninterpretable patterns, such as image, video, sound, and text [43], are now widely used for the various model developments for the classification, prediction, and detection tasks [31]. It is expected that such emerging models developed based on unstructured or semi-structured information with non-numeric organizations, such as data from eye trackers and EEG data, will expand the horizons of MMLA.

Log-Based Data Collection

Log data, collected through learners' interaction with learning management systems via mouse clicks, keyboard inputs, and touch, in quantified forms (e.g., number, frequency) [26], have been the traditional sources of data in LA. Such data collection is mainly done in online platforms, such as MOOCs [18], with bigger sample scales and broader demographics than the sensor-based data collection. Although the collection of log data is often more accessible due to the absence of complex hardware infrastructure and sensors and can be interpreted with relative ease [36], the insights from log data have been subject to criticism for its superficial interpretations [33]. Also, its smaller computation requirements make it suitable for extensive data collection at larger scales. With the emergence of generative AI, the log data, such as the discourse between learners and the system, will become much more valuable due to its potential for personalized chat-based learning assistants, which will become more common with current advancements in Transformer-based Natural Language Processing (NLP) models (e.g., GPT-4) [27].

Questionnaire Data Collection

The questionnaire is one traditional data collection method for learning analytics: evaluating learning on objective (e.g., knowledge gain) and subjective levels (e.g., learning experience). One common approach has been a pre-post questionnaire to measure the objective learning outcomes (e.g., knowledge gain) through task performances. With increasing emphasis on the User Experience (UX) in computer-assisted systems, more measures are developed and implemented for gauging the UX of the system (e.g., System Usability Scale (SUS) [8], Attrakdiff questionnaire [22]). Most existing measures have been developed especially for Human-Computer Interaction (HCI), which focus primarily on computer-based artifacts [2]. However, with the expansion of the physical and virtual ecosystems of TEL, there are emerging necessities for more standardized measures for evaluating the UX of various peripheral devices (e.g., AR/VR, conversational agents) and agents (e.g., virtual robots) [31]. Deciding the timing of questionnaire-based data collection (e.g., real-time, post-hoc) is one challenge, where researchers should balance the timely aspect and obstructiveness of the data collection.

Observation-Based Data Collection

Observation-based data collection is typical where the targeted learners are not fully capable of expressing their own perspectives (e.g., children with intellectual disability) or experts' opinion takes an essential role in evaluation (e.g., evaluating collaborative learning [9]). In such cases, observers' evaluation of observable indicators becomes the means of gauging learners' learning progress and performances [25]. The evaluation objectives are often learners' internal states, such as affects, attention, and perceived experiences [14,30,31], that influence learning experiences and potential learning outcomes. Since the evaluation is dependent on third-person observation, having clear annotation standards and frameworks is essential for the validity of the data. However, in some cases, practitioners often design and execute the measures themselves without having solid standards or frameworks [2]. Another challenge comes from individual differences: behaviors occur differently due to cultural backgrounds and individual differences [14], such as behavioral or emotional expressiveness. Alternative methods of combining human annotations with other layers of ground truths are suggested to compensate for such limitations: implementation of biosensor data (e.g., eye tracker [31] electroencephalography (EEG) [14]) and collecting self-reported ground truths [30] from learners.

4.2 RQ2. How Is Learner Feedback Designed in the Context of Multimodal Learning Systems?

Multimodal learning feedback in the form of in situ real-time feedback has often been provided via physical components, such as touch-based devices, wearables, haptic devices, physical prototypes, and speakers. In our literature search, in situ real-time feedback was more predominant than post-hoc feedback, while some took the hybrid approach. Such feedback often employed intuitive pictograms, color-coding, sound effects, vibration, and force feedback to provide immediate responses as learning interventions. In the meantime, post-hoc feedback has often

Multimodal Feedback			
Feedback Modality	Visual	Auditory	Tactile
Feedback Characteristics	Spacial / Temporal	Temporal	Temporal
Feedback Timing	Post-hoc / Real-time		Real-time
Feedback Functions	Semantic / Intuitive		Intuitive
Feedback Types	-Graphics -Dashboards -Text	-Sound Effects -Music -Voice	-Physical Movements -Vibrations

Fig. 1. Multimodal feedback involves decision-making regarding the feedback modalities, characteristics, timing, functions, and specific types of feedback.

been provided as dashboards, narrative text, and personalized voice feedback. Learner dashboards continue to be a prominent tool for supporting self-regulated learning in LA and MMLA. Dashboards in LA provide an easy-to-understand visual representation of complex learning data in real-time, which allows educators and students to make informed decisions. Generally, the feedback design in MMLA includes the following design elements: feedback modalities, characteristics, timing, types, and functions (see Fig. 1). In the following sections, we investigate the feedback elements found in the previous studies concerning their modalities.

Visual

Graphics are the primary visual element with intuitive delivery. The realistic graphical features have often been combined with engaging virtual environments [16,45], gamification elements [4,9,16] for specific learning objectives and contexts with enhanced immersion [54]. The symbolic features of the graphic have been used to communicate complex constructs. Symbolic pictograms, icons, and emojis are used [15,46] to help reinforce or correct learners' behaviors. Visual effects, such as 2D/3D effects and color coding [7,15,19,24,48], are used for highlighting specific information in the visual message delivery. Additionally, motion graphics/animations are used to convey dynamic information, such as a reference for the model trajectory and movements [24,45].

Dashboards commonly use post-hoc visual language with extensive and collective information. For example, statistical analysis of learning progress and performances has been shown through data visualization via graphs [1,5,47], tables [1,5], and gauge bars [35]. Multimodal learning systems track more sophisticated data from sensors capable of monitoring latent constructs in learners. Video [10,32] and audio recordings [52] are used as feedback for summative evaluation via dashboards so learners can reflect on their learning.

Text is used for its descriptive nature, capable of delivering narratives and details. It is a distinctive feature compared to other visual languages since the text relies on its semantic nature and the meaning layer, while visual languages mainly depend on intuitive understanding. Thanks to its clarity in message delivery, text feedback has often been used in dashboards for written descriptions [15,46] and message alerts [7]. To differentiate the information hierarchy, some visual traits, such as font size [19], highlighting [48], and colors [15,48], have partially been applied to texts.

Auditory

Sound effects refer to types of auditory stimuli that are artificially made. Sound effects are used for positive feedback in dashboards for showing approval and rewards (e.g., bell chime [29]), while alerting sound effects are used for intuitively signaling learners for behavior corrections (e.g., dog barks [29]). Sound effects are also used for in situ real-time feedback [32] in multimodal learning systems for better immersion in certain educational scenarios (e.g., golf putting sound with different pitches [24]).

Voice feedback has been commonly implemented for its semantic and phonetic features. Since lexical meaning can be delivered through voice messages, vocal instructions are given for the concept delivery [6], guidance [37], and dialogue simulations [1]. The acoustic features have been mainly emphasized for assisting pronunciations of second language learners and young learners [1]. Various tonal differences were applied to the vocal feedback to highlight specific information or certain sound units.

Music has been implemented for musical education [34,52] and context-giving for the immersions. Musical traits of learners' instrumental play, such as tempo, pitch, and timbre, have been corrected by providing specific parts of the musical recording as guidance. Music can also create a certain ambiance with immersive visual aids.

Tactile

Physical movements have often been used for providing feedback on the psychomotor aspects of complex skill learning. For instance, model movements have been demonstrated for sports training (e.g., rowing [35,45]) and delivering abstract concepts [6,16,41,54]. Fine motor movements were given for handwriting education with the trajectory (e.g., handwriting [7,32,42]). The syringe prototype provided the force feedback [29], intertwining with physical probes for more effective veterinary training. Movement feedback has often been helpful for learners with visual impairments for compensating their limitations in visual knowledge acquisition [6].

Vibrations constitute the majority of tactile feedback found in literature, often referred to as vibrotactile feedback, in the form of small vibrations and frictions.

Vibrations are simplistic and are not able to encode complex information. Vibrations have been implemented for concept delivery (e.g., texture rendering [23]), guidance (e.g., haptic trajectory [7]), and as corrective feedback (e.g., vibration buzzers [16,46]). All vibration feedback, and other tactile feedback, have mostly been adopted as real-time feedback due to their temporal context-specific nature and, therefore, not used in the dashboards.

4.3 RQ3. What Are the Considerations for Implementing Multimodal Learning Systems in Various Learning Domains?

To answer RQ3, we analyzed the multimodal learning systems found in our literature according to the three learning domains from revised Bloom's taxonomy [28]: cognitive, psychomotor, and affective domains. The *cognitive domain* involves the development of our mental skills and acquiring knowledge. The *Psychomotor domain* relates to discreet physical functions, reflex actions, and interpretive movements of the human body, while the *affective domain* involves our feelings, emotions, and attitudes. Furthermore, we also cluster the learning systems according to their specific application domain and learning goals and present some of the largest clusters. It should be noted that it is not our intention to present learning systems as exclusive to one domain, and we only seek to categorize the learning systems according to their primary learning objective.

Cognitive Domain

Conceptual Learning: Multimodal feedback loops for conceptual learning primarily focus on facilitating knowledge delivery and comprehension. Providing haptic feedback, in addition to visual-oriented course content, to demonstrate various physical phenomena has shown an enhanced understanding of the phenomena in learners [16,23]. The inclusion of additional modalities in instructions of conceptual learning can assist learners with visual impairments (e.g., haptic feedback from a stylus on Phantom Omni[2] [6]).

Language Learning: Multimodality is also beneficial in various aspects of language learning, which has traditionally been considered a predominately cognitive domain. Improving pronunciation and intonation in learning a foreign language has been a commonly targeted learning objective through various methods, such as visual aids with ideal mouth movements [48] and audio feedback with standard pronunciation [1]. Children and learners with disabilities have been the main end user of learning systems for first-language learning. For children, teaching how to read [19], write with characters [7], and improve handwriting skills [7] has been the main focus. For writing tasks, force feedback has been commonly given through stylus [42,53,54] and colored trajectory feedback [7] to indicate learners' errors intuitively.

[2] http://www.immersion.fr/.

Medical Education: Multimodal learning systems for medical education have been implemented to compensate for textbook-oriented education, aiming at more practice-based learning. Yeom et al. [53] suggested a 3D visual and tactile education system offering vivid visuals and tactile structures of human organs for gross anatomy class. Similarly, Palpation education tools [4], ultrasonography simulator [50], injection simulators for human patients [38], and animals [29] have been designed to promote authentic real-life practices of such complex skills with mock-ups. Those mock-ups have embedded collective sensors and software for learning analytics and feedback so that learners can receive real-time feedback during their learning practices [4,29]. Medical education systems also tend to involve physical props, mainly for tactile data collection and embedded performance assessment algorithms to provide real-time instructions and feedback.

Affective Domain

Clear Communication Skills: Systems have been developed to improve clear communication skills during learners' presentations. With real-time evaluation, learners were asked to reflect on their performances and improve their skills over practice [15,37,46,51]. Combining visual and auditory data collected from a webcam, microphone, and Kinect [15,46,51], learners' posture, gaze, facial expression, and voice traits for clear communication have been evaluated. Systems gave the correction in real-time, by short written descriptions [15,46], real-time posture analysis [46,51], and performance analysis on the dashboards as post-hoc feedback [15,37,46].

Psychomotor Domain

Sports Education: In sports education or training, learning goals are predominantly psychomotor. As such, during sporting activities, real-time physical features have been evaluated: posture and strike patterns [24] for the golf swing, body orientation and posture [35] for rowing, and body movement [20] for dancing. These learning systems aim to correct learner errors in real time and offer actionable plans to improve learners' motor skills. As motor-skills development demands conscious repetitive practices [17] where learners rely on apprenticeship-based education, systems can computationally model experts or mentors [32] and use ML to provide real-time feedback.

Musical Education: Systems in musical education were implemented to support human-machine ensemble [34] and violin play [52]. Based on visual and auditory indicators collected from a camera and a microphone, the phasing of violin play was analyzed on the dashboard [52]. To support the human-machine play [34], the shadow visual of the pianist and pre-recorded music piece has been played along with the learner's play during repetitive practices. Through visual aid, learners were taught to understand the current issues, correct errors, and internalize better techniques in an analytical and reflective manner.

4.4 Challenges and Opportunities

Generalization vs. Personalization of Multimodal Learning Systems. While most systems aim at the best generalizability in the application, more and more learning systems target feedback provisions with personalization since one system should be general enough to cover targeted user groups while it should effectively reflect individuals' critical learning necessities. In this regard, future studies for refining the generalizability and personalization of critical learning necessities, timing, frequencies, and effects in multimodal learning system design would greatly benefit the community.

Overarching MMLA Frameworks for Higher-Level Learning Objectives. Multimodal learning systems are often modeled as domain-specific and context-based since most systems aim to improve concrete learning activities with clear system goals. However, in many cases, such goals are set based on fragmentary frameworks, lacking overarching models for higher-level learning objectives that can be universally applied to general domains or even domain-specific instructional design. Having such an overarching framework could work as a common ground where practitioners and researchers can exchange and share their knowledge and grow as a community while defining learning features is often the biggest challenge in MMLA with advancements in a data-driven approach.

Closing the Feedback Loop in MMLA. Our findings suggest that despite the advances in AI and ML algorithms, multimodal learning systems often fail to close the feedback loop. Though the systems we examined in our study included feedback in the system loop, most MMLA systems in the field need to take the current analytics into the context of the next round of feedback provision. In this sense, closing the feedback loop based on various modalities and evaluating the effect of the feedback loop for further optimization seems to be an essential challenge in the field.

5 Conclusion

In this scoping review, we investigated multimodal learning systems, which is an integral extension of modern TEL systems. We investigate systems in three stages as an extension to the MLeAM framework: 1) multimodal data collection and processing, 2) multimodal feedback design decisions, and 3) multimodal system implementation for various learning domains. The result indicates the necessity of a more holistic understanding of the whole process in order to design effective systems and multimodal instruction patterns. We also identified critical challenges in multimodal learning systems, such as defining learning indicators, balancing the generalization and personalization of analytics and interventions, and closing the feedback loop in multimodal learning systems. Our paper provides an overview of the role multimodality plays in defining the potential of the next generations of TELs and outlines important considerations for data collection, feedback design, and MMLA design for adaptive TEL system implementations.

With more evidence-based, data-driven approaches taken in LA, the quality of data is getting increasingly important, especially in the context of MMLA. Although data is becoming more accessible through sensors on commercialized devices (e.g., laptops, webcam [30]) and increasing public datasets, engineering competencies are becoming more critical in MMLA [44] as how data is collected and processed impacts the quality of data and therefore, the predictions it makes. Based on our analysis of RQ1, MMLA builds upon, rather than replacing, traditional LA but using data from multiple modalities. By doing so, MMLA is able to make more robust predictions about learners' performance across multiple domains, as evidenced by RQ3, and can also provide more personalized feedback. However, even with the increased roles of data engineering and advancements in AI, researchers' insights, experiences, and domain knowledge are still critical [44]. For example, the black-box nature of ML models makes decisions and predictions in MMLA often not explainable and requires human interpretations. Explainable AI (e.g., tree-based models) [43] can supplement the current MMLA in partially addressing this issue by providing better interpretability of such analysis. This also holds true for the LA dashboards, as evidenced by RQ2, with the majority of multimodal learning systems still relying on the affordances of traditional LA dashboards, which support necessities for the stronger MMLA and feedback design based on multimodalities.

Acknowledgements. This work was supported by Leiden-Delft-Erasmus Centre for Education and Learning (LDE-CEL).

References

1. Ai, R., et al.: Sprinter: language technologies for interactive and multimedia language learning. In: Proceedings of the Ninth International Conference on Language Resources and Evaluation (LREC 2014), pp. 2733–2738 (2014)
2. Alenljung, B., Lindblom, J., Andreasson, R., Ziemke, T.: User experience in social human-robot interaction. In: Rapid automation: concepts, methodologies, tools, and applications, pp. 1468–1490. IGI Global (2019)
3. Arksey, H., O'Malley, L.: Scoping studies: towards a methodological framework. Int. J. Soc. Res. Methodol. **8**(1), 19–32 (2005)
4. Asadipour, A., Debattista, K., Chalmers, A.: Visuohaptic augmented feedback for enhancing motor skills acquisition. Vis. Comput. **33**(4), 401–411 (2017)
5. Asadipour, A., Debattista, K., Patel, V., Chalmers, A.: A technology-aided multimodal training approach to assist abdominal palpation training and its assessment in medical education. Int. J. Hum. Comput. Stud. **137**, 102394 (2020)
6. Bernareggi, C., Ahmetovic, D., Mascetti, S.: μgraph: haptic exploration and editing of 3D chemical diagrams. In: The 21st International ACM SIGACCESS Conference on Computers and Accessibility, pp. 312–317 (2019)
7. Brondi, R., Satler, M., Avizzano, C.A., Tripicchio, P.: A multimodal learning system for handwriting movements. In: 2014 International Conference on Intelligent Environments, pp. 256–259. IEEE (2014)

8. Brooke, J., et al.: SUS-A quick and dirty usability scale. Usability Eval. Ind. **189**(194), 4–7 (1996)
9. Chen, H., Tan, E., Lee, Y., Praharaj, S., Specht, M., Zhao, G.: Developing AI into explanatory supporting models: an explanation-visualized deep learning prototype. In: The International Conference of Learning Science (ICLS) (2020)
10. Chollet, M., Ghate, P., Neubauer, C., Scherer, S.: Influence of individual differences when training public speaking with virtual audiences. In: Proceedings of the 18th International Conference on Intelligent Virtual Agents, pp. 1–7 (2018)
11. Cope, B., Kalantzis, M., Group, N.L.: Multiliteracies: Literacy Learning and the Design of Social Futures. Literacies (Routledge), Routledge (2000). https://books.google.nl/books?id=a6eBiUQLJu4C
12. Cukurova, M., Giannakos, M., Martinez-Maldonado, R.: The promise and challenges of multimodal learning analytics. Br. J. Educ. Technol. **51**(5), 1441–1449 (2020)
13. Di Mitri, D., Schneider, J., Specht, M., Drachsler, H.: From signals to knowledge: a conceptual model for multimodal learning analytics. J. Comput. Assist. Learn. **34**(4), 338–349 (2018)
14. D'Mello, S., Graesser, A.: Mining bodily patterns of affective experience during learning. In: Educational data mining 2010 (2010)
15. Domínguez, F., Chiluiza, K.: Towards a distributed framework to analyze multimodal data. In: Proceedings of Workshop Cross-LAK-held at LAK 2016, pp. 52–57 (2016)
16. Edwards, B.I., Bielawski, K.S., Prada, R., Cheok, A.D.: Haptic virtual reality and immersive learning for enhanced organic chemistry instruction. Virtual Reality **23**(4), 363–373 (2019)
17. Ericsson, K.A., Krampe, R.T., Tesch-Römer, C.: The role of deliberate practice in the acquisition of expert performance. Psychol. Rev. **100**(3), 363 (1993)
18. Ezen-Can, A., Boyer, K.E., Kellogg, S., Booth, S.: Unsupervised modeling for understanding MOOC discussion forums: a learning analytics approach. In: Proceedings of the Fifth International Conference on Learning Analytics and Knowledge, pp. 146–150 (2015)
19. Fan, M., Antle, A.N., Cramer, E.S.: Design rationale: opportunities and recommendations for tangible reading systems for children. In: Proceedings of the The 15th International Conference on Interaction Design and Children, pp. 101–112 (2016)
20. Françoise, J., Fdili Alaoui, S., Schiphorst, T., Bevilacqua, F.: Vocalizing dance movement for interactive sonification of Laban effort factors. In: Proceedings of the 2014 Conference on Designing Interactive Systems, pp. 1079–1082 (2014)
21. Frolova, E.V., Rogach, O.V., Ryabova, T.M.: Digitalization of education in modern scientific discourse: new trends and risks analysis. Eur. J. Contemp. Educ. **9**(2), 313–336 (2020)
22. Hassenzahl, M., Wiklund-Engblom, A., Bengs, A., Hägglund, S., Diefenbach, S.: Experience-oriented and product-oriented evaluation: psychological need fulfillment, positive affect, and product perception. Int. J. Hum. Comput. Interact. **31**(8), 530–544 (2015)
23. Hightower, B., Lovato, S., Davison, J., Wartella, E., Piper, A.M.: Haptic explorers: supporting science journaling through mobile haptic feedback displays. Int. J. Hum. Comput. Stud. **122**, 103–112 (2019)
24. Jakus, G., Stojmenova, K., Tomažič, S., Sodnik, J.: A system for efficient motor learning using multimodal augmented feedback. Multimedia Tools Appl. **76**(20), 20409–20421 (2017)

25. Järvelä, S., Malmberg, J., Haataja, E., Sobocinski, M., Kirschner, P.A.: What multimodal data can tell us about the students' regulation of their learning process? Learn. Instruct. **72**, 101203 (2021)
26. Jia, J., He, Y., Le, H.: A multimodal human computer interaction system and its application in smart learning environments. In: Cheung, S.K.S., Li, R., Phusavat, K., Paoprasert, N., Kwok, L.F. (eds.) ICBL 2020. LNCS, vol. 12218, pp. 3–14. Springer, Cham (2020). https://doi.org/10.1007/978-3-030-51968-1_1
27. Kasneci, E., et al.: ChatGPT for good? On opportunities and challenges of large language models for education. Learn. Individ. Differ. **103**, 102274 (2023)
28. Krathwohl, D.R.: A revision of bloom's taxonomy: an overview. Theor. Pract. **41**(4), 212–218 (2002)
29. Lee, J., et al.: An intravenous injection simulator using augmented reality for veterinary education and its evaluation. In: Proceedings of the 11th ACM SIGGRAPH International Conference on Virtual-Reality Continuum and its Applications in Industry, pp. 31–34 (2012)
30. Lee, Y., Chen, H., Zhao, G., Specht, M.: WEDAR: webcam-based attention analysis via attention regulator behavior recognition with a novel E-reading dataset. In: 24th ACM International Conference on Multimodal Interaction (ICMI), pp. 319–328. ACM (2022)
31. Lee, Y., Specht, M.: Can we empower attentive E-reading with a social robot? An introductory study with a novel multimodal dataset and deep learning approaches. In: LAK23: 13th International Learning Analytics and Knowledge Conference (LAK 2023). ACM (2023)
32. Limbu, B.H., Jarodzka, H., Klemke, R., Specht, M.: Can you ink while you blink? Assessing mental effort in a sensor-based calligraphy trainer. Sensors **19**(14), 3244 (2019). https://doi.org/10.3390/s19143244
33. Liu, S., d'Aquin, M.: Unsupervised learning for understanding student achievement in a distance learning setting. In: 2017 IEEE Global Engineering Education Conference (EDUCON), pp. 1373–1377. IEEE (2017)
34. Maezawa, A., Yamamoto, K.: MuEns: a multimodal human-machine music ensemble for live concert performance. In: Proceedings of the 2017 CHI Conference on Human Factors in Computing Systems, pp. 4290–4301 (2017)
35. Maria, K., Filippeschi, A., Ruffaldi, E., Shorr, Y., Gopher, D.: Evaluation of multimodal feedback effects on the time-course of motor learning in multimodal VR platform for rowing training. In: 2015 International Conference on Virtual Rehabilitation (ICVR), pp. 158–159. IEEE (2015)
36. Mathew, A., Amudha, P., Sivakumari, S.: Deep learning techniques: an overview. Adv. Mach. Learn. Technol. Appl.: Proc. AMLTA **2020**, 599–608 (2021)
37. Ochoa, X., Domínguez, F., Guamán, B., Maya, R., Falcones, G., Castells, J.: The rap system: automatic feedback of oral presentation skills using multimodal analysis and low-cost sensors. In: Proceedings of the 8th International Conference on Learning Analytics and Knowledge, pp. 360–364 (2018)
38. Ortegon, T., et al.: Prototyping interactive multimodal VR epidural administration. In: 2019 IEEE International Conference on Consumer Electronics (ICCE), pp. 1–3. IEEE (2019)
39. Oyedotun, T.D.: Sudden change of pedagogy in education driven by COVID-19: perspectives and evaluation from a developing country. Res. Globalization **2**, 100029 (2020)
40. Pardo, A., Jovanovic, J., Dawson, S., Gašević, D., Mirriahi, N.: Using learning analytics to scale the provision of personalised feedback. Br. J. Educ. Technol. **50**(1), 128–138 (2019)

41. Pires, A.C., et al.: Learning Maths with a tangible user interface: lessons learned through participatory design with children with visual impairments and their educators. Int. J. Child-Comput. Interact. **32**, 100382 (2022)
42. Plimmer, B., Reid, P., Blagojevic, R., Crossan, A., Brewster, S.: Signing on the tactile line: a multimodal system for teaching handwriting to blind children. ACM Trans. Comput. Hum. Interact. (TOCHI) **18**(3), 1–29 (2011)
43. Rahman, M.A., Brown, D.J., Shopland, N., Burton, A., Mahmud, M.: Explainable multimodal machine learning for engagement analysis by continuous performance Test. In: Antona, M., Stephanidis, C. (eds) Universal Access in Human-Computer Interaction. User and Context Diversity. HCII 2022. Lecture Notes in Computer Science. vol 13309. Springer, Cham (2022). https://doi.org/10.1007/978-3-031-05039-8_28
44. Romero, C., Ventura, S.: Educational data mining and learning analytics: an updated survey. Wiley Interdisc. Rev. Data Min. Knowl. Discov. **10**(3), e1355 (2020)
45. Ruffaldi, E., Filippeschi, A., Avizzano, C.A., Bardy, B., Gopher, D., Bergamasco, M.: Feedback, affordances, and accelerators for training sports in virtual environments. Presence: Teleoperators Virtual Environ. **20**(1), 33–46 (2011)
46. Schneider, J., Börner, D., Van Rosmalen, P., Specht, M.: Presentation trainer, your public speaking multimodal coach. In: Proceedings of the 2015 ACM on International Conference on Multimodal Interaction, pp. 539–546 (2015)
47. Sebkhi, N., Desai, D., Islam, M., Lu, J., Wilson, K., Ghovanloo, M.: Multimodal speech capture system for speech rehabilitation and learning. IEEE Trans. Biomed. Eng. **64**(11), 2639–2649 (2017)
48. Shukla, S., Shivakumar, A., Vasoya, M., Pei, Y., Lyon, A.F.: iLEAP: a human-AI teaming based mobile language learning solution for dual language learners in early and special educations. In: International Association for Development of the Information Society (2019)
49. Silva, M.J.: Children using electronic sensors to create and use knowledge on environmental health. First Monday (2020)
50. Sokolowski, J.A., Garcia, H.M., Richards, W., Banks, C.M.: Developing a low-cost multi-modal simulator for ultrasonography training. In: Proceedings of the Conference on Summer Computer Simulation, pp. 1–5 (2015)
51. Van Rosmalen, P., Börner, D., Schneider, J., Petukhova, O., Van Helvert, J.: Feedback design in multimodal dialogue systems. In: International Conference on Computer Supported Education (CSEDU). vol. 2, pp. 209–217 (2015)
52. Volpe, G., et al.: A multimodal corpus for technology-enhanced learning of violin playing. In: Proceedings of the 12th Biannual Conference on Italian SIGCHI Chapter, pp. 1–5 (2017)
53. Yeom, S., Choi-Lundberg, D.L., Fluck, A.E., Sale, A.: Factors influencing undergraduate students' acceptance of a haptic interface for learning gross anatomy. Interact. Technol. Smart Educ. **14**(1), 50–66 (2017)
54. Yiannoutsou, N., Johnson, R., Price, S.: Exploring how children interact with 3D shapes using haptic technologies. In: Proceedings of the 17th ACM Conference on Interaction Design and Children, pp. 533–538 (2018)
55. Yu, Z., Li, X., Niu, X., Shi, J., Zhao, G.: AutoHR: a strong end-to-end baseline for remote heart rate measurement with neural searching. IEEE Sig. Process. Lett. **27**, 1245–1249 (2020)

Broader and Deeper: A Multi-Features with Latent Relations BERT Knowledge Tracing Model

Zhaoxing Li[1(✉)], Mark Jacobsen[1], Lei Shi[2], Yunzhan Zhou[1], and Jindi Wang[1]

[1] Department of Computer Science, Durham University, Durham, UK
{zhaoxing.li2,mark.jacobsen,yunzhan.zhou,jindi.wang}@durham.ac.uk
[2] Open Lab, School of Computing, Newcastle University, Newcastle upon Tyne, UK
lei.shi@ncl.ac.uk

Abstract. Knowledge tracing aims to estimate students' knowledge state or skill mastering level over time, which is evolving into an essential task in educational technology. Traditional knowledge tracing algorithms generally use one or a few features to predict students' behaviour and do not consider the latent relations between these features, which could be limiting and disregarding important information in the features. In this paper, we propose MLFBK: A Multi-Features with Latent Relations BERT Knowledge Tracing model, which is a novel BERT based Knowledge Tracing approach that utilises multiple features and mines latent relations between features to improve the performance of the Knowledge Tracing model. Specifically, our algorithm leverages four data features (*student_id*, *skill_id*, *item_id*, and *response_id*, as well as three meaningful latent relations among features to improve the performance: individual *skill mastery*, *ability profile* of students (learning transfer across skills), and *problem difficulty*. By incorporating these explicit features, latent relations, and the strength of the BERT model, we achieve higher accuracy and efficiency in knowledge tracing tasks. We use t-SNE as a visualisation tool to analyse different embedding strategies. Moreover, we conduct ablation studies and activation function evaluation to evaluate our model. Experimental results demonstrate that our algorithm outperforms baseline methods and demonstrates good interpretability.

Keywords: Knowledge Tracing · BERT · Multi-Features · Latent Relations

1 Introduction

In recent years, Technology Enhanced Learning (TEL) has become an essential research field, mainly due to the increasing need for innovative solutions in the education sector. One of the most promising approaches to this problem is Intelligent Tutoring Systems (ITS), which could provide personalised learning experiences for each student. To achieve this personalisation, ITS requires a reliable method for estimating students' knowledge state and learning progress. This

O. Viberg et al. (Eds.): EC-TEL 2023, LNCS 14200, pp. 183–197, 2023.
https://doi.org/10.1007/978-3-031-42682-7_13

method is known as Knowledge Tracing (KT). KT estimates students' knowledge state or skill mastering level based on the student's interaction data collected from ITS [15]. Accurate and efficient KT models are essential for ITS and educators to provide personalised learning experiences and support to students, such as tailored feedback, targeted hints, and relevant additional learning resources.

Generally, there are three kinds of KT models. Bayesian Knowledge Tracing (BKT), Logistic KT models, and Deep Learning based Knowledge Tracing (DKT) [16]. BKT is one of the earliest and most influential KT models. It uses a probabilistic framework to model student knowledge and learning state over time [2]. Logistic KT models are developed based on the concept of logistic regression, a statistical technique utilised to model the probability of a binary outcome by utilising one or more predictor variables. While BKT and Logistic models have achieved significant success in predicting student performance, they have also been criticised for their inability to capture the complex relationships between different skills and concepts [18]. To address this limitation, the more recent DKT models have utilised deep learning techniques to capture the complex interactions between student responses, skills, and questions [23]. DKT models have achieved state-of-the-art performance on benchmark datasets but require a large amount of training data to achieve good results.

Previous KT models have often been limited by their reliance on a single or few features, which could fail to capture the complexity of student learning behaviour data. Numerous studies have demonstrated that incorporating one or two additional features could enhance the performance of KT models [8,32]. Additionally, Minn *et al.* suggested that identifying latent features could further improve the performance of KT [20]. However, to date, there has been no research that has investigated the effectiveness of combining multiple features and latent relations to improve the performance of KT models.

Therefore, the research question of this paper is: *Whether incorporating multiple features and mining the latent relations between features together could improve the accuracy and efficiency of KT models?*

In this paper, we present the **M**ulti-**L**atent **F**eature **B**ERT **K**nowledge Tracing model that is both "broader" and "deeper" than the previous models to address the above-mentioned limitation by incorporating multiple features with mined latent relations that provide richer and more diverse contextual information. By "broader", we incorporate four different types of features into our model: *student_id*, *skill_id*, *question_id*, and *response_id*. These features provide additional contextual information to help the model better capture individual differences in learning and problem-solving strategies. By "deeper", we employ a feature engineering method to extract three meaningful latent relations important for representing student's behaviour: *skill mastery*, *ability profile* of students (learning transfer across skills), and *problem difficulty*. We utilise a monotonic convolutional multi-head self-attention mechanism to combine the above explicit features and latent relations. By incorporating these explicit features and latent relations, our model could better account for the nuances and complexities of student learning and achieve superior performance compared to existing KT models. The experimental results show that MLFBK outperforms the four baseline models on five benchmark datasets. Furthermore, the t-SNE as the visualisation tool was used to analyse the interpretability of MLFBK and the embedding strategies. The experimental results show that MLFBK outperforms the baseline models and could effectively enhance the interpretability of deep learning based KT models.

The main contributions of our paper lie in the following three aspects:

1. We propose MLFBK, a novel **M**ulti- **F**eatures with **L**atent relations **B**ERT **K**nowledge Tracing model, which not only considers the multiple explicit features but also deeply mines the latent relations between the features by using a feature engineering method.[1]
2. Our model achieves state-of-the-art performance, outperforming four existing state-of-the-art models on five benchmark datasets. Moreover, we conduct ablation experiments and demonstrate different embedding strategies with a visualisation tool to investigate the contribution of different latent relations.
3. MLFBK exhibits good interpretability as a deep learning based KT method and has advantages in training efficiency.

2 Related Work

This paper aims to present a novel BERT-based KT model that incorporates multi-features and latent relations. Therefore, we first review the cornerstone of the BERT model – the Transformer based models and their applications. Then we review the development of KT methods in general. At last, we review existing KT methods from the perspective of the number of integrated features.

2.1 Transformer-Based Models and Application

The Transformer architecture, proposed by Vaswani *et al.* [28], is a type of neural network that has gained widespread popularity in natural language processing (NLP), and other domains due to its ability to effectively model long-range dependencies and capture complex patterns in sequential data. Transformers have been used in various NLP tasks, including language translation, question answering, and text classification, and have achieved state-of-the-art performance on many benchmarks [13].

In addition to NLP, Transformers have also been applied in other domains, such as computer vision [10], speech recognition [22], and recommendation systems [30]. For example, the Vision Transformer (ViT) has recently been proposed as an alternative to convolutional neural networks (CNNs) for image classification tasks, achieving competitive performance on several benchmark datasets.

Besides the basic Transformer models, many powerful evolutions of Transformer-based methods were proposed, such as the GPT [6] and BERT [3]. The well-known ChatGPT originated from GPT [19]. BERT (Bidirectional

[1] Source code and datasets are available at https://github.com/Zhaoxing-Li/MLFBK.

Encoder Representations from Transformers), introduced by Devlin *et al.* [3], is a pre-trained Transformer-based language model that has achieved state-of-the-art performance on various NLP tasks. BERT utilises self-attention and masked language modelling (MLM) techniques to train the Transformer bidirectionally. Its remarkable ability to process natural language text effectively and generate high-quality embeddings has made it a popular choice and a superior performer in many Deep Learning tasks [14]. BERT has also been adapted to various other fields with excellent results. For instance, ConvBERT utilises the original BERT architecture in image processing task [9], BERT4Rec enhances the performance recommendation systems [25], and LakhNES improves the quality of music generation by incorporating BERT [4].

2.2 Knowledge Tracing

Knowledge Tracing is a technique utilised in educational data mining that aims to model students' knowledge state and mastering level of the learning concepts or subjects [31]. Generally, the KT models could be classified into three categories based on the different structures of the modelling approach that the model used: probabilistic models, logistic regression KT models, and deep learning-based models [18].

Probabilistic KT models assume a student's learning process follows a Markov process. They use a probabilistic graphical model such as Hidden Markov Model (HMM) or Bayesian Belief Network to track their changing learning states. Bayesian Knowledge Tracing (BKT) is a classic probabilistic model that has been used for this purpose, but it has several limitations: BKT does not account for the complexity or difficulty of concepts and skills and assumes that each question requires only one skill. This makes it difficult to process complex problems involving multiple skills and complex relationships between concepts, questions, and skills. To address these limitations, researchers have proposed models including Dynamic BKT (DBKT), which uses Dynamic Bayesian Network (DBN) to model prerequisite hierarchies and dependencies of multiple skills [5]. The logistic KT models are based on the principle of logistic regression, which is a statistical method used to estimate the probability of a binary outcome by using one or more predictor variables. However, both BKT and logistic KT models struggle to process multiple topics or skills and fail to account for other features that may impact student learning.

To overcome these limitations, researchers have turned to deep learning technologies to develop Deep Knowledge Tracing (DKT) [14]. DKT models a knowledge tracing task as a sequence prediction problem and has shown promise in achieving better performance than BKT and logistic KT models. The self-attention mechanisms were widely used in deep learning architectures, which have also been applied to KT models, resulting in models such as SAKT and SAINT+ [24]. These methods have achieved higher performance than traditional DL-based methods. More recently, several BERT-based methods were proposed that achieved state-of-the-art performance. BEKT [27] is a deep knowledge tracing with bidirectional encoder representations from transformers. MonaconBERT [12] utilised the monotonic attention based ConvBERT to improve the knowledge tracing.

2.3 KT Models with Different Feature Numbers

Single feature KT models Single-feature KT models use only one feature, usually exercise or skill, to predict a student's knowledge or mastery of a particular skill or concept. Deep Knowledge Tracing (DKT) and Self-Attentive Knowledge Tracing (SAKT) [26] are examples of single-feature models that have been proposed to improve performance by using different techniques, such as LSTM networks and attention mechanisms to deal with the sparsity of exercise data.

Double-feature KT models Double-feature KT models use both exercise and skill features, resulting in significant performance gains compared to single-feature models. Deep Hierarchical Knowledge Tracing (DHKT) [29], Bi-Interaction Deep Knowledge Tracing (BIDKT) [11], and Attentive Knowledge Tracing (AKT) [7] are examples of double-feature models that have been proposed to improve performance by modelling the hierarchical relations between skills and exercises and proposing new attention mechanisms and embedding methods.

Multi-feature KT models Multi-factor KT models integrate multiple learning-related factors into the model to improve performance. Exercise-aware Knowledge Tracing (EKT) [17] and Relation-aware self-attention Knowledge Tracing (RKT) [21] are examples of multi-feature models that have been proposed to integrate information such as the exercise-making sequence, the relations between skills and time delay since the last interaction, and the text information of the exercise content.

3 Methodology

3.1 Problem Statement

The goal of knowledge tracing is to use a series of interaction data from Online Learning Systems (OLS) or Intelligent Tutoring Systems (ITS) to predict the correctness of a student's next answers. The student's interactions are represented by a data sequence, denoted as $x_1, ..., x_t$, where $t - th$ is represented as $x_t = (qt, at)$. Here, q_t refers to the $t - th$ question and indicates whether the student's answer is correct (1) or not (0).

3.2 Proposed Model Architecture

We propose a novel Knowledge Tracing model, Multi Features with Latent Relations BERT Knowledge Tracing (MLFBK), to improve the traditional KT models by incorporating multi-features and mining latent relations between different features in the student historical interaction data. Figure 1 shows the architecture of MLFBK, which consists of three parts: embedding on the left; BERT-based architecture in the middle; the correctness sequence output on the right. The embedding part on the left further contains two components: the Multi-Features embedding on the top, and the Latent-Relations embedding at the bottom.

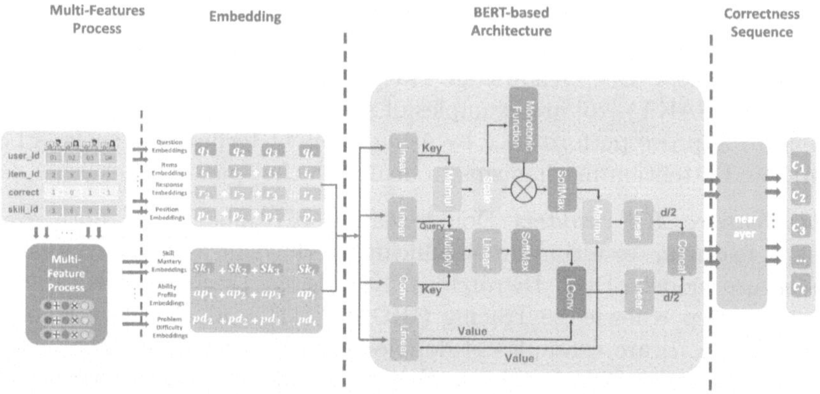

Fig. 1. The architecture of MLFBK. MLFBK consists of three parts: 1) the multi-features process (on the left), 2) the BERT-based architecture (in the middle), and 3) the correctness sequence output part(on the right).

Multi-Features Embedding. In the Multi-Features Embedding part, we incorporate four different types of features into our model: *student_id*, *skill_id*, *question_id*, and *response_id*. Particularly, *student_id* is utilised to generate the interaction sequences. It is also used in the Latent Relation Embedding component for calculating the *skill mastery* embedding and the *ability profile* embedding. These features need *student_id* to keep track of a single student.

Latent Relations Embedding. In the Latent Relations Embedding component, we use a feature engineering method proposed by work [20]. Using this method, we mine three different meaningful latent relations among the behaviour data of individual students: *skill mastery*, *ability profile* (learning transfer across skills), and *problem difficulty*.

Skill Mastery. The formulation of skill mastery is based on the Bayesian Knowledge Tracing (BKT) model, which uses four parameters to represent probabilities related to a student's mastery of a skill. These parameters include $P(L_o)$, the probability that a student masters the skill before attempting the first problem associated with it; $P(T)$, the probability that a student will master the skill after the next practice opportunity; $P(G)$, the probability that a student guesses the correct answer to a question despite not knowing the skill; and $P(S)$, the probability that a student answers a question incorrectly despite knowing the skill. Skill mastery is the probability of learning a skill rather than the probability that a student applies the skill correctly. A BKT model is trained for each skill, and the inputs to each skill model are the binary responses of a student on that single skill. Figure 2 shows the Skill Mastery mining process.

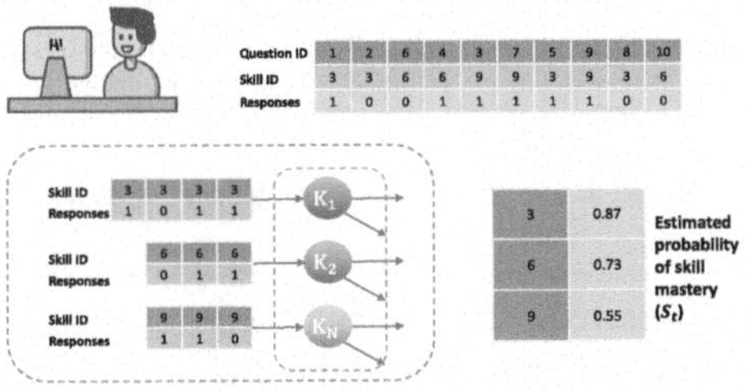

Fig. 2. Estimated the probability of skill mastery at each timestamp.

Ability Profile. Students' interactions are divided into multiple time intervals, and past performance is encoded to estimate their ability profile. The ability profile is encoded as a cluster ID and updated after each time interval using all previous attempts on each skill. The K-means algorithm is used to evaluate the temporal long-term learning ability of students in both training and testing at each time interval. Figure 3 shows the ability profile extraction process.

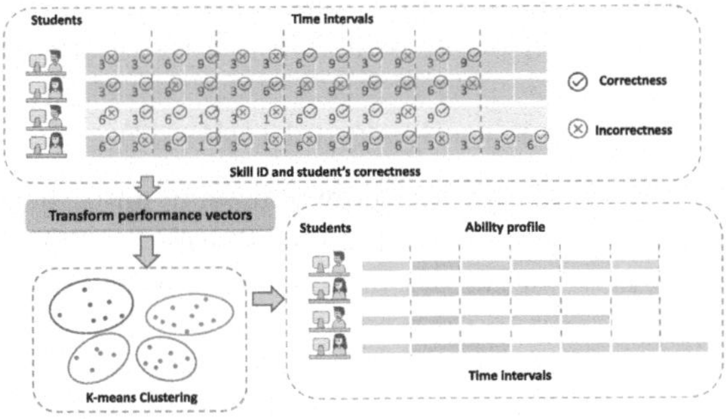

Fig. 3. Estimated the probability of skill mastery at each timestamp.

Problem Difficulty. This is calculated on a scale between 1 and 10, with 1 being the easiest and 10 being the most difficult. We use function 1 to map the average success rate of a problem onto the 10-level scale. The problem difficulty (p_j) could be calculated as:

$$\delta\left(p_j\right)=\left\lfloor\frac{\sum_i^{|N_j|} O_i\left(p_j\right)}{|N_j|}\cdot 10\right\rfloor \tag{1}$$

where P_j is the jth problem. N_j is the set of the students who tried to solve problem p_j. $O_i(p_j)$ is the first attempt of student i to solve problem p_j. Problems with a higher success rate are considered easier, while problems with a lower success rate are considered more difficult.

Overall, in the first part of our model, we incorporate question embedding E_q, items embedding E_i, response embedding E_r, learnable positional embedding E_{pos}, skill mastery embedding E_{SK}, ability profile embedding E_{AP}, and problem difficulty embedding E_{PD}. The final input embedding is denoted as:

$$E_{\text{input}} = E_q + E_i + E_r + E_{pos} + E_{SK} + E_{AP} + E_{PD}. \tag{2}$$

BERT Based Architecture. The second part of our proposed architecture is a BERT-based method (shown in Fig. 1). First, the encoder blocks use the pre-LN Transformer architecture with 12 layers to normalise the input vectors E_{input}. The pre-LN can be formulated as follows:

$$z = LN_{\text{pre}}(E_{\text{input}}) \tag{3}$$

The normalised value z is then transformed into the query, key, and value of monotonic convolutional multi-head attention. This result is passed through a dropout layer and added to the embedding vectors as a residual connection.

$$a = x + D(\text{MonoConvMulAttn}(z, z, z)) \tag{4}$$

The output is normalised and passed through fully connected layers with a LeakyReLU activation function. The results are again normalised through a dropout layer, and the second result is added as a residual connection.

$$fc = W_{fc2}(\text{LeakyReLU}(W_{fc1})) \tag{5}$$

Moreover, we utilise a monotonic convolutional multi-head attention proposed by [12], which is combined with mixed-attention and monotonic attention, to represent forgetting in sequence data. Monotonic multi-head attention uses an exponential decay mechanism to measure the distance between sequences, while span-based dynamic convolution uses a lightweight convolution to combine query and key vectors.

3.3 Experiment Setting

Datasets. We adopted four benchmark datasets to validate the performance of the MLFBK model, including EdNet [1][2], assist09[3], assist12[4], algebra06[5].

[2] https://github.com/riiid/ednet.
[3] https://sites.google.com/site/assistmentsdata/home.
[4] https://sites.google.com/site/assistmentsdata/home.
[5] https://pslcdatashop.web.cmu.edu/KDDCup.

Baseline Models. In this study, we evaluated the performance of our MLFBK model by comparing it with three state-of-the-art models: MonaCoBERT [12], BEKT [27], and AKT [7], as well as the top two baseline models (SSAKT and LTMTI) in the Riiid Answer Correctness Prediction Competition hosted on Kaggle[6].

Evaluation Metrics and Validation. We used the area under the curve (AUC) as the evaluation metric to compare the model's performance on four benchmark datasets. After that, we conducted an activation function evaluation to compare the different activation functions. We also conducted an ablation study to identify the contribution of different latent relations. Furthermore, we applied t-SNE as the visualisation tool to evaluate our method's embedding strategies and interpretability.

Hyperparameters for Experiments. For a fair comparison, all baseline models were trained using the same set of parameters. Specifically, training was conducted with a batch size of 64 and a train/test split ratio of 0.8/0.2. The model was trained for 100 epochs with the Adam optimiser and a learning rate of 0.001. The loss function used was binary cross-entropy, and the model utilised a total of 12 encoder layers with a hidden size of 512 and 8 attention heads. The data was preprocessed by splitting it into interaction sequences with a maximum length of 100. In cases where a student had less than 100 interactions, the remaining sequence was padded with zeros. For students with more than 100 interactions, the sequence was split into multiple subsequences of length 100.

4 Results and Discussion

4.1 Overall Performance

Table 1 presents the comparison results of MLFBK with five other KT models, including MonaCoBERT, BEKT, AKT, SSAKT, and LTMTL, on four benchmark datasets, including EdNet, assist09, algebra06, and assist12. It is clear from Table 1 that MLFBK outperforms the other five KT models on all four datasets in terms of AUC, indicating that MLFBK is a promising method for KT. Take the algebra06 dataset as an example: MLFBK achieves an AUC of 0.8327, which is 1.4%, 2.9%, 3.9%, 5.2%, and 2.2% higher than the AUC values of MonaCoBERT, BEKT, SSAKT, LTMTI, and AKT, respectively. The average improvement on this dataset is 3.12%. MonaCoBERT and BEKT also perform relatively well, with AUC values close to those of MLFBK on some datasets. SSAKT and LTMTI, on the other hand, have lower AUC values, indicating weaker performance. The results suggest that MLFBK is a competitive method for knowledge tracing and could potentially improve the accuracy of student modelling by incorporating more student action features and mining latent relations.

[6] https://www.kaggle.com/code/datakite/riiid-answer-correctness.

Table 1. Comparison of different KT models on five benchmark datasets. The best performance is denoted in bold.

Dataset	Metrics	MLFBK	Monaco	BEKT	SSAKT	LTMTI	AKT
EdNet	AUC	**0.8278**	0.7336	0.8204	0.7981	0.8023	0.7982
assist09	AUC	**0.8524**	0.8059	0.8227	0.6754	0.8132	0.7691
algebra06	AUC	**0.8412**	0.8201	0.8165	0.7937	0.7915	0.8143
assist12	AUC	**0.8350**	0.8132	0.7167	0.7356	0.6834	0.8034

4.2 Ablation Study

In order to identify the contribution of each latent relation in the MLFBK model to the overall performance, we conducted an ablation study. The results are summarised in Table 2. MLFBK* in the table indicates the basic model structure with explicit features. *ap* represents ability profile, *sm* represents skill mastery, and *pd* represents problem difficulty. Table 2 also shows the AUC values for different versions of MLFBK* that were trained with different combinations of latent relations. It is clear that the performance of the MLFBK model is influenced by the different embedding strategies used for different relations. The models incorporating all three latent relations achieved the highest AUC values on three of the four datasets, except the assist09. Nevertheless, it also achieved the second-highest score in the assist09.

The *problem difficulty* contributed significantly to the model's performance, with the models that used only the problem difficulty embedding achieving the highest AUC values on four datasets compared to other single latent relation embeddings. The combination of *problem difficulty* and *ability profile* achieved the best performance on the assist09 dataset and the second-highest performance on EdNet, indicating that the combination of these two latent relations has more weight in the predictions. The *skill mastery* feature had a comparatively lower impact on the model's performance, with the models that used only the *skill mastery* feature achieving the lowest AUC values on four datasets. However, the models that used a combination of features achieved higher AUC values than the models that used a single feature, indicating that the three latent relations are complementary to each other.

Overall, the ablation study results suggest that the MLFBK model's performance could be effectively improved by incorporating multi-features and multiple latent relations. The more features and/or latent relations embeddings were incorporated, the higher AUC scores could be achieved.

4.3 Activation Function Evaluation

To investigate the impact of activation functions on the performance of our MLFBK model, we conducted a study where we tested our model with three different activation functions: Leaky ReLU, Sigmoid, and Linear. Figure 6 shows the results of activation function evaluation. We trained and validated the models

Table 2. Ablation Study of MLFBK. The abbreviations used in there are as follows: *ap* for ability profile, *sm* for skill mastery and *pd* for problem difficulty. The best performance is denoted in bold.

Model	EdNet	assist09	algebra06	assist12
MLFBK*	0.7221	0.8002	0.7997	0.8065
MLFBK* + *ap*	0.7503	0.7922	0.8139	0.7713
MLFBK* +*sm*	0.7454	0.7891	0.7983	0.7611
MLFBK* +*pd*	0.8194	0.8411	0.8256	0.8304
MLFBK* +*ap* + *sm*	0.7429	0.8078	0.8201	0.7989
MLFBK* +*ap* + *pd*	0.8270	**0.8560**	0.8344	0.8287
MLFBK* +*sm* + *pd*	0.8233	0.8445	0.8362	0.8216
MLFBK* +*ap* + *sm* + *pd*	**0.8278**	0.8524	**0.8412**	**0.8350**

for 50 epochs with early stopping. Upon analysing the results, we found that all three activation functions produced similar results in terms of both training and validation behaviour. However, the Linear activation function performed slightly better than the other two. Specifically, it had the highest accuracy and AUC score on the validation set, which indicates that it may be the most suitable activation function for our MLFBK model. It is worth noting that the Leaky ReLU activation function stopped early during the training process, which may be due to its high learning rate. Overall, our findings suggest that the choice of an activation function has a relatively minor impact on the performance of our MLFBK model, but using the Linear activation function may lead to slightly better results.

4.4 Analysis of Embedding Strategy

We conducted a t-SNE analysis to visualise the entire embedding vector created in our MLFBK model. The results show the good interpretability of our methods' embedding strategies. Figure 4 shows the comparison of general embedding and MLFBK embedding strategies, utilising t-SNE as the visualisation method. Here, we take the embedding strategy of AKT as an example (on the left) and our MLFBK embedding strategy (on the right) on the assistments09 dataset. Each data point in the plot represents a learning interaction associated with a student, question, response, correctness, item, ability profile, skill mastery, and problem difficulty. The data points were coloured based on the ability profile value associated with them, specifically the transfer across skills value for the relevant student at the relevant time.

The left part of Fig. 4 shows the general embedding could not distinguish different features as all the features mixed together. In contrast, the right part of Fig. 4 shows that the MLFBK embedding strategy could distinguish different embedding with different colours well. The t-SNE plot shows that the students with small ability profile values at the current interaction were grouped together

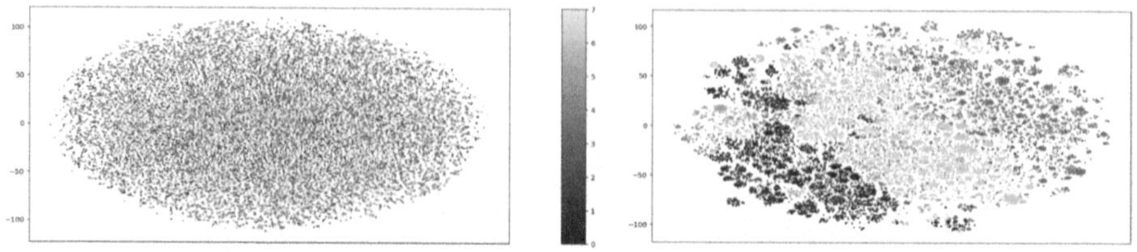

Fig. 4. The comparison of general embedding (Left) and MLFBK embedding (Right) strategies, utilising t-SNE as the visualisation method.

by the embedding, as were students with large values. This grouping could be used by the model to differentiate between interactions with correct responses and incorrect responses. The ability profile values provide additional information about students' performance, which could be useful for predicting their future performance. Overall, the t-SNE analysis demonstrated the effectiveness of the MLFBK model in capturing and utilising complex student interaction data.

Figure 5 shows the different embedding strategies of different single latent relations. The left is the embedding for the ability profile. It is the embedding without the additional features and then coloured according to the problem difficulty. It is easy to see that the problem difficulty feature is heavily considered in the feature embedding. The middle is embedding for problem difficulty. It only colours the learning interactions based on the problem difficulty of the relevant question. In this figure, the embedding doesn't seem to generate groupings, but more of a constant gradient, where the more difficult problems are in the top left and the easier problems are in the bottom right. The right image is the embedding for skill mastery. Here the skill mastery of the student on the relevant *item* is highlighted. This feature is multiplied by 100 and rounded to convert it to a categorical feature instead of a continuous one. The embedding also seems to be a gradient instead of groupings.

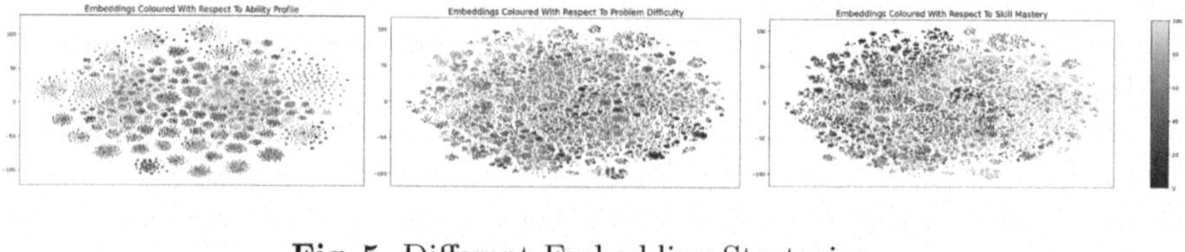

Fig. 5. Different Embedding Strategies.

4.5 Analysis of Estimating Problem Difficulty

We compared our model with MonaCoBERT regarding estimating problem difficulty for specific questions in the assistments2009 dataset. While MonaCoBERT uses a classical test theory (CTT) approach to estimate difficulties, our model calculates problem difficulty as a feature to use as input for the BERT model.

The comparison is visually represented in Fig. 7, with difficulty levels on the x-axis and the number of students answering correctly (green) or incorrectly (red) on the y-axis. Common sense dictates that harder questions should have more incorrect answers, although there may be exceptions. Surprisingly, the MonaCoBERT method showed that many students answered easy questions incorrectly but answered more difficult questions correctly, which seemed unlikely given the number of students evaluated. In contrast, our model revealed that as question difficulty increased, fewer students answered correctly, aligning with expectations. The results show that our method of estimating problem difficulty is far superior to the CTT difficulty estimation used by MonaCoBERT. Our method provides much more predictive value in estimating problem difficulty. This highlights the effectiveness of using our MLFBK model in predicting student performance in educational settings.

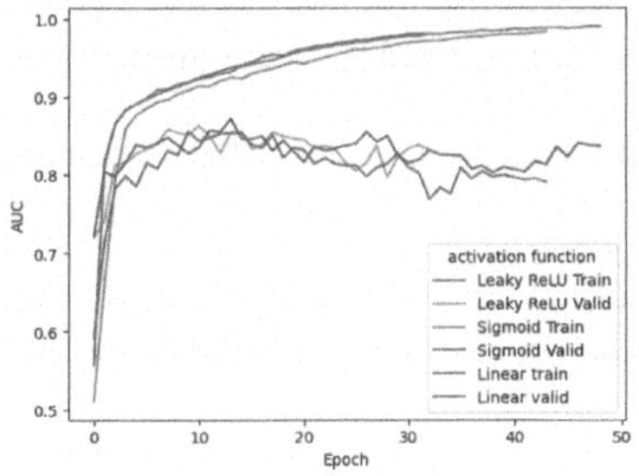

Fig. 6. Activation Function evaluation.

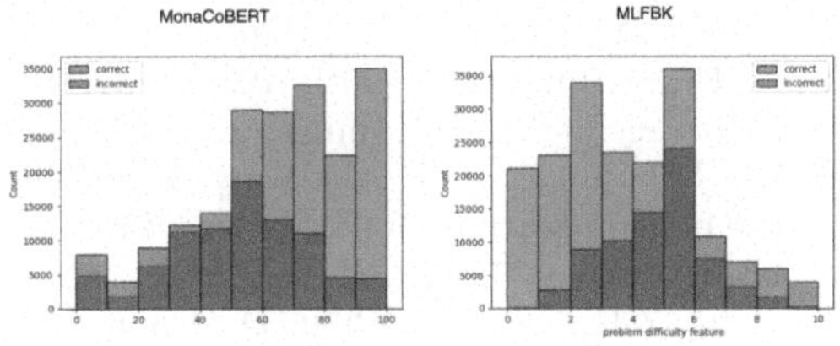

Fig. 7. Estimating Problem Difficulty.

5 Conclusion and Future Work

In this paper, we have proposed the MLFBK, which employs a BERT-based architecture incorporating multi-features and latent relations to improve the performance of Knowledge Tracing models. Experimental results show that MLFBK outperforms the five baseline models in every benchmark dataset on the metric of AUC. Moreover, we conducted an ablation study for different embedding strategies. The results indicate that combining different features and latent relations could improve performance effectively. Incorporating additional embeddings resulted in increased AUC scores. Moreover, we utilise the t-SNE as the visualisation tool to compare different embedding strategies. The results show that our method not only improves the performance of the models but also improves the model's interpretability. In future work, we plan to improve the architecture to process more comprehensive features and latent relations to satisfy the sustainable development requirement of Knowledge Tracing. Moreover, we will develop a model that could enhance memory efficiency as it handles growing amounts of multi-features and latent relations.

References

1. Choi, Y., et al.: EdNet: a large-scale hierarchical dataset in education. In: Bittencourt, I.I., Cukurova, M., Muldner, K., Luckin, R., Millán, E. (eds.) AIED 2020. LNCS (LNAI), vol. 12164, pp. 69–73. Springer, Cham (2020). https://doi.org/10.1007/978-3-030-52240-7_13
2. Corbett, A.T., Anderson, J.R.: Knowledge tracing: modeling the acquisition of procedural knowledge. User Model. User-Adap. Inter. **4**(4), 253–278 (1994)
3. Devlin, J., Chang, M.W., Lee, K., Toutanova, K.: Bert: pre-training of deep bidirectional transformers for language understanding. arXiv preprint arXiv:1810.04805 (2018)
4. Donahue, C., Mao, H.H., Li, Y.E., Cottrell, G.W., McAuley, J.: Lakhnes: improving multi-instrumental music generation with cross-domain pre-training. arXiv preprint arXiv:1907.04868 (2019)
5. Drass, J.A., Muir-Nash, J., Boykin, P.C., Turek, J.M., Baker, K.L.: Perceived and actual level of knowledge of diabetes mellitus among nurses. Diabetes Care **12**(5), 351–356 (1989)
6. Floridi, L., Chiriatti, M.: Gpt-3: its nature, scope, limits, and consequences. Mind. Mach. **30**(4), 681–694 (2020)
7. Ghosh, A., Heffernan, N., Lan, A.S.: Context-aware attentive knowledge tracing. In: Proceedings of the 26th ACM SIGKDD International Conference on Knowledge Discovery and Data Mining, pp. 2330–2339 (2020)
8. He, L., Tang, J., Li, X., Wang, P., Chen, F., Wang, T.: Multi-type factors representation learning for deep learning-based knowledge tracing. World Wide Web **25**(3), 1343–1372 (2022)
9. Jiang, Z.H., Yu, W., Zhou, D., Chen, Y., Feng, J., Yan, S.: Convbert: improving BERT with span-based dynamic convolution. Adv. Neural. Inf. Process. Syst. **33**, 12837–12848 (2020)
10. Kalyan, K.S., Rajasekharan, A., Sangeetha, S.: Ammus: a survey of transformer-based pretrained models in natural language processing. arXiv preprint arXiv:2108.05542 (2021)
11. Krishnan, R., Singh, J., Sato, M., Zhang, Q., Ohkuma, T.: Incorporating wide context information for deep knowledge tracing using attentional bi-interaction. In: L2D@ WSDM, pp. 1–13 (2021)
12. Lee, U., Park, Y., Kim, Y., Choi, S., Kim, H.: Monacobert: monotonic attention based convbert for knowledge tracing. arXiv preprint arXiv:2208.12615 (2022)
13. Li, Z., Shi, L., Cristea, A., Zhou, Y., Xiao, C., Pan, Z.: SimStu-transformer: a transformer-based approach to simulating student behaviour. In: Rodrigo, M.M., Matsuda, N., Cristea, A.I., Dimitrova, V. (eds.) Artificial Intelligence in Education. Posters and Late Breaking Results, Workshops and Tutorials, Industry and Innovation Tracks, Practitioners' and Doctoral Consortium. AIED 2022. Lecture Notes in Computer Science, vol. 13356, pp. 348–351. Springer, Cham (2022). https://doi.org/10.1007/978-3-031-11647-6_67
14. Li, Z., Shi, L., Cristea, A.I., Zhou, Y.: A survey of collaborative reinforcement learning: interactive methods and design patterns. In: Designing Interactive Systems Conference 2021, pp. 1579–1590 (2021)
15. Li, Z., Shi, L., Zhou, Y., Wang, J.: Towards student behaviour simulation: a decision transformer based approach. In: Frasson, C., Mylonas, P., Troussas, C. (eds.) Augmented Intelligence and Intelligent Tutoring Systems. ITS 2023. Lecture Notes in Computer Science, vol. 13891, pp. 553–562. Springer, Cham (2023). https://doi.org/10.1007/978-3-031-32883-1_49

16. Lin, T., Wang, Y., Liu, X., Qiu, X.: A survey of transformers. AI Open (2022)
17. Liu, Q., et al.: Ekt: exercise-aware knowledge tracing for student performance prediction. IEEE Trans. Knowl. Data Eng. **33**(1), 100–115 (2019)
18. Liu, Q., Shen, S., Huang, Z., Chen, E., Zheng, Y.: A survey of knowledge tracing. arXiv preprint arXiv:2105.15106 (2021)
19. Lund, B.D., Wang, T.: Chatting about chatGPT: how may AI and GPT impact academia and libraries? Library Hi Tech News **40**, 26–29 (2023)
20. Minn, S., Vie, J.J., Takeuchi, K., Kashima, H., Zhu, F.: Interpretable knowledge tracing: simple and efficient student modeling with causal relations. In: Proceedings of the AAAI Conference on Artificial Intelligence, vol. 36, pp. 12810–12818 (2022)
21. Pandey, S., Srivastava, J.: Rkt: relation-aware self-attention for knowledge tracing. In: Proceedings of the 29th ACM International Conference on Information and Knowledge Management, pp. 1205–1214 (2020)
22. Parmar, N., et al.: Image transformer. In: International Conference on Machine Learning, pp. 4055–4064. PMLR (2018)
23. Piech, C., et al.: Deep knowledge tracing. Adv. Neural Inf. Process. Syst. **28** (2015)
24. Shin, D., Shim, Y., Yu, H., Lee, S., Kim, B., Choi, Y.: Saint+: integrating temporal features for EdNet correctness prediction. In: LAK21: 11th International Learning Analytics and Knowledge Conference, pp. 490–496 (2021)
25. Sun, F., et al.: Bert4rec: sequential recommendation with bidirectional encoder representations from transformer. In: Proceedings of the 28th ACM International Conference on Information and Knowledge Management, pp. 1441–1450 (2019)
26. Tan, W., Jin, Y., Liu, M., Zhang, H.: BiDKT: deep knowledge tracing with BERT. In: Bao, W., Yuan, X., Gao, L., Luan, T.H., Choi, D.B.J. (eds.) ADHOC-NETS/TridentCom -2021. LNICST, vol. 428, pp. 260–278. Springer, Cham (2022). https://doi.org/10.1007/978-3-030-98005-4_19
27. Tiana, Z., Zhengc, G., Flanaganb, B., Mic, J., Ogatab, H.: Bekt: deep knowledge tracing with bidirectional encoder representations from transformers. In: Proceedings of the 29th International Conference on Computers in Education (2021)
28. Vaswani, A., et al.: Attention is all you need. Adv. Neural Inf. Process. Syst. **30** (2017)
29. Wang, T., Ma, F., Gao, J.: Deep hierarchical knowledge tracing. In: Proceedings of the 12th International Conference on Educational Data Mining (2019)
30. Wu, L., Li, S., Hsieh, C.J., Sharpnack, J.: SSE-PT: sequential recommendation via personalized transformer. In: Proceedings of the 14th ACM Conference on Recommender Systems, pp. 328–337 (2020)
31. Yudelson, M.V., Koedinger, K.R., Gordon, G.J.: Individualized Bayesian knowledge tracing models. In: Lane, H.C., Yacef, K., Mostow, J., Pavlik, P. (eds.) AIED 2013. LNCS (LNAI), vol. 7926, pp. 171–180. Springer, Heidelberg (2013). https://doi.org/10.1007/978-3-642-39112-5_18
32. Zhang, C., Jiang, Y., Zhang, W., Gu, C.: Muse: multi-scale temporal features evolution for knowledge tracing. arXiv preprint arXiv:2102.00228 (2021)

Why You Should Give Your Students Automatic Process Feedback on Their Collaboration: Evidence from a Randomized Experiment

Lukas Menzel[1(✉)], Sebastian Gombert[2], Joshua Weidlich[2], Aron Fink[3], Andreas Frey[3], and Hendrik Drachsler[1,2]

[1] studiumdigitale, Goethe University, Frankfurt am Main, Germany
menzel@sd.uni-frankfurt.de

[2] DIPF: Leibniz Institute for Research and Information in Education, Frankfurt am Main, Germany
{s.gombert,j.weidlich,h.drachsler}@dipf.de

[3] Pedagogical Psychology, Goethe University, Frankfurt am Main, Germany
{a.fink,frey}@psych.uni-frankfurt.de

Abstract. In Computer-Supported Collaborative Learning (CSCL), students learn in small groups to achieve learning benefits outside what would be possible for individual students. As in other forms of learning, students need feedback on the quality of their work. Still, writing high-quality informative feedback requires time on the part of educators. This makes it less feasible to provide quality feedback at scale. Given the importance of group dynamics in CSCL, quality feedback should also contain information about group processes and discussion quality. Emergent roles provide a natural anchor point for this.

We propose a method to automatically deliver highly informative, textual process feedback for CSCL forum discussion tasks in an introductory teacher education class, focusing on individual students' group communication. This feedback is generated from several discourse indicators, that are used to derive emergent roles of the students. From that we derive feedback about strengths and potential for improvement. In a randomized control trial, we show that the highly informative feedback generated with our method is preferred by the students. Implications and avenues for future research are discussed in light of these findings.

Keywords: Automated Textual Feedback · AI-assisted Agents · Collaborative Learning · Learning Analytics

1 Introduction

In higher education, researchers and educators often find themselves in a position where high student-to-teacher ratios make it difficult to provide personalized support to students. There are two main ways to resolve this: (1) Students

O. Viberg et al. (Eds.): EC-TEL 2023, LNCS 14200, pp. 198–212, 2023.
https://doi.org/10.1007/978-3-031-42682-7_14

can learn with their peers in social learning environments. (2) Teaching personnel can be supported in reaching more students at once. To combine these approaches, methods from Computer-Supported Collaborative Learning (CSCL) can be accompanied by Learning Analytics (LA), leading to cycles of social knowledge building and data-informed self-reflection. To move from LA towards informing learners' self-reflection, LA data must be interpreted and brought into a form that learners can understand, like well-phrased textual feedback [23]. By pre-selecting and contextualizing data, textual feedback can overcome the drawbacks of other forms of data display like learning dashboards, which often only visualize learning data without proper context [18]. Showing relevant information with an interpretation makes such feedback highly informative [11] and helps students to become competent agents within their reflection processes.

Providing students with feedback on their writing and discourse structure during and after their discussion assignments bears the potential to support them in reflecting on their collaboration quality. Ideally, this would improve their metacognition in communicative situations and thus help to make their learning groups more effective. Our goal is thus to advance the methods for automatically providing feedback to students (1) *by evaluating the use of mostly linguistic measures (indicator candidates) to assess qualities of educational forum discourse* and (2) *by providing highly informative feedback based on language and communication analysis.* We apply various means of discourse analysis, including readability assessment, psycholinguistic measurements, and group communication analysis to a data set of educational discourse. The data set was collected during a CSCL task in a teacher education lecture. The assignments were specifically designed for a project that aimed to provide automatically generated feedback to students. Finally, we provide preliminary evidence from a randomized control study that our feedback is liked by students both in comparison to less informative feedback and in absolute terms.

2 Background

CSCL as a discipline often draws from the *socio-constructivist framework* [15, p. 17], which also serves as a basis for the research at hand. Constructivists argue that knowledge is built actively and all knowledge is constructed in a cycle of acting (construction), perceiving (reconstruction) and reflecting (deconstruction). In socio-constructivism, this idea is taken one step further by arguing that the knowledge construction process developing the human intellect mostly takes place in social environments and is therefore heavily influenced by those [e.g., 9]. This is supported by psychological findings that all parts of the knowledge construction process are influenced by social environments [e.g., 7, 12]. Social environments and the emerging role constellations that prevail within them hence play a decisive role in the quality of learning outcomes. Emergent (social) roles therefore provide a natural anchor point when aiming to support knowledge construction processes. Dowell, Nixon, and Graesser [10] operationalize the identification of emergent roles on a linguistic level through their Group Communication Analysis method and provide evidence that supports the theory.

In CSCL, educators create social contexts using technology such as discussion forums. They do this by integrating the knowledge construction cycle phases into CSCL apps, with assignments following a macro script of learning activities, which in turn follow a micro script [8]. To aid learners in cognitive regulation between phases, technology can either mediate human intervention or intervene automatically. As group dynamics are so important in CSCL, *Data-enriched Learning Activities* [11] for CSCL should stimulate the learners' metacognition, enabling them to reflect on their group role and to self-regulate if required.

To achieve this, we can give process feedback to learners. Data-informed, personalized, and textual feedback for learners brings Learning Analytics and socio-constructivist thinking together by creating a formative learning environment [27], moving us further towards *Highly Informative LA* [11]. Such feedback should be concise, actionable [4], and in line with learners' goals [18]. The automatic observation of collaborative knowledge construction and deconstruction can be achieved by analyzing group communication patterns and identifying emergent roles. In any CSCL task, role identification reveals profiles of learners, with their communicative strengths and weaknesses. This knowledge helps us to focus on important information for each role and tailor feedback accordingly. Such highly informative process feedback can then inform learner reflections.

3 Research Questions and Methodology

For the present research, we collected forum posts and forum metadata from a CSCL discussion assignment. We collected the data from a first cohort of students, so that we could then analyze it before running same assignment again with another cohort. Our goal was to automatically create LA-informed feedback for the second cohort of students using the insights that we gained from the analysis of the first cohort's data. Our analysis in this paper is mainly based on linguistic process indicators derived from the forum messages in the data set and their interrelations.

The research questions that we want to answer in the present research are:

RQ1a What are useful indicators for analyzing CSCL discussion assignments?
RQ1b Using a select set of indicators, what emergent roles can we identify in the data set?
RQ2a How can the examined indicators and emergent roles inform personalized, textual process feedback in the context of the given assignments?
RQ2b Do students find the provided feedback useful to reflect and self-regulate?

We describe each indicator candidate in detail and provide a rationale for its potential use in an educational discourse analysis. Based on normative, as well as evidence-supported argumentation, we select the indicators that we want to use for our emergent role analysis and in our feedback texts (RQ1a). To assess how each selected indicator should influence the feedback texts (RQ2a), we test the indicators for the stability of their correlations over the assignment phases. Thereafter, to detect emergent roles (RQ1b), we carry out a cluster analysis.

Indicator candidates that had significant impact on the formation of the clusters will be singled out for phrasing personalized feedback (RQ2a).

We then suggest feedback texts for each cluster. Some indicators might only be relevant for certain groups of students, for example depending on the cluster they belong to. They will thus be included into the feedback conditionally. In a randomized control trial, we gave feedback texts generated using this method to a new cohort of students. Those texts also contained generated product feedback on the group outcome. We show that the highly informative feedback generated with our new method is preferred by the students (RQ2b). Implications and avenues for future research are discussed in light of these findings.

4 The CSCL Discourse Data Set

The data set under examination was created within one of our research projects. The project aims towards analyzing the manifold data that is generated during the course of online learning to give automated, artificial intelligence (AI) based feedback to learners.

Part of this project was a forum discourse assignment, where first semester student teachers had to discuss two videos of teaching lessons in three assignment phases. 689 students contributed 8115 posts in total to the discourse forum. The students were put into groups with three up to six students, most of which had four (31 groups) or five (144 groups) participants. This resulted in a total count of 187 groups. The assignment was split into three phases[1]:

1. In phase 1, the students had to watch the two videos and then collect two to six teaching activities (group work, class discussion, etc.) for each video. Every student had to contribute at least one activity here and contribute at least one additional comment to the forum. (2849 posts)
2. Next, in phase 2, the students had to analyze the collected activities regarding their potential for cognitive activation of the students shown in the video. Members of the group would then either agree to the analysis of their peers or provide their own alternative analysis. (3861 posts)
3. In the last phase, the students were to formulate a collective statement based upon their analyzes from phase two. One or more students would draft a statement and the others would then comment their improvements on that statement, until every student agreed on the final solution. (1405 posts)

All three phases had a strong script on how to use the forum. The students had to place each statement in a separate comment. Also, to express affirmation, students had to use (in German) the phrases "this statement reflects my opinion" and "I agree with the assessment".

[1] The assignment texts, as well as other supplemental material, like statistics about the data, the database schema, formulas, algorithms, our evaluation data, and the feedback templates can be found in our OSF.io repository.

5 The Indicator Candidates

5.1 Group Communication Analysis

Group Communication Analysis (GCA) is a method that combines computational linguistic analysis techniques with time series analysis[2]. It was invented by Dowell, Nixon, and Graesser [10], who used it to detect emergent social roles in two large data sets of educational chat discussions. The method combines several measures which are mainly based on semantic vectors and vector space calculations with a post count based participation measure.

We made two changes to the original method: first, we used Sentence BERT [24] instead of Latent Semantic Analysis (LSA) to generate our vectors. This allowed us to skip the corpus expansion and model training steps. Also, output vectors from large neural models like Sentence BERT are known to yield better results for semantic analyses, than LSA does. Secondly, the original GCA method worked for chat data, which has no additional information about the relations of posts, other than the order of their arrival. Our forum data was structured as a post-reply-tree. We took this into account by only comparing posts that had a child or sibling relation within that tree[3].

Participation The participation measure is there to "signif[y] a willingness and readiness for participants to externalize and share information and thoughts" [3,10, p. 1010]. The measure sets the post count of a participant in relation to the post count of the discussion. It rewards participants with a high post count share relative to the whole conversation. We used the improved participation measure that the authors supply [10, fn. 1].

Responsivity The internal cohesion, responsivity and social impact all describe how participants interact with each other and with themselves on a semantic level. The responsivity of a participant signifies how they reflect on other participant's contributions [e.g. 16]. It is measured by comparing the content of all posts a participant made to all previous posts by the other participants.

Social Impact The social impact then is the flip side of a participant's responsivity: it shows how other's reflected on a participant's posts by comparing a post to all posts that were made later in time by other participants. The responsivity and the social impact are therefore a quantification method for collective knowledge construction.

Internal Cohesion The *internal cohesion* of a participants posts was constructed to quantify their reflection process and therefore self-regulation [e.g. 30]. It works by comparing the content of each post of a participant to all previous posts that a participant made. The measure's value rises in proportion to the semantic similarity of the posts of an individual.

---

[2] you can find all the formulas we used in the supplemental material but if you are interested in the topic, go read the original paper. It's really a masterpiece.

[3] See the supplemental material for more information on how we transformed the graph.

Newness The newness quantifies the tendency of a participant to share new information, rather than to discuss mostly the information that has already been shared (*biased information sharing*) [6] and to pass over critique or alternatives to the current consensus [17]. It is measured by averaging over the distance of each of a participants posts to the semantic space of the previous posts in a discussion, which is represented by a linear hull.

Communication Density This measure describes how dense a participant communicates. With the changes we made to the original method, we couldn't implement this measure as originally described. We thus had to replace it later with the Flesch Reading Ease score. Still, in future research, we might try to replace Flesch with another measure that can capture the density on a semantic level.

5.2 Affirmation Detection

It was an integral part of all assignments that the students explicitly affirmed the statements of their group members. Affirming peer contributions was the central mechanism to keep the discussion vivid and to settle on statements and on assertions alike. To detect affirmation, we created semantic vectors for a list of common affirmative comments. We then took the average vector $\vec{a}$ of these and compared the vectors of all sentences in a post to $\vec{a}$. When a sentence vector had a cosine distance below a threshold of 0.461 (chosen by manually examining the data), the post was marked as containing an affirmation. The affirmation rate of a student is the share of their posts which contain an affirmation.

5.3 Readability

Evidence that the reading ease of a text plays an important role for a reader's engagement with its content exists for a very long time by now. Reading ease has therefore played a role in field of psycholinguistics for nearly a century by now [cf. 13]. We expected that the readability of a participants contributions in a text-based online discussion does influence the engagement of other participants with a contribution as well.

To measure readability, we implemented the Flesch Reading Ease score [13]. The parameters of the Flesch formula has to be recalculated for every language. We thus use the formula from Amstad [1] as an indicator candidate.

In Sect. 5.1, we mentioned that we could not implement the *communication density* from the GCA. We still wanted a measure that served a similar purpose. Explaining complex matter using simple words usually makes texts less dense but more readable. Therefore, we deemed the Flesch score to represent an inverse of the idea behind the *communication density* and used it as a somewhat imperfect replacement measure. It is imperfect, because it doesn't capture the density on a semantic level, but only based on sentence and word lengths.

5.4 Uncertainty

For educational and scientific discourse, the presence of uncertainty poses a key feature. Chen, Benus, and Hernandez [5] even argue that science in general is about the management of uncertainty. They expound the problems of presenting merely the final result of science – a knowledge product – as being the science itself instead of acknowledging that science is mostly about the process of constructing knowledge. This process is about transitioning from an uncertain idea of how something could be – i.e., a hypothesis – to certain knowledge about the examined matter. While science is about using a methodology for constructing new, formerly "unknown knowledge", education is about reconstructing "known knowledge". In education, uncertainty therefore needs to be managed, too. Albeit implicitly, it has to play a key role in any well-designed didactic method. Observing uncertainty in discourses within science education settings is therefore an important factor for gaining an understanding of the discourse quality.

In natural language, there are certain cue words and phrases, but also semantic structures beyond those that signal hedging and semantic uncertainty [21]. Cues of uncertainty in language have highly contextual semantics. Hence, the cues have to be contextually disambiguated [32]. We used a custom transformer model based on RoBERTa [22] to detect four types of uncertainty: *epistemic*, *doxastic*, *investigative* and *conditional* [31]. For each student, we then used the mean rate of uncertainty tokens per post as an indicator.

5.5 Other Candidates

There were several indicator candidates which we also considered but which did not turn out to be too useful for us. To keep the cluster analysis to a manageable amount of indicators, we decided to rule out these indicators from the analysis. Still, we kept the option to use them in the feedback templates if they would turn out to be distinctive for a certain cluster *after* the cluster analysis.

Activity Based Collaboration Analysis This set of indicators, including *initiative*, *responsiveness*, *presence*, and *productivity*[4], were derived by Scheffel *et al.* [29] from forum metadata and used to predict and influence student performance. While they serve as a baseline for comparison with the linguistic indicators in this paper, they are not included in the cluster analysis as they are not based on language properties. Additionally, the *participation* measure from the GCA method implements the same concepts.

Affective Norms Affective norms are psycholinguistic attributes of words. We speculated that the affective properties of communication would indicate the emotional involvement of a leaner, which among other things plays a significant role for their social presence [26]. On the lexical level, using the dictionary from Köper and Schulte im Walde [20], we examined the *abstractness*, *imageability*, *valence* and *arousal* of the language used by each student.

[4] as the students were in fixed groups, implementing the *connectedness* indicator [29] did not make sense for our data set.

Keyword Simple Word Rates Keywords are words that are of low frequency in common parlance but of higher frequency in the examined corpus. The keywords of our CSCL discourse corpus are primarily technical terms that relate to the assignment. We hence assumed that students' use of keywords could indicate the level of confidence with which they navigate the field. Simple words are the flip side of this coin. By the our definition, these are words that occur at a comparatively high frequency in common parlance. Here, we used the 200 most common words in a subset of the German Colossal, Cleaned Common Crawl Corpus [25][5].

Mean post depth in the discussion graph For each student, we calculated the average relative depth of their posts in the discussion graph with $0 \leq$ depth ≤ 1. This would allow us to observe where the posts of a student concentrate in the discussion. We did not use this measure in the cluster analysis itself, though it turned out that this measure helps with explaining some of the emergent roles that we found later.

Length measures Lastly, we also measured the sentences per post, the ratio of accessory to main clauses and the sentence length in tokens.

6 Selecting and Evaluating The Indicators

To identify emergent roles using a cluster analysis (RQ1b), we had to make sure that we could assess the cluster composition. In addition, we needed to limit the effect of a potentially too similar set of variables to skew the cluster centroid distances. Students want concise, actionable feedback [4]. We can deliver this by concentrating only on those features that really matter. This meant that we now had to reduce the feature space by carefully selecting the indicators which we would use to determine the emergent roles.

Before we carried out any analysis, we normalized all the data by (1) winsorizing each indicator candidate for their upper and lower percentiles, as well as (2) z-score-normalizing it. Both steps were more important for the cluster analysis than for the correlation analysis, as Spearman's r_s can deal well with outliers and differing variable scales.

We then computed correlation matrices, using Spearman's correlation coefficient for all indicators on the participant level and taking the mean values of all candidates that were computed on the post level. We generated one matrix for all discussions of a group, as well as one for each discussion phase. We also inspected the correlations between well-founded candidates and those that were not as well-founded to see if we could gain insights into the usefulness of the latter ones. But as we did not have information about how these candidates would influence the group outcome, this turned out to be a rather impractical approach. By combining the correlation analysis and a normative evaluation of the indicator candidates, in the end, we included the set of indicators into the cluster analysis that are described in Sects. 5.1 to 5.4.

[5] The procedure to retrieve the simple words and the keywords is described in the supplemental material.

To answer RQ2a, we also needed to figure out how each indicator would influence the phrasing of our feedback. Each indicator candidate could potentially behave differently depending on the micro script of the assignment phase (RQ1a). Hence, we needed to assert the stability of the indicators over the phases. For unstable indicators, we will need to collect empirical data on their behavior with regard to a specific micro script in the long run. For the work at hand, we might have to assert them per phase in the feedback text, instead of just reporting, e.g., on an overall mean value. To assert the indicator stability, we computed paired t-tests over the raw correlation values between all indicator candidates and each phase. This produced a matrix for each of the candidates which showed the significance of the changes in an indicators correlations between each phase.

Only the affirmation rate and uncertainty indicators were unstable among phases. Uncertainty in phase 2 significantly differed ($p < 1\%$) from phases 1 and 3, likely due to the distinct tasks assigned in each phase: collecting information in phase 1, discussing in phase 2, and summarizing findings in phase 3. The affirmation rate also significantly varied ($p < 0.2\%$) between all phases, correlating with the amount of prompted interactions in each phase. This means that (1) the affirmation rate and uncertainty depend on the assignment's micro script, and feedback on these indicators can't be transferred to different micro scripts. Norms for these indicators would need recalculating for new micro scripts. Also, (2) derived clusters would be specific to these indicators. (3) Feedback given on these indicators should consider the given micro script.

7 Finding the Emergent Roles

The emergent roles (RQ1b) are inferred from the results of a hierarchical clustering analysis. Hierarchical (or agglomerative) clustering can support selecting an adequate cluster size visually, through dendrograms. This method helped us with selecting a feasible number of clusters by setting a minimum distance for the centroids and in naming the resulting roles by considering the proximity of the clusters. We set the cluster distance to 15.5, as we noticed that the last two clusters that emerge from that distance are very distinct. Unifying them by setting the distance just a little higher made the clusters more difficult to explain. We then made an independent t-test for each of the selected indicators comparing all clusters with each other, to determine which indicators are most distinctive between the clusters (sample groups). In the final written exam on the lecture, students were given a task on cognitive activation related to our CSCL discussion assignment. Their score on this task was included in our data set. As we wanted to know how the clusters relate to student performance, we also examined the relationship between clusters, exam points, and dropout rates.

Cluster 1 members contributed moderately but shared the most new and relevant information (as seen by their social impact), despite not always communicating clearly. They had high internal cohesion and low affirmation rates, often posting lengthy messages (.21 SDs above average) at the beginning of discussions (mean relative tree depth of .85 SDs below average). Their communication style

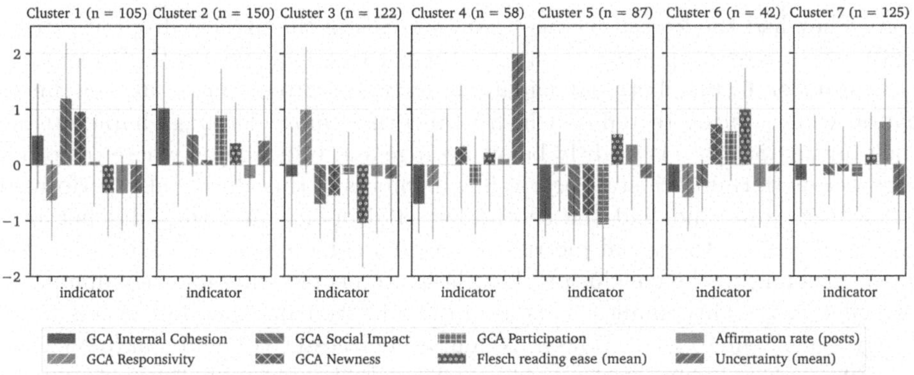

Fig. 1. Participant Cluster Centroids (hand-selected features; SD as error bar)

was very certain, similar to cluster 6. They are comparable to the *Influential Actors* from Dowell, Nixon, and Graesser [10].

Cluster 2 students had outstanding participation rates. They communicated using simpler language and had a similar affirmation rate to cluster 3, while displaying some uncertainty in their communication style. Their social impact was high and their responsivity about average. This aligns them with the *Drivers* group from Dowell, Nixon, and Graesser [10] Interestingly, they were also high performers on the cognitive activation exam assignment (.25 points; SD .76) and had the lowest dropout rate at 4% (as defined by if they attended the exam).

Cluster 3 members, dubbed *Summarizers*, displayed high responsivity and frequently rephrased their peers' information. They had low scores for newness and social impact, second only to cluster 5. Their participation tended to be late in the conversation (mean post depth: .57 SDs above average; SD 1.21), with less readable messages and a similar affirmation rate to cluster 2, but with little uncertainty. Cluster 3 often co-occurred with *Influential Actors* or *Drivers*, indicating an inter-dependency of these roles.

Cluster 4 stands out by having the most uncertain students while its members' posts have the second-highest newness on average. Members of this cluster don't participate very much and communicate with a low internal cohesion. Their social impact is near the average. These seem to be rather cautious students who are otherwise doing relatively average in most of the other measures. We refer to members of cluster 4 as *Cautious Learners.*

Cluster 5, or *Left-Behinds*, rarely participated in discussions and tended to join late. They didn't bother much to refer to their peers posts. Instead, they often only made affirmations accompanied by an excuse, giving them the second-highest affirmation rate. Their internal cohesion is to be taken with a grain of salt: this value drops if a participant does not make too many posts. *Left-Behinds* typically co-occurred with *Drivers* (co-occurrence in 27% of all groups; 78.16% of all cases where cluster 5 occurred). This also drove down their participation score. They had the lowest average exam scores and the highest dropout rate at 25.3%, with most dropouts (19 out of 22) occurring in groups with *Drivers*.

In **cluster 6**, members participate actively and often contribute new information while writing readably, which is also their most defining characteristic. Their affirmation rate is slightly below average and thus among where the other more well-performing clusters are. While members of this cluster also performed well in the exam and had the second-lowest dropout rate, they did not perform very well on the social metrics of internal cohesion, responsivity or social impact, leading to the conclusion that these are people who don't communicate very effectively. This smallest cluster of only 42 students therefore seems to be mostly equivalent to what Dowell, Nixon, and Graesser [10] call *Chatterers*.

Cluster 7 members participated moderately, having high affirmation rates and typically contributed in the middle of the conversation, with a near average mean post depth. They waited until others had made their points, before affirming them and confidently adding their own information, with the lowest uncertainty among *Influential Actors*. Most of their scores were slightly below average, making them distinct from *Followers* from Dowell, Nixon, and Graesser [10], but more effective communicators than *Chatterers*. We call them *Deferrers*.

The emergent roles that we found in this analysis are not only to be viewed on an individual level. Instead, by pairing the findings about the behavior of the cluster members with a co-occurrence matrix[6], we could show that the behavioral patterns of one student produce those of another. Saqr and López-Pernas [28] propose that individual disposition influences emergent roles, yet group dynamics also steer students towards specific roles. When formulating feedback, it could severely demotivate students who took a less active or beneficial role in the face of, e.g., their peers being high performers that are already hard to keep up with. Therefore, all feedback should have a motivational component to it.

8 Feedback Design and Evaluation

We used our insights about the emergent roles and the indicators to create feedback for another cohort of students who worked on the same assignment. The feedback structure drew from Brooks *et al.* [2], who provide key questions for recalling learning goals (*feeding up*), reflecting on performance (*feeding back*), and providing tips for improvement (*feeding forward*). Brooks *et al.* [2] also identified four *levels* of feedback. First, the feedback should inform about a learners understanding of the task. For this, we developed a separate method to generate feedback on the product of phase 3. It draws from experiences we've made before [14] and is out of scope for the work at hand. Here, we focus on the *process*, the *self-regulation* and *self levels*. We gave students positively phrased feedback based on their role and helped them with self-regulation regarding their group behavior. As our method needs a fair amount of data and we didn't want students to try and manipulate indicators without us providing an interpretation, we sent them our feedback after the assignment finished.

[6] You can find the co-occurrence matrix in the supplemental material.

Each emergent role got its own feedback template. The *feeding up* part – a short description of the assignment to recall the learning goal – was the same for all students. We then combined *feeding back* and *feeding forward* for indicators that actually mattered to the specific roles, as well as to the students in general. We guarded most of the clauses in the templates by conditionals. The condition for a clause to appear was usually a fixed deviation of the individuals from the z-score normalized mean value over the full sample, but sometimes also over a single phase. The conditionals and phrases were fine tuned so that no student would get an empty feedback text. We also added some clauses that addressed the co-occurrence of another role within the group, to address the emergence of certain roles in the light of another role being present.

Shortly after we designed the feedback, the new cohort of first semester teacher students finished the described CSCL assignment. Using the previous year's cluster centroids, we executed our analysis code to obtain indicator values and emergent roles. For half the students, we generated the process feedback texts described here[7] and combined this with the product feedback from our second feedback generation method. Students could receive either this *highly informative feedback* (HIF), or the *feedback as usual* (FAU), which was the same that the first cohort received. Besides the *feedup*, the FAU only showed basic information about the process. That included the *message count* for each phase and if they had participated enough so that the assignment could be counted as being solved. We included this information in the HIF, too. We now carried out a randomized experiment, where we presented the HIF to about half ($n = 202$) of the students and the FAU to the other half ($n = 206$).

We showed the resulting feedback texts to the students in our Learning Management System. To assert whether we should continue pursuing our course, we asked them to fill out a survey on the feedback, just below the feedback text. On a four point Likert-scale[8], we asked the students if the feedback (1) was comprehensible, (2) was helpful for their further learning, (3) made them aware of their progress, (4) helped them with reflecting their learning behavior, (5) helps them to self-regulate in the future, and (6) motivates them to learn. When compared to the FAU, all of these improved substantially. Not only that but the students liked our *highly-informative feedback* absolute terms: 79 % found the HIF to be helpful or very helpful ($+28\%$to FAU; $U = 3236; p < 0.01\%$), two thirds found it helpful or very helpful for their reflection ($+23\%; U = 3576.5; p = 0.01\%$) and 71 % replied that it would help them to self-regulate ($+30\%; U = 3140; p < 0.01\%$). As this paper is about process feedback, these values are the most important ones here. In a Mann-Whitney U test, the differences between HIF and FAU of those three variables were highly significant ($p < 0.1\%$), showing that the students perceived the HIF to be an improvement over the FAU.

---

[7] again, the feedback templates can be found in our OSF.io repository.

[8] (strongly) disagree, (strongly) agree.

9 Conclusion and Outlook

We now have evidence that using linguistic indicators and GCA is a viable option to create data-informed, personalized, textual process feedback for learners (RQ1a). The analysis revealed emergent roles and gave us a glance at their interplay (RQ1b). It also revealed a path towards highly informative process feedback (RQ2a) that is based on a deeper language-based analysis of group dynamics, as well as individual writing styles. We need to give special care to the CSCL micro script when designing feedback based on such indicators and when analyzing emergent roles, as its influence is high for some indicators.

While our study was designed to give generated process feedback to all students alike, we think that there are some cases, like *Left Behinds*, where it would be better to redirect students to teachers instead. Adding to that, as the process feedback can be manipulable by students, our method should not be used to assess them summatively, but only to provide formative feedback.

Our preliminary survey results indicate that we're making progress towards providing useful automated feedback (RQ2b) through our presented method. Jivet *et al.* [18] demanded that LA-informed feedback would need to be contextualized in order to be relevant to students. They demanded this in the light of LA dashboards which back then were often missing the context needed to make sense of the presented indicators. Our concise, actionable, and contextualized textual feedback meets this demand. Of course, the students' self-reported value judgments have their limitations. We now have to test whether the students actually adapt their behavior in response to the feedback. This could show in improvements in single indicators as well as in the role they take in a discussion.

Again, we ran assignments with one cohort of students so that we could find indicators and create models that would be helpful to create feedback for another cohort doing the same assignment. This advances on prior methods for LA-informed feedback and sets the path for our future research trajectory. Regarding the process feedback, using our proposed method, we will need to find more indicators that are stable across different micro scripts and create sets of indicators and their empirical values that are specific to certain micro scripts as well. This will bring us towards process feedback that is not only useful for a certain assignment macro script, but which will also be composable and reusable across different assignments.

Lowering the integration barrier of automated feedback into teaching practice remains a challenge. Under our current method, LA experts must laboriously identify process indicators, contextualize them and phrase feedback accordingly. To scale this up, we will need a technical infrastructure as well as processes in place that support us in collecting empirical values of experience on the indicators. The results must also be of obvious value to teachers. In the long run, we hence need to support them in the authoring process. Integrated into tools that provide teachers information on their students performance [e.g., 19], we should deliver recommendations of indicators and role-specific feedback texts, that are tailored to their assignments automatically.

References

1. Amstad, T.: Wie Verständlich Sind Unsere Zeitungen? ETH Zürich (1978)
2. Brooks, C., Carroll, A., Gillies, R., Hattie, J.: A matrix of feedback. AJTE **44**(4), 14–32 (2019). https://doi.org/10.14221/ajte.2018v44n4.2
3. Care, E., Scoular, C., Griffin, P.: Assessment of collaborative problem solving in education environments. Appl. Measur. Educ. **29**(4), 250–264 (2016). https://doi.org/10.1080/08957347.2016.1209204
4. Cha, H.-J., Park, T.: Applying and evaluating visualization design guidelines for a MOOC dashboard to facilitate self-regulated learning based on learning analytics. KSII TIIS **13**(6), 2799–2823 (2019). https://doi.org/10.3837/tiis.2019.06.002
5. Chen, Y., Benus, M.J., Hernandez, J.: Managing uncertainty in scientific argumentation. Sci. Ed. **103**(5), 1235–1276 (2019). https://doi.org/10.1002/sce.21527
6. Dennis, A.R.: Information exchange and use in group decision making: you can lead a group to information, but you can't make it think. MIS Q. **20**(4), 433 (1996). https://doi.org/10.2307/249563
7. Dijksterhuis, A.: Automatic social influence the perception-behavior links. In: Social Influence: Direct and Indirect Processes, p. 95. Psychology Press (2001)
8. Dillenbourg, P., Hong, F.: The mechanics of CSCL macro scripts. Comput. Support. Learn. **3**(1), 5–23 (2008). https://doi.org/10.1007/s11412-007-9033-1
9. Doise, W.: On the social development of the intellect. In: Shulman, V.L., Restaino-Baumann, L.C.R., Butler, L. (eds.) The Future of Piagetian Theory. Springer, Boston, MA (1985). https://doi.org/10.1007/978-1-4684-4925-9_5
10. Dowell, N.M.M., Nixon, T.M., Graesser, A.C.: Group communication analysis: a computational linguistics approach for detecting Sociocognitive roles in multiparty interactions. Behav. Res. Methods **51**(3), 1007–1041 (2018). https://doi.org/10.3758/s13428-018-1102-z
11. Drachsler, H.: Towards Highly Informative Learning Analytics. Open Universiteit, Heerlen (2023). https://doi.org/10.25656/01:26785
12. Ferguson, M.J., Bargh, J.A.: How social perception can automatically influence behavior. Trends Cogn. Sci. **8**(1), 33–39 (2004). https://doi.org/10.1016/j.tics.2003.11.004
13. Flesch, R.: A new readability yardstick. J. Appl. Psychol. **32**(3), 221 (1948)
14. Gombert, S., et al.: Coding energy knowledge in constructed responses with explainable NLP models. Comput. Assist. Learn. (2022). https://doi.org/10.1111/jcal.12767
15. Haake, J., Schwabe, G., Wessner, M.: CSCL - Kompendium: Lehr- Und Handbuch Zum Computerunterstützten Kooperativen Lernen. Oldenbourg Wissenschaftsverlag GmbH (2004)
16. Hesse, F., Care, E., Buder, J., Sassenberg, K., Griffin, P.: A framework for teachable collaborative problem solving skills. In: Griffin, P., Care, E. (eds.) Assessment and Teaching of 21st Century Skills. Educational Assessment in an Information Age, pp. 37–56. Springer, Dordrecht (2015). https://doi.org/10.1007/978-94-017-9395-7_2
17. Janis, I.L.: Groupthink: Psychological Studies of Policy Decisions and Fiascoes. Houghton Mifflin School (1982)
18. Jivet, I., Scheffel, M., Drachsler, H., Specht, M.: Awareness is not enough: pitfalls of learning analytics dashboards in the educational practice. In: Lavoué, É., Drachsler, H., Verbert, K., Broisin, J., Pérez-Sanagustín, M. (eds.) EC-TEL 2017. LNCS, vol. 10474, pp. 82–96. Springer, Cham (2017). https://doi.org/10.1007/978-3-319-66610-5_7

19. Karademir, O., Ahmad, A., Schneider, J., Di Mitri, D., Jivet, I., Drachsler, H.: Designing the learning analytics cockpit - a dashboard that enables interventions. In: De la Prieta, F., et al. (eds.) MIS4TEL 2021. LNNS, vol. 326, pp. 95–104. Springer, Cham (2022). https://doi.org/10.1007/978-3-030-86618-1_10
20. Köper, M., Schulte im Walde, S.: Automatically generated affective norms of abstractness, arousal, imageability and valence for 350 000 German lemmas. In: Proceedings of the Tenth International Conference on Language Resources and Evaluation (LREC 2016), pp. 2595–2598. European Language Resources Association (ELRA), Portorož (2016)
21. Lakoff, G.: Hedges: a study in meaning criteria and the logic of fuzzy concepts. J. Philos. Logic **2**(4), 458–508 (1973)
22. Liu, Y., et al.: RoBERTa: A robustly optimized BERT pretraining approach. CoRR abs/1907.11692 (2019)
23. Ramos-Soto, A., Lama, M., Vazquez-Barreiros, B., Bugarin, A., Mucientes, M., Barro, S.: Towards textual reporting in learning analytics dashboards. In: 2015 IEEE 15th International Conference on Advanced Learning Technologies, pp. 260–264. IEEE, Hualien (2015). https://doi.org/10.1109/ICALT.2015.96
24. Reimers, N., Gurevych, I.: Sentence-BERT: sentence embeddings using siamese BERT-networks. In: Proceedings of the 2019 Conference on Empirical Methods in Natural Language Processing. Association for Computational Linguistics (2019)
25. Reißel, P., May, P.: The German Colossal, Cleaned Common Crawl Corpus, German NLP Group. (2020). https://german-nlp-group.github.io/projects/gc4-corpus.html (visited on 08/10/2022)
26. Rourke, L., Anderson, T., Garrison, D.R., Archer, W.: Assessing social presence in asynchronous text-based computer conferencing. J. Distance Educ./Rev. Distance **14**(2), 50–71 (1999)
27. Sansone, N., Cesareni, D.: Which learning analytics for a socio-constructivist teaching and learning blended experience? J. e-Learning and Knowl. Soc. (2019). https://doi.org/10.20368/1971-8829/1135047
28. Saqr, M., López-Pernas, S.: How CSCL roles emerge, persist, transition, and evolve over time: a four-year longitudinal study. Comput. Educ. **189**, 104581 (2022). https://doi.org/10.1016/j.compedu.2022.104581
29. Scheffel, M., Drachsler, H., Kreijns, K., de Kraker, J., Specht: Widget, M.: Widget as you lead, i am performing well indeed!: using results from an exploratory offline study to inform an empirical online study about a learning analytics widget in a collaborative learning environment. In: Proceedings of the Seventh International Learning Analytics and Knowledge Conference, pp. 289–298. ACM, Vancouver British Columbia (2017). https://doi.org/10.1145/3027385.3027428
30. Stahl, G.: Rediscovering CSCL. In: Koschmann,T., Hall, R., Miyake, N.(eds.) CSCL 2: Carrying Forward the Conversation, pp. 169–181 (2002)
31. Szarvas, G., Vincze, V., Farkas, R., Móra, G., Gurevych, I.: Cross-genre and cross-domain detection of semantic uncertainty. Comput. Linguist. **38**(2), 335–367 (2012). https://doi.org/10.1162/COLI_a_00098
32. Velldal, E., Øvrelid, L., Read, J., Oepen, S.: Speculation and negation: rules, rankers, and the role of syntax. Comput. Linguist. **38**(2), 369–410 (2012). https://doi.org/10.1162/COLI_a_00126

Interactive Web-Based Learning Materials Vs. Tutorial Chatbot: Differences in User Experience

Behzad Mirzababaei[1(✉)], Katharina Maitz[2,3], Angela Fessl[1,2], and Viktoria Pammer-Schindler[1,2]

[1] Know-Center GmbH, Graz, Austria
bmirzababaei@know-center.at
[2] Graz University of Technology, Graz, Austria
{afessl,viktoria.pammer-schindler}@tugraz.at
[3] Private University College for Teacher Education Augustinum, Graz, Austria
katharina.maitz@pph-augustinum.at

Abstract. Today's learning platforms make content available and enable social interaction between humans. Tomorrow, such platforms could also host computational tutors that support learning through dialogues. In this work, we explore how user experience differs between learning via web-based interactive content and learning within a dialogue led by a computational tutorial agent. To this purpose, we conducted a study with 31 master students of inclusive education. One group interacted with web-based textual learning materials (DIGIVIDget condition, $n = 14$). The other group interacted with a tutorial agent (DIGIBOT condition, $n = 17$). Both groups received the same text-based content on formulating search queries for the Internet. Using the standard System Usability Scale, the DIGIBOT's usability was rated as slightly higher than the DIGIVIDget's, but not significantly (Mann-Whitney-U-Test, $U = 166.5, p = .06$). Subsequently, two focus group discussions were carried out with participants who had also tested the respective other technology ($n = 12$). Focus group participants highlighted positively the interactive nature of DIGIBOT, the motivational effect of receiving immediate feedback, and that DIGIBOT requires and facilitates more concentration than DIGIVIDget. Freely navigable web-based content may be more suitable to give an overview over a large area of knowledge and allow punctual access to it. The dialogic interaction is therefore particularly interesting when prior knowledge about the learning domain is small or for users with special needs, who especially benefit from good structure, interactivity to focus, and dialogic interaction as a further motivational factor.

Keywords: learning management system · computational tutor · educational conversational agent · inclusive education

O. Viberg et al. (Eds.): EC-TEL 2023, LNCS 14200, pp. 213–228, 2023.
https://doi.org/10.1007/978-3-031-42682-7_15

1 Introduction

Learning management systems (LMS) are the standard educational technology used in education. LMS typically offer functionalities to share multimedia content, quizzes with different question formats, and social features like message boards and discussion forums. LMS are web-based and via responsive design work across all kinds of devices. Due to their widespread use, they now also have the advantage of being very common and well-established.

Other educational technologies, such as educational conversational agents, are much newer and much less widespread; they have become possible through advances in natural language processing. Agents' responses could be generative or retrieval. In generative models, the responses are generated based on the user's inputs, for example, OpenAI's ChatGPT which uses (large-) language models. However, in retrieval models, the best response has been selected from a pre-defined list of responses (e.g. [18]). While educational conversational agents can take multiple roles, in this work, we are particularly interested in tutorial conversational agents. These typically (are programmed to) convey content and to ask questions to learners or answer questions of learners.

Clearly, these two types of technologies are very different. However, they can complement each other, such that we see tutorial conversational agents as a type of technology that could be added to current's LMS. Subsequently, LMS could continue to share multimedia content and interactive quizzes, and host social activities between human users, but in addition, would provide access to computational tutors. LMS would continue their move from sharing content to hosting learning activities (now: by social features; future: in addition by providing access to computational tutors). In this work, we delve more deeply into the obvious, namely that these two types of technologies are very different, and explore based on a user study in which we compare learning via features typically found in an LMS with learning via features typically found in a tutorial agent in terms of usability and overall user experience (e.g. [2,15]).

2 Related Work

2.1 Learning Management Systems

Learning management systems (LMS) are an educational technology offering functionalities for creating, managing, and delivering course material [26]. Such functionalities include sharing of (multimedia) learning content, personalised user experience, flexible analytics, a variety of quiz formats and adaptive assessments, and social features including message boards or discussion forums [24]. Popular LMS for universities are for example Moodle (*moodle.com*), ATutor (*atutor.github.io*), Blackboard (*blackboard.com/teaching-learning/*), and OLAT (*olat.org*). LMS are used in various ways to support teaching and to teach a wide range of learners. Additionally, LMS are applicable in different instructional settings supporting face-to-face, fully remote and blended learning.

Typically, LMS are implemented as online learning technology using responsive design and are therefore working on all kinds of devices (e.g. smartphones, tablets). This leads to their widespread use in different learning contexts, and thus, LMS are well-known and well-established.

Depending on the environment in which the LMS is embedded, its usage requires more or less self-regulated learning capabilities. In traditional learning settings (face-to-face), instructors design the duration, the pace or the learning sequence of the course, thus, there is no self-regulated learning for students [25]. In contrast, in higher education, where the support and guidance of an instructor are limited, the set of skills subsumed under the term self-regulated learning is essential [7]. Self-regulated learning is defined as "the strategies that students use to regulate their cognition (i.e., use of various cognitive and meta-cognitive strategies) as well as the use of resource management strategies that students use to control their learning" [20]. Students are seen as active participants in the learning process, and they need to construct their own goals, criteria, or standards [21]. Monitoring their own learning progress towards these goals, criteria, or standards allows students to assess whether the learning process should continue as is or if some type of change is necessary [21].

The utilisation of LMS provides the possibility to easily navigate through online content. Learners also need to self-pace their learning in line with their self-regulated learning strategies, which is often a challenge. At the same time, such learning settings allow learners to be very flexible in their learning; thus they appreciate well-designed LMS and learning materials in this regard.

2.2 Educational Conversational Agents

Educational conversational agents refer to software with which users interact in a dialogic manner, typically with the look and feel of a chat that serves an educational purpose. Educational conversational agents represent a dialogic interaction metaphor (i.e. way how users interact with the technology). In some sense, they continue the long tradition of research on intelligent tutoring systems, in the general sense of constituting AI-enabled technology that aims to provide individualised support for learning, including giving feedback.

They have been studied to take on different roles in learning: they can act as a tutor (e.g., [18]), a peer (e.g., [12]), a moderator (e.g., [19]) or as a teachable agent in educational settings [3]. As a tutor, the agent can provide expert knowledge and guidance. For instance, Mirzababaei and Pammer-Schindler [18] developed an agent that asks an argumentative question and then gives feedback on the learners' responses and guides them to build a complete argument. As a peer, the agent can provide support and guidance similar to a fellow student. In [12], they simulated peer interaction with an agent which acted as a peer with different emotions and genders and its impact on social judgements, interest, self-efficacy, and learning. As a moderator, the agent can facilitate discussions between users and provide feedback. For instance, Neto and Fernandes [19] developed an agent to increase engagement and collaboration in discussion among students. As a teachable agent, it takes the role of a student who learns from the user. In [3], a teachable agent was developed to investigate the impact of the agent's feedback and actions on the users' motivation.

Educational conversational agents also have been used for a range of learning domains and subjects, such as mathematics (e.g., [10]), computer programming concepts (e.g., [30]), argumentation skills (e.g., [28]) and the GDPR (General Data Protection Regulation) (e.g., [17]). In terms of the target groups, educational conversational agents have been studied with primary school students (e.g., [6]), apprentices (e.g., [29]), university students (e.g., [18]) or learners with disabilities (e.g., [11]). Conversational agents can also utilise individualised learning and interactive feedback. Their features enable them to create inclusive learning environments for students with diverse living environments or learning disorders. For example, Gupta and Chen [11] created an agent that interviewed students around questions about design opportunities and challenges in using conversational agents to support inclusive learning. As an example, based on the interviews, it was revealed that for students with learning disabilities, the learning periods should be short and concise.

Typical characteristics of a tutorial agent include conveying content, giving individualised responses and feedback to learners' responses, and proactive guidance through a learning/teaching path. Interaction, as one of the main characteristics of this technology, increases learners' motivation compared to a more traditional learning system [23]. In relationship to LMS, educational conversational agents are typically more prescriptive in terms of how to navigate through the content via their dialogue structure (e.g., [10]). For example, Grossman et al. [10] created an educational conversational agent - called MathBot - which acted as a tutor with scripted dialogue. Their goal was to compare MathBot, as an automated text-based tutor, with Khan Academy, as an LMS which used videos and written tutorials, in terms of user preferences and learning outcomes. As for user preferences, 53% of participants preferred Khan Academy with videos to MathBot (42%). However, compared to text-based Khan Academy, 47% preferred MathBot, which was more than 44% of Khan Academy which used only text. The difference was not significant in learning outcomes, although the MathBot performed slightly better.

3 DIGIVIDget and DIGIBOT

This study aims to evaluate and contrast the user experience related factors such as usability and user preferences between two educational technologies - DIGIVIDget and DIGIBOT which convey the same text-based materials. Subsequently, we present the design of both.

Learning domain: 21st-century skills include a broad spectrum of digital competences and skills, including information and data literacy as suggested by the DigComp 2.2 [27] and the DigCompEdu [22] frameworks. Being able to search for information on the Internet [8] or formulating appropriate search queries is one crucial digital competence. In this regard, our goal was to convey the skills of formulating concrete and meaningful search queries that can be applied in common search engines such as Google or Bing. Search engines usually offer a set of search operators in the form of words or symbols that allow users to find more refined and targeted results but are hardly used in practice. The search operators covered by both tools are quote (“”), or (OR), asterisk (*), range (..), site (*site:*), filetype (*filetype:*), intitle (*intitle:*) and exclusion (-).

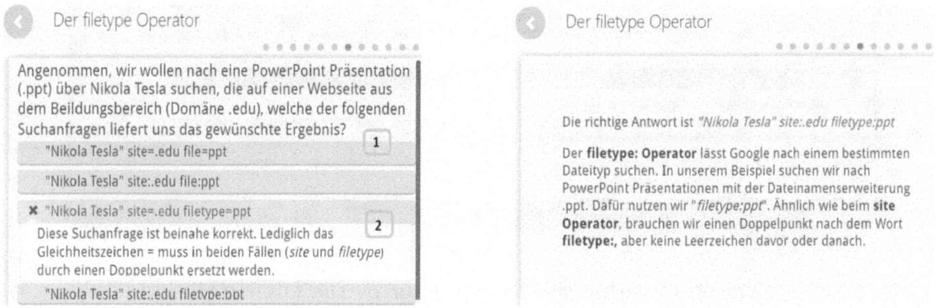

(a) Slide 1 (b) Slide 2

Fig. 1. Covering the filetype operator by the DIGIVIDget

In this work, we formulated the intended learning outcomes in the form of competence-oriented learning goals [9]. Both tools convey content related to the same learning goal, which is “You are able to search for information on the Internet in a targeted way.” but each tool conveyed it differently.

DIGIVIDget: The DIGIVIDget is a learning platform implemented in an adapted version of Moodle 3.11.3. The adaptations refer especially to the look and feel of the platform: i) the user interface does not resemble Moodle, ii) the content is structured along teaching units, each consisting of one or more competence-oriented learning goals [9], and iii) teaching units convey the learning content in the form of micro-learning cards implemented using H5P (*h5p.org*). Generally, the DIGIVIDget offers a set of teaching units on digital competences. One is the formulation of targeted search queries using search operators.

To convey the learning content about how to formulate targeted search queries, we have prepared the content as a set of 13 micro-learning cards. After a general introduction presented on the first micro-learning card, we introduce each search operator in the form of a presentation with integrated quizzes on two slides (see Fig. 1): On the first slide (Fig. 1a, point 1), the user receives a question related to the current introduced search operator, *filetype*. After answering the question, the user receives feedback on the correctness of the given answer (Fig. 1a, point 2). In the second slide (see Fig. 1b), the user is presented with the correct answer and an additional explanation about the operator.

The DIGIVIDget allows learners to freely navigate through the micro-learning cards and by going through all the micro-learning cards and learning the respective content, users can achieve the learning goal.

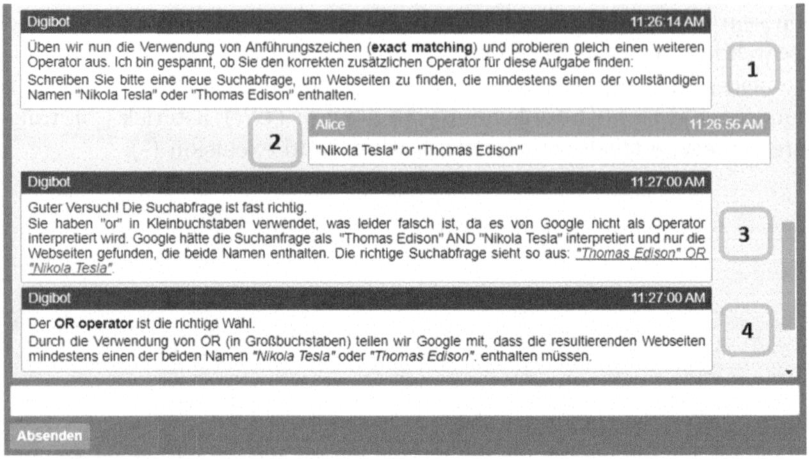

Fig. 2. Covering the OR operator by the DIGIBOT

DIGIBOT: The DIGIBOT is an educational conversational agent that acts as a tutor. It is designed to convey the same learning materials with the same wording and order as DIGIVIDget but in a dialogic form. The dialogue starts with a general introduction and greeting. Then, the agent talks about each operator one by one in the form of a dialogue, including asking questions (multiple choice or free-text question) about operators, giving adaptive feedback, and an explanation about the operators. Figure 2, a screenshot of the DIGIBOT, shows how the agent covers the content related to the OR operator. In Fig 2, point 1, the user, called Alice, receives a free-text question related to the OR operator. The user can answer it by writing the answer in the textbox at the button. After having answered the question by the user (point 2), the agent gives adaptive feedback on the correctness of the given answer (point 3). The agent's responses differ based on the user's responses. Finally, the agent gives a general explanation about the search operator (point 4). The DIGIBOT covers the learning materials by asking questions and giving adaptive feedback in a dialogic manner. The DIGIBOT was implemented upon the Bazaar framework [1].

The main difference between the DIGIVIDget and the DIGIBOT is how they convey the learning materials. The DIGIVIDget presents the content with micro-learning cards enabling the learners to freely navigate through them. However, the DIGIBOT conveys the same content through a conversation with learners.

4 Research Questions

Above, we have described both tools. They materialise different interaction metaphors in the sense that users (=learners) can interact in different manners with what should be learned through this interaction. The DIGIVIDget's metaphor is that of technology showing content to the learner, and the learner actively reading it and navigating through the content. The DIGIBOT's metaphor is that of an active entity (=the tutor) that engages the learner in a conversation around the learning content. As DIGIVIDget and DIGIBOT materialise different strategies for providing learners with the knowledge they need to reach (the same) learning goals, user experience is expected to differ.

In this work, we structure our exploration of how user experience differs into research questions that target different user-experience related constructs such as usability and user preference (RQs 1–3). Further, we aimed to explore the potential of each approach in inclusive educational contexts (RQ4), in line with our selection of study participants (see next Sect. 5 on methodology.)

- RQ1: *How was the DIGIVIDget perceived by the participants regarding its usability and usefulness?*
- RQ2: *How was the DIGIBOT perceived by the participants regarding its usability and usefulness?*
- RQ3: *What are users' preferences towards the DIGIVIDget and the DIGIBOT?*
- RQ4: *What is the potential of the different approaches for application in inclusive educational contexts from experts' point of view?*

5 Methodology

5.1 Participants

Study participants were recruited in a master's program on inclusive education at an Austrian university and they were asked to participate in the study as part of a mandatory course in the winter term 2022/2023. Study participation was not mandatory and in no way required to pass the course. 31 students out of 36 students in the course participated in the study. The majority of the participants (87.1%) were female. All of them had at least a Bachelor's degree in educational science or a related field (psychology, social work, pedagogy). At least 19 out of the 31 have practical experience as teaching assistants or personal assistants in working with people with disabilities and/or young people with special learning needs (for the others, this is not known).

5.2 Procedure and Instruments

We answered the above research questions with an explorative study carried out in January 2023. The study was divided into two phases: In the first phase, the 31 study participants were randomly assigned to two groups. One group used the DIGIVIDget ($n = 14$) and the other group used the DIGIBOT ($n = 17$). Immediately after their learning experience, the participants filled in a questionnaire comprising 10 items regarding the system (System Usability Scale (SUS), ten items) [4] and six items regarding their evaluation of the learning content.

The SUS consists of five items representing negative aspects (even-numbered items, for example, "*I feel the system is unnecessarily complex.*") and five items representing positive aspects (odd-numbered items, for example, "*I can very well imagine using the system on a regular basis.*") of a system's usability. The additional six questions were developed by the authors and concerned the participants' evaluation of the delivery of the content, learning activities and learnability, for example, *"Even without or with little previous knowledge, the content can be well understood."*. All questions were rated on a scale ranging from 1 ("I completely disagree") to 5 ("I completely agree"). The internal consistency of the SUS in our sample (re-coded negative items) was good (Cronbach's alpha of .89) and the internal consistency of the self-developed scale was sufficient (Cronbach's alpha at .84). The quantitative data collected through the questionnaires forms the basis for answering RQs 1 and 2.

At the end of the questionnaire, we added one free-text question asking *"What did you like most about the DIGIVIDget/DIGIBOT and the learning activity? What did you not like so much?"*, where only either DIGIVIDget or DIGIBOT was presented. This question aimed to contribute to answering RQs 1, 2 and 3.

In the second phase, a smaller sample of six participants was drawn from each group. These twelve participants were also asked to try the technology they had not used in the first phase and participate in a focus group discussion one week later. All six focus group participants drawn from the DIGIBOT group also tried the DIGIVIDget and participated in the focus group discussion. From the DIGIVIDget group, one participant did not join the focus group discussion. The following questions guided the focus group discussion: (1) How did participants like each learning experience as a whole (trying both approaches one after the other), and what did they like in particular, what not so much? (2) What (if any) effect do participants see in the order of the two approaches when working through both? (3) What advantages and disadvantages do participants see (when comparing both approaches)? (4) Which approach did participants prefer and why? (5) What is the potential of both tools in the field of inclusive education in terms of competence and knowledge gain as well as learning engagement and motivation? (6) What are possible barriers to use?

Both focus group discussions took place online and lasted around 40 min; they were recorded, transcribed verbatim, and analysed applying qualitative content analysis [14]. Qualitative analysis of the discussions was used to give additional insight into RQs 1 and 2, and to answer RQs 3 and 4.

6 Results

6.1 Perceived Usability and Usefulness (RQs 1 and 2)

To answer RQ1 and RQ2, we use the results of the questionnaires regarding the usability of the DIGIVIDget and the DIGIBOT. Table 1 shows the median and the interquartile range for each question in both groups.

We can summarise that the median scores of odd questions (positive aspects, higher median means higher perceived better usability) for the DIGIVIDget group are between $MD = 3$ ($IQR = 1$) and $MD = 4$ ($IQR = 1$), and for the DIGIBOT group, all median scores were at 4 (IQR between 1 and 2). For the even questions (negative aspects, higher median means lower perceived poorer usability), the median scores in the DIGIVIDget group are between $MD = 1.5$ ($IQR = 2$) and $M = 2$ ($IQR = 2$), and in the DIGIBOT group between $MD = 1$ ($IQR = 0$) and $MD = 2$ ($IQR = 1.5$).

Table 1. The median (MD) and the interquartile range (IQR) for each SUS question and the overall mean (M) and standard deviation (SD) are shown.

#	Question	DIGIVIDget ($n = 14$) MD (IQR)	DIGIBOT ($n = 17$) MD (IQR)
1	I can very well imagine using the system on a regular basis	3 (1)	4 (1)
2	I feel the system is unnecessarily complex	2 (1)	1 (1)
3	I feel the system is easy to use	4 (2)	4 (2)
4	I think I would need technical support to use the system	2 (2)	2 (1.5)
5	I find that the various features of the system are well integrated	4 (1)	4 (1)
6	I find that there are too many inconsistencies in the system	2.5 (1)	2 (1)
7	I imagine most people will learn to master the system quickly	4 (1)	4 (2)
8	I find the operation to be very cumbersome	2 (2)	1 (1)
9	I felt very confident using the system	4 (2)	4 (1.5)
10	I had to learn a lot of things before I could work with the system	1.5 (2)	1 (0)
Overall		$M = 3.58$ ($SD = 0.77$)	$M = 4.12$ ($SD = 0.72$)

To compute an overall mean score for the SUS, we re-coded the scores of even-numbered questions or negative aspect items (by subtracting the given scores from 5 and adding 1 to them). The results showed that the overall SUS score for the DIGIVIDget group was $M = 3.58$ ($SD = 0.77$) while the score for the DIGIBOT group was $M = 4.12$ ($SD = 0.72$), indicating slightly higher perceived better usability of the DIGIBOT. However, the difference between the two groups is statistically not significant based on the Mann-Whitney-U-Test ($U = 166.5, p = 0.06$).

Besides the questions regarding usability and usefulness, the participants were asked six questions related to the content and the learning activities. Table 2 shows the median and the interquartile range for each of the questions related to the content and the learning activities. Similar to the SUS, we calculated a mean score for the overall scale. The overall scores for the DIGIVIDget groups and the DIGIBOT groups are $M = 3.31$ ($SD = 0.89$) and $M = 3.66$ ($SD = 0.83$) respectively, indicating that both systems were perceived as appealing and supporting learning (as shown by the rather high medians). There is only a small, statistically not significant difference in this regard between the two approaches ($U = 146.5, p = 0.28$).

Finally, we report results on a free-text question to participants that asked what they liked most and what least of the tool they had used in their condition

Table 2. The median (MD) and the interquartile range (IQR) for each question related to the content and learning activities and the overall mean (M) and standard deviation (SD) are shown.

#	Question	DIGIVIDget ($n = 14$) MD (IQR)	DIGIBOT ($n = 17$) MD (IQR)
1	The contents are presented in an appealing way	3.5 (2)	4 (1.5)
2	Even without or with very little previous knowledge, the content can be well understood	3 (3)	4 (3)
3	The content is presented in a way that what has been learned can easily be applied to similar situations in practical use	3.5 (1)	4 (2)
4	The learning activity is designed in varied ways	3 (2)	3 (2)
5	The learning activity is designed in such a way that it motivates to stick with it and complete it in one piece	3.5 (2)	3 (1)
6	I find that learning activities that are prepared like this one supports self-directed learning	4 (2)	4 (2)
Overall		$M = 3.31$ ($SD = 0.89$)	$M = 3.66$ ($SD = 0.83$)

(which could be the DIGIVIDget or the DIGIBOT). 21 out of 31 participants answered this question (DIGIVIDget group: $n = 8$; DIGIBOT group: $n = 13$).

As for DIGIVIDget, the participants liked the navigability and being able to try different answers before receiving the correct answer. In addition, the most negative aspect, mentioned by three participants, was the lack of enough introductory explanation to the topic and how to proceed through the content. As for the DIGIBOT, study participants liked the agent's responses, which were found to be short, concise and helpful. The most negatively mentioned aspects of the DIGIBOT were related to the user interface design. For instance, it was mentioned that *"Maybe the design could be made a little more lively and appealing"*.

6.2 Users' (Comparative) Preferences (RQ3)

Two focus group discussions were held as a follow-up after the participants used the tools. In focus group 1, the participants used the DIGIVIDget first and then the DIGIBOT, while in the second focus group, they used first the DIGIBOT and then the DIGIVIDget. Participants of the first focus group are referred to as P1 - P5, and participants of the second focus group as P6 - P11.

In the first question, the participants were asked to briefly summarise their impressions of both tools. Overall, the participants liked both tools, the DIGIVIDget and the DIGIBOT: Regarding the DIGIVIDget, P5 stated: *"I thought both contents were actually cool. I found that even with "this classic" [DIGIVIDget], there were already many different methods inside. So it was already quite varied designed. "*. referring to the DIGIVIDget and the different types of presenting the content (e.g. quizes, slides) Besides the mentioned diversity of activities in the DIGIVIDget, users also liked that with the DIGIVIDget they can take as much time as they need to deepen and strengthen the knowledge *"If you have the classic learning platform [DIGIVIDget], you can take more time and adjust to it and repeat it"* (P3). In contrast, the dialogic structure of the DIGIBOT potentially put some time pressure on them, as was mentioned in both focus groups. Another positive aspect of the DIGIVIDget mentioned in one of the focus group discussions was the clear structure of the content, while the DIGIBOT might become confusing *"if it is a large quantity [of information] that should be conveyed"* (P6). In both focus group discussions, the interactivity of the DIGIBOT was highlighted as a very positive aspect and, for example, P10 stated that learning with the DIGIBOT was a lot of fun *"So it was kind of very funny and at the same time you really learned something because it was so constructive and you had to write something into it yourself. And this was somehow a lot of fun."*. Some participants even indicated a clear preference for the DIGIBOT on an affective level, such as P11, who said *"I personally liked that one [DIGIBOT] better. I found this interactive element totally enjoyable"* or on the level of learning effect, such as P1 who stated *"the DIGIBOT alone would have been sufficient"*. In particular, direct feedback was mentioned by all participants and they agreed that this was a particularly motivating and encouraging aspect of the DIGIBOT; for example, P1 found the DIGIBOT very exciting as his learning situation changed completely and turned into *"a more motivated learning through the very positive and very appreciative feedback, so I felt like I was more motivated, but also somehow more eager to interact with the tool [DIGIBOT]"*.

Note that interacting with an educational conversational agent was a new experience for all focus group participants. This is illustrated by the following statement from P8 *"I found it [DIGIBOT] nice that it was something different and that there was simply some variety in it"*.

In the second question, we asked focus group participants about the order in which they had used both tools, and whether they had any preference regarding this. In focus group 1, the participants had used the DIGIVIDget first and the DIGIBOT afterwards. Three of the participants in this group explicitly stated that they liked the order in which they used the tools. P4, for example, said *"I actually think it's great. I noticed that at first with the classical system [DIGIVIDget] it was so that I could try it out and grasp, also in terms of content, what is it actually about and how does it actually work? And then through the bot [DIGIBOT] actually the idea to repeat once again for deepening"*.

In focus group 2, the participants had used the DIGIBOT first and the DIGIVIDget afterwards. Opinions regarding the order differed, such as P7: *"I find the classic [DIGIVIDget] good so that you learn with it at the beginning to get prior knowledge and then can start with the other [DIGIBOT]"*. Another participant from this group, P8, contradicts this: *"So I think that basically both will work, but I would also say the DIGIBOT first, [...] this interactive is, I think, good to get into. And later, when you have the slides, you can actually learn very well with it"*. P11 supports this but qualifies that there may have been a bias towards this order as it was the actual order in which tools were used for P11.

Regarding concentration, in both focus groups the predominant experience reported was that the participants were more focused and concentrated when learning with the DIGIBOT. For example, P5 stated *"I was more concentrated with the DIGIBOT because it was more interactive in my eyes and required more concentration"* and P6 said *"simply that one has the feeling [that] it reacts situational to me at the moment is conducive to attention"*. Only P10 disagreed with the prevailing opinion and said that *"I learn more concentrated when learning as typical with a text or slides [...] there I am more concentrated than with a chatbot, because I think this is somehow more relaxed"* - implicitly pointing to a potential (time) pressure perceived when working with the DIGIBOT.

6.3 DIGIVIDget and DIGIBOT in Inclusive Education (RQ4)

Finally, in both focus groups, we discussed the potential of both tools for inclusive education (RQ4). As study participants are doing their masters in inclusive education this was a reasonable discussion to lead. Almost all participants saw potential for tutorial agents in inclusive education, based on their comparative experience with both types of technology. For example, P5 stated that *"[...] the DIGIBOT has great potential for inclusion because in the context of learning difficulties, I would say, it is easier to use than the classic system [DIGIVIDget]"*. Other participants from both focus groups pointed out that children and young people (e.g. from disadvantaged backgrounds), who are hard to get excited about learning, are typical learner groups in inclusive education. They could benefit from DIGIBOT, or conversational agents in general, as it is a technology that is seen as *"very close to life worlds of the younger generation"*. P4 who works with children stated that *"Especially where there is a learning disability or especially reading difficulties, or comprehension difficulties, I thought that it would appeal well to exactly these girls, would motivate them"*. Also P11 pointed to the potential of tutorial agents to positively impact motivation: *"With children and young people, I can totally imagine that the motivation to learn increases insanely because they simply have fun with it [DIGIBOT]"*.

7 Discussion and Conclusion

We have developed and investigated two educational tools, DIGIVIDget and DIGIBOT, regarding usability and preferences by conducting a study with 31 master students in inclusive education. In this investigation, DIGIVIDget stands in for how traditional learning platforms that have developed from learning management systems (LMS), support learning by providing (interactive) learning materials in a web-based and freely navigable manner. DIGIBOT stands in for tutorial agents as a new interaction paradigm in which content and interaction are integrated into a dialogue.

Regarding usability (RQs 1 and 2), the DIGIBOT achieved better System Usability Scale (SUS) results than the DIGIVIDget. However, the difference was not statistically significant. To this knowledge, we can contribute via the discussions led within the focus groups, which further compared DIGIVIDget with DIGIBOT. Our guiding research questions for the focus group discussions were to understand user preferences towards the two technologies (RQ3) and thoughts about applicability and ways of using them (potentially in different ways) in inclusive education.

Regarding the degree of concentration, the focus group discussions indicate that participants were more focused and concentrated when using the DIGIBOT. This is in line with the findings of Cai et al. [5] in which the conversational agent kept the learners focused as they talked to and received feedback from the agent. In general, an interactive learning process needs and facilitates more concentration. Concretely, DIGIBOT asks questions and immediately gives personalised feedback to users' responses. Contrasting this, DIGIVIDget does not require as much interaction and makes skimming through content easier.

Opinions varied regarding the preferred order of usage. Discussions point to individual preferences with underlying agreement about main user experience characteristics of the two technology types: some participants referred to the DIGIVIDget as their preferred first tool to cover the whole content because they are allowed to repeat each part and can freely navigate through the whole content. These participants would use DIGIBOT subsequently to practice the content through open questions in DIGIBOT's dialogue structure. Other participants considered the DIGIBOT a better first tool to get into the topic as it clearly structures the content and facilitates, and would then use the DIGIVIDget to practice and focus on more challenging parts of the content.

Note that a suitable or preferred order of usage might also depend on the learners' domain knowledge or cognitive capability (relevant in inclusive education). In this regard, a tutorial agent (in our case: DIGIBOT) is more suitable for those having less domain knowledge and hence needing and benefitting more from guidance (cp. [13]). On the other hand, the LMS-style way of supporting learning towards the set learning goals (in our case: DIGIVIDget) allows free navigation. While this requires more self-regulated learning competence as it less strongly requires concentration and interaction, this allows learners to cover content at their own pace, and also to select content. This all points to more suitability for learners with an overall higher self-regulated learning competence or motivation, more domain knowledge, or more punctual interests (as is typical for instance for professionals as learners, cp. [16]).

Finally, the focus group discussion also addressed the potential of the tools in inclusive education, especially the DIGIBOT mentioned by both focus groups. In line with the above discussions regarding user experience and a priori suitability of tutorial agents vs. interactive and freely navigable web-based content, discussions highlighted especially two aspects: Learners with learning difficulties could benefit from tutorial agents due to their characteristic of being more interactive hence both requiring and facilitating more concentration, and due to their characteristic of more strongly requiring to follow the predetermined structure than freely navigable web-based content. Further, also children and the younger generation in more general, as well as learners who have difficulty getting excited about learning are typical target groups in inclusive education. These target groups could benefit from tutorial agents because according to the experts participating in the focus group discussion, they are potentially more motivating. Some of this may be reduced as conversational agents become more usual (now, their novelty helps make them more motivating), but the dialogic nature of interaction with tutorial agents may be intrinsically more motivating for these target groups.

Concludingly, we see that the two types of explored technologies constitute different interaction metaphors, in the sense that they allow different ways of learning through interacting with technology and content made available through it. Today's learning platforms have already moved forward from platforms that primarily share content to platforms that host learning activities (now: by social features that connect humans). This move could be continued to provide access to computational tutors and thereby support a different type of learning activity. Educational technology research now needs to think of how to combine and use the different interaction metaphors, and for what kinds of user groups which is more suitable. This work is an (early) investigation of these questions and points to follow-up work that explores the same overarching question in different domains, over time as the novelty of conversational agents is reduced, and specifically with user groups that have been identified as being different in terms of preferable interaction metaphor.

Acknowledgements. This work was supported by the "DDAI" COMET Module within the COMET-Competence Centers for Excellent Technologies Program, funded by the Austrian Federal Ministry (BMK and BMDW), the Austrian Research Promotion Agency (FFG), the province of Styria (SFG) and partners from industry and academia. The COMET Program is managed by FFG.

References

1. Adamson, D., Dyke, G., Jang, H., Rosé, C.P.: Towards an agile approach to adapting dynamic collaboration support to student needs. Int. J. AIED **24**(1), 92–124 (2014)
2. Bansah, A.K., Darko Agyei, D.: Perceived convenience, usefulness, effectiveness and user acceptance of information technology: evaluating students' experiences of a learning management system. Technol. Pedagogy Educ. **31**(4), 431–449 (2022)
3. Borjigin, A., Miao, C., Lim, S.F., Li, S., Shen, Z.: Teachable agents with intrinsic motivation. In: Conati, C., Heffernan, N., Mitrovic, A., Verdejo, M.F. (eds.) AIED 2015. LNCS (LNAI), vol. 9112, pp. 34–43. Springer, Cham (2015). https://doi.org/10.1007/978-3-319-19773-9_4
4. Brooke, J., et al.: SUS-a quick and dirty usability scale. Usability Eval. Ind. **189**(194), 4–7 (1996)
5. Cai, W., et al.: MathBot: a personalized conversational agent for learning math. ACM (2019)
6. Catania, F., Spitale, M., Cosentino, G., Garzotto, F.: Conversational agents to promote children's verbal communication skills. In: Følstad, A., et al. (eds.) CONVERSATIONS 2020. LNCS, vol. 12604, pp. 158–172. Springer, Cham (2021). https://doi.org/10.1007/978-3-030-68288-0_11

7. Cicchinelli, A., et al.: Finding traces of self-regulated learning in activity streams. In: Proceedings of the 8th International Conference on Learning Analytics and Knowledge, pp. 191–200 (2018)
8. Fessl, A., Apaolaza, A., Gledson, A., Pammer-Schindler, V., Vigo, M.: Mirror, mirror on my search...: data-driven reflection and experimentation with search behaviour. In: Scheffel, M., Broisin, J., Pammer-Schindler, V., Ioannou, A., Schneider, J. (eds.) EC-TEL 2019. LNCS, vol. 11722, pp. 83–97. Springer, Cham (2019). https://doi.org/10.1007/978-3-030-29736-7_7
9. Fessl, A., Maitz, K., Dennerlein, S., Pammer-Schindler, V.: The impact of explicating learning goals on teaching and learning in higher education: evaluating a learning goal visualization. In: De Laet, T., Klemke, R., Alario-Hoyos, C., Hilliger, I., Ortega-Arranz, A. (eds.) EC-TEL 2021. LNCS, vol. 12884, pp. 1–15. Springer, Cham (2021). https://doi.org/10.1007/978-3-030-86436-1_1
10. Grossman, J., Lin, Z., Sheng, H., Wei, J.T.Z., Williams, J.J., Goel, S.: MathBot: transforming online resources for learning math into conversational interactions. AAAI 2019 Story-Enabled Intelligence (2019)
11. Gupta, S., Chen, Y.: Supporting inclusive learning using chatbots? a chatbot-led interview study. J. Inf. Syst. Educ. **33**(1), 98–108 (2022)
12. Kim, Y., Baylor, A.L., Shen, E.: Pedagogical agents as learning companions: the impact of agent emotion and gender. J. Comput. Assist. Learn. **23**(3), 220–234 (2007)
13. Kirschner, P.A., Sweller, J., Clark, R.E.: Why minimal guidance during instruction does not work: an analysis of the failure of constructivist, discovery, problem-based, experiential, and inquiry-based teaching. Educ. Psychol. **41**(2), 75–86 (2006)
14. Kuckartz, U.: Qualitative inhaltsanalyse : Methoden, praxis, computerunterstützung (2018)
15. Leong, P.H., Goh, O.S., Yogan, J.K., Sam, Y.H., Fong, C.W.: The evaluation of user experience testing for retrieval-based model and deep learning conversational agent. Inter. J. Adv. Comput. Sci. Appl. **12**(4) (2021)
16. Littlejohn, A., Pammer-Schindler, V.: Technologies for professional learning. In: Harteis, C., Gijbels, D., Kyndt, E. (eds.) Research Approaches on Workplace Learning. PPL, vol. 31, pp. 321–346. Springer, Cham (2022). https://doi.org/10.1007/978-3-030-89582-2_15
17. Mirzababaei, B., Pammer-Schindler, V.: An educational conversational agent for GDPR. In: EC-TEL, pp. 470–476. Springer (2022). https://doi.org/10.1007/978-3-031-16290-9_38
18. Mirzababaei, B., Pammer-Schindler, V.: Learning to give a complete argument with a conversational agent: an experimental study in two domains of argumentation. In: EC-TEL, pp. 215–228. Springer (2022). https://doi.org/10.1007/978-3-031-16290-9_16
19. Neto, A.J.M., Fernandes, M.A.: Chatbot and conversational analysis to promote collaborative learning in distance education. In: 2019 IEEE 19th International Conference on Advanced Learning Technologies (ICALT), vol. 2161, pp. 324–326. IEEE (2019)
20. Pintrich, P.R.: The role of motivation in promoting and sustaining self-regulated learning. Int. J. Educ. Res. **31**(6), 459–470 (1999)
21. Pintrich, P.R.: A conceptual framework for assessing motivation and self-regulated learning in college students. Educ. Psychol. Rev. **16**(4), 385–407 (2004)
22. Redecker, C., et al.: European framework for the digital competence of educators: Digcompedu. Tech. rep, Joint Research Centre (Seville site) (2017)

23. Ruan, S., et al.: QuizBot: a dialogue-based adaptive learning system for factual knowledge. In: Proceedings of the 2019 CHI, pp. 1–13 (2019)
24. Sankey, M.D., Marshall, S.J.: Perspective chapter: the learning management system of 2028 and how we start planning for this now. In: Higher Education-Reflections From the Field. IntechOpen (2023)
25. Shirk, J.: Designing a self-paced learning experience to support learner self-regulation. J. Teach. Learn. Technol. **9**(1) (2020)
26. Turnbull, D., Chugh, R., Luck, J.: Issues in learning management systems implementation: a comparison of research perspectives between Australia and China. Educ. Inf. Technol. **26**(4), 3789–3810 (2021)
27. Vuorikari Rina, R., Kluzer, S., Punie, Y.: Digcomp 2.2: the digital competence framework for citizens-with new examples of knowledge, skills and attitudes. Tech. rep., Joint Research Centre (Seville site) (2022)
28. Wambsganss, T., Kueng, T., Soellner, M., Leimeister, J.M.: ArgueTutor: an adaptive dialog-based learning system for argumentation skills. In: Proceedings of the CHI, pp. 1–13 (2021)
29. Wolfbauer, I., Pammer-Schindler, V., Maitz, K., Rosé, C.P.: A script for conversational reflection guidance: a field study on developing reflection competence with apprentices. IEEE Trans. Learn. Technol. **15**(5) (2022)
30. Zhao, J., Song, T., Sun, Y.: APIHelper: helping junior android programmers learn API usage. IAENG Int. J. Comput. Sci. **47**(1), 92–97 (2020)

Assessing the Quality of Multiple-Choice Questions Using GPT-4 and Rule-Based Methods

Steven Moore(✉), Huy A. Nguyen, Tianying Chen, and John Stamper

Carnegie Mellon University, Pittsburgh, PA 15213, USA
StevenJamesMoore@gmail.com

Abstract. Multiple-choice questions with item-writing flaws can negatively impact student learning and skew analytics. These flaws are often present in student-generated questions, making it difficult to assess their quality and suitability for classroom usage. Existing methods for evaluating multiple-choice questions often focus on machine readability metrics, without considering their intended use within course materials and their pedagogical implications. In this study, we compared the performance of a rule-based method we developed to a machine-learning based method utilizing GPT-4 for the task of automatically assessing multiple-choice questions based on 19 common item-writing flaws. By analyzing 200 student-generated questions from four different subject areas, we found that the rule-based method correctly detected 91% of the flaws identified by human annotators, as compared to 79% by GPT-4. We demonstrated the effectiveness of the two methods in identifying common item-writing flaws present in the student-generated questions across different subject areas. The rule-based method can accurately and efficiently evaluate multiple-choice questions from multiple domains, outperforming GPT-4 and going beyond existing metrics that do not account for the educational use of such questions. Finally, we discuss the potential for using these automated methods to improve the quality of questions based on the identified flaws.

Keywords: Question evaluation · Question quality · Rule-based · GPT-4

1 Introduction

Multiple-choice questions (MCQs) are a widely used form of assessment in higher education, both for formative and summative evaluations. MCQs are advantageous because of their efficiency to score, objective grading, ability to generate item-analysis data, and the shorter time required for students to respond [5]. In recent years, the task of authoring educational MCQs is no longer specific to instructors, and the popularization of automatic question generation (AQG) systems further scaled up this process [21]. Another method for scaling the creation of educational MCQs is having students take part in the process of question creation, commonly referred to as a form of learnersourcing [35]. Student-generated questions often have higher quality, and target more complex cognitive processes compared to AQG [14]. The process of generating questions also has educational benefits for students and can lead to positive learning outcomes, such as improved retention and transfer [19].

O. Viberg et al. (Eds.): EC-TEL 2023, LNCS 14200, pp. 229–245, 2023.
https://doi.org/10.1007/978-3-031-42682-7_16

While student-generated questions typically have higher quality than those created through automated methods, their quality may widely vary due to multiple uncontrollable factors [28]. On one hand, poorly designed MCQs may exhibit characteristics that can be exploited by pattern recognition and guessing, thus leading to shallow learning [9]. On the other hand, ensuring high-quality MCQs, whether created by AQG or students, is itself a challenging task. Common evaluation methods used by previous research include using experts, other students, or automated methods [25]. Even though automatic methods are most efficient, they come with important caveats. Notably, existing automated methods often rely on the surface-level features of a question, such as the readability of text length, without considering the pedagogical value it adds to the assessment [2]. Additionally, these methods are often applied to datasets consisting of questions targeted at lower academic grade levels, such as basic reading comprehension, or questions that are not used in an educational context at all [14]. While the use of human experts might provide the most accurate assessment of question quality, the manual evaluation process often lacks standardization and efficiency [21]. However, human evaluation can provide a more in-depth analysis, considering the question's potential to support learning. For instance, the Item-Writing Flaws (IWFs) rubric is an effective evaluation method which considers the pedagogical value of the question and its answer choices through various criteria [3, 8]. This rubric typically consists of 19 items that assess whether an educational MCQ is acceptable for use in the classroom or not. However, applying this rubric to a large number of questions can be time-consuming and often requires human expertise.

To address this gap, we explored two automatic methods to evaluate educational MCQs using the IWF rubric. The first method utilizes a rule-based approach to apply the rubric, making it easy to modify and maintain interpretability, while not requiring a large training dataset. Our second method relies on GPT-4, a large multimodal model capable of processing text inputs and producing text outputs, which has achieved human-level performance on various professional and academic benchmarks [30]. This second method prompts GPT-4 to apply the IWF criteria to the provided questions one at a time. Using student-generated questions from four distinct subject areas, we evaluated both methods and compared them to human expert evaluation that also utilized the IWF rubric. We investigate to what extent a rule-based multi-label classifier and GPT-4 can accurately identify IWFs in student-generated MCQs. With this setting, our research questions are as follows:

RQ1: How does automatic evaluation of educational MCQs using the IWF rubric compare to human evaluation?

RQ2: How does the performance of the automatic application of the IWF rubric vary across subject areas?

RQ3: Which IWFs are the most common in student-generated educational questions?

2 Related Work

2.1 Evaluating Assessment Questions with Student Data

Educational MCQs generated by instructors, students, or through automated methods are all susceptible to flaws that impact their efficacy and quality [33]. One challenge in evaluating MCQs' quality lies in determining what criteria are sufficient to indicate that a question has high quality and is effective for use in an educational context. To overcome this subjectivity, different item response theory and statistical methods have been utilized to evaluate student-generated MCQs, such as the Item Difficulty Index and the Discrimination Index [18, 21]. These techniques require post-hoc analysis of student performance data on the questions, as they use the percentage of students that answered the question correctly and measure the question's ability to differentiate between students who have a high level of knowledge and those who do not. However, this can be detrimental to the learning process, because if the questions being used have not been first vetted for their quality, then they may be poorly constructed which can negatively impact students' performance and achievement, causing these analyses to be inaccurate [6]. To avoid potential harm to student learning and save them time from answering questions with potentially low quality, questions should be evaluated prior to classroom usage. Towards this goal, recent research has investigated different methods for evaluating educational MCQs that utilize smaller amounts of student data, or no student data at all, to achieve a higher quality evaluation [7]. For instance, work by [39] utilized small amounts of student data along with their perceptions of certain questions to acquire a comprehensive evaluation of questions in an educational context.

2.2 Human Evaluation of Assessment Questions

The use of the IWF rubric is effective at evaluating educational questions, yet the application often requires substantial human effort and is time-consuming, especially when evaluating a large number of questions across multiple subject areas [16]. Human evaluation of both AQG and student-generated MCQs often serves as a benchmark for comparing how well a method classified the quality of the educational questions [4, 21]. This evaluation consists of one or more experts judging the questions based on "best practice" conventions, which can include their pure subjective judgment, such as indicating if they would use the question in their class, or the more formal application of a standardized rubric [11]. The most common human evaluation methods involve the application of a rubric. This practice helps to standardize the process, improve replicability, and decrease subjectivity [31]. While different rubrics have been employed for this process, the Item-Writing Flaws (IWFs) rubric containing 19 criteria for assessing educational questions has been standardized and evaluated via previous research [3, 28, 33]. One such study that utilized this 19-item rubric assessed the quality of over two thousand MCQs [37]. Utilizing two human evaluators, they determined that nearly half of the questions were deemed unacceptable for educational usage, due to having more than one IWF. In this case, the question difficulties may be skewed to be too easy or too hard, which in turn misleads students and related learning analytics [9].

2.3 Automatic Evaluation of Assessment Questions

The automatic evaluation of questions usually employs metrics such as readability and explainability, based on natural language processing (NLP) metrics like BLEU and METEOR [34]. However, recent research has shown that these metrics do not correlate with human evaluation and do not consider the pedagogical value of the questions [22]. To improve the classification accuracy of a question's quality, recent efforts have focused on training classification models using large datasets of student responses [29, 32]. These methods rarely utilize questions from complex domains that go beyond the cognitive process of recall [21]. Additionally, the model architectures used in these methods are often difficult to interpret because they have black-box evaluation criteria. For instance, a recent study achieved an 81.22% accuracy in classifying question quality using recurrent neural networks [32]. However, the classification criteria used a single label based on how "shallow" or "deep" human raters found the question to be, which may be subjective and hard to replicate. In another study, GPT-3 was used to assess the quality of short answer questions in post-secondary education and often overestimated the quality [27]. The authors proposed that this overestimation was due to the high complexity of the input questions, but verifying this conjecture was difficult due to the black-box model. To improve interpretability and accuracy, prior research has turned to rule-based classification methods, which can offer feedback on why a question was classified a certain way [40]. Rule-based methods break down the classification criteria into smaller components, making it easier to identify specific patterns and features within the data, and achieving similar or greater success than black-box models, such as deep learning methods [41].

3 Methods

3.1 Dataset

The datasets used in this study were collected from a digital learning platform used by several public universities and community colleges in the western United States. The data comes from students using the platform in their respective courses during the 2020 and 2021 academic years. The four courses are introductory Chemistry, introductory Biochemistry, introductory Statistics, and a course on learning how to effectively collaborate, referred to as CollabU. Students in these courses were undergraduates, towards the beginning of their studies, and pursuing either a two- or four-year degree.

As students worked through the digital learning materials on the platform in their respective courses, they were prompted to create a multiple-choice question (MCQ). The prompt asked students to create a single MCQ about a topic they had recently learned in their course. Each MCQ consists of a question text, known as the *stem*, and four answer choices, one of which must be denoted as correct. The creation of this MCQ was done directly in the digital learning platform with no additional tools utilized. Students did not receive any assistance or feedback as they created their questions. Additionally, it was presented in the same visual manner as the other activities found on the platform. From each of these four courses, we randomly selected 50 student-generated questions to utilize for this study, resulting in a total of 200 MCQs.

3.2 Human Evaluation

In order to assess the quality of the student-generated MCQs, we utilized a series of guidelines for identifying Item-Writing Flaws (IWFs), which are based on a taxonomy of 31 multiple-choice item-writing guidelines [10]. The exact rubric we used for the study was a modified version that consists of 19 unique items and has been used and validated in previous studies [3, 8, 28]. Following [37], a question with 0 or 1 flaw identified by the rubric is considered *acceptable* and any questions with 2 or more flaws is considered *unacceptable*. This distinction is used to determine if a question could be utilized in a class as a formative assessment that the instructor would trust. A full description of the 19 items that make up the rubric can be found in Table 1.

Two item raters evaluated each student-generated MCQ, following the 19 IWF guidelines. Both raters had content-area expertise across all four domains, ample experience developing multiple-choice questions, and multiple prior training sessions in writing high quality assessments. Using the IWF rubric, the raters went through each of the 200 student-generated MCQs and applied the rubric to the question text and accompanying answer choices for each student contribution. The inter-rater reliability (IRR) values between the two evaluators for each rubric item are also reported in Table 1. It includes the percentage agreement and Cohen's Kappa κ statistic [26] as a measure of IRR for all rubric items. All items were at either a near perfect or substantial level of agreement between the raters. The two evaluators then met to resolve any disagreements in their evaluations and discussed discordant questions until they reached a consensus on the coding. We acknowledge that, despite the two expert evaluators' backgrounds and high IRR, they could still interpret the student-generated questions differently, based on their prior knowledge and linguistic preferences [2].

Table 1. The rubric of 19 Item-Writing Flaws used to evaluate the student-generated multiple-choice questions. The bracketed numbers indicate agreement percentage between raters and Cohen's κ value for each item.

Item-Writing Flaw	Attributes of questions that do not contain the flaw
Ambiguous or unclear information (87.50%, $\kappa = 0.66$)	Questions and all options should be written in clear, unambiguous language
Implausible distractors (96.00%, $\kappa = 0.82$)	Make all distractors plausible as good items depend on having effective distractors
None of the above (100%, $\kappa = 1.00$)	Avoid none of the above as it only really measures students ability to detect incorrect answers
Longest option correct (97.00%, $\kappa = 0.83$)	Often the correct option is longer and includes more detailed information, which clues students to this option
Gratuitous information (89.50%, $\kappa = 0.71$)	Avoid unnecessary information in the stem that is not required to answer the question
True/false question (100%, $\kappa = 1.00$)	The options should not be a series of true/false statements
Convergence cues (89.50%, $\kappa = 0.70$)	Avoid convergence cues in options where there are different combinations of multiple components to the answer

(continued)

Table 1. (*continued*)

Item-Writing Flaw	Attributes of questions that do not contain the flaw
Logical cues (88.00%, $\kappa = 0.68$)	Avoid clues in the stem and the correct option that can help the test-wise student to identify the correct option
All of the above (100%, $\kappa = 1.00$)	Avoid all of the above options as students can guess correct responses based on partial information
Fill-in-blank (100%, $\kappa = 1.00$)	Avoid omitting words in the middle of the stem that students must insert from the options provided
Absolute terms (100%, $\kappa = 1.00$)	Avoid the use of absolute terms (e.g. never, always, all) in the options as students are aware that they are almost always false
Word repeats (97.00%, $\kappa = 0.83$)	Avoid similarly worded stems and correct responses or words repeated in the stem and correct response
Unfocused stem (94.50%, $\kappa = 0.79$)	The stem should present a clear and focused question that can be understood and answered without looking at the options
Complex or K-type (94.00%, $\kappa = 0.78$)	Avoid questions that have a range of correct responses, that ask students to select from a number of possible combinations of the responses
Grammatical cues (92.50%, $\kappa = 0.76$)	All options should be grammatically consistent with the stem and should be parallel in style and form
Lost sequence (97.50%, $\kappa = 0.89$)	All options should be arranged in chronological or numerical order
Vague terms (98.50%, $\kappa = 0.93$)	Avoid the use of vague terms (e.g. frequently, occasionally) in the options as there is seldom agreement on their actual meaning
More than one correct (100%, $\kappa = 1.00$)	In single best-answer form, questions should have 1, and only 1, best answer
Negative worded (100%, $\kappa = 1.00$)	Negatively worded stems are less likely to measure important learning outcomes and can confuse students

3.3 Rule-Based Evaluation

The task of automatically applying the Item-Writing Flaws rubric to MCQs is a multi-label classification problem, as each question may be matched with several criteria [1]. In order to implement this automated method, we followed a rule-based approach that applies each individual rubric criteria via its own logic. Rule-based approaches have been used in similar educational tasks such as classifying the Bloom's Taxonomy of a question [12]. Such an approach is particularly effective when the problem suffers from a lack of training data, as is the case in the present study, due to a lack of public datasets containing questions that are evaluated for their educational quality [15]. Furthermore, a rule-based approach allows for vastly improved interpretability compared to traditional black-box classification approaches, such as neural networks [41].

Working alongside the human evaluators, we constructed a script that is composed of a programmatic method for each of the 19 IWF rubric criteria. It uses several Python libraries and three different pre-trained large language models (LLMs) to implement the 19 different criteria. The logic for many of the criteria involved string manipulation, such as checking if the *longest option was the correct answer*. Other criteria involved the use of standard NLP techniques, such as Named Entity Recognition or Part-of-Speech tagging [36] to help identify if a *word is repeated* between the question's stem and correct answer. The more challenging and advanced criteria, such as identifying if a question contains *implausible distractors*, involved the use of LLMs. For instance, a RoBERTa classifier pretrained on the Corpus of Linguistic Acceptability (CoLA) was utilized to help identify *ambiguous or unclear information* in a question's stem [20]. To determine if a question contained *more than one correct answer*, we leveraged GPT-4's capabilities for question answering [30]. For a more detailed explanation of the programmatically implemented 19 IWFs criteria, the final code is made publicly available[1], however the student question data is currently private and can be made available upon request.

3.4 GPT-4 Evaluation

The second automatic evaluation method utilizes GPT-4, a transformer-based multi-modal model pre-trained to predict the next token in a document [30]. We utilize GPT-4 as our second automated method as it has achieved human-level performance on academic tasks, such as standardized college-level exams in Psychology, History, and Math. It has also achieved state-of-the-art performance on traditional machine learning benchmarks, such as the MMLU, which consists of 57 tasks from a variety of domains that are used to demonstrate a model's extensive world knowledge and problem-solving ability [13]. What also makes GPT-4 unique compared to many other language models, is the ability to follow natural language prompts to perform specific tasks [24]. These prompts serve as instructions for the model to perform, such as providing the model with a rubric and multiple-choice question and then prompting it to apply the rubric criteria to the question.

The exact wording of the prompts provided to GPT-4 can drastically influence the output the model provides [23]. Towards this end, our task involved providing GPT-4 with a single IWF rubric criteria at a time and having it state if the provided question satisfied that given criteria or not. The names of the criteria we used as well as their definitions are nearly identical to the ones shown in Table 1. We opted to directly use the prompts rather than continually engineering prompts to determine the best output. While we believe refinement of the prompts is valuable future work, we wanted to see how well GPT-4 would perform applying the same IWF rubric and giving it instructions akin to what would be provided to a human evaluator. Specifically, the prompt we provided GPT-4 for each IWF rubric criteria and question states: *Begin your response with yes or no, does this multiple-choice question satisfy the criteria relating to {criteria}: {definition}? Explain why. {question}*. The rubric criteria, definition of the criteria, and the multiple-choice question including all answer options are input into the prompt respectively.

[1] https://github.com/StevenJamesMoore/ECTEL23/blob/main/IWF.ipynb.

Additionally, we utilized the default parameters of the model and accessed it using the GPT-4 API via the Python programming language.

Note, the prompt instructions also asked GPT-4 to provide an explanation as to why a question satisfies or violates the criteria, which was done to encourage a more thorough and accurate response from the model [17]. A human evaluator went through each of the responses and coded them as GPT-4 indicating if the criteria was satisfied or violated. Although we had originally intended to use a simple "Yes" or "No" response to indicate whether the criteria were met, we found that this approach was not always clear in distinguishing whether the criteria had been violated or satisfied.

4 Results

4.1 Automatic Methods versus Human Identification

The 19 IWF criteria were automatically applied to all 200 student-generated questions, resulting in a total of 3800 classifications. The rule-based method matched 90.87% of human classifications, achieving an exact match ratio of 15%, where all of the 19 IWF criteria matched the human evaluation for the question. The GPT-4 method matched 78.89% of human classifications, achieving an exact match ratio of 12%. We also considered the Hamming loss, which is a measure of the difference between two sets of binary labels and calculated as the fraction of labels that are incorrectly predicted [38]. The rule-based method achieved a Hamming Loss of 0.09 and the GPT-4 method achieved a Hamming Loss of 0.21, indicating that on average 9% and 21% of the flaws were misclassified respectively. Table 2 displays the number of IWFs assigned to questions for each evaluation method grouped by counts. A paired t-test showed a small significant difference in the number of IWFs identified for each question by the human ($M = 1.6$, $SD = 1.3$) and rule-based ($M = 2.1$, $SD = 1.4$) methods, $t(199) = 5.59$, $p < .001$. The rule-based evaluation method more commonly identified potential flaws in the questions compared to the humans. Another paired t-test showed a significant difference in the number of IWFs identified for each question by the human ($M = 1.6$, $SD = 1.3$) and GPT-4 ($M = 4.2$, $SD = 3.4$) methods, $t(199) = 11.8$, $p < .001$. The GPT-4 evaluation identified even more potential flaws in the questions compared to both the human and rule-based methods. While the human and rule-based methods never found more than six IWFs per question, the GPT-4 method found up to thirteen.

Table 2. Counts of IWFs per question from all three evaluation methods.

Number of Flaws	0	1	2	3	4	5	6	7	8	9	10	11	12	13
Human Evaluation	39	72	42	28	9	6	2	0	0	0	0	0	0	0
Rule-based Evaluation	23	49	56	34	27	8	1	0	0	0	0	0	0	0
GPT-4 Evaluation	30	23	25	24	13	17	7	19	11	11	9	7	1	1

When the quality of the questions were labeled as acceptable (< 2 IWFs) or unacceptable ($\geq$ 2 IWFs), a chi-square test revealed there was a significant relationship between the question quality and three evaluation methods, $\chi^2(2, N = 200) = 36.64, p < .001$. Between the three methods, GPT-4 was more likely to evaluate a question as having unacceptable quality. The human evaluation identified 111 acceptable and 89 unacceptable questions, while the rule-based evaluation matched 130 (65%) of these (57 acceptable, 73 unacceptable). The GPT-4 evaluation matched 123 (62%) of the human quality evaluations (44 acceptable, 79 unacceptable). Figure 1 shows the confusion matrices for the quality classifications based on the number of IWFs found in each question between the human and rule-based evaluation and the human and GPT-4 evaluation.

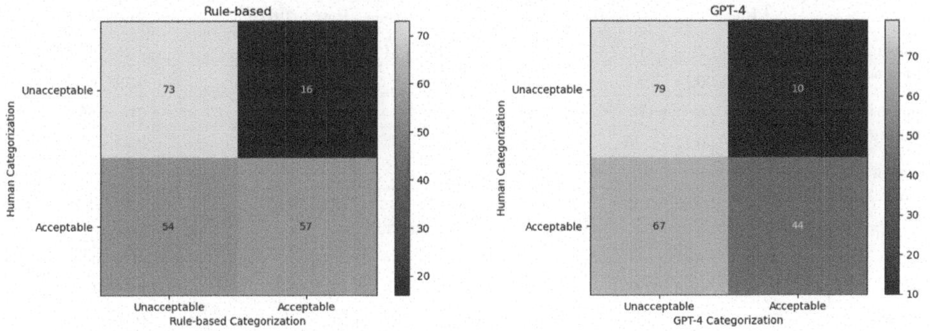

Fig. 1. Confusion matrices for the classification of a question's quality for the rule-based method (left) and the GPT-4 method (right).

4.2 Impact of the Domain

The automatic evaluation methods, rule-based and GPT-4, performed differently across criteria and domains, with the rule-based method outperforming GPT-4 on all four domains. Table 3 shows the performance of all three evaluation methods across all four domains. Between the datasets, we use F1 scores to evaluate success. Since a majority of the questions meet the criteria rather than violate them, the F1 score provides a better measure over accuracy, as it includes false negatives and false positives. From Table 3, we observe that the rule-based and GPT-4 methods commonly matched human evaluation for some criteria, such as *none of the above* and *negative worded*, and performed poorly for other criteria, such as *logical cues* and *more than one correct*. In particular, the rule-based method achieves high F1 scores for *longest option correct* and *true/false question* compared to GPT-4. Note, the rules for these two criteria can be easily implemented programmatically, as they only check for text length and keywords.

Both the rule-based and GPT-4 methods have a lower micro-average F1 score, the computed proportion of correctly classified observations out of all observations, for the Chemistry and Biochemistry courses compared to Statistics and CollabU. This may be in part due to the similar domains of these science courses, where the human evaluators focused more on the objective of the questions, rather than the grammar, while the automated methods did not. Additionally, some of the poor performance related to F1 scores is due to the small number of that flaw being found in the questions. For instance, *gratuitous information* and *vague terms* have poor performance by F1 score, but those flaws are quite rare across all four courses. Ultimately, the rule-based method outperformed GPT-4, by measure of micro-average F1 score, across all four domains.

Table 3. The count of flaws (N) and performance (F1) of the human evaluation (Hum) compared to both the rule-based (Rule) and GPT-4 (GPT) methods across all four domains. A dash (-) in the table indicates that the flaw was not present in any question of that dataset based on human evaluation and therefore no F1 score is computed.

Item-Writing Flaws		Chemistry			Biochemistry			Statistics			CollabU		
		Hum	Rule	GPT	Hum	Rule	GPT	Hum	Rule	GPT	Hum	Rule	GPT
ambiguous information	N	12	2	11	7	4	25	14	11	25	7	7	40
	F1	–	0.14	0.61	–	0.00	0.25	–	0.40	0.41	–	0.29	0.30
implausible distractors	N	10	6	17	3	9	16	8	9	17	25	21	29
	F1	–	0.12	0.30	–	0.33	0.11	–	0.82	0.16	–	0.83	0.78
none of the above	N	7	8	6	3	3	3	1	1	1	1	1	1
	F1	–	0.80	0.62	–	1.00	0.67	–	1.00	0.00	–	1.00	1.00
longest option correct	N	5	5	6	2	2	11	3	3	6	9	10	13 implePara>
	F1	–	0.80	0.18	–	1.00	0.00	–	1.00	0.44	–	0.95	0.36
gratuitous information	N	0	0	2	7	5	25	3	0	18	0	0	19
	F1	–	–	0.00	–	0.67	0.38	–	0.00	0.29	–	–	0.00
true/false question	N	2	3	1	6	11	11	1	1	3	3	3	4
	F1	–	0.80	0.67	–	0.59	0.24	–	1.00	0.00	–	1.00	0.29
convergence cues	N	2	12	12	12	36	13	9	11	18	10	16	16
	F1	–	0.14	0.14	–	0.50	0.24	–	0.80	0.30	–	0.77	0.23
logical cues	N	2	2	9	2	6	15	3	1	18	10	0	23
	F1	–	0.00	0.00	–	0.00	0.00	–	0.00	0.10	–	0.00	0.36
all of the above	N	2	0	1	3	0	2	1	0	1	2	1	3
	F1	–	0.00	0.67	–	0.00	0.80	–	0.00	1.00 implePara>	–	0.67	0.80
fill-in-the-blank	N	2	2	3	4	3	2	0	0	0	1	1	4
	F1	–	1.00	0.00	–	0.86	0.67	–	–	–	–	1.00	0.40
absolute terms	N	2	6	1	6	19	9	0	2	1	7	10	6
	F1	-	0.00	0.00	–	0.40	0.27	–	0.00	0.00	–	0.71	0.62
word repeats	N	0	0	2	8	0	7	0	0	6	3	2	5
	F1	–	–	0.00	–	0.00	0.13	–	–	0.00	–	0.00	0.25
unfocused stem	N	0	2	7	5	4	15	7	3	17	4	4	28
	F1	–	0.00	0.00	–	0.44	0.30	–	0.40	0.50	–	0.75	0.25
complex or K-type	N	2	0	6	6	9	6	3	2	14	1	1	27
	f1	–	0.00	0.25	–	0.53	0.50	–	0.80	0.24	–	1.00	0.07
grammatical cues	N	1	3	17	13	24 implePara>	14	5	13	20	11	18	36
	F1	–	0.00	0.11	–	0.65	0.30	–	0.44	0.32	–	0.76	0.38
lost sequence	N	0	2	12	2	0	12	11	11	17	0	0	7
	F1	–	0.00	0.00	–	0.00	0.29	–	0.91	0.43	–	–	0.00

(continued)

Table 3. (*continued*)

Item-Writing Flaws		Chemistry			Biochemistry			Statistics			CollabU		
		Hum	Rule	GPT	Hum	Rule	GPT	Hum	Rule	GPT	Hum	Rule	GPT
vague terms	N	0	0	0	2	0	4	0	0	3	0	0	10
	F1	–	–	–	–	0.00	0.00	–	–	0.00	–	–	0.00
more than one correct	N	0	13	5	0	4	14	0	20	16	4	10	22
	F1	–	0.00	0.00	–	0.00	0.00	–	0.00	0.00	–	0.43	0.15
negative worded	N	0	0	0	8	14	15	2	3	2	6	7	6
	F1	–	–	–	–	0.64	0.70	–	0.80	1.00	–	0.92	1.00
micro-avg		–	0.30	0.25	–	0.48	0.28	–	0.56	0.30	–	0.70	0.36
totals		49	66	118	99	149	219	71	91	203	104	112	299

4.3 Common Item-Writing Flaws

The most frequently identified violated criteria varied across the three methods, although in some domains the rule-based and GPT-4 methods had similar classifications to the human evaluation. Table 3 shows that the *implausible distractor* criteria was violated the most across all questions in human evaluation, whereas *vague terms* was the least violated. On the other hand, the rule-based method found *convergence cues* to be the most commonly violated criteria and *vague terms* to also be the least violated. As for the GPT-4 method, the most commonly violated criteria was *ambiguous unclear information*, and *all of the above* was the least violated. Although the most frequently violated criteria varied across all three methods, the rule-based and GPT-4 methods shared similar results with human evaluation. Specifically, the rule-based method's most violated criteria ranked as the third most violated criteria in human evaluation, while the GPT-4 method's most violated criteria ranked second.

A Pearson correlation coefficient showed there was a significant positive correlation between the number of flaws identified for each criteria between the rule-based and human evaluations for Biochemistry ($r(17) = .747, p < .001$), Statistics ($r(17) = .496, p < .05$), and CollabU ($r(17) = .833, p < .001$). However, this correlation was not found to be significant for Chemistry ($r(17) = .191, p = .433$). A Pearson correlation coefficient was also computed for the number of flaws identified for each criteria between the GPT-4 and human evaluations. There was a significant positive correlation found for Statistics ($r(17) = .756, p < .001$), and CollabU ($r(17) = .4702, p < .05$). No significant correlation was found for Chemistry ($r(17) = .443, p = .057$) and Biochemistry ($r(17) = .262, p = .278$). This suggests that for Statistics and CollabU, both automated methods identified similar trends in the violated criteria – i.e., if a flaw was commonly found by human evaluation, it was also likely to be commonly found by the automated methods.

5 Discussion

In this work, we developed an automatic rule-based method and assessed its performance compared to GPT-4 and human annotation for evaluating the quality of educational MCQs using the IWF rubric. In contrast to prior research, we employed criteria that pertain directly to the pedagogical value of the question across multiple dimensions. We found that this method can perform at a level comparable to human evaluation for certain rubric criteria and outperforms GPT-4 in the same task across all rubric criteria. The rule-based method was effective in evaluating questions across four distinct subject areas, even with the presence of domain-specific jargon. When comparing the results of our automatic evaluation methods to human evaluation, we identified commonly found IWFs in student-generated questions across the four subject areas. Our results suggest that using a rule-based multi-label classification method can achieve a high level of accuracy while also maintaining interpretability, which the GPT-4 method lacks.

Both of the automatic methods' classifications were stricter, in the sense that they assigned many more IWFs to the student-generated questions than human experts, particularly GPT-4. However, this is preferable to being less strict, as guaranteeing high-quality questions during the evaluation process is crucial so as to not disrupt student learning. Additionally, both of the automatic methods could easily help filter out questions whose quality is too low for human review, e.g., if a question has four or more IWFs, it would likely take substantial time to review and could be dropped. This filtering capability of the rule-based method is supported by our results showing that it matches 65% of human classification when categorizing questions as *acceptable* or *unacceptable*, based on the IWF count. This method of binary classification of quality is commonly used in MCQ evaluation and has a performance level comparable to other models using similar educational datasets [29, 32]. Additionally, these automatic methods could be identifying criteria that were missed by the human evaluators, rather than misclassifying questions with the IWF rubric criteria.

While GPT-4's training data included material from the four course domains used in this study, its black-box nature poses challenges in interpreting why it might be misclassifying specific IWF criteria [30]. For instance, the GPT-4 method achieves extremely low F1 scores for *gratuitous information*, *unfocused stem*, and *vague terms*, all of which relate to the question's stem being unnecessarily verbose. Our analysis revealed that GPT-4 identifies a significantly high number of these three flaws across questions in each domain compared to the human and rule-based methods. This could mean that GPT-4 is mistakenly combining these criteria due to their similarity, marking them all as violated based on a single flaw. In contrast, the rule-based method can be designed to implement each criteria explicitly without overlapping with other flaws.

Across the four different subject areas utilized in this study, we found that both the rule-based and GPT-4 methods performed better on Statistics and CollabU, compared to Chemistry and Biochemistry. This may be in part due to the latter two domains containing questions that use more terminologies and jargon, making some of the NLP techniques less effective [7]. Interestingly, the rule-based method achieved more than double the micro-average F1 score of the GPT-4 method in CollabU. GPT-4's worse performance in this case may be due to proper nouns being included in the question text. The human evaluators familiar with the course content would find the usage of the proper nouns acceptable and the rule-based method does not leverage proper nouns in many of the criteria. However, GPT-4 may identify these as errors in the question as it lacks the necessary context to know if they are essential to the question or not.

Compared to the other course domains, CollabU, a course on learning how to effectively collaborate, may have more recall-level student-generated questions. In contrast, the other domains may include more complex questions that involve formulas or numbers that are challenging to decipher for the automatic methods. Criteria such as *lost sequence* are also more applicable to domains such as Chemistry or Statistics as they may include question options that are purely numerical, causing the arrangement of options to matter. Additionally, both automatic methods performed the worst in Chemistry and Biochemistry, two closely related science courses. IWF criteria such as *grammatical cues* and *convergence cues* were excessively identified by both methods compared to the human evaluators. With the subjectivity that arises from human evaluation, even when applying a standardized rubric, it is possible the evaluators were less focused on grammar in this domain and more focused on the objective of the question, prioritizing *what* was being asked more than *how* it was being asked. This highlights the need for automatic evaluation methods that can focus on both the syntax and the question's content that is critical to the domain and pedagogy. In contrast to human evaluation, automatic methods scale easier, reduce human subjectivity leading to enhanced replicability, and can be used by individuals without domain expertise.

Finally, the rule-based method demonstrated effectiveness in identifying IWFs that are common in accordance with human evaluation in each of the datasets analyzed. In line with previous research, *ambiguous or unclear information* and *implausible distractors* were two of the most identified flaws across all questions by the human, rule-based, and GPT-4 methods [33, 37]. Our analysis revealed that 50% of the questions in the CollabU dataset exhibited the *implausible distractors* flaw. Again, this may be attributed to the recall-based nature of the material in this domain, which could make it challenging for students to generate plausible alternative options for the questions. In contrast to [33, 37], our datasets contained a high percentage of questions with the *convergence cues* flaw. This might be a result of the digital interface that students used to construct MCQs in our study, as it might have encouraged them to copy the correct answer and then modify it, leading to the prevalence of this flaw. In turn, these findings can inform teachers of the common flaws that they should focus on when refining student-generated MCQs and providing them with feedback on the task.

We expected both automatic methods to perform highly on the IWF criteria *more than one correct*, as they both leverage GPT-4, which has achieved success in these course domains [30]. However, the presence of different flaws, such as incorrect grammar or the inclusion of proper nouns, may cause the question to be confusing, potentially misleading GPT-4 into incorrectly answering some of the questions. Additionally, while criteria such as *none of the above* and *fill-in-the-blank* might initially appear to be easy to achieve near perfect accuracy on, they can give both the rule-based and GPT-4 methods difficulty. For instance, the rule-based method, which uses keyword matching, might not properly detect *none of the above* if there is a spelling mistake or if there are extra words amongst the given option. Similarly, GPT-4 was often overzealous at detecting these flaws, as at times it interpreted different answer options as effectively containing text akin to *none of the above*, despite it not explicitly being an option.

6 Limitations and Future Work

We identified several limitations to our study that may be addressed in future research. First, our study relies on several datasets of student-generated questions, whose quality may vary by the subject area and individual students. Analyzing educational MCQs from other domains that contain a different variety of flaws could lead to more holistic and generalizable findings. It should be noted that the classification of questions in our study is inherently subjective due to the nature of human evaluation. To mitigate this, we employed a standardized IWF rubric and achieved a high inter-rater reliability (IRR) for each criteria. However, it is possible that different evaluators may arrive at different results. The code implementation used to identify the item-writing flaws could be adjusted to achieve different results. For example, variations in threshold for cosine similarity, utilizing an alternative implementation of a method from a different library, or rewording the GPT-4 prompts could affect the outcome.

Finally, the use of GPT-4 poses challenges with replicability, despite providing the prompts and default hyperparameters used in this research. One challenge is that the output of GPT-4 still requires human evaluation to interpret and verify what the model intended, as even when it is prompted for specific phrasing, it may still respond in a conflating manner. Another related challenge is that the model is both inherently random to some degree and still under development, meaning at a future point in time it might perform differently given the same tasks as this research. In order to promote transparency and reproducibility of our research, we have open-sourced our code. This allows for full visibility into the logic used for classifying each item-writing flaw and maintains interpretability so that other researchers can easily make any desired modifications. A promising future direction of this work is to both improve the classification accuracy of these flaws and extend the automatic methods to also provide suggestions for addressing the identified flaws. While GPT-4 may have not been as accurate as the rule-based method for identifying the flaws, it can provide explanations and suggest improvements to the questions.

7 Conclusion

In this paper, we proposed a novel rule-based method for automatically evaluating the quality of educational multiple-choice questions using criteria from the Item-Writing Flaws rubric. The results indicate that the rule-based method accurately assesses the quality of student-generated questions across multiple distinct subject areas and highlights the occurrence of different flaws in questions across these domains. It outperforms GPT-4 in applying the Item-Writing Flaws rubric across all four domains when compared to human evaluation. Both automated methods demonstrate how certain flaws may be easier or harder to identify, depending on the subject area. We contribute a categorization and comparison of item-writing flaws found in student-generated questions across four different subject areas. These results provide a valuable baseline performance measure for future research. This work also opens further opportunities for developing open and interpretable methods for evaluating educational questions by pedagogical values.

References

1. Alazaidah, R., Thabtah, F., Al-Radaideh, Q.: A multi-label classification approach based on correlations among labels. Int. J. Adv. Comput. Sci. Appl. **6**, 52–59 (2015)
2. Amidei, J., Piwek, P., Willis, A.: Rethinking the agreement in human evaluation tasks. In: Proceedings of the 27th International Conference on Computational Linguistics (2018)
3. Breakall, J., Randles, C., Tasker, R.: Development and use of a multiple-choice item writing flaws evaluation instrument in the context of general chemistry. Chem. Educ. Res. Pract. **20**, 369–382 (2019)
4. Brown, G.T., Abdulnabi, H.H.: Evaluating the quality of higher education instructor-constructed multiple-choice tests: Impact on student grades. In: Frontiers in Education. Frontiers Media SA, p. 24 (2017)
5. Butler, A.C.: Multiple-choice testing in education: are the best practices for assessment also good for learning? J. Appl. Res. Mem. Cogn. **7**, 323–331 (2018)
6. Clifton, S.L., Schriner, C.L.: Assessing the quality of multiple-choice test items. Nurse Educ. **35**, 12–16 (2010)
7. Cochran, K., Cohn, C., Hutchins, N., Biswas, G., Hastings, P.: Improving automated evaluation of formative assessments with text data augmentation. In: Rodrigo, M.M., Matsuda, N., Cristea, A.I., Dimitrova, V. (eds.) Artificial Intelligence in Education: 23rd International Conference, AIED 2022, Durham, UK, July 27–31, 2022, Proceedings, Part I, pp. 390–401. Springer International Publishing, Cham (2022). https://doi.org/10.1007/978-3-031-11644-5_32
8. Danh, T., et al.: Evaluating the quality of multiple-choice questions in a NAPLEX preparation book. Curr. Pharm. Teach. Learn. (2020)
9. Downing, S.M.: The effects of violating standard item writing principles on tests and students: the consequences of using flawed test items on achievement examinations in medical education. Adv. Health Sci. Educ. **10**, 133–143 (2005)
10. Haladyna, T.M.: Developing and Validating Multiple-choice Test Items. Psychology Press (2004)
11. Haladyna, T.M., Downing, S.M., Rodriguez, M.C.: A review of multiple-choice item-writing guidelines for classroom assessment. Appl. Meas. Educ. **15**, 309–333 (2002)
12. Haris, S.S., Omar, N.: A rule-based approach in Bloom's Taxonomy question classification through natural language processing. In: 2012 7th International Conference on Computing and Convergence Technology (ICCCT), pp. 410–414. IEEE (2012)
13. Hendrycks, D., et al.: Measuring massive multitask language understanding. In: International Conference on Learning
14. Horbach, A., Aldabe, I., Bexte, M., de Lacalle, O.L., Maritxalar, M.: Linguistic appropriateness and pedagogic usefulness of reading comprehension questions. In: Proceedings of The 12th Language Resources and Evaluation Conference, pp 1753–1762 (2020)
15. Hüllermeier, E., Fürnkranz, J., Mencia, E.L., Nguyen, V.-L., Rapp, M.: Rule-based multi-label classification: challenges and opportunities. In: Gutiérrez-Basulto, V., Kliegr, T., Soylu, A., Giese, M., Roman, D. (eds.) RuleML+RR 2020. LNCS, vol. 12173, pp. 3–19. Springer, Cham (2020). https://doi.org/10.1007/978-3-030-57977-7_1
16. Ji, T., Lyu, C., Jones, G., Zhou, L., Graham, Y.: QAScore—an unsupervised unreferenced metric for the question generation evaluation. Entropy **24**, 1514 (2022)
17. Kasneci, E., et al.: ChatGPT for good? On opportunities and challenges of large language models for education. Learn. Individ. Differ **103**, 102274 (2023)
18. Khairani, A.Z., Shamsuddin, H.: Assessing item difficulty and discrimination indices of teacher-developed multiple-choice tests. In: Tang, S.F., Logonnathan, L. (eds.) Assessment for Learning Within and Beyond the Classroom, pp. 417–426. Springer, Singapore (2016). https://doi.org/10.1007/978-981-10-0908-2_35

19. Khosravi, H., Demartini, G., Sadiq, S., Gasevic, D.: Charting the design and analytics agenda of learnersourcing systems. In: LAK21: 11th International Learning Analytics and Knowledge Conference, pp. 32–42 (2021)
20. Krishna, K., Wieting, J., Iyyer, M.: Reformulating unsupervised style transfer as paraphrase generation. In: Proceedings of the 2020 Conference on Empirical Methods in Natural Language Processing (EMNLP), pp. 737–762 (2020)
21. Kurdi, G., Leo, J., Parsia, B., Sattler, U., Al-Emari, S.: A systematic review of automatic question generation for educational purposes. Int. J. Artif. Intell. Educ. **30**, 121–204 (2020)
22. van der Lee, C., Gatt, A., van Miltenburg, E., Krahmer, E.: Human evaluation of automatically generated text. Comput. Speech Lang. **67**, 101151 (2021)
23. Lee, P., Bubeck, S., Petro, J.: Benefits, limits, and risks of GPT-4 as an AI chatbot for medicine. N. Engl. J. Med. **388**, 1233–1239 (2023)
24. Liu, Y., Iter, D., Xu, Y., Wang, S., Xu, R., Zhu, C.: GPTEval: NLG Evaluation using GPT-4 with Better Human Alignment. ArXiv Prepr ArXiv230316634 (2023)
25. Lu, O.H., Huang, A.Y., Tsai, D.C., Yang, S.J.: Expert-authored and machine-generated short-answer questions for assessing students learning performance. Educ. Technol. Soc. (2021)
26. McHugh, M.L.: Interrater reliability: the kappa statistic. Biochem. Medica. **22**, 276–282 (2012)
27. Moore, S., Nguyen, H.A., Bier, N., Domadia, T., Stamper, J.: Assessing the quality of student-generated short answer questions using GPT-3. In: Hilliger, Is., Muñoz-Merino, P.J., De Laet, T., Ortega-Arranz, A., Farrell, T. (eds.) Educating for a New Future: Making Sense of Technology-Enhanced Learning Adoption: 17th European Conference on Technology Enhanced Learning, EC-TEL 2022, Toulouse, France, September 12–16, 2022, Proceedings, pp. 243–257. Springer International Publishing, Cham (2022). https://doi.org/10.1007/978-3-031-16290-9_18
28. Moore, S., Nguyen, H.A., Stamper, J.: Examining the effects of student participation and performance on the quality of learnersourcing multiple-choice questions. In: Proceedings of the Eighth ACM Conference on Learning@ Scale, pp. 209–220 (2021)
29. Ni, L., et al.: Deepqr: Neural-based quality ratings for learnersourced multiple-choice questions. In: Proceedings of the AAAI Conference on Artificial Intelligence, pp. 12826–12834 (2022)
30. OpenAI: GPT-4 Technical Report (2023). http://arxiv.org/abs/2303.08774
31. Pugh, D., De Champlain, A., Gierl, M., Lai, H., Touchie, C.: Can automated item generation be used to develop high quality MCQs that assess application of knowledge? Res. Pract. Technol. Enhanc. Learn. **15**, 1–13 (2020)
32. Ruseti, S., et al.: Predicting question quality using recurrent neural networks. In: Rosé, C.P., et al. (eds.) AIED 2018. LNCS (LNAI), vol. 10947, pp. 491–502. Springer, Cham (2018). https://doi.org/10.1007/978-3-319-93843-1_36
33. Rush, B.R., Rankin, D.C., White, B.J.: The impact of item-writing flaws and item complexity on examination item difficulty and discrimination value. BMC Med. Educ. 1–10 (2016)
34. Scialom, T., Staiano, J.: Ask to learn: a study on curiosity-driven question generation. In: Proceedings of the 28th International Conference on Computational Linguistics, pp. 2224–2235 (2020)
35. Singh, A., Brooks, C., Doroudi, S.: Learnersourcing in theory and practice: synthesizing the literature and charting the future. In: Proceedings of the Ninth ACM Conference on Learning@ Scale, pp 234–245 (2022)
36. Straková, J., Straka, M., Hajic, J.: Open-source tools for morphology, lemmatization, POS tagging and named entity recognition. In: Proceedings of 52nd Annual Meeting of the Association for Computational Linguistics: System Demonstrations, pp 13–18 (2014)
37. Tarrant, M., Knierim, A., Hayes, S.K., Ware, J.: The frequency of item writing flaws in multiple-choice questions used in high stakes nursing assessments. Nurse Educ. Today (2006)

38. Tsoumakas, G., Katakis, I.: Multi-label classification: an overview. Int. J. Data Warehous Min. IJDWM **3**, 1–13 (2007)
39. Van Campenhout, R., Hubertz, M., Johnson, B.G.: Evaluating AI-generated questions: a mixed-methods analysis using question data and student perceptions. In: Rodrigo, M.M., Matsuda, N., Cristea, A.I., Dimitrova, V. (eds.) Artificial Intelligence in Education: 23rd International Conference, AIED 2022, Durham, UK, July 27–31, 2022, Proceedings, Part I, pp. 344–353. Springer International Publishing, Cham (2022). https://doi.org/10.1007/978-3-031-11644-5_28
40. van der Waa, J., Nieuwburg, E., Cremers, A., Neerincx, M.: Evaluating XAI: a comparison of rule-based and example-based explanations. Artif Intell **291**, 103404 (2021)
41. Wang, Z., Zhang, W., Liu, N., Wang, J.: Scalable rule-based representation learning for interpretable classification. Adv. Neural Inf. Process Syst. **34**, 30479–30491 (2021)

Early Prediction of Learners At-Risk of Failure in Online Professional Training Using a Weighted Vote

Mohamed Mouaici(✉)

Logipro Company, Le Puy-en-Velay, France
mouaici.med@gmail.com, mohamed.mouaici@logipro.com

Abstract. Professional training involves the acquisition of knowledge, skills, and expertise required to perform specific job roles. It can take various forms, including classroom instruction, practical experience, and online training. While online training has the potential to reach a wider audience, a lack of interaction and support may lead to low engagement and high risk of failure. In this paper, we propose a solution to predict, as early as possible, the risk of failure in online professional training. To achieve this, we use a dataset of 13,719 observations, including 912 learners and 182 online courses delivered through an LMS from 2017 to 2022. Our data analysis led us to define the risk of failure based on three classes: low risk, medium risk, and high risk. The objective is to predict the class of each observation when the learner reaches the halfway point in each course. Initially, we tested nine predictive models, which revealed discrepancies in their results across the three classes. To address this gap, we propose a new solution that employs a weighted vote to improve classifications. This solution applies the Borda method to rank the nine models based on their predictive performance in each class. Then, the weight assigned to each model is calculated by considering both its rank and its F1 score in each risk of failure class. Finally, we apply a weighted majority vote involving the nine models. On average, and compared to the baseline models, our solution improves the F1 score by 1.2% for the three risk classes.

Keywords: Online Professional Training · Failure Risk · Early Prediction · Weighted vote

1 Introduction

Professional training refers to the acquisition of knowledge and skills required for specific job roles [1–4]. It is typically designed to equip individuals with the necessary competencies to succeed in their professional careers. Taking advantage of technology, this learning is often delivered through blended or online courses using virtual environments, such as Learning Management Systems (LMS). Digital traces collected by the LMS can be analyzed using Learning Analytics (LA) solutions [5, 6]. LA is a field that involves the collection, analysis, and interpretation of data generated by learners as they interact with courses in digital learning environments [7]. LA uses data mining,

O. Viberg et al. (Eds.): EC-TEL 2023, LNCS 14200, pp. 246–262, 2023.
https://doi.org/10.1007/978-3-031-42682-7_17

machine learning techniques to identify patterns in learner behavior, performance, and engagement. These techniques can be used to provide personalized feedback, develop more effective teaching strategies, and identify at-risk students [7]. In this paper, we explore the use of LA solutions to predict, as early as possible, learners at risk of failure in the context of online professional training. For this purpose, we start by examining the existing literature that addresses this objective in online learning contexts.

1.1 Prediction of Learners At Risk of Failure in Online Courses

Several LA techniques have been applied to identify learners at risk of failure in online courses [8–10]. Different types of data are used to build predictive models, including clickstream data, discussion forum data, and demographic data. Predictive solutions are studied based on various machine learning and deep learning algorithms [8–10].

The authors in [11] propose a solution to predict failure based on student activity on the Internet: LMS data, internet access log, and demographic information. They considered five methods: decision tree, Bayes naive, Logistic Regression, Random Forest, and Artificial Neural Network. The results show that the Random Forest provides the best performance to predict students at risk of failure. In [12], the authors use a dataset from the UCI Machine Learning Repository to compare 14 Tree-based and Rule-based classification techniques to predict student performance. Three test cases are performed: a dataset with all attributes (33 attributes); a dataset with the best attributes; and a dataset with oversampling using SMOTE (Synthetic Minority Oversampling Technique). The results show that the Tree-based algorithms, such as Random Forest, performed better than the other categories, in particular by using oversampling. In [13], the authors aim to identify meaningful behavioral indicators of learning using LMS data relating to the success in an online course. The authors study the relationship between behavioral features and course scores through correlation analyses and hierarchical regression analysis. The results demonstrated that students' regular study, late submissions of assignments, and proof of reading the course information packets significantly predicted their course achievement.

The authors in [14] focus on applying Deep Learning algorithms to study the learning behavior of students in a Virtual Learning Environment. They try to predict learners' performance to prevent the risk of failure. The proposed model is implemented using the Bidirectional Long-Short Term Memory algorithm (BLSTM) and applied to the Open University Learning Analytics Dataset. The BLSTM has achieved good results compared to other models by obtaining an accuracy score of 97%. The study in [15] proposes connectionist approaches to predict learning outcomes by combining Convolutional Neural Networks (CNN) and sequence models (LSTM). The authors develop a hyper-model combining CNN and LSTM to extract features from MOOCs data and predict whether each student will drop out or complete courses.

The authors in [16] investigate the performance of LSTM to predict learners at risk of failure in a course provided in a self-paced mode of online education. The study uses the Open University Learning Analytics Dataset including 22,437 learners with 69% of success and 31% of failure cases. The LSTM model shows the highest predictive results with an accuracy of 84.57%, precision of 82.24%, and recall of 79.43%.

1.2 Limitations

To summarize, prior studies suggest that data collected by LMS platforms can be used to detect learners at risk in online courses. However, the definition of learners at risk of failure is contingent upon the studied context, leading to a lack of consensus among researchers [8, 9]. According to certain studies, learners are deemed to be at risk of failure if they do not complete a certain percentage of assessments (e.g., 50%) [8, 17]. Other researches consider learners at risk if they have been inactive for a certain number of consecutive days or if they failed to pass the course evaluation [18]. The varying definitions of at-risk learners highlight the importance of carefully considering the risk of failure to take into account the specific characteristics of the studied context [12].

Moreover, the majority of studies that propose solutions to predict learners at risk of failure focus on the prediction at the end of the course [8, 10, 19], leaving little time for educators to intervene to help learners overcome their difficulties. Only a few studies have considered the prediction of learners at risk of failure as early as possible.

Finally, several studies use public datasets, making it unwarranted to reuse their approaches on real-world data, as is the case in our online professional training context.

1.3 Contribution and Research Questions

This research is conducted in collaboration with a French training company that offers several types of online professional training through an LMS. The company has a pedagogical team who design and implement training courses and provide support to learners. The pedagogical team analyze learners' behavior to identify those at risk of failure. But this task is challenging with a large number of learners enrolled in multiple courses. Therefore, the objective of this research is to provide them with a solution to detect, as early as possible, learners at risk of failure in online professional training. Considering the limitations identified in the state-of-the-art, the main contributions of this work are:

- Definition of learners at risk of failure in the online professional training context based on the learners' behavior captured by the data collected by the LMS.
- A new algorithm which combines nine well-known predictive models to improve predictions. It relies on a weighted voting approach using the Borda count method and the predictive performance of each model.
- Investigation of the most important factors to predict learners at risk of failure.

These contributions aim to address the following research questions:

RQ1. What are the most effective predictive models to predict, as early as possible, learners at risk of failure in online professional training, and how can the combination of these models be optimized to enhance predictions?

RQ2. What are the key factors that impact the prediction of learners at risk of failure in online professional training?

2 Datasets Description and Learners At-Risk Definition

In our professional training context, courses are provided as e-learning content packages through the LMS. The courses are designed according to the SCORM standard, either SCORM 1.2 or 2004 [20]. Each course comprises various educational content such as videos, texts, and exercises, culminating in a quiz-based evaluation to assess skill acquisition. The pedagogical team offer two learning scenarios: a sequential scenario that presents the course contents in a linear step-by-step manner, and a self-directed scenario that allows learners to choose their preferred educational contents in each course. Regardless of the learning scenario, learners must use the LMS to complete the courses, with the condition of passing each course's quiz evaluation to advance to the subsequent course. The data collected by the LMS are presented below.

2.1 Data Collection, Preprocessing and Features Extraction

Learning traces collected by the LMS from 2017 to 2022 are used in this work. These traces include 182 e-learning courses and 912 learners. Using the available learning traces in our LMS and drawing from previous research in e-learning courses [8–10], we have identified four categories of learning features to study at-risk learners:

A. **Learner Profile:** information related to learners and their skills
B. **Course features:** meta-data related to the course
C. **Course visualization**: information about learners' interactions with the course
D. **Quiz-related features:** learners' results obtained in the course evaluation
E. **Platforms connection:** learners' connection to the LMS and the Forum

Table 1 provides a description of all the features grouped in these four categories.

Table 1. Features description

Cat	Feature	Feature Description	Type
A	FA1	The learner's gender	Factor
	FA2	The age of the learner	integer
	FA3	Whether or not the learner has the course prerequisites	Binary
B	FB1	The course duration estimated by the pedagogical team	Integer
	FB2	Is the course in scorm 2004 or scorm 1.2	Factor
	FB3	The learning scenario of the course	Factor
C	FC1	The total time spent on the course	Integer
	FC2	The number of (re)visualization of the course contents	Integer
	FC3	The number of days spent to complete the course	Integer
	FC4	The average time spent per day on the course	Float
	FC5	The average time spent per content (re)visualization	Float
	FC6	The learner's connection habit to the course: 1. At work (8 a.m. to 12 p.m.; 2 p.m. to 5 p.m.) 2. During the break (from 12 p.m. to 2 p.m.) 3. After work (from 5 p.m. to 7 p.m.) 4. In the evening (after 7 p.m.)	Factor

(*continued*)

Table 1. (*continued*)

Cat	Feature	Feature Description	Type
D	FD1	The total time spent on the quiz	Integer
	FD2	The number of attempts made on the quiz	Integer
	FD3	The average time spent by attempt	Float
	FD4	The best score obtained by the learner on the quiz	Float
	FD5	The average score obtained including all attempts	Float
E	FE1	The number of connections to the LMS home page	Integer
	FE2	The number of connections to the forum of the course	Integer

The features depicting a duration time are in seconds. The learning time is managed by the LMS, which specifically tracks the time learners spend on the content of the course provided through the LMS. While learners are expected to engage during regular working hours, some individuals access the course contents outside of these designated times, such as during lunch breaks or in the evenings. To capture this behavior, we introduce the variable FC6. Demographics information (FA1 to FA3) are used to gain insights into the characteristics of individuals and understand how they may influence the outcomes being predicted [8–10]. By including demographics information, we try to identify patterns between these factors and the predicted outcomes to understand how different subgroups may behave in the given context, leading to more targeted and tailored predictions or interventions. In our study, the 19 features (in Table 1) are used as explanatory variables to build models to predict learners at risk of failure. Hence, numeric features are normalized, while categorical features are encoded. The estimated duration (FB1) is used to normalize features indicating a duration, while the minimum and maximum values are used to normalize all other numerical features.

2.2 Risk of Failure Definition

Initially, to pass a course, learners must obtain a minimum score of 60% on the quiz assessment. If they make several attempts, the best score is recorded. This initial threshold is defined by the pedagogical team. This may allow us to consider a binary definition to predict learners at risk of failure (failure/not failure). However, relying on a binary definition may have limitations. Indeed, the binary definition may not be appropriate for all learners, as those who score just below or above the threshold of 60% may still require support. In other words, are learners who score 59% really at risk? And have learners who score 60% or 62% really passed the course?

To address this limitation, we analyze the learners' behavior by observing their performance evolution over a course sequence. The purpose is to determine whether learners who score close to the 60% threshold in one course face difficulties in passing the subsequent course. In our dataset containing 912 learners and 182 courses, we observed that 55% of learners scored below 60% in at least one course during the training. Furthermore, we discovered that the majority of learners (almost 85%) who scored between 60%

and 72% in a course tend to score below the 60% threshold in the subsequent courses. In contrast, some learners who scored below 60% in certain courses have demonstrated consistency in their performance and success in the subsequent courses.

Figure 1 depicts the performance evolution of 6 learners over a sequence of 5 courses.

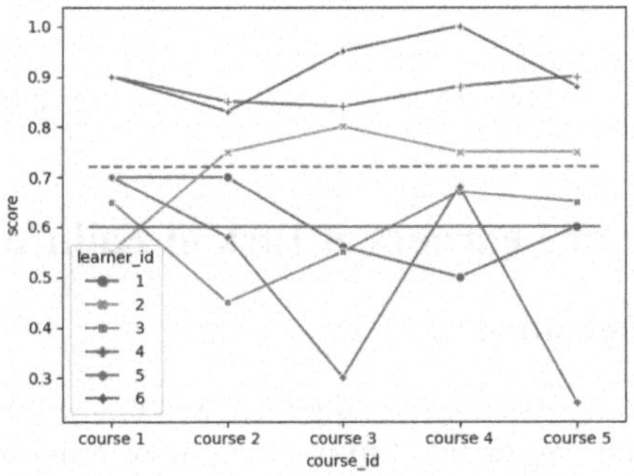

Fig. 1. Example of Learners Performance Evolution

For clarity reasons, Fig. 1 illustrates a representative example of our analysis with only 6 learners and a sequence of 5 courses. The horizontal red line represents the initial minimum threshold required to pass a course (60%). The blue horizontal dotted line represents the threshold of 72% identified in our analysis. Learners 1, 3, and 5 who scored slightly above the 60% threshold in the first course faced difficulties passing the subsequent courses (course 2,3 and 4), while learners 4 and 6 who scored above 90% in their first courses passed all the quizzes without difficulty. Based on this analysis, we define the risk of failure using three classes: low, medium, and high risk; denoting it as "Y," which is determined based on the best score obtained in the quiz-type evaluation of each course (FD4 in Table 1).

$$Risk\ of\ failure: \begin{cases} Y = 0\ for\ Low\ risk \overset{\text{def}}{=} \text{FD4} > 72\% \\ Y = 1\ for\ Medium\ risk \overset{\text{def}}{=} \text{FD4} \in [60\%, 72\%] \\ Y = 2\ for\ High\ Risk \overset{\text{def}}{=} \text{FD4} < 60\ \% \end{cases}$$

This definition has been approved by the pedagogical team involved in this work.

2.3 Descriptive Analysis of the dataset

Our dataset consists of 912 learners and 182 e-learning courses provided from 2017 to 2022 through an LMS. It contains 13,719 observations, with 33.8% of low risk of failure (best score > 72%), 11.1% of medium risk (best score between 60% and 72%), and 55.2% of high risk (best score less than 60%). This dataset is presented in Table 2.

The data exhibits an imbalance among the three risk of failure classes. The high risk of failure class comprises the majority with 55.2% of observations, while the low and medium risk classes represent the minority with 33.8% and 11.1% of observations, respectively. Predicting observations accurately for these minority classes can be challenging due to this data imbalance. We will address this issue in the upcoming section.

Table 2. Dataset description

Data	#Learners	#courses	#Observations
All	912	182	13,719 (100%)
Low risk	657	125	4,631 (33.8%)
Medium risk	399	92	1,516 (11.1%)
High risk	905	180	7,572 (55.2%)

3 Early Prediction of Learners at Risk of Failure

3.1 Early Prediction Definition

Our objective is to predict learners at risk of failure as early as possible. After consulting with the pedagogical team, we decided to focus on predicting the risk of failure when learners complete half of the estimated duration (FB1) of the course. Therefore, we can formulate our prediction problem as follows:

$$Y = f(FA1 \ldots FA3, FB1 \ldots FB3, FC1 \ldots FC6, FD1 \ldots FD5, FE1, FE2)_T$$

$$With\ T = \frac{1}{2} * FB1$$

Y is our target variable with the three failure risk classes. T is the time at which the prediction of Y must be made. FB1 is the course estimated duration. Hence, our objective is to predict the value of Y (0, 1 or 2) using the 19 features (FA1...FE2) calculated when the learner would have reached a learning duration equal to half the estimated duration of the course. To do this, we use the date indicated in the learning traces to calculate the 19 features at T = 1/2*FB1 for each learner on each course in the dataset.

3.2 Data Splitting and Oversampling using SMOTE

As mentioned above, the 19 explanatory features are calculated at T = 1/2*FB1, and the Y variable's values at the course end are kept. The obtained dataset (13,719 observations) is split randomly with stratification into two subsets: 75% to train predictive models and 25% to evaluate them. Table 3 describes these two data subsets.

Table 3. Data train and data evaluation description

Data subset	Low risk	Medium risk	High risk
Train models	3,458 (33.6%)	1,148 (11.2%)	5,683 (55.2%)
Evaluate them	1,173 (34.2%)	368 (10.7%)	1,889 (55.1%)

Table 3 displays an imbalance in data between the three failure risk classes. This can be problematic especially for the training dataset because it may lead to an under-fitting issue in the predictive models [12]. Indeed, the minority classes may be under-considered by the predictive models. To address this, SMOTE (Synthetic Minority Oversampling Technique) is used to oversample the low and medium risk classes by generating dummy observations to match the number of observations in the high risk class. This balances the training dataset with an equal number of observations in the three classes: 5,683 observations in each failure risk class. The evaluation dataset is not resampled to evaluate the models in real-world conditions without any sampling biases.

3.3 Predictive Models and Evaluation Metrics

We can use different supervised learning models that are suitable for predicting the three classes of our target variable (Y). Initially, we test nine commonly used models: Multinomial Logistic Regression **(MLR)**; Decision Tree **(DT)**; Random Forest **(RF)**; eXtreme Gradient Boosting **(XGB)**; Adaptive Boosting **(AdB)**; Bagging Classifier **(BC)**; Naive Bayes Classifier **(NB)**; K-nearest neighbors **(KNN)**; Artificial Neural Network **(ANN).** Once these nine models are trained on the oversampled training dataset, their performance are evaluated using the evaluation dataset. The predicted class of each observation is compared with its actual class to compute three evaluation metrics:

- **Precision**: the proportion of true positives among all the predicted positives.
- **Recall:** the proportion of true positives among all actual positives.
- **F1 score:** the harmonic mean of precision and recall, which is useful in situations where minimizing both false positives and false negatives is important.

In our study, a particular importance is given to the F1 score which combines precision and recall to enhance accurate classifications while minimizing misclassifications. This choice is also motivated by the requirements of the pedagogical team, which ask to minimize false alarms while maximizing true positive classifications.

3.4 Training Models and Initial Evaluation Results

We use a 10-folds cross-validation process to train the nine predictive models on the oversampled training dataset. Then, we evaluate them on the evaluation dataset containing 3,430 observations. To compare the results, we calculate precision (Pre), recall (Rec), and F1 score (F1). The comparison of the evaluation results is shown in Table 4.

Table 4. Initial evaluation results.

Models	Low risk			Medium Risk			High Risk		
	Pre.	Rec.	F1	Pre.	Rec.	F1.	Pre.	Rec.	F1
MLR	.855	.629	.725	.259	.377	.307	.774	.830	.801
KNN	.535	.578	.556	.198	.515	.286	.772	.485	.595

(continued)

Table 4. (*continued*)

Models	Low risk			Medium Risk			High Risk		
	Pre.	Rec.	F1	Pre.	Rec.	F1.	Pre.	Rec.	F1
NB	.583	.481	.527	.171	.884	.287	.850	.233	.365
DT	.794	.826	.810	.529	.688	.598	.882	.807	.843
RF	.857	.815	**.836**	.590	.694	.638	.874	.869	**.871**
ADB	.885	.762	.818	.481	.717	.575	.870	.858	.864
XGB	.837	.823	.830	.603	.689	**.643**	.879	.862	.870
BC	.874	.513	.647	.230	.593	.331	.788	.737	.762
ANN	.920	.625	.744	.310	.617	.407	.811	.787	.799

Table 4 shows that DT, RF, ADB and XGB models obtain high precision and F1 scores for the low and high risk of failure classes (greater than 80%). The best F1 score for these two classes is obtained by RF (Random forest), with 83.6% for the low risk class and 87.10% for the high risk class. However, the performance for the medium risk class is lower for all models, with XGB achieving the best F1 score of 64.3%. Even with the use of oversampling, the limited number of observations in this class restricted the models' capacity to learn from learners' behaviors, resulting in a medium risk of failure. Nonetheless, the F1 score of 64.3% obtained by XGB is encouraging, highlighting the importance of considering this medium risk of failure class.

Conversely, the KNN and NB models yield lower precision and F1 scores for all three classes. However, it is worth mentioning that the NB model shows higher sensitivity to the medium risk class, as indicated by its recall score of 88.4%. Hence, in the case where the false positive predictions are not a major concern, the NB model may be considered as the preferred option for the medium risk class prediction.

Our initial analysis corroborates previous research works on the effectiveness of ensemble methods, such as Random Forest and boosting algorithms, in predicting at-risk learners in online courses using LMS data [11, 13]. Furthermore, our findings validate the challenges documented in the literature regarding the accurate identification of at-risk learners in the minority classes [12]. Building upon these promising results and recognizing the variability in predictions across the three risk classes, we investigated the potential of employing meta-models to improve our predictive capabilities.

4 Meta-Models and the Proposed Weighted Vote Algorithm

A meta-model combines multiple models' predictions to enhance the overall prediction accuracy. A Meta-model is built by training several base models and then aggregating their predictions using a specific algorithm. The idea is to leverage the advantages of diverse base models and offset their limitations to provide more accurate predictions. Our study investigates two meta-models, the majority vote and Borda count method, and introduces a novel algorithm that combines the nine previous models through a weighted majority vote mechanism based on the Borda count method.

4.1 Majority Vote

Initially, we explore the majority vote method to aggregate the predictions of the nine models. This method gives equal weight to each model, and the final class for each observation is determined by the class with the most votes. Nevertheless, there are other variations of the majority vote that can assign different weights to each model based on their performance, such as the Borda count method.

4.2 Borda Count Method Applied with the Majority Vote

The Borda count method [21] is used to assign scores to each model based on their performance on the test dataset during the k-folds cross-validation process. In each k-fold iteration, the nine models are ranked in each risk of failure class based on their F1 score, and they are given a certain number of points based on their rank. The model ranked first receives 9 points; the model ranked second receives 8 points, and so on until the model ranked last receives 1 point. The points for each model are summed across all k-folds iterations, and the model with the highest total number of points in a failure risk class is considered as the best model for that class. Our study applies the Borda count method with the majority vote, where the weight of each model corresponds to its total number of points obtained during the k-fold cross-validation. The majority vote is then applied with these voting weights, and the final class of each observation is determined by the class with the highest total number of weights.

By developing this method with the majority vote and by analyzing their results and their limitations, we had the idea to propose a new weighted vote algorithm.

4.3 Proposed Weighted Vote Algorithm

The Borda count method, while useful, can have limitations in accurately reflecting the performance differences between predictive models. It only considers the rank ordering of the models and assigns points based on it. Consequently, differences in the performance among models may not be adequately reflected, leading to some models receiving different number of points despite the small/large difference in their performance. Suppose we have two models, A and B, with F1 scores of 90% and 60%, respectively. Despite the significant difference in their F1 scores (0.9 vs. 0.6), the Borda count method assigns 2 points to the model A and 1 point to the model B. The application of this method with the majority vote does not solve the problem because the weight of each model will correspond to its total number of points without taking into account the differences in performance with the other models. Therefore, we propose a new algorithm that uses a weighted majority voting approach, based on the Borda count method and the F1 scores to account for performance differences between models. Our solution is presented by the Algorithm 1.

Algorithm. 1. Proposed Weighted Vote Algorithm

```
1.  Input. DT = Oversampled training dataset, DE: Evaluation dataset, K=10
2.  Output. Final_class: final class of each observation in DE.
3.  Initialize W= matrix (3 x 9) = [low, medium, high]x[the nine models]
4.  For i in 1 to k
5.      Dtr, Dts = Split DT into training and testing sets for the ith fold
6.      Tmodels = Train the nine models (Dtr)
7.      Results = Test the nine models (Dts)
8.      For each risk class j in (low risk, medium risk, high risk)
9.          Rank[i, j] = Rank the nine models according to their F1 scores (Results,j)
10.         Points[i, j] = Allocate points to each model (Rank (i, j))
11. AvgF1 = Get the average F1 score of each model in each risk class across all k-folds
12. AvgF1= Normalize the F1score of each model in each risk class using the min max values
13. Total points = Sum the points of each model across all k-folds in each risk class
14. Final rank = rank the nine model in each class (Total points)
15. W = Final rank[] x AvgF1[]
16. For each observation O in DE
17.     S_low = Sum the weights of all the models predicting O as low risk of failure (O,W)
18.     S_med= Sum the weights of all the models predicting O as medium risk (O,W)
19.     S_high = Sum the weights of all the models predicting O as high risk of failure (O,W)
20.     Final_class[O] = max (S_low, S_med, S_high)
21. Return Final_class
```

Our algorithm takes as input the oversampled training dataset (DT), the evaluation dataset (DE), and the number of the k-folds for the cross-validation. Line 3 initializes the matrix which will contain the voting weight of each model in each failure risk class.

For each K-fold, we extract the data to train and test the 9 models; then we calculate their F1 score (lines 4 to 7). This allows us to rank them in each risk class according to their F1 score; and to assign them a certain number of points: the best model will have 9 points, the second one will have 8 points, and so on (lines 8 to 10).

At the end of the k-fold cross-validation process, the average F1 score is retrieved for each model in each failure risk class (line 11). Then, in line 12, the average F1 score of each model is normalized within each risk class using the min and max values of that class. Normalizing the F1 score of the 9 models in each class allows for a fair comparison of their performance, preventing any penalties for the class with the lowest performance (medium risk of failure) during the weighted vote. Next, in line 13, the total number of points for each model in each risk class is calculated by summing their points from the k iterations. This allows, in line 14, to rank the models in each risk class based on their total number of points in that class. Line 15 calculates the vote weight of each model for each class by multiplying its average normalized F1 score with its final rank in that class. The voting weight of the best model in a class is 9: obtained by multiplying 9 points (allocated to the best model in that risk class) with its average normalized F1 score of 1. On the other hand, the weight of the last model is 0 because its average normalized F1 score is 0. This approach considers both the rank and normalized F1 score of each model in each class, allowing for a more accurate assignment of voting weight that accounts for both small and large differences between the models.

Finally, the 9 models are used to predict the class of each observation of the evaluation dataset (DE); and the voting weights of the models corresponding to the predicted class are summed (lines 16 to 19). The highest weight sum determines the risk class of each observation (line 20), and these classifications are returned in line 21.

5 Evaluation Results and Research Questions Answers

We assess our algorithm on the evaluation dataset: 3,430 observations with 34.2% of the observations in the low failure risk class, 10.7% in the medium risk class, and 55.1% in the high risk. We compare the predictive performance of our algorithm with those obtained by the previous best models (RF and XGB). We also compare our algorithm with the two meta-models investigated in this work: the majority vote and the Borda count method applied with the majority vote. Table 5 displays this comparison.

Table 5. Evaluation Results of the Proposed Algorithm and Comparison

Models	Low risk			Medium Risk			High Risk		
	Pre.	Rec.	F1	Pre.	Rec.	F1	Pre.	Rec.	F1
RF	.857	.815	.836	.590	.694	.638	.874	.869	.871
XGB	.837	.823	.830	.603	.689	.643	.879	.862	.870
Majority Vote (MJ)	.895	.759	.822	.390	.673	.493	.849	.803	.825
MJ with Borda	.887	.800	.841	.572	.705	.631	.869	.880	.874
Our algorithm	.897	.816	**.855**	.620	.694	**.655**	.889	.886	**.887**

Table 5 shows that our algorithm outperforms all other models and meta-models in terms of precision, recall and F1 score for the three risk of failure classes. The majority vote (MJ) does not improve the prediction results for any risk class, indicating the negative impact of assigning equal weights to models with significant performance discrepancies. However, the majority vote with the Borda count method enhances the results for RF and XGB models, surpassing the majority vote in all three risk classes. Nevertheless, the Borda count method overlooks performance differences between the models. To overcome this limitation, our algorithm incorporates a weighted voting mechanism, by assigning weights that account for these performance differences. Therefore, for the low risk of failure, our algorithm achieves the highest F1 score of 85.5%, improving the results of the majority vote with the Borda count method by 1.4%. In the medium risk of failure class, our algorithm achieves an F1 score of 65.5%, which is a 1.2% improvement over the XGB model. In the high risk class, our algorithm improves the F1 score by 1.3%. Additionally, our algorithm yields notable improvements in precision and recall across all three risk classes. During the evaluation of our algorithm through the 10-fold cross-validation, we consistently observed slight improvements across the 10 iterations.

On average, our algorithm showed a 1.3% enhancement in the F1 score for the three risk classes. Furthermore, our algorithm achieved a macro F1 score of 79.9%, while the majority vote with the Borda count method scored 78.2%. These slight improvements obtained by our algorithm are valuable and can be attributed to various factors, including the initial performance of the baseline models. If the baseline models already exhibit high performance, there may be limited room for significant improvement. Nevertheless, even small advancements contribute to enhancing overall performance and demonstrate progress in predicting at-risk learners in professional training. In the existing literature, various ensemble methods and weighting approaches have been explored to improve predictions [13–15]. Our algorithm's contribution is a weighted voting approach that incorporates F1 scores and a normalization step to account the performance differences between models, leading to improved classifications compared to the baseline models and meta-models.

5.1 Extraction of Failure Risk Factors

We use Shapely Additive Explanation (SHAP) to analyze the significance and contribution of each feature in the output predictions of our solution [16]. The SHAP values are the average contribution of each feature to the prediction of our algorithm across all possible combinations of features. Figure 2 depicts the top ten features (obtained using SHAP) for predicting learners at risk of failure in online professional training.

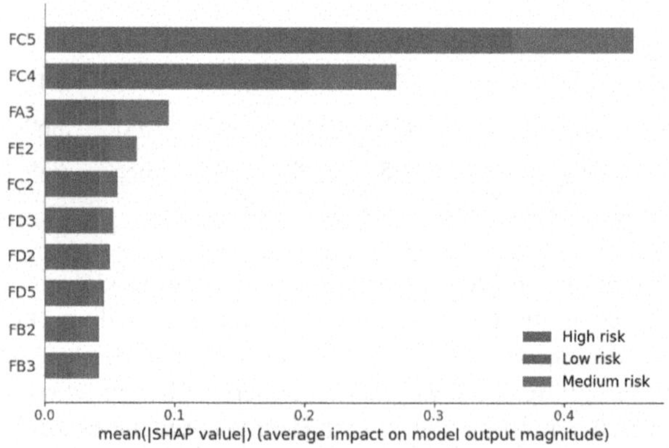

Fig. 2. Features importance identification through SHAP

The two most significant features are the average time spent on the course contents (FC5) and the average time spent per learning day (FC4). FC5 is highly important for predicting the high and low risk of failure. Its importance decreases for the medium risk class as indicated by the size of the three bars: blue, pink and green. FC4 shows dominant importance in the high risk class, and balanced importance for the medium and low risk classes. The third most important factor is the possession or not of the necessary prerequisites for the course (FA3), with a greater impact on the prediction of learners at medium and high risk of failure. Then, the consultation of the course forum (FE2) is the fourth factor with a more dominant importance for the high failure risk class. The remaining six factors have a low importance in predicting learners at risk of failure in the three classes. Our results align with prior research conducted in various online learning contexts [11–13], emphasizing the importance of regularity and active engagement for achieving success in courses. Additionally, our study confirms that learners with prior knowledge or course-related prerequisites have a higher likelihood of success, which is consistent with previous research on at-risk learners [11]. These findings highlight the significance of prerequisite knowledge in facilitating successful learning outcomes and underscore the importance of addressing the needs of learners with diverse levels of prior knowledge to enhance their chances of success in professional training programs. These results allowed us to provide answers to our research questions.

5.2 Discussion and Answers of the Research Questions

Our research aims to develop a solution for early prediction of learners at risk of failure in online professional training. For this purpose, we formulated two research questions:

RQ1. What are the most effective predictive models to predict, as early as possible, learners at risk of failure in online professional training, and how can the combination of these models be optimized to enhance predictions?

RQ2. What are the key factors that impact the prediction of learners at risk of failure?

Based on the evaluation results, the most effective models to predict learners at risk of failure at halfway through the course are the Random Forest (RF) and the Gradient Boosting (XGB). However, identifying learners at medium risk of failure was more challenging. This may be due to the smaller number of observations in this class. Despite oversampling, the minority class may not have had enough representation in the training data to effectively capture its characteristics and patterns. The difference in the performance between the best models in the three risk of failure classes led us to assume that the use of meta-models such as the majority vote and the Borda count method can improve predictions. The majority vote did not improve the predictive performance of any risk of failure class. Assigning equal weight to the nine models despite their considerable performance differences seems to be a limited approach that led to poor classifications. To address the limitations of the majority vote method, we have investigated the Borda count method. This method assigns points to each model based on its rank in predicting the observations of each risk class, and the majority vote is then applied using these points as weights. This has remarkably improved the results obtained by RF and XGB in the three risk of failure classes. Although the Borda count method improved the results, it has a limitation: it doesn't account for the differences in predictive performance among the models. Instead, it only assigns to each model a certain number of points based on its rank and uses these points as the weight in the vote. To address this, we proposed a weighted majority vote algorithm which assigns a weight to each model based on its rank in the Borda method and its average F1 score in the k-folds cross-validation process. This algorithm leverages the strengths of each model while considering their performance differences. The evaluation showed the effectiveness of our solution by improving the prediction results for all three risk of failure classes.

Regarding **RQ2**, our experiments results and the use of SHAP revealed that the regularity in learning and the possession of the necessary prerequisites are the key factors to study the risk of failure. Regularity in learning refers to regular consultation/review of the course contents, which allows better acquisition/consolidation of knowledge and better success. The possession of the necessary prerequisites factor highlights the importance of ensuring that students have the required knowledge and skills before taking a course to minimize the risk of failure. These factors' importance may vary across different risk classes, with a more significant effect in the low and high risk classes.

6 Conclusions, Limitations and Future Work

This research work is conducted in collaboration with a pedagogical team from a training center in France. The objective is to provide this team with a solution to predict, as early as possible, learners at risk of failure in online professional training.

For this purpose, the learning traces collected by the training center's LMS between 2017 and 2022 are retrieved. This allows us to construct a dataset containing 13,719 observations with 912 learners and 182 courses. The analysis of learners' behavior through this data led us to propose a definition of the risk of failure with three classes: low risk, medium risk, and high risk. The data imbalance between these three risk classes is addressed by applying SMOTE-based oversampling.

Afterward, nine well-known predictive models are trained to predict the observations of each risk of failure class at halfway through the course. The initial evaluation results show that the random forest is the best model for the low and high risk classes with an F1 score of 83.6% and 87.1%, respectively. For the medium risk of failure class, the XGboost model obtains the best F1 score of 64.3%. This shows a difference between the best models in the three risk classes and a difficulty to predict the medium risk of failure. This divergence led us to explore two meta-models to combine predictions: the majority vote and the Borda count method. The majority vote did not improve the results of any risk class, but the application of the Borda count method slightly improved the F1 score for the low and high risk of failure.

The analysis of these results and the identification of the limits of these two meta-models led us to propose a new weighted majority voting algorithm. Our algorithm assigns a weight to each model based on its rank in the Borda count method and its average F1 score in the k-folds cross-validation process. This algorithm allows to leverage the strengths of each individual model while taking into account the difference in their predictive performance. Our algorithm improves the results for the three risk of failure classes compared to all other models and meta-models. The F1 score is improved by 1.4% in the low risk class, by 1.2% for the medium risk class, and by 1.3% for the high risk class. These results led us to explore the most important factors in these predictions using SHAP. The regular consultation of the educational contents and the possession of the necessary prerequisites for the course are the most important factors to study the risk of failure in our professional training context.

Similar to other research in predicting at-risk learners, our study is limited by the data collected and analyzed, primarily gathered from an LMS. Consequently, our understanding of learner behaviors may be incomplete as activities outside the LMS, such as accessing external resources and interactions on other platforms, are not captured. Additionally, the findings are based on a specific dataset from online professional training, potentially limiting their generalizability to other contexts. Like any predictive solution, it is essential to note that the performance of our algorithm may vary depending on the dataset and underlying models employed. Therefore, these limitations should be taken into account when interpreting the results and making broader implications of our study. Our future work will focus on integrating new data sources and evaluating the effectiveness of our algorithm in diverse contexts. We also aim to investigate the impact of our solution on learning outcomes in the online professional training context.

References

1. Lambert, M., Vero, J., Zimmermann, B.: Vocational training and professional development: a capability perspective. Int. J. Train. Dev. **16**(3), 164–182 (2012)
2. Mouaici, M., Vignollet, L., Galez, C., Etienne, M.: Learning analytics dashboards for professional training - challenges and proposal. In: CEUR Workshop Proceedings (2018)
3. Littlejohn, A.: Learning and work: professional learning analytics. In: Handbook of Learning Analytics, Society for Learning Analytics Research (SoLAR), pp. 269–277 (2017)
4. Ruiz-Calleja, A., Prieto, L.P., et al.: Learning analytics for professional and workplace learning: a literature review. In: Lecture Notes in Computer Science (2017)
5. Daumiller, M., Rinas, R., Olden, D., Dresel, M.: Academics' motivations in professional training courses: effects on learning engagement and learning gains (2020)
6. Singh, V., Thurman, A.: How Many ways can we define online learning? a systematic literature review of definitions of online learning (1988-2018). Am. J. Distan. Educ. **33**(4), 289–306 (2019). https://doi.org/10.1080/08923647.2019.1663082
7. Elias, T.: Learning analytics : definitions , processes and potential. Learning (2011)
8. Alhothali, A., et al.: Predicting student outcomes in online courses using machine learning techniques: a review. Sustain. **14**, 6199 (2022)
9. Katarya, R., Gaba, J.: A review on machine learning based student's academic performance prediction systems. In: Proceedings. - International Conference on Artificial Intelligence and Smart Systems, ICAIS (2021)
10. Adnan, M., et al.: Predicting at-risk students at different percentages of course length for early intervention using machine learning models. IEEE Access (2021)
11. Trakunphutthirak, R., Cheung, Y., Lee, V.: Detecting student at risk of failure: A case study of conceptualizing mining from internet access log files. In: ICDMW (2019)
12. Senthil, S., Lin, W.M.: Applying classification techniques to predict students' academic results. In: ICCTAC 2017, vol. 2018, pp. 1–6 (2018)
13. You, J.W.: Identifying significant indicators using LMS data to predict course achievement in online learning. Internet High. Educ. **29**, 23–30 (2016)
14. Souai, W., Mihoub, A., Tarhouni, M., Zidi, S., Krichen, M., Mahfoudhi, S.: Predicting at-risk students using the deep learning BLSTM approach. SMARTTECH (2022)
15. Mubarak, A.A., Cao, H., Hezam, I.M.: Deep analytic model for student dropout prediction in massive open online courses. Comput. Electr. Eng. (2021)
16. Waheed, H., et al.: Early prediction of learners at risk in self-paced education: a neural network approach. Expert Syst. Appl. **213**, 118868 (2023)
17. Burgos, C., et al.: Data mining for modeling students' performance: a tutoring action plan to prevent academic dropout. Comput. Electr. Eng. **66**, 541–556 (2018)

18. Hong, B., Wei, Z., Yang, Y.: Discovering learning behavior patterns to predict dropout in MOOC. In: ICCSE 2017 - 12th International Conference on Computer Science and Education, pp. 700–704 (2017)
19. Kustitskaya, T.A., et al.: Early student-at-risk detection by current learning performance and learning behavior indicators. Bulg. Acad. Sci. Cybern. Inf. Technol. (2022)
20. What is SCORM and How it Works. https://scorm.com/. Accessed 05 Apr 2023
21. Zahid, M.A., De Swart, H.: The borda majority count. Inf. Sci. (Ny). (2015)

How to Characterize and Analyze the Computational Thinking Skills of a Learning Game?

Mathieu Muratet[1,2](✉)

[1] Sorbonne Université, CNRS, LIP6, 75005 Paris, France
[2] INSEI, 58–60 avenue des Landes, 92150 Suresnes, France
mathieu.muratet@lip6.fr
https://webia.lip6.fr/ muratetm/

Abstract. Computational thinking is a discipline poorly mastered by elementary school teachers. To help teachers address these skills with their students, we develop the SPY game. In this paper we conduct a didactic analysis of the game and we propose a tool to describe the competencies targeted by the game based on game mechanics. The proposed tool has been applied to describe 21 of the 26 PIAF skills (a skills base on computational thinking). We show how these descriptions provide to teachers and designers micro information about the active skills in a level or macro information about the evolution of a game scenario complexity.

Keywords: Serious Game · Learning Game · Computational Thinking · Modeling · Competency · Didactic

1 Introduction and Positionning

For a few years now, computer science has been teached again in school in France [2], known as computational thinking [4]. According to Wing [16], computational thinking involves five cognitive abilities: (1) algorithmic thinking, (2) abstraction, (3) evaluation, (4) decomposition, and (5) generalization. Based on this definition, Parmentier *et al.* [13] proposed a fine division of computational and algorithmic thinking skills for basic education (the PIAF framework). They also provided pedagogical scenarios helping teachers to teach these skills to their students. This question of the appropriation of these skills by elementary school teachers is complex to address. Indeed, teaching this new discipline requires an important investment on their side [5], notably because of the lack of training (initial and in-service). For instance, teachers have difficulties in constructing their pedagogical scenarios or in judging the relevance of tools to train their students on these skills.

We assume that even if elementary school teachers do not master these skills, they foresee the interest for their students when they are presented in skills base; and thus a tool based on these references would be usable for the teachers.

O. Viberg et al. (Eds.): EC-TEL 2023, LNCS 14200, pp. 263–277, 2023.
https://doi.org/10.1007/978-3-031-42682-7_18

Our proposal: Proposing a skill-driven learning game that will assist teachers in developing computational thinking learning sessions with their students.

Today, several dozen learning games on the theme of computer science exist [7,10] but very few explain how the underlying skills are worked on and even fewer provide tools for teachers to help them adapt the games to their context [15].

The research problem is: how to help teachers who are not familiar with computational thinking to identify the skills involved in game situations (which they could create themselves)? This research problem includes two research questions:

- How can we formalize the skills base on computational thinking from the ludic features of a learning game?
- How to exploit this formalization to analyze the levels of the learning game and extract the skills involved?

In order to answer these research questions we will present the theoretical foundation in Sect. 2. Then, in Sect. 3, we will present the SPY game we use in this research and outline its didactic features. In Sect. 4, we will propose a formalization to describe computational thinking skills depending on game functionalities. And we will illustrate the application of this formalization on some computational thinking skills in Sect. 5. At the end, we will present results on the SPY game in Sect. 6 before concluding.

2 Theoretical Foundation

In 1994, Balacheff [1] identified the "computational transposition" process. It aims at identifying the links between the internal and external[1] universe of the device through an interface. This interface plays a particular role when it becomes "a reference for the user in relation to which knowledge is built"[2] [1]. Thus, the design choices of an interface influence the knowledge build process.

Designing a learning game with an intrinsic metaphor consists in putting learnings at the heart of the gameplay [9]. In this context, the designers of learning games propose gameplay mechanisms in harmony with the content to be taught, building game features which are mostly didactic. However, the computational transposition of the learnings targeted is not always explicit. Branthiome [3] developed the idea of "adidactical situations" in a learning game on programming. In this game, the students can program an initial solution that is not very efficient and, with the feedback from the system, update its solution to switch to a winning procedure. Then, the game features proposed are didactic in order to allow the students to progress in their learning path even if they are not aware of it during the game.

[1] The user is in the external universe of the device.

[2] translated from french "une référence pour l'utilisateur relativement à laquelle la connaissance est cons-truite".

The player interacts with the learning game and develops usage patterns that transform the game from an artifact to an instrument [6]. The schemas thus developed depend on the properties of the interactive artifact (in our case, the game functionalities available in a given situation). The theory of semiotic mediation develops the idea of the semiotic potential of an artifact [8]. This potential is defined by a double link "which may occur between i) an artifact, and the personal meanings emerging from its use to accomplish a task, and ii) at the same time the mathematical meanings evoked by its use and recognizable as mathematics by an expert" [8]. We focused on this second link, where we look for characterizing the links between a learning game (the artifact) and the signs resulting from its use, recognizable as knowledge, in our case computational thinking.

3 Analysis of Didactic Features of the SPY Game

SPY[3] (see Fig. 1) is a learning game on computational thinking. It has been designed for high school students (grades 9–12). It is an open-source project[4] developed by Sorbonne University. The goal of the game is to program the actions of an agent to reach a precise position. These actions are represented as blocks that the player has to arrange in sequences executed by the agent.

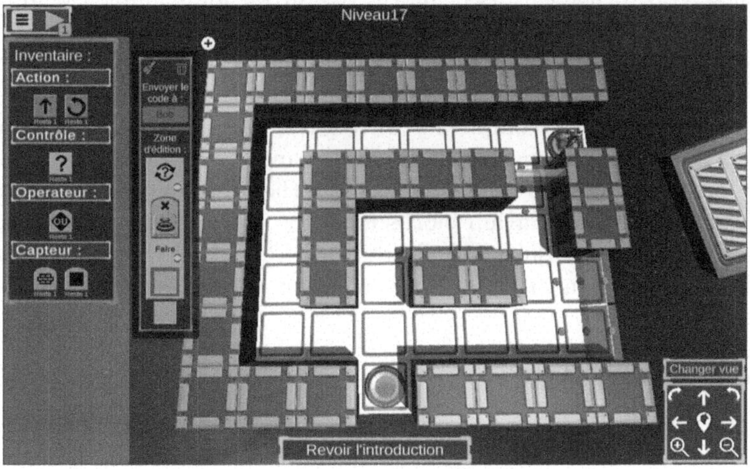

Fig. 1. Example of a SPY level.

The mobilization of computational thinking skills relies on a set of game features. We will detail here the analysis of this artifact to identify all its playful features and to study the links with the knowledge to be taught: computational thinking.

[3] SPY: https://spy.lip6.fr/, accessed on March 6, 2023.
[4] SPY source code: https://github.com/Mocahteam/SPY, accessed on March 6, 2023.

3.1 Programming Blocks

The programming blocks are the fundamental elements of SPY, they constitute the basic bricks of the programs executed by the agents. The programming blocks are divided into four categories:

- **Action blocks:** These blocks allow the player to define the actions executed by the agents: "Move forward", "Turn left", "Turn right", "Wait", "Activate a terminal" and "Turn around". Note that all these actions are atomic except for the "Turn around" action which can be broken down in two actions "Turn right" or "Turn left".
- **Control blocks:** These blocks allow the player to control the action blocks to be executed: "If Then", "If Then Else", "Repeat n times", "While" and "Forever".
- **Sensors:** These blocks give information about the environment around the agents. The sensors return Boolean values that can be used in the "If Then", "If Then Else" and "While" control blocks. The sensors allow the agent to know whether a wall is in front of it, to its left, or its right; whether a pathway is in front of it, to its left, or its right; whether a guard, a guarded area, or a door is in front of it; and whether a terminal or an exit is on its position.
- **Operators:** These blocks allow the player to combine sensors. We find the classic Boolean operators: "No", "Or" and "And". Note that some sensors can be expressed by other sensors using the operators, for example "Wall in front" is equivalent to "No Pathway in front".
- **Blocks limitation:** SPY gives the possibility for each level to define available resources (quantity of each programming blocks). This feature is useful to reduce or increase the complexity of a level. For example, an introductory level could contain only useful blocks for solving the level, thus preventing the player to choose between useless blocks. On the other hand, restricting access to (or the quantity of) certain blocks force the player to use other blocks. For example, we can give only one "Move forward" block to force the usage of "Repeat n times" control block for moving an agent several squares forward.

3.2 Programming Area

The programming area is the second fundamental functionality of SPY. It hosts the programming blocks allowing the player to build solutions.

By default, each agent is associated with a programming area. It is however possible to break this association to ask the player to define it. In this case, the player has to indicate in the programming area the name of the agent linked. Thus, on execution, the program will be sent to the linked agent.

A programming area can contain an initial program, which can be optimal, non-optimal, or buggy. The player will therefore have to complete or correct it if necessary.

Finally, SPY allows to associate several agents to a unique programming area. This gives the opportunity to designers to build levels where the player will have to find a solution not only for one agent but for several agents. The player will have to design generic solutions.

3.3 Drag and Drop

Drag and drop is the third fundamental functionality in the SPY game because it allows the player to edit programming areas. However, it is possible to disable this feature, in this case, the level has to offer one or more pre-built programs. This feature allows designers to build levels where the player does not have to program but has to read several programs, understand them and choose which one to send to the agent(s) (see Fig. 2).

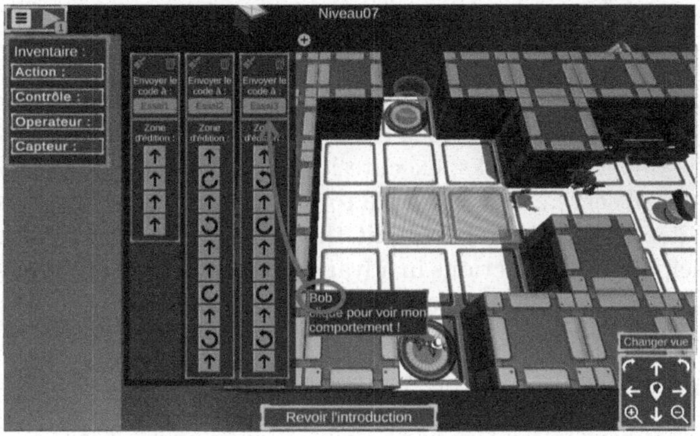

Fig. 2. Example level where drag an drop is disabled. The player has to replace one of the *Essai1*, *Essai2* or *Essai3* with the name of the robot (Bob). In this example the right solution is *Essai3*.

3.4 Obstacles

To solve the different levels of the game, the player must program one or more agents for them to reach a particular position while avoiding obstacles. These obstacles have been designed with a didactic intention.

Guards monitor areas of the maze (see red squares on the ground in Fig. 2). If an agent is detected by a guard, the player loses. Also, as for the agents, the guards can have pre-built program that makes the monitored areas dynamic. The player can select each guard in the game, observe the program that composes it, understand this program, anticipate the guard's movements, and program the agent accordingly.

Doors can be opened and closed using terminals. This feature was introduced to initiate a stepwise resolution process. When a door blocks the pathway, the player must break down his/her solution into steps (objective 1: activate the terminal to open the door; and objective 2: reach the exit). Doors also allow the manipulation of objects with changing state (open or closed).

3.5 Control Execution

When the player wants to test his/her solution s/he clicks on the start button. Each programming area sends its program to the target agent if it exists and each agent/guard executes its actions in parallel. The player can follow the execution of the programs by observing the agents/guards moving in the scene. The ongoing action is highlighted in the program execution panel. The player can pause the simulation at any time and execute the programs step by step.

3.6 Number of Executions

Finding a program, that moves the agent directly from the starting point to the ending point, in one attempt can be a complex task, especially on levels with moving guards. SPY authorizes to solve a level in several moves. The player can define a first sequence of blocks, execute it, observe the new situation, add new blocks, execute, observe... It is possible to find the solution step by step.

However, it can be relevant to limit this number of executions to force the player to anticipate several actions in advance. For each level of SPY, it is possible to define the authorized number of executions to solve it.

3.7 Fog and Briefing

In a default SPY level, the player has an omniscient view of the situation which allows him/her to plan his/her actions to reach the objective described in the briefing. The fog allows modifying this rule by limiting the view of an agent to its close environment In this case, the briefing plays a fundamental role, as it should contain clues allowing the player to find the solution. For example, the algorithm can be given in the briefing in natural language and the player has to translate it using the formal language of the game.

3.8 Synthesis of the Game Functionalities

The analysis of the different functionalities of SPY shows us that each of them is didactic. Some of them are obvious, such as the control blocks that allow to manipulate the associated programming notions. Others are hidden, such as i) the associated program of a guard that will require the player to understand it and to anticipate its execution, or ii) the use of a single programming area to control two agents that will force the player to generalize his/her solution.

From a macro point of view, the different features of SPY allow covering the skills of computational thinking as defined by Wing [16]. The player has to observe and model the simulation (abstraction), break down his/her strategy into steps (decomposition), determine the best solution (evaluation), plan the actions (algorithmic thinking), and reuse and adapt previous solutions to new problems (generalization). But how do we identify if a particular skill is involved in a given level? How combinations of features influence skills involved?

4 Linking Skills to Game Features

To describe a skill we define constraints based on game features that we evaluate with a Boolean expression. If this rule is true because the set of constraints is satisfied, then we consider that the skill is involved in the analyzed level. The rules and constraints defined for each skill are based on the level structure described in XML format. Table 1 shows the tags we reference in this article. A complete and commented level model is given in [11].

Table 1. Main tags description structuring a SPY level.

Tag	Description
<dragdropDisabled>	If present, disables drag and drop functionality
<blockLimit blockType="X" limit="Y">	If present, defines the quantity Y of blocks of type X available in the inventory (if Y = -1 ⇒ block is unlimited)
<player inputLine="X">	Defines an agent controlled by the player. This agent listens to the communication channel X
<enemy inputLine="X">	Defines a guard. This guard listens to the communication channel X
<script outputLine="X" editMode="Y" type="Z">	Defines a programming area that will send its content on communication channel X (see <player> and <enemy> tag). The **editMode** property indicates whether or not the player can change the communication channel. The **type** property indicates whether this programming area contains an optimal, non-optimal, buggy, or undefined pre-built program

The identification of a skill is then based on the evaluation of a set of constraints. Table 2 describes the set of parameters that can be applied to a constraint. In the following section, we give some examples of constraints that we have defined to characterize some PIAF skills.

5 Application of the PIAF Skills Formalization

As we presented in the introduction, we choose to base our work on the PIAF framework. It is focused on computational thinking and proposes six main skills. Each of these skills is broken down into a set of sub-skills for a total of 26 sub-skills [14].

The six main skills are: C1 - Abstracting away/generalizing; C2 - Compose/decompose a sequence of actions; C3 - Control a sequence of actions; C4 - Evaluate objects or sequences of actions; C5 - Translate between representations; and C6 - Build a sequence of actions iteratively. In the rest of the article we refer to the PIAF skills as follows: CX.Y means that sub-skill Y of skill X is involved, e.g. C2.4 refers to the fourth sub-skill of C2.

Table 2. Description of possible constraints.

$TAG \in$ set of XML tags
$ATTR \in$ set of valid attributes for TAG
$OPP \in \{=, <, \leq, >, \geq, \neq\}$
$VAL \in \mathbb{N}$

Constraint	Description
TAG	Filters TAG tags
$TAG\ ATTR\ OP\ VAL$	Filters TAG tags that have an attribute $ATTR$ equal/different... to an integer value
$TAG\ ATTR$ *include* SET	Filters TAG tags that have an attribute $ATTR$ whose value is included in a set of values (SET)
$TAG\ ATTR$ *sameValue* TAG_2 $ATTR_2$	Filters TAG tags that have an attribute $ATTR$ whose value is equal to the value of the attribute $ATTR_2$ of tag TAG_2
TAG *hasChild*	Filters TAG tags that contain at least one child tag

The description of all PIAF skills is not exhaustively developed here. The set of rules and constraints used to characterize the PIAF skills according to the game features is available in [12]. Here, we describe with precision three PIAF skills and we summarize the others.

5.1 C1.1 - Name Objects and (sequences of) Actions

Skill C1.1 is defined as follow: "Being able to give names to objects, actions and sequences of actions" [14, p. 2].

In SPY we consider that this skill is involved when the player can link a programming area with an agent. Indeed, in this case, he has to name his/her program so that it is executed by the right agent.

We describe this skill using the constraint "**TAG ATTR OP VAL**" which is instantiated as follow: "**script editMode** = **2**". This constraint means: "filters'script' tags that have an 'editMode' attribute 'equal' to the value 2". The boolean expression that defines the complete rule is then $C1.1 = Card(scripteditMode = 2) \geq 1$ which means: "Skill C1.1 is involved in the level if the cardinal of the constraint is greater than 0", in other words "if the level contains at least one nameable programming area".

5.2 C1.5 - Predict the Outcome of a Sequence of Actions

Skill C1.5 is defined as: "Being able to tell, from a sequence of actions, what will happen if it is executed. In contrast to competency 1.4, this competency is about providing a prediction without actually executing the sequence of actions" [14, p. 5].

In SPY, this skill is involved when a level contains a guard with a pre-built program. In this case, the player has to anticipate the movements of the guard. The player will have to propose a first solution to see the guard movements and check his/her predictions.

To describe this skill, it is necessary to check that a programming area is linked with a guard and contains at least one action.

The rule is described using a double parameter: (P1) "**TAG ATTR** sameValue **TAG2 ATTR2**" on one hand and (P2) "**TAG** hasChild" on the other hand.

The first parameter ensures that a guard ("enemy" tag) listens to the same communication line ("inputLine" attribute) as a programming area ("script" tag and "outputLine" attribute). P1 is instantiated as follow: "**enemy inputLine** sameValue **script outputLine**".

The second parameter ensures that the programming area ("script" tag) contains at least one action. P2 is instantiated as follow: "**script** hasChild".

The Boolean expression that defines the complete rule is the intersection of the two parameters: $C1.5 = Card(P1 \cap P2) \geq 1$.

5.3 C2.1 - Order a Sequence of Actions to Reach a Goal

Skill C2.1 is defined as: "Given an unordered list of actions and a goal, being able to combine these actions in a valid order to build a sequence that achieves the goal. [...] So, the learner does not need to identify all the parts needed to achieve the goal, but only their correct order" [14, p. 7].

In SPY, this is a situation where the player has only useful blocks available to solve the problem. The player has to simply arrange them in the right order to solve the level.

To describe this skill, it is necessary to fulfil the following constraints: (R1) drag and drop is activated to allow the player to combine actions; (R2) no unlimited block is available; and (R3) there is at least one action available in the inventory.

Rule R1 is described using the constraint "**TAG**" which is instantiated with the tag "**dragdropDisabled**". We want to check that drag and drop is active and therefore that the "dragdropDisabled" tag is not in the level description. R1 is defined as $Card(dragdropDisabled) = 0$.

Rule R2 is described using the constraint "**TAG ATTR OP VAL**" which is instantiated as follow: "**blockLimit limit = -1**". This constraint means: "filters'blockLimit' tags that have a 'limit' attribute 'equal' to the value -1". We want to check that there is no unlimited amount of blocks, so R2 is defined as $Card(blockLimit\ limit = -1) = 0$.

The rule R3 is described using a double parameter: (P1) "**TAG ATTR OP VAL**" on one hand and (P2) "**TAG ATTR** include **SET**" on the other hand. The first parameter identifies whether a block is available in the inventory ("**blockLimit limit ≥ 1**") and the second whether this block is an action block ("**blockLimit blockType** include **{Forward, TurnLeft, TurnRight, Wait, Activate, TurnBack}**"). The cardinal of the intersection of these two parameters counts the number of action blocks available in the inventory. R3 is defined as follow: $Card(P1 \cap P2) \geq 1$.

The Boolean expression that defines the complete rule is then: $C2.1 = R1 \ \&\& \ R2 \ \&\& \ R3$.

5.4 Summary of Skills Encoded

To simplify the description of skills in this section, we name recurring rules and parameters as follows: $NPA()$: number of **N**ameable **P**rogramming **A**rea $\rightarrow Card(script\ editMode = 2)$; $CPA()$: number of **C**orrect **P**rogramming **A**reas $\rightarrow Card(script\ type = 0)$; $NOPA()$: number of **N**on **O**ptimal **P**rogramming **A**reas $\rightarrow Card(script\ type = 1)$; $BPA()$: number of **B**ugged **P**rogramming **A**reas $\rightarrow Card(script\ type = 2)$; $IBQ(B, Q)$: true if level **I**ncludes at least one **B**lock B in **Q**uantity Q, false otherwise $\rightarrow Card((blockLimit\ blockType = B) \cap (blockLimit\ limit \geq Q)) \geq 1$; $ISQ(S, Q)$: true if level **I**ncludes at least one item of the **S**et S in **Q**uantity Q, false otherwise $\rightarrow Card((blockLimit\ blockTypeinclude\ S) \cap (blockLimit\ limit \geq Q)) \geq 1$; $DD()$: true if **D**rag&**D**rop is enabled, false otherwise $\rightarrow Card(dragdropDisabled) = 0$.

C1.1 Name objects and (sequences of) actions: if a level contains at least one nameable programming area; $C1.1 = NPA() \geq 1$.

C1.2 Differentiate (i) object and action, and (ii) atomic actions and non-atomic actions: if a level contains non-atomic actions ("Turn back" action (IBQ_1)) which can be decomposed into two atomic actions ("Turn left" actions (IBQ_2) or "Turn right" actions (IBQ_3)) or if a level contains actions (ISQ_1) and captors (ISQ_2) that illustrate the concept of expressions and instructions; $C1.2 = (IBQ_1(TurnBack, 1) \ \&\& \ (IBQ_2(TurnLeft, 2) \ || \ IBQ_3(TurnRight, 2))) || \ (ISQ_1(\{AllActions\},\ 1) \ \&\& \ ISQ_2(\{AllCaptors\}, 1))$.

C1.3 Identify the input parameters of a sequence of actions: No game mechanics for this skill; $C1.3 = \varnothing$.

C1.4 Describe the outcome of a sequence of actions: No game mechanics for this skill; $C1.4 = \varnothing$.

C1.5 Predict the outcome of a sequence of actions: if a level contains a guard with a pre-built program; $C1.5 = Card\ (enemy\ inputLine\ sameValuescript\ outputLine\ \cap\ script\ hasChild) \geq 1$.

C1.6 Using objects whose value can change: if a level contains conditional control structure (ISQ_1) and captors (ISQ_2) whose value varies according to the context or if a level makes it possible to control (IBQ) the state of a door ($R1$); **Rule:** $R1 \rightarrow Card(door\ slotId\ sameValue\ slot\ slotId) \geq 1$; $C1.6 = (ISQ_1(\{While, IfThen, IfElse\}, 1) \ \&\& \ ISQ_2(\{AllCaptors\}, 1)) \ ||(IBQ(Activate, 1) \ \&\& \ R1)$.

C1.7 Recognize existing objects and (sequences of) actions that can be used to reach a similar goal: if a level only provides nameable programming areas ($R1$) of which at least one is a correct pre-filled solution ($R2$) that the payer must recognize and cannot modify (DD); **Rules:** $R1 \rightarrow NPA() = Card(script)$; $R2 \rightarrow CPA() \cap (script\ hasChild)) \geq 1$; $C1.7 = R1 \ \&\& \ R2 \ \&\& \ !DD$.

C2.1 Order a sequence of actions to reach a goal: if a level allows the player to combine actions (DD) without unlimited blocks ($R1$) and with at least one action available in the inventory (ISQ); **Rule:** $R1 \rightarrow Card\ (blockLimitlimit = -1) = 0$; $C2.1 = DD\ \&\&\ R1\ \&\&\ ISQ(\{AllActions\}, 1)$.

C2.2 Complete a sequence of actions to reach a simple goal: if a level allows the player to combine (DD) only actions (ISQ_1) without control structures (ISQ_2) and only provides bugged pre-filled solutions ($R1$) for the player to complete; **Rule:** $R1 \rightarrow BPA() \cap (script\ hasChild)) = Card(script)$; $C2.2 = DD\ \&\&\ ISQ_1(\{AllActions\}, 1)\ \&\&\ !ISQ_2(\{ControlList\}, 1)\ \&\&\ R1$.

C2.3 Create a sequence of actions to reach a simple goal: if a level allows
the player to combine (DD) only actions (ISQ_1) without control structures (ISQ_2); $C2.3 = DD\ \&\&\ ISQ_1(\{AllActions\}, 1)\ \&\&\ !ISQ_2(\{ControlList\}, 1)$.

C2.4 Create a sequence of actions to reach a complex goal: if a level allows the player to combine (DD) actions (ISQ_1) and control structures (ISQ_2); $C2.4 = DD\ \&\&\ ISQ_1(\{AllActions\}, 1)\ \&\&\ ISQ_2(\{ControlList\}, 1)$.

C2.5 Combine sequences of actions to reach a goal: No game mechanics for this skill; $C2.5 = \varnothing$.

C2.6 Decompose goals into simpler subgoals: if a level does not limit the number of execution to 1; $C2.6 = Card(executionLimit\ amount = 1) = 0$.

C3.1 Repeat a sequence of actions a given number of times: if a level allows the player to combine (DD) For loops (IBQ); $C3.1 = DD\ \&\&IBQ(ForLoop, 1)$.

C3.2 Repeat a sequence of actions until a goal has been reached: if a level allows the player to combine (DD) While loops (IBQ) with captors (ISQ_1) and without operators (ISQ_2); $C3.2 = DD\ \&\&\ IBQ(WhileLoop, 1)\ \&\&ISQ_1(\{AllCaptors\}, 1)\ \&\&\ !ISQ_2(\{OperatorList\}, 1)$.

C3.3 Integrate a simple condition into a sequence of actions: if a level allows the player to combine (DD) If statements (ISQ_1) with captors (ISQ_2) and without operators (ISQ_3); $C3.3 = DD\ \&\&\ ISQ_1(\{If Then, IfElse\}, 1)\ \&\&ISQ_2(\{AllCaptors\}, 1)\ \&\&\ !ISQ_3(\{OperatorList\}, 1)$.

C3.4 Integrate a complex condition into a sequence of actions: if a level allows the player to combine (DD) conditionnal statements (ISQ_1) with captors (ISQ_2) and operators (ISQ_3); $C3.3 = DD\ \&\&\ ISQ_1(\{While, IfThen, IfElse\},\ 1)\ \&\&\ ISQ_2(\{AllCaptors\}, 1)\ \&\&\ ISQ_3(\{OperatorList\}, 1)$.

C4.1 Compare two objects according to a given criterion: No game mechanics for this skill; $C4.1 = \varnothing$.

C4.2 Compare two sequences of actions according to a given criterion: if a level only provides nameable pre-filled solutions ($R1$) with at least one correct solution and non-optimal solutions ($R2$) that the player cannot modify (DD); **Rules:** $R1 \rightarrow NPA() = Card(script)$; $R2 \rightarrow CPA() \geq 1\ \&\&\ (CPA() + NOPA()) = Card(script)$; $C4.2 = R1\ \&\&\ R2\ \&\&\ !DD$.

C4.3 Improve a sequence of actions according to a given criterion: if a level only provides pre-filled non-optimal solutions ($R1$) that the player must fix (DD); **Rule:** $R1 \rightarrow NOPA() \geq 1$ && $NOPA() = Card(script)$; $C4.3 = R1$ && DD.

C5.1 Represent objects or sequences of actions through one formal representation: if a level asks the player to combine (DD) action blocks (ISQ); $C5.1 = DD$ && $ISQ(\{AllActions\}, 1)$.

C5.2 Translate objects or sequences of actions between formal representations: if a level hides the exit position; $C5.2 = Card(fog) \geq 1 \, || Card(hideExits) \geq 1$.

C6.1 Verify if a sequence of actions reaches a given goal: if a level contains a robot to be programmed; $C6.1 = Card(player) \geq 1$.

C6.2 Notice errors in a sequence of actions: No game mechanics for this skill; $C6.2 = \varnothing$.

C6.3 Fix a sequence of actions for reaching a given goal: if a level only provides pre-filled bugged solutions ($R1$) that the player must fix (DD); **Rule:** $R1 \rightarrow BPA() \geq 1$ && $BPA() = Card(script)$; $C6.3 = R1$ && DD.

C6.4 Extend or modify a sequence of actions to reach a new goal: if a level requires the player to combine (DD) action blocks (ISQ) to control multiple robots with the same program ($R1$); **Rule:** $R1 \rightarrow Card(player\ inputLinesameValue\ player\ inputLine) \geq 2$; $C6.4 = DD$ && $ISQ(\{AllActions\}, 1)$ && $R2$.

6 Results

We have summarized the description of PIAF skills with the proposed formalization and we have illustrated in detail the description of three of them. In addition to the PIAF skills, we have tested our formalization with another skills base. We have described the 5 levels of the "3.4 Programming" skill from the CRCN domain 3 "Content creation"[5]. Finally, we have used the formalization to describe the set of playful functionalities of SPY (called SPY functionalities base). All these descriptions are available in [12].

Thus we can analyze each level with respect to the different skills bases. Table 3 illustrates the analysis of one level with the 3 skills bases. This visualization gives to the teacher the skills involved according to the skills base. In this example, the level 1 of CRCN skill 3.4 has been identified. It is defined as "Read and construct an algorithm with simple instructions"[6]. CRCN skills base is less precise than the PIAF ones but gives a overall view of skills involved. With these different levels of information, the teacher will determine if the level is an interesting candidate to integrate his/her pedagogical scenario.

[5] CRCN (*Cadre de Référence des Compétences Numériques*) is a french skills base inspired by the DigComp 2.1: https://eduscol.education.fr/document/20389/download, accessed April 7, 2023.

[6] translated from french "Lire et construire un algorithme qui comprend des instructions simples".

Table 3. Analysis of one level with the different skills bases

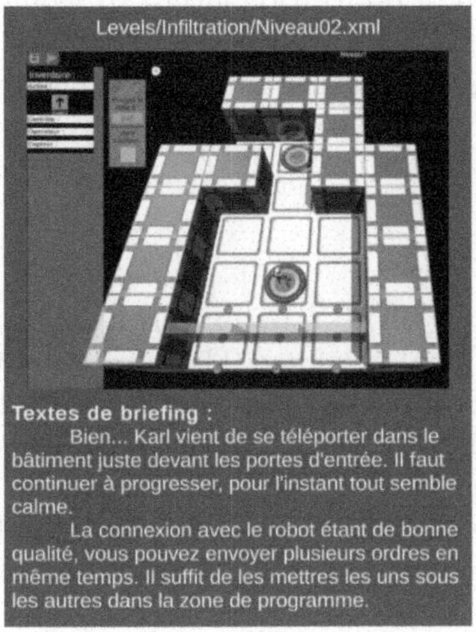

PIAF skills base: C2.1 - Order a sequence of actions to reach a goal C2.3 - Create a sequence of actions to reach a simple goal C2.6 - Decompose goals into simpler sub-goals C5.1 - Represent objects or sequences of actions through one formal representation C6.1 - Verify if a sequence of actions reaches a given goal
CRCN skills base: Level 1
SPY skills base: F1 - Solve a problem in several steps F10 - unlimited blocks F11 - action block "Move forward"

We can also use these descriptions to analyze the complexity of a game scenario. SPY contains two scenarios: an original SPY called "Infiltration" consisting of 20 levels and a copy of the BlocklyMaze game[7] consisting of 10 levels. Teachers can also build their own scenarios by composing them from the existing level library. We used the PIAF skills base to characterize the didactic dimension of the different scenarios and the SPY functionalities base to characterize their playful dimension. The combination of skills and playful features in each level gives an indicator of its complexity (see Fig. 3). We observe the progressive evolution of the complexity and the appearance of the different skills during the two scenarios. This visualization allows to compare the complexity of scenarios based on common criteria. We can see that Infiltration starts lower and ends higher than BlocklyMaze but the progression is smoother on BlocklyMaze. This visual-

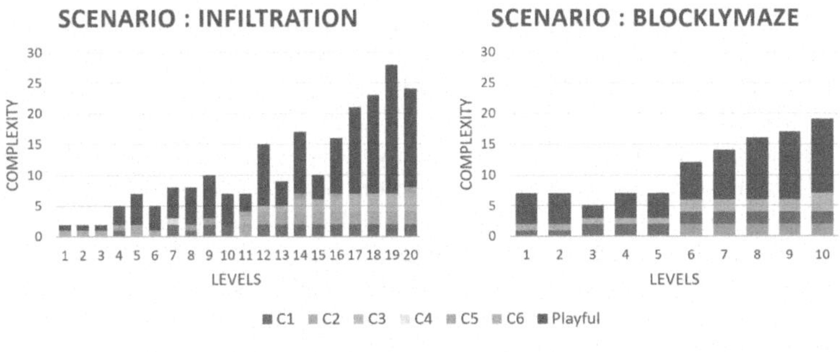

Fig. 3. Analysis of two scenarios.

[7] BlocklyMaze: https://blockly.games/maze, accessed April 10, 2023.

ization is also useful for designers to detect uncovered skills or unbalanced levels. For instance we can see that C4 is only covered in Infiltration level 7. It would be interesting to create levels focused on PIAF skills C4.2 and C4.3. This analysis also reveals some complexity peaks (levels 12 and 14 of Infiltration). These are interesting indicators to study these levels and considering adjustments.

7 Conclusion and Perspectives

In this paper we performed a didactic analysis of SPY by exploring the main features of the game in relation to computational thinking. Then, we proposed a formalization to describe skills from game features. We used this formalization to propose a description of i) the 21 PIAF skills involved in SPY, ii) the 5 levels of CRCN skills base and iii) the 35 game features of SPY. All the results are presented in [12]. We have shown that the proposed formalization is independent of skills bases. We have detailed in this article an extract of these results using the C1.1, C1.5 and C2.1 skills of the PIAF base.

Finally, we have shown how these descriptions can be used to build metadata on existing levels. These descriptions provide to teachers and designers micro information about the active skills in a level or macro information about the evolution of the game scenario complexity.

Currently the SPY game does not contain a level editor. The creation or modification of levels is not very accessible (editing XML files by hand). One perspective for this work is to propose an editor allowing teachers to create their own game levels. This will give autonomy to teachers as they will get an automatic skill analysis of their own levels.

Acknowledgements. The author acknowledges the support of the French Agence Nationale de la Recherche (ANR), under grant ANR-18-CE38-0008 (project IECARE) and Stéphanie Chane Chick Te for her proofreading of this article.

References

1. Balacheff, N.: La transposition informatique, un nouveau problème pour la didactique. In: Artigue, M., Gras, R., Laborde, C., Tavignot, P., Balacheff, N., (ed.) colloque "Vingt ans de didactique des mathématiques en France", 15–17 juin 1993, pp. 364–370. Recherches en didactique des mathématiques, La Pensée Sauvage, Paris, France (1993). https://telearn.archives-ouvertes.fr/hal-00190646
2. Baron, G.L., Drot-Delange, B., Grandbastien, M., Tort, F.: Computer science education in french secondary schools: historical and didactical perspectives. ACM Trans. Comput. Educ. **14**(2) (2014). https://doi.org/10.1145/2602486
3. Branthôme, M.: Pyrates: a serious game designed to support the transition from block-based to text-based programming. In: European Conference on Technology Enhanced Learning (EC-TEL 2022). Lecture Notes in Computer Science, vol. 13450, pp. 31–44 (2022)

4. Chiprianov, V., Gallon, L.: Introducing computational thinking to K-5 in a French context. In: 21st Annual Conference on Innovation and Technology in Computer Science Education (ITiCSE 2016). ACM Press, Arequipa, Peru (2016). https://doi.org/10.1145/2899415.2899439, https://hal-univ-pau.archives-ouvertes.fr/hal-01908224
5. Kradolfer, S., Dubois, S., Riedo, F., Mondada, F., Fassa, F.: A sociological contribution to understanding the use of robots in schools: the thymio robot. In: Beetz, M., Johnston, B., Williams, M.A. (eds.) Soc. Robot., pp. 217–228. Springer International Publishing, Cham (2014). https://doi.org/10.1007/978-3-319-11973-1_22
6. Laisney, P., Chatoney, M.: Instrumented activity and theory of instrument of Pierre Rabardel. In: Philosophy of Technology for Technology Education to Sense/Brill (2018). https://hal-amu.archives-ouvertes.fr/hal-01903109
7. Lindberg, R.S.N., Laine, T.H., Haaranen, L.: Gamifying programming education in k-12: a review of programming curricula in seven countries and programming games. British J. Educ. Technol. **50**(4), 1979–1995 (2019). https://doi.org/10.1111/bjet.12685, https://bera-journals.onlinelibrary.wiley.com/doi/abs/10.1111/bjet.12685
8. Mariotti, M.A., Maracci, M.: resources for the teacher from a semiotic mediation perspective, pp. 59–75. Springer, Netherlands, Dordrecht (2012). https://doi.org/10.1007/978-94-007-1966-8_4
9. Marne, B., Wisdom, J., Huynh-Kim-Bang, B., Labat, J.M.: The six facets of serious game design: a methodology enhanced by our design pattern library. In: Seventh European Conference on Technology Enhanced Learning (EC-TEL 2012). Lecture Notes in Computer Science, vol. 7563, pp. 208–221. Springer, Berlin/Heidelberg, Saarbrücken, Germany (Sep 2012). https://doi.org/10.1007/978-3-642-33263-0_17, https://hal.sorbonne-universite.fr/hal-00739124
10. Miljanovic, M.A., Bradbury, J.S.: A review of serious games for programming. In: Göbel, S., et al. (eds.) Serious Games, pp. 204–216. Springer International Publishing, Cham (2018). https://doi.org/10.1007/978-3-030-02762-9_21
11. Muratet, M.: Complete and commented level model in XML format (2023). https://github.com/Mocahteam/SPY/blob/master/Doc/LevelModel.xml. Accessed 19 Jun 2023
12. Muratet, M.: Description of PIAF skills using the SPY game features (2023). https://github.com/Mocahteam/SPY/blob/master/Assets/StreamingAssets/Competencies/competenciesReferential.json. Accessed 19 Jun 2023
13. Parmentier, Y., et al.: PIAF: developing computational and algorithmic thinking in fundamental education. In: EdMedia+ Innovate Learning, Association for the Advancement of Computing in Education (AACE), pp. 315–322 (2020)
14. PIAF Project: the complete list of the 26 PIAF skills and their description (2021). https://piaf.loria.fr/wp-content/uploads/2021/09/PIAF-Referential-of-Competencies-Description-and-Examples.pdf. Accessed 19 Jun 2023
15. Saddoug, H., Rahimian, A., Marne, B., Muratet, M., Sehaba, K., Jolivet, S.: Review of the adaptability of a set of learning games meant for teaching computational thinking or programming in France. In: Special Session on Gamification on Computer Programming Learning, vol. 1, pp. 562–569. SCITEPRESS - Science and Technology Publications, Prague, Czech Republic (Apr 2022). https://doi.org/10.5220/0011126400003182, https://hal.science/hal-03668918
16. Wing, J.M.: Computational thinking. Commun. ACM **49**(3), 33–35 (2006)

Evaluating ChatGPT's Decimal Skills and Feedback Generation in a Digital Learning Game

Huy A. Nguyen[1](✉), Hayden Stec[1], Xinying Hou[2], Sarah Di[1], and Bruce M. McLaren[1]

[1] Carnegie Mellon University, Pittsburgh, PA 15213, USA
hn1@cs.cmu.edu
[2] University of Michigan, Ann Arbor, MI 48104, USA

Abstract. While open-ended self-explanations have been shown to promote robust learning in multiple studies, they pose significant challenges to automated grading and feedback in technology-enhanced learning, due to the unconstrained nature of the students' input. Our work investigates whether recent advances in Large Language Models, and in particular ChatGPT, can address this issue. Using decimal exercises and student data from a prior study of the learning game *Decimal Point*, with more than 5,000 open-ended self-explanation responses, we investigate ChatGPT's capability in (1) solving the in-game exercises, (2) determining the correctness of students' answers, and (3) providing meaningful feedback to incorrect answers. Our results showed that ChatGPT can respond well to conceptual questions, but struggled with decimal place values and number line problems. In addition, it was able to accurately assess the correctness of 75% of the students' answers and generated generally high-quality feedback, similar to human instructors. We conclude with a discussion of ChatGPT's strengths and weaknesses and suggest several venues for extending its use cases in digital teaching and learning.

Keywords: ChatGPT · Decimal Numbers · Automated grading · Self-Explanation

1 Introduction

As Large Language Models (LLMs) have become more accessible in recent years, questions have risen across scientific domains about the potential applications of these powerful tools. Within the field of education, there is noticeable excitement about the possibility of incorporating LLMs into digital learning platforms [14, 18, 23, 28]. Past research in the area of assessment and evaluation has yielded promising results from LLMs [20, 28], and with the availability of more powerful and generalizable models like ChatGPT [32], it is now feasible to ask whether these technologies can go beyond traditional classification tasks to generating high-quality, human-like feedback that benefit both students and teachers alike.

O. Viberg et al. (Eds.): EC-TEL 2023, LNCS 14200, pp. 278–293, 2023.
https://doi.org/10.1007/978-3-031-42682-7_19

Our work explores one such use case in the context of *Decimal Point*, a game that teaches decimal numbers and operations to middle school students. *Decimal Point* features a series of mini-games, where the player solves a decimal problem (e.g., placing 0.456 on a number line between -1 and 1) and then responds to a self-explanation prompt (e.g., "Is 0.456 to the left or right of the number line? How do you know?"). The game has been deployed in many classroom studies to explore a variety of learning game topics [9, 10, 17], with a recent study showing that open-ended self-explanation prompts yielded the best learning outcomes, compared to multiple-choice and drag-and-drop formats, without disrupting the game play experience [17]. However, grading the open-ended responses was highly labor-intensive and could not be carried out in real-time [21], thus limiting the students' opportunities to learn from timely feedback. This drawback motivates our current work, which explores the capabilities of ChatGPT to serve as a "teaching assistant" tasked with grading and generating feedback for students' self-explanations in the game. In particular, we focused on three research questions:

RQ1: Can ChatGPT correctly answer the problem-solving and self-explanation questions in the game *Decimal Point*?

RQ2: Can ChatGPT accurately rate the correctness of students' self-explanation answers?

RQ3: Can ChatGPT provide *instructionally meaningful* feedback to incorrect self-explanation answers?

Through the investigation of these questions, our work makes the following contributions to the area of technology-enhanced learning. First, we report the evaluation results of a state-of-the-art LLM on a large volume of real student data, with actionable insights into its strengths and weaknesses. Second, we introduce a generalizable workflow for assessing the pedagogical value of ChatGPT's outputs, including a 6-category coding rubric that can be applied to other knowledge domains. Finally, we have open sourced our ChatGPT querying scripts to support reproducibility and assist other researchers in their own explorations of LLMs' potential.

2 Background

2.1 Self-explanation in Digital Learning Games

Prompted self-explanation has been shown to support meaningful learning and help develop metacognitive skills within digital learning games. For instance, [11] reported that multiple-choice self-explanation prompts within a digital learning environment aimed towards helping students acquire scientific concepts about light and shadow led to higher learning gains than no self-explanation. Additionally, [22] found that within a middle school fractions game, menu-based self-explanation prompts aimed towards helping students draw connections between game terminology and mathematics terminology were more effective for learning than no self-explanation prompts.

However, not all studies support incorporating self-explanation into learning games. [1] reported that in the game *Newtonian Game Dynamics*, there were no learning differences between students in the self-explanation condition with explanatory feedback and the control condition with neither self-explanation nor explanatory feedback. In addition, students in the experimental condition completed fewer game levels than the control group, demonstrating that self-explanation has the potential to disrupt game flow and introduce extraneous cognitive processing. Wylie and Chi [31] posit that this inconsistency in learning differences can be attributed to the *type* of prompted self-explanation used in digital learning games. In particular, there are five main types of self-explanation cast along a continuum from *unconstrained self-explanation* prompts, where learners create their own explanations without guidance, to *highly constrained self-explanation* prompts (i.e., *menu-based self-explanations*), where learners choose from a given set of explanations. According to Johnson & Mayer [12], highly constrained self-explanations present less cognitive load to learners and could therefore lead to better learning outcomes. On the other hand, Wylie and Chi [31] argue that less constrained self-explanation prompts foster more *constructive* and *active* engagement with the learning material, whereby the learner is prompted to generate their own explanations (constructive) and type or write them down (active). In turn, these activities enable learners to connect their prior knowledge, fill in gaps of understanding and achieve better learning outcomes.

Other than their cognitive loads, a major difference between these self-explanation formats lies in the ability to provide feedback to students. Highly constrained questions typically correspond to a fixed set of solutions that can be checked by a computer system, thus enabling real-time feedback generation. On the other hand, unconstrained self-explanations are difficult to grade in an automated manner, due to challenges in understanding student inputs in the presence of varied writing styles, grammatical errors and misspellings [25]. Even so, automated grading of open-ended answers remains a crucial area of research, as it can enable timely feedback that helps students improve their learning [33]. More recently, the development of large language models may provide a pathway towards this capability in a wide range of learning platforms. In the following sections, we further describe recent advances in language models and our evaluation of this hypothesis.

2.2 Large Language Models in Education

Large language models (LLMs) generally function by leveraging massive corpora of textual data as input to transformer-based models, consisting of hundreds of billions of parameters [7]. The hallmark of the transformer architecture is the attention mechanism, which helps these models make better predictions by focusing on specific parts of the text that are relevant to the task at hand. Among the prominent LLMs is the Generative Pretrained Transformer (GPT) series developed by OpenAI, with the recent introduction of their GPT-3.5 model, released publicly as ChatGPT [32]. This model has been shown to excel at question-answering and various reasoning tasks, while demonstrating superior generalization compared to previous LLMs [24].

The release of ChatGPT has prompted a new wave of research on how it can be best applied in educational contexts [28]. Recent work has shown that ChatGPT can act as a tutor to reduce students' cognitive load in medical education [14], or generate algebra hints that improve student learning [23]. At the same time, there have been concerns about potential cheating or plagiarism in writing assignments, fueled by the ease at which ChatGPT can generate human-like writing within seconds [5]. While much of this debate centers around how students should and should not use ChatGPT, less attention has been paid to whether teachers and instructors can benefit from this technology. For example, [18] has shown that a GPT-3 model is able to help teachers detect high-quality student-generated questions that can be incorporated into future iterations of a college-level chemistry course. Our work seeks to further explore use cases in this direction, especially those that involve reviewing a significant amount of text data and typically require considerable efforts from human experts. In particular, we investigate whether ChatGPT can provide accurate assessments of, and high-quality feedback to, more than 5,000 self-explanation responses produced by students who play a digital learning game for decimal numbers. To our knowledge, this is the first rigorous evaluation of ChatGPT on a large volume of real student data. We elaborate on the data source and our evaluation criteria below.

2.3 The Learning Game *Decimal Point*

Decimal Point is a single-player, non-competitive learning game targeted at helping middle school students practice decimal numbers and operations [15]. The game specifically targets common decimal misconceptions held by students, such as longer decimals are larger than shorter decimals (e.g., 0.234 > 0.9). In the game, the student travels through a fictional amusement park with alien friends and completes a series of 24 mini-games. Each mini-game features two problem-solving questions, followed by a self-explanation prompt designed to address common decimal misconceptions and reinforce student learning (Fig. 1). There are five types of problem-solving questions; each type corresponds to specific templates for the self-explanation prompt that follows (Table 1). Throughout their game play, the student gets immediate feedback about the correctness of their answers, and can make any number of attempts to arrive at correct answers. In addition, they must answer all questions correctly to advance to the next mini-game round.

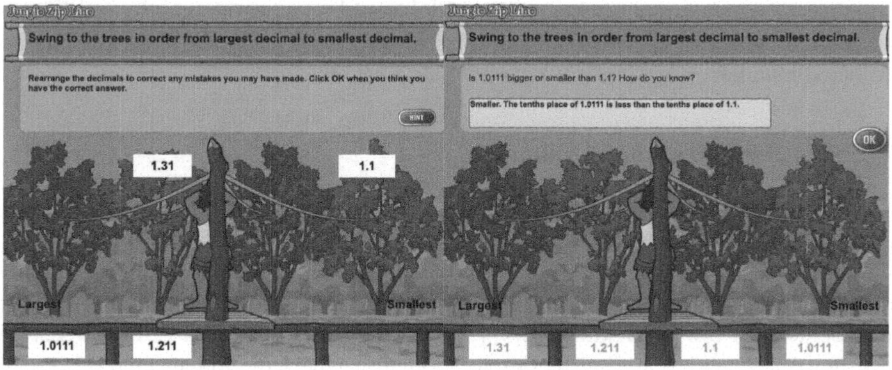

Fig. 1. A problem-solving question (left) and self-explanation prompt (right) in the mini-game Jungle Zipline. The student sorts a sequence of decimal numbers and then explains how to compare two numbers in this sequence.

Table 1. The types of problem-solving activities and the corresponding examples for self-explanation prompts.

Problem Type	Description	Self-explanation templates
Addition	Enter the carry and result digits when adding two decimal numbers	What should you do when there are more than 10 in any column?
Bucket	Label each given number as "bigger than" or "smaller than" a threshold	Is number X bigger or smaller than number Y? How do you know?
Number Line	Locate the position of a number on a number line between -1 and 1	Is number X closer to 0 or to −1/0.5/1? How do you know?
Sequence	Find the next two terms in an increasing or decreasing arithmetic sequence	What should you remember to find the next number in the sequence? When should you carry/how do you know?
Sorting	Sort the given decimal numbers in increasing or decreasing order	Is number X bigger or smaller than number Y? How do you know?

Decimal Point has been used in many classroom studies to explore different learning game topics, including, for instance, gender effects [10], open student models [9], and the benefits of self-explanation [17]. While most of these prior studies implemented multiple-choice self-explanation questions, we also experimented with two other formats, drag-and-drop and open-ended, in a study reported in [17]. Our results indicated that open-ended self-explanation prompts led to the best learning outcomes; however, because the students' responses are unstructured text, they could not be graded in real-time. Instead, we implemented a keyword matching heuristic, where the student's answer was considered acceptable if it contained more than three words, with at least one of the words matching a set of keywords that might be found in a correct explanation [17]. In this work, we investigate whether ChatGPT could address this gap by grading the students' answers and providing meaningful instructional feedback in a real-time and automated manner.

2.4 Types of Feedback and Evaluation

White the positive effects of feedback in digital learning platforms is well known [30], its benefits can be impacted by a variety of factors, including the timing and content of the feedback [29]. In particular, immediate feedback allows students to quickly identify and correct any mistakes or misconceptions they may have, which is especially helpful for students with low prior knowledge [26]. At the same time, delayed feedback has been shown to benefit learning in complex domains, where the longer intervals enable more time for reflection and knowledge assimilation [4].

Feedback content typically consists of a verification component – i.e., a simple "right" or "wrong" statement – and an elaboration component, which justifies the verification [13]. The elaboration may contain different kinds of information, including (1) task-specific information, such as the correct answer and relevant rubric items, (2) instruction-based information, which explains why an answer is correct or incorrect, and (3) extra-instructional information, which provides further worked examples or analogies not included in the original learning materials. Under this categorization schema, prior research has reported that feedback messages with both the verification and elaboration components can lead to better learning than those that only feature verification [30]. At the same time, the affective nature of the language used in feedback messages may also play a role in its effectiveness – for instance, encouraging and polite language can help students improve their learning, especially those with low prior knowledge [16].

In the context of *Decimal Point*, as the decimal exercises focus on addressing common decimal misconceptions [15], the use of immediate feedback with clear elaborations and positive language would provide the greatest benefit to students. Thus, with the introduction of ChatGPT, we are interested in whether the game can generate feedback messages with the desired qualities. In what follows, we further describe the properties of the decimal exercises in the game and our rubric for assessing ChatGPT's responses.

3 Methods and Materials

3.1 Dataset

We employed student data from a classroom study conducted by McLaren and colleagues [17] in the spring of 2021. In this study, 357 5th and 6th graders were randomly assigned to play the learning game *Decimal Point* with either multiple-choice, drag-and-drop, or open-ended self-explanation questions. For the purpose of our analysis, we focused on students' open-ended self-explanations and ChatGPT's capability in evaluating them. Thus, our final dataset contains 117 students who generated 5,142 open-ended self-explanation answers in total. Based on the manual coding of these answers, as reported in [21], there were 1,000 correct, 4,076 incorrect, and 66 off-topic answers, which we also treated as incorrect.

3.2 ChatGPT Queries

Our data collection with ChatGPT took place in the conversational web interface at https://chat.openai.com/chat, using the March 23 version of ChatGPT[1] and with GPT-3.5 as the underlying model [32]. We also utilized the ChatGPT Wrapper library[2] to automate the process of sending questions to ChatGPT and recording its responses. For RQ1 – whether ChatGPT can correctly answer the problem-solving and self-explanation questions in *Decimal Point* – ChatGPT's answers were evaluated by a researcher in the team who is experienced with middle school math education.

For RQ2 – whether ChatGPT can correctly label students' open-ended self-explanations as correct or incorrect – we made use of the student answers from [17] and the rubric for grading them from [21]. In particular, we constructed a query template (Fig. 2) that provides ChatGPT with the following information:

[1] https://help.openai.com/en/articles/6825453-chatgpt-release-notes.

[2] https://github.com/mmabrouk/chatgpt-wrapper.

- The self-explanation prompt (`se_prompt`), for example: "When adding two decimal numbers, how should you line up the numbers and add them?"
- The student's answer (`student_answer`), for example: "On top of the same values."
- The relevant grading rubric items (`rubric_items`) for this prompt, for example: "A correct response should mention aligning numbers by either the decimal point or decimal place values."

```
Given a student's self-explanation response after they've played an educational game about
decimal numbers, label each response as CORRECT or INCORRECT according to the
following guidelines.
    • INCORRECT responses deviate from the correct answer, use incorrect reasoning,
      are irrelevant, or do not directly answer the question.
    • If a response gives correct reasoning but does not explicitly answer the question it
      should still be labeled as CORRECT.
Note: Typos or grammatical errors should not be considered unless they affect the
correctness of the answer.
Here is the self-explanation question: se_prompt
Here is the student's response: student_answer
Here is the rubric for grading this question: rubric_items
Please answer with only a single word: 'CORRECT' or 'INCORRECT'. Do not include any
additional information.
```

Fig. 2. The query template for asking ChatGPT to grade a student's self-explanation answer. The placeholder fields `se_prompt`, `student_answer` and `rubric_items` are to be substituted for the actual data in each query.

For RQ3 – whether ChatGPT can provide instructionally meaningful feedback to incorrect self-explanation answers – we similarly constructed a query template, shown in Fig. 3, which contains the self-explanation prompt (`se_prompt`), grading rubric items (`rubric_items`), and the student's answer (`student_answer`). After collecting ChatGPT's feedback responses for all 4,142 incorrect answers in the dataset, based on the human labeling from [21], we carried out a qualitative coding process [6] to evaluate them as follows. First, one researcher analyzed 1.5% of the responses to develop a coding rubric. Three members of the team then independently coded 20% of the responses based on this rubric, with an inter-rater reliability (IRR) score of at least 60% in each category. Next, the three members met to resolve disagreements in their codes and refine the rubric. Finally, they applied the updated rubric to code the remaining 80% of the data. The final rubric is included in Table 2.

Suppose you are a middle school math teacher and you are currently teaching decimals. You want to grade students' explanations for how they solved a decimal question, as directed by a prepared question you wrote ahead of time. Given that question, a small rubric explaining the requirements for a correct answer, and the student's incorrect answer, please provide a clear and concise 1-3 sentences of feedback to the student about why their answer is incorrect and direct them to the correct answer.
Here is the self-explanation question: `se_prompt`
Here is the rubric for grading this question: `rubric_items`
Here is the student's response: `student_answer`

Fig. 3. The query template for asking ChatGPT to provide feedback to a student's incorrect self-explanation. The placeholder fields `se_prompt`, `rubric_items` and `student_answer` are to be substituted for the actual data in each query.

Table 2. The final coding rubric for evaluating ChatGPT's feedback to incorrect answers.

Category & Codes	Description	Cohen's κ
Accuracy (Yes, No, N/A)	Does ChatGPT accurately distinguish between partially correct and fully incorrect answers? Label N/A for questions with no partial credit	61.7%
Fluency (Yes, No)	Is the feedback written in grammatically correct and natural-sounding English?	99.8%
Regulation (Yes, No, N/A)	Does the feedback address all decimal misconceptions reflected in the answer? Label N/A for answers that do not clearly reflect any misconception	87.3%
Solution (Yes, No, Incorrect)	Does the feedback tell the student the correct answer?	69.9%
Rationale (Yes, No, Incorrect)	Does the feedback quote the appropriate rubric item(s) or provide a rationale to explain why an answer is incorrect?	94.2%
Encouragement (Yes, No)	Does the feedback provide any form of encouragement?	79.6%

4 Results

4.1 Evaluation of ChatGPT's Decimal Skills

We observed that the ChatGPT interface provides the option to re-generate the response to a previous question, which leads to a different answer due to a change in the underlying random seed. To account for this variability, we had ChatGPT answer each of the 48 problem-solving questions and 24 self-explanation prompts in *Decimal Point* ten times and observed how consistently its answers were correct. Figure 4 shows ChatGPT's problem-solving and self-explanation performance in each problem type, as evaluated by a researcher in the team. Among the problem-solving questions, ChatGPT was able to correctly solve most of the *Bucket* and *Sorting* exercises, which both involve decimal number comparisons. However, it tended to claim that longer negative decimals were greater than shorter negative decimals (e.g., $-1.701 > -1.7$) and longer positive decimals were less than shorter positive decimals (e.g., $0.299 < 0.29$), resulting in low correct rates at two *Bucket* problems. For decimal addition problems in the *Sequence* and *Addition* types, the majority of ChatGPT's numeric outputs were correct, but it did not provide the carry digits in *Addition* problems. Finally, ChatGPT struggled with *Number Line* problems the most, likely due to the need to visualize spatial distances that extends beyond text generation. Interestingly, in many cases ChatGPT could draw a valid number line and even correctly state where the given number should be located, but it still placed the number marker at an incorrect location.

With the self-explanation prompts, using the same rubric employed by [21] to grade student answers, we observed that ChatGPT was able to answer most questions correctly across all five problem types. There were only two questions in the *Sorting* type where ChatGPT provided incorrect reasoning. In particular, ChatGPT claimed that 9.222 is bigger than 9.2111 because "the digit 2 in the thousandths place of 9.222 is larger than the digit 1 in the hundredths place of 9.2111" and that 1.1 is bigger than 1.0111 "because both numbers have the digit 1 in the tenths place but the following digits are smaller in 1.0111 than in 1.1." These errors can be attributed to incorrect applications of decimal comparison by place values, and to mis-identifications of the values at each decimal place.

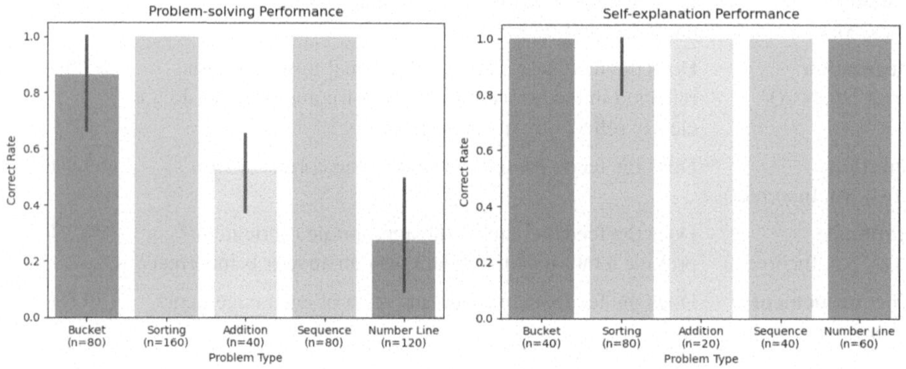

Fig. 4. ChatGPT's rate of correctness in the problem-solving and self-explanation questions, aggregated by problem type. Error bars denote the 95% confidence interval.

4.2 Evaluation of ChatGPT's Grading

Compared to the 1,000 correct and 4,142 incorrect labels of the self-explanation responses assigned by human graders in [21], ChatGPT identified 1,948 correct and 3,194 incorrect responses. Using the human labels as ground truth, we computed ChatGPT's accuracy as 0.75, ROC-AUC score as 0.78, and IRR as Cohen's $\kappa = 41.2\%$, with the full confusion matrix included in Table 3. We observed that most of the mismatches were due to ChatGPT grading an incorrect answer as correct, suggesting that it did not follow the grading rubrics as closely as human graders.

Table 3. The confusion matrix between humans' and ChatGPT's labels of the 5,142 self-explanation responses.

	Human: Correct	Human: Incorrect
ChatGPT: Correct	830	1,118
ChatGPT: Incorrect	170	3,024

The 1,118 cases of false positives are distributed across problem types as follows: 101 in *Bucket*, 174 in *Sorting*, 218 in *Addition*, 441 in *Sequence*, and 184 in *Number Line*. When analyzing the mismatches in each problem type, we observed the following patterns. For *Bucket* and *Sorting* self-explanation prompts, ChatGPT tended to focus on the presence of keywords such as "bigger" and "smaller" to determine correctness, regardless of whether the student provided an explanation or answered the question correctly (e.g., "−0.9 is smaller than 0.6 because it is smaller" was rated as correct by ChatGPT). In *Addition* problems, where the self-explanation prompts involve describing the process to line up two decimal numbers before adding them, ChatGPT tended to label student responses that included positional and directional words such as "underneath," "above," "left," and "right" (e.g. "underneath each other") as correct, even if they did not mention lining up by the decimal point or place values. In *Sequence* problems, students were asked to describe the general rule for finding the next numbers in a sequence, but many answers that were overly specific to the current mini-game (e.g. "to add 1.3 to whatever the last decimal is.") were regarded as correct by ChatGPT. Finally, we observed from *Number Line* responses that the provision of an answer, without the accompanying reasoning, was sufficient to get a correct label from ChatGPT. In general, ChatGPT appeared to rely on particular keywords extracted from the rubric to determine correctness, rather than the content of the explanations.

4.3 Evaluation of ChatGPT's Feedback

The 4,142 feedback paragraphs generated by ChatGPT had an average length of 3.4 sentences ($SD = 0.9$) and contained 64.5 words on average ($SD = 19.5$). Figure 5 shows the evaluation results of these feedback messages, based on the categories included in Table 2. We observed that all of ChatGPT's outputs demonstrated proficient English usage, with a 100% rating of YES in the *Fluency* category. 716 of its feedback messages also contained some forms of encouragement, including "your answer is on the right track," "great job" and "keep practicing," but there were no clear patterns for when ChatGPT decided to provide encouragement. Additionally, ChatGPT was able to detect 9 cases of offensive or disrespectful language that students used in their self-explanations, likely due to their frustration, and reminded them to maintain an appropriate attitude in class.

For the *Accuracy* category, among the 2,607 incorrect answers to the self-explanation questions where partial credit is available (e.g., "Is 0.456 to the left or right of the number

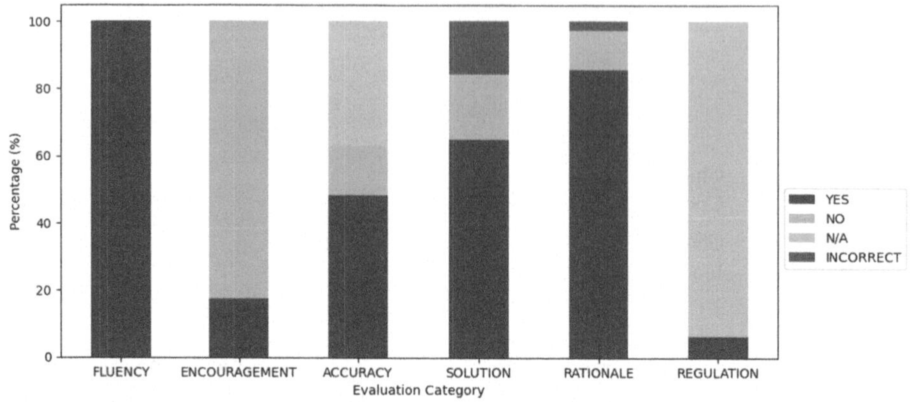

Fig. 5. The distribution of code labels for ChatGPT's feedback in each evaluation category.

line? How do you know?"), ChatGPT was able to distinguish between partially correct answers and fully incorrect answers 1,994 times. Partially correct answers are those that provide a correct statement (e.g., "to the right") but incorrect or missing explanations, or vice versa. However, there were 110 cases where ChatGPT mistook a partially correct answer for being fully correct and simply congratulated the student, instead of explaining their mistakes. These answers typically lacked the explanation component required in the grading rubric, suggesting that ChatGPT was sometimes unable to apply all of the rubric criteria in its feedback generation.

Additional instances of ChatGPT not following the input query are observed in the *Solution* category, where it did not provide the solution in its feedback to 794 incorrect answers, even though it was explicitly requested to do so (Fig. 3). In these cases, we observed that the students' answers were either empty, very brief or off-topic (e.g., "idk," "subtract," "by adding up"). In response, ChatGPT chose to remind the student of the relevant rubric items, instead of giving them the solution. However, there were also 659 cases where ChatGPT provided a solution that was incorrect. These cases predominantly fell into the *Sorting*, *Bucket* and *Number Line* problem types, where ChatGPT's solutions demonstrated similar issues as those in its responses to the problem-solving and self-explanation questions. In particular, with *Bucket* and *Sorting* problems, ChatGPT either mis-identified the decimal place values (e.g., "0.22 is bigger because it has a 2 in the tenths place value, whereas 0.2 only has a 0 in that place") or applied place values incorrectly in its comparisons ("9.222 is bigger than 9.2111 because the digit in the thousandths place is larger"). Likewise with *Number Line* problems, ChatGPT showed misconceptions about the number placement, even when its rationale was correct (e.g., "0.456 is a decimal number between 0 and 1, and since it is less than 0.5, it must be to the left of 0 on the number line").

While ChatGPT had occasional issues with generating its own solutions, it demonstrated good capabilities in understanding the students' answers and explaining the rationale for their incorrectness, as observed in 3,549 cases in the *Rationale* category. Our analysis showed that ChatGPT was able to provide a wide range of nuanced explanations to students, such as "your answer is not specific enough" or "good effort, but the reason why -8.517 is smaller than 8.5 is not explained in your answer." In many cases, it was able to directly reference the incorrect components of the students' answers. For instance, when responding to an incorrect answer, "[-0.07 is] closer to 0 because it has more digits," ChatGPT correctly pointed out that "the number of digits does not determine the closeness of a decimal number to 0 or -1." In general, while the majority of incorrect answers did not clearly reflect any misconceptions, due to students omitting the reasoning or not clearly expressing their thoughts, when misconceptions did manifest, ChatGPT was effective at addressing them in its feedback, as can be seen by the results of the *Regulation* category.

5 Discussion and Conclusion

In this work, we examined ChatGPT's capabilities as a "teaching assistant" to support student learning of decimal numbers in the digital learning game *Decimal Point*. Our goal was to derive actionable insights on the strengths and weaknesses of ChatGPT, and to identify its appropriate use cases in the classroom. Our first analysis of ChatGPT's responses to the problem-solving and self-explanation questions in the game revealed varying performance levels across decimal problem types. ChatGPT generally did well in decimal comparisons, but tended to make errors with numbers having three or more decimal digits. It could perform decimal additions and carrying correctly, but could not express when carrying took place. Finally, just as *Number Line* problems have been identified as the most difficult for students in prior studies [19], so did they pose the stiffest challenge to ChatGPT. Across the *Number Line* problems in the game, ChatGPT only answered one or two correctly out of ten, indicating a performance worse than chance. While identifying the cause of this poor performance can be difficult, as is typical with black-box neural networks, a feasible high-level explanation is that, as a probabilistic language model [2], ChatGPT is trained to output the most likely responses, rather than relying on internal mathematical rules. Thus, if a setting frequently appears in its training data, such as drawing a number line from -1 to 1, ChatGPT will be able to replicate it well, but will encounter problems with more specific tasks, such as locating 0.579 on the drawn number line. This line of reasoning also explains why ChatGPT had better performance in the self-explanation questions, where it could make better use of its language skills. We observed that ChatGPT was able to cite several textbook mathematical procedures almost verbatim (e.g., "if the sum of the digits in any column is greater than 9, you need to carry over the excess to the next column") to deliver satisfactory explanations, although it would still have occasional issues with applying these procedures to rarely occuring numbers such as 1.0111. Thus, at the moment, ChatGPT may be more suited for more conceptual rather than procedural math questions, and teachers should always double check its answers before sharing with their students.

Our second research question tests ChatGPT's comprehension skill, as we provide it with data from multiple sources – including the grading context, rubric items, input question and student's answer – and ask it to determine the correctness of the answer. Comparing ChatGPT's labels to ground-truth human labels from [21], we found that

ChatGPT had low false negatives (170) but high false positives (1,118). Further analyses showed that these mismatches are likely due to shallow keyword matching with the grading rubric, rather than a rigorous application of the provided rubric items. Because this correctness classification task is fairly specific to the questions and answers in the learning game *Decimal Point*, it is possible that ChatGPT, as a general-purpose task solver [24], could not detect all of the nuances in the grading rubric. In this case, its performance can be improved by fine-tuning the underlying model (GPT-3.5) on a portion of the human-labeled data from [21] to acquire more accurate domain embeddings; however, doing so would take away ChatGPT's ease of use and require deep learning expertise to scale to other knowledge domains and learning contexts.

Next, we performed a thorough analysis of ChatGPT's feedback messages to all of the 4,142 incorrect self-explanations in the dataset. Our most interesting insight is that ChatGPT exhibited several behaviors that fit the "suppose you are a middle school math teacher" setting in our input query, even though some of these behaviors were not explicitly specified, or even contradicted our other requests. First, it demonstrated fluent English communication, provided various forms of encouragement, and also called out students' usage of inappropriate language. Second, although we had asked ChatGPT to provide the solution in its feedback, ChatGPT only reminded students about the rubric and prompted them to try again when it detected low-effort submissions, i.e., answers that were empty, too brief or off-topic. This behavior is consistent with prior research reporting that, instead of being shown the solution right away, students should go through a stage of productive struggle to attain deep learning [27]. Third, despite the frequent grammatical errors and misspellings made by students, ChatGPT demonstrated a good understanding of the students' answers and was frequently able to point out which components were incorrect, as well as to address the underlying misconceptions. The primary weakness of ChatGPT's feedback lies in its provision of the solutions, which exhibit several patterns of incorrectness, as discussed above.

Given the above insights, we propose that ChatGPT can assist teachers in the initial review and feedback generation stage, where it can point out prominent errors, misconceptions and suggest a general feedback outline. However, due to potential inaccuracies in its mathematical statements, ChatGPT is not yet ready to be used as a standalone student-facing application, and all of its outputs should be double checked by a domain expert. At the same time, several improvements to ChatGPT, including the GPT-4 model with superior mathematics performance [3], are already released or under active development. Thus, future research should closely monitor the progress of these LLMs to identify the best opportunity to integrate them in digital learning platforms.

Finally, we should note the limitations of this current work. First, we have only investigated ChatGPT's performance in the domain of decimal numbers. While other research has tested ChatGPT on a wider range of mathematical tasks [8], due to the complexities underlying LLMs, it is difficult to infer whether ChatGPT's good performance in one domain will transfer to another domain. Thus, researchers and instructors should perform their own assessments to determine the appropriate use cases of ChatGPT in their respective domains. Second, because ChatGPT's outputs depend on a set of random seeds which the user does not have access to, our current results may suffer from a lack of replicability. We expect that the development and release of future LLMs will be more streamlined and offer users more control over their interaction with such models. In the meantime, we have shared our scripts for querying ChatGPT on GitHub[3] to support the research community in reproducing our data collection process. We envision this work as a foundational step towards more rigorous benchmarks for assessing the roles of LLMs in education. Ultimately, the field of LLMs would greatly benefit from the inputs of both AI researchers and educators alike to ensure its contribution towards scalable, equitable and effective technology-enhanced learning.

Acknowledgements. This work was supported by NSF Award #DRL-2201796. Thanks to Injila Adil for assisting with the coding of the self-explanation feedback.

References

1. Adams, D.M., Clark, D.B.: Integrating self-explanation functionality into a complex game environment: keeping gaming in motion. Comput. Educ. **73**, 149–159 (2014)
2. Bengio, Y., Ducharme, R., Vincent, P.: A neural probabilistic language model. Adv. Neural Inform. Process. Syst. **13** (2000)
3. Bubeck, S., et al.: Sparks of artificial general intelligence: early experiments with gpt-4. arXiv preprint arXiv:2303.12712 (2023)
4. Corral, D., Carpenter, S.K., Clingan-Siverly, S.: The effects of immediate versus delayed feedback on complex concept learning. Quar. J. Exper. Psychol. **74**(4), 786–799 (2021)
5. Cotton, D.R.E., Cotton, P.A., Shipway, J.R.: Chatting and Cheating: Ensuring academic integrity in the era of ChatGPT. EdArXiv, 1–11 (2023)
6. DeCuir-Gunby, J.T., Marshall, P.L., McCulloch, A.W.: Developing and using a codebook for the analysis of interview data: an example from a professional development research project. Field Meth. **23**(2), 136–155 (2011)
7. Devlin, J., Chang, M.-W., Lee, K., Toutanova, K.: Bert: Pre-training of deep bidirectional transformers for language understanding. arXiv preprint arXiv:1810.04805 (2018)
8. Frieder, S., et al.: Mathematical capabilities of chatgpt. arXiv preprint arXiv:2301.13867 (2023)
9. Hou, X., Nguyen, H.A., Richey, J.E., Harpstead, E., Hammer, J., McLaren, B.M.: Assessing the effects of open models of learning and enjoyment in a digital learning game. Int. J. Artif. Intell. Educ. **32**(1), 120–150 (2022)
10. Hou, X., Nguyen, H.A., Elizabeth Richey, J., McLaren, B. M.: Exploring how gender and enjoyment impact learning in a digital learning game. In: Bittencourt, I.I., Cukurova, M., Muldner, K., Luckin, R., Millán, E. (eds.) Artificial Intelligence in Education: 21st International Conference, AIED 2020, Ifrane, Morocco, July 6–10, 2020, Proceedings, Part I, pp. 255–268. Springer International Publishing, Cham (2020). https://doi.org/10.1007/978-3-030-52237-7_21
11. Hsu, Chung-Yuan., Tsai, Chin-Chung.: Investigating the impact of integrating self-explanation into an educational game: A pilot study. In: Chang, Maiga, Hwang, Wu-Yuin., Chen, Ming-Puu., Müller, Wolfgang (eds.) Edutainment 2011. LNCS, vol. 6872, pp. 250–254. Springer, Heidelberg (2011). https://doi.org/10.1007/978-3-642-23456-9_49
12. Johnson, C.I., Mayer, R.E.: Applying the self-explanation principle to multimedia learning in a computer-based game-like environment. Comput. Hum. Behav. **26**(6), 1246–1252 (2010)

[3] https://github.com/McLearn-Lab/ECTEL2023-DP-SE.

13. Kulhavy, R.W., Stock, W.A.: Feedback in written instruction: the place of response certitude. Educ. Psychol. Rev. **1**, 279–308 (1989)
14. Kung, T.H., et al.: Performance of ChatGPT on USMLE: potential for AI-assisted medical education using large language models. PLoS Digital Health **2**, 2, e0000198 (2023)
15. McLaren, B.M., Adams, D.M., Mayer, R.E., Forlizzi, J.: A computer-based game that promotes mathematics learning more than a conventional approach. Int. J. Game-Bas. Learn. **7**(1), 36–56 (2017)
16. McLaren, B.M., DeLeeuw, K.E., Mayer, R.E.: Polite web-based intelligent tutors: can they improve learning in classrooms? Comput. Educ. **56**(3), 574–584 (2011)
17. McLaren, B.M., Richey, J.E., Nguyen, H.A., Mogessie, M.: Focused self-explanations lead to the best learning outcomes in a digital learning game. In: Proceedings of the 17th International Conference of the Learning Sciences, pp. 1229–1232 ISLS (2022)
18. Moore, S., Nguyen, H.A., Bier, N., Domadia, T., Stamper, J.: Assessing the quality of student-generated short answer questions using GPT-3. In: Educating for a New Future: Making Sense of Technology-Enhanced Learning Adoption: 17th European Conference on Technology Enhanced Learning, EC-TEL 2022, Toulouse, France, September 12–16, 2022, Proceedings, pp. 243–257. Springer (2022)
19. Nguyen, H., Hou, X., Stamper, J., McLaren, B.M.: Moving beyond test scores: analyzing the effectiveness of a digital learning game through learning analytics. In: Proceedings of the 13th International Conference on Educational Data Mining (2020)
20. Nguyen, H.A., Bhat, S., Moore, S., Bier, N., Stamper, J.: Towards generalized methods for automatic question generation in educational domains. In: Educating for a New Future: Making Sense of Technology-Enhanced Learning Adoption: 17th European Conference on Technology Enhanced Learning, EC-TEL 2022, Toulouse, France, September 12–16, 2022, Proceedings. pp. 272–284. Springer (2022)
21. Nguyen, H.A., Hou, X., Stec, H., Di, S., Stamper, J., McLaren, B.: Examining the benefits of prompted self-explanation for problem-solving in a decimal learning game. In: Proceedings of the International Conference on Artificial Intelligence in Education. Springer
22. O'Neil, H.F., Chung, G.K., Kerr, D., Vendlinski, T.P., Buschang, R.E., Mayer, R.E.: Adding self-explanation prompts to an educational computer game. Comput. Hum. Behav. **30**, 23–28 (2014)
23. Pardos, Z.A., Bhandari, S.: Learning gain differences between ChatGPT and human tutor generated algebra hints. arXiv preprint arXiv:2302.06871 (2023)
24. Qin, C., Zhang, A., Zhang, Z., Chen, J., Yasunaga, M., Yang, D.: Is chatgpt a general-purpose natural language processing task solver? arXiv preprint arXiv:2302.06476 (2023)
25. Ramesh, D., Sanampudi, S.K.: An automated essay scoring systems: a systematic literature review. Artif. Intell. Rev. **55**(3), 2495–2527 (2022)
26. Razzaq, R., Ostrow, K.S., Heffernan, N.T.: Effect of immediate feedback on math achievement at the high school level. In: Bittencourt, I.I., Cukurova, M., Muldner, K., Luckin, R., Millán, E. (eds.) AIED 2020. LNCS (LNAI), vol. 12164, pp. 263–267. Springer, Cham (2020). https://doi.org/10.1007/978-3-030-52240-7_48
27. Richey, J.E., et al.: More confusion and frustration, better learning: The impact of erroneous examples. Comput. Educ. **139**, 173–190 (2019)
28. Rudolph, J., Tan, S., Tan, S.: ChatGPT: bullshit spewer or the end of traditional assessments in higher education? J. Appl. Learn. Teach. **6**, 1 (2023)
29. Swart, E.K., Nielen, T.M., Sikkema-de Jong, M.T.: Supporting learning from text: a meta-analysis on the timing and content of effective feedback. Educ. Res. Rev. **28**, 100296 (2019)
30. Van der Kleij, F.M., Feskens, R.C., Eggen, T.J.: Effects of feedback in a computer-based learning environment on students' learning outcomes: a meta-analysis. Rev. Educ. Res. **85**(4), 475–511 (2015)

31. Wylie, R., Chi, M.T.: The self-explanation principle in multimedia learning. The Cambridge Handbook of Multimedia Learning, vol. 413 (2014)
32. Ye, J., et al.: A Comprehensive Capability Analysis of GPT-3 and GPT-3.5 Series Models. arXiv preprint arXiv:2303.10420 (2023)
33. Zhu, M., Lee, H.-S., Wang, T., Liu, O.L., Belur, V., Pallant, A.: Investigating the impact of automated feedback on students' scientific argumentation. Int. J. Sci. Educ. **39**(12), 1648–1668 (2017)

Designing a Revision System: An Exploratory Qualitative Study to Identify the Needs of French Teachers and Students

Denis Ollivier[1,3](✉), Franck Silvestre[1,2], Jean-Baptiste Raclet[2], Emmanuel Lescure[3], and Julien Broisin[2]

[1] IRIT, Université Toulouse Capitole, Toulouse, France
denis.ollivier@irit.fr
[2] IRIT, Université Toulouse III - Paul Sabatier, Toulouse, France
[3] Kosmos Education, Nantes, France

Abstract. The design of interactive systems leveraging testing and spacing effects has been poorly studied in ecological contexts. This paper presents an exploratory qualitative study conducted with French middle school and high-school teachers and students to identify hypotheses to guide the design of this kind of system. The resulting hypotheses are: (1) students will access the interactive system with a variety of devices; (2) the presence of a revision system will induce more testing activity during revision but (3) still massively before exams. (4) Teachers would like to have access to nominative indicators to set up personalised monitoring. (5) Students and parents will consent to share personal data with teachers. These hypotheses will be tested with a quantitative study based on data collected through the first version of the revision tool.

Keywords: Testing effect · Spacing effect · Revision · Interactive system · Qualitative method

1 Introduction

According to the French national education program, as stated in its official bulletin N°27 of 2 July 2015, the "accompagnement personnalisé" ["personal support"] lessons aim to equip students with the necessary learning methods, including the practice of revision. To work on this revision activity, we propose the following definition provided by the Cambridge dictionary[1] : "study of work you have done, in order to prepare for an exam".

Different studies have shown that revising knowledge is more effective by testing oneself on that knowledge [17,20], that is the testing effect. Furthermore, spacing out work sessions [7,9,19] is more effective than a massed effort in a single session, called the spacing effect. These effects are both beneficial for longer retention of information and could be used to help students throughout their revision.

[1] https://dictionary.cambridge.org/fr/dictionnaire/anglais/revision.

O. Viberg et al. (Eds.): EC-TEL 2023, LNCS 14200, pp. 294–307, 2023.
https://doi.org/10.1007/978-3-031-42682-7_20

We, therefore, ask how technology can support revisions by promoting the best use of these effects. The literature already questions the support of these effects through several digital tools [14,21]. However, these tools are not designed in a school setting and have not been tested in middle-school or high-school ecological contexts, as highlighted in Latimier's thesis [14]. Our research, therefore, focuses on the design of an interactive revision system that takes advantage of test and spacing effects in a high-school environment. This paper presents the exploratory qualitative study conducted with teachers and students to identify hypotheses to explore to design a tool adapted to their needs. We seek to answer the following research questions:

RQ1. What hypotheses will help design a revision tool that meets teachers' needs?
RQ2. What hypotheses will help design a revision tool adapted to students' needs?

This article is structured as follows. Section 2 presents the work on which our research is based. Section 3 describes the methodology of this study. Section 4 presents the study context. Section 5 presents the results obtained. Section 6 discusses the results. Finally, the last section summarises the study and how it fits in with further work on this system.

2 State of the Art

Several studies, such as that of Phelps [17] and Rowland et al. [20], show that it is more effective to test oneself than to simply reread the information one wishes to remember: this is the testing effect. More generally, the literature identifies an improvement in knowledge retention over the long term when this effect is used [18,25]. Roediger et al. [18] have shown that the tests can be repeated several times for greater benefit.

Various studies have shown that spacing out revision sessions instead of concentrating them at the same time also has a beneficial effect on the memorisation of long-term information [9,19]. This effect, called the spacing effect, has been studied in several disciplines such as language learning [7] or mathematics [15] and has shown that the more test sessions are spaced out, the more likely it is to remember the information for a longer period. Carpenter's work in 2012 [9] confirms that the beneficial effect tends to have a longer impact as spacing is increased but warns that too much spacing should not be used as the learner may forget the knowledge. This work emphasises the need to tailor spacing to the learning conditions and objectives.

In her thesis, Latimier studied the articulation of the test and spacing effects and underlined that their effects are additional [14]. Thus, it seems relevant to apply these two effects jointly within the same tool to hope to maximise the results of school learning. To this end, the study carried out in Latimier's thesis [14] underlines the interest in mobilising digital tools. Thus, in the literature, we find several tools that mention test and spacing effects, such as Anki or Didask, which are essentially designed for language learning or simple knowledge [14,21]. However, most of these tools have been tested with university students or adults [10,14,21], in a context that does not correspond to the ecological reality. In her experimental study with Didask [14], Latimier specifies on pages 144 to 147 that the experimental conditions do not correspond to an ecological context since the students were adults in perfect autonomy, essentially motivated by financial compensation and without interaction with a teacher or other students. Thus, Latimier [14] points out that younger populations are rarely tested in studies of test and spacing effects and that it would be interesting to do so.

Our work is in line with Biggs' constructivist alignment [6]. In order to align pedagogical objectives with learning activity and assessment activity, revisions aimed at preparing a summative assessment must be based on formatively assessed classroom activities. This is why we decided to build a tool based on Elaastic[1], formerly known as Tsaap-Notes. This tool has already been studied in ecological contexts in higher education [4,22] and in secondary education [3]. The recycling of classroom activities with Elaastic to semi-automatically generate review tests has been the subject of previous work [4,23]. This work, conducted in higher education only, highlighted the widespread use of review tests by students but did not explore in detail the modalities of review. For example, no data on test spacing is provided.

3 Research Method

In order to design a tool adapted to pedagogical needs and students, we wish to follow a human-centred design with teachers and students. Our work is part of design-based research [2,16], and we approach each of our iterations through mixed methods to capitalise on the contributions of qualitative and quantitative results. For the first iteration of this research project, we follow the exploratory sequential model of Creswell and Clark [12]. In line with this model, we have therefore conducted a qualitative study with volunteer teachers and students to identify hypotheses that will help in the design of an interactive revision system adapted to the needs of teachers and students. The hypotheses identified will be investigated quantitatively through the collection of objective data through the first version of the tool.

4 The Qualitative Study

The qualitative study is based on interviews with teachers and students. These interviews focus on the first (RQ1) and second (RQ2) research questions, respectively. The study was conducted in French, with French participants. Therefore all materials and results shown in this paper are translated into English for a better understanding.

[1] https://www.irit.fr/elaastic/.

4.1 Participants

For this study, we interviewed eight volunteer teachers from middle school and high school who had already been trained in the use of Elaastic. Despite the participation of 8 teachers in these interviews, only six valid recordings could be kept for this study. Indeed, one damaged recording, as well as an interview for which written permission to use the data was not given, had to be excluded from the results.

In the second phase, we were able to obtain four individual interviews with students who had recently completed their secondary education or were in their final year to ask them about their practices in secondary school.

4.2 Data Collection Procedure

The qualitative study that is the subject of this paper was based on semi-structured individual interviews with participants lasting approximately 45 min. They were based on questionnaires developed in team meetings, stating the purpose of each question for the current study, guided by UTAUT2 for some aspects regarding technology acceptance. Some closed questions aimed to only start the subject without giving any hints and leaving the door open for the participants to argue their answers freely. Sometimes, follow-up questions were asked to get more information on a specific subject if the participants didn't mention it themselves. Each of these interviews consisted of three phases. The first phase (about 20 min.) aimed to gain a better understanding of the participants' working environment. The second phase was the presentation (about 5 min.) of a prototype revision tool in order to make the subject concrete for the participants, helping them to imagine the tool and its potential uses. Finally, the last phase (about 20 min.) consisted in questioning the participants about the prototype presented and the various aspects that could impact the use of the target system positively or negatively.

A thematic analysis was carried out on each of the interviews, the results of which are detailed below. The encoding of the themes was carried out by only one person, the same one that conducted the interviews. However, each theme has been reviewed by the team to ensure the relevance of the coding done. Then, the formulation of hypotheses has been done as a group while analysing the results of the encoded transcriptions.

Data on the teachers' profiles were collected in advance by online survey and is summarised in Table 1. We gathered in Table 2 the results of the teachers' feeling of proficiency with different technologies, asked through the online survey with a 5-point Likert scale going from "Pas à l'aise du tout" ["Not at ease at all"] to "Très à l'aise" ["Very at ease"]. The interview used the questionnaire presented in Table 3. Information on the students was collected in interviews with the questionnaire in Table 4 and their profiles are summarised in Table 5. The original data in French are accessible in an Open Science Framework repository[2], with the questionnaires, and full transcriptions of the interviews.

[2] https://osf.io/cz7fe/?view_only=cc64c8417d184a9298efc638a54cde34.

Table 1. Profile of teachers participating in the study

Identity			Professional experience			
Id	**Age**	**Gen.**	**Years**	**Disciplines**	**Grade teached**	**Nb stud.**
T1	44	F	18	Biology	7th, 8th, 9th	315
T2	48	F	23	History, MEC, Geography	6th, 7th, 8th, 9th, 10th	170
T4	59	M	38	Mathematics, IT	6th, 7th, 8th, 9th, 10th, 1re, 12th	150
T5	35	M	12	Mathematics, IT	6th, 7th, 8th, 9th, 10th, 11th, 12th	150
T6	43	F	20	Mathematics, IT	6th, 7th, 8th, 10th, 1re, 12th	150
T8	49	M	23	Physics-Chemistry	6th, 7th, 8th, 9th, 10th	300

Table 2. Technological proficiency declared by teachers

Id	Internet	Computer	Smartphone	Electrical tablet
T1	at ease	neither at ease nor uncomfortable	uncomfortable	at ease
T2	at ease	at ease	very uncomfortable	neither at ease nor uncomfortable
T4	at ease	at ease	at ease	at ease
T5	very at ease	very at ease	at ease	at ease
T6	at ease	at ease	neither at ease nor uncomfortable	neither at ease nor uncomfortable
T8	very at ease	very at ease	at ease	at ease

Table 3. Questionnaire used with teachers

Questions asked
Among your teaching practices, do you use one more frequently than the others?
Do you provide out-of-class work for your students? If so, in what form?
How do you ask students to prepare a summative assessment?
Are you comfortable using digital tools for teaching? Which ones do you use?
Do you use social networks to share with students? And to share with other teachers?
— *Presentation of prototype* —
Do you think that such an application is pedagogically relevant for students? For the teachers?
Would you have any reservations about using such a tool? With regard to teachers? With regard to the students?
What indicators could be useful in such an application?
Would you like to intervene before such an application? How would you do that?

Table 4. Questionnaire used with students

Questions asked
How old are you?
What gender do you identify with?
What course of study and/or specialisation did you pursue in high school?
During the past school year, did you have access to the following tools at home in the evening?
How did you interact with your teachers last year? With your classmates?
How do you use technology? Of the school uses, do you use it directly in the classroom as well? If so, have you ever used any particular tools that you recall?
Do you already use a revision application? If so, which one? Can you describe it? If not, can you see what it looks like?
What should a revision app look like for you? What tools would you expect it to offer?
— *Presentation of prototype* —
Do you think a revision application like this would be useful in your work?
If you were to use a revision application, do you think you would get better grades?
On average, how much time per week would you use such an application?
What elements might slow you down in using the presented application?
What elements would you like to see in such an application? To help you work better? To appreciate the tool / be motivated to use it?
Would you like your parents to be able to see the work done on this application?
Do you feel more motivated to use the app if you can interact with other students on it?
What role do you think teachers should have around this application?
What information would you be willing to share with the teacher? Automatically or on demand (with action on your part)? Nominally or anonymously?

Table 5. Profile of students participating in the study

Students	Age	Gender	Specialisation
S1	17	M	Physics, Biology
S2	17	F	Maths, Physics
S3	17	M	Maths, IT
S4	17	F	Arts, Literature

The non-functional, high-fidelity-looking prototype presented in **Fig.** 1 was designed with the idea of offering content already worked on in the classroom through the use of the online tool Elaastic [4]. The prototype was first envisaged with a mobile-first approach, assuming that this was a suitable format for students. It takes the form of 9 static screens (4 main, 5 altered states), inspired by the functioning and shape of Elaastic. The interviews were analysed by coding theme to group the common elements mentioned by the participants.

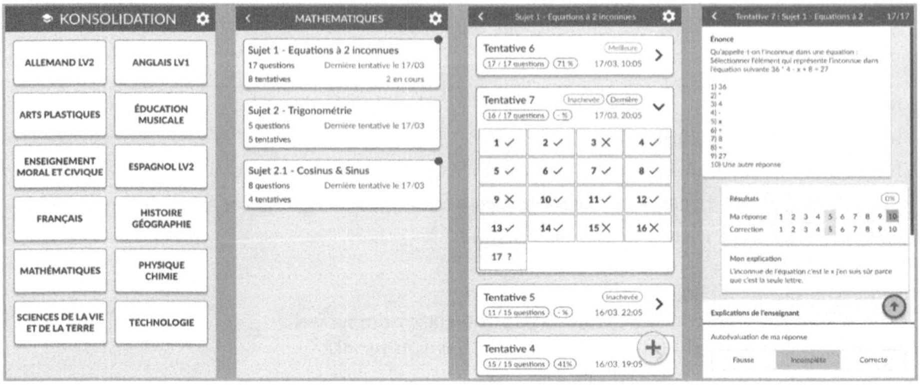

Fig. 1. 4 main screens of the prototype presented during the interview

5 Results

The result of this analysis is a fairly large number of themes that cannot all be mentioned here. Therefore, the elements presented here will be those that were most mentioned in the interviews or considered relevant for the formulation of hypotheses that could guide the design of a first version of the target system.

5.1 Having the Tool Available on Devices Other Than the Smartphone

First of all, when teachers were asked about their eventual reservation regarding the tool and mentioned it could concern the tool itself or the device it was presented on, it emerged that there was a need to access the tool via various devices. This idea was expressed by several teachers, sometimes in opposition to the mobile: T1-"... [the tool should be accessible on different devices because they don't have smartphones but they may have an electronic tablet or access to a computer at home", and on the other hand, sometimes in favour of the mobile: T4-"We would have said it's on the computer necessarily it would have been difficult, but strangely the pupils know how to use the computer less today than the tablet or the phone". The interviews with the students brought out the same need for other reasons. While teachers were worried about fairness and material issues, some students simply stated they prefer the computer to the mobile when it comes to working: S3-"So frankly it depends on the students I know that some are much more likely to work with their phone, others with their computer. As a student I mainly use the computer, after that both platforms are good I think."

5.2 Regulating the Use of Smartphones in the Context of Education

To further delve into the topic of the use of smartphones in education, two teachers emphasised the need to remain vigilant about the use of digital tools because of the abuses that can arise from them: T4-"I agree less and less with the use of smartphones in high school regarding the damages that it may bring", but they consider that the problem is not the tool in itself but the control we can have on it: T5-"And for me there is a real need for support ... to explain that it is a pedagogical tool and that it must therefore be supervised". While the students may appear not as concerned as the teachers regarding the use of smartphones to work, one of them still mentioned some limits regarding eventual distractions that may come out while using smartphones, which caught our attention : S1-"If it's ever going to be an application that's going to be on the phone, what would be good is that it's usable without the internet because I know that ... if I get a notification, it will make me want to get out of the application to check, to see what it is."

5.3 The Motivation Around Digital and the Use of the Tool

However, even though some limits are highlighted, some teachers stated that using digital tools motivates students, which influences their teaching methods: T2-"All my lessons are systematically illustrated by a slide show . .. I know that they appreciate it very much; every year at the end of the year, I check with my students", T1-"... I know they like it when there are little videos or extra things, or LearningApps for example...". While this intrinsic motivation with digital tools has been observed by the teachers, the presentation of the prototype was intended to allow the pupils to imagine the possible functionalities of the tool and to project themselves into its possible use. Thus, the pupils expressed a certain enthusiasm specifically toward the tool : S2-"So I find it very interesting, especially the fact that the pupils can progress by seeing the arguments of their classmates; I really find it very interesting", S1-"... [I think that it could be very interesting to have an application of this kind, yeah frankly, it's cool".

5.4 Staying Cautious with the Eventual Need for Extrinsic Motivation

Nonetheless, some teachers stressed that such a tool might not be sufficient if it is not accompanied by a grade as extrinsic motivation: T4- "... at first perhaps we will have to find a carrot to make them want to go spontaneously...". In opposition, when the students were asked specifically about the possibility of integrating a grade into the tool, they all expressed the negative feeling that the grade would be perceived as a hindrance: S4-"Erm, I would see it more as a percentage like there was on the model rather than a grade. It's true that a mark can demoralise the pupil depending on the type, and he can say to himself, 'I'm stuck at such and such a mark,' and that can be particularly frustrating".

5.5 Supervising Students' Revision with Indicators

Finally, after the presentation of the prototype, when teachers were asked about the indicators they would find relevant, many expressed an interest in indicators on the use of the tool by pupils. These indicators were mentioned as relevant tools for generating individual monitoring: En5-"So what could be interesting is to know the rate of use of the application during the sequence and up to the evaluation in fact ... to help them better distribute their workload". However, one teacher emphasised that this possibility can lead to a workload that needs to be considered: T8"The time or workload I think, is really on the analysis of the feedback, which is done more or less individually, where there can be a workload that is indeed substantial." These needs echoed the students' statements when we asked them about the role they think the teachers should have regarding the revision tool; it first appeared that a supervisory role was expected: S2-"At the high school, we are always very sheltered, so we refer a lot to the teachers, to what they really tell us to do, so I think that encouraging them is the most important thing". On the other hand, by specifically mentioning the possibility of having indicators, the students also mention the interest in taking advantage of it to make a personalised follow-up: S4-"I think that it could help the teacher to see what the student produces to try to correct it afterwards in addition to the corrections with the arguments and to see where the student is and to see his progress".

6 Discussion

The purpose of the individual interviews in this study was to identify hypotheses to guide the design of a teacher and student-friendly revision system. Each hypothesis will be accompanied by the implications it brings to the conception of the first version of the revision system. All hypotheses are regrouped in the **Table** 6 at the end of the discussion.

6.1 Access the Tool via Different Devices

First, understanding the context and the devices used refers to UTAUT2 Model and the facilitating conditions, which is a prerequisite for us: the first step to help students benefit from the testing and spacing effect through our system is for them to use it. The interviews helped us hypothesise that **(H1)** the students will access the system through a variety of devices, as opposed to our first assumption about smartphone being a sufficient device considering that literature shows that it is a motivational source for students [5,11]. However, even if teachers observed the same effect, they argued in favour of multi-device accessibility, as students in early high school (6th to 9th grade) may not have a smartphone but access to another device at home. In addition, a good number of students stressed that the use could vary and stated some inconveniences related to smartphone use while revising. Referring to others' research [1,13], it seems relevant to us to develop a first version accessible on several types of devices. We then need to set up appropriate markers, which will allow us to identify the devices used by the students in a revision context. The system should also be developed keeping in mind the regulation that could be needed to help the student avoid the distractions that could occur while using digital tools. Even though no specific feature will be implemented at first, the structure of the tool must already be done considering such evolution.

6.2 Making a Testing Tool Available Encourages Students to Test Themselves More to Revise

Ensuring the accessibility to the tool was a prerequisite to benefit from students' enthusiasm. Teachers' observations and students' reactions to the tool presented indicate that the introduction of a digital tool seems to have a positive impact on student's motivation. Using this motivation as a starting point, we hypothesise that **(H2)** providing students with a digital revision tool that exploits the testing effect will already have a beneficial effect on their use of the test as a revision method. This hypothesis will be investigated by comparing the uses of the first version of the revision system with the use of Elaastic as a revision tool by students. This hypothesis also implies that we will not try to incite the students through any other means than providing the application and the eventual initial formation to use it, as we want to observe their behaviour with as less solicitation as possible.

6.3 Pupils Revise Especially in the Run-Up to Evaluations

Despite the motivation highlighted, it was pointed out by some teachers that it might not be sufficient for use in the absence of marking. Considering the opinion of students who said marking the revision could harm the activity, we would like to add none. Then, we can refer to some studies of students' attitudes towards revision, which show a tendency for students to revise massively in the run-up to evaluations [8]. It can therefore be hypothesised that **(H3)** the use of the revision system will be particularly marked in the vicinity of evaluations, and this hypothesis will be studied with the data collected via the system. The system should therefore make it possible to collect the dates of students' work and the dates of students' exams in the subjects worked on. With the system gathering these data, we shall then study the question of regulation through the scope of the planning of the students' revision. Echoing the previous hypothesis, the same parameter of no solicitation is needed here to observe the students' behaviour without further action from the system.

6.4 Nominal Indicators on Student Activity

When asked about the kind of indicators teachers would like to see if they find any relevant ones, many of them responded positively to the idea of using the tool to set up personalised monitoring, even though they did not provide many different indicators ideas. However, a need to remain vigilant regarding the time that such monitoring can cost was highlighted. We, therefore, assume that **(H4)** teachers will use the nominative data on pupils' work to improve individualised monitoring despite the workload involved if we provide some relevant indicators to do so. The workload mentioned seems quite important, so we will try to verify this hypothesis by proposing different depths of indicators and tracing how teachers use them.

Such data collection to build indicators brings our attention toward privacy and ethics [24] regarding the students. Given the students' expressed need for monitoring, we are confident in assuming that **(H5)** students and their parents will agree to the collection of personal data to build indicators for teachers. However, to test that hypothesis, we will ensure the system implements privacy by design, allowing students and their parents to choose at any time which nominative data they transmit or not to teachers and to trace these choices.

6.5 A Perspective on Out-of-Class Regulation

Finally, when we summarise the elements that emerge from these interviews, both students and teachers seem to think that secondary school students are not able to fully regulate themselves. Thus, we think it would be interesting to work on this tool from the perspective of teacher regulation of out-of-class work. By seriously studying the literature about self-regulation as well as teacher-directed learning, we believe that we could reconsider this tool as an assistance to the regulation of students' revisions. We, therefore, intend to explore further the idea of a tool that helps teachers to regulate students' out-of-class work in the first instance and which could evolve in the longer term into a tool that simplifies the transition to self-regulated learning for students.

6.6 Limits

In the context of this study, some limitations must be pointed out concerning the lack of diversity among the participants. Indeed, the teachers interviewed have rather similar profiles, with more than ten years of teaching experience, generally scientific disciplines, and a marked technological fluency. This first approach with a voluntary audience allows us to guide our reflections, but it is necessary to gather more various data to obtain more representative ones. On the other hand, students showed some difficulty in developing ideas on open questions. The limited spectrum of the interrogated audience is an issue that we will correct through the gathering of data with the first version of the tool with the quantitative study following this one.

Another limit regarding our method shall be mentioned. The transcriptions and thematic encoding being done by the same person that interviewed the participants may raise issues regarding eventual bias during the study. However, as we conducted an exploratory study, our aim was solely to identify hypotheses for later verification through a quantitative study, so the eventual bias seemed acceptable, considering these resulting hypotheses will be tested with objective data.

Table 6. Hypotheses identified through the interviews

	Hypotheses
H1	The students will access the system through a variety of devices (smartphones, computers, tablets)
H2	Providing students with a digital revision tool that exploits the testing effect will already have a beneficial effect on their use of the test as a revision method
H3	The use of the revision system will be particularly marked in the vicinity of evaluations
H4	The teachers will use the nominative data on pupils' work to improve individualised monitoring despite the workload involved
H5	The students and their parents will agree to the collection of personal data to build indicators for teachers

7 Conclusion

In our research, we are asking ourselves how to design an interactive system adapted to the revision activity, taking advantage of the test and spacing effects. We decided to interview teachers and students to identify the hypotheses that will guide the quantitative study that will allow the design of a relevant tool. As a result of these interviews, we assume that students will naturally test themselves more **(H2)** with a multi-platform tool at their disposal **(H1)**, but still massively before exams **(H3)**. We also assume that by providing teachers with dashboards, they will work to improve individualised monitoring despite the workload involved **(H4)**. As these dashboards imply the collection of students' personal data, we finally assume that the students and their parents will accept to show the students' nominative data to build more precise individual indicators for teachers **(H5)**. According to the exploratory sequential method, this qualitative study helped us design the tool for it to be adapted to test the different assumptions made with this study. Through the tool, we will collect objective data and analysis of these results will serve as a basis for reflection in the development of future versions of the tool, which should ultimately lead to the identification of recommendations for the design of revision tools adapted to the needs of students and teachers.

References

1. Amadieu, F., Mulet, J., Van der Linden, J., Lombard, J., Van de Leemput, C.: Acceptabilité des technologies d'apprentissage mobile: le cas des tablettes. Éducation permanente **2**, 31–40 (2019)
2. Anderson, T., Shattuck, J.: Design-based research: a decade of progress in education research? Educ. Res. **41**(1), 16–25 (2012)

3. Andriamiseza, R.: Learning Analytics-Based Formative Assessment Recommendations for Technology-Enhanced Learning Practices. Ph.D. thesis, Université de Toulouse, Université Toulouse III-Paul Sabatier (2022)
4. Andriamiseza, R., Silvestre, F., Parmentier, J.-F., Broisin, J.: Recommendations for orchestration of formative assessment sequences: a data-driven approach. In: De Laet, T., Klemke, R., Alario-Hoyos, C., Hilliger, I., Ortega-Arranz, A. (eds.) EC-TEL 2021. LNCS, vol. 12884, pp. 245–259. Springer, Cham (2021). https://doi.org/10.1007/978-3-030-86436-1_19
5. Bai, H.: Pedagogical practices of mobile learning in k-12 and higher education settings. TechTrends **63**(5), 611–620 (2019)
6. Biggs, J.: Enhancing teaching through constructive alignment. High. Educ. **32**(3), 347–364 (1996)
7. Bird, S.: Effects of distributed practice on the acquisition of second language English syntax-erratum. Appl. Psycholinguist. **32**(2), 435–452 (2011)
8. Blasiman, R.N., Dunlosky, J., Rawson, K.A.: The what, how much, and when of study strategies: comparing intended versus actual study behaviour. Memory **25**(6), 784–792 (2017)
9. Carpenter, S.K., Cepeda, N.J., Rohrer, D., Kang, S.H., Pashler, H.: Using spacing to enhance diverse forms of learning: review of recent research and implications for instruction. Educ. Psychol. Rev. **24**(3), 369–378 (2012)
10. Carvalho, P.F., Sana, F., Yan, V.X.: Self-regulated spacing in a massive open online course is related to better learning. NPJ Sci. Learn. **5**(1), 1–7 (2020)
11. Cavanaugh, C., Maor, D., McCarthy, A.: K-12 mobile learning. ETC Press (2014)
12. Creswell, J.W., Plano Clark, V.L., Gutmann, M.L., Hanson, W.E.: Advanced mixed methods research designs. In: Handbook of Mixed Methods in Social and Behavioral Research **209**(240), 209–240 (2003)
13. Farrah, M., Abu-Dawood, A.: Using mobile phone applications in teaching and learning process (2018)
14. Latimier, A.: Optimisation de l'apprentissage par récupération en mémoire pour promouvoir la rétention à long terme de nouvelles connaissances. Ph.D. thesis, Université Paris sciences et lettres (2019)
15. Lyle, K.B., Bego, C.R., Hopkins, R.F., Hieb, J.L., Ralston, P.A.: How the amount and spacing of retrieval practice affect the short-and long-term retention of mathematics knowledge. Educ. Psychol. Rev. **32**(1), 277–295 (2020)
16. Mandran, N., Vermeulen, M., Prior, E.: Comment guider les doctorants dans l'utilisation du design-based research? In: 10e Conférence sur les Environnements Informatiques pour l'Apprentissage Humain, pp. 130–141 (2021)
17. Phelps, R.P.: The effect of testing on student achievement, 1910–2010. Int. J. Test. **12**(1), 21–43 (2012)
18. Roediger, H.L., III., Karpicke, J.D.: Test-enhanced learning: taking memory tests improves long-term retention. Psychol. Sci. **17**(3), 249–255 (2006)
19. Rohrer, D., Taylor, K.: The effects of overlearning and distributed practise on the retention of mathematics knowledge. Appl. Cogn. Psychol.: Official J. Soci. Appl. Res. Memory Cogn. **20**(9), 1209–1224 (2006)
20. Rowland, C.A.: The effect of testing versus restudy on retention: a meta-analytic review of the testing effect. Psychol. Bull. **140**(6), 1432 (2014)
21. Seibert Hanson, A.E., Brown, C.M.: Enhancing L2 learning through a mobile assisted spaced-repetition tool: an effective but bitter pill? Comput. Assist. Lang. Learn. **33**(1–2), 133–155 (2020)

22. Silvestre, F.: Conception et mise en oeuvre d'un système d'évaluation formative pour les cours en face à face dans l'enseignement supérieur. Ph.D. thesis, Université de Toulouse, Université Toulouse III-Paul Sabatier (2015)
23. Silvestre, F., Vidal, P., Broisin, J.: Online tests based on contributions provided by teachers and students during face to face lectures. In: 2015 IEEE 15th International Conference on Advanced Learning Technologies, pp. 29–33. IEEE (2015)
24. Willis, J.E., Slade, S., Prinsloo, P.: Ethical oversight of student data in learning analytics: a typology derived from a cross-continental, cross-institutional perspective. Educ. Technol. Res. Dev. **64**, 881–901 (2016)
25. Zaromb, F.M., Roediger, H.L.: The testing effect in free recall is associated with enhanced organizational processes. Memory Cogn. **38**(8), 995–1008 (2010)

Evaluation of a Hybrid AI-Human Recommender for CS1 Instructors in a Real Educational Scenario

Filipe Dwan Pereira[1,5](✉), Elaine Oliveira[3], Luiz Rodrigues[4], Luciano Cabral[5,6], David Oliveira[3], Leandro Carvalho[3], Dragan Gasevic[7], Alexandra Cristea[2], Diego Dermeval[4], and Rafael Ferreira Mello[5,7]

[1] Federal University of Roraima, Boa Vista, Brazil
filipe.dwan@ufrr.br
[2] Durham University, Durham, England
[3] Federal University of Amazonas, Manaus, Brazil
[4] Federal University of Alagoas, Maceió, Brazil
[5] CESAR School, Recife, Brazil
[6] Federal Institute of Pernambuco, Recife, Brazil
[7] Monash University, Melbourne, VI, Australia

Abstract. Automatic code graders, also called Programming Online Judges (OJ), can support students and instructors in introduction to programming courses (CS1). Using OJs in CS1, instructors select problems to compose assignment lists, whereas students submit their code solutions and receive instantaneous feedback. Whilst this process reduces the instructors' workload in evaluating students' code, selecting problems to compose assignments is arduous. Recently, recommender systems have been proposed by the literature to support OJ users. Nonetheless, there is a lack of recommenders fitted for CS1 courses and the ones found in the literature have not been assessed by the target users in a real educational scenario. It is worth noting that hybrid human/AI systems are claimed to potentially surpass isolated human or AI. In this study, we adapted and evaluated a state-of-the-art hybrid human/AI recommender to support CS1 instructors in selecting problems to compose variations of CS1 assignments. We compared data-driven measures (e.g., time students take to solve problems, number of logical lines of code, and hit rate) extracted from student logs whilst solving programming problems from assignments created by instructors versus when solving assignments in collaboration with an adaptation of cutting-edge hybrid/AI method. As a result, employing a data analysis comparing experimental and control conditions using multi-level regressions, we observed that the recommender provided problems compatible with human-selected in all data-driven measures tested.

Keywords: Hybrid systems evaluation · recommender system · introductory programming

O. Viberg et al. (Eds.): EC-TEL 2023, LNCS 14200, pp. 308–323, 2023.
https://doi.org/10.1007/978-3-031-42682-7_21

1 Introduction

Programming Online Judge (OJ) is an auto-grader system capable of providing instantaneous feedback about the accuracy of a code solution [11,21,30]. Typically, these systems offer programming problems of different topics related to computer science subjects [11,30,34]. Computer Science 1 (CS1) instructors are increasingly adopting OJ to enhance the learning experience in the offerings of this introductory course [15,22,30,33]. For the instructor, it reduces the workload due to the automatic evaluation provided by the OJ [20,30]. For the student, it allows them to readily correct their code errors (due to the instantaneous feedback) and receive a fair assessment ([16] demonstrate that OJ assessment is fairer than the human one). The OJ feedback can highlight the strengths and weaknesses of the learners' solutions, allowing them to improve their skills and knowledge.

Nonetheless, there is much room for improvement in OJ systems to support CS1 classes [20,30,34]. To illustrate, due to the wide variety of problems provided in these systems, it is hard for the instructors to select appropriate problems to compose assignments. As such, it could take much time for the instructors to create the assignments. In such situations (overload of options – problems), the combination of OJ and recommendation systems are suggested in the literature [20,30,32,34].

Despite calls from literature [15,17,28,30,33] for research about recommending problems in OJs, only a few works have proposed methods for this task. Furthermore, the few methods available are generally suitable for expert students, but not for novices [20,30,32,34]. It is worth noting that proposing methods to assist instructors of CS1 is claimed to be crucial for the advancement of learning to program [17,27].

In this work we replicated, adapted and validated a cutting-edge method [24] to help instructors select problems in a CS1 course, where the instructors submit a list of problems to a recommender system, which suggests similar problems that the instructors can use, for instance, to avoid plagiarism. The method was validated in a novel data-driven setting, with two conditions: one where students received problems generated by the instructors, and one where students receive problems selected by the instructors using the AI recommendations.

2 Related Work

The methods proposed in the literature to recommend problems in OJ typically investigate only shallow features based on the students' submissions and attempts to perform the recommendation. For instance, Fantozzi and Laura [9] proposed a recommender system for expert users who are training for the International Collegiate Programming Contest (ICPC)[1]. The method employs students' attempts at an OJ and uses an autoencoder neural network to recommend problems. Similarly, Saito and Watanobe [28] proposed a recommender

[1] urlhttps://icpc.global/.

that applies a recurrent neural network to produce students' learning paths based on their attempts. Yera and Martínez [32] also applied students' attempts and feature engineering to create a recommender system for OJs. All these works [9,28,32] demonstrated results only in a synthetic scenario based on machine learning performance metrics (e.g., F1-score). Evaluations with real users were not carried out. Moreover, these methods are best suited for expert learners, particularly those who are training for the ICPC.

Recent works [7,20] suggest tracking log information (instead of only collecting the number of attempts) when students are solving problems in an Integrated Development Environment (IDE) to extract fine-grained features that depict the effort students take to solve the problems. Carter et al. [7] explain that IDE offers researchers the widest spectrum of student process data, as this is where learners spend a large majority of their time problem-solving. An example is [20], which proposed a recommender system in OJs based on the effort required to solve problems focused on CS1 students. The features employed were based on a data-driven analysis of how students solved problems whilst they were developing their code in an IDE. Despite finding satisfactory results when compared with a baseline, the authors pointed out limitations related to the lack of information about the problems' topics. That is, they observed that it was necessary to detect the topic of the problem and associate this information with the effort required to solve the problem.

In this sense, a recent work [24] extended the work proposed in [20], adding a topic detector and caring out a validation of the recommender with 35 CS1 instructors. The results surpassed the baseline (an adaptation of Yera and Martínez's work [32]) in the measures experimented. The validation was carried out through a questionnaire in which the instructors estimated the coding effort, hit rate and resolution time expected to solve the automatically recommended problems versus questions recommended by their baseline [32]. Nonetheless, despite the importance of validation with instructors and their satisfactory results in a laboratory setting, Fincher et al. [10] explain that it is critical to evaluate educational methods in real scenarios (scarcity of proposed methods evaluated in real scenarios), and with students. Schwartz and Gurung [29] claim that it is imperative to go beyond questionnaires and validate methods available in the literature using data-driven evidence as well.

In this regard, de Oliveira et al. [19] evaluated whether extended feedback from an OJ system would improve the students' motivation using data-driven evidence collected from the students' side. Still, Quille and Bergin [26] evaluated how a performance prediction system associated with an OJ could impact the students' outcomes. Both works performed that analysis in a controlled experiment in a real educational scenario. However, there is a lack of studies evaluating how recommendation systems from a data-driven perspective work in a real educational scenario with CS1 students.

Furthermore, previous works [19,26] imply learning improvements when the hybrid human/AI methods were associated with instructor mediation. That is, the AI method might recommend options for the instructor who decides how the AI information should be applied to enhance the students' outcome. Moreover, the instructors could also enhance the AI method capabilities. To understand deeply the importance of those methods, the students' perspective must have been observed and analysed [13,24]. However, to the best of our knowledge, there is no work that evaluates a recommender system to support CS1 students from the perspective of the students, and with data-driven evidence.

3 Contributions and Novelty

The study described in the current paper adapted the state-of-the-art recommendation method proposed in [24] and validated it in a real scenario, with 7 CS1 classes, and 196 students. Our proposal performs a detailed analysis of the recommender system under different aspects: i) employing a data-driven evaluation of the method by collecting fine-grained data whilst students solved the recommended problems in an IDE embedded in the OJ; ii) comparing the problems recommended by the method with problems recommended by humans; and iii) adapting a hybrid approach for the recommendation, in which the instructor validates and rectifies the recommendations provided by the AI and also enhance the AI capabilities. As such, this study is an incremental work that represents a step towards validating and employing a cutting-edge method available in the literature, by, for the first time, to the best of our knowledge, replicating their work [24] using their open dataset and validating their method in a real-life scenario over a data-driven perspective from the students' perspective.

Thus, the main contribution of the paper is the practical application of an educational method available in the literature [24] in a real-world educational scenario and testing and evaluating their effectiveness with data-driven approaches. This allows for refining and improving the method, and ensuring that it is effective in diverse settings and for a wide range of users. Moreover, this offers valuable evidence for the future of OJ systems to support CS1 instructors and students.

4 Educational Scenario

Introduction to Programming is offered at the Federal University of Amazonas as part of several undergraduate courses. The objective of the discipline is to help students learn to solve algorithmic problems and to offer the ability to elaborate, verify and implement algorithms in a high-level programming language.

Since 2020, the research developed in this area is being supported by the SUPER Project, which has funding from Samsung, using resources from the Informatics Law for the Western Amazon.

These CS1 courses cover 7 topics in the CS1 assignments. As the topics are cumulative, content from earlier topics appears in later topics. Each assignment contains an average of 12 problems related to the following topics: (i) sequential structure; (ii) simple conditionals (if-then-else); (iii) nested conditionals (if-then-else nested); (iv) while loops; (v) vectors and strings; (vi) for loops; and (vii) matrices. Exams generally are composed of 2 questions. To avoid plagiarism in the assignments, the instructors create variations of assignments each semester, using distinct questions. The methodology (e.g., pedagogical material and notes) used in CS1 classes is the same, regardless of the instructor who teaches the course. The assignments are carried out using the tool CodeBench[2], an online judge system used by instructors from different universities that performs an automatic evaluation of the students' code solutions. After instructors post the assignments to CodeBench, students solve problems in an IDE embedded into CodeBench. Python is used as the target programming language of the course.

5 Recommendation Method

For the recommendation, we adapted the hypothesis presented in [24]: *if students have solved a given problem (Target Problem (TP)) and there are problems similar to TP in terms of topic and effort required, thus these problems can be used as potential Recommended Problems (RPs) to replace TP in new assignments.* To validate that hypothesis and replicate the work in [24], we used the CodeBench open dataset, which is described in the next section.

5.1 Dataset

CodeBench provides a freely anonymised dataset[3] with fine-grained information on programming students' behaviours. Whilst students are solving problems in an IDE embedded in the CodeBench system, the students' logs are collected. In short, the dataset contains each character typed by the students and the timestamps. It is also possible to know such information as when the students stopped typing, when they pasted content in the IDE, and when they clicked outside the IDE.

Following the proposal given in [24], we extracted 22 features from the students' logs to feed the recommender system. The features include the hit rate students take to get problems accepted, the average lines of code per problem, the average time students take to solve problems, the average cyclomatic complexity of the solutions per problem, etc. The entire list of features is available in [24].

Moreover, we used the problem descriptions to detect the problem topics based on the CS1 syllabus, as suggested in [23,24]. To feed the recommender, we used the data from 2016 to 2019 (before the pandemic[4]), as can be seen in Table 1. Furthermore, the number of different problems from CodeBench we used in this work is 1,026, as shown in Table 2. The table shows the problems segregated by the CS1 topics. These are the problems the recommender system can choose from.

[2] https://codebench.icomp.ufam.edu.br/.

[3] https://codebench.icomp.ufam.edu.br/dataset/.

[4] During the pandemic, the course stopped for a while and after 1 year, it was reoffered remotely, instead of face to face. That's why we do not use the data during the pandemic, since it is in different educational conditions.

Table 1. CodeBench's data set segregated by term. Assig. Probs means number of assignment problems, whereas Ex. Probs. means Exam problems.

Term	Students	Assig. Probs.	Ex. Probs.	Code	Attempts
2016-1	471	681	124	30140	154163
2016-2	172	447	110	9501	38933
2017-1	463	1278	163	38304	119370
2017-2	177	556	103	10942	27613
2018-1	465	1550	182	47969	148775
2018-2	180	893	107	13458	46765
2019-1	489	1559	176	38417	140537
2019-2	297	1116	138	28348	36632
Total	2714	8080	1103	217079	712788

Table 2. Description of CodeBench Topics.

Topic	Description	N
sequential structure	arithmetic operations and use of variables	157
if-then-else	conditional structure	136
if-then-else (nested)	nested conditionals structure	161
while-loop	loops using the structure while	114
for-loop	loops using the structure for	117
vectors and strings	unidimensional vectors and string operations	207
matrices	bidimensional matrices operation	134
Total		1,026

5.2 Recommendation Steps

Figure 1 shows how the recommendation is performed by this recommender method. To summarise, the instructor defines the TP that will be used as a reference problem to perform the recommendation. In practice, the TP is a given problem previously used by the instructor in an assignment provided by classes from previous semesters. The recommender first detects the topic of the TP, based on the CS1 syllabus (see Table 2). The method then recommends an RP that is associated with the same topic as the TP and that requires a similar effort to be solved. For example, if the TP is associated with the conditional structure (if-then-else), then the recommender suggests a conditional structure problem as well that requires a similar effort to be solved.

To detect the topic of problems, we use the pipeline proposed in [23], which combines Natural Language Processing (NLP) techniques with shallow and deep machine learning models (a similar NLP pipeline was effectively used in other cutting-edge works [3,4]). As a result, the best model (which was a Convolutional

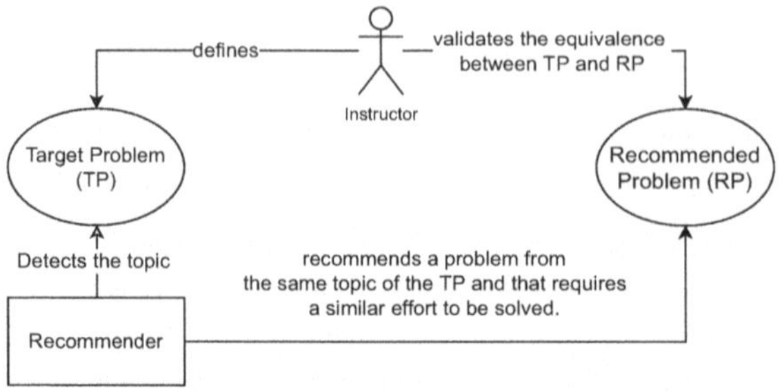

Fig. 1. How the recommendation is performed.

Neural Network) reached 90% F1-score. In this case, the need to use a predictive model is that most questions from OJs are not annotated with the CS1 topics.

6 Experimental Study

The focus of this paper is to evaluate the method presented in Sect. 5 in a real scenario, using data-driven evidence from the students' perspective, instead of applying a questionnaire for instructors. This evaluation was divided into two steps: i) the instructors' selection of the problems in collaboration with the AI recommender system (detailed in Sect. 6.2); and ii) the data-driven evaluation of the students' logs when solving the recommended problems, versus when solving problems selected manually by the instructors (detailed in Sect. 6.3).

The data utilised for this data-driven evaluation was collected during the first term of 2021. The course methodology aligns with the pattern outlined in Sect. 4. It is important to note that we have two distinct sources of log data: i) to support the functioning of the recommender system, which was collected between 2016 and 2019 (Sect. 5.1); ii) to conduct the data-driven evaluation from the students' perspective, which was gathered specifically during the first term of 2021.

6.1 Conditions (Controlled Vs Experimental)

The instructors of the CS1 courses that participated in this experiment created seven assignments for the course, one assignment for each topic (see the seven topics in Sect. 4). For the controlled condition, we used the assignments composed by these instructors. For the experimental condition, we used the problems recommended by the method specified in Sect. 5, as illustrated in Fig. 1. The assignment lists used in the control condition contained 12 problems. For the sake of simplicity, we adopted the first six problems in these lists to be used as TPs. In this way, the recommender selected the nearest neighbour of each TP to compose the first six problems in the assignment lists in the experimental condition.

More formally, we were interested to assess whether the variation assignments (let us call them List B) were equivalent to the Master List in terms of the effort required to solve the lists and the topic of the problems. Let us call *Master Lists*, the assignments created by CS1 instructors. Our intention, thus, was to assess whether a List B, which is a variation of a Master List, in which the problems from both (Master List and List B) must be equivalent in terms of the topic associated and the effort required to solve the problems. To illustrate, if the first six problems from the Master List are $L_{master} = \{TP_1, TP_2, TP_3, TP_4, TP_5, TP_6\}$ then List B must contain the problems $L_B = \{RP'_1, RP'_2, RP'_3, RP'_4, RP'_5, RP'_6\}$, where each pair of questions (TP_i, RP'_i), i varying from 1 to 6, must require a similar effort and topic to be solved by the students.

6.2 Hybrid Human/AI Recommendation

Attending a call from the literature [1,8,13], we adapted the method from [24], to employ the concept of hybrid intelligence, where we combine instructor knowledge with our AI method, to collaboratively create assignments in real classes of CS1. In total, 7 instructors participated in this study. The instructors were responsible for the courses of the control and experimental condition. Following the recommendation steps presented in Sect. 5, the instructors evaluated the problems provided by the recommendation method according to the following criteria: i) if the topics of both problems (TP vs RP) were equivalent; ii) if the estimated time for the resolution of both (TP vs RP) were equivalent; iii) if the estimated coding effort for the resolution of both (TP vs RP) were equivalent; iv) if the estimated hit rate for the resolution of both (TP vs RP) were equivalent; and v) whether the instructors thought the problems (TP vs RP) were interchangeable. These criteria were defined in line with the work of [24]. The criteria under ii) to v) were employed to estimate the effort required to solve the problems and their equivalence, as suggested in [24]. The last criterion (v) was central to the instructor's decision to keep the problem on the assignment list. In total, 10 problems were replaced by the instructors, 5 of them because the pair of problems were from different topics, and 5 because of incompatibility in terms of effort required to solve the problems (one of the items from i) to iv)).

In case of the instructor not accepting the AI method recommendation, a justification is given by the instructor, explaining the reason why the RP was not kept on the assignment list. The justification is given based on the above five criteria (i-v). The justification is then used to adjust the recommender, i.e., to improve the AI. For example, a source of error for the recommender is when the topic detector misclassifies a given problem (this occurs 10% of the time since the model is 90% accurate). When this happens, the instructor can adjust the AI, by relabelling the problems with the correct topic , so that the next time, this RP will be associated with the correct topic. Notice that after the instructor not accepting the RP, a new recommendation is performed.

Regarding criteria i-iv, the system recommends the i-th closest neighbour of the TP, starting the variable i from 2 (that is, from the second nearest neighbour[5]) and increasing this value if the substitution was not accepted by the instructor (for more information about the recommendation process itself, please check [24]). In case of a not accepted recommendation here, the instructor does not rectify the AI-method recommendation. We just use the following nearest neighbour of the TP as the RP. The proposal of instructor adjustments of the AI, in this case, will be made in future work.

As such, human/AI collaboration is performed in three sequential steps: i) the instructor provides as input an assignment (we call it, as said, the Master List - controlled condition), ii) the AI method returns one or several recommended problem(s) for each problem of that Master List to be used in the assignment variation(s) (List B - experimental condition), iii) the instructor validates each recommendation and decides whether they can be used in the assignment/exam variation(s), and iv) AI is adjusted in case of RP replacement (for topic incompatibility).

6.3 Evaluation with Students

For the method evaluation, we collected fine-grained data from the students (during the first term of 2021) whilst they were solving the assignment problems of the controlled (Master Lists) and experimental conditions (Lists B). An example of the fine granularity data collected is given in Fig. 2, when a student was writing a print command.

The total of problems in all assignments was 42 (6 problems x 7 topics). Fine-grained data (see an example in Fig. 2) was collected from students, whilst they were writing their solutions in the CodeBench IDE. A total of 196 students participated in the study, 130 in the control group and 66 in the experimental group. All the data was anonymised and consent for data collection analysis and publication was given by all students who participated in this experiment.


```
27/5/2016@8:34:42:871:focus
27/5/2016@8:34:43:475:change:{"from":{"line":0,"ch":0},"to":{"line":0,"ch":0},"text":["p"],"removed":[""],"origin":"+input"}
27/5/2016@8:34:43:615:change:{"from":{"line":0,"ch":1},"to":{"line":0,"ch":1},"text":["r"],"removed":[""],"origin":"+input"}
27/5/2016@8:34:43:677:change:{"from":{"line":0,"ch":2},"to":{"line":0,"ch":2},"text":["i"],"removed":[""],"origin":"+input"}
27/5/2016@8:34:43:811:change:{"from":{"line":0,"ch":3},"to":{"line":0,"ch":3},"text":["n"],"removed":[""],"origin":"+input"}
27/5/2016@8:34:43:884:change:{"from":{"line":0,"ch":4},"to":{"line":0,"ch":4},"text":["t"],"removed":[""],"origin":"+input"}
27/5/2016@8:34:43:884:change:{"from":{"line":0,"ch":5},"to":{"line":0,"ch":5},"text":["()"],"removed":[""],"origin":"+input"}
```


Fig. 2. Logs collected when the learner was writing a *print* command.

From such data, we extracted the following measures to evaluate whether the TPs and RPs from each condition was equivalent:

- *Resolution Time*: time the student took to solve the question, not counting downtime (more than 2 min).

[5] Notice that the first nearest neighbour of a given TP is itself and that is why we start i from the number 2.

- *codeEffort*: whether the expected coding effort (number of lines of code, number of control structures used) to solve both TP and RP problems are equivalent.
- *hitRate*: if the hit rate expected to solve both TP and RP problems are equivalent. The hit rate is the proportion of code solutions accepted (correct) divided by problems attempted, for a given problem.

6.4 Data Analysis

We compared experimental and control conditions using multi-level regressions [14] because such regression models are aligned to our numeric measures as well as handle dependent data (i.e., multiple answers from the same students). Standard t-tests, for instance, do not handle more than two repeated measures, whilst ANOVAs suffer with unbalanced datasets such as ours [6] and standard regressions assume data points are independent [12]. Differently, multi-level regression models handle dependent data because, loosely speaking, they create a number of standard regression models (e.g., one for each level), and then group them together. In our case, for instance, the grouping factor was *users*. The algorithm took group differences (e.g., from one person to another) into account by, oftentimes, having one intercept per group. These are known as the *random coefficients* [18].

Additionally, multi-level regressions calculate *fixed coefficients*. These can be seen as overall properties of the dataset that do not vary across groups but are calculated considering group (dis)similarities [18]. Thereby, using multi-level regressions is imperative to properly reach the goal of the proposed study given our experimental design. Note that we were interested in understanding the overall effect of the recommendation method compared to human selections. Therefore, we focused on fixed coefficients, which provide this overall perspective while controlling for data dependency. Thus, we ran three multi-level regressions, one with each measure as dependent variable, and users as the grouping factor (i.e., random coefficients) and condition (control vs experimental) as the independent variable (i.e., fixed coefficients) for all.

Importantly, multi-level regressions have assumptions similar to those of standard regression [14]. Residuals normality, for instance, is one of them [12]. However, testing this and similar assumptions is subject to new assumptions and threads to validity as well [6]. Then, we opted to additionally conduct robust analyses. These are considered to address limitations of the standard approaches in the presence of, for instance, outliers, and yield similar results when original assumptions are met [31]. Therefore, we ran standard and robust multi-level analyses – one pair for each measure – using the *lme4* and *robustlmm* R libraries, respectively. Then, we compared the standard's and robust's results to identify possible differences among them aiming to maximise conclusion validity. We did not correct *p*-values because these tests represent a small number of comparisons planned apriori [5] and use 95% confidence intervals for our comparisons and *p*-values, which were calculated using the *lmerTest* R package.

7 Results

Table 3 and Fig. 3 summarise our results. First, they show the mean and standard deviation values of each condition for all three measures. Next, they show the multi-level regression results, focusing on the fixed coefficient (experimental vs control) (see Sect. 6.4). Specifically, the table reports the coefficient and its standard error, t statistic, and *p*-value. Finally, the table reports the 95% confidence intervals estimated for each condition.

Table 3. Results summary for all measures. *Condition* shows descriptive statistics as Mean (Standard Deviation) for experimental (EXP) and control (CTR) groups. *Multi-level Regressions* shows the condition coefficient (Coef) and its standard error (SE), t statistic, p-value, and conditions' Confidence Intervals.

	Condition		Multi-level Regressions				
Measure	EXP	CTR	Coef (SE)	t stat	p-val	CI Exp	CI Ctr
Hit Rate	0.39 (0.22)	0.43 (0.26)	0.02 (0.03)	0.47	0.63	[0.37 - 0.47]	[0.40 - 0.47]
Res Time	40.7 (34.7)	45.9 (43.5)	5.32 (3.95)	1.35	0.18	[34.0 - 46.6]	[41.1 - 50.2]
Code Eff.	191 (131)	212 (149)	21.3 (14.0)	1.52	0.13	[166 - 211]	[194 - 226]

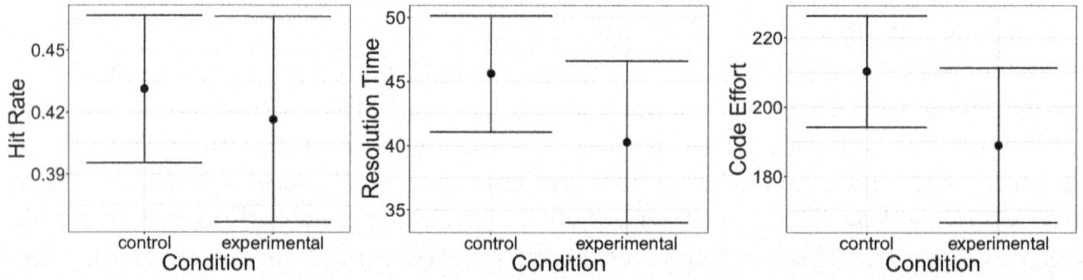

Fig. 3. Outcomes of measures comparing the experimental setting versus the control setting.

As Table 3 demonstrates, all p-values were greater than the alpha level (0.05). Accordingly, the CIs of experimental and control groups overlapped for all measures. Hence, we could not reject the null hypothesis that the condition coefficient significantly affected any of the three measures. Similarly, the robust analyses yielded the same conclusions for hit rate (Coef = 0.01; SE = 0.03; t = 0.245; EXP CI: [0.36 - 0.46]; CTR CI: [0.38 - 0.46]), resolution time (Coef = 2.09; SE = 3.35; t = 0.624; EXP CI: [32.4 - 43.64]; CTR CI: [36.0 - 43.6), and code effort (Coef = 19.6; SE = 13.8; t = 1.428; EXP CI: [158 - 202]; CTR CI: [183 - 215]). Thus, these findings suggest that the recommendation method recommended problems that required resolution times and coding efforts, as well as led to hit rates, similar to those of problems selected by instructors.

8 Pedagogical Implications

Here we provide an important step towards the employment of a method provided in the literature [24], which is crucial [15,25] since many AI methods provided in conference and journal papers end up not being used in real educational scenarios. Indeed, our study provides advantages in terms of employing a practical application of an AI method to allow for testing and evaluation of their effectiveness in real-world situations critical for refining and improving this method, and ensuring that they are effective in diverse settings and for a wide range of users. Still, our study enables instructors to tailor and adapt the AI method validated to meet the unique needs of their learners and their specific context. The original work [24] provided general guidelines and principles for the use of their method. However, the implementation of their method requires customisation and adaptation for different contexts, learners, and learning goals. As such, our work allows for such customisation and adaptation, leading to more effective implementation of that educational method.

We strongly believe that the practical application of educational methods available in the literature in real-world educational scenarios is critical for improving educational practice and ensuring that learners receive high-quality and effective education.

Furthermore, a practical implication of our findings is the reduction of instructors' workload in the problem selection task, to compose assignments lists using OJs. That is, save the instructors time and effort by filtering through a vast amount of programming problems and presenting them with only the most relevant ones. This makes room for freeing the instructors' time, enhancing their methodological and pedagogical planning, and reducing the high failure rates that are common in CS1 classes [15,27].

Moreover, our adaption to employ hybrid human/AI intelligence to the work presented in [24] has opened room for enhancing instructors and AI capabilities for the benefit of both sides. Overall, the combination of AI and human expertise has the potential to enhance the effectiveness and efficiency of education, leading to improved learning outcomes and increased student satisfaction. As such, hybrid human/AI systems are becoming increasingly important in education, and are likely to play a major role in the future of education [13].

Moreover, another possible application for this work is the creation of a pool of similar questions that could be used to identify students with *fragile learning* [27]. Fragile learning refers to a situation where a student may have solved an exercise by chance, without possessing all the necessary skills and concepts needed to solve the problem, or may have found the solution online. A more reliable way to confirm whether the student has actually acquired the skills associated with the exercise is to ask them to solve a similar question, which is similar in terms of topic, estimated time of resolution, and level of effort required. If the student fails to solve a similar problem, it could be an indication of fragile learning, which is important to detect for the evolution of the computer education field [17,27]. Similarly, asking students to solve similar problems could also be used to identify signs of plagiarism, which is a common issue in CS1 classes [2].

By enabling the creation of tools for detecting fragile learning and preventing plagiarism based on the solving of multiple similar problems, our method offers a valuable contribution to the field.

The current study provided empirical evidence that might help computing education researchers. The method might be also useful to design pre- and post-tests, by creating two or more assignments that require similar effort, and resolution time, and will produce similar hit rates for those with similar knowledge. The challenge to find pairs of equivalent questions to be used in pre- and post-tests of experiments in the area of computer education is well known. Thereby, the method could be intuitively employed for this purpose.

9 Final Remarks

In this work, we assessed a recommendation system used in real-life classes of CS1, to help the instructors in the selection of problems to compose assignment lists. We demonstrated that the humanly validated recommendations (hybrid human/AI approach) are compatible with the humanly selected problems. The method was tested in an environment with real classes, in which students in the control group solved the humanly selected questions, while students in the experimental group solved the selected questions through a collaboration between the instructor and the AI method. As such, it is believed that the human/AI hybrid method can be employed in online judge systems to reduce the workload of CS1 instructors.

As a limitation, we collected data from a single institution, which brings external threats to the method's validity. Moreover, we obtained the data from our intervention from a single semester, in a teaching cycle of 14 weeks. As such, how our intervention affects the time the instructor takes to select problems, and if it poses more or less challenging problems for students is one aspect that merits more investigation.

Our adaptation of the work from [24] does not provide an alternative in cases where the recommendation is not useful, because of incompatibility between the effort required to solve the TP and RP. In our future work, we plan to enhance our approach by soliciting feedback (or rating) from instructors who choose not to accept a recommendation due to the aforementioned reason (incompatibility between the effort from TP and RP). By asking for a rating of the recommendation, we can gain deeper insight into the extent of its shortcomings and make necessary adjustments to the recommender model accordingly. Additionally, we aspire to conduct a more extensive analysis of CS1 classes to further validate our findings. Indeed, validating research findings with a wider sample is essential for ensuring that the results are reliable and generalisable. By including a larger and more diverse sample, we can improve the representativeness of our findings, and enhance the likelihood that the results will be applicable to other contexts and populations.

Finally, the proposed recommender method could be applied to any programming course. To understand its power of generality in-depth, future research should carry out new experiments in other courses other than CS1.

Acknowledgements. This research, carried out within the scope of the Samsung-UFAM Project for Education and Research (SUPER), according to Article 39 of Decree n°10.521/2020, was funded by Samsung Electronics of Amazonia Ltda., under the terms of Federal Law n°8.387/1991 through agreement 001/2020, signed with UFAM and FAEPI, Brazil. This study was financed in part by Conselho Nacional de Desenvolvimento Científico e Tecnológico - Brasil - CNPq (Process 308513/2020-7) and Fundação de Amparo a Pesquisa do Estado do Amazonas - FAPEAM (Process 01.02.016301.02770/2021-63). This study was financed in part by the Acuity Insights under the Alo Grant program.

References

1. Akata, Z., et al.: A research agenda for hybrid intelligence: augmenting human intellect with collaborative, adaptive, responsible, and explainable artificial intelligence. Computer **53**(08), 18–28 (2020)
2. Albluwi, I.: Plagiarism in programming assessments: a systematic review. ACM Trans. Comput. Educ. (TOCE) **20**(1), 1–28 (2019)
3. Alrajhi, L., Alamri, A., Pereira, F.D., Cristea, A.I.: Urgency analysis of learners' comments: an automated intervention priority model for MOOC. In: Cristea, A.I., Troussas, C. (eds.) ITS 2021. LNCS, vol. 12677, pp. 148–160. Springer, Cham (2021). https://doi.org/10.1007/978-3-030-80421-3_18
4. Alrajhi, L., Alharbi, K., Cristea, A.I., Pereira, F.D.: Extracting the language of the need for urgent intervention in MOOCs by analysing text posts. In: International Conference on Web-Based Learning. pp. 161–173. Springer, Cham (2022). https://doi.org/10.1007/978-3-031-33023-0_14
5. Armstrong, R.A.: When to use the Bonferroni correction. Ophthalmic Physiol. Optics **34**(5), 502–508 (2014)
6. Cairns, P.: Doing Better Statistics in Human-Computer Interaction. Cambridge University Press, Cambridge (2019)
7. Carter, A., Hundhausen, C., Olivares, D.: Leveraging the integrated development environment for learning analytics. In: The Cambridge Handbook of Computing Education Research, chap. 23, pp. 679–706. Cambridge University Press, Cambridge (2019)
8. Dellermann, D., Ebel, P., Söllner, M., Leimeister, J.M.: Hybrid intelligence. Bus. Inf. Syst. Eng. **61**(5), 637–643 (2019)
9. Fantozzi, P., Laura, L.: Recommending tasks in online judges using autoencoder neural networks. Olympiads Inform. **14**, 61–76 (2020)
10. Fincher, S., Tenenberg, J., Dorn, B.: H.C., McCartney, R., Murphy, L.: Computing education research today. In: The Cambridge Handbook of Computing Education Research, chap. 2, pp. 40–55. Cambridge University Press, Cambridge (2019)
11. Fonseca, S.C., Pereira, F.D., Oliveira, E.H., Oliveira, D.B., Carvalho, L.S., Cristea, A.I.: Automatic subject-based contextualisation of programming assignment lists. Int. Educ. Data Min. Soc. (2020)
12. Gelman, A., Hill, J.: Data Analysis Using Regression and Multilevel/Hierarchical Models. Cambridge University Press, Cambridge (2006)
13. Holstein, K., Aleven, V., Rummel, N.: A conceptual framework for human–AI hybrid adaptivity in education. In: Bittencourt, I.I., Cukurova, M., Muldner, K., Luckin, R., Millán, E. (eds.) AIED 2020. LNCS (LNAI), vol. 12163, pp. 240–254. Springer, Cham (2020). https://doi.org/10.1007/978-3-030-52237-7_20

14. Hox, J.J., Moerbeek, M., Van de Schoot, R.: Multilevel Analysis: Techniques and Applications. Routledge (2010)
15. Ihantola, P., et al.: Educational data mining and learning analytics in programming: literature review and case studies. In: Proceedings of the 2015 ITiCSE on Working Group Reports, pp. 41–63. ACM (2015)
16. Kurnia, A., Lim, A., Cheang, B.: Online judge. Comput. Educ. **36**(4), 299–315 (2001). https://doi.org/10.1016/S0360-1315(01)00018-5
17. Luxton-Reilly, A., et al.: Introductory programming: a systematic literature review. In: Proceedings Companion of the 23rd Annual ACM Conference on Innovation and Technology in Computer Science Education, pp. 55–106 (2018)
18. Mirman, D.: Growth Curve Analysis and Visualization Using R. CRC Press (2016)
19. de Oliveira, J., Salem, F., de Oliveira, E.H.T., Oliveira, D.B.F., de Carvalho, L.S.G., Pereira, F.D.: Os estudantes leem as mensagens de feedback estendido exibidas em juízes online? In: Anais do XXXI Simpósio Brasileiro de Informática na Educação, pp. 1723–1732. SBC (2020)
20. Pereira, F.D., et al.: A recommender system based on effort: towards minimising negative affects and maximising achievement in CS1 learning. In: Cristea, A.I., Troussas, C. (eds.) ITS 2021. LNCS, vol. 12677, pp. 466–480. Springer, Cham (2021). https://doi.org/10.1007/978-3-030-80421-3_51
21. Pereira, F.D., et al.: Using learning analytics in the Amazonas: understanding students' behaviour in introductory programming. Brit. J. Educ. Technol. **51**(4), 955–972 (2020)
22. Pereira, F.D., et al.: Explaining individual and collective programming students' behavior by interpreting a black-box predictive model. IEEE Access **9**, 117097–117119 (2021)
23. Pereira, F.D., et al.: Toward supporting CS1 instructors and learners with fine-grained topic detection in online judges. IEEE Access **11**, 22513–22525 (2023)
24. Pereira, F.D., et al.: Towards human-AI collaboration: a recommender system to support CS1 instructors to select problems for assignments and exams. IEEE Trans. Learn. Technol., 1–14 (2022). https://doi.org/10.1109/TLT.2022.3224121
25. Pereira, F.D., de Souza, L.M., de Oliveira, E.H.T., de Oliveira, D.B.F., de Carvalho, L.S.G.: Predição de desempenho em ambientes computacionais para turmas de programação: um mapeamento sistemático da literatura. In: Anais do XXXI Simpósio Brasileiro de Informática na Educação, pp. 1673–1682. SBC (2020)
26. Quille, K., Bergin, S.: Cs1: how will they do? how can we help? a decade of research and practice. Comput. Sci. Educ. **29**(2–3), 254–282 (2019)
27. Robins, A.V.: Novice programmers and introductory programming. In: The Cambridge Handbook of Computing Education Research, chap. 12, pp. 327–376. Cambridge University Press, Cambridge (2019)
28. Saito, T., Watanobe, Y.: Learning path recommendation system for programming education based on neural networks. Int. J. Dist. Educ. Technol. (IJDET) **18**(1), 36–64 (2020)
29. Schwartz, B.M., Gurung, R.A.: Evidence-based teaching for higher education. American Psychological Association (2012)
30. Wasik, S., Antczak, M., Badura, J., Laskowski, A., Sternal, T.: A survey on online judge systems and their applications. ACM Comput. Surv. (CSUR) **51**(1), 3 (2018)
31. Wilcox, R.R.: Introduction to robust estimation and hypothesis testing. Academic Press (2011)
32. Yera, R., Martínez, L.: A recommendation approach for programming online judges supported by data preprocessing techniques. Appl. Intell. **47**(2), 277–290 (2017)

33. Zhao, W.X., Zhang, W., He, Y., Xie, X., Wen, J.R.: Automatically learning topics and difficulty levels of problems in online judge systems. ACM Trans. Inf. Syst. (TOIS) **36**(3), 27 (2018)
34. Zhou, W., Pan, Y., Zhou, Y., Sun, G.: The framework of a new online judge system for programming education. In: Proceedings of ACM Turing Celebration Conference-China, pp. 9–14. ACM (2018)

Evaluating the Impact and Usability of an AI-Driven Feedback System for Learning Design

Gerti Pishtari[1(✉)], Edna Milena Sarmiento-Márquez[2], María Jesús Rodríguez-Triana[2], Marlene Wagner[1], and Tobias Ley[1,2]

[1] University for Continuing Education Krems, Krems an der Donau, Austria
{gerti.pishtari,marlene.wagner,tobias.ley}@donau-uni.ac.at

[2] Tallinn University, Tallinn, Estonia
{msm,mjrt}@tlu.ee

Abstract. Despite the momentum that Artificial Intelligence (AI) is gaining in education, its role and impact on teachers' learning design practices are still underexplored. This paper reports an experimental study (N = 38) taking place in a teacher training where an AI-driven feedback system aided teachers in the creation of learning designs. The study analyses the impact that using the AI feedback had on the quality of designs that teachers created, and the usability evaluation of the system. We noticed statistically significant differences between the designs created by the randomly assigned teachers in the experimental (using AI) and control group (without AI), suggesting that AI algorithms specialized to perform specific tasks related to the learning design could help teachers to better meet their design goals. While teachers graded the usability of the feedback system as above average, they also found it easy to use and its functions well integrated. In open-ended questions, teachers expressed doubts about their trust in AI systems and the impact that they may have in school communities, suggesting that future work should explore not only the long-term impact that using AI can have on teachers' design practices, but also on their perceptions and understanding of the technology.

Keywords: Artificial Intelligence · Learning Design · Design Analytics · Mobile Learning · Inquiry-Based Learning · Teacher Training

1 Introduction

Artificial Intelligence (AI) is transforming the way we access and process information, and education is at the forefront of this transformation. AI tools, such

This research has been partially funded by the European Union in the context of Twinning (EuropeAid/160712/ID/ACT/ACT/DZ), and the Estonian Research Council's Personal Research Grant (PRG1634).

O. Viberg et al. (Eds.): EC-TEL 2023, LNCS 14200, pp. 324–338, 2023.
https://doi.org/10.1007/978-3-031-42682-7_22

as ChatGPT, are already being used by students, and this has required a shift in teaching practices and curriculum development for educators and schools [26]. AI has been widely discussed in Technology Enhanced Learning (TEL), especially in the context of Learning Analytics (LA). Despite valid concerns on data privacy, bias, and ethical implications of using AI in education, research also highlights its potential to enable automated feedback [2], identify students at risk [13], or personalize the learning experience [26].

Recently, there has been a growing consensus in TEL that a productive partnership should be sought between teachers and AI through hybrid teacher-AI systems [12]. Rather than relying solely on AI that autonomously adapts the instructional process, this approach involves integrating AI systems with teacher expertise for more effective and efficient learning experiences. Apart from the existing AI works aiming at supporting decision-making during and after the learning experience, to close the loop of a successful teacher-AI partnership it will be necessary to understand the impact that using AI in real settings has on teachers' learning design practices. Although some related research has been conducted on the use of AI in Learning Design (LD), it has mainly focused on how AI can help with automatic content analysis of learning designs [20,24].

Therefore, in this paper, we explore one aspect of this teacher-AI partnership, namely when AI provides support for teachers during the learning design by automatic content analysis and feedback. We report on an experimental study that explored the impact that using an AI-driven feedback system had on participants of an in-service teacher training. The system analyzed the textual content of a learning design and checked if it reached specific design goals. More concretely, we randomly assigned teachers to the experimental (using AI) or control group (without AI), and compared the quality of designs created by them, guided by specific design goals that had to be achieved (see Sect. 4). We also report on the usability evaluation of the feedback system that followed.

The rest of this paper is organized as follows. In Sect. 2, we present the related work on LD and AI in education. In Sect. 3, we provide an overview of the context of the study, followed by the methodology (Sect. 4) and results (Sect. 5). In Sect. 6, we discuss the implications of this study for both research and practice. Finally, in Sect. 7, we conclude the paper and outline potential avenues for future research.

2 Related Work

In this section, we first describe relevant definitions, research, and open topics in the field of LD. Next, we present a snapshot of the current research on AI in TEL, and discuss the role that AI can have in LD.

2.1 Learning Design and the Need to Provide High-Level Guidance to Teachers

The field of LD aims to support teachers in developing, implementing, and sharing effective learning activity plans [16]. To achieve this goal, research in LD has contributed with multiple design representations, methodologies, frameworks, and authoring tools [18]. Learning design is a term also used to describe the process of designing a learning activity and the various artifacts created during this process by teachers [16]. The process is typically described as cyclic, involving the phases of conceptualization, authoring, implementation, and reflection [19]. During the conceptualization phase, teachers define the learning objectives and consider the necessary resources. In the authoring phase, teachers define the sequence, structure, and content of the learning activity. This is followed by the implementation of the design (i.e., its enactment), as well as an a posteriori reflection on its outcome, often closing the loop by leading to a re-conceptualization. The design artifacts produced during this lifecycle typically consist of the sequence of learning tasks, resources, and supports developed by teachers to facilitate the achievement of the learning objectives [9].

The adoption of authoring tools promoted by the field of LD remains low [16]. Even in more successful cases, designing learning activities remains a demanding task, as teachers need both technical expertise and pedagogical knowledge related to the specific context targeted by the tool (e.g., m-learning, collaborative, or inquiry learning) to design meaningful activities. For instance, [20] report that a community of teachers behind an m-learning tool struggled to design contextualized learning activities. Indeed, in several cases, teachers designed activities supposed to happen in a thematic park outdoors, but that did not include tasks requiring students to use the information found in their surroundings. Moreover, in multiple cases, the designed activities did not promote higher-order thinking skills in students (such as requiring them to perform analysis, evaluations, or creative tasks) [20]. [22] also report that teachers that used an authoring tool tailored for Inquiry-Based Learning (IBL) rarely included collaborative activities, despite the emphasis of IBL on promoting interactive engagement among students, or even skipped some of the IBL phases, putting at risk the IBL structure of the design.

Teacher training has traditionally been the primary method for improving teachers' ability to design effective and context-specific learning activities, but they can be expensive and time-consuming [20]. Also, while teachers may grasp LD practices in a training (as a "one-shot intervention"), adopting them in practice may require a long-term effort, where teachers receive feedback on their designs. Therefore, it is important to provide ongoing support to teachers to ensure that the learning designs they create align with their defined goals. Historically, this kind of high-level, pedagogically-guided analysis has been carried out manually by researchers or teacher trainers. For example, the Revised Bloom Taxonomy [7] has been used to evaluate whether a learning design fosters higher-order thinking skills in students. Since recent advances in AI have made it possible to accurately automate these analyses (see, for instance [17]), the next step would be to integrate them in authoring tools for feedback purposes, providing constant support to teachers during the design process.

2.2 Towards a Hybrid Teacher-AI Partnership

The use of AI in TEL has seen a significant increase in recent years [11]. Intelligent tutors are the traditional context where unsupervised and supervised machine learning have long been used to profile students or to assess their knowledge and automatically adapt learning activities to meet their needs. Recent developments in software, mobile, and sensor technologies have made it possible to track and analyze learning activities in new ways and contexts, leading to the emergence of the field of LA. AI in LA has been mainly used to measure student knowledge and skills, such as through predictive analytics that identify at-risk students [13]. Nevertheless, emerging research purposes include, among others, supporting pedagogical approaches such as collaborative learning, self-regulated learning, or project-based learning [15,25]. From the technical point of view, AI in LA has enabled the automatic processing and sense-making of large amounts of data, that would have otherwise required some manual human interpretation, even when they come from different data streams, such as in the case of multi-modal LA [4].

There is a growing consensus in TEL that the integration of AI technologies and human capabilities can leverage the unique strengths of both [6]. For instance, a teacher-AI partnership can be developed to take advantage of teacher intuition, derived from their experience and knowledge of their students, and AIs' ability to process large amounts of data and identify patterns [12]. It is becoming increasingly apparent that relying solely on AI systems that autonomously adapt learning and instruction processes may have adverse consequences, particularly with regard to learners [12]. Therefore, it is important to establish an alternate control mechanism that would impede AI to take over critical skills from learners, but that can balance AI usage to their abilities and skills [6]. Similarly, a shared responsibility between teachers and AI can take on various forms, ranging from teachers having complete control while AI provides support information, to AI automating most tasks while teachers monitor the process [12]. While the exact balance of the shared decision-making between teachers and AI will depend on the context, to advance successful teacher-AI partnerships it will be necessary to consider the entire aforementioned LD lifecycle.

Although existing research has produced several hybrid teacher-AI systems that demonstrate different levels of shared responsibility [6,12], the main focus has been on the enactment and (to a lesser extent) reflection phases of LD (e.g., AI that helps teachers with learning orchestration, and the related reflection that follows). The impact that AI can have on the LD phases of conceptualization and authoring remains underexplored. Indeed, the few related papers about AI in LD have focused on the role that AI can play in our understanding of the learning design outcomes, by using AI algorithms to automatically analyze and classify the textual content of learning designs, such as in the context of online higher education [24], or in m-learning [20]. Similar algorithms, if embedded in authoring tools, could foster guiding systems that can provide automatic feedback to teachers during the authoring phase. As a first step in this direction, in this paper, we investigate the impact that an AI-driven feedback system for

LD, designed to assist teachers in creating effective learning activities (during the authoring phase), has on the quality of the designs that teachers produce. The AI system can inform teachers if their learning designs meet specific m-learning and IBL criteria and it is further discussed in Sect. 4. Moreover, we report the usability evaluation that followed.

3 Context of the Study

Broader Context of the Study. This study is part of a broader Designed-Based Research initiative that aims to support teachers in their learning design practices. In previous work, we have focused on the contexts of m-learning and IBL. Namely, we have inquired about teacher practices and needs when designing for these contexts, and the support that LA and AI can provide. Moreover, we have designed an authoring tool and dashboards that help teachers to design and monitor effective learning activities outdoors (see, for instance [21]). Additionally, we have developed a machine learning algorithm that can automatically classify the textual content of learning designs [17,19]. Specifically, the algorithm identifies for each learning task (and consequently, for the entire learning design containing them) if it requires (or not) from students to:

- Perform higher-order thinking (that corresponds to the levels of *analyze*, *evaluate* and *create* of Blooms' Revised Taxonomy [7]).
- Have knowledge about the specific outdoor contextual environment where the learning activity is happening, or if students need to be in the contextual environment to perform the task (also called *about-context* and *in-context* knowledge according to Sharples [23]).
- Follow any of the phases of *conceptualization*, *investigation*, or *conclusion* of the IBL model (proposed by [14]).

The algorithm is based on BERT [3] and proved to be reliable on each of the binary-classification tasks, with Cohens' Kappa between 0.69–0.82, Accuracy between 0.86–0.95, and Recall between 0.74–0.96 [17]. In this study, we made use of this algorithm to provide feedback to teachers while designing learning activities (further explained in Sect. 4).

The Teacher-Training Context. The current study was conducted during an in-service teacher training with over 140 participants from K-12 schools in Algeria. The training happened online and lasted 4 days, between April 17–22, 2022. It focused on good practices of implementing LD, LA, and m-learning in teaching and learning practices. Each topic had a total of 4 sessions, each with a duration of 180 min, distributed on different days. The activities described in this paper happened as part of the first two LA sessions, and the instructor was the first author of this paper.

Participants. While we invited all the teachers attending the training, 38 accepted to participate in the study, from which 31 (81.6%) were female and 7 (18.4%) male. The sample consisted of teachers who taught students in 8th grade or higher, while also including 4 teacher trainers. Teachers participating had different domains of expertise, including science (i.e., biology, chemistry, physics) (11 participants); literature and language (7); foreign language (6); mathematics (3); or informatics (3). Only 5 (13.2%) had less than 5 years of experience. For further details, see the extended summary of the participants available online[1].

4 Methodology

Research Questions (RQ). This study aims to investigate the impact that an AI-driven feedback system had on the quality of designs created by teachers, and teachers' perceived usability of the feedback system. To accomplish this, we formulated the following research questions (RQ):

- **(RQ1)** Is there any difference in the quality of learning designs created by teachers using the AI-driven feedback system vs. teachers not using it?
- **(RQ2)** How do teachers perceive the usability of the feedback system?

In the rest of this section, we will describe the procedure used to conduct the study, the criteria that we considered to assess the quality of a learning design, and the data analysis approach followed to respond to the RQs.

Study Design and Procedure. Mainly due to the nature of RQ1, we adopted an interventional, analytic, and exploratory research approach that led us towards an experimental study, introducing an intervention and studying the effects. The study involved two phases, we will refer to them as phases A and B, which happened accordingly during the first and second LA sessions of the training (see Sect. 3 for a description of the training context). During phase A, participants:

- Were informed about the goals of the study and filled out the consent form.
- Filled out a form with questions about their age, gender, domain of expertise, and working experience (available online[2]).
- Had 40 min to design one m-learning activity.

Regarding the last point, each participant was asked to design an m-learning activity intended to happen outdoors. They were free to choose the topic of the activity and the mobile technology that teachers or students had to use (e.g., sensors, mobile devices, or specific applications). The activity had to contain a minimum of five different tasks intended to be performed by students. The design had to achieve the following criteria (i.e., design goals):

[1] https://bit.ly/2023ai4lPparticipants.
[2] https://bit.ly/2023ai4ldGeneralForm.

1. All the tasks part of the same design (learning activity) had to be meaningfully related, creating a connected learning narrative (i.e., an activity with disconnected tasks, which asked students to inquire about aspects that were not connected to each other, did not match this goal).
2. Tasks had to nudge students to perform higher-order thinking (represented by the levels of Analysis, Evaluation, and Creation of Revised Blooms' Taxonomy [7]).
3. The activity had to follow an IBL strategy (i.e., involving the IBL phases of Conceptualization, Investigation, and Conclusion [14]).
4. The activity had to make use of the contextual environment (as discussed in Sect. 3).

Participants used Google Docs to share the activity (only) with the first author of this paper.

The objective of this first design activity was to evaluate participants' design skills prior to phase B (i.e., the intervention). The designs created by teachers were graded with a score from 0 to 4 (one point for each of the goals mentioned above). We used the AI algorithm described in Sect. 3 to automatically evaluate if an activity achieved goals 2–4, while the first author of this paper manually evaluated each activity regarding goal 1 (the meaningful learning narrative).

We randomly assigned participants into the experimental or control group, by controlling that the participants that received a score higher than 3 in the design activity of phase A were equally distributed. We will call these participants high-score (vs. low-score) designers. Each group included a total of 19 participants, with 7 high-score designers in the experimental and 8 in the control group.

During phase B each participant had to design a learning activity following the same guidelines and goals as in phase A, but the activity had to include a different narrative and tasks. While the control group followed exactly the same steps as in phase A, participants in the experimental group had access to a Google Form where they could upload the learning activity (available online[3]). Once uploaded, the participant received an email with a report about their activity, including details on whether it fulfilled goals 2–4, and for the ones that were not reached, tips on how to achieve them. It should be noted that the control group also had access to the same design tips, as we had shared them in previous training sessions. No feedback was provided regarding goal 1 (the meaningful learning narrative). The email included a disclaimer explaining that results should be interpreted with caution, as despite its reliability, the algorithm could make errors. It was up to the participants to consider or disregard the feedback.

We used a Python script to automatically check the input of a Google Spreadsheet synchronized with the Form. The script had the machine learning model discussed in Sect. 3 preloaded, and for each new entry in the spreadsheet, it created a report using predefined textual templates and sent it as an email to the

[3] https://bit.ly/2023ai4ldAIfeedbackForm.

address included in the form (see the online document for a flowchart of the feedback system and an example of the report[4]).

After the sessions, (only) members of the experimental group filled out a form with questions from the System Usability Scale (SUS) [1], plus three open-ended questions about their user experience, and one general question about their perception of the role that AI could play in learning design practices. Specifically, the open ended-questions included:

- What was your overall impression of the AI system used to provide feedback, and why?
- Can you describe any specific aspects of the system that you found particularly helpful or frustrating?
- Based on your experience using the system, what changes or improvements would you suggest?
- What are your general perceptions of using AI for learning design practices?

Data Analysis. To respond to RQ1, we explored if the AI-driven feedback, which is our independent variable (IV) representing the intervention, had an effect on the score that teachers received for their learning designs. Thus our dependent variables (DV) are represented by the 4 goals of the learning design sessions discussed previously (we will call them ***DV1. Narrative***, ***DV2. Bloom***, ***DV3. IBL***, and ***DV4. Context***). These are all dichotomous variables (taking the value 1 when the goal is met and 0 otherwise). We also considered ***DV5. Design Score***, represented by the cumulative score of all the achieved objectives in a given design (an ordinal variable with a value between 0 and 4).

We selected the statistical tests based on the nature of our variables (dichotomous or ordinal), and our relatively small sample size ($N = 38$ for between-groups, and $N = 19$ for within-group comparisons). We used Fishers' Exact Test for between-group comparisons (experimental vs the control) when considering each of the dichotomous variables (DV1-4), and Mann-Whitney U Test for the ordinal variable (DV5). We also used McNemars' test for within-group comparisons (e.g., between designs from phases A and B for participants of the same group) based on each of the dichotomous variables (DV1-4), and Wilcoxon Signed-Rank Test for the ordinal variable (DV5). We used an alpha level of .05 for all the tests. We also compared the frequencies of achieving the specific goals (our DVs), per group (experimental and control) and phase (A and B) (see Sect. 5).

Regarding RQ2, we explored descriptive statistics for the cumulative SUS score (i.e., mean, standard deviation), and for each of its questions (i.e., median). We combined these analyses with a thematic analysis of the four open-ended questions. The thematic analysis was conducted by the first two authors of this paper, following the guidelines proposed by [10], namely, including the phases of: a) becoming familiar with the data, b) generating initial codes, c) searching for themes, d) reviewing themes, and e) defining themes. Figure 1 summarizes the experimental study design.

[4] https://bit.ly/2023ai4ldFlowchartReportexample.

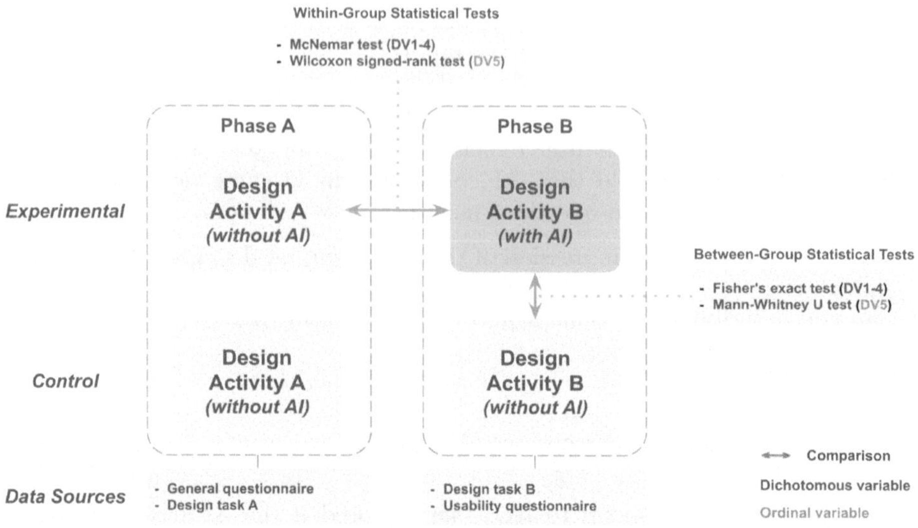

Fig. 1. Experimental study design, including the phases (A and B), statistical tests used, and data sources. The statistical tests are grouped into within-group and between-group ones.

5 Results

This section describes the results alongside the RQs.

5.1 RQ1. Impact of Using AI on the Designs Created by Teachers

As it can be noticed in Fig. 2, the most significant change in terms of frequencies (i.e., the total number of designs that achieved a specific goal) was between the learning designs created by low-score designers of the experimental group in phase A and phase B, as well as between the low-score designers of both the experimental and control groups in phase B. We did not notice differences between the participants in terms of their working experience, age, or domain of expertise (as reported in the general questionnaire filled in phase A). See the extended table of the results available online[5] for further details.

Regarding the comparison of the experimental (n = 19) and control (n = 19) groups in phase B. The Fishers' exact tests showed that there was a statistically significant association between the use of the AI-driven feedback system and the achievement of the Bloom (p = *.005*), IBL (p = *.008*); and Context (p = *.038*) goals. There was no statistically significant association for the achievement of the Narrative goal (p = *.515*). See Fig. 3 for the related odds ratio and intervals of confidence. Concerning the Design Score, we used a Mann-Whitney U test. Distributions of the design scores for experimental and control groups were not

[5] https://bit.ly/2023ai4ldFullDataset.

		Phase A			Phase B		
		High-score Designers	Low-score Designers	All	High-score Designers	Low-score Designers	All
Experimental	DV1. Narrative	5 (71.4%)	3 (25%)	8 (42.1%)	6 (85.7%)	4 (33.3%)	10 (53.6%)
	DV2. Bloom	7 (100%)	3 (25%)	10 (53.6%)	7 (100%)	10 (83.3%)	17 (89.5%)
	DV3. IBL	6 (85.7%)	0	6 (31.6%)	6 (85.7%)	7 (58.3%)	13 (68.4%)
	DV4. Context	7 (100%)	3 (25%)	10 (53.6%)	7 (100%)	9 (75%)	16 (84.2%)
Control	DV1. Narrative	5 (62.5%)	1 (9.1%)	6 (31.6%)	5 (62.5%)	2 (18.2%)	7 (36.8%)
	DV2. Bloom	8 (100%)	1 (9.1%)	9 (47.4%)	7 (87.5%)	3 (36.4%)	8 (42.1%)
	DV3. IBL	7 (87.5%)	0	7 (36.8%)	4 (50%)	0	4 (21.1%)
	DV4. Context	7 (87.5%)	2 (18.2%)	9 (47.4%)	7 (87.5%)	2 (18.2%)	9 (47.4%)

Fig. 2. Frequencies (i.e. where each count represents a design that achieved a specific objective, such as following an IBL strategy) clustered per group (experimental or control), phase (A or B), and dependent variable (DV1-4). Results are shown separately for high- and low-score designers (named based on the first design activity), as well as for all the participants together.

similar, as assessed by visual inspection. Median design scores for the experimental group (Median = 3) were statistically significantly higher compared to the control group (Median = 1), U = 278, z = 2.922, $p = .003$. The effect size was moderate (r = .047).

Apropos the comparisons of the designs created by the experimental group in phases A and B. An exact McNemars' test determined that there was a statistically significant association between the use of the AI-driven feedback system and the achievement of the Bloom ($p = .016$) and IBL ($p = .039$) goals, but not for the Narrative ($p = .727$) and Context ($p = .109$) goals. See Fig. 3 for the corresponding φ coefficients (with higher positive values indicating a stronger association between the IV and the DV). Regarding the Design Score, we used a Wilcoxon signed-rank test. The difference scores were approximately symmetrically distributed, as assessed by a histogram with a superimposed normal curve. There was a statistically significant median increase (MD = 1) in the design scores from phase A (Median = 1) to phase B (Median = 3), z = 2.956, $p = .003$. The effect size was large (r = .67)

Figure 3 provides a summary of the results for all the discussed tests. See its online version[6] for a detailed description and interpretation of each test (also including results for within-group comparisons for the control group, and between-group comparisons for the first design activity in phase A).

[6] https://bit.ly/2023ai4ldStatisticalTests.

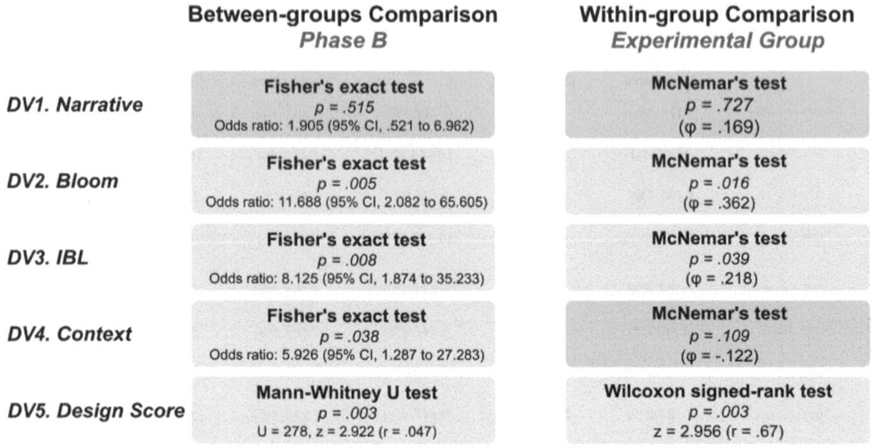

Fig. 3. Results from the statistical tests. With green the statistically significant. (Color figure online)

5.2 RQ2. Perceived Usability of the AI-Driven Feedback System

The mean SUS score was 61.6, with a standard deviation of 8.1, suggesting that while the AI-driven feedback system received an average score, there were some differences between the participants. We did not notice differences in terms of high- vs. low-score designers, experience, age, or domain of expertise. The system was also perceived as not being hard to use and its functions were considered as being well integrated. See the online table[7] about the SUS evaluation for more details, including anonymous individual responses and the median score for each question.

Results from the 3 open-ended questions about the user experience supported the ones from SUS. Moreover, we identified three main themes:

1. *Integration*: Teachers perceived the feedback as useful (15 participants mentioned it), but considered the overall process (from filling out the form to receiving an email with the report) as unnecessarily long. One participant suggested having *"one single system that integrates everything"*, such as an authoring tool (instead of Google Docs) with an integrated feedback system.
2. *Trust*: Teachers were not sure whether to trust the assessment of the algorithm or not. For instance, one participant explained that *"the fact that the email included a disclaimer about the accuracy of the algorithm made me doubt its results"*.
3. *Technical issues*: Eight participants reported that the system did not always work properly. Indeed, sometimes the script took longer than expected to generate and send the report, while emails were sent manually twice.

[7] https://bit.ly/2023ai4ldSUS.

Regarding the fourth open-ended question (the general perceptions of using AI for learning design). Only 4 optimistic answers emphasized the fact that AI could help teachers to improve the quality of learning activities that they create, while most of the teachers expressed doubts. This could be grouped into *privacy issues* (e.g., how AI systems will treat their data), *trust concerns* (e.g., how reliable and unbiased AI could be in this context), and fear of an increasing *digital divide* (e.g., one participant raised concerns that *"a broad implementation of AI in education could increase the digital gap between rich and poor schools"*).

6 Discussion

Regarding RQ1 (the impact of the AI-driven feedback), teachers of the experimental group (using AI) scored better results when comparing their designs in Phase B with their previous designs in Phase A, as well as with their peers in the control group in Phase A. These differences were also statistically significant for most of the design goals (our DVs). We can also deduce that this difference was mainly due to the increased performance of low-score designers in phase B (as seen in Fig. 2). The fact that there were no changes for DV1. Narrative (the only design goal for which the AI system did not provide feedback), on the one hand, enhances the evidence that the improvement for the other goals was due to the usage of the AI-driven feedback. On the other hand, it highlights the complexity of supporting teachers to design meaningful activities with AI, as it is necessary to consider multiple pedagogical and context-dependent aspects [22,23]. This highlights the need to explore other good LD practices for which AI can provide support. Moreover, while our results show that similar AI for LD tools can help teachers to improve their design skills, they are related to a specific setting (i.e., online teacher training) and contexts (m-learning and IBL). Thus, future research could explore the impact that the same AI-driven feedback system can have in different settings. One such case could be the IBL community behind Graasp [22]. Moreover, future research could also explore other contexts apart from m-learning and IBL, such as helping teachers to design for collaborative learning or flipped classroom, or even take a case-independent approach by targeting community of teachers behind authoring tools that are agnostic to specific contexts or pedagogical approaches (such as ILDE [5]).

We started this paper by emphasizing the current research trends advocating for a teacher-AI partnership. While our study provides an example of this partnership (targeting the authoring phase of the learning design, with an AI-driven feedback system that informs teachers if they are meeting specific good LD practices), it is just a snapshot in a broader and more complex pool of practices, where the long term impact that using AI can have on teachers design practices and behavior remains unknown. For instance, many "gut-feeling" decisions that teachers make regarding their designs are indeed the result of cumulative experience over the years [27]. In the long term, longitudinal studies should explore whether and how the usage of AI will impact this expertise formation.

Concerning RQ2 (the usability evaluation), the AI-driven feedback system received an average SUS score, but it was also perceived as useful (as seen from the open-ended responses). These results might be due to the early-stage implementation of the system through a Google Form and automatic emails. Thus, our future iterations will include a fully functional prototype, exploring how teachers perceive a feedback system that is integrated into an authoring tool. Furthermore, teachers' answers to our open-ended questions emphasize the importance of topics such as trust, data privacy, and the impact that AI can have in different school communities. These issues need to be tackled to advance successful teacher-AI partnerships, not only in the context of AI for LD, but in the broader context of education. In the short term, research could explore how teachers' perceptions related to these issues change once teachers start adopting AI tools.

Limitations of this study include the small sample size. Results should be interpreted with caution, and as related to the specific context and study. We did not control for covariates and moderator variables (this would have required statistical tests not suitable for our dataset). Nevertheless, we did equally distribute high-score designers between the groups to avoid having groups with unbalanced design expertise. Future studies, with bigger sample sizes, might explore the effect that variables like the domain of expertise, experience, technical skills, age, or gender might have on the impact that using AI can have on design practices. Our context, an online training, made it difficult to control for other factors that might have influenced teachers during the design sessions. The short duration of the study is another limitation. Indeed, future work could explore how AI impacts teachers' design behaviors through longer studies that alternate the usage and absence of AI (e.g., ABAB studies [8]). In our study the control group received nothing, but future work might also explore what happens when the control group receives human feedback instead. Regarding the LD analyses, we automatically evaluated the design goals related to DV2-4 with an AI algorithm. Despite the reliability of the algorithm [17], a human evaluation might have produced different results. Also, only one person evaluated whether the learning designs achieved the Narrative goal (DV1) which may be subject to personal interpretation. Last but not least, the thematic analysis of the open-ended questions relies on the subjectivity of the researchers, which might have led to oversimplification or overlooking of important details.

7 Conclusion and Future Work

This paper explored the impact that using an AI-driven feedback system for LD had on the designs that teachers created, and presented the related usability evaluation of the system. We noticed statistically significant differences between designs from teachers that used AI and the ones that did not on most of the design goals that we considered (represented by our dependent variables). The same was true for within-group comparisons (i.e., comparison between the designs created by teachers in the experimental group in the sessions with and without AI). The AI-driven feedback system received an average SUS score of 61.6, but it was perceived as easy to use and its functions well integrated.

This paper provides an example of how experimental studies could be integrated as part of broader research initiatives that follow a Design-Based Research approach. Indeed, in our future iterations, we will make use of the gathered feedback when developing a system that integrates both the authoring tool and the AI-driven feedback. Moreover, to advance successful teacher-AI partnerships, future research not only should inquire about the long-term impact that using AI could have on teachers' design practices, but should also tackle open issues about trust, data privacy, or the impact that AI usage can have in school communities.

References

1. Brooke, J., et al.: SUS - a quick and dirty usability scale. Usabil. Eval. Ind. **189**(194), 4–7 (1996)
2. Cavalcanti, A.P., et al.: Automatic feedback in online learning environments: a systematic literature review. Comput. Educ. Artif. Intell. **2**, 100027 (2021)
3. Devlin, J., Chang, M.W., Lee, K., Toutanova, K.: BERT: pre-training of deep bidirectional transformers for language understanding. arXiv preprint arXiv:1810.04805 (2018)
4. Di Mitri, D., Schneider, J., Specht, M., Drachsler, H.: From signals to knowledge: a conceptual model for multimodal learning analytics. J. Comput. Assist. Learn. **34**(4), 338–349 (2018)
5. Hernández-Leo, D., et al.: An integrated environment for learning design. Front. ICT **5**, 9 (2018)
6. Holstein, K., Aleven, V., Rummel, N.: A conceptual framework for human–AI hybrid adaptivity in education. In: Bittencourt, I.I., Cukurova, M., Muldner, K., Luckin, R., Millán, E. (eds.) AIED 2020. LNCS (LNAI), vol. 12163, pp. 240–254. Springer, Cham (2020). https://doi.org/10.1007/978-3-030-52237-7_20
7. Krathwohl, D.R.: A revision of bloom's taxonomy: an overview. Theory Pract. **41**(4), 212–218 (2002)
8. Kratochwill, T.R., et al.: Single-case intervention research design standards. Remedial Spec. Educ. **34**(1), 26–38 (2013)
9. Lockyer, L., Heathcote, E., Dawson, S.: Informing pedagogical action: aligning learning analytics with learning design. Am. Behav. Sci. **57**(10), 1439–1459 (2013)
10. Maguire, M., Delahunt, B.: Doing a thematic analysis: a practical, step-by-step guide for learning and teaching scholars. All Ireland J. High. Educ. **9**(3) (2017)
11. Mavrikis, M., Cukurova, M., Di Mitri, D., Schneider, J., Drachsler, H.: A short history, emerging challenges and co-operation structures for artificial intelligence in education. Bildung und Erziehung **74**(3), 249–263 (2021)
12. Molenaar, I.: Towards hybrid human-AI learning technologies. Eur. J. Educ. **57**(4), 632–645 (2022)
13. Moreno-Marcos, P.M., Muñoz-Merino, P.J., Maldonado-Mahauad, J., Perez-Sanagustin, M., Alario-Hoyos, C., Kloos, C.D.: Temporal analysis for dropout prediction using self-regulated learning strategies in self-paced MOOCs. Comput. Educ. **145**, 103728 (2020)
14. Pedaste, M., et al.: Phases of inquiry-based learning: definitions and the inquiry cycle. Educ. Res. Rev. **14**, 47–61 (2015)
15. Perez-Alvarez, R., Jivet, I., Pérez-Sanagustin, M., Scheffel, M., Verbert, K.: Tools designed to support self-regulated learning in online learning environments: a systematic review. IEEE Trans. Learn. Technol. (2022)

16. Persico, D., Pozzi, F.: Informing learning design with learning analytics to improve teacher inquiry. Br. J. Edu. Technol. **46**(2), 230–248 (2015)
17. Pishtari, G., Prieto, L.P., Rodríguez-Triana, M.J., Martinez-Maldonado, R.: Design analytics for mobile learning: scaling up the classification of learning designs based on cognitive and contextual elements. J. Learn. Anal. **9**(2), 236–252 (2022)
18. Pishtari, G., et al.: Learning design and learning analytics in mobile and ubiquitous learning: a systematic review. Br. J. Educ. Technol. **51**(4), 1078–1100 (2020)
19. Pishtari, G., Rodríguez-Triana, M.J.: An analysis of mobile learning tools in terms of pedagogical affordances and support to the learning activity life cycle. In: Gil, E., Mor, Y., Dimitriadis, Y., Köppe, C. (eds.) Hybrid Learning Spaces. UTLP, pp. 167–183. Springer, Cham (2022). https://doi.org/10.1007/978-3-030-88520-5_10
20. Pishtari, G., Rodríguez-Triana, M.J., Prieto, L.P., Ruiz-Calleja, A., Väljataga, T.: What kind of learning designs do practitioners create for mobile learning? Lessons learnt from two in-the-wild case studies. J. Comput. Assist. Learn. (2022)
21. Pishtari, G., Rodríguez-Triana, M.J., Väljataga, T.: A multi-stakeholder perspective of analytics for learning design in location-based learning. Int. J. Mob. Blend. Learn. (IJMBL) **13**(1), 1–17 (2021)
22. Rodríguez-Triana, M.J., Prieto, L.P., Pishtari, G.: What do learning designs show about pedagogical adoption? An analysis approach and a case study on inquiry-based learning. In: De Laet, T., Klemke, R., Alario-Hoyos, C., Hilliger, I., Ortega-Arranz, A. (eds.) EC-TEL 2021. LNCS, vol. 12884, pp. 275–288. Springer, Cham (2021). https://doi.org/10.1007/978-3-030-86436-1_21
23. Sharples, M.: Making sense of context for mobile learning. In: Mobile Learning, pp. 140–153. Routledge, London (2015)
24. Sie, R.L., et al.: Artificial intelligence to enhance learning design in UOW online, a unified approach to fully online learning. In: 2018 IEEE International Conference on Teaching, Assessment, and Learning for Engineering (TALE), pp. 761–767. IEEE (2018)
25. Spikol, D., Ruffaldi, E., Dabisias, G., Cukurova, M.: Supervised machine learning in multimodal learning analytics for estimating success in project-based learning. J. Comput. Assist. Learn. **34**(4), 366–377 (2018)
26. Tlili, A., et al.: What if the devil is my guardian angel: Chatgpt as a case study of using chatbots in education. Smart Learn. Environ. **10**(1), 15 (2023)
27. Vanlommel, K., Van Gasse, R., Vanhoof, J., Van Petegem, P.: Teachers' decision-making: data based or intuition driven? Int. J. Educ. Res. **83**, 75–83 (2017)

Single or Multi-page Learning Analytics Dashboards? Relationships Between Teachers' Cognitive Load and Visualisation Literacy

Stanislav Pozdniakov(✉), Roberto Martinez-Maldonado, Yi-Shan Tsai, Namrata Srivastava, Yuchen Liu, and Dragan Gasevic

Monash University, Melbourne, Australia
stanislavpoznyakof@gmail.com

Abstract. There has been a proliferation of learning analytics (LA) interfaces designed to support teachers, such as LA dashboards. However, although teacher dashboards have been extensively studied, there is limited understanding of the relationship between single-page or multi-page dashboard designs and the cognitive demands placed on teachers to use them. Additionally, teachers typically have varying levels of visualisation literacy (VL), which may make it easier or more difficult for them to engage with single-page versus multi-page dashboard designs. In this paper, we explore how teachers, with varying VL, use single-page and multi-page LA dashboards. We conducted a quasi-experimental study with 23 higher education teachers of varied VL inspecting single and multi-page LA dashboards. We used an eye-tracking device to measure cognitive load while teachers inspected the LA dashboards in online group work. We investigated how proxy metrics derived from eye-tracking data related to teachers' cognitive load varied depending on the type of the dashboard teacher used and the level of VL teachers have. Our findings suggest that the design of the LA dashboard had an impact on the cognitive load experienced by the teachers. Post-hoc analysis revealed that teachers with low VL had a marginally lower cognitive load when using single-page dashboards. We argue that the LA dashboard design for teachers should account for teachers' levels of VL and provide design recommendations.

Keywords: data literacy · learning analytics · dashboards · eye-tracking

1 Introduction

Learning analytics (LA) dashboards are garnering more attention as a way to provide technology-enhanced support for teachers [36,39]. There is a range of learning contexts in which dashboards are deployed to assist teachers with monitoring student progress, including online learning [13], MOOCs [11], collaborative learning [3], and K-12 classrooms [7]. However, despite the growing efforts

O. Viberg et al. (Eds.): EC-TEL 2023, LNCS 14200, pp. 339–355, 2023.
https://doi.org/10.1007/978-3-031-42682-7_23

to design and implement effective teacher-facing dashboards, there is no unanimous consensus regarding their effectiveness in supporting the teachers' monitoring capabilities [8,30,44]. Typical explanations for the lack of consensus include dashboard designs that do not align with teachers' needs [18,38] and teachers' lack of proficiency in effectively using dashboards [17,40], including key data and visualisation literacy skills [34].

Data literacy is typically linked with specialised skills required for teachers to effectively use dashboards. It encompasses the teachers' ability to organise, collect, analyse and draw inferences from students' data [26]. The existing body of literature suggests that teachers with low data literacy are prone to misinterpretation of students' data and might make wrong decisions [32]. Nonetheless, there is a lack of empirical research investigating how teachers' data literacy is intertwined with their dashboard use. As most LA dashboards commonly make extensive use of advanced visualisations, there is a more appropriate construct to represent the relevant skills teachers need to use LA dashboards, which is often overlooked in the existing LA literature: visualisation literacy (VL). VL refers to the ability to effectively interact with visualisations [23] (i.e., interpreting and making conclusions about students' progress).

In parallel, numerous attempts have been made to explore how different dashboard designs can better support teachers' monitoring efforts. For example, Echeverria et al. [14] and van Leeuwen and Rummel [41] have explored the potentially positive effects of augmenting single-page dashboards with visual explanations to enhance teachers' interpretive capabilities. Fernandez Nieto et al. [15] suggested the use of text and tables as a viable alternative to single-page visualisations. In a similar vein, Chen et al. [10] examined how structuring visualisations in the form of slides spread across multiple pages could enhance teachers' understanding of students' learning data. Furthermore, Martinez-Maldonado et al. [27] designed and evaluated a layered dashboard, employing a multi-page approach to simplify the exploration of learners' data. Despite these efforts, the question of whether visualisations should be consolidated on a single page or distributed across multiple pages has not been thoroughly investigated.

In this paper, we address the above gap and respond to the call for experimental studies on the effects of LA dashboard designs, as suggested in a recent review by Sahin et al. [35]. Specifically, we investigate how the design of the dashboard impacts teachers' cognitive load, taking into account their VL. Unlike previous studies, we explicitly compare how teachers with varying levels of VL use single- and multi-page LA dashboards. Our research examines how a proxy metric related to cognitive load vary depending on the type of dashboard and the level of VL of the teacher. To achieve this, we conducted a quasi-experimental study with 23 teachers of different VL levels inspecting single and multi-page dashboards while using an eye-tracking device. The dashboards presented data on online synchronous breakout groups.

2 Background

2.1 Teacher's Dashboard Design in Learning Analytics

Teacher-focused learning analytics (LA) dashboards often incorporate design elements aimed at simplifying the interpretation of data visualisations for monitoring students' progress. To aid in the formulation of takeaways from the charts and assist teachers in their daily tasks, explanatory annotations are often included. Echeverria et al. [14] conducted an eye-tracking study to investigate the impact of explicit visual explanations on teachers' interpretation skills. In their study, teachers were presented with single-page dashboards with and without explanatory annotations, and the authors analysed how the annotations guided teachers' attention, reduced colour variation, and explained trends with text. The authors found evidence that adding annotations reduced the cognitive effort required to interpret visualisations [14]. Van Leeuwen and Rummel [41] similarly examined single-page dashboards with and without explanatory annotations and found that enriching a dashboard with advisory text helped teachers feel more confident and required less effort when making decisions about identifying groups of students that need more help.

In some cases, tables and text may be used as an alternative to visualisations, as it is assumed that some teachers may lack the necessary skills to effectively interpret student data using visualisations. Fernandez Nieto et al. [15] examined the extent to which non-visual techniques, such as tabular visualisations or written reports, could support teachers in understanding data insights. They presented qualitative evidence that these alternative dashboards may be sufficient for some teachers' needs.

Finally, structuring visualisations based on the specific needs of teachers can help them focus on the aspects of student monitoring that are relevant at a given time. For example, Chen et al. [10] designed and evaluated multi-page dashboards for teachers to navigate various data views generated from MOOC data. Although the design approach was evaluated through expert interviews, there is no indication as to whether it helped lower the overview load for teachers. Martinez-Maldonado et al. [27] proposed and evaluated an approach to structure visualisations into multi-page dashboards based on the main pedagogical needs of teachers. This design approach aimed to simplify the representation of multimodal data to reduce the cognitive load of teachers who monitor students' progress in healthcare simulations. The authors indicated that the resulting dashboard helped teachers focus on how students were progressing towards specific learning outcomes.

Yet, the effectiveness of basic dashboard designs in reducing teachers' cognitive load has not been sufficiently investigated. Bach et al. [2] suggest that dashboard design can be categorized in terms of both *content-based* design, which refers to the data and visualisations used, and *composition-based* design patterns, which include the placement of visualizations across multiple pages, their structure and interaction techniques, and the colour semantics used. Existing reviews on dashboards for technology-enhanced learning [28] and teaching [32,37] position existing dashboards in terms of *content-based* design features and omit the *composition-based* ones.

While previous works have provided evidence of the effectiveness of various dashboard patterns in enhancing teachers' monitoring capabilities, a recent review on LA dashboard research [35] indicates a lack of experimental designs investigating *composition-based* design features. To the best of our knowledge, there is no explicit evidence on whether single or multi-page dashboard designs [2], which are composition-based dashboard design features that have been implicitly explored in separate previous studies [10,14,15,27,41], are related to teachers' ability to monitor students' progress. Such a distinction is becoming prominent in the human-computer interaction literature (e.g., [2,9]) but has not yet been conceptualised in educational technology literature. This is important because teachers typically have varying visualisation literacy skills, and it is unclear whether differences in VL levels might impede teachers' monitoring of students' progress, depending on the *composition-based* design features of LA dashboards (e.g., single or multiple-page interfaces).

2.2 Data and Visualisation Literacy

The need to scaffold teachers' abilities to use data and data visualisations has been previously flagged in the literature [1,24,32]. The teachers' ability to collect, analyse and interpret data to produce actionable insights is referred to as *data literacy* [26]. A recent review on teachers' data literacy [32] indicates emerging interest in improving teachers' data-related skills, such as the ability to identify patterns, trends and outliers in the data, to generate hypotheses about student behaviour and performance, and to validate or refute these hypotheses through further analysis [42], to enable technology-enhanced teaching. However, the concept of data literacy incorporates the ability to perform many low-level data tasks, most of which are not necessarily typical for teachers' everyday practices [42].

Instead of being involved in the data organisation and data wrangling tasks, teachers commonly access visualisations through LA dashboards. That is why the concept of *visualisation literacy* (VL) [23] may be more relevant as it focuses specifically on the abilities that teachers need to effectively use visual data interfaces. VL refers to the skillset required to comprehend and analyse visual representations of data, extract meaningful insights, and draw conclusions based on the information displayed [16]. This competency is essential for educators because of the increasing demand for teachers to work with the data, particularly, in the form of LA visual interfaces. Understanding teachers' VL skills could enable designers to create LA interfaces targeted to additionally support teachers with low VL. Several approaches to measuring visualisation literacy have been proposed recently. Burns et al. [6] suggested using Bloom's taxonomy of educational objectives to investigate how users interact with visualisations and complete tasks targeted at specific levels of comprehension. Lee et al. [23] developed and validated an assessment tool, the visualisation literacy assessment test (VLAT), to evaluate and quantify an individual's VL.

Although recent studies have attempted to elicit how users with varying VL use narrative visualisations [21], the exploration of the role of teachers' VL in relation to how they use LA dashboards is still emerging. Donohoe and Costello [12] conducted a study using VLAT, comparing teachers' visualisation literacy with their self-reported skills to interpret visualisations. They found that teachers are typically overconfident about their skills. In another study, Pozdniakov et al. [34] investigated how teachers with varying VL used two single-page dashboards. They found that high VL teachers adopted more complex strategies, while low VL teachers benefited from combining text descriptions with corresponding visualisations.

In summary, the literature has not provided any conclusive evidence on the effectiveness of single or multi-page dashboard designs. Additionally, it is uncertain how challenging it would be for teachers with varying VL to use these dashboard designs. To bridge this gap in knowledge, we have formulated the following research question (RQ): To what extent do teachers with varying levels of VL exhibit differences in cognitive load when using single and multi-page LA dashboards?

3 Methods

In this section, we outline the study procedure implemented to address the research question. The study was conducted in the context of a teacher-centric dashboard, deployed as part of a graduate course at Monash University, aimed at aiding teachers in monitoring synchronous online learning tasks. In this course, students participated in weekly 3-hour online classes facilitated by two instructors. These classes typically involved a range of tasks, with students forming small groups of 4–6 members and using audio-visual and text-based tools such as Zoom and Google Docs. Three versions of the dashboard were designed to assist teachers in monitoring student groups when the students entered breakout rooms in Zoom to work on group tasks. A laboratory experiment was set up to emulate teachers monitoring student groups during remote online classes, which was conducted in the university lab. We provide a summary of the study tasks and procedure below.

3.1 Participants and Study Procedure

A total of 24 teachers (13 females, 10 males) between 22 and 60 years old ($M = 31$, $SD = 8$) participated in the study. All teachers except one had completed a postgraduate degree (7 masters, 12 PhD students, 2 with a PhD degree), held a STEM degree, and were either currently employed as teachers in the university or had on average three years of teaching experience ($M = 3$, $SD = 3.4$).

The study procedure consisted of three parts: i) an eyetracking session where participants were asked to answer questions using three different dashboards; and ii) a VL (visual literacy) assessment was sent via email to participants to complete within one or two days after the study. All participants were reimbursed with $50 for their time and effort.

The eye-tracking component (i) of the study comprised a session lasting approximately 40 min. The process began with a calibration of the Tobii Pro Nano 60 Hz eye-tracker, placed at the bottom of a 24" desktop monitor with a resolution of 1920 × 1200 and a sampling rate of 60 Hz. The screen luminance was kept constant for all participants. An external video camera was set up to capture audio data, and a stationary chair was provided to participants to ensure consistent positioning. The lab maintained moderate and consistent illumination throughout the study for all participants.

Participants underwent a brief onboarding session for all conditions, where they were given an explanation of every element, colour, and text displayed on the screen. They then completed a short training activity to simulate the tasks they would be performing. For the task itself, participants were presented with a screenshot of the dashboard and asked to assess students' engagement. To guide the interpretation of visualisations, six tasks were provided to teachers. These tasks included questions like: "Which group or groups have the most inactive students?", "Which group is the most engaged in the discussion?", and "In your opinion, which group or groups might have experienced issues with progressing in the learning activity?". The study utilized a within-subject design, meaning all participants were asked the same set of questions for all dashboard versions.

All participants interacted with two single-page and one multi-page LA dashboards (refer to Figs. 2, 3, and Subsect. 3.2 for details), totalling three versions. To counter any order effect (i.e., participants showing a preference for the first version presented), we employed a three-by-three Latin square matrix design, which pseudo-randomly determined the order in which the versions were shown. To mitigate any carry-over effect (i.e., participants memorising the data after exposure to the first LA dashboard and thus confounding the use of subsequent dashboards), each exposure to a new LA dashboard presented data from a different classroom session to the participant. Consequently, data from three random classes, with students' names pseudonymised, was used in the study.

During the study, we collected the eye-tracking data with Tobii Pro Software. We followed the recommendations for preprocessing pupil dilation data as suggested in [19,29]. The samples with absent data about the pupil diameter of one of the eyes and blinks were removed. The noise reduction using Butterworth smoothing filter was applied to the raw data with a second-degree filter with a critical frequency of 1/8 of the sampling period. Next, we averaged pupil diameter over the left and right eyes to obtain a "cyclopean eye". Lastly, we use a baseline correction, i.e., using measures of pupil dilation with respect to the period where participants were not working on the main task.

Once the lab study was completed, the validated VLAT test [23] consisting of 53 multiple-choice questions that require the interpretation of various data charts (e.g., bar and lines charts among several others) was used to assess teachers' VL. We followed the recommendations provided by Lee et al. [23] by setting a limit of 40 s per question to make it a standardised test and to allow participants to skip a question if they were unsure about the correct answer. Since VLAT could activate or improve VL skills because teachers get exposed to several charts, we administered the test 1–3 days after completion of the task to minimise bias (Fig. 1).

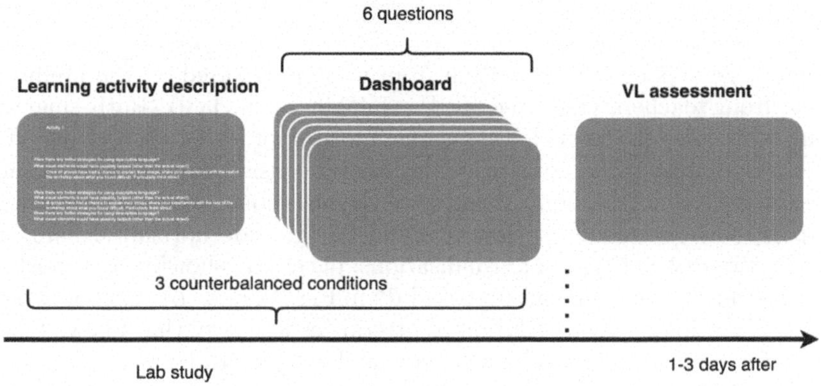

Fig. 1. Outline of the study procedure.

3.2 Design of Single and Multi-page Dashboards

Here we summarise the main visualisations used in the dashboards. The dashboards were initially designed and deployed to help teachers overcome the current monitoring limitations in Zoom. The dashboards use the data captured by an open-source analytics system called ZoomSense [4]. The software deploys virtual agents to each Zoom breakout room to automatically capture which student is speaking at each moment. Given the configuration done in advance by the teachers, these agents automatically create a Google Doc associated with each room and emit the link to students. This paper focuses on two single-page dashboards – version 1 and version 2 (see Fig. 2), and a one multi-page dashboard (Fig. 3)). The latter was the pre-existing dashboard that was an original component of ZoomSense.

A timeline chart shown at the top of the interface was included in all dashboard versions and depicts the activity where the class was, containing three activities and the start and final times of the class. The single-page dashboards consist of the following charts:

- a narrative-based chart classifying students based on the Zoom speech data as active (if the student was talking), inactive (not talking) and dominant/quiet (if one was doing most of the talk or not talking much compared to the others, respectively) (see *V1* in Fig. 2);
- a horizontal state bar signalling the progress in the Google Docs (see *V2* in Fig. 2);

- two horizontal bar charts, respectively, depicting the amount of students' speech detected in each group, and illustrating the total amount of time a teacher spent in a breakout room (see *V3* and *V5* in Fig. 2);
- sociogram charts, one per breakout room, where each node depicts a student or a teacher, while the thickness of a link between two nodes represents the amount of time two participants communicated after each other (see *V4* in Fig. 2).

Single-page version 2 is a revision from version 1, based on the preliminary feedback from teachers (reported by Pozdniakov et al. [33]). Both single-page version 1 and version 2 provided the same information using six and five visualisations, respectively. The multi-page dashboard consisted of four visualisations as presented in Fig. 3. Among them, two visualisations were also present in a single-page dashboard, i.e., sociograms and Google doc horizontal bars, while there were two distinct types of visualisations: pie charts showing a proportion of time each student spoke in a group (see *V6** in Fig. 3); and (b) timeline sequence diagrams depicting the constellation of utterances in a way that allows teachers to see the dynamic of turn-taking behaviour between students in a group (see *V7** in Fig. 2). To navigate between different views, participants used navigation buttons (see *N* in Fig. 3).

3.3 Measures

Visualisation literacy. Once the participants completed the VL test, the individual score for each participant was computed. If participants skipped the question or ran out of time, the answer was marked as wrong. The median value of VL scores for all participants ($Mdn = 39$) was used as a threshold to classify participants to *low* or *high* VL groups. There were 12 participants in the low VL ($Q1 = 30$, $Mdn = 35$, $Q3 = 37$, $min = 17$, $max = 39$) group and 11 participants in the high VL ($Q1 = 43.5$, $Mdn = 45$, $Q3 = 46$, $min = 40$, $max = 48$) group.

Pupil dialation. We used pupil dilation as a proxy to the cognitive load of participants when they used various dashboards [43]. We followed recommendations suggested in [19,29] and used subtractive baseline corrections for pupil diameter. We used the period before the dashboards were shown when participants were reading learning activity as a baseline period, i.e., the period when participants were not working on the main task. This resulted in two measures of pupil diameter. *Intra-Trial Change in Pupil Dilation* – indicates pupil diameter changes over the course of dashboard use respective to the measures taken during the period before the participant started using a dashboard. Since such a baseline period was taken before each dashboard was used, it accounts for the cognitive load participants experienced when they used the dashboard in the previous inspections. This measure was computed similarly to how it is reported in [19]. The running mean was computed over a corresponding baseline period. The measure was then computed as a mean difference between pupil diameter and the average over a baseline period. Typically, a high pupil dilation is a proxy for a higher cognitive load.

3.4 Analysis

In order to answer the research question, the measure of pupil dilation described above was selected as the dependent variable, where interface type was used as an independent variable, and visualisation literacy was a covariate. We used Linear Mixed Effects Model (LMEMs) to conduct the analysis as recommended in [29]. y_{ij} is the dependent variable for the j-th observation within the i-th participant, two independent variables ,x_{1ij} and x_{2ij}, were used as fixed effects, and a random

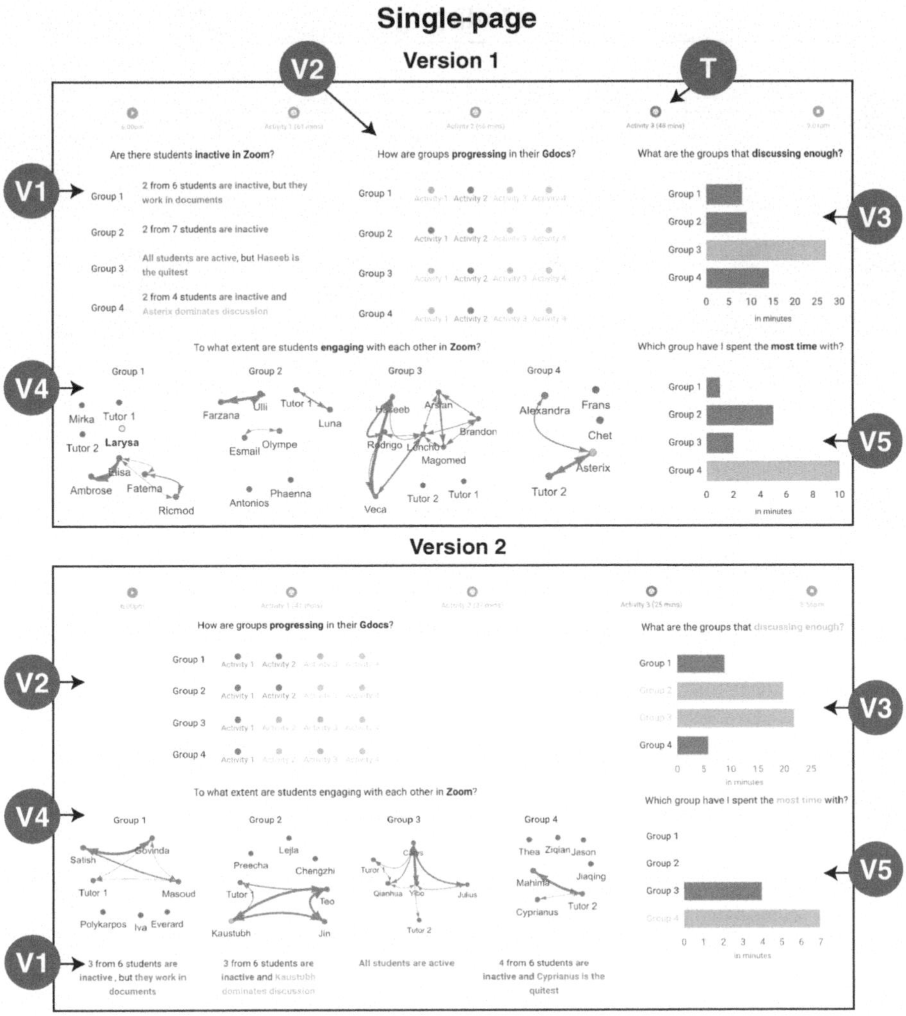

Fig. 2. Single-page dashboards version 1 and version 2 used in the study.

effect (random intercept only, u_i, for each participant was introduced into the model. The following equation describes the model we used:

$$y_{ij} = \beta_0 + \beta_1 x_{1ij} + \beta_2 x_{2ij} + \beta_3 (x_{1ij} \cdot x_{2ij}) + u_i + e_{ij}$$

The model was fitted using a bidirectional stepwise algorithm for model selection based on AIC. We used the *lmerTest* R package [20], because it computes trustworthy p-values for fixed effects, provides correct Type III ANOVA tables

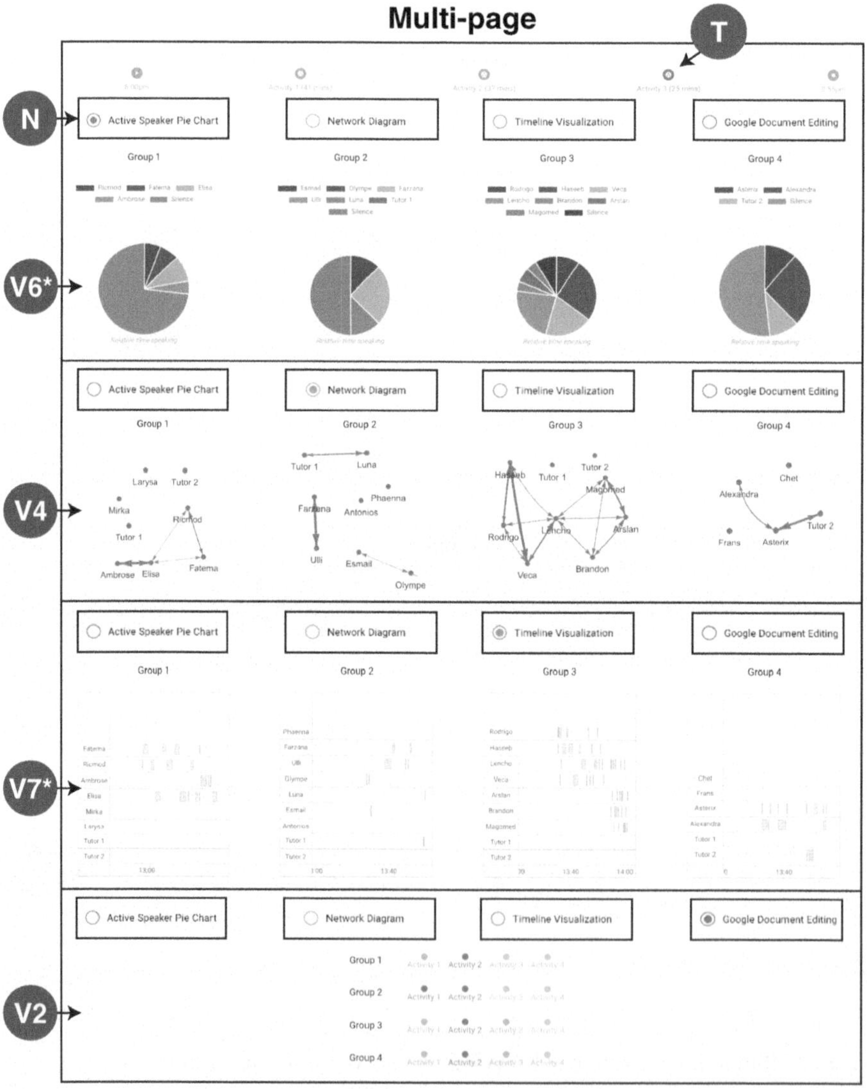

Fig. 3. Multi-page dashboard used in the study.

via the Satterthwaite approximation, and does backward stepwise elimination correctly.

Post-hoc analysis was used to demonstrate the direction and magnitude of the difference in the interaction effect. It was conducted via computing marginal means for interaction effects using the *emmeans* R package [25]. The Benjamini-Hochberg false discovery rate procedure [5] was used to account for family-wise error. We applied this procedure when computing pairwise marginal contrasts for interaction effects. Thus, the reported p-values are presented after such adjustments were applied.

4 Results

Descriptive statistics for the baseline corrected pupil dilation measure per interface were as follows: multi-paged dashboard $M = 0.121$, $SD = 0.109$, single-page dashboards version 1 $M = 0.081$, $SD = 0.128$, and version 2 $M = 0.096$, $SD = 0.123$. We conducted a stepwise backward elimination and used ANOVA to check whether the model with an interaction effect between the interface inspected and VL had a significantly higher Akaike information criterion (AIC) than the simpler model without an interaction effect. The introduction of the interaction effect between the interface used and VL was found to be significantly contributing to the model fit ($\chi^2(2) = 8.7, p < 0.0128$). Table 1 presents the main effect and interaction effects for the model regressed over pupil dilation measure.

Table 1. Results of LMEM for teachers' baseline-corrected pupil dilation depending on interface type used and teachers' VL.

term	NumDF	DenDF	F	p.value	sig	Cohen's f	CI
VL_group_gen	1	21	1.182	0.289	nan	0.237	[0, Inf]
interface	2	387	8.769	0.000	***	0.213	[0.12, Inf]
VL_group_gen:interface	2	387	4.366	0.013	*	0.150	[0.051, Inf]

Cohen's f partial effect sizes are: >= .10 (small), >= .25 (medium), >= .40 (large). [a] *Significance: *** = 0.001, ** = 0.01, * = 0.05, nan = <0.05.* [* *]

Interaction Effect on Pupil Diameter. The interaction effect between VL and type of the interface used by teachers was found to be significant ($F(2{,}387) = 4.4$, $p < 0.013$, $f = 0.15$) as indicated in Table 1. The main effect of VL showed to be insignificant, while the type of the interface used in the study indicated a significant main effect. In order to interpret the direction and magnitude of the interaction effect, we computed pairwise comparisons. Figure 4 shows the overall differences for pupil dilation between VL and interface type and describes significant pairwise comparisons and the direction of effect.

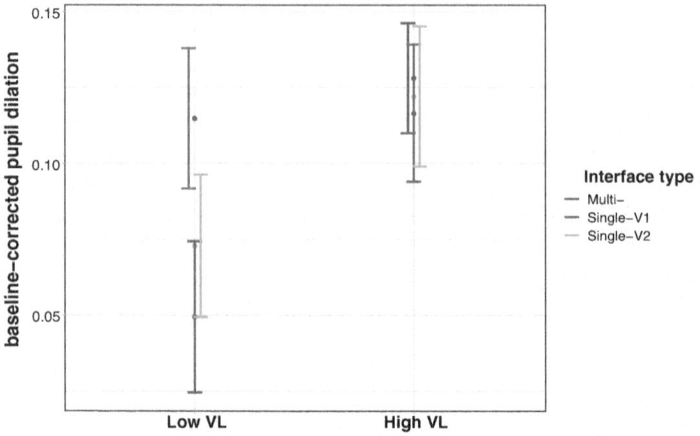

Fig. 4. Interaction effect of teachers' VL with interface type for the measure of teachers' cognitive load was found to be statistically significant ($\chi^2(2) = 4.4$, $p < 0.013$).

Pairwise comparisons between teachers' VL splits for interfaces showed no statistically significant differences in pupil diameter for all interfaces, i.e., multi-page ($t(24) = -0.3$, $p < 0.749$, $d = -0.173$, 95% CI $[-1.28, 0.93]$), single-page version 1 ($t(24) = -1.6$, $p < 0.116$, $d = -0.872$, 95% CI $[-1.98, 0.23]$), and version 2 ($t(24) = -1.2$, $p < 0.243$, $d = -0.64$, 95% CI $[-1.74, 0.47]$)[1]. That means that, in general, when teachers with high and low visualisation literacy were presented with a single-page dashboard, they would not exhibit considerable differences in cognitive load.

However, pairwise comparisons within each VL split indicated that for *teachers with low VL*, there were significant differences in pupil diameter depending on whether they used single-page or multi-page dashboards. As shown in Fig. 4, teachers with low VL had lower pupil diameter when they used both single-page interfaces version 1 ($M_{high} = 0.116$, $M_{low} = 0.049$, $t(387) = 5.1$, $p < 0.001$, $d = 0.849$, 95% CI $[0.52, 1.18]$) and version 2 ($M_{high} = 0.122$, $M_{low} = 0.072$, $t(387) = 3.3$, $p = 0.001$, $d = 0.545$, 95% CI $[0.22, 0.88]$) compared to the multi-page interface ($M_{high} = 0.128$, $M_{low} = 0.114$). **This means teachers with low visualisation literacy (VL) were more likely to be influenced by multi- or single-page dashboards in comparison to the teachers with high VL.** Teachers with low VL exhibited more variation in terms of cognitive load in response to the dashboard type.

5 Discussion

Summary of results. We found that there were differences in teachers' cognitive load depending on whether they used single-page or multi-page LA dash-

[1] Cohen's d effect sizes are interpreted as follows: >= 0.2 (small), >= 0.5 (medium), and >= 0.8 (large).

boards. Specifically, the study found that **teachers with low VL experienced increased cognitive load when using multi-page dashboards to monitor students in a simulated class**. We see two reasons for this. Firstly, when teachers with low VL were inspecting the multi-page dashboard, they might have experienced high uncertainty when deciding which dashboard view was the most appropriate for the learning task, hence switching between multiple views. Secondly, teachers with low VL might have issues when using evidence from multiple dashboard pages to complete the tasks required during the study.

Implications for Research and Practice. Based on our findings, we would argue that in situations where teachers experience a high monitoring load [22], designers of learning analytics (LA) can prioritise single-page dashboard designs. This is particularly important for teachers with low VL, as our study found that they experienced significantly higher cognitive load when using a multi-page LA dashboard compared to a single-page one. By using a single-page dashboard design, teachers with low VL may find it easier to process and interpret the information presented, leading to more effective monitoring and intervention strategies. Additionally, a single-page design can help reduce the uncertainty associated with selecting different dashboard views, which can be a major source of cognitive load for teachers with low VL.

However, when teachers have limited screen space on their devices for the monitoring dashboard, such as when using tablets or mobile phones, or when teachers are exposed to a larger number of student groups, LA dashboard designers might opt for the multi-page dashboard design.

Our study's results are partly in line with previous research on dashboard designs [10,15,27,41]. These studies suggested that while it may be beneficial for teachers to have separate, yet interconnected, dashboard views, the ultimate decision on dashboard design should be based on teachers' pedagogical goals. However, our study also adds to this body of literature by highlighting the importance of considering teachers' visualisation literacy when designing LA dashboards. Specifically, our findings suggest that teachers with low VL may experience a higher cognitive load when using a multi-page dashboard, which could negatively impact their decision-making processes.

However, we did not observe any statistically significant differences in cognitive load for high VL teachers. This suggests that teachers with high VL were able to effectively use both single-page and multi-page LA dashboards by employing appropriate strategies. This could also indicate that the current VL categorisation of low and high may have not fully captured the complexity of teachers' VL skills, and an alternative instrument, such as the one proposed by Burns et al. [6], might be necessary to evaluate high VL teachers' competencies. Alternatively, it could be that for teachers with high VL other characteristics, such as technological skills or years of professional experience [24], would better explain the corresponding variation in cognitive load.

Limitations. Our study has a few limitations that can provide direction for future research. Firstly, the LA dashboards used in this study included different types of visualizations, making it difficult to disentangle the effects of the dashboard composition from the effects of the dashboard content. Future research is required to fully isolate such effects. Secondly, alternative established measures of cognitive load, including self-reported ones, could be used to validate the cognitive load measurements we used. Thirdly, a detailed analysis of tasks, which teachers had been asked to complete when they were inspecting the dashboards, is required. This would allow us to elicit differences in how accurately teachers with low and high VL used the dashboards for each task, and might explain why teachers with high VL have a high cognitive load regardless of the particular interface they used. Moreover, our study was conducted in a particular setting where teachers had a high monitoring load during remote online synchronous classes conducted through Zoom. Future research should investigate whether similar results can be obtained in different teaching environments. Lastly, it is unclear how variations in teachers' VL skills would play out in non-simulated, real-world settings. Therefore, further research is needed to explore how differences in teachers' VL skills could affect or moderate the activation of their professional knowledge, as suggested by [31].

6 Conclusion

Our study findings demonstrate that the type of dashboard interface can affect the cognitive load of teachers when monitoring students using LA dashboards. Post-hoc analysis revealed that teachers with low VL experienced lower cognitive load when using single-page dashboards. Based on these results, we recommend that LA designers should consider teachers' VL skills when designing dashboards. Specifically, in situations where teachers face high monitoring loads, we suggest that a single-page LA dashboard design may better support teachers with low visualisation literacy.

Acknowledgements. This research was at least in part funded by the Australian Research Council (DP210100060) and Jacobs Foundation (Research Fellowship).

References

1. Ahn, J., Nguyen, H., Campos, F.: From visible to understandable: designing for teacher agency in education data visualizations. Contemp. Issues Technol. Teach. Educ. **21**(1), 155–186 (2021)
2. Bach, B., et al.: Dashboard design patterns, August 2022. arXiv:2205.00757 [cs]
3. Bao, H., Li, Y., Su, Y., Xing, S., Chen, N.S., Rosé, C.P.: The effects of a learning analytics dashboard on teachers' diagnosis and intervention in computer-supported collaborative learning. Technol. Pedagog. Educ. **30**(2), 287–303 (2021)
4. Bartindale, T., Chen, P., Marshall, H., Pozdniakov, S., Richardson, D.: ZoomSense: a scalable infrastructure for augmenting zoom. In: Proceedings of the 29th ACM International Conference on Multimedia, pp. 3771–3774 (2021)
5. Benjamini, Y., Hochberg, Y.: Controlling the false discovery rate: a practical and powerful approach to multiple testing. J. Roy. Stat. Soc.: Ser. B (Methodol.) **57**(1), 289–300 (1995)

6. Burns, A., Xiong, C., Franconeri, S., Cairo, A., Mahyar, N.: How to evaluate data visualizations across different levels of understanding, September 2020. arXiv:2009.01747 [cs]
7. Knoop-van Campen, C.A., Wise, A., Molenaar, I.: The equalizing effect of teacher dashboards on feedback in K-12 classrooms. Interact. Learn. Environ. 1–17 (2021)
8. Campos, F., Ahn, J., DiGiacomo, D.K., Nguyen, H., Hays, M.: Making sense of sensemaking: understanding how K-12 teachers and coaches react to visual analytics. J. Learn. Anal. 1–21 (2021)
9. Charleer, S., Gerling, K., Gutiérrez, F., Cauwenbergh, H., Luycx, B., Verbert, K.: Real-time dashboards to support esports spectating. In: Proceedings of the 2018 Annual Symposium on Computer-Human Interaction in Play, pp. 59–71 (2018)
10. Chen, Q., Li, Z., Pong, T.C., Qu, H.: Designing narrative slideshows for learning analytics. In: 2019 IEEE pacific visualization symposium (PacificVis), pp. 237–246 (2019)
11. Dipace, A., Fazlagic, B., Minerva, T.: The design of a learning analytics dashboard: Eduopen MOOC platform redefinition procedures. J. E-learn. Knowl. Soc. **15**(3), 29–47 (2019)
12. Donohoe, D., Costello, E.: Data visualisation literacy in higher education: an exploratory study of understanding of a learning dashboard tool. Int. J. Emerg. Technol. Learn. (iJET) **15**(17), 115 (2020)
13. Dourado, R.A., Rodrigues, R.L., Ferreira, N., Mello, R.F., Gomes, A.S., Verbert, K.: A teacher-facing learning analytics dashboard for process-oriented feedback in online learning. In: LAK21: 11th International Learning Analytics and Knowledge Conference, pp. 482–489 (2021)
14. Echeverria, V., Martinez-Maldonado, R., Buckingham Shum, S., Chiluiza, K., Granda, R., Conati, C.: Exploratory versus explanatory visual learning analytics: driving teachers' attention through educational data storytelling. J. Learn. Anal. **5**(3) (2018)
15. Fernandez Nieto, G.M., Kitto, K., Buckingham Shum, S., Martinez-Maldonado, R.: Beyond the learning analytics dashboard: alternative ways to communicate student data insights combining visualisation, narrative and storytelling. In: LAK22: 12th International Learning Analytics and Knowledge Conference, pp. 219–229. Online , March 2022
16. Firat, E.E., Joshi, A., Laramee, R.S.: Interactive visualization literacy: the state-of-the-art. Inf. Vis. **21**(3), 285–310 (2022)
17. Herodotou, C., Rienties, B., Boroowa, A., Zdrahal, Z., Hlosta, M.: A large-scale implementation of predictive learning analytics in higher education: The teachers' role and perspective. Educ. Technol. Res. Dev. **67**(5), 1273–1306 (2019)
18. Kaliisa, R., Mørch, A.I., Kluge, A.: 'My Point of Departure for Analytics is Extreme Skepticism': implications derived from an investigation of university teachers' learning analytics perspectives and design practices. Technol. Knowl. Learn. **27**(2), 505–527 (2022)
19. Krejtz, K., Duchowski, A.T., Niedzielska, A., Biele, C., Krejtz, I.: Eye tracking cognitive load using pupil diameter and microsaccades with fixed gaze. PLoS ONE **13**(9), e0203629 (2018)
20. Kuznetsova, A., Brockhoff, P.B., Christensen, R.H.B.: lmerTest package: tests in linear mixed effects models. J. Stat. Softw. **82**(13), 1–26 (2017)
21. Lalle, S., Toker, D., Conati, C.: Gaze-driven adaptive interventions for magazine-style narrative visualizations. IEEE Trans. Vis. Comput. Graph. **27**(6), 2941–2952 (2021)

22. Lawrence, L.E.M., et al.: Teachers' orchestration needs during the shift to remote learning. In: De Laet, T., Klemke, R., Alario-Hoyos, C., Hilliger, I., Ortega-Arranz, A. (eds.) EC-TEL 2021. LNCS, vol. 12884, pp. 347–351. Springer, Cham (2021). https://doi.org/10.1007/978-3-030-86436-1_33
23. Lee, S., Kim, S.H., Kwon, B.C.: VLAT: development of a visualization literacy assessment test. IEEE Trans. Vis. Comput. Graph. **23**(1), 551–560 (2017)
24. van Leeuwen, A., Knoop-van Campen, C.A., Molenaar, I., Rummel, N.: How teacher characteristics relate to how teachers use dashboards: results from two case studies in K-12. J. Learn. Anal. **8**(2), 6–21 (2021)
25. Lenth, R.V.: emmeans: Estimated Marginal Means, aka Least-Squares Means (2022), r package version 1.8.2
26. Mandinach, E.B., Abrams, L.M.: Data literacy and learning analytics. In: Lang, C., Siemens, G., Wise, A.F., GaÅ¡eviÄ‡, D., Merceron, A. (eds.) The Handbook of Learning Analytics, 2 edn, pp. 196–204. SoLAR (2017)
27. Martinez-Maldonado, R., Echeverria, V., Fernandez Nieto, G., Buckingham Shum, S.: From data to insights: a layered storytelling approach for multimodal learning analytics. In: Proceedings of the 2020 CHI Conference on Human Factors in Computing Systems, pp. 1–15. Honolulu HI USA, April 2020
28. Matcha, W., Ahmad Uzir, N., Gasevic, D., Pardo, A.: A systematic review of empirical studies on learning analytics dashboards: a self-regulated learning perspective. IEEE Trans. Learn. Technol. **13**(2), 226–245 (2020)
29. Mathôt, S., Vilotijević, A.: Methods in cognitive pupillometry: design, preprocessing, and statistical analysis. Behav. Res. Methods (2022)
30. Molenaar, I., Knoop-van Campen, C.A.N.: How teachers make dashboard information actionable. IEEE Trans. Learn. Technol. **12**(3), 347–355 (2019)
31. Molenaar, I., Knoop-van Campen, C.: Teacher dashboards in practice: usage and impact. In: Lavoué, É., Drachsler, H., Verbert, K., Broisin, J., Pérez-Sanagustín, M. (eds.) EC-TEL 2017. LNCS, vol. 10474, pp. 125–138. Springer, Cham (2017). https://doi.org/10.1007/978-3-319-66610-5_10
32. Ndukwe, I.G., Daniel, B.K.: Teaching analytics, value and tools for teacher data literacy: a systematic and tripartite approach. Int. J. Educ. Technol. High. Educ. **17**(1), 1–31 (2020)
33. Pozdniakov, S., et al.: The Question-driven Dashboard: How Can We Design Analytics Interfaces Aligned to Teachers' Inquiry? p. 11 (2022)
34. Pozdniakov, S., Martinez-Maldonado, R., Tsai, Y.S., Echeverria, V., Srivastava, N., Gasevic, D.: How do teachers use dashboards enhanced with data storytelling elements according to their data visualisation literacy skills? In: LAK23: 13th International Learning Analytics and Knowledge Conference. LAK2023, New York, NY, USA, pp. 89–99 (2023)
35. Sahin, M., Ifenthaler, D.: Visualizations and dashboards for learning analytics: a systematic literature review. In: Sahin, M., Ifenthaler, D. (eds.) Visualizations and Dashboards for Learning Analytics. AALT, pp. 3–22. Springer, Cham (2021). https://doi.org/10.1007/978-3-030-81222-5_1
36. Salas-Pilco, S.Z., Xiao, K., Hu, X.: Artificial intelligence and learning analytics in teacher education: a systematic review. Educ. Sci. **12**(8), 569 (2022). Multidisciplinary Digital Publishing Institute
37. Schwendimann, B.A., et al.: Perceiving learning at a glance: a systematic literature review of learning dashboard research. IEEE Trans. Learn. Technol. **10**(1), 30–41 (2017)

38. Sergis, S., Sampson, D.G.: Teaching and learning analytics to support teacher inquiry: a systematic literature review. In: Learning Analytics: Fundaments, Applications, and Trends, pp. 25–63 (2017)
39. Sousa, E.B.d., Alexandre, B., Ferreira Mello, R., Pontual Falcão, T., Vesin, B., Gašević, D.: Applications of learning analytics in high schools: a systematic literature review. Front. Artif. Intell. **4**, 737891 (2021). publisher: Frontiers Media SA
40. Tsai, Y.S., Gasevic, D.: Learning analytics in higher education - challenges and policies: a review of eight learning analytics policies. In: Proceedings of the Seventh International Learning Analytics and Knowledge Conference, pp. 233–242. Vancouver British Columbia Canada, March 2017
41. Van Leeuwen, A., Rummel, N.: Comparing teachers' use of mirroring and advising dashboards. In: Proceedings of the Tenth International Conference on Learning Analytics and Knowledge, pp. 26–34 (2020)
42. Voithofer, R., Golan, A.M.: Data sources for educators: mining meaningful data for course and program decision making. In: Responsible Analytics and Data Mining in Education, pp. 83–100 (2018)
43. van der Wel, P., van Steenbergen, H.: Pupil dilation as an index of effort in cognitive control tasks: a review. Psychonomic Bull. Rev. **25**(6), 2005–2015 (2018)
44. Wise, A.F., Jung, Y.: Teaching with analytics: towards a situated model of instructional decision-making. J. Learn. Anal. **6**(2), 53–69 (2019)

Designing Technology for Doctoral Persistence and Well-Being: Findings from a Two-Country Value-Sensitive Inquiry into Student Progress

Luis P. Prieto[1(✉)], María Jesús Rodríguez-Triana[2], Yannis Dimitriadis[1], Gerti Pishtari[3], and Paula Odriozola-González[4]

[1] Universidad de Valladolid, Valladolid, Spain
{luispablo.prieto,ioannis.dimitriadis}@uva.es
[2] Tallinn University, Tallinn, Estonia
mjrt@tlu.ee
[3] University for Continuing Education Krems, Krems an der Donau, Austria
gerti.pishtari@donau-uni.ac.at
[4] Universidad de Cantabria, Santander, Spain
paula.odriozola@unican.es

Abstract. Doctoral education suffers from widespread dropout and well-being problems, for which we have not yet found scalable and generalizable interventions. This paper characterizes these problems as amenable to technology-enhanced learning (TEL) intervention and derives design knowledge for such solutions. We conducted two iterations of design-based research using a value-sensitive design approach to understand how technology could support doctoral progress, well-being, and persistence, with 19 doctoral students from multiple disciplines in Estonia and Spain. Our quantitative and qualitative analysis of questionnaires, interviews, and diary data confirms prior research about the importance of perceiving progress in the dissertation materials. They also highlight the uniqueness and self-direction of the doctoral journey, and particular (but well-defined) external factors that could be targeted by TEL support. Our design-oriented findings can inform the development of multiple TEL solutions to address these problems. Further, the particular methods used to elicit these findings both illustrate the added value of value-sensitive design for the field of TEL and provide examples of techniques that can be used to be mindful of stakeholder values when designing learning technologies.

Keywords: Design knowledge · Value-sensitive design · Cultural probes · Human-centered design · Doctoral education · Dropout · Well-being

---

The present work has been supported by grants RYC2021-032273-I and PID2020-112584RB-C32, funded by MCIN/AEI/10.13039/501100011033 and the European Union's "NextGenerationEU/PRTR". It has also been supported by the Estonian Research Council's Personal Research Grant (PRG) under grant number PRG1634.

O. Viberg et al. (Eds.): EC-TEL 2023, LNCS 14200, pp. 356–370, 2023.
https://doi.org/10.1007/978-3-031-42682-7_24

1 Introduction

A large proportion of the manpower we train to research solutions for the global challenges we face towards a more responsible and sustainable future (i.e., doctoral students), never finish their degrees [22]. Indeed, research has recently documented a large incidence of dropout and emotional well-being problems (e.g., anxiety or depression) [6,17] among doctoral candidates. These problems are widespread on a global scale, as shown by studies in multiple countries/institutions [17,22]. However, few interventions exist to address these two intertwined problems [11,14]. Further, most of these isolated initiatives occur on a local basis, with few multi-country interventions.

Aside from demographic and socioeconomic factors [20], recent doctoral education research has uncovered critical motivational factors related to doctoral persistence and well-being, over which candidates have more influence [5]. The everyday perception of one's own progress in the dissertation materials has been found as the strongest of these motivational factors [4].

This paper draws inspiration from the fields of human-computer interaction (HCI), social psychology, and quantitative ethnography [19], applying a value-sensitive design (VSD) perspective. VSD emphasizes that culture [21], and especially values (i.e., what a person or group of people consider important in life) are critical to the adoption and transfer of new technologies [8]. To eventually design acceptable TEL support for the aforementioned doctoral problems, we set out to understand doctoral student values and their experience of progress, by integrating VSD techniques in a two-iteration empirical investigation following a design-based research methodology. N = 19 doctoral students from different disciplines and doctoral stages in two universities in Estonia and Spain provided us with quantitative and qualitative evidence through questionnaires, interviews, and diaries.

The contribution of this paper is thus threefold: 1) it formally articulates doctoral dropout and well-being as an important and wicked global problem, potentially amenable to TEL solutions; 2) it reports design insights extracted from a two-iteration value-sensitive empirical investigation carried out in two countries; and 3) it provides a (so far, scarce) methodological example of how VSD methods can be adapted for TEL solution design, which could serve as a blueprint for further TEL studies.

2 Related Work

Doctoral Well-Being and Dropout: A Worldwide Problem (with No TEL Solution). Doctoral education research has documented an increasing incidence of well-being and dropout problems. Recent estimates suggest that about 24% of doctoral students suffer from depression and 17% from anxiety [17], higher than in the general population. An even greater proportion never finish their PhD, with commonly-cited estimates of dropout rates around 50%.

Research has also documented a wide variety of factors relating to these two intertwined phenomena: from socio-demographic factors (e.g., gender, academic discipline), economic ones (e.g., availability of a doctoral scholarship), individual, institutional, and inter-personal issues (e.g., writing skills, department culture, or relationship with the supervisor) and a long et cetera [20]. It is worth noting that many of these factors are outside the control of the doctoral candidate, which makes them difficult targets for supportive interventions. An exception to this trend are recently-discovered motivational factors and processes [5], of which *the perception of one's own progress in the dissertation materials* seems to be the strongest [4].

Despite the richness of research in understanding doctoral dropout and well-being, the research on *interventions* (including technological or socio-technical solutions) to address these problems is scarce. Recent reviews show only a handful of intervention strategies for doctoral well-being and dropout [11,14], often supported by only cursory evaluations in a single context or requiring long-term institutional reforms spanning decades [10]. A key factor in this lack of generalizable interventions is the inherent uniqueness of each doctoral topic and process which, along with the students' and their contexts' uniqueness [12], make it hard to propose one-size-fits-all solutions. Only very recently, training actions targeting motivational factors such as progress, have shown promising initial results in multi-country doctoral student samples [15].

We suggest that this situation could be changed by the TEL research community. While TEL has shown the potential to adapt and personalize learning at scale (e.g., through adaptive systems or personal learning environments), there exist very few TEL solutions for doctoral students.

Human-Centered and Value-Sensitive Design in Technology-Enhanced Learning. There have been recent calls for a more human-centered design of different kinds of TEL, e.g., human-centered learning analytics [2]. Part of this trend towards more human-centered TEL solutions are recent calls for more culturally-aware TEL solutions (e.g., culturally-aware LA, see [21]), which suggest that it is essential to consider the different cultures where the TEL solution will potentially be applied, to be able to better transfer the solution from its original place of development to other countries/cultures. This line of reasoning is influenced by cross-cultural and social psychology research which, for example, highlights the existence of *values* (i.e., what is important to people in their lives [7]) that seem to appear and structure behavior across cultures, but which members of different cultures seem to assign different levels of importance to. A typical example is Schwartz's theory of basic values [18], defined as trans-situational goals, varying in importance, which serve as guiding principles in the life of a person or group (e.g., seeking pleasure, wealth, or caring for one's own family). Despite the importance of these cultural values to drive attitudes and behavior, it is worth noting that there often exists variability and tension between group/culture values and each individual's values (e.g., a person that values tradition, even if they belong to a culture that generally values novelty more) [21]. This emphasis on understanding and addressing explicitly the values of stakeholders when designing technology has been labeled "value-sensitive design" (VSD) [8], and it is not only a philosophical stance on designing technology: over the years it has developed its own toolkit of methods for inquiring and understanding human stakeholder values during solution design [7].

Yet, despite the increasing interest in the design of culturally-aware and value-sensitive TEL solutions, there exist still few examples of *exactly how* we can do that, and whether the methods from VSD can be directly adapted for the design of learning technologies [3]. We aim to continue addressing this gap, by providing a detailed account of how we inquired into the culture and values of doctoral students from two different countries/institutions with the aim of designing technologies that support doctoral progress, persistence, and well-being.

3 Method

In order to enable *multiple* TEL solutions for doctoral progress, persistence, and well-being, we involved doctoral candidates in an inquiry to extract *design knowledge*, mirroring the first step in the value-sensitive design process suggested by [3]. Our inquiry was driven by one main research question: "What values should a technology to support doctoral progress embody?" [RQ1]

To illuminate this broad design research question from a value-sensitive perspective, we need to take into account that human values are *contextual*: doctoral student actions and attitudes when using TEL solutions will be shaped not only by their basic (i.e., transcontextual) values but also their doctorate-related values (i.e., what they value from the doctoral experience/degree) and technology use values. Acknowledging this and the uniqueness of each doctoral student and thesis process, we defined two sub-questions: "What do doctoral students value at the basic, doctorate and technology use levels?" [RQ1.1] and "How do doctoral students experience progress at the group-level and individually?" [RQ1.2].

We followed an iterative mixed-methods *design-based research* (DBR) as our overall methodology, in two iterations that drew inspiration and concrete research methods from VSD [7]. In the first iteration, we aimed to understand the everyday experience of doctoral progress and to elicit initial values, while the second one delved more deeply into such values at different levels, and confirmed findings from the first iteration about the doctoral progress experience.

Context and Participants. Following a *purposeful sampling* strategy to maximize the variety of viewpoints in terms of country, research discipline, and doctoral stage, we recruited volunteer doctoral candidates from two public universities in Estonia and Spain, independently for the two DBR iterations. All participants had participated in a doctoral training about doctoral persistence and well-being, thus ensuring that they considered such problems important/relevant. n = 9 doctoral students (all female, 5 Spanish, and 4 Estonian) from multiple disciplines and at different doctoral stages participated in the first iteration. n = 10 *different* doctoral students (4 female, 6 male, 5 from each institution), also from multiple stages and disciplines, participated in the second one. In both cases, informed consent was sought before starting the data-gathering activities.

Data Gathering. In the first iteration, we used a form of *cultural probe* [9], a participatory design technique in which the participants collaborate actively in the data gathering of everyday data, with a particular research focus (in our case, doctoral progress). Doctoral students engaged in a *daily self-tracking and journaling* exercise, in which students tracked quantitatively how much time they had slept, the time spent working on both their thesis and other work tasks, their subjective perception of progress that day (in a 7-step Likert scale from Very unsatisfactory to Very satisfactory), as well as additional quantitative variables defined by students themselves as important for their progress. Each daily entry also included a narrative journal entry about the events of the day. *Two semi-structured interviews* were conducted before and after the use of the probe to discuss overall motivations, customize the questions in the probe, and delve into the events and reasons behind the data gathered using the probe. 270 daily entries were gathered through this method, over about two months.

In the second iteration, participants filled in a *questionnaire* about their motivations and challenges with progress. The questionnaire measured basic values using the Portrait Values Questionnaire (PVQ). The PVQ is based on Schwartz's theory of basic values, which was designed to study values across contexts and cultures [18]. The questionnaire also asked students to rank doctorate-related (i.e., specific to what they value in the doctoral experience/degree) and technology use values elicited from the analysis of the first iteration interviews. Then, a *co-design interview* was held with each student, in which they were further asked about their motivations and challenges, and the evaluation of *value scenarios* (scenarios of technologies and technology use embodying a certain value [7]) representing highly-ranked values (as per the PVQ results of each participant)[1]. Finally, the co-design interview also delved deeper into the results of their value ranking exercises.

Data Analysis. We followed a concurrent triangulation mixed methods strategy to analyze the data from both iterations. To answer RQ1.1 we analyzed the evidence from Iteration 1 interviews to elicit potential values at the basic, doctorate-related and technology-use levels, through a process of *(inductive) reflexive thematic analysis* [1] (by a single researcher using techniques such as prolonged engagement, persistent observation to increase trustworthiness). These were triangulated (and quantitative trends extracted through *descriptive statistics*) with the evidence from the PVQ and value-ranking questionnaires in Iteration 2, further supported by the co-design interviews' evidence. To answer RQ1.2 both qualitatively (e.g., finding factors related to doctoral progress) *and* quantitatively (i.e., understand the relative strength of those factors) we have used a quantitative ethnography [19] approach. The first author

[1] For example, a scenario featuring a personalizable system in which doctoral students gather and delve into data about their everyday progress on the thesis materials (to emphasize the value of *Self-Direction*, which includes aspects like curiosity and autonomy). The value scenarios used in the present study can be found at https://tinyurl.com/ECTEL23-VSD-scenarios.

performed another (inductive) reflexive thematic analysis (again using prolonged engagement and persistent observation) of the 270 journal entries that accompanied the self-tracking quantitative data in Iteration 1. The codes from this qualitative analysis, along with the quantitative self-tracking data were then used to build *stepwise linear regression models* trying to predict the students' satisfaction with that day's progress on the basis of such quantitative and qualitative (i.e., whether a code was present or absent in that day's data) predictors. Akaike Information Criterion (AIC) was used in both forward and backward variable selection to obtain the most predictive and parsimonious models of student progress. Finally, to triangulate these linear models and further understand the connections between factors that are distinctive of days with positively- and negatively-evaluated progress, we performed an *epistemic network analysis* (ENA [19]) discarding the neutrally-valued entries (leaving 202 journal entries) and comparing the code co-occurrence networks of positive and negative progress days. All these quantitative trends have been triangulated with the qualitative data from the interviews following the probe in Iteration 1. Then, to understand the experience of progress *for each individual student*, we have built similar stepwise linear regression and ENA models, using only that student's data.

Finally, design insights about how technologies could be designed to support doctoral progress, persistence, and well-being (as an answer to the overall RQ1, see Sect. 5) have been extracted from all the aforementioned analyses, through discussions among the research team using particular VSD heuristic tools such as *value dams and flows*, which foregrounds features considered important by a large proportion of stakeholders, removing those unacceptable even for a small proportion of them [7].

4 Results

4.1 RQ1.1 What Do Doctoral Students Value at the Basic, Doctorate and Technology Use Levels?

Basic Values. The analysis of interview data from the first iteration suggested aspects that doctoral students may find generally valuable (e.g., emotional stability, or learning new things). The results of the PVQ in the second iteration suggest that there are three key basic (i.e., transcontextual) values, as we can see in Fig. 1. Our international, multi-disciplinary sample of n=10 doctoral students held *Self-Direction* (independent thought and action-choosing, creating, exploring) as the most important value ($\mu = +1.075$), with *Universalism* (understanding, appreciation, and protection for the welfare of all people/nature) and *Benevolence* (enhancement of the welfare of people with whom one is in frequent personal contact) as second- and third-highest ($\mu = +0.708$ and $\mu = +0.700$, respectively). The small spread in those values' scores suggests an uniformity of values in the participant group, despite their different national, gender, and disciplinary backgrounds. The co-design interviews in the same iteration triangulated and further qualified the PVQ results of each student (e.g., participant 3016's high *Security* score being was related to the Russia-Ukraine conflict).

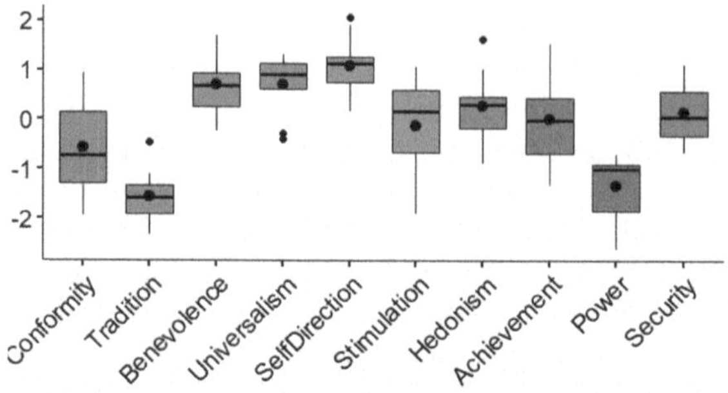

Fig. 1. Results of the Portrait Values Questionnaire of n = 10 doctoral students in our second iteration.

Further triangulation of these basic value results can be gleaned from the desirability scores that participants gave to the value scenarios in the co-design interviews later on (see technology-related values below), where the *Self-Direction* scenario was more highly scored in general.

Doctorate-Related Values. The first iteration interviews served to elicit valuable aspects of the doctoral experience. This included notions like being motivated/energized about their PhD, being able to concentrate, doing the thesis in a short time, or making progress. In the questionnaire of our second iteration, we asked doctoral students to compare (i.e., rank) these elicited values. The results in Fig. 2 (left) further confirm that the notion of *Making progress* is very important to doctoral students in our sample (avg. rank $\mu = 2.2$), followed by *Feeling motivated/energized* by their PhD topic (avg. rank $\mu = 3.3$). Yet, we can also observe a wider variability in most of the doctorate-related values, suggesting that, beyond these two, individual students have quite heterogeneous priorities to what they value about the doctoral experience.

Further information about what students consider important in the doctorate can be inferred from the "custom quantitative variables" that doctoral candidates chose to self-track in the reflective probe of Iteration 1. Students chose to self-track a total of 28 variables, which we could cluster into 5 coarse areas: 1) Particular thesis activities the students want to focus on (or do more of) (11 variables); 2) Features of the emotional/motivational experience of doing the dissertation (6 variables); 3) Ways of working on the thesis that students have found especially (in)effective; 4) Other activities (i.e., not related to the thesis) which the students still want to remember doing; and 5) Activities that actively detract from their ability to do the thesis. It is worth noting the focus on *activities* that most of the variables show, specifically the *time spent* on them.

RQ1.1.3 Technology-Related Values. From the interviews in Iteration 1, we elicited several aspects mentioned as important in using the technological probe or future versions of supportive doctoral technology (e.g., that it should

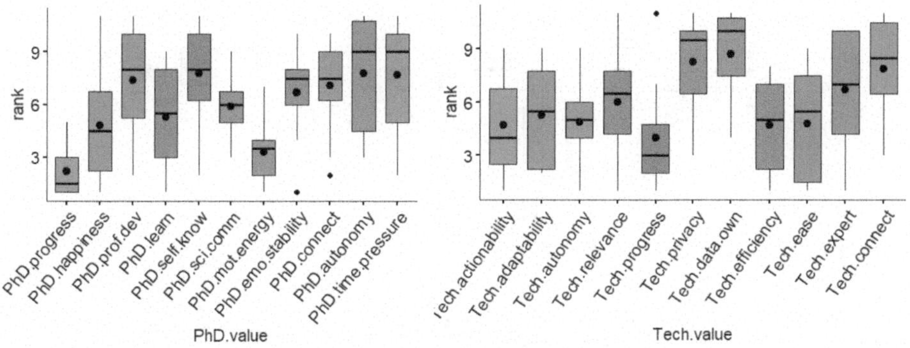

Fig. 2. Results of the value-ranking exercise for values related to the doctorate (left) and values related to technology use (right), of N = 10 doctoral students in our second iteration. *NB: Lower values denote higher importance.*

be personalizable, easy to use, or concerns about data access and privacy). These technology use values were then ranked by the doctoral students in Iteration 2 (see Fig. 2, right). Being able to observe one's own progress was considered most important, on average (avg rank $\mu = 4.0$), with a comparatively small spread. We can also observe that most values have mid-range average rank values and a wide spread, signaling a large heterogeneity in hierarchies of importance among doctoral candidates in our multi-country sample. The distribution of values shows only minor differences when slicing the data by country or gender, suggesting that the heterogeneity is not due to these reasons alone. Interestingly, concerns about data privacy and ownership were ranked as less important by students from both countries. The interview data from Iteration 2 also served to triangulate and qualify these tech-related values. For instance, students suggested specific visualizations that would make the technology *Easy to use* and *Perceive progress* (e.g., a very simple, color-coded calendar view of the days she had written her dissertation), or specific thresholds for the *Efficiency* value (e.g., the app should be usable in under one minute each day).

In these co-design interviews, we also asked doctoral candidates to assess the acceptability of different value scenarios of TEL solutions embodying basic values like *Self-Direction* or *Benevolence*. All three scenarios were quite highly valued in terms of usefulness, ease of use, and intention of use (overall average $\mu = 7.83$ in a 0–10 scale, see Fig. 3), with a small advantage for the *Self-direction* scenario over the *Benevolence* one. The additional discussion with doctoral students about the reasons for such scores helped elicit additional useful features for future technologies supporting doctoral well-being and persistence. For instance, several students mentioned that their higher ease of use scores in the *Benevolence* scenario was mainly due to the appearance of motivational tips and strategies, recommended from an analysis of other doctoral students' data.

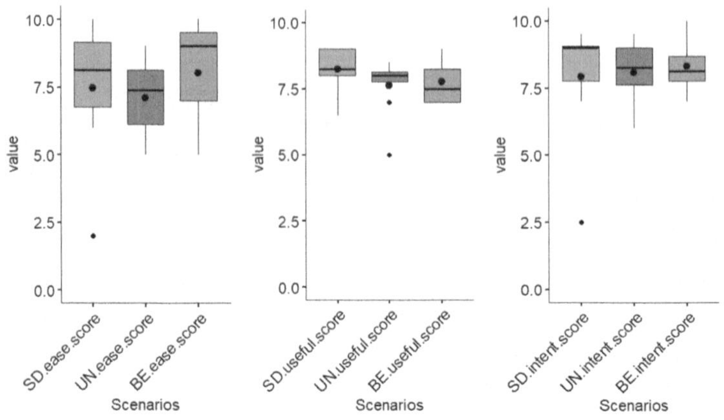

Fig. 3. Scores given to different value-oriented technology scenarios, of N = 10 doctoral students in our second iteration. Left: Ease of use; Center: Usefulness; Right: Intention of use.

4.2 RQ1.2 How Do Doctoral Students Experience Progress at the Group-Level and Individually?

From Evidence at the Group-Level. To understand how doctoral students experience progress in their everyday life, we built stepwise linear regression models using both the *quantitative* self-tracking data and additional predictors based on the presence/absence of a code from our *qualitative* inductive coding of narrative diary entries, from the probe in Iteration 1. As we can see in Fig. 4 (purple color), only the time spent on thesis-related tasks (*Time.Thesis*) and the hours slept the preceding day (*Time.Sleep*) were significant (and positive) predictors of such perception of progress among the quantitatively self-tracked variables. Among the predictors coming from the qualitative analysis of unstructured diary entries, we can see that entries that mentioned the use of *Productivity Techniques* (e.g., the "Pomodoro method"), *Learning* new things, or completing tasks (without specifying whether they are thesis-related or not, i.e., *GenericTasks*) were, on average, occurring more frequently on days with better progress. Conversely, being interrupted (or having others interfere in one's work, *InterruptionsInterferences*) or spending time doing housework, personal or family-related tasks (*HouseworkFamilyPersonal*), were experiences more often happening on days with less progress. We can also see how certain kinds of feelings/emotions (a sense of *Lacking Time* to do one's tasks or the sense that the tasks were taking too much *Effort*) are also associated with lower progress in a day. Here again, the directional relationship between these features of a student's daily experience and the perception of progress is not as interesting as the *relative amount* of influence these predictors seem to exert on such perception of progress.

To triangulate this view of progress and delve even deeper into how different features of the doctoral experience interact with each other and relate to the perception of progress, we can turn to ENA, comparing the co-occurrence of codes

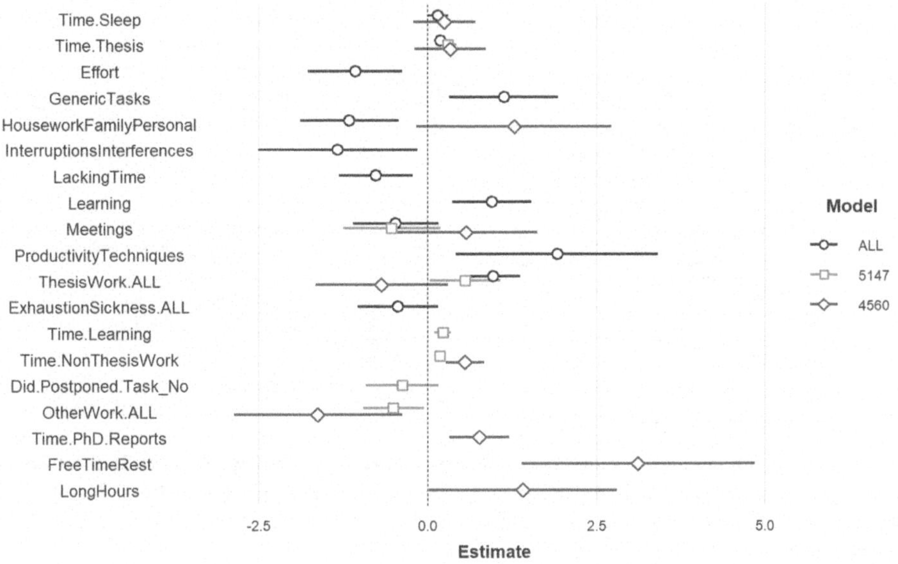

Fig. 4. Coefficient estimates and standard errors of stepwise linear regression models trying to estimate doctoral students' perception of progress as a function of variables from Iteration 1's self-tracking/diary probe. Legend: ALL refers to a model based on all students' data, and numbered models are based on different single students' data. (Color figure online)

in "good progress" vs. "bad progress" days. As we can see in Fig. 5 (left) new codes (and their relations) appear as pivotal for distinguishing days with positive vs. negative progress. For instance, mentions of postponing tasks and procrastinating (*PostponeProcrastinate*) appear frequently on both kinds of days, but co-occur with mentions to *Learning* new things and working on specific thesis tasks (*ThesisWork.ALL*) on positive progress days, maybe denoting a final overcoming of the procrastination or finding a productive way to procrastinate by learning things considered useful down the road. However, on negative progress days, such procrastination appears along with a sense of time pressure (*LackingTime*) or dedicating time to rest or do leisure activities (*FreeTimeRest*). Thesis-related tasks (*ThesisWork.ALL*) are quite central to the "positive progress" days' network of codes, strongly linked with *Learning* and non-thesis work tasks (*OtherWork.ALL*), indicating good progress on days that students manage to balance their different obligations (and their thirst for learning, related to the *Self-direction* value in RQ1.1 above). Yet, even this very clear predictor of satisfactory progress also appears on negative progress days, when doctoral students are somehow interrupted or external forces interfere with their work (*InterruptionsInterferences*).

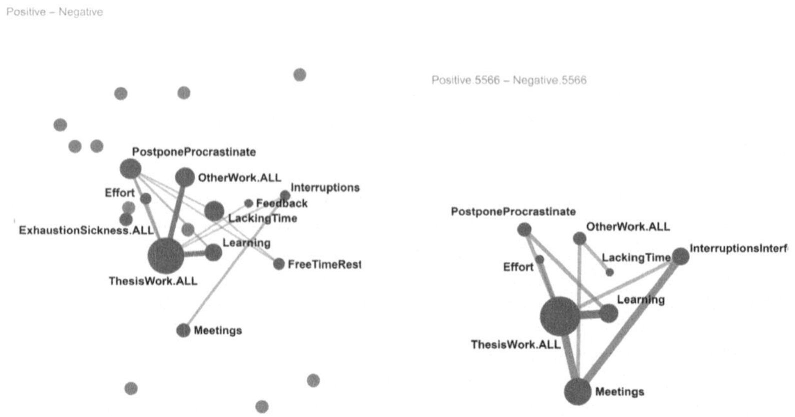

Fig. 5. Epistemic network analysis comparing codes appearing in Iteration 1 diaries, on days with positive vs. negative perception of students' progress. Left: Using data from the whole group (N = 9 students, m = 202 diary entries); Right: Using data from a particular student (m = 27 diary entries)

From Evidence at the Individual-Level. To understand how heterogeneous this purposefully-selected group of students is in their experience of progress (i.e., how wide the spread around the average group trends above is), we built similar stepwise linear regression models to predict progress as a function of the quantitative and qualitative data in the diaries of every single doctoral student in Iteration 1, including the custom quantitative variables defined by each student. The resulting individual models are much more predictive, as measured by standard metrics like R-squared or root mean squared error (see our previous work [16]). Further, these models show that in some cases the individual trends go *in the opposite direction* to the group-level trends, and the strength of predictors widely varies, and that new predictors appear. For instance, for student 4560 (Fig. 4, red color) mentioning *Meetings* in a day was found as a positive predictor of progress (counter to the group-level trend), while mentions to working on thesis-related tasks (*ThesisWork.ALL*) was found a negative predictor, signaling some kind of blockage with those activities. For student 5147, predictors that are not found in the group-level models include the mentioning of working on non-thesis work tasks (OtherWork.ALL) or not doing tasks that she normally postpones (*Did.Postponed.Task_No*), both as negative predictors. This indicates that, for her particular situation, the conflict with other work tasks (e.g., teaching) and her tendency to postpone thesis-related tasks, are central challenges in her experience of doctoral progress.

Similar individual analyses can be performed using the same kind of ENA comparing good vs. bad progress days. For each individual student, again we find trends that differ from the group-level ones and add further nuance and specificity of each students' situation and challenges. For instance, in the case of student 5566 (Fig. 5, right), we see that *Meetings* and interruptions (*Interrup-*

tionsInterferences) play a stronger role in her bad progress days (compared to the group-level network). Furthermore, in her case, the role of non-thesis work tasks (*OtherWork.ALL*) is more unambiguously linked to the bad progress days' network (while in the group-level network it was rather associated with the good progress days' network), indicating a stronger level of disruption/conflict from such activities into her dissertation progress.

5 Discussion

Designing to Support Doctoral Progress (and Persistence and Well-Being). Aside from *confirming the importance of perceiving one's own progress in the dissertation* (as per the doctorate- and technology-related value ranking exercises), we can use the evidence from our inquiry into doctoral values and the experience of doctoral progress to derive design insights for the development of future TEL solutions to the problems of doctoral well-being and persistence:

- *Self-direction (including autonomy, curiosity, and learning) as a key basic value of doctoral culture (with Benevolence and Universalism as additional key values).* This insight, stemming from the PVQ and the value scenario evaluations in RQ1.1, could be used in TEL solutions that exploit doctoral students' curiosity and thirst for self-direction (e.g., an interactive LA dashboard that lets students investigate data about their progress and what strategies work specifically for them)[2].
- *Time tensions and task conflicts.* The group-level ENA comparison of good/bad progress days and the predictors of progress in the linear regression model of RQ1.2 suggest that the time conflict between thesis work and other kinds of work (including family/housework) is a key feature of students' struggle for progress. This is also supported by the high ranking of ease and efficiency of use in RQ1.1's technology-related values. This should be exploited in future TEL solutions not only by making such technologies minimalistic and quick to use. They could also specifically focus on time/task management skills (and self-regulated learning more broadly).
- *The quest for focus.* The pivotal role of procrastination, as well as the negative influence of interruptions and meetings (including self-interruption) in the models of RQ1.2 suggest that finding uninterrupted time and mental energy to do the hard work of producing new scientific knowledge, is a key challenge for many students' progress. This again could be a target for TEL solutions designed, e.g., to help them focus on central parts of their dissertation while managing these external disruptors.
- *Progress as uniquely experienced.* The wide variety of contextual factors related to progress, as well as their varying directionalities and relative strengths in the individual models of RQ1.2 reinforces the idea that not only

[2] More design ideas for TEL solutions embodying the high-ranked doctoral values can be found at https://tinyurl.com/ECTEL23-VSD-scenarios.

each dissertation and student is different, but also the path to navigate doctoral challenges (like the two mentioned above) will be unique. This suggests adaptive systems and personalization as potentially important technological features of TEL solutions for doctoral dropout and well-being (see [16] for a concrete proposal of a personalizable system for doctoral education).
- *Motivational tips and strategies as a useful device.* This "value flow" [7] from participants' evaluations of the value scenarios suggests that providing evidence-based strategies to foster student progress would be valuable, pointing to recommender systems using either social filters or based on individualized analyses of the student's own data.

A Methodological Blueprint. The methods used in this inquiry borrow from human-computer interaction, quantitative ethnography, and social/cross-cultural psychology to try to make the development of value-sensitive and culturally-aware TEL more concrete (in line with recent calls like [2,21]). Notable methodological elements of this new way of initiating a TEL design cycle include:

- The use of the PVQ and Schwartz's theory of basic values [18] to investigate core values of a group of learners (which may shape their actions and usage of the TEL solutions we propose) in a way that is cross-culturally consistent.
- The use of technological reflective cultural probes [9,13] to gather longitudinal unstructured data, and the quantitative exploration of the combined quantitative and qualitative evidence from such probes, to understand the complex relationship between multiple contextual factors of the learner experience and the central focus of our exploration. In this regard, stepwise linear models are just one potential option that has the advantage of being both interpretable for researchers and comparatively parsimonious due to variable selection.
- The combination of value scenarios, value dams and flows, and other methods from value-sensitive design [7] of which there exist few examples in TEL [3].

Limitations. The study presented here, however, is not without limitations and should be understood as the first of a series of studies into the complex issue of doctoral dropout and well-being. Albeit our samples come from two countries and multiple disciplines, it cannot be assumed to be representative of the doctoral student population (e.g., note its gender imbalance), and we cannot thus suggest that the group-level trends above will generalize to other cultures or institutions. Further studies in other countries/cultures would be needed to validate and refine these results. Also, the inductive coding process was done by a single researcher. While this is not considered a problem in reflexive thematic analysis [1], it may subtract from the external validity of our results. Finally, we should note that, due to space limitations, participant quotes have been removed from the reporting of evidence, which limits the grounding of the insights to the raw data that generated them.

Conclusion... or a New Beginning. We are currently facing many wicked global problems, yet much of our human talent to solve them is wasted due to the dropout and well-being problems that afflict doctoral education. In this paper, we have articulated doctoral persistence and well-being as important, unsolved educational problems, amenable to TEL support. We have performed a value-sensitive, culturally-aware inquiry in two iterations, with 19 doctoral students from multiple disciplines in two different countries, focusing on students' perception of progress. Rather than proposing a single solution to these problems, we have decided to expose our mixed-methods analysis of evidence from this initial inquiry and our design-oriented conclusions from it (a common contribution in HCI which is still rare TEL). We hope this newfound evidence and knowledge will spark a host of TEL proposals focusing on doctoral progress to address these dire global problems – as well as further studies into doctoral culture and experience in different settings, using a similar methodological blueprint.

References

1. Braun, V., Clarke, V.: One size fits all? What counts as quality practice in (reflexive) thematic analysis? Qual. Res. Psychol. **18**(3), 328–352 (2021). https://doi.org/10.1080/14780887.2020.1769238
2. Buckingham Shum, S., Ferguson, R., Martinez-Maldonado, R.: Human-centred learning analytics. J. Learn. Anal. **6**(2), 1–9 (2019)
3. Chen, B., Zhu, H.: Towards value-sensitive learning analytics design. In: Proceedings of the 9th International Conference on Learning Analytics & Knowledge, pp. 343–352. ACM, Tempe AZ USA, March 2019. https://doi.org/10.1145/3303772.3303798
4. De Clercq, M., Frenay, M., Azzi, A., Klein, O., Galand, B.: All you need is self-determination: investigation of Ph.d students' motivation profiles and their impact on the doctoral completion process. Int. J. Doctoral Stud. **16**, 189–209 (2021). https://doi.org/10.28945/4702
5. Devos, C., Boudrenghien, G., Van der Linden, N., Azzi, A., Frenay, M., Galand, B., Klein, O.: Doctoral students' experiences leading to completion or attrition: a matter of sense, progress and distress. Eur. J. Psychol. Educ. **32**(1), 61–77 (2017)
6. Evans, T.M., Bira, L., Gastelum, J.B., Weiss, L.T., Vanderford, N.L.: Evidence for a mental health crisis in graduate education. Nat. Biotechnol. **36**(3), 282–284 (2018)
7. Friedman, B., Hendry, D.G., Borning, A., et al.: A survey of value sensitive design methods. Found. Trends Hum.-Comput. Interact. **11**(2), 63–125 (2017)
8. Friedman, B., Kahn, P.H., Borning, A.: Value sensitive design and information systems. The handbook of information and computer ethics, pp. 69–101 (2008)
9. Gaver, B., Dunne, T., Pacenti, E.: Design: cultural probes. Interactions **6**(1), 21–29 (1999). https://doi.org/10.1145/291224.291235
10. Geven, K., Skopek, J., Triventi, M.: How to Increase PhD completion rates? an impact evaluation of two reforms in a selective graduate school, 1976–2012. Res. High. Educ. **59**(5), 529–552 (2018). https://doi.org/10.1007/s11162-017-9481-z
11. Jackman, P.C., Jacobs, L., Hawkins, R.M., Sisson, K.: Mental health and psychological wellbeing in the early stages of doctoral study: a systematic review. Europ. J. High. Educ. **12**(3), 293–313 (2021). https://doi.org/10.1080/21568235.2021.1939752

12. Lahenius, K., Martinsuo, M.: Different types of doctoral study processes. Scand. J. Educ. Res. **55**(6), 609–623 (2011)
13. Loi, D.: Reflective probes, primitive probes and playful triggers. In: Ethnographic Praxis in Industry Conference Proceedings 2007(1), pp. 232–245 (2007). https://doi.org/10.1111/j.1559-8918.2007.tb00079.x
14. Mackie, S.A., Bates, G.W.: Contribution of the doctoral education environment to PhD candidates' mental health problems: a scoping review. High. Educ. Res. Dev. **38**(3), 565–578 (2019). https://doi.org/10.1080/07294360.2018.1556620
15. Prieto, L., Odriozola-González, P., Rodríguez-Triana, M.J., Dimitriadis, Y., Ley, T.: Progress-oriented workshops for doctoral well-being: evidence from a two-country design-based research. Int. J. Doctoral Stud. **17**, 39–66 (2022). https://doi.org/10.28945/4898
16. Prieto, L.P., Pishtari, G., Dimitriadis, Y., Triana, M.J.R., Ley, T., Odriozola-González, P.: Single-case learning analytics: feasibility of a human-centred analytics approach to support doctoral education. Accepted at the Journal of Universal Computer Science (in press). https://doi.org/10.31219/osf.io/ku6mv
17. Satinsky, E.N., et al.: Systematic review and meta-analysis of depression, anxiety, and suicidal ideation among Ph.D. students. Sci. Rep. **11**(1), 14370 (2021). https://doi.org/10.1038/s41598-021-93687-7
18. Schwartz, S.H., et al.: An overview of the schwartz theory of basic values. Online Readings Psychol. Culture **2**(1), 2307–2919 (2012)
19. Shaffer, D.W.: Quantitative Ethnography. Lulu.com (2017)
20. Sverdlik, A., Hall, N.C., McAlpine, L., Hubbard, K.: The PhD experience: a review of the factors influencing doctoral students' completion, achievement, and well-being. Int. J. Doctoral Stud. **13**, 361–388 (2018). https://doi.org/10.28945/4113
21. Viberg, O., Jivet, I., Scheffel, M.: Designing culturally aware learning analytics: a value sensitive perspective, pp. 177–192. Springer, Cham (2023). https://doi.org/10.1007/978-3-031-27646-0_10
22. Wollast, R., et al.: Who are the doctoral students who drop out? Factors associated with the rate of doctoral degree completion in universities. Int. J. High. Educ. **7**(4), 143–156 (2018). https://doi.org/10.5430/ijhe.v7n4p143

A Critical Consideration of the Ethical Implications in Learning Analytics as Data Ecology

Paul Prinsloo[1], Mohammad Khalil[2(✉)], and Sharon Slade[3]

[1] Department of Business Management, University of South Africa, Pretoria, South Africa
prinsp@unisa.ac.za
[2] Centre for the Science of Learning and Technology (SLATE), University of Bergen, Bergen, Norway
mohammad.khalil@uib.no
[3] Independent Researcher, Oxford, UK

Abstract. Over the past decade or so, learning analytics (LA) has matured as a research field and as operational practice within many educational institutions, mostly in the Global North. Learning analytics is commonly defined as the measurement, collection, analysis and use of students' data to improve students' learning. Until recently, the main sources of data for LA were restricted to institutional datasets gathered from, for example, learning management systems (LMSs) registration data, etc. Since such data gathering took place within a relatively closed digital ecosystem, institutions held the responsibility to maintain student privacy and to restrict their data collection to that needed to carry out their educational duties. The increasing digitisation and datafication of higher education combined with increased commercialisation of teaching and learning support systems and applications, acts to destabilise this understanding of learning analytics as a digital ecosystem. Given these continuing changes, agreements with plat-form providers and the roles of social media, applications, plugins, and mobile learning in teaching and learning now prompt us to consider learning analytics as data ecology rather than as a 'closed' ecosystem. This paper first maps learning analytics as data ecology before illustrating the need to think differently about its ethical implications.

Keywords: data ecology · ethics · data interests · privacy · learning analytics

1 Introduction

Concerns around students' rights to privacy and the notion of consent have been fundamental to learning analytics (LA) research and praxis since 2011 (e.g., [7, 8, 11]). The main source of student learning data is often the institutional learning management system (LMS) in combination with other institutional data sources such as registration systems, assessment and examinations systems, library records and services under the umbrella of 'student support'. As such, it is safe to say that the collection, analysis

O. Viberg et al. (Eds.): EC-TEL 2023, LNCS 14200, pp. 371–382, 2023.
https://doi.org/10.1007/978-3-031-42682-7_25

and use of student data has mainly taken place behind institutional firewalls and largely governed by institutional data governance and, on occasion, by ethical review boards [36].

As higher education becomes more digitised and datafied [35], students' learning "spills over" into other spaces [26] as that learning is supplemented by a number of different but increasingly linked spaces such as Massive Open Online Courses, social media, YouTube, Google Docs and mobile applications such as WhatsApp (e.g., [3, 18]). As a result of this expansion into other spaces, the boundaries of the LMS as the "walled garden" of data [1] become less secure - and this has implications not only for the fiduciary duty of institutions to ensure data privacy, but also for students' rights to have their data protected [23]. We acknowledge the asymmetrical power relations between students and higher education institutions (HEIs), and that HEIs have both a moral and a legal duty to protect student data. However, students' individual and collective data practices and "digital promiscuity" also impact on the ability of HEIs to maintain that protection [25].

In this paper we map the ethical considerations and implications of understanding learning analytics as part of a data ecology rather than as a closed data ecosystem.

2 The Expanding Data Gaze

Even before the emergence of LA as a distinct research focus and praxis, there were suggestions that educational data analysis was being seen as surveillance [13, 14]. Such 'surveillance' has become a constant theoretical or heuristic lens in research about student privacy in the context of LA (e.g., [6, 27, 29]). In a recent article by [1], Arnold refers to LA as "Surveillance machines in ivory towers" by which students and academics alike are abstracted. Arnold suggests that this has led to "a politics in which people are addressed as digital artefacts - instances of when, what and how they have interacted online rather than being respected as people who are more than a data point on an educational social graph" (p. 70). Students have no option but to be surveilled and cannot leave LMS as "the walled garden" (p. 76). He concludes that "Universities are part of a global surveillance economy" (p. 84).

Arnold's [1] earlier concerns link well to evidence of an intensification of the "data gaze" and an expansion of that gaze to new data frontiers [4, 21]. The notion of the data gaze can be loosely defined as the pervasive surveillance and scrutiny of individuals' digital activities and personal data by various entities, often driven by data-driven technologies and algorithms. In his work, Beer [4] refers to this as "powerful analytic, constitutive and performative social presence" (p. 8) that promises "speedy, accessible, revealing, panoramic, prophetic and smart" (p. 22) insights. Data surveillance as a form of capitalism [37], invites an increasing number of venture capitalists, online platform providers and data cartels to exploit the increasing datafication of life [16]. And, as Skinner-Thompson [38] points out, it is those who are already vulnerable due to gender, culture, class or race that are most at risk.

Higher education is not exempt from this intensification and expansion of the data gaze [32, 33]. Post-Covid higher education has positively embraced digitisation and the new opportunities to datafy teaching and learning [5]. Not only has student surveillance within institutional boundaries increased, there are also examples that LA follows students when their learning 'spills over' into other spaces. For example, Jones, Rubel and LeClere [39] report on the collection of students' geolocation data which is then combined with biometric and learning engagement data. These authors indicate that the US Family Educational Rights and Privacy Act of 1974 (FERPA) offers no protection to students when data is gathered from their "smart phones, chat rooms, online discussion lists, social media sites, and web browser data" (p. 277). Additionally, there is evidence of institutions using radio-frequency identification (RFID) via students' access cards, tracking their social media and collecting data from wearable devices [2]. Although this may predominantly relate to a research context seeking to further our understanding of learning theory and practice, this expansion of data collection has generated the notion of 'seamless' LA, that is, the tracking of students across multiple informal and formal platforms [40].

Thompson and Prinsloo [29] state that the data gaze is anything but "linear and unidirectional – from the one with power who gazes to the gazed-upon" (p. 156) and introduce the concept of sousveillance; that we each surveil one another (see [20]). It may therefore be more useful to think about the data gaze as 'manyfolded', referring to "'different versions, different performances, different realities, that co-exist in the present' ([41] in [29, p. 156]).

In the light of the expansion of the data gaze, the 'spilling over' of learning into previously private spaces, and institutional tracking of students via a range of technologies outside of the "walled garden", Prinsloo, Khalil, and Slade [24] suggest that LA should be understood as part of a data ecology rather than as part of a secure and bounded data ecosystem. As such, we should recognise that student privacy has become both more fragile and its protection is becoming increasingly difficult and outwith the control of HEIs [43].

3 Learning Analytics as Ecology

Institutions collect data from students throughout their learning journeys: from pre-enrolment, enrolment, their engagement with lecturers, peers, student support and student administration, as well as during re-enrolment processes or as alumni. Students access learning materials and engage with tasks and peers using a variety of devices, such as laptops, tablets, and mobile phones, all the while leaving digital traces. Their uses of other devices, e.g., wearables, library cards etc., offer further opportunities for institutional data collection (see Fig. 1).

It is this complexity of inter-connected data sources that led Prinsloo et al. [24] to propose that we might better understand LA as an ecosystem. "Central to data ecosystems are the relations and transactions between its autonomous but interrelated actors (human and non-human) flowing from and constituting varying degrees of interdependency." Essential characteristics of data ecosystems are that (1) there are different actors (e.g., data users, re-users, service providers, policies, laws, consultants, etc.); (2) data flows through the system engaging with other data (eco)systems; (3) value is created for and through each of the data flows depending on the data interests of the different actors/systems. (see a full discussion in [24]). Figure 2 below illustrates how LA might be seen as a data ecosystem.

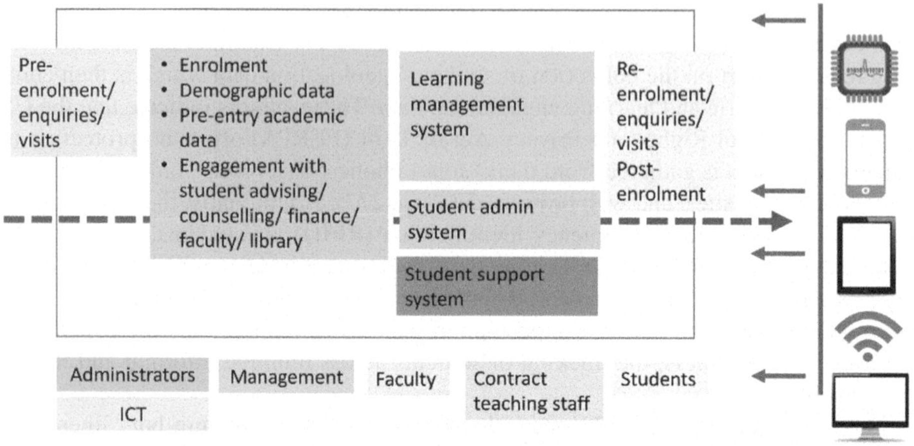

Fig. 1. The student data journey

An integral part of understanding the student data journey is to consider the different types of data that are found and shared during students' learning journeys. A useful description of the different data types is proposed by Kitchin [41] who refers to directed data, automated data and gifted data.

- *Directed* data, in the context of Fig. 1, refers to data gathered for a specific reason at specific points such as pre-enrolment and registration (e.g., demographic and prior learning data). Assessments (formative and summative), surveys, opinion polls and research projects may also be directed data.
- *Automated* data collection and analysis refers to the harvesting of data from multiple sources without human intervention. For example, student's login and engagement data, the download of resources, clicker and library access data, etc.
- *Gifted* data refers to data and information that students share voluntarily in discussion forums and email communication.

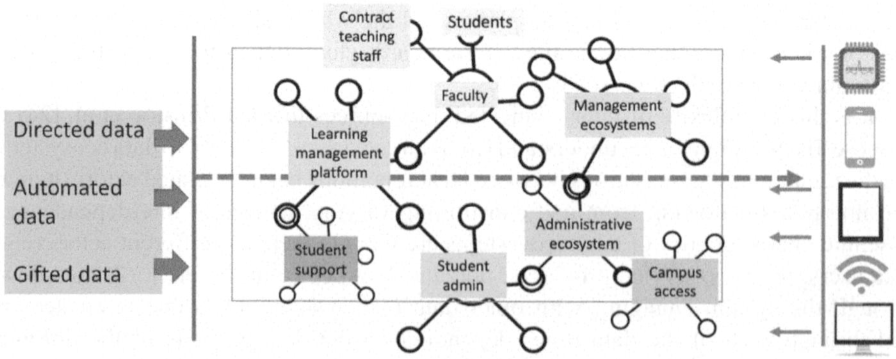

Fig. 2. LA as data ecosystem

As can be seen in Fig. 2, while students use a variety of devices (on the right of the diagram) to access their learning resources and engage with faculty and other students, most, if not all, of their learning takes place behind the institutional firewall and within the LMS. Collated data (whether directed, automated or gifted) is shared with other institutional data ecosystems and stakeholders, depending on stakeholder interests and perceived value of that data. As such all the collection, analysis and use of student data takes place within the mandate and fiduciary duty of institutions and is largely governed by institutional policy and processes and, in some cases, by Ethical Review Boards.

Central to this paper is consideration of the ethical implications in the event that learning 'spills over' into students' private spaces. Such spaces are increasingly included in the intensification and expansion of institutional and commercial data gazes. What is the impact of the consideration of LA not as a (closed) data ecosystem but rather as a data ecology? And what are the ethical implications for LA in terms of student data privacy; institutional data governance; institutional contracts with external providers and teaching assistants; the use of social media in teaching and learning; the inclusion of MOOCs as support for or as part of formal courses, to mention but a few?

Prinsloo et al. [24] map the main characteristics of LA as data ecology as follows:

- (May) include a variety of ecosystems.
- Evidence of links between these different ecosystems, and/or links to data stakeholders or data interests outside of the institutional LA data ecosystem
- Evidence of a multidirectional flow of information and values between non-human, humans, institutions and technology
- Evidence of sharing of data with stakeholders outside of the institutional LA data ecosystem (e.g. platform and analysis providers, governments, regulatory bodies, MOOC platforms, apps and service providers)
- Evidence of importing of data from stakeholders outside of the institutional LA data ecosystem (e.g., social media, multimodal data from multiple devices, and service providers).

As can be seen in Fig. 3, LA has become part of a broader network of data interests - such as social media (shown on the right), and a range of other role players and data interests such as national higher education data ecosystems, national security ecosystems, learning platform providers and textbook and tablet/phone providers. For example, the Predictive Analytics Reporting (PAR) Framework in the United States is a collaborative initiative involving multiple higher education institutions and technology providers. It aims to leverage learning analytics to improve student success and retention rates. Participating institutions share data and collaborate on research projects to identify effective interventions and support strategies. Additionally, we have networks and data flows involving a range of commercial interests and data brokers or cartels.

Figure 3 makes apparent that this entanglement of higher education institutions with a fluid range of other data interests, data flows, providers (e.g. platform providers, electronic textbook providers, etc.) makes the protection of student data privacy very difficult, if not impossible. Adding to this complexity of protecting student data is our recognition of students as active rather than passive data subjects. Students now participate in a variety of networks outside of the institutional LMS, in self-organised groups or as individuals, in which their own or fellow students' personal data may be (un)intentionally

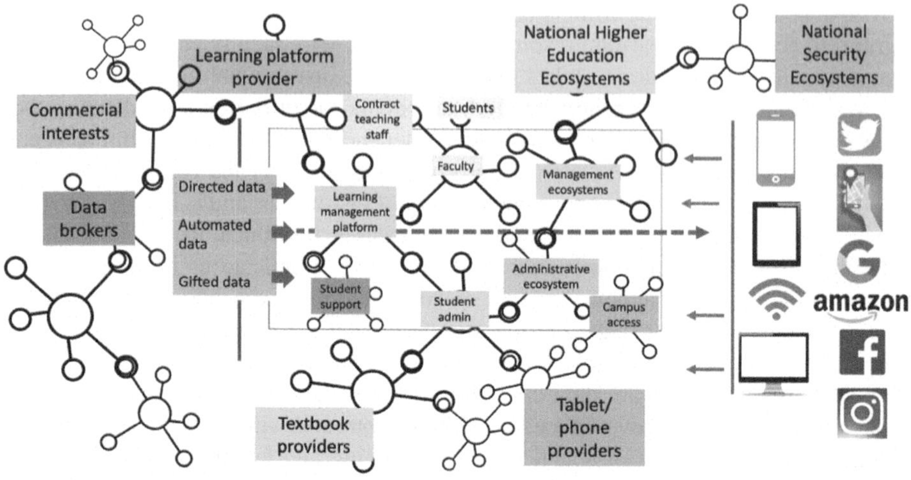

Fig. 3. LA as data ecology

leaked. Given the move toward sousveillance [20] - where surveillance-of-each-other is becoming normalised, and in which personal information (and the personal information of others) may be shared in digitally promiscuous ways [25], the task of higher education institutions and student data governance has just become much more difficult.

Would privacy enhancing technologies be (part of) the solution - whether as institutional or individual strategy? Prinsloo et al. [23] make the argument that privacy and student data are much more than just technical issues, but need to be understood as, as [41] suggest as also "... legal, economic, social, relational, ethical, temporal, spatial and philosophical" (p. 3). They continue to make the case that we should consider student privacy as a social problem and that student data privacy should be considered in the nexus of "the complex assemblages that produce, circulate, share/sell and utilise data in diverse ways; ... and how they interact to form intersecting data products, services and markets and shape policy and regulation" [12, p. 5]. If we consider student data privacy and its protection as only technological, we run the risk of naivety and techno-solutionism. Of particular interest here is Prinsloo et al.'s [23] consideration of alternative approaches to understanding individual data privacy, such as considering contextual integrity; data privacy as ontological; group privacy; marginal privacy; and indigenous understandings of privacy. While it falls outside of the scope of this paper to examine these, we briefly reflect on their discussion of data-as-commodity before returning to the notion of group privacy.

At the core of the changing landscape of data in general and adding a layer of complexity to LA as ecology is data-as-commodity. The commodification of data and the commercial value of data contribute to the intensification and expansion of the data gaze as discussed earlier. It is also important to note that the commercial value of data does not (necessarily or directly) lie in the scope of the original collection of data, but increasingly in selling that data to be combined with other data sources outside the original scope and purpose of its collection [9, 15]. "Data about people produces revenue in three ways: companies can sell it directly, use it to improve services, or use it to predict, change, or modify behaviour. Of these three options, behavioural use represents by far the biggest source of revenue for technology companies" [31, p. 13].

In the same way that technology cannot yet provide sufficient privacy and data protections, there are concerns that the answer does not lie in legal protection. Skinner-Thompson [38] is clear that in order for a person to trade their personal information in return for something else, they must first have control over their data, and increasingly they don't. The digitisation and datafication of our lives means that it is simply impossible for individuals to be aware of or control every data processing activity, to assess the scope of collection, or even to assess whether there are any legal concerns around the collection and use of their data.

There is ample research setting out the costs and benefits of sharing personal data (e.g., see [10]). Additionally, it is well established that individuals are anything but rational when they routinely accept a platform's Terms and Conditions without reading them [30]. In the context of higher education, one example of this is the complexities of ensuring the protection of student data (and awareness of the scope and purpose of the downstream use of student data by a range of actors) when students are required to enrol for Massive Open Online Courses (MOOCs) through their institutional portals as a pre-requirement for continuing with their studies at a particular institution or as additional support [22, 42].

Of particular interest here is Prinsloo et al.'s [23] discussion of *group privacy*. In contrast to legal and regulatory frameworks focusing on *individuals'* responsibility to protect their own and others' personal information, group privacy may facilitate not only a better comprehension of the complexities of ensuring individual privacy in a data ecology, but also allow individuals to assume responsibility for the privacy of others. The argument for considering group privacy is twofold.

Firstly, analyses of student data are often category-based whereby the engagement, demographic, gender, race, or other identity constructs of individuals are used to group that individual with others who share a particular characteristic or identity construct. For example, when a particular student shares a pattern of engagement with other individuals, they may be categorised and grouped as 'at-risk' despite any differences in socio-economic income, culture, prior learning experiences and demographic data. Taylor, Floridi and van der Sloot [28] state that this "result[s] in decisions that pose real risks on the aggregate level, for groups of, or rather grouped people" [28, p. 10]. These authors further point out that such grouping practises "challenges the very foundations of most currently existing legal, ethical and social practices and theories" [28, pp.13–14].

Consideration of LA as part of a data ecology recognises that individual students' data could be combined with other individuals' data based on a particular characteristics or behaviours. These 'data group profiles' can extend beyond the educational sphere and may impact on future life choices.

The second part of the argument relates to humans as relational beings who are part of a broader context. Prinsloo et al. [23] uses the example of a 'selfie' which captures (and potentially identifies) others nearby. There is evidence of such images being used by repressive regimes to trace individuals taking part in protests (e.g., [17]). As [23] point out, it is no longer possible to say "what happens in Vegas, stays in Vegas" as information shared with one person may inadvertently result in wider sharing than expected. Individual privacy is only as safe as the safest person in a circle of influence and contacts. Loi and Christen [19] also discuss "inferential privacy" meaning "inferences that can be made about a group of people defined by a feature, or combination thereof, shared by all individuals in the group" (p. 207). The earlier example of a selfie taken within a group in a particular context can effectively label any in the background of that image as sharing the purpose, agenda and intentions of the picture taker.

4 Learning Analytics as an Ecosystem or Ecology - What are the Implications?

In their analysis of 11 learning analytics implementation frameworks, Prinsloo et al. [24] found ample evidence that LA is predominantly considered as a data ecology. Only one framework [27] linked LA to other data ecosystems and multidirectional data flows. There was no evidence of "an awareness of how LA functions as an ecosystem in a larger ecology of data networks and assemblages" [24]. Of specific interest to this paper are the authors' concerns about the ethical and privacy implications when institutional data ecosystems become part of external data ecosystems. As there is ample evidence of increasing commercial interests in student data coupled with the absorption of many institutional LMSs and analytical services into commercial data ecologies, we should consider the implications for data stewardship, student privacy and ethics.

Having introduced the complexities of effectively managing student data privacy and protection as a result of the expansion of the data gaze, we turn to consideration of the ethical implications for learning analytics for a range of key stakeholders.

Implications for students:

- Students should be aware that their (learning analytics) data could be shared with stakeholders outside of the institutional LA data ecosystem. This includes platform and analysis providers, governments, regulatory bodies, digital learning environments, and service providers. As a result, they should be mindful of the information they share and how it might be utilised.
- Students should understand that their data is not limited to a single system but can be part of a larger ecosystem where data is conveyed and consumed. This means that student data could be ingested by for example sensors, social media, and provider cookies.
- Students should be informed that their trace data can be imported from stakeholders inside and outside of the institutional data ecosystem. This means that their data could be collected by and/or reported to administrators, managers, student support counsellors, and even external bodies such as commercial providers and governments.
- Students should understand the implications of sharing other's data without consideration.

Implications for institutions.

- It is no longer sufficient to rely on traditional data protection and privacy policies. Educational institutions must broaden their policy scope to explicitly reference (and

set boundaries around) external stakeholders who may be able to access and process student data.
- All HEIs should ensure that their uses of student data are clearly established and are transparent to students (and other stakeholders). This should include the scope of data collected (as well as what is out of bounds), the purpose(s) of data collection, the technologies used, analytical techniques and access to explanations of their development and data training sets.
- HEIs have a fiduciary duty to ensure that their students' data is secure and unexploited.
- Institutions should enable students to review and correct inaccurate data and to challenge decisions based on flawed data or assumptions (and, vice versa, students should bear some responsibility for ensuring that their data is appropriate and complete.

Implications for teaching staff.

- Teaching staff may opt to introduce greater variety into their courses, using for example, MOOCs or externally hosted blogs and wikis, as well as other social media platforms. In doing so, they should be cognisant of the privacy and data sharing practices of these providers, ensuring that student data is not unwittingly exposed to third party users.
- Teaching and faculty staff will often communicate to a group of students as part of their teaching. Care should be taken to maintain the privacy of individual students by not sharing personal or confidential information with the wider group (or with platform providers).

Implications for relationships with third party providers.

- When creating relationships with third party providers, e.g., for marketing, software or hardware provision, data analysis purposes, institutions must set clear boundaries on the uses of data provided - both in terms of the designated task and potential downstream uses.
- Third party providers of learning analytics systems will have necessarily trained their learning platforms on datasets. HEIs will need to understand how meaningful and relevant those training datasets are for their own contexts and take a view on the possibilities of introducing bias to their own contexts [34].

Although much of this is included in existing legislation, e.g., GDPR, certain aspects or nuances are not specifically included, for example:

- Where student data is not limited to a single system but is part of a larger ecosystem, While GDPR focuses on the protection of personal data within specific contexts, it does not explicitly address the broader data ecosystem.
- It is suggested above that students should understand the implications of sharing others' data without consideration. While GDPR addresses the sharing and processing of individuals' personal data, it does not specifically discuss the implications of sharing data related to other individuals.
- GDPR sets requirements for data processing by educational institutions, but does not specifically address the responsibilities and considerations of individual teaching staff regarding data privacy.

- Finally, while GDPR requires data controllers to have appropriate data processing agreements in place with third parties, the emphasis here on establishing clear boundaries goes beyond the specific requirements of that legislation.

It is important to note that the GDPR provides a comprehensive framework for data protection and privacy in the European Union. While some aspects mentioned in the text may not be explicitly covered by GDPR, the regulation sets a strong foundation for safeguarding individuals' personal data and requires organizations to ensure transparency, security, and individual rights in the processing of such data.

5 Conclusions

This study highlights several particular issues, including:

- The expansion of learning analytics beyond the institutional (LMS) such that it now encompasses a variety of digital spaces such as social media, Massive Open Online Courses (MOOCs), and mobile applications. This expansion challenges the notion of the LMS as a "walled garden" of data and raises concerns about the protection of student data in these additional spaces.
- The concept of LA as a form of surveillance, with students and academics abstracted as digital artefacts and higher education institutions as increasingly part of the global surveillance economy.
- The increasing challenges to student data privacy given the collection of a much broader range of student data, e.g., geolocation data, biometric data, and data from wearable devices, social media, online discussions, and web browsing no longer protection by existing legislation.
- The limitations of relying solely on technological or legal solutions for protection of privacy, and the need to consider social, ethical, economic, and philosophical dimensions.

As a result, we argue that LA has moved from being a data ecosystem to being part of a broader data ecology where data flows between human and non-human actors, spilling over institutional firewalls and data governance and where individual student data seems to have escaped and have become available, often intentionally, to others.

While we are convinced that it is more productive (and sobering) to consider LA as part of a broader data ecology, we question whether the LA (research and practice) community feel the same. Amid the reality of surveillance and sousveillance, assuming LA to be part of a closed (or at least protected) ecosystem may leave student data ripe for the picking.

References

1. Arnold, B.B.: Surveillance machines in ivory towers? surveillance capitalism, dignity and learning management systems. Canberra Law Rev. **19**(1), 70 (2022)
2. Arriba Pérez, F., Santos, J., Rodriguez, M.: Analytics of biometric data from wearable devices to support teaching and learning activities. J. Inform. Syst. Eng. Manage. **1**(1), 41–54 (2016)
3. Barrot, J.S.: Using social networking sites as a language teaching and learning environment. Lang. Teach. 1–16 (2022)
4. Beer, D: The Data Gaze. Safe, London, UK (2019)
5. Beetham, H., et al.: Surveillance practices, risks and responses in the post pandemic university. Digital Culture Educ.n **14**(1), 16–37 (2022)
6. Drachsler, H., et al.: Ethical and privacy issues in the application of learning analytics. In: Proceedings of the 5th International Conference on Learning Analytics and Knowledge, pp. 390–391 (2015)
7. Ferguson, R.: Learning analytics: drivers, developments and challenges. Int. J. Technol. Enhan. Learn. **4**(5–6), 304–317 (2012)
8. Greller, W., Drachsler, H.: Translating learning into numbers: a generic framework for learning analytics. J. Educ. Technol. Soc. **15**(3), 42–57 (2012)
9. Hudson, J.: The world's most liveable city—for Māori: data advocacy and Māori wellbeing in Tāmaki Makaurau (Auckland). In: Kukutai, T., Taylor, J. (eds.) Data sovereignty for indigenous peoples: Current practice and future needs, pp. 179–191. ANU Press (2016)
10. Khalil, M., Ebner, M.: De-identification in learning analytics. J. Learn. Anal. **3**(1), 129–138 (2016)
11. Khalil, M.: Learning analytics in massive open online courses. arXiv preprint arXiv:1802.09344 (2018)
12. Kitchin, R., Lauriault, T.: Towards critical data studies: Charting and unpacking data assemblages and their work. The Programmable City Working Paper 29th July 2014 (2014)
13. Knox, D.: A good horse runs at the shadow of the whip: surveillance and organisational trust in online learning environments. Can. J. Media Stud. **7**, 07–1 (2010)
14. Knox, D.: Spies in the house of learning: a typology of surveillance in online learning environments. Paper presented at Edge2010, St. Johns, Canada (2010b)
15. Komljenovic, J.: The rise of education rentiers: digital platforms, digital data and rents. Learn. Media Technol. **46**(3), 320–332 (2021)
16. Lamdan, S.: Data Cartels: The Companies that Control and Monopolise Our Information. Stanford University Press, Redwood City, CA (2022)
17. Lindau, J.D.: Surveillance and the Vanishing Individual: Power and Privacy in the Digital Age. Rowman & Littlefield, London, UK (2022)
18. Loglo, F.S., Zawacki-Richter, O.: Learning with digital media: a systematic review of students' use in African higher education. J. Learn. Develop. **10**(1), 1–23 (2023)
19. Loi, M., Christen, M.: Two concepts of group privacy. Philos. Technol. **33**(2), 207–224 (2020). Retrieved from
20. Mann, S., Nolan, J., Wellman, B.: Sousveillance: inventing and using wearable computing devices for data collection in surveillance environments. Surveill. Soc. **1**(3), 331–355 (2003)
21. Prinsloo, P.: Data frontiers and frontiers of power in (higher) education: a view of/from the Global South. Teach. High. Educ. **25**(4), 366–383 (2020)
22. Prinsloo, P., Slade, S., Khalil, M.: Student data privacy in MOOCs: a sentiment analysis. Distan. Educ. **40**(3), 395–413 (2019)
23. Prinsloo, P., Slade, S., Khalil, M.: The answer is (not only) technological: considering student data privacy in learning analytics. Br. J. Edu. Technol. **53**(4), 876–893 (2022)

24. Prinsloo, P., Khalil, M., Slade, S.: Learning analytics as data ecology: a tentative proposal. J. Comput. High. Educ. 1–29 (2023)
25. Prinsloo, P., Slade, S.: Student vulnerability, agency, and learning analytics: an exploration. J. Learn. Anal. **3**(1), 159–182 (2016)
26. Slade, P., Khalil, M.: (under review). Multimodal learning analytics - in-between student privacy and encroachment: a systematic review. British J. Educ. Technol.
27. Slade, S., Prinsloo, P.: Learning analytics: ethical issues and dilemmas. Am. Behav. Sci. **57**(10), 1510–1529 (2013)
28. Taylor, L., Floridi, L., van der Sloot, B. (Eds.). (2016). G*roup Privacy: New challenges of data technologies* (Vol.126). Springer
29. Thompson, T.L., Prinsloo, P.: Returning the data gaze in higher education. Learn. Media Technol. 1–13 (2022)
30. Trepte, S., Reinecke, L.: The reciprocal effects of social network site use and the disposition for self-disclosure: a longitudinal study. Comput. Hum. Behav. **29**, 1102–1112 (2013)
31. Viljoen, S.: Democratic data: a relational theory for data governance. Yale Law J. 573–654 (2021)
32. Williamson, B.: Education technology seizes a pandemic opening. Current History **120**(822), 15–20 (2021)
33. Williamson, B.: Making markets through digital platforms: pearson, edu-business, and the (e) valuation of higher education. Critical Stud. Educ. **62**(1), 50–66 (2021)
34. Williamson, B.: Smarter learning software: Education and the big data imaginary. Big Data - Social Data, 10 Dec, University of Warwick (2015)
35. Williamson, B., Bayne, S., Shay, S.: The datafication of teaching in Higher Education: critical issues and perspectives. Teach. High. Educ. **25**(4), 351–365 (2020)
36. Willis, J.E., Slade, S., Prinsloo, P.: Ethical oversight of student data in learning analytics: a typology derived from a cross-continental, cross-institutional perspective. Educ. Tech. Res. Dev. **64**, 881–901 (2016)
37. Zuboff, S.: The Age of Surveillance Capitalism. The Fight for a Human Future at the New Frontier of Power. Public Affairs, New York, NY (2019)
38. Skinner-Thompson, S.: Privacy at the Margins. Cambridge University Press (2020)
39. Jones, K.M., Rubel, A., LeClere, E.: A matter of trust: Higher education institutions as information fiduciaries in an age of educational data mining and learning analytics. J. Am. Soc. Inf. Sci. **71**(10), 1227–1241 (2020)
40. Moon, J., Lee, D., Choi, G.W., Seo, J., Do, J., Lim, T.: Learning analytics in seamless learning environments: a systematic review. Interact. Learn. Environ. 1–18 (2023)
41. Mol, A.: The Body Multiple: Ontology in Medical Practice. Duke University Press (2002)
42. Khalil, M., Prinsloo, P., Slade, S.: The unbearable lightness of consent: Mapping MOOC providers' response to consent. In: Proceedings of the Fifth Annual ACM Conference on Learning at Scale, pp. 1–11 (2018)
43. Khalil, M., Wong, J., Er, E., Heitmann, M., Belokrys, G.: Tweetology of learning analytics: what does Twitter tell us about the trends and development of the field*?*. In: LAK22: 12th International Learning Analytics and Knowledge Conference, pp. 347–357 (2022)

Learning to Give Useful Hints: Assistance Action Evaluation and Policy Improvements

Robin Schmucker[1](✉), Nimish Pachapurkar[2], Shanmuga Bala[2], Miral Shah[2], and Tom Mitchell[1]

[1] Carnegie Mellon University, Pittsburgh, PA, USA
{rschmuck,tom.mitchell}@cs.cmu.edu
[2] CK-12 Foundation, Palo Alto, CA, USA
miral.shah@ck12.org

Abstract. We describe a fielded online tutoring system that learns which of several candidate assistance actions (e.g., one of multiple hints) to provide to students when they answer a practice question incorrectly. The system learns, from large-scale data of prior students, which assistance action to give for each of thousands of questions, to maximize measures of student learning outcomes. Using data from over 190,000 students in an online Biology course, we quantify the impact of different assistance actions for each question on a variety of outcomes (e.g., response correctness, practice completion), framing the machine learning task as a multi-armed bandit problem. We study relationships among different measures of learning outcomes, leading us to design an algorithm that for each question decides on the most suitable assistance policy training objective to optimize central target measures. We evaluate the trained policy for providing assistance actions, comparing it to a randomized assistance policy in live use with over 20,000 students, showing significant improvements resulting from the system's ability to learn to teach better based on data from earlier students in the course. We discuss our design process and challenges we faced when fielding data-driven technology, providing insights to designers of future learning systems.

Keywords: intelligent tutoring systems · multi-armed bandits

1 Introduction

Intelligent tutoring systems (ITSs) are part of everyday life for millions of students worldwide. ITSs promote accessible learning experiences that can narrow the educational achievement gap [24] and that, in some cases, can be as effective as human tutoring [13]. In their effort to create effective learning systems, ITS designers are confronted with a plethora of design decisions ranging from specifying general instructional design principles [12] to the creation of individual learning and practice materials. Designers rely on their domain expertise and

O. Viberg et al. (Eds.): EC-TEL 2023, LNCS 14200, pp. 383–398, 2023.
https://doi.org/10.1007/978-3-031-42682-7_26

consider effects of different design choices, but in many cases it is difficult to predict which exact choice will benefit students the most [18], and often thousands of design decisions have to be made on a case by case basis (e.g., which exact hint is most effective for this specific question). In this context, the promise of data-driven design approaches is that they can leverage system usage data to evaluate the effects of different design choices inside the ITS on student learning and can improve learning outcomes by refining the ITS automatically over time.

This work describes an online tutoring system that embraces a data-driven design approach by using large-scale student data to learn which of several candidate assistance actions to provide to students after they answer a practice questions incorrectly. We report results from a study–analysing data from over 190,000 students in a Biology course–evaluating the impact of individual assistance actions and assistance policies on different measures of learning outcomes. We discuss rationales behind our methodology and provide insights for the design of future learning systems. The main contributions of this work include:

- *Quantifying effects of assistance.* We evaluate effects of over 7,000 individual assistance actions on a variety of student learning outcome measures (e.g., practice completion). We study the relationship among different measures and design an assistance policy training algorithm that for each question decides on the most suitable policy training objective to optimize the student's success at the current question as well as their overall session performance.
- *Offline policy optimization.* We compute statistically significant estimates on the effects of multi-armed bandit policies trained to optimize different learning outcome measures. Studying assistance actions selected by these policies, we find that there is no single best assistance type (e.g., hint, vocabulary).
- *Live A/B evaluation.* We evaluate the assistance policy trained using our algorithm in comparison to a randomized assistance policy in live use with over 20,000 students. The system's ability to learn to teach better using data from prior students improves learning outcomes of future students significantly.

2 Related Work

2.1 Evaluating Treatment Effects Inside ITSs

Initially the effects of ITSs on student learning were evaluated at the *system level* by comparing a group of students that uses the ITS to a control group in a post-test [13]. Later research focuses on studying the effects of individual *instructional design choices* [12] and conducts experiments with students that interact with different configurations of the same learning system (e.g., [16,17]). With the ever increasing popularity of online ITSs, large-scale student log data becomes available, which enables investigating the effects of increasingly detailed system design choices, up to the choice of individual *practice questions* and *hints*.

As part of this development, ASSISTments introduced AXIS [27], the E-TRIALS TestBed [19] and the TeacherASSSIST system [20] to allow educators and researchers to create and evaluate the effectiveness of different problem sets and *on-demand* assistance materials. In the context of massive open online courses (MOOCs), DynamicProblem [28] was introduced as a proof-of-concept system that supports bandit algorithms [14] to collect feedback from students regarding the helpfulness of individual assistance materials. Relatedly, the MOOClet framework [23] allows instructors to specify multiple versions of educational resources and to evaluate them in A/B tests using randomization and bandit algorithms. The UpGrade system [8] was introduced as a flexible A/B testing framework designed for easy integration into various learning systems.

This work describes a fielded online tutoring system at CK12.org that learns to provide effective assistance actions (e.g., choose one of multiple available hints) to support students after they answer practice questions incorrectly. We use offline evaluation techniques [15] to leverage log data capturing over 4,800,000 assistance requests from over 190,000 students in a Biology course. The unprecedented scale of this data enables us to compute statistically significant estimates on the effects of *individual* assistance actions and assistance policies on different measures of learning outcomes. We further evaluate the effectiveness of the learned assistance policy in live use with over 20,000 students.

2.2 Data-Driven Assistance Policies

Here, we provide a concise overview of related research that uses data-driven techniques to support students during the problem solving process via bandit and reinforcement learning (RL) algorithms. For a comprehensive review on RL in the education domain we refer to a survey by Doroudi et al. [6].

Barnes and Stamper [3] induced a Markov decision process (MDP) based on hundreds of student solution paths and used RL to generate new hints inside a logic ITS. Chi et al. [4] modeled a physics tutor via an MDP with 16 states and learned a RL policy to improve student learning outcomes by deciding whether to ask the student to reflect on a problem or to tell them additional information. Georgila et al. [9] used Least-Squares Policy Iteration to learn a feedback policy for an interpersonal skill training system using data describing over 500 features from 72 participants. Ju et al. [10] identified critical pedagogical decisions based on Q-value and reward function estimates derived from logs of 1,148 students inside a probability ITS. Relatedly, Ausin et al. [1,2] explored Gaussian Process- and inverse RL-based approaches to address the credit assignment problem inside a logic ITS. A recent series of works [7,25,26] used a random policy to collect data from 500 students in an operational command course and explored offline RL techniques to learn adaptive scaffolding policies based on the ICAP framework.

A recent study by Prihar et al. [21] compared a multi-armed bandit algorithm based on Thompson Sampling to a random assistance policy with respect to their ability to increase students' *success on the next question*. In a two-month long experiment with 2,923 questions they find the bandit algorithm to be only slightly more effective than the random policy and argue that this is due to sample size limitations (on average 6.5 samples per action). In contrast, this work accurately estimates the impact of individual actions on *different measures of learning outcomes* by leveraging hundreds of samples per action (Table 1).

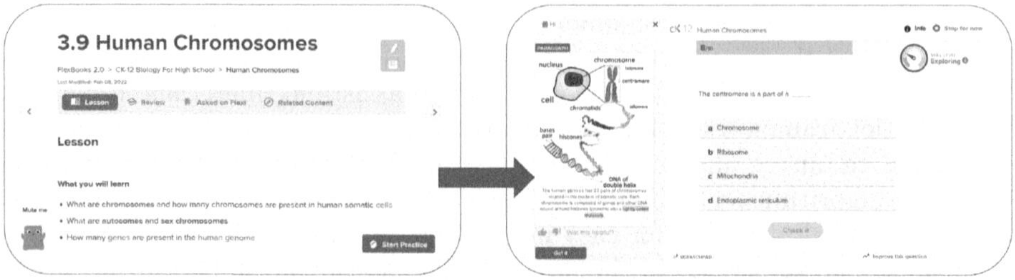

Fig. 1. Example views from the concept *Human Chromosomes.* [Left] In the *Lesson* section the student interacts with multi-modal learning materials. [Right] During *Adaptive Practice* the student develops and tests their understanding by answering practice questions. In the shown example the system displays a paragraph with illustration to assist the student before they reattempt the question after an initial incorrect response.

Further, in contrast to Prihar et al. [21], we quantify treatment effects by automatically providing assistance in response to incorrect student responses which avoids self-selection effects when assistance is only shown upon student request.

3 CK-12 FlexBook 2.0 System

The CK-12 Foundation is a non-profit organization that provides millions of students worldwide with access to free educational resources. CK-12's Flexbook 2.0 system[1] is a web-based ITS that offers a large variety of courses for different subjects and grade levels. Each course consists of a sequence of *concepts.* Each concept has a *Lesson* section with learning materials and an *Adaptive Practice* (AP) section where students can develop and test their understanding (Fig. 1).

The AP section features item response theory (IRT)-driven question sequencing and tries to select practice questions matching the student's ability level (*Goldilocks* principle [12]). After the system selects a question, the student can request a hint before submitting a first response. If the first response is incorrect, the system provides immediate feedback by displaying one *assistance action* (e.g., a hint or vocabulary) and the student reattempts the question. Afterwards, the system uses the student's first response to update the student's ability estimate and selects the next practice question. This process repeats until the student completes the AP session successfully by achieving 10 correct responses or until the question pool is exhausted in which case the student can try again.

This paper centers on the question of how we can employ data-driven techniques to learn an *assistance policy* that selects the most effective assistance action as feedback for each individual question. We focus on CK-12's *Biology for High School* course which is used by hundreds of thousands of students each year and whose content has been developed and refined for over ten years. The course covers hundreds of concepts and features over 12,000 questions corresponding

[1] https://www.ck12.org.

to five categories: *multiple-choice*, *select-all-that-apply*, *fill-in-the-blank*, *short-answer* and *true-false*. The AP system associates each question with a set of potential assistance actions. An exception are true-false questions which students only attempt once. The average non-true-false question is associated with 4.8 different actions. Each action falls into one of six categories: *hint*, *paragraph* (short text from lesson), *vocabulary* (keyword definitions), *remove distractor* (removes multiple-choice/select-all-that-apply response option), *first letter* (shows initial of fill-in-the-blank/short-answer solution) and *no assistance* (as baseline).

4 Methodology

4.1 Formal Problem Statement

We denote the set of practice questions inside the system as $Q = \{q_1, \ldots, q_k\}$. Each question $q \in Q$ is associated with a set of n_q assistance actions $A_q = \{a_{q,1}, \ldots, a_{q,n_q}\}$ that the system can use to support students after their first incorrect response. In this work, we approach the problem of learning one effective assistance policy for the entire practice system by learning one question-specific multi-armed bandit policy π_q for each practice question $q \in Q$. During deployment, π_q responds to each assistance query for question q by selecting one assistance action $a_q \in A_q$ and in return receives a real-valued reward $r_q \in \mathbb{R}$ which is assumed to be sampled from an action-specific and time-invariant distribution R_{a_q} with mean μ_{a_q}. The optimal question-specific assistance policy π_q^* maximizes the expected reward by always selecting action $a_q^* = \arg\max_{a_q \in A_q} \mu_{a_q}$.

For us, multi-armed bandits are a framework that enables our system to automatically make design decisions by learning from the observed behavior of earlier students. It is difficult for experts to predict the most effective design ahead of time [18] and the bandit framework enables the system to estimate the effects of potential design choices using student data to refine the ITS automatically over time. Section 6 discusses benefits and limitations of our bandit formulation.

4.2 Data Collection

This work focuses on an online high-school Biology course that has been in continuous refinement for over ten years. Because of this, its content base features *multiple* assistance actions for individual questions. This raises the question of *what type* of assistance action is most effective for a particular question (e.g., should one provide hints or keyword definitions?). Even if the domain experts decide on a specific type of assistance, it is still unclear *what action* from the reduced action set is most effective (e.g., which exact hint should one show?).

To address these questions, we conduct an experiment to quantify the impact of *individual* assistance actions on different measures of learning outcomes. Starting from Aug 23rd, 2022, a randomized assistance policy was deployed. Each time this policy is queried to provide assistance for a question $q \in Q$, it uniformly (with same chance) chooses one action at random from the set A_q. An overview of the data collected up to Jan 11th, 2023, is provided by Table 1.

4.3 Measures of Learning Outcomes

One key question in this work is how to define a reward function that takes as input information about a student practice session and that outputs a reward value that quantifies the degree to which the assistance provided by the system led to successful learning. This reward function is central as it serves as objective during policy training and thus directly affects the experience of future students.

Table 1. Data collection overview. The *Overall* column shows statistics on the raw data collected for all content in the Biology course. The *Offline/Online Evaluation* columns show statistics on the data that went into the offline/online evaluation experiments.

	Overall	Offline Eval.	Online Eval.
# of questions	12,496	1,336	4,521
# of assistance actions	36,354	7,707	11,406
# of concepts	470	166	166
# of students	191,554	164,516	27,268
# of practice sessions	1,274,072	1,007,850	62,464
# of student responses	20,425,691	17,081,054	953,185
# of shown actions	4,842,856	3,266,171	234,178
average correctness	63.3%	60.0%	61.1%
average completion	75.1%	77.1%	69.4%
collection period (days)	142	142	9

The designers of the practice system want to promote growth in *student knowledge* as well as *student engagement.* Unfortunately, student knowledge and engagement are both unobservable variables and the system is limited in that it can only access data that describes the student's observable interactions with the website interface. Because of this, we compiled a list specifying different measures of learning outcomes that can be computed from the observed log data:

- *Reattempt correct*: Binary indicator ($\{0, 1\}$) of whether the student is correct on the reattempt directly after the assistance action.
- *Student Ability*: 3-Parameter item response theory (IRT)-based ability estimate using all first attempt responses computed at end of session. IRT is a logistic model that explains response correctness by fitting student- (ability) and question-specific (difficulty, discrimination, guessing) parameters [5].
- *Session success*: Binary indicator ($\{0, 1\}$) of whether the student achieves 10 correct responses in the practice session.
- *Future correct rate*: Proportion of student's correct responses on first attempts on other practice questions following the assistance action.
- *Next question correct*: Binary indicator ($\{0, 1\}$) of whether the student is correct on the next question following the assistance action (used in [21]).

- *Future response time*: Measures the student's average response time on questions after an assistance action in seconds (individual question response time values are capped at 60 s (95% percentile) to mitigate outliers).
- *Student confidence*: Tertiary indicator ($\{1, 2, 3\}$) of the student's self-reported confidence level at the end of the practice session.

In the experiments we study the relationships between these individual outcome measures (Sect. 5.1) which leads us to defining our final reward function R as

$$R(s, q) = 0.4 \cdot \text{reattempt\_correct}(s, q) + 0.6 \cdot \text{student\_ability}(s). \quad (1)$$

Here, s represents information about a student's entire practice session and q indicates the question for which the student received assistance. The reward value is computed as a weighted sum that considers the student's success at reattempting question q as well as their overall practice session performance.

4.4 Offline Policy Optimization and Evaluation

Preprocessing. Before policy optimization and evaluation we perform the following preprocessing steps: (i) To avoid early dropouts, we only consider practice sessions in which students respond to at least five different questions. (ii) To avoid memorization effects, we only consider each student's first practice attempt for each concept. (iii) To avoid confounding, we estimate the effects of individual assistance actions using only practice sessions in which the student did not request a hint before their first attempt. (iv) To achieve high confidence in our effect estimates we focus on practice questions with at least 100 samples per assistance action. As a result, we consider a set of 1,336 unique questions from 166 concepts associated with 7,707 assistance actions and draw from over 3,200,000 assistance queries occurring in over 1,000,000 different practice sessions (Table 1).

Optimization. To train and evaluate the effects of different assistance policies without conducting repeated live experiments we rely on offline policy optimization [15] and leverage log data collected by the randomized exploration policy. First, we estimate the effectiveness of individual assistance actions by computing the mean value for each learning outcome measure across all relevant practice sessions. From there, our experiments study various multi-armed bandit policies trained to optimize different outcome measures. In preliminary experiments, we found that when using measures with high variance as training objectives (i.e., *student ability* and *session success*), the conventional policy optimization approach–that for each question selects the assistance action estimated to be optimal–struggles to reliably identify actions that perform well in the evaluation on separate test data. For the average question we found optimizing policies for *reattempt correctness*–a measure with focus on a single question and thus lower variance–to be the most effective way to also boost *student ability* and *session success* due to its positive correlations to the other measures (Fig. 3 left).

Still, for a sizeable number of questions the conventional approach yielded better policies when directly optimizing for the measure of interest (Sect. 5.2). These tended to be questions with more available data or with larger differences in the effects of individual assistance actions. This motivated the design of a training algorithm that for each question automatically decides whether we have sufficient data to optimize the measure of interest (e.g., *reward*) directly or whether we should use the low variance *reattempt correctness* measure. We first use the training data to identify the two actions that optimize the measure of interest and *reattempt correctness.* We then conduct a one-sided Welch T-Test to decide whether the former has a significantly larger effect on the measure of interest than the *reattempt correctness* action and if not select the low variance *reattempt correctness* measure as the question-specific training objective.

Evaluation. In the offline evaluation experiments we report mean performance estimates derived from a 20 times repeated 5-fold cross validation. In each fold 80% of practice sessions are used for policy training and the remaining 20% are used for testing. This process yields a statistically unbiased estimate of the bandit policy's performance as it simulates a series of interactions with different students inside the system and avoids overfitting effects of sampling with replacement-based approaches [15]. For the significance test we determine a suitable p-value for each individual outcome measure by evaluating $p \in \{0.01, 0.02, \ldots, 0.1\}$ via cross-validation. The final policy used in live A/B evaluation is trained using data from all practice sessions and optimizes our reward function (Eq. 1).

5 Results

5.1 Assistance Action Evaluation

We estimate the effects of individual assistance actions on different measures of learning outcomes by leveraging the student log data collected by the randomized assistance policy (Sect. 4.2). One example of the results of this evaluation process is provided by Fig. 2. It shows the question text, the set of available assistance actions and estimates on how each action affects different outcome measures. We can see how the *paragraph* that provides detailed information leads to the highest reattempt correctness rate. In comparison, *hint 1* leads to a lower reattempt correctness, but conveys insights that improve overall session performance as captured by the final student ability score. We can also identify actions that are not helpful. For example, *hint 2* and *vocabulary* both lead to worse outcomes than showing *no assistance.* Overall, these estimates are very compelling for the content creators, as they allow them to reflect on how the individual resources they designed affect the student experience in different ways.

To study the relationships between the different learning outcome measures we analyse average within question correlations across the 1,336 questions (Fig. 3). We focus on within question correlation instead of total correlation to be more robust towards effects caused by systematic differences between individual questions (e.g., difficulty). We observe that reattempt correctness is most correlated with the IRT-based student ability estimates ($r = 0.27$) and that it is mostly uncorrelated with next question correctness ($r = 0.04$). This shows that while assistance actions can improve students' overall session performance, due to differences between individual questions, it is not enough to focus only on the next question. Matching our intuition, ability estimates correlate with session success ($r = 0.35$), future correctness ($r = 0.64$) and next question correctness rates ($r = 0.36$). This is because these measures all consider first attempt response correctness. Student response time has a low positive correlation to student ability ($r = 0.23$) and self-reported student confidence shows very low correlations with the other considered measures.

Before moving on to training assistance policies we quantify the degree to which we can differentiate the effects of assistance actions for individual questions based on the available log data via analysis of variance (ANOVA). Compared to the bandit problem which tries to identify the single most effective action, ANOVA focuses on the simpler question of whether there are statistically significant differences in mean effects between individual actions. For a p-value of 0.05 ANOVA rejects the null hypothesis for *reattempt correctness* for 83.2% ($n = 1,111$), for *student ability* for 13.3% ($n = 178$) and for *session success rate* for 9.6% ($n = 128$) of questions. We can explain this by studying sample variance and the effect size gaps between the most and least effective assistance

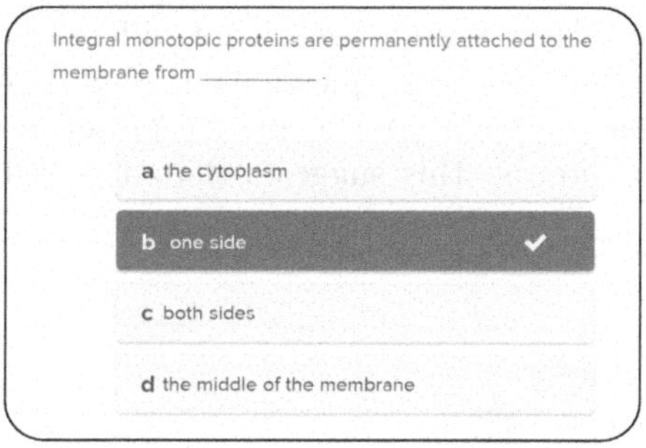

(a) Practice Question.

- *hint 1*: The prefix **mono-** means **single** or **alone.**
- *hint 2*: The word **integral** means **essential** or **necessary to make whole.**
- *paragraph*: Transmembrane proteins span the entire plasma membrane. Transmembrane proteins are found in all types of biological membranes. Integral monotopic proteins are permanently attached to the membrane from only one side.
- *vocabulary*:
  - cytoplasm: Material inside the cell membrane, including the watery cytosol and other cell structures except the nucleus if one is present.
  - protein: A peptide that is greater than one hundred amino acids in length.

(b) Assistance Actions.

	n	Reward	Reatt. Cor.	Stud. Abil.	Sess. Succ.
no assist.	872	0.025 ±.079	0.313 ±.031	-0.167 ±.125	0.925 ±.017
hint 1	986	**0.394** ±.077	0.693 ±.029	**0.195** ±.121	0.934 ±.015
hint 2	940	-0.029 ±.081	0.255 ±.028	-0.219 ±.130	0.920 ±.017
paragraph	940	0.363 ±.078	**0.774** ±.027	0.088 ±.121	**0.935** ±.016
vocabulary	936	-0.033 ±.078	0.259 ±.028	-0.228 ±.126	0.929 ±.016

(c) Action Performance Estimates.

Fig. 2. Example of assistance action evaluation for one individual question.

action for each outcome measure. By only focusing on the current question, *reattempt correctness* exhibits on average across the 1,336 question a better ratio between action effect gaps and sample variance ($\delta = 0.230$, $\sigma^2 = 0.229$) compared to the *student ability* ($\delta = 0.302$, $\sigma^2 = 3.665$) and *session completion rate* ($\delta = 0.042$, $\sigma^2 = 0.085$) measures which describe overall session performance.

5.2 Offline Policy Evaluation

While ANOVA finds significant differences in mean action effects on *reattempt correctness* for most questions, it only detects differences on *student ability* and *session completion* for a smaller subset of questions. For our offline policy evaluation process this suggests that it is difficult to reliably identify the optimal

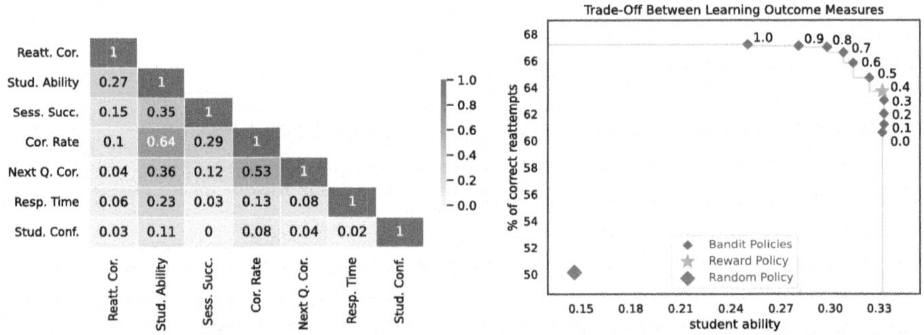

Fig. 3. [Left] Average within question correlations between individual measures of learning outcomes across 1,336 questions. [Right] Pareto front visualizing the estimated average performance of policies optimized to increase the final student ability estimates (x-axis) and reattempt correctness rate (y-axis) across 178 questions. Each bandit policy is marked with a number that indicates how it weights the two objectives.

Table 2. Offline evaluation of various policies across the 178 questions for which ANOVA indicated significant differences ($p < 0.05$) in mean action effects on student ability. The first two rows show no assistance and randomized policies as baselines. The following four rows are bandit policies optimized directly for different outcome measures and the reward function. We report mean values and 95% confidence intervals.

policy/measure	Reward	Reatt. Cor.	Stud. Abil.	Sess. Succ.
no assistance	0.241 ±.064	0.433 ±.023	0.113 ±.106	0.801 ±.039
random	0.288 ±.067	0.501 ±.021	0.146 ±.109	0.806 ±.039
reattempt correct	0.419 ±.071	**0.672** ±.020	0.250 ±.115	0.816 ±.038
student ability	0.442 ±.068	0.606 ±.025	**0.332** ±.109	0.819 ±.038
session success	0.371 ±.068	0.573 ±.025	0.237 ±.109	0.817 ±.037
reward	**0.454** ±.068	0.637 ±.023	**0.332** ±.108	**0.820** ±.038

assistance actions for the latter two measures even when having access to hundreds of samples per action. Indeed, in preliminary experiments we found that action effect rankings based on training data often deviate from rankings based on separate test data. For the average question we found training assistance policies based on *reattempt correctness* estimates to be the most effective way to boost all three outcome measures. This is due to its lower variance and the fact that improvements in *reattempt correctness* are positively correlated with improvements in *student ability* and *session completion rates* (Fig. 3 left).

Still, for 178 (13.3%) of the 1,366 questions ANOVA detected significant differences in action effects on *student ability* which is a core measure of interest. To study the relationship between *reattempt correctness* and *student ability* for these 178 questions, we train bandit policies for different objectives. Here, analog to the reward function (Eq. 1), we assign each policy a weight $w_1 \in \{0, 0.1, \ldots, 1.0\}$ and compute its reward values by linearly weighting *reattempt correctness* with w_1 and *student ability* with $1 - w_1$. We visualize the Pareto front defined by the resulting policies (Fig. 3 right) and observe performance estimates that range in *reattempt correctness* rates from 60.6% to 67.2% and in *student ability* from

Table 3. Offline evaluation of various policies across 1, 336 questions. The first two rows show no assistance and randomized policies as baselines. The following four rows are bandit policies optimized with our algorithm for different learning outcome measures and the reward function. We report mean values and 95% confidence intervals.

policy/measure	Reward	Reatt. Cor	Stud. Abil.	Sess. Succ.
no assistance	0.218 ±.026	0.498 ±.008	0.032 ±.042	0.815 ±.014
random	0.255 ±.026	0.551 ±.007	0.058 ±.042	0.820 ±.013
reattempt correct	0.327 ±.026	**0.666** ±.007	0.101 ±.043	**0.827** ±.013
student ability	0.327 ±.026	0.660 ±.007	**0.105** ±.043	**0.827** ±.013
session success	0.326 ±.026	0.663 ±.007	0.101 ±.043	**0.827** ±.013
reward	**0.328** ±.026	0.664 ±.007	0.104 ±.043	**0.827** ±.013

Table 4. Types of assistance actions selected by the multi-armed bandit policy learned using our reward function for all 1,336 questions. The individual columns show how the policy focuses on different types of assistance actions for different types of questions.

action/question	Mult.-Choice	All-That-Apply	Fill-Blank	Short-Answ.
no assistance	5.0%	7.3%	1.8%	3.4%
hint	11.4%	15.6%	6.6%	5.6%
paragraph	51.2%	43.1%	57.9%	55.1%
vocabulary	5.7%	16.5%	1.8%	3.4%
hide distractor	26.8%	17.4%	-	-
first letter	-	-	31.7%	32.6%

0.250 to 0.332. All learned policies outperform the *random* policy significantly. In collaboration with domain experts we select $w_1 = 0.4$ as reward function to train the assistance policy for live evaluation as it improves both measures substantially. Table 2 provides detailed performance statistics for policies trained to optimize different outcome measures across the 178 questions.

To train an assistance policy for all 1,366 questions we designed an algorithm that for each question decides whether we have sufficient data to optimize the measure of interest (e.g., *reward*) directly or whether we should use the low variance *reattempt correctness* measure (Sect. 4.4). Table 3 shows average performance metrics across 1,336 questions for a policy that always selects the *no assistance* action, the *random* policy, and four policies trained using our algorithm to optimize *reattempt correctness* rates, *student ability*, *successful session completion* rates, and *reward* function. The algorithm resolves the variance issue and the trained policies enhance the student experience in different ways.

Lastly, we study for which types of questions the final policy offers which types of assistance actions to maximize the *reward* objective. Table 4 shows for each question type for what proportion of questions the policy finds a certain assistance type to be most effective. We find that the policy utilizes a diverse blend of different assistance types for each type of question and that paragraph actions are selected most frequently overall. Because of this, we compare the effects of a policy that always selects *paragraph* actions to the trained *reward* policy in an additional experiment. Across the 1,175 questions with paragraphs, we find that the *reward policy* outperforms the *paragraph* policy in all outcome measures (*reward:* 0.336/0.299, *reattempt correctness:* 67.3%/61.5%, *student ability:* 0.112/0.089, *session success:* 84.0%/83.7%). Thus, the data-driven approach benefits by selecting effective teaching actions on a question-by-question basis.

Table 5. Live policy evaluation. We randomly assign student practice sessions to the randomized policy ($n = 31,527$) and the learned bandit policy ($n = 30,937$) condition, track various outcome measures and report mean values and 95% confidence intervals.

policy/measure	Reward	Reatt. Cor.	Stud. Abil.	Sess. Succ.
random	0.753 ±.016	0.585 ±.004	0.866 ±.026	0.676 ±.005
bandit	**0.881** ±.015	**0.683** ±.004	**1.013** ±.024	**0.712** ±.005

5.3 Online Policy Evaluation

To evaluate the policy optimized using our training algorithm we compare its ability to provide students with effective assistance actions to the randomized assistance policy. For this a nine-day long A/B evaluation (Apr 5th to Apr 13th, 2023) was conducted in which practice sessions for the 166 studied concepts were randomly assigned to the bandit and the randomized policy condition. During this period we collected log data describing over 62,000 sessions from over 20,000 different students (Table 1). Even though the learned assistance policy implemented only 1,336 question-specific bandit policies, it was able to provide learned actions for 87,721 (74.9%) of the 117,180 queries and only needed to default to random action selection in 29,459 (25.1%) cases. This is because the majority of incorrect responses occur on a smaller number of questions.

Table 5 reports average performance for the two different policies. The trained assistance policy outperforms the randomized policy significantly in all outcome measures, achieving on average a 9.8% improvement in reattempt correctness rate and a 0.147 higher student ability estimate. The session success rate improvement from 67.6% to 71.2% corresponds to a 11.1% reduction in sessions in which students did not achieve the practice target. We note that in contrast to the offline evaluation (Sect. 5.2) where we estimate effects based on individual assistance queries, here we compute metrics based on the session level.

6 Discussion

The results show how the offline evaluation approach can leverage large-scale student log data to quantify the impact of individual assistance actions (e.g., hints and keyword definitions) for each question on different measures of student learning outcomes (e.g., reattempt correctness, practice completion). This allows ITS designers to monitor and reflect on fine-grained design decisions inside the system (e.g., which assistance action for which question) and enables a data-driven design process in which the designers can specify a reward function to train an assistance policy that promotes the desired student learning experience. The live use evaluation confirms that this process provides the system with the ability to learn to teach better automatically over time, by showing how the actions selected by the learned multi-armed bandit policies lead to significant improvements in learning outcomes compared to a randomized assistance policy.

By studying the assistance actions selected by our optimized policy (Fig. 4) we observe that there is no single best type of assistance that is always most effective. This emphasizes the importance of algorithms that can identify the most effective teaching action for each individual practice question based on observational data. Interestingly, the policy blends more informative (e.g., paragraphs) with less informative assistance actions (e.g., hints) and decides for some questions to provide no additional help at all. This indicates a trade-off between giving and withholding information during the learning process which is a phenoma that has been described as *assistance dilemma* in prior research [11].

Our methodology combines multi-armed bandit and offline policy evaluation techniques [15] with large-scale student log data to compute high confidence estimates on the effects of individual assistance actions. One inherent property of our multi-armed bandit formulation of the problem is that it focuses on selecting the teaching action that is most effective for the *average* student and does not attempt to provide assistance conditioned on the *individual* student, and does not capture synergies that could occur when certain combinations of assistance actions are shown to a student in the same practice session. While a reinforcement learning approach could be used to address both of these shortcomings, the volume of training data required for such an approach would increase dramatically, and it would be much harder to compute statistically significant estimates on the effects of individual policies before deployment. We will explore the potential of personalized assistance policies via contextual bandit and reinforcement learning algorithms [7,22] in future work. Another future direction is the integration of online bandit algorithms [14] into the current system to keep enhancing the assistance policies by adaptively sampling individual actions based on evolving effect estimates in live deployment. Adaptive sampling is of particular interest to us as the pool of questions and assistance actions is continuously refined.

7 Conclusion

In this paper we discussed a large-scale online tutoring system that uses student log data to learn which of several candidate assistance actions (e.g., hints and paragraphs) to provide to students when they answer a particular practice question incorrectly. We used offline policy evaluation to leverage data from over 1,000,000 student practice sessions to evaluate the effects of individual assistance actions and multi-armed bandit policies on various measures of learning outcomes. We studied relationships among outcome measures and designed an algorithm to train an assistance policy that optimizes the student's success at answering the current question, as well as their overall practice session performance. In a live evaluation with over 20,000 students we compared the trained assistance policy to a randomized assistance policy finding that the system's ability to learn to select more effective teaching actions automatically over time enables significant improvements in learning outcomes of future students. The trained policy now supports thousands of students practicing Biology each day.

Acknowledgements. This research was supported by the AFOSR under award FA95501710218.

References

1. Ausin, M.S., Azizsoltani, H., Barnes, T., Chi, M.: Leveraging deep reinforcement learning for pedagogical policy induction in an intelligent tutoring system. In: Proceedings of the 12th International Conference on EDM, pp. 168–177. EDM, Montréal, Canada (2019)
2. Ausin, M.S., Maniktala, M., Barnes, T., Chi, M.: Tackling the credit assignment problem in reinforcement learning-induced pedagogical policies with neural networks. In: Roll, I., McNamara, D., Sosnovsky, S., Luckin, R., Dimitrova, V. (eds.) AIED 2021. LNCS (LNAI), vol. 12748, pp. 356–368. Springer, Cham (2021). https://doi.org/10.1007/978-3-030-78292-4_29
3. Barnes, T., Stamper, J.: Toward automatic hint generation for logic proof tutoring using historical student data. In: Woolf, B.P., Aïmeur, E., Nkambou, R., Lajoie, S. (eds.) ITS 2008. LNCS, vol. 5091, pp. 373–382. Springer, Heidelberg (2008). https://doi.org/10.1007/978-3-540-69132-7_41

4. Chi, M., VanLehn, K., Litman, D.: Do micro-level tutorial decisions matter: applying reinforcement learning to induce pedagogical tutorial tactics. In: Aleven, V., Kay, J., Mostow, J. (eds.) ITS 2010. LNCS, vol. 6094, pp. 224–234. Springer, Heidelberg (2010). https://doi.org/10.1007/978-3-642-13388-6_27
5. De Ayala, R.J.: The Theory and Practice of Item Response Theory. Guilford, New York, NY, USA (2013)
6. Doroudi, S., Aleven, V., Brunskill, E.: Where's the reward? Int. J. AIED **29**(4), 568–620 (2019)
7. Fahid, F.M., Rowe, J.P., Spain, R.D., Goldberg, B.S., Pokorny, R., Lester, J.: Adaptively scaffolding cognitive engagement with batch constrained Deep Q-networks. In: Roll, I., McNamara, D., Sosnovsky, S., Luckin, R., Dimitrova, V. (eds.) AIED 2021. LNCS (LNAI), vol. 12748, pp. 113–124. Springer, Cham (2021). https://doi.org/10.1007/978-3-030-78292-4_10
8. Fancsali, S., Murphy, A., Ritter, S.: Closing the loop in educational data science with an open source architecture for large-scale field trials. In: Proceedings of the 15th International Conference on EDM, pp. 834–838. EDM, Durham, UK (July 2022)
9. Georgila, K., Core, M.G., Nye, B.D., Karumbaiah, S., Auerbach, D., Ram, M.: Using reinforcement learning to optimize the policies of an intelligent tutoring system for interpersonal skills training. In: Proceedings of the 18th International Conference on Autonomous Agents and MultiAgent Systems, pp. 737–745. AAMAS, Richland, SC (2019)
10. Ju, S., Zhou, G., Barnes, T., Chi, M.: Pick the moment: identifying critical pedagogical decisions using long-short term rewards. In: Proceedings of the 13th International Conference on EDM, pp. 126–136. EDM, Virtual (2020)
11. Koedinger, K.R., Aleven, V.: Exploring the assistance dilemma in experiments with cognitive tutors. Educ. Psychol. Rev. **19**(3), 239–264 (2007)
12. Koedinger, K.R., Booth, J.L., Klahr, D.: Instructional complexity and the science to constrain it. Science **342**(6161), 935–937 (2013)
13. Kulik, J.A., Fletcher, J.D.: Effectiveness of intelligent tutoring systems: a meta-analytic review. Rev. Educ. Res. **86**(1), 42–78 (2016)
14. Lattimore, T., Szepesvári, C.: Bandit Algorithms. Cambridge University Press, Cambridge, UK (2020)
15. Li, L., Chu, W., Langford, J., Wang, X.: Unbiased offline evaluation of contextual-bandit-based news article recommendation algorithms. In: Proceedings of the 4th International Conference on WSDM, pp. 297–306. WSDM '11, ACM, New York, NY, USA (2011)
16. McLaren, B.M., Richey, J.E., Nguyen, H., Hou, X.: How instructional context can impact learning with educational technology: Lessons from a study with a digital learning game. Comput. Educ. **178**, 1–20 (2022)
17. Nagashima, T., et al.: How does sustaining and interleaving visual scaffolding help learners? a classroom study with an intelligent tutoring system. In: Proceedings of the Annual Meeting of the Cognitive Science Society, vol. 44 (2022)
18. Nathan, M.J., Koedinger, K.R., Alibali, M.W.: Expert blind spot: When content knowledge eclipses pedagogical content knowledge. In: Proceedings of the 3rd International Conference on Cognitive Science, vol. 3, pp. 644–648. USTC Press, Beijing, China (2001)
19. Ostrow, K., Heffernan, N., Williams, J.J.: Tomorrow's edtech today: establishing a learning platform as a collaborative research tool for sound science. Teach. Coll. Rec. **119**(3), 1–36 (2017)

20. Patikorn, T., Heffernan, N.T.: Effectiveness of crowd-sourcing on-demand assistance from teachers in online learning platforms. In: Proceedings of the 7th International Conference on Learning @ Scale, pp. 115–124. L@S '20, ACM, New York, NY, USA (2020)
21. Prihar, E., Haim, A., Sales, A., Heffernan, N.: Automatic interpretable personalized learning. In: Proceedings of the 9th International Conference on Learning @ Scale, pp. 1–11. L@S '22, ACM, New York, NY, USA (2022)
22. Prihar, E., Patikorn, T., Botelho, A., Sales, A., Heffernan, N.: Toward personalizing students' education with crowdsourced tutoring. In: Proceedings of the 8th International Conference on Learning @ Scale, pp. 37–45. L@S '21, ACM, New York, NY, USA (2021)
23. Reza, M., Kim, J., Bhattacharjee, A., Rafferty, A.N., Williams, J.J.: The MOOClet framework: unifying experimentation, dynamic improvement, and personalization in online courses. In: Proceedings of the 8th ACM Conference on Learning @ Scale, pp. 15–26. L@S '21, ACM, New York, NY, USA (2021)
24. Roschelle, J., Feng, M., Murphy, R.F., Mason, C.A.: Online mathematics homework increases student achievement. AERA Open **2**(4), 1–12 (2016)
25. Spain, R., Rowe, J., Goldberg, B., Pokorny, R., Lester, J., Rockville, M.: Enhancing learning outcomes through adaptive remediation with gift. In: Proceedings of the I/ITSEC, pp. 1–11. I/ITSEC, Orlando, Florida (2019)
26. Spain, R., et al.: A reinforcement learning approach to adaptive remediation in online training. J. Defense Model. Simul. **2**(19), 173–193 (2021)
27. Williams, J.J., et al.: AXIS: generating explanations at scale with learner sourcing and machine learning. In: Proceedings of the 3rd ACM Conference on Learning @ Scale, pp. 379–388. L@S '16, ACM, New York, USA (2016)
28. Williams, J.J., Rafferty, A.N., Tingley, D., Ang, A., Lasecki, W.S., Kim, J.: Enhancing online problems through instructor-centered tools for randomized experiments. In: Proceedings of the CHI Conference on Human Factors in Computing Systems, pp. 1–12. CHI '18, ACM, New York, NY, USA (2018)

Understanding Peer Feedback Contributions Using Natural Language Processing

Mayara Simões de Oliveira Castro[1], Rafael Ferreira Mello[2,6(✉)], Giuseppe Fiorentino[1], Olga Viberg[3(✉)], Daniel Spikol[4], Martine Baars[5], and Dragan Gašević[6]

[1] Universidade Federal Rural de Pernambuco, Recife, PE, Brazil
[2] CESAR School, Rua Bione, Cais do Apolo, 220, CEP: 50030-390 Recife, PE, Brazil
rflm@cesar.org.br
[3] KTH Royal Institute of Technology, Stockholm, Sweden
oviberg@kth.se
[4] University of Copenhagen, Copenhagen, Denmark
ds@di.ku.dk
[5] Department of psychology, education and child studies, Erasmus University Rotterdam, Rotterdam, Netherlands
baars@essb.eur.nl
[6] Monash University, 20 Exhibition Walk, Clayton VIC, 3800, Australia
dragan.gasevic@monash.edu

Abstract. Peer feedback has been widely used in computer-supported collaborative learning (CSCL) setting to improve students' engagement with massive courses. Although the peer feedback process increases students' self-regulatory practice, metacognition, and academic achievement, instructors need to go through large amounts of feedback text data which is much more time-consuming. To address this challenge, the present study proposes an automated content analysis approach to identify relevant categories in peer feedback based on traditional and sequence-based classifiers using TF-IDF and content-independent features. We use a data set from an extensive course (N = 231 students) in the setting of engineering higher education. In particular, a total of 2,444 peer feedback messages were analyzed. The CRF classification model based on the TF-IDF features achieved the best performance. The results illustrate that the ability to scale up the automatic analysis of peer feedback provides new opportunities for student-improved learning and improved teacher support in higher education at scale.

Keywords: Content Analysis · Peer Feedback · Natural Language Processing · Computer Supported Collaborative Learning · Higher Education

O. Viberg et al. (Eds.): EC-TEL 2023, LNCS 14200, pp. 399–414, 2023.
https://doi.org/10.1007/978-3-031-42682-7_27

1 Introduction

Peer assessment and peer feedback are key components in the collaborative learning setting [20]. Peer assessment has been shown to increase learning performance [24], and peer feedback can help students reflect on their contributions and identify areas for improvement [26]. The instructor's participation in orchestrating the peer feedback process is necessary. However, this task is time-consuming and often impossible to keep track of the feedback given by each student in a group in a large-enrolment course (more than 100 students) [45]. Therefore, there is a need to develop tools and methods that would allow for automated feedback analysis to improve teacher support and, ultimately, learning.

Recent studies have applied machine learning methods to automate content analysis in educational settings [7,13,14]. More specifically, previous research proposed the development of tools and models to automate content analysis of instructor-provided feedback to support improved learning practices [7,35]. Nevertheless, to the best of our knowledge, no previous study focused on analysing peer feedback in large enrolment courses aiming to understand how students provide peer assessment/feedback.

Therefore, this paper presents the results of a study that examined machine learning algorithms trained based on a combination of traditional and state-of-the-art natural language processing features for the automated content analysis of peer feedback. The features analysed included (i) TF-IDF, (ii) content-independent features from Linguistic Inquiry Word Count (LIWC, [43]) and Coh-Metrix [16], (iii) sequential content-independent features approach [14] that considers the sequence of the text to extract features, and (iv) BERT linguistic model. This study uses a dataset from a massive introductory course (N = 231 students) at a large engineering university in Sweden. The course was run in a computer-supported collaborative learning setting. The best algorithm evaluated reached Cohen's κ of 0.43 in the feedback analysis. Further, we report on the results of a detailed analysis of the most predictive features for each category extracted from the CRF model. This information could ultimately increase our understanding of the nature and role of peer feedback in the students' learning process in a computer-supported collaborative learning setting.

2 Background

2.1 Peer Assessment and Feedback in Computer-Supported Collaborative Learning

Collaborative learning has been shown to relate to student learning performance (e.g., [48]). In CSCL settings, collaborative learning processes are supported by technology [11]. Harnessing the technological affordances and pedagogical strategies, learners are supported in their learning process as a group, knowledge sharing, and co-construction [21]. In their meta-analysis on the effects of key elements (e.g., the role of collaboration, computer use, learning settings and supporting strategies) and in CSCL settings, Chen et al. [8] identified that peer assessment and peer feedback moderately affected knowledge gains, perception, and social interaction in these environments.

In the CSCL setting, peer assessment and feedback are key factors of success [20]. Peer assessment has been found to affect student learning positively [24]. Generally, students are shown to exhibit positive attitudes towards peer assessment (e.g., [38]), and they find that peer assessment practices help them to divide tasks equally [27]. In this context, peer feedback is understood as the communication process between students, providing each other with information to increase learning performance [37]. Peer feedback has often been considered an educational activity for enhancing students' learning opportunities. Moreover, peer feedback aims to bridge the gap between a student's current performance and desired level of performance [25]. In higher education, peer assessment and feedback have been found to enhance student learning, academic achievement, and metacognition [40].

Moreover, earlier research on peer feedback has demonstrated that various kinds and levels of specificity of the information provided in feedback lead to different learning outcomes [42]. Among the different types of feedback specificity, scholars argue that supporting comments and suggestions are important since they could provide further understanding of how different types of feedback could promote further improvement to inform future feedback training and practices [10]. Additionally, affective feedback (e.g., in the form of text messages) uses affective language to support or bestow praise or criticism by demonstrating positive or negative feelings about the work [10].

Researchers have also stated that formative feedback examines affective and cognitive feedback practices [33]. In this direction, cognitive feedback involves the content of the work, and the feedback comment could include specifying and explaining aspects of the work under review; it highlights problems, explanations and suggestions and could influence the receiver's performance in various ways. Others categorized and studied peer feedback in terms of cognitive and metacognitive (i.e., such feedback is evaluative and reflective that helps students develop peer feedback nature [10]), demonstrating that affective feedback is essential. However, it has not been confirmed by the later studies that showed that affective feedback does not necessarily influence post-feedback behavior [15].

Although the benefits of understanding the nature of peer feedback, the task of analysing the whole content generated by students in peer feedback activities becomes challenging and time-consuming for the instructor, especially in large enrolment courses [45]. Extracting the main information from peer feedback is important as it could help instructors to understand the main questions and students' mistakes, which supports instructors' feedback and could lead to a change in the course design [45]. Thus, the development of tools to support this process is extremely valuable.

In short, the previous studies listed in this section synthesised the key aspects of peer feedback into five distinct categories: (i) Management, which pertains to the students' contributions during project development; (ii) Affect, encompassing the affective messages conveyed in the feedback by students; (iii) Interpersonal factors, referring to positive and negative interactions that occur during group work; (iv) Suggestions for improvement, including explicit recommendations for enhancing the proposed activity; and (v) Cognition, covering reflective and evaluative messages. Additionally, a Miscellaneous category was included to capture any messages that did not fit into the other categories.

2.2 Computational Approaches to Automated Content Analysis

Several studies have developed and applied computational approaches for automated content analysis in different educational contexts to automatically analyse large amounts of textual data, including student essays, forum posts, and feedback [7,13,14]. In the context of feedback analysis, Lee and Lim [23] propose an automated analysis of feedback about university courses to highlight students' main concerns with the institution based on their feedback's key terms. The authors created several graph representations based on the top words in the feedback message. This study has demonstrated that processing and understanding a large amount of unstructured data generated using text analytics is possible.

Recently, several studies have applied natural language processing methods and linguistic tools (e.g., LIWC and Coh-Metrix) for extracting specific categories from feedback messages provided by instructors [7,35]. The initial study proposed several models to automatically identify the feedback levels proposed in [17] (e.g., task, process, self-regulation and self). The random forest classifier, the best-performing algorithm, reached Cohen's κ of 0.39 [7]. Osakwe et al. [35] evaluated the same categories, but the authors also used several sampling methods and an ablation study to overcome the limitations in the previous paper. In the best-case scenario, Cohen's κ increased to 0.42. In both papers, the authors presented the best predictive features.

In addition to traditional machine learning models, deep learning approaches have been proven effective for text classification in educational settings [12]. An example is the work of [3] that evaluated the performance of random forest-based algorithms and the BERT deep learning linguistic model for automatic detection of social presence in online discussions. The authors compare the approach with traditional text mining and linguistic features like LIWC and Coh-metrix with the approach using the fine-tuned BERT language model for social presence classification. The results demonstrate that the XGBoost and AdaBoost (Adaptive Boosting) algorithms outperformed the BERT model in the automated classification of online discussion messages.

Finally, we highlight the research performed by Ferreira et al. [14] that proposed a new approach for automated content analysis of written essays, called sequential content-independent features, using the features from adjacent sentences and not only from the analysed sentences to incorporate information [14]. The authors suggested that this approach could be useful when the classification task is related to a sentence in a large text (e.g., a sentence in a feedback message). They evaluated traditional machine learning algorithms combined with

TF-IDF, content-independent, and sequential content-independent features. In this study, the best classifiers' performance was the XGBoost and CRF models based on the proposed sequential content-independent feature set, demonstrating the potential of using the sequence in the text as a key extracting factor in this type of analysis.

3 Research Questions

The previous studies demonstrate the potential of automated content analysis of educational feedback. This study proposes the evaluation of traditional TF-IDF and content-independent features combined with traditional machine learning algorithms and BERT for the automated content analysis of peer feedback according to the six categories described in Sect. 2.1: Management, Affect, Interpersonal factors, Suggestions for improvement, Cognition, and Miscellaneous. As such, this study aims to answer the following research question:

Research Question 1 (RQ1): To what extent can natural language processing algorithms automatically identify categories of peer feedback?

Although automated content analysis of feedback messages could facilitate the instructors' interactions with the students in the course [40], the classification per se does not provide insights into the most relevant features. Previous studies demonstrated the potential of further unpacking details about the most important features in the educational settings [7,14]. Therefore, we utilised the best-performing classifier developed in this study to address the second research question:

Research Question 2 (RQ2): Which features are the most predictive of peer feedback categories?

4 Method

4.1 Course Design and Dataset

In the studied context, students conducted project-based tasks as a part of a design project, performed in groups of four to six students along with seminars and lectures. To support both students in their collaborative learning process as well as teaching assistants and the examiner in the assessment process, a CSCL assessment system (CLASS) has been introduced in the course (for details, see [46]). The CLASS system has three key modules: i) peer assessment, 2) self-reflection, and 3) examiner feedback. Peer assessment and self-reflection tasks were a mandatory part of the individual assessment process during formative and summative assessment steps. More specifically, each student was asked to write anonymous feedback to four-five more peers/students that were constituting the same project group. This was a part of the student individual assessment and contributed to the student grade, both during the formative and summative assessment steps. In the CLASS system context, students could read their peers' self-reflections, which, together with their personal experiences from the project group work, were used to provide anonymous feedback to their peers in a group of four to six students. Each student needed to formulate eight to 12 pieces of peer feedback throughout the course. The teacher assistant and the examiner read the feedback (anonymous) for each student to assess each student's contribution to the project work.

In this context, a dataset containing 2,444 feedback messages written in English created by 231 students was collected. These feedback messages were divided into 10,319 sentences, extracted from peer feedback written by students for a university class from Sweden and annotated in different categories. The data annotation followed the exploratory approach proposed by Boyatzis [5], where no predetermined set of categories was adopted. The main idea of this approach is to let the annotators identify categories that surface directly from the text data. The annotation used the sentences as the unit of analysis and followed four steps: (i) two annotators assessed 3% of all feedback messages (n = 120). After this analysis, six categories emerged from this process: (1) 'management', (2) 'suggestions for improvement', (3)' interpersonal factors', (4) 'cognition', (5) 'affect', and (6) 'miscellaneous'. (ii) a sample of 500 individual students' feedback entries was coded by two annotators separately. This sample aligned well with the recommended size (10% to 25% of the dataset) proposed in [36]. Cohen's kappa values of this stage achieved 0.65, which suggests a moderate level of agreement [22], which also validated the categories identified in the previous step. (iii) based on the disagreements, the annotators discussed the discrepancies and re-annotated the divergent texts. In this stage, Cohen's kappa values were calculated at 0.86 (strong level of agreement [22]). (iv) the rest of the dataset was coded independently by the annotators.

Table 1 provides a comprehensive overview of each category, including its rationale, an illustrative example sentence, and the number of instances (sentences) belonging to that category. By examining this table, you can better understand the categories and the criteria used to classify them.

4.2 Features

The natural language processing step has been performed based on TF-IDF features commonly applied in text classification problems [13] and content-independent features based on linguistic resources to classify different students' texts [7,13,31]. Furthermore, Ferreira et al. [14] proposed a new approach, called sequential content-independent features, that demonstrated the potential to classify educational texts. Thus, we defined the following features for this study:

TF-IDF: Term Frequency - Inverse Document Frequency (TF-IDF) is a content-based text feature extraction approach commonly used in classification models [28]. It transforms a textual document to an array containing the term counts [28]. We adopted the traditional TF-IDF technique [28].

LIWC features: LIWC is a text analysis resource that counts words in psychologically meaningful categories [43]. The distribution of those categories in the text can give insight into the psychological state of its author or can reflect the author's personal condition [44]. In this study, we extracted a total of 94 LIWC features. In the problem of peer feedback, these features are relevant for two main reasons: they provide structural characteristics of text and features related to emotions which can be useful to identify the sentences [7].

Table 1. Dataset Peer Feedback Categories descriptions

Category	Description	Example	Number of sentences
Management	All contributions to the group and the student's tasks during the project. No emotional opinion. All task-related behaviours	You contribute to the blog on time and are always present during our group meetings	4,014
Affect	Affect of the student on the group or the feedback giving person	He brings much energy to the group meetings, something that I appreciate very much. I am glad that we had [student] on our team!	721
Interpersonal factors	All interaction, both positive and negative, and the process of working in a group	[student] is always willing to collaborate with the rest of the group and actively participates in the discussions	2,811
Suggestions for improvement	Suggestions on how to improve on a certain domain	The only thing he, and we, could do better is to be more ready on the course literature during both the exercises and the group meetings as we have not always used the information from it when we work.	897
Cognition	Feedback related to thinking and inspiration	He has had a lot of good ideas regarding different solutions to our design	1,289
Miscellaneous	Interesting feedback that does not fit the other categories	I don't think much has changed since the previous peer feedback, and therefore I don't have much to add regarding the performance and contribution to the project	240

Coh-Metrix features: Coh-Metrix is a computational linguistic tool that measures text cohesion and difficulty on a range of word, sentence, paragraph, and discourse dimensions [32]. It is extensively used in the educational field to evaluate the coherence and structure of text (e.g., [7,14]). In this study, we have extracted a total of 83 Coh-Metrix features.

Sequential content-independent features: This feature incorporates the neighbouring features of a sentence, meaning that the features vector of a sentence S_i contains its own features plus those of the sentences S_{i-1} and S_{i+1} when these exist [14]. As this study focuses on analysing individual sentences in a larger text (e.g., feedback message), this approach could potentially improve the final classification as it considers the sequence of sentences in the text [14].

For the initial Content-independent features space used in this study, considering LIWC and Coh-Metrix only, we had 177 features. After incorporating the features from the previous and subsequent sentences, resulting in the sequential content-independent features, the final features vector of each sentence contained 531 features - 3×177 features.

4.3 Model Selection and Evaluation

We trained the evaluated different machine learning classifiers used by previous works [7,14,31]: Gaussian Kernal SVM (SVM), Gaussian Naive Bayes (NB), Logistic Regression (LR), K-nearest neighbours (KNN) AdaBoost, XGBoost, Random Forest(RF) and Conditional Random Fields (CRF). The SVM algorithm attempts to find a hyperplane with the maximum distance from the positive and negative examples [2]. In the case of a multi-classification problem, the outcome is a combination of several SVM classifiers [14]. The KNN algorithm finds the k nearest neighbours among the training documents (e.g., sentences in feedback messages) and uses the categories of the k neighbours to weigh the category candidates using the similarity score between each neighbour document and the test document [47]. NB uses the joint probabilities of words and categories to estimate the probabilities of categories given a document (e.g., sentences in the feedback messages) [47]. The Logistic Regression algorithm is used to assess the effects of predictor variables on categorical outcomes [34]. It estimates the probability of an event occurring based on a given data and a set of independent variables [18].

Another family of algorithms evaluated was the decision tree ensembles. Random forest is a technique that combines tree predictors based on the values of a random vector sampled independently from all trees in the forest, and each tree has a unit vote for the most relevant category at a given input [6]. AdaBoost and XGBoost are state-of-the-art decision tree approach [14]. These algorithms use the boosting technique to enhance the performance of individual models. It works by training a sequence of weak models and combining this information to an accurate classification [29]. Lastly, the CRF algorithm creates a graph model to analyse the neighbourhood of the instances in the categorisation process [14].

Finally, we also evaluated the performance of the BERT language model. BERT generates embeddings that vary according to the textual context of each occurrence of a lexicon, which allows capturing variations of meaning [12]. This work uses the pre-trained BERT model provided by the simpletransformers library[1].

To address research question RQ1, we measured the performance of the classifiers using a 10-fold cross-validation sampling approach in combination with two measures widely used in the literature [1,14]: (I) **F1-score** is the geometric mean of precision and recall, where *Precision* measures the percentage of correct instances among the identified positive instances and *Recall* measures the percentage of correct instances that can be identified among all the positive instances [19]; (ii) **Cohen's κ** coefficient is a statistical measure of inter-rater agreement for qualitative items [30].

To tackle research question RQ2, we evaluated the significance of the top 20 features concerning their relevance to predicting the categories examined in the present study (see table 1). We focused on the analysis using the best-performing model (CRF) pinpointed in the evaluation carried out to address the first research question. The Transition Feature Coefficients (TFC) [41], a largely used measure for this goal, was applied to estimate the importance of the individual features for the CRF model.

5 Results

5.1 RQ1: Performance of the Proposed Models

RQ1 aimed to compare the performance of different machine learning algorithm that aimed to identify relevant categories of peer feedback. Table 2 presents the results of the machine learning algorithms introduced in Sect. 4.3, that were

Table 2. Results for the analysed algorithms in terms of F1 and Cohen's κ.

	Content-Based Features		Content-independent		Sequential Features	
Algorithm	F1	κ	F1	κ	F1	κ
SVM	0.56	0.40	0.23	0.00	0.24	0.00
NB	0.22	0.08	0.13	0.09	0.10	0.06
KNN	0.34	0.15	0.36	0.12	0.32	0.05
LR	0.54	0.38	0.52	0.34	0.52	0.34
RF	0.54	0.38	0.51	0.32	0.46	0.27
AdaBoost	0.46	0.27	0.48	0.29	0.47	0.28
XGBoost	0.34	0.16	0.38	0.16	0.38	0.16
CRF	0.58	0.43	0.52	0.35	0.52	0.34
BERT	0.51	0.32	–	–	–	–

[1] https://simpletransformers.ai/docs/classification-specifics/supported-model-types.

trained using content-based features (TF-IDF and BERT), content-independent features, and sequential content-independent features (Sect. 4.2), respectively. The table shows the results of F1 and Cohen's κ using a 10-fold cross-validation described in 4.3. We also note that, in the case of the BERT classifier, the results based on content-independent and sequential features could not be obtained, as it focused on the analysis of feedback content based on the pre-trained embeddings in the language model of BERT.

The results indicated that the models based on TF-IDF features outperformed those based on content-independent features considering the majority of the classifiers in the analysis. The exceptions were AdaBoost and XGBoost, where the content-independent features reached better results. It is important to highlight that the results for the content-independent and sequential content-independent features were comparable for KNN, LR, RF, and CRF. Finally, using sequential features did not increase the performance of any model assessed. CRF, the best-performing classifier, reached 0.43 (moderate agreement [22]) and 0.35 of Cohen's κ when applied with TF-IDF and content-independent features, respectively. CRF combined with TF-IDF also performed better in terms of F1. Logistic regression and Random forest classifiers also reached results higher than 0.3 of Cohen's κ, which indicates a fair level of agreement [22].

5.2 RQ2: Feature Importance

To answer research question RQ2, we analysed the most relevant features of the CRF classifier, as this was the best-performing classifier. Moreover, we extract the main features for the TF-IDF and content-independent analysis in order to get different insights. The main goal of this part of the study was to provide insights into the most predictive features and their contributions to each category assessed.

Table 3 presents the top 20 most predictive TF-IDF features for the CRF classifier, the better-performing model in our experiments, ranked based on the TFC index. It also shows the average (and standard deviation) of the features for each category. The table lists the most significant words for the model. In general, the relevant word could be related to the categories extracted (more details in Sect. 6). However, the frequency distribution for many category was not different (including many columns with 0), which diminishes the possible interpretation of the influence of specific features for specific categories.

Similarly, Table 4 shows the importance analysis for the CRF in combination with the content-independent features. Again, the features were ranked according to the TFC measure. The key findings of this table are: (i) Coh-Metrix and LIWC have 10 features each within the top-20; (ii) features related to the number of pronouns (cm.WRDPRP2, cm.WRDPRP3p), the incidence of linguistics elements (cm.CNCCaus, cm.WRDNOUN, cm.DRGERUND, cm.CNCAdd) and average/standard deviation measures related to words, sentences, and paragraphs (cm.DESSLd, cm.DESSLd, cm.WRDFRQa, cm.DESWLsyd) were the relevant features for coh-metrix; (iii) for LIWC features related to Personal Concerns (liwc.money, liwc.relig, liwc.death), Cognitive Processes (liwc.discrep,

Table 3. Top-20 most important TF-IDF features and their values for each category using the CRF classifier (see Table 1 for the category names).

#	Feature	TFC	Management	Affect	Inter. factors	Improvement	Cognition	Misc.
1	idea	5.990	0.01 (0.05)	0.01 (0.05)	0.05 (0.10)	0.03 (0.08)	0.13 (0.15)	0.02 (0.06)
2	discussion	5.264	0.01 (0.06)	0.00 (0.03)	0.04 (0.11)	0.03 (0.09)	0.03 (0.08)	0.00 (0.02)
3	improvement	4.450	0.00 (0.02)	0.00 (0.03)	0.00 (0.03)	0.02 (0.09)	0.01 (0.06)	0.01 (0.08)
4	maybe	4.284	0.00 (0.02)	0.00 (0.01)	0.00 (0.02)	0.02 (0.10)	0.00 (0.03)	0.01 (0.05)
5	little	4.196	0.00 (0.02)	0.00 (0.05)	0.01 (0.04)	0.05 (0.13)	0.00 (0.03)	0.02 (0.07)
6	knowledge	4.138	0.00 (0.05)	0.00 (0.00)	0.00 (0.02)	0.00 (0.02)	0.02 (0.10)	0.00 (0.02)
7	involve	4.086	0.01 (0.07)	0.00 (0.03)	0.01 (0.06)	0.00 (0.03)	0.01 (0.05)	0.01 (0.04)
8	take	4.066	0.03 (0.10)	0.00 (0.04)	0.02 (0.08)	0.01 (0.05)	0.01 (0.04)	0.00 (0.03)
9	stateoftheart	4.059	0.00 (0.04)	0.00 (0.00)	0.00 (0.01)	0.00 (0.02)	0.00 (0.03)	0.00 (0.03)
10	good	4.058	0.05 (0.11)	0.09 (0.21)	0.05 (0.10)	0.02 (0.07)	0.08 (0.12)	0.02 (0.07)
11	improve	4.044	0.00 (0.04)	0.01 (0.05)	0.01 (0.05)	0.04 (0.12)	0.01 (0.05)	0.01 (0.06)
12	collaborate	3.991	0.00 (0.02)	0.00 (0.02)	0.01 (0.08)	0.00 (0.03)	0.00 (0.03)	0.00 (0.00)
13	easy	3.967	0.00 (0.04)	0.00 (0.04)	0.02 (0.11)	0.00 (0.03)	0.00 (0.03)	0.00 (0.01)
14	creative	3.943	0.00 (0.04)	0.01 (0.06)	0.00 (0.04)	0.00 (0.03)	0.03 (0.12)	0.00 (0.00)
15	design	3.878	0.03 (0.09)	0.00 (0.03)	0.02 (0.06)	0.02 (0.07)	0.05 (0.11)	0.01 (0.05)
16	theory	3.861	0.02 (0.08)	0.00 (0.01)	0.01 (0.04)	0.04 (0.10)	0.05 (0.12)	0.01 (0.04)
17	thank	3.812	0.00 (0.03)	0.02 (0.11)	0.00 (0.04)	0.00 (0.00)	0.00 (0.02)	0.01 (0.09)
18	future	3.752	0.00 (0.02)	0.01 (0.07)	0.00 (0.01)	0.02 (0.08)	0.00 (0.01)	0.00 (0.02)
19	group	3.670	0.04 (0.09)	0.05 (0.10)	0.08 (0.11)	0.04 (0.08)	0.03 (0.07)	0.03 (0.07)
20	expect	3.596	0.00 (0.04)	0.00 (0.00)	0.00 (0.01)	0.00 (0.00)	0.00 (0.01)	0.00 (0.00)

Table 4. Top-20 most important Content-Independent features and their values for each category using the CRF classifier (see Table 1 for the category names).

#	Feature	Description	TFC	Management	Affect	Inter. factors	Improvement	Cognition	Misc.
1	cm.WRDPRP2	Number of second person pronouns	0.603	0.08 (0.30)	0.28 (0.62)	0.09 (0.33)	0.27 (0.50)	0.07 (0.29)	0.29 (0.51)
2	cm.WRDPRP3p	Number of third person pronouns in plural form	0.303	0.35 (0.71)	0.40 (0.67)	0.37 (0.76)	0.53 (0.95)	0.34 (0.69)	0.35 (0.82)
3	cm.CNCCaus	Causal connectives incidence	0.300	0.07 (0.28)	0.07 (0.30)	0.12 (0.37)	0.27 (0.52)	0.07 (0.29)	0.25 (0.47)
4	cm.WRDNOUN	Noun incidence	0.291	0.06 (0.26)	0.03 (0.20)	0.05 (0.24)	0.14 (0.38)	0.07 (0.27)	0.06 (0.24)
5	liwc.money	Personal Concerns, money (audit, cash)	0.269	0.06 (0.63)	0.05 (0.50)	0.05 (0.55)	0.07 (0.81)	0.03 (0.38)	0.00 (0.00)
6	liwc.relig	Personal Concerns, religion (altar, church)	0.215	0.01 (0.22)	0.19 (1.42)	0.03 (0.56)	0.01 (0.15)	0.01 (0.16)	0.12 (1.66)
7	cm.DESSLd	Standard deviation of the mean length of sentences	0.206	0.02 (0.43)	0.01 (0.20)	0.01 (0.31)	0.00 (0.14)	0.00 (0.03)	0.02 (0.31)
8	liwc.discrep	Cognitive Processes, discrepancy (should, would)	0.197	0.64 (2.08)	0.76 (2.37)	0.83 (2.30)	0.58 (1.78)	4.59 (4.53)	1.56 (3.29)
9	liwc.colon	Number of Semicolons	0.172	0.04 (0.80)	0.18 (2.32)	0.03 (0.63)	0.11 (1.19)	0.01 (0.19)	0.04 (0.55)
10	cm.DRGERUND	Gerunds incidence	0.168	0.25 (0.69)	0.09 (0.39)	0.17 (0.58)	0.30 (0.78)	0.22 (0.70)	0.36 (0.90)
11	cm.DESPLd	Standard deviation of the mean length of paragraphs	0.160	0.02 (0.52)	0.04 (0.55)	0.01 (0.16)	0.01 (0.20)	0.02 (0.42)	0.00 (0.00)
12	liwc.sad	Affective Processes, sadness (grief, cry)	0.141	0.12 (1.04)	0.06 (0.54)	0.09 (0.75)	0.15 (1.03)	0.03 (0.46)	0.35 (1.84)
13	liwc.insight	Cognitive processes, insight (think, know)	0.137	2.34 (4.08)	2.09 (4.74)	3.31 (4.80)	3.65 (4.25)	8.17 (6.51)	3.03 (4.70)
14	liwc.death	Personal Concerns, death related words (bury, coffin)	0.133	0.02 (0.31)	0.09 (1.20)	0.02 (0.39)	0.00 (0.09)	0.01 (0.21)	0.11 (1.66)
15	cm.WRDFRQa	Average word frequency for all words	0.130	0.03 (0.19)	0.01 (0.09)	0.04 (0.21)	0.07 (0.28)	0.04 (0.22)	0.05 (0.21)
16	liwc.ingest	Biological processes, ingestion (dish, eat)	0.126	0.03 (0.60)	0.02 (0.25)	0.06 (0.67)	0.06 (0.54)	0.04 (0.52)	0.00 (0.00)
17	cm.CNCAdd	Additive connectives incidence	0.123	0.13 (0.44)	0.14 (0.45)	0.22 (0.56)	0.43 (0.71)	0.11 (0.43)	0.51 (0.74)
18	liwc.compare	Cognitive processes, comparison (more, less)	0.120	1.57 (3.49)	1.69 (4.25)	1.70 (3.41)	1.46 (4.12)	5.77 (5.30)	3.03 (4.57)
19	liwc.filler	Spoken categories, fillers (blah, you know, I mean)	0.112	0.00 (0.08)	0.01 (0.35)	0.00 (0.11)	0.01 (0.25)	0.00 (0.00)	0.00 (0.00)
20	cm.DESWLsyd	Syllables in the words standard deviation	0.111	0.77 (0.33)	0.58 (0.35)	0.71 (0.29)	0.69 (0.25)	0.73 (0.26)	0.68 (0.31)

liwc.insight, liwc.compare), Affective Processes (liwc.sad), Biological processes (liwc.ingest), and Spoken categories (liwc.filler) were relevant.

6 Discussion

The results for the automatic categorisation of peer feedback messages (RQ1) revealed that the CRF classifier reached the best performance when applied in combination with TF-IDF and content-independent features. CRF reached 0.43 (TF-IDF) and 0.35 (Content-independent) of Cohen's κ, which represents a moderate and fair level agreement rate [22], respectively. This result aligns with the literature as CRF usually outperforms other models when applied to tasks related to categorising individual sentences within significant texts (e.g., feedback messages) [14,39]. Moreover, previous studies on the analysis of feedback messages (using different categories) also reached similar results, Cohen's κ 0.39 [7] and 0.42 [35]. On the other hand, XGBoost did not achieve good values. The unbalanced nature of the dataset could have influenced this outcome [9], but further investigation is required to understand this result better.

Moreover, TF-IDF features generally reached better results. This indicates that the vocabulary (e.g., words) used by students was relevant. The low performance of BERT and the low relevance of features related to vocabulary richness (from Coh-Metrix) suggest that the students did not employ a varied language when providing feedback to their peers, always using similar words [12,16,31]. This finding is aligned with the literature as peer feedback usually is designed for specific tasks with focused vocabulary [37,38,40]. Finally, it is important to mention that previous studies [14] have shown a lack of generalizability of TF-IDF across different domains, which can impact the performance of models with these features when applied to the same task (e.g., peer feedback analysis), but for different courses.

Our second research question aimed to analyse the important features extracted using the best-performing classification model (CRF) measured based on the Transition Feature Coefficients (TFC) [41]. The results showed that the top-ranked features for TF-IDF included words related to the categories analysed. For instance, the discussion and improvement of the word could be an indication of "suggestion for improvement"; collaboration and design are words related to "management"; good and thanks to "affective"; and idea, creativity, and knowledge to "cognition". However, it is hard to interpret the differences in the frequency of these words per category. In this sense, previous works [4,7] have suggested that the analysis of content-independent features could provide more actionable insights.

For example, Table 4 shows that a higher number of second-person pronouns (cm.WRDPRP2) were associated to affect, suggestion for improvement, and miscellaneous categories, while low occurrences of these pronouns were related to management, interpersonal factors and cognition. Furthermore, the LIWC categories were well aligned with the peer feedback category suggested as the features related to the cognitive process (liwc.discrep, liwc.insight, liwc.compare) had higher values for the feedback cognition category; and the number of LIWC personal concerns related words had higher values for the affect category.

Finally, this paper makes important educational contributions in several ways. First, the automatic classification of peer feedback content could assist instructors during peer feedback assessment. Specifically, by utilizing the automatically identified categories and most relevant features, instructors could provide targeted feedback to students on how to improve their messages. For instance, the instructor could recommend the students provide more personal (affective category) or reflective (cognition category) feedback. Additionally, these findings could serve as a foundation for developing technology-supported systems, such as chatbots, that offer timely guidance to students throughout the peer feedback process. For example, the chatbot could send nudges to the students while they write the feedback message suggesting improvement in the content. Furthermore, our research sheds light on key aspects of students' relationships with their peers, their contributions to group work, and their interactions with others. This information could help reduce the time that human reviewers spend supporting computer-supported collaborative learning (CSCL) interactions. Overall, the contributions of this paper have important implications for improving the effectiveness and efficiency of peer feedback in educational settings.

7 Limitation and Future Directions

We acknowledge the following limitations of the study. First, the data used in the study contained just the categories of the sentences within each feedback generated by a sample of students at one of the Swedish universities. Although this can help instructors to fasten their evaluation by knowing where to focus in each feedback message, this study did not ensure the generalizability of the proposed approach. Future research should aim to evaluate the automated classification of similar categories in diverse datasets, potentially encompassing different languages. Second, the dataset used in the study had a very imbalanced number of instances per class. This could impact the outcome of the evaluated models. Therefore, it is important to evaluate over/under sampling algorithms to optimize the machine learning models used in future research. Finally, this study did not intend to evaluate the integration of the final model with the CLASS [46], from where we extracted the dataset in use. Such integration is a promising line of future work.

References

1. Aggarwal, C.C., Zhai, C.: A survey of text classification algorithms. In: Aggarwal, C., Zhai, C. (eds), Mining Text Data. Springer, Boston, MA (2012). https://doi.org/10.1007/978-1-4614-3223-4_6
2. Allahyari, M., et al.: A brief survey of text mining: Classification, clustering and extraction techniques. arXiv preprint arXiv:1707.02919 (2017)
3. André, M., Mello, R.F., Nascimento, A., Lins, R.D., Gašević, D.: Toward automatic classification of online discussion messages for social presence. IEEE Trans. Learn. Technol. **14**(6), 802–816 (2021)

4. Barbosa, G., et al.: Towards automatic cross-language classification of cognitive presence in online discussions. In: Proceedings of the Tenth International Conference on Learning Analytics & Knowledge, pp. 605–614 (2020)
5. Boyatzis, R.E.: Transforming Qualitative Information: Thematic analysis and code development. sage (1998)
6. Breiman, L.: Random forests. Mach. Learn. **45**(1), 5–32 (2001)
7. Cavalcanti, A.P., Diego, A., Mello, R.F., Mangaroska, K., Nascimento, A., Freitas, F., Gašević, D.: How good is my feedback? A content analysis of written feedback. In: Proceedings of the Tenth International Conference on Learning Analytics & Knowledge, pp. 428–437 (2020)
8. Chen, J., Wang, M., Kirschner, P.A., Tsai, C.C.: The role of collaboration, computer use, learning environments, and supporting strategies in CSCL: a meta-analysis. Rev. Educ. Res. **88**(6), 799–843 (2018)
9. Chen, T., Guestrin, C.: XGBoost: a scalable tree boosting system. In: Proceedings of the 22nd ACM SIGKDD International Conference on Knowledge Discovery and Data Mining, pp. 785–794 (2016)
10. Cheng, K.H., Liang, J.C., Tsai, C.C.: Examining the role of feedback messages in undergraduate students' writing performance during an online peer assessment activity. Internet High. Educ. **25**, 78–84 (2015)
11. Cress, U., Rosé, C., Wise, A.F., Oshima, J. (eds.): International Handbook of Computer-Supported Collaborative Learning. CCLS, vol. 19. Springer, Cham (2021). https://doi.org/10.1007/978-3-030-65291-3
12. Devlin, J., Chang, M.W., Lee, K., Toutanova, K.: BERT: Pre-training of deep bidirectional transformers for language understanding. arXiv preprint arXiv:1810.04805 (2018)
13. Ferreira-Mello, R., André, M., Pinheiro, A., Costa, E., Romero, C.: Text mining in education. Wiley Interdisc. Rev. Data Min. Knowl. Discov. **9**(6), e1332 (2019)
14. Ferreira Mello, R., Fiorentino, G., Oliveira, H., Miranda, P., Rakovic, M., Gasevic, D.: Towards automated content analysis of rhetorical structure of written essays using sequential content-independent features in portuguese. In: LAK22: 12th International Learning Analytics and Knowledge Conference, pp. 404–414 (2022)
15. Fong, C.J., Schallert, D.L., Williams, K.M., Williamson, Z.H., Lin, S., Kim, Y.W., Chen, L.H.: Making feedback constructive: the interplay of undergraduates' motivation with perceptions of feedback specificity and friendliness. Educ. Psychol. **41**(10), 1241–1259 (2021)
16. Graesser, A.C., McNamara, D.S., Kulikowich, J.M.: Coh-metrix: providing multilevel analyses of text characteristics. Educ. Res. **40**(5), 223–234 (2011)
17. Hattie, J., Timperley, H.: The power of feedback. Rev. Educ. Res. **77**(1), 81–112 (2007)
18. IBM: What is logistic regression? https://www.ibm.com/topics/logistic-regression (2023). Accessed 3 Jan 2023
19. Jiang, J.: Information extraction from text. In: Aggarwal, C., Zhai, C. (eds), Mining Text Data. Springer, Boston, MA (2012). https://doi.org/10.1007/978-1-4614-3223-4_2
20. Kollar, I., Fischer, F.: Peer assessment as collaborative learning: a cognitive perspective. Learn. Instr. **20**(4), 344–348 (2010)
21. Kreijns, K., Kirschner, P.A., Jochems, W.: Identifying the pitfalls for social interaction in computer-supported collaborative learning environments: a review of the research. Comput. Hum. Behav. **19**(3), 335–353 (2003)

22. Landis, J.R., Koch, G.G.: The measurement of observer agreement for categorical data. biometrics **33**(1), 159–174 (1977)
23. Lee, A., Lim, T.M.: Mining opinions from university students' feedback using text analytics. Inf. Technol. Ind. **4**(1), 26–33 (2016)
24. Li, H., Xiong, Y., Hunter, C.V., Guo, X., Tywoniw, R.: Does peer assessment promote student learning? A meta-analysis. Assess. Eval. High. Educ. **45**(2), 193–211 (2020)
25. Lizzio, A., Wilson, K.: Feedback on assessment: students' perceptions of quality and effectiveness. Assess. Eval. High. Educ. **33**(3), 263–275 (2008)
26. Luo, Y., Liu, Y., et al.: Comparison between peer feedback and automated feedback in college English writing: a case study. Open J. Mod. Linguist. **7**(04), 197 (2017)
27. Ma, Z., Yan, X., Wang, Q.: Assessing individual contribution in collaborative learning through self-and peer-assessment in the context of china. Innovations Educ. Teach. Int. **57**(3), 352–363 (2020)
28. Manning, C., Schutze, H.: Foundations of Statistical Natural Language Processing. MIT Press, Cambridge (1999)
29. Mayr, A., Binder, H., Gefeller, O., Schmid, M.: The evolution of boosting algorithms. Methods Inf. Med. **53**(06), 419–427 (2014)
30. McHugh, M.L.: Interrater reliability: the kappa statistic. Biochemia Med. **22**(3), 276–282 (2012)
31. McNamara, D.S., Crossley, S.A., McCarthy, P.M.: Linguistic features of writing quality. Written Commun. **27**(1), 57–86 (2010)
32. McNamara, D.S., Louwerse, M.M., McCarthy, P.M., Graesser, A.C.: Coh-metrix: capturing linguistic features of cohesion. Discourse Process. **47**(4), 292–330 (2010)
33. Nelson, M.M., Schunn, C.D.: The nature of feedback: how different types of peer feedback affect writing performance. Instr. Sci. **37**, 375–401 (2009)
34. Nick, T.G., Campbell, K.M.: Logistic regression. Top. Biostatistics **404**, 273–301 (2007)
35. Osakwe, I., Chen, G., Whitelock-Wainwright, A., Gašević, D., Cavalcanti, A.P., Mello, R.F.: Towards automated content analysis of educational feedback: a multi-language study. Comput. Educ. Artif. Intell. **3**, 100059 (2022)
36. O'Connor, C., Joffe, H.: Intercoder reliability in qualitative research: debates and practical guidelines. Int. J. Qual. Methods **19**, 1609406919899220 (2020)
37. Phielix, C., Prins, F.J., Kirschner, P.A.: Awareness of group performance in a CSCL-environment: effects of peer feedback and reflection. Comput. Hum. Behav. **26**(2), 151–161 (2010)
38. Prins, F.J., Sluijsmans, D.M., Kirschner, P.A., Strijbos, J.W.: Formative peer assessment in a CSCL environment: a case study. Assess. Eval. High. Educ. **30**(4), 417–444 (2005)
39. dos Santos, K.S., Soder, M., Marques, B.S.B., Feltrim, V.D.: Analyzing the rhetorical structure of opinion articles in the context of a Brazilian college entrance examination. In: Villavicencio, A. (ed.) PROPOR 2018. LNCS (LNAI), vol. 11122, pp. 3–12. Springer, Cham (2018). https://doi.org/10.1007/978-3-319-99722-3_1
40. Simonsmeier, B.A., Peiffer, H., Flaig, M., Schneider, M.: Peer feedback improves students' academic self-concept in higher education. Res. High. Educ. **61**, 706–724 (2020)
41. Sutton, C., McCallum, A.: An introduction to conditional random fields for relational learning. Introduction Stat. Relational Learn. **2**, 93–128 (2006)
42. Tan, J.S., Chen, W.: Peer feedback to support collaborative knowledge improvement: what kind of feedback feed-forward? Comput. Educ. **187**, 104467 (2022)

43. Tausczik, Y.R., Pennebaker, J.W.: The psychological meaning of words: LIWC and computerized text analysis methods. J. Lang. Soc. Psychol. **29**(1), 24–54 (2010)
44. Van Wissen, L., Boot, P.: An electronic translation of the LIWC dictionary into Dutch. In: Electronic Lexicography in the 21st Century: Proceedings of eLex 2017 Conference, pp. 703–715. Lexical Computing (2017)
45. Viberg, O., Mavroudi, A., Fernaeus, Y., Bogdan, C., Laaksolahti, J.: Reducing free riding: CLASS – a system for collaborative learning assessment. In: Popescu, E., Belén Gil, A., Lancia, L., Simona Sica, L., Mavroudi, A. (eds.) MIS4TEL 2019. AISC, vol. 1008, pp. 132–138. Springer, Cham (2019). https://doi.org/10.1007/978-3-030-23884-1_17
46. Viberg, O., Mavroudi, A., Fernaeus, Y., Bogdan, C., Laaksolahti, J.: Reducing free riding: CLASS – a system for collaborative learning assessment. In: Popescu, E., Belén Gil, A., Lancia, L., Simona Sica, L., Mavroudi, A. (eds.) MIS4TEL 2019. AISC, vol. 1008, pp. 132–138. Springer, Cham (2020). https://doi.org/10.1007/978-3-030-23884-1_17
47. Yang, Y., Liu, X.: A re-examination of text categorization methods. In: Proceedings of the 22nd Annual International ACM SIGIR Conference on Research and Development in Information Retrieval, pp. 42–49 (1999)
48. Zhang, S., Chen, J., Wen, Y., Chen, H., Gao, Q., Wang, Q.: Capturing regulatory patterns in online collaborative learning: a network analytic approach. Int. J. Comput. Support. Collaborative Learn. **16**(1), 37–66 (2021). https://doi.org/10.1007/s11412-021-09339-5

AI and Narrative Scripts to Educate Adolescents About Social Media Algorithms: Insights About AI Overdependence, Trust and Awareness

Emily Theophilou[1(✉)], Francesco Lomonaco[2], Gregor Donabauer[2,3], Dimitri Ognibene[2], Roberto J. Sánchez-Reina[1], and Davinia Hernàndez-Leo[1]

[1] Universitat Pompeu Fabra, Barcelona, Spain
emily.theophilou@upf.edu
[2] Università degli Studi di Milano-Bicocca, Milan, Italy
[3] University of Regensburg, Regensburg, Germany

Abstract. Social Media Artificial Intelligence algorithms provide users with engaging and personalized content. Yet, the personalization of algorithms may have a negative impact on users who lack AI literacy. The limited understanding of SM algorithms among the population suggest that adolescents are more likely to place blind trust in the information they consume, exposing them to negative consequences (misinformation, filter bubbles and echo chambers). We therefore propose an intervention with a narrative scripts approach to raise awareness of AI algorithms in SM. To foster an authentic learning experience and question adolescents' trust in AI, we deploy a low-accuracy AI image classifier. A quasi-experimental study was conducted among 144 high-school students in Barcelona, Spain. The results show that the narrative scripts intervention improved students' awareness of SM algorithms and shaped more critical attitudes towards them. A comparison of students' choices between human predictions and those produced by a low-accuracy AI classifier shows a lack of AI overdependence. Information about predictions' source did not affect students' trust or learning about AI. These findings contribute towards SM algorithms education and share insight into the effect of deploying low-accuracy detectors in learning technology interventions.

Keywords: Social media algorithms education · Low-accuracy image classification · Adolescents AI trust · AI overdependence

1 Introduction

The technological advances in machine learning algorithms have seen significant development in the generation, curation and delivery of content. Techniques such as user profiling, data mining, and tracking users' actions identify the patterns in

O. Viberg et al. (Eds.): EC-TEL 2023, LNCS 14200, pp. 415–429, 2023.
https://doi.org/10.1007/978-3-031-42682-7_28

user behavior with the aim of delivering content preferences and increasing user engagement [36]. With algorithms influencing the information and content users consume, new concerns emerge about their adverse effects on users' experiences. The filtering of content based on user's preferences and online behavior can eventually lead to negative consequences such as polarization, the creation of echo chambers, reality distortion, and social media addiction [14,19].

The invisibility of AI-based algorithms deepens the problem, as users are often unaware of the mechanisms behind the content they consume [27] and are unaware of its homogeneity. According to [3], young adults are aware of the consequences of SM algorithms, such as filter bubbles, but fail to take action against them. Conversely, [27] suggest that younger generations, who have grown up surrounded by personalized AI systems, tend to trust AI but are unaware of its potential negative consequences. This highlights the need for interventions that educate adolescents on SM algorithms and provide strategies for dealing with them [27,36].

Additionally, it emphasizes the potential risk of relying too heavily on algorithms and prompts questioning of the uncritical trust placed in AI. Therefore, this study proposes an intervention to raise awareness of the algorithms behind SM platforms for high school students. In particular, the study analyzes the implementation of the narrative scripts [16], an authentic learning approach, situated in teaching about filter bubbles and body image distortion. To foster an authentic learning experience towards AI algorithms, the study utilizes and evaluates a low-accuracy image classifier. The implementation of the AI classifier allowed us to challenge adolescents' trust towards AI and explore AI overdependence. The study addresses a threefold objective (a) assess the narrative scripts approach as an intervention tool for SM algorithms education, (b) challenge adolescents trust in AI and enhance their awareness with the deployment of a low accuracy AI classifier, and (c) investigate if the use of low-accuracy AI classifier can result in adverse educational outcomes.

2 Social Media Algorithms and Adolescents

SM use among adolescents has become increasingly prevalent in recent years, with a notable increase after the COVID-19 lockdown [9]. Visual platforms such as YouTube, TikTok, and Instagram serve as key sources of social interaction, entertainment, and self-expression [37]. These types of platforms typically utilize proprietary personalization algorithms to curate and present content that matches a user's preferences. SM algorithms aim to improve navigation/online experience by displaying content that is both relevant and engaging to each individual user. As a result, no two users have the same SM experience [8]. In spite of the effectiveness/efficacy of AI algorithms, there is a potential for adverse outcomes, such as the creation of echo chambers that reinforce a homogeneous content while creating a (statistically) distorted or biased perception of reality [14,20].

The negative effects of AI algorithms can generate harmful effects that may impact the users' attitudes, behaviors, and well-being [6,32]. Concerning adolescents' body image, filter bubbles can shape young users' exposure to idealistic body images affecting their perceptions of a healthy body [10,14] and potentially lead to lower body satisfaction [5]. It is therefore important to recognize the functions and impacts of algorithms on social media platforms and interact with them consciously and critically [11]. A study investigating how Instagram's body type-specific filter bubbles are understood by female adolescents found that the effect was attributed to individual preferences rather than an adverse effect of an AI algorithm [35]. Even though content recommendation is based on individual preference, preference magnification and the exclusion of contrasting content can create a disclosed environment that can isolate the user. This demonstrates how an increase in algorithms and AI technologies can significantly impact young people's understanding of the world around them [34]. As [33] note, children are growing up with AI applications, including chatbots and recommendation tools, without necessarily understanding the basic principles behind them. Despite their lack of awareness of AI technologies, adolescents tend to trust AI [27] and have uncritical attitudes towards AI-based assistants [31].

A study conducted among the Finnish population to assess awareness of AI algorithms found that adolescents aged 15 to 19 have a positive attitude towards algorithm-driven recommendations despite low algorithmic awareness levels [11]. These findings highlight the potential issue that younger generations may not fully understand how algorithms work or where they are present. Yet, adolescents tend to trust and have a favorable view of their outputs and recommendations. Trust in information technology tools involves the acceptance of potential vulnerabilities that might affect an output [24]. However, AI algorithms outputs are often found biased or unfair [1,28]. Hence an insufficient knowledge among adolescents regarding algorithms' functionality and potential vulnerabilities leaves them open to accepting falsified information without being critical about it. This could raise concerns about the overreliance on algorithm-generated recommendations without critical evaluation which could potentially contribute to the propagation of systemic biases [2].

Overdependence on algorithms and AI can be a significant concern, mainly if individuals rely too heavily on these technologies without understanding their limitations. Additionally, overreliance on algorithms and AI can lead to a lack of critical thinking skills, as individuals may not question the results they receive or understand how these results were generated. Overall, the literature suggests that adolescents' knowledge towards SM algorithms is often lacking, yet they tend to trust AI algorithms and overdependence on these technologies can lead to adverse effects. Consequently, it is crucial to develop interventions to challenge adolescents' blind trust towards AI algorithms and raise awareness of potential consequences that can arise and provide them with strategies to counteract them.

2.1 Social Media Algorithms Education

Interventions aimed at enhancing information literacy and resistance to manipulation can help exert greater control over users' online environment [18]. The implementation of AI literacy courses in school curriculums has been advocated by researchers and educators in the last few years and saw the design, development and evaluation of different curriculum proposals [17,21,33]. According to [17], an AI curriculum should have four stages depending on the student's age. For younger students (kindergarten and primary school), the initial stage should involve a playful exploration of AI topics to build awareness. As students grow older and move into middle school, they should engage in more critical thinking approaches through experimentation and familiarisation with AI topics. By reaching high school, students should cover more advanced AI topics to promote independent thinking and apply their knowledge. Overall, [17] model suggests that AI education should be tailored to a student's developmental stage, focusing on building awareness, critical thinking, and applied knowledge as they progress through their education.

While [17] model suggests a gradual exposure to AI concepts, [21] explores an approach that targets middle school students without prior experience on computer science-related topics. Both approaches have common aspects that see students familiarization with the dynamics behind AI algorithms and explore machine learning topics at different paces. Besides the content covered in the AI literacy curriculum, it is also important to consider the methods and types of learning being encouraged. For example, [17] applied methods such as discovery and inquiry learning alongside techniques of storytelling and educational robotic tools whereas [21] saw the incorporation of hands-on games, discussions, and building projects that utilise AI functionalities. Both types of interventions have proven successful in raising awareness of AI algorithms and demonstrate that AI literacy can take different forms, regardless of the educational tools used.

The use of algorithms to support and illustrate their functionality, can help students understand the impact of algorithms on users' actions, behaviors, and well-being [26]. Demonstrations of how SM invincible algorithms work can help understand algorithms at work [12] and promote awareness of their capabilities and limitations [4]. Interventions that deconstruct SM algorithms and demonstrate them to students at work saw a rise in the last few years. For instance, [23] replicated machine learning mechanisms through interactive classroom activities to raise awareness of negative algorithmic consequences, such as echo chambers.

In addition to demonstrating how algorithms function, previous research has investigated the potential of using algorithmic predictions to increase awareness of SM risks. For instance, a study replicated AI-based labeling of image classifications in a controlled photo-sharing platform. It found that it helped adolescents develop a critical stance towards body image representations on SM [29]. However, this raises the question of whether demonstrating how machine learning algorithms work requires genuine AI predictions or if human-made predictions can suffice in conveying the message. We believe that the type of activity to be performed determines the appropriate approach. When conducting experimental work, AI algorithms may be used to deceive participants in order to explore their decision-making or preferences [38,39]. Conversely, in educational settings, AI predictions can be used to demonstrate the workings of algorithms in an attempt to spark students' curiosity, and provide insights into the capabilities and limitations of AI. Advanced interventions can even offer a hands-on environment where students can manipulate algorithm parameters and experience authentic learning opportunities.

2.2 The Present Study

This study proposes the design of an intervention aimed at adolescents to raise awareness of how SM algorithms work, their potential consequences and strategies to overcome them. Based on the literature presented, the intervention will cover AI media topics as suggested by [36], interactive classroom activities that replicate machine learning algorithms as outlined by [23], and the use of real machine learning algorithms predictions to prompt critical questioning of AI algorithms. To provide an engaging educational experience towards SM education, we implement the proposed activities within the Narrative Scripts environment [16,22]. In particular, the NS approach sees the deployment of a simulated SM platform that delivers learning material to students through educational scripts guided by narratives. The use of the narrative script approach will provide an opportunity to frame the learning material within a storyline to explore AI algorithms' negative consequences in social media through the eyes of a fictional user.

As a component of the intervention, our proposal involves the demonstration of actual predictions made by machine learning algorithms to stimulate critical thinking in relation to AI algorithms. The deployment of AI algorithms for educational purposes is a challenging task however it can provide an authentic learning scenario where students are exposed to their realistic capabilities. While AI has shown impressive performance in several benchmarks [15], the accuracy of AI predictions depends upon the quality of data available for model training and relies on task-specific datasets that are difficult to locate. However, when replicating accurately human behaviors, such AI machinery would go undetected in learning settings. While the employment of a low-accuracy algorithm can hinder the behavioral trust of participants [39], it could potentially work as a tool to question adolescents' uncritical trust towards these systems and possibly foster critical thinking towards their use. Given the limited research exploring the potential impact of low-performing AI algorithms in educational contexts, this study aims to address this gap and provide valuable insights. Hence, the following research questions have been formulated:

RQ1: What effect does an intervention on SM algorithms within the NSs have on adolescents' awareness and attitudes towards SM algorithms?
RQ2: Does the exposure to a low accuracy detector affect students' awareness, attitudes and trust towards AI in general (as vs human predictions)?
RQ3: Can we use low accuracy AI recommendations to evaluate the impact of the educational activity on students AI overdependence?

3 Methodology

3.1 Participants and Study Design

The study was conducted across high schools in Barcelona. In total, 144 students participated (n = 144; 54.86% male, 45.14% female; Ages 12 to 19, mean age = 14.8, SD = 1.71). The study was done as part of a SM literacy workshop and was conducted in two sessions. It took place in the spring semester of the academic year 2022, with schools participating in one session per month. As part of the research protocol, students and parents were briefed on the research objectives and the purpose of the workshop prior to its commencement. Both students and their families were requested to sign an electronic consent form to consent to their participation in the study.

3.2 Procedure

Our learning approach saw a combination of the different stages proposed by [17]. Students initially became involved in playful storytelling techniques to engage with the context of AI in social media, and saw the deployment of interactive classroom activities to engage into critical thinking approaches to become familiar with algorithms (see Fig. 1). Students were introduced to topics related to filter bubbles, recommender systems and image classification under the theme of body image.

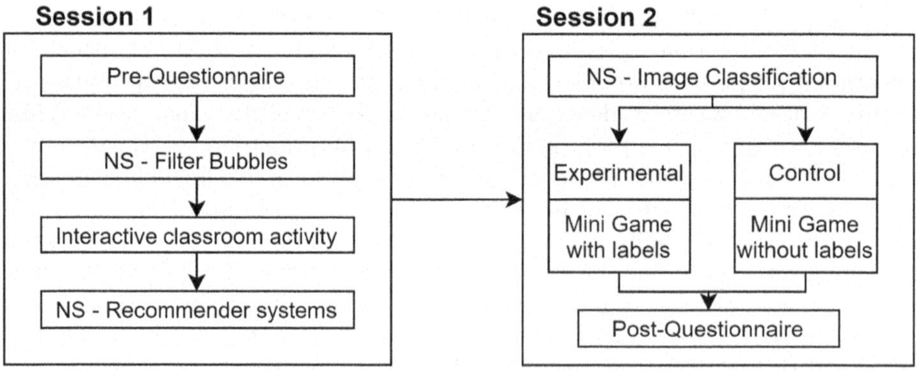

Fig. 1. Learning design and procedure of the study.

During the first session of the workshop, students completed the pre questionnaire and then accessed material through the Narrative Script platform. Then the teacher initiated an interactive classroom activity where students were exposed to a filter bubble scenario and the negative effect it can have on one's body image. After the activity, students returned to the Narrative Scripts platform and were introduced to the topic of recommender systems.

The second session revolved around a mission to help the fictional CEO of the platform to employ a new "AI agent" with the goal to help monitor the types of images uploaded to the platform. To begin with, students were explained how an image classification system works. Then they were given access to a mini-game with the goal of evaluating an image classification system.

During the mini-game, a randomized controlled experimental design was applied to evaluate the potential effects of an AI classifier with low accuracy. To achieve this, we presented two predictions to students: one generated by a low-accuracy algorithm and the other by humans. The game interface displayed an image of a person, two sets of predictions (human and AI), the predictions (gender and BMI), and a button to select the decorations they found more suitable (see Fig. 2). In the control group, students were not informed whether the prediction was made by AI or human, while it was reported to the experimental group (see Fig. 1). The conditions were randomly assigned. Students were shown ten images and the set of predictions was randomly placed each time. After the game was over, students completed the post questionnaire.

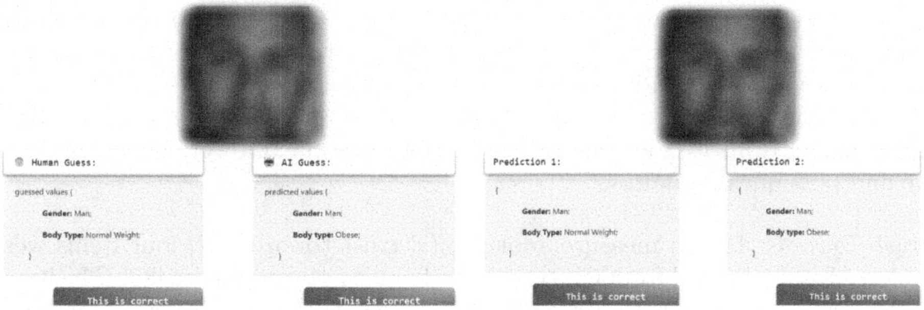

Fig. 2. The interface of the mini-game. The interface on the left corresponds to the experimental group, where participants could see which prediction was made by AI or humans. The right interface corresponds to the control group. The images have been blurred in this paper for privacy reasons.

3.3 AI Model: Architecture and Training

To generate the AI predictions we developed a machine learning model based on multiple pre-trained convolutional neural networks (CNN) and fine tuned it on a dataset that consists of face images annotated with their associated BMI values. The pretrained models we use as part of our fully-connected BMI prediction model are adopted from the DeepFace library [30] and we adapt four different versions (VGGFace, age, gender, race) as hidden components. We also used the hidden gender model out-of-the-box for gender prediction in our experiments. The training of the BMI model was performed using the Reddit-HWBMI dataset [13]. During the training stage the model was underfitted on the data, leading to BMI outputs that are in the majority of the cases higher than the ground truth (so predictions are skewed towards higher BMI values). To get AI-predictions for the experiments we use MTCNN to crop images around a person's face and resize this cutout to a dimension of 224×224 (model input size). Afterwards we feed them inside our BMI model which predicts the person's BMI as a scalar. We use these values during the experiments as the AI condition.

3.4 Measurements

Social Media Algorithms (SMA) Awareness: To measure participants' awareness of algorithmic functions in SM, the question "When I navigate social media, algorithms influence the content I see" was included as part of the pre and post questionnaire. It was measured with a 5-point Likert scale ranging from 1 - Very untrue to 5 - Very true. Moreover, the question "I have heard of the concept Artificial intelligence algorithms" was included to measure students' experience with AI algorithms.

SMA Attitude: Attitude items were formulated based on the AI divide study by [11], and questions were developed to measure students' attitudes towards algorithmic functions and effects. In particular, two items were formulated to measure students' attitudes towards algorithm recommendations in SM and the addictive consequences of SM use. Both items were measured with a 5 Likert scale ranging from 1 - I love it and 5 - It frustrates me and were included in the pre and post questionnaires.

Trust Towards AI: To measure adolescents' trust towards AI, four items were extracted and adjusted from the trust in technology questionnaire [25]. The items were based on the Institution-Based Trust questions and covered the dimensions of competence, trusting intentions, integrity and benevolence. The items were measured with a Likert scale ranging from 1- Strongly disagree and 5 - Totally agree. Trust towards AI was measured as part of the post questionnaire.

AI Overdependence: AI overdependence occurs when individuals excessively rely on AI systems, disregarding their limitations and potential errors. In our study, we measured this variable by observing students' choices of predictions during the mini-game phase, which served as an indicator of the extent to which students exhibited excessive dependence on AI-generated predictions.

3.5 Data Analysis

To minimize the effect of considering data from students not paying attention to the images and classifications shown to them, a misleading image labeling was given to them halfway through the experiment (a female was classified as a male (photo 6)). Consequently, we excluded participants who responded incorrectly to the image during the analysis. This resulted in 23 students being removed and the final sample size being 121 students.

To calculate the human predictions of the BMI values, an internal study was conducted before the main study with 39 participants (n = 39; 54% male, 46% female; Ages 19 to 61, mean age = 26.3, SD = 8.2). The participants were asked to classify a set of images from the VIP dataset [7] regarding the gender and BMI they believed the person in the image had.

4 Findings

The final sample included the data of 121 students (n = 121; 52.9%male, 47.1% female; Ages 12 to 19, mean age = 14.6, SD = 1.69). In regards to RQ1, the intervention showed to be effective in raising adolescents' awareness of SM algorithms. A paired t-test showed significant differences between the pre and post-questions ($p \leq .01$) as the participants' awareness was higher in the post-questionnaire (mPost = 3.72) than in the pre (mPre = 3.27). The intervention also influenced students' attitudes towards AI in SM with a significant effect on algorithms recommending them content in SM (mPre = 2.21, mPost = 2.61,$p \leq .01$) and becoming hooked in SM (mPre = 3.21, mPost = 3.63, $p \leq .01$). Figure 3 displays the findings concerned with the effect of the intervention on students' awareness and attitudes of AI in SM. An independent t-test showed significant differences between the two genders previously hearing about AI algorithms, with male students (mMales = 2.77) reporting hearing more about it than female students (mFemales = 2.21). However, no significant differences were found between the two genders regarding how SM algorithms work. Concerning AI attitudes, female adolescents shared a more significant initial concern of becoming hooked in SM than male adolescents (mFemales = 3.5, mMales = 3.08, p = $p \leq .05$). However, this difference decreased after the intervention and showed no significant differences (mFemales = 3.8, mMales = 3.5, $p \geq .05$).

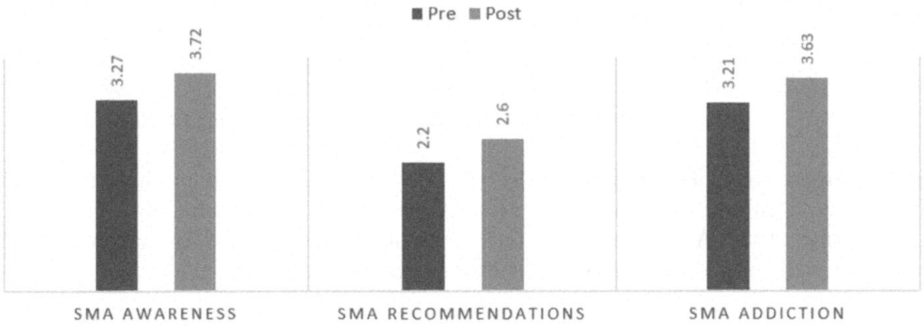

Fig. 3. Students' SMA awareness and attitudes before and after the intervention.

Regarding RQ2, the exposure to a low-accuracy image classification did not affect students' learning. The final sample saw 61 students under the control condition and 60 under the experimental. An independent t-test showed significant

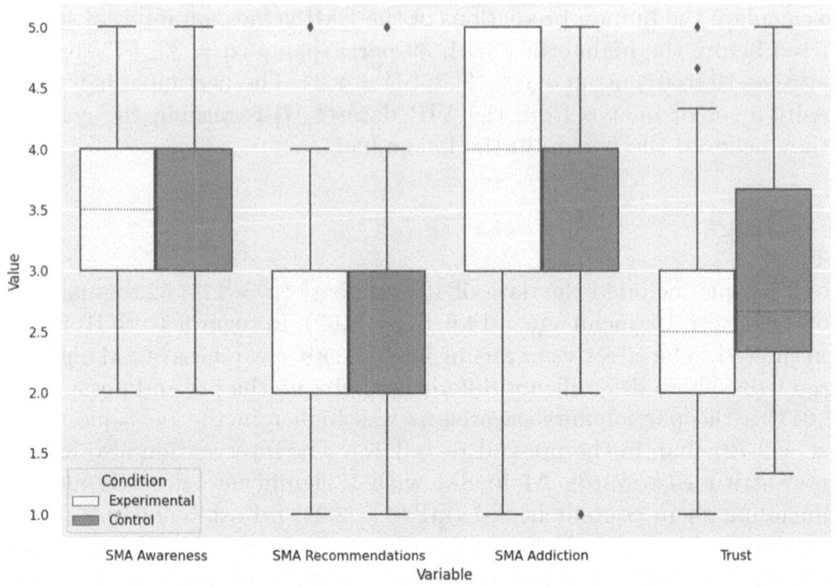

Fig. 4. Students performance under each condition in the post questionnaire.

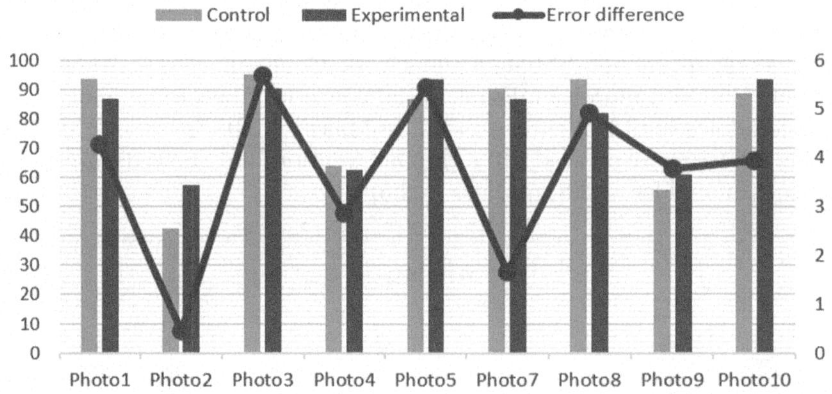

Fig. 5. Percentage of participants' selections of human-generated predictions during the mini-game. In addition, the graph visually compares the participants' choices with the error rate of the AI detector in relation to the human inputs. An error difference less than 1 indicates a high agreement between AI and human-prediction.

differences between the two groups' initial awareness of how SM algorithms work (mControl = 3.65, mExperimental = 3.27, $p \leq .05$). Therefore, we conducted an independent t-test on the students' learning gains instead, where no significant differences were found ($p \geq .05$). Concerning AI attitudes and AI trust, no significant differences were found between the two conditions. Figure 4 displays the impact of the intervention on students' awareness and attitudes per condition.

Regarding RQ3, an exploratory analysis was conducted to examine students' selections during the mini-game. Findings showed that students under both conditions selected similar predictions. Students' human prediction selection under the control condition was 78% in comparison to experimental condition students, where it was 80%. An independent t-test showed no significant differences ($p \geq .05$). Figure 5 depicts students' human-generated prediction selection for each photo.

5 Discussion and Conclusion

This study utilized a narrative scripts approach to educate adolescents about social media AI algorithms and challenge their trust using a low-accuracy image detector. Three research questions were formulated to examine algorithmic awareness, trust, and over-dependence. RQ1 assessed the effectiveness of the narrative scripts approach as an intervention tool. RQ2 investigated the impact of a low-accuracy detector on adolescents' learning and trust. Lastly, RQ3 explored adolescents' AI overdependence. The findings provide valuable insights into the educational outcomes influenced by a low-accuracy image classifier.

The use of the narrative scripts as an intervention tool effectively increased awareness of SM algorithms and fostered critical attitudes towards them. Following the intervention, students demonstrated improved awareness of how SM algorithms work. Additionally, the intervention led to students becoming more critical regarding algorithm-recommended content and the addictive nature of SM. This aligns with previous work that saw interactive interventions as an effective approach towards raising awareness of AI algorithms [21,23]. This finding carries significant importance in today's rapidly evolving AI-driven world. The increased awareness and critical thinking skills towards AI algorithms can empower students to make informed decisions while navigating in online platforms and ultimately help prevent harmful situations. Female adolescents' self-reported awareness of AI algorithms was lower than that of male students, consistent with previous findings [11]. However, their understanding of how the algorithms work was not significantly different from male participants. This suggests that gender overconfidence may contribute to the lower self-reported awareness among females, as suggested by [11]. In terms of AI attitudes, female adolescents exhibited a significantly more critical view of social media addiction compared to males. This could be attributed to their higher tendency towards social media addiction [40], leading to greater scrutiny.

Regarding RQ2, the study found that students' learning and attitudes improved regardless of their exposure to low-quality image classification. This suggests that the intervention itself was effective in enhancing student outcomes, independent of the additional factor of low-quality image classification. Thus, the implementation of low-accuracy image classification for demonstrative purposes does not have a negative impact on learning about SMA. However, the use of low-accuracy image classifications to challenge students' trust remains questionable. Our results indicated that students in the experimental condition had slightly lower levels of trust compared to the control group, but no significant differences were observed. This could be attributed to the specific AI algorithm used and the sample size of our study.

Finally, RQ3 examined students' AI overdependence by comparing low accuracy predictions to human-made predictions. Our findings indicate that students' selections were similar in both conditions, suggesting that students in the experimental condition did not demonstrate AI overdependence. Notably, in photo 2, where the AI classifier's accuracy was close to human predictions, students in the control condition blindly preferred the AI prediction, while those in the experimental condition chose the human prediction. This contrasts with the findings of [39], where participants showed a stronger preference for AI decisions over human decisions. Although this may indicate potential AI aversion, no significant differences were observed, warranting further investigation of secondary variables that might influence the results. To delve deeper, we analyzed students' selections and trust levels under the experimental condition, but no significant differences were found. This could be attributed to the accuracy level of our deployed AI algorithm. While low-accuracy algorithms can be used to raise awareness of AI limitations, more research is needed to determine the ideal accuracy level that can challenge students' beliefs without promoting AI aversion.

To conclude, we remark on a few limitations that future researchers should take into consideration. The use of low-accuracy classifiers to challenge adolescents' trust in AI does not affect learning outcomes; however, we find that such classifiers need to be closer to adolescents' day-to-day activities to make them more critical of their outcomes. Also, accuracy levels should not be at the lowest to not promote AI aversion. Finally, the design of our study evaluated the low-accuracy detector through a mini-game interface. With no previous work having a similar design, we find that this could have potentially influenced the results and further work needs to be done to establish its accuracy. Lastly, our study had a low sample size.

This study's intervention effectively raised participants' awareness and critical thinking about social media AI algorithms, promoting responsible use of social media. Low-accuracy classifiers can be used as educational tools to provoke discussions about AI overdependence and trust among adolescents without impacting learning outcomes.

Acknowledgement. This work has been partially funded by the Volkswagen Foundation (COURAGE project, no. 95567). TIDE-UPF also acknowledges the support by AEI/10.13039/ 501100011033 (PID2020-112584RB-C33, MDM-2015-0502), ICREA under the ICREA Academia programme (D. Hernández-Leo, Serra Hunter) and the Department of Research and Universities of the Government of Catalonia (SGR 00930).

References

1. Angwin, J., Larson, J., Mattu, S., Kirchner, L.: Machine Bias *. Auerbach Publications, Mar 2022. https://doi.org/10.1201/9781003278290-37

2. Banker, S., Khetani, S.: Algorithm overdependence: how the use of algorithmic recommendation systems can increase risks to consumer well-being. J. Public Policy Marketing **38**, 500–515 (2019). https://doi.org/10.1177/0743915619858057
3. Burbach, L., Halbach, P., Ziefle, M., Calero Valdez, A.: Bubble trouble: strategies against filter bubbles in online social networks. In: Duffy, V.G. (ed.) HCII 2019. LNCS, vol. 11582, pp. 441–456. Springer, Cham (2019). https://doi.org/10.1007/978-3-030-22219-2_33
4. Cai, C.J., Jongejan, J., Holbrook, J.: The effects of example-based explanations in a machine learning interface. In: International Conference on Intelligent User Interfaces, Proceedings IUI Part F147615, 258–262 (2019). https://doi.org/10.1145/3301275.3302289
5. Cataldo, I., et al.: Fitspiration on social media: body-image and other psychopathological risks among young adults. A narrative review. Emerging Trends Drugs Addictions Health **1**, 100010 (2021). https://doi.org/10.1016/j.etdah.2021.100010
6. Coyne, S.M., et al.: Contributions of mainstream sexual media exposure to sexual attitudes, perceived peer norms, and sexual behavior: a meta-analysis. J. Adolescent Health **64**, 430–436 (2019). https://doi.org/10.1016/j.jadohealth.2018.11.016
7. Dantcheva, A., Bremond, F., Bilinski, P.: Show me your face and i will tell you your height, weight and body mass index. In: 2018 24th International Conference on Pattern Recognition (ICPR), pp. 3555–3560 (2018). https://doi.org/10.1109/ICPR.2018.8546159
8. Eg, R., Özlem Demirkol Tønnesen, Tennfjord, M.K.: A scoping review of personalized user experiences on social media: the interplay between algorithms and human factors. Comput. Hum. Behav. Rep. **9**, 100253 (2023). https://doi.org/10.1016/j.chbr.2022.100253
9. Fernandes, B., Biswas, U.N., Tan-Mansukhani, R., Vallejo, A., Essau, C.A.: The impact of covid-19 lockdown on internet use and escapism in adolescents. Revista de Psicologia Clinica con Ninos y Adolescentes **7**, 59–65 (2020). https://doi.org/10.21134/RPCNA.2020.MON.2056
10. Fioravanti, G., Benucci, S.B., Ceragioli, G., Casale, S.: How the exposure to beauty ideals on social networking sites influences body image: A systematic review of experimental studies. Adolescent Res. Rev. **7**, 419–458 (2022). https://doi.org/10.1007/s40894-022-00179-4
11. Gran, A.B., Booth, P., Bucher, T.: To be or not to be algorithm aware: a question of a new digital divide? Inf. Commun. Soc. **24**, 1779–1796 (2021). https://doi.org/10.1080/1369118X.2020.1736124
12. Hamilton, K., Karahalios, K., Sandvig, C., Eslami, M.: A path to understanding the effects of algorithm awareness. In: CHI '14 Extended Abstracts on Human Factors in Computing Systems, CHI EA 2014, pp. 631–642. Association for Computing Machinery, New York (2014). https://doi.org/10.1145/2559206.2578883,https://doi.org/10.1145/2559206.2578883
13. Haritosh, A., Gupta, A., Chahal, E.S., Misra, A., Chandra, S.: A novel method to estimate height, weight and body mass index from face images. In: 2019 Twelfth International Conference on Contemporary Computing (IC3), pp. 1–6 (2019). https://doi.org/10.1109/IC3.2019.8844872
14. Harriger, J.A., Evans, J.A., Thompson, J.K., Tylka, T.L.: The dangers of the rabbit hole: reflections on social media as a portal into a distorted world of edited bodies and eating disorder risk and the role of algorithms. Body Image **41**, 292–297 (2022). https://doi.org/10.1016/j.bodyim.2022.03.007

15. He, K., Zhang, X., Ren, S., Sun, J.: Delving deep into rectifiers: Surpassing human-level performance on imagenet classification (2015)
16. Hernández-Leo, D., Theophilou, E., Lobo, R., Sánchez-Reina, R., Ognibene, D.: Narrative scripts embedded in social media towards empowering digital and self-protection skills. In: De Laet, T., Klemke, R., Alario-Hoyos, C., Hilliger, I., Ortega-Arranz, A. (eds.) EC-TEL 2021. LNCS, vol. 12884, pp. 394–398. Springer, Cham (2021). https://doi.org/10.1007/978-3-030-86436-1_42
17. Kandlhofer, M., Steinbauer, G., Hirschmugl-Gaisch, S., Huber, P.: Artificial intelligence and computer science in education: from kindergarten to university. In: 2016 IEEE Frontiers in Education Conference (FIE), pp. 1–9 (2016). https://doi.org/10.1109/FIE.2016.7757570
18. Kozyreva, A., Lewandowsky, S., Hertwig, R.: Citizens versus the internet: confronting digital challenges with cognitive tools. Psychological Sci. Public Interest **21**, 103–156 (2020). https://doi.org/10.1177/1529100620946707
19. Lazer, D.M.J., et al.: The science of fake news. Science **359**(6380), 1094–1096 (2018). https://doi.org/10.1126/science.aao2998
20. Lee, E., Karimi, F., Wagner, C., Jo, H.H., Strohmaier, M., Galesic, M.: Homophily and minority-group size explain perception biases in social networks. Nature Hum. Behav. **3**, 1078–1087 (2019). https://doi.org/10.1038/s41562-019-0677-4
21. Lee, I., Ali, S., Zhang, H., DiPaola, D., Breazeal, C.: Developing middle school students' ai literacy. In: Proceedings of the 52nd ACM Technical Symposium on Computer Science Education, SIGCSE 2021, pp. 191–197. Association for Computing Machinery, New York (2021). https://doi.org/10.1145/3408877.3432513D
22. Lobo-Quintero, R., Sánchez-Reina, R., Theophilou, E., Hernández-Leo, D.: Intrinsic motivation for social media literacy, a look into the narrative scripts. In: Fulantelli, G., Burgos, D., Casalino, G., Cimitile, M., Lo Bosco, G., Taibi, D. (eds.) Higher Education Learning Methodologies and Technologies Online, pp. 419–432. Springer, Cham (2023)
23. Lomonaco, F., Ognibene, D., Trianni, V., Taibi, D.: A game-based educational experience to increase awareness about the threats of social media filter bubbles and echo chambers inspired by "wisdom of the crowd": preliminary results. In: 4th International Conference on Higher Education Learning Methodologies and Technologies Online (2022)
24. Mcknight, D.H., Carter, M., Thatcher, J.B., Clay, P.F.: Trust in a specific technology. ACM Trans. Manage. Inf. Syst. **2**, 1–25 (2011). https://doi.org/10.1145/1985347.1985353
25. McKnight, D.H., Choudhury, V., Kacmar, C.: Developing and validating trust measures for e-commerce: an integrative typology. Inf. Syst. Res. **13**, 334–359 (2002). https://doi.org/10.1287/isre.13.3.334.81
26. Ognibene, D., et al.: Moving beyond benchmarks and competitions: towards addressing social media challenges in an educational context. Datenbank-Spektrum, February 2023. https://doi.org/10.1007/s13222-023-00436-3
27. Okkonen, J., Kotilainen, S.: Minors and Artificial Intelligence - Implications to Media Literacy, vol. 918. Springer (2019). https://doi.org/10.1007/978-3-030-11890-7_82
28. Pagano, T.P., et al.: Bias and unfairness in machine learning models: a systematic literature review (2022)
29. Rodríguez-Rementería, A., Sanchez-Reina, R., Theophilou, E., Hernández-Leo, D.: Actitudes sobre la edición de imágenes en redes sociales y su etiquetado: un posible método preventivo (2022)

30. Serengil, S.I., Ozpinar, A.: Lightface: a hybrid deep face recognition framework. In: 2020 Innovations in Intelligent Systems and Applications Conference (ASYU), pp. 1–5 (2020). https://doi.org/10.1109/ASYU50717.2020.9259802
31. Serholt, S., et al.: The case of classroom robots: teachers' deliberations on the ethical tensions. AI Soc. **32**, 613–631 (2017). https://doi.org/10.1007/S00146-016-0667-2
32. Sherlock, M., Wagstaff, D.L.: Exploring the relationship between frequency of Instagram use, exposure to idealized images, and psychological well-being in women. Psychol. Popular Media Culture **8**, 482–490 (10 2019). https://doi.org/10.1037/ppm0000182
33. Su, J., Ng, D.T.K., Chu, S.K.W.: Artificial intelligence (ai) literacy in early childhood education: the challenges and opportunities. Comput. Educ. Artif. Intell. **4**, 100124 (2023). https://doi.org/10.1016/j.caeai.2023.100124
34. Swart, J.: Experiencing algorithms: How young people understand, feel about, and engage with algorithmic news selection on social media. Social Media + Society **7**, 205630512110088 (2021). https://doi.org/10.1177/20563051211008828
35. Sánchez-Reina, J.R., Theophilou, E., Hernández-Leo, D., Medina-Bravo, P.: The power of beauty or the tyranny of algorithms. How do teens understand body image on instagram? Editorial Dykinson S.L (2021)
36. Valtonen, T., Tedre, M., Mäkitalo, K., Vartiainen, H.: Media literacy education in the age of machine learning. J. Media Literacy Educ. **11**, September 2019. https://doi.org/10.23860/JMLE-2019-11-2-2
37. Vogels, E.A., Gelles-Watnick, R., Massarat, N.: Teens, social media and technology 2022. Tech. rep, Pew Research Center (2022)
38. Warwick, K., Shah, H.: Can machines think? a report on turing test experiments at the royal society. J. Exp. Theoretical Artif. Intell. **28**, 989–1007 (2016). https://doi.org/10.1080/0952813X.2015.1055826
39. Zhang, G., Chong, L., Kotovsky, K., Cagan, J.: Trust in an AI versus a human teammate: the effects of teammate identity and performance on human-ai cooperation. Comput. Hum. Behav. **139**, 107536 (2023). https://doi.org/10.1016/j.chb.2022.107536
40. Žmavc, M., Šorgo, A., Gabrovec, B., Crnkovic, N., Cesar, K., Špela Selak: the protective role of resilience in the development of social media addiction in tertiary students and psychometric properties of the slovenian bergen social media addiction scale (bsmas). Int. J. Environ. Res. Public Health **19**, 13178 (2022). https://doi.org/10.3390/ijerph192013178

Analyzing Learners' Perception of Indicators in Student-Facing Analytics: A Card Sorting Approach

Esteban Villalobos[1(✉)], Isabel Hilliger[2], Mar Pérez-Sanagustín[1], Carlos González[2], Sergio Celis[3], and Julien Broisin[1]

[1] IRIT, Université Toulouse III - Paul Sabatier, Toulouse, France
{esteban.villalobos,mar.perez-sanagustin,julien.broisin}@irit.fr
[2] Pontificia Universidad Católica de Chile, Santiago, Chile
{ihillige,cgonzalu}@uc.cl
[3] Universidad de Chile, Santiago, Chile
scelis@uchile.cl

Abstract. Many studies have explored using different indicators to support students' self-monitoring. This has motivated the development of student-facing analytics, such as dashboards and chatbots. However, there is a limited understanding of how learners interpret these indicators and act on that information. This study evaluates different indicators from a student perspective by adapting the card sorting technique, which is employed in Human-Centered Design. We chose eight indicators based on different comparative reference frames from the literature to create 16 cards to present both a visual and a text representation per indicator. Qualitative and quantitative data were collected from 21 students of three majors at two Latin American universities. According to the quantitative results, students' agreement level about the indicators' interpretability and actionability was relatively low. Nonetheless, the indicators that included temporality were found to be less interpretable but more actionable than those that did not. The analysis indicates that several students would use this information to improve their study habits only if their performance in the course is lower than expected. These findings might be used as a starting point to design student-facing analytics. Also, adapting the card sorting technique could be replicated to understand learners' use of indicators in other TEL contexts.

Keywords: Self-monitoring · Learning Analytics Dashboards · Indicators

1 Introduction

Researchers in the area of technology-enhanced learning (TEL) have proposed solutions to support students' self-monitoring based, mainly, on Learning Analytics Dashboards (LADs). LADs are "single displays that aggregate different indicators about learner(s), learning processes(es), and/or learning context(s) into one or multiple visualizations" [6] to help students interpret their learning strategies and produce effective changes for their

O. Viberg et al. (Eds.): EC-TEL 2023, LNCS 14200, pp. 430–445, 2023.
https://doi.org/10.1007/978-3-031-42682-7_29

learning [1]. However, to know how students make sense of dashboard indicators is still a challenge for TEL designers and researchers [2], which might affect the appropriation of LADs and, therefore, their impact on learners' strategies. Recent literature stresses the importance of providing actionable (knowing how to use the information to adapt their behavior) and interpretable (being able to understand the information being presented) indicators for generating actual behavioral changes [3, 4]. This article aims to understand which indicators are interpretable and actionable to advance the support of autonomous learning strategies. Specifically, the following research question is addressed: What type of self-monitoring indicators are more actionable for higher education students and which way of delivery are more interpretable?

1.1 Challenges when Defining Indicators for Self-monitoring Learning Analytics Dashboards

Researchers have been studying indicators to guide students in their learning process. These indicators are computed from trace data and delivered as LADs [5]. LADs transform raw data into 'actionable insights', usually delivered through indicators, to produce student behavioral changes [3]. Several proposals using different indicators are found in the literature, especially for MOOC-based platforms [5]. However, the proposed indicators have not been shown to be very effective in activating students' behavioral changes. To be effective, indicators have to be interpretable and actionable to students, so they can use this information to adapt their behavior [3, 4].

According to Vytasek et al. [7], one of the main challenges in supporting students through Learning Analytics (LA) is selecting appropriate reference frames for the indicators. Reference frames are defined as the comparison point of an individual's engagement activities to some standard or benchmark when giving analytics to students [8]. Thus, careful selection of reference frames is crucial, as they act as mediators between analytics and students' motivation to enhance engagement [9].

To guide the selection of reference frames, Jivet et al. [10] describe three types that differ in when the anchor for comparison is set (past-, present- and future-directed). Past-directed indicators focus on the student's progress so far, anchoring the learner on a past state to evaluate their performance. Present-directed indicators focus on a social reference frame, as learners compare their current state to the performance levels of their peers at the same point in time. Future-directed indicators outline goals and a future state that learners aim for and how far they are from this goal. This classification highlights the importance of time as a key dimension in reference frames.

Molenaar and Wise [11] provide another framework that conceptualize temporal indicators regarding position, duration, rate, or frequency. They classified indicators as being expressed as an absolute value (e.g., "There were 3 planning actions") and relative terms (e.g., "Planning actions were 33% of all the actions taken"). In a similar line, Schwendimann et al. [6] classified indicators into six groups: action-related, learner-related, content-related, result-related, context-related, and social-related. A subsequent review by Pérez-Álvarez et al. [5] found that action-related indicators were the most commonly used to support students in online environments.

Regarding the representation of the indicators, Schwendimann et al. [6] found that the most common representation for indicators were, in descending order of usage, bar charts, line graphs, tables, pie charts, and scatterplots. Méndez et al. [12] suggested that some representations to show the indicators are vaguer than others. For example, they found that textual representations, despite being considered more vague than other visualizations, were preferred by students.

Despite the existing approaches and frameworks proposed for providing indicators to learners, there is still a limited understanding of how learners interpret them and act on their information [3]. This work aims to understand how students make sense of different indicators and use them to change their behavior. We take as a basis the action-based indicators, proposed by Schwendimann et al. [16], and organize them according to the reference frames proposed by Jivet et al. [3] and Molenaar and Wise [20]. We then distinguish between absolute and relative indicators [20], and between indicators with social comparison or without it [3]. Finally, we also compare textual with visual representations of the data, in the line of Méndez et al. [12] studies.

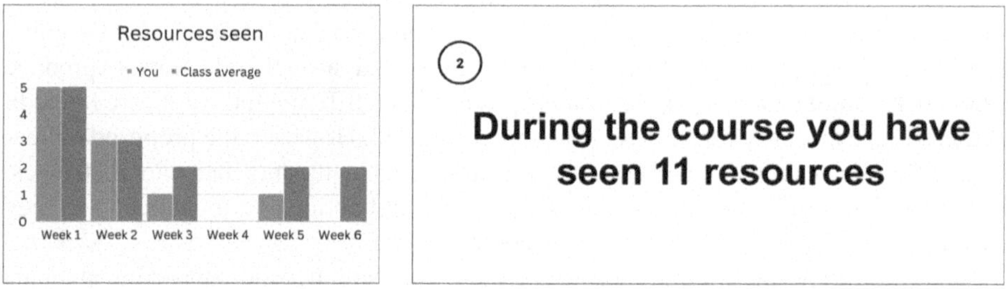

(a) (b)

Fig. 1. (a) Example of a card with a visual representation of a self-monitoring indicator. (b) Example of a card with a text representation of a self-monitoring indicator.

2 Methods

A concurrent mixed-methods design was selected as the main methodological approach [13]. The aim was to collect quantitative and qualitative data to understand how higher education students interpret and act on different indicators. To design more effective indicators, some researchers are applying Human-Centered Design approaches to Learning Analytics (HCLA) [14, 15] to help stakeholders think about indicator design choices systematically. In the same line, we selected the card sorting technique to evaluate all indicators in parallel. This technique has been extensively used in Human-Computer Interaction (HCI) as a user-centered design method. It is an eliciting technique that explores how different items could be classified. It aims to identify consistent patterns in how people think about particular items [16]. We followed the suggestions by Spencer [16] for designing and implementing the card sorting sessions.

(1) Deciding what you want to learn. The aim of this study was to examine whether students could make sense of different indicators described in the literature for identifying patterns in students' perceptions about the interpretability and actionability of indicators to support changes in their learning strategies.

(2) Selecting the method. Students received a predetermined set of category names in individual cards made of paper so that they can manipulated (i.e., self-monitoring indicators), and they were asked to organize the individual cards according to their level of actionability and interpretability. We conducted in-person sessions that lasted one hour and thirty minutes, using laminated paper cards and bid sheets of paper to sort the cards according these two parameters. One researcher moderated the activity, while two research assistants took notes and pictures. All sessions were audio recorded.

(3) Choosing the cards' content. We chose action-related indicators as defined Schwendimann et al. [6], as these are the most commonly found in LADs for students [5]. Then, we took the comparative reference frame proposed by Jivet et al. [10] and Molenaar and Wise [11] (see details about these frameworks in Sect. 2) to organize and classify the indicators into three categories:

- Temporal versus non-temporal,
- Absolute versus relative,
- Social versus non-social.

We then proposed a textual and a visual representation for each indicator. We chose these two representations because, according to [12], students can prefer text-based indicators to receive feedback. The result was 16 cards to be used in the sessions with the students. Figure 1 shows an example of how one of the indicators was presented as a text and visual graph, while Table 1 summarizes all the indicators considered in the study.

Table 1. Classification of self-monitoring indicators evaluated in this study.

	Non-temporal (do not use time as a frame of reference)	Temporal (use time as a frame of reference)
Absolute	Number of resources viewed	Number of resources viewed per week
Relative	Percentage of resources viewed of the total available	Percentage of resources viewed of the total available per week
Social absolute	Number of resources viewed compared to the rest of the class	Number of resources viewed per week compared to the rest of the class
Social relative	Percentage of resources viewed of the total available compared to the class	Percentage of resources viewed of the total available per week compared to the class
Absolute	Non-temporal (do not use time as a frame of reference)	Temporal (use time as a frame of reference)

(4) Choosing and inviting participants. Study participants were selected by using a convenience sampling method among students from two different universities: U1 and U2. U1 is a non-profit private university, while U2 is a public institution. Both universities are large and selective institutions in Latin America. They are part of a large research project that aims to analyze the experience of higher education students in post-pandemic learning environments. Out of these universities, we selected a purposive sample of students affiliated with different degrees. Purposive sampling is a non-probabilistic strategy widely used in social sciences, which consists of selecting study participants from a particular section of the population of interest who have different characteristics that you need in your sample [17, 18]. In this study, these characteristics consisted of exposure to different learning technologies and different learning experiences. Students affiliated with U1 use a different LMS than those affiliated with U2, exposing them to different LMS features and reporting. Within U1, students enrolled in social science courses are exposed to different learning and teaching methods than those enrolled in STEM courses. Students withing this sample received an email inviting them to participate in this study, and they voluntarily registered in the card sorting sessions through a form. 21 undergraduate students participated in the card sorting ses (see Table 2), who signed a written consent form at the beginning of each session. As a compensation for their participation on the study, they opted to a gift card that was raffled among participants.

Table 2. Purposive sample of card sorting participants

Higher education degree	Course	Course enrollment	Card sorting participants
Education (U1)	Education and society	35	6
Physiotherapy (U1)	Research unit in physiotherapy	70	5
Engineering (U1)	Anthrodesign	16	2
Engineering (U2)	Leadership and social innovation	26	8

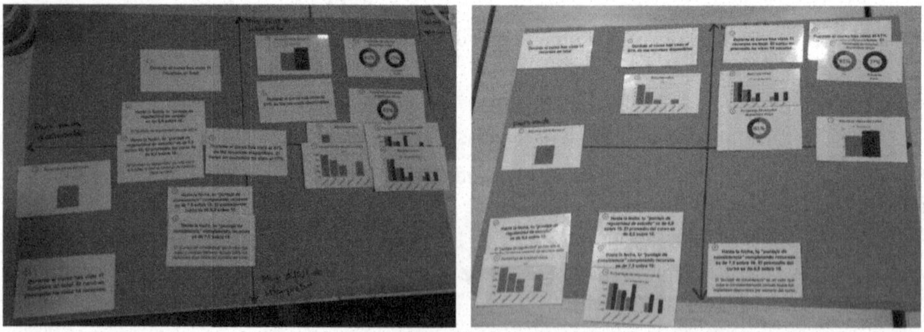

Fig. 2. Examples of how different students sorted different indicators according to their interpretability (horizontal axis) and their actionability (vertical axis).

(5) Running the card sorting and recording the data. Four card sorting sessions were held; one per higher education degree (see Table 2). Each session was organized into five phases, following steps suggested by Spencer [16].

a. **Introducing the activity.** Researchers in charge of moderating the card sorting sessions introduced the activity by exposing a fictional scenario:

> "You are a student in a course of your degree, with 30 students and one professor. It is a course that has both face-to-face and online activities held synchronously and asynchronously, using the institutional LMS. Data can be captured from your behavior in the LMS, deriving different indicators to support your learning."

b. **Handing out the materials.** After the introduction, researchers provided students with 16 paper cards with all the selected indicators (see Table 1). The moderator presented the materials to the students in the following way:

> "You will be shown a series of cards, each card with an indicator based on your actions in the course. These indicators were obtained directly from the LMS data and could be updated whenever you click on a resource."

c. **Sorting the cards.** After five minutes of reviewing the indicators, participants were required to rank them in a 2D grid. The horizontal axis went from "Not at all actionable" to "Very actionable," and the vertical axis went from "Not at all interpretable" to "Very interpretable" (see Fig. 2).
d. **Asking follow-up questions.** After the card sorting, students asked to justify their decisions in a 10-minute discussion session: Could you explain why you ordered the indicators this way?
e. **Recording the outcomes.** Two research assistants were in charge of recording both qualitative and quantitative data (see Subsect. 3.2). Qualitative data gathering implied recording the session's audio, which was later transcribed verbatim through a paid software and reviewed by the researcher in charge of moderating each card sorting session. For gathering quantitative data, pictures were taken for each one of the cards sorting grids (see examples in Fig. 2). Grids were analyzed by a researcher who translated the position of each card into rank scores from 1 (lowest preference) to 16 (highest preference).

(6) Analyzing outcomes. To analyze the qualitative outcomes (i.e., transcriptions of audio sessions), we conducted a thematic analysis as proposed by Nowell et al. [19]:

1. Getting familiarized with the data (the researcher and the two research assistants involved in the card sorting sessions read each transcript individually)
2. Generating initial categorical codes concerning the types of codes evaluated (see Table 1): (a) text vs visual, (b) absolute versus relative, (c) social versus non-social reference frames, and (d) temporal versus non temporal.
3. Searching for themes: the three researchers met to discuss potential themes based on the categorical codes established step (2).
4. Reviewing themes' adequacy by extracting quotes from the raw data
5. Naming themes: (a) Actionability, (b) Interpretability, (c) Prioritized indicators, (d) Relationship between indicators and academic performance, and (e) Self-monitoring support interventions

6. Producing a report. The two research assistants wrote a 7-page manuscript with the principal findings for each theme, including the quotes extracted from sessions' transcripts.

Regarding quantitative data, we analyzed the preferences elicited from students in their grids. We computed (1) which type of indicators were ranked higher on average, and (2) the level of agreement across students. We computed a score for each axis for each card based on where it was placed from 1 (ranked as the lowest preference) to 16 (ranked as the highest preference). Since students ranked preferences in a 2D grid, there was the possibility that some cards could tie on either axis. In these cases, the score assigned was the average rank of the group. To determine which type of indicators students preferred, we computed the mean score of its corresponding cards that we called the *rank score*. To compute the agreement between two students, we computed the Kendall Tau-b correlation coefficient [20]. The values for the Tau-b correlation can go from -1 (meaning perfectly inverted preferences) to 1 (perfectly aligned preferences). For all pairs of participants in the study, we computed their agreement regarding the interpretability and actionability of the indicators. Both qualitative and quantitative results were triangulated by contrasting findings to answer the research question.

3 Findings

Table 3 reports the three main findings obtained from the quantitative and qualitative analysis of card sorting information.

3.1 Results Regarding the Actionability of Indicators

The quantitative analysis indicates that **Visual elements** (rank score = 9.9/16) **were preferred over text elements** (rank score = 7.1/16). According to the quantitative analysis, visual elements help some students understand the indicators, which leads them to plan and change their study habits. Most students agreed that the most actionable indicators were those that contain a visual element (e.g., bar chart or pie chart). As one of the students points out:

> "I also found it (visual indicators) much easier to interpret and kind of actionable at the same time. Graphs and percentages tell you more than words. For example, you have seen 11 resources in total. Doesn't tell you anything. It's nothing relevant because it doesn't even tell you a number." [Physiotherapy Student, Female, U1].

Regarding **temporality, indicators with temporal information** (rank score = 9.2/16) **were found to be more actionable than non temporal indicators** (rank score = 7.8/16). The qualitative analysis indicates that students would like to know how they progress week by week to monitor their progress during the semester and visualize their failures, in order to set up a study plan for the following weeks:

> "If this week I have a test, that week my bar will be very high and the following week it will be zero because I already had the test and I'm not going to study it...

I'm interested in knowing, especially if I have a neurology test one week, the next week my bar will be high and the next week it's the other way around. So that kind of pays me back a bit, I direct my study according to the time I manage." [Physiotherapy Student, Female, U1]

Regarding **relative indicators**, participants perceived **percentages to be much clearer and much more engaging**. According to the qualitative analysis, having a **relative or a social frame** of reference allows students to know how far they are regarding their studies concerning an upcoming evaluation. The frame of references indicate that something needs to be improved as indicated by the following student:

"The comparison with the course, I still find it good, because perhaps it makes you think, if your study is paying off, if you are doing well, because maybe you are not. Maybe I am not doing so well and I feel like I'm studying super well but I realize that studying for the course requires having required 80% of the resources, I'm 30 and there's the answer." [Physiotherapy Student, Female, U1]

Some students said **they would be prompted to act only if their course performance was lower than expected**. For example, when asked about their preferences, one student answered:

"Personally, I wouldn't care. I mean, if I'm doing badly, I would mind. But if I'm doing well, even if I have already seen ten PDFs, if I have a good grade, then I wouldn't mind." [Engineering Student, U2]

Table 3. Table 2. Main findings regarding the actionability and interpretability of self-monitoring indicators. For qualitative results, the rank score goes from 1 (ranked at the lowest preference) to 16 (ranked as the highest preference).

Findings	Quantitative results	Qualitative results
F1. Students tend to find more actionable:		
• Visual over text • Temporal over non temporal (but less interpretable) • With social comparison over no social comparison • Relative indicators over absolute indicators Indicators that are less actionable require greater attention and effort for its understanding	The rank score for actionability was *higher* for: • Visual elements (9.9) over text elements (7.1) • Temporal indicators (9.2) over non temporal (7.8) • Elements with social comparison (9.1) over no comparison (7.9) • Relative indicators (9.4) over absolute indicators (7.6)	• Visual elements were perceived to be more actionable • Temporal indicators allow students to review their progress and failures • Relative and social indicators were perceived to be more motivating

(*continued*)

Table 3. (*continued*)

Findings	Quantitative results	Qualitative results
F2. Students tend to find more interpretable: • Visual over text • Non temporal over temporal (but could generate confusions) • With social comparison over no social comparison • Relative indicators over absolute indicators Indicators that are less interpretable usually contain a greater amount of text and images	The rank score for interpretability was *higher* for: • Visual elements (10.5) over text elements (6.5) • Non temporal indicators (9.1) over temporal (7.9) • Elements with social comparison (8.8) over no comparison (8.2) • Relative indicators (8.8) over absolute indicators (8.2)	• Visual elements were perceived to be easier to understand • Relative indicators provided students with a frame of reference, as well as social indicators
F3. Regarding self-monitoring interventions: • Students emphasized the need for customization and being able to review the indicators whenever they wanted • Students appreciated hints that were applicable to their courses • Students who received mailing generally did not see it • Students who received text messages valued their closeness	• The average level of agreement across pairs of students was overall weak for both actionability (0.14) and interpretability (0.16) • Several pairs of students reported inverted preferences for actionability (31.6%) and interpretability (26.46%)	Students like to have data about their progress using learning resources during the semester, but students report different preferences about images or nudges to improve their performance

Despite the observed trends, there was much variability in both qualitative and quantitative sources, and we observed a weak level of agreement between students. The mean correlation coefficient was 0.14, considered a weak level of agreement (see Fig. 3a). Furthermore, several pairs of students (31.62%) had inverted preferences, since they had a negative correlation. Concerning **text indicators**, some students claim that text can work as a motivator for their learning but as a complement to indicators that contain charts or images. Students also perceive that absolute indicators can work like text indicators to complement relative indicators. Regarding **temporal indicators**, some students perceive them to be confusing to understand. In other words, these indicators might be less interpretable, making them less actionable. Finally, some students indicated that they do not like the comparison with the course average but rather compete with themselves, looking for other frames of reference, such as, for example, the total number of resources they viewed.

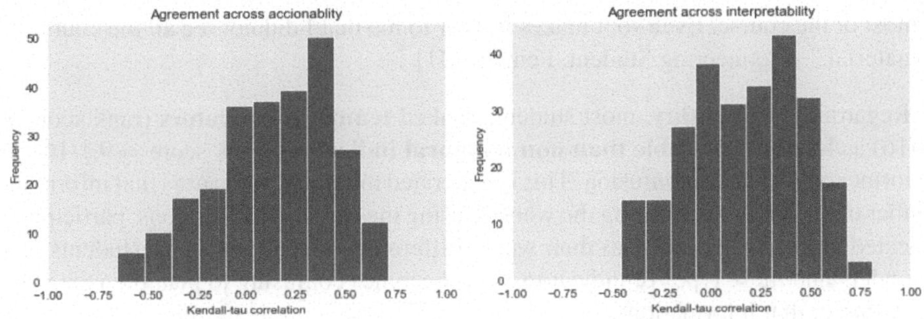

(a) (b)

Fig. 3. Ranking correlation between pairs of students regarding (a) actionability and (b) interpretability. (−1 is perfectly inverted preferences, 1 is perfectly aligned preferences, and 0 is no correlation).

3.2 Results Regarding the Interpretability of Indicators

Most students perceive **visual indicators** (rank score = 10.5/16) **as easier to interpret than text-based ones** (rank score = 6.5/16). Some students mentioned that cards with text took longer to understand, which turned out to be not very actionable, as described by the following students:

> "Pure text, it really bothered me a lot. It is difficult to interpret and for the same reason, it is not actionable for me, because I can't take advantage of the mation" [Engineering Student, U2]
>
> "I divided the cards between the most actionable side, what is proper and at least, what is actionable compared to the course, and what is easier to interpret is graphic " [Physiotherapy Student, U1].

Regarding the use of **relative indicators**, some students indicated that the use of percentages was key for greater interpretability of the data because it gave them a frame of reference of the total (100%):

> "The percentages are much easier to interpret and I also feel that they give you how, I don't know how to say it, just that one can, how to relate it to something." [Physiotherapy Student, U1]
>
> "Percentage of seen resources makes it clear to me that I have not seen the total. So it is much easier for me to interpret how today I have not reviewed the total, so I could organize myself better to see what resources I have reviewed." [Engineering Student, U1]

Concerning **social comparisons**, students tend to consider those with social comparison more interpretable (rank score = 8.8/16) than those witout (rank score = 8.2/16), because it gives them a standard to be achieved:

> "The same as seeing the course average. I don't know whether it would help me, maybe because the competition would encourage me to do more as I did less than

most of the course. Even so it makes it clear to me that I did not see all the course material." [Engineering Student, Female, U1]

Regarding **temporality**, most students ranked **temporal indicators** (rank score = 7.9/16) as **less interpretable than non temporal indicators** (rank score = 9.1/16), as the former could lead to confusion. This is generated mainly by indicators that inform the number of resources seen during the week. During the card sorting sessions, participants indicated that each student plans their weeks differently. This is why some students may misunderstand these types of indicators, so it becomes confusing to plan the next steps in relation to that information:

"For example, you may have reviewed four additional resources than the average, but those resources can be like 5% of the total. So you may have a false idea that you are more advanced without having reviewed all the resources" [Education Student, U1]

"Because there are people who, I don't know, one week may study a lot because they don't like to study week by week, so information by week may not be found useful." [Kinesiology Student, U1].

As for what the students considered **less interpretable**, they tend to disregard indicators that contain more text than images and dismiss indicators that contain absolute numbers rather than percentages.

3.3 Results Regarding Self-monitoring

Students agreed that self-monitoring indicators tend to be more actionable when they have lower performance in their courses. By comparing with the rest of the course, students can evaluate whether they are performing above or below the average. Some students perceive that the most actionable and relevant indicators are those that inform the resources viewed week by week:

"It could be useful to see the comparison with the course, because I don't know if there was a test one day or one week and my classmates reviewed a specific resource a lot. (...) Maybe I could provide information on why I didn't do so well" [Physiotherapy Student, Female, U1]

Finally, we asked about how they would like to have access to this information. Students indicated that they would value the data to be directly accessible (for example, when entering a platform, they could see it in the home page) and during the whole semester, in the course's own platforms. Not so much through mail messaging, which would rather be complementary). In addition, in some cases, students note that they would like to customize these indicators. One education student mentioned:

"(...) if I could change the colors, customize it and, in my own case, I would really like to move things. In [the LMS] you can, I like that because you can move it around and I like things in alphabetical order" [Education student, Male, U1].

4 Discussion

This study contributes to the existing body of knowledge regarding the design of student-facing analytics by illustrating students' preferences on self-monitoring indicators. Both qualitative and quantitative findings obtained from the analysis of the card sorting outcomes indicate that students find more actionable: (1) visual indicators over text, (2) temporal indicators over non-temporal, (3) social comparisons rather than without them, and (4) relative indicators over absolute metrics. Regarding interpretability, some students found temporal indicators less interpretable, as they could lead to confusion. Still, our work suggests that there is a connection between the type of indicators and their interpretability and actionability, which have some implications at different levels.

4.1 Implications About the Relationship Between Indicators and Self-regulated Learning

Prior research on LA identified self-regulated learning (SRL) as a primary focus of LADs. However, recent literature indicates that few analytical efforts are grounded in SRL theories [1]. Theories of learning play a key role in the development of these initiatives as they provide frameworks to understand students' actions better and, thus, adjust support. The findings of this study are discussed concerning these theories and highlight some hypotheses that could inspire future work.

First, indicators provided within a temporal frame could potentially promote metacognitive monitoring strategies. Our findings suggest that embedding indicators within a temporal frame are key to providing students with a reference for their progression in the course. This aligns with what some SRL models call the "performance phase" [21] or cognitive regulatory strategies [22], in which students perform metacognitive monitoring of their progress. These indicators could help students recognize their temporal evolution and change their behavior accordingly.

Second, indicators embedded within a social context are perceived as more actionable and, therefore, could promote self-reflection and more strategic learning strategies. Our findings show that students perceive the indicators as more actionable when provided with social comparisons with their course companions, especially if their course results are under their expectations. This relates to the forethought phase, as defined by Zimmerman [21], in which students reflect on their goals and evaluate their outcomes and expectations.

In summary, we observe potential relationships that should be further evaluated when analyzing our results concerning SRL theories. Future experimentations could be conducted to evaluate the analyzed indicators' potential to support learning strategies.

4.2 Implications in the Design of LADs

This Study Illustrates How Reference Frames Work as a Mechanism to Support the Interpretation of Indicators from the Perspective of Students. Students who participated in card sorting sessions justified their interpretation of indicators with a similar lens to the reference frames proposed by Jivet et al. [10]. Mainly, students viewed indicators displaying weekly information to understand their prior progress (past-directed).

For example, some students remarked that they would like to have this information to see if there were any changes they could make to their study habits. Non-temporal indicators, such as the percentage of total resources seen, tended to be associated with future-directed behavior. Students usually associated these indicators with the amount of work to be done. Our work suggests that students found past-directed indicators less interpretable but more actionable. In particular, past-directed indicators were seen valuable if they were unsatisfied with their performance.

Still, It Is Important to Consider Designing Flexible Lads to Embrace Students' Diversity and Needs. Most students indicated that comparing the rest of the course would motivate them to take action. However, some students perceived comparisons as less actionable, as they put them in a situation of anxiety or demotivation because they were not at the same level as their classmates. As Vytasek et al. [7] note, using social comparison as a reference frame might be challenging, as it can promote negative emotions such as frustration or hopelessness, likely further disengaging struggling students. This partly explains why some students argue that, despite finding this reference frame interpretable and actionable, they would not like to have access to this information.

Some students said they would be prompted to act only if their course performance was lower than expected. This relation between student performance and the actionability of indicators can be linked to the goal-directed behavior of students. In particular, Jivet et al. [2] showed that students' goals could shape what reference frames students find relevant for their particular situation. They found that students that aim to master the subject prefer different indicators compared with those whose goal was just to pass the course. In our study, several students reported that their goal was to pass their courses. This could explain why students reported that they would act upon indicators only if they saw that they were at risk of having a bad performance in the course.

It is worth considering that although the students mentioned indicators that could be useful concerning their performance, this arose spontaneously and in a limited group of participants, so it was not possible to go deeper on the characteristics of such indicators. This would be interesting to be explored in future studies, especially considering the variability of the answers. New insights on this regard could lead to recommendations or information for students according to their performance to help them to take action and plan their study.

Regardless of identifying students' predominating preferences towards specific indicators, our findings also revealed variability in the general agreement across students' rankings. Prior research has already seen that students' preferences for indicators can vary across students depending on their goals [2]. The 'one-size-fits-all' design philosophy has already been under question, as numerous external and internal factors may affect the impact of an intervention [23, 24]. In line with previous HCLA efforts [14, 15], implementing a user-centered design method such as the card sorting technique was useful for collecting nuanced information about how students think about different types of indicators for different academic scenarios.

5 Conclusions and limitations

Our work provides insight into what types of indicators students find actionable and interpretable. The findings suggest that visual indicators, temporal indicators, social comparisons, and relative indicators are more actionable and interpretable. However, the study also highlights that no one-size-fits-all approach exists, and students' goals and individual factors can significantly impact their preferences. The card sorting method proved useful for understanding learners' use of indicators and could be replicated in other Technology-Enhanced Learning (TEL) contexts. These findings could be valuable for designers of student-facing analytics, as it provides insight into what indicators could effectively promote students' self-monitoring and academic success. Additionally, this research emphasizes the importance of a user-centered design approach and highlights the need to consider individual differences in the design of student-facing analytics.

The main limitation of this study is the use of non-probabilistic sampling, which can introduce potential self-selection bias. Jivet et al. [2], for example, show that there exists a relationship between SRL skills and students' preferences for some indicators. When selecting students, we did not control for SRL skills, which could have introduced bias in our result or explained the variability of the responses. Furthermore, while card sorting intends to go beyond self-reported by alluding to students' mental models, most findings still rely on prompts given by students based on their perception. This means that some students' preferences elicited in this study might not align with what they would be interested in during an entire course. These preferences could also change depending on the system used to access the information, the indicators' availability, and the course's instructional design.

Acknowledgments. This paper has been funded by the ANR LASER (156322) and the Chilean National Agency for Research and Development (ANID), under the 'Student Experience in Higher Education in Chile: Expectations and Realities' Millennium Nucleus. The authors acknowledge PROF-XXI, which is an Erasmus+ Capacity Building in the Field of Higher Education project funded by the European Commission (609767-EPP-1-2019-1- ES-EPPKA2-CBHE-JP). This publication reflects the views only of the authors and funders cannot be held responsible for any use which may be made of the information contained therein.

References

1. Matcha, W., Ahmad Uzir, N., Gasevic, D., Pardo, A.: A systematic review of empirical studies on learning analytics dashboards: a self-regulated learning perspective. IEEE Trans. Learn. Technol. 1 (2019). https://doi.org/10.1109/TLT.2019.2916802
2. Jivet, I., Scheffel, M., Schmitz, M., Robbers, S., Specht, M., Drachsler, H.: From students with love: an empirical study on learner goals, self-regulated learning and sense-making of learning analytics in higher education. Internet High. Educ. **47**, 100758 (2020). https://doi.org/10.1016/j.iheduc.2020.100758
3. Jørnø, R.L., Gynther, K.: What constitutes an 'Actionable Insight' in learning analytics? J. Learn. Anal. **5** (2018). https://doi.org/10.18608/jla.2018.53.13
4. van Leeuwen, A., Teasley, S.D., Wise, A.F.: Teacher and student facing learning analytics. In: Handbook of Learning Analytics, p. 11 (2022)

5. Pérez-Álvarez, R., Jivet, I., Perez-Sanagustin, M., Scheffel, M., Verbert, K.: Tools designed to support self-regulated learning in online learning environments: a systematic review. IEEE Trans. Learn. Technol. **15**, 508–522 (2022). https://doi.org/10.1109/TLT.2022.3193271
6. Schwendimann, B.A., et al.: Perceiving learning at a glance: a systematic literature review of learning dashboard research. IEEE Trans. Learn. Technol. **10**, 30–41 (2017). https://doi.org/10.1109/TLT.2016.2599522
7. Vytasek, J.M., Patzak, A., Winne, P.H.: Analytics for student engagement. In: Virvou, M., Alepis, E., Tsihrintzis, G.A., Jain, L.C. (eds.) Machine Learning Paradigms: Advances in Learning Analytics, pp. 23–48. Springer International Publishing, Cham (2020). https://doi.org/10.1007/978-3-030-13743-4_3
8. Wise, A.F.: Designing pedagogical interventions to support student use of learning analytics. In: Proceedings of the Fourth International Conference on Learning Analytics And Knowledge, pp. 203–211. ACM, Indianapolis Indiana USA (2014). https://doi.org/10.1145/2567574.2567588
9. Lim, L., Dawson, S., Joksimovic, S., Gašević, D.: Exploring students' sensemaking of learning analytics dashboards: does frame of reference make a difference? In: Proceedings of the 9th International Conference on Learning Analytics & Knowledge, pp. 250–259. ACM, Tempe AZ USA (2019). https://doi.org/10.1145/3303772.3303804
10. Jivet, I., Scheffel, M., Drachsler, H., Specht, M.: Awareness is not enough: pitfalls of learning analytics dashboards in the educational practice. In: Lavoué, É., Drachsler, H., Verbert, K., Broisin, J., Pérez-Sanagustín, M. (eds.) Data Driven Approaches in Digital Education, pp. 82–96. Springer International Publishing, Cham (2017). https://doi.org/10.1007/978-3-319-66610-5_7
11. Molenaar, I., Wise, A.F.: Temporal Aspects of Learning Analytics - Grounding Analyses in Concepts of Time. In: Handbook of Learning Analytics, p. 11 (2022)
12. Mendez, G., Galárraga, L., Chiluiza, K.: Showing academic performance predictions during term planning: effects on students' decisions, behaviors, and preferences. In: Proceedings of the 2021 CHI Conference on Human Factors in Computing Systems, pp. 1–17. ACM, Yokohama Japan (2021). https://doi.org/10.1145/3411764.3445718
13. Creswell, J., Guetterman, T.: Educational Research: Planning, Conducting, and Evaluating Quantitative and Qualitative Research, 6th Edn (2018)
14. Chatti, M.A., et al.: How to design effective learning analytics indicators? a human-centered design approach. In: Alario-Hoyos, C., Rodríguez-Triana, M.J., Scheffel, M., Arnedillo-Sánchez, I., Dennerlein, S.M. (eds.) Addressing Global Challenges and Quality Education: 15th European Conference on Technology Enhanced Learning, EC-TEL 2020, Heidelberg, Germany, September 14–18, 2020, Proceedings, pp. 303–317. Springer International Publishing, Cham (2020). https://doi.org/10.1007/978-3-030-57717-9_22
15. Dimitriadis, Y., Martínez-Maldonado, R., Wiley, K.: Human-centered design principles for actionable learning analytics. In: Tsiatsos, T., Demetriadis, S., Mikropoulos, A., Dagdilelis, V. (eds.) Research on E-Learning and ICT in Education: Technological, Pedagogical and Instructional Perspectives, pp. 277–296. Springer International Publishing, Cham (2021). https://doi.org/10.1007/978-3-030-64363-8_15
16. Spencer, D.: Card Sorting: Designing Usable Categories. Rosenfeld Media, Brooklyn, New York (2009)
17. Guarte, J.M., Barrios, E.B.: Estimation under purposive sampling. Commun. Stat. Simul. Comput. **35**, 277–284 (2006). https://doi.org/10.1080/03610910600591610
18. Purposive Sample. In: Encyclopedia of Survey Research Methods. Sage Publications, Inc., 2455 Teller Road, Thousand Oaks California 91320 United States of America (2008). https://doi.org/10.4135/9781412963947.n419

19. Nowell, L.S., Norris, J.M., White, D.E., Moules, N.J.: Thematic analysis: striving to meet the trustworthiness criteria. Int. J. Qual. Methods. **16**, 160940691773384 (2017). https://doi.org/10.1177/1609406917733847
20. Kendall, M.G.: The treatment of ties in ranking problems. Biometrika **33**, 239–251 (1945). https://doi.org/10.2307/2332303
21. Zimmerman, B.J.: Attaining self-regulation. In: Handbook of Self-Regulation, pp. 13–39. Elsevier (2000). https://doi.org/10.1016/B978-012109890-2/50031-7
22. Boekaerts, M.: Self-regulated learning at the junction of cognition and motivation. Eur. Psychol. **1**, 100–112 (1996). https://doi.org/10.1027/1016-9040.1.2.100
23. Teasley, S.D.: Student facing dashboards: one size fits all? Technol. Knowl. Learn. **22**(3), 377–384 (2017). https://doi.org/10.1007/s10758-017-9314-3
24. Jivet, I., Wong, J., Scheffel, M., Valle Torre, M., Specht, M., Drachsler, H.: Quantum of choice: how learners' feedback monitoring decisions, goals and self-regulated learning skills are related. In: LAK21: 11th International Learning Analytics and Knowledge Conference, pp. 416–427. ACM, Irvine CA USA (2021). https://doi.org/10.1145/3448139.3448179

Here or There? Differences of On-Site and Remote Students' Perceptions of Usability, Social Presence, Engagement, and Learning in Synchronous Hybrid Classrooms

Marlene Wagner[1](✉), Gerti Pishtari[1], and Tobias Ley[1,2]

[1] University for Continuing Education Krems (Danube University Krems), Dr. Karl Dorrek Straße 30, 3500 Krems an der Donau, Austria
{marlene.wagner,gerti.pishtari,tobias.ley}@donau-uni.ac.at
[2] Tallinn University, Narva mnt 25, 10120 Tallinn, Estonia

Abstract. Synchronous hybrid classrooms, where on-site and remote learners participate simultaneously in instruction, offer organizational and pedagogical advantages, but are also associated with pedagogical and technological challenges. To date, there are few empirical studies which investigated the use and perceived impact of synchronous hybrid classrooms on students' engagement and learning. Prior studies have primarily targeted higher education contexts and often involved emergency scenarios during the pandemic. The aim of the present study is to evaluate a non-pandemic related, systematically developed implementation of the synchronous hybrid classroom in four Austrian vocational high schools. This paper presents results from students' perspective about the perceived usability, social presence and the perceived impact that the synchronous hybrid classroom had on their engagement and learning. We collected data from 241 students who either participated on-site ($n = 129$) or remotely ($n = 112$). Results from independent samples t-tests showed significantly higher perceived levels of usability, social presence, and learning for on-site students as compared to their remote peers. Students' sense of social presence and their usability perceptions turned out to be significant predictors of students' perceived learning. Enhancing social presence in synchronous hybrid classrooms and improving the usability of the technology used can therefore be seen as important steps for maximizing its impact. In the short term, there are some techniques to achieve these steps; in the long term, however, research should also focus on teacher practices to foster successful implementations of synchronous hybrid classrooms.

Keywords: synchronous hybrid classroom · secondary education · usability · social presence · engagement · perceived learning

1 Introduction

During the COVID-19 pandemic and the accompanying school closures and social distancing regulations, teaching formats such as distance education and hybrid learning have become the "new normal" [18, 32]. Thanks to digital technologies students had access to

O. Viberg et al. (Eds.): EC-TEL 2023, LNCS 14200, pp. 446–458, 2023.
https://doi.org/10.1007/978-3-031-42682-7_30

educational resources and could participate in instruction, despite quarantine measures in place. Hybrid learning environments can be defined as learning environments that utilize "the process of hybridisation to create hybridity in learning through dissolving or fusing traditional dichotomies between for instance offline/online, digital/analogue or formal/informal learning" (p. 1714) [18]. The synchronous hybrid classroom or also called "Here or There (HOT) instruction" is a special form of hybrid learning and refers to a learning environment in which both on-site ("here") and remote ("there") students simultaneously participate in instruction [20]. While this learning environment was considered a typical emergency scenario during the pandemic, some educational institutions have decided to keep implementing synchronous hybrid classrooms to provide broader access to educational opportunities. They are more often implemented in higher education contexts [15], whereas implementations in K-12 schools are still rare [20].

The aim of the present study is to evaluate a non-pandemic related, systematically developed implementation of the synchronous hybrid classroom in four Austrian vocational high schools. This paper presents results from an online survey designed to explore students' perceptions about the usability, social presence and the perceived impact that the synchronous hybrid classroom had on their engagement and learning. Evaluating the usability of new digital learning environments such as the synchronous hybrid classroom is crucial, since "user-friendly technology systems tend to be more effective, efficient and satisfying to learners" (p. 1952) [17]. Social presence, i.e., the "realness" of other persons in the interaction, is also an important construct in online learning environments because it affects learning and social outcomes [14]. In what follows, we present the theoretical and empirical background of the study (Sect. 2), which includes an overview of the current state of the art of research, focusing on benefits and challenges of synchronous hybrid classrooms and the variables used in this study (i.e., perceived usability, social presence, engagement and learning). The section ends with the research questions of the present study. In the methodology section (Sect. 3), a description of the participants, procedure, and measures is provided. Section 4 presents the results of the study and in Sect. 5, we discuss the results in relation to previous findings and suggest implications for future research and practice. Finally, the main conclusions are presented in Sect. 6.

2 Theoretical and Empirical Background

2.1 Synchronous Hybrid Classrooms

Synchronous hybrid classrooms can be implemented in different ways, like for example as a "Remote Classroom" or "Hybrid Virtual Classroom" [20]). Zydney et al. [34] distinguish between the "Virtual Flipped Classroom Approach", the "Student-Facilitated Approach", and the "Hybrid Approach". What all learning environments have in common is that both on-site and remote students simultaneously participate in instruction. In the literature, several other terms are used to describe this type of instruction, including *blended synchronous learning* [5], *HyFlex* [1], *multi-access learning* [11], *synchromodal learning* [4], *synchronous hybrid learning* [20], and *Here or There Instruction* [34]. Synchronous hybrid learning environments usually involve a combination of the following technological setup [34]:

1. Use of a videoconferencing tool (e.g., Zoom, Microsoft Teams, WebEx): The video conference is projected in the physical classroom so that on-site students see the video of remote students, the chat and the slides shared by the teacher. On-site students may or may not be logged in to the video conference, depending on whether mixed group work (on-site together with remote students) is planned. Remote students view the video, chat, and slides on their personal computers either at home or from another campus location, and they use their own headsets and webcams when speaking. The chosen video conferencing tool should be easy to use, and a fast, interruption-free internet connection is essential for the success of synchronous hybrid classrooms [34].
2. Audio-visual hardware: Microphones, speakers and cameras are integral components of synchronous hybrid classrooms. On-site students can communicate with remote students via USB connected omnidirectional speakerphones that are connected to the teacher's audio input and output. Video of the physical classroom can be created using fixed or movable webcams, so-called Swivls. High-quality audio is a vital prerequisite for the success of synchronous hybrid classrooms [34].
3. Presentation computer: Teachers can either use classroom-based computers or bring their personal devices. Classroom-based computers may have the advantage that audio, video, and projection can be set up in advance [34].

Prior research has shown that synchronous hybrid classrooms offer organizational and pedagogical benefits but are also associated with pedagogical and technological challenges. *Organizational benefits* include increased flexibility in terms of course attendance (also in case of illness or job- or family-related commitments), access to education regardless of location and thereby addressing a larger number of potential learners, easier invitation of external experts, and reduction of workload, since courses only need to be offered once [20, 34]. *Pedagogical benefits* comprise richer learning experiences due to the possibility to include expertise outside the institution, strengthening of social relations among on-site and remote students as well as the teacher (and maybe also international relations), continuity in instruction (particularly in times of crises), more guidance and support from the teacher as compared to online asynchronous courses, and promotion of students' digital skills [20].

Despite the above-mentioned benefits, synchronous hybrid classrooms are associated with several challenges. *Pedagogical challenges from the teacher perspective* include a radical change of pedagogical methods, requirement of digital skills, willingness to try out new things and evaluate the results, and higher coordination effort and mental load as the teacher must pay attention to both on-site and remote students [20]. *Pedagogical challenges from the student perspective* entail unequal learning experiences for on-site and remote students, risk that remote students feel excluded, and the demand for more self-discipline among remote students [20]. Finally, *technological challenges* mostly refer to maximizing social presence of remote students, technical difficulties (mainly audio and video), the need of continuous updates, and technology may be seen as an imposition for both the teacher and on-site students in terms of positioning cameras or speaking into a microphone [20].

2.2 Usability

Usability is an essential concept when evaluating educational technologies [17]. The International Organization for Standardization [10] defines usability as the "extent to which a product can be used by specified users to achieve specific goals with effectiveness, efficiency and satisfaction under a specific context of use". Usability research has shown that the three dimensions (effectiveness, efficiency, and satisfaction) are weakly correlated, and that it is particularly important to evaluate perceived usability (satisfaction) next to the other two, more objective dimensions, since it has a significant impact on students' learning experience and their learning outcomes [29].

As synchronous hybrid classrooms require a certain technological setup (see Sect. 2.1), which is still relatively new, it is important to evaluate its usability. Raes, Vanneste et al. [21] investigated the usability of a hybrid virtual classroom implementation by conducting classroom observations and focus groups with students and found that it was relatively straightforward for the students to use the functionalities of their platform. However, some technical assistance was needed at the start of the lesson when students had to log in to the system and remote students had to ensure that their headsets are working properly. In a mixed-methods study, Shi et al. [24] found that the technical affordance (i.e., usability) of their blended synchronous learning environment significantly predicted students' deep cognitive engagement.

2.3 Social Presence

Social presence is a central construct in online learning environments [23]. The term "social presence" was coined by the communication researchers Short et al. [25], referring to the degree to which another person is perceived as a "real person" in computer-mediated communication (CMC). In a recent comprehensive review on social presence, Kreijns et al. [14] reformulated the Short et al. definition, stating that social presence is "a psychological phenomenon in which, to a certain extent, the others are perceived as physical "real" persons in technology-mediated communication enabled by CMC tools and electronic platforms" (p. 156). Meta-analytic evidence [23] shows that social presence is significantly associated with students' satisfaction and perceived learning in online learning environments. Beyond that, indicators of social presence turned out to be important predictors of students' academic performance in some empirical studies (e.g., [12, 33]).

Social presence also plays a key role in synchronous hybrid classrooms. Szeto and Cheng [26], for example, found in their qualitative case study that on-site and remote students had varying social presence experiences related to interaction. In their case, remote students reported that multi-screen projections of the teacher and the face-to-face group helped to create a "real" sense of participating in face-to-face instruction; however, interactions were perceived as indirect, and students missed hand gestures and social cues. In a mixed-methods study, Butz and Stupnisky [6] investigated the relationships among students' need satisfaction, motivation, and achievement in synchronous hybrid learning environments by applying self-determination theory and showed that peer relatedness (i.e., authentic social connections between on-site and remote students) has a major impact on synchronous hybrid learning.

2.4 Impact of Synchronous Hybrid Classrooms on Engagement and Learning

Engagement is a multifaceted construct, which can be defined in three ways [9]. *Behavioral engagement* refers to the involvement and participation of students in academic and extracurricular activities. *Emotional engagement* relates to students' positive and negative reactions to teachers, classmates, and scholarly activities. *Cognitive engagement* concerns students' willingness to invest effort to understand complex ideas and to cope with difficult tasks. Engagement is considered to be a "messy construct", as some of the definitions overlap with other constructs, for example on-task behavior (*behavioral*), student attitudes (*emotional*) or self-regulated learning (*cognitive*) [9] Nevertheless, meta-analytic results show that there is a moderately strong and positive relationship between overall student engagement and academic achievement [16].

The concept of *perceived learning* relates to "changes in the learner's perceptions of skill and knowledge levels before and after the learning experience" (p. 406) [2]. In a similar fashion, students' perceived learning outcomes can also be classified into the categories of cognitive, behavioral and affective outcomes [30]. Evaluating how students perceive their learning is important for teachers because it can improve the quality of instruction, thereby enhancing students' learning experience [3].

As noted in the literature review by Raes, Detienne et al. [20] there are only a few empirical studies which have examined the use and impact of synchronous hybrid classrooms on students' engagement and learning. Prior studies mainly focused on researching benefits, challenges, and design principles of synchronous hybrid classrooms, by employing exploratory and qualitative research methods. Most studies were conducted in higher education contexts, especially in times of the COVID-19 pandemic.

In an experimental study, Raes, Vanneste et al. [21] compared four different learning environments (pure face-to-face, pure virtual, hybrid face-to-face and hybrid virtual) and found that the hybrid virtual setting is the most challenging to learn in as a remote participant; relatedness to peers and intrinsic motivation was lowest in this setting. However, findings of their study indicate that launching quizzes has a positive impact on students' motivation. Shi et al. [24] investigated the relationships among blended synchronous learning environments, high school students' motivation, and cognitive engagement and found that pedagogical affordance of the synchronous hybrid classroom had a positively direct effect on deep cognitive engagement. However, the authors also warned that remote students are often faced with the problem of lower cognitive engagement. In the context of higher education, Raes [19] examined the effect of level of presence (on-site vs. remote, with or without interaction) on conceptual and affective learning outcomes and found no significant differences between physical and remote presence regarding conceptual understanding, albeit significant differences regarding affective engagement (e.g., interest, sense of presence) in favor of on-site students.

2.5 The Present Study

The literature review has shown that prior studies related to synchronous hybrid classrooms were either conducted several years before the COVID-19 pandemic, when video conferencing tools such as Zoom or Microsoft Teams were not yet popular, or during the COVID-19 pandemic as a form of emergency remote teaching [27]. Most studies were undertaken in the context of higher education, while studies in K-12 education are still rare. Moreover, earlier studies mainly evaluated the effects of single or a couple of lessons in the synchronous hybrid classroom, but do not consider the synchronous hybrid classroom as a long-term and institutional strategy. If students and teachers are not yet familiar with this instructional approach and if the technology used is not mature enough, it is likely that the results are more negative (in the sense that remote students are disadvantaged) than they necessarily would be. Research results of longer-term, large-scale and more systematic and deliberate implementations of synchronous hybrid classrooms are needed because these may offset some of the negative consequences observed in shorter studies.

The aim of the present study is therefore to evaluate a non-pandemic related, systematically developed implementation of the synchronous hybrid classroom in four Austrian vocational high schools. In this paper, we focus on students' perspective about the perceived usability, social presence and the perceived impact that the synchronous hybrid classroom had on students' engagement and learning, as these variables are considered crucial for successful implementations of synchronous hybrid classrooms.

We are guided by the following research questions:

RQ1. How do students evaluate the use of the synchronous hybrid classroom in terms of usability, social presence and the impact on engagement and learning?
RQ2. Are there differences between on-site and remote students' perceptions regarding usability, social presence and the impact on engagement and learning?
RQ3. How well does students' sense of social presence predict their perceived learning?
RQ4. How well do students' usability perceptions predict their perceived learning?

Since there are no prior studies with the exact same setting, we did not formulate any hypotheses to the above-mentioned research questions.

3 Methodology

3.1 Context of the Study, Participants and Procedure

The study was conducted in four Austrian vocational high schools, which have teamed up and jointly offer different educational specializations (e.g., health care management and sports) since the school year 2020/21. Each school site offers one educational specialization and students can choose one of the four specializations (taught from grade 11 to 13, two lessons of 50 min per week). If the specialization is not taught at the school they attend, they can still participate in instruction via the virtual classroom, which is organized using the platform Microsoft Teams. To sum up, the four educational specializations are taught in a synchronous hybrid classroom, as some students participate on-site and some students remotely from another school campus location. Students attend all lessons in the same modality (either online or remotely from another school campus location), depending on whether their chosen specialization is offered at their school location. Since the synchronous hybrid classroom is quite a new instructional approach, school leaders wanted to evaluate its implementation. A total of 241 students (68% female) from all four school sites (grades 11 – 13) and with an average age of $M = 17.45$ years ($SD = 1.11$) participated in the online survey. Approximately half of the students participate online in the synchronous hybrid classroom ($n = 112$; 46.5%) and the other half participates on-site ($n = 129$; 53.5%). The online survey was administered in December 2022 and January 2023 in their regular school lessons of the specialization and under the guidance of their teachers.

3.2 Measures

Evaluation of the Synchronous Hybrid Classroom. An adapted version of the CriSP questionnaire (classroom response system perceptions questionnaire) by Richardson et al. [22], which consists of three scales with a total of 18 items, was used to capture students' perceptions of the synchronous hybrid classroom: (1) *Usability* (example item: "There were too many technical problems with the use of the virtual classroom" (-), 5 items, Cronbach's $\alpha = .69$), (2) impact on *engagement* (example item: "The virtual classroom increased my motivation to learn", 7 items, Cronbach's $\alpha = .92$), (3) impact on learning (*perceived learning*) (example item: "I believe that I can learn better with the virtual classroom than in lessons without the virtual classroom", 5 items, Cronbach's $\alpha = .75$). Agreement with the statements was recorded using a five-point rating scale from 1 (not at all true) to 5 (exactly true). The CriSP questionnaire was originally developed to assess student perceptions of classroom response systems; however, Richardson et al. [22] state that—with minor changes—the instrument can be used to evaluate the impact of other classroom technologies on learning as well. Accordingly, we changed the term "classroom response systems" to "virtual classroom", referring to the Microsoft Teams platform that was used to realize the synchronous hybrid classroom. In addition, four translated items of the usability scale were taken from the "Perceived Ease of Use" scale by Venkatesh [28]. *Usability* items refer to the dimension of "perceived usability" (satisfaction), as introduced in the theoretical background section. *Engagement* items can be mostly classified as behavioral and emotional engagement, while cognitive engagement is represented in the *perceived learning* items [22].

Social Presence. Students' sense of social presence in the synchronous hybrid classroom was captured using an adapted version of the social presence measure developed by Kreijns et al. [13], which consists of 10 items (example item: "In the virtual classroom, it feels like we are a face-to-face discussion group", Cronbach's $\alpha = .91$). Students responded to the items using a five-point rating scale from 1 (not at all true) to 5 (exactly true).

Figure 1 provides a summary of the research questions, instruments, and data analysis methods used in the present study.

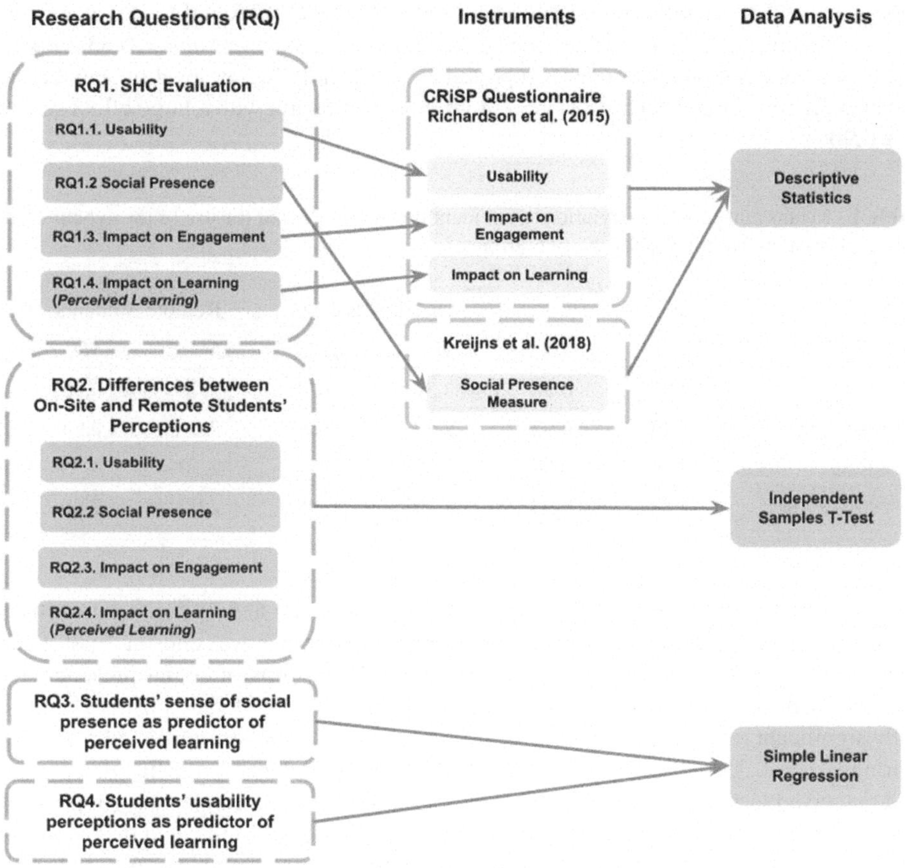

Fig. 1. Research questions, instruments, and data analysis.

4 Results

Descriptive findings (i.e., means and standard deviations) regarding students' perceptions of the use of the synchronous hybrid classroom are shown in Table 1. Students' evaluations of the usability and the impact on engagement and perceived learning were average to tendentially negative. Results for the usability subscale were higher compared to the perceived impact on engagement and learning. Students' sense of social presence in the synchronous hybrid classroom was also rather low.

To check whether there are differences in the evaluation of the synchronous hybrid classroom between on-site and remote students, independent samples t-tests were conducted. Results indicate that on-site students perceived a significantly higher level of usability than remote students, $t(191) = -2.70$, $p = .008$. The effect size according to Cohen [8]) is $d = 0.85$, corresponding to a large effect size. On-site students reported a higher perceived impact on engagement than their remote peers, but this difference did not reach statistical significance, $t(225) = -1.71$, $p = .088$. However, a statistically significant difference between on-site and remote students was found for the perceived impact on learning, $t(183) = -2.22, p = .027$, with a large effect size of $d = 0.83$. Finally, results indicate that on-site students reported a significantly higher level of social presence than their remote peers, $t(231) = -4.49, p < .001$, again with a large effect size of $d = 0.90$.

Table 1. Means and standard deviations of student perceptions about the use of the synchronous hybrid classroom overall and for the two groups

	Overall		On-Site Students		Remote Students	
	M	*SD*	*M*	*SD*	*M*	*SD*
Usability	3.22	0.86	3.36	0.77	3.05	0.95
Engagement	2.12	0.92	2.22	0.89	2.01	0.94
Learning	2.45	0.84	2.56	0.71	2.30	0.95
Social Presence	2.34	0.93	2.59	0.98	2.07	0.80

To examine how well students' sense of social presence and usability perceptions predict perceived learning, a simple linear regression approach was chosen. First, Pearson correlations were conducted to examine the relationships of social presence and usability with students' perceived learning. Results indicate moderate, positive, statistically significant relationships between students' sense of social presence and perceived learning, $r = 0.35$, $n = 223$, $p < .001$, and between students' usability perceptions and perceived learning, $r = 0.32$, $n = 222$, $p < .001$. Second, simple linear regression analyses were conducted for each of the two factors. The results indicated that students' sense of social presence statistically significantly predicts perceived learning, $F(1, 221) = 30.82$, $p < .001$, and social presence accounted for 11.8% of the variance in perceived learning. Students' usability perceptions also statistically significantly predict perceived learning, $F(2, 224) = 65.94$, p < .001, and usability accounted for 22.4% of the variance in perceived learning. Results of the simple linear regression analyses are summarized in Table 2.

Table 2. Summary of simple linear regression analysis for social presence and usability predicting perceived learning

Variable	B	SE	T	95%CI	
				LL	UP
Social presence	0.31***	.05	5.55	0.20	0.42
Usability	0.46***	.06	8.12	0.35	0.57

Note. *** p < .001; B = unstandardized regression coefficient; SE = standard error, T = t-statistic value, CI = confidence interval; LL = lower limit; UL = upper limit

5 Discussion

The aim of the present study was to evaluate a non-pandemic related, systematically developed implementation of the synchronous hybrid classroom in secondary education in terms of its perceived usability and its perceived impacts on student engagement and learning, considering the important role of social presence. Descriptive findings show that students evaluate the use of the synchronous hybrid classroom in terms of its perceived usability and the perceived impact on engagement and learning as average to negative. The usability of the synchronous hybrid classroom was rated slightly higher than the perceived impact on engagement and learning, meaning that it was easy for students to use the technology associated with the synchronous hybrid classroom and that there were not too many technical problems. Students' sense of social presence was remarkably low in both groups. Findings of the study highlight that the use of the synchronous hybrid classroom is not always perceived positively among high school students. This result contrasts with the empirical findings from Shi et al. [24] who also investigated a longer-term implementation of blended synchronous learning in a Chinese high school and found higher levels of pedagogical, social and technical affordance. However, in their case, all subjects were taught in a synchronous hybrid classroom. Further empirical research is needed to delineate which design and implementation characteristics of the synchronous hybrid classroom result in better acceptance and satisfaction by this target group. Future studies may take a participatory design approach involving both researchers and practitioners, including teachers, students, and school managers, to iteratively design, implement, and assess the synchronous hybrid classroom [35].

Also in our specific setting, we found differences between on-site and remote students' perceptions. On-site students reported statistically significantly higher levels of usability, social presence, and perceived learning. Thus, it can be deduced that on-site students had a clear advantage over remote students in this implementation of the synchronous hybrid classroom. We did not find a significant difference between on-site and remote students' engagement; however, descriptive findings indicate that on-site students were also more engaged in the synchronous hybrid classroom. These results still need to be complemented with qualitative data such as observations in real settings and interviews or focus groups like in the study by Raes, Vanneste et al. [21] to provide meaningful explanations. Understanding the reasons underlying these differences is crucial for creating successful implementations of synchronous hybrid classrooms.

Results of the simple linear regression analyses pointed towards the important role of social presence and usability in predicting students' perceived learning. Enhancing social presence in synchronous hybrid classrooms and improving usability of technology used can therefore be seen as important steps for maximizing its impact. These two factors can also be interpreted as having *independent* effects on perceived learning, meaning that very likely measures taken to improve usability may not have an impact on improving social presence and vice versa. Usability might be a factor that improves with longer engagement in a hybrid learning setting and students and teachers growing more accustomed to learning in such a setting, but social presence may stay a strong predictor independently of usability.

To increase the usability, teachers could be supported by teaching assistants who overview the technology and take care of technical problems [31, 34]. The employment of a "technology navigator" was also suggested by Cain [7], arguing that such a person can provide both pre-teaching and while teaching support for both students and the teacher. Particular attention should be paid to the audio, ensuring that remote students get the same audio quality as on-site students [20].

Even if usability may be addressed by these measures and may also be something that is improved over time by getting used to, our study clearly shows that perceived social presence needs separate and deliberate consideration. In the short term, there are some techniques that can be used to enhance students' sense of social presence, for example by mixing on-site and remote students during group work [34], by asking several questions throughout the lesson (e.g., using online quizzes and polls), and by being particularly attentive to remote students [20]. The main challenge of teachers is to evenly balance their attention between on-site and remote students, as too much attention to the online group is also not ideal [26]. Using polls and quizzes could cognitively activate both on-site and remote students, thereby also increasing their engagement [5]. From a technical perspective, students' sense of social presence could be increased by using multi-screen projections [26] so that on-site and remote students can see each other and by employing chatrooms and discussion forums.

In the long term, however, research should also focus on teacher practices to foster successful implementations of synchronous hybrid classrooms. In the end, the success of the synchronous hybrid classroom depends on its technical and pedagogical implementation. Designing synchronous hybrid learning activities is not trivial for teachers, as apart from technical expertise, teachers are required to adapt, or drastically change their teaching practices to provide a meaningful and similar learning experience for on-site and remote students. Due to the novelty of this instructional approach, teachers do not have access to the same pool of related good practices as for other, more well-established teaching approaches. Future research should therefore explore teachers' needs and practices, when designing for synchronous hybrid learning settings.

The present study also has some limitations which must be acknowledged. First, and although our sample included students with considerable experience in this teaching setting, we still only collected self-report data using a cross-sectional design. Future studies may employ a longitudinal, quasi-experimental design to test causal relationships between design characteristics of the synchronous hybrid classroom and student learning outcomes [20]. Additionally, empirical real-time data should be collected, for example by using multimodal learning analytics approaches, to capture students' engagement and social presence in the moment of learning [20]. In the present study, students had to reflect on their learning experiences in retrospect. Also, studies should include academic performance measures such as achievement tests or grades in order to gain more objective insights on actual learning.

6 Conclusion

This paper presented evaluation results of a synchronous hybrid classroom implementation in four Austrian vocational high schools. Results showed that there is still some potential for improvement in terms of design and implementation characteristics of the synchronous hybrid classroom to enhance students' learning experience. Maximizing students' sense of social presence and increasing the usability of the technology used in the synchronous hybrid classroom are important first steps, as these turned out to be significant predictors of students' perceived learning.

References

1. Abdelmalak, M.M.M., Parra, J.L.: Expanding learning opportunities for graduate students with HyFlex course design. Int. J. Online Pedagog. Course Des. **6**(4), 19–37 (2016)
2. Alavi, M., Marakas, G.M., Yoo, Y.: A comparative study of distributed learning environments on learning outcomes. Inf. Syst. Res. **13**(4), 404–415 (2002)
3. Alqurashi, E.: Predicting student satisfaction and perceived learning within online learning environments. Distance Educ. **40**(1), 133–148 (2019)
4. Bell, J., Sawaya, S., Cain, W.: Synchromodal classes: designing for shared learning experiences between face-to-face and online students. Int. J. Designs for Learning **5**(1), 68–82 (2014)
5. Bower, M., Dalgarno, B., Kennedy, G.E., Lee, M.J., Kenney, J.: Design and implementation factors in blended synchronous learning environments: outcomes from a cross-case analysis. Comput. Educ. **86**, 1–17 (2015)
6. Butz, N.T., Stupnisky, R.H.: A mixed methods study of graduate students' self-determined motivation in synchronous hybrid learning environments. The Internet and Higher Educ. **28**, 85–95 (J2016)
7. Cain, W.: Technology navigators: an innovative role in pedagogy, design and instructional support. In: Redmond, P., Lock, J., Danaher, P.A. (eds.) Educational Innovations and Contemporary Technologies, pp. 21–35. Palgrave Macmillan UK, London (2015)
8. Cohen, J.: A power primer. Psychol. Bull. **112**(1), 155–159 (1992)
9. Fredricks, J.A., Blumenfeld, P.C., Paris, A.H.: School engagement: potential of the concept, state of the evidence. Rev. Educ. Res. **74**(1), 59–109 (2004)
10. International Organization for Standardization. ISO/DIS 25062(en), Systems and software engineering—Systems and Software Quality Requirements and Evaluation (SQuaRE)—Common Industry Format (CIF) for usability: Quantitative usability test report. https://www.iso.org/obp/ui/#iso:std:iso:25062:dis:ed-1:v1:en
11. Irvine, V., Code, J., Richards, L.: Realigning higher education for the 21st-century learner through multi-access learning. MERLOT J. Online Learn. Teach. **9**(2), 172–186 (2013)
12. Joksimović, S., Gašević, D., Kovanović, V., Riecke, B.E., Hatala, M.: Social presence in online discussions as a process predictor of academic performance. J. Comput. Assist. Learn. **31**(6), 638–654 (2015)
13. Kreijns, K., Weidlich, J., Rajagopal, K.: The psychometric properties of a preliminary social presence measure using rasch analysis. In: Pammer-Schindler, V., Pérez-Sanagustín, M., Drachsler, H., Elferink, R., Scheffel, M. (eds.) Lifelong Technology-Enhanced Learning. LNCS, vol. 11082, pp. 31–44. Springer, Cham (2018)
14. Kreijns, K., Xu, K., Weidlich, J.: Social presence: conceptualization and measurement. Educ. Psychol. Rev. **34**, 139–170 (2022)
15. Lakhal, S., Mukamurera, J., Bédard, M., Heilporn, G., Chauret, M.: Students and instructors perspective on blended synchronous learning in a Canadian graduate program. J. Comput. Assist. Learn. **37**(5), 1383–1396 (2021)
16. Lei, H., Cui, Y., Zhou, W.: Relationships between student engagement and academic achievement: a meta-analysis. Soc. Behav. Personal. Int. J. **46**(3), 517–528 (2018)
17. Lu, J., Schmidt, M., Lee, M., Huang, R.: Usability research in educational technology: a state-of-the-art systematic review. Education Tech. Res. Dev. **70**, 1951–1992 (2022)

18. Nørgård, R.T.: Theorising hybrid lifelong learning. Br. J. Edu. Technol. **52**(4), 1709–1723 (2021)
19. Raes, A.: Exploring student and teacher experiences in hybrid learning environments: does presence matter? Postdigital Sci. Educ. **4**(1), 138–159 (2022)
20. Raes, A., Detienne, L., Windey, I., Depaepe, F.: A systematic literature review on synchronous hybrid learning: gaps identified. Learning Environ. Res. **23**(3), 269–290 (2020)
21. Raes, A., Vanneste, P., Pieters, M., Windey, I., Van Den Noortgate, W., Depaepe, F.: Learning and instruction in the hybrid virtual classroom: an investigation of students' engagement and the effect of quizzes. Comput. Educ. **143**, 103682 (2020)
22. Richardson, A.M., Dunn, P.K., McDonald, C., Oprescu, F.: CRiSP: an instrument for assessing student perceptions of classroom response systems. J. Sci. Educ. Technol. **24**(4), 432–447 (2015)
23. Richardson, J.C., Maeda, Y., Lv, J., Caskurlu, S.: Social presence in relation to students' satisfaction and learning in the online environment: a meta-analysis. Comput. Hum. Behav. **71**, 402–417 (2017)
24. Shi, Y., Tong, M., Long, T.: Investigating relationships among blended synchronous learning environments, students' motivation, and cognitive engagement: a mixed methods study. Comput. Educ. **168**, 104193 (2021)
25. Short, J., Williams, E., Christie, B.: The Social Psychology of Telecommunications. Wiley, London (1976)
26. Szeto, E., Cheng, A.Y.N.: Towards a framework of interactions in a blended synchronous learning environment: what effects are there on students' social presence experience? Interact. Learn. Environ. **24**(3), 487–503 (2016)
27. Ulla, M.B., Perales, W.F.: Hybrid teaching: Conceptualization through practice for the post COVID19 pandemic education. Frontiers in Education **7**, 924594 (2022)
28. Venkatesh, V.: Determinants of perceived ease of use: integrating control, intrinsic motivation, and emotion into the technology acceptance model. Inf. Syst. Res. **11**(4), 342–365 (2000)
29. Vlachogianni, P., Tselios, N.: Perceived usability evaluation of educational technology using the System Usability Scale (SUS): a systematic review. J. Res. Technol. Educ. **54**(3), 392–409 (2022)
30. Wei, X., Saab, N., Admiraal, W.: Do learners share the same perceived learning outcomes in MOOCs? identifying the role of motivation, perceived learning support, learning engagement, and self-regulated learning strategies. The Internet and Higher Educ. **56**, 100880 (2023)
31. White, C.P., Ramirez, R., Smith, J.G., Plonowski, L.: Simultaneous delivery of a face-to-face course to on-campus and remote off-campus students. TechTrends **54**(4), 34–40 (2010)
32. Willermark, S., Islind, A.S.: Seven educational affordances of virtual classrooms. Computers and Education Open **3**, 100078 (2022)
33. Zhan, Z., Mei, H.: Academic self-concept and social presence in face-to-face and online learning: perceptions and effects on students' learning achievement and satisfaction across environments. Comput. Educ. **69**, 131–138 (2013)
34. Zydney, J.M., McKimmy, P., Lindberg, R., Schmidt, M.: Here or there instruction: lessons learned in implementing innovative approaches to blended synchronous learning. TechTrends **63**(2), 123–132 (2019)
35. Zydney, J.M., Warner, Z., Angelone, L.: Learning through experience: using design based research to redesign protocols for blended synchronous learning environments. Comput. Educ. **143**, 103678 (2020)

Exploring the Potential of Immersive Virtual Environments for Learning American Sign Language

Jindi Wang[1(✉)], Ioannis Ivrissimtzis[1], Zhaoxing Li[1], Yunzhan Zhou[1], and Lei Shi[2]

[1] Department of Computer Science, Durham University, Durham, UK
{jindi.wang,ioannis.ivrissimtzis,zhaoxing.li2,yunzhan.zhou}@durham.ac.uk
[2] Open Lab, School of Computing, Newcastle University, Newcastle upon Tyne, UK
lei.shi@newcastle.ac.uk

Abstract. Sign languages enable effective communication between deaf and hearing people. Despite years of extensive pedagogical research, learning sign language online comes with a number of difficulties that might be frustrating for some students. Indeed, most of the existing approaches rely heavily on learning resources uploaded on websites, assuming that users will frequently consult them; however, this approach may feel tedious and uninspiring. To address this issue, several researchers have started looking into learning sign language in a game-based environment. However, the majority of the existing work still relies on website-based designs, with only a very few proposed systems providing an immersive virtual environment, and there are no user studies comparing website-based and immersive virtual environments. In this paper, we present an immersive environment for learning numbers 0–9 in American Sign Language (ASL). Our hypothesis is that an immersive virtual environment can provide users with a better learning experience and that users will show a higher level of engagement compared to website-based learning. We conducted a questionnaire-based user survey, and our initial findings suggest that users prefer to learn in an immersive virtual environment.

Keywords: Human Computer Interaction (HCI) · Interaction Design · Empirical Studies in Interaction Design · ASL Learning

1 Introduction

The World Health Organization (WHO)[1] predicts that, by 2050, about 2.5 billion people will have some degree of hearing loss, and at least 700 million of them will need some sort of hearing rehabilitation. The rehabilitation training procedures for people with hearing loss include the use of sign language and

[1] https://www.who.int/zh/news-room/fact-sheets/detail/deafness-and-hearing-loss.

O. Viberg et al. (Eds.): EC-TEL 2023, LNCS 14200, pp. 459–474, 2023.
https://doi.org/10.1007/978-3-031-42682-7_31

various alternative sensory techniques such as voice reading, writing with fingers on the palm of the hearing-impaired, and vibration sensing. While the most common form of communication for those who are deaf is sign language, most people without hearing loss have never studied sign language, making communication between these two groups challenging. Thus, the learning of sign language has become a key topic in educational research to break down communication barriers between diverse groups.

In the past years, face-to-face teaching of sign languages has been severely affected by the COVID-19 restrictions, with alternative online approaches filling in the gap. The majority of the latest approaches to teaching sign languages [10,11,20] employ website-based tools, while approaches based on immersive virtual reality (VR) technology [29] are more sparse in the literature. The following are some of the few studies on the VR-based approach. Adamo *et al.* [1] proposed the use of an immersive 3D learning environment to increase the mathematical skills of deaf children by teaching mathematical concepts and ASL's math terminology through user interaction with fantasy 3D virtual signers and environments. Schioppo *et al.* [24] proposed a sign language recognition method using features extracted from data acquired by a Leap Motion controller from an egocentric view. The method was tested on the 26 letters of the ASL alphabet. In a related development, Phan *et al.* [21] used motion tracking to trial a number of different methods for providing user feedback in a sign language learning system.

For the purposes of our study, we created a learning environment employing widely used VR technology to provide users with an immersive environment for learning numbers 0–9 in American Sign Language (ASL). Several issues with existing website-based and immersive approaches were identified and addressed in the design of our system, including small datasets for training the gesture recogniser, a lack of real-world settings, and most importantly, a lack of user satisfaction for sustained engagement with the system. To improve user experience, inspired by the ASL Sea Battle [7], a sign language game that was created by Bragg *et al.* to facilitate the gathering of user data, we developed and introduced into the system a Whack-a-Mole type of game.

To the best of our knowledge, no previous user studies are focusing on comparing website-based with VR-based systems, especially for learning 0–9 in ASL. Hence, we conducted a user study based on the survey scheme proposed by Schrepp *et al.* [26], aiming at comparing differences in user experience between an immersive and a website-based environment. The website-based environment was developed by Quizlet[2]. To make fair comparisons, the design aimed at maximising the consistency between the two environments.

Summarising, the main research question motivating our work: ***"Does an immersive ASL learning environment provide better user experience to learn ASL compared to a web-based environment?"***, was looked into within the context of an immersive environment for learning numbers between 0 and 9 in ASL. Our main contributions are as follows:

[2] https://quizlet.com/560702085/asl-numbers-0-9-flash-cards/.

1. We implemented a novel immersive virtual environment for ASL learning with a Whack-a-Mole type of game.
2. We provide initial evidence that immersive virtual environments can enhance users' learning experience and engagement when compared to website-based learning environments for ASL. This suggests that incorporating immersive elements into ASL education may be a promising direction for improving learning outcomes and user satisfaction.

2 Related Work

First, we briefly review sign language recognition, which is a crucial technology for computer-assisted sign language learning and an important technical part of our system. Then, we go over some current research on web-based sign language learning, concentrating on the issues of effectiveness and usability of the website's features. Finally, we review research on sign language as a communication tool in general, going beyond the learning of the language.

Sign Language Recognition: Bheda *et al.* [4] proposed a method based on deep convolutional neural networks (CNNs) to recognize images of gestures of the letters and digits in ASL. Kim *et al.* [16] proposed a novel sign language recognition method, which employs an object detection network for a region of interest (ROI) segmentation to preprocess the input data. Battistoni *et al.* [3] described a method for ASL alphabet recognition based on CNNs, which allows for monitoring the users' learning progress. Jiang *et al.* [13] proposed a novel fingerspelling identification method for Chinese Sign Language via AlexNet-based transfer learning and evaluated four different methods of transfer learning. Camgoz *et al.* [8] introduced a novel transformer-based architecture that jointly learns Continuous Sign Language Recognition and Translation while being trainable in an end-to-end manner. Zhang *et al.* [31] proposed MediaPipe Hands, a real-time on-device hand tracking pipeline to compute hand landmark positions from a single RGB camera frame for AR/VR applications. Goswami *et al.* [12] created a new dataset for ASL recognition and used it to train a CNN-based model for hand gesture recognition and classification. Finally, Pallavi *et al.* [18] presented a deep learning model based on the YOLOv3 architecture, reporting high recognition rates on the ASL alphabet.

Having reviewed the existing work on sign language recognition, we concluded that Mediapipe is the most suitable tool for the purposes of this paper, and thus, we used it for sign language recognition, benefiting from its highly accurate, real-time detection of hand landmark points. Moreover, as an open-source hand gesture detection framework from Google, it is well-documented and supported.

Website-Based Sign Language Learning: Kumar *et al.* [17] proposed a sign language translation system based solely on visual input, employing deep learning for accurate translation. Joy *et al.* [15] proposed SignQuiz, a finger-spelt sign learning application for Indian sign language (ISL), utilizing automatic sign language recognition techniques. Vaitkevičius *et al.* [28] presented a system capable of learning gestures using the data from the Leap Motion device and classifying them with Hidden Markov Classification (HMC). Bird *et al.* [5] used a late fusion approach for sign language recognition from multi-modal data. They significantly improved the overall accuracy compared to single-modality image classification (88.14%) and Leap Motion data classification (72.73%). John *et al.* [14] proposed a system aiming at handling regional variations in vocabulary and grammar through a common vision-based platform. Empe *et al.* [10] developed a smartphone app called SimboWika to help deaf primary school kids learn Filipino Sign Language. They were motivated by the observation that communication between those who have hearing loss and those who do not can be challenging, especially when considering the unique perspective of persons with hearing loss language, and the lack of proficiency in sign language by those without hearing loss. Estrada *et al.* [11] proposed a web tool aimed at kids with and without hearing difficulties. They used a game to help children learn sign language through play. Patricks *et al.* [20] developed the interactive website application Sign2Sign, integrating real-time sign language detection AI, dynamic 3D avatars, and conversation-focused sign language instruction to support sign language education.

We note that, despite the significant size of some of the research projects behind these proposed methods and systems, there is no systematic evaluation of how users are affected by their interactions with these systems and, ultimately, how well the sign language students are progressing. Thus, we argue that user research is necessary, and the questionnaire interview format seems to be appropriate for an initial investigation.

Sign Language Applications: Bantupalli *et al.* [2] presented a vision-based application for translating sign language to text, thus aiding communication between signers and non-signers. Their recognition model takes video sequences and extracts temporal and spatial features from them. Schnepp *et al.* [25] argued that an animated sign language dictionary is a valuable resource for caregivers learning to communicate with residents who use sign language. They developed such a tool using a human-centred design methodology. Samonte [23] developed an e-tutor system, assisting instructors with course delivery and assessment. Economou *et al.* [9] developed a Serious Game (SG) aiming at closing the communication gap between the able hearing people and those with hearing impairment. Their tool facilitates sign language learning, specifically targeting the adult population. Wang *et al.* [30] developed a gamified sign language environment with characteristics that users could personalise. They found that gamification improved user experience. The research we reviewed on sign language applications shows that dictionary searches and gamification can improve users' motivation, which informed our choice to include such features in our system design.

Our survey of the literature verified that, as we have already noted, the majority of the existing work utilizes web-based solutions for the creation of sign language learning interfaces. This is often the most convenient solution, making it easy for the user to access all the learning materials. However, on the other hand, such an approach can lead to users developing a sense of repetitiveness and feelings of boredom. This is an observation supported by user feedback on such systems, and in fact, some users would drop out of the learning process altogether due to a lack of motivation [19].

Thus, the main objective of our work is to investigate whether virtual environments can provide a better user experience in sign language learning. We built a VR-based system that provides users with an immersive experience and added a quiz and a small game to stimulate users' interest and improve their experience. We note that recent advances in VR technology mean that there is a more general trend of migration of online tasks from web-based systems on the 2D planar screen to the immersive 3D space [22]; our system does something similar for sign language learning. Moreover, noting the absence of user research on the subject, in order to determine if an immersive learning environment can indeed improve the user experience when learning a sign language, we invited two groups of users to undertake an interview survey. Our aims were to evaluate our system and compare the user experience of learning 0–9 in ASL with a website-based learning environment.

3 User Interface of Immersive Environment and Website

This section provides an overview of the key components of the proposed immersive environment and the main features and user interfaces to compare with the web-based learning environment, as shown in Fig. 1.

3.1 The Immersive Learning Environment

Figure 1(a) shows the learning resources and the game in the immersive learning environment, from the user's perspective 45° to the left. The whole scene was created in Unity (2020.3.32f1). Regarding the user's interaction with the system, we track their eye position with the HTC Vive Pro's eye-tracking feature and enable the functions of clicking or picking an object after 3 s of fixed attention by the user.

The image acquisition was done by an integrated camera, linked to a PC using openCV (3.4.2) [6]. Regarding gesture recognition, Mediapipe was used to detect the user's hand and extract a sequence of 21 feature points (p_0, p_1, p_2,...,p_{20}), corresponding to landmarks on the detected hand. We set p_0, the point at the bottom of the palm near the user's wrist, as the origin of the frame's coordinate system. Let (x_i, y_i) be the coordinates of the point p_i. They are normalized by

$$x_i = \frac{x_i - x_0}{x_{max}}, \quad y_i = \frac{y_i - y_0}{y_{max}}, \qquad i = 1, 2, \ldots, 20. \tag{1}$$

where

$$\begin{aligned} x_{max} &= max(\,|x_1 - x_0|, |x_2 - x_0|, \ldots, |x_{20} - x_0|\,) \\ y_{max} &= max(\,|y_1 - y_0|, |y_2 - y_0|, \ldots, |y_{20} - y_0|\,) \end{aligned} \tag{2}$$

and are then fed as a feature vector to the classifier. The classifier is a multilayer perceptron consisting of three fully connected layers, implemented in Python 3.6 and Tensorflow 2.6.0. We trained the classifier on a commodity PC with an RTX3080 GPU. The obtained recognition accuracy rates were above 90%, a result that was deemed sufficient for the purposes of this study as it is expected to support an overall smooth user experience.

The implemented user interfaces comprise four different modules: **Instructions**, **Sign Language Dictionary**, **Quiz**, and **Whack-a-Mole Game**, respectively. Each module is described in more detail below.

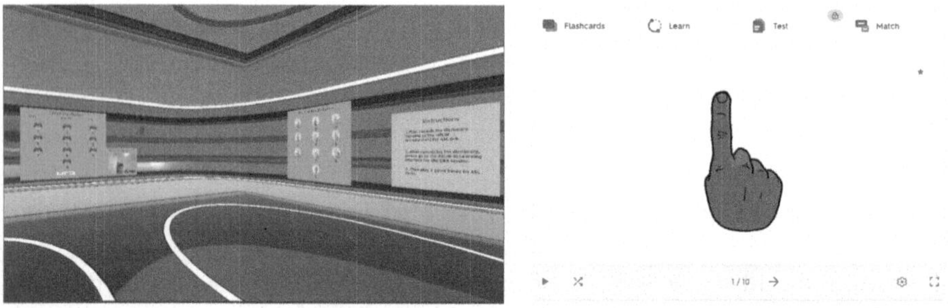

(a) (b)

Fig. 1. (a) The implemented immersive environment for 0–9 ASL learning. (b) The website-based 0–9 ASL learning environment.

Instructions. In order to make the system easy to use, we created an **Instructions** interface, which also serves as the point of entry when the user logs into the system. In this interface, the user is introduced to the following three basic steps of the learning process, see also Fig. 2 (right).

1. Consulting the numbers 0–9 in an ASL dictionary (located to the left of the **Instructions**) to familiarise themselves with ASL 0–9 for about 5 min.
2. Users can self-assess their study of ASL 0–9 by accessing the **Quiz** module.
3. Users can engage in a game of Whack-a-Mole.

Sign Language Dictionary. We created an ASL dictionary for users to search. Figure 2 shows illustrations of how the user can sign/express the numbers 0 to 9 (to the left of the Instructions).

Quiz. To improve the efficacy of the learning process, we integrated into the system a question-answer module that allows the users to assess their level of competence and, at the same time, exercise their signing skills by responding to a series of questions generated at random from a data bank. In the example shown in Fig. 3(a), the system pulled from the data bank the question "Can you

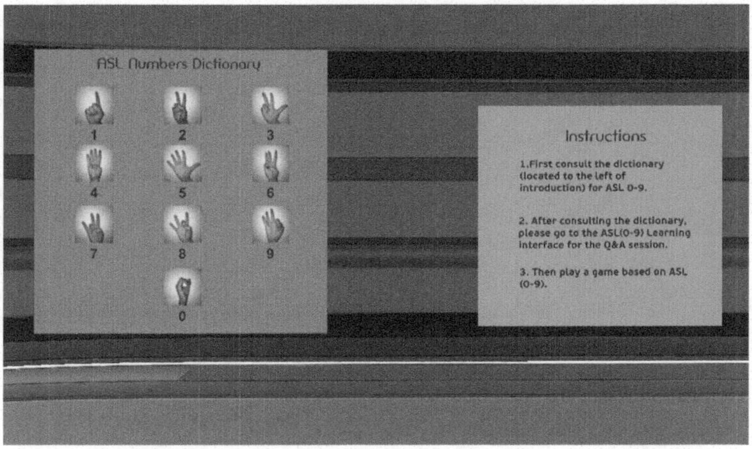

Fig. 2. The user's initial perspective of 0–9 ASL **Dictionary** and **Instructions**.

sign for 9?". After perhaps consulting the dictionary, and if they have developed the appropriate skill, the user can sign the word "9". Alternatively, they can select the "I don't know" option, and the system will demonstrate to them the appropriate expression. In that case, the user will also be advised to continue exercising until they indicate that they feel comfortable signing that digit by pressing the relevant button.

Whack-a-Mole Game. We adopted the Whack-a-Mole game and implemented a sign language-based version of it, aiming to engage users and improve their learning experience. In our game, as shown in Fig. 3(b), each location is marked by a unique identifier. If the user signs correctly the current position of the gopher, one point is added; otherwise, no point is awarded. By default, if the user does not sign the gopher's location within 3 s, a new gopher will appear. The total duration of the game is 30 s.

3.2 Website Environment

Figure 1(b) shows the user interface of learning 0–9 ASL in a website environment, which includes **Flashcards**, **Learn** and **Match**.

The **Flashcards** corresponds to the user interface of the sign language dictionary in the VR environment so that users can quickly become familiar with the representation of 0–9 numbers. Besides, the **Learn** module, like the Quiz interface, is used to further enhance the user's familiarity with the 0–9 ASL as shown in Fig. 3(c). Moreover, the **Match**, module as shown in Fig. 3(d), like the Whack-a-Mole game, is a match game used to enhance the entertainment of learning 0–9 in ASL.

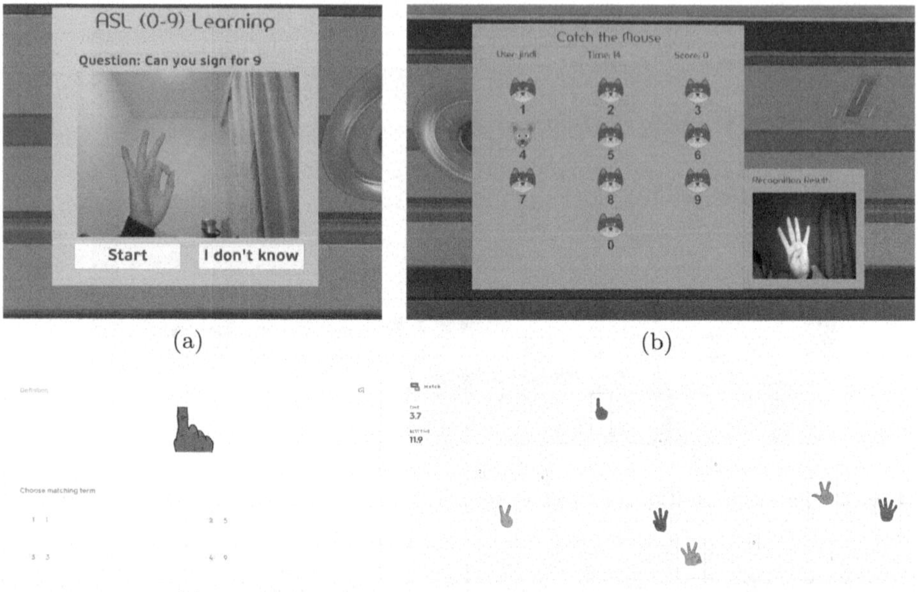

(a) (b) (c) (d)

Fig. 3. (a) The 0–9 ASL learning quiz module in a VR environment. (b) The 0–9 ASL learning game in a VR environment. (c) The 0–9 ASL learning quiz module in a website environment. (d) The 0–9 ASL learning game in a website environment.

4 Methodology

With the intention of collecting user feedback, which would serve as the study's data source, we invited 15 users (M = 8, F = 7) to test the immersive sign language learning environment we developed, and 15 different users (M = 8, F = 7) to test the website-based ASL learning environment. Most users have minimal to no prior knowledge of ASL or other sign languages.

Users of the immersive environment first read the Instructions interface to become familiar with the learning procedure and then moved to the 0–9 ASL dictionary to spend 5 min studying the representations of the 0–9 digits. Users were encouraged to use the Quiz interface and take quizzes after they felt comfortable with them, and to use the Whack-a-Mole interface to play the game when they considered themselves familiar with them. In the website-based environment, users first queried the **Flashcards** for 5 min to get familiar with 0–9 in ASL, then they were encouraged to click the "Learn" button to take quizzes that contain multiple choice questions, and finally to click the "Match" button to enter the match game.

We adopted the user survey scheme proposed by Schrepp *et al.* [26], which is commonly used for evaluating the user experience in interactive systems, comprising six *scales*, each one representing a distinct user experience aspect: **Attractiveness**, **Efficiency**, **Perspicuity**, **Dependability**, **Stimulation**,

Novelty. Each scale is divided into either six or four more specific items, as shown in Table 1. Following the recommended protocol, we evaluated the user experience, on each of the 26 items, on a 7-point Likert scale ranging from -3 (fully agree with a negative term) to +3 (fully agree with a positive term). After the completion of the questionnaire, qualitative feedback was collected through follow-up interviews with the users.

Table 1. User experience questionnaire.

Attractiveness	Perspicuity
A1: annoying / enjoyable	**P1**: not understandable / understandable
A2: good / bad	**P2**: easy to learn / difficult to learn
A3: unlikable / pleasing	**P3**: complicated / easy
A4: unpleasant / pleasant	**P4**: clear / confusing
A5: attractive / unattractive	
A6: friendly / unfriendly	
Efficiency	**Dependability**
E1: fast / slow	**D1**: unpredictable / predictable
E2: inefficient / efficient	**D2**: obstructive / supportive
E3: impractical / practical	**D3**: secure / not secure
E4: organized / cluttered	**D4**: meets expectations / does not meet expectations
Stimulation	**Novelty**
S1: valuable / inferior	**N1**: creative / dull
S2: boring / exciting	**N2**: inventive / conventional
S3: not interesting / interesting	**N3**: usual / leading edge
S4: motivating / demotivating	**N4**: conservative / innovative

5 Result Analysis

In this section, we present the analysis of the data collected from the two groups, aiming at a comparison of user experience between the VR and the Web-based environments. Figure 4 shows the distribution of scores for each question in the two learning environments.

Figure 4 shows mean value scores for each item in the two learning environments. Clearly, the distribution of the mean scores of VR is more favourable than that of the web-based environment, indicating higher user satisfaction when using the former. We also notice that all mean scores for the VR are positive, while those for the Web are mixed. From qualitative user feedback, we found that the items with negative mean scores are mostly because users felt bored during the Web learning sessions (Fig. 5).

To further compare the user experience in the two learning environments, we studied user feedback against the benchmark proposed in [27]. In that paper,

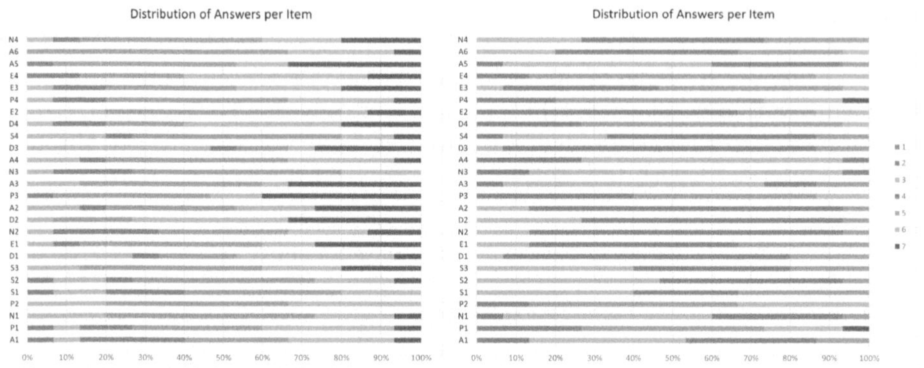

Fig. 4. The score distributions for the VR (left), and the Web (right) environments.

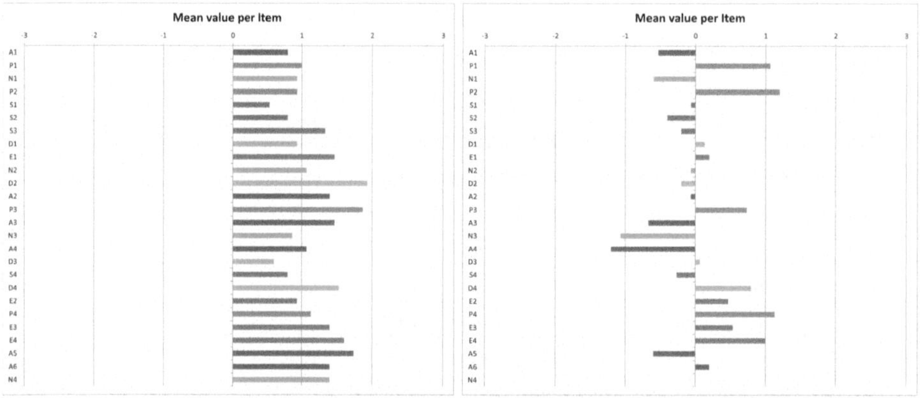

Fig. 5. Mean value scores for each item, in VR (left), and the Web (right) environments.

the authors analysed a large database of questionnaire responses and proposed the benchmark intervals in Table 2.

- **Excellent**: In the range of the 10% best results.
- **Good**: 10% of results better, 75% of results worse.
- **Above average**: 25% of results better, 50% of results worse.
- **Below average**: 50% of results better, 25% of results worse.
- **Bad**: In the range of the 25% worst results.

Figure 6 depicts the distribution of six scales in Benchmark intervals, in which different colours represent different benchmark intervals. We can observe that the mean values of six scales except **Stimulation** in the VR environment are above average; this indicates that a large number of users can accept learning ASL 0–9 in VR, while in the Web environment, the mean values of six scales are almost below the average, indicating that users have a low acceptance of learning ASL 0–9 on website. The six scales in the two learning environments are analysed below.

Table 2. Benchmark intervals for the user experience scales.

	Attractiveness	Perspicuity	Efficiency	Dependability	Stimulation	Novelty
Excellent	≥ 1.75	≥ 1.78	≥ 1.90	≥ 1.65	≥ 1.55	≥ 1.40
Good	[1.52, 1.75)	[1.47, 1.78)	[1.56, 1.90)	[1.48, 1.65)	[1.31, 1.55)	[1.05, 1.40)
Above average	[1.17, 1.52)	[0.98, 1.47)	[1.08, 1.56)	[1.14, 1.48)	[0.99, 1.31)	[0.71, 1.05)
Below average	[0.70, 1.17)	[0.54, 0.98)	[0.64, 1.08)	[0.78, 1.14)	[0.50, 0.99)	[0.30, 0.71)
Bad	<0.70	<0.54	<0.64	<0.78	<0.50	<0.30

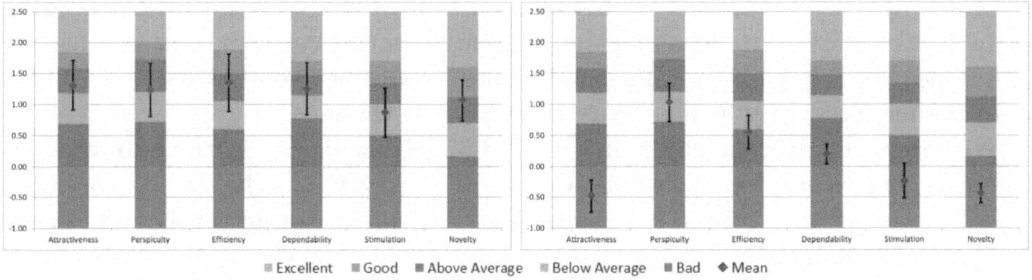

Fig. 6. Benchmark intervals for the six scales, in VR (left), and the Web (right).

Attractiveness: the average score in VR is 1.311 (SD = 0.791) in the "above average" category, while for Web it is -0.478 (SD = 0.511) in the "Bad" category. This suggests that users find the VR environment more attractive for them to learn sign language. However, it received low scores from several users in terms of "annoying/enjoyable", as shown in Fig. 4. This could be due to the fact that the user needs to wear a headset which increases their learning burden. Besides, for the web-based environment, it received low scores in terms of "unpleasant/pleasant", as shown in Fig. 4. This may be because the content they were learning is not interesting enough.

Perspicuity: the average score for VR is 1.233 (SD = 0.848) in the "above average" category, while for Web it is 1.033 (SD = 0.611) in the "Below average" category. The two platforms have similar scores on this scale and are both around the average, indicating that the perspicuity of both platforms is well-received by users.

Efficiency: the average score for VR is 1.350 (SD = 0.915) in the "above average" category, while for Web it is 0.550 (SD = 0.536) in the "Bad" category. Although the score of VR is higher than that of the Web, the standard deviation of VR is also larger than that of the Web, indicating that VR fluctuates greatly under the efficiency scale. The possible reason is that some users have used VR equipment before and did not need to re-learn the use of VR equipment; while some users had no experience in using VR before and needed to learn the use of VR, which might increase their learning load.

Dependability: the average score in VR is 1.250 (SD = 0.829) in the "above average" category, while for Web it is 0.200 (SD = 0.316) in the "Bad" category. Although the standard deviation of VR on this scale is large, it means that some users feel that VR needs to be strengthened in terms of Dependability. Several users thought they executed the right gesture but were judged as being wrong. The back-end gesture recognition algorithm may be underperforming due to inadequate training data for particular gestures, resulting in low recognition accuracy rates. Future developments are planned to train recognition models to better generalize to user hand physiological variances.

Stimulation: the average score in VR is 0.867 (SD = 0.784) in the "Below average" category, while for Web it is -0.233 (SD = 0.563) in the "Bad" category. The score of VR on this scale is higher than that of the Web, because according to the feedback of users, learning sign language on the Web was only a selection with a mouse click, while in VR, sign language could be used to express numbers in an immersive way, which is more attractive to them.

Novelty: the average score in VR is 1.067 (SD = 0.651) in the "above average" category, while for Web it is -0.433 (SD = 0.306) in the "Bad" category. Today's users are acclimated to searching and learning content on the web, hence the Web's score on this scale is low. VR scores higher than the Web because many people have never learned in VR and find it novel.

In [27], the scales of the user experience questionnaire are grouped into *pragmatic quality* (Perspicuity, Efficiency, Dependability), and *hedonic quality* (Stimulation, Novelty), while Attractiveness is a pure valence dimension. Pragmatic quality describes task-related quality aspects, and hedonic quality describes the non-task-related quality aspects. Table 3 shows the mean scores for the two environments over these grouped scales, and the corresponding p-values. We note that, in all cases, we have statistically significant differences, especially regarding attractiveness and hedonic quality.

Table 3. Means and p-values for the three groups of scales.

Pragmatic and Hedonic Quality	VR	Website	P-Value
Attractiveness	1.31	−0.48	5.73216E-20
Pragmatic Quality	1.28	0.59	1.86984E-09
Hedonic Quality	0.97	−0.33	1.23737E-18

6 Discussion

We used VR technology to create an immersive environment for learning numbers in ASL and conducted a user study on it. We investigated whether immersive environments can provide a better user experience. Our hypothesis that users prefer to learn ASL 0–9 in an immersive, rather than a website-based environment, was tested with a questionnaire-based study on two groups of users.

We employed six assessment scales - **Attractiveness**, **Efficiency**, **Perspicuity**, **Dependability**, **Stimulation**, **Novelty** - on which users judged the system's design. The results show that our immersive ASL learning system performs effectively and can essentially meet user requirements for ASL learning. Thus, we were able to answer affirmatively the research question of whether an immersive ASL learning environment provides a better user experience to learn ASL. The analysis of environmental experience reveals that most users prefer to learn sign language in an immersive VR environment, probably because it is more experiential, while only very few users prefer to learn ASL via the web-based learning environment, primarily because they find it convenient and user-friendly to search for sign language information on web pages.

We note that, even though most users prefer immersive VR learning environments, the technology is still in its early stages of development. The system needs to be further streamlined and tweaked for specific functions to enhance the user experience. In particular, qualitative user feedback revealed the following limitations of the immersive VR learning environment.

6.1 Limitations

For each assessment scale, the main limitations of the system's design and implementation were as follows. **Attractiveness**: some users complained that there weren't any animated hints when sign language was correctly deciphered. The user's experience could be improved by including animated hints. **Efficiency**: some users have complained that our interface is not sufficiently automatic because playing the sign language game requires them to press the start button actively. **Perspicuity**: some users have reported that they did not know how to move around in the scene. **Dependability**: some users reported that they had made the correct sign language while playing the game, but the system judged that it was wrong, resulting in a lower score for the user. **Stimulation**: from the analysis of the stimulation scale results, a small number of users gave low scores, indicating that our system needs to be designed more creatively. **Novelty**: a small number of users thought that the system was not innovative enough, perhaps because they perceived the learning model as too easy.

Additionally, there were several methodological issues with our study that need to be considered. Firstly, with only 30 people taking part in the user survey, the sample size is relatively small and may not give an accurate representation of the intended audience. Secondly, as our study included only Chinese participants, the findings might not apply to people from different cultural backgrounds. To ensure broader validity of the findings, future studies should be based on larger and more varied samples.

7 Conclusion

We developed a virtual setting that gives users an immersive experience for learning ASL. We created four user interfaces corresponding to four distinct types of functionality, enabling users to easily comprehend the system's workflow and each phase of ASL learning: an instruction module, an ASL dictionary, a quiz module, and an ASL game based on Whack-a-Mole. To determine the acceptability of our UIs and evaluate user satisfaction with the virtual environment design, the findings of a user questionnaire were analysed (N = 30). The results indicated that users were generally satisfied with the virtual environment we built, and they preferred it against the website-based learning mode. Overall, the outcome supports our initial hypothesis that immersive virtual environments can improve users' experience of learning ASL.

In the future, we plan to include in our immersive environment more interactive elements such as backdrop movement, scene changes, and animation prompts. We also plan to implement various automatic settings to minimize the need for user interaction for the control of the system, and a follow-through user interface will be created so that the user can comprehend how to move the items in the scene. Furthermore, a more robust sign recognition model will be created, allowing us to include more sophisticated sign language learning material.

References

1. Adamo-Villani, N., Carpenter, E., Arns, L.: An immersive virtual environment for learning sign language mathematics. In: ACM SIGGRAPH 2006 Educators Program, pp. 20-es (2006)
2. Bantupalli, K., Xie, Y.: American sign language recognition using deep learning and computer vision. In: Proceedings of ICBD, pp. 4896–4899. IEEE (2018)
3. Battistoni, P., Di Gregorio, M., Sebillo, M., Vitiello, G.: Ai at the edge for sign language learning support. In: Proceedings of HCC, pp. 16–23. IEEE (2019)
4. Bheda, V., Radpour, D.: Using deep convolutional networks for gesture recognition in American sign language. arXiv:1710.06836 (2017)
5. Bird, J.J., Ekárt, A., Faria, D.R.: British sign language recognition via late fusion of computer vision and leap motion with transfer learning to American sign language. Sensors **20**(18), 5151 (2020)
6. Bradski, G., Kaehler, A.: Opencv. Dr. Dobb's J. Softw. Tools **3**, 120 (2000)
7. Bragg, D., Caselli, N., Gallagher, J.W., Goldberg, M., Oka, C.J., Thies, W.: ASL sea battle: gamifying sign language data collection. In: Proceedings of CHI-HFCS, pp. 1–13 (2021)
8. Camgoz, N.C., Koller, O., Hadfield, S., Bowden, R.: Sign language transformers: joint end-to-end sign language recognition and translation. In: Proceedings of CVPR, pp. 10023–10033 (2020)
9. Economou, D., Russi, M.G., Doumanis, I., Mentzelopoulos, M., Bouki, V., Ferguson, J.: Using serious games for learning british sign language combining video, enhanced interactivity, and VR technology. J. Univ. Comput. Sci. **26**(8), 996–1016 (2020)
10. Empe, N.A.A., Echon, R.C.L., Vega, H.D.A., Paterno, P.L.C., Jamis, M.N., Yabut, E.R.: SimboWika: a mobile and web application to learn filipino sign language for deaf students in elementary schools. In: Proceedings of R10-HTC, pp. 1–6. IEEE (2020)
11. Estrada-Cota, I., Carreño-León, M.A., Sandoval-Bringas, J.A., Leyva-Carrillo, A.A., Quiroz, H.X.C.: Design of a Web tool for teaching-learning of states and capitals of México through the Mexican sign language. In: Proceedings of ICITE, pp. 174–179. IEEE (2021)

12. Goswami, T., Javaji, S.R.: CNN model for American sign language recognition. In: Kumar, A., Mozar, S. (eds.) ICCCE 2020. LNEE, vol. 698, pp. 55–61. Springer, Singapore (2021). https://doi.org/10.1007/978-981-15-7961-5_6
13. Jiang, X., Hu, B., Chandra Satapathy, S., Wang, S.H., Zhang, Y.D.: Fingerspelling identification for Chinese sign language via alexnet-based transfer learning and adam optimizer. Scientific Programming 2020 (2020)
14. John, A., Krishnan, R.H., Vinitha, A.M.: Language Recognition System: An Application Based Study with Special Reference to Sociolinguistics and Computational Linguistics (2021)
15. Joy, J., Balakrishnan, K., Sreeraj, M.: Signquiz: a quiz based tool for learning finger spelled signs in Indian sign language using ASLR. IEEE Access **7**, 28363–28371 (2019)
16. Kim, S., Ji, Y., Lee, K.B.: An effective sign language learning with object detection based ROI segmentation. In: Proceedings of IRC, pp. 330–333. IEEE (2018)
17. Kumar, S.S., Wangyal, T., Saboo, V., Srinath, R.: Time series neural networks for real time sign language translation. In: Proceedings of ICMLA, pp. 243–248. IEEE (2018)
18. Pallavi, P., Sarvamangala, D.: Recognition of sign language using deep neural network. Int. J. Adv. Res. Comput. Sci. **12**, 92–97 (2021)
19. Park, J.H., Choi, H.J.: Factors influencing adult learners' decision to drop out or persist in online learning. J. Educ. Technol. Soc. **12**(4), 207–217 (2009)
20. Patricks, A.: Developing an accessible learning application for sign language (c) (2022)
21. Phan, H.D., Ellis, K., Dorin, A., Olivier, P.: Feedback strategies for embodied agents to enhance sign language vocabulary learning. In: ACM-IVA, pp. 1–8 (2020)
22. Reisoğlu, I., Topu, B., Yılmaz, R., Karakuş Yılmaz, T., Göktaş, Y.: 3d virtual learning environments in education: a meta-review. Asia Pac. Educ. Rev. **18**, 81–100 (2017)
23. Samonte, M.J.C.: An assistive technology using fsl, speech recognition, gamification and online handwritten character recognition in learning statistics for students with hearing and speech impairment. In: Proceedings of ICFET, pp. 92–97 (2020)
24. Schioppo, J., Meyer, Z., Fabiano, D., Canavan, S.: Sign language recognition: Learning American sign language in a virtual environment. In: Extended Abstracts of the CHI Conference on Human Factors in Computing Systems, pp. 1–6 (2019)
25. Schnepp, J., Wolfe, R., Brionez, G., Baowidan, S., Johnson, R., McDonald, J.: Human-centered design for a sign language learning application. In: Proceedings of PETRAE, pp. 1–5 (2020)
26. Schrepp, M., Hinderks, A., Thomaschewski, J.: Applying the User Experience Questionnaire (UEQ) in different evaluation scenarios. In: Marcus, A. (ed.) DUXU 2014. LNCS, vol. 8517, pp. 383–392. Springer, Cham (2014). https://doi.org/10.1007/978-3-319-07668-3_37
27. Schrepp, M., Thomaschewski, J., Hinderks, A.: Construction of a benchmark for the user experience questionnaire (UEQ). Int. J. Interact. Multimed. Artif. Intell. **4**(4), 40–44 (2017)
28. Vaitkevičius, A., Taroza, M., Blažauskas, T., Damaševičius, R., Maskeliūnas, R., Woźniak, M.: Recognition of American sign language gestures in a virtual reality using leap motion. Appl. Sci. **9**(3), 445 (2019)
29. Wang, J., Ivrissimtzis, I., Li, Z., Zhou, Y., Shi, L.: Developing and evaluating a novel gamified virtual learning environment for ASL. In: INTERACT 2023. LNCS. Springer (2023)

30. Wang, J., Ivrissimtzis, I., Li, Z., Zhou, Y., Shi, L.: User-defined hand gesture interface to improve user experience of learning American sign language. In: International Conference on Intelligent Tutoring Systems, pp. 479–490. Springer (2023)
31. Zhang, F., et al.: Mediapipe hands: on-device real-time hand tracking. arXiv:2006.10214 (2020)

Towards Improving the Reliability and Transparency of ChatGPT for Educational Question Answering

Yongchao Wu(✉), Aron Henriksson, Martin Duneld, and Jalal Nouri

Stockholm University, NOD-huset, Borgarfjordsgatan 12, 16455 Stockholm, Sweden
{yongchao.wu,aronhen,xmartin,jalal}@dsv.su.se

Abstract. Large language models (LLMs), such as ChatGPT, have shown remarkable performance on various natural language processing (NLP) tasks, including educational question answering (EQA). However, LLMs generate text entirely based on knowledge obtained during pre-training, which means they struggle with recent information or domain-specific knowledge bases. Moreover, only providing answers to questions posed to LLMs without any grounding materials makes it difficult for students to judge their validity. We therefore propose a method for integrating information retrieval systems with LLMs when developing EQA systems, which in addition to improving EQA performance grounds the answers in the educational context. Our experiments show that the proposed system outperforms vanilla ChatGPT with a significant margin of 110.9%, 67.8%, 43.3%, and 9.2% on BLEU, ROUGE, METEOR and BERTScore. In addition, we argue that the use of the retrieved educational context enhances the transparency and reliability of the EQA process, making it easier to determine the correctness of the answers.

Keywords: AI · NLP · ChatGPT · LLMs · Educational Question Answering

1 Introduction

Large language models (LLMs), such as BERT [2] and the GPT [12] family models, have made significant strides in advancing the Natural Language Processing (NLP) field by surpassing previous state-of-the-art benchmarks on numerous tasks. ChatGPT [10], a recently developed LLM pre-trained on extensive datasets using reinforcement learning with human feedback, has further highlighted the potential of LLMs to generate high-quality, natural and fluent conversation responses based on natural language formatted input, which has brought attention to LLMs from both academia and industry. Furthermore, the capability of ChatGPT to perform NLP tasks without the need for adding specific training data by utilizing a prompt message that includes either a few examples (few-shot) or no examples (zero-shot) of the user's intention, facilitates the scalability of artificial intelligence (AI) based applications in various domains,

O. Viberg et al. (Eds.): EC-TEL 2023, LNCS 14200, pp. 475–488, 2023.
https://doi.org/10.1007/978-3-031-42682-7_32

including education. An example of such an application is the educational question answering systems (EQA) that can automatically provide answers to queries from educators or learners. EQA systems are particularly advantageous in normal classes and Massive Open Online Courses (MOOCs), where there are many students but limited educators are available to answer their queries. EQA systems enable learners to get prompt answers to their questions, reducing wait times and enabling them to solve problems immediately, [4] which not only enhances the learning experience but also eases the heavy burden on educators [17].

The integration of responsible AI into education is crucial [9]; however, building responsible LLM-based EQA systems is challenging for several reasons. Firstly, LLMs have the limitation of being inclined to hallucinate [5], which might lead to misconceptions. Secondly, LLMs generate answers based on the knowledge they acquire during pre-training, which limits their ability to access up-to-date information [7] and specific educational knowledge bases, which, in turn, can affect the reliability of the models. Furthermore, since ChatGPT is not a open-source system, its retrieving process is concealed from end users. This lack of transparency makes it difficult for users to verify the grounding material behind the provided answers.

To address these challenges, this study proposes a novel method that combines an Information Retrieval System (IRS) and an LLM for performing EQA. Firstly, we utilize an IRS to index learning materials as a knowledge base. When a student poses a query, the IRS first retrieves the relevant educational context. This context serves two purposes: i) it explicitly provides grounding material for generated answers, ii) it constructs a context-aware prompt message to assist the LLM in providing context-related answers. By incorporating this approach, we aim to improve the reliability and transparency of EQA systems, thus ensuring that students receive more accurate and trustworthy answers to their queries.

The layout of this paper is structured as follows. In Sect. 2, the formulation of the proposed EQA approach and information about the SciQ datasets are presented. Section 3 describes the experimental settings, evaluation metrics, and results for the EQA performance. Lastly, Sect. 4 concludes the paper and suggests possible avenues for future research.

2 Data and Method

This section begins by providing an overview of the dataset utilized in this study, followed by a description of our proposed EQA approach.

2.1 Data

We deploy the open dataset, SciQ [15], to evaluate our proposed approach for EQA. An example of the SciQ dataset is shown in Fig. 1. The SciQ dataset encompasses more than 10,000 science questions in a multiple-choice format, where each *educational question* is accompanied by a human-labelled correct

SciQ Dataset Example	
Supporting Material	Today, most living things use oxygen to make ATP from glucose. However, many living things can also make ATP without oxygen. This is true of some plants and fungi and also of many bacteria. These organisms use aerobic respiration when oxygen is present, but when oxygen is in short supply, they use anaerobic respiration instead. Certain bacteria can only use anaerobic respiration. In fact, they may not be able to survive at all in the presence of oxygen.
Educational Question	What do most living things use to make ATP from glucose?
Answer	oxygen

Fig. 1. Example of SciQ dataset for question answering. SciQ provides an educational question, the correct answer to the question, and supporting material for each example.

answer. This dataset was developed with a specific emphasis on the education domain, including subjects related to physics, chemistry, and biology, and has been rigorously evaluated for its educational efficacy in real-world science examinations. To aid in the identification of the correct answer, the supplementary *supporting material* is provided for the majority of questions. In this work, the collection of supplementary *supporting materials* serves as the knowledge base for the EQA task, where the correct *answers* are utilized as gold labels.

2.2 Method

In an EQA scenario, frozen LLMs, like ChatGPT, solely present an answer to an educational question without indicating the underlying source on which the answer is based, negatively impacting their reliability and transparency. Figure 2 illustrates the workflow of our proposed EQA approach. Our approach differs from vanilla ChatGPT in that it not only generates answers but also explicitly presents the educational contexts that serve as a reference to the knowledge base, which enables teachers and students to understand the basis upon which the answers are generated. Before querying frozen LLMs for question answering, two essential preliminary procedures are designed: educational context retrieval and prompt message construction.

Educational Context Retrieval. An LLM-based IRS is utilized to retrieve the most relevant learning materials for a particular educational question. In this study, the state-of-the-art LLM-based IRS, ColBERTv2 [6], was used due to its demonstrated ability to conduct searches with high precision in zero-shot settings. First, all supporting materials are indexed by ColBERTv2 as the learning material knowledge base L in the format of encoded vectors. Then, ColBERTv2

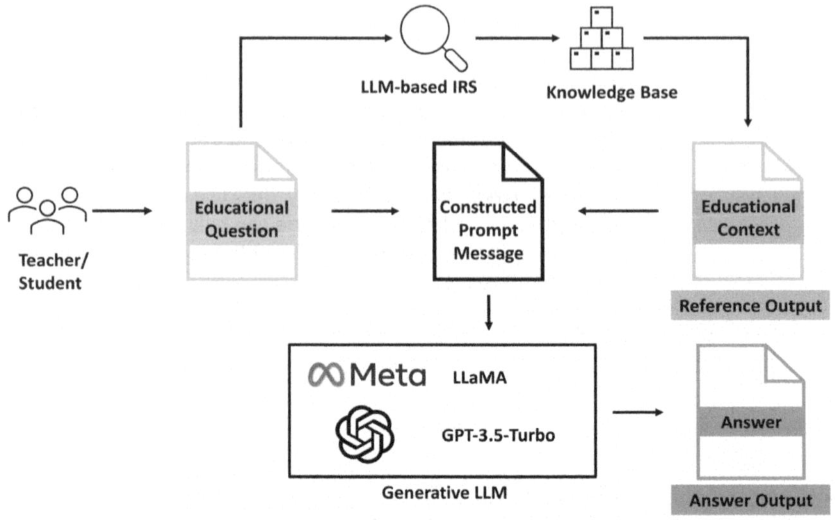

Fig. 2. The EQA workflow of our proposed approach. The proposed EQA system has two outputs: the educational context as the reference output (colored green) and the predicted answer (colored orange) (Color figure online)

is employed to handle the natural language format educational question Q posed by a student or a teacher. The top-k (K=*1* in this study) most relevant educational context, denoted as C, is retrieved based on the largest cosine similarity between Q and all available learning materials in L.

$$C = \mathit{ColBERTv2}(Q, L) \tag{1}$$

The retrieved educational context C serves a dual purpose. Firstly, it provides a reference for the generated answer, and secondly, it plays a key role in constructing the prompt message in conjunction with the educational question Q.

Prompt Message Construction. In order to prompt the LLM to generate the answer $A(a_1, a_2, \cdots, a_n)$ for the educational question Q within the knowledge base of the educational context C, we first construct the prompt message X containing textual information of both Q and C,

$$X = PM(A, C) \tag{2}$$

Prompt messages were generated using both zero-shot and few-shot settings, as few-shot generally outperforms zero-shot and can further improve EQA performance. For few-shot experiments, we utilize five-shot as it is commonly used on question answering tasks using LLMs [3,13,14]. In the zero-shot prompt message construction, a brief task instruction *"question answering based on context, please give a short answer, often between 1 and 4 words"* is provided alongside Q and C. With the question answering prompt template from LLaMA [14], we design the prompt message to generate short answers because the gold answers in SciQ vary from 1 to 4 words. In contrast, the five-shot prompt message includes an additional five examples that explicitly "instruct" the LLM to produce desired answers. We illustrate the prompt message without educational context information, as well as the zero-shot and five-shot prompt messages with context information in Fig. 3.

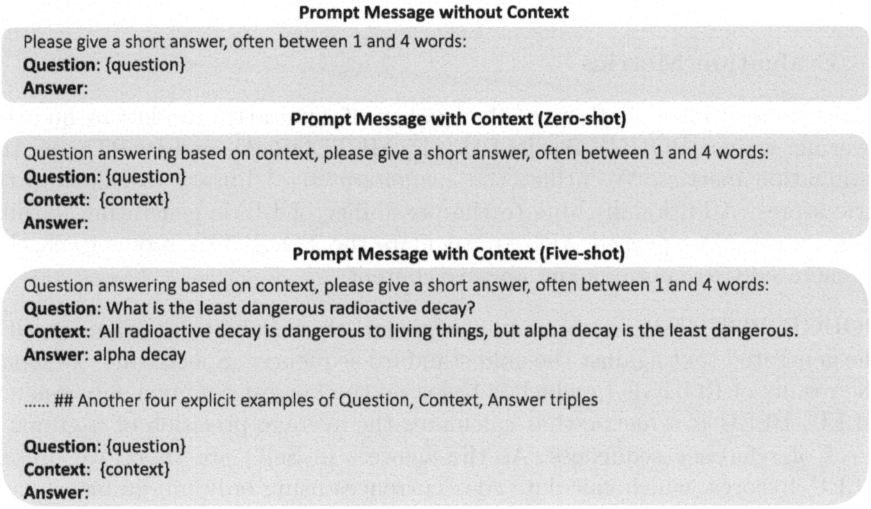

Fig. 3. Prompt message examples. The value in curly brackets is variable, e.g. {context} is the context retrieved for a specific {question}.

The constructed prompt message X will serve as the input to the frozen LLM and generate the predicted answer tokens autoregressively in the following formula:

$$P_{LLM}(A|X) = \prod_{i=1}^{n} P_{LLM}(a_i|PM(A,C); a_{1:i-1}) \quad (3)$$

which indicates that the proposed constructed prompt message could help the frozen LLM to generate answers with the consideration of information from educational context C and knowledge base L, as well as the explicit instruction examples.

3 Experiments

This section outlines the experimental setup, which encompasses the implementation details, evaluation metrics and comparison systems.

3.1 Implementation Details

For experiment data, we employ the *Datasets*[1] library to obtain and preprocess the SciQ dataset. Specifically, we eliminate the examples that do not have *supporting materials* as well as the examples used for few-shot learning, and ultimately use 11,523 examples to evaluate the performance of different systems. We deployed two of the latest LLMs, ChatGPT (GPT-3.5-Turbo[2]) and LLaMA[3] to perform EQA.

3.2 Evaluation Metrics

Like previous studies that assess the quality of generative models in question answering, we use ROUGE [8], BLEU [11], METEOR [1], and BERTScore [16] as evaluation metrics. We utilize the *evaluate-metric*[4] library to calculate the metric scores. Additionally, due to the possibility of LLMs generating harmful content, we use Perspective API[5] to calculate the TOXICITY scores to check if the generated text contains any abusive content.

- ROUGE. ROUGE is a commonly used metric that evaluates n-grams recall of the generated text against the gold standard sequences. Specifically, we report the results of ROUGE-L, which is based on the longest common subsequence.
- BLEU. BLEU is a metric that calculates the average precision of n-grams in a set of reference sequences. As the answers in SciQ are short, we present BLEU-1 scores, which calculate co-occurrences using only uni-grams.
- METEOR. METEOR is a metric that emphasizes recall and calculates how similar the generated sequence is to the actual sequence by taking into account synonyms, stemming, and paraphrasing.
- BERTScore. BERTScore utilizes contextual embeddings from pre-trained BERT models and determines the similarity between words in the generated and reference sentences using cosine similarity. The BERTScore outputs values of Precision, Recall and F1. In this work, we report F1 as its proved reliable performance in difference evaluation setting [16].
- TOXICITY. TOXICITY score is in the form of a probability, which signifies the likelihood of a reader perceiving the text as abusive content, and the value falls between 0 and 1. A lower score indicates a smaller chance that the content is abusive.

[1] https://huggingface.co/docs/datasets/index. Last access 15 March 2023.

[2] https://openai.com/blog/introducing-chatgpt-and-whisper-apis. Last accessed 15 March 2023.

[3] Due to the computational power limitation, we experimented with the 7B version in this project. https://github.com/facebookresearch/LLaMA. Last accessed 10 March 2023.

[4] https://huggingface.co/evaluate-metric. Last Access 15 March 2023.

[5] https://perspectiveapi.com/how-it-works/. Last Access 15 March 2023.

3.3 Comparison Systems

To evaluate how well IRS and few-shot learning can enhance EQA, we compare Vanilla ChatGPT, ChatGPT-IRS zero-shot, and ChatGPT-IRS five-shot. We also include two different generative LLMs when evaluating our approach, in this case by also adding LLaMA five-shot and LLaMA-IRS five-shot to our evaluation. To perform the five-shot approach, we randomly select five examples from the SciQ dataset to create a prompt message, and these five examples are excluded during evaluation for all comparison systems. Since ChatGPT was originally trained with question answering capabilities, there is no need for additional instruction to perform EQA. On the other hand, LLaMA was not specifically trained for question answering tasks. As a result, Vanilla LLaMA cannot perform EQA without instruction. Consequently, we do not include Vanilla ChatGPT five-shot and Vanilla LLaMA in the experiments. We exclude non-generative QA methods since they treat QA as tasks formulated as detecting answer spans, which involve different evaluation metrics.

- **Vanilla ChatGPT.** Vanilla ChatGPT is the original OpenAI ChatGPT that does not use IRS, and its prompt message only contains information about the educational question.
- **ChatGPT-IRS zero-shot.** ChatGPT-IRS zero-shot incorporates IRS and uses a zero-shot constructed prompt message. This message includes information about both the educational question and the retrieved educational context.
- **ChatGPT-IRS five-shot.** ChatGPT-IRS five-shot utilizes IRS and a five-shot constructed prompt message. This message contains information about both the educational question and retrieved educational context, as well as five examples of question answering based on context.
- **LLaMA five-shot.** LLaMA five-shot refers to LLaMA, a generative LLM that employs a five-shot constructed prompt message. This message includes five examples of question answering without context information.
- **LLaMA-IRS five-shot.** LLaMA-IRS five-shot integrates IRS and a five-shot constructed prompt message. This message contains five examples of question answering with context information.

4 Result and Analysis

In this section, we will first scrutinize the EQA results produced by all comparison systems. Then, we will elaborate on the impact that the IRS has on the effectiveness and transparency of EQA.

4.1 Educational Question Answering Result and Analysis

Table 1 presents the EQA results for all the comparison systems. Vanilla ChatGPT is outperformed by ChatGPT-IRS in zero-shot learning by significant margins of 85.5%, 58.7%, 38.0% and 8.4% for BLEU-1, ROUGE-L, METEOR and

Table 1. Educational Question Answering performance of all comparison models measured by BLEU-1, ROUGE-L, METEOR and TOXICITY. The best scores are marked in bold.

Model	BLEU-1	ROUGE-L	METEOR	BERTScore	TOXICITY
Vanilla ChatGPT	0.275	0.444	0.379	0.841	0.0592
ChatGPT-IRS zero-shot	0.510	0.705	0.523	0.912	0.0569
ChatGPT-IRS five-shot	**0.580**	**0.745**	**0.543**	**0.919**	0.0553
LLaMA five-shot	0.135	0.3505	0.210	0.769	**0.0453**
LLaMA-IRS five-shot	0.393	0.544	0.367	0.867	0.0541

BERTScore, respectively. By providing five examples for instruction, ChatGPT-IRS five-shot achieves the highest performance in educational question answering, obtaining BLEU-1, ROUGE-L, METEOR and BERTScore of 0.580, 0.754 and 0.543, outperforming Vanilla ChatGPT by 110.9%, 67.8%, and 9.2%, respectively. This outcome serves as a direct demonstration that ChatGPT can produce answers that are closer to the correct answers by leveraging the educational context obtained through IRS and explicit instructions. Furthermore, the results suggest that LLaMA typically has lower performance than ChatGPT on EQA. For instance, LLaMA five-shot falls significantly behind Vanilla ChatGPT. The primary reason for this difference is that LLaMA was trained without consideration for QA tasks. Nevertheless, LLaMA-IRS five-shot exhibited superior performance over Vanilla ChatGPT with the support of contextual information obtained from the IRS, which further highlights the effectiveness of combining an IRS with an LLM for EQA tasks. The TOXICITY score for all systems is low and comparable to the TOXICITY score of the correct answers (0.0537), indicating that both ChatGPT and LLaMA are unlikely to produce abusive content when answering educational questions.

4.2 The Impact of the IRS on Educational Question Answering

Due to the inherent imperfections of the IRS, there may be instances in which the educational context is not accurately retrieved, potentially resulting in repercussions for the EQA accuracy. This subsection presents a detailed discussion of the influence that the IRS has on the field of EQA.

Table 2. The performance of IRS on retrieving educational context.

	Rank 1	Rank 2	Rank 3	Rank 4	Rank 5
IRS Performance	0.766	0.882	0.919	0.938	0.947

Table 2 indicates the outcome of the IRS performance evaluation. We evaluated the efficacy of the IRS in accurately retrieving the educational context by quantifying the probability of retrieving the correct context within a specified rank *k*. For instance, there is a 0.947 probability of the correct educational context being retrieved within the first five documents obtained from the IRS. The findings demonstrate that the utilized IRS is not flawless. Particularly, when only utilizing the top-ranked material as the educational context, there is a 23.4% likelihood of an incorrect context being retrieved. However, the performance of the IRS improves as the number of returned documents increases. For example, compared to using only the top-1 document, the probability of correctly retrieving the educational context rises to over 90% when considering the top three retrieved documents.

Table 3. The performance ChatGPT-IRS five-shot with correctly and incorrectly retrieved educational context. For comparison, we include ChatGPT-IRS five-shot with top-1 retrieved context (correct and incorrect) and Vanilla ChatGPT.

	BLEU-1	ROUGE-L	METEOR	BERTScore
ChatGPT-IRS five-shot + top-1 retrieved context	0.580	0.745	0.543	0.919
ChatGPT-IRS five-shot + Correctly retrieved context	0.617	0.781	0.571	0.928
ChatGPT-IRS five-shot + Incorrectly retrieved context	0.467	0.636	0.453	0.893
Vanilla ChatGPT	0.275	0.444	0.379	0.841

We examined the performance results of the best system, ChatGPT-IRS five-shot, in answering educational questions with correctly and incorrectly retrieved educational context in Table 3. The results demonstrate that a higher question-answering performance can be achieved through the use of a correctly retrieved educational context, achieving 0.617, 0.781, 0.571 and 0.928 on BLEU-1, ROUGE-L, METEOR and BERTScore. On the other hand, if the educational context is not retrieved correctly, the EQA performance is inferior compared to using the top-1 retrieved context. However, an intriguing observation was made when analyzing the data presented in both Tables 1 and 3: despite having an educational context that was retrieved incorrectly, ChatGPT-IRS five-shot still performs better than Vanilla ChatGPT in terms of BLEU-1 (0.467 compared to 0.275), ROUGE-L (0.636 compared to 0.444), METEOR (0.453 compared to 0.379) and BERTScore (0.893 compared to 0.841).

To quantify the impact of retrieved educational context on EQA performance, we plotted the distribution of metric scores for BLEU-1, ROUGE-L, METEOR and BERTScore of ChatGPT-IRS five-shot with both correctly and incorrectly retrieved educational context, as well as Vanilla ChatGPT with no context in Fig. 4. The results indicate that Vanilla ChatGPT generally obtains lower metric scores, whereas ChatGPT-IRS five-shot, whether with correctly or incorrectly retrieved educational context, tends to achieve higher metric scores. For instance, in the case of BLEU-1 and BERTScore, Vanilla ChatGPT can only produce 20% perfect answers that achieve a BLEU-1 and BERTScore of 1. On the other hand, more than 50% of the answers generated by ChatGPT-IRS five-shot with correctly retrieved educational context are a perfect match.

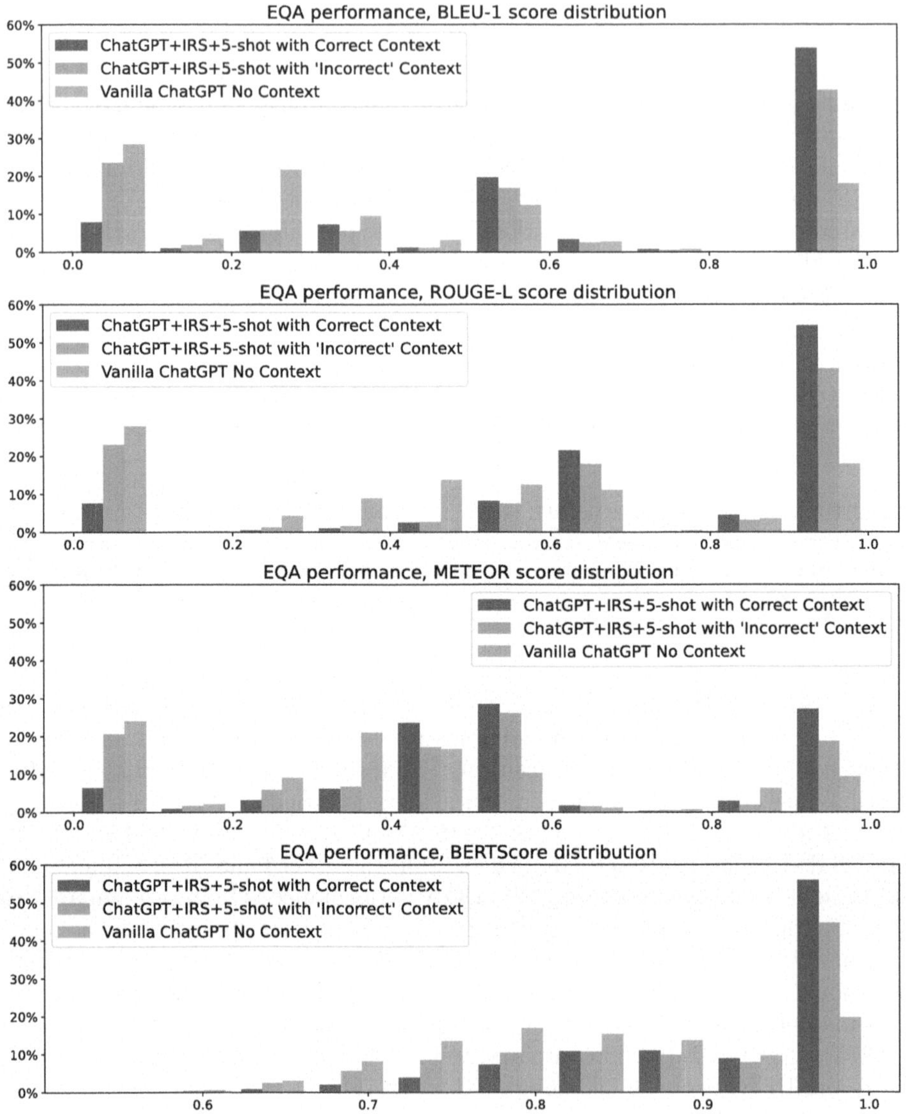

Fig. 4. The BLEU-1, ROUGE-L, METEOR and BERTScore distributions of Vanilla ChatGPT (orange), as well as ChatGPT-IRS five-shot with correctly (green) or incorrectly (blue) retrieved educational context. The metric scores are shown on the x-axis, while the y-axis shows the proportion or percentage of those scores in the distribution. (Color figure online)

With incorrectly retrieved educational context, 40% of the answers produced by ChatGPT-IRS five-shot still achieved a perfect match with the reference answer. When considering BERTScore, Vanilla GPT generates answers that primarily range from 0.5 to 0.8 in terms of BERTScore distribution. On the other hand, ChatGPT-IRS generates answers that achieve BERTScore scores mostly between 0.8 and 1. This outcome indicates that ChatGPT-IRS, through the use of retrieved context, is capable of generating answers that are more similar to the reference (gold) answers. When examining the lower BLEU-1 scores, it was found that ChatGPT-IRS five-shot produced less than 10% of answers that were completely different from the gold answers when using the correct educational context. However, this percentage increased to over 20% when incorrect educational context was used. Vanilla GPT, on the other hand, produced almost 30% of answers with a BLEU-1 score of 0. The results suggest that for the SciQ dataset, there may be multiple relevant supporting materials that can serve as educational context for the same question, which can help EQA. However, non-relevant retrieved contexts could mislead ChatGPT and result in incorrect answers.

Furthermore, we conducted a manual review of the retrieved documents and discovered that the documents retrieved as incorrect are often[6] still relevant to the corresponding educational context. For instance, when answering the question "*What do we call the predictable distribution of molecular speeds found in gas of many molecules?*", the "correct context" is " *...However, a gas of many molecules has a predictable distribution of molecular speeds, known as the Maxwell-Boltzmann distribution.*" while the retrieved context is "*... a gas of many molecules has a predictable distribution of molecular speeds, This distribution is called the Maxwell-Boltzmann distribution*". In this case, there are multiple relevant educational contexts for one question in the domain-specific knowledge base that can aid ChatGPT to provide correct answers. There are, of course, cases where based on the incorrectly and non-relevant retrieved educational context, the produced answer is wrong. In the instance of the question, "*What is the number of chambers in a crocodile's stomach?*" the retrieved context pertains to "*ruminants*", leading to an erroneous response of 4 instead of the correct answer of 2. Similarly, ChatGPT commits the same error by also producing an erroneous response of 4. However, by introducing an alternative response based on the rank-2 retrieved context, our proposed approach demonstrates the capacity to furnish the correct response of 2. This underscores the potential utility of leveraging relevant educational materials when refining EQA, thus minimizing the incidence of inaccuracies due to inadequate or irrelevant contextual information.

The following is a summary of the findings from the analysis of the impact of IRS on EQA. In general, the use of educational context retrieved by the IRS enhances the reliability of ChatGPT for EQA. Nevertheless, as the IRS is not perfect, ChatGPT may be misled by an incorrect or irrelevant educational context. To address this, providing ChatGPT with multiple top-k retrieved educational contexts could improve the likelihood of feeding ChatGPT with a correct

[6] Although there are many comparable instances in the SciQ datasets, we only present two single examples as part of the current project's scope. However, we plan to conduct an extensive quantitative analysis as future work.

educational context, resulting in more desirable answers. Additionally, explicitly outputting the retrieved educational context would make it easier for students or teachers to evaluate whether the produced answer is correct or incorrect. Finally, we include the above examples in Fig. 5 to illustrate the improvement brought by our approach.

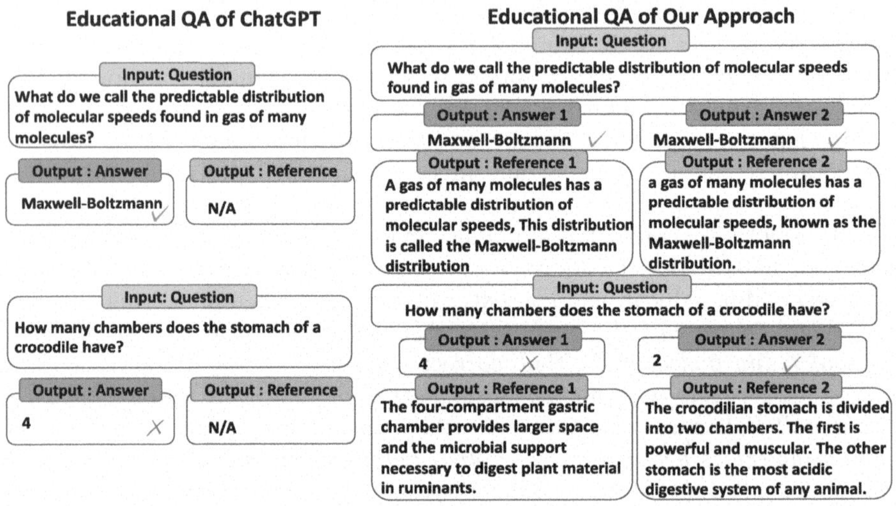

Fig. 5. Examples question answering performed by vanilla ChatGPT and our proposed approach. Vanilla ChatGPT solely produces answers while our proposed approach attaches the educational context as a reference.

5 Conclusion, Limitations and Future Work

In this study, we have introduced a novel approach that combines an information retrieval system with large language models to enhance the reliability and transparency of educational question answering systems. With the provided educational context information retrieved by the information retrieval system, the educational question answering performance is significantly improved. Moreover, the educational context explicitly serves as output, making it easier for students to assess the viability of generated answer. By integrating the information retrieval system with large language models, educators can have the opportunities to develop educational question answering systems that are founded on up-to-date and specialized knowledge aiming at various study groups and exceed general knowledge limitation of large language models, such as ChatGPT. We acknowledge that our work has some limitations. The evaluation metrics we used mainly assess how closely the generated answers match the reference answers. While these metrics can effectively evaluate the quality of text generated by LLMs on a large scale, they may not be able to fully capture the quality of longer or rephrased answers. Therefore, in future work, we intend to incorporate human evaluation to address this issue. In future studies, we plan to experiment with other datasets and conduct an in-depth analysis of the relationship between the performance of the information retrieval system and the performance of the educational question answering system. Additionally, our plan is to apply this method in practical situations, such as creating a knowledge base for educational materials that can categorize sections and paragraphs, and assess whether it can provide advantages for both teachers and students.

Acknowledgement. This research was funded by Swedish Research Council with grant number 2019-05049. The computations/data handling were enabled by resources provided by the National Academic Infrastructure for Supercomputing in Sweden (NAISS) at C3SE partially funded by the Swedish Research Council through grant agreement no. 2022-06725.

References

1. Banerjee, S., Lavie, A.: METEOR: an automatic metric for MT evaluation with improved correlation with human judgments. In: Proceedings of the ACL Workshop on Intrinsic and Extrinsic Evaluation Measures for Machine Translation and/or Summarization, pp. 65–72. Association for Computational Linguistics, Ann Arbor, Michigan, June 2005. https://aclanthology.org/W05-0909
2. Devlin, J., Chang, M.W., Lee, K., Toutanova, K.: BERT: Pre-training of deep bidirectional transformers for language understanding. In: Proceedings of the 2019 Conference of the North American Chapter of the Association for Computational Linguistics: Human Language Technologies, Volume 1 (Long and Short Papers), pp. 4171–4186. Association for Computational Linguistics, Minneapolis, Minnesota, June 2019. https://doi.org/10.18653/v1/N19-1423. https://aclanthology.org/N19-1423
3. Hoffmann, J., et al.: Training compute-optimal large language models (2022)
4. Hsu, H.H., Huang, N.F.: Xiao-shih: a self-enriched question answering bot with machine learning on Chinese-based moocs. IEEE Trans. Learn. Technol. **15**(2), 223–237 (2022). https://doi.org/10.1109/TLT.2022.3162572
5. Ji, Z., et al.: Survey of hallucination in natural language generation. ACM Comput. Surv. **55**(12) (2023). https://doi.org/10.1145/3571730
6. Khattab, O., Zaharia, M.: Colbert: efficient and effective passage search via contextualized late interaction over bert. In: Proceedings of the 43rd International ACM SIGIR Conference on Research and Development in Information Retrieval, SIGIR 2020, pp. 39–48. Association for Computing Machinery, New York (2020). https://doi.org/10.1145/3397271.3401075
7. Komeili, M., Shuster, K., Weston, J.: Internet-augmented dialogue generation. In: Annual Meeting of the Association for Computational Linguistics (2021)
8. Lin, C.Y.: ROUGE: a package for automatic evaluation of summaries. In: Text Summarization Branches Out, pp. 74–81. Association for Computational Linguistics, Barcelona, July 2004. https://aclanthology.org/W04-1013
9. Ocaña-Fernández, Y., Valenzuela-Fernández, L.A., Garro-Aburto, L.L.: Artificial intelligence and its implications in higher education. J. Educ. Psychology-Propositos y Representaciones **7**(2), 553–568 (2019)

10. OpenAI: Chatgpt: Optimizing language models for dialogue (2022). https://openai.com/blog/chatgpt/
11. Papineni, K., Roukos, S., Ward, T., Zhu, W.J.: Bleu: a method for automatic evaluation of machine translation. In: Proceedings of the 40th Annual Meeting of the Association for Computational Linguistics. pp. 311–318. Association for Computational Linguistics, Philadelphia, Pennsylvania, USA, July 2002. https://doi.org/10.3115/1073083.1073135. https://aclanthology.org/P02-1040
12. Radford, A., Narasimhan, K., Salimans, T., Sutskever, I., et al.: Improving language understanding by generative pre-training (2018)
13. Rae, J.W., et al.: Scaling language models: Methods, analysis and insights from training gopher (2022)
14. Touvron, H., et al.: Llama: open and efficient foundation language models (2023)
15. Welbl, J., Liu, N.F., Gardner, M.: Crowdsourcing multiple choice science questions. In: Proceedings of the 3rd Workshop on Noisy User-generated Text, pp. 94–106. Association for Computational Linguistics, Copenhagen, Denmark, September 2017. https://doi.org/10.18653/v1/W17-4413
16. Zhang, T., Kishore, V., Wu, F., Weinberger, K.Q., Artzi, Y.: Bertscore: evaluating text generation with bert (2020)
17. Zylich, B., Viola, A., Toggerson, B., Al-Hariri, L., Lan, A.: Exploring automated question answering methods for teaching assistance. In: Bittencourt, I.I., Cukurova, M., Muldner, K., Luckin, R., Millán, E. (eds.) AIED 2020. LNCS (LNAI), vol. 12163, pp. 610–622. Springer, Cham (2020). https://doi.org/10.1007/978-3-030-52237-7_49

How Do Teachers Search for Learning Resources? A Mixed Method Field Study

Elad Yacobson(✉) and Giora Alexandron

Weizmann Institute of Science, 234 Herzl St., 7610001 Rehovot, Israel
elad.yacobson@weizmann.ac.il

Abstract. Teachers using Open Educational Resource (OER) repositories face the challenge of searching and selecting learning resources (LRs) that match their pedagogical goals and teaching preferences. However, teachers are often overwhelmed by the multitude of LRs in such repositories. One way of aiding teachers is providing them with search mechanisms that rely on semantic information describing different properties of the materials, and peer-generated reviews and feedback ('social recommendations'). Previous studies of teachers' search and select strategies in such systems were usually conducted in controlled settings, limiting their generalization to real-life contexts. The literature also lacks systematic evaluations of the usefulness of semantic information and social recommendations to teachers' search processes. To address these gaps, we conducted a study with physics teachers who use a nation-wide blended-learning environment containing an OER repository and social network features. We applied a mixed-method approach, first interviewing teachers and observing them performing authentic search tasks, and then triangulating these findings with quantitative analysis of log files containing data about teacher interaction with the learning environment. Our findings demonstrate the value that teachers ascribe to social-based information, especially from peers who are perceived as credible or like-minded, when searching and selecting LRs. We discuss possible implications for stake-holders and designers of OER repositories for blended instruction in K-12 environments.

Keywords: Open Educational Resources · Semantic Information · Learning Analytics

1 Introduction

Blended-Learning environments usually rely on repositories of digital Open Educational Resources (OERs), such as lesson plans, interactive activities, presentations, videos and more. The term 'open' is derived from the fact that the

The work of EY was partially supported by the Israeli Council for Higher Education via the Weizmann Data Science Research Center. GA's research was generously supported by the Estate of Emile Mimran and by the Maurice and Vivienne Wohl Biology Endowment. The authors wish to thank Dr. Moriah Ariely for her assistance with the qualitative part of this research.

O. Viberg et al. (Eds.): EC-TEL 2023, LNCS 14200, pp. 489–503, 2023.
https://doi.org/10.1007/978-3-031-42682-7_33

resources in these repositories are usually available to teachers free of charge, allowing teachers to choose from a large variety and amount of learning materials, suitable for different students and different learning situations [11]. However, the large amount of resources these repositories contain can be overwhelming for teachers, and make it difficult for them to find appropriate learning materials that suit their pedagogical goals and teaching preferences [8]. Therefore, in order to assist teachers in the process of searching and selecting learning materials, these repositories need to provide search mechanisms, which most commonly rely on meta-data that provides semantic information about the digital content [3].

1.1 Semantic Information

The term 'semantic information' (in the context of OER repositories) refers to information describing the content and different attributes of the learning resources (LRs) in the repository, such as the topic, the level of difficulty, its intended use – whether as a test, class practice or homework, which grade it is appropriate for, the estimated amount of time it takes to complete the activity, the technological aids required for it (e.g., mobile devices), and more. It is represented as structured meta-data used to catalog LRs and make the process of finding and selecting resources more efficient [27]. In addition to supporting search and select, this information, combined with student performance data, can provide teachers with learning analytics that can assist them in making informed pedagogical decisions. For example, it can help teachers diagnose individual needs and plan personalized learning sequences [15,18]. Search mechanisms based on semantic information can also reduce the workload for teachers, learners and content-providers [16] and help people with learning disabilities or even physical disabilities (such as visually impaired individuals) in navigating through the digital learning environment [10]. Therefore, there is a need for solutions for defining, creating, and managing meta-data that describe the contents of OER repositories. There have been past attempts at defining standardized schemes of meta-data to describe OERs (such as the ieee LOM [6] and the DCMI [28]). However, these were criticized for being overly complicated and for focusing mostly on technological considerations rather than pedagogical ones [21]. Therefore, it is essential that we first understand teacher needs regarding semantic information for describing OERs, before we try to devise new schemes and standards for such information and search mechanisms that rely on them.

1.2 Teachers' Search and Select Strategies

Surprisingly, only a few studies have examined teachers' strategies for searching and selecting digital LRs in OER repositories [25]. Findings regarding the considerations that guide teachers when selecting LRs, and the different search strategies they employ, showed heterogeneous behavior: teachers employ different search routines [4,7,21,25], look for different types of LRs [4,25], and take into account different considerations. For example, in [21], teacher focus was on finding resources that are age-appropriate, aligned with core standards, and engaging and interactive. In [13], teachers emphasis was given to resources that could be easily modified and adjusted to teachers' personal instructional style. In contrast to that, in [19] it was reported that teachers prioritized efficiency and thus preferred resources that could be administered 'as-is', without need for further time-consuming adjustments. Not surprisingly, cost is also a factor that teacher may consider, with reported preference to open resources that can be used free of charge [19]. Classifying such considerations into categories, Siedel and Stylianides [25] proposed six types of categories: student-driven, teacher-driven, mathematics-driven, constraints-driven, resource-driven, and culture-driven.

Another aspect in which teachers differ is the semantic information they use during their search [7]: while some teachers start by filtering existing activities according to the intended role of the activity in a teaching sequence (e.g., opening a new subject), other teachers may prefer searching according to curricular relevance or the type of skill required from students to complete the activity, such as drawing conclusions or making inferences. Other studies have underlined the importance teachers attribute to evaluative meta-data, such as recommendations from peers [1,2,21,22,24].

1.3 Gaps in Existing Literature

However, reviewing the body of literature on the topic reveals some significant gaps: first, some of these studies are two-decade old (e.g., [4,20–22]), possibly rendering at least part of their findings and conclusions irrelevant to the current time. Another gap concerns the generalizability of some of the findings to real-life settings. As some of these studies were conducted in small-scale, research-oriented learning environments (e.g., [7,20–22]), the ecological validity of the findings may be limited. Third, most of these studies relied on self-reported data collection methods such as surveys, questionnaires or interviews as their main source of data [4,8,9,13,19,25]. One major drawback of such methods is that there are often substantial differences between subjects' self reports and their actual behavior [17]. And finally, only a handful of studies focused on the role of semantic information in teachers' search processes. Most relevant to our research is the work of [1,2,24], who applied a quantitative methodology to investigate teachers' behavior in marketplace resource repositories. By analysing interaction log data, they examined the relations between different attributes of the LRs and teachers' choices. However, these studies focused only on the impact of *evaluative*, peer-generated meta-data on teachers' choice of LRs, and did not consider other types of semantic information.

Altogether, there is lack of up-to-date, methodologically-robust research about teachers' search strategies in real-life educational settings, focusing on the type and role of the semantic information that teachers utilize.

1.4 Research Overview, Questions and Contribution

To address the above-mentioned gaps, we used a mixed method approach: first, we interviewed teachers (n = 14) who are active users of a blended-learning environment that includes an OER repository with a few thousands LRs. The teachers were interviewed individually, and demonstrated their search routine during the interview. The focus of these interviews was on their use of semantic information about the LRs during their search. Second, to triangulate our findings, we employed quantitative analysis of log files documenting teachers' interaction with the learning environment.

Concretely, the present research seeks to answer the following:

- **RQ1:** What are the goals and considerations that guide teachers when searching for learning materials?
- **RQ2:** What are the different search strategies that teachers employ in order to achieve these goals?
- **RQ3:** What are the different types of semantic information teachers' rely on during their search process?

The main contribution of this paper is extending our understanding, based on qualitative and quantitative analysis of real-world data, of how teachers search and select resources in OER repositories, and especially, the role of semantic and social information in this process.

2 Methodology

2.1 Learning Environment

The learning environment used in this study is called *PeTeL* (**Pe**rsonalized **Te**aching and **L**earning)[1]. PeTeL is an open environment that is available at no cost to all the science teachers in Israel. It is both a shared repository of OERs and a learning management system (LMS) that also includes social network features for teachers, peer-to-peer sharing mechanisms, and learning analytic tools. It is implemented on top of a Moodle LMS, and is divided into separate modules for each of the subject matters that it covers: biology, chemistry, physics, math, and computer science.

The OER Repository. Each module in PeTeL includes an OER repository that offers a large variety of LRs. These LRs are created and uploaded to the system by either PeTeL's content developers, or by the teachers themselves. The repository's interface, exemplified in physics, is shown in Fig. 1. Teachers search the repository for LRs in the following manner: first, they choose one of the three main subject matter categories in physics (mechanics, electromagnetism

[1] https://stwww1.weizmann.ac.il/petel/en/home-en/.

or radiation and matter), using the left-hand side tool bar (marked with 'A'). They can use the same tool bar to define a finer-grained sub-category for their search. The results of their search are presented in the middle part of the screen, each relevant LR in a separate rectangle (e.g., the rectangle marked with 'D'). The teacher can then filter the results according to several predefined criteria, such as type of activity (e.g. diagnostic questionnaire, interactive task, home assignment, etc.), pedagogical goals, type of feedback given to the students, and more (see filter menu bar marked with 'B'). Teachers can decide to present the search results in a different order, according to several criteria - the date the LR was added to the system (new LRs presented first), alphabetical order of the LR's title, recommendations from the PeTeL team first, and more (see sorting tool marked with 'D'). Another possibility is searching using a free-text window (marked with 'C'). After choosing an activity, the teacher can download the activity into his/her own personal environment inside PeTeL (see download button marked with 'E'), and use it during the lesson or as homework. After the students completed the tasks assigned to them by their teacher, the teacher receives a detailed report of students' achievements.

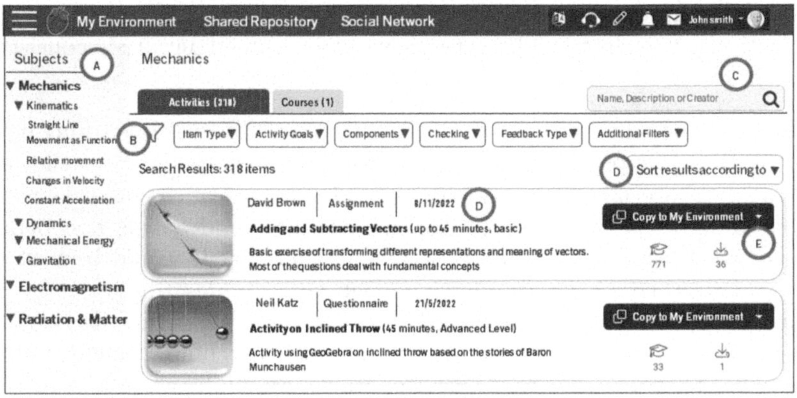

Fig. 1. The physics OER Repository in PeTeL

The Social Network. In addition, PeTeL also includes social network features, enabling teachers to share with their peers insights and recommendations, teaching materials, learning sequences, and even complete courses.

2.2 Research Population

The research population consists of 465 active physics teachers using PeTeL. For the purpose of this research, we define an 'active teacher' as one who logged into PeTeL and searched for an LR in the repository at least once during the 18 months examined in this study (August 2021 – January 2023). Out of this pool of teachers, we sampled and interviewed fourteen teachers: seven women and seven men. Their experience in teaching ranged between two to thirty years (M = 12, SD = 9.8), and their experience in using PeTeL was between one to four years (M = 2.4, SD = 1.3). Most of the teachers had extensive technological experience: two of them have a Master's degree in engineering, five worked in the Hi-Tech industry prior to becoming a teacher, and one taught computer science in high-school before switching to teach physics.

2.3 Research Tools

As previously described, we applied a mixed-method approach, using both qualitative methods (interviews) and quantitative methods (log-file analysis). Data gathered from the interviews was used to answer all three RQs. The log-file analysis was focused on teachers' use of different components of the search mechanism, as an indication of their interest in various types of semantic information. It was therefore used only in the context of the third RQ, which concerns the semantic information teachers require during their search process.

Interviews. All interviews were held through Zoom, recorded, fully transcribed and selectively translated. The interviews were semi-structured, consisting of three main parts:

- In the first part, the teachers were asked to open the PeTeL learning environment on their computer, share their screen, and demonstrate how they search for learning materials. The rationale behind this part of the interview was the understanding that teachers' professed intentions and beliefs do not always co-align with their actual practices [17,26], therefore it would be best to *see* their search process instead of letting them verbally describe it.
- In the second stage, the researcher asked the teachers: "If we had no budget or technological limits, what would be the ideal searching mechanism in your opinion?". This question was based on the methodology applied in [14]. In their research, as part of a participatory design process conducted with high-school math teachers, the researchers asked the teachers what super-powers they would want to possess while working in their classrooms. The rationale underlying such a question is that in order to reveal teachers' true needs, without constraining their thinking to the limitations of the existing technology, we must ask broad and open questions allowing teachers' imagination to run freely.
- The third part included questions referring to the teachers' personal background: their experience in teaching, their technological background, and their experience with PeTeL in particular.

Log Files of Teachers' Actions. Teachers' interactions with the learning environment are stored in the system's log files. Logged actions include logging in or out of the system, search and select-related actions such as using a search

Table 1. Examples of search-related events extracted from the log files

Time	Teacher ID	Subject Matter	Filters Used	Sorting Used	Free Text
2021-08-09 06:38:30	9753	Mechanics			
2021-08-09 06:38:39	9753	Dynamics			"friction"
2021-08-09 06:38:46	9753	Dynamics		#Downloads	
2021-08-10 11:29:47	1028	Radiation & Matter			
2021-08-10 11:30:01	1028	Light: experiments			
2021-08-10 11:32:17	1028	Light: experiments	Type=Quiz		
2021-08-10 11:32:56	1028	Light: experiments			"Dave Brown"

filter, downloading an LR, or giving feedback on an existing LR. For this research, we used the following attributes of teachers' search-related interactions: teachers' identification number, the time in which the search-related action took place, the subject matter being searched for, the search filters being used (such as type of activity, level of difficulty, type of feedback given to the students, etc.), sorting the search results, and using free-text search queries. A few examples of data points extracted from the log files are shown in Table 1.

The log files used in this research contained 29,625 search-related actions performed by 465 physics teachers. These actions took place during a time period of eighteen months (August 2021 – January 2023).

2.4 Data Analysis

Interviews. Teachers' responses were analyzed using a bottom-up approach in order to identify categories and subcategories that emerged during the interviews. The unit of analysis was any sentence or part of sentence that related to teachers' considerations during their search, to their search strategies or to their reliance on semantic information. Teachers' responses that were irrelevant to the subject of the search process were omitted. A total of 335 relevant responses were analyzed. In order to validate the analysis, a second researcher (holding a PhD in science education) was given 67 responses (20% of the total number of responses) generated by three different teachers, and analyzed them according to the defined categories and subcategories. The coding of the two researchers was compared, reaching a 88% level of agreement (Cohen's Kappa = 0.73).

Log File Analysis. Teacher search and select sessions are typically composed of the following sequence of actions: defining the relevant subject matter, applying filtering criteria (such as type of activity), ranking the search results according to some criterion, investigating the top elements, and eventually selecting a resource. Our assumption was that actions that belong to the same search session would occur within a narrow time window. Therefore, we defined a time threshold of maximum sixty minutes (determined following a manual inspection of the log files) between two consecutive actions that would still be considered as belonging to the same session. This yielded 4,482 teacher search sessions, with an average of 6.6 actions per session.

For each of these sessions, we examined whether the teacher used the following search-related features: filtering of the search results, sorting the search results, and free text search. Our assumption was that through the analysis of teachers' use of these features during their search, we would gain a better understanding of the semantic information that is important to them in their search process. For example, if a large number of teachers filter their search results according to the duration of the LR, it suggests that such meta-data about LRs is important for them. Regarding the use of filtering and sorting, since the categories available to teachers are finite and predefined, we looked into which were used most frequently. Regarding the use of free text search, teachers' search words were classified into six categories:

- *Curricular:* this category included words pertaining to subjects and concepts in physics (e.g., "friction").
- *Item type:* this category included words defining the type of item the teacher was looking for (e.g. "diagnostic question").
- *Author:* this category consisted of names of teachers (e.g., "David Brown"). When a teacher writes the name of another teacher in the search line, it means they are searching for activities that were created by that teacher.
- *Applications used:* this category included words describing the use of technological applications in the LR (e.g., "Geogebra").
- *LR's title:* this category included words that were taken from the LR's title (e.g., "turtles" - the teacher used this search word to find a specific LR containing an activity about a competition between turtles).
- *Other:* this category included search words that were gibberish, numbers, or that could not be determined as belonging to either one of the previous categories (e.g., "book").

To resolve cases of ambiguity concerning the classification of a certain search term, we conducted a search in the system using the same search words that the teacher used. We then examined the search results to see if only a specific LR was returned containing the search words in its title, implying that the teacher was searching for that exact LR according to it's title; or that the search yielded multiple LRs, suggesting that this is a broader search term pertaining to other categories of classification. In cases where the ambiguity could not be resolved, we classified the search word as belonging to the 'Other' category.

3 Results

3.1 RQ1: Teacher Considerations When Searching for LRs

The analysis of teachers' interviews yielded three main factors that teachers consider when searching for LRs: (a) Curricular considerations; (b) Teaching objectives; (c) Reliability.

Curricular Considerations: By 'curricular considerations' we refer to the fact that teachers were first and foremost guided by domain knowledge and conceptual understanding considerations that target the learning goals defined by the curriculum. All fourteen teachers that were interviewed referred to this aspect: "I go to the repository and look for an activity according to the subject matter" (teacher #2). These considerations also appeared in teacher response to the question: "If we had no budget or technological limits, what would be the ideal searching mechanism in your opinion?", to which three of the teachers indicated that they would like to be able to search according to even more fine-grained categories and concepts in physics.

Teaching Objectives: Twelve of the teachers (85%) testified that when they search for LRs, one of the things they take into account is the teaching objective that the LR should help them achieve. Some of the objectives mentioned by the teachers were more of an administrative nature, such as: "I use it as a tool to check student attendance" (teacher #1). Some talked about the manner in which they use the LRs: "I use it mainly for exercising the material[...] but I also use it for tests and evaluation purposes" (teacher #2). However, most of the objectives that teachers described in their responses revolved around the need to facilitate student learning or improve their learning experience. Two teachers stressed their intention to promote active learning through problem solving. Three teachers emphasized their need to monitor students' progress and their state of knowledge. Two teachers mentioned the need to align between the nature of the LR and the needs of the class. Finally, one teacher raised her need to find activities that meet the personal needs of individual students: "Each student has her own 'channel' that she finds more comfortable for learning. Therefore, I try to give several options so that each one of them will find what's most suitable for her" (teacher #10).

Reliability: The OER repository in PeTeL allows teachers to upload LRs that they have created themselves, so that other teachers could download and use them in their own courses. This results in a situation where some of the activities in the repository contain errors or technical malfunctions (the content created by the development team goes through a quality assurance process). During the interviews, ten teachers (70%) referred to the reliability of the items as an important factor that should be verified prior to administering a resource to the students: "I try and perform an initial activation of the LR to see that it's working properly. Because I came across activities that look great at first, but in the end don't work as planned..." (teacher #2).

3.2 RQ2: Teachers' Search Strategies

Regarding teachers' search strategies, we found that the majority of the teachers that were interviewed (ten out of fourteen) followed a similar search pattern, which consisted of 2–3 stages: First, they entered the repository and filtered it by their current curricular learning goals (e.g., "Mechanics", and within it, "Kinematics"). The next stage depended on the number of results that the curricular-oriented search returned: if there were only a few matching options (up to ten), they opened each of them and examined whether it was suitable for their needs. But in case that the search returned a large number of LRs that fit the curricular goals (sometimes several dozens), they scanned the results while relying on several cues and heuristics in order to narrow down the number of LRs to obtain a smaller set that they can examine in detail. We note that this observation is inline with the "hybrid" search strategy described by Cooper et al. [7], in the sense that teachers used both the existing categories of semantic information and their own personal considerations during the search process. However, due to the large number of resources that exist in PeTeL, filtering according to the existing categories did not always produce a manageable size search results, small enough that teachers could carefully examine each resource. To bridge this gap, teachers developed a stage that we refer to as 'quick scanning' to quickly discard unpromising resources, and remain with those the are "worth" inspecting.

3.3 RQ3: Semantic Information Teachers Use During Search

To answer RQ3, we rely on results from both the qualitative part of our research (i.e., the interviews) and the quantitative part (analysis of the teacher interaction log files).

Qualitative Research - Interviews: As can be expected, teachers differ from one another in the semantic information that they use during their search sessions. For example, three teachers said that the graphic image helps them to understand whether a certain activity is suitable or not, while five others said it could be misleading. Contradicting opinions also appeared with respect to level of difficulty: while four of the teachers considered the LR's level of difficulty, three other teachers said that they did not trust other teachers' classification, or that 'easy' and 'difficult' where context-dependent. A similar approach was found towards the duration of time needed to complete an LR: two teachers said it helps them to make a decision about the relevance of the LR, one said that she takes it into consideration despite knowing that this attribute may be inaccurate, and two said that they do not consider this information at all. Three of the teachers relied on the LR's title, two teachers filtered LRs according to the device it runs on (mobile or computer), and four teachers looked at the type of activity contained in the LR (questionnaire, test, diagnostic questions, exercise, etc.).

However, *the most commonly used information was social-based*: the identity of the LR's creator and the number of times that the LR had been downloaded. Twelve teachers (85% of the teachers) said that the identity of the LR's creator is of great importance to them, and some even indicated that it is the first thing that they look at. Teachers looked for LRs created by teachers that they know and trust: "First of all, I look if there is someone I know. For instance, [name of teacher], I know that the content he creates is good" (teacher #12). Others indicated that they avoid using activities created by certain teachers, because they know that they are not suitable for them: "There is this one teacher, and I know him and that his activities lack interactivity" (teacher #8).

As for the number of times an LR has been downloaded, eight teachers said that they take it into account when searching for LRs. Interestingly, the reasons for looking at this statistic were diverse: some said that if many teachers downloaded a certain activity, it probably means that it is good. Other regarded a large number of downloads as an indication that this activity is probably free of technical problems: "If there is a mistake in a question, and only two people downloaded it, it is less likely that someone had noticed it" (teacher #10).

In addition, when asked to describe the ideal search mechanism, ignoring technical or budget constraints, seven teachers (50%) again emphasized the importance of social-based information, such as peer-based recommendations on LRs.

Quantitative Analysis of System Log Files. As previously described, in order to understand what is the semantic information that assists teachers in their search process, we looked at three aspects of teachers' searches: free-text searches, filters, and sorting.

Free Text Search: free text was used in 936 searches (21% of searches) conducted by 234 teachers (50% of teachers). The search words were divided into six categories (see Sect. 2.4). Table 2 presents the number of searches in which each category was used. Words belonging to the 'curricular' category (i.e. pertaining to subjects or concepts in physics) were used most frequently. The second most used category was the 'LR type', which could point to the teaching objectives of the teacher – whether he/she is searching for a diagnostic question, an exam, exercises for the students, etc. The third most used category was the 'author' category. We note that these three categories are in alignment with our findings from the qualitative part of this research, that emphasized the importance of curricular and pedagogical considerations for teachers, as well as their reliance on social-based information.

Table 2. Free text searches

	Category	number of searches
1	Curricular	603
2	LR type	134
3	Author	117
4	LR's title	78
5	Applications used	23
6	Other	89

Filters: filters were used in 545 searches (12% of searches) conducted by 193 teachers (41.5% of teachers). 50 different filters were used. The most frequently used filters were those describing the type of resource – quiz (137 searches), questionnaire (133 searches), or assignment (101 searches). Filters defining the teaching objectives of the resource were also frequently used: summary of subject (61 searches), opening a new subject (57 searches), exposing existing knowledge (45 searches) or implementation of knowledge (40 searches). Amongst the filters revolving around social aspects, the most frequently applied was the filter showing whether an LR was validated by the PeTeL team (39 searches)[2]

Sorting: sorting of search results was used in 89 searches (2% of searches) conducted by 41 teachers (9% of teachers). There were six different sorting criteria available to teachers: 1) The time that the LR was added to the repository; 2) The number of times that the LR was downloaded; 3) Alphabetical order by LR title; 4) Alphabetical order by LR author; 5) Show first LRs that were recommended by the PeTeL team; 6) Rank LRs according to the number of student responses to the LR items. Criterion #1 (time LR was added to the repository) is the default sorting criterion for searches in PeTeL, and therefore was used in all the searches. Thus, we omitted it from our analysis. Table 3 contains the number of searches in which the other five criteria were used (in descending order). We note that the most frequently used criterion is social-based – the number of times an LR was used (downloaded) by other teachers.

Table 3. Sorting criteria used in searches

	Sorting criterion	number of searches
a	Number of times activity was used	47
b	Title of resource	18
c	Name of content creator	18
d	Recommendations of PeTeL team	6
e	Number of students' answers	0

4 Discussion and Conclusions

In this research, we examined teachers' search strategies in OER repositories, focusing on how they utilize semantic and social information within the search and select process. We found that teachers consider three main factors when searching and choosing learning materials: curricular requirements, teaching objectives, and reliability of the resource. To achieve these goals, most teachers rely on a search strategy that consists of three stages: filtering according to

[2] A full list of all filters used, in descending order, can be found in https://shorturl.at/sIP18.

pre-defined meta-data categories offered by the search mechanism of the learning environment (mainly according to curricular learning goals), performing an initial scan of the search results in order to decide which LRs seem suitable for their needs, thus narrowing down the number of LRs to a manageable size, and finally thoroughly inspecting the content of each of the remaining learning resources, then selecting the LR that seems most suitable to their need.

As was demonstrated in previous studies (e.g., [7]), the semantic information that teachers use during their search is varied, with different teachers relying on different aspects. However, what was common to almost all of the teachers who participated in this study, was the great importance that they attributed to social-based information: the identity of the teacher who created the LR, the resource popularity (the number of times it was downloaded by other teachers), and peer recommendations. Teachers relied on this information when evaluating LRs with respect to both suitability to teaching objectives and reliability. Teachers used different sources of information to assess peers: some peers were known to them personally from professional development communities; some where connected to them through PeTeL's social network; some where highly reputed teachers; and in some cases, their trust in peers' resources was based on positive experience with content created or recommended by those teachers.

One possible implication of this result is that social-based mechanisms that build on the collective wisdom of the teacher community can increase the value that online learning environments offer to teachers. This is not surprising: The advantages of communities of practice have been repeatedly demonstrated in the past (for example, in [29]). Some of the benefits that were associated with communities of practice are their ability to create, retain and exchange knowledge within the community (ibid), to foster feelings of confidence and self-efficacy among their participants [23], and to encourage diversity, inclusion and awareness [12]. Specifically with respect to teachers' use of OER repositories, Clements et al. [5] showed how the quality of the resources in a repository can improve through collaborative efforts of teachers. However, most OER repositories are primarily designed as one-to-many unidirectional storage and retrieval information systems, whereas OER systems that are designed to encourage collaboration among teachers and to foster digital community building are not common. Our study extends our understanding of the value that collaborative environments offer to teachers, focusing on the role of social-based information in supporting effective search and select of LRs.

Therefore, designers and developers of blended learning environments who wish to build on the affordances that communities of practice offer teachers, should consider implementing features that support the establishment of digital communities, for example by adding social network features. Based on the results of the present study, social-based information such as the identity of the content creator; evaluative meta-data such as the number of downloads, comments and recommendations; and perhaps even the identity of teachers who downloaded certain LRs and recommended them (though this raises concerns about possible infringements to teacher privacy), should be made available for teachers and presented to them in a clear and noticeable fashion.

References

1. Abramovich, S., Schunn, C.D.: Studying teacher selection of resources in an ultra-large scale interactive system: does metadata guide the way? Comput. Educ. **58**(1), 551–559 (2012)
2. Abramovich, S., Schunn, C.D., Correnti, R.J.: The role of evaluative metadata in an online teacher resource exchange. Educ. Tech. Res. Dev. **61**(6), 863–883 (2013)
3. Anderson, T., Whitelock, D.: The educational semantic web: Visioning and practicing the future of education. J. Interactive Media Educ. (2004)
4. Carlson, B., Reidy, S.: Effective access: Teachers' use of digital resources (research in progress). OCLC Syst. Serv. Int. Digital Library Perspectives **20**(2), 65–70 (2004)
5. Clements, K., Pawlowski, J., Manouselis, N.: Open educational resources repositories literature review-towards a comprehensive quality approaches framework. Comput. Hum. Behav. **51**, 1098–1106 (2015)
6. Committee, I.L.T.S., et al.: Learning object metadata (2002). http://ltsc.ieee.org/wg12/
7. Cooper, J., Olsher, S., Yerushalmy, M.: Didactic metadata informing teachers' selection of learning resources: boundary crossing in professional development. J. Math. Teacher Educ. **23**(4), 363–384 (2020)
8. Diekema, A.R., Olsen, M.W.: Personal information management practices of teachers. Proc. Am. Soc. Inf. Sci. Technol. **48**(1), 1–10 (2011)
9. Diekema, A.R., Olsen, M.W.: The notion of relevance in teacher information behavior. Proc. Am. Soc. Inf. Sci. Technol. **49**(1), 1–9 (2012)
10. Doush, I.A., Alkhateeb, F., Maghayreh, E.A., Alsmadi, I., Samarah, S.: Annotations, collaborative tagging, and searching mathematics in e-learning. arXiv preprint arXiv:1211.1780 (2012)
11. Downes, S.: Models for sustainable open educational resources. Interdisciplinary J. E-Learning Learn. Objects **3**(1), 29–44 (2007)
12. Dutton, K.: Increasing diversity, awareness, and inclusion in corporate culture: investigating communities of practice and resource groups among employees. Dev. Learn. Organizations Int. J. **32**, 19–21 (2018)
13. Gueudet, G., Trouche, L.: Towards new documentation systems for mathematics teachers? Educ. Stud. Math. **71**, 199–218 (2009)
14. Holstein, K., McLaren, B.M., Aleven, V.: Intelligent tutors as teachers' aides: exploring teacher needs for real-time analytics in blended classrooms. In: Proceedings of the Seventh International Learning Analytics & Knowledge Conference, pp. 257–266 (2017)
15. Holstein, K., McLaren, B.M., Aleven, V.: Co-designing a real-time classroom orchestration tool to support teacher-ai complementarity. Grantee Submission (2019)
16. Koper, R.: Use of the semantic web to solve some basic problems in education: Increase flexible, distributed lifelong learning; decrease teacher's workload. J. Interact. Media Educ. **2004**(1), 1–23 (2004)
17. Li, Q., Baker, R., Warschauer, M.: Using clickstream data to measure, understand, and support self-regulated learning in online courses. Internet High. Educ. **45**, 100727 (2020)
18. Nazaretsky, T., Bar, C., Walter, M., Alexandron, G.: Empowering teachers with ai: co-designing a learning analytics tool for personalized instruction in the science classroom. In: LAK22: 12th International Learning Analytics and Knowledge Conference, pp. 1–12 (2022)

19. Quentin, I., Bruillard, É.: Explaining internal functioning of online teacher networks: between personal interest and depersonalized collective production, between the sandbox and the hive. In: Society for Information Technology & Teacher Education International Conference, pp. 2627–2634. Association for the Advancement of Computing in Education (AACE) (2013)
20. Recker, M., Dorward, J., Dawson, D., Mao, X., Liu, Y., Palmer, B., Halioris, S., Park, J.: Teaching, designing, and sharing: a context for learning objects. Interdisc. J. E-Learning Learn. Objects **1**(1), 197–216 (2005)
21. Recker, M.M., Dorward, J., Nelson, L.M.: Discovery and use of online learning resources: case study findings. J. Educ. Technol. Soc. **7**(2), 93–104 (2004)
22. Recker, M.M., Walker, A., Lawless, K.: What do you recommend? implementation and analyses of collaborative information filtering of web resources for education. Instr. Sci. **31**(4), 299–316 (2003)
23. Regalla, M., Davies, A., Grissom, D., Losavio, A.: Classroom to communities of practice: benefits for English learners and teacher candidates through partnerships. Multicult. Perspect. **20**(1), 25–32 (2018)
24. Shelton, B.E., Duffin, J., Wang, Y., Ball, J.: Linking open course wares and open education resources: creating an effective search and recommendation system. Procedia Comput. Sci. **1**(2), 2865–2870 (2010)
25. Siedel, H., Stylianides, A.J.: Teachers' selection of resources in an era of plenty: An interview study with secondary mathematics teachers in England. Research on mathematics textbooks and teachers' resources: Advances and issues, pp. 119–144 (2018)
26. Speer, N.M.: Issues of methods and theory in the study of mathematics teachers' professed and attributed beliefs. Educ. Stud. Math. **58**, 361–391 (2005)
27. Stojanovic, L., Staab, S., Studer, R.: elearning based on the semantic web. In: WebNet2001-World Conference on the WWW and Internet, pp. 23–27. Citeseer (2001)
28. Weibel, S.L., Koch, T.: The dublin core metadata initiative. D-lib magazine **6**(12), 1082–9873 (2000)
29. Wenger, E., et al.: Communities of practice: learning as a social system. Syst. Thinker **9**(5), 2–3 (1998)

Automated Detection of Students' Gaze Interactions in Collaborative Learning Videos: A Novel Approach

Qi Zhou[1(✉)], Amartya Bhattacharya[2], Wannapon Suraworachet[1], Hajime Nagahara[2], and Mutlu Cukurova[1]

[1] UCL Knowledge Lab, University College London, London, UK
qtnvqz3@ucl.ac.uk
[2] Osaka University, Suita, Japan

Abstract. Gaze behaviours have been considered important social signals to explore human learning. Over the past decade, previous research showed positive relationships between certain features of gaze behaviours and the quality of collaborative learning. However, most studies focus on detecting students' gaze behaviours with eye-tracking tools which are costly, logistically challenging, and can be obtrusive in real-world physical collaboration spaces. This study presents a novel approach to detecting students' gaze behaviours from videos of real-world collaborative learning activities. Pre-trained computer vision models were used to detect objects on the scenes, students' faces, and their gaze directions. Then, a rule-based approach was applied to detect gaze behaviours that are associated with peer communication and resource management aspects of collaborative learning. In order to test the accuracy of the proposed approach, twenty collaborative learning sessions, each lasting from 33 min to 67 min, from five groups in a 10-week-long higher education course were analysed. The results showed that the proposed approach achieves 66.57% overall accuracy at automatically detecting students' gaze interactions in collaborative learning videos. The implications of these findings for supporting students' collaborative learning in real-world technology-enhanced learning environments are discussed.

Keywords: Social signal processing · Face-to-face collaborative learning · Gaze behaviours · Computer Vision

1 Introduction

In recent years, with the development of AI and learning analytics techniques, an increasing number of researchers tried to gain insights into collaborative learning through the analysis of video data. Various engineered features were extracted from video data and then related to the outcomes of collaborative learning [1–4]. However, black box methods which directly correlate computer observable features with learning constructs may oversimplify the representation of the real complexity of collaborative learning and cannot provide enough educationally meaningful information for the development of

O. Viberg et al. (Eds.): EC-TEL 2023, LNCS 14200, pp. 504–517, 2023.
https://doi.org/10.1007/978-3-031-42682-7_34

learning and teaching practice [5]. To improve the transparency and interpretability of the system, a few studies tried to explore the potential of human-observable behaviours which can be extracted from computationally detectable features to provide insights for collaborative learning [5–7]. Yet, the identification of such behaviours still relied heavily on manual human coding which is time and resource intensive and cannot be scaled. There is a need for automated approaches to detect educationally meaningful behaviours from video data in collaborative learning. This would allow opportunities for real-time intervention and feedback to improve students' collaborative interactions and their associated learning outcomes.

Although gaining significant attention from computer vision researchers, the detection of students' gaze behaviours from video data is still an understudied area for AI in Education. Particularly, existing research has two significant limitations. First, the detection of gaze behaviours heavily relies on the use of eye trackers, which are cumbersome, obtrusive, and costly. Second, though there are computer vision studies that have succeeded in detecting gaze behaviours from videos in formally constructed structured contexts such as meetings with high accuracy, these studies are mainly carried out in laboratory settings and lack transferability to real-world, complex educational settings.

In this study, we propose a novel approach using computer vision models to detect students' gaze behaviours in real-world collaborative learning settings. The results indicate the potential of using this approach to identify meaningful gaze interactions in collaborative learning videos automatically and generate real-time interventions for students.

2 Background Research

2.1 Detection of Gaze Behaviours

Gaze behaviours are considered to be an important element to study shared understanding in collaborative learning activities. Existing literature argues that the effective use of gaze behaviours during collaborative learning may help students with streamlining speech [8], co-presenting [9], as well as disambiguating and directing others' attention to particular reference points [10]. Most existing gaze behaviours research in collaborative learning utilised eye-tracking tools which were mainly used to capture students' attentive regions. Measurements extracted from this attentive region, such as joint visual attention (JVA) [11], gaze overlap [12], and attention similarity [13] have been shown to have a positive relationship with the quality of collaborative learning. Previous research emphasized more on visual attention in collaborative working space rather than gaze behaviours among students, which also has been illustrated to be an important indicator of social interactions during collaborative learning [14, 15]. However, limited by technology, resources, and equipment, most studies were carried out in digital learning environments rather than investigating students' real-world collaborative learning interactions [16]. Although a few studies tried to explore students' gaze interactions in physical collaborative learning contexts, the detection of gaze behaviours in these studies still relied heavily on human annotation [17]. In addition, as eye-tracking equipment is hard to be applied in ecologically valid settings, an overwhelming majority of published studies were conducted in laboratory settings [18, 19]. Most studies reviewed here were carried out in controlled laboratory settings, and some computer vision research even required participants to sit in a fixed position and have specific postures without excessive head movement [30]. Therefore, whether the identified proxies of previous research can be captured automatically with high accuracy and whether they can effectively reflect the quality of collaborative learning in real-world settings requires further research.

With the development of recent deep learning techniques, recent studies from the computer vision community have been focusing on this problem of the automatic detection of gaze behaviours from video data [20–23]. Both, head direction extracted from postures [23], and eye direction extracted from appearance [20], were used to estimate where the group members are gazing at. To optimize the accuracy of detection, previous research explored the data collection settings with different numbers of cameras [24], cameras with different angles [25], and cameras with special functions, such as 3D cameras [26], IR cameras [27], and Near-eye cameras [28]. Traditionally, due to interest in detecting human-human interactions, these studies only considered gaze behaviours among humans but neglected the gaze behaviours of looking at objects in the environment. However, humans' interactions with educational resources in their immediate environment are equally important to be able to interpret their learning outcomes. A few studies explored gaze behaviours towards both humans and objects [29] trying to detect the gaze behaviours which require both visual attention to the objects and eye communication between humans. Yet, to the best of our knowledge, none of the existing approaches achieved the detection of these complex gaze dynamics in the context of education and with more than three participants. In this paper, we present an approach to address this significant research challenge.

2.2 Gaze Behaviours and Collaborative Learning

In the past decade, many research studies have explored gaze behaviours' potential as indicators of collaboration quality. Some studies found that Joint Visual Attention (JVA) can be a good predictor of group performance in collaborative learning [19, 31, 32]. Schneider and Pea [33] explored how JVA can be used to enhance collaborative learning and illustrated that visualizing real-time JVA for students could improve their quality of collaboration. Furthermore, they extended their work by using network analysis for eye-tracking data [33] and found that different aspects of collaborative learning, such as mutual understanding, division of tasks, signs of coordination, and dialogue management can be associated with different network metrics for JVA. In addition to the studies focused on gaze behaviours in remote settings, Zhou and colleagues [17] explored gaze behaviours in real-world collaborative learning activities. For instance, they have identified four types of gaze behaviours, namely gazing at peers, gazing at laptops, gazing at tutors and gazing at other objects, and explored different patterns of gaze interactions that have been used by groups during the process of collaboration. Their results showed that the use of different gaze patterns can be related to the groups' differences in shared understanding in collaborative learning. However, the detection of such gaze behaviours was carried out by researchers with manual annotation and potential automated detection of such gaze behaviours was presented as a future research opportunity.

In this paper, we present a novel approach to detecting gaze interactions in collaborative learning videos. Automated detection of such gaze behaviours has significant implications for developing tools to provide meaningful and timely insights to educators, interventions for improving students' collaborative learning skills and outcomes, as well as supporting researchers' painstaking video analysis of collaborative learning interactions.

3 Context

3.1 Education Context

The study was conducted in a postgraduate module in the UK. Thirty-four students were divided into groups of four or five. The groups were assigned by the teaching team with consideration to creating mixed-gendered, interdisciplinary, and varied first languages. Before the study started, ethical approval was received from the institution and individual consent was given by students. Participation had no relation to the summative assessment of the module. Students were able to opt-out at any time during the study.

During the 10-week course, students were asked to collaborate in groups to design a technological solution to overcome an educational challenge chosen by the group. For each week, students had to 1) read literature related to the weekly topic; 2) view the pre-recorded lectures; 3) participate in the online asynchrony class debate via Moodle forum; 4) participate in a one-hour face-to-face tutorial; 5) participate in face-to-face group discussions to work on their weekly collaborative group tasks, and 6) reflect on their weekly learning experience individually via Google Docs. This study focused on data collected on the fifth task, students' face-to-face group discussions on collaborative learning tasks.

3.2 Data Collection

During the face-to-face group discussion sessions, students were seated as a group around a T-shaped table (Fig. 1). Each student accessed an online collaboration platform, Miro, through their own laptop/tablet. An Intel RealSense camera was set at the far end of the T-shaped table to capture video data. The video data was captured as.bag files and then has been transferred to .mp4 files. Twenty collaborative learning sessions, lasting from about 33 min to 67 min, have been analysed in this study.

Fig. 1. Data collection setting of the collaborative learning activity

4 Methodology

4.1 Gaze Object Detection

Gaze object detection is the task of detecting the objects that one or multiple persons are looking at in an image or video. This task was done in 3 steps i) person head tracking ii) prediction of gaze position ii) detection of the corresponding object. The whole architecture has been given below in Fig. 2.

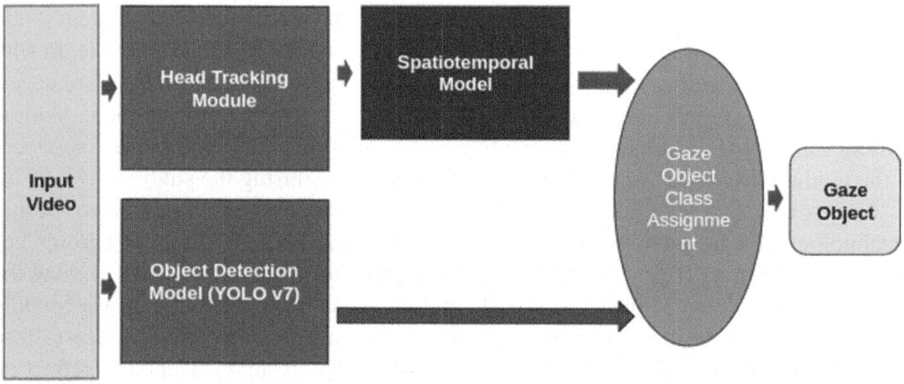

Fig. 2. Gaze Object Detection Framework

i) **Head Tracking.** Head tracking is essential in order to obtain the bounding boxes of the people present in the video, whose gaze behaviours we want to observe. The bounding boxes obtained through the head tracking module served as an input to the gaze prediction module.

For tracking the heads, initially, the head bounding boxes are obtained using a pre-trained YOLOv7 model on the Crowdhuman dataset [34]. In order to track the bounding boxes in a series of frames, after obtaining the head bounding boxes for the first frame, the task was to distribute all the head bounding boxes into random classes and then for the subsequent frames we needed to assign the bounding boxes obtained into the classes based on the nearest neighbour principle.

The whole intuition was to find the "distance" between the head bounding box corresponding to the previous frame and the head bounding box, obtained in the current frame as shown in Fig. 3. The trivial method was to compare the distance between the bounding boxes but this trivial solution proved to be ineffective in cases where occlusions were observed. The occlusion problem was solved by using features generated from the portion of the image encapsulated by the head bounding box.

This problem was analogous to the person re-identification task, thus a model for the re-identification task was selected for feature generation of the image inside the bounding box. As proposed by Zhou et al. [17] a model for person reidentification in which the problem was solved by taking into account the features learned at multiple

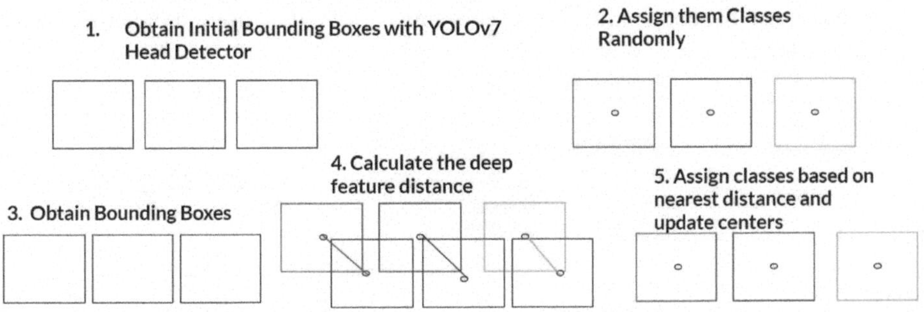

Fig. 3. Head Tracking Framework

scales or omni-scale features. This model was used to generate the features from the image inside the bounding boxes.

The value obtained using the distance between the features obtained using the omni-scale model was called the deep feature distance. The features obtained using the omni-scale feature representation was a vector of the shape of (512*1) and thus the sum of the element-wise difference of the vector corresponding to the previous frame and that of the current frame, was taken as the deep feature distance.

ii) **SpatioTemporal Model for Gaze Estimation.** The bounding boxes corresponding to each of the persons present in the video served as input to the Gaze Prediction module responsible for predicting the coordinates of the gaze point. The Gaze estimation problem was first addressed by Recasens et al., [27] using scene information as well as head position information for a single image. There were improvements in the task of gaze estimation in the subsequent years. Chong et al. [35] proposed a model for gaze estimation in videos using head features, head bounding box coordinates and a video. The spatiotemporal model proposed by the authors which uses Convolutional LSTM layers in order to transfer information learned from the previous frame for evaluating the next frames proved to be fruitful in predicting the gaze points. Since this model was the only model that was dealing with videos and had state-of-the-art results, this model was chosen as our model for the prediction of the gaze point. In our work, the spatio-temporal model is trained on VideoAttention Dataset [35]. The model received the position of the head bounding box coordinates as well as the whole frame as input. The head image was obtained from the bounding boxes. Feature maps of both the head as well as the whole image were obtained separately using convolutional filters. The image features were then multiplied by the attention weights, calculated from the head feature maps. The head feature map was then concatenated with the scene feature map which was then encoded as shown in Fig. 4, and was given as input to the decoder as shown in Fig. 5. Upon obtaining the encoded features, the temporal information was integrated into the model using convolutional Long Short-Term Memory layers [37]. The encoded features were then decoded using four deconvolutional layers which helped in upsampling the features. The final deconvolutional layer gave output in the form of a heatmap from which the exact gaze coordinates were obtained by selecting the pixel corresponding to the maximum heatmap value. These coordinates were then used in the task of gaze object detection.

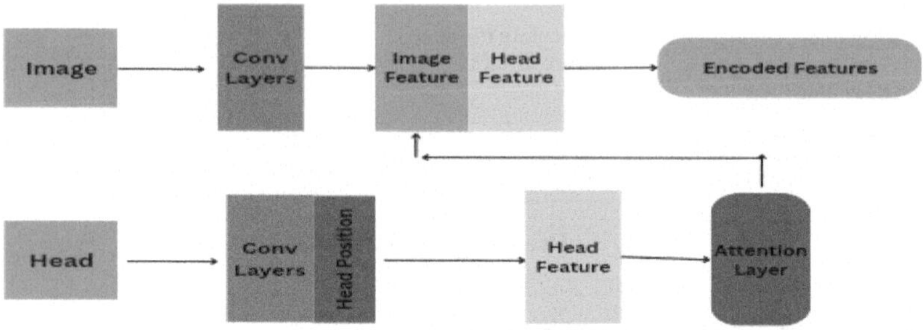

Fig. 4. Feature Encoder

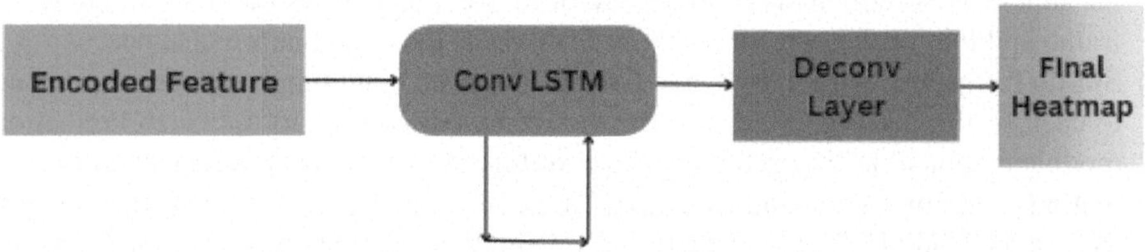

Fig. 5. Feature Decoder

iii) **Object Detection and Assignment.** In parallel, the object bounding boxes present in a video were detected using a pre-trained YOLOv7 model. The objects corresponding to gaze points were determined in two consecutive manners.
   a) If there are no overlaps between multiple objects bounding boxes and the gaze point, the object is chosen within whose bounding box the gaze point lies,
   b) Else if the gaze point lies at an intersection of multiple bounding boxes, the box whose centre is closest to the gaze point in terms of Euclidean distance is chosen as the given gaze object.

This was achieved by the following algorithm:

For a single frame, upon obtaining the gaze point (x, y) coordinate, the number of bounding boxes that enclose the gaze point was found by the following computation.

For every object bounding box, "i" (obtained from YOLOv7) having coordinates (xi, yi, xi + wi, yi + hi), if $xi < x < xi + wi$, also if $yi < y < yi + hi$, then gaze point (x, y) is confirmed to be inside the bounding box. The object bounding box coordinates corresponding to the gaze point were stored.

Now, if for a gaze point, there is only a single object bounding box that encloses it, the object label corresponding to the bounding box is inferred as the gaze object.

And if there are multiple bounding boxes associated with the gaze point, the centre of every object bounding box having coordinates as $(xi, yi, xi + wi, yi + hi)$ are obtained by calculating $(xi + wi/2, yi + hi/2)$. Then the gaze object is found by taking the label associated with the bounding box whose centre has the minimum Euclidean distance from the gaze point.

4.2 Gaze Annotation

Two types of gaze behaviours, namely gazing at peers and gazing at laptops were identified and labelled manually from the video data to test the accuracy of the auto-detection model build. These two gaze behaviours were illustrated to have the potential of distinguishing the process of collaborative learning for groups with different learning outcomes [17]. The first frame of each second from a particular session was extracted to generate a new video for labelling gaze behaviours. Computer Vision Annotation Tool (CVAT)(cvat.org) was used for video annotation. The coding work was conducted by two researchers. Before they worked separately, a sample video of 1000 frames was coded by both of them to test the reliability of the coding process. Inter-rater reliability of double coding presented very high-reliability values (Cohen's Kappa = 0.98).

5 Results

The overall accuracy of the proposed model for automatically detecting gaze behaviours in collaborative learning was calculated as 66.57%. The laptop gaze behaviour class precision was 78.44% while the class recall was 75.28%, and the F1 score is 76.83%. It shows the approach's effectiveness to detect the students' behaviour of gazing at laptops during collaborative learning activities. Whereas the performance of detecting the behaviours of gazing at students was relatively low at 42.31% and 38.04% in class recall and precision respectively (Table 1).

Table 1. Confusion Matrix for Automated Gaze Detection Model

		Annotation			
		L(Laptop)	S(Student)	Overall	Class Precision
Detection	L(Laptop)	3368	926	4294	78.44%
	S(Student)	1106	679	1785	38.04%
	Overall	4474	1605	6079	
	Class Recall	75.28%	42.31%		66.57%

There might be several reasons for the approach's low performance in detecting gazing behaviours associated with peer communication. Firstly, the approach's detection of gaze behaviours was based on a single picture while the human annotation of these gaze behaviours took the consecutive frames into consideration. In other words, the proposed computer vision approach only considered the behaviour of gazing at students as an instantaneous action but neglected the gaze behaviour as a coherent contextual movement.

One possible way to improve the performance might be using algorithms such as team-Long short-term memory (LSTM) to process both single data points and the entire sequences of data [36].

Fig. 6. An example of mislabeled data

Secondly, the detection of gaze direction only takes students' head and body postures into account. To be more specific, this approach detects students' gaze direction through their body key points which only change with their head and body postures. However, during the process of annotation work, it is found that many students gaze at others by only moving their eyes but not moving their heads or bodies towards others. In these cases, the algorithm made the wrong decisions (as Fig. 6 shown, person1 was still facing his laptop, though he was gazing at person 2 in the group).

Previous literature showed that head orientation contributes ~ 68.9% to the gaze direction in meetings, which is similar to the accuracy of the approach proposed in this study [23]. It was suggested that eye blinks can also be considered during the detection of gaze points. To address this, more key points about eyes should be extracted when detecting students' gaze direction. Thirdly, it would be harder to match students' gaze directions with other students' faces due to the different spaces occupied by students' faces and laptops in the scenes. As Fig. 7 shows, since students often sat behind their laptops, the box of the head might be overlapped with the boxes of other objects. As a result, students were more likely to be detected as gazing at an object which occupied a larger area. To solve this, the camera angles and students' laptops area in the scenes may be tried to be limited to the screen area. Also, the adjudication area of students needs to be adjusted from the head to face area only.

Fig. 7. An example of mislabeled data

6 Discussion

This study presents a novel approach to detect students' gaze behaviours among peers and towards objects by using pre-trained models in a real-world collaborative learning context. The YOLOv7 model is used to detect objects and to track heads that appeared in the scenes. Then, based on the head tracking box, a spatiotemporal model was used to estimate students' gaze points. At last, a rule-based method was applied to assign the gaze object. The result shows that the proposed approach can achieve 66.57% in detecting students' behaviours of gazing at peers and gazing at their laptops in real-world teaching and learning contexts. Given the fact that the gaze behaviours detection task in this study considered both humans and objects in face-to-face collaboration, which has not been explored in previous studies, we compared the performance with baselines in similar contexts. For instance, Stiefelhagen and colleagues [39] reported an approach of detecting the focus of attention for the meeting by analysing video data from a panoramic camera with an accuracy of 73.9%. Müller et al., [40] tried to detect participants' eye contact, which was similar to the gazing at peers behaviour in this study, by analysing videos from eight cameras for four participants. They have achieved 54% accuracy with a no-training model. Moreover, Sabuncuoglu and Sezgin [43] developed models with up to 71% percent accuracy of predicting group-level activity based on video inputs. Although the performance of detecting gaze behaviours towards laptops is comparable to existing state-of-the-art algorithms used in different real-world contexts, further suggestions for improvement of gaze behaviours among peers were also suggested by analyzing the decisions made by the proposed algorithm. Also, the proposed approach reduces the technical costs of data collection by using only one RGB camera for a collaborative group.

The use of automated detection of these gaze behaviours from video data has broad educational research and practice implications. First, the proposed approach provides a reliable and efficient approach for analyzing gaze behaviours in real-world collaborative learning settings, which can assist researchers and educators in understanding the dynamics of group interactions from video data. It can break through the limit of eye trackers, and extend the use of previous gaze indicators, such as JVA, gaze overlap, and gaze similarity from digital collaborative learning settings to physical collaborative learning contexts. To be more specific, by detecting each individual's gaze object in physical collaboration, whether the members of a group were gazing at the same object or a similar area can also be estimated. These estimations may help with further exploring the effectiveness of these indicators in face-to-face collaborative learning contexts. Moreover, this study proposed a more practical method of gaze detection in real-world learning contexts. It is argued that the scalability, sustainability [41], evidence of impact and ethics [42] of MMLA design might all influence the potential adoption in authentic learning situations. Compared to the traditional gaze detection using eye trackers, the proposed method is less invasive, low-cost, and easy-adapt, especially in a complex collaborative learning scenario. It makes gaze detection in real-world collaborative learning practice more realistic. However, it is also worth noting that the proposed method has some limitations compared with the eye trackers. On the one hand, the accuracy of the proposed method can be still not promising enough, especially when detecting the gaze behaviours between peers. On the other hand, the types of gazed objects that can be detected by this method are not complex enough. This may limit the adoption of this method in other contexts. It is worth exploring the trade-offs between the "high practicality" and the "performance" of gaze detection in MMLA design.

Second, the results of this study provide opportunities for the automated detection of gaze behaviours that can be used as predictors of collaborative learning outcomes. Previous research showed that two distinct types of gaze patterns (peer-interaction-focused type and resource-interaction-focused type) are associated with students' shared understanding, and can be identified by whether students were gazing at peers, laptops, and tutors [17]. The proposed automatic detection approach here can provide the possibility for this kind of study to be conducted with a larger sample size in a variety of contexts, which would test the generalisability of findings from previous small-scale research with human-labelled gaze behaviours. At the very least, with the help of this automated gaze behaviour detection, manual analysis of video data can be done with less effort in a more reliable manner. Lastly, as Schneider and Pea [19] illustrated, students might benefit from knowing where other students in the group were gazing in both virtual and co-located collaborative learning contexts. Therefore, it is worth exploring how visualizations generated from the automatic detection of gaze behaviours in physical collaborative learning settings can be used to support collaboration. This line of investigation has the potential to contribute to both the research and practice of collaborative learning.

Limitations

There are also some limitations of this study that should be noted. Firstly, the proposed approach only tracks the positions of heads but does not involve a face recognition function (due to ethical concerns associated with the use of face recognition in classrooms [38]), so it is hard to estimate the identity of the person gazed at by peers. Therefore, the alignment of gaze behaviours from different students needed to be conducted manually initially. It is important to improve the proposed approach's accuracy without exacerbating its associated ethical and privacy implications. Secondly, the analysed data set contains more behaviours of gazing at laptops than gazing at students. This unbalanced data may have affected the results of the analysis. More annotated data with gazing at students should be included to improve accuracy and reliability. Lastly, the current approach only takes two gaze behaviours into consideration. Although these gaze behaviours are associated with important aspects of collaborative learning (i.e. resource management, and peer interactions) future studies should include more types of gaze behaviours to gain insights into the complex process of collaborative learning.

7 Conclusion

In this paper, we proposed a novel approach to automatically detect students' gaze behaviours in real-world collaborative learning activities using pre-trained models and a rule-based method. Considering the accuracy of the model on novel video data, we conclude that the approach has the potential to be used in diverse real-world contexts in the future. The approach presented has significant implications for studying gaze interactions in physical collaborative learning activities from videos as well as developing automated feedback interventions for collaborative learning activities.

Acknowledgement. This research was partially funded by UCL-CDI AWS Doctoral Scholarship in Digital Innovation and the European Union's Horizon 2020 research and innovation programme under grant agreement No 101004676.

References

1. Spikol, D., Ruffaldi, E., Dabisias, G., Cukurova, M.: Supervised machine learning in multimodal learning analytics for estimating success in project-based learning. J. Comput. Assist. Learn. **34**, 366–377 (2018). https://doi.org/10.1111/jcal.12263
2. Spikol, D., Ruffaldi, E., Landolfi, L., Cukurova, M.: Estimation of success in collaborative learning based on multimodal learning analytics features. In: 2017 IEEE 17th International Conference on Advanced Learning Technologies (ICALT), pp. 269–273 (2017). https://doi.org/10.1109/ICALT.2017.122
3. Cukurova, M., Luckin, R., Millán, E., Mavrikis, M.: The NISPI framework: analysing collaborative problem-solving from students' physical interactions. Comput. Educ. **116**, 93–109 (2018). https://doi.org/10.1016/j.compedu.2017.08.007
4. Spikol, D., Ruffaldi, E., Cukurova, M.: Using multimodal learning analytics to identify aspects of collaboration in project-based learning. In: proceedings of the International Conference on Computer Supported Collaborative Learning (CSCL) (2017)
5. Cukurova, M., Zhou, Q., Spikol, D., Landolfi, L.: Modelling collaborative problem-solving competence with transparent learning analytics: is video data enough? In: Proceedings of the Tenth International Conference on Learning Analytics & Knowledge, pp. 270–275. Association for Computing Machinery, New York, NY, USA (2020). https://doi.org/10.1145/3375462.3375484
6. Martinez-Maldonado, R., Gaševic, D., Echeverria, V., Fernandez Nieto, G., Swiecki, Z., Buckingham Shum, S.: What do you mean by collaboration analytics? a conceptual model. J. Learning Analytics **8**, 126–153 (2021)
7. Wise, A.F., Knight, S., Shum, S.B.: Collaborative learning analytics. In: International handbook of computer-supported collaborative learning, pp. 425–443. Springer (2021). https://doi.org/10.1007/978-3-030-65291-3_23

8. Monk, A.F., Gale, C.: A look is worth a thousand words: full gaze awareness in video-mediated conversation. Discourse Process. **33**, 257–278 (2002)
9. Gupta, K., Lee, G.A., Billinghurst, M.: Do you see what I see? the effect of gaze tracking on task space remote collaboration. IEEE Trans. Visual Comput. Graphics **22**, 2413–2422 (2016)
10. Staudte, M., Crocker, M.W.: Investigating joint attention mechanisms through spoken human–robot interaction. Cognition **120**, 268–291 (2011)
11. Schlösser, C., Schlieker-Steens, P., Kienle, A., Harrer, A.: Using real-time gaze based awareness methods to enhance collaboration. In: CYTED-RITOS International Workshop on Groupware, pp. 19–27. Springer (2015). https://doi.org/10.1007/978-3-319-22747-4_2
12. D'Angelo, S., Gergle, D.: An eye for design: gaze visualizations for remote collaborative work. In: Proceedings of the 2018 CHI Conference on Human Factors in Computing Systems, pp. 1–12 (2018)
13. Papavlasopoulou, S., Sharma, K., Giannakos, M., Jaccheri, L.: Using eye-tracking to unveil differences between kids and teens in coding activities. In: Proceedings of the 2017 Conference on Interaction Design and Children, pp. 171–181 (2017)
14. Sharma, K., Olsen, J., Verma, H., Caballero, D., Jermann, P.: Challenging joint visual attention as a proxy for collaborative performance: ISLS annual meeting 2021 (virtual): international society of the learning sciences. International Society of the Learning Sciences, Proceedings, pp. 91–98 (2021). https://doi.org/10.22318/cscl2021.91
15. Fan, L., Wang, W., Huang, S., Tang, X., Zhu, S.-C.: Understanding human gaze communication by spatio-temporal graph reasoning. In: Proceedings of the IEEE/CVF International Conference on Computer Vision, pp. 5724–5733 (2019)
16. D'angelo, S., Schneider, B.: Shared gaze visualizations in collaborative interactions: past, present and future. Interact. Comput. **33**, 115–133 (2021)
17. Zhou, Q., Suraworachet, W., Celiktutan, O., Cukurova, M.: What does shared understanding in students' face-to-face collaborative learning gaze behaviours "look like"?. In: Rodrigo, M.M., Matsuda, N., Cristea, A.I., Dimitrova, V. (eds.) Artificial Intelligence in Education, pp. 588–593. Springer International Publishing, Cham (2022). https://doi.org/10.1007/978-3-031-11644-5_53
18. Sung, G., Feng, T., Schneider, B.: Learners learn more and instructors track better with real-time gaze sharing. Proceedings of the ACM on Human-Computer Interaction **5**, 1–23 (2021)
19. Schneider, B., Pea, R.: Real-time mutual gaze perception enhances collaborative learning and collaboration quality. In: Educational Media and Technology Yearbook, pp. 99–125. Springer (2017)
20. Cheng, Y., Wang, H., Bao, Y., Lu, F.: Appearance-based gaze estimation with deep learning: A review and benchmark. arXiv preprint arXiv:2104.12668 (2021)
21. Mukherjee, S.S., Robertson, N.M.: Deep head pose: gaze-direction estimation in multimodal video. IEEE Trans. Multimedia **17**, 2094–2107 (2015)
22. Robertson, N., Reid, I.: Estimating gaze direction from low-resolution faces in video. In: European conference on computer vision, pp. 402–415. Springer (2006). https://doi.org/10.1007/11744047_31
23. Stiefelhagen, R., Zhu, J.: Head orientation and gaze direction in meetings. In: CHI'02 Extended Abstracts on Human Factors in Computing Systems, pp. 858–859 (2002)
24. Tonsen, M., Steil, J., Sugano, Y., Bulling, A.: Invisibleeye: mobile eye tracking using multiple low-resolution cameras and learning-based gaze estimation. Proceedings of the ACM on Interactive, Mobile, Wearable and Ubiquitous Technol. **1**, 1–21 (2017)
25. Wright, R., Ellis, T., Makris, D.: Measuring inferred gaze direction to support analysis of people in a meeting. Expert Syst. Appl. **169**, 114398 (2021). https://doi.org/10.1016/j.eswa.2020.114398

26. Lian, D., et al.: RGBD based gaze estimation via multi-task CNN. In: Proceedings of the AAAI Conference on Artificial Intelligence, pp. 2488–2495 (2019)
27. Recasens, A., Vondrick, C., Khosla, A., Torralba, A.: Following gaze in video. In: Proceedings of the IEEE International Conference on Computer Vision, pp. 1435–1443 (2017)
28. Kim, J., et al.: Nvgaze: An anatomically-informed dataset for low-latency, near-eye gaze estimation. In: Proceedings of the 2019 CHI Conference on Human Factors in Computing Systems, pp. 1–12 (2019)
29. Li, Y., Shen, W., Gao, Z., Zhu, Y., Zhai, G., Guo, G.: Looking here or there? gaze following in 360-degree images. In: 2021 IEEE/CVF International Conference on Computer Vision (ICCV), pp. 3722–3731. IEEE, Montreal, QC, Canada (2021). https://doi.org/10.1109/ICCV48922.2021.00372
30. Huang, Q.: TabletGaze: dataset and algorithm for unconstrained appearance-based gaze estimation in mobile tablets. In: Machine Vision and Appl. **28**(5–6), 445–461 (2015)
31. Richardson, D.C., Dale, R.: Looking to understand: the coupling between speakers' and listeners' eye movements and its relationship to discourse comprehension. Cogn. Sci. **29**, 1045–1060 (2005). https://doi.org/10.1207/s15516709cog0000_29
32. Jermann, P., Mullins, D., Nüssli, M.-A., Dillenbourg, P., Nuessli, M.-A.: Collaborative gaze footprints: correlates of interaction quality. In: International Conference on Computer Supported Collaborative Learning (2011)
33. Schneider, B., Pea, R.: Toward collaboration sensing. Intern. J. Comput.-Support. Collab. Learn. **9**, 371–395 (2014). https://doi.org/10.1007/s11412-014-9202-y
34. CrowdHuman Dataset. https://www.crowdhuman.org/. Accessed 16 Jan 2023
35. Chong, E., Wang, Y., Ruiz, N., Rehg, J.M.: Detecting attended visual targets in video. In: 2020 IEEE/CVF Conference on Computer Vision and Pattern Recognition (CVPR), pp. 5395–5405. IEEE, Seattle, WA, USA (2020). https://doi.org/10.1109/CVPR42600.2020.00544
36. Kasparova, A., Celiktutan, O., Cukurova, M.: Inferring student engagement in collaborative problem solving from visual cues. In: Companion Publication of the 2020 International Conference on Multimodal Interaction, pp. 177–181. Association for Computing Machinery, New York, NY, USA (2020). https://doi.org/10.1145/3395035.3425961
37. Shi, X., Chen, Z., Wang, H., Yeung, D.-Y., Wong, W.-K., Woo, W.-C.: Convolutional lstm network: a machine learning approach for precipitation 5405 nowcasting. In: Advances in Neural Information Processing Systems, pp. 802–810
38. Holmes, W., et al.: Ethics of AI in education: towards a community-wide framework. International J. Artificial Intelligence Educ. pp. 1–23 (2021)
39. Stiefelhagen, R., Yang, J., Waibel, A.: Modeling focus of attention for meeting indexing based on multiple cues. IEEE Trans. Neural Networks **13**(4), 928–938 (2002)
40. Müller, P., Huang, M.X., Zhang, X., Bulling, A.: Robust eye contact detection in natural multi-person interactions using gaze and speaking behaviour. In: Proceedings of the 2018 ACM Symposium on Eye Tracking Research & Applications, pp. 1–10 (2018)
41. Yan, L., Zhao, L., Gasevic, D., Martinez-Maldonado, R.: Scalability, sustainability, and ethicality of multimodal learning analytics. In: LAK22: 12th International Learning Analytics and Knowledge Conference, pp. 13–23 (2022)
42. Alwahaby, H., Cukurova, M., Papamitsiou, Z., Giannakos, M.: The evidence of impact and ethical considerations of multimodal learning analytics: a systematic literature review. The Multimodal Learning Analytics Handbook, pp. 289–325 (2022)
43. Sabuncuoglu, A., Sezgin, T.M.: Multimodal Group Activity Dataset for Classroom Engagement Level Prediction. arXiv preprint arXiv:2304.08901 (2023)

Pedagogically-Informed Implementation of Reinforcement Learning on Knowledge Graphs for Context-Aware Learning Recommendations

Hasan Abu-Rasheed(✉), Christian Weber, Mareike Dornhöfer, and Madjid Fathi

University of Siegen, Siegen, Germany
hasan.abu.rasheed@uni-siegen.de

Abstract. Context-aware recommender systems are important tools to address the learning context in technology enhanced learning. However, the contextual factors of learning, as well as the mechanisms of integrating them into the recommendation, are mostly defined from a technical perspective, rather than a pedagogical one. In this paper, we introduce a new approach for generating pedagogically informed, context-aware, learning recommendations. We build on the context definition in situated and subject-oriented learning theories. Then, we utilize a knowledge graph structure to build the environment for a path exploration and ranking algorithm, which is influenced by agent exploration in reinforcement learning (RL), for creating sequential learning-path recommendations. Our design of the agent's reward function integrates learning-context factors in the recommender system. We evaluate the proposed solution qualitatively with domain experts, and quantitatively using semantic-similarity measures to compare our recommended paths to expert-curated learning content. Our evaluation shows an enriched recommendation based on the learners' context, as well as a better discovery of relevant educational content.

Keywords: Knowledge graphs · Context-aware · Recommender system · TEL · Learning path · Situated learning · Pedagogy-based learning recommendations

1 Introduction

In modern digital learning, the large target group of open, online, learning resource providers makes it impossible for one learning-offer to fit the needs and goals of different learners alike. Therefore, concepts of personalized and adaptive learning (PAL) became essential foundations for enhancing the learners' performance and motivation [1, 2]. In technology enhanced learning (TEL), personalization is not purely a technical process, but one that is greatly dependent on the pedagogical foundations of learning [3]. Therefore, TEL approaches define and utilize technologies that can model learners, learning materials and learning settings, to enable, e.g., a recommendation system,

O. Viberg et al. (Eds.): EC-TEL 2023, LNCS 14200, pp. 518–523, 2023.
https://doi.org/10.1007/978-3-031-42682-7_35

of generating personalized learning suggestions. This concept has its roots in learning theories, such as constructivism, situated learning, and student-centered approaches. In situated learning theory, the context in which learning happens is not separable from knowledge acquisition during the learning process [4]. Learning in this sense is situated in a real-world context, which points out the importance of representing the learner within a defined context if personalization is to be accomplished. To that end, several technologies, including ontologies and knowledge graphs (KG), have been addressed in the literature to model the learning context. KGs have shown promising results for creating knowledge maps that represent the cognitive maps learners create in their minds, within a certain learning context [5]. While embedding the learner's context and the context of the educational resource in the KG is key to enabling contextual personalization, the recommendation algorithm should still address the pedagogical learning requirements, and utilize the knowledge structure effectively, to generate the personalized learning recommendation. Therefore, we propose in this paper an approach to utilize KGs and RL to model the context of the learner and generate context-aware learning-path recommendations, through graph exploration and path ranking. Our proposed solution aims to provide a pedagogically informed contextualization of the path recommendation through: 1) identifying and integrating learner context-factors in the KG, which were selected here based on situated learning theory, and 2) utilizing a graph-exploration approach that is based on RL, with a contextually defined reward function, to rank the potential paths between a learner and their learning goal, and thus, recommending the top-ranking learning path.

2 Background

KG is a knowledge modeling method that is composed of a network of entities represented by nodes, and relations that connect them [6]. KG is defined by the triple $\{(h, r, t)|h, t \in E, r \in R\}$, where h is the head entity, r is the relation, t is the tail entity, E is the entity group and R is the relation group. KGs have been used in recent years for supporting context-aware recommendation systems, as in [7] and [8]. KGs provide rich semantic information about items and their relationships, which can be used to enhance the quality of recommendations. Yang et al. [9] utilize that feature to enhance fact mining from the KG. Syed et al. [10] use domain-KGs to support context-aware recommendations, where they segment user queries and reason over the segmented logical triples to create contextual recommendations.

The main challenge in context-aware recommendations over KGs is to incorporate the learner's context into the KG and the recommendation algorithm. To that end, several researchers, such as Xian et al. [11], utilized RL to generate graph-based recommendations. The authors proposed a policy-guided path reasoning and design a soft reward function for the RL agent, which interacts with the KG environment to maximize a cumulative reward function. They formulate the RL problem and as a Markov decision process, in which an agent takes actions in a stateful environment to optimize the reward over time. Although the authors address the role of reward function design to enhance the exploration and path ranking of the KG, they do not address the role of context in that navigation. Therefore, while the proposed solution in [11] proved an excellent performance on product datasets from Amazon, its implementation in a TEL environment is still limited, since the reward is not only dependent on the similarity between two consecutive items on the graph-path, but rather on the relevance of both items to the learner's goal and learning context. Therefore, we build on that concept and propose an RL-based recommendation algorithm that utilizes the context factors embedded in the KG structure, through the design of a unique contextual reward function that focuses on the pedagogical requirements for path ranking over the KG.

3 Methodology

The first step of implementing the recommendation and designing the reward function is defining the contextual factors that will describe the learning from a pedagogical point of view. From the contextual factors surveyed in [12–14], we select three factors with the highest effect size in the evaluation use case of vocational education and training (VAT), namely: *Learner's background knowledge, time available for learning*, and the *learning exploration preference*. This contextual information is integrated into the user- and learning resource nodes in the KG.

The recommendation system is then designed as a KG exploration and path ranking algorithm. In our approach, the KG defines the environment that the agent explores. KG nodes are considered states of the environment, and KG relations are considered the transition actions between environment states. After defining all possible paths between the learner and their learning goal in the KG, the agent explores the paths in the respective RL environment iteratively, see Fig. 1. Here, we consider our implementation influenced by RL and not a direct adoption of the algorithm, since the agent in our approach is not meant to learn the KG environment for, e.g., an autonomous-navigation or maze-solving task. Through its exploration, the agent ranks the paths based on the reward function. With each transition from one state to another, the reward function is used to update the value of the respective state-action pairs of nodes and relations in each explored path. The exploration then stops when all paths are explored at least once, and the maximum iteration limit is reached.

To update the state-action values contextually, we embed the contextual factors in the reward function. This approach allows the system to utilize the KG structure and the embedded contextual information in reflecting the learner's context on the path-ranking process. In comparison to other exhaustive implementations of RL over KG, our approach represents a lighter implementation, which does not compromise the pedagogical aspect of ranking the potential learning paths, while reducing the required computational load on the agent exploration.

Building on the definition of a state-action value function from RL (Eq. 1), we define the reward function as shown in Eq. 2 and Eq. 3.

$$\mathrm{Q(s, a)} \leftarrow \sum\nolimits_{s' \in S} P^a_{ss'}\left[R^a_{ss'} + \gamma \max_{a'} Q\left(s', a'\right)\right] \tag{1}$$

$$R^a_{ss'} = F\left(ExP, DfG, BK, T_p\right) \tag{2}$$

$$R^a_{ss'} = W_{BK} * f_{BK}\left(BK, txt\left(s'\right)\right) + W_{ExP} * f_{ExP}(ExP, DfG) + W_T * f_T\left(T_p, t\left(s'\right)\right) \tag{3}$$

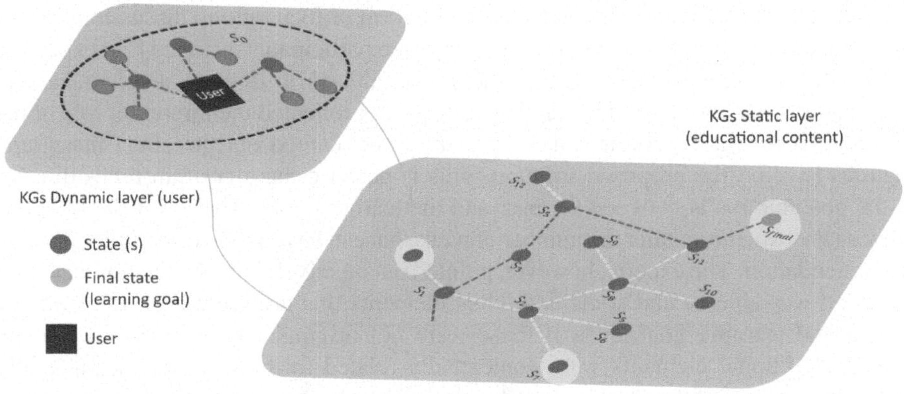

Fig. 1. KG as an environment for the agent exploration. The blue path illustrates the highest ranked learning-path based on the agent exploration, where s_i: state i, s_{final}: goal state.

where $Q(s, a)$ is the value of state s when taking the action a. $P^a_{ss'}$ is the transition model. $R^a_{ss'}$ is the reward function. *ExP* is the exploration factor. *DfG* is the graph distance from the learning goal. *BK* is the background knowledge factor. T_p is the time factor. The contextual factors (*ExP*, *BK* and T_p) play the main role in updating state-action values. Those values are then used to calculate the overall learning path rank. The path with the highest rank corresponds to the states and actions that offer the highest contextual gain from learning. This path is then recommended to the learner.

4 Evaluation and Results

The proposed solution has been evaluated qualitatively and quantitatively in the vocational education and training domain, namely in the fields of elderly care and transferable-skills training. This use case was selected due to the availability of users, domain experts, and expert-curated learning materials, from which the KG was constructed.

For the quantitative evaluation, a sample of 5 user profiles has been created and fed to the recommender system with a fixed learning goal. The profiles covered a range of potential learner contexts expected in an elderly-care home, including experienced personnel, newly hired ones, nursing staff, cleaning staff, and management. The resulting recommendations were then compared to expert-defined recommended paths for the same user contexts. The comparison aimed to identify: 1) the overlap between the system- and expert-recommendations, i.e., coverage, and 2) the new material recommendations introduced by the contextual recommender, which was not considered by the experts. The results showed 83% coverage with the expert recommended path. 17% of the expert recommendation was not covered by the system. We were able to track the reason to the amount of textual content provide for a part of the learning materials, which revealed a limitation in creating sufficiently accurate relations in the KG. On the other hand, our recommender was able to identify additional learning materials in the KG, which was added to the learning path. The additional materials were then evaluated qualitatively by the domain experts.

Qualitative evaluation was conducted in the form of focus-group discussions with a sample of domain experts and learners. Focus group participants included four experts in the elderly-care domain, six experts in the transferable-skills domain, and five learners from multiple backgrounds. The qualitative feedback reflected the important role of the user context for the recommendation. Experts have pointed out the effect that graph relations have on the proposed solution. This is because the algorithm relies directly on the potential paths between the user and the learning goal. The fewer the relations between the two, the smaller the number of paths that can be found to offer a personalized recommendation. The experts, however, pointed out positively that the recommendation algorithm was able to find some additional elements that are relevant to the learner's context and learning goal, even if those were not originally defined by the content curator. Additional elements were contextually related to the user, and semantically similar to elements of the recommended path, which reflects directly the effectiveness of our proposed contextualization approach. To support the evaluation within this ongoing research with statistical results, a large-scale A/B test has been designed to measure the difference in learners' performance based on the contextual recommendation. Future steps also include supporting the recommendation algorithm with an explanation module, to elaborate to the user why the recommendation has been generated.

5 Conclusion

In this poster paper, we describe a knowledge graph-based, context-aware, recommender system algorithm. Our approach is designed based on pedagogical foundations of learning context in the situated learning theory. We select three key contextual factors from a literature survey. We then utilize the KG structure to embed the contextual information in the metadata of the KG nodes. This information is then used by a context-aware recommendation algorithm, which is developed based on a light implementation of RL over KGs. Our design of the reward functions, which affects the values of state-actions, allows utilizing the context factors for ranking the learning path in the KG without the need for exhaustive RL computations over the KG environment. The proposed solution has gone through preliminary evolution, qualitatively and quantitatively. The results showed the effectiveness of the solution in contextualizing the recommendation. Results also pointed out some risks due to the large dependency of path finding phase on the KG relations. Further larger-scale evaluation is the next step to test the proposed approach statistically, in terms of its influence on the learner's performance.

References

1. Taylor, D.L., Yeung, M., Bashet, A.Z.: Personalized and adaptive learning. In: Ryoo, J., Winkelmann, K. (eds.) Innovative Learning Environments in STEM Higher Education: Opportunities, Challenges, and Looking Forward, pp. 17–34. Springer International Publishing, Cham (2021). https://doi.org/10.1007/978-3-030-58948-6_2
2. Rajabalee, Y.B., Santally, M.I.: Learner satisfaction, engagement and performances in an online module: implications for institutional e-learning policy. Educ Inf Technol. **26**, 2623–2656 (2021). https://doi.org/10.1007/s10639-020-10375-1

3. Daniela, L.: Smart pedagogy as a driving wheel for technology-enhanced learning. Technol. Knowl. Learn. **26**(4), 711–718 (2021). https://doi.org/10.1007/s10758-021-09536-z
4. Lave, J., Wenger, E.: Situated Learning: Legitimate Peripheral Participation. Cambridge university press (1991)
5. Shin, H.S., Jeong, A.: Modeling the relationship between students' prior knowledge, causal reasoning processes, and quality of causal maps. Comput. Educ. **163**, 104113 (2021). https://doi.org/10.1016/j.compedu.2020.104113
6. Fensel, D., et al.: Introduction: what is a knowledge graph? In: Knowledge Graphs, pp. 1–10. Springer International Publishing, Cham (2020). https://doi.org/10.1007/978-3-030-37439-6_1
7. Abu-Rasheed, H., Dornhöfer, M., Weber, C., Kismihók, G., Buchmann, U., Fathi, M.: Building contextual knowledge graphs for personalized learning recommendations using text mining and semantic graph completion. In: The 23rd IEEE International Conference on Advanced Learning Technologies (ICALT 2023). IEEE Computer Society Publications, IEEEXplore, Utah, USA (2023)
8. Lv, P., Wang, X., Xu, J., Wang, J.: Intelligent personalised exercise recommendation: a weighted knowledge graph-based approach. Comput. Appl. Eng. Educ. **29**, 1403–1419 (2021). https://doi.org/10.1002/cae.22395
9. Yang, Y., Li, Y., Karras, P., Tung, A.K.H.: Context-aware outstanding fact mining from knowledge graphs. In: Proceedings of the 27th ACM SIGKDD Conference on Knowledge Discovery & Data Mining, pp. 2006–2016. ACM, Virtual Event Singapore (2021). https://doi.org/10.1145/3447548.3467272
10. Syed, M.H., Huy, T.Q.B., Chung, S.-T.: Context-aware explainable recommendation based on domain knowledge graph. Big Data and Cognitive Comput. **6**, 11 (2022). https://doi.org/10.3390/bdcc6010011
11. Xian, Y., Fu, Z., Muthukrishnan, S., de Melo, G., Zhang, Y.: Reinforcement knowledge graph reasoning for explainable recommendation. In: Proceedings of the 42nd International ACM SIGIR Conference on Research and Development in Information Retrieval, pp. 285–294. ACM, Paris France (2019). https://doi.org/10.1145/3331184.3331203
12. Verbert, K., et al.: Context-aware recommender systems for learning: a survey and future challenges. IEEE Trans. Learning Technol. **5**, 318–335 (2012). https://doi.org/10.1109/TLT.2012.11
13. Hemmler, Y.M., Ifenthaler, D.: Indicators of the learning context for supporting personalized and adaptive learning environments. In: 2022 International Conference on Advanced Learning Technologies (ICALT), pp. 61–65. IEEE, Bucharest, Romania (2022). https://doi.org/10.1109/ICALT55010.2022.00026
14. Ahmad, A., et al.: What indicators can i serve you with? an evaluation of a research-driven learning analytics indicator repository. In: CSEDU (I), pp. 58–68 (2022). https://doi.org/10.5220/0010995800003182

Teacher Professional Development to Help Students Manage Stress: Barriers and Enablers

Laia Albó and Marc Beardsley(✉)

Universitat Pompeu Fabra, Barcelona, Spain
marc.beardsley@upf.edu

Abstract. This research work seeks to better understand barriers and enablers in addressing student stress in school settings using a continuing professional development (CPD) approach informed by research on teacher needs in the post-pandemic educational ecosystem. A survey study was conducted in which 91 teachers from 3 countries (Spain, Denmark, and Cyprus) participated. Preliminary results indicate that teachers hold negative stress mindsets – which presents a barrier the CPD must address across regions. Secondly, an emphasis on stress management techniques emerges as a focal point for the program. Thirdly, among elements that comprise the CPD approach, Learning Design and Digital Technologies for teaching and learning are topics generating the most interest from teachers whereas Open Educational Resources and Universal Design for Learning the least. Results are to inform the design and evaluation of a CDP approach and contribute to our understanding of teacher needs in the post-pandemic educational ecosystem.

Keywords: Learning design · Teacher professional development · Stress management

1 Introduction

Schools provide an appealing environment for teaching about and practicing stress management. School situations are often shared sources of stress for students [1] while classrooms offer safe spaces for learning and opportunities to provide co-regulation support through nurturing, instruction, and coaching [2]. Thus, having teachers teach students about stress and scaffold their practice of stress management techniques in a situated manner, presents a potential way in which stress management interventions can reach many students and contribute to improvements in health literacy [3]. Further, facilitating the implementation of interventions with digital technologies such as online community platforms, open educational resources (OER), and cloud-based tools can contribute to their scalability.

With the above in mind, a European project (RemixED) focused on teacher continuing professional development (CPD) was created to help teachers improve student knowledge of stress and use of stress management techniques. However, for teachers to implement interventions, according to the Fogg Behavior Model [4], teachers must have adequate motivation and ability to deliver such interventions. Hence, to tap into

O. Viberg et al. (Eds.): EC-TEL 2023, LNCS 14200, pp. 524–530, 2023.
https://doi.org/10.1007/978-3-031-42682-7_36

teacher motivation, the design of the CPD approach was informed by research conducted after emergency response teaching (ERT) – i.e., post-COVID lockdowns. Collaborative work, pedagogical uses of technology, and inclusion were identified as areas of interest among teachers [5, 6]. Open Educational Resources (OER) were also included in the CPD design for the potential they offer in fostering equity by reducing barriers to accessing quality education [7]. The integration of the above areas led to the conceptualization of a team-based learning design CPD approach. This approach involves having teachers collaboratively design, test, and share learning activities that involve the pedagogical use of technologies and open resources related to student stress.

In relation to investigating teacher ability to deliver the intervention, the program first selected evidence-based stress management techniques as focal points for the CPD program. A key technique identified was cognitive reappraisal. A recent intervention with college students based on cognitive reappraisal was found to positively affect students when facing stressful situations [8]. The intervention focused on student beliefs about stress (i.e., stress mindsets). The aim was to shift student beliefs from stress-is-debilitating to stress-is-enhancing – as adopting a more positive stress mindset is associated with greater perceived health and well-being [9]. Research related to mindsets (albeit intelligence mindsets rather than stress mindsets) has found that teacher mindsets directly affect the sustainability of changes in student mindsets [10]. Hence, a teacher's stress mindset can affect their ability to deliver stress management interventions to students that have lasting effects.

This research work seeks to better understand potential barriers and enablers in addressing student stress and anxiety in the post-pandemic educational ecosystem. On the one hand, results will inform the final design of the CPD program and its evaluation. On the other hand, results will contribute to our understanding of teacher stress mindsets and their preferences related to CPD involving digital technologies in the post-pandemic educational ecosystem. The research questions we aim to address are:

RQ1. Do teachers have a positive (enabler) or negative stress mindset (barrier)?
RQ2. What reasons do teachers provide for wanting to learn about student stress (enablers)?
RQ3. Are there CPD elements that teachers find more appealing (enablers) than others? (See the list of elements in the 2.1 section).
RQ4. Are there differences in teacher preferences for CPD elements based on teacher contexts (e.g., where participant teachers live and work)?

2 Methods

2.1 Instruments and Data Collection

A survey form was distributed to school teachers in Spain, Cyprus, and Denmark in the 2022–23 school year. An analysis of four items from the survey are being reported. The first item is the Stress Mindset Measure (SMM) [11]. SMM is a closed-ended questionnaire that asks respondents to rate 8 statements about stress on a five-point scale ranging from 0 (strongly disagree) to 4 (strongly agree). The instrument includes both affirmative and negative statements. SMM scores are obtained by reverse scoring the four negative items and then taking the mean of all 8 items. Higher scores (above

2) represent a positive, stress-is-enhancing mindset whereas lower scores represent a stress-is-debilitating mindset.

The second item is an open-ended question that asks respondents to indicate, in relation to the topic of student stress, what they would be most interested to learn more about. The third item is a closed-ended question using a Likert scale that ranges from 0 (not interested at all) to 7 (extremely interested). The aim is to better understand teacher preferences toward CPD topics related to digital technologies in the post-pandemic educational ecosystem. Respondents were asked to indicate how interested they were in learning about the following topics:

A. Stress (e.g. the science of stress and stress management strategies);
B. UDL: Universal Design for Learning (e.g. inclusive teaching guidelines);
C. OER: Open Educational Resources (e.g. creating reusable resources for the educational community);
D. LD: Learning design (e.g. a methodology for designing and reflecting upon student learning experiences);
E. CoP: Communities of practice (e.g. collaboration with peers for professional development);
F. DT: Internet technologies (digital technologies) for teaching and learning.

Finally, the fourth item is an open-ended question that asks respondents to select among the CPD topics the one they would be most interested to learn more about and to explain why. Once translated into local languages, the survey was disseminated by school partners in the research project to their teachers and school networks. Consent was obtained from participants and ethical approval received for the research.

2.2 Participants

In total, 91 teachers answered the survey questions, 63 (69.2%) female, 27 (29.7%) male, and one preferred not to respond. Five (5.5%) were under 30 years old (y/o), 18 (19.8%) 30–39 y/o, 33 (36.3%) 40–49 y/o, 20 (22.0%) 50–59 y/o, and 15 (16.5%) were more than 60 y/o. Teachers lived and worked in three different countries: 38 (41.8%) in Spain, 37 (40.7%) in Cyprus, and 16 (17.6%) in Denmark. Years of teaching experience varied as 13 (14.3%) had 5 years of experience or less, 13 (14.3%) 6–10 years, 20 (22.0%) 11–15 years, 15 (16.5%) 16–20 years, 13 (14.3%) 21–25 years, and 17 (18.7%) had 26 years or more. Attitudes toward the use of new internet technologies for teaching and learning also varied: 13 (14.3%) were cautious toward new technologies and only use them when necessary; 13 (14.3%) were usually among the last in their circle to use a new technology; 18 (19.8%) usually decide to use a new technological tool when most people they know are already using it; 28 (30.8%) like new technologies and use them before most people in their circle do; and 19 (20.9%) love new technologies and are among the first to experiment with them. No statistically significant differences were found among the three country groups regarding teacher age, years of teaching experience, and attitudes toward using new technologies for teaching and learning.

3 Preliminary Results and Discussions

3.1 Teacher Stress Mindsets

Answering RQ1, the SMM average of responding teachers is 1.69 (SD = 0.43) out of 4 which indicates that, overall, respondents have a negative stress mindset (stress-is-debilitating). No statistically significant differences were found when comparing the SMM average across countries. Respondents from Spain obtained a SMM average of 1.73 (SD = 0.45), those from Denmark had a SMM of 1.78 (SD = 0.29), and those from Cyprus had a SMM of 1.61 (SD = 0.76). Results are consistent with studies conducted with professionals in the United States [11]. This result uncovers a possible barrier for the CPD program as teachers are to teach students about stress management techniques that often involve helping students reframe stressful academic situations as challenges rather than threats. Moreover, to help reinforce positive stress mindsets, teachers are encouraged to model embracing academic stress in how they present, orchestrate, and give feedback on stressful tasks such as tests, presentations, and conflicts. If teachers hold negative stress mindsets, they may inadvertently model avoidance behaviors, reinforce negative beliefs towards stress, and reverse gains made during the intervention [10]. Thus, a common element of the CPD program (across countries), involves working to develop and support positive stress mindsets among participating teachers – e.g., providing evidence and communicating the benefits of a positive stress mindset to teachers.

3.2 Reasons Given for Learning About Student Stress

In total, 44 responded to the second question which has been analyzed through thematic coding [12]. The primary reason teachers gave (RQ2) was to learn "stress management" techniques (in general, for the students and for class management). This reason appeared in 40.9% of responses. The second most common reason given, in 11.4% of responses, was "everything", meaning that they are interested in learning everything about the topic of student stress. To "enhance performance/productivity" and "stress should be avoided" both appeared in 6.8% of responses. The latter confirms the negative stress mindsets of some respondents. "Stress and health" (e.g., how stress affects students' sleep) and "emotions management" were the next most common reasons given with a 4.5% of responses each. Other reasons appearing include inclusive teaching, stress and workloads, stress and learning processes, how to help students deal with stress during evaluations or when facing new activities, conflict management, habits of study, and stress and the relationships in the school environment (teacher-students; students-students). While there seems to be a broad interest among respondents in learning about the topic of student stress, an emphasis on stress management techniques emerges as a focal point for the CPD program.

3.3 Teachers' Interest in the Elements that Conform the PD Program

To address RQ3, responses to the third question which reports teacher level of interest in learning about topics selected for the CPD program were analyzed. Results shows that teacher interest was highest for LD (M = 4.67, SD = 2.11), followed by DT (M = 4.60, SD = 2.09), stress (M = 4.54, SD = 2.05), OER (M = 4.53, SD = 2.13), CoP (M = 4.51, SD = 2.09) and lastly, UDL (M = 4.42, SD = 2.07). Moreover, Fig. 1 presents the results of an analysis of the open question responses related to the aforementioned topics. The number of times a topic was mentioned as the most preferred topic to learn about is presented. In total, 53 out of 91 participants answered the open question. 3 participants expressed an interest in more than one topic (2 respondents wrote "all" and 1 listed 3 of the 6 topics). Thus, the number of times topics were listed as a preferred topic is 65.

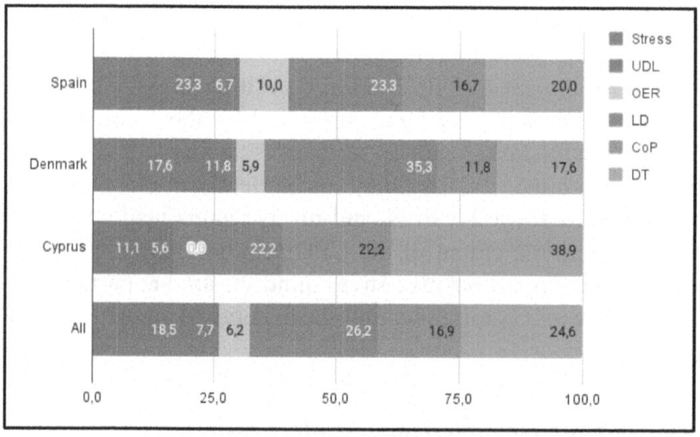

Fig. 1. Frequency in percentages that CPD topics were listed as preferred topics (n = 65).

In line with results from question 3, LD is the topic mentioned most often (26.2%). The second most mentioned is DT (24.6%), followed by stress (18.5%). Yet, unlike the interest ratings from question 3, CoP (16.9%) appeared in more responses than both UDL (7.7%) and OER (6.2%). Furthermore, preferences differed by country. The most preferred topic for Cypriot respondents was DT (38.9%), followed by CoP (22.2%) and LD (22.2%). No Cypriot respondents mentioned OER as a preferred topic and UDL was minimally mentioned (5.6%). Thus, the gap between the most preferred and least preferred topics was large. Danish respondents preferred learning about LD (35.3%), DT (17.6%) and Stress (17.6%). Spanish respondents preferred LD (23.3%), Stress (23.3%) and DT (20%). These country differences combined with the gaps between the most and least preferred topics suggest that flexibility needs to be built into the CPD program so that the way it is presented to teachers and implemented can be adjusted to teacher preferences – e.g., emphasizing the preferred topics among others to help participants better engage with training.

4 Conclusions and Future Directions

This research work seeks to better understand potential barriers and enablers in addressing student stress in school settings using a CPD approach that applies team-based LD and integrates inclusive uses of DT and OER. Firstly, survey results indicate that teachers hold negative stress mindsets – which presents a barrier the program must overcome in all participating regions. Secondly, while there seems to be a broad interest among teachers in learning about the topic of student stress, an emphasis on stress management techniques emerges as a focal point for the program. Thirdly, among the elements that comprise the CPD approach, LD, DT and Stress are the topics generating the most interest. Although, topics of interest vary by country. Thus, flexibility needs to be built into the CPD program so that the way it is presented to teachers and implemented can be adjusted to align with teacher preferences. Results contribute to our understanding of teacher stress mindsets and their preferences related to CPD. Our contribution can inspire technology-enhanced learning researchers and practitioners who aim to improve teacher CPD involving digital technologies in the post-pandemic educational ecosystem. Future work is to involve widening investigations to examine teacher knowledge and behavior (i.e., baselines) related to stress and stress management techniques, LD, UDL, OER, DT, and CoP; and conducting post-CPD program investigations to assess the impact of the program on teachers.

Acknowledgements. The authors would like to thank the RemixED project members for their contributions to the survey design. This work was partially funded by Erasmus+ (2021–1-ES01-KA220-SCH-000032801), the Department of Research and Universities of the Government of Catalonia (SGR 00930), and the Spanish Ministry (PID2020-112584RB-C33 funded by MICIN/AEI/10.13039/501100011033).

References

1. Pascoe, M.C., Hetrick, S.E., Parker, A.G.: The impact of stress on students in secondary school and higher education. Int. J. Adolesc. Youth **25**(1), 104–112 (2020)
2. Murray, D.W., Rosanbalm, K.D., Christopoulos, C., Hamoudi, A.: Self-regulation and Toxic Stress: Foundations for Understanding Self-Regulation from an Applied Developmental Perspective. OPRE Report #2015–21, Washington (2015)
3. Nutbeam, D., Lloyd, J.E.: Understanding and responding to health literacy as a social determinant of health. Annu Rev Public Health **42**(1), 159–173 (2021)
4. Fogg, B.J.: A behavior model for persuasive design. In: Proceedings of the 4th international Conference on Persuasive Technology, pp. 1–7. ACM, NY (2009)
5. Albó, L., Beardsley, M., Martínez-Moreno, J., Santos, P., Hernández-Leo, D.: Emergency remote teaching: capturing teacher experiences in Spain with SELFIE. In: Alario-Hoyos, C., Rodríguez-Triana, M.J., Scheffel, M., Arnedillo-Sánchez, I., Dennerlein, S.M. (eds) Addressing Global Challenges and Quality Education. EC-TEL 2020. Springer, Cham. (2020)
6. Beardsley, M., Albó, L., Aragón, P., Hernández-Leo, D.: Emergency education effects on teacher abilities and motivation to use digital technologies. Br. J. Edu. Technol. **52**(4), 1455–1477 (2021)
7. Ford, A., Alemneh, D.: Equitable educational planning: embracing open educational resources for the post-pandemic era. Educational Planning **28**(3), 21–30 (2021)

8. Goyer, J.P., Akinola, M., Grunberg, R., Crum, A.J.: Thriving under pressure: the effects of stress-related wise interventions on affect, sleep, and exam performance for college students from disadvantaged backgrounds. Emotion **22**(8), 1755 (2022)
9. Crum, A.J., Akinola, M., Martin, A., Fath, S.: The role of stress mindset in shaping cognitive, emotional, and physiological responses to challenging and threatening stress. Anxiety Stress Coping **30**(4), 379–395 (2017)
10. Yeager, D.S., et al.: Teacher mindsets help explain where a growth-mindset intervention does and doesn't work. Psychol. Sci. **33**(1), 18–32 (2022)
11. Crum, A.J., Salovey, P., Achor, S.: Rethinking stress: the role of mindsets in determining the stress response. J. Pers. Soc. Psychol. **104**(4), 716 (2013)
12. Gibbs, G.R.: 4 Thematic Coding and Categorizing. Analyzing Qualitative Data. SAGE Publications, London (2007)

Lateral Reading Against Misinformation: The Cognitive Processing Level Mediates the Intervention Effect on the News Credibility Assessment Performance

Benedikt Artmann(✉), Christian Scheibenzuber, Marvin Fendt, and Nicolae Nistor

Ludwig-Maximilians-Universität München, Leopoldstr. 13, 80802 München, Germany
Benedikt.Artmann@psy.lmu.de

Abstract. Approaching the problem of fake news with media literacy and fake news training, lateral reading training improves the discernment between truthful and fake news. How this improvement is achieved remains to be proven. Assuming that the level of cognitive processing mediates the effect of news literacy training on news evaluation skills, changes in cognitive processing need to be examined. Addressing this gap, this poster paper presents the development of a category system as a content analysis tool, aiming to analyze the cognitive processing level applied to assessing news. The new instrument is tested with data from an information literacy training using the lateral reading training approach in three different training conditions including a control group. Data from $N = 179$ participants were coded using the proposed category system and analyzed using regression analysis to examine mediation effects between the training groups, cognitive processing level and test scores. The results of this analysis show a mediation effect of cognitive processing level on news evaluation test scores, suggesting that enhancing the cognitive processing may improve the ability to evaluate information. Furthermore, these preliminary results will be supplemented with results from more participants to reach a sample size of $N = 344$.

Keywords: Misinformation · Information Literacy Training · Level of Cognitive Processing

1 Introduction

Misinformation is one of the central challenges of this century. For example, medical or political misinformation distorts public discourse on serious issues, leading to unscientific and falsified debates [4]. Governments and independent organizations are calling for explicit interventions to educate citizens. Misinformation is defined as information that imitates legitimate news but is intentionally or unintentionally false and misleading [8]. Misinformation is quickly spread for example by people sharing it on social media, which potentially leads to problems in many areas of social life. To counteract such misinformation, intervention measures are necessary.

O. Viberg et al. (Eds.): EC-TEL 2023, LNCS 14200, pp. 531–535, 2023.
https://doi.org/10.1007/978-3-031-42682-7_37

Conducting information literacy training, multiple training approaches are available, such as lateral reading or inoculation. Among the possible interventions, the most popular, inoculation, seems to induce generic skepticism towards all news, rather than improving participants' ability to discern between real and fake news [6]. Interventions with a stronger cognitive character, such as lateral reading, seem to be more likely to have this desired effect.

Providing an alternative, a promising approach to foster information literacy is lateral reading. Lateral reading encourages readers to read the positions of other trustworthy sources on questionable topics [5]. Readers should stop reading a news article, leave the current site, and look what other digital sources say about the topic. Hence, knowledge of, for example, trustworthy sources or search engines is required. Additionally, the information literacy training encourages readers to investigate the role of the author, the background of the article, and possible interests.

To evaluate such training approaches, training effects are measured and compared. Within previous lateral reading intervention studies, the effectiveness of specific training approaches are shown to be statistically significant, while leaving open the explanation of how the improvement is achieved [2, 5]. The explanation of this training effect, how the performance improvement was achieved, remained open. This performance improvement can be expected to be a result of improved cognitive processing while assessing news. When evaluating news, people may vary in their level of cognitive processing [7]. Resisting persuasion attempts is assumed to be the result of analytical news processing, such as thorough investigation of information on author or sources [1, 7]. Falling for misinformation, in contrast, is associated with intuitive cognitive processing, like decision making based on feelings or under influence of biases.

Accordingly, it is assumed that cognitive processing mediates the intervention effect on performance. This assumption is not sufficiently proven yet. Thus, this poster paper presents preliminary results on the role of cognitive processing within evaluating news credibility. Therefore, a new category system is developed, aiming to categorize cognitive processes involved in news evaluation. Applying that instrument, the results of an information literacy training will be analyzed according to cognitive processing.

2 Research Question

To address the above mentioned research gap, two research questions are investigated.

1. To what extent does a lateral reading intervention influence the level of cognitive processing?
2. To what extent does the level of cognitive processing mediate the lateral reading intervention effect on the ability to correctly assess online news?

3 Methods

As a research design a 3x2 factorial experiment was chosen. The first factor was the training condition, which included one control group and two experimental groups. The second factor was the education of the trainers, some were freshmen, and some were graduated educational science students. The principles of group equivalence were followed. Data were collected by university students conducting the information literacy training. We analyzed a subsample of $N = 179$ participants from the total sample of $N = 344$ and provide preliminary results. A Kruskal-Wallis H test indicated there was no significant difference between the different groups in the pretest.

As independent variable, the intervention was conducted on 3 levels, including a control group and two experimental groups. While the *control group* received no training, participants in the first experimental group, the *written instruction group*, learned about lateral reading by reading an instruction, whereas within the second experimental group, the *training group*, the participants were instructed by a trainer. Within the training group, the trainers applied cognitive apprenticeship. Throughout the learning process, the trainers utilized modelling, scaffolding, and fading. The trainers modelled lateral reading by showing its usage. During the further training the participants were coached evaluating news, including the continuous fading out of the provided support.

The dependent variable consists of the test scores achieved in the posttest. The test score was measured showing examples of online news and asking for assessment of credibility, on a Likert scale from 1 = not credible at all to 7 = entirely credible [7]. The scale was reversed for the fake news examples.

Representing the mediator variable, the level of cognitive processing (CPL) was assessed by content analysis of justifications of the news assessment. Therefore, a new category system was created. Developing the instrument for content analysis, categories were derived from the literature, combined with sighting of the material and consensual coding [7]. Within the category system, a higher level of cognitive processing is associated with more analytical reasoning, while a lower level of cognitive processing is associated with more intuitive reasoning. The category system was newly developed for this purpose. Four categories were used to code the data. Overall, the categories from no answer to research represent the increasing level of cognitive processing. The lowest category *no answer* resembles no given justification for the assessment, such as writing nothing, or just typing any letters to complete the form. An intuitive decision is labeled as *intuitive*. For example, the comment "Unserious headline(.) There I do not read the article at all" supports an intuitive decision. Rising in cognitive processing, the category *analytic* suggests an analytical decision. Therefore, the comment "(Author name) is known to have spread misinformation at the beginning of the pandemic" is exemplary. The highest category is *inquiry*, a decision includes further research that leads to a decision. For example, "After looking up (source name), it seems to be more trustworthy than first thought", would be an inquiry.

The data were consensually coded by two coders, while further developing the category system and coding guideline aiming for a high intercoder reliability. The agreement was substantial, as Cohen's kappa was $\kappa = .76$. The data were analyzed using IBM SPSS Statistics version 28 and Process for SPSS version 4.2 [3].

4 Results

The descriptive analysis of levels of cognitive processing are presented in Table 1, showing the different means and standard deviation for each group and each level of cognitive processing. The highest means in the categories analytic processing ($M =$

2.77) and inquiry based processing ($M = .83$) were achieved by the training group, while the lowest values in categories analytic processing ($M = 1.87$) and inquiry based processing ($M = .13$) were reached by the control group. Considering the intuitive processing category, the highest mean was achieved by the control group ($M = 3.52$), while the lowest mean was scored by the training group ($M = 1.77$). Within the no answer category, the values are in the range of $M = .42$ in the reader group to $M = .57$ in the training group.

Table 1. Means and standard deviations of frequencies of applied CPL in the Posttest

Group	Level of cognitive processing				n
	n/a	intuitive	analytic	inquiry	
Control	.48 (1.35)	3.52 (1.67)	1.87 (1.31)	.13 (.47)	61
Written instruction	.42 (1.31)	2.49 (1.86)	2.48 (1.71)	.62 (1.17)	65
Training	.57 (1.67)	1.77 (1.49)	2.77 (1.69)	.83 (1.22)	53
Total	.48 (1.43)	2.63 (1.83)	2.36 (1.61)	0.51 (1.04)	179

Following, the results of the mediation analysis are described. A bootstrap confidence interval was calculated for a level of confidence = 95,000 on 10,000 bootstrap samples. The category no answer had no significant mediation effect for either of the training group comparisons, as the confidence interval for each includes 0 (written instruction group: CI = [–.232, .230]; training group: CI = [–.175, .387]). Intuitive processing had a significant mediation effect for the written instruction group ($a_{1,2}b_2 = -.470$, CI = [–.781, –.159]), as well as for the training group ($a_{2,2}b_2 = -.790$, CI = [–1.122, –.477]). While the mediation effect of analytic processing was not significant for the written instruction group (CI = [–.002, .618]), it was significant for the training group ($a_{2,3}b_3 = .430$, CI = [.088, .743]). Inquiry based cognitive processing had a significant mediation effect for the written instruction group ($a_{1,4}b_4 = .305$, CI = [.110, .522]), as well as for the training group ($a_{2,4}b_4 = .436$, CI = [.209, .677]). In total, the variance accounted for in the present mediation model is $R^2 = .418$ ($F(3,175) = 41.953$, $p < .001$).

5 Conclusion

The descriptive data show that the highest cognitive processing, associated with analytic processing and inquiry based processing, was used most frequently by the training group, while lower cognitive processing, as intuitive processing, was used most frequently by the control group. Correspondingly, intuitive processing as a lower CPL occurred most frequently in the control group, less frequently in the reader group, and least frequently in the training group. Regarding the category no answer, there was no trend visible.

The mediation analysis also showed that giving no answer had no significant effect, confirming that not providing justification is not related to a specific test score. Intuitive processing had a negative mediation effect on test scores for both intervention groups, showing that intuitive judgments lead to lower test scores, implying that lower CPL leads to more false news judgments. The highest form of CPL, inquiry based processing, also had an effect on test scores in both group comparisons. However, analytic processing had also a significant effect for the training group, while the effect was not significant for the reader group. In total, the mediation model examining the different levels of CPL explained 42% of the differences in posttest scores.

The results suggest that the intervention had an effect on CPL. Moreover, as there was a mediation effect for the different levels of cognitive processing on the news test score, these mediation effects indicate that higher CPL might lead to better information evaluation. Overall, these findings are consistent with results from lateral reading intervention studies, which show significant improvements in news test scores with training approaches, compared to significantly less improvements in control groups.

In conclusion, it seems insightful for new information literacy training to focus on improving CPL. Interventions with a stronger cognitive character, such as lateral reading, are more likely to have this desirable effect and might provide better results than other interventions, like inoculation. Within this contribution a new category system for evaluating information literacy training was proposed and tested. In the next steps, the category system will be further evaluated, and it will be applied to the full sample $N = 344$, to test if these preliminary results can be confirmed.

References

1. Faragó, L., Krekó, P., Orosz, G.: Hungarian, lazy, and biased: the role of analytic thinking and partisanship in fake news discernment on a Hungarian representative sample. Sci. Rep. **13**(1), 178 (2023). https://doi.org/10.1038/s41598-022-26724-8
2. Fendt, M., Nistor, N., Scheibenzuber, C., Artmann, B.: Sourcing against misinformation: effects of a scalable lateral reading training based on cognitive apprenticeship. Computers in Human Behavior, 107820 (2023). https://doi.org/10.1016/j.chb.2023.107820
3. Hayes, A.F.: Introduction to Mediation, Moderation, and Conditional Process Analysis: A Regression-Based Approach. Guilford Press (2018)
4. Lewandowsky, S., et al.: When science becomes embroiled in conflict: recognizing the public's need for debate while combating conspiracies and misinformation. The Annals of the American Academy of Political and Social Science **700**(1), 26–40 (2022). https://doi.org/10.1177/00027162221084663
5. McGrew, S.: Learning to evaluate: an intervention in civic online reasoning. Comput. Educ. **145**, 103711 (2020). https://doi.org/10.1016/j.compedu.2019.103711
6. Modirrousta-Galian, A., Higham, P.A.: Gamified inoculation interventions do not improve discrimination between true and fake news: reanalyzing existing research with receiver operating characteristic analysis. J. Experimental Psychology: General (2023). https://doi.org/10.1037/xge0001395
7. Pennycook, G., Rand, D.G.: The psychology of fake news. Trends Cogn. Sci. **25**(5), 388–402 (2021). https://doi.org/10.1016/j.tics.2021.02.007
8. van der Linden, S.: Misinformation: susceptibility, spread, and interventions to immunize the public. Nat. Med. **28**(3), 460–467 (2022). https://doi.org/10.1038/s41591-022-01713-6

Exploring Students' Problem-Solving Challenges in Self-regulated Learning Through Training Video Prompts

Guy Cohen(✉) and Anat Cohen

Tel Aviv University, Tel Aviv, Israel
guycohen2@mail.tau.ac.il, anatco@tauex.tau.ac.il

Abstract. In the rapidly changing digital era, schools face the challenge of developing self-regulated learning (SRL) skills, particularly problem-solving, which is crucial for lifelong learning. Literature often discusses learners' difficulties in problem-solving and measuring SRL strategies. This study explores students' challenges during the problem-solving process. A video-assisted SRL training program was developed, including a digital toolkit with materials like checklists, interactive videos, and problem-solving tasks. Analyzing 1,417 responses from 13–16-year-old students, the study revealed difficulties in time planning, problem identification, exploration, providing solutions, and solution evaluation. Interestingly, there were significant differences between students' pre-questionnaire reports and their video prompt responses. These findings can inform the development of feedback-based technologies like chatbots and virtual assistants to enhance efficient problem-solving for learners.

Keywords: Self-Regulated Learning · Problem-Based Learning · Video-Based Learning · Video-Based Prompt · K-12 Education

1 Introduction

Self-regulated learning (SRL) is crucial for effective learning, adaptability, and goal achievement, particularly for young adolescents' lifelong learning [1]. Video-based technology has been recommended to enhance SRL strategies and the learning process. However, its use for SRL training among young adolescents is limited [3]. Scaffolding support, such as prompts, can help learners during online learning by guiding their actions [7]. Prompt usage in SRL training often focuses on metacognitive processes and reflection [10].

Problem-solving is a key aspect of SRL, requiring diverse skills to learning challenges [6]. Feedback is essential for improving SRL skills, enabling learners to track progress, identify areas for improvement, and adjust strategies [3]. Effective feedback mechanisms should be integrated into instructional practices, particularly in SRL training [2, 10]. To provide effective feedback on problem-solving, challenges associated with strategies need to be defined, measured, and evaluated [4, 9]. Two main challenges are coping

O. Viberg et al. (Eds.): EC-TEL 2023, LNCS 14200, pp. 536–541, 2023.
https://doi.org/10.1007/978-3-031-42682-7_38

with difficulties during problem-solving and measuring strategy usage [4, 8]. Due to the complexity of SRL, combining various data sources is crucial for understanding and measuring it. Further research is needed to explore new forms of data integration in assessing SRL strategies [5, 6].

This study investigates challenges faced by students during problem-solving; creating a comprehensive map for identifying these challenges. It will measure and identify specific steps and tasks where students struggle within the problem-solving process, using video prompts (reflection questions) to gather data on student responses. The resulting map can inform the development of targeted SRL training programs that provide feedback to help learners overcome the identified challenges, whether from a human or technology-based source.

2 The Current Research

2.1 Research Objective and Question

This study aims to understand the specific difficulties students face during the problem-solving process and identify gaps in their SRL skills. By analyzing students' responses to video prompts, the research provides insights into the practical implementation of SRL training programs, highlighting areas that may require additional support to promote effective problem-solving strategies. The research question is, "What are the difficulties that students encounter when engaging in the process of problem-solving during self-regulated learning?".

2.2 Research Context

In this study, a student intervention program was conducted alongside teacher training to improve students' SRL skills using a problem-solving framework called VAST (Video Assisted SRL Training). VAST incorporates specific SRL strategies such as time management, feedback, elaboration, and critical thinking. It presents a step-by-step approach to problem-solving through a digital toolbox that includes interactive videos, checklists, and problem-solving tasks. To assess students' SRL skills related to problem-solving, a pre-questionnaire was distributed before the intervention program. Students watched the videos in a specific order based on the step number of the problem-solving process. They then worked in groups to apply the framework to solve a given problem, with the option to re-watch the videos.

2.3 Research Tool

SRL-PS questionnaire. An integrative (SRL and problem-solving) questionnaire was used to assess students' problem-solving activities within the VAST framework. Students rated their agreement with statements that described various problem-solving tasks using a 5-point Likert-type scale. The questionnaire's reliability is $\alpha = 0.94$.

Video prompts. Video prompts presented at the beginning of each video, asked students to describe their approach to specific strategies when faced with past problems. This information was used to gather insights into students' typical strategies and difficulties encountered during problem-solving. Students' responses were anonymous to the research team.

2.4 Research Population

205 students in grades 6–11 (in the field of Humanities and STEM) participated in the video-based training program. This study analyzed the responses of 177 students who addressed the prompts (reflective questions) integrated in the videos.

2.5 Research Method and Procedure

This paper presents primary findings on student difficulties based on their responses to video prompts and the questionnaire. The research employed both qualitative and quantitative methodologies, with a focus on the quantitative results in this paper. Descriptive measures were calculated for each step in the problem-solving framework using the pre-questionnaire to determine the difficulties students encounter during self-regulated learning. Video prompt records of students' initial views were analyzed to capture their past activities before the current learning process about relevant strategies. Students' responses to the video prompts were qualitatively analyzed to identify difficulties faced during problem-solving. The difficulties were categorized based on the specific tasks in the problem-solving framework. Two experts conducted the filtering process independently, and the results were consolidated and compared. Difficulty was defined as a reported challenge or a lack of reference to a particular strategy. The occurrence of each difficulty was calculated for each task within the framework, and the percentage of total difficulties among respondents was determined. Quartiles were calculated to compare the percentage of difficulties across tasks. Data analysis was performed using JASP 17.01 software.

3 Findings

The analysis of the questionnaire responses showed that most students self-identified as having high SRL skills. Students rated the statements related to the implementation of various strategies throughout the problem-solving process with a score of at least 4 out of 5, suggesting that they did not encounter significant difficulties while completing these steps. Specifically, the mean scores for *time planning*, *problem identification*, *problem exploration*, *time management*, *solution development*, and *solution evaluation* steps were high ($M = 3.67$, $SD = 1.02$; $M = 4.28$, $SD = 0.69$; $M = 4.33$, $SD = 0.67$; $M = 3.49$, $SD = 1.36$; $M = 4.24$, $SD = 0.73$; and $M = 4.27$, $SD = 0.69$, respectively).

The analysis of the video prompts showed that out of 1718 records, 1212 were related to the first viewing of the videos. The responses were categorized based on the different problem-solving steps and tasks involved in the framework. Notably, certain difficulties, such as those related to motivation, emotions, and technology, did not correspond to any specific step or task in the framework and were excluded from the analysis. In order to understand which tasks posed greater difficulties for students, the frequency of reported difficulties in each task was compared using quartile calculation. The results of this analysis are presented in Table 1.

Table 1. Quartile calculation of percentage number of difficulties in 32 problem-solving tasks within the VAST framework

	Valid	Missing	Mean	Std. Deviation	Minimum	Maximum	25th percentile	50th percentile	75th percentile
Percentage of difficulties among video prompt responders	32	0	94.40	5.37	79.82	100	91.25	95.96	98.9

According to the analysis, many students faced difficulties while performing various tasks involved in the problem-solving process. The percentage of students who encountered difficulties across different tasks ranged from 79.82% to 100%. Specifically, managing time posed significant challenges for students, including *time planning* (79.82% to 90.35%), *time management* (91.36% to 92.59%), and *time management evaluation* (100%). During the *problem identification* step, a higher number of students expressed difficulties related to identifying constraints and defining solution criteria compared to other tasks in this step (96.04% and 97.03%, respectively). Similarly, during the *problem exploration* step, more students struggled with identifying information gaps and operational questioning tasks than other tasks (97.73% and 96.59%, respectively). Additionally, the majority of students encountered difficulties within the *solution development* step (ranging from 90.41% to 100%), while the first task in this step, the 'candidate solution identification' task, was reported to be relatively less difficult. Moreover, the 'process monitoring' and 'process improvement' tasks in the *solution evaluation* step were particularly challenging for most students (98.53% and 97.06%, respectively). Furthermore, compared to other tasks in each step, more students expressed difficulties in the reflection tasks during the *problem identification*, *problem exploration*, and *solution evaluation* steps (99.01%, 98.86% and 100%, respectively).

Student difficulties encountered during problem-solving were analyzed using responses to video prompts, compared across different tasks within the framework, and represented as a PS-SOS map using the previously mentioned calculation. This map summarizes the specific tasks and steps in the problem-solving framework where students faced difficulties. Each quartile represents a level of difficulty for a specific task in the problem-solving framework, with the color scale indicating the number of difficulties associated with that task. The darkest color within the scale represents a high number of difficulties, while the brightest indicates relatively few difficulties. Figure 1 presents the PS-SOS Map, which illustrates the difficulties experienced by students based on their responses to the video prompts.

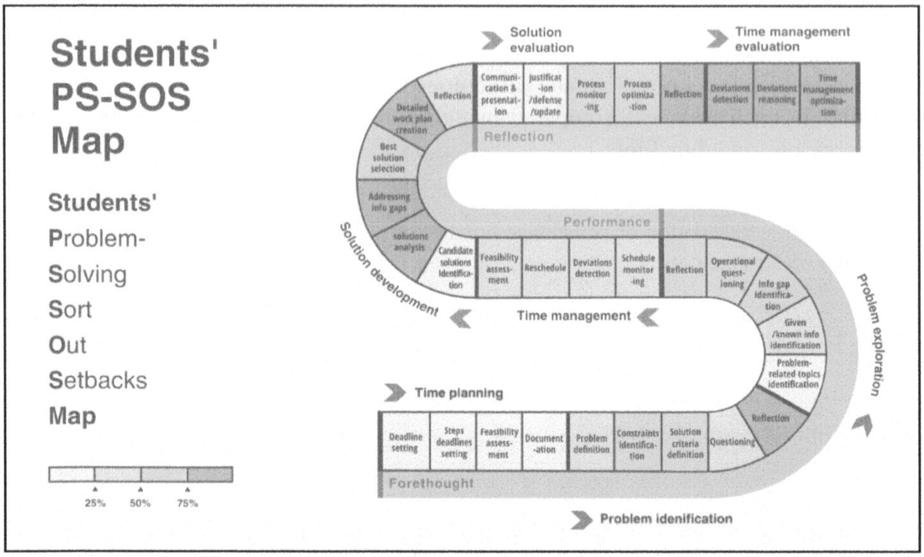

Fig. 1. Students' PS-SOS Map: The relative share of students' difficulties in each task of the problem-solving framework. For example, the percentage number of difficulties in the task 'Constraints identification' (indicated by the brightest orange color) is higher than 50% of the other tasks.

4 Discussion and Conclusion

Understanding how students learn and solve problems is important, but it can be difficult to measure their strategies, especially with new types of data streams [5]. This study aimed to address this research challenge by examining the difficulties students face while solving problems using their responses video prompts. This study revealed that despite reporting high levels of problem-solving skills in a questionnaire, they encountered difficulties in their prompt responses in the context of their past experience. This highlights the importance of employing diverse research tools and collecting data during the problem-solving process [6]. This study classified the challenges based on specific steps and tasks, providing a framework that combines problem-solving and self-regulated learning strategies. The problem-solving framework and the generated PS-SOS map can help identify difficult steps and tasks during self-regulated learning.

It is worth noting that the lack of familiarity among students with the problem-solving framework and video-based training emphasizes the need for further investigation and implementation. The challenges associated with linking motivation, emotions, and technology to specific tasks or steps underscore the importance of conducting additional research. This research should primarily focus on identifying motivational and emotional strategies that can enhance the mapping framework and gather precise data on task-specific difficulty levels. To overcome the limitations of self-reported data, it is crucial to actively seek feedback from multiple sources and teachers throughout the process. By addressing these challenges, future training programs can effectively enhance problem-solving skills. Additionally, exploring how teachers or technology, such as chatbots or virtual assistants, can provide feedback based on the difficulty level will further facilitate the learning process for students.

Acknowledgement. This research is supported by the Chief Scientist of the Israeli Ministry of Education.

References

1. Alderman, M.K., MacDonald, S.: A self-regulatory approach to classroom management: empowering students and teachers. Kappa Delta Pi Record **51**(2), 52–56 (2015). https://doi.org/10.1080/00228958.2015.1023145
2. Araka, E., Maina, E., Gitonga, R., Oboko, R.: Research trends in measurement and intervention tools for self-regulated learning for e-learning environments—systematic review (2008–2018). Res. Pract. Technol. Enhanc. Learn. **15**, 1–21 (2020). https://doi.org/10.1186/S41039-020-00129-5
3. Cohen, G., et al.: Video-assisted self-regulated learning (SRL) training: COVID-19 Edition. In: Hilliger, I., Muñoz-Merino, P.J., De Laet, T., Ortega-Arranz, A., Farrell, T. (eds) Educating for a New Future: Making Sense of Technology-Enhanced Learning Adoption. EC-TEL 2022. Lecture Notes in Computer Science, pp. 59–73 (2022). Springer, Cham. https://doi.org/10.1007/978-3-031-16290-9_5
4. Liu, T., Israel, M.: Uncovering students' problem-solving processes in game-based learning environments. Comput. Educ. **182**, 104462 (2022). https://doi.org/10.1016/j.compedu.2022.104462
5. Molenaar, I., de Mooij, S., Azevedo, R., Bannertd, M., Järveläe, S., Gaševićf, D.: Measuring self-regulated learning and the role of AI: five years of research using multimodal multichannel data. Computers in Human Behavior, 107540 (2022). https://doi.org/10.1016/j.chb.2022.107540
6. OECD. OECD Skills Outlook 2021: Learning for Life. OECD Publishing, Paris (2021). https://doi.org/10.1787/0ae365b4-en
7. Rowe, F.A., Rafferty, J.A.: Instructional design interventions for supporting self-regulated learning: enhancing academic outcomes in postsecondary e-learning environments. MERLOT J. Online Learn. Teach. **9**(4), 590–601 (2013)
8. Tissenbaum, M.: I see what you did there! divergent collaboration and learner transitions from unproductive to productive states in open-ended inquiry. Comput. Educ. **145**, 1–15 (2020). https://doi.org/10.1016/j.compedu.2019.103739
9. Yavuz, G., Yasemin, D., Arslan, Ç.: Elementary school students perception levels of problem-solving skills. Universal J. Educational Res. **5**(11), 1896–1901 (2017). https://doi.org/10.13189/ujer.2017.051106
10. Zheng, L.: The effectiveness of self-regulated learning scaffolds on academic performance in computer-based learning environments: a meta-analysis. Asia Pac. Educ. Rev. **17**(2), 187–202 (2016). https://doi.org/10.1007/s12564-016-9426-9

Facilitating and Hindering Aspects of Technology-Enriched Challenge-Based Learning in ECIU University, a European University International Network Initiative

Asta Daunorienė[1] and Dorothea Ellinger[2](✉)

[1] Kaunas University of Technology, K. Donelaicio St. 73, 44244 Kaunas, Lithuania
[2] Technische Universität Hamburg, Am Schwartzenberg-Campus 1, 21073 Hamburg, Deutschland
dorothea.ellinger@tuhh.de

Abstract. In 2018 The European Union launched an initiative of pilot networks of the European Universities Initiative. The European Union-funded initiative described here focuses on the implementation of challenge-based learning (CBL) as an educational model in the13 European universities that formed the alliance. The aim of the 13 European universities was to implement CBL as an international action rather than doing it independently. This provided a special understanding of the use of digital technologies to support and enhance teaching and learning activities. This has generated considerable interest in a better understanding of the facilitating and hindering aspects of technology-enriched CBL. Interviews and surveys conducted while implementing CBL helped to identify the shortcomings of technology-enhanced learning in a cross-border CBL environment. The data revealed that the obstacles of technology-enriched CBL are related to technical problems, time management in preparing and presenting online materials and reducing the personal interaction between teachers and students. It was also found that using digital tools for implementing CBL may be a difficult task. Nonetheless there are several steps an international network should consider when wanting to promote successful teaching and learning experiences. In particular, the use of digital technologies can support collaborative learning in CBL and enable students to work together in virtual teams using tools such as online discussion forums and video conferencing. It can also enable students to receive feedback on their work from both teachers and peers through online assessment and feedback tools.

Keywords: Challenge-Based Learning · Technology-Enriched Learning · European Universities · International Network

1 Introduction

Challenge-Based Learning (further CBL) is an approach to education that focuses on solving real-world problems through interdisciplinary collaboration and inquiry-based learning. CBL engages students in authentic and meaningful learning experiences that challenge them to apply their knowledge and skills to solve complex problems.

O. Viberg et al. (Eds.): EC-TEL 2023, LNCS 14200, pp. 542–547, 2023.
https://doi.org/10.1007/978-3-031-42682-7_39

In 2001 Giorgio and Brophy described CBL as a specific Problem-Based Learning methodology supported by Digital Experimentation Toolkits, which include materials, initial instructions, references to web resources and specific software tools [1]. In 2009, Johnson et al. [2] published a report highlighting the importance of interdisciplinarity, real-world problem-solving, student freedom, excitement, creativity and community engagement, which opened the era of CBL. It was further argued that CBL could increase student motivation [3] and helps to understand and solve the problems being addressed [4].

Difficulties of CBL however, may be that the planning of challenges involves multidisciplinary knowledge, that challenges are usually implemented outside the subject of the curriculum and the effectiveness of the results may not be immediately apparent [5].

Starting in 2018, research results revealed that educational Technology-enriched learning (further TEL) may support CBL by providing students with access to information, resources and tools [6, 7]. In addition, TEL can support collaborative learning in CBL by enabling students to work together in virtual teams with instructors and peers, using tools like online discussion forums and video conferencing [6].

Overall, TEL and CBL can work together to create engaging, authentic and meaningful learning experiences for students in higher education. By combining the benefits of both approaches, students can develop skills such as problem-solving, collaboration and communication, which are key skills in the 21st century.

Due to the numerous benefits of TEL CBL highlighted by many scholars, in 2020–2022, the 13 European universities aimed to implement CBL as an educational model and this coincided with the onset of the COVID-19 pandemic. This gave a special notion to the use of digital educational technologies to support and enhance teaching and learning activities. The paper aims to examine the facilitating and hindering aspects of technology-enriched CBL in the ECIU University emphasizing the potential of digital tools for collaborative learning and feedback in cross-border CBL.

2 Methodology

The research methodology used to analyze facilitating and hindering aspects of TEL transnational CBL is based on a mixed-method study. It combined explorative semi-structured expert interviews [8] conducted between January 2021 and June 2022 with online surveys. The qualitative part captured a sample of 13 interviews with a total of 23 teachers (9 pair interviews and 4 single interview) and 14 students in nine group interviews. Interview scripts for teacher and students differed slightly while one focused on teaching and the other on learning and corresponding frameworks as well as administrative conditions. Similar in the survey while students were requested to state about their self-reception of gained competences teachers were asked about their description of students gained competencies. The different groups' interviews were conducted and recorded in video conferences, shortly after the respective challenges cycle completed. The Challenges were offered to students from the 13 universities consortium. Most of the Challenges were offered extracurricular but about half of the students were able to have the achievement acknowledged as part of their degree program. Students could choose a Challenge that interested them and solve it together as a team in one semester. The four

Challenge cycles took place between December 2020 and June 2022, which implies that three CBL cycles where held when most Universities were forced to do the teaching fully digital, and traveling was strictly regulated due to Corona prevention regulations. The fourth CBL cycle was held online or in a hybrid way. The connection of transnational CBL with TEL was therefore not only for didactic reasons, but also determined by the external necessities. Following the completion of each CBL cycle, students participated in interview sessions, which were recorded and transcribed for further analysis.

Based on qualitative findings of the first interview round and on publications addressing factors that support or hinder the implementation of teaching innovations [9, 10], a survey for teachers and one for students was set up to raise quantitative data. In total 50 teachers from eight consortium universities and 82 students from ten partners took part in the research. Collecting data via online forms started in January 2021 and ended in June 2022. Each survey round started shortly after the respective CBL cycle has been completed. In closed-ended and open questions the surveys captured personal attitudes towards CBL, hindering and supporting technology-enriched CBL factors and students' additional self-statements about learning goals and acquired key competencies.

The transcribed and anonymized data were coded by applying Qualitative Content Analysis that combined deductive and inductive categorization [11] assisted by the software MAXQDA [12]. The online forms' data were processed in Excel.

3 Results

3.1 Hindering Aspects of Technology-Enriched Challenge-Based Learning

The research findings and suggestions about TEL CBL in a transnational network of 13 European universities are based on four investigated pilot cycles in which students could take part in Challenges offered by the network. Given the interdisciplinary and international composition of students' team members, (most of them) not being familiar with CBL, organizing as a team usually seemed to take some effort and time. Time issues e.g., unexpected high workload, missing fit with schedule and curricula at home university, working in different time zones, as well as team issues e.g., problematic team dynamics, and conflicts with roles and responsivities, were, therefore, most mentioned by CBL cycle participants in the surveys.

Student interviewees who had the chance to participate in a hybrid TEL CBL cycle agreed in that instead of spending most of the sessions and teamwork online, it could have been beneficial to have met each other earlier and longer face-to-face throughout the process: "*Online, we lose a little bit. I know that of course at the beginning, since we are people from other universities and all over the world, we have to do some first meetings online, but I think having the opportunity to spend a few days together and hands on the problem and like 24/7 altogether [...] it's great. Also, for the results of the Challenge [...], we didn't have a lot of time to work together. We're a little bit more online and we lost a little bit of the good of the team working.*" (P4, S4: 51)

Whenever online or hybrid mode were mentioned explicitly the used video conferencing, video chat or content management system were addressed. In the investigated TEL CBL cycles, no shared video conferencing used by all 13 partners was available and all universities had their regulations about accessibility to students from other universities and data and privacy regulations. However, several dedicated teachers had the experiences as described by one in the second challenge cycle, stating: "*[…] even yesterday when I had these evening courses, everybody was without cameras and I didn't force them because they didn't listen to me and just a few people were talking, I don't know if working or somewhere else. And you know, for them this distance learning and this online course is a little bit tricky. I think for them it's an advantage, because you know they can do whatever they want and they can also participate in the course, even though it's just with their names on the screen. But when you want to discuss, it seems they are absent.*" (P2_Int1_T, Pos. 24). Although there was a shared Content Management System (based on Moodle), it was rarely used; primarily because teachers preferred to use the systems and tools they were familiar with, although it was complicated and sometimes impossible to provide access for students from other network partners. Teacher surveys results revealed that some teachers complained about a lack of knowledge of digital tools for team working by students, which was not at all addressed by the students.

3.2 Facilitating Aspects of Technology-Enriched Challenge-Based Learning

Notably, video conferencing also was mentioned in surveys and interviews as an enabling and facilitating tool, when combined with good collaboration among students as well as with the teacher or external stakeholder to receive feedback and support. For example, one interviewed student spots considerable advantages in a digital setting: "*On the part of the teacher and organization and everything, it was easier online. For example, the challenge providers could stay at their office and still be, instead of saying 'Oh, I can't come because it is two hours away from my office'. […] That was helpful. Also, the fact that we were just on Moodle. And that we could just go and click and check what we have to do, etc., instead of sending an e-mail, what we would have done if it were in presence.*" (P2, Int 4, S2)

Next to Moodle, online whiteboards turned out to be one of the favorite tools for learners and teachers to facilitate collaboration in Challenges as stated by one teacher: "*Yeah, and they had fun with the boards. It was online so we had this online board where they actually put all the information and we can see all the time how they are working, how they are doing and they can see as well. So, everything at this point was quite smooth because they used this board, they, of course, did not contact us as much as we may be expected, but still, they had this option.*" *(P3_ Int5_T, Pos. 33)*. It was mostly the teachers who suggested digital tools for collaboration, communication, data analysis and investigation, data storage or creative thinking. One summarized the experiences with those tools:" *Everything works nicely in the online environment, but I think for the brainstorming part, it would be nice to have either a hybrid or in presence, completely.*" (P3_Int5_T, Pos. 28).

3.3 Teachers Perspective to Cope with Identifies Aspects of Technology-Enriched Challenge-Based Learning

TEL CBL teachers have to adapt their way of teaching to the ambiguities that come along with this format. This means they have to set time and resources for coaching, feedback sessions and other types of support for the student teams. They had to guide and coach students who might find the way forward unclear, the criteria for grading vague or the demands for subject-specific knowledge demanding. TEL CBL pedagogy puts a higher demand on teams being fully functional than other courses do. Research results showed that during the challenge rounds more than 80% of the teachers agreed (1) that TEL CBL placed high demands on them and their knowledge of the teaching and learning process but also (2) that it has been worthwhile or rewarding to them. Notably, two third agreed that it was easy to switch the role from being an expert to being a coach and one third did not agree with this statement.

4 Discussion and Conclusion

Research results identified some drawbacks of using TEL in a transnational CBL setting for the teachers and the learners. Those include: (1) technical issues such as connectivity problems between different network partners and device compatibility issues that can disrupt the learning experience, (2) preparing and delivering online materials can be time-consuming and requires additional effort on the part of the teacher next to the efforts needed to react adequately in the international and interdisciplinary learning setting and (3) reduce personal interaction between teachers and students, making it more difficult to build relationships and provide individualized support. Several limitations exist in this study. The data collected from the ECIU university network may not generalize to other networks. Thus, expanding the study to include diverse university networks and analyzing their experiences in implementing CBL is recommended. This broader scope would enhance our understanding of CBL in higher education. Furthermore, comparing technology-enriched CBL practices across various educational contexts would be valuable.

According to the interviewed students, face-to-face meetings strongly enhance the group dynamics and teamwork, this calls for new concepts and resources for inclusive mobility to be provided. Based on our experiences of the first three years, there are several steps that a transnational network can take to foster a successful teaching and learning experience. Here are some recommendations:

1. Identify and integrate appropriate digital tools and platforms to support the CBL projects that are user-friendly, accessible and secure to most of the partners in the network and that support collaboration, communication, and knowledge sharing.
2. Encourage collaboration and communication among students, teachers and other stakeholders across the network. This can be achieved through regular virtual meetings, online discussion forums and other forms of digital communication.
3. Ensure that all participants have the necessary training and support to effectively use the digital tools and platforms and that there is ongoing support available throughout the duration of the CBL projects.
4. Regularly evaluate the effectiveness of the CBL projects and reflect on what is working well and what could be improved. Use this feedback to refine the design and implementation of future projects and to continuously improve the teaching and learning experience.

References

1. Baloian, N., Breuer, H., Hoeksema, K., Hoppe, U., Milrad, M.: Implementing the challenge based learning in classroom scenarios. In: Proceedings of the symposium on Advanced Technologies in Education, vol. 4 (2004)
2. Johnson, L.F., Smith, R.S., Smythe, J.T., Varon, R.K.: Challenge-Based Learning: An Approach for our Time, pp. 1–38. The New Media Consortium (2009)
3. Binder, F.V., Nichols, M., Reinehr, S., Malucelli, A.: Challenge based learning applied to mobile software development teaching. In: 2017 IEEE 30th Conference on Software Engineering Education and Training (CSEE&T), pp. 57–64. IEEE (2017)
4. Detoni, M., Sales, A., Chanin, R., Villwock, L.H., Santos, A.R.: Using challenge based learning to create an engaging classroom environment to teach software startups. In: Proceedings of the XXXIII Brazilian Symposium on Software Engineering, pp. 547–552 (2019)
5. Fidalgo-Blanco, Á., Sein-Echaluce, M.L., García-Peñalvo, F.J.: Integration of the methods CBL and CBI for their application in the management of cooperative academic resources. In: 2016 International Symposium on Computers in Education (SIIE), pp. 1–6. IEEE (2016)
6. Gibson, D., Irving, L., Scott, K. Technology-enabled challenge-based learning in a global context. In: Collaborative learning in a global world, pp. 25–40 (2018)
7. Smith, C., Onofre-Martínez, K., Contrino, M. F., Membrillo-Hernández, J.: Course design process in a technology-enhanced learning environment. Comput. Electr. Eng. **93**, 107263 (2021)
8. Bogner, A., Littig, B., Menz, W.: Interviews mit Experten. Springer Fachmedien Wiesbaden, Wiesbaden (2014)
9. Beyerlin, S., Gotzen, S., Linnartz, D.: Herausforderungen für Lehrende beim Forschenden Lernen: Ergebnisse einer qualitativen Studie an der TH Köln. In: Forschendes Lernen: Theorie, Empirie, Praxis, pp. 160–173 (2020)
10. Bulmann, U., Bornhöft, S., Ellinger, D.: Barriers and enabling factors for engaging engineering students in research. a multi-perspective approach. In: Proceedings of the 47th Annual SEFI Conference. Annual Conference of European Society for Engineering Education (SEFI), Budapest (Hungary), pp. 1458–1468 (2019)
11. Mayring, P.: Qualitative content analysis: theoretical foundation, basic procedures and software solution. Klagenfurt. https://nbn-resolving.org/urn:nbn:de:0168-ssoar-395173. Accessed 30 Mar 2023
12. Rädiker, S., Kuckartz, U.: Analyse qualitativer Daten mit MAXQDA: Text. Audio und Video. (2018). https://doi.org/10.1007/978-3-658-22095-2

Digitally Supported Learning Processes in Schools: Teachers' Implicit Theories on Learning Activities with Technology

Nadine Esterl(✉), Sonja Berger, and Nicolae Nistor

Faculty of Psychology and Educational Sciences, Ludwig-Maximilians-Universität München, Leopoldstr. 13, 80802 Munich, Germany
esterl.nadine@campus.lmu.de, sonja.berger@psy.lmu.de, nic.nistor@uni-muenchen.de

Abstract. Technology is often not used profitably to promote teaching and learning processes. Implicit theories influence the use of technology in teaching. So far, these have been insufficiently explored against the background of the ICAP framework. This study addressed this research gap and investigated teachers' implicit theories of quality use of technology. Semi-structured expert interviews were conducted with $N = 12$ teachers from different types of secondary schools in Germany. The results show that the use of technology for passive engagement is justified by the format of the technology, the active engagement by the learning outcome, the constructive engagement by information and communication technology (ICT) literacy promotion and the interactive engagement by students' cooperation. Further research should describe implicit theories by the way learner-centered teaching is implemented with technology.

Keywords: Technology in teaching · Cognitive activation · Implicit theories

1 Introduction

The current discourse in educational research shows that various factors have an influence on teaching with technology [11, 12]. Despite existing models that take these factors into account and examine the quality of technology use, the so-called fidelity of implementation [3] of methods and measures in practice is low and teachers often use technology at a level that is not very conducive to learning [11].

Studies that addressed the quality of technology use in the classroom rarely considered teachers' perspectives and how they justify the use [11]. Implicit theories of teachers about technology describe these perspectives and are lay theories that determine what goals and plans teachers define [1], how situations are interpreted, and teachers respond to them in the classroom [7]. Implicit theories can be viewed in terms of the belief of the changeability of students' attributes [4], which can be differentiated from a pedagogical perspective. This spans a continuum between a transmissive orientation and a constructivist orientation of teachers [4]. In the transmissive orientation, implicit theories

O. Viberg et al. (Eds.): EC-TEL 2023, LNCS 14200, pp. 548–553, 2023.
https://doi.org/10.1007/978-3-031-42682-7_40

of teachers contain the belief that students should be clearly given the solution, or they learn better when something is demonstrated. Teachers with a constructivist orientation argue that students learn the best independently and in an active appropriation process through problem solving [4].

Diverse studies have already considered implicit theories of teachers on the use of technology in the classroom [10], without a particular focus on the type of learning activities used including underlying instructional principles. Against this backdrop, we explored the implicit theories of teachers about teaching with technology.

The choice of learning activities is a complex decision-making process conditioned by many factors [11]. In the German didactic tradition, these factors are based on teaching principles, such as self-activity and self-control or differentiation and individualization [13]. Teachers select a particular learning activity because it is appropriate for a particular phase of instruction and in terms of the cognitive learning objective [6]. A possible synthesis of this purpose and goal is the ICAP framework [5, 6]. It distinguishes four different ways of engaging with learning material that can be performed for a specific purpose in order to trigger different learning processes [5].

Passive engagement does not require students to engage in any visible activity. They are merely expected to absorb information, for example, by watching a video [5, 11]. The learning process assumed here corresponds to the isolated storing of information [5]. *Active engagement* involves reproducing previously learned knowledge or visibly manipulating the material by, for example, taking a digital quiz [5, 11]. This type of engagement leads to the activation of prior knowledge and the new knowledge can be linked with prior knowledge and be stored [5]. *Constructive engagement* goes beyond this activation, linkage to prior knowledge, and storage by additionally independently inferring new knowledge from the activated prior knowledge or from the knowledge integrated by the new material. The generated knowledge can be integrated into existing knowledge structures [5]. Finally, *interactive engagement* means that students are expected to generate ideas beyond the material in groups. All the learning processes of constructive engagement are integrated, and in addition, new knowledge is inferred in co-construction [5]. The depth of processing, and hence the profitability increases across the different types of engagement from passive to interactive [5].

The distinction between transmissive and constructivist orientation can be linked to the ICAP framework and the will, skill, tool and pedagogy model, which distinguishes between attitudes (will component), skills, technical framework (tool component) and pedagogy. The pedagogy component corresponds to the pedagogical approach, which can be, for example, transmissive or constructivist [8]. Further, the transmissive orientation can be associated with passive engagement, when teachers assume that this is the best way to learn with technology [4, 5]. In contrast, the constructivist orientation is different, to which the definitions of active, constructive, and interactive engagement are more applicable [4, 5]. One possible conclusion is that teachers have implicit theories that align with the types of engagement with the learning material and are located on a continuum between constructivist and transmissive. So far, implicit theories have rarely been related to models for the use of technology in a way that promotes learning by quality of technology use.

2 Research Questions

This study was based on the above identified gap in research and explored the following research question: How do teachers justify the use of technology to achieve different types of engagement with learning materials?

3 Methods

Twelve teachers ($N = 12$) from different types of schools in Germany were recruited by e-mail and participated in semi-structured expert interviews. Of these, 7 were consultants for digital education in Bavaria. The remaining teachers were selected based on their commitment to using technology in the classroom. The guideline for the semi-structured expert interviews was structured according to the different ways of engaging with the learning material described in the ICAP framework [5]. Teachers were asked to identify which technology should be used for the types of engagement with the learning material. If they were unfamiliar with the ICAP framework, a description of it was given at the beginning. After the first question, they were then asked to explain how this technology was used and to justify this. Finally, the teachers should conclude what characterizes good teaching with technology. The interviews took between 70 min and 128 min. The interview transcriptions were analyzed using the method of thematic content analysis with the procedure of content structuring according to Mayring's [9] specifications. If the category system formed was not sufficient to classify the teachers' statements and the main categories did not adequately represent the material, additional (sub-)categories were formed inductively [9]. This resulted in a total of 26 main categories and one sub-category.

4 Results

4.1 Implicit Theories About *Passive* Engagement

Seven teachers described the *format of the digital medium* as a major factor influencing how and for what purpose they use technology. It was crucial that learning material can be presented differently through different media and possibilities within the medium. *Goal orientation* in terms of learning objectives to be achieved by students played different roles for five teachers. By using technology, teachers manage to explain complex issues, can exercise more control, and work towards a set goal. Some teachers explained that a passive use of technology is suitable for *structuring lessons* by leading to a topic area, *developing a subject matter* or *conveying learning content*.

4.2 Implicit Theories About *Active* Engagement

According to six teachers interviewed, active engagement is particularly suitable for *ensuring learning success*. Teachers not only mentioned that results can be secured, but also that active engagement is suitable for practicing and repeating learning content. Five teachers explained that active engagement using technology is suitable for *differentiation and individualization.* Not only can students and their requirements be addressed individually, but work can also be done inclusively. As for passive engagement, the aspect of *structuredness* plays a role for active engagement. Students can acquire the learning material or can collect content in a structured way.

4.3 Implicit Theories About *Constructive* Engagement

According to eight teachers, constructive engagement is particularly suitable for *promoting students' ICT competencies* in the use of technology. The use of technology also contains the possibility to create a *relation to students' everyday life* and prepare them for their future careers. The majority of teachers described that students can *work through the learning content on their own.* A teacher explained that this type of engagement allows students to combine learning materials with knowledge from long-term memory. In addition to active engagement, according to half of the teachers, constructive engagement is suitable for *differentiation and individualization* in that students and their learning requirements can be addressed individually.

4.4 Implicit Theories About *Interactive* Engagement

All teachers mentioned the reason for using technology for interactive engagement is to enable students to *work cooperatively. Structuredness* plays a role as students can work through the learning material in a structured way and teachers can use technology to introduce a topic or to convey content in a structurally consistent way. Seven teachers stated that interactive technology use enables them *to work in a goal-oriented manner.* Technology therefore not only leads to the achievement of goals, but also to the efficient achievement of goals. According to four teachers' technology usage *promotes ICT competencies* in dealing with them. *Relation to students' everyday life* can be also established and they can be prepared for future life through competence training. Interactive engagement using technology was also targeted by six teachers to let *students work out learning content or create something on their own.*

5 Discussion and Conclusions

The purpose of this study was to investigate what implicit theories teachers have about teaching and learning with technology. The teachers justified the passive engagement with the format of the digital medium. On the one hand, the use of technology was explained by the digital medium itself. This highlights the proximity to the tool component described in the will, skill, tool and pedagogy model [8]. On the other hand, teachers argued for methodological-didactic aspects, such as structuredness and goal orientation. With the finding of goal orientation, a connection can be made to the basic distinction of implicit theories into transmissive and constructivist orientation. Aldahdouh et al. [2] found in their study that innovativeness is mediated by goal orientation. Passive engagement is often less innovative, as the transmissive approach is more likely to be followed, with re-reception anchored in its goal orientation [2, 4]. As these justification factors seem to describe a teacher-centered perspective, the pedagogical approach taken for passive engagement is transmissive [4, 5, 8].

Active engagement was mainly justified with regard to secure learning success, differentiation and individualization and structuredness. While for the passive engagement the structuredness was described more in terms of guidance, supplementation and as a basis for further elaboration, for active engagement, the principle of structuredness for teachers was described more for the elaboration and collection of materials, with focus on the students' own activity. Learner success assurance, differentiation and individualization can be explained by the pedagogy component of the will, skill, tool and pedagogy model and describe teachers' assumptions that the use of technology would promote learning through these aspects. In contrast to passive engagement, the focus is more on the students, whose learning success is to be ensured and who can be brought to active engagement. The parallelism of the reasoning factors to the manipulative activity of the students becomes clear and the active engagement seems to describe more the constructivist orientation [4, 5, 8].

This constructivist orientation becomes clearer for constructive engagement. This type of engagement was predominantly justified by teachers in terms of ICT competence promotion and self-activity. Similar to the findings of Esterl, Berger and Nistor [6], it was shown that constructive engagement enables a creative and independent way of working by allowing students to control their own learning process and become active themselves. Further, constructive engagement was justified as promoting competencies in dealing with technology. This can be interpreted as promoting the development of coherent knowledge structures through constructive engagement [11].

The teachers often justified interactive engagement with cooperation or collaboration. This finding is consistent with the explanation of the ICAP framework, which focuses on collaborative work for this type of engagement [5]. The reasoning factor of goal orientation can be traced back to the finding of Aldahdouh et al. [2]. Opportunities for interactive engagement are more innovative because a more constructivist approach is followed by teachers, with students' own activity anchored in their goal orientation [2, 4]. The results show the proximity to the pedagogical approach of constructivist orientation [4] for the interactive engagement.

Since the fidelity of implementation [3] of methods in practice is low, teachers need more practice-oriented approaches. Teachers can especially draw on the findings of this study on the high-quality use of technology for constructive and interactive engagement but also identify for which purposes passive and active engagement are more appropriate. They can also implement the related teaching principles. Thus, teachers can find a practice-oriented starting point for themselves to increasingly integrate aspects of existing models and to elaborately develop their implicit theories. Future research should focus on one type of engagement with the learning material to better relate teachers' explanations to the way students engage. Further research can also build on the results of this study, which showed that teachers' implicit theories should not only be explained by their transmissive and constructivist orientation. Rather, the ways in which students engage with the learning material and the underlying instructional principles should also be addressed. Future research on implicit theories will hopefully benefit from this proposed broader perspective and help to understand more precisely how teachers think. Models for high-quality use of technology in the classroom can be adapted to better reflect reality.

References

1. Abelson, R.P.: Differences between belief and knowledge systems. Cogn. Sci. **3**(4), 355–366 (1979). https://doi.org/10.1207/s15516709cog0304_4
2. Aldahdouh, T.Z., Nokelainen, P., Korhonen, V.: Innovativeness of staff in higher education. Do implicit theories and goal orientation matter? Int. J. High. Educ. **7**(2), 43–57 (2018). https://doi.org/10.5430/ijhe.v7n2p43
3. Arneson, J.B., Woodbury, J., Offerdahl, E.G.: Fidelity of implementation as a guiding framework for transitioning research-based instructional practices from on site to online. J. Microbiol. Biol. Educ. **23**(1), 1–6 (2022). https://doi.org/10.1128/jmbe.00337-21
4. Chan, K.-W., Elliott, R.G.: Relational analysis of personal epistemology and conceptions about teaching and learning. Teach. Teach. Educ. **20**(8), 817–831 (2004). https://doi.org/10.1016/j.tate.2004.09.002
5. Chi, M.T.H., Wylie, R.: The ICAP framework: linking cognitive engagement to active learning outcomes. Educ. Psychol. **49**(4), 219–243 (2014). https://doi.org/10.1080/00461520.2014.965823
6. Esterl, N., Berger, S., Nistor, N.: Digital media in schools during the covid-19 lockdown: teachers‘ experiences with choosing teaching strategies. In: 17th European Conference on Technology Enhanced Learning, EC-TEL 2022, pp. 507–513. Springer Nature, Cham (2022). https://doi.org/10.1007/978-3-031-16290-9
7. Furnham, A.: Lay theories. Everyday understanding of problems in the social sciences. Pergamon Press, Oxford (1988)
8. Knezek, G., Christensen, R.: Extending the will, skill, tool model of technology integration: adding pedagogy as a new model construct. J. Comput. High. Educ. **28**, 307–325 (2016). https://doi.org/10.1007/s12528-016-9120-2
9. Mayring, P.: Qualitative Inhaltsanalyse. 12th edn. Beltz, Weinheim, Basel (2015)
10. Mertala, P.: Teachers‘ beliefs about technology integration in early childhood education: a meta-ethnographical synthesis of qualitative research. Comput. Hum. Behav. **101**, 334–349 (2019). https://doi.org/10.1016/j.chb.2019.08.003
11. Sailer, M., Schultz-Pernice, F., Fischer, F.: Contextual facilitators for learning activities involving technology in higher education: the C♭-model. Comput. Hum. Behav. **121**, 1–13 (2021). https://doi.org/10.1016/j.chb.2021.106794
12. Scherer, R., Siddiq, F., Howard, S.K., Tondeur, J.: The more experienced, the better prepared? New evidence on the relation between teachers' experience and their readiness for online teaching and learning. Comput. Hum. Behav. **139**, 1–14 (2023). https://doi.org/10.1016/j.chb.2022.107530
13. Wiater, W.: Unterrichtsprinzipien. Prüfungswissen – Basiswissen Schulpädagogik. Auer Verlag, Augsburg (2018)

Transferring Digital Competences for Teaching from Theory into Practice Through Reflection

Angela Fessl[1,2(✉)], Monica Divitini[3], and Katharina Maitz[1,4]

[1] Institute of Interactive Systems and Data Science, Graz University of Technology, Sandgasse 36, 8010 Graz, Austria
afessl@tugraz.at
[2] Know-Center GmbH, Sandgasse 36, 8010 Graz, Austria
[3] Norwegian University of Science and Technology, Trondheim, Norway
[4] Private University College of Teacher Education Augustinum, Graz, Austria

Abstract. Teachers must continuously develop their digital proficiency by acquiring digital competences and transferring them into practice. This requires to enhance teachers' self-regulated learning skills and to foster reflective learning. In this work, we present the results of an evaluation that was conducted with six in-service teachers attending five workshops of a professional development training. The teachers used a learning platform called DIGIVIDget that offers micro-learning content related to basic digital competences for teaching. Reflective learning was induced by presenting different types of reflective questions in the DIGIVIDget and by conducting dedicated reflection sessions in the workshop series. The results show reflective learning among the participants and that the transfer of newly acquired digital competences (theory) into class (practice) took place, but only rarely.

Keywords: Reflective learning · Prompts · Digital Competences

1 Introduction

Teachers must acquire digital competences and be able to transfer them into practice for educating their students [7]. This requires to enhance their self-regulated learning skills and to foster reflective learning. Regulating one's own learning process is a vital skill, especially when the support and guidance of an instructor is limited [2]. Reflective learning, i.e., the conscious re-evaluation of past experiences to learn from them and to guide future behaviour [1] is another crucial skill and used to close the theory-practice gap [4]. There exist a plethora of research on how to support self-regulated and reflective learning with the help of technology, especially with the help of prompts. However, findings regarding the impact of prompts are ambiguous [8,9].

The learning platform DIGIVIDget offers learning material on basic digital competences [7] relevant in the educational context and aims to support teachers in the self-regulated acquisition of digital competences. In this poster paper we

O. Viberg et al. (Eds.): EC-TEL 2023, LNCS 14200, pp. 554–559, 2023.
https://doi.org/10.1007/978-3-031-42682-7_41

present the evaluation of DIGIVIDget with focus on transferring acquired competences to practice through reflection. The study was conducted in the context of a professional development training, in which digital competences were conveyed using the DIGIVIDget and in an accompanying five-part workshop series. Reflective learning was fostered by offering different types of reflective questions in the DIGIVIDget and by conducting dedicated reflection sessions in the workshop series. In this paper, we address the following research questions: (RQ1) How did the participants experience reflection in both contexts? (RQ2) In which of the contexts did the teachers reflect more in-depth about the learning content, possible connections between learning and practice, and a possible transfer into practice? (RQ3) To what extent might transfer of newly acquired digital competences (theory) into class (practice) have taken place?

2 DIGIVIDget: The System and Its Evaluation

2.1 Reflection Prompts in DIGIVIDget

The DIGIVIDget content is structured along learning units for achieving competence oriented learning goals [5]. The content of each unit is presented in a sequence of micro-learning cards presenting rich interactive content. In each sequence, we added up to two reflective questions. All learning units have one reflective question at the end. Additionally, if a learning unit consists of more than 12 micro learning cards, we added an in-between reflective question. In-between reflective questions are open-ended questions consisting of meta cognitive prompts and motivational regulation prompts inspired by Daumiller and Dresel [3]. One of these prompts is for example *"Think about: where could you apply this content in practice?"*. Reflective questions at the end of each learning unit refer back to the content of the unit and prompt to either reflect on past experiences or to think about how to apply the content (in future) in practice. For example *"In this learning unit, you were introduced to the following 6 tips to [..]. Think about which tip you would like to try in the future and when."*

2.2 Methodology

Procedure. The evaluation was conducted in Styria, Austria as part of a professional development course for in-service teachers consisting of 5 workshops in October/November 2022.

In the first workshop the participants received an introduction to DIGIVIDget, then they were introduced to some content. At the end, the participants received their homework, i.e., they were asked to go through the relevant unit in the DIGIVIDget, to reflect about the content and answer the reflective questions in the system, and to apply the newly gained knowledge in school. The subsequent workshops all followed a similar structure, starting with a shared reflection session about the homework. The reflection was guided by some prompting questions and answers collected with Padlet (padlet.com). Afterwards, the participants were introduced to new content and received their homework. Workshop 5 also included a final reflection on the course.

Coding Schema. For analysing the answers given to the reflective questions in both contexts, i.e., within the system and during the workshops, we developed a coding schema inspired by Boud et al. [1]. The schema was developed combining a deductive (top-down) and inductive (bottom-up) approach. It consists of 3 categories of codes and corresponding sub-codes. Category 1 consists of *general codes* where answers given refer to the learning content, provide feedback, or indicate some learning constraints, however, these answers cannot be seen as real reflections but help to return to possible experiences. Category 2 consists of *transfer codes* for answers that consist of reflection about the learning or teaching process, attend to emotions or attitude, or connect theory with practice or vice versa. Category 3 consists of *outcomes/impact codes* emphasising achieved outcomes or impact in practice. All material was coded by two researchers. Agreement was achieved either in a first step of coding the answers independently, or in a second step after discussion.

Participants. Six secondary school teachers participated in the workshops. All of them were female, 50 years old or older ($M = 55, SD = 4.472$), and they had up to 30 years of experience as teachers ($M = 18.9, SD = 13.698$).

3 Results

Overall, at the end of the course there were 44 meaningful answers to the different reflective questions in the DIGIVIDget, 17 (39%) of them were given to in-between reflective questions and 27 (61%) to questions at the end of a learning unit. In addition, there were 70 meaningful answers collected in the reflection sessions (written in Padlet). In the following we present a short description of the analysis results, divided in the three main categories of the coding schema, with number in parenthesis indicating percentages.

Category 1: General Codes. In the DIGIVIDget, we received more answers that were coded as comments about the content or annotations than in the workshops. All answers related to feedback about the DIGIVIDget (11.43%), the learning content (14.29%), the workshop (11.43%), the reflection sessions (4.29%), or the overall experience of the training (8.57%) were provided in the workshop series only. No feedback was given in the DIGIVIDget. Also all possible constraints (time: 14.29%, competences: 5.71%, and interest: 1.43%), but one (related to one participants' competences), were mentioned in the workshops only. One example of feedback about the workshops with time constraints is *"With this wealth of knowledge that you have given us, it is now clear that we had little time on the online afternoon for practical things. Unfortunately, I largely lacked the time to 'learn along' at home at my leisure."*

Category 2: Transfer Codes. In both contexts, we received several answers that contain reflection about participants' teaching practice (DIGIVIDget: 9.1%; Workshops: 7.14%), their learning process (DIGIVIDget: 11.36%; Workshops: 25.71%), or were related to emotions or attitudes (DIGIVIDget: 9.1%; Workshops: 2.86%). In the workshops, several answers that include reflection about the own learning process were combined with constraints. For example *"I read through topics 1 and 2 and took the quizzes. I was able to follow the content well. However, this was very time-consuming for me, so I could not delve further. The content is very interesting and informative. I think you get a good overview."* We also received in both contexts answers that either create a connection from learning to practice through reflection (DIGIVIDget: 18.8%; Workshops: 7.14%) or create a connection from practice to learning (DIGIVIDget: 2.27%; Workshops: 2.86%). One example of an answer we received in the DIGIVIDget that combines reflecting about the learning process and connecting it to practice is *"I have already gained a good overview of how to critically examine Internet content. I can use different search engines and enter search terms more specifically to get the information I want."*.

Category 3: Outcome/Impact Codes. We received several answers that were coded as an outcome of reflection, 50% of such answers were given in the DIGIVIDget, but only 17.14% of such answers were found in the workshop series. *"I will talk more often at home with my children or at school with the children, if the topic fits."*. The answers present for example different plans in the future e.g. to either try out a newly acquainted platform on the Internet or to talk more often with children about difficult topics. Altogether 4 answers were coded to mention an impact in relation to teaching/learning practices, one was provided in the DIGIVIDget and three in the workshop series. In the DIGIVIDget one person reflected on the tips offered about how to critically evaluate information for its truth and quality: *"I find the page'Check credibility on the Internet' good, I immediately forward this link to my computer science colleagues"*. In the reflection session in the second workshop, one participant wrote *"Activity: padlet: I created a padlet for my students. They liked it a lot"*. Although Padlet was not introduced in Workshop 1, the participant went, as part of their homework, through the respective learning goal in the DIGIVIDget and applied the content learned directly in their teaching practice. These answers show some impact regarding the participants' teaching practice and that the transfer of acquired theoretical knowledge into teaching practice (to a certain extent) has taken place.

4 Discussion and Conclusion

Overall, the feedback from our participants regarding the workshop series and the DIGIVIDget was very positive.

Reflection Possibilities (RQ1). All participants confirmed that the reflection at the beginning of each workshop was more effective than reflecting alone in a self-regulated way in the DIGIVIDget, in line with existing literature [3,6,8,9]. This was connected by some to the collaborative nature of the reflection in the workshops.

Reflection in Both Contexts (RQ2). Answers coded with *general codes* cannot be seen as real reflection, they only help to return to possible experiences [1].

The general code *Comments* was more often assigned to answers given in the DIGIVIDget than in the workshop series. This could be explained with the fact, that all reflective questions offered in the DIGIVIDget were related to one specific learning goal and asked to think about either the own learning process directed towards this goal (in-between questions/meta cognitive questions) or about the content of the learning goal (reflective questions at the end of a learning unit). The codes about *Feedback* and *Constraints* were only (but one) assigned to answers received in the workshop. This might be connected to how questions were formulated and not explicitly addressing feedback and constraints in the DIGIVIDget. More interesting is that we received many answers related to different constraints regarding the participants' self-regulated learning with the DIGIVIDget in the workshops. Again, we have not explicitly asked about constraints in the reflection sessions, however, in the social context of the workshops the participants might have had the need to explain/justify why they did not apply (that much of) the learned content in practice.

Attending to emotions or attitude is higher in the context of the DIGIVIDget. The number of answers related to the reflection about their learning process is higher in the workshops than in the DIGIVIDget. One reason for this finding could be that in the reflection sessions the participants were motivated to participate and to think about what they have learned to contribute to the discussions and to share their experiences with other colleagues. In contrast, the number of answers relating learning to practice is higher in the DIGIVIDget. One explanation could be that the reflective questions posed in the DIGIVIDget are referring to concrete learning content and relating practice to it is easy to do and mirrored back in the results.

Outcomes and Impact in Both Contexts (RQ3). As known from literature, achieving in-depth reflection that is leading to concrete outcomes or impact is challenging [6,8]. The number of answers coded as showing an outcome is higher in the DIGIVIDget than in the workshops. This shows that the participants reflecting in the DIGIVIDget have identified some learning content that they would like to look at in more detail after the training or intent to put into practice. The number of answers mentioning an achieved impact in both contexts is rather low. However, three out of four answers coded in this category were detected in the workshops showing evidence of concrete transfers of the newly acquired digital competences into practice.

Self-regulated and Reflective Learning. Initiating reflective learning is challenging, especially when trying to initiate reflective learning with the help of reflective prompts throughout self-regulated learning [3,6,8,9]. Reflective learning in the DIGIVIDget was rather superficial, it was more seen as a possibility for note taking than really thinking about the presented content in depth or to transfer or envisioning the application in practice. Additionally, learning cards asking for reflection can easily be clicked away, especially when having the feeling to be able to come back to the respective learning card and fill it in at a later point in time. In contrast, dedicated reflective sessions in the workshop series could have lead to deeper reflection due to its social character, since the explanation or justification of reflective answers given in the group was possible. All answers inserted in the Padlet were visible to all fellow learners, thus, deeper reflection by comparing own experiences to the experiences of others was possible. Additionally, in the workshops the participants had a clear timeframe for reflection without the possibility to postpone it. Summing up, systems supporting self-directed reflective learning should not be seen in isolation, but together with the learning context in which they are embedded in.

The work presented in this poster is an exploration to be extended in a study with more participants. We also plan to investigate the applicability of the developed coding schema in different contexts for analyzing individual reflection texts in terms of transfer from newly gained theoretical knowledge into practice.

Acknowledgement. The "DIGIVID" Erasmus+ project (grant number: 2020-1-AT01-KA226-HE-092590) is co-funded by the Erasmus+ Programm of the European Union. Know-Center is a COMET Centre within the COMET - Competence Centers for Excellent Technologies Programme and funded by BMK, BMAW as well as the co-financing provinces Styria, Vienna and Tyrol. COMET is managed by FFG.

References

1. Boud, D., Keogh, R., Walker, D.: Promoting Reflective Learning: A Model. Open University, London (1996)
2. Cicchinelli, A., et al.: Finding traces of self-regulated learning in activity streams. In: Proceedings of the 8th International Conference on Learning Analytics and Knowledge, pp. 191–200 (2018)
3. Daumiller, M., Dresel, M.: Supporting self-regulated learning with digital media using motivational regulation and metacognitive prompts. J. Exp. Educ. **87**(1), 161–176 (2019)
4. Fessl, A., Bratic, M., Pammer, V.: Continuous learning with a quiz for stroke nurses. Int. J. Technol. Enhanced Learn. **6**(3), 265–275 (2014)
5. Fessl, A., Maitz, K., Dennerlein, S., Pammer-Schindler, V.: The impact of explicating learning goals on teaching and learning in higher education: evaluating a learning goal visualization. In: De Laet, T., Klemke, R., Alario-Hoyos, C., Hilliger, I., Ortega-Arranz, A. (eds.) EC-TEL 2021. LNCS, vol. 12884, pp. 1–15. Springer, Cham (2021). https://doi.org/10.1007/978-3-030-86436-1_1
6. Fessl, A., Wesiak, G., Rivera-Pelayo, V., Feyertag, S., Pammer, V.: In-app reflection guidance: lessons learned across four field trials at the workplace. IEEE Trans. Learn. Technol. **10**(4), 488–501 (2017)
7. Redecker, C., et al.: European framework for the digital competence of educators: Digcompedu. Technical report, Joint Research Centre (Seville site) (2017)
8. Rivera-Pelayo, V., Fessl, A., Müller, L., Pammer, V.: Introducing mood self-tracking at work: empirical insights from call centers. ACM Trans. Comput.-Hum. Interact. (TOCHI) **24**(1), 1–28 (2017)
9. Schumacher, C., Ifenthaler, D.: Investigating prompts for supporting students' self-regulation-a remaining challenge for learning analytics approaches? The Internet and Higher Education **49**, 100791 (2021)

"Feedback is not Embarrassing but Helpful :)"

An Exploratory Study on the Applicability of Constructive Feedback Checklists for Lecturers in Online Learning Settings

Robin Gleeson[1(✉)], Larissa Bartok[1], and Carla Souta Barreiros[2]

[1] University of Vienna, Universitätsring 1, 1010 Vienna, Austria
robin.gleeson@univie.ac.at

[2] Graz University of Technology, Rechbauerstraße 12, 8010 Graz, Austria

Abstract. Feedback about students' learning process and behaviour is one of the most effective strategies to immediately impact learning progress. Learning analytics and other educational technologies often provide automatic feedback to students. Therefore, it is critical to address automatic feedback's potential positive and negative impacts on students' well-being.

This research paper discusses the development and implementation of a checklist for creating constructive and actionable feedback in online learning settings. We refined our literature-based checklist during expert workshops and an online focus group and applied it to a higher education course. The course used a flipped classroom approach, and students were asked to create videos, complete quizzes, and engage in self-reflection. The quizzes were followed by automatic detailed feedback based on our developed feedback guidelines.

We collected qualitative data on emotional valence and activation potential and gathered opinions from students using open-ended questions. Quantitative data was collected using an online evaluation questionnaire, and the interaction patterns with the self-assessment quizzes and other materials on Moodle were analysed. The preliminary results suggest that students perceived the employed feedback elements positively, but the feedback may not be activating enough for well-performing students. Lastly, we discuss the value of the suggested checklist in light of emerging AI chatbots like ChatGPT and consider possible venues to improve it.

Keywords: Automatic feedback · Constructive feedback · Learning analytics

1 Introduction

Feedback is a crucial component of the learning process, as it allows students to recognise their strengths and weaknesses, identify areas that need improvement, and develop strategies for success. Higher education students and educators often refer to challenges related to feedback practices, contextual constraints and individual capacity [11, 12].

R. Gleeson, L. Bartok and C. S. Barreiros—Contributed equally.

O. Viberg et al. (Eds.): EC-TEL 2023, LNCS 14200, pp. 560–565, 2023.
https://doi.org/10.1007/978-3-031-42682-7_42

Automatic feedback addresses some of these challenges, as it can be provided in real-time and personalised to students' needs and preferences. Also, it can help reduce educators' workload in traditional or hybrid settings and are essential in online courses. With the digital transformation at higher education institutions, automatic feedback has become ubiquitous and is often generated by technologies such as learning analytics and AI-powered tools.

The interactions of feedback and emotions are still an under-explored area of research [10, 14], even-more-so for emotions in automatic feedback systems.

Our research focuses on designing, developing, and evaluating learning analytics technologies that support higher education students to gain and improve self-regulated learning skills. We are particularly interested in understanding the impact of automated written feedback on higher education students based on formative assessment data.

This article proposes a literature-based checklist for constructive and actionable feedback, consisting of ten items to consider when generating feedback. Moreover, we present preliminary empirical results of the checklist evaluation and discuss the main findings.

2 Checklist for Constructive and Actionable Feedback

Based on a literature research [1, 2, 4, 6, 7], we developed an initial draft for constructive and actionable feedback (particularly in learning analytics settings). Next, we conducted workshops and an online focus group with participants with expertise in pedagogy, learning analytics, psychology, ethics, data privacy, and educational technology from three higher education institutions. Based on this work, we further refined and condensed the initial draft into easy-to-understand, concise guidelines in the form of a checklist (see Fig. 1), which is meant to assist in creating feedback elements.

3 Pilot Study

We present a pilot study with our two-fold research question:

i) Do the feedback elements meet our checklist criteria from the students' point of view?
ii) How does the checklist-derived automatic feedback impact on students' affective well-being?

3.1 Research Methodology

For our study, we conducted an online post-questionnaire with six sections: 1) information about the goals of the study, 2) questions regarding the participants' demographics, 3) Self-regulated learning, 4) questions about the quizzes, the feedback provided, and the emotions related to the feedback, 5) the System Usability Scale, and the 6) questions about instructional feedback perception. In addition, we collected the participants' interaction data with the formative quizzes.

Checklist for constructive & actionable feedback (in learning analytics settings)		
☐	1	**It is accurate.** Feedback should be based on first-hand data and free from bias.
☐	2	**It is immediate.** Feedback is most useful at the earliest opportunity after the related behavior.
☐	3	**It is specific rather than general.** Generalizations and mentioning broad character traits are less helpful than referring to specific behavior.
☐	4	**It suggests plans for improvement.** Feedback should be actionable, focusing on behavior that the person receiving feedback can do something about.
☐	5	**It is solicited rather than imposed.** Feedback is most useful when the person receiving it feels that they need and want it.
☐	6	**It is confidential.** Feedback should be given in private, including other parties only after the explicit approval of the recipient.
☐	7	**It is provided by a trusted party.** The feedback provider needs to be credible in the eyes of the recipient.
☐	8	**It uses descriptive, non-judgmental language.** By avoiding evaluative language, feedback reduces the need for the individual receiving feedback to react defensively.
☐	9	**It is tailored to the recipient's needs.** In order to be perceived as relevant and helpful, feedback must meet the needs (and the tone) of its target audience.
☐	10	**It is checked to ensure clear communication.** Feedback that isn't understood (or, worse, misunderstood) by the recipient will have un-predictable, likely undesirable, effects.

Fig. 1. Checklist for constructive & actionable feedback.

3.2 Course and Participants Characterisation

The feasibility of the checklist in guiding feedback was empirically tested in an exploratory design with one seminar course offered at a higher education institution (Bachelor study program Philosophy and Psychology teaching degree) during the Spring semester of 2022. 36 students were enrolled in the seminar "Research Methods and Statistics". The course was designed using a flipped classroom approach, exposing each topic and corresponding learning goals. Students were asked to answer formative quizzes and self-reflection questions. Afterwards, live online classes took place, and all seven topics were discussed.

The quizzes were created on the Learning Management System Moodle. Each quiz consisted of five (open-ended & multiple-choice) questions. After taking the quiz, the system automatically provided detailed feedback, composed by the lecturer and following the checklist guidelines. Students were able to answer the formative quizzes as many times as they wished, and their final grade was determined by a group video presentation

(40%), a critique (2 pages) on a scientific article provided (30%) and a statistical task analysing data using the software SPSS (30%).

3.3 Preliminary Results

Did Students Interact with the Formative Quizzes?

Most students answered the online quizzes at least once. On average, the students answered the quiz 1.5 times. The majority of trials happened before the content was discussed in class. Table 1 presents the students' interaction data with the formative quizzes.

Table 1. Students' interaction data with the formative quizzes.

	Number Students	Mean trials	Median trials	Max trials	Min trials	Trials after class
Quiz 1	35	1,65	1	8	1	10
Quiz 2	36	1,71	1	8	1	24
Quiz 3	35	1,76	1	6	0	16
Quiz 4	35	1,41	1	4	0	17
Quiz 5	34	1,60	1	8	1	23
Quiz 6	35	1,49	1	5	0	22
Quiz 7	35	1,54	1	7	0	21

What are Our Students' Affective Responses to the Feedback Elements?

We gathered information on emotional valence and activation ("call-to-action") potential by asking students about their affective response to feedback elements included in the formative quizzes, accordingly with [3, 9], albeit only 8 students completed the questionnaire. Figure 2 depicts on the left the two-dimensional framework of emotions emphasising emotional valence and activation, and on the right, the students' emotional responses to our feedback elements.

Do the Online Feedback Elements Meet or Fail Our Checklist Criteria From Our Students' Point of View?

We gathered qualitative information on our feedback elements with open-ended questions and analysed responses with a deductive category system [5] based on the criteria of our checklist for constructive & actionable feedback. Codes are further defined on either positive (+) or negative (–) valence. Our coding system can readily be applied to open-ended student responses, but more data is needed before we can report meaningful results (see Fig. 3). Even with the limited number of answers ($N = 8$) we could verify a positive tone with regards to the provided feedback.

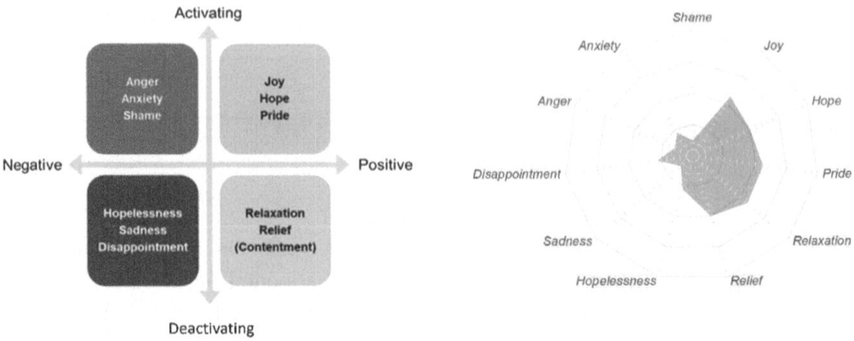

Fig. 2. Left: Two-dimensional framework of emotions emphasising emotional valence and activation [3, 9]. Right: "Please share how frequently you experienced the following emotions while reading the feedback provided in the course quizzes." Average response on 5-Point Likert Scale (Never – Rarely – Sometimes – Often – Always, N = 8).

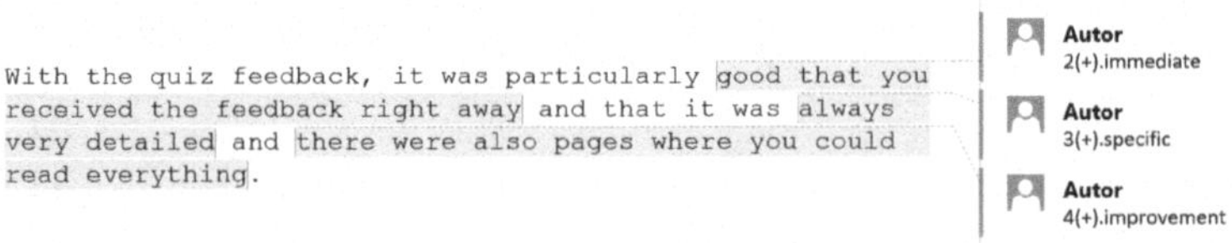

Fig. 3. Snippet from a coded student response to our feedback elements, three matched codes with positive valence.

4 Discussion

Based on preliminary results, the feedback elements are perceived positively by our students, but not necessarily as activating. The endeavour to maintain a positive atmosphere (and foster student well-being) might lead to student inactivation, especially for students on a good track so far. This might require revising our checklist to also address (and avoid inactivating) well-performing students.

Preliminary results from our qualitative content analysis confirm the viability of the coding system based on our feedback checklist, but more qualitative data is needed to either adapt the online feedback elements or rework our checklist.

In addition to the above-discussed checklist's application in human-to-human feedback, emerging AI chatbots like ChatGPT could provide interesting new opportunities for generating AI-assisted feedback to students in conjunction with tailored templates like our feedback checklist. This new generation of Chatbots are already being used in higher education settings [13], and many more publications can be expected in the coming months.

The checklist items can be integrated directly as prompts (input) for ChatGPT to consider when formulating feedback to students, along with the student responses to be assessed. We would expect this prompt design to improve ChatGPT's output and reduce manual postprocessing before the lecturer can pass the task feedback on to their students, and initial trial runs indicate that student task feedback created by ChatGPT

4.0 will consistently adhere to our feedback checklist guidelines if prompted to do so in the initial prompt. This streamlined process can reduce time investment on behalf of the teacher, though we do not recommend passing on AI-generated task feedback to students without prior plausability check, at least for the current generation of AI Chatbots.

Future challenges include integrating our ongoing research into current standard models and feedback frameworks for digital learning environments [4, 8].

References

1. Brooke, J.: SUS: a quick and dirty usability scale. In: Jordan, P.W., Thomas, B., Weerdmeester, B.A., McClelland, A.L., (eds.). Usability Evaluation in Industry. London: Taylor and Francis (1996)
2. Center for Teaching and Learning (2019). Teacher Feedback. Infopool better teaching. University of Vienna, February 2019. https://infopool.univie.ac.at/en/start-page/teaching-advising/feedback/teacher-feedback/
3. Lim, L.-A., et al.: Students' perceptions of, and emotional responses to, personalised learning analytics-based feedback: an exploratory study of four courses. Assess. Eval. High. Educ. **46**(3), 339–359 (2021)
4. Maier, U., Klotz, C.: Personalized feedback in digital learning environments: classification framework and literature review. Comput. Educ. Artif. Intell. **3**, 100080 (2022)
5. Mayring, P.: Qualitative content analysis: theoretical foundation, basic procedures and software solution. Klagenfurt (2014). https://nbn-resolving.org/urn:nbn:de:0168-ssoar-395173
6. Mill, C.R.: Feedback: the art of giving and receiving help. In: Porter, L., Mill, C.R., (Eds.), The Reading Book for Human Relations Training, pp. 18–19. Bethel: ME: NTL Institute for Applied Behavioral Science (1976)
7. Omer, A.A.A., Abdularhim, M.E.: The criteria of constructive feedback: the feedback that counts. J. Health Spec. **5**(1), 45–48 (2017)
8. Panadero, E., Lipnevich, A.A.: A review of feedback models and typologies: towards an integrative model of feedback elements. Educ. Res. Rev. **35**, 100416 (2022)
9. Pekrun, R.: The control-value theory of achievement emotions: assumptions, corollaries, and implications for educational research and practice. Educ. Psychol. Rev. **18**, 315–341 (2006). https://doi.org/10.1007/s10648-006-9029-9
10. Rowe, A.D.: Feelings about feedback: the role of emotions in assessment for learning. Scaling Assess. Learn. High. Educ. 159–172 (2017)
11. Jensen, L., Bearman, M., Boud, D.: Feedback encounters: towards a framework for analysing and understanding feedback processes. Assess. Eval. High. Educ. **48**(1), 121–134 (2023). https://doi.org/10.1080/02602938.2022.2059446
12. Henderson, M., Ryan, T., Phillips, M.: The challenges of feedback in higher education. Assess. Eval. High. Educ. **44**(8), 1237–1252 (2019). https://doi.org/10.1080/02602938.2019.1599815
13. Rudolph, J., Tan, S., Tan, S.: ChatGPT: bullshit spewer or the end of traditional assessments in higher education?. J. Appl. Learn. Teach. **6**(1) (2023). https://doi.org/10.37074/jalt.2023.6.1.9
14. Värlander, S.: The role of students' emotions in formal feedback situations. Teach. High. Educ. **13**(2), 145–156 (2008)

Enhancing Learning Mobility with a Community-Based Micro-Credential e-Portfolio Platform Service for Higher Education

Rika Ikeda(✉), Andrey Ferriyan, Keiko Okawa, and Achmad Husni Thamrin

Keio University, 2-15-45, Mita, Minato-ku, Tokyo, Japan
rika.ikeda@keio.jp, andrey@sfc.wide.ad.jp, keiko@kmd.keio.ac.jp, husni@sfc.keio.ac.jp

Abstract. This paper reports on the design of Inxignia: Community-Based Micro-Credential e-Portfolio Platform Service in collaboration with SOI Asia (School on Internet Asia). It aims to connect fragmented learning opportunities in the Landscape of Practice (LoP). Inxignia enables learners to navigate the three modes of the LoP framework: Engagement, Imagination, and Alignment. This research answers the research question: What are the focal elements for each mode in SOI Asia? Inxignia has three components corresponding to the modes: engage with communities of practice, reflect learning experiences on a continuous and overarching basis, and codesign learning pathways with multiple stakeholders. The results indicated that Inxignia supported each mode.

Keywords: Learning Mobility · Landscape of Practice · Micro-Credentials

1 Introduction

1.1 Research Background

Learning mobility is defined as the mobility of learners (transnationally, regionally, or online) within a specific period, consciously organized for educational purposes [1], and it is a learning experience where individuals go outside of their everyday contexts [2]. Learning Mobility enhances employability and career network [3,4]. However, learning mobility programs experience challenges in motivation and recruitment of learners [5].

SOI Asia is a consortium of universities in the Asia-Pacific Region. SOI Asia offers learning mobility programs in collaboration with partner universities such as the Asia Pacific Internet Engineer (APIE) Program to build Internet Engineering skills, knowledge, and a community [6]. The programs combine short-term face-to-face and online activities such as three months and one week, providing opportunities to connect with professional internet engineer communities

O. Viberg et al. (Eds.): EC-TEL 2023, LNCS 14200, pp. 566–572, 2023.
https://doi.org/10.1007/978-3-031-42682-7_43

in the region. Smaller-scale learning mobility programs are more accessible for students. However, there is a need for participation in the programs to utilize subsequent learning and career opportunities. Accumulating small-scale learning offered in different locations and disciplines is becoming necessary in a rapidly changing society and for acquiring a new skill [7].

1.2 Landscape of Practice

Lave and Wenger define learning as a participation process in a Community of Practice (CoP). The Landscape of Practice (LoP) concept compares participation in multiple CoPs to a landscape and that learning is the path one follows in that landscape. The identity formed while traversing this landscape is the learning outcome [8]. The following are modes for building identity in LoP [8,9]:

- Engagement: To participate in an activity by working or talking with people in the communities of practice.
- Imagination: Using our imagination to situate ourselves in the world, identify different ways of thinking, reflect on our situation, and search for new possibilities.
- Alignment: A two-way process of adjusting firms, perspectives, interpretations, and contexts so that actions have the expected effects.

In the LoP Framework, SOI Asia has the Engagement that connects with the CoPs. However, it needs more support for Imagination and Alignment. There is a need to research designing an integrated process and environment for learners to navigate the three modes and leverage participation in a small-scale learning mobility program into the subsequent learning and career.

This research aims to design the process and environment as well as answer the research question: What are the focal elements for each mode in SOI Asia? For Imagination and Alignment, the proposal will be newly designed to support each mode. In the Engagement mode, the requirements are defined by evaluating learning mobility programs already offered in SOI Asia. Next, a literature review explores the possibilities of Imagination and Alignment in SOI Asia.

2 Literature Review

2.1 Reflection in the Field of Education

Imagination in the context of SOI Asia means reflecting on experiences, including small-scale learning to imagine where they stand and future learning and career possibilities. A tool that was often used for reflection in education is an e-Portfolio. An e-Portfolio is electronic data that continuously accumulate all possible learning evidence to support learning and career development [9]. However, they contain a large amount of information, making them less likely to be reviewed on an ongoing and overall basis.

Life storytelling is telling one's life story as a reflection method and an act performed to understand oneself and the world [10]. It is also used in e-Portfolio to reflect on the past and plan for the future [9]. Arima [11] proposed the Life Storytelling Board, a tool designed to be consistent in life storytelling, even to create opportunities for continuous and overarching reflection on life. Combining blocks with keywords related to the episode of the user's life supports continuous reflection on the whole life and its relationships without information overload with text.

2.2 Codesign of Learning with Multiple Stakeholders

Alignment in the context of SOI Asia means coordinating with stakeholders to achieve the desired learning and career pathways. Codesign is one of customer co-creation, which can facilitate understanding user needs in service design [12]. The involvement of key users through Codesign can lead to the development of design concepts with more significant user benefits than a team composed solely of in-house experts.

Micro-credential can create a learning pathway by combining learning opportunities from different entities. The credential certifies learning outcomes acquired in smaller modules than traditional degrees. Its role makes learning outcomes visible and provides a common language within the communities while simultaneously resolving the fragmentation of small-scale learning [13]. Micro-credentials are often provided as digital badges that are visual and digital representations of credentials as a badge. There are micro-credential services that provide the ability to create, issue, collect, and share digital badges, such as Credly. Some of the services provide a Learning Pathway function that combines different badges to visualize learning pathways.

3 Design

3.1 Design Concept

This research proposes Inxignia: A Community-Based Micro-Credential e-Portfolio Platform Service that enables learners to navigate Engagement, Imagination, and Alignment. Figure 1 gives a whole picture of Inxignia. Inxignia consists of an e-Portfolio platform and the process around it that are three initiatives corresponding to each mode. The figure shows who is involved in which process. Three community members join the process proposed in the research: Learners (students and alumni), Faculties, and Working Professionals. The arrows represent the relationship in which platform data is utilized in each process, and the results of each process are stored in the platform. In addition to the features of other micro-credentialing services, the platform will offer the Life Storytelling Board function. The platform will be updated to integrate and manage micro-credential data from other sources so that learners can use it for their next study or career move. Inxignia uses an Open-Badge to maintain compatibility with other micro-credential systems and works on adaptation with version 3.0. It unifies the information to be included in Open-Badge with other micro-credential services. Quality assurance standards will also be aligned.

For the process around the platform, first, learners will participate, sustain their learning, engage, and deepen their relationships with the communities of practice in different locations and study fields. Digital badges are issued and stored on the platform to prove those learning achievements. Second, they reflect and imagine where they stand and their future possibilities in an overview and ongoing manner using Life Storytelling Board. Then, the Learning Pathway Codesign for learners to collaborate with stakeholders to design their learning.

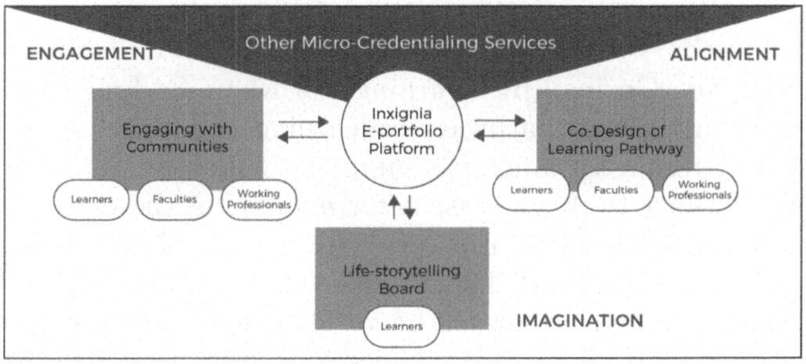

Fig. 1. Scheme of Inxignia

3.2 Components

Engaging with Communities. SOI Asia provides opportunities to engage with communities that are included in or connected to SOI Asia, such as APIE Program. This study assess whether learners engage and gain a deeper understanding of the community and the requirements of that already provided Engagement opportunity and identify what other interventions are needed.

Reflection. Reflection is conducted by using Life Storytelling Board. Figure 2 shows an example of a completed board and the components to create the board. Two or three Learners are paired up and divided into a speaker and a listener, and the speaker describes their formal and non-formal educational and professional history. There is one speaker, and the rest are listeners. Those keywords are written in a block and placed on the board. Each block of formal and non-formal educational history is color-coded. After placing the blocks about the past, the speaker set a goal in 5–10 years and thought about the steps to bridge that goal and the present while placing the transparent blocks. Any comments or ideas they want to add should be noted and placed in the support block. The listener looks at the blocks and asks questions of the speaker, digging deeper into past and future stories and offering ideas. As they reflect on the past and plan for the future, they can use previously earned digital badges and other badges associated with them so that it helps to leverage participation in a small-scale learning mobility program for their future learning and career.

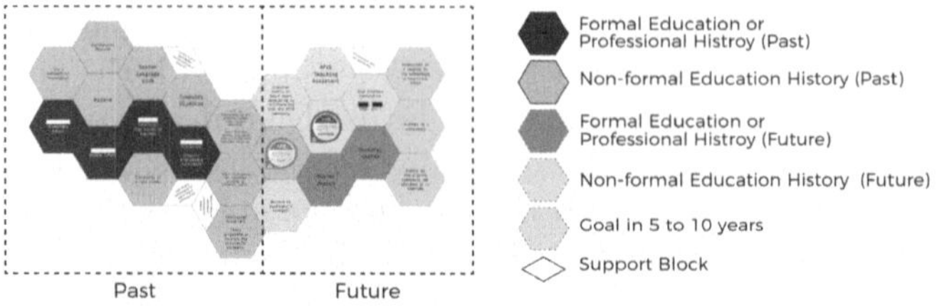

Fig. 2. An Example of Life Storytelling Board

Learning Pathway Codesign. Learning Pathways Codesign is an opportunity for designing integrated pathways of learning and career opportunities by sharing ideas and resources among community members, including Learners, Faculties, and Working Professionals. After explaining the objectives and how to proceed, they will be divided into several groups based on sub-project in SOI Asia. Subsequently, each team defines the Knowledge, Skills, and Attitudes that each project wants human resources to have. They determine the very first learning step, the last learning step, and intermediate steps to get those knowledge, skills, and attitudes. The young faculties and graduate students became facilitators to support the discussion. The actual process of creating the course is then done primarily by the faculty and Working Professionals, and it will be applied to the Learning Pathway feature on the platform.

4 Preliminary Results

Engaging with Communities. A survey of the 12 students who participated in the APIE showed that engagement was generally high. APIE consists of self-paced online courses, synchronous online sessions, an onsite camp, and an internship. The survey was conducted with students who had completed the APIE camp up to the end of the program. All students agree or strongly agree that they could confidently explain to others the objective and content of the APIE program, and they are willing to have been more involved in the APIE community by participating in internships and as a TA. The most significant impact on their motivation is having a clear idea of how they can utilize the experience for their future learning and career or enjoyment of the learning process. The interview results indicate that both reasons were greatly influenced by the ability to meet and interact with learners from different contexts, working professionals, and faculties in the field.

Reflection. The Life Storytelling Board was implemented with 11 students who participated in APIE. In the survey, all speakers answered that they gained a clearer idea of their short and long-term learning plans after creating the Life Storytelling Board. In addition, four speakers who previously did not state plans to utilize APIE mentioned ideas for the future to take advantage of APIE opportunities, such as participating in an APIE Internship and getting deeper involvement with the APIE community after creating the Life Storytelling Board.

Learning Pathway Codesign. The first trial of the Learning Pathway Codesign was conducted with 20 learners, faculty members, and working professionals. The observation and interview results indicate that mechanisms are needed to design learning from the learner's perspective and to incorporate learner opinions. While students and faculty members had different opinions, the team reflected the opinions of the faculty members rather than those of the students. Also, the team that designed the learning pathway that the students rated highly was seen to promote discussion from the learner's perspective. The second trial reflected improvements from the previous test and was conducted with two learners and two faculty who were involved in APIE Program. This trial incorporated post-its to write personal opinions and the element of learner interviews to develop concrete personas to design learning experiences for specific target audiences. Multiple learning activities were predefined to provide enjoyable learning pathways for learners and incorporate opportunities to engage with the community, ensuring a balanced utilization of these activities. Working Professionals' opinions were collected in advance and shared with the trial participants. The interview and the observation indicate that it supported customer insights into latent user needs and faculties' conversion of promising new ideas into viable concepts.

5 Conclusion

The first run of Inxignia is conducted in APIE Program and is reported in this study. The preliminary results indicated that Inxignia supported Engagement, Imagination, and Alignment modes for SOI Asia Learners. Improvements will be made based on the evaluation and applied to other educational programs offered at SOI Asia. Integration with existing activities in the SOI Asia community will be considered to make this approach sustainable.

References

1. European Platform on Learning Mobility. https://pjp-eu.coe.int/en/web/youth-partnership/european-platform-on-learning-mobility. Accessed 5 Apr 2023
2. Learning mobility for all. https://lllplatform.eu/policy-areas/skills-and-qualifications/learning-mobility-for-all/. Accessed 5 Apr 2023
3. Brandenburg, U., Berghoff S., Taboadela O.: The Erasmus Impact Study, pp. 1–10. European Commission Education and Culture (2014)
4. Babcock, E.: Mobility Mentoring, pp. 1–15. A Publication of Crittenton Women's Union (2012)
5. Devlin, M.: Learning Mobility, Social Inclusion, and Non-formal Education, pp. 5–202. Council of Europe (2017)
6. APIE. https://apie.soi.asia/. Accessed 5 Apr 2023

7. Brown, M.: The global micro-credential landscape. J. Learn. Dev. **8**(2), 228–254 (2021)
8. Wenger, E.: Learning in Landscapes of Practice. Routledge, London (2014)
9. Morimoto, Y., Nagata, T., Ogawa, K., Yamakawa, O.: e-Portfolio in Education. Minervashobo (2017)
10. Trentham, B.: Life storytelling, occupation, social participation and aging. Occup. Therapy Now **9**(5), 23–26 (2007)
11. Arima, S.: Design of Fermentational Reflection Model, pp. 1–199. Keio University Graduate School of Media Design (2021)
12. Trischler, J., Pervan, S., Scott, D.: The value of codesign. J. Serv. Res. **21**(1), 75–100 (2018)
13. Yonezawa, A. https://www.mext.go.jp/content/20201125-mxt_koutou01-1422495_04.pdf. Accessed 5 Apr 2023

On Extended Reality Objective Performance Metrics for Neurosurgical Training

Alessandro Iop[1(✉)], Olga Viberg[1], Adrian Elmi-Terander[3,4], Erik Edström[2,4], and Mario Romero[1]

[1] EECS, KTH Royal Institute of Technology, Stockholm, Sweden
{aiop,oviberg,marior}@kth.se
[2] Department of Clinical Neuroscience, Karolinska Institutet, Stockholm, Sweden
[3] Department of Surgical Sciences, Uppsala University, Uppsala, Sweden
[4] Capio Spine Center Stockholm, Löwenströmska Hospital, Stockholm, Sweden

Abstract. The adoption of Extended Reality (XR) technologies for supporting learning processes is an increasingly popular research topic for a wide variety of domains, including medical education. Currently, within this community, the metrics applied to quantify the potential impact these technologies have on procedural knowledge acquisition are inconsistent. This paper proposes a practical definition of standard metrics for the learning goals in the application of XR to surgical training. Their value in the context of previous research in neurosurgical training is also discussed. Objective metrics of performance include: spatial accuracy and precision, time-to-task completion, number of attempts. The objective definition of what the learner's aims are enables the creation of comparable XR systems that track progress during training. The first impact is to provide a community-wide metric of progress that allows for consistent measurements. Furthermore, a measurable target opens the possibility for automated performance assessments with constructive feedback.

Keywords: Extended Reality · Surgical Simulation · Neurosurgical Education · Procedural Knowledge · Performance Metrics

1 Introduction

Surgical education is lengthy. It takes medical students from textbooks in the classroom to performing surgeries on live patients. There are currently numerous opportunities for surgical *residents*, i.e. doctors in training, to acquire nominal knowledge on human anatomy and physiology by means of both analog and digital tools. Conversely, hands-on practice of operations tends to be limited prior to the learner stepping into a real operating room (OR). In the traditional educational path, gaining the know-how about a specific operation happens directly

Supported by InfraVis, Swedish Research Council grant 2021-00181.

O. Viberg et al. (Eds.): EC-TEL 2023, LNCS 14200, pp. 573–579, 2023.
https://doi.org/10.1007/978-3-031-42682-7_44

in front of a live patient: residents start by observing a senior surgeon performing the operation, then they operate on their own while being under supervision of an expert until they gain the independence to operate on their own. Before entering the OR, opportunities for honing manual dexterity and hand-eye coordination are rare and expensive. Residents might be able to gain access to animal and/or human cadavers in a handful of occasions and with limited possibilities for repeated training sessions. In this context, what is lacking is the possibility for residents to quickly and independently assess their own performance after a surgical *simulation*, as well as compare it with the performance of experts or their own past performance, with the aim of analyzing their own learning curve over time. In recent years, researchers in medicine and engineering have come together to address this lack of resources for surgical practice by proposing numerous novel tools and environments targeting residents as individual learners who wish to hone their skills in a risk-free, controlled and accessible environment.

Table 1. Systematic review of metrics used in XR cranial neurosurgical training classified by educational setting. Based on [11].

Metric type	*Learning*	*Practicing*	*Skill assessment*	Total (freq.)
Space-time	[10]	[2,6,12,22,27]	[1,3,8,16,18,19,24,25]	14 (54%)
Force	[10]	[6,22]	[1,3,5,8,18,19,24,26]	11 (42%)
Outcome	[4,10,14]	[6,7,22,27]	[1,3,5,8,16,19,21,24–26]	17 (65%)
Qualitative	[13,17,20]	[2,15,23]	[16,26]	8 (31%)

The adoption of anatomically realistic *phantom* models, as well as of XR technologies, such as augmented and virtual reality, are two of the most prolific avenues of research from this perspective [9]. By combining virtual with real imagery, and integrating it with accurate replicas of human anatomy, numerous possibilities for interactive, realistic and adaptable simulation scenarios are enabled. One of the greatest benefits of employing these accessible and easy-to-develop emerging technologies is arguably the versatility of the resulting learning environments to fit different types of surgical practices. Furthermore, through sensors and automatic data collection, assessing simulation performance improvements over time is greatly facilitated by modern applications. A consequence of this research windfall is the need for common learning-measuring criteria. To enable a full exploration of the versatility, scalability and accessibility of newly developed XR tools for surgical education, there needs to be a common set of metrics that quantify simulation performance as a measure of *procedural knowledge* acquisition and transfer. With widespread adoption of standard performance metrics by the research community, it may be possible to compare learning achievements both across different technologies and between different actors, potentially distantly located and with varying degrees of expertise. In the present paper, we propose a set of metrics for the assessment of outcomes in XR simulations of surgical operations, specifically in the field of cranial neurosurgery. From this perspective, this narrower field of research comes with a partially different set of challenges when compared to, for instance, spinal neurosurgery, and, as we have previously shown, has so far been relatively uncharted territory for educational XR technologies [11]. Nevertheless, our proposed set of metrics can be applied to other types of surgery where procedural knowledge acquisition and transfer involves precise and efficient hand-eye coordination and manual dexterity.

2 Survey of the Domain of Practice

In a recent systematic review, we surveyed the adoption of XR technologies, with varying degrees of augmentation, in cranial neurosurgical education [11]. There, we defined education as a combination of learning, practicing and skill assessment, with the goal of acquiring the necessary knowledge to successfully perform a surgical procedure. Table 1 highlights the variability in the metrics considered among the 26 studies that measured user performance. Studies are grouped by education type according to the definition above, while performance metrics are arbitrarily categorized based on complexity, degree of aggregation and collection method (automatic vs. non-automatic) into the following:

- **Space-time** metrics include time, position and orientation measures in the surgical performance, i.e. kinematic measures that can be related to both the surgical simulation as a whole or only part of it. Examples are time to completion, instrument position, entry point location.
- **Force** metrics include measures of forces applied by test subjects onto the instrument or onto the apparatus being used as a proxy for the patient (e.g. a phantom). Examples are bandwidth, ratio and sum of the forces applied.
- **Outcome** metrics include frequencies and patterns of accuracy, errors, precision and consistency in the simulation. Metrics derived from comparisons with the intended outcome or an existing benchmark are also included. Examples are number of attempts, frequency of complications and success rate.
- **Qualitative** metrics include non-automatic evaluations made by experimenters or experts to evaluate surgical simulation performance, according to either standard or arbitrary criteria. Examples are grades based on scales, answers to questions and scores given to operative dictation.

As shown in Table 1, despite a broad arbitrary categorization of performance metrics considered in the studies, there is no clear consensus on a common type of metric. There appears to be notable variance in the frequency distribution of the single metric categories considered here. The outcome category, while being the most frequent (65%), still falls short of being labeled as "widely adopted". This is surprising, considering that simple measures of success, accuracy and precision fall into this category. Possible reasons may be the nature and scale of the research questions investigated, as well as the alternative adoption of more qualitative methods for assessing performance, i.e. the fourth category of metrics. In other words, not all the studies present data related to, for instance, time to completion or distance to the target, because an approximate estimate of outcome was performed by experts. This qualitative category, on the other hand, is the least representative among the 26 studies (31%). It involves non-automatic assessment from senior surgeons grading through validated forms, ensuring systematic scoring. Finally, quantity and variability of metrics also noticeably vary between different types of education under scrutiny. In particular, while only a handful of distinct "learning" studies employ performance metrics at all (n=7), the "skill assessment" studies present considerably richer data (n=12). In the latter case, more than one category of metric is often considered simultaneously.

3 PARENT Metrics for Objective Assessment

As previously discussed, one of the many benefits of adopting XR technologies in surgical education is their versatility and scalability in different settings. By enabling asynchronous, distributed, and independent procedural knowledge acquisition and transfer, the learning opportunities for a resident surgeon increase compared to traditional education. Given the traditional co-located, synchronous learning in this field, portable and relatively inexpensive XR technologies can thus complement training through automatically assessed performance metrics. Such metrics need not be limited to low-dimension measures of e.g. kinematics and forces; "advanced" computed metrics can also be considered, such that multiple "simple" ones can be aggregated into meaningful indexes. Furthermore, the absence of a teacher during this mediated learning experience entails that subjective evaluations of surgical performance are not scalable in space and time. That is, the need for an expert surgeon assessing and grading simulation performance is unwarranted by the ability for residents to practice "anytime, anywhere".

In order to propose a set of metrics that can reach consensus across multiple domains of expertise, their usefulness should be balanced with their scalability. While metrics that suit a specific surgical operation are effective in providing the necessary data to inform reliable evaluations, this approach is very sensitive to small variations in the learning scenario. This means that, for instance, the total volume of tumor removed may be relevant in tumor resection tasks, but not applicable at all in ventriculostomy tasks. On the other hand, metrics that are too abstract for the scenario may fall short of being informative enough for a learner aiming at assessing their own performance by comparing it to the intended one (e.g. as performed by experts) or to their past performances. A simple grade on an arbitrary and opaque A–F scale is an example: the grade does not tell why the performance was graded as such or what the student may have done correctly or not. The following proposed metrics should therefore act as a concrete origin for the automatic collection and aggregation of relevant performance indicators. If kept agnostic to the specific surgical procedure, they can be robust enough to enable cross-domain comparisons, and sufficient for a preliminary real-time assessment.

- **P***recision of distances and angles*: how close the measured values are to each other, i.e. their variability across multiple simulation trials. This can be inferred by calculating Euclidean and angular distances between surgical instruments at equivalent time frames in two or more trials.
- **A***ccuracy of distances and angles*: how close the measured values are to the intended (target) value, i.e. their correctness for each simulation trial, inferred by comparing against benchmark baselines.
- **R***ate of success*: ratio between the number of successful simulation trials and total number of trials. It is complementary to the rate of error, the ratio between the number of unsuccessful trials and total number of trials. A clear definition of a threshold between success and error is warranted here.
- **E***rrors of measurement*: robustness of the hardware in measuring performance indicators, expressed as the minimal detectable difference between two distinct observations over the range of values across all observations.
- **N***umber of attempts*: count of simulation trials. This metric needs a clear definition distinguishing a re-start from a continuation of a previous attempt.
- **T***ime to completion*: total time elapsed between the start and the end of a single simulation trial. A clear definition for procedure start and end, either as a location in space and/or a moment in time, is warranted here.

4 Conclusions and Future Work

Growing research on XR technologies in neurosurgical training calls for consensus one learning metrics. By observing current trends in the field and carefully balancing scalability and efficacy, we have proposed six concrete metrics for objective quantification of procedural knowledge acquisition and transfer. Consensus over them and, ultimately, their adoption throughout the broader field of surgical education will potentially enable more impactful research results that are comparable across different application domains. In future research, these metrics may afford rigorous and quantitative comparison between participant populations, simulated procedures, and XR tools. For validation, we plan to disseminate them in future workshops and surveying the research community.

References

1. Alotaibi, F.E., et al.: Assessing bimanual performance in brain tumor resection with NeuroTouch, a virtual reality simulator. Neurosurgery **11**, 89–98 (2015)
2. Ansaripour, A., et al.: P56 virtual reality simulation in neurosurgical training: a single blinded randomised controlled trial & review of all available training models. J. Neurol. Neurosurg. Psychiatry **90**(3), e38 (2019)
3. Azarnoush, H., et al.: Neurosurgical virtual reality simulation metrics to assess psychomotor skills during brain tumor resection. Int. J. Comput. Assist. Radiol. Surg. 603–618 (2015)
4. Azimi, E., Molina, C., Chang, A., Huang, J., Huang, C.-M., Kazanzides, P.: Interactive training and operation ecosystem for surgical tasks in mixed reality. In: Stoyanov, D., et al. (eds.) CARE/CLIP/OR 2.0/ISIC -2018. LNCS, vol. 11041, pp. 20–29. Springer, Cham (2018). https://doi.org/10.1007/978-3-030-01201-4_3

5. Bugdadi, A., et al.: Automaticity of force application during simulated brain tumor resection. J. Surg. Ed. 104–115 (2018)
6. Bugdadi, A., et al.: Is virtual reality surgical performance influenced by force feedback device utilized? J. Surg. Ed. 262–273 (2019)
7. Cutolo, F., et al.: A new head-mounted display-based AR system in neurosurg. ONC.: a study on phantom. Comput. Assist. Surg. 39–53 (2017)
8. Gelinas-Phaneuf, N., et al.: Assessing performance in brain tumor resection using a novel virtual reality simulator. Int. J. Comput. Assist. Radiol. Surg. 1–9 (2014)
9. Herur-Raman, A., et al.: Next-generation simulation-integrating extended reality technology into medical education. Front. Virtual Real. 115 (2021)
10. Holloway, T., et al.: Operator experience determines performance in a simulated computer-based brain tumor resection task. Int. J. Comput. Assist. Radiol. Surg. 1853–1862 (2015)
11. Iop, A., et al.: Extended reality in neurosurgical education: a systematic review. Sensors **22**(16), 6067 (2022)
12. Ledwos, N., et al.: Assessment of learning curves on a simulated neurosurgical task using metrics selected by AI. J. Neurosurg. 1–12 (2022)
13. Lin, W., Zhu, Z., He, B., Liu, Y., Hong, W., Liao, Z.: A novel virtual reality simulation training system with haptic feedback for improving lateral ventricle puncture skill. Virtual Real. 1–13 (2021)
14. Patel, A., et al.: Neurosurgical tactile discrimination training with haptic-based virtual reality simulation. Neurol. Res. **36**(12), 1035–1039 (2014)
15. Perin, A., et al.: The "stars-cascade" study: VR simulation as a new training approach in vascular neurosurgery. World Neurosurg. **154**, e130–e146 (2021)
16. Roitberg, B.Z., et al.: Evaluation of sensory and motor skills in neurosurgery applicants using a virtual reality neurosurgical simulator: the sensory-motor quotient. J. Surg. Educ. **72**(6), 1165–1171 (2015)
17. Ros, M., et al.: Applying an immersive tutorial in virtual reality to learning a new technique. Neuro-Chirurgie, 212–218 (2020)
18. Sawaya, R., et al.: Virtual reality tumor resection: the force pyramid approach. Oper. Neurosurg. **14**(6), 686–696 (2018)
19. Sawaya, R., et al.: Development of a performance model for virtual reality tumor resections. J. Neurosurg. 192–200 (2019)
20. Schirmer, C.M., et al.: Virtual reality-based simulation training for ventriculostomy: an evidence-based approach. Neurosurgery, 66–73 (2013)
21. Shakur, S.F., et al.: Usefulness of a VR percutaneous trigeminal rhizotomy simulator in neurosurgical training. Op. Neurosurg. 420–425 (2015)
22. Teodoro-Vite, S., et al.: A high-fidelity hybrid virtual reality simulator of aneurysm clipping repair with brain sylvian fissure exploration for vascular neurosurgery training. Simul. Healthc. 285–294 (2021)
23. Thawani, J., et al.: Resident simulation training in endoscopic endonasal surgery utilizing haptic feedback technology. J. Clin. Neurosci. 112–116 (2016)
24. Winkler-Schwartz, A., et al.: Bimanual psychomotor performance in neurosurgical resident applicants assessed using NeuroTouch, a virtual reality simulator. J. Surg. Educ. 942–953 (2016)
25. Winkler-Schwartz, A., et al.: Machine learning identification of surgical and operative factors associated with surgical expertise in virtual reality simulation. JAMA Netw. Open (2019)
26. Winkler-Schwartz, A., et al.: A comparison of visual rating scales and simulated virtual reality metrics in neurosurgical training: a generalizability theory study. World Neurosurg. **127**, e230–e235 (2019)

27. Yudkowsky, R., et al.: Practice on an augmented reality/haptic simulator and library of virtual brains improves residents' ability to perform a ventriculostomy. Simul. Healthc. **8**(1), 25–31 (2013)

Multimodal Analytics for Collaborative Teacher Reflection of Human-AI Hybrid Teaching: Design Opportunities and Constraints

Shamya Karumbaiah[1(✉)], Pinyang Liu[2], Alisa Maksimova[3], Lea De Vylder[2], Nikol Rummel[3], and Vincent Aleven[2]

[1] University of Wisconsin-Madison, Madison, USA
shamya.karumbaiah@wisc.edu
[2] Carnegie Mellon University, Pittsburgh, USA
{pinyangl,ldevylde}@andrew.cmu.edu, aleven@cs.cmu.edu
[3] Ruhr-Universität Bochum, Bochum, Germany
alisa.maksimova@cais-research.de, nikol.rummel@rub.de

Abstract. Past research shows that teachers benefit immensely from reflecting on their classroom practices. At the same time, adaptive and artificially intelligent (AI) tutors are shown to be highly effective for students, especially when teachers are involved in supporting students' learning. Yet, there is little research on how to support teachers to reflect on their practices around AI tutors. We posit that analytics built on multimodal data from the classroom (e.g., teacher position, student-AI interaction) would be beneficial in providing effective scaffolding and evidence for teachers' collaborative reflection on human-AI hybrid teaching. To better understand the design opportunities and constraints of a future tool for teacher reflection, we conducted storyboarding sessions with seven in-service teachers. Our analysis revealed that certain modalities (e.g., position v. video) might be more beneficial and less constrained than others in identifying reflection-worthy moments and trends. We discuss teachers' needs for reflection in classrooms with AI tutors and their boundaries in using multimodal analytics.

Keywords: Teachers · Multimodal Analytics · Storyboards · Reflection · Human-AI Partnerships · Collaboration

1 Introduction

Teacher reflections on their classroom practices are shown to be effective for teachers' beliefs, practices, and reflection, and in turn, their students' learning [1]. *Reflections* are a form of deliberative thinking (c.f. [2]) that teachers do as part of either their everyday practice (reflection-in-action) or continuous professional development (reflection-on-action), with an aim to improve their classroom practices. While past empirical research on reflection highlights its benefits to teacher practices and student learning, there is a lack of consensus on how to support teachers effectively during their reflection, especially leveraging any benefits technology may have to offer [1]. Supporting effective teacher

O. Viberg et al. (Eds.): EC-TEL 2023, LNCS 14200, pp. 580–585, 2023.
https://doi.org/10.1007/978-3-031-42682-7_45

reflection involves providing scaffolds and evidence to induce perplexity about their practices and support problem-solving [4]. Currently, deriving evidence from classroom teaching predominantly relies on videos, with technology supporting manual video annotation or capturing of reflection-worthy snippets during class [5]. Videos afford teachers the opportunity to look back on their practice, without relying on their memory during the often fast-paced nature of classroom orchestration. However, past research has also suggested that browsing through hours of video, potentially multiple times, to identify relevant evidence tends to be time-consuming [6], which may make it hard for in-service teachers due to their limited time.

In classrooms with adaptive and artificially intelligent (AI) tutors, teachers' classroom practices such as conceptual guidance, socio-emotional support, and monitoring are related to improved student learning and engagement with the AI tutor [3]. Yet, there is little research on how to support teachers to reflect on *human-AI hybrid teaching*, wherein the instructional role is shared between teachers and AI [7]. While current teacher-facing tools in AI tutors mostly include analytics on students [3], such tools could also be developed for teacher reflections, especially if they could augment teachers' intelligence about their own practices. Hence, we aim to build a reflection tool that will extract and show trends in students' learning and teachers' practices in classrooms with AI tutors and illustrate them with strategically selected examples from class sessions. However, it is underexplored how best to design such a tool.

We adopt two primary design stances: multimodality and collaboration. It is shown that multimodal access to the learning situations helps to enable teachers' reflection [8]. Accordingly, recent research in non-AI classrooms has explored how multimodal analytics from classroom data could help identify effective scaffolds for teacher reflection, what we call *reflection-worthy* moments and trends. This includes analytics built on teacher video, position, and interaction. Similarly, opportunities to collaborate with peers to co-construct better solutions are considered effective in teacher learning [9]. A review by Clarke and colleagues [1] reported that an overwhelming majority of teacher reflections are structured to be collaborative.

While multimodal analytics can open new possibilities, multimodal sensing could raise stakeholder concerns over the issues of privacy and the possibility of creating surveillance systems monitoring students' and teachers' behavior [10]. Therefore, it is critical to examine teachers' views on constraints on the ways to collect and use multimodal data. Moreover, data ownership and the ethical use of data need to be established with stakeholders to avoid the potential misuse of student and teacher data [11]. Similarly, our design stance on collaboration may raise additional social constraints for teachers while sharing their personal recordings with a colleague (e.g., awkwardness in viewing themselves on screen). While evidence from classrooms that don't match teachers' beliefs about themselves or their students may trigger effective moments of reflection with a colleague, it may need a supportive culture [12].

Thus, the two research questions that guide our analysis are: 1) *What are teachers' needs for reflecting on their practices in classrooms with AI tutors?* 2) *What are their boundaries and perceptions in using multimodal analytics for collaborative reflection of human-AI hybrid teaching?*

2 Methods

To understand teachers' needs, preferences, and boundaries for multimodal collaborative reflection of human-AI hybrid teaching, we designed a speed dating study with storyboards. The speed dating method allows us to validate teachers' needs, discover new ideas through participants' observations and suggestions, test and understand the boundaries of the tool through riskier solutions, and receive direct feedback from the primary user group to identify possible design directions.

We designed twelve storyboards to document cohesive storylines with different class scenarios with AI tutors and corresponding teacher interactions with the reflection tool. Specifically, each storyboard consists of three panels with the following outline: a description of the problem or class scenario, how a (future) tool reacts to the scenario (i.e., what data it collects and/or how it collects data), and what the tool presents to the user. We identified topics for storyboards that illustrate our key design stances: multimodality and collaboration (see Sect. 1). The topics correspond to the content of the reflection (e.g., teaching practice, student learning), multimodality (e.g., sensors, privacy), collaboration (e.g., with whom to reflect, data sharing), and reflection method (e.g., when to reflect, data to display, platform).

Seven teachers participated in the speed dating study. They were all math teachers from middle and high schools in the United States (6) and Croatia (1), with teaching experience ranging from 5 to 21 years. They taught a range of math topics such as algebra, statistics, geometry, and calculus. Six of them use some form of educational technology in their everyday teaching. Each session lasted for around 60 min. In total, we extracted 189 such quotes from the seven sessions. After grouping all the quotes by the topics, we formed 3 top-level and 14 mid-level clusters.

3 Results

3.1 Aligning Multimodality with Reflection Needs

Our analysis reveals teacher needs and priorities for reflection that can inform the modalities that could maximize the benefits for teachers (see discussion in Sect. 4).

Teachers Need Data on Their own Classroom Practices to Reflect on How Effective They Are. Three teachers wanted to know whether their interventions and any new activity they try in the classroom is effective for student learning. One teacher expressed an interest in seeing how their help-giving supports students' learning with the AI tutor. While explaining struggles with their current approach, they said: "Usually, they'll ask me a question, and I'll answer it. And I'll come back in a few minutes to see [if] they are answering more questions. Are they still stuck in the same spot? Are they still making the same mistake? Then maybe my help wasn't too effective, and maybe I've got to come up with another way to explain that problem."

Teachers Need Data That Would Help Them Reflect on Their Students' Needs For Support. Teachers said that they needed data to reflect on how students are doing: do several people in the class struggle with something that should be explained in more detail? Three teachers suggested that other content-related data, such as common misconceptions among their students, would be helpful in reflecting on the improvements they need to make. Similarly, they wanted to know which students they were helping the most and whether they were ignoring anyone who may need them.

Data About Student *Well-Being and Stress* Could be Helpful if it Were Accurate and the Causes Were Reliably Interpreted. The majority of the teachers (4 out of 7) were interested in reflecting on their students' well-being. While data-driven evidence of student well-being was appreciated by teachers, one teacher raised concerns about the accuracy of inferring students' mental states and the factors associated with them.

3.2 Boundaries of Multimodal Data Collection and Sharing

Besides the financial cost, there could be logistical (e.g., device setup and maintenance) and social (e.g., awkwardness in hearing one's own voice, the feeling of surveillance, and data sharing) constraints in introducing multimodal sensors to classrooms.

Cameras are Perceived as too Invasive and Untrustworthy. The majority of the teachers (5 out of 7) emphasized that cameras are not allowed in their classrooms. The two common reasons cited were privacy and trust. As one teacher explained, "You feel you don't want your kids to be filmed during school, and as a teacher, I feel like I don't want to be filmed during school. I'd like to have some bigger level of trust." Still, two teachers expressed their inclination to have their classes videotaped, especially in their bigger classrooms. However, the goal was not to reflect on their classroom practices. Rather, they were interested in cameras as a surveillance tool to observe students who tended to be off-task and "mischief." This shows that teachers may have contradictory notions of privacy and invasiveness.

Collecting Data on Teacher Positions, Student-AI Interaction, and Demographic is Acceptable. As an alternative to cameras, teachers (5 out of 7) suggested that the AI tutor log data would be useful and "non-invasive," to monitor student learning and progress. Log data was also considered helpful in providing evidence for further investigations on the concept students may be struggling with. To reflect on their own practices, collecting data on their position was perceived as non-invasive and helpful. One teacher said, "I think this [teacher position data] is very helpful - like teachers tend to not emphasize or tend to support a kind of students than the other." Relatedly, all teachers objected to having any sensor that may distract the class. Half the teachers were comfortable sharing their students' demographic information, as long as it was one-time and not too time-consuming.

Physiological Data is Seen as a Way to Detect what they Cannot Otherwise Monitor, but There are Concerns About their Accuracy and Lack of Context. Having multimodal data, potentially including physiological data, meant for teachers that they can reflect on students' learning and mental states that are not accessible in other ways. One teacher noted how younger students sometimes are not very good at expressing their feelings. However, teachers were concerned that the accuracy of the physiological data collected may be questionable and that "[they] could be very easily skewed based on something that happened in a previous period that you're not even aware of."

Teachers Want to be Able to Decide Who to Share their Data with, and Some are Wary of their Colleagues' Potential Misuse and Misinterpretation of Them. Four teachers objected to sharing their class data with their school administrators. One of them said, "The supervisor is a person that doesn't know what's going on, and then still tries to micromanage things, and that will make the teacher want to leave." In contrast, teachers were relatively more comfortable in sharing their data with a colleague. Opinions on this split. Three teachers suggested that it could provide great opportunities to reflect together on their teaching practices and learn from each other. Yet, the other three teachers expressed concerns about sharing class data as they feel uneasy about the situation of comparing themselves and their class to the others. Nevertheless, one thing that all the teachers agreed on, is to have control over their own class data. If someone wants access to their data, they should ask for permission first.

3.3 Opportunities and Constraints in Multimodal Collaborative Reflection

In addition to understanding teacher needs for reflection and potential boundaries in data collection and sharing, our analysis revealed teachers' desires and constraints about how they would like to reflect with multimodal data and the role of collaboration.

Collaborative Reflections Are More Effective, but the Nature of Collaboration May Vary. The majority of teachers (4 out of 7) expressed interest in reflecting collaboratively with colleagues, recognizing its benefits in improving their classroom practices. One participant said, "You know it's good to have someone else look at it from a different perspective to help you with reflections." While some teachers shared a preference for paired reflection on specific problems, others were comfortable with discussing best practices more generally as a bigger group. Two participants, in particular, suggested doing reflection with teachers in the same subject or department. In contrast, another teacher stated that student differences might limit how useful data from another class could be, despite being the same grade and subject.

Effective Collaborative Reflection Needs a Positive Relationship. Teachers also expressed some constraints in making collaborative reflection work and highlighted how important it is to have a positive relationship with the collaborator. One teacher reasoned out the potential tension arising from viewing collaboration as competition. Only one teacher preferred doing reflections alone. They expressed feeling socially awkward when suggesting improvements to a teacher who may not be doing well.

4 Discussion

Several instances in our storyboarding sessions highlighted the "state of perplexity or doubt" and the need for "subsequent inquiry" that teachers express during reflection about their classroom practices. Such deliberative thinking separates the kind of support teachers need for reflection from what is available now in teacher-facing orchestration tools in AI tutors. Overall, all teachers expressed a strong interest in collecting classroom data to reflect on how effective their classroom practices are in general and how well they meet individual student needs. However, teachers varied (sometimes even contradicted one another) in their perceptions of how useful or constraining the different modes of data collection would be in supporting their reflection needs. The majority, if not all, teachers shared the opinion that cameras are too invasive. This finding raises serious concerns about the over-reliance on videos for teacher reflections. Our findings revealed a few alternatives for classrooms with AI tutors (e.g., position, interaction log, physiological data) that tend to be acceptable to teachers, some of which may also apply to traditional classrooms. Other ethical concerns around sensors collecting biometric data did not come up in the study as relevant for the teachers. However, it needs to be taken into account that these approaches are highly debated. Lastly, since the majority of the teachers in this study found collaboration to be effective in general and already a part of their everyday practice, our tool should foster collaborative. As per teachers' strong preference for data control, the tool needs to be designed to allow teachers to own and share their data with those they trust. While data-driven reasoning was appreciated by all teachers, they also realized that a few cases might be beyond an AI tool's capabilities (e.g., external factors that may be causing student stress). Past research on AI-based teacher tools has noted the benefit of human-AI synergy, wherein teachers make sense of a situation alerted by a tool using their rich contextual knowledge and gathering more information by talking to the students [6]. Hence, an open question for future design activities is how to design for effective AI-teacher complementarity in reflection tools.

References

1. Clarke, S., Gates, Z., Foster, M., et al.: Mapping the Design Space for Teacher Learning Through Reflection (2020). https://repository.isls.org//handle/1/6535
2. Dewey, J.: How We Think. Lexington, MA: D.C. Heath and Company (1910)
3. Holstein, K., McLaren, B.M., Aleven, V.: Student learning benefits of a mixed-reality teacher awareness tool in AI-enhanced classrooms. In: Penstein Rosé, C., et al. (eds.) AIED 2018. LNCS (LNAI), vol. 10947, pp. 154–168. Springer, Cham (2018). https://doi.org/10.1007/978-3-319-93843-1_12
4. Kori, K., Pedaste, M., Leijen, Ä., Mäeots, M.: Supporting reflection in technology-enhanced learning. Educ. Res. Rev. **11**, 45–55 (2014)
5. Fleck, R., Fitzpatrick, G.: Teachers' and tutors' social reflection around sensecam images. Int. J. Hum Comput Stud. **67**(12), 1024–1036 (2009)
6. Santagata, R., Bray, W.: Professional development processes that promote teacher change: the case of a video-based program focused on leveraging students' mathematical errors. Prof. Dev. Educ. **42**(4), 547–568 (2016)
7. Karumbaiah, S., et al.: A spatiotemporal analysis of teacher practices in supporting student learning and engagement in an AI-enabled classroom. In: Artificial Intelligence in Education, pp. 450–462 (2023). https://doi.org/10.1007/978-3-031-36272-9_37
8. Porayska-Pomsta, K.: AI as a methodology for supporting educational praxis and teacher metacognition. Int. J. Artif. Intell. Educ. **26**, 679–700 (2016)
9. Darling-Hammond, L., Richardson, N.: Teacher learning: What matters? Educational Leadership (2009)
10. Cukurova, M., Giannakos, M., Martinez-Maldonado, R.: The promise and challenges of multimodal learning analytics. Br. J. Edu. Technol. **51**(5), 1441–1449 (2020)
11. Ogan, A.: Reframing classroom sensing: promise and peril. Interactions **2**(6), 26–32 (2019)
12. Prilla, M., Blunk, O., Chounta, I.A.: How does collaborative reflection unfold in online communities? an analysis of two data set. Comput. Support. Coop. Work **29**, 697–741 (2020)

Computational Analysis of Audio Recordings of Piano Performance for Automatic Evaluation

Norihiro Kato[1], Eita Nakamura[2], Kyoko Mine[3], Orie Doeda[1], and Masanao Yamada[1](✉)

[1] National Institute of Technology, Kushiro College, Kushiro, Japan
ym@kushiro-ct.ac.jp
[2] Kyoto University, Kyoto, Japan
[3] Osaka Ohtani University, Tondabayashi, Japan

Abstract. We developed a computational evaluation method for piano performance with the goal of building a practice support system for beginners. We recorded students' performances as audio data and applied several recent methods for audio-to-MIDI transcription based on deep neural networks to extract the pitch, onset time, and offset time of musical notes. To determine the correctness of the performance, we aligned the extracted MIDI data with the musical score using a hidden Markov model (HMM). We compared the audio-to-MIDI transcription methods and optimized the weight on different types of performance errors to conform to teacher's assessment. Our experiments showed a strong correlation between the rate of performance errors obtained from the alignment and the evaluation by a teacher who listened to the performance. The results that indicate performance errors and tempo stability can be used in a practice support system that provides feedback to learners.

Keywords: Computational performance evaluation · Hidden Markov model · Audio-to-MIDI transcription

1 Introduction

Effective performance evaluation plays a crucial role in music education, as it enables learners to receive valuable feedback for improving their skills [7]. However, traditional methods often fall short in providing timely and personalized feedback, particularly in large classrooms or for remote learning situations. In recent years, there has been a growing interest in applying technology to evaluate the performance of musical instruments [2,7]. Research efforts have explored various approaches, aiming to support learners in their musical journey. One of these methods includes visualization of performances [8], which has seen advancements in incorporating augmented reality technology [1,4].

This work was supported by JSPS KAKENHI Grant Numbers 21K02846, 21K12187, 22H03661.

O. Viberg et al. (Eds.): EC-TEL 2023, LNCS 14200, pp. 586–592, 2023.
https://doi.org/10.1007/978-3-031-42682-7_46

Among the diverse range of musical instruments, the piano has many performers at varying skill levels, which results in differing performance evaluation criteria across studies—from basic elements such as pitch and rhythm in beginners, to musical expression in advanced players. In previous research [12], an overall evaluation was performed for each full piece performed by beginners using acoustic data and support vector regression (SVR) models. Despite these advancements in performance evaluation techniques, challenges still remain in leveraging technology for effective formative assessment. Formative assessment, an evaluation of learning achievement during the instructional process, allows for adjustments in learning activities and teaching methods. As each individual has different performance aspects that need to be improved, it can be difficult for teachers to provide sufficient advice to every student in a class.

In response to these challenges, our study aims to enhance formative assessment in piano performance education for beginners by contrasting score data with transcriptions of audio recordings in MIDI (Musical Instrument Digital Interface) format. Our focus is on individual elements of performance such as wrong touch, re-playing, and tempo consistency for personalized evaluation. With these considerations in mind, our central research question is: How closely can computationally analyzed performance errors align with teachers' evaluations? This investigation could pave the way for a feedback system that utilizes computationally analyzed errors for formative assessment.

2 Related Work

Active research on performance evaluation of piano has explored various methods to provide feedback to learners within the music education context [5]. Fukuda et al. [3] developed a system that detects mistakes in the user's performance and simplifies challenging sections of a musical score based on the user's skill level. Wang et al. [11] proposed two audio-based piano performance evaluation systems for beginners using deep neural networks (DNN). DNN-based piano performance evaluations use end-to-end processing, eliminating the need for sheet music. However, for formative evaluation, which requires assessing each note, musical note information needs to be transformed from the audio signal to compare with sheet music.

Extracting musical note information from audio performance data is a challenging problem in the area of music information retrieval, especially for polyphonic music such as piano music. Recently, accurate methods have been realized using machine learning techniques, including PovNet [10] based on a dual DNN architecture for pitch estimation and onset and velocity (intensity) estimation, and the high-resolution MIDI transcription (HighReso) method [6] based on convolutional-recurrent neural network. While these MIDI transcription methods are usually evaluated on relatively "clean" piano recording data, their performance for low-quality recordings common in practical situations of music education has not been investigated well in the literature. In this study, we use both two methods as a part of the automatic evaluation method and compare the results.

3 Method

The data we used in this study comes from the final exam of group piano lessons conducted in the Early Childhood Education major at a certain university's Faculty of Education. In the exam, the students perform one piece each from Beyer Op. 101 and children's songs, and one instructor evaluated their performances. The criteria for this exam were (a) wrong touch and re-playing, (b) rhythm, and (c) dynamics on a scale from A to C (A+, A, A–, B+, B, B–, C).

The performances in the exam were recorded as audio data using an iPad, which was placed in a concert hall with a total area of 1,741 square meters and 217 seats, positioned 3.23 m in front of the grand piano and at a height of 0.65 m. To convert the audio data into MIDI, we employed two recent methods for MIDI transcription, PovNet [10] and HighReso [6].

After the transcription, we prepared the MIDI data of the sheet music manually, and an HMM was employed to align the MIDI data from both the performance and the sheet music. Benefitting from the HMM's ability to discern correctly and incorrectly played notes [9], we calculated their proportions relative to the total number of played notes. Since the wrong touches and re-playing of evaluation criterion (a) corresponds to pitch errors and extra notes, respectively, we define the evaluation score E as

$$E = w_p E_p + (1 - w_p) E_e, \tag{1}$$

where E_p denotes the pitch error rate, E_e the extra note rate, and w_p the weight for pitch errors. We measured the correspondence between the teacher's evaluation and the evaluation score E using the Spearman's rank correlation coefficients while varying the weight w_p.

For the variation in rhythm, we calculated the relative speed of each note in the performance locally by dividing the aligned sheet music's Inter-Onset Interval (IOI), by the performance IOI. IOI is the time interval between the onsets of consecutive musical notes. We took the median of this local tempo list as the reference tempo for the performance, and used the root mean square of the relative errors between the local tempo and the reference tempo as an indicator of playing speed consistency. Extra notes that did not have corresponding sheet music notes were excluded from this calculation.

4 Results and Discussion

A total of 29 students from three classes took the exam. The results of comparison between the transcription methods, PovNet and HighReso, are shown in Fig. 1. The results for PovNet consistently showed a high correlation with teacher evaluations, with the correlation coefficient reaching its maximum value of 0.86 when $w_p = 0.58$. For HighReso, the maximum value was 0.77 when $w_p = 0.905$. In the following discussions, PovNet with $w_p = 0.58$ is used.

The relationship between the evaluation score E and the teacher evaluations is shown in Fig. 2. Overall, performances with a lower score have higher teacher

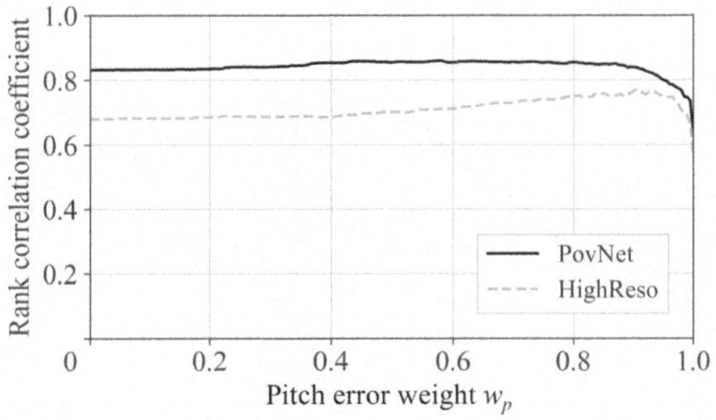

Fig. 1. Comparison of audio-to-MIDI transcription methods

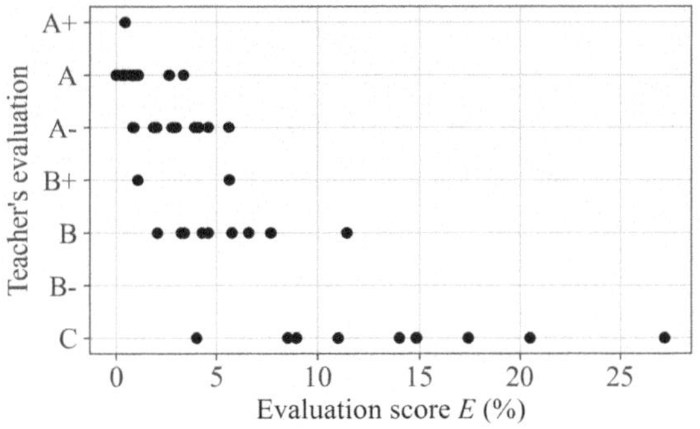

Fig. 2. Relationship between incorrect notes and teacher's evaluation

evaluations, and vice versa. Below, we discuss some of the performances that deviate from this trend.

The performance at the right end of the B evaluation (Bayer Op.101, No.78) has a higher evaluation than some of C-graded performances, despite having more performance errors indicated by the score E. To examine the cause, Fig. 3 displays the progression of the performance compared to the sheet music. Consecutive extra notes indicate re-plays, and blue plus signs scattered among black dots are due to pitch detection errors by PovNet. Extra notes that cannot be associated with a position in the sheet music are plotted at the zero point of score time. In the figure, a significant number of extra notes are detected because of re-playing at approximately 23 s of score time. It is likely that the teacher considered this as a single mistake, and despite the large number of detected errors, still awarded a B evaluation.

The rightmost data point in the C evaluation of Fig. 2, representing the children's song 'Crickets', is another intriguing case. Although the performance errors are comparable to the average of B-rated performances, it falls into the C

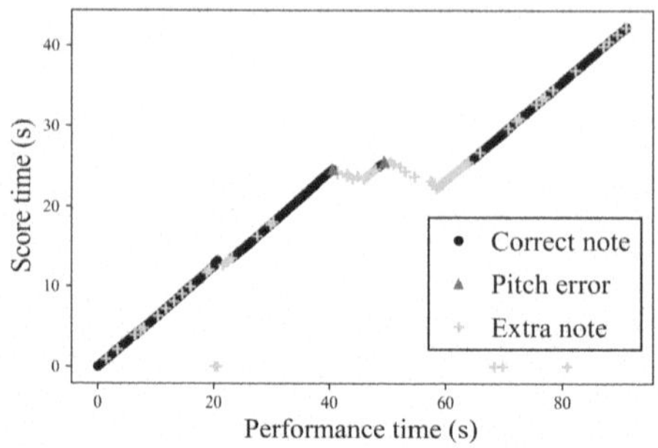

Fig. 3. Performance progression of Bayer Op.101, No.78

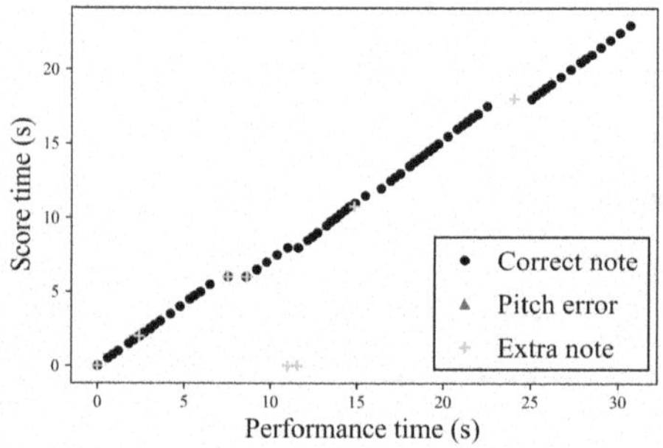

Fig. 4. Performance progression of “Crickets”

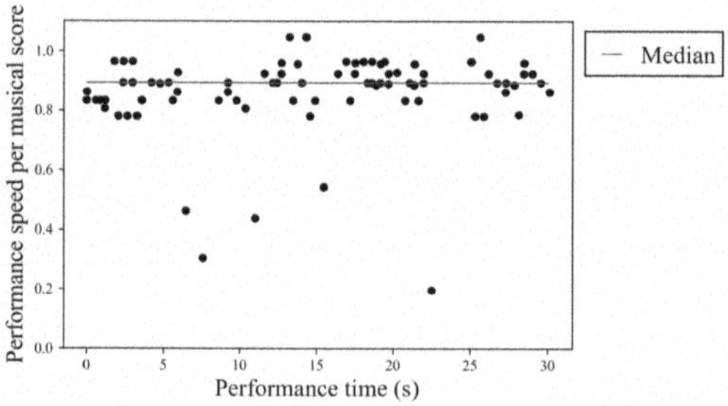

Fig. 5. Tempo deviation of “Crickets”

rating category. Figure 4 illustrates the progression of this performance, which contains hardly any extra notes, but reveals gaps starting at approximately the 7-s and 23-s in the performance time. To illustrate this brief pause clearly, Fig. 5 shows the rhythmic variability calculated by the method described in the previous section, for the same performance. The values below 1 indicating a slower performance than the sheet music. From this figure, it is easy to discern the points where the hands have momentarily stopped.

5 Conclusion

In this research, we explored a novel approach to piano performance evaluation by utilizing advanced machine learning methods, applying PovNet and HighReso for audio-to-MIDI transcription in real-world classroom settings. We found that PovNet demonstrated superior performance and a significant correlation with teacher evaluations. We also observed deviations through the data analysis, and were able to identify and visualize contributing factors to these deviations, such as re-plays and brief pauses. Our findings demonstrate the potential of machine learning in performance evaluation to provide personalized and timely feedback.

Future research directions include developing an interactive feedback system for music practice, aiding learners in error identification and correction. Additionally, conducting a multi-year longitudinal study can assess the long-term effects of technology-enhanced formative assessment on students' musical development, achievement, motivation, self-efficacy, and engagement.

References

1. Deja, J.A.: Piano learning and improvisation through adaptive visualisation and digital augmentation. In: Companion Proceedings of the 2022 Conference on Interactive Surfaces and Spaces, pp. 41–45 (2022)
2. Dorfman, J.: Theory and Practice of Technology-based Music Instruction. Oxford University Press, Oxford (2022)
3. Fukuda, T., Ikemiya, Y., Itoyama, K., Yoshii, K.: "A score-informed piano tutoring system with mistake detection and score simplification" within the music education contexts. In: Proceedings of the 12th Sound and Music Computing Conference (SMC), vol. 1, pp. 105–110 (2015)
4. Heyen, F., Ngo, Q.Q., Kurzhals, K., Sedlmair, M.: Data-driven visual reflection on music instrument practice. In: ACM CHI Conference on Human Factors in Computing Systems (2022)
5. Kim, H., Ramoneda, P., Miron, M., Serra, X.: An overview of automatic piano performance assessment within the music education contexts. Proc. Int. Soc. Music Inf. Retrieval **1**, 465–474 (2017)
6. Kong, Q., Li, B., Song, X., Wan, Y., Wang, Y.: High-resolution piano transcription with pedals by regressing onset and offset times. IEEE/ACM Trans. Audio Speech Lang. Process. **29**, 3707–3717 (2021)
7. Lerch, A., Arthur, C., Pati, A., Gururani, S.: An interdisciplinary review of music performance analysis. Trans. Int. Soc. Music Inf. Retrieval **3**(1), 221–245 (2021)
8. Lima, H.B., Santos, C.G.R.D., Meiguins, B.S.: A survey of music visualization techniques. ACM Comput. Surv. (CSUR) **57**(7), 1–29 (2022)
9. Nakamura, E., Yoshii, K., Katayose, H.: Performance error detection and post-processing for fast and accurate symbolic music alignment. IN: Proceedings of the International Society for Music Information Retrieval, pp. 347–353 (2017)
10. Shibata, K., Nakamura, E., Yoshi, K.: Non-local musical statistics as guides for audio-to-score piano transcription. Inf. Sci. **566**, 262–280 (2021)

11. Wang, W., Pan, J., Yi, H., Song, Z., Li, M.: Audio-based piano performance evaluation for beginners with convolutional neural network and attention mechanism. IEEE/ACM Trans. Audio Speech Lang. Process. **29**, 1119–1133 (2021)
12. Wu, C.W., Gururani, S., Pati, A., Vidwans, A.: Towards the objective assessment of music performances. In: International Conference on Music Perception and Cognition (ICMPC), pp. 99–103 (2016)

Barrier-Free Dissemination of Medical Knowledge: Challenges and Solutions for Individuals with Visual Impairments

Sarah Langer(✉), Andrea Balz, and Iris Nemec

University of Applied Sciences Technikum Wien, 1200 Vienna, Austria
Sarah.langer@technikum-wien.at

Abstract. Visual impairments affect 60% of adults, 8% of whom suffer from color vision deficiencies. Furthermore, contrast sensitivity decreases with age. Accordingly, teaching and training materials must be adapted to these needs. Thus, a web-moodle course with medical content developed internally was used. The aim was to check whether this course is suitable for people with reduced color contrast sensitivity or color vision deficiencies. Furthermore, the usability was tested. For this purpose, 44 participants answered out a questionnaire. This showed that the preferred learning formats were videos and pictures, with drawn pictures being preferred. For checking knowledge, memory cards and self-checks are the preferred choices. The laptop/PC (66%) clearly emerges as the increasingly preferred end device. The verification of color contrast was done through an open-source website. It can be seen that the color works well only in selected combinations. When reviewing possible difficulties related to color vision deficiencies, some problems came to light. For example, a link with a monochromaticity would not be recognized.

Keywords: Color vision deficiency · Color contrast sensitivity · Universal Design in Teaching

1 Introduction

It is hard to imagine a society without the use of digital media. Thus, a change is also evident in the field of education and training, such as at universities. As early as the 1990s, digitization was at the center of innovations in various areas of human life. This is also the case in medicine. Here, one of the most important fields is the training of competent medical professionals and the continuing education and training of those already trained [1].

In addition to the content, the preparation of the documents is also important. Worldwide, 2.2 billion people suffer from near or distance vision impairment [2]. To be able to work as a physician only a certain degree of vision loss is tolerated. To narrow this down, only the impairment of color vision deficiency and the decrease of color contrast sensitivity will be discussed in the following.

O. Viberg et al. (Eds.): EC-TEL 2023, LNCS 14200, pp. 593–598, 2023.
https://doi.org/10.1007/978-3-031-42682-7_47

Color vision deficiency is one of the most common diseases, preceded by red-green deficiency. In European Caucasians about 8% of men and 0.4% of women are affected. In Chinese and Japanese ethnicity between 4% and 6.5% of men are affected [3].

They are classified according to the type of cones affected. Trichromacy is the mildest and is divided into protanomaly (red cones are affected), deuteranomaly (green cones are affected), and tritanomaly, in which the blue cones are affected. Individuals with dichromacy have a reduced dimension of color vision. Dichromacy is further divided into protanopia (no functionality of the red cones), deuteranopia (no functionality of the green cones) and tritanopia (no functionality of the blue cones). In monochromacy, color discrimination is completely absent [4].

Another factor which often appears due to age is the decrease of contrast sensitivity. Thus, the reduction of the ability to distinguish and interpret color nuances [5]. For example, a study by Berninger [6] showed that the peripheral color sense in the protan and tritan axis have a statistically significant difference with increasing age. Crassini [7] showed similar results in contrast sensitivity in peripheral presentation of the stimuli. Here, it was also examined how age affects the observation of sharp edges. It was shown that the ability decreases with age as well.

Depending on these two common visual impairments, the media provided must be prepared accordingly. The baseline was a web Moodle course with medical content developed. The aim was to check whether this course is suitable and usable for people with reduced color contrast sensitivity or color vision deficiencies.

2 Methods

The course to be tested was developed internally within the e-learning platform Moodle (version 4.1). It contains both theoretical content and interactive parts to build up and expand knowledge about selected medical use cases. The course is divided into three levels of fidelity. Level 1 deals with theoretical knowledge. In this section, the participants are provided with various materials about the use case related topics ranging from anatomy to practical application. The used learning formats were videos, pictures, self-checks, pdf, hotspot images, drag and drop quizzes, flash cards and active books. In Level 2 – the interactive training section – the participants are able to train the workflow steps of different medical scenarios in a hospital. This involves both equipment organization (e.g. in an emergency crash cart) and decisions during patient treatment. The organization and details about the usage of specific medical equipment is presented in the form of an interactive book and the knowledge can be consolidated by performing an interactive test. In the last level a virtual environment provides immersive insight to parts of the selected use cases. Here, the participants can take a closer look at the previously presented equipment and workflow steps in a virtual environment. At the example of the emergency crash cart, the individual stores can be opened and more details about the devices can be obtained. In addition, a multiple-choice test, implemented directly in the virtual environment, allows for a quick knowledge check. This course was created in the context of a research project and is to be understood as a prototype. Special focus was on didactic concepts and supportive design of the content.

To test the usability of the course, two different questionnaires were performed. The first questionnaire was completed by 24 students. Beforehand, they completed the course during a one-week Learning, Teaching and Training Event. Another questionnaire was sent out three months later to students and professionals in medical engineering and to medical professionals. A total of 19 people completed this questionnaire. Before completing this questionnaire, the participants who were not part of the training week got an overview of the course and its features via video guide. The following questions were included in both questionnaires:

- Did you use an e-learning platform equal or similar to Moodle before?
- How do you rate the orientation in the course structure? (1 = very bad; 5 = very good)
- What type of images do you find more appealing and enlightening?
- What learning formats would you like to see in general?

The following questions were asked in only one questionnaire. The first questionnaire was addressed to the group that learned about the course via the video, the second questionnaire was addressed to the students group that worked through the course by their own. This questionnaire was filled out anonymously.

- I would take advantage of this course type. (yes/no)
- Do you prefer to read large texts in your PC or laptop, or do you prefer to read them using tablets or phones?

As next step the course was checked for accessibility regarding color vision deficiency and reduction of color contrast sensitivity. It was ensured that those colors did not appear on grey background or in combination. Furthermore, it was determined whether the graphics used were color-independent. In addition to the manual check, a color weakness simulator was used [8]. For this, screenshots of parts of the course were taken and the different color deficiencies were simulated.

The contrast analysis was performed using the open source program TPGi Color Contrast Analyser v3.2.1 (Clearwater, USA). The six different colors in use were compared with each other. It was considered whether the minimum contrast (4.5:1) was present when using text in normal size and with large font (18pt/24px) (3:1). Furthermore, whether an increased contrast was achieved with normal font size (7:1) and with large font size (4.5:1). Finally, it was tested whether the visual representation of user interface components and graphical objects had a contrast ratio of at least 3:1 for non-text [9].

Thus, the question arose whether the example course to be reviewed is suitable for people with the mentioned visual impairments. In other words, in which areas the future developers would have to focus their attention. Furthermore, the usability test should show whether the basic structure and the materials used in the course have found approval or where there is potential for improvement and change.

3 Results

The evaluation of the questionnaire shows that the use of PDFs was most desired with 24%, followed by videos (21%). The option for self-review was requested in the form of self-checks (15%), memory games (9%), and flash cards (11%). 14% of respondents preferred images to convey knowledge. 36% preferred pictures, 39% preferred drawings, and for 25% this was irrelevant. A wiki was found desirable by 6% of respondents. General orientation within the course was rated 4 out of 5 by almost half of the respondents. In the choice of the terminal device, laptop/PC emerged as the preferred choice with 66%, tablet with 24%, and mobile phone with 10%.

Table 1 shows the comparison of the specified colors in terms of their color contrast to each other. It shows that black has good contrast for all requirements except with dark blue. Grey is compatible with black, with dark blue at minimal contrast in normal-sized type, and graphic objects. Dark blue has good contrast with white and can be used with green and light blue except for increased contrast in normal-sized type. Grey can only be used in this combination with normal-sized type for the minimum contrast needed. Both green and white have sufficient contrast with black. White can also be combined with dark blue.

Table 1. Contrast analysis of the colors used in the course

	Black (#000000)	Grey (#aca8a8)	Dark blue (#253d87)	Light blue (#8ad0db)	Green (#86c547)	White (#ffffff)
Black	1:1	8.9:1	2.1:1	12.1:1	10.1:1	21:1
Grey	8.9:1	1:1	4.3:1	1.4:1	1.3:1	2.4:1
Dark blue	2.1:1	4.3:1	1:1	5.8:1	4.81:1	10.0:1
Light blue	12.1:1	1.4:1	5.8:1	1:1	1.2:1	1.7:1
Green	10.1:1	1.1:1	4.8:1	1.2:1	1:1	2.1:1
White	21:1	2.4:1	10.0:1	1.7:1	2.1:1	1:1

When analyzing which barriers are present when color vision deficiency is present, the following was found out. In the course it is possible to document the personal progress. To do this, click on a check mark next to the medium (Fig. 1b). Here it shows on the one hand that the grey color (not yet clicked) on the white background forms a bad contrast. On the other hand, the choice of the color (green) with confirmed success for persons with a green weakness could be difficult to recognize. On a positive note, in addition to the color showing success, a check mark also indicates it. This can also be seen when using the images, where the color indicates which path is positive or negative (Fig. 1a). In case of red or green color vision deficiency or even monochromaticity, the differentiation would not be possible. However, in this case an additional text description for each path is available. Furthermore, the selected display of links is not recognizable with a monochromaticity (Fig. 1c).

In the interactive training in the case of the selected medical scenario, the patient's condition is conveyed by means of a picture. Depending on the condition, the patient is shown with normal, blue or grey colored skin. This is not recognizable for persons with color vision impairment. In addition, the vital parameters like heart rate, blood pressure and oxygen saturation are shown. The Active Book of the ventilator was displayed with pictures. As these were shown using grey color on a white background, there is

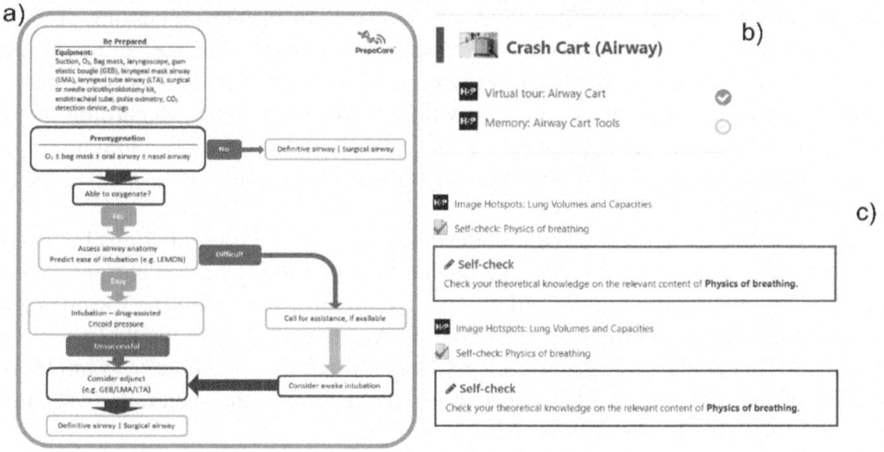

Fig. 1. Examples which would cause difficulty with color vision deficiency

insufficient contrast. When used in virtual reality, it can be seen that the resolution of the objects is blurred. In addition to the materials shown, a description of them has been added. In this one, a red font on a grey background was used. In the quiz which is included in the virtual environment, the marked answers are highlighted in dark blue while the font remains grey. If a question is answered incorrectly, it is highlighted in red and the font color does not change. In addition, it is recorded in writing whether the answer was correct or incorrect.

4 Discussion

The aim was to test the Moodle course with medical content developed internally. The usability study showed that the majority of the participants were satisfied with the orientation. Thus, it can be assumed that the structure in the three levels in combination with the provided materials was well chosen. The fact that drawings and photographs were the clearly preferred choice in the selection of images shows how important it is to represent them appropriately. In the e-learning course, the colors red and green were sometimes used to indicate a positive and negative path, respectively. However, this is not recognizable for persons with a red-green weakness. Here it can be accentuated positively that in addition to the color, there was always a text to describe the situation. However, this only applied to the classic traffic light colors. For someone with a blue weakness, distinguishing between different shades of blue is very difficult. Thus, it can be assumed that when the designers of the course used light and dark blue to distinguish content parts, the participant would not recognize this. This problem can also be found with linked text. People with monochromaticity would not be able to distinguish links from normal text. Here it would be helpful, for example, if the links were additionally underlined. For persons with a weakened color contrast sensitivity, the given colors seem to be contrasty enough only in a few used combinations. Therefore, only five combinations are possible to use without restrictions. Thus, the designer is either very limited in his choice or another color choice should be made in further processing. That the participants with a limited color contrast sensitivity can hardly recognize the progress button is to be assumed by the bright grey on a white background. This is an internal Moodle feature and can only be changed with administrator rights. Regarding the VR solution only little time has been spent on the graphics, since it is only a first prototype. Thus, the edges are heavily pixelated and might therefore be harder to identify by people at an advanced age.

In general, the analysis showed that the course is usable with limitations but should be adapted for optimal use. So that the developers of future courses can make them accessible from the outset, it would be, for example, a possibility to formulate the findings of this research project as a handbook. Another possibility would be to create a checklist. This could be customized for specific impairments. In order to implement this in a meaningful way, further courses and the activities and materials that can be integrated into Moodle would have to be considered.

References

1. ZAVA, Der Digitale Arzt - welche Rolle spielt Digitalisierung in der medizinischen Ausbildung? (2023). https://www.zavamed.com/de/digitalisierung-in-der-medizinischen-ausbildung.html
2. WHO-World Health Organization, Blindness and vision impairment (2022). https://www.who.int/en/news-room/fact-sheets/detail/blindness-and-visual-impairment
3. Birch, J.: Worldwide prevalence of red-green color deficiency. Opt. Soc. Am. **29**(3), 313–320 (2012)
4. Simunovic, M.P.: Colour vision deficiency. Nat. Eye **24**(5), 747–755 (2010). https://doi.org/10.1038/eye.2009.251
5. Christiaen, M.-P., Bohn, F.: Sehen - Erkennen – Orientieren (2020)
6. Berninger, T., Drobner, B., Hogg, C., Rudolph, G., Arden, G.B., Kampik, A.: Farbensehen in Abhängigkeit vom Alter: eine Normwertstudie. Klin Monbl Augenheilkd **215**(07), 37–42 (1999)
7. Crassini, B., Brown, B., Bowman, K.: Age-related changes in contrast sensitivity in central and peripheral retina. Perception **17**(3), 315–332 (1988). https://doi.org/10.1068/p170315
8. Colorblind Guide, Colorblind Simulator (2022). https://www.colorblindguide.com/color-blindness-simulator
9. TPGi, Color Contrast Analyser (CCA) (2023). https://www.tpgi.com/color-contrast-checker/

Process Mining on Students' Web Learning Traces: A Case Study with an Ethnographic Analysis

Roberto Nai[1(✉)], Emilio Sulis[1], Elisa Marengo[1], Manuela Vinai[2], and Sara Capecchi[1,3]

[1] Department of Computer Science, University of Turin, Turin, Italy
roberto.nai@unito.it
[2] Department of Philosophy and Education Sciences, University of Turin, Turin, Italy
[3] Laboratorio CINI Informatica e Scuola, Rome, Italy

Abstract. The study of learning processes can benefit from examining the digital traces left by students while browsing educational platforms. In this work, we propose an analysis of how process mining techniques can be combined with online educational technologies. In particular, we describe a process discovery experiment based on students' movements between the web pages' paragraphs of a tutorial specifically built for teaching the programming language Python. In addition, we explore the ethnographic and conceptual genealogy of a learning project focused on a programming tutorial. Observations of the digital traces are accompanied by qualitative reflections with three objectives: human-machine interactions in a learning laboratory, the relationship between individuals and the environment, and the relationship between disciplines (alliance between computer science and anthropology) through the concept of consilience.

Keywords: Educational process mining · E-learning · Learning process discovery · Ethnography

1 Introduction

Student pathways during learning can be monitored from multiple perspectives. The success of a learning process is influenced by several factors, including attention, duration, classroom environment, and motivation. The learning outcome can be the subject of quantitative analysis (e.g., the number of positive responses to a test) or qualitative analysis (e.g., the degree of appreciation and feedback left by students during the course). Technologies make it possible to track students behavior during learning through computer instrumentation. In this work, we exploit digital traces left by students in a web-based tutorial. The content of each page can be divided into paragraphs, so it can be monitored to understand students' movements between parts, as well as clicks or mouse movements.

O. Viberg et al. (Eds.): EC-TEL 2023, LNCS 14200, pp. 599–604, 2023.
https://doi.org/10.1007/978-3-031-42682-7_48

Timed events can then be examined using appropriate techniques to appreciate the learning process. The discipline of Process Mining (PM) perfectly fits for this purpose, and in this paper we explore process discovery techniques. As a matter of fact, observational techniques have already shown the possibility of analysing a learning situation. This paper also introduces an exploration of the learning context with classical observational techniques, peculiar to ethnology. We consider as a case study a web tutorial of ten pages on the programming language Python[1]. The use of PM and observational techniques during the execution of the tutorial is twofold. First, to provide useful insights for improving the tutorial itself; aggregated data can be used to suggest how and where to improve the tutorial, to find bottlenecks in the sequence of activities, delays, nonlinear paths. Second, the analysis of the collected data can be used as an evaluation tool for teachers: results can provide suggestions for the improvement of student learning by identifying outliers and learning differences among students. In the following, Sect. 2 provides the background of our work by introducing some related work and the case study. Section 3 explores the process analysis, also with an ethnographic perspective. Finally, Sect. 4 presents conclusions.

2 Background and Related Work

Educational process mining (EPM) is a relatively new discipline which aims at studying students learning behaviours. This information is then used in various ways such as to correlate learning paths with performances or automatically extract learning preferences [2,8]. One of the key aspects contributing to the application of EPM is the availability of data which is supported by the number of courses and learning material available over the web or through Learning Management Systems (LMS) [3], among which Moodle [6]. Etinger et al. [4] and Real et al. [9] compared learning paths of different students and classify them according to their performances. We add an observation from the ethnographical perspective [11]. A LMS offers advantages for teachers and users. It supports data collection, organization, and user-friendliness. In this paper we propose an approach which goes in the direction of supporting the personalization and leaving a student the possibility of selecting the preferred learning path.

2.1 Web Tutorial

We proposed a web tutorial of ten pages (in Italian) to introduce Python programming language to newcomers. Between two web-pages, a test asks for a quick answer to check learning. Each page includes three or four paragraphs (sections), up to a total of 34 paragraphs in the tutorial. Finally, the user is invited to complete a satisfaction survey. To investigate the role of the activities order in the learning process, we propose three different sequences. The tutorial has two fixed parts: first, the INTRODUCTION lessons of three web-pages, including a presentation, the meaning of a program, and variables. Second,

[1] https://www.python.org.

the last page (FUNCTIONS). For the middle part of the tutorial, students can select one out of three paths, as in Fig. 1. Each lesson on DATA TYPES, DATA STRUCTURES, and CONTROL STRUCTURES includes two web pages. To prevent order to influence students, the three topics are presented in a web page as rotating blocks, as in Fig. 2.

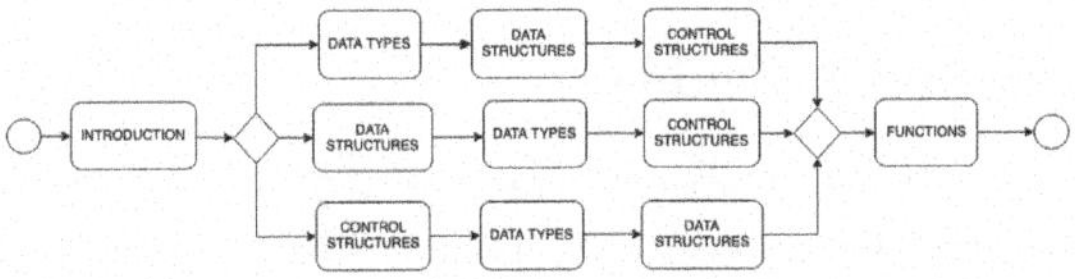

Fig. 1. The three different learning paths; on the top, the standard learning flow. Full size image available at https://github.com/roberto-nai/ectel2023

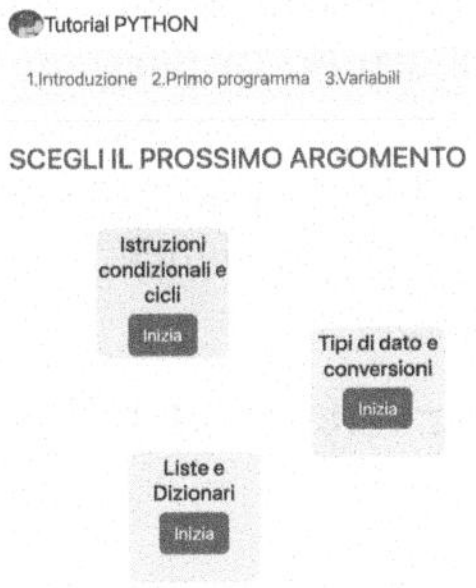

Fig. 2. The rotating blocks allowing students to select next lessons (web-page in Italian). Full size image available at https://github.com/roberto-nai/ectel2023

2.2 Case Study

The tutorial has been proposed to students of an Italian university course, not expert in computer science. During the tutorial, an observational study was conducted by an ethnologist. The data collected via the web tutorial are: entering a page, scrolling through a paragraph (section) of the page, exiting the page, accessing the quiz related to the page, and as last activity accessing the satisfaction survey.

2.3 Process Mining

The PM discipline is oriented toward timed events in which the sequence of activities is important [1]. Process discovery algorithms are of particular interest to this case study since they allow us to reconstruct the students learning paths. The data described in Sect. 2.2, used for process discovery, were collected through the web tutorial and saved in a SQL relational database. Each *event record* (*event*) in an event log includes at least three basic features [1]: 1) the identifier of the process instance it belongs to; 2) the name of the activity which generated the event; 3) the execution timestamp. The sequence of events generated by the same process forms a *trace* or *case* [1]. To analyse the event logs we used academically licensed Apromore [7][2].

2.4 Ethnography and Learning

The idea of adding traditional observations to digital observations, applies first and directly to the classroom context. Direct observation is used as a source of ethnographic information, enables contextual data collection and leads to a descriptive type of restitution of the setting (in which project activities take place). Here *ethnographic research* is proposed, alongside the proposition of the tutorial by the computer scientists involved. At the theoretical level, an effort has been made to study how science is produced. We introduce concepts that can help contextualize the case study. In particular, qualitative reflections have three objectives: human-machine interactions in a learning laboratory, the relationship between individuals and the environment, and the relationship between disciplines through the concept of consilience.

3 Results of the Observational Study

3.1 Event Log

Following Sect. 2.3, in our case the session ID (an alphanumeric string generated for each http connection to the web tutorial) is the process instance identifier, while the different activities involved in the process are 11, starting from the INTRODUCTION up to FUNCTIONS and then the survey page (Sect. 2.1). Each event includes the timestamp at the granularity level of day, hour, minute and second on which the event occurred. Two event logs were analysed: one at the page level and one at the level of individual paragraphs within pages. In both cases, we focused on complete traces, i.e. cases reaching FUNCTIONS or survey page. We have 70 valid cases, with an average duration of 37.7 min, a median of 31.6, and a standard deviation of 24.6. Variability of duration is high, in a range from 3 min up to one hour and a half. Sampling data is available[3].

3.2 Observation from Digital Traces

Process discovery outputs described in Fig. 3, show the case frequency: the paths by users after the third page (VARIABLES) are fairly evenly distributed (36% for route A, 27% for route B, and 37% for route C). We can explore meaningful research directions, i.e. by considering students reaching good or bad results

[2] https://apromore.com.

[3] https://github.com/roberto-nai/ectel2023.

in quizzes. We considered the correct answers to obtain two balanced subsets of cases, the one with a percentage of correct quizzes below 70% (i.e. 31 cases of *low performance*) and above 70% (i.e. 39 cases of *good performance*). The aggregate learning processes appear immediately different: Fig. 4.a shows a quite linear learning process for *low performance* cases, where the mean case duration is 28.4 min. Figure 4.b suggests how best students have a more complicated learning process, having a mean duration of 43.6 min. The comparison suggests that who spent more time on the tutorial pages and visited some pages more than once, also answered the quizzes better.

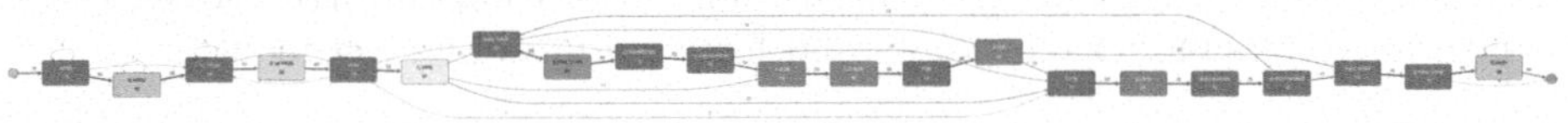

Fig. 3. Discovered process of paths among pages and quizzes. Full size image available at https://github.com/roberto-nai/ectel2023

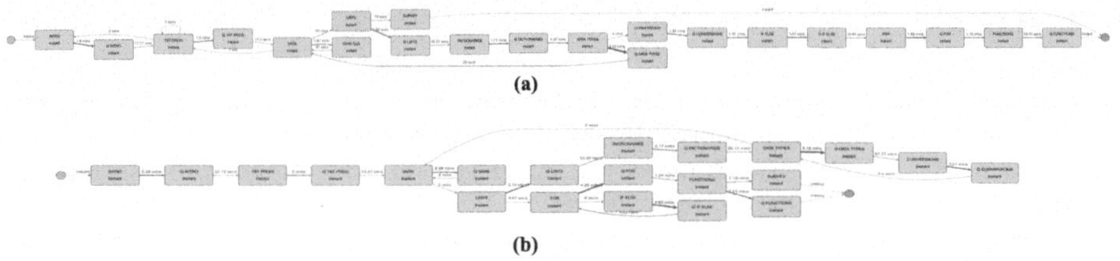

Fig. 4. Processes of low performing students (a) and good performing ones (b). Full size image available at https://github.com/roberto-nai/ectel2023

3.3 An Ethnographic Insight

The ethnographic exploration of the study project is well represented by *truthfulness function* identified by Cassin [5], which investigates the stages of data production. The observation of the classroom's context in which the tutorial was administered highlights the variables of interest, namely, the numerosity of students, the distribution in space, and the possibilities for comparison. The presence of the lecturer providing support for students in case of doubts facilitated the conduct of the tutorial. The proximity among students fostered a positive climate for discussions aiming at overcoming minor difficulties. Accordingly to the concept of consilience [10], the observation suggests to take into account the twofold direction between the need for informatics to consider the technical construction of the tutorial, and the anthropological one to focus on the context, i.e. the type of classroom, the noisiness or quietness of the environment, the time of performance, and finally the relationality aspects.

4 Conclusions

This study combines digital traces and ethnographic observation to investigate students' behaviors during learning. The method is useful for discovering navigation processes on web-tutorial to identify meaningful patterns. Event logs can be used to study user experience, e.g. when students stop navigating after a series of events. PM also helps understand students' learning processes by separating students based on their performance. The timing of learning processes lead to higher achievement and recommending them to other students. Future work plans include increasing the number of students involved, verifying learners' conformance to typical direct paths, and restitution through ethnographic narrative style, including interviews and focus groups among students.

Acknowledgements. This research has been partially carried out within the projects "AI-LEAP" and "Circular Health for Industry", funded by the "Compagnia di San Paolo".

References

1. van der Aalst, W.: Process Mining: Data Science in Action, vol. 2. Springer, Heidelberg (2016). https://doi.org/10.1007/978-3-662-49851-4
2. Bogarín, A., Cerezo, R., Romero, C.: A survey on educational process mining. WIREs DM Knowl. Discov. **8**(1) (2018)
3. Cavus, N.: Distance learning and learning management systems. Procedia Soc. Behav. Sci. **191**, 872–877 (2015)
4. Etinger, D.: Discovering and mapping LMS course usage patterns to learning outcomes. In: Ahram, T., Karwowski, W., Vergnano, A., Leali, F., Taiar, R. (eds.) IHSI 2020. AISC, vol. 1131, pp. 486–491. Springer, Cham (2020). https://doi.org/10.1007/978-3-030-39512-4_76
5. Fassin, D.: If Truth be Told: The Politics of Public Ethnography. Duke University Press, Durham (2017)
6. Gogan, M.L., Sirbu, R., Draghici, A.: Aspects concerning the use of the Moodle platform-case study. Procedia Technol. **19**, 1142–1148 (2015)
7. La Rosa, M., et al.: Apromore: an advanced process model repository. Expert Syst. Appl. **38**(6), 7029–7040 (2011)
8. Racca, A.R., Sulis, E., Capecchi, S.: Behavioral web tracking in e-learning: an educational process mining application. In: E.B., et al. (ed.) 26th International Conference Information Visualisation, IV 2022, Vienna, Austria, 19–22 July 2022, pp. 269–274. IEEE (2022). https://doi.org/10.1109/IV56949.2022.00053
9. Real, E., Pimentel, E., Oliveira, L., Braga, J., Stiubiener, I.: Educational Process Mining for Verifying Student Learning Paths in an Introductory Programming Course, pp. 1–9 (2020)
10. Slingerland, E., Collard, M.: Creating Consilience: Integrating the Sciences and the Humanities. Oxford University Press, Oxford (2011)
11. Wilson, S.: The use of ethnographic techniques in educational research. Rev. Educ. Res. **47**(2), 245–265 (1977)

"TRINE 4D Pedagogical Model": Designing Teaching Scenarios for Using Telepresence Robots in Education

Maria Perifanou(✉)

University of Macedonia, Egnatia 156, Thessaloniki 546 36, Greece
mariaperif@gmail.com

Abstract. This paper proposes the "TRinE 4D Pedagogical Model" which is a 4-step design process that aims at guiding teachers, practitioners or instructional/course designers to design their own activities or lesson plans in which they will use one or more Telepresence Robots (TR). Our research has shown that there are specific pedagogical factors that have a major impact on the design of a teaching scenario or an activity in which a teacher integrates a TR that will facilitate the participation of one or more students or the lesson delivery by a teacher. These pedagogical factors are a) the Educational Context, b) the Educational TR Settings, and c) the Teaching Methods and Tools. A number of pilots have run during the period 2022–23 in order to test the validity of the "TRinE 4D Pedagogical Model".

This paper presents the theoretical philosophy behind the 4-step design process of the "TRinE 4D Pedagogical Model", and the pilots' results. The teaching scenarios that have been applied in different educational settings provided us with valuable feedback for the effective integration of TR in education.

Keywords: Telepresence Robots · Pedagogical Models · Instructional Design

1 Introduction

Nowadays, especially after COVID 19, we can watch an increasing shift towards distance education and online learning at all levels of education and especially in higher education. A high number of emerging innovative technologies give to educators the opportunity to support their students' learning process as never before even when students or teachers cannot attend the classroom physically. Such an example of emerging technology is the use of Telepresence Robots (TR) in education which has dramatically changed the way that teachers can deliver a lesson or students attend a course that requires a hands-on experience, a lab and field work or outdoor learning activities [1–5]. A Telepresence Robot is a type of robot that allows a user to remotely interact with a distant environment or location. TR are video-conferencing devices on wheels with wireless connectivity that are controlled remotely via a computer, tablet or smartphone. Typically, telepresence robots are equipped with cameras, speakers, microphones, wheels, battery, software, sensors, wireless connectivity and more features [3] allowing the user

O. Viberg et al. (Eds.): EC-TEL 2023, LNCS 14200, pp. 605–610, 2023.
https://doi.org/10.1007/978-3-031-42682-7_49

to see and hear what the robot sees and hears, and to communicate with people in the remote location.

In the context of the Erasmus + KA2 project "TRinE – Telepresence Robots in Education" (Project Reference: 2020–1-MT01-KA227-SCH-092408) which addresses the use of TR in educational institutions at upper secondary and higher education levels, such as in classrooms and other (e-)learning settings, we tried to answer the questions of how the education sector can benefit from this technology, what challenges we face, and what projects and research already exist in this area. We also investigated if there is any prior research on specific didactic methodologies that could better enhance the use of TR in education. Based on our findings, we aimed to design and propose a didactic framework that could facilitate the integration of TR in Education. In the following sections, we will present the theoretical philosophy behind the 4-step design process of the "TRinE 4D Pedagogical Model" and the first pilots' results.

2 "TRinE 4D Pedagogical Model"

2.1 The Design of the "TRinE 4D Pedagogical Model"

The "TRinE 4D Pedagogical Model", is based on the "Action Research" philosophy and methodology that is generally applied in the social sciences and it includes the long recognised four-stage problem-solving approach of the cycle (spiral) of collectively planning, acting, observing and reflecting [6–8]. The whole research process consists of three phases and each step of the process is well-designed and has a specific aim (see Fig. 1):

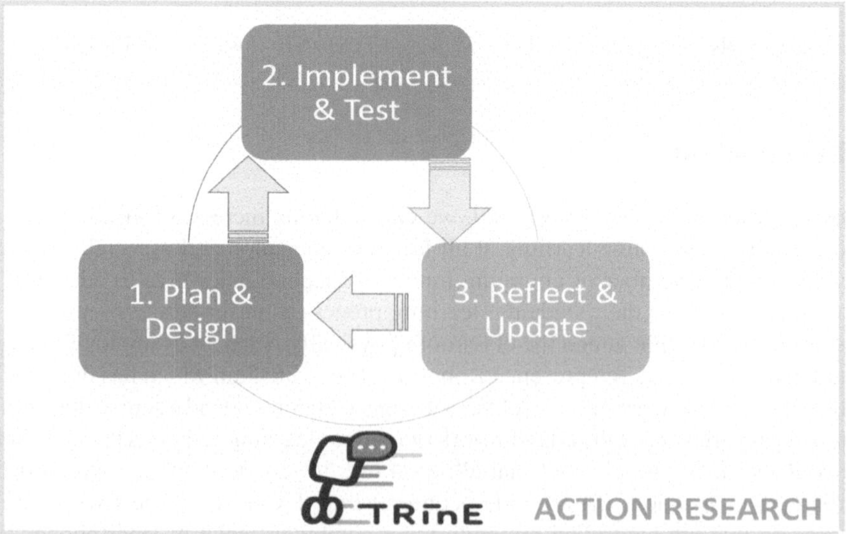

Fig. 1. Step by Step process of the TRinE "Action Research"

- "Plan and Design": The first phase of the research proposed a series of actions (steps) that lead to the design of the "TRinE 4D Pedagogical Model".
- "Implement and Test": The second phase included the practical implementation of the "TRinE 4D Pedagogical Model" in real classrooms, with teachers who applied the proposed didactic model and provided their useful feedback.
- "Reflect and Update": The third phase included the analysis and reflection on collected data and the update of the initial design of the "TRinE 4D Pedagogical Model".

The first phase of planning and designing of the "TRinE 4D Pedagogical Model" included six basic steps (see Fig. 2). Each step of the process was very important and had specific aims.

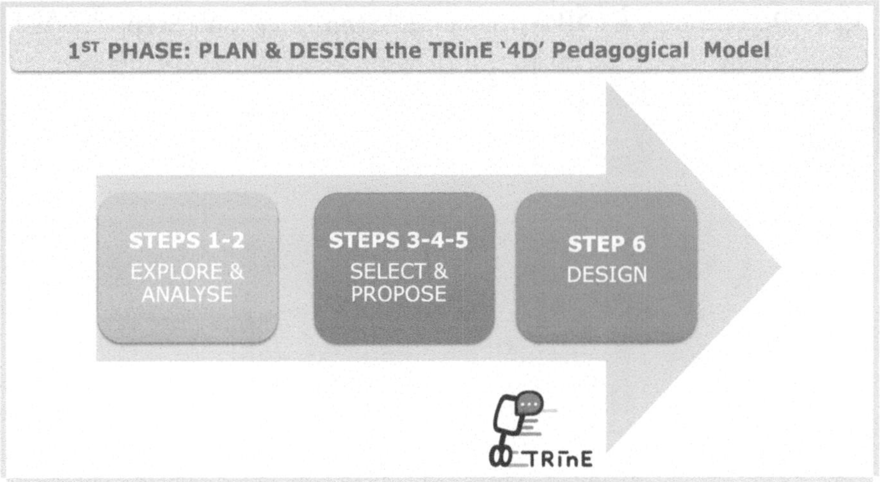

Fig. 2. The "TRinE 4D Pedagogical Model"

The first two steps of this research phase focused on the exploration and analysis of the didactic TR uses and teaching methodologies/ approaches, while the steps 3, 4, and 5 had as main objective the final evaluation, selection, and proposal of the most efficient didactic methodologies for TR in education. The final step of this research phase was the design of the "TRinE 4D Pedagogical Model" taking under consideration all previous research findings.

2.2 The "TRinE 4D Pedagogical Model" Action Phases

The "TRinE 4D Pedagogical Model" is a proposal of a 4-step design process (see Fig. 3) that aims at guiding any practitioner or instructional/course designer who intent to design his/her own activities or lesson plans in which he/she will use one or more TR in his/her course.

Previous studies have shown [4] that there are specific pedagogical factors that have a major impact on the design of a teaching scenario, an activity in which we plan to integrate a TR that will facilitate the participation of one or more students or the lesson delivery by the teacher. These pedagogical factors are: a) *the Educational Context, b) the Educational TR Settings, c) the Teaching Methods and Tools.* All these specific factors are interconnected and all of them "affect and interact" with each other. That means that the "*Educational Context"* can affect the choice of the "*Educational TR Settings"* and the "*Teaching Methods* and *Tools"*. The same applies for the "*Educational TR Settings"* that can also affect the choice of the "*Teaching Methods* and *Tools"* and finally the design of the TR teaching scenario or activity.

More specifically, the "TRinE 4D Pedagogical Model" invites teachers, practitioners and instructional designers to take the following 4-step design process (see Fig. 3):

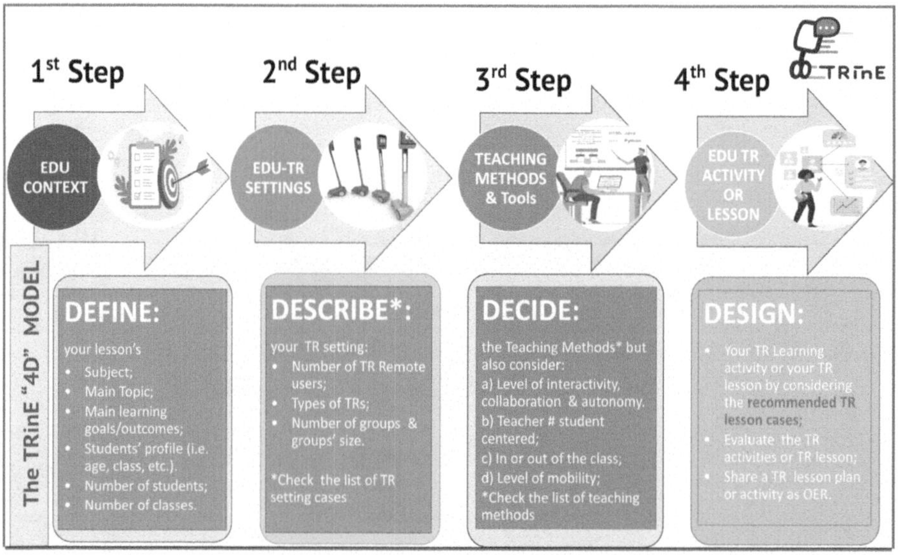

Fig. 3. The "TRinE 4D Pedagogical Model"

a) "Define the Educational Context": As soon as educators start designing any teaching scenario it is essential to define the course's subject, main topic, main learning goals/outcomes, students' profile (i.e., age, class, etc.), number of students, or collaborating classes.
b) "Describe the Educational TR Settings": The TR settings vary depending on who is the controller of the TR and the place where the TR is located: 1) A remote teacher or expert teaches a class; 2) A remote student participates in a class; 3) A remote student interacts with a local teacher; 4) A remote student collaborates with a local student; 5) A remote class communicates with a local teacher or expert; 6) A remote class communicates with a local class.
c) "Decide the Teaching Methods and Tools": A TR should be used preferably in cases where it is necessary. At this step, it is recommended that teachers, practitioners and instructional designers to choose collaborative and student-centered methodologies proposing TR activities that could promote group work, interaction, and fun. It is also

important teachers to consider very well the following design factors: 1) the level of interactivity, collaboration and autonomy; 2) the type of methodology; 3) the type of activity ("In or out of the class"); 4) the level of mobility. Furthermore, in this step, educators should consider the tools that they plan to use during their course. Technical factors should be also taken into consideration.
d) "Design the TR activity, lesson or course": Teachers, practitioners and instructional designers should also consider all the valuable information collected during the previous design steps and consult the list of TR teaching scenarios developed by the consortium and shared as OERs on the TRinE platform.

2.3 First Results of Piloting the "TRinE 4D Pedagogical Model"

A list of 15 TRinE Teaching Scenarios have been developed by all the partners of the TRinE Erasmus +KA2 project (https://www.trine-platform.com/) based on the "TRinE 4D Pedagogical Model". The TRinE Teaching Scenarios focused on promoting and practising linguistic skills, intercultural skills, ICT skills, as well as social and communication skills, preparing students for telework and telelearning environments. The "TRinE 4D Pedagogical Model" was piloted by all partners during two training sessions that took place in Iceland and in Austria during 2022. All partners worked in groups in order to evaluate each phase of the designing process and finally provided their feedback. Following that introductory piloting phase, two scenarios were tried out at each partners' institution and the results were discussed in the final project's meeting in Germany in January 2023. A major research finding is that the teaching methodologies that promote collaboration via group/pair work or gamification can really support the efficient integration of TR in Education. Also, it is confirmed in practice that the a) *Educational Context,* b) the *Educational TR Settings*, c) the *Teaching Methods and Tools* are all interconnected factors and all of them "affect and interact" with each other. Several updates occurred (e.g., including the "tools" component in the 3rd step) to the final version of the "TRinE 4D Pedagogical Model" until the conclusion of all running pilots.

3 Conclusions

This paper presented the theoretical philosophy behind the 4-step design process of the "TRinE 4D Pedagogical Model" as well as the initial pilots' results. The main aim of this pedagogical framework is to guide and support teachers, practitioners and instructional designers in designing efficient TR teaching scenarios that could facilitate the successful integration of TR in education. Student-centered methodologies as well as collaborative and game-based approaches are preferable when teachers wish to use TR in their teaching practice. A variety of TR teaching scenarios are openly accessible under creative common licenses at the TRinE platform (https://www.trine-platform.com/trine-ideas/) and ready to be used by anyone interested in using them. The TRinE team envisages to build an open community of educators across Europe who wish to use, create and share their TR scenarios. We also hope to help students who want to use TR in order to facilitate their studies, as well as all institutions that are going through a digital transformation.

Finally, in light of our literature review findings, it is crucial to highlight that no other initiative, either in Europe or across the globe, has ever proposed or implemented a pedagogical model for integrating TR in education. With this paper, we aim to address this research gap comprehensively, and we envision it as just the starting point for a series of significant contributions in this particular field.

References

1. Kristoffersson, A., Coradeschi, S., Loutfi, A.: A review of mobile robotic telepresence. Adv. Human-Comput. Interact. **3** (2013). https://doi.org/10.1155/2013/902316
2. Ahumada-Newhart, V., Olson, J.S.: Going to school on a robot: robot and user interface design features that matter. ACM Trans. Comput.-Human Interact. (TOCHI) **26**(4), 1–28 (2019). https://doi.org/10.1145/3325210
3. Perifanou, M., Häfner, P., Economides, A.A.: Users' experiences and perceptions about telepresence robots in education. In: Proceedings of EDULEARN 2022, 14th International Conference on Education and New Learning Technologies, pp. 9870–9879. Palma de Mallorca, Spain, IATED (2022). https://doi.org/10.21125/edulearn.2022.2379
4. Häfner, P., et al.: Limits and benefits of using telepresence robots for educational purposes. In: Proceedings of the ICL 2022 "Learning in the Age of Digital and Green Transition", 25th International Conference on Interactive Collaborative Learning and 51st International Conference on Engineering Pedagogy, Vienna, Austria, 27–30 September 2022. Lecture Notes in Networks and Systems, vol. 634. Springer, Cham (2023). https://doi.org/10.1007/978-3-031-26190-9_3
5. Wernbacher, T., et al.: TRinE: telepresence robots in education. In: Proceedings of the 16th Annual International Technology, Education and Development Conference (INTED) 2022, 7–8 March 2022, pp. 6514–6522. IATED (2022). https://doi.org/10.21125/inted.2022.1653
6. Price, J.N.: Action research, pedagogy and change: the transformative potential of action research in pre-service teacher education. J. Curric. Stud. **33**(1), 43–74 (2001)
7. Annison, J.: Action research: reviewing the implementation of a distance-learning degree program utilizing communication and information technologies. Innov. Educ. Teach. Int. **39**(2), 95–107 (2002)
8. Lloyd, C.: Developing and changing practice in special educational needs through critically reflective action research: a case study. Eur. J. Spec. Needs Educ. **17**, 109–127 (2002)

Traceability *by Design*: Design of an Interactive System to Improve the Automatic Generation of Git Traces During a Learning Activity

Mika Pons[1](✉), Jean-Michel Bruel[2], Jean-Baptiste Raclet[3], and Franck Silvestre[1]

[1] IRIT, Université Toulouse Capitole, Toulouse, France
mika.pons@irit.fr
[2] IRIT, Université Toulouse 2 Jean Jaurès, Toulouse, France
[3] IRIT, Université Toulouse 3 Paul Sabatier, Toulouse, France

Abstract. *Learning Analytics* (LA) is collecting and analyzing traces of learners' activities in order to understand and improve learning. This paper focuses on traces generated using the version control system Git. Existing works on the topic have limitations regarding the quality of the traces they analyze: (1) the quantity and content are not always sufficient for in-depth analysis of student behavior, (2) their limited reliability can lead to a loss of exploitable data, and (3) the method of generating these traces is not generic. We propose a new interactive system based on Git and the observation of file modifications to generate automatically reliable and rich traces. This interactive system will soon be experimented with in an ecological context and is intended for diversified teaching contexts.

Keywords: Learning analytics · Git · Traces · Interactive system

1 Introduction

If the use of version control tools, like Git, is widespread in the software industry, it is also used in an educational context, mainly in computer science training [2,3]. Integrating such tools in teaching constitutes a simple means of obtaining traces of the activity of the students thanks to the actions of *commits* carried out during the progress of the activities to version the work. More particularly, Git works using a decentralized architecture which allows to work with local copies and thus to synchronize with the main remote copy. It helps teachers collect students' work. Also, Git can store in an optimized way the modifications made by the students, called *diff*.

O. Viberg et al. (Eds.): EC-TEL 2023, LNCS 14200, pp. 611–617, 2023.
https://doi.org/10.1007/978-3-031-42682-7_50

At the crossroads of *Learning Analytics* and version management software, we see the emergence of work based on the analysis of traces produced using version management software in computer learning [8]. Some works exploit *Process Mining* techniques for trace analysis by extracting metrics related to students' learning behavior [4].

However, these studies have limitations concerning the traces generated by version control software (VCS) such as Git. Indeed, the content of these traces is not sufficient for certain analyses requiring more precise temporal information to be known. For example, we can't make an analysis on the duration of the resolution of exercises because there is not enough information available for that. Between the beginning of a work session and the resolution of an exercise, the time actually spent working is unknown. Also, these traces may lack reliability when their generation is based on a declarative and open process by the student. Finally, these traces are generated with methods that are difficult to apply in fields that do not fall within the field of computer science.

To overcome these limitations, we wonder how to design an interactive Git trace generation system for students, and more specifically: (RQ1) How to increase the quantity of Git traces using an interactive system? (RQ2) How to increase the quality of Git traces using an interactive system? (RQ3) How can an interactive system make the process of generating Git traces usable for an audience unfamiliar with Git?

First, we will provide an overview of works that use Git traces to improve teaching in Sect. 2, while highlighting their limitations. Secondly, in Sect. 3, we will present the interactive system LAWG designed to answer the issues raised by our research questions. Finally, we'll explain how the features of LAWG address this in the Sect. 4.

2 State of the Art

Several papers [2,3] have experimented with integrating VCS into computer science learning and show the benefits. The integration of VCS into practical sessions gives the teacher the ability to centralize the distribution of course material for all students and to easily monitor and collect their work [1]. In the field of *Process Mining* (PM), several works [5] focus on analyzing Git traces generated in the context of software development courses. In 2021, Macak et al. [4] proposed a method to analyze Git traces of student projects using PM. This article shows it is possible to identify student learning behaviors using PM technique. However, only the information provided by Git in a commit is considered for analysis. Git traces do not contain contextual information about a student's progress in a learning activity, such as solving a well-identified question. There is no temporal information concerning the dates of the start of resolution activity for a question and therefore does not address (RQ1). Finally, this method of analysis does not deal with the issues of reliability and easy of use of the traces generation, as referred to in (RQ2, RQ3).

In 2018, Silvestre et Raclet [10] developed a learning protocol based on code review and test-guided development. To help orchestrate its different phases, a dashboard, G4S [7], is used. Based on the commits made and the milestones (reviews, corrections) filled in by the teacher, this dashboard provides a number of indicators, such as the progress of students within their group. The dashboard also makes it possible to export the traces enhanced by the context of the resolution of the questions. We exported the dashboard data and analyzed it using PM techniques [6]. Unfortunately, we couldn't extract any indicators of students' behavior because the traces didn't contain enough information for that. More precise information on students' real-time activity (RQ1) was lacking, the process of marking questions as solved depended too much on the students, leading to errors in the data (RQ2), and the process was difficult to operationalize for an audience not very proficient with Git (RQ3).

A 2022 study [9] explores an alternative way to automatically generate and visualize student activity traces during practical sessions. To automate the generation of the traces, Rodriguez-Rivera et al. integrated the commit commands into a Makefile, generating a Git trace for each compilation. But, compilations are infrequent, leading to coarse tracing granularity (RQ1). Using a Makefile is restrictive for a non-Git-competent audience (RQ3).

In conclusion, to our knowledge, there is a lack of prior work on an interactive system capable of overcoming the identified limitations in quantity, quality, and ease of use. We sought a compromise between G4S and EnCourse. To address this, we have designed an interactive system that generates traces in real-time, considering the contextual information of students' progress, while maximizing reliability and ease of use.

3 The Interactive System LAWG and Its Features

To answer our research questions, we designed an interactive system, called LAWG, written in Python and open-source, available for Windows, MacOS, and Linux[1]. Our interactive system offers three main functionalities that we explain in the following sections: (1) Supervise work sessions, saving all resources at the end of each session (2) Observe all changes made to files in the workspace to save them in real-time (3) Provide a command-line interface for students to mark a question as solved.

The context in which LAWG is used is as follows: students work during *work sessions* on *worksheets* made up of several exercises, each consisting of one or more *questions*. Students flag questions as solved by making a *commit* (with an associated message) and synchronize their remote workspace using the `push` command[2]. Finally, the sequence of commits constitutes a *branch*.

Before using the interactive system, the teacher and then each student must configure it[3]. The system manages the student's workspace and automatically traces the start and the end of a work session. When the student opens and

[1] Available on GitHub at this address: https://github.com/git4school/LAWG.
[2] Local and remote workspaces are managed with the VCS Git.
[3] This part is explained in the longer version published here: https://hal.science/hal-04141003.

closes the system, it opens and closes the workspace, saving the latest changes. These events generate the respective ``Resume'' and ``Pause'' commits.

When LAWG is launched, changes to workspace files are observed. Each event causes a commit to be produced in the `auto` branch. The events observed are: *modification*, *creation*, *deletion*, *move* and *renaming* of a file. For these commits, we have defined a minimalist message form to facilitate further processing:

- `"[moved] <path_file> -> <path_new_folder>"`
- `"[renamed] <path_file> -> <new_name_file>"`
- `"[<event>] <path_file>"`

LAWG offers the student a command-line interface. The commands available are easily expandable thanks to a modular design and are suggested as a list to the student. This allows the student to mark a question as solved with the `fix` command, whose questions are also suggested. Using this command generates a commit of the form ``Fix <question>''.

Last, some limitations of our system have been identified. First, there is still a dependency between the student and the expertise in Git (initial cloning of the repository and SSH key). Moreover, the system is not designed to work with multiple branches as yet.

4 What are the Benefits of Using the Interactive System?

Concerning the question (RQ1). The generation of traces when each file is modified provides a more detailed overview of student activity. This gives us greater coverage of their actual activity. To test the system, we generated traces of a student using the system to answer questions on an worksheet from a real course[4]. The Fig. 1 shows an extract of the generated traces. New traces generated thanks to the system are in red. We can see that the volume of traces is significantly increased and covers a more extensive range of time than without using the system.

Through the generation of a trace for each file modification, it is possible to identify information about students' behavior via the name of these files. A concrete example of this, in the case of the Fig. 1, is the identification of the good following of the Test-Driven-Development (TDD). We can see in lines 62 and 61 that the student integrates the test `ArticleTest`, then modifies the associated class `Article` thanks to the naming convention of the tests. This is, therefore, representative of TDD. On the other hand, we can see that the student modifies the classes `IndexController` on line 67 before the associated test `IndexControllerTest` on line 66. Here we see that the TDD is not followed, and a simple comparison of the file names would make it possible to automate this identification from these traces.

In addition, the management of work sessions makes integrating the beginning and end of these sessions in the logs possible. This can be observed in the

[4] The anonymized dataset is available on OSF at this address: https://osf.io/t3wqr/?view_only=69907570f39046edba382a5e855ed26a.

Fig. 1 at the lines 44 and 74 with the commits ``Resume'' and ``Pause''. Also, the associated mechanism, which empties and restores the workspace, allows us to ensure the systematic use of the interactive system for each work session and, therefore, the completeness of the traces.

44	fbf16ec	Mon, 10 Apr 2023 18:28:55 +0200	Pause
45	**ea3f9d1**	**Mon, 10 Apr 2023 18:26:46 +0200**	**Fix #2b**
46	19c7009	Mon, 10 Apr 2023 18:26:06 +0200	[modified] src/test/java/doremi/doremi/BandTest.java
47	6890448	Mon, 10 Apr 2023 18:23:36 +0200	[modified] src/main/java/doremi/domain/Band.java
48	89a6b70	Mon, 10 Apr 2023 18:23:31 +0200	[modified] src/main/java/doremi/domain/Band.java
49	1157e96	Mon, 10 Apr 2023 18:23:15 +0200	[modified] src/test/java/doremi/doremi/BandTest.java
50	fa4054a	Mon, 10 Apr 2023 18:23:13 +0200	[created] src/test/java/doremi/doremi/BandTest.java
51	fa0c6fa	Mon, 10 Apr 2023 18:22:39 +0200	[modified] src/main/java/doremi/domain/Album.java
52	ce3c3bd	Mon, 10 Apr 2023 18:22:23 +0200	[modified] src/main/java/doremi/domain/Album.java
53	1c5090f	Mon, 10 Apr 2023 18:21:47 +0200	[modified] src/test/java/doremi/AlbumTest.java
54	2312a58	Mon, 10 Apr 2023 18:21:34 +0200	[modified] src/test/java/doremi/AlbumTest.java
55	533580e	Mon, 10 Apr 2023 18:21:33 +0200	[created] src/test/java/doremi/AlbumTest.java
56	**ce3dd1d**	**Mon, 10 Apr 2023 18:19:26 +0200**	**Fix #2a**
57	be88b27	Mon, 10 Apr 2023 18:19:11 +0200	[modified] src/main/java/doremi/domain/Article.java
58	6e9899f	Mon, 10 Apr 2023 18:19:07 +0200	[modified] src/main/java/doremi/domain/Article.java
59	6b853e4	Mon, 10 Apr 2023 18:18:21 +0200	[modified] src/main/java/doremi/domain/Article.java
60	6da0f26	Mon, 10 Apr 2023 18:17:59 +0200	[modified] src/main/java/doremi/domain/Article.java
61	ecb0a7a	Mon, 10 Apr 2023 18:17:29 +0200	[modified] src/test/java/doremi/ArticleTest.java
62	151e5c2	Mon, 10 Apr 2023 18:17:20 +0200	[created] src/test/java/doremi/ArticleTest.java
63	**c13b362**	**Mon, 10 Apr 2023 18:16:09 +0200**	**Fix #1**
64	fe51014	Mon, 10 Apr 2023 18:15:52 +0200	[modified] src/main/java/doremi/controllers/IndexController.java
65	e42f65f	Mon, 10 Apr 2023 18:14:54 +0200	[modified] src/test/java/doremi/IndexControllerTest.java
66	81bfb45	Mon, 10 Apr 2023 18:14:47 +0200	[created] src/test/java/doremi/IndexControllerTest.java
67	55f182b	Mon, 10 Apr 2023 18:14:22 +0200	[modified] src/main/java/doremi/controllers/IndexController.java
68	9f3e898	Mon, 10 Apr 2023 18:14:05 +0200	[modified] src/main/java/doremi/controllers/IndexController.java
69	424e099	Mon, 10 Apr 2023 18:13:43 +0200	[modified] src/main/java/doremi/controllers/IndexController.java
70	dff1b1d	Mon, 10 Apr 2023 18:13:28 +0200	[created] src/main/java/doremi/controllers/IndexController.java
71	3191ec0	Mon, 10 Apr 2023 18:12:33 +0200	[modified] src/main/resources/templates/index.html
72	9c8158d	Mon, 10 Apr 2023 18:12:24 +0200	[modified] src/main/resources/templates/index.html
73	79bbdbd	Mon, 10 Apr 2023 18:12:17 +0200	[created] src/main/resources/templates/index.html
74	8a0b7c7	Mon, 10 Apr 2023 18:10:07 +0200	Resume

Fig. 1. Extract of the traces generated with the system

Concerning the question (RQ2). With the question resolution interface, we went from declarative and open trace generation to declarative but closed trace generation. Indeed, the command `fix` generates a trace whose message is normalized. Validating the command prevents the student from marking as solved a question that is not in the list given to the configuration. In this way, errors from the students are avoided. Thanks to its partial automation, traces generation becomes semi-automatic and closed. Many of the traces generated by LAWG are no longer dependent on student declaration, reducing the possibility of omissions.

Concerning the question (RQ3). The interactive system makes it easier to integrate into non-computer science areas. It abstracts the use of Git for trace generation so that it can be used for an audience unfamiliar with Git. The triggering of the automatic generation of traces when simply modifying a file makes it usable in all areas that require working on a computer, especially when the expected contributions are text productions.

5 Conclusion

We addressed the limitations of trace generation tools through Git repositories and introduced our interactive system, LAWG. This system automatically generates traces when students modify files and includes a command for validating questions resolution. Our contribution improves the quantity, quality and easy of use of activity trace production. In future experiments, we plan to apply process mining techniques or analyze student behavior in relation to target behaviors. Our interactive system will be tested in computer learning courses this year, and we are prioritizing the collection of personal data, ensuring compliance with GDPR regulations. Access to personal data is restricted to teachers via the G4S dashboard, and anonymized data is made available to researchers. To simplify the process and ensure GDPR compliance, data anonymization will be integrated into the export feature of G4S.

References

1. Clifton, C., Kaczmarczyk, L.C., Mrozek, M.: Subverting the fundamentals sequence: using version control to enhance course management. ACM SIGCSE Bull. (2007)
2. Laadan, O., Nieh, J., Viennot, N.: Teaching operating systems using virtual appliances and distributed version control. In: Proceedings of the 41st ACM Technical Symposium on Computer Science Education (2010)
3. Lawrance, J., Jung, S., Wiseman, C.: Git on the cloud in the classroom. In: Proceeding of the 44th ACM Technical Symposium on Computer Science Education - SIGCSE '13 (2013)
4. Macak, M., Kruzelova, D., Chren, S., Buhnova, B.: Using process mining for Git log analysis of projects in a software development course. Educ. Inf. Technol. (2021)
5. Mittal, M., Sureka, A.: Process mining software repositories from student projects in an undergraduate software engineering course. In: Companion Proceedings of the 36th International Conference on Software Engineering (2014)
6. Pons, M., Bruel, J.M., Raclet, J.B., Silvestre, F.: Finding behavioral indicators from contextualized commits in software engineering courses with process mining. Front. Softw. Eng. Educ. Springer (2023, to be published)
7. Raclet, J.-B., Silvestre, F.: Git4School: a dashboard for supporting teacher interventions in software engineering courses. In: Alario-Hoyos, C., Rodríguez-Triana, M.J., Scheffel, M., Arnedillo-Sánchez, I., Dennerlein, S.M. (eds.) EC-TEL 2020. LNCS, vol. 12315, pp. 392–397. Springer, Cham (2020). https://doi.org/10.1007/978-3-030-57717-9_33
8. Robles, G., González-Barahona, J.M.: Mining student repositories to gain learning analytics. an experience report. In: 2013 IEEE Global Engineering Education Conference (EDUCON) (2013)

9. Rodriguez-Rivera, G., et al.: Tracking large class projects in real-time using fine-grained source control. In: Proceedings of the 53rd ACM Technical Symposium on Computer Science Education, vol. 1 (2022)
10. Silvestre, F., Raclet, J.B.: Développement dirigé par les tests et revue de code par les pairs pour l'apprentissage de la programmation. In: Ludovia CH: 1ère édition sur le thème" Émanciper l'école et la société avec le numérique?" (2018)

Towards Designing and Evaluating an Adaptable Assistance System for Technology-Enhanced Vocational Education

Antje Proske[1], Hermann Körndle[1], Kristin Drexler[1], Julia Kirsten[1], Klara Schröder[1], Sebastian Kucharski[2(✉)], Tommy Kubica[2], and Iris Braun[2]

[1] Faculty of Psychology, Technische Universität Dresden, Dresden, Germany
{antje.proske,hermann.korndle,kristin.drexler, julia.kirsten,klara.schroder}@tu-dresden.de
[2] Faculty of Computer Science, Technische Universität Dresden, Dresden, Germany
{sebastian.kucharski,tommy.kubica,iris.braun}@tu-dresden.de

Abstract. Intelligent tutoring systems collect learners' traces in technology-enhanced learning environments with the aim of guiding and improving their learning in real time. Research has succeeded in developing data models that optimize the prediction of learning outcomes. Accurate prediction, however, does not provide information on how to achieve the desired learning outcomes. Recent approaches emphasize an interdisciplinary design process using human-computer interaction and learning engineering methods. Accordingly, this paper introduces an adaptable assistance system for vocational education that is developed in an interdisciplinary collaboration between learning and computer science experts. The assistance system supports both the processes of self-regulated learning and collaborative knowledge building by enabling learners to individually choose from topic-specific and/or interaction-specific recommendations. The chatbot recommendations are derived from a learning suggestion middleware that evaluates xAPI statements. It is based on explanatory learner models that provide not only accurate predictions, but also interpretable and actionable insights into learners' activities and their learning process. A graphical knowledge structure provides an overview of the learning content, learner's progress and allows free navigation. Ideas on how to evaluate the assistance system in scenarios of self-regulated learning and workplace learning will be outlined.

Keywords: Technology-Enhanced Learning Environments · Vocational Education and Training · Intelligent Tutoring System · Recommendations · Chatbot

1 Theoretical Background

The acquisition of knowledge and skills that are flexible transferable to everyday (work) life plays a main role in vocational education and training (VET). In dig-

O. Viberg et al. (Eds.): EC-TEL 2023, LNCS 14200, pp. 618–623, 2023.
https://doi.org/10.1007/978-3-031-42682-7_51

ital learning scenarios at the workplace, Intelligent Tutoring Systems (ITS) [3] can provide valuable assistance towards boosting learners' skills and competencies. However, developing ITSs is very time-consuming and costly [4]. Therefore, this paper addresses the question how an low effort assistance system that individually supports learners can be designed. We present an adaptable assistance system that - in contrast to typical ITSs - allows learners to individually choose from topic-specific and/or interaction-specific recommendations in order to improve their learning. In this way, the effort required to develop the system can be reduced, while at the same time the possibility can be established to generate interpretable and actionable insights into learners' activities (see [4]).

The paper is structured as follows, Sect. 2 presents the psychological learning concept behind the system. Afterwards, Sect. 3 describes the realization of the conceptualized ITS. Finally, Sect. 4 outlines the planned case studies and concludes the paper.

2 Psychological Learning Concept

The psychological learning concept is based on different complex so-called *work-related learning tasks* that center learning on real-world work tasks and problems. These learning tasks model reality and aim at the integration of skills, knowledge, and attitudes [5]. Learners apply their knowledge and skills to fulfill the tasks. At the same time, they learn while completing the task(s) [5]. The *assistance system* is developed in an iterative process of design and improvement.

2.1 General Idea

A key part of the design process was to develop an explanatory learner model [4] that enables the insight-driven use of learning analytics to guide and improve learning in the learning environment. The explanatory learner model is based on the psychological Co-Evolution Model [2], which describes how knowledge is constructed through cognitive and social processes that mutually influence each other. As such, it provides the basis for deriving measurable indicators of knowledge-building behavior that is conducive to learning - both at the individual level and in shared knowledge construction (i.e. co-evolution of knowledge).

The idea of the project is to grant learners a larger degree of autonomy in regulating their learning process than it is usually the case with current ITSs. To this end, the system considers three control loops for learning regulation [1]: The *outer loop* establishes a connection between learners and the content demands of the learning modules. Learning modules combine work-related learning tasks of different degrees of complexity with information and media on a particular topic in the form of text, graphics, or video. The outer loop generates feedback on learning behavior and progress in a module. The *inner loop* generates feedback on learning behavior and progress for the individual elements of a learning module (e.g., on steps of a work-related learning task). In this way, learner's selection from the elements of a learning module as well as a deeper engagement with these elements is supported. Finally, the *workplace loop* ensures that the assistance system can access digital components of the workplace to use its digital data for completion of a work-related learning task.

Taking into account these three loops allows to reduce the high overhead of AI-based ITSs as follows: Diagnostic learner information is obtained directly from the completion of work-related learning tasks whose solution steps are supported by the assistance system in form of a wide range of different information (e.g. solution examples, videos, feedback). Learners can choose from this information and learn which choice provides the best cognitive and motivational support.

2.2 Components of the Assistance System

To ensure the co-evolution of learners' knowledge as well as the regulation of learning via the loops mentioned above, the assistance system will consist of two essential elements: a) a structured visualization of the learning content, and b) opportunities for learners to interact with the system as well as with other learners.

Structuring and Visualization of Content. In order to provide learners with recommendations as to which learning modules are suitable for which learning objectives or which information can be used to solve different complex work-related learning tasks, the assistance system must access the content in a structured way. To this end, a polyhierarchical taxonomy can be used which facilitates a clear description not only of the content requirements of a particular learning module, but also of the work-related learning tasks. In addition, by explicitly defining the content necessary for task solution, the requirement profile of a particular learning task can be visualized via the taxonomy. Thus, the visualization provides a global orientation about the overall content as well as about the localization of the requirement profile of a particular learning task. Such a visualization can invite learners to consider how work-related learning tasks bridge separate learning modules and whether review or inspection of particular learning modules is necessary [8]. Furthermore, possible paths through a learning module can be represented in a manageable way.

Interactivity. Since work-related learning tasks are typically solved by a learner in several, qualitatively different steps, the assistance system will need to register the products a learner generates while performing these steps. In response, the assistance system can interactively support learners by, for example, providing them opportunities for collaborative exchange, explicating solution steps, providing further information, or by providing feedback. However, providing supportive information for improvement of learning such as formative feedback in real-time is one of the challenging tasks in technology-enhanced learning environments [6]. Recent research suggests that chatbots could serve as an effective means to empower students to actively control and regulate their learning process [7].

3 Technical Realization

Following the presented psychological learning concept, the ITS is conceptualized as a modular system with two components responsible for providing assistance. This architecture allows teachers to syntonize it to their individual scenarios by configuring components and even dynamically activating or deactivating them.

3.1 Chatbot Acting Proactively and Reactively

A chatbot is used to emulate an intelligent tutor with whom the learner can interact dynamically and who is able to bring together like-minded learners to collaborate on group tasks, for example. This virtual tutor can provide the learner with information as well as assistance such as suggestions regarding the learning process. The interaction can take place in two forms. The first is proactive, where the learner initiates the interaction by actively asking for assistance. An example of such an interaction scenario is that the learner has a certain time slot in which learning can take place and asks for learning content that is appropriate for the specified time with respect to the user's learning state. Second, reactively, in which case the virtual tutor reacts to learning actions that are indicators, with regard to the respective learning state, that the provision of assistance is appropriate. An example of such a trigger could be that the learner's navigation and interaction behavior deviates from a specified, psychologically grounded learning path. Accordingly, the virtual tutor would point this out and would suggest the learning action that would bring the learner back to the defined path.

As Learning Management System (LMS) we use the an open source project *ILIAS*[1] for authoring and presenting the learning materials and quizzes to the learners. The chatbot is implemented as a web application independent of ILIAS using *Botpress*[2], an open source framework for building conversational AI applications. The integration into ILIAS is done by a plugin, that is responsible for the communication with the Botpress server, where the functional logic is encapsulated and from where a suitable chatbot frontend is loaded.

3.2 Graphical Knowledge Structure

A graphical structure gives an overview of the learning topic, i.e. the knowledge structure. Its purpose is to visualize the learning content, the connections and dependencies between this content, and the learner's progress within it. Moreover, it serves as a means for the learner for navigation through the learning material, either freely or by following predefined learning paths. The learning material is, according to the ILIAS content structure, organized hierarchically with topics and learning modules as the top-level elements and *work related learning tasks*, as the leaf elements of the resulting knowledge structure tree.

[1] https://www.ilias.de/, visited on 03/06/2023.
[2] https://botpress.com, visited on 03/04/2023.

The current learning content is automatically loaded from ILIAS. Moreover, the teacher can use the graphical structure to parameterize the ITS, for example, by specifying, assistance scenarios in detail.

The knowledge structure component is implemented as a *Vue.js* application independent of ILIAS using *diagram-js*, an open source toolbox for building web-based diagram editors. The integration into ILIAS is done by a plugin, that is responsible for the integration of the JavaScript code into the ILIAS user frontend and for the communication with the ILIAS-core, e.g., for requesting the current learning content.

3.3 ITS Architecture

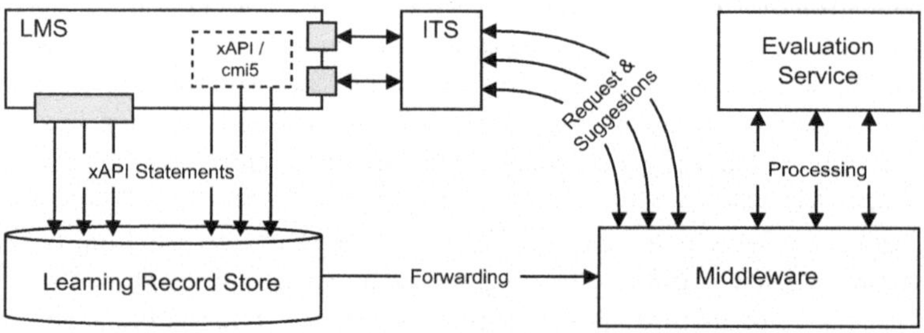

Fig. 1. Architectural overview of the ITS components and how they communicate.

The conceptualized ITS is implemented as an ecosystem of self-contained microservices as shown in Fig. 1. In this way, the intended modular character of the system is taken into account and the system is largely independent of version-specific changes in the LMS around which it is built (i.e., ILIAS). The interaction of the user with the learning content is either observed within ILIAS or within a connected *Content Management Systems* (CMS), depending on where the learning process takes place. The performed learning actions are sent as *xAPI* statements to a *Learning Locker* server[3], an open source *Learning Record Store* (LRS), for recording. From there, the statements are forwarded to a middleware component that is responsible for coordinating the ITS-side control of the user interaction components of the ITS. The middleware is a simple communication and information buffering component. The psychological concept is implemented by a second component, the *Suggestion Generator*, which is parameterized and invoked by the middleware. This component holds the psychological ITS concept, deduces the user's learning state from the incoming learning action statements, and initiates assistance actions when the processing of both in mutual dependence makes it seem appropriate. Using this architecture will not only allow to support different learning scenarios, which may include self-regulated or collaborative activities, but should also allow to transfer the approach to different learning environments.

[3] https://learningpool.com/learning-record-store/, visited on 03/04/2023.

4 Conclusion and Future Work

To summarize, the paper depicts the potential of an intelligent assistance system in digital learning environments in order to foster individual, self-regulated as well as collaborative learning processes. Future research should investigate the acceptance and effects of the assistance system in multiple scenarios of VET.

The assistance system will be tested in scenarios of self-regulated learning and collaborative knowledge construction as well as in scenarios, in which learners use digital tools to create themselves an interactive learning environment. The topics of the case studies will range from scenarios of continuing vocational training in the field of electrical engineering, workplace training in the use of CNC machines, to the training of interdisciplinary skills for the cross-company planning of automated solutions. Even though, preliminary results can not yet be presented, it is expected that the use of the assistance system will increase learner acceptance and engagement in technology-enhanced VET learning environments.

This allows us to provide a transferable tool that can help educators to develop and improve digital training programs with low effort as well as the learner to study more efficiently.

References

1. Aleven, V., Sewall, J., Andres, J.M., Sottilare, R., Long, R., Baker, R.: Towards adapting to learners at scale: integrating MOOC and intelligent tutoring frameworks. In: Proceedings of the Fifth Annual ACM Conference on Learning at Scale (2018)
2. Cress, U., Kimmerle, J.: The interrelations of individual learning and collective knowledge construction: a cognitive-systemic framework. In: Schwan, S., Cress, U. (eds.) Psychol. Digit. Learn., pp. 123–145. Springer, Cham (2017). https://doi.org/10.1007/978-3-319-49077-9_7
3. Graesser, A.C., Conley, M.W., Olney, A.: Intelligent tutoring systems. APA educational psychology handbook, vol. 3, pp. 451–473. Application to learning and teaching (2012)
4. Rosé, C.P., McLaughlin, E.A., Liu, R., Koedinger, K.R.: Explanatory learner models: why machine learning (alone) is not the answer. Br. J. Edu. Technol. **50**(6), 2943–2958 (2019)
5. Van Merriënboer, J.J., Kirschner, P.A.: Ten steps to complex learning: a systematic approach to four-component instructional design. Routledge (2017)
6. Vijayakumar, B., Höhn, S., Schommer, C.: Quizbot: exploring formative feedback with conversational interfaces. In: Draaijer, S., Joosten-ten Brinke, D., Ras, E. (eds.) TEA 2018. CCIS, vol. 1014, pp. 102–120. Springer, Cham (2019). https://doi.org/10.1007/978-3-030-25264-9_8
7. Winkler, R., Söllner, M.: Unleashing the potential of chatbots in education: a state-of-the-art analysis. In: Academy of Management Annual Meeting (AOM) (2018)
8. Winne, P.H., et al.: nstudy: software for learning analytics about processes for self-regulated learning. J. Learn. Analyt. **6**(2), 95–106 (2019)

Learning with the School Library: Mapping Technology-Enhanced Learning Underpinnings

Eduarda Ribeiro Mota[1,2(✉)], Teresa Margarida Loureiro Cardoso[1,3], Ana Carolina Ferreira da Cruz[1,2], and Filomena Pestana[1]

[1] Rede WEIWER®, LE@D, Laboratório de Educação a Distância e eLearning, Universidade Aberta, Lisbon, Portugal
904536@estudante.uab.pt, {teresa.cardoso,maria.coelho}@uab.pt, carolina.cruz@mail-rbe.org

[2] Rede de Bibliotecas Escolares, Ministério da Educação, Portugal

[3] Departamento de Educação e Ensino a Distância, Universidade Aberta, Lisbon, Portugal

Abstract. Technology-enhanced learning has been at the center of any global educational agenda for the past decades. More recently, with the COVID-19 pandemics, it has (re)gained a wider interest. However, it has been at the core of the Portuguese School Libraries Network since its creation in 1996, with the mission of promoting learning scenarios that enhance essential literacy skills for 21st-century learners. Therefore, in Portugal, the school library plays an important role in fostering such technology-enhanced learning environments. But, which underpinnings on technology enhanced-learning are evidenced in the main documents of the Portuguese School Libraries Network, namely in its *Learning with the School Library* Referential? The objective of our study is to map the underpinnings of technology-enhanced learning present in this framework, particularly in terms of how digital literacy is approached in relation to other literacies. To this end, we will use a qualitative methodology approach in a case study supported by content analysis with a focus on digital literacy. Ultimately, we will conclude that digital literacy is addressed transversally in the Referential, reflecting the innovative use of tools, technologies and learning environments to enhance students' literacy skills.

Keywords: School Library · Technology-Enhanced Learning · Digital literacy · Pedagogical Innovation · Collaborative Practices · Mapping K-12 Underpinnings

1 Introduction

In a pandemic context that has reinforced and accelerated the exponential use of technology in education, the inevitability of incorporating the digital component into pedagogical practices is widely recognised, with its implications for the definition of social and educational policies, which necessarily include the professional development of teachers with the intended impact of improving students' literacy. In Portugal, the School Libraries Network plays an essential role in this regard, contributing to the lines of action set out in the *National Digital Skills Initiative e.2030* [1], by promoting digital

O. Viberg et al. (Eds.): EC-TEL 2023, LNCS 14200, pp. 624–629, 2023.
https://doi.org/10.1007/978-3-031-42682-7_52

literacy among teachers, teacher librarians and students, reflecting the main guidelines of the *European Framework for the Digital Competence of Educators: DigCompEdu* [2] and the *Students' Profile by the End of Compulsory Schooling* [3], which is currently the main theoretical basis for the action of the Portuguese education programmes. It is, therefore, essential to analyse the foundations and guidelines of one of the main structuring documents of the School Libraries Network, of the Portuguese Ministry of Education, the *Learning with the School Library* Referential, showing how it reflects the creation of technology-enhanced learning environments and the promotion of digital literacy among students at all levels of education.

Thus, the main objective of our study is to map the technology-enhanced learning underpinnings perceived in the *Learning with the School Library* Referential, through a content analysis that allows us to contribute to the definition of the state of the art in Portugal regarding the action of school libraries in the promotion of learning scenarios that enhance the development of essential literacies for 21st-century learners, namely digital literacy.

2 Learning with the School Library: Strengthening the Curriculum Through a Literacy-Based Approach

2.1 The Conceptual Framework: Knowledge, Skills and Values

Since its publication in 2012 and its update in 2017 to include secondary education, the *Learning with the School Library* Referential has served as a strategic tool for improving the literacy skills of Portuguese students at all school levels. This guiding document is based on the assumption that the curriculum in all school years, from kindergarten to grade 12, is enhanced and enriched by its intersection with multiliteracies and it emphasises collaborative work between the teacher librarian and teachers of curricular areas in schools. It is grounded in a theoretical and conceptual framework that defines the knowledge, skills and values associated with three key areas of literacy – reading, media and information –, which are translated into descriptors of student performance at the end of each school cycle.

The performance descriptors are presented sequentially, given the 'progressive and cumulative nature of the knowledge and skills to be developed throughout the educational levels on which it focuses' [4]. With regard to digital literacy, it does not appear in the document as a specific area to which skills are linked but as a cross-cutting area to all the others, manifested both in the respective descriptors and in operationalisation strategies based on learning scenarios characterised by digital environments and the use of tools and technologies in formal and informal learning contexts. The descriptors associated with the expected performance are formally presented in tables that allow a sequential reading across school cycles within a literacy domain or a holistic analysis of the expected performance across the three literacy domains in each school cycle.

Alongside the tables of descriptors for the different literacies are the values and attitudes to be developed in each area of literacy, but, in this case, there is no division or sequence by cycle. For example, with regard to information literacy, there are nine attitudes/values that should be fostered at all levels of education, such as 'respecting copyright and related rights', 'showing initiative and creativity in problem-solving' or 'accepting criticism' [4].

For each literacy area, a wide range of suggestions for operationalisation strategies is also provided, complemented at the end of the document with examples of activities to support teachers in developing these competences in their students in a strategic and integrated way in the specific context of their schools.

2.2 Empowering Students with Technology-Enhanced Learning

As mentioned above, the transversal nature of digital literacy is emphasised throughout the *Learning with the School Library* Referential, whose glossary defines digital literacy as 'the ability to use technologies, networks and digital tools ethically, effectively and safely to find, use, produce and communicate information' [4]. It is thus perceived across the different areas of literacy and is linked to the skills to be developed in reading, media and information literacy, in relation to the learning to be achieved in the curriculum areas in each cycle.

The focus on innovative learning scenarios involving digital strategies, technologies and tools is evidenced in the proposed operationalisation strategies at the end of each of the sections of the Referential dedicated to the three literacy areas. The analysis of these proposed strategies allows us to draw some conclusions:

- The diversity of purposes and educational contexts for using digital scenarios and tools is noteworthy;
- Some of the strategies are associated with only one literacy area, and it is possible to recognise the adequacy between the suggested strategy and the specificity of the literacy competence to be developed, e.g., the use of digital tools to improve reading fluency (reading literacy), media conversion activities (media literacy) and citation, referencing and bibliography (information literacy);
- Some of the strategies are common to two or more literacy areas, such as the collaborative creation of transmedia narratives, combining diverse languages, formats and media (reading and media literacy) or the use of digital book libraries, online catalogues, digital repositories, directories, search engines (reading, media and information literacy);
- Resorting to digital technologies favours strategies that involve operations of active use and elaboration, such as the creation of transmedia narratives or the production of concept/mind maps;
- In digital-based strategies, collaborative work is valued, either through the collaborative production of content or by encouraging participation in platforms such as wikis and blogs or participation in online reader communities;
- Some types of media, tools or multimodal products are suggested (e.g., podcasts, book trailers and citation management tools such as Zotero or Mendeley). However, even these are included as suggestions in lists that open up to other possibilities to be selected by pedagogical teams according to the class profile, the specific context of the schools and the objectives of the work to be developed with the students.

Our exploratory analysis also allows us to confirm that most of the proposals presented require the active involvement of students in their learning process, including, as mentioned above, their participation in collaborative work processes. The implications for the teaching process are direct, namely for teachers, teacher librarians and other educators who are challenged to work together to design scenarios that promote meaningful learning activities for students in contexts that are increasingly hybrid learning ecosystems.

3 Designing Technology-Enhanced Learning Environments Through the Referential: Achievements and Limitations

The *Learning with the School Library* Referential, as of 2020, also counts on the online resource *Learning with the School Library: Activities and Resources* hosted on the official portal of the School Libraries Network [5], to complement its scope. This resource corresponds not only to a repository of activities and tools provided by the School Libraries Network Coordination Office to support the implementation of the Referential, but also to a virtual platform for interaction and exchange, where teacher librarians from all over the country can share their activity plans. Unsurprisingly, these plans are in line with those prepared by the Coordinating Office, as they have to follow the template provided and show that, regardless of the focus of the joint activity, teachers and teacher librarians favour collaborative work and implement active learning methodologies, with an emphasis on exploratory activities and experimentation, often framed in hybrid learning scenarios.

Collaborative practice is also at the core of the WEIWE(R)BE project, which is the result of a partnership between the School Libraries Network and the WEIWER® Network, based at the Laboratory of Distance Education and eLearning (LE@D) of the Open University (Portugal). This project, whose main objective is to develop the information literacy skills of secondary school students through the strategic articulation between the library and the classroom, also has the *Learning with the School Library* Referential as one of its main frameworks, focusing on aspects related to information literacy and to the transversality in the approach to digital literacy [6]. Furthermore, this is a project that has had as technical and pedagogical support an ongoing training course aimed at teachers who take part in the project in its first year of implementation, allowing their monitoring in the field, as well as the sharing of experiences, practices and resources, mainly through the LMS platform used in the training course. The participation of each school in the project involves the development of a work plan corresponding to a practical learning situation, designed in collaboration between the teacher librarian and at least one teacher of a curricular area, relying on the operationalisation strategies recommended in the *Learning with the School Library* Referential. In their work plans, most schools opt for collaborative work and active learning methods supported by digital environments and tools.

Notwithstanding the achievements presented above, and taking into account the national coverage of the libraries network, the comparative analysis of the monitoring reports on the implementation of the *Learning with the School Library* Referential in recent years shows a decrease in the number of school libraries implementing it in 2021–2022, namely: 1601 (out of a total of 2525) compared to 1824 (out of a total of 2469) registered in the pre-pandemic school year [7, 8]. However, in terms of the impact of implementing the Referential in schools, teachers' perceptions maintained the same trend of perceiving a significant impact on learning and educational success, with the agreement with this perception ranging from 96%–98% in 2018–2019 [8] to 97%-99% in 2021–2022 [7].

Apart from the fact that the number of participating schools is lower than before the pandemic, which could be explained, for instance, by the extraordinary workload that we all had to face, the teachers' perceptions of the impact of the Referential reveal the need to invest in the literacy-approach to the curriculum that this framework entails and, consequently, highlight the need for more teacher training as a means of promoting the implementation of the Referential in more schools across the country. In response to this need, the School Libraries Network published the guide *Learning with the school library: a programme for developing literacy* [9] to support teachers in developing a strategic, systematic and comprehensive approach to applying the Referential in their schools.

4 Conclusion

Given the challenges facing education in today's world, characterised by the ubiquity of digital technologies and a high degree of uncertainty about the future [10], education systems must define policies that encourage pedagogical innovation. In the case of the Portuguese education system, the School Libraries Network programme has contributed to a dynamic of innovation in schools by relying on teacher librarians to apply in their local contexts the national guidelines, which focus on a literacy-based approach to the curriculum that integrates learning with multiple literacies. Through the national coverage of the libraries network, a significant number of schools have applied the *Learning with the School Library* Referential, whose conceptual framework and suggested practical activities have enabled the implementation of technology-enhanced learning based on active learning methodologies and centred both on collaborative work and the strategic mobilisation of digital environments and tools, thus contributing to the digital empowerment of both students and teachers.

Considering, on the one hand, teachers' perceptions of the positive impact of the activities of the Referential on students' learning and educational success and, on the other hand, the recent decline in the number of schools implementing it, it is essential to ensure that its implementation in schools becomes even more comprehensive, integrated and systematic. Ultimately, this is also due to the fact that digital literacy is a transversal literacy that reflects 'the presence of technologies, tools and digital environments in all contexts and domains, formal and informal, of learning' [4].

References

1. Portugal INCoDe.2030. Action Lines. https://www.incode2030.gov.pt/en/eixos-en
2. Punie, Y., Redecker, C.: European Framework for the Digital Competence of Educators: DigCompEdu. Publications Office of the European Union (2017).https://doi.org/10.2760/178382

3. Martins, G.: (Coord.): Students' Profile by the End of Compulsory Schooling. Ministério da Educação (2017). https://cidadania.dge.mec.pt/sites/default/files/pdfs/students-profile.pdf
4. Rede de Bibliotecas Escolares: Aprender com a biblioteca Escolar. Referencial de aprendizagens associadas ao trabalho das bibliotecas escolares na educação pré-escolar e nos ensinos básico e secundário (2017). https://www.rbe.mec.pt/np4/AcBE.html?newsId=99&fileName=referencial_2017.pdf
5. Rede de Bibliotecas Escolares: Aprender com a Biblioteca Escolar: Atividades e Recursos. Portal RBE. https://www.rbe.mec.pt/np4/AprendercBE.html
6. Cardoso, T., Pestana, F., Cruz, A., Mota, E.: O Programa WEIWE(R)BE no ecossistema da escola digital. In: T. Cardoso (Org.) Educação: Saberes em Movimento, Saberes que Movimentam, Volume III, Capítulo 4, pp. 43–55. ARTEMIS Editora (2023). https://doi.org/10.37572/EdArt_2802237744
7. Rede de Bibliotecas Escolares: Referencial Aprender com a biblioteca escolar: Relatório de implementação 2021–22 (2022). https://www.rbe.mec.pt/np4/%7B$clientServletPath%7D/?newsId=3317&fileName=relatorio_final_2021.22.pdf
8. Rede de Bibliotecas Escolares: Referencial Aprender com a biblioteca escolar: Relatório de implementação 2018–19 (2019). https://www.rbe.mec.pt/np4/%7B$clientServletPath%7D/?newsId=99&fileName=relatorio_18.19_.pdf
9. Rede de Bibliotecas Escolares: Guia orientador. Aprender com a biblioteca escolar: programa para o desenvolvimento de literacias (2022). https://www.rbe.mec.pt/np4/%7B$clientServletPath%7D/?newsId=2716&fileName=guia_orientador_acbe2022.pdf
10. UNESCO [Comissão Internacional sobre os Futuros da Educação]: Reimagining our futures together: a new social contract for education (2021). https://unesdoc.unesco.org/ark:/48223/pf0000379381

Learning Path Recommendation from an Inferred Learning Space

Madjid Sadallah and Grégory Smits(✉)

IMT Atlantique, Lab-STICC UMR CNRS 6285, 29238 Brest, France
{madjid.sadallah,gregory.smits}@imt-atlantique.fr

Abstract. Defining a learning space of reference may be a challenging task for the concerned tutor(s). However, once formalized, such a representation of possible learning sequences may serve as a norm to evaluate the current state of a learner and to potentially derive recommendations about the next learning state to target. A pragmatic strategy is introduced in this article to ease the definition of a subjective learning space from a few tutor(s)-provided examples of representative learning paths. A measure is then also inferred from these representative paths that can then be used to evaluate an ongoing learning path. The learning space and the evaluation measure, combined together, are then used to suggest the learning activity the learner should address next.

Keywords: Learning space inference · Learner evaluation · Fuzzy measure inference · Recommendation

1 Introduction

Massive Open Online Courses (MOOC) have been largely adopted to provide a flexible access to a collection of learning activities. It makes sense to consider that, within a same platform, learners may follow different learning sequences to reach a same goal [3] which is to master a targeted set of skills.

A Learning Space (LS), as defined by Doignon and Falmagne in [4], is a formal model used to describe the knowledge states of learners. It consists in learning states representing families of problems a learner is able to solve at a given time that are linked by prerequisite relationships. The practical applications of LSs are wide-ranging and it has been shown that they may improve both teaching and learning outcomes. ALEKS [2] is an example of a web-based intelligent tutoring system that employs LSs to assess student knowledge and instruct them in various scientific fields by providing personalized feedbacks.

The construction of an appropriate LS is a highly demanding task that generally relies on the expertise of one or several competent tutors. To ease the construction of an LS, a cooperative approach called *QUERY* [5] question experts about the dependencies between the learning activities. The present article introduces a novel approach to construct a LS that then serves as a basis for providing learners with feedbacks on their ongoing learning process. Unlike

O. Viberg et al. (Eds.): EC-TEL 2023, LNCS 14200, pp. 630–635, 2023.
https://doi.org/10.1007/978-3-031-42682-7_53

the traditional approach, which requires tutors to answer questions about the prerequisites between learning activities, the proposed strategy seeks examples of representative learners from the concerned tutors. These tutor-given examples serve to illustrate a possible learning trajectory to achieve a complete mastery of the skills targeted in the course. While inferring LS from a few learning paths is not a new concept, the main contribution of this work is to infer an evaluation measure from the tutor(s)-provided examples, which is then used to assess and complete an ongoing learning path. This approach has several benefits over the traditional approach to constructing LSs. First, it is less time-consuming and resource-intensive since tutors do not need to provide explicit information on the prerequisite relationships between states. Second, the proposed approach may be used to provide learners with personalized suggestions about the way to address the different problems and to give them a quantitative feedback about the gap between their ongoing learning sequence and learners of reference.

Section 2 provides a detailed account of the proposed approach, outlining the LS construction phase and the inference of the evaluation measure, which are then used to recommend the learning paths. Section 3 finally illustrates how the approach could be integrated in an online learning environment.

2 Proposed Approach

In this section, the fundamental properties of an LS are first recalled before showing how this structure is used in the proposed approach.

2.1 Learning Space Inference from a Few Sequences

Let Q be a set of problems that can be addressed during a given course. Especially if the course holds in a flexible learning platform as a MOOC can be, then it is generally considered that different paths may be envisaged to master Q, despite the existence of prerequisites to solve some of these problems. An LS [4] is a formal structure defined by a couple $(Q, \mathcal{K})$, $\mathcal{K}$ being a family of subsets of Q that organizes the different knowledge states that describe what a learner is able to solve at a given stage of its learning process. Two axioms make such a formal structure relevant to model a learning domain:

1. learning smoothness (i.e. step-by-step learning), if $K \subset L \subseteq Q$ then it must exist a chain of states $K_0 = K \subset K_1 \subset \ldots \subset K_n = L$ with $K_i = K_{i-1} \bigcup \{q_i\}, q_i \in Q$,
2. learning consistency, if $K \subset L \subseteq Q$ and $q \in Q \setminus K$, then $K \bigcup \{q\} \in \mathcal{K}$ implies $L \bigcup \{q\} \in \mathcal{K}$.

A singularity of the proposed approach is to ask the tutor(s) managing the course to provide a few examples of learners who have been identified as particularly outstanding in the way they have addressed the different problems Q to serve as references. Let $\mathcal{E} = \{e_1, \ldots e_m\}$ be this set of representative learners. It is imposed that each learner e is associated with a sequence, denoted by S_e,

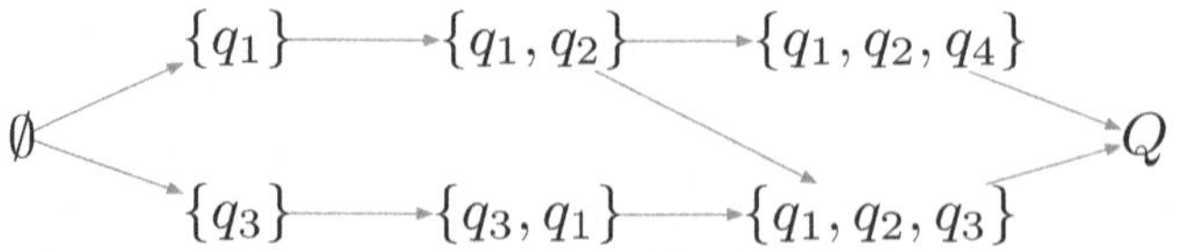

Fig. 1. LS built from the three learning sequences S_{e_1}, S_{e_2} and S_{e_3}

describing the order in which he/she has addressed all the problems in Q. Each $S_e, e \in \mathcal{E}$, being a complete learning sequence, forms a complete chain of step-by-step learning states from $\emptyset$ to Q. It has been proved in [4] (Theorem 13.5.5 in Chap. 13) that given a set of learning sequences (i.e. $\{S_{e_1}, \ldots, S_{e_m}\}$) the union of their prefixes forms an LS.

To illustrate this LS construction step, let us consider that $Q = \{q_1, q_2, q_3, q_4\}$ and that three representative learning sequences are provided by the tutor(s): $S_{e_1} = q_1 \prec q_2 \prec q_3 \prec q_4$, $S_{e_2} = q_1 \prec q_2 \prec q_4 \prec q_3$ and $S_{e_3} = q_3 \prec q_1 \prec q_2 \prec q_4$. Figure 1 depicts the obtained LS.

2.2 Learner's Evaluation Wrt. a LS of Reference

In addition to serve as a basis to build the LS, the set $\mathcal{E}$ of representative learners is also used to infer an evaluation measure. This measure may then be used to set up normative evaluations confronting an ongoing learning process with the learning sequences of reference that constitute the norm. To infer the evaluation function from the set $\mathcal{E}$, an adaptation of the approach named CHOCOLATE introduced in [7] is proposed. It aims at inferring the characteristic function of a disjunctive concept from a few user-provided representative examples. This approach is particularly relevant in this context as, first, it takes as input a tiny set of positive examples, thus reducing the cognitive load of the concerned tutor(s). These examples are treated in a non-contrastive way, i.e. without considering negative examples nor discriminating wrt. other concepts. Finally, and probably the most important property in our case, CHOCOLATE captures generalization situations when properties are shared among a subset of representatives examples (i.e. common subsequences in the tutor(s)-provided learning sequences) but without discarding singular examples. CHOCOLATE, that is an automatic learning method from a tiny set of positive examples [8], draws its theoretical foundation in the cognitive approach called the Exemplar View [6] that advocates for a disjunctive interpretation of the representative examples.

The inference mechanism of CHOCOLATE and its underlying weighting measures are revisited to handle sequences of items as input, instead of sets of items, and to fit the behavior expected in an online learning context.
A function $\delta : Q \rightarrow [0, 1]$ is first used to quantify the importance of each problem taken individually. It is considered here that the higher the number of states in which a problem q appears, among the states in $\mathcal{K}$, the more important the problem. This weighting strategy is justified by the fact that a problem that

frequently appears in the different knowledge states is a prerequisite to solve many other problems. More formally, the δ function is defined as follows:

$$\delta(q) = \frac{|\{k \in \mathcal{K} \text{ st. } q \in k\}|}{|Q|}, \tag{1}$$

where k is a knowledge state in $\mathcal{K}$.

Considering the toy example depicted in Fig. 1, $\delta(q_1) = \frac{6}{7}$, $\delta(q_2) = \delta(q_3) = \frac{4}{7}$ and $\delta(q_4) = \frac{2}{7}$.

A second function denoted by μ is used to quantify the relevance of a sequence of problems. A sequence S to evaluate is considered relevant if it matches one of the possible learning sequences involved in the considered LS. The comparison between S and the representative examples from $\mathcal{E}$ cannot rely on their longest common subsequence, as it would not take into account the relations of prerequisite between problems, but rely on the identification of the longest prefix of the examples that is a subsequence of S, hence the following μ function:

$$\mu(S) = \max_{e \in \mathcal{E}} \max_{i=1}^{|S_e|} \frac{|S_e^i| \times (S_e^i \blacktriangleleft S)}{|S_e|}, \tag{2}$$

where S_e^i is the prefix of size i of the sequence S_e, $|S|$ the length of a sequence S and $(S_e^i \blacktriangleleft S)$ a Boolean predicate indicating if S_e^i is a subsequence of S. It is straightforward to show that μ possesses the properties of a fuzzy measure:

1. $\mu(S = \emptyset) = 0$ as $(S_e^i \blacktriangleleft \emptyset)$ always equals 0 whatever the prefix S_e^i,
2. $\mu(S \in \mathcal{E}) = 1$ as $|S_e^i| \times (S_e^i \blacktriangleleft S')$ equals $|S_e|$ when $S = S_e$,
3. $\mu(S) \leq \mu(S')$ if $(S \blacktriangleleft S')$. Let S_e^i be the longest prefix of S among the examples in $\mathcal{E}$, then by transitivity S_e^i is also a prefix of S'. The length of the longest prefix of S_e^i that is also a subsequence S can only increase when new activities are added to S.

To illustrate the way the relevance of a sequence is quantified, let us consider an ongoing sequence $S = q_1 \prec q_3 \prec q_2$ and its comparison wrt. the LS in Fig. 1. Then, $\mu(S) = \frac{2}{4}$ as the longest prefix among the examples in $\mathcal{E}$ that is a subsequence of S is $q_1 \prec q_2$ from e_1 and e_2. Considering now a learner addressing the problems in the following order $S = q_3 \prec q_2$, then this sequence gets the following relevance degree $\mu(S) = \frac{1}{4}$ as the prerequisite of q_2 have not been addressed.

μ is a fuzzy measure that quantifies the matching of any (sub)sequence of problems wrt. the examples in S. The Choquet integral, as a sub(sup)-additive aggregation function, is particularly relevant to aggregate the individual weights of the problems (given by the δ function) when the way they are combined matters (the μ function). However, the discrete version of the Choquet integral takes as input a set whose elements are processed in a decreasing order of their individual weight to quantify the overall weight of their combinations, but does not consider any temporality. This is why, in order to also take into account the temporal order the problems are addressed in the evaluated sequence, a temporal criteria is added to the aggregation function given in Eq. 3:

$$\mathcal{C}(S) = \sum_{j=1}^{|S|} [\mu(H_j(S)) - \mu(H_{j-1}(S))] \times (H_j(S) \triangleleft S) \times \kappa_j(S), \quad (3)$$

where $\kappa_j(S)$ returns the j^{st} most important, in terms of prerequisite, problem of the sequence S and $H_j(S)$ is the sequence composed of the j most important problems in S ranked in a decreasing order of their δ score. The Boolean predicate $(H_j(S) \triangleleft S)$ returns 1 if $H_j(S)$ is a subsequence of S, which means that the evaluated sequence $H_j(S)$ has been actually approached this way. In other words, the function $\mathcal{C}(S)$ identifies the longest sequence of the most important problems that appears in S but also checking that they are addressed according to their relations of prerequisite defined in the inferred LS.

As an illustration, let us consider the sequence $S = q_1 \prec q_4 \prec q_2$ to evaluate and the LS in Fig. 1. Its score is computed as follows: $\mathcal{C}(S) = \frac{1}{4} \times \frac{6}{7} \times 1 + (\frac{2}{4} - \frac{1}{4}) \times \frac{4}{7} \times 1 + (\frac{3}{4} - \frac{2}{4}) \times \frac{2}{7} \times 0 = \frac{5}{14}$.

2.3 Recommending the Next Learning Activity

A first quantitative feedback, using the $\mathcal{C}(S)$ function, can be given to the learner about the relevance of his/her ongoing learning process compared to a LS of reference. It is now shown how the LS and the function $\mathcal{C}(S)$, combined together, may be used to provide the learner with suggestions about the next learning activity to address.

Let $N(S) = \{q \in Q \setminus S\}$ be the set of problems the learner still has to address. This set may be reduced to the what is called the outer fringe in [4] of the knowledge states mastered by the concerned learner. The outer fringe is the set of problems that are directly reachable from a given knowledge state. Let $q \in N(S)$ be a reachable problem, then the function C is used to evaluate the gain for the learner of addressing q, this gain is denoted by $\gamma(q, S)$ and is computed as follows:

$$\gamma(q, S) = \mathcal{C}(S \prec q) - \mathcal{C}(S). \quad (4)$$

The next problem q that the proposed strategy suggests to address is such that $\gamma(q, S) = \max_{q' \in N(S)} \gamma(q', S)$.

As an illustration, let us consider that the learner has completed only one activity $S = q_1$ from the space in Fig. 1. Then, the next reachable problems are $\{q_2, q_3\}$. As $\mathcal{C}(q_1 \prec q_2) = \frac{5}{14}$ and $\mathcal{C}(q_1 \prec q_3) = \frac{3}{14}$, q_2 is suggested.

Such a fuzzy-measure-guided recommendation may be seen as a positive, thus opposite, definition of the Shapley value. The Shaley value is often used to quantify and explain the overall importance of an item q wrt. a fuzzy measure. Instead of determining the importance of q as the mean loss observed when q is removed from all the states it appears in, the gain caused by adding q determines the importance of learning q next. This recommendation strategy may be seen as a positive counterfactual-based explanation method in the field of explainable AI [1]. The problem q that is suggested is the minimal reachable improvement of the learning sequence S that allows the learner to get closer to the target class formed by the representative examples used to build the LS.

3 Ongoing Works

This paper describes recent theoretical works on the cooperative definition of an LS of reference from few examples. Experimentations are currently in progress so as to assess the relevance of the proposed evaluation strategy and the recommendations it generates. These experimentations are conducted in a MOOC platform of a French engineering school. It has first been observed on a given course involving 13 problems that, despite its linear structure, 12 different learning paths have been followed by learners who performed well (final grade $\geq \frac{7}{10}$). The 5 first learning steps of these 12 paths are always the same. The proposed methodology gives a significant weight to this sequence shared among these 12 paths of reference but then also takes into consideration all the possible ways to build a sequence that covers all the remaining problems.

Our current research aims to leverage the inferred LS and the assessment metric to provide learners with personalized feedbacks tailored to their current state of knowledge and the learning goal. An underlying research question is that such a learning goal may be inferred from few teacher(s)-selected examples of successful learners. Next step will be to assess the impact of the provided recommandation on learners' achievement.

References

1. Byrne, R.M.: Counterfactual thought. Annu. Rev. Psychol. **67**, 135–157 (2016)
2. Canfield, W.: Aleks: a web-based intelligent tutoring system. Math. Comput. Educ. **35**(2), 152 (2001)
3. Davis, D., Chen, G., Hauff, C., Houben, G.J.: Gauging mooc learners' adherence to the designed learning path. In: International Educational Data Mining Society (2016)
4. Doignon, J.P., Falmagne, J.C.: Knowledge Spaces. Springer, Cham (2012)
5. Kambouri, M., Koppen, M., Villano, M., Falmagne, J.C.: Knowledge assessment: tapping human expertise by the query routine. Int. J. Hum. Comput. Stud. **40**(1), 119–151 (1994)
6. Smith, E.E., Medin, D.L.: The exemplar view. In: Foundations of Cognitive Psychology: Core Readings, pp. 277–292 (2002)
7. Smits, G., Yager, R.R., Lesot, M.-J., Pivert, O.: Concept membership modeling using a choquet integral. In: Lesot, M.-J., et al. (eds.) IPMU 2020. CCIS, vol. 1237, pp. 359–372. Springer, Cham (2020). https://doi.org/10.1007/978-3-030-50146-4_27
8. Wang, Y., Yao, Q., Kwok, J.T., Ni, L.M.: Generalizing from a few examples: a survey on few-shot learning. ACM Comput. Surv. (CSUR) **53**(3), 1–34 (2020)

Exploring Barriers for the Acceptance of Smart Learning Environment Automated Support

Sergio Serrano-Iglesias(✉), Eduardo Gómez-Sánchez, Miguel L. Bote-Lorenzo, Víctor Alonso-Prieto, and Vanesa Gallego-Lema

GSIC-EMIC Research Group, Universidad de Valladolid, Valladolid, Spain
{sergio,victor,vanesa.gallego}@gsic.uva.es, {edugom,migbot}@tel.uva.es

Abstract. Smart Learning Environments (SLEs) can detect learning opportunities, personalized and contextualized for each student, both in traditional and out-of-class learning settings. This can help to promote learning that is more meaningful in a scalable fashion. However, instructors may be reluctant to loose control by letting SLEs autonomously decide this. Moreover, students may not accept to use learning systems in their free time, when they are out-of-class. This paper presents an exploratory study based on two learning experiences supported by an SLE. The findings show that the involved instructors desire a large degree of control over the recommendations made by the SLE, and that students are mostly (but not completely) positive about using such a system.

Keywords: smart learning environments · teacher agency · out-of-class learning · automated recommendations

1 Introduction

Smart Learning Environments (SLEs) are Technology Enhanced Learning (TEL) environments that seek to provide a personalized support to learners adequate for their individual learning needs and context [6]. Thanks to the advances in Learning Analytics and the availability of data related with the actions performed by students across physical and virtual spaces, SLEs can intervene autonomously at any time to call the attention of learners about relevant resources and activities related to the courses they are enrolled in. Several researchers see in this feature of SLEs their potential to connect what happens in traditional (class, virtual learning environments...) and out-of-class (places in the city...) learning environments, since SLEs can be aware of the topics that are dealt in the formal lessons, monitor learning interactions with institutional applications, and then propose personalized learning tasks when students are wandering around in their leisure time. For example, [2] proposes a system for learning Japanese in which students can use an app to annotate elements they learn in a specific context outside the class (e.g. the supermarket), practice them with examples,

O. Viberg et al. (Eds.): EC-TEL 2023, LNCS 14200, pp. 636–641, 2023.
https://doi.org/10.1007/978-3-031-42682-7_54

and also receive suggestions when they are in a physical or social context that is relevant to their previous learning (e.g. in a restaurant where someone has labelled a related item). In our previous work [5], we have described scenarios in which students enrolled a course about History of Art watch videos, read PDFs and answer quizzes in the institutional Moodle. The SLE tracks their progress and, when they are in the city, it proposes tasks related to nearby historical buildings (e.g. a Gothic cathedral or a Renaissance palace).

In spite of the optimistic view of researchers, the adoption of SLEs in real practice may be hindered by the expectations and preconceptions of stakeholders, particularly learners and instructors. One concern comes from instructors feelings about the SLE acting autonomously but in relation to their formal learning design. For SLEs to be scalable, all the feedback they provide (learning tasks or resources) cannot be generated by the instructors of each course: they may be looked up in the web (e.g. a YouTube video), generated automatically (e.g. quizzes derived from Linked Open Data) or proposed by communities of instructors or domain experts and stored in public repositories. However, instructors may wonder whether such learning resources align well with the learning goals set by them (e.g. a video related to "gothic" may not be about the architectural style or that a true-false quiz may have debatable options), or dislike the frequency or moments chosen to provide recommendations (e.g. they might like to limit the number of them per day or bound them to a specific city or neighborhood). These concerns are part of a broader issue, namely the agency of instructors [4] when introducing autonomous support systems such as SLEs to their students.

Another issue is the acceptance of students of learning activities to be carried out of class, in the leisure time, but connected to what they learn in class. While situated learning can be more meaningful and engaging [1], and if connected to what was part of the formal lessons allows for a deeper reflection and understanding of the contents of the curricula [3], we may encounter that students feel that a system that makes such learning recommendations is a kind of homework, and may thus reject the usage of SLEs when they are out of class.

With the aim of shedding some light on these issues, this paper presents an exploratory study addressing the following general research question (GRQ): *Are there relevant barriers for the acceptance by teachers and students of Smart Learning Environments?* This question will be particularized in two specific research questions: RQ1: *Will autonomous SLE performance be perceived as a threat to teacher agency?*, and RQ2: *Will out-of-class learning recommendations made by SLEs be rejected by students?* While other issues may hinder the adoption of SLEs (e.g. data privacy, integration with institutional platforms, application usability, etc.), these are left out of the scope of this study.

2 Research Approach and Context

Due to the exploratory nature of this study, it was carried out as a multiple case study analyzed with mixed methods. The participants in two learning situations carried out in a Faculty of Education, supported by an SLE, were surveyed and interviewed by the end each learning situation to gain insight of their perceptions.

2.1 Smart Learning Environment

In this study, we made use of SCARLETT [5] as the supporting SLE. SCARLETT is capable of providing context-aware personalized recommendations across different environments and spaces to learners in different learning situations. It collects learning traces from the environments, tools and devices involved in the learning situation (e.g., Moodle or Kahoot!); analyzes them and generates learning indicators to conform a student model (e.g., which is the level of performance of each student in each topic); and, using this model, triggers recommendations (e.g., take a picture, answer a short text question or do a quiz). SCARLETT can support multiple learning situations by reading the learning design created by the teacher (i.e. the learning activities and resources to be carried out during the formal lesson, annotated with the topics they deal with), which influences the operation of the rest of its components.

By architectural design, SCARLETT provides feedback driven by a set of recommendation rules stored in a database so that they can be tailored. Further, activities recommended by SCARLETT are taken from an external repository that offers a retrieval interface so that multiple resource providers could be used in order to achieve scalabillity. In order to properly contextualize the findings concerning teacher agency in this study, it is important to remark that both recommendation rules and activities to be recommended by SCARLETT were co-designed by the instructors of the course and the researchers.

Although the study focuses on two learning experiences supported by SCARLETT, the research questions are not dependent on the actual choice of SLE, and thus the findings may be generalized to other SLEs capable of providing autonomous recommendations to learners.

2.2 Learning Situations and Participants

Both scenarios took place the first year of the Degree of Education, lasting 3 weeks each. The first one (S1) was in a course on School Organization, focused in a unit about playgrounds (their design, inclusiveness, educational potential, etc.), while the second (S2) was part of a course on ICTs for Education, in a unit centered on the impact of advertising campaigns. Teacher T1 (female, around 10 years of experience) co-designed and instructed both courses, while teacher T2 (male, over 30 years of experience) was also instructor in S2. In S1, students were in one single class, while S2 had two classes (each with an instructor). A total of 212 students (53 male, 159 female) participated in the study.

Both scenarios started after content of the unit had been delivered with lectures and seminars. In S1, happening in May 2022, students performed a questionnaire with Kahoot! for revising the concepts worked in class, and the SLE collected the results to build an initial model of students and, after that, students were invited to carry out geo-localized tasks at their own pace during two weeks. Tasks were open-ended questions related with the features present in playgrounds in primary schools throughout the city. In the third week, they did an orienteering activity in the campus, with the supervision of the teacher.

Students performed tasks available through QR codes, derived from the student model considering their performance in the Kahoot! and the geo-localized tasks. By the end of the third week, the SLE published in Moodle a reinforcement quiz that was personalized for each student (i.e. each had a different set of questions).

Scenario S2 took place in November 2022. It also started with a Kahoot! monitored by the SLE. After that, during the first week they located and took photos of advertising campaigns present in the city, which served the teachers to generate multiple choice questions (MCQs). These MCQs were stored in a repository used by the SLE to make personalized recommendations of geo-localized tasks along the second and third weeks. Similarly to S1, by the end of the scenario students received a personalized quiz in Moodle.

To carry out tasks in the city, students made use of SCARLETTApp, a tool that sends the position and id of the student to the SLE, which in turn proposes personalized and contextualized learning tasks. Recommendations rules (both for geo-localized tasks and the quiz in Moodle) promoted the selection of tasks on topics in which the student had less competence.

Despite the similarities between scenarios, there were relevant differences. In S1, the activity was encouraged but not graded. Due to the open-ended nature of the tasks, students did not receive direct feedback by the application once they submitted the answer. Instead, a collaborative portfolio collected all answers for discussion in class. In contrast, in S2 students had to complete a minimum of 4 recommended tasks in different locations, and results were graded. Each MCQs had a correct answer, so students got feedback after they submitted their answer.

2.3 Data Sources

An anonymous survey was administered after each experience (17 questions in S1, 23 in S2) and 109 answers were collected in total. Focus groups were also carried out with a selection of students, combining active and less active profiles, with a total of 18 students interviewed in three sessions (one for S1, two for S2). Teacher T1 was interviewed at the end of S1, and both T1 and T2 were jointly interviewed at the end of S2.

3 Results

Concerning the perception of the autonomous operation of the system in relation to teacher agency (RQ1), teachers were explicitly asked during the interviews at the end of each scenario. Though they both perceived benefits of the enactment of activities in informal contexts, specially to improve student motivation and reflection (T1: "*They have seen a connection [of real world] with the contents*" or T2: "*What is most important is the motivation it generated*"), this satisfaction was conditioned to the control of the recommended resources. When asked if they would allow the SLE to recommend third party resources, both of them were against it, regardless to the source. T1 stated "*The use of collaborative platforms and public resources [...] is convenient, but I would need to revise them*",

"*The content [created by other instructors] can be fantastic. It is not that I don't trust it, but each teacher has their own way of teaching*", "*I'd recommend SCARLETT [in fact, the support given to that scenario] as I know how it behaves. If I didn't know what type of feedback it can offer to the student, like external videos [...] it could cause conceptual conflicts*". Both teachers understood, however, the resulting workload and lack of scalability of such level of control as the number of resources and students increases. Interestingly, T2 also stated that he would like to be informed "*from time to time*" of the recent recommendations made by the SLE (what tasks to whom and where) "*in order to have a selection of perceptions, and build from it my interpretation*".

As for RQ2, the appropriate informants are students. In the survey, after S1 they were asked the following open-ended question: "*SCARLETT can help you discover learning opportunities while you are wandering around in the city. Do you consider valuable to unintentionally find out about these opportunities? Why?*". All 32 were positive. Arguments included fun, more dynamic learning, learning at their own pace or effortlessly, or gaining awareness of the environment. They also point out that they can have the control, as they can close the app. In S2 we separated this question into 1–5 agreement scale for a simpler "*I would like to receive recommendations from SCARLETT in my free time*" and an open-ended explanation question. The former collected 78 answers, with 36 in disagreement (1–2) and 15 in agreement (4–5). Positive comments were similar to those in S1, while negative comments referred mostly to the lack of time in general (i.e. they feel they are very busy). Only four students explicitly stated that this was something they would not do in their free time, while a few others showed positive or negative interest in the advertising domain in particular (i.e. in their mind, the SLE would only support this domain).

The focus group added evidences to this parted attitude towards receiving learning recommendations in their free time. For example, in S1 they were mentioning minor inconveniences of receiving recommendations during their free time, but they were laughing and clearly there was not a negative attitude: "*I live by a school and received recommendations while having breakfast, I thought I would never finish breakfast!*" or "*A concert was about to start and I was doing a task [about a nearby school]*" but they immediately added "*Anything that is learning without being sitting on your chair is so cool*". In one of the S2 focus groups one student stated that "*I started using SCARLETT because it was mandatory, but then I liked it*". When the researcher inquired whether they would use it in other courses (with tasks adapted to another domain) if it was fully voluntary, some said "*I would use it sometimes*", other "*It depends on the topic. Maybe [the topic] does not motivate me*", two agreed on "*If it helps you to prepare for the exam, I would use it*", two mentioned that "*This is less boring than learning at home with paper [the book]*", and one was forthright to state that "*I would not do it if it is not mandatory, this or anything else*". In the other S2 focus group, the ambiance was more against using the SLE in their free time: "*I used it because it was mandatory*", "*It is tiring, I wouldn't do it on my own will*", "*And me, to be honest*", but this latter student also added "*But then [when he had completed the number of mandatory activities] you see another one and think, I'm going to do it, it's not that hard*", and the rest also agreed that they went beyond what was required because, once started, "*it is neither that hard nor that boring*".

4 Discussion and Limitations

Both instructors and students involved in this study valued the fact the SLE offers with contextualized learning opportunities in a location related to the topic of study, resulting in a more meaning, engaging and dynamic process. Still, there are barriers to be addressed for its adoption. Teachers want further control over the recommended resources, while students have parted feelings about using the SLE voluntarily at first glance, though their attitude is positive once they have tried it. These conclusions are undoubtedly biased by the small sample and homogeneity of participants, and more studies (in other domains, educational levels, and with other instructors) are needed to generalize. However, our findings should be a word of caution for overoptimistic expectations on the acceptance of systems, such as SLEs, that autonomously provide learning recommendations in both institutional and out-of-class environments.

Acknoledgements. This research was partially funded Grant PID2020-112584RB-C32 funded by MCIN/AEI/10.13039/501100011033.

References

1. Ley, T., et al.: Scaling informal learning at the workplace: a model and four designs from a large-scale design-based research effort. Br. J. Educ. Technol. **45**, 1036–1048 (2014)
2. Mouri, K., Ogata, H.: Ubiquitous learning analytics in the real-world language learning. Smart Learn. Environ. **2**, 1–8 (2015)
3. Pimmer, C., Mateescu, M., Gröhbiel, U.: Mobile and ubiquitous learning in higher education settings. A systematic review of empirical studies. Comput. Hum. Beh. **63**, 490–501 (2016)
4. Priestley, M., Biesta, G., Robinson, S.: Teacher Agency: What Is It and Why Does It Matter? In: Flip the System. Routledge (2015)
5. Serrano-Iglesias, S., Gómez-Sánchez, E., Bote-Lorenzo, M.L., Asensio-Pérez, J.I., Ruiz-Calleja, A., Vega-Gorgojo, G.: Demonstration of SCARLETT: a smart learning environment to support learners across formal and informal contexts. In: De Laet, T., Klemke, R., Alario-Hoyos, C., Hilliger, I., Ortega-Arranz, A. (eds.) EC-TEL 2021. LNCS, vol. 12884, pp. 404–408. Springer, Cham (2021). https://doi.org/10.1007/978-3-030-86436-1_44
6. Tabuenca, B., et al.: Affordances and core functions of smart learning environments: a systematic literature review. IEEE Trans. Learn. Technol. **14**(2), 129–145 (2021)

FAMS: A Formative Assessment Management System for Generating Individualised Feedback

Raja Khurram Shahzad(✉), Erik Ström(✉), and Peter Mozelius(✉)

Mid Sweden University, Ostersund, Sweden
{raja-khurram.shahzad,erik.strom,peter.mozelius}@miun.se
http://www.miun.se

Abstract. Virtual learning environments offer new possibilities for technology enhanced teaching and learning, but providing rapid, individualised feedback for complex assignments in large student groups remains challenging. This paper presents a Formative Assessment Management System (FAMS), a computer-based tool for teachers to generate written feedback at scale with minimal overhead. FAMS leverages archived feedback fragments and thematic identifiers to create pertinent feedback while consistently maintaining quality and fairness. The system has been implemented in programming courses and yielded promising results, including reduced feedback delivery time and maintained feedback quality. Future research will evaluate FAMS from student and teacher perspectives, conforming to educational action research, continuous quality improvements, and investigating correlations between aspect-based assessment and learning outcomes.

Keywords: Formative assessment · Individualised feedback · Archived feedback · Technology enhanced learning · Educational action research

1 Introduction

Formative learning is a critical component of effective teaching and learning in higher education, as it focuses on providing students with continuous and constructive feedback throughout the learning process [1]. This approach enables students to understand their strengths and areas for improvement, allowing them to adjust their learning strategies [2]. Research has consistently demonstrated the positive impact of formative learning on student engagement, motivation, and performance [6]. However, providing individualised, timely, and effective written feedback for large student groups can be significantly challenging and is a long-standing weakness for educators [8]. Delays in feedback can hinder the formative process, as students may have difficulty recalling the relevant context or may have already moved on to new tasks or topics.

In the 21st century, online learning and virtual learning environments have opened up new possibilities for formative assessment, both in humanities [5]

O. Viberg et al. (Eds.): EC-TEL 2023, LNCS 14200, pp. 642–647, 2023.
https://doi.org/10.1007/978-3-031-42682-7_55

and STEM subjects [4,12]. Thus, this demonstration paper presents the Formative Assessment Management System (FAMS) to address the challenge and take advantage of new possibilities. FAMS is designed to streamline the grading process and facilitate creating and managing personalised feedback for each student, leveraging the benefits of aspect-based assessments to align with formative learning principles. Moreover, this paper also presents the design and implementation of FAMS, possible integration with existing learning management systems, and its potential for enhancing the quality and efficiency of feedback delivery.

2 Aspect-Based Assessment

Aspect-based assessment approach aligns well with formative learning, as it focuses on breaking down assignments into smaller aspects, each addressing specific skills, knowledge areas, or learning objectives [3]. This facilitates targeted feedback, allowing students to better understand their strengths and weaknesses [1,7]. Key benefits of integrating aspect-based assessments into formative learning include:

- Focused evaluation and feedback: Concentrating on specific aspects of an assignment allows teachers to provide more precise feedback [9], helping students identify areas where they excel or need improvement [2].
- Streamlined grading process: Simplifying grading with binary outcomes for each aspect (pass or fail) can make the evaluation process more efficient, particularly for large classes.
- The clarity in learning objectives: Breaking down assignments into aspects helps to clarify learning objectives, improving alignment between instruction, assessment, and learning goals [3].
- Data-driven insights: Tracking student performance on individual aspects can provide valuable data for teachers [11], helping them identify common misconceptions and weaknesses and tailor their instruction accordingly.
- Facilitated growth and development: Aspect-based assessments enable targeted interventions and support, promoting growth and development in areas where students may be struggling [2].

By incorporating aspect-based assessments into formative learning, educators can enhance the educational process [3,10]. Thus, as described in the following sections, the FAMS system leverages the advantages of aspect-based assessments to streamline the grading process and enable individualised feedback generation for large student groups.

3 The FAMS Solution

3.1 Design and Implementation

FAMS provides a versatile environment for maintaining digital archives of categorised feedback. For this purpose, FAMS uses a database of feedback fragments.

The fragments can be classified into categories to make the database reusable across different subjects. In each category, fragments are stored with two pieces of information, i.e., thematic identifier and content. The thematic identifier links fragments in the grading document and interlinks between fragments within the database to create composite feedback for more complex and nuanced feedback scenarios.

FAMS provides a simple graphical interface with two options, i.e., Feedback Management View (FMV) and Grading View. FMV allows users to add, sort and filter fragments based on categories and modify their content and its associated thematic identifiers. Grading View is further divided into student focus and aspect focus. The student focus view displays a list of students and a frame containing all aspects to be graded (please see Fig. 1a). The aspect focus view shows a list of aspects with a frame displaying all students to be graded for the selected aspect. This flexibility is designed to accommodate different grading workflows and user preferences.

For using FAMS, a grading protocol is created, which comprises aspects with binary outcomes for assessment. A grading project is created to use the protocol, which may contain zero to many students. Users can select relevant feedback fragments for each aspect, add free text or restrict fragment alternatives to certain categories. Users can also preview, edit, or create new fragments without accessing FMV. FAMS generates feedback for all or selected students by retrieving relevant content from the database and creating individual feedback documents for each student (please see Fig. 1b). The supported output file formats for feedback include PDF, Markdown, and simple text.

(a) Protocol View (b) Output View

Fig. 1. Different views of FAMS

3.2 Analytics and Reporting

FAMS provides comprehensive analytics and reporting features, allowing educators to make data-driven decisions. The system tracks performance data for each aspect associated with learning objectives, enabling the identification of bottlenecks and areas for improvement. By analysing this data, educators can quickly identify trends and patterns that reveal which aspects students struggle with most or which course components require additional attention or resources.

In addition to tracking performance data for each aspect, FAMS monitors the number of attempts students make for each assignment. This information provides valuable insight into student engagement, perseverance, and the effectiveness of the feedback provided. By comparing the number of attempts across different student batches, educators can identify changes in student performance over time and the impact of any adjustments made to the course content, teaching strategies, and feedback process. Some key benefits of monitoring assignment attempts and comparing performance data across different student batches are as follows:

- Continuous improvement: By identifying trends and patterns in student performance, educators can make informed decisions on refining course content and adjusting teaching strategies to support student learning better.
- Early intervention: Tracking the number of attempts students make for each assignment allows educators to identify struggling students early on and provide timely support or additional resources to help them succeed.
- Evaluation of feedback effectiveness: Analysing the impact of feedback on student performance helps educators determine if the feedback provided is constructive and helpful, allowing them to refine and improve their feedback processes.
- Cross-group comparisons: Comparing performance data across different student batches can reveal the impact of changes made to the course, highlighting the success of specific interventions or adjustments and informing future course development.

3.3 Integration and Bias Mitigation

FAMS can be integrated with popular Learning Management Systems like Canvas, Blackboard, and Moodle for submission retrieval, feedback publishing, and ensuring up-to-date student information. Moreover, maintaining fairness and impartiality in the feedback process, including that given through FAMS, is crucial. To achieve this, it is crucial to regularly review and revise feedback fragments to eliminate any discriminatory language or assumptions that may lead to biases. Furthermore, promoting collaboration among educators in creating and managing feedback fragments is crucial to ensure a comprehensive approach that considers diverse perspectives.

3.4 Initial Implementation and Observations

The usage of FAMS required minor preparations, such as ensuring that the assignment's requirements could be broken down into concise aspects aligned with learning objectives. The database of feedback fragments was primarily populated with feedback gathered from past course iterations and supplemented with fresh fragments generated during each assignment's evaluation. Existing fragments were refined whenever edge cases were identified. Thus, the process of generating feedback was streamlined by FAMS, resulting in a significant reduction in the providing feedback time from weeks to days.

Due to FAMS, the process of generating feedback was streamlined, resulting in a significant reduction in the providing feedback time from weeks to days. Students appreciated the shorter response time and the quality of feedback in the course evaluations, although this batch of students had not experienced delays similar to past years. An unforeseen side effect of the reduced delay was a significant increase in students' attempts before passing assignments in the first course. In the first course, students could submit lab assignments unlimited times, leading to minor changes for additional feedback. This issue was addressed in the second course by limiting the number of attempts for assignments. It is noteworthy that courses utilizing the FAMS system have shown a higher rate of student success compared to previous years. However, this observation can only be directly attributed to the FAMS system with further research. The FAMS usage in programming courses was a positive experience, showcasing its potential to enhance formative assessment processes in this educational context.

4 Evaluation and Future Research

To assess FAMS' effectiveness, a comprehensive evaluation involving students and teachers is necessary, employing quantitative and qualitative methods like surveys, interviews, and focus groups. Comparing traditional grading methods with FAMS can help evaluate time efficiency, consistency, and feedback quality. Additionally, researchers can investigate FAMS' impact on student learning outcomes, such as performance improvement, engagement, and satisfaction.

Future research related to FAMS could focus on several topics, including:

- Continuous quality improvements: Refine and expand FAMS to better support users by focusing on aspects like the feedback database, user interface, and analytics capabilities.
- Correlations between aspect-based assessment and learning outcomes: Investigate the relationship between FAMS' aspect-based assessment approach and student learning outcomes. Examine whether the focused evaluation and feedback lead to better performance, understanding, or retention.
- Adaptability to other educational contexts: Explore FAMS' application in settings like K-12 education, vocational training, or professional development courses, and potential modifications for these contexts.

Conducting evaluations and investigating these topics will help FAMS evolve and adapt, providing more efficient and effective formative feedback in diverse educational settings and contributing to understanding its capabilities and applications.

5 Conclusion

This paper discussed the challenges of providing individualised, timely, and constructive written feedback in formative learning in higher education. The Formative Assessment Management System has been introduced as a potential solution to address these challenges, leveraging the benefits of aspect-based assessments to align with formative learning principles. FAMS streamlines the grading process and facilitates the creation and management of personalised feedback for each student, offering integration possibilities with existing learning management systems. The initial implementation of FAMS showcased its potential for enhancing feedback delivery. The system reduced the delay in providing feedback, maintained quality, and potentially increased students' success rates. Future research and evaluation can contribute to FAMS' ongoing refinement and expansion, ultimately enhancing its impact in various educational contexts and ensuring that all students receive the support they need to thrive.

References

1. Black, P., Wiliam, D.: Inside the black box: raising standards through classroom assessment. Phi Delta Kappan **80**(2), 139–148 (1998)
2. Hattie, J., Timperley, H.: The power of feedback. Rev. Educ. Res. **77**(1), 81–112 (2007)
3. Wiliam, D.: Embedded formative assessment. Bloomington, IN: Solution Tree Press (2011)
4. Barana, A., Marchisio, M.T.: good reasons to adopt an automated formative assessment model for learning and teaching Mathematics and scientific disciplines. Procedia. Soc. Behav. Sci. **228**, 608–613 (2016)
5. Wilson, J., Roscoe, R., Ahmed, Y.: Automated formative writing assessment using a levels of language framework. Assess. Writ. **34**, 16–36 (2017)
6. Dolin, J., Black, P., Harlen, W., Tiberghien, A.: Exploring relations between formative and summative assessment. In: Dolin, J., Evans, R. (eds.) Transforming Assessment. CSER, vol. 4, pp. 53–80. Springer, Cham (2018). https://doi.org/10.1007/978-3-319-63248-3_3
7. Zhu, M., Liu, O. L., Lee, H.-S.: The effect of automated feedback on revision behavior and learning gains in formative assessment of scientific argument writing. Comput. Educ. **143**, 103668 (2020)
8. Lu, C., Cutumisu, M.: Integrating deep learning into an automated feedback generation system for automated essay scoring. In: Proceedings of The 14th International Conference on Educational Data Mining, pp. 573–579. International Educational Data Mining Society, France (2021)
9. Burlacu, N.: Aspects of assessment of students' activity in the seminar classes: problems and solutions. J. Soc. Sci. **4**(4), 63–74 (2021)
10. Hao, Q., et al.: Towards understanding the effective design of automated formative feedback for programming assignments. Comput. Sci. Educ. **32**(1), 105–127 (2022)
11. Panadero, E., Lipnevich, A.A.: A review of feedback models and typologies: towards an integrative model of feedback elements. Educ. Res. Rev. **35**, 100416 (2022)
12. Mekterović, I., Brkić, L., Horvat, M.: Scaling automated programming assessment systems. Electronics **12**(4), 942 (2023)

The Added Value of Simulations in 3D Virtual Worlds for Professional Training of First Aid Medical Teams

Tamar Shamir-Inbal(✉), Talia Or-Griff, and Ina Blau

The Open University of Israel, 4353701 Ra'anana, Israel
tamaris@openu.ac.il

Abstract. Virtual worlds are based on a virtual reality technology, which allows three-dimensional realistic situations within a digital environment. The study framework is based on the Activity Theory and the model of Serious Games. These frameworks emphasize the interrelationships between the virtual worlds' various components, including user activity, training design, and their formal definition as Serious Games. This study examined the teaching and learning characteristics which take place in three-dimensional virtual world environments (3DVW) and focused on a training pilot for emergency medical personnel of the Israeli First Aid medical teams (IFA). Semi-structured interviews were conducted through video-conferencing with 27 volunteers and employees of the IFA who participated in 3D virtual worlds training simulations. These interviews provided an understanding of their training experience in virtual worlds in general and the various medical simulation experience in particular. The findings showed that learning effectiveness was the main added value in immersive 3D virtual worlds training. The VW simulator has the ability to make learning more efficient and results in improvement and acquisition of professional skills in medical teams with an emphasis on following medical protocols. In addition, the virtual environment can enhance motivation and enjoyment in the context of medical training. Moreover, the virtual environment enables safe practice of complex medical procedures. These findings strengthen the positive trend of 3D virtual worlds technology implementation in medical training.

Keywords: VR-Virtual reality · VW-Virtual world · SBL-Simulation based learning · Immersive first aid training · 3D Virtual worlds

1 Introduction

In recent years, we have witnessed an increasing use of virtual world technology in the field of medical training, mainly because these worlds are able to simulate reality through simulations (Liaw et al., 2021). Virtual worlds are based on virtual reality technology that allows the presentation of three-dimensional realistic situations within a computerized environment. These environments include realistic virtual reality simulations to the point of a sense of immersion. (Çakiroğlu & Gökoğlu, 2019). Virtual worlds, in many cases,

O. Viberg et al. (Eds.): EC-TEL 2023, LNCS 14200, pp. 648–655, 2023.
https://doi.org/10.1007/978-3-031-42682-7_56

also include the concept of a digital game. Digital games in 3D virtual environments were initially intended for the younger generation for purposes of learning and as a social tool (Danforth et al., 2009). Virtual world game structures should be precise in order to distinguish between entertainment and serious games (Ulmer et al., 2022). The platform examined in this study is an example of a serious game whose purpose is to develop relevant professional skills for the trainees.

With the outbreak of the COVID-19 pandemic, conditions were created to accelerate the use of 3D virtual worlds (D3VW) in medical training. These environments allow learners to take part in a virtual simulation, while maintaining social distance in an easy and safe way. This takes place in order to maintain a learning sequence and to use the technology during emergency times (Liaw et al., 2021).

The use of virtual worlds for training purposes allows interactions and immersion. Thus, it has been adopted over the years by various organizations, such as for military training, especially simulations for pilots, and the training of medical teams (Messinger et al., 2009). It seems that the use of simulations in virtual worlds has helped to move the training of medical staff from passive exposure to the content and procedures to active learning. The implementation of teaching approaches based on advanced technologies has created an opportunity for innovative learning and has led to high student satisfaction and motivation (Danforth et al., 2009). For example, it was found that the element of competitiveness, which is common in digital games, is a central element for increasing the motivation and participation of students in 3D virtual worlds training (Liaw et al., 2021). This component positively affects the learners' performance, which results in fewer errors in the application of training content and skills in the real world (Ulmer et al., 2022). These advantages have led to the fact that today this technology serves innovative purposes in the medical field, and its use increases the learners' involvement and motivation to learn (Izard et al., 2018).

1.1 The Goals of the Study

The study examined the characteristics of teaching and learning that exist in educational environments in a three-dimensional virtual world. This training was conducted with Israeli First Aid (IFA) personnel in the field of emergency medicine. During the study, we examined how teaching and learning in a 3D virtual worlds environment enables active involvement of the learners and provides experience in collaborative learning processes. This paper relates to the perspectives of the participants in the context of teaching and learning processes experienced by IFA teams using a 3D environment in virtual professional training (see illustration in Fig. 1). Accordingly, the research question was: What are the perspectives of the study participants on the added value of conducting training in an innovative 3D virtual environment in the field of emergency medicine?

2 Methodology

The study was conducted using the qualitative research approach. This approach enabled an in-depth understanding of the users' experience in virtual worlds as a training environment.

Fig. 1. Illustration of the 3D environment for professional training in emergency medicine

2.1 The Participants

The participants consisted of 27 employees and volunteers serving in different positions within the IFA organization. The majority of the participants were male (56%). A significant portion of the participants were youth volunteers (70%) aged 16–20 years learning to provide first-aid. As part of their professional development, all participants had completed "Course 60". Additionally, 67% of the participants had taken part in the Multi-Casualty Incident course, while 34% had participated in the Paramedic course (see details below). The choice of this group of participants was based on a pilot that was conducted in the IFA organization.

2.2 The Research Context

The participants were exposed to 3D virtual worlds (3DVWs) as part of the professional training required for their work in the organization, as detailed in the above section. Course 60 is a 60-hours face-to-face training course that includes diverse topics in emergency medicine, such as basic CPR and equipment use, identifying emergency situations, cardiovascular diseases, treating trauma victims, and use of ambulance equipment.

The Ambulance as a Multi-Casualty Incident course trains participants to handle multi-casualty incidents in IFA ambulances that have additional equipment. It also includes training on complex medical situations and various degrees of injuries.

The Paramedic course for emergency medicine at IFA includes 227 hours of theoretical and practical training in ambulances at IFA stations, while studying various first aid fields and obtaining a permit to drive an ambulance-type security vehicle.

The 3D virtual training was conducted in two different environments. The first environment allowed experience in medical simulation and was defined as 3D virtual space (3DVW), although it did not require VR optical equipment. The representation of the objects in this environment was three-dimensional, therefore even without the equipment it provided a sense of immersion. This was a multi-player immersive virtual world (IVW) with the ability to represent each player through an avatar.

The second environment was a 3D environment, and it usually used VR headsets. This environment created the sense of immersion through both the use of VR headsets and an avatar representation in the form of hands. Similar to the previous environment, this environment also offered medical simulations with an emphasis on emergency medicine. It demonstrated the sequence of resuscitation techniques and inserting an infusion as well as enabling practice of these processes.

2.3 Instruments and Procedure

Semi-structured interviews were conducted with employees and volunteers of the IFA organization to assess the effectiveness of the virtual simulations. Interviews included three main sections: 1) participants' background, such as age, gender, professional training, and position in the organization, 2) 3D learning processes and characteristics, including comparison to traditional simulations, assessment of skill improvement, or acquisition of new skills, and 3) collaboration and communication processes, such as feedback provided by the training coordinators and peers. The interviews lasted 30–60 min each. The interviews were coded bottom-up, defining categories and subcategories according to the research question. A content unit was a statement by an interviewee referring to a certain topic (and not to the participants themselves). Each statement could belong to more than one category. About 25% of the transcripts were checked by another rater, and inter-rater reliability was satisfactory. The raters were experts in digital learning technologies and trained in conducting qualitative analysis.

3 Findings

3.1 The Added Value of the 3D Virtual Worlds

Tables 1 and 2 describe the added value that participants found in the context of their learning experience in general and in the context of the effectiveness of the medical training in particular.

The data indicates that the simulator experience provides valuable improvements in both the learning process in general and for medical training in particular. A third of the participants (35%) reported a significant learning effectiveness with the simulator. Although there were few statements about pleasure and motivation, the training still stimulated these elements and contributed to a positive experience. Additionally, participants highlighted the acquisition and improvement of essential professional skills for medical staff in the IFA ambulance through the simulations.

Table 2 refers to the detailed presentation of the simulator's added value in medical training.

Table 2 highlights the enhanced value of the 3D virtual world simulator for medical training. Participants recognized the simulator as a tool that provided professional and medical advantages, facilitating better and easier understanding of medical protocols. Trainers emphasized the simulator's ability to enable medical procedures that are not feasible in traditional face-to-face training, such as experimenting on mannequins or colleagues. About 50% of participants acknowledged the simulator's advantage in performing a range of procedures, and 23.5% appreciated the opportunity to practice identical medical situations through simulations, avoiding potential harm (17%).

Table 1. The added value of the simulator for learning. (N = 130)

Subcategory	Number of statements	Percentage of number of interviewees	Example statement
Effectiveness of learning	45	35%	"You learn how to recognize the various situations which you perfected in the simulator." (R)
Acquisition and improvement of skills	34	26%	"I know that the simulations helped me learn the order of procedures, which is the most important - skills of inserting an infusion and of all the required steps in treating a patient." (C)
Pleasure/motivation for youth	25	19%	"In the end it's cool to be with the VR headset and equipment." (A)
Autonomous study	19	15%	"Because of the simulations I didn't have to stop learning; for example, now with Covid-19 learning doesn't stop". (L.D.)
Social interaction	7	5%	"It was nice to be with your friends in the course. We learned and 'played' together." (AP)

Table 2. The added value of the simulator for medical training. (N = 81)

Subcategory	Number of statements	Percentage of the total number of interviewees	Example statement
Simulation of medical treatment	40	50%	"The simulator presents and shows things just like in reality, which is quite different from reading information to learn. The simulator helped me understand and learn the procedures." (C)
Practice of medical procedures	19	23%	"It gives more complete exposure [to medical procedures that need to be practiced] and the ability to do more things." (AS)
Safe training procedures	14	17%	"When it's with a real patient, I would be more afraid. With the simulator I feel more confident and it's possible to learn through a 3D virtual environment and practice safely. I'm sure now that I will feel better able to use the procedures on real patients after this training." (AS)
Saving resources	8	10%	"With the simulator I can learn virtually how to use expensive medical equipment. If it were real equipment, I would be afraid to ruin it." (P)

4 Discussion

The research question examined the added value of using 3DVW in the context of training emergency medical teams in the IFA. The findings show an extensive added value in the use of a virtual reality simulator in the IFA organization's training. The added value is reflected in two main components: the added value for learning in general and for professional medical training in particular.

About one third of the training participants stated that the simulator increased the effectiveness of learning for them, and about a quarter of the participants felt an improvement in their professional skills regarding medical procedures. It was also found that enjoying learning experience in the virtual environment increased trainees' motivation to practice procedures frequently, while saving resources of time and money. This finding is consistent with previous studies (Danforth et al., 2009; Izard et al., 2018) which have shown that the use of a simulator promotes practice and thus enhances active learning processes. In medical training, the learner must take an active role in applying the learning content and skills. This practice can be relatively easy when conducted in innovative environments such as 3D virtual worlds. Moreover, treatment of a "virtual patient" through various medical simulations encourages mental flexibility among the training participants. Hence, the possibility of experimenting with numerous test cases in 3D virtual worlds, makes it possible to create improved medical training for paramedics and medics.

Beyond that, the participants mentioned the importance of being able to train in a simulator without causing harm and to practice medical procedures that are difficult to practice frequently in traditional training, such as inserting an infusion. The ability of the 3D virtual worlds technology to demonstrate medical situations in a realistic way, for example chest pressure, asthma attacks, etc., was also emphasized. In addition, some participants stated that the confidence they acquired as a result of using the simulator allowed them to participate in role-playing in order to practice the actions as senior medical team members. Thus, the advantage of medical training in 3D virtual environments lies in the ability to practice situations that cannot be practiced in reality. Nevertheless, virtual worlds can help medical professionals improve their skills and knowledge, become familiar with using different tools, and understand additional roles in medical teams (Izard et al., 2018).

These findings may help policy makers in the IFA and other organizations that train medical teams at various levels through simulations in 3D virtual worlds. This environment can achieve professional goals in terms of positive user experience, learning, and professional training. Additionally, it enables exploration and application of Activity Theory and Serious Games approaches as these provide a safe, realistic, and tailored environment for medical teams to practice.

References

1. Çakiroğlu, Ü., Gökoğlu, S.: Development of fire safety behavioral skills via virtual reality. Comput. Educ. **133**, 56–68 (2019)

2. Danforth, D.R., Procter, M., Chen, R., Johnson, M., Heller, R.: Development of virtual patient simulations for medical education. J. Virtual Worlds Res. 2(2) (2009). https://doi.org/10.4101/jvwr.v2i2.707
3. Izard, S.G., Juanes, J.A., García Peñalvo, F.J., Estella, J.M.G., Ledesma, M.J.S., Ruisoto, P.: Virtual reality as an educational and training tool for medicine. J. Med. Syst. **42**, 1–5 (2018). https://doi.org/10.1007/s10916-018-0900-2
4. Liaw, S.Y., et al.: Wow, woo, win"-Healthcare students' and facilitators' experiences of interprofessional simulation in three-dimensional virtual world: a qualitative evaluation study. Nurse Educ. Today **105**, 105018 (2021)
5. Messinger, P.R., et al.: Virtual worlds—past, present, and future: new directions in social computing. Decision Support Syst. **47**(3), 204–228 (2009)
6. Ulmer, J., Braun, S., Cheng, C.T., Dowey, S., Wollert, J.: Gamification of Virtual Reality assembly training. Effects of a combined point and level system on motivation and training results. Int. J. Hum.-Comput. Stud. 102854 (2022)

Support Mechanisms and Value Creation in Multi-Stakeholder Networks for Digital Innovation in Education: A Cross-Country Study

Pirgit Sillaots[1(✉)], Raquel Coelho[2], Kairit Tammets[1], Mutlu Cukurova[3], Linda Helene Sillat[1], Minna Lakkala[4], Heli Aru-Chabilan[5], Kirke Kasari[5], Madona Mikeladze[6], Tatia Nakashidze-Makharadze[6], Valentina Dagienė[7], Vaida Masiulionytė-Dagienė[7], and Cecilie Hansen[8]

[1] Tallinn University, Narva Road 25, 10120 Tallinn, Estonia
pirgit.sillaots@tlu.ee
[2] Stanford University, 450 Jane Stanford Way, Stanford, CA 94305–2004, USA
[3] University College London, Gower Street, London WC1E 6BT, UK
[4] University of Helsinki, P.O. Box 4 (Yliopistonkatu 3), 00014 Helsinki, Finland
[5] Education and Youth Board, Lõõtsa 4, 11415 Tallinn, Estonia
[6] Batuma Shota Rustaveli State University, 32/35 Rustaveli/Ninoshvili Street, 6010 Batumi, Georgia
[7] Vilnius University, 3 University Street, 01513 Vilnius, Lithuania
[8] University of Bergen, P.O.Box 7800, 5020 Bergen, Norway

Abstract. This study investigates the impact of support mechanisms on enhancing the participation of network members in diverse multi-stakeholder networks with a primary focus on digital innovation in education. The study was conducted in collaboration with national networks from partner countries of a H2020 project, which aims to accelerate digital innovation in and across schools. Twenty-six international stakeholders from various backgrounds, including teachers, school leaders, mentors, educational technologists, policy makers, and a researcher were interviewed (n = 14) or surveyed (n = 12). Using Wenger et al.'s [1] value creation framework, the study identified participants' perceptions of various activities, interactions, and structures that enable network members to generate value. The results indicated overarching values for members to be associated with capacity building opportunities, joint projects, opportunities for expanding impact through recognized expertise, access to personalized support and guidance, and knowledge sharing platforms.

Keywords: multi-stakeholder networks · digital innovation · support mechanisms · value creation

O. Viberg et al. (Eds.): EC-TEL 2023, LNCS 14200, pp. 656–661, 2023.
https://doi.org/10.1007/978-3-031-42682-7_57

1 Introduction

Recently the concept of networks as learning communities has gained traction as a promising catalyst for innovation in the education sector. Characterized by their flexibility, lack of boundaries, and focus on members' interests, these networks present platforms for transformative change [2]. While the term "networks" often refers to connections among people, terms such as "learning communities" or "communities of practice" emphasize collaborative learning partnerships and dedication to a shared domain [1]. In this study, we adopt the term "networks as learning communities" and use the shorthand "network" to underscore the interconnected nature of these two elements in the networks under examination., Number of networks have been established in Europe to promote innovation within and across schools by connecting schools, research institutes, policy makers, and other public and private institutions. Some recent examples include the SALL ('Schools as Living Labs') project [3], the OSOS ('Open Schools for Open Societies') project [4], and the Hypatia project [5].

The success of these networks hinges on members deriving value from their involvement; otherwise, they may disengage, leading to network disintegration [1]. Value creation stems from various activities and interactions, yielding short or long-term benefits for participants, such as problem-solving, skill development, social connections, and access to resources. Wenger et al.'s value creation framework [1] examines the value generated by individuals through their involvement in social learning activities, consisting of five cycles revealing how network participation contributes to value creation [1]. Assessing value creation should link specific activities and interactions to desired outcomes. In this study, we refer to these activities and interactions as network-embedded support mechanisms, which may include, for example, professional development opportunities and knowledge-sharing platforms.

This study aimed to investigate the support mechanisms among members of national stakeholder networks, given their critical importance for network success. We sought to contribute to the growing knowledge on the importance of support mechanisms and value creation in implementing educational innovation initiatives in multi-stakeholder networks. While not establishing a causal link between support mechanisms and value creation, our findings offer insights for the broader education community focused on digital innovation and inform future endeavours. We collaborated with national networks from partner countries of the iHub4Schools project that aims to accelerate digital innovation in and across schools. The study focused on the research question: Which support mechanisms, including knowledge sharing, collaboration, and external expertise, do network members perceive as crucial for generating value from their participation in professional multi-stakeholder networks?

2 Method

In total, 26 members of five national stakeholder networks in each pilot country were recruited to participate in the study. Participants were recruited by collaborators in partner countries through their professional networks, employing a convenience sampling method. Nine stakeholders from Estonia, five from Lithuania, seven from Finland, four from Georgia, and one from Norway participated in the study.

We developed a structured interview protocol based on the work of Wenger et al. [1] with the aim to explore the perceived values of stakeholder networks for members as well as significant activities, interactions, and structures within the network. Additionally, we designed an open-question survey to gather the same information, which was administered in Finland, Norway, and Georgia. Both the interview and survey questions were translated into the native language of the country. The interviews were conducted online, and recorded, and the same approach was used for survey responses. Collaborators translated quotes that were relevant to the research question from interviews and surveys back into English with the help of experienced native-speaker researchers to reduce the potential bias introduced in the process.

We used a combination of deductive and inductive approaches in the data analysis. We developed a codebook based on the Value Creation Framework [1]. It included codes for values related to the cycles of immediate and potential value creation (e.g., access to new knowledge and information sources), as well as support mechanisms grounded in the authors' knowledge of practices in networks, such as training and knowledge sharing platforms. The first two authors independently coded the data, incorporating unanticipated values and support mechanisms into the codebook as needed. Following this, a tentative thematic analysis was conducted to identify the most significant support mechanisms that emerged from the data. Preliminary findings were shared with collaborators to validate and revise our findings accordingly.

3 Preliminary Findings and Discussion

Our preliminary analysis identified five support mechanisms that contribute to the generation of both immediate and potential values in these networks: capacity building opportunities, joint projects, opportunities for expanding impact through recognized expertise, access to personalized support and knowledge sharing platforms. The abbreviations have been used to indicate the members' networks in the quotes: E (Estonia), F (Finland), G (Georgia), L (Lithuania), N (Norway). It is important to note that no causal relationship is implied between the support mechanisms identified and value creation, due to the methodological limitations of our investigation.

3.1 Capacity Building Opportunities

Many network members stressed the significance of participating in events such as trainings, seminars, workshops, regular meetings, conferences, seasonal schools, and networking gatherings. The following quotes from two networks illustrate the diverse benefits of participating in various events: *Through these additional trainings and meetings, I aim to improve my job performance by bringing new skills to my school. Teaching can often be monotonous and numbing, so these events serve as a lifeline amid daily routines. It's refreshing to meet like-minded individuals and exchange up- dates from various schools (Teacher 3, F); The training received through the program, as well as seminars and other events involving mentor networks, has been incredibly useful for sharing experiences and acquiring tips and tricks (Mentor 1, E).*

These insights reveal the value derived from participating in various events, including improved knowledge, skills and the opportunity to share experiences with professionals. Furthermore, members emphasized the importance of certain characteristics that enhance the value of capacity building events, such as in-person interaction and diverse expertise and backgrounds. For instance, the following quotes emphasize the preference for a diverse pool of stakeholders joining these events: *Different people, different schools - I observed others using technology. I gained valuable examples from other schools, seeing how others use it, and adapted those ideas. If you stay within your own bubble, you won't progress. You may think you know everything, but when you see others, you grow... (Educational technologist 1, E).*

Most participants stressed the importance of diverse stakeholders in network events, as their presence leads to a richer learner experience, broader perspectives, and enhanced collaboration. Key aspects highlighted include a) exposure to varied practices from different schools, enabling members to implement these in their own contexts; b) interdisciplinary collaboration with experts from various levels of education, edtech companies, and municipalities; c) holistic understanding through the inclusion of developer teachers, experts, and government representatives, promoting a comprehensive grasp of the issues at hand. Additionally, members highlighted the importance of hands-on activities such as individual assignments and collective problem-solving during events. Incorporating these elements allows members to gain practical insights that directly support their everyday work. As one member shared: *Participating in training sessions and engaging with activities such as homework between training sessions have been significant events for me* (School leader 2, E). In addition to formal opportunities, the members stressed the value of creating dedicated spaces for casual networking during these events; for example: *While lectures at events were important, informal table discussions during coffee breaks were even more significant. (...) These casual interactions have helped clarify my thoughts, provide alternative solutions to problems, and allowed me to share tips or ideas on how I've addressed issues myself.*" (Teacher 1, F).

Finally, the significance of practical aspects in enhancing the value derived from network members' participation in these events is evident in their responses. Participants highlighted aspects such as obtaining certifications, receiving financial support, having events scheduled during their work hours, and providing learning opportunities: *I value obtaining new knowledge and skills, as well as having certificates to validate that new knowledge. (Teacher 1, E); The financial aspect, such as receiving extra money, is valuable to me (Mentor 1, E).*

The quotes suggest that practical considerations are crucial to maximize the benefits of participation. These factors complement other key dimensions, such as in-person events, diverse stakeholder involvement, sharing and networking opportunities.

3.2 Joint Projects

While capacity building opportunities, such as workshops or conferences, were acknowledged by network members as highly valuable to their professional growth and expanding their professional network, they also pointed out that extended opportunities for collaboration can augment these experiences, leading to more meaningful learning. One member noted the benefits of extended collaborative opportunities: *The most influential experiences for me have involved collaboration with digital pedagogy development teachers from other schools in planning and implementing various tasks. Through these interactions, I've become acquainted with teachers in almost every school in my municipality and have had the opportunity to observe diverse practices across many different schools. (Teacher 3, F).* This quote highlights the significance of extended collaboration, which goes beyond one-time events, in enhancing the depth and continuity of learning experiences. It emphasizes the importance of fostering sustainable relationships, ongoing dialogue, and a comprehensive understanding of diverse practices within multi-stakeholder networks.

3.3 Opportunities to Expand Impact Through Recognized Expertise

In national networks, gaining a reputation is vital, and many network members emphasized its importance. They stressed the significance of expertise recognition through broader impact opportunities. This recognition can occur through invited talks, collaboration, consultations, and workshops. For example: *As an expert, recognition and consultation opportunities naturally follow. You will be invited to various workshops to conduct sessions and share experiences (Educational technologist 1, E); While recognition of excellence in mentoring is not very important to me, invitations to participate in various events may serve as evidence of my expertise (Mentor 1, L).*

These quotes exemplify the importance network members place on gaining a reputation and having their expertise recognized. Such recognition, often through invitations and opportunities, not only validates their skills but also allows them to contribute meaningfully to the broader educational community. These valuable opportunities serve as crucial support mechanisms, benefiting individual members and fostering the overall development of the network. In addition to verbal praise and recognition, networks should consider implementing practical mechanisms that enable members to make a broader impact, such as pairing experienced members with newcomers or organizing regular workshops led by network members. By integrating these support mechanisms, networks can enhance the creation of member value, leading to more successful and sustainable networks.

3.4 Access to Personalized Support and Guidance

Members from national stakeholder networks also stressed the significance of personalized approaches to complement capacity building opportunities. This is particularly important for teachers who may be less tech-savvy or resistant to change. One mentor underscored the benefits of customized training and forming personal connections with teachers, stating: *I feel differently about consulting and mentoring. I think it is im- important to listen to people and be there for them as a person. For those who are not highly skilled or are resistant to change, training alone may not be effective. Instead, a more personalized approach through mentoring and/or consulting can be more meaningful for these individuals" (Mentor 2, E).* This perspective suggests that a one-size-fits-all approach to professional development in these networks might not be sufficient for addressing the diverse needs and backgrounds of teachers. By incorporating personalized approaches, such as mentoring and consulting, educational stakeholders can better support teachers with varying levels of technology proficiency and openness to change.

3.5 Knowledge Sharing Platforms

Many network members noted the use of social media groups and local engagement platforms as key mechanisms for sharing information and receiving support. These tools offer benefits such as allowing members to access information at their own pace. A teacher from an Estonia network explained: *Facebook groups remain an effective and neutral platform for our generation. Information posted on the group's wall offers flexibility - if I have time today, I can check for updates; if not, I can choose not to visit the page and read the content. Additionally, we used a Messenger chat group among the teachers to discuss problems and support one another* (Teacher 1, E). In general, the participants suggested that digital channels allow network members to engage in meaningful discussions, share information, and stay connected beyond formal network activities, providing an additional layer of ongoing support.

4 Conclusion

This study aimed to investigate the support mechanisms perceived as significant in helping network members generate value from participating in different national networks, given their critical importance for network success. Our preliminary analysis identified five primary support mechanisms that contribute to the generation of value in these networks, ultimately contributing to their sustainability: capacity building opportunities, joint projects, opportunities for expanding impact through recognized expertise, access to personalized support and guidance, and knowledge sharing platforms. The insights into the support mechanisms identified here have the potential to help network members generate further value from participating in different national networks focused on digital innovation. By incorporating these mechanisms, future digital innovation initiatives can enhance collaboration, promote ongoing learning, and ultimately contribute to the sustainable growth of these networks.

Acknowledgement. The work was funded by EC funded project iHub4Schools, grant nr:101004676.

References

1. Wenger, E., Trayner, B., De Laat, M.: Promoting and assessing value creation in communities and networks: a conceptual framework (2011)
2. Lieberman, A.: Networks as learning communities: shaping the future of teacher development. J. Teach. Educ. **51**(3), 221–227 (2000)
3. School as Living Labs: About. https://www.schoolsaslivinglabs.eu/ (2021)
4. Open Schools for Open Societies: Home. https://www.openschools.eu/OSOS (2021)
5. Hypatia: About. https://www.ecsite.eu/activities-and-services/projects/hypatia (2020)

Towards Live Coding and Instant Feedback on Common Issues in Large Lectures

Sven Strickroth(✉)

LMU Munich, Oettingenstr. 67, 80538 München, Germany
sven.strickroth@ifi.lmu.de
https://www.tel.ifi.lmu.de/

Abstract. Learning programming requires practice. Timely feedback is one of the main drivers for learning and overcoming obstacles. In large lectures, however, social interactions and feedback are rather limited. Currently, there are no satisfactory ways for lecturers to detect and react on the most pressing issues directly in a lecture for various reasons such as students not daring to ask questions or too many erroneous submissions to inspect. This article proposes to combine Audience Response Systems and E-Assessment systems to tackle these issues. Within a lecture, students work on small programming assignments, upload their solutions, and then the lecturer can request a nearly instant overview of the correctness as well as the most common errors. This overview can help the lecturer to discuss different solutions strategies as well as the most common issues. Preliminary results of a case study with a prototype indicate that the approach is usable and formed useful clusters. Further development and research possibilities are outlined.

Keywords: Audience Response · Just-in-Time Teaching · Programming Education · Live Feedback · Learning Analytics · Formative Assessment

1 Motivation

Learning programming has found its way into many curricula outside of traditional computer science and mathematics study programs such as engineering, science, or economics. An inherent problem is, however, that learning programming is often perceived as difficult by beginners [9]. Programming consists of several abilities that learners have to master at the same time, including understanding of the syntax of the formal programming language, problem solving, computational thinking as well as testing and debugging skills [3]. Particularly, working on exercises and timely feedback are important for learning [5]. Weekly assignments are widely used, however, there is a longer period of time between teaching a concept, applying it, and finally getting feedback (e.g., after a few days when the concept was taught and/or a week after the submission deadline).

O. Viberg et al. (Eds.): EC-TEL 2023, LNCS 14200, pp. 662–667, 2023.
https://doi.org/10.1007/978-3-031-42682-7_58

Introductory programming courses are often attended by several hundred students [2,7]. With such large classes, frontal lectures are often the last resort. Here, students are usually only passively listening and might not dare to ask a potentially "dumb" question in front of a large audience or might be intimidated by more sophisticated questions of more advanced fellow students [7]. Hence, social interactions, discussions, and feedback (for both, the students and the teacher) become rather limited abetting inactive students and high dropout rates [2,7]. Particularly, it is important to get an overview of issues that affect many students in order to be able to discuss the most pressing issues.

In this paper a higher-education teaching approach using educational technology for more practical lectures in which the students program live and get instant feedback from the lecturer is presented. For this an algorithm is proposed that groups and ranks the most common errors enabling the teacher to discuss these.

2 Related Research

A common way to activate students or to increase interactivity in (large) classes are audience/classroom response systems (CRS, ARS) or "clickers" [4]. The key aspect of an ARS is to pose a question as a lecturer in class, to automatically collect the answers of the students, and to immediately present an evaluation of the (anonymous, aggregated) results. There is a wide variety of didactic scenarios such as knowledge checks, group interactions, or competitions that have shown to be effective [4,8,10,11]. Still, most of these systems focus on multiple-choice questions for simple voting [10]. Hence, it is hard to reach higher levels of Bloom's taxonomy such as working on programming assignments. Particularly for programming education, there are four notable approaches: Mader and Bry used puzzles in their ARS to assess coding skills in Haskell [10]. There are two approaches by Hauswirth and Adamoli [6] as well as Robbins [12] that implemented each an ARS to support teaching programming in Java. Both systems support traditional multiple-choice questions and small fill-in-the-gap programming tasks (using a simple text field inside the ARS). The teachers can inspect the submissions, however, there seems to be no automatic evaluation of the submissions and no overview of the most common errors. Additionally, there is an approach by Ebert and Ring [3] that can collect and present common syntax errors of Python assignments in-class. However, that approach cannot handle functional or other run-time errors.

To support teaching in large classes, many (semi-)automated e-assessment systems have been developed [15]. An advantage of such tools is that timely feedback can be provided 24/7 without involving teachers. An example is the GATE system [14] in which students can upload their solution attempts and can request tests within the deadline to get feedback. Additionally, all submissions are tested automatically after the deadline to support teaching assistants grading the submissions. To assist the teaching assistants, GATE can suggest already used feedback snippets of similar submissions [13]. However, current systems are not designed to support in-class activities but for assessing formative homework assignments, summative examinations or competitions. Such systems provide aggregated overviews on the numbers of correct and incorrect submissions or lists of all submissions showing their evaluation results.

There also is research on common (syntax) errors (e.g., [1]), that needs to be considered for the clustering. However, there is no system for in-class usage.

Summing up, e-assessment systems provide capabilities for assessing and testing (mass) student submissions. However, they don't provide special overviews to support live lectures. ARS are designed for live feedback but can't be used for programming as they don't provide automatic evaluation and specific result aggregation capabilities. Therefore, there is a research gap on how to enhance e-assessment systems with special overview features for supporting live lectures.

3 Teaching Approach and System Requirements

The central idea of the teaching approach is that students are activated and encouraged to work on programming problems directly in class. This goes beyond typical live-coding sessions by the teacher or the presentation of worked examples. Particularly, in the first case the students are just passive consumers and might not dare to ask questions. Furthermore, students should see alternative solution strategies. In both "traditional" cases, only a very limited number of different solution strategies can be discussed that are (primarily) prepared by the lecturer. As the students do not program themselves or only on their own devices, there is no feedback for the teacher on common prevailing problems to support just-in-time teaching. In general, a comparison of the own performance with the overall class performance can also help students to get a better sense of their learning progress.

The proposed teaching approach demands that students attend the lectures with a laptop in presence or can use their normal computer for hybrid lectures. The lecturer prepares small coding problems before the lecture, e.g. code skeletons that need to be filled with (simple) algorithms addressing a specific topic of the lecture. This way higher-order thinking skills such as problem-solving can be addressed compared to simple multiple-choice questions. These assignments are then presented in class and students work on them synchronously within a time limit of approx. 10 min. While the students are working on the assignments either alone or in pair programming, they can talk to their seat neighbors, and the lecturer can walk around in the lecture hall to answer questions and to look for common problems. As soon as the students finish their work, they upload it to the used e-assessment system. When the time is up, the teacher closes the submission and triggers the automatic evaluation of all submissions. The submissions are now automatically checked in the background and the typical ARS features move into the focus: An ARS provides an overview of the results for both the lecturer and the students that can be presented on a projector. A key point of the proposed approach is that the lecturer gets an overview of the most common errors for discussion in class.

The key requirements for such a system are: 1) providing code templates to students; 2) upload and automatic test capabilities for programming assignments; 3) tests need to be triggered on-demand and finish within a few minutes; 4) the system should provide an overview of the number of submissions that passed the tests and a ranking of the most common errors (in a clustered way with links to submissions, including both syntax and functional errors) that can be shown on a projector; 5) access for the teacher to all (erroneous and correct) submissions for in-class discussion without disclosing specific students.

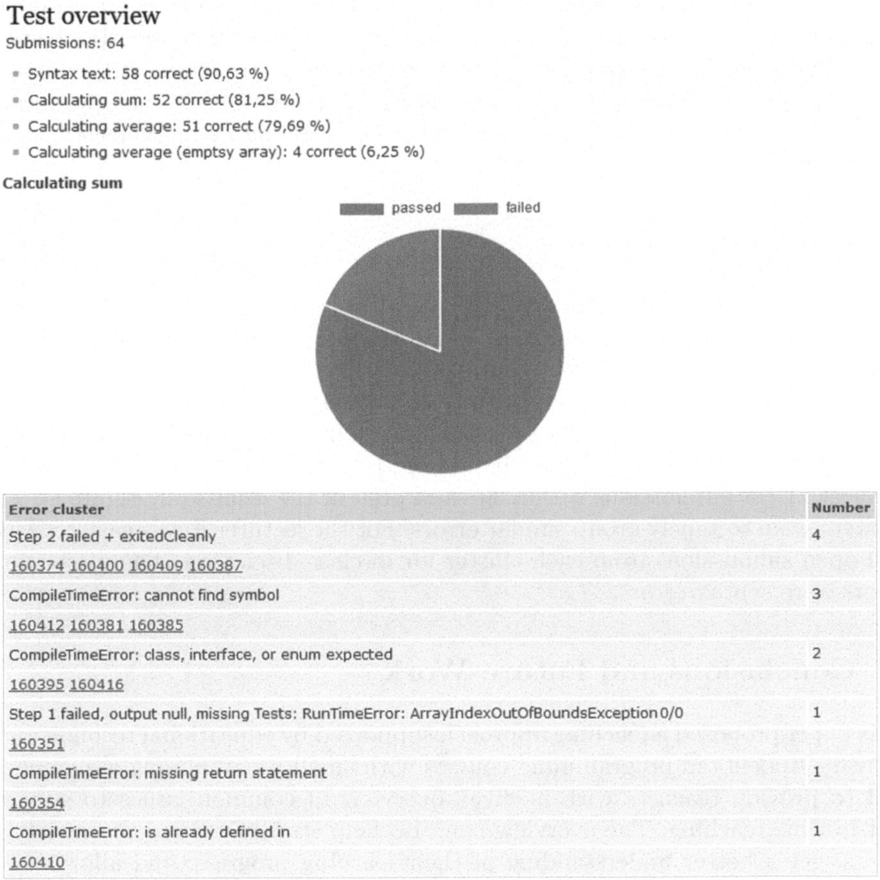

Fig. 1. Screenshot of the test result overview with grouped common errors and links to the corresponding submissions based on their IDs

4 Implementation of the Prototype

The requirements identified in the previous section were implemented in the GATE system [14]. For this research a simple text-based clustering approach was used which is an optimized version based on the idea presented in [13]: After all tests are automatically executed, the outputs of all failed tests are parsed to detect Java exceptions, and syntax errors. Also, the failed test steps are taken into account to localize the error.

Figure 1 shows the user interface of the developed prototype. At the top, there is an overview of the number of submissions (64 here), the four executed tests (a syntax test and three function tests for calculations on an array), and the number of correct submissions for each test. Below, there is the output for the test named "Calculating sum". As in ARS, there is a prominent pie chart showing the correctness of the submissions, followed by a table comprising the found clustered errors of the submissions. In the figure there are six clusters. The first cluster is a runtime error where the second test step failed (i.e., wrong calculation on a non-empty array) consisting of 4 submissions and the second cluster is a syntax error (i.e., typo in the class/variable name) consisting of 3 submissions.

5 Preliminary Results

The proposed teaching approach and algorithm was used in a first-semester introductory programming course at LMU Munich, Germany, in the last winter term. Approx. 900 students were enrolled for that course of which approx. 300-450 students attended the hybrid course in presence regularly.

In the first test, 64 students took part in the live coding and submitted their solution attempts within approx. 10 min of given time. The prototype was able to check all the submissions within 30 s and present the results (cf. Figure 1). The clusters seem to sanely group similar errors. For the lecturer it was easy to select and open submissions from each cluster for in-class discussion. The majority of errors were syntax errors.

6 Conclusions and Future Work

This paper proposed a teaching approach supported by educational technology to activate students in programming courses with small programming assignments and to provide teachers with a "live" overview of common issues to support just-in-time teaching. The overview can also help students to see the variety of errors, get a better understanding of their learning progress, and allows them to compare with their fellow students. Still, the overview is primarily intended for the teacher here. For this teaching approach technical requirements were compiled and a prototype implemented.

In a first test in a course, the clustering approach formed sensible and usable clusters for in-class discussion in an appropriate time.

Further research needs to be conducted to optimize the clustering approach and to systematically evaluate the teaching approach in practice. Based on this approach didactic questions such as when and how to use it optimally in lectures can be investigated (e.g, how much time to allot, should templates be provided to students, how should these look like, should students also be able to open different solutions on their own). Also, the general grouping approach can be used in different scenarios such as (group) programming practicals to get a better overview of the progress and common issues, and showing the clusters to tutors as an aid for their preparation of exercise sessions or (semi-)automatic grading (e.g., batch feedback provisioning for submissions with similar errors).

References

1. Becker, B.A.: An effective approach to enhancing compiler error messages. In: Proceedings SIGCSE TS. ACM (2016). https://doi.org/10.1145/2839509.2844584
2. Strickroth, S., Bry, F.: The future of higher education is social and personalized! experience report and perspectives. In: Proceedings CSEDU, vol. 1, pp. 389–396. INSTICC, SciTePress (2022). https://doi.org/10.5220/0011087700003182
3. Ebert, M., Ring, M.: A presentation framework for programming in programing lectures. In: Proceedings EDUCON, pp. 369–374. IEEE (2016)
4. Fies, C., Marshall, J.: Classroom response systems: a review of the literature. J. Sci. Educ. Technol. **15**(1), 101–109 (2006). https://doi.org/10.1007/s10956-006-0360-1
5. Hattie, J., Timperley, H.: The power of feedback. Rev. Educ. Res. **77**(1), 81–112 (2007). https://doi.org/10.3102/003465430298487
6. Hauswirth, M., Adamoli, A.: Solve & evaluate with informa: a java-based classroom response system for teaching java. In: Proceedings PPPJ. ACM (2009). https://doi.org/10.1145/1596655.1596657
7. Heller, N., Bry, F.: Organizing peer correction in tertiary stem education: an approach and its evaluation. iJEP **9**(4), 16–32 (2019)
8. Kay, R.H., LeSage, A.: Examining the benefits and challenges of using audience response systems: a review of the literature. Comput. Educ. **53**(3), 819–827 (2009). https://doi.org/10.1016/j.compedu.2009.05.001
9. Luxton-Reilly, A., et al.: Introductory programming: a systematic literature review. In: Proceedings ITiCSE, pp. 55–106 (2018). https://doi.org/10.1145/3293881.3295779
10. Mader, S., Bry, F.: Audience response systems reimagined. In: Herzog, M.A., Kubincová, Z., Han, P., Temperini, M. (eds.) ICWL 2019. LNCS, vol. 11841, pp. 203–216. Springer, Cham (2019). https://doi.org/10.1007/978-3-030-35758-0_19
11. Mazur, E., Somers, M.D.: Peer instruction: a user's manual. Am. J. Phys. **67**(4), 359–360 (1999). https://doi.org/10.1119/1.19265
12. Robbins, S.: Beyond clickers. In: Proceedings SIGCSE TS. ACM (2011). https://doi.org/10.1145/1953163.1953347
13. Strickroth, S., Holzinger, F.: Supporting the semi-automatic feedback provisioning on programming assignments. In: Proceedings MIS4TEL, pp. 13–19 (2022). https://doi.org/10.1007/978-3-031-20617-7_3
14. Strickroth, S., Olivier, H., Pinkwart, N.: Das GATE-System: qualitätssteigerung durch Selbsttests für Studenten bei der Onlineabgabe von Übungsaufgaben? In: Proceedings DeLFI, pp. 115–126 (2011). https://dl.gi.de/handle/20.500.12116/4740
15. Strickroth, S., Striewe, M.: Building a corpus of task-based grading and feedback systems for learning and teaching programming. iJEP **12**(5), 26–41 (2022). https://doi.org/10.3991/ijep.v12i5.31283

Supporting Remote Students Through Utilizing Web-Based Exercise-Templates and a Mobile Learning Chatbot for Creating and Interacting with Learning Materials

Hasan Abu-Rasheed[1](✉), Yannis Efthymiou[2], Madjid Fathi[1], Parvin Ghadamighalandari[1], Julián López Medina[3], Covadonga Ordoñez García[3], Gregory Tsardanidis[2], Johannes Zenkert[1], and Giannis Zgeras[2]

[1] University of Siegen, Siegen, Germany
hasan.abu.rasheed@uni-siegen.de
[2] Open Lab Athens, Athens, Greece
[3] University of Alicante, Alicante, Spain

Abstract. During COVID-19 pandemic, and in the post-pandemic era, the dependency on digital learning tools and integrating them into regular teaching practices revealed several challenges and requirements from those tools. Such tools are needed to accommodate existing learning materials that teachers use, and deliver them to students who are learning remotely. In this paper, we demonstrate a mobile learning approach for supporting remote students and teachers. Our proposed approach utilizes a pedagogically informed design of exercise templates to construct learning materials as stand-alone exercises. A web application is designed to enable teachers of creating those exercises. On the learner's side, a Chatbot-based mobile application is developed to ensure an easy and understandable interaction with the system for young students. Students could engage in a conversation with the Chatbot, solve exercises and get predefined teacher feedback on their solutions, all without a direct contact with the teacher who created those exercises. We implement our system and test it in three European contexts, in Spain, Greece and Germany. Our evaluation reveals high acceptance of the system's ability to integrate existing materials to offer them to remote students; high student engagement with the learning Chatbot; and several lessons-learned from the user interaction with the system.

Keywords: M-learning · Post-pandemic Digital Learning · Chatbot · Exercise-based Learning Materials

1 Introduction

In the post-pandemic era, lessons learned from the digital, remote, learning practices during the pandemic have emphasised the role of regular use of technology in classrooms and home-schooling. An increased number of teachers were subject to a situation where

O. Viberg et al. (Eds.): EC-TEL 2023, LNCS 14200, pp. 668–673, 2023.
https://doi.org/10.1007/978-3-031-42682-7_59

they needed to select a suitable learning application for their students, which led to an increased amount of pedagogical feedback on the suitability of such learning applications to the classroom and remote earning settings.

Mobile learning was one of the most used approaches within those settings, due to the wide availability of mobile devices among learners, either privately owned or provided by their schools. However, creating, and editing the learning materials on a mobile phone or a tablet, with a relatively small screen and low performance, was not as simple and easy as on a personal computer. Therefore, a mobile learning solution that is easy to use for both learners and educators was necessary.

On the learner side, the interaction with the learning software was also challenged by the ease of use of the learning application. As interaction support means, Chatbots were used in education to improve connectedness, efficiency, and interactional uncertainty [1]. They could quickly create an environment for online learning that is targeted, customized, and goal-driven [1].

In this research, we utilize Chatbots as interaction support tools, and address at the same time the pedagogical requirements from the teachers to create educational materials and offer them to students through the Chatbot. We analyse the pedagogical requirements extensively with domain experts, and design a comprehensive learning tool, which provides teachers and students with the required support for material curation, transfer, and then remote learning, keeping the feedback from teachers available to students even without direct access to the teacher or the classroom.

2 Related Work

The use of mobile devices and Chatbots in education has a relatively short history [1]. However, in recent years, the rapid advancements in mobile technology and artificial intelligence have led to increased integration of these tools in educational settings [2]. The convenience and accessibility of mobile devices have made it possible for learners to access educational resources and engage in virtual learning experiences anytime and anywhere. Similarly, Chatbots have proven to be effective in delivering personalized and interactive learning experiences, as well as providing instant feedback and support. The use of Chatbots in education was mainly focused on learning tasks, rather than assessment or content authoring. Several authoring tools have been introduced in the market during the pandemic years. Teacher feedback on those tools showed the importance of considering pedagogical aspects in designing the tool functions and components, alongside the usability of the tool [3, 4]. While solutions introduced in the literature and industry focus on either the learner or the teacher, ecosystems for supporting both at the same time were seldom addressed. We, therefore, build on the pedagogical requirements addressed by teaching experts and introduce a system that supports teachers and learners in transferring knowledge through exercises. The proposed approach is developed as a support to the learning process through remote exercise-based interaction, which builds on the existing learning materials that teachers already developed and regularly use, and simplifies the task of digitalizing those materials, as well as interacting with them by the learners.

3 Methodology

To design the proposed ecosystem, a series of interviews have been conducted with educational experts to decide the pedagogical functions needed in the learning. Alongside the interviews, a literature survey was conducted to analyse existing solutions. Based on this phase of requirements analyses, the proposed system was designed through three main components: 1) Authoring tool for exercise-based materials. 2) Mobile learning app for material delivery. 3) Chatbot system for facilitating the interaction with the learning materials on the mobile app. Teachers interact with the system through the web application. When the student sends a message from the mobile application, it is directed to the API Gateway as a POST request, which is then forwarded to the respective language model for language understanding and response generation. Four language models are created, one for each language. The services were hosted on Amazon Web Services (AWS) instance, which is connected to Android through Amazon API Gateway. The mobile application is then connected to the Chatbot server and the exercise database, to identify the learner intent, retrieve the corresponding exercise, and display it interactively on the mobile device.

3.1 Authoring Tool for Material Creation

A web application authoring tool is built using Angular framework based on the functional requirements from teaching experts. Through the authoring tool, teachers can create "topics" in different learning subjects. Inside a topic, different types of "activities" can be defined. The activity here refers to a singular exercise. For the exercises, five question types are defined: Multiple choice questions, Open-ended, True/False, and Matching-pairs questions. The authoring tool offers the teacher to freely arrange the order and layout of the activity. For open-ended questions, the web application also contains an admin panel to retrieve the digitally submitted answers on the mobile app, where the teacher can assess them and provide feedback back in classroom when needed. A preview of the interface from the web application is shown in Fig. 1.

Template-Based Learning Materials:
The design of the exercises and their activities in the proposed solution was accomplished through the pedagogical requirements of the mobile learning and the technical requirements of a re-usable structure that educators can dynamically adjust to their own materials. A set of exercise templates has been therefore developed to describe the combinations of question types, the layout of the activities in one topic, and the essential components for each question type.

Since remote learners, who have limited or no access to teachers, are the target group, material templates included an introduction component to offer a brief theoretical background about the information relevant to the exercise activities. Multimedia elements were introduced to support showing videos, images, or webpages in the introduction, alongside the textual content.

For each activity, an activity prompt was also provided with multimedia components. The activity was equipped with fields to offer feedback to the students based on their answers. Teachers could add hints, corrections, or motivational comments in the feedback fields, which correspond to a correct answer or a wrong answer from the student. Students get this feedback then on the mobile application based on the correctness of their answers. For open-ended questions, the feedback was potentially given by the teacher based on manual analysis of the answer, to avoid incorrect automatic assessment of the student's free-text answers.

3.2 Educational Chatbot

The Chatbot is designed to support the remote learning scenario. After the student logs in to the mobile app, they can start interacting with the Chatbot through text or by using clickable buttons. The conversation on this screen is managed through a RASA-based Chatbot pipeline. After requesting a learning topic, the Chatbot identifies the corresponding activities in the database and forwards their identifiers to the mobile app, where they are then retrieved and displayed to the learner.

The Chatbot interaction with the student is governed by a careful dialogue management approach, which ensures that the student will be able to reach the target exercises easily and offers at the same time some motivational sentences to encourage the student to continue learning. The conversation is also protected against dead ends, to reduce the chances of students getting frustrated or not being able to reach their goal. Re-prompting and alternative suggestions are used for that purpose. The Chatbot also offers functionality for the student to observe their progress and allows for basic recommendations about redoing exercises that were not solved correctly in the past.

3.3 Learning Mobile App

In the first step of using the mobile application, learners sign up and create a profile, Fig. 1. After entering all the required information, a profile will be created, and the system will return the user to the login screen. Registered students require only a username. The device ID is stored in the database. Both information pieces provide an anonymous log-in process, with no personal information about the student. Once the Chatbot defines the requested activities, students can solve them and get feedback regarding the completed activity. Activities are displayed interactively, and the answer triggers the system to show if the answer was accurate or not based on the predefined feedback. After finishing all activities of a topic, a total score is calculated and displayed on the screen to indicate the success. For a learning review, learners can see all the completed activities and revisit a previous exercise if they want.

4 Evaluation and Results

For the evaluation of the proposed system, three multiplier events were held with teachers and students of elementary and secondary schools. A total of 36 teachers and 8 students participated from a primary and a secondary schools in Spain. In, Greece, a total of 50 teachers from a high school, as well as a Solidarity School participated. In addition, a workshop on the future of Pedagogy was held to discuss the use of the applications. In Germany, 2 teachers and 38 pupils from the 4th grade tested mainly using the Chatbot with previously created materials.

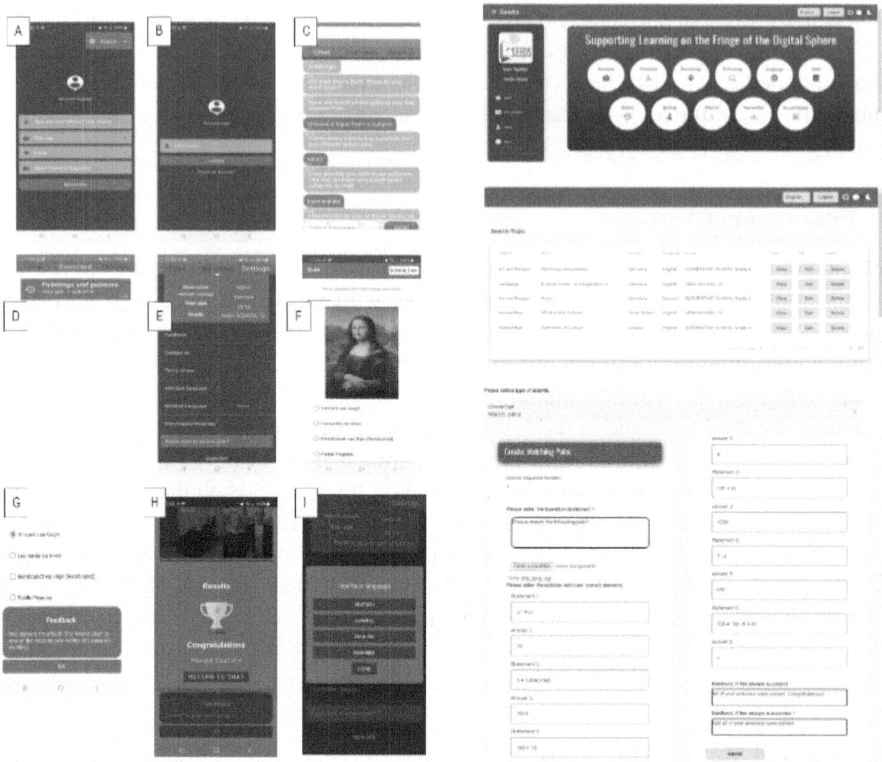

Fig. 1. Mobile App Interfaces (left): A: Registration, B: Log in, C: Chatbot main screen, D: saved exercises, E: Settings, F, Activity screen, G Feedback screen, H: Score and reward screen, I: Change language setting. Web Application Interfaces (right): Subject selection, topic editing, activity editing screens.

We use the Unified Theory of Acceptance and Use of Technology (UTAUT) model [5] for collecting the users' input on SEEDS Apps. A questionnaire with 18 questions was developed. 15 questions used a (1–5) Likert scale and aimed to assess the technology acceptance on four factors: Performance expectancy Effort expectancy, Social influence, Facilitating Conditions. Three overall Likert-scales questions addressed user adoption, and two open-ended questions were also used to collect qualitative feedback. The results showed that SEEDS apps scored an average of 4/5 in all factors, except for effort expectancy that scored 4.6/5. Teachers found the system generally useful to their students, with hints on limitations of the usability side of the mobile app. From the students who used the apps, a high level of engagement was recorded. Students also pointed out the usefulness of interacting with the Chatbot, with partial difficulty in recognizing the meaning of some sentences they wrote. Detailed documentation of the evaluation results is published on the ERASMUS + result platform. Based on the evolution results, future steps for further developing interfaces have been planned.

5 Conclusion

In this paper, we demonstrate an exercise-based learning ecosystem, which is designed to support teachers and students in remote learning settings. The proposed solution was based on a pedagogical foundation through requirements analysis with teachers. It is then designed with three main components: a web application for exercise material authoring, an educational Chatbot system for managing the interaction with students, and a mobile application that offers an interactive means of accessing the exercises, solving them, and getting direct, predefined feedback on their solutions. The system has been evaluated with users in three countries: Germany, Spain and Greece. Teachers and learners highlighted the positive role the app played in supporting exercise-based learning and accommodating existing materials in the system. Students also showed high engagement and interest in the features of the system and the chat functionality. Users also highlighted limitations in the interaction model, related to some transitions between the screens, and the potential to add more dynamic features for material creation.

References

1. Okonkwo, C.W., Ade-Ibijola, A.: Chatbots applications in education: a systematic review. Comput. Educ. Artif. Intell. **2**, 100033 (2021). https://doi.org/10.1016/j.caeai.2021.100033
2. Kuhail, M.A., Alturki, N., Alramlawi, S., Alhejori, K.: Interacting with educational chatbots: a systematic review. Educ. Inf. Technol. **28**, 973–1018 (2023). https://doi.org/10.1007/s10639-022-11177-3
3. Abdulrahaman, M.D., et al.: Multimedia tools in the teaching and learning processes: a systematic review. Heliyon **6**, e05312 (2020). https://doi.org/10.1016/j.heliyon.2020.e05312
4. Antón-Sancho, Á., Vergara, D., Lamas-Álvarez, V.E., Fernández-Arias, P.: Digital content creation tools: american university teachers' perception. Appl. Sci. **11**, 11649 (2021). https://doi.org/10.3390/app112411649
5. Venkatesh, M., Davis, D.: User acceptance of information technology: toward a unified view. MIS Q. **27**, 425 (2003).https://doi.org/10.2307/30036540

An Evaluation System to Trace the Usage of the OER Conversion Tool (convOERter)

Lubna Ali[1(✉)], Sven Judel[1], Deekshith Shetty[2], and Ulrik Schroeder[1]

[1] Learning Technologies Research Group, RWTH Aachen University, Aachen, Germany
{ali,judel,schroeder}@cs.rwth-aachen.de
[2] RWTH Aachen University, Aachen, Germany
deekshith.shetty@rwth-aachen.de

Abstract. Open Educational Resources (OER) are available resources for teaching, learning, and research distributed under an open license. They are considered essential building blocks in educational systems, as they can be freely used, modified, and shared. However, there are still many challenges that hinder the proper utilization of OER at schools as well as in higher education institutions. One of these challenges is the lack of technical tools that support producing OER or converting existing educational materials to OER. In order to overcome this problem, the OER Conversion Tool *convOERter* has been developed at the Learning Technologies Research Group of RWTH Aachen University. The main functionality of the tool is to support converting existing educational materials to OER by extracting images from the input files and replacing them with OER-compliant images retrieved from OER image portals. Since it is crucial to understand the tool's usage and to trace the interaction between the tool and the end users, an evaluation system, consisting of a logging module, analytics engines, and a dashboard has been developed and integrated. In this paper, we will introduce the system's conceptual design and illustrate its main modules. We will also highlight how and to which extent convOERter is being used by tracing and analyzing the interaction logs of the integrated system. Additionally, we will summarize the results of a usability study that was conducted to assess the effectiveness of the evaluation system.

Keywords: OER · Evaluation System · convOERter · Learning Analytics · Open Educational Resources

1 Introduction

The term Open Educational Resources (OER) has been defined by the UNESCO as "learning, teaching and research materials in any format and medium that reside in the public domain or are under copyright that have been released under an open license, that permit no-cost access, re-use, re-purpose, adaptation and

O. Viberg et al. (Eds.): EC-TEL 2023, LNCS 14200, pp. 674–679, 2023.
https://doi.org/10.1007/978-3-031-42682-7_60

redistribution by others".[1]. There are many advantages to apply and utilize OER within the educational practices in higher education. One of these advantages is that OER support providing more equal access to knowledge to many traditionally disadvantaged potential users, who would not otherwise have such access due to geographical, demographical, financial, or cultural reasons [8]. Additionally, appropriate use of OER can improve the quality of learning and teaching processes [8] and the potential financial savings from reducing effort duplication in the development of learning materials [3]. Since OER help in facilitating access to high-quality digital educational materials, they have the potential to play a significant role in enhancing education around the world and increasing the sharing and open practice that results from OER usage [7].

However, there are still many obstacles that hinder the proper deployment of OER in the educational context. D'Antoni outlined many of the obstacles that OER advocates must consider, including the existence of copyrighted information in OER, which obstructs their use [4]. There is a huge challenge to determine the right way to obtain proper resource from the vast number of available resources. Moreover, when producing OER, the usage of open license models raises legal concerns and uncertainty. The construction of OER itself necessitates a significant amount of effort. Basic image editors as well as specialized tools such as H5P[2] or GitBook[3] help in producing new OER. In addition to this, popular search engines such as Google, DuckDuckGo, and Bing allow users to find images under creative commons license. However, huge challenges in converting existing educational materials to OER can be observed.

Since there is a vast amount of already produced and well-tested educational materials, it could be useful for educators to convert these materials to OER instead of producing new content from scratch. As means to mitigate this challenge, the Learning Technologies Research Group at RWTH Aachen University has developed a web-based tool *convOERter* [1] that supports converting already existing materials to OER with as much automation as possible. The OER conversion tool extracts all image elements from an imported file and then searches for OER-complaint images in OER image portals such as Openverse[4] and Flickr[5]. Afterward, the tool presents viable replacements, and the user can choose the most proper one among the suggested. This step is repeated until all the images in the input file have proper replacements. In the last step, the selected images are replaced automatically in the original file, licensed according to the TASLL rule[6] and the edited file is exported with the requested changes. Since it is necessary to understand how the tool is being used by the end users and to trace the possible interactions between the tool and the users, an evaluation system has

1 https://www.unesco.org/en/open-educational-resources, Last accessed: 13.04.2023.
2 https://h5p.org/, Last accessed: 11.04.2023.
3 https://www.gitbook.com/, Last accessed: 11.04.2023.
4 https://openverse.org/eu/, Last accessed: 11.04.2023.
5 https://www.flickr.com/creativecommons/, Last accessed: 11.04.2023.
6 https://www.oercommons.org/courseware/lesson/97649/overview?section=3/, Last accessed: 13.04.2023.

been developed and integrated within the tool[7]. In this paper, we will present this system, illustrate its modules and highlight its usage. In the following section, we will introduce the conceptual design followed by introducing its components. Then, we will present the results of a small evaluation study conducted with a couple of OER-interested people to evaluate its functionality. Finally, we will demonstrate briefly the usage of convOERter during the previous months.

2 Conceptual Design and Implementation

In order to understand user interactions with the system, we have applied hybrid techniques of web analytics and task modeling. Accordingly, we have set up the operations needed to understand and analyze the log files and displaying the corresponding results graphically on a dashboard. These can be summarized as follows: 1. Identifying a defined set of user interactions to log. 2. Performing various types of analysis on these user logs and comparison of user interaction pathways with a defined ideal task flow. 3. Displaying the analysis results on a dashboard. Figure 1 shows an overview of the evaluation system's architecture.

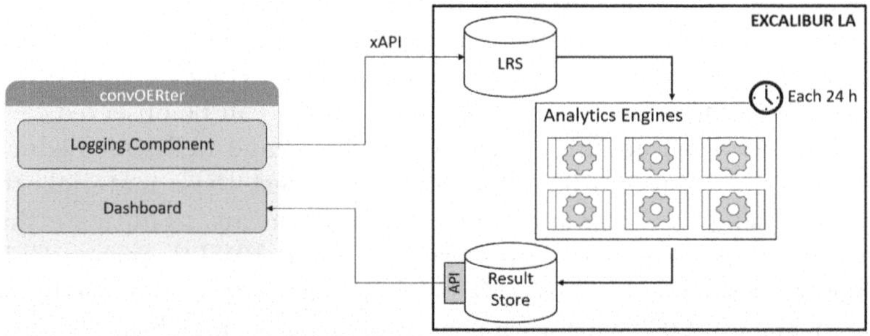

Fig. 1. The evaluation system's data analysis infrastructure

Interaction logs collected in convOERter are sent to a Learning Record Store (LRS) within the existing analytics infrastructure Excalibur LA [5] as xAPI statements[8]. Although Excalibur was originally designed for Learning Analytics, the periodic data analysis serves the needs for the intended evaluation. Further, no implementation of an own infrastructure was required and only the analytics engines had to be developed, enabling to bring the whole system live faster. The Rights Engine of Excalibur was omitted in this setup as logging consent was handled directly within convOERter and no account management is given which settings could be stored for later sessions. In total, 36 engines were developed to analyze different aspects including the usage of image search methods, session durations and how often sessions lead to publishing new OER. Further,

[7] https://convoerter-eval.elearn.rwth-aachen.de/en/. Last accessed 14.04.2023.
[8] https://xapi.com/, Last accessed 11.04.2023.

engines also analyzed the responses to an integrated feedback form. These analysis results are stored in a result store such that a dashboard, directly included in convOERter, can retrieve them constantly via various endpoints. More technical details of this evaluation system are given in [6].

3 System Evaluation

The developed evaluation system was evaluated in terms of usability and functionality by five university educators in individual sessions of 60 min. At the beginning of the meeting, the participants were welcomed and thanked for their participation. Then, convOERter was introduced and its functionality was illustrated. After that, the evaluation system has been presented to the participants, including its dashboard and visualizations. During this presentation, a set of task questions were shared with the participants, where they were asked to answer loudly and their answers have been documented. Then the participants have been asked to fill out the System Usability Scale (SUS) to collect their overall satisfaction about the dashboard. Figure 2 shows the single responses of the five participants (P1 to P5) as well as the calculated SUS Score, according to [2]. The scores ranged from 77.55 to 95 with an average score of 85.5, which slightly takes it to the excellent category. A final questionnaire asked users to list the most negative and positive aspects of the dashboard in two free-text input sections, respectively. These open feedback make it possible to pinpoint places, where the convOERter tool needs to be improved further. The task questions and the usability questionnaire have been analyzed and showed that the participants' attitudes regarding the system were overall positive.

	P1	P2	P3	P4	P5	SUS Score	0-64: Not Acceptable
Q1	4	4	4	3	4		65-84: Acceptable
Q2	3	4	4	4	4		85-100: Excellent
Q3	2	4	3	3	4		
Q4	4	3	3	4	4		
Q5	3	3	4	3	3		
Q6	3	4	4	3	4		
Q7	3	3	3	3	3		
Q8	4	3	4	3	4		
Q9	4	3	3	2	4		
Q10	3	3	3	3	4		
SUS Score	82.5	85	87.5	77.5	95	Average	85.5

Fig. 2. System Usability Scale questionnaire results overview

4 convOERter Usage

The evaluation system has been integrated within convOERter and deployed in August 2022. Since then, we have utilized the evaluation system to trace the usage of the conversion tool and to gain some insights on how the tool is being used. Mentoring the usage of the tool will provide us with valuable information that will support us with the further development of the tool. Different usage aspects can be logged, analyzed and displayed on the admin dashboard such as the origin of the geographic traffic, number of manual replacements, number of external searches, type of imported files as well as chosen licenses. Additionally, the task model for each session can be traced. This enables us to understand the workflow of each session and highlight where potential difficulties have been encountered. The following two figures illustrate two examples of tracing the usage of convOERter in the period between August - December, 2022. Figure 3 presents an example of a task model for a specific session. It can be noticed that the workflow for this session started by importing the file and displaying the images. Then, an image was selected to be processed, where the user chose the external image search and entered the query for the respective image manually. Next, the image was edited by the user and replaced. Figure 4 shows another example of the admin panel. Here, an overview about the type of imported files and the number of total exported and processed images are displayed. It can be noticed that .ppt files are more frequently used compared to .doc files. Additionally, the figure shows a visualization of the number of processed images compared to the total number of images.

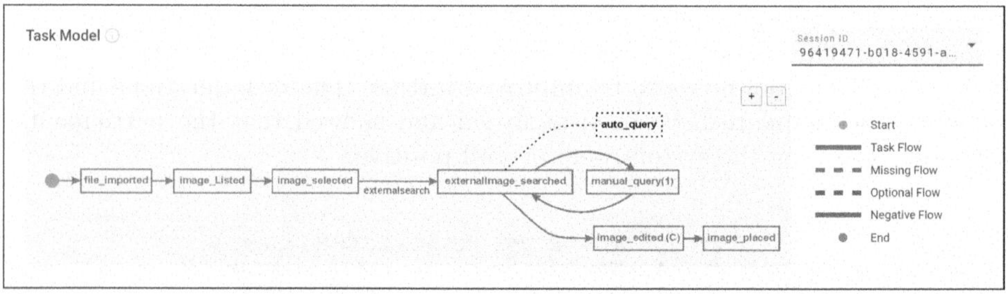

Fig. 3. An example of a task model for a specific session

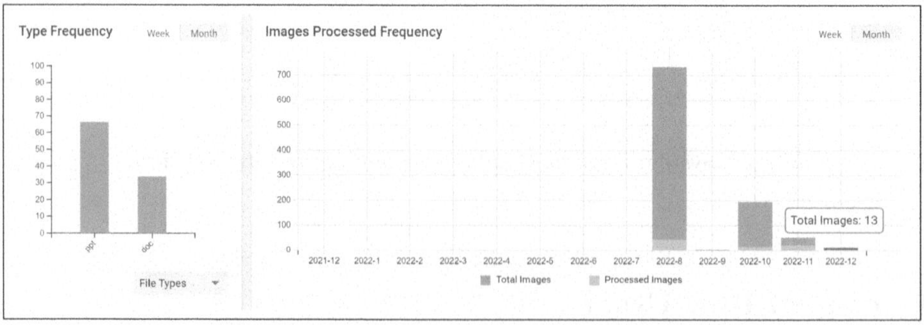

Fig. 4. An example of the imported file types and no. of images

5 Conclusion and Future Work

In this paper, we have introduced the components of the evaluation system that has been designed and developed to trace the possible interactions between the end user and the conversion tool. The evaluation system includes a logging module to identify user interaction, multiple analytics engines to analyze these interactions, and a dashboard for displaying the analysis results. Additionally, we have presented the results of an evaluation study that has been conducted with a small number of participants to evaluate the usability of the evaluation system. The evaluation results showed that the participants' attitudes regarding the system were overall positive and the participants were satisfied with the system functionality. As a future work, we are planning to further trace the usage of convOERter in order to gain more insights into how and to which extent it has been utilized by the community. Additionally, we are planning to further investigate participants' feedback and analyze their open feedback regarding the evaluation system and convOERter. Furthermore, the evaluation study could be repeated with a larger sample of participants to collect further information about the effectiveness of the evaluation system.

References

1. Ali, L., Schroeder, U.: A tool to enhance the utilization of OER in higher education. In: 11th International Conference on Education and New Learning Technologies, pp. 7321–7325. IATED Academy, Palma, Mallorca (2019). https://doi.org/10.21125/edulearn.2019.1752
2. Brooke, J.: SUS: A quick and dirty usability scale. Usability Eval. Ind. **189**, 4–7 (1995)
3. Commonwealth of Learning and UNESCO: Survey on Governments' Open Educational Resources (OER) Policies. In: Commonwealth of Learning. Vancouver, Canada (2012)
4. D'Antoni, S.: Open educational resources: reviewing initiatives and issues. Open Learn. J. Open Distance e-Learn. **24**, 3–10 (2009)
5. Judel, S., Schroeder, U.: EXCALIBUR LA - an extendable and scalable infrastructure build for learning analytics. In: 2022 International Conference on Advanced Learning Technologies (ICALT), pp. 155–157. IEEE, Bucharest, Romania (2022). https://doi.org/10.1109/ICALT55010.2022.00053
6. Shetty, D.R.: Design and implementation of an evaluation system for OER conversion tool (convOERter). Master's thesis, RWTH Aachen University (2022)
7. Welle, M., de los Arcos, B., Farrow, B.P., McAndrew, P.: The impact of OER on teaching and learning practice. In: Open Praxis, pp. 351–361. International Council for Open and Distance Education (2015). https://doi.org/10.5944/openpraxis.7.4.227
8. Yuan, L., MacNeill, S., Kraan, W.: Open educational resources - opportunities and challenges for higher education. In: The Battle for Open, How Openness Won and Why It Doesn't Feel Like Victory, pp. 1–34. (JISC) CETIS (2008)

Technology Enhanced Training in Medical Multi-User Scenarios

Andrea Balz(✉) and Mathias Forjan

University of Applied Sciences Technikum Wien, Vienna, Austria
andrea.balz@technikum-wien.at

Abstract. Simulation and training became a standard activity in several fields of education. These include also the medical sector. The training of complex procedures, or rarely occurring situations, helps to improve the performance of medical professionals under stressful situations. Over the last years, mixed reality solutions grew in importance and made their way into medical training setups. The focus is usually put on the medical process itself, whereas the environment and the used equipment are of secondary importance. The approach of the presented results of the research project MedTech-mR are showing the possibilities of using real life scenarios including room setup and equipment. The solution is based on a virtual reality approach, using the Oculus Quest 2 and hand-tracking mode. The produced and tested solution includes a multiuser setup and therefore allows to train team communication skills with up to five persons actively engaged into one scenario. The observing facilitator guides the users and performs the consecutive debriefing. The evaluation showed that putting the trainees into a realistic medical environment and equipping them with digital clones of actually used devices helps the users to immerse into the simulation scenario and focus more on the tasks themselves.

Keywords: Healthcare · Training · Simulation · AR/VR

1 Introduction

The healthcare sector is one of the most sensitive and vulnerable areas worldwide [1]. The COVID-19 pandemic further underlined this and demonstrated that medical professionals have to deal with high loads and low resources at the same time. Especially the emergency department experienced increased workloads and stressful situations. However, they are amongst the first and therefore most important contact points for a patient's survival. Highly critical situations, which in addition might occur very rarely in daily routine, require profound knowledge about each single step in the medical workflow. Therefore, regular training of such clinical scenarios is indispensable [2].

Simulation of medical use cases is nowadays seen as the golden standard. However, the on-site procedure binds resources such as rooms, staff members and financial expenses for the (high-fidelity) mannequins. Furthermore, the simulation process does not only consist of the hands-on performance, but also the briefing and debriefing phases

O. Viberg et al. (Eds.): EC-TEL 2023, LNCS 14200, pp. 680–685, 2023.
https://doi.org/10.1007/978-3-031-42682-7_61

for preparation and evaluation. This represents one of the main reasons to include novel technological approaches with the aim of partially or completely digitalizing training workflows. During the last few years increased research focus was put on this field, including augmented-, mixed- and virtual reality solutions [3]. Lockdowns and reduced mobility options during the COVID-19 pandemic also limited the educational sector. Therefore, there was the need for finding new ways to improve distant learning [4], also in the healthcare sector [5].

The research project MedTech-mR focuses on development of Augmented Reality (AR) and Virtual Reality (VR) setups for healthcare. This includes medical room planning, medical and technological processes and medical trainings. The developed solutions for support of medical trainings ranges from short ECG electrode positioning, over digital versions of a lung simulator up to the VR simulation of complete medical workflows, which is presented within the scope of this paper.

2 Methods

The selected use case for medical workflow simulation represents the scenario of a difficult airway management. The problem definition itself was provided by medical professionals from the emergency department of a European regional hospital. The tasks for the participating group of medical professionals (physicians, nurses and assistants) include anamnesis, examination of different vital parameters, decisions of different actions and distribution of tasks among the team. A selected section of the workflow's underlying decision tree is represented in Fig. 1.

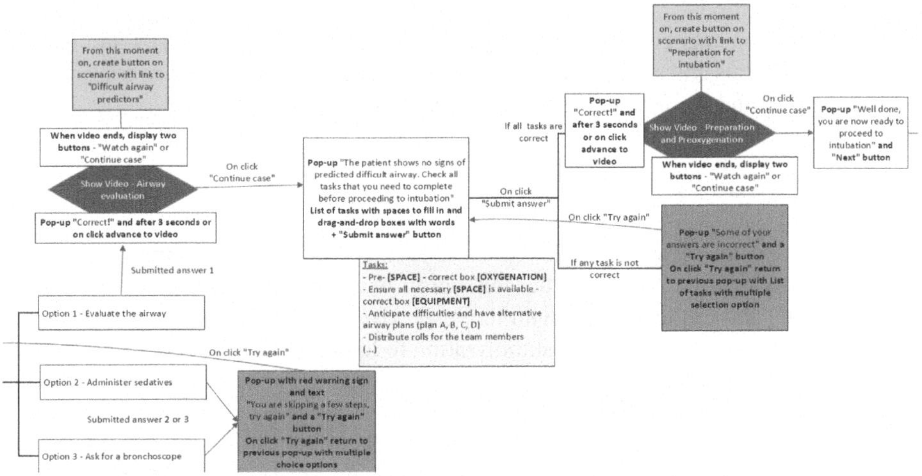

Fig. 1. Selection of the decision tree for the implemented difficult airway management workflow including two action branching settings (blue rhombus)

The VR solution of the presented scenario was developed in the Unity environment. The main configuration of the training is performed by using a customized node-based editor. This editor allows the creation of workflows which consist of names, actions defining change of vital parameters and used medical devices. As those actions are linked to a change of the simulated vital parameters of the patient, the Pulse Physiology Engine was implemented to allow realistic simulation of vital parameters, such as heart rate, blood pressure, respiratory frequency, oxygenation rate and one ECG lead. The vital parameters are of the same importance in the virtual reality as in reality. For this reason, the trend and change of the parameters has to be observed by the trainee during the simulation and is visually represented on selected digital copies of realistic medical devices. Those devices were created based on a) either custom-built digital objects or b) object files coming from actual manufacturers of such devices. To facilitate and mainstream the VR development, the popular Virtual Reality Tool Kit (VRTK) Version 4 was included. VRTK does not only provide ready-to-go assets, but also focuses on unity-event-driven structure allowing for easy implementation of new features. Additionally, Pun2 was used as networking framework and the Oculus Integration Package served as basis for hand tracking.

In order to create a realistic training setup, a moderator role was implemented. Such moderator is usually also part of the on-site training scenario including the classic briefing and de-briefing processes. The moderator role has the task to continuously monitor the trainees via a PC application which contains a communication option based on a voice chat functionality, which was implemented by using Photon Voice 2. Trainees can enter the simulation via their VR headsets. For the purpose of this training scenario the following requirements have led to the selection of the Oculus Quest 2 headset: 1) low-cost hardware solution, 2) good networking opportunities, 3) opportunity to select either controller-based or hand tracking based usage. As realistic working procedures are put into focus of this solution, the use of controllers has been discarded in favor of hand tracking methods.

The simulation was evaluated by 20 medical professionals (physicians and nurses) with a training focus and additional 23 students of three universities and two knowledge sectors (nursing and medical engineering) with the focus on education.

3 Results

The resulting virtual environment covers three levels of integration: a) the configurator app which provides the basis for the generation of individual training setups, b) the moderator role, and c) the VR app with the respective simulated scenario.

Thereby, the moderator has the authorization to load and start a simulation, observe the trainees' performance, change the patient's vital situation in accordance with the correctness of the chosen decisions, and give additional support via voice input if required. Additionally, visual and textual feedback is provided to the trainees during the whole simulation procedure. This includes (graphical and numerical) change of vital parameters on the monitor (e.g. change of heart rate and blood oxygen saturation), behavior of the patient (e.g. change of skin color in case of low oxygenation) and textual feedback on a second simulated monitor. This textual feedback is based on the decision tree and the activities of the trainees. It displays information if a decision was correct or why a decision was insufficient or incorrect. Additionally, a single warning lamp is mounted at the virtual bedside, which signals if a wrong decision was taken. By these means immediate feedback for the users is provided within the simulation setting.

The VR application also enables multiple users to train collaboratively within the same room and scenario. They are displayed as 3D characters in different shirt colors and can navigate through the room either physically or by teleportation. Furthermore, mobile objects – such as monitors, lamps and the patient data clipboard – can be moved in position and rotation by the touch and pinch gestures. The positions of the characters and the devices are continuously synchronized. Hence, all users (including the moderator) can observe the relative position of the team members to the patient in accordance with their task in the simulation procedure. This multiplayer mode is an essential realistic simulation option as emergency treatment of a patient is performed as team effort. Figure 2 shows the final setup of the medical scenario with two collaborating users.

Fig. 2. Patient treatment training in VR in multiplayer mode (two users and the view of the moderator during simulation) and insight to real setting while participants being in VR mode (lower right corner).

4 Discussion

The need of resource saving training solutions for medical professionals is indisputable and therefore virtual environments are gaining importance in the medical educational sector. The presented virtual training simulation brings together different aspects of a medical scenario, such as adequate patient assessment and treatment, communication pathways within a team being in a potentially stressful situation, and continuous evaluation and feedback opportunity. The examination is provided in a safe environment and can be repeated regularly, independent of location and time. Therefore, the training frequency and intensity can be increased while saving valuable resources, which represents one of the main advantages.

The high potential of the developed training solution was also underlined by the mainly positive feedback of the evaluating participants, consisting of professionals and students in the medical and engineering field. Minor drawbacks, such as difficulties with gestures at first use and overlaying audio tracks can be easily solved by a short initial pretraining phase on the distinct hand gestures and different physical locations for the participants. Since the implemented voice chat function was evaluated to be well working, it is expected to be very useful for future applications with decentralized team settings. The medical equipment for performance of the whole training procedure is currently available in another training environment focusing on the localization and selection of correct devices and will be implemented in the upcoming version of the virtual workflow training. Concerning fidelity level of the room and equipment the evaluation showed further potential of improvement. Especially medical professionals argued that the training should include a more realistic surrounding and a higher level of fidelity. For most of the students the environment was sufficient for first training experiences, however, single students mentioned that they would also prefer more realistic visualization.

Overall, the solution proves to provide valuable support for the target group in many different aspects. It is easy to use, can be performed and repeated at any time and with multiple users, the requirements are low (one VR headset per participant and a PC including the software for the facilitator) and offers navigation and handling without being bound to charging cables and controllers. However, there is still potential for enhancements within the current training solution and extension to other scenarios within the health sector. A training environment for a pediatric use case is already being planned and further smaller training settings for single parts of structural hospital processes are under development. The stand-alone solutions could in future be individually combined by users in order to create customized training environments according to their needs.

References

1. Parzonka, K., Ndayishimiye, C., Domagała, A.: Methods and tools used to estimate the shortages of medical staff in European countries-scoping review. Int J Environ Res Public Health **20**(4), 2945 (2023)
2. de Ribaupierre, S., Kapralos, B., Haji, F., Stroulia E., Dubrowski A., Eagleson, R.: Healthcare training enhancement through virtual reality and serious games. In: Ma, M., Jain, L., Anderson, P. (eds) Virtual, Augmented Reality and Serious Games for Healthcare 1. Intelligent Systems Reference Library, vol. 68. Springer, Berlin, Heidelberg (2014)

3. Javaid, M., Haleem, A.: Virtual reality applications toward medical field. Clinical Epidemiology and Global Health **8**(2), 600–605 (2020)
4. Chen, F.-Q., et al.: Effectiveness of virtual reality in nursing education: meta-analysis. JMIR **22**(9), e18290 (2020)
5. Dyer, E., Swartzlander, B.J., Gugliucci, M.R.: Using virtual reality in medical education to teach empathy. J Med Libr Assoc **106**(4), 498–500 (2018)

A Teacher Professional Development Tool for Creating and Sharing Research Lessons on Evidence-Based Teaching Strategies

Marc Beardsley(✉), Laia Albó, and Davinia Hernández-Leo

Universitat Pompeu Fabra, Barcelona, Spain
marc.beardsley@upf.edu

Abstract. This demo paper presents a teacher professional development (PD) tool aimed at increasing educator adoption of evidence-based teaching and learning strategies such as retrieval practice, distributed practice, spaced learning, and reframing. The tool, evolving from Learning Design and online communities of teachers' technologies, is an online platform centered on a teacher-led inquiry design template. The template, developed to scaffold teacher creation of research lessons (i.e., case studies) based on their use of the strategies, presents a 5-step teacher inquiry process: (1) lesson planning, (2) data planning, (3) activity and materials, (4) sense-making, and (5) communication. In addition to enabling teachers to create their own research lessons, document the lesson effects, and share their work with other teachers; the tool provides teachers with content and resources to deepen their understanding of the strategies and to support their usage. Furthermore, exemplar research lessons that teachers can duplicate and adapt to their contexts are offered to facilitate teacher learning and creation of case studies. The tool was co-designed with teachers as part of a European project that ran a series of workshops for teachers in four countries during the academic year 2021–2022 – and has been integrated into a 20-h teacher PD program.

Keywords: Learning design · Teacher professional development · Teacher inquiry · Lesson study

1 Pedagogical Background

As Guskey [1] writes, "of all aspects of professional development, sustaining change is perhaps the most neglected. It is clear that, to be successful, professional development must be seen as a process, not an event." Process-focused approaches to teacher professional development (PD) such as Teacher Inquiry [2] and Japanese Lesson Study [3] have the potential to deliver sustainable changes to teacher practices. However, obstacles including time constraints and a lack of research (i.e. procedural) knowledge have slowed adoption [4]. A recent survey study found that teachers have a greater affinity for learning about evidence-based teaching and strategies such as retrieval practice [5] and distributed practice [6] over learning teacher inquiry for PD [7]. Furthermore, research suggests that educational responses to COVID-19 resulted in teachers not only rapidly

O. Viberg et al. (Eds.): EC-TEL 2023, LNCS 14200, pp. 686–691, 2023.
https://doi.org/10.1007/978-3-031-42682-7_62

adopting technology but also increasing peer support and sharing of resources and recognizing the need to advance their pedagogical usage of technologies [8]. Adapting to these recent teacher experiences and preferences, this demo paper presents a teacher PD tool that facilitates educator creation and sharing of research lessons on their use of evidence-based teaching strategies and supporting technologies; and scaffolds their adoption of a collaborative teacher inquiry approach.

2 Technological Background

The tool has its technological background in Learning Design (LD) [9] and online communities of teachers (OC) [10]. LD tools are primarily intended to support educators in designing their lessons for learning [10]. They support educators in making design decisions related to teaching and learning such as deciding the types of activities that students must carry out, the order of lessons and/or lesson activities, the technologies to use, the data to collect, and, sometimes, they provide a scaffolding for pedagogical orientation [9]. OC platforms intend to provide an online space for sharing resources and exchanging ideas among a community of teachers. They facilitate teachers learning from each other and usually act as informal learning environments for teacher professional development [10]. Our tool is an online platform centered on a web-based, teacher-led inquiry design template. The template has been specifically developed to support the design of evidence-based case studies, also referred to as research lessons [3]. The template has been integrated into the LdShake/ILDE [11] community tool. LdShake provides social features allowing registered users to create, share and build upon the work of others [12]. The current platform is realized as a website and - as is common for this type of application - consists of a frontend written in HTML, JavaScript, and jQuery, as well as a backend with a MySQL database and PHP code.

3 Description of the Prototype

The tool has three main parts: a LD tool, a community platform, and a space for resources. The tool enables teachers to create their own research lessons for selected evidence-based strategies, document lesson effects, and share work with other teachers. The community platform contains articles and videos that introduce strategies and example research lessons teachers can copy and adapt to their contexts. The examples include those created by teachers and exemplars (i.e., model lessons) created by an expert team. The aim of the examples is to support a community of mutual inspiration among educators. The resources space hosts resources aimed at facilitating the integration of the platform into teacher PD programs.

The LD tool consists of a template that guides teachers through a 5-step teacher inquiry process (Fig. 1): (1) lesson planning, (2) data planning, (3) activity and materials, (4) sense-making, and (5) communication. The template includes text input fields (e.g., see Lesson theme and Instructional goals fields in Fig. 1), multi-select dropdowns (e.g., see Primary strategy field in Fig. 1), and multi-select checkboxes (e.g., see Strategies field in Fig. 1). Each step contains several fields detailed in Fig. 2 scheme.

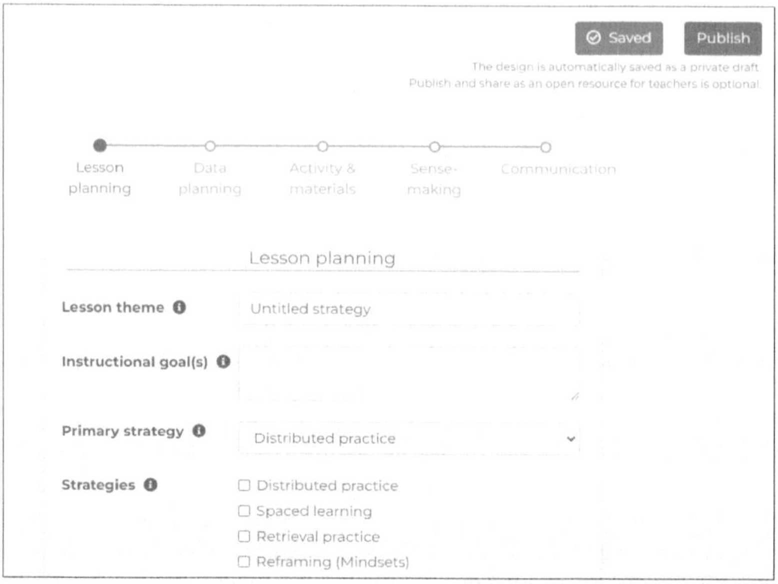

Fig. 1. Screenshot of the teacher-led inquiry design template comprising five steps.

Lesson planning shows the theme of the lesson, its instructional goals, and also specifies the teaching and learning evidence-based strategies that the lesson applies. Currently, there are four available strategies: distributed practice, spaced learning, retrieval practice, and reframing.

Distributed practice is a strategy that involves spreading out learning over time rather than massing the learning into a single session. It does not require more learning time but rather the time dedicated to learning is spread out which produces better long-term learning gains [6].

Spaced learning is a strategy, derived from neuroscientific studies on long-term memory formation [13], consisting of three memory activations separated by two 10-min breaks. In other words, the same content (with slight variations) is repeated three times in the same session. Between each repetition is a 10-min 'distractor' break in which students do an activity unrelated to the target content.

Retrieval practice is a strategy that involves having students reconstruct their knowledge (i.e., taking practice tests, doing free recall activities). It has been shown to lead to meaningful gains in learning when compared to restudying (i.e., reviewing one's notes or rereading articles) and concept mapping [5].

Reframing is a strategy that involves intentionally working toward changing one's point of view or set of beliefs (i.e., mindset) on a topic. Reframing can be helpful in changing student views of academic challenges and the resulting stress from being negative to positive [14]. This can help students better self-regulate, manage stressful situations, and embrace learning.

Data planning (second step of the template) specifies the methods in which data will be collected by teachers to check the effects of the strategies implemented. *Activity and materials* (third step) describe the activities of the lesson (lesson sequence) and materials to be used by students and teachers. The *sense-making* section (fourth step) scaffolds teacher reflections by providing questions for reflecting and making sense of the data collected from the lesson implementation. Lastly, the *communication* section (fifth step), asks teachers to share their work with the educational community by providing a public summary, links to shared files (lesson materials, presentation files), and to mark descriptors of the case study characteristics (e.g., student ages, language of instruction, etc.; see Fig. 2) to facilitate discovery of the work by others via the tool.

The community platform presents an information page for each strategy (Fig. 3) that contains a brief explanation of the strategy, a video overview of the strategy, and a selection of academic references. Moreover, the bottom half of each page displays the example research lessons – both the exemplars and teacher-contributed lessons.

The resources space hosts a digital handbook to deepen theoretical and practical knowledge of the strategies, classroom materials to support the use of the strategies such as videos and posters to show students, and a digital toolkit for educational trainers. The toolkit consists of materials needed to run a multi-session teacher PD program that makes use of the tool. A working prototype is available [https://illumine.upf.edu/] and screen captures of each main part are in an open repository [https://bit.ly/llum].

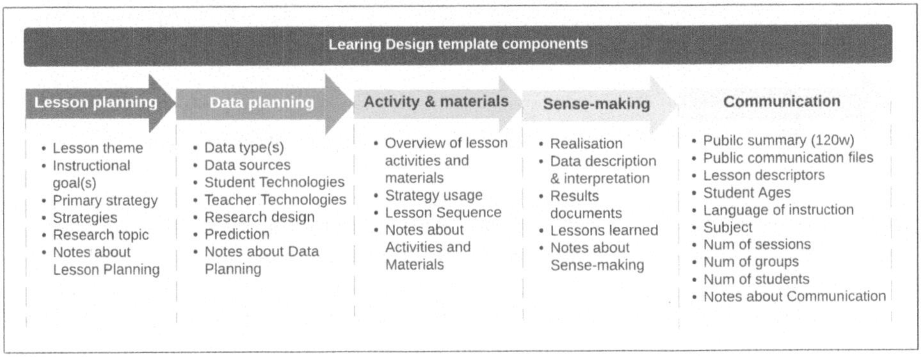

Fig. 2. Teacher-led inquiry design template components' scheme.

4 Use Case, Preliminary Results and Future Work

The Illumine research project was the context for developing, testing, and using the tool following a design-based research approach [15]. Illumine is an Erasmus + co-funded project that aims to support school education teachers in implementing evidence-based teaching practices with technology and in understanding science of learning theory (cognitive science, neuroscience) that underlies these practices. The tool and a corresponding 20-h teacher PD program were developed across a series of workshops for teachers carried out in four countries (Spain, Portugal, Estonia and Serbia) during the academic year 2021–2022. Overall, 45 teachers participated in the conceptualization and testing of the tool across three rounds of testing: initial template (paper prototype), initial website,

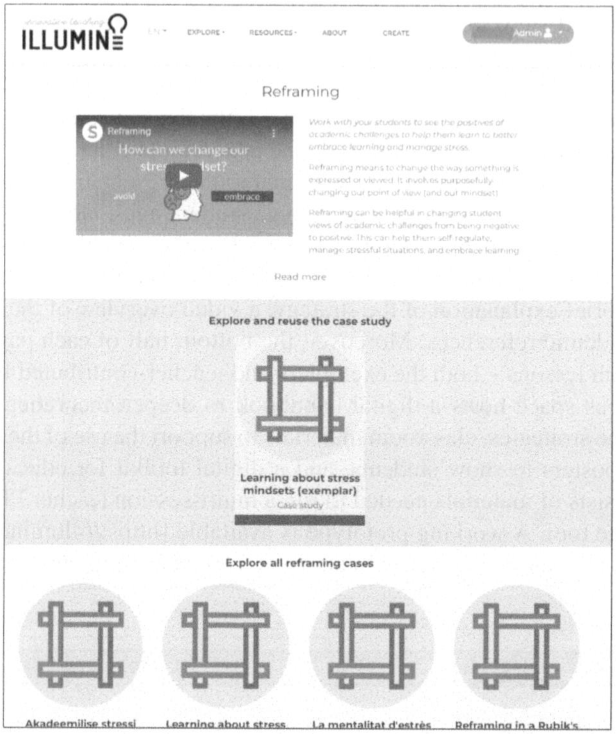

Fig. 3. Screenshot of the evidence-based strategy page of *Reframing*.

alpha web-based template and beta website. At first, some teachers found the template to be long and tedious, and the messaging on the tool unclear. Revisions such as better separating and ordering the 5-steps, using terminology more familiar to teachers, and adding hints to provide examples of how to complete each field has led to positive evaluations of the beta version. Work on the tool is still advancing. More examples from teachers are being added, improvements are being made to how visitors to the tool discover and engage with research lessons, and, in the future, additional teaching and learning strategies are to be added.

All in all, the tool facilitates teacher learning of evidence-based strategies, use of teacher inquiry, and works to recognize and disseminate the efforts of teachers via their research lessons and video case studies. It provides relatable content and examples that make the strategies understandable to educators; and it contributes open resources to the educational community.

Acknowledgements. The authors would like to thank the Illumine project members and participants for their contributions to the tool design (https://illumine.upf.edu/). This work was partially funded by Erasmus+ (2020–1-ES01-KA201–082504), the Department of Research and Universities of the Government of Catalonia (SGR 00930), and the Spanish Ministry (PID2020-112584RB-C33 funded by MICIN/AEI/https://doi.org/10.13039/501100011033). D. Hernández-Leo (Serra Húnter) acknowledges the support by ICREA under the ICREA Academia program.

References

1. Guskey, T.R.: Professional development and teacher change. Teachers and Teach. **8**(3), 381–391 (2002)
2. Mertler, C.A.: Action research as teacher inquiry: a viable strategy for resolving problems of practice. Pract. Assess. Res. Eval. **26**, 19 (2021)
3. Doig, B., Groves, S.: Japanese lesson study: Teacher professional development through communities of inquiry. Math. Teach. Educ. Dev. **13**(1), 77–93 (2011)
4. Chokshi, S., Fernandez, C.: Challenges to importing Japanese lesson study: concerns, misconceptions, and nuances. Phi Delta Kappan **85**(7), 520–525 (2004)
5. Karpicke, J.D., Blunt, J.R.: Retrieval practice produces more learning than elaborative studying with concept mapping. Science **331**(6018), 772–775 (2011)
6. Weinstein, Y., Sumeracki, M., Caviglioli, O.: Understanding How We Learn: A Visual Guide. Routledge, New York (2018)
7. Beardsley, M., Albó, L., Teacher motivation toward professional development following emergency remote teaching experiences. In: Proceedings of the 15th International Conference on Computer-Supported Collaborative Learning, pp. 561–562 (2022)
8. Beardsley, M., Albó, L., Aragón, P., Hernández-Leo, D.: Emergency education effects on teacher abilities and motivation to use digital technologies. Br. J. Edu. Technol. **52**(4), 1455–1477 (2021)
9. Wasson, B., Kirschner, P.A.: Learning design: european approaches. TechTrends **64**, 815–827 (2020)
10. Michos, K., Hernández-Leo, D.: Supporting awareness in communities of learning design practice. Comput. Hum. Behav. **85**, 255–270 (2018)
11. Hernández-Leo, D., et al.: An integrated environment for learning design. Frontiers in ICT **5**, 9 (2018)
12. Hernández-Leo, D., Moreno, P., Chacón, J., Blat, J.: LdShake support for team-based learning design. Comput. Hum. Behav. **37**, 402–412 (2014)
13. Kelley, P., Whatson, T.: Making long-term memories in minutes: a spaced learning pattern from memory research in education. Front. Hum. Neurosci. **7**, 589 (2013)
14. Crum, A.J., Akinola, M., Martin, A., Fath, S.: The role of stress mindset in shaping cognitive, emotional, and physiological responses to challenging and threatening stress. Anxiety Stress Coping **30**(4), 379–395 (2017)
15. Cole, R., Purao, S., Rossi, M., Sein, M.: Being proactive: where action research meets design research. In: ICIS 2005 Proceedings, p. 27 (2005)

CERSEI: Cognitive Effort Based Recommender System for Enhancing Inclusiveness

Geoffray Bonnin[1,2(✉)], Vaclav Bayer[2], Miriam Fernandez[2], Christothea Herodotou[2], Martin Hlosta[3], and Paul Mulholland[2]

[1] Loria - Université de Lorraine, Nancy, France
bonnin@loria.fr
[2] The Open University, Milton Keynes, UK
{geoffray.bonnin,vaclav.bayer,miriam.fernandez,christothea.herodotou, paul.mulholland}@open.ac.uk
[3] Swiss Distance University of Applied Sciences, Brig, Switzerland
martin.hlosta@ffhs.ch

Abstract. Awarding gaps have been commonly observed between different socio-demographic categories of students, especially in the domains of sociology and learning science. Recent research has shown that using Learning Analytics models could be exploited to reduce these gaps, and therefore contribute to making the learning process more inclusive and equitable. This demonstration paper presents CERSEI, a new web-based learning prototype that aims to enhance inclusiveness by exploiting two Learning Analytics models: a cognitive effort model and an activity recommender built upon the cognitive effort model. Previous research has indeed shown a strong interplay between socio-economic status, effort and motivation, e.g., families from higher socio-economic status tend to mobilize more resources to prevent their children from falling down the social ladder. Some categories of students might therefore have fewer sources of motivation and exert less effort, or a higher tendency to exert effort on specific activities that are not the most relevant for succeeding. CERSEI allows students to track their effort by assigning ratings on their activities using the RSME scale and to receive engaging recommendations of learning activities. This will allow us to collect the relevant data to better understand how effort is exerted by different categories of students and how recommendations can impact them. Based on the outcomes of the related analysis, we will then aim at creating better Learning Analytics models. We expect that these models will help to provide more inclusive and equitable learning.

Keywords: Cognitive Effort · Activity Recommendation · Inclusiveness

1 Introduction

According to research, students from privileged backgrounds generally have a greater chance of success compared to their underprivileged peers [1,2]. The

O. Viberg et al. (Eds.): EC-TEL 2023, LNCS 14200, pp. 692–697, 2023.
https://doi.org/10.1007/978-3-031-42682-7_63

phenomenon of different socio-demographic groups having different learning outcomes is generally referred to as the awarding gap [3], also called achievement gap [4]. One means of reducing this gap is to exploit the potential of Learning Analytics models. Recently, Hlosta et al. [5] studied the effects of asking teachers to contact students based on predictions from a Learning Analytics model that indicated which students were likely to fail. Using this method increased the learning success of ethnic minority students by 10% and that of students from low IMD (Index of Multiple Deprivation) band by 4%.

We believe that effort modeling is one very promising Learning Analytics approach towards that goal, especially because effort and motivation have been found to be particularly important factors of the success of students from privileged backgrounds [2]. The underlying hypothesis, called compensatory advantage hypothesis, states that the achievement gap is stronger among students with a lower ability and can be explained in terms of effort and motivation, i.e., students from a privileged background tend to exert more effort and to have more sources of motivation [6]. Providing students with a means to give feedback about their effort and receive effort-based educational recommendations could therefore contribute to reduce this gap.

We therefore developed CERSEI (Cognitive Effort based Recommender System for Enhancing Inclusiveness), a learning platform that allows students to assign effort ratings to the activities they complete on a Virtual Learning Environment (VLE) and to receive effort-based recommendations. More precisely, students can use CERSEI to keep track of the effort they exerted on previous activities and to estimate how much effort they think would be required for them to complete the next available activities. Based on these ratings and on students' behavioral data (mouse and keyboard usage, page views, submitted work, etc.), the platform computes predicted effort ratings and provides activity recommendations that the students can choose to accept or reject. When they accept, they are directed to a local Moodle-based VLE deployed on the same server on which they can perform the corresponding activity and submit their work.

From a research point of view, CERSEI allows us to collect behavioral data and subjective effort ratings that can be used to train our effort model. The first version of our effort model is built upon the work of Moissa et al. [7], which focused on modelling students' cognitive effort using similar learning data collected during 45-minute series of activities. The study demonstrated the relevance of using mouse and keyboard usage data as a means of measuring and predicting the effort, and the even higher relevance of also incorporating longer-term past student data as input of the models, i.e., mouse and keyboard usage data from previous activities.

Overall, our goal is to test the hypothesis that the effort is different for different categories of students (as indicated previously in the literature), to have a better understanding of how different categories of students exert effort while learning, and to have a better understanding of the extent to which engaging recommendations of learning activities can be useful depending on the categories of students. As a first step however, we are currently preparing a pre-study to assess the usability and design of the platform, and to make sure it is fully functional, especially in terms of data access. This process includes applications for ethical and data privacy approvals from our university, which are currently being conducted. A separate study will be made in a future work, which will be built upon the results of the pre-study.

2 Overview of CERSEI

CERSEI takes the form of a web platform that can be linked to a VLE to connect students' learning data to our effort model and recommender system. The platform has three main functionalities: (1) Online Activities, (2) Effort Tracking and (3) Activity Recommendations.

2.1 Online Activities

In order to have a pool of activities that can be used as recommendations by the recommender system, CERSEI includes a simple Moodle-based learning environment on which activities can be created by teachers. Students can then access these activities and submit their work using the Moodle online interface. Currently, the platform only contains a few initial activities for the purpose of evaluating the usability of the platform. These activities are related to the topic of web technology, and go from short HTML and CSS exercises to the development of advanced PHP and JavaScript applications.

While students perform these online activities, their behavioral data is recorded (mouse and keyboard usage). These data are then used by our effort model to predict effort ratings of future activities. These activities can be accessed from the different views of the platform related to effort tracking and activity recommendations, which are presented next.

2.2 Effort Tracking

CERSEI categorizes the activities that the student can perform according to two dimensions: the type of learning environment (the VLE to which CERSEI is linked, or CERSEI itself) and the completion of these activities (whether an activity was completed or not). In other words, four views are related to effort tracking: (1) Completed from VLE, (2) Remaining from VLE, (3) Completed from CERSEI and (4) Remaining from CERSEI, see Fig. 1. Initially, all VLE activities are in the second category, and all activities from CERSEI are in the fourth category. Each time an activity from the VLE is completed, it becomes visible in the first category, and each time an activity from CERSEI is completed it becomes visible in the third category.

Students can use these views to provide effort estimates for remaining activities, and perceived effort rating for the completed ones. Both types of ratings can be changed or removed any time. When no ratings have been provided by a student to an activity, the value predicted by our effort model is displayed

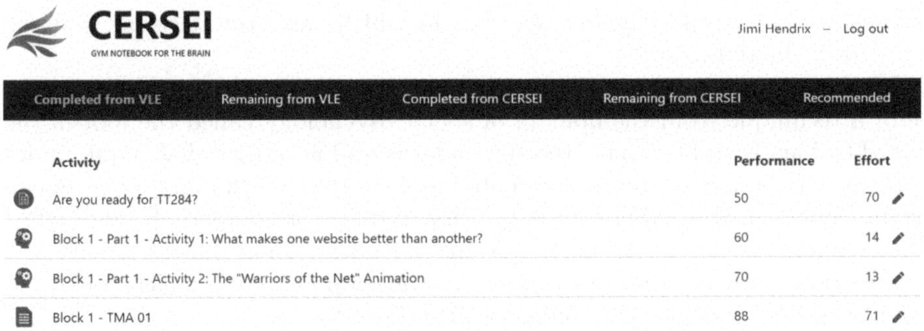

Fig. 1. The different views of CERSEI. Students can click on the pen icons to change the effort ratings and the individual activity links to access them either on the VLE or on the local Moodle.

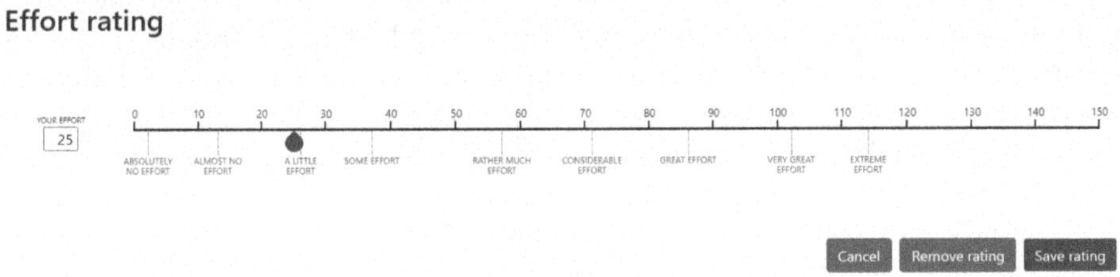

Fig. 2. The RSME modal window used to assign ratings. The modal window appears when students click on the pen icons from the effort tracking views and allows them to assign, change or remove their ratings.

instead. The platform therefore handles three types of effort ratings: estimated ratings, perceived ratings and predicted ratings, which are all stored separately in our database. Making this distinction is important because some low effort tasks may seem to require a high effort and vice versa, which could have an impact on the acceptance of recommended activities.

All estimated and perceived effort ratings are assigned by students using the RSME, see Fig. 2. This instrument provides students with a scale from 0 to 150 on which several verbal labels were precisely positioned based on a user study [8]. Compared to the more widespread NASA-TLX instrument [9], it is similar to the "Effort" dimension of the instrument, but has the advantage of being precise in terms of intervals between the labels. Predicted ratings are currently computed based on the effort model from Moissa et al. [7].

2.3 Activity Recommendations

The last view of the platform is dedicated to activity recommendations. Recommendations are displayed in a relatively large box that contains a precise description together with an illustration. Students can either accept the recommendation, in which case they are directed to the corresponding online Moodle interface, or reject the recommendation, in which case, the decision is simply recorded in the database.

The recommendations are computed based on the effort based model and use of a technique from the domain of social psychology called the foot-in-the-door. The idea is to first make recommendations of activities that require a low effort, and if these activities are accepted and completed, to make a subsequent recommendation of a similar activity[1] that requires a comparably high effort. This technique seems particularly relevant for educational purposes because it is compatible with the the zone of proximal development [10], which states that activities should increase the challenge little by little.

3 Pre-study

We are currently preparing a user study to assess the usability and design of the first version of the platform using the AttrakDiff questionnaire[2]. We are recruiting students of the current presentation of a module on Web technologies from our university. The learning data of the student will be sent to our servers once a day, and will be used to determine the list of activities the students have completed and the ones they still have to complete.

The study will start in May 2023 and will last until June 2023. The main axes of the experimental protocol are the following:

- Step 1: The student accesses the platform and creates an account
- Step 2: The student provides effort ratings to 20 - 30 of his previously completed VLE activities
- Step 3: The system provides the student with a first low effort recommendation
  - Step 3a: The student assigns an estimated rating (how much effort will be required)
  - Step 3b: The student accepts or rejects the recommendation
  - Step 3c: If the recommendation is accepted and completed, then the effort rating is refined by the student
- Step 4: The system provides the students with a second higher effort recommendation
  - Step 4a: The student assigns an estimated rating (how much effort will be required)
  - Step 4b: The student accepts or rejects the recommendation
  - Step 4c: If the recommendation is accepted and completed, then the effort rating is refined by the student
- Step 5: The student answers the AttrakDiff questionnaire.

[1] Currently, the similarity between the activities is a simple cosine similarity based on their meta-data and text content.

[2] https://www.attrakdiff.de/index-en.html.

4 Conclusion

The current version of CERSEI is able to be connected to the VLE of a university, and allows students to track their effort and receive activity recommendations. At this stage, our models are still relatively rudimentary, as our current goal is only to assess the usability and design of the platform.

In future work, we will undertake a larger study with a much higher number of students from the next presentation of the same module. The number of students who register each year to this module is around 1,500. We hope that more than 300 students will participate, which will allow us to collect a high amount of effort ratings. We will also collect socio-demographic data from the data repository of the university and will study how effort is exerted by different categories of students and how recommendations can impact them. Based on the outcomes of the related analysis, we will then propose different effort models that we will test using the usual offline information retrieval methodology. Subsequently, we will use the best-performing model to study different aspects related to our recommender system, such as the influence of the elapsed time between consecutive recommendations and of different effort gap values between subsequent recommendations.

References

1. Herbaut, E.: Overcoming failure in higher education: social inequalities and compensatory advantage in dropout patterns. Acta Sociologica. **64**(4), 383–402 (2021)
2. Gil-Hernández, C.: The (Unequal) Interplay between cognitive and noncognitive skills in early educational attainment. Am. Behav. Sci. **65**(11), 1577–1598 (2021)
3. Wong, B., El Morally, R., Copsey-Blake, M.: 'Fair and square': what do students think about the ethnicity degree awarding gap? J. Further High. Educ. **45**(8), 1147–1161 (2021)
4. Jeynes, W.: A meta-analysis: the effects of parental involvement on minority children's academic achievement. Educ. Urban Soc. **35**, 202–218 (2003)
5. Hlosta, M., Herodotou, C., Bayer, V., Fernandez, M.: Impact of predictive learning analytics on course awarding gap of disadvantaged students in STEM. In: Roll, I., McNamara, D., Sosnovsky, S., Luckin, R., Dimitrova, V. (eds.) AIED 2021. LNCS (LNAI), vol. 12749, pp. 190–195. Springer, Cham (2021). https://doi.org/10.1007/978-3-030-78270-2_34
6. Bernardi, F., Triventi, M.: Compensatory advantage in educational transitions: yrivial or substantial? Simulated Scenario analysis. Acta sociológica. **63**(1), 40–62 (2020)
7. Moissa, B., Bonnin, G., Boyer, A.: Measuring and predicting students' effort: a study on the feasibility of cognitive load measures to real-life scenarios. In: Proceedings of EC-TEL 2021, pp. 363–367 (2021)
8. Zijlstra, F., van Doorn, L.: The Construction of a Scale to Measure Perceived Effort. University of Technology (1985)
9. Hart, S., Staveland, L.: Development of NASA-TLX (Task Load Index): Results of empirical and theoretical research. Adv. Psychol. **52**, 139–183 (1988)
10. Vygotsky, L., Cole, M.: Mind in Society: Development of Higher Psychological Processes. Harvard University Press (1978)

A Student-Centered Learning Analytics Dashboard Towards Course Goal Achievement in STEM Education

Sebastian Buvari, Olga Viberg(✉), Alessandro Iop, and Mario Romero

EECS, KTH Royal Institute of Technology, Stockholm, Sweden
{buvari,oviberg,aiop,marior}@kth.se

Abstract. Online learning has become an everyday form of learning for many students across different disciplines, including STEM subjects in the setting of higher education. Studying in these settings requires students to self-regulate their learning to a higher degree as compared to campus-based education. A vital aspect of self-regulated learning is the application of goal-setting strategies. Universities act to support students' goal-setting through the achievement of course learning outcomes, which work both as a promise and metric of academic achievement. However, a lack of clear integration between course activities and course learning outcomes leaves a dissonance between students' study efforts and the course progress. This demo study presents a student-centered learning analytics dashboard aimed at assisting students in their achievement of course learning goals in the setting of STEM higher education. The dashboard was designed using a design science methodological approach. Thirty-seven students have contributed to its development and evaluation during different stages of the design process, including the conceptual iterative design and prototyping. The preliminary results show that students found the tool to be easy to use and useful for the achievement of the course goals.

Keywords: Learning Outcomes · Learning Analytics Dashboard · STEM Higher Education · Participatory Design

1 Introduction

Online education requires learners to self-regulate their work, yet many of them are poor at self-regulated learning (SRL) [1]. SRL refers to the extent to which learners are active participants of their own learning progress by means of monitoring and controlling their motivation, metacognition, cognition, and behavior towards achieving their learning goals [2]. Research has shown that engaging in strategies related to SRL, such as goal settings and visualization of the student learning progress towards the achievement of the course learning goals, positively affects academic success in online learning settings [3,4]. However, current SRL support aiming at assisting students in their progression towards the course

O. Viberg et al. (Eds.): EC-TEL 2023, LNCS 14200, pp. 698–704, 2023.
https://doi.org/10.1007/978-3-031-42682-7_64

goals has so far been limited [5]. The present demo study aims to fill this gap by presenting a learning analytics dashboard (LAD) aimed at assisting students in visualising their learning progress in relation to the achievement of the course learning objectives. Achievement of goals is one of the crucial determinant of students' learning progress and has impact on academic outcomes [9].

Previous research stresses the importance of designing quality courses for students' learning success and satisfaction [6]. One of the critical course learning design practices is articulating easily comprehensible learning objectives and their sequence to obtain the desired learning outcomes [7]. Learning objectives in a course refer to specific skills, knowledge and dispositions that students are expected to acquire or demonstrate at the end of the course [7,8].

Today, higher education institutions are increasingly adopting digital technologies such as learning management systems (LMSs). Students using these systems produce activity logs which can be used to track and visualise their study efforts as a progression towards the achievement of course learning objectives.

Deployment of analytics technologies is becoming increasingly important in higher education. According to Susnjak et al. [10], analytics in this sector focuses on maximizing student retention rates by identifying at-risk individuals early on, and initiating interventions whilst improving the quality of the overall educational experience. One of such analytics innovation tools are LADs, which aim to provide learners with a "snapshot of how they are progressing in their courses" [10]. Overall, analytics tools such as LADs reveal learner insights that could prompt a reflection process that would not be realised in other way. In this study, we draw on the advances in visualisation technologies and learning analytics to present how a student-facing LAD, aiming to raise student awareness of how they progress toward the achievement of course learning objectives, could be designed and implemented in the setting of engineering higher education.

2 Case Study Settings

We use a second-cycle course on Information Visualization as a case study. The course gives six higher education credits, roughly mapping to 160 h of work, including attending lectures, reading, programming, presenting, testing, developing group projects, critiquing, discussing, and writing journals. For all the course learning activities, Canvas (the LMS) is used. Approximately 50 students register for the course every year. The course participants meet face-to-face in a visualization studio over the course of 16 two-hour meetings, half of which are lectures and the other half are student presentations and discussions. Of particular interest are the learning journals the students need to keep. The focus of the self-reflection learning journal are the individual intended learning outcomes (ILOs) of the students. The students submit three journal entries, one after each group project deliverable. Each journal entry is worth 10% of the final grade. In the journal entries, students must state their personal intended learning objectives. In each journal entry, they evaluate and reflect on what they have done, learned and planned for the next stage of work. They also reflect on the plans and actions that did not succeed towards advancing the project and the lessons learned from them. The students receive prompt feedback to their journal entries with a focus on the learning objectives and the reflections.

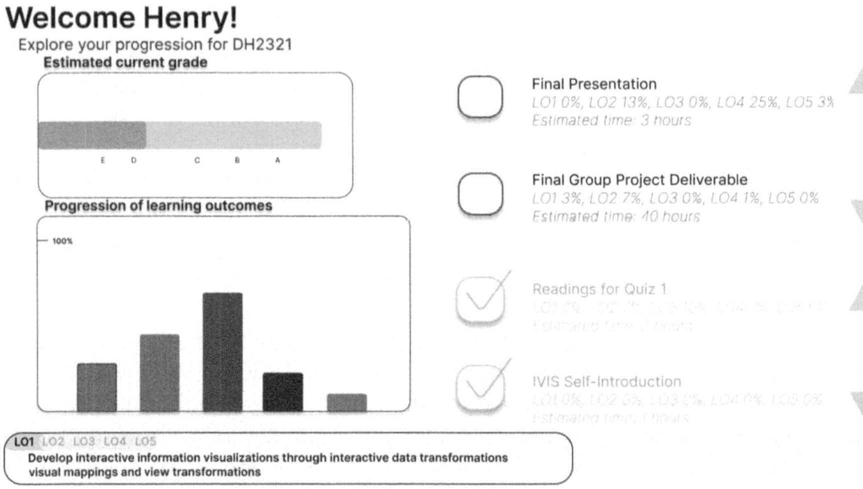

Fig. 1. A tentative Figma design of the learning analytics dashboard (LAD).

3 Design Science Research Approach

When developing the student-facing LAD, we followed a Design Science Research methodology [11], which divides the design process into five major steps: 1. problem awareness; 2. suggestion; 3. development; 4. evaluation; and 5. conclusion. In this study, problem awareness (step 1) can be described as the recognition of segregation between ILOs and course activities. The suggestion (step 2) was the development of a student-facing LAD. We employed *participatory design* to define a LAD that met students' needs, as suggested by previous studies [12–14]. Thirty-seven students in the targeted course participated in a F2F workshop in February 2023, where they were briefly introduced to the dashboard idea by the authors. The students were then asked to work in smaller groups to brainstorm what functionality the dashboard should deliver to meet their needs and preferences. The students submitted their suggestions through the tool Menti. The final part of the workshop involved the entirety of the audience further developing submitted suggestions, by providing useful insights into how they would like the dashboard to function and look like in terms of the interface design. The analysis of the student suggestions led to the development in Figma of the tentative design shown in Fig. 1.

This design was presented to a group of three students who provided their feedback. Major suggestions, such as removing the cluttered ILO distribution as presented under each assignment and adding the presentation for each assignment's due date, were gathered and implemented for the final dashboard design. With the student feedback, we developed a functional prototype presented in the following section.

4 The 'Learning Progress' Dashboard

The dashboard, named 'Learning Progress', was developed using react.js, material UI and nivo, which is a library built on d3.js. Data from the LMS (Canvas) used in the case study course was included, with due dates and estimated time per assignment. The resulting implementation, using the tentative design and student feedback from the group session as blueprint, is shown in Fig. 2. The four major components of the dashboard include: 1. the *assignment handler*; 2. the *learning outcome tracker*; 3. the *grade progression chart*; and 4. the *learning outcome description box*.

The *assignment handler* (Fig. 2A) starts the workflow. Here, students are able to see the assignment. Through this component, students are able to view completed assignments at the bottom, deadlines for future assignments, and the teacher's estimated completion time. The two lists of incomplete and completed assignments are scroll-able, allowing the student to monitor their assignments within one interface. Clicking on an incomplete assignment's checkbox marks it as completed and moves the assignment into the completed list. Clicking on a completed assignment's checkbox returns the assignment to incomplete status. Through this simple interaction, students are able to keep track of completed and incomplete assignments, how much time they should approximately set aside for each assignment, and when each assignment needs to be completed. Completed assignments feed the data stream, which is connected to and visualized in the *learning outcome tracker* and *grade progression chart*.

The *learning outcome tracker* (Fig. 2B) is the core of the visualization. It displays a student's progression towards each ILO. This allows students to gauge their course progression in a previously unexplored manner, by directly connecting each assignment to relevant ILOs. Each assignment is credited with varying percentage values in respect to each learning outcome. By marking an assignment as complete, those values are directly displayed and added in the learning outcome tracker. As the values are percentage based, the maximum value a student can reach in each learning outcome is 100%.

The *grade progression chart* (Fig. 2C) displays an estimated current grade for students based on their completed assignments. Visualizing this progression allows students to readily assess the distance between grades and to experiment with combinations of assignments to reach a target grade. The *learning outcome description box* (Fig. 2D) provides students with immediate access to the ILOs. This reminds students of the learning outcomes and encourages them to actively review them as they complete assignments, thus giving assignments a new value

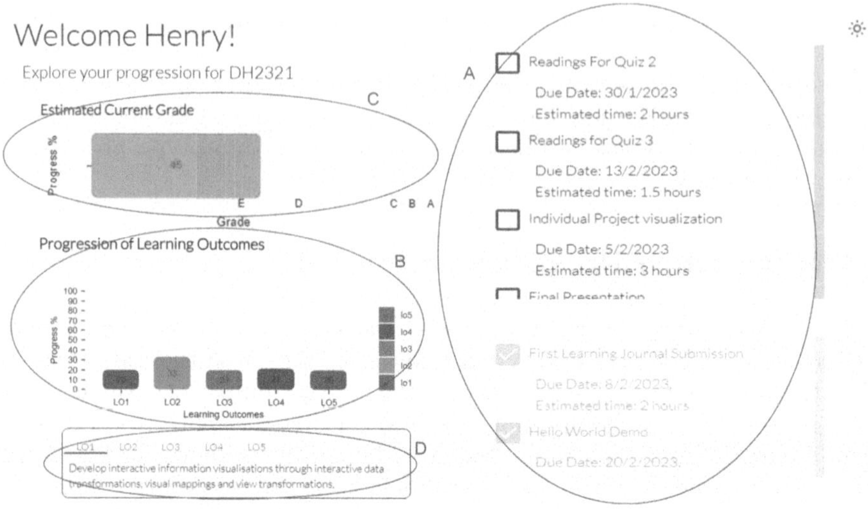

Fig. 2. The four components. A: *assignment handler*; B: *learning outcome tracker*; C: *grade progression chart*; and D: *learning outcome description box.*

prospective. Before, it was difficult to track the course ILOs through the details of the assignments.

5 Conclusions and Future Development

Based on initial usability evaluation results, future development of the 'Learning Progress' dashboard will explore new visualizations, which would further increase clarity and accessibility of student progression towards the course ILOs. Other development paths will enable personalized customizations of the learning dashboard. This could include simple features such as color, as well as more advanced ones such as adding personally developed goals to the assignment section. Other features will support students' creativity when approaching assignments, such as allowing them to split assignments into arbitrary sub-tasks. Further development of the new features will be conducted through participatory design. The next step of this project is to apply the principles of Privacy by Design to address students' possible privacy concerns in learning analytics, and to finally introduce the dashboard to all the students participating in the next course iteration [15]. This demonstration paper presented a student-centered learning analytics dashboard to assist students in their course goals' achievement, in the setting of STEM higher education. Based on the rigorous course learning design, the designed dashboard shows the potential to support students in their regulation of learning, ultimately leading to improved learning outcomes.

References

1. Wong, J., et al.: Facilitating goal setting and planning to enhance online self-regulation of learning. Comput. Hum. Behav. **124**, 106913 (2021)
2. Boekaerts, M., Cascallar, E.: How far have we moved toward the integration of theory and practice in self-regulation? Educ. Psychol. Rev. **18**, 199–210 (2006)
3. Förster, N., Souvignier, E.: Learning progress assessment and goal setting: effects on reading achievement, reading motivation and reading self-concept. Learn. Instruct. **32**, 91–100 (2014)
4. Kizilcec, R.F., et al.: Self-regulated learning strategies predict learner behavior and goal attainment in Massive Open Online Courses. Comput. Educ. **104**, 18–33 (2017)
5. Perez-Alvarez, R., et al.: Tools designed to support self-regulated learning in online learning environments: a systematic review. IEEE Trans. Learn. Technol. **15**(4), 508–522 (2022)
6. Jaggars, S.S., Xu, D.: How do online course design features influence student performance? Comput. Educ. **95**, 270–284 (2016)
7. Adams, N. E.: Bloom's taxonomy of cognitive learning objectives. J. Med. Libr. Assoc. JMLA **103**(3), 152 (2015)
8. Combs, K.L., et al.: Enhancing curriculum and delivery: linking assessment to learning objectives. Assess. Eval. High. Ed. **33**(1), 87–102 (2008)
9. Hulleman, C.S., et al.: A meta-analytic review of achievement goal measures: different labels for the same constructs or different constructs with similar labels? Psychol. Bull. **136**(3), 422 (2010)
10. Susnjak, T., et al.: Learning analytics dashboard: a tool for providing actionable insights to learners. Inter. J. of Educational Technology in Higher Ed. **19**(1), 12 (2022)
11. Vaishnavi, V.K., Kuechler, W.: Design Science Research Methods and Patterns: Innovating Information and Communication Technology. CRC Press, Boca Raton (2015)
12. Revano, T.F., Garcia, M.B.: Designing human-centered learning analytics dashboard for higher education using a participatory design approach. In: IEEE 13th International Conference on Humanoid, Nanotechnology, Information Technology, Communication and Control, Environment, and Management (HNICEM). Manila, Philippines. vol. **2021**, pp. 1–5 (2021)
13. Dimitriadis, Y., Martínez-Maldonado, R., Wiley, K.: Human-centered design principles for actionable learning analytics. In: Tsiatsos, T., Demetriadis, S., Mikropoulos, A., Dagdilelis, V. (eds.) Research on E-Learning and ICT in Education, pp. 277–296. Springer, Cham (2021). https://doi.org/10.1007/978-3-030-64363-8_15
14. Jivet, I.: The dashboard that loved me: Designing adaptive learning analytics for self-regulated learning (2021)
15. Mutimukwe, C., et al.: Students' privacy concerns in learning analytics: model development. Br. J. Educ. Technol. **53**(4), 932–951 (2022)

Augmented Intelligence in Tutoring Systems: A Case Study in Real-Time Pose Tracking to Enhance the Self-learning of Fitness Exercises

Nghia Duong-Trung(✉), Hitesh Kotte, and Miloš Kravčík

Educational Technology Lab, German Research Center for Artificial Intelligence (DFKI), Alt-Moabit 91C, 10559 Berlin, Germany
{nghia_trung.duong,hitesh.kotte,milos.kravcik}@dfki.de

Abstract. In technology enhanced learning is development of psycho-motor skills an area with a lot of potential, which is enabled by rapid improvements of sensors and wearable devices, combined with artificial intelligence. Here we focus on fitness exercises and present a novel approach based on computer vision techniques to track the practitioner's pose and provide automatically real-time feedback for improvement, based on the input from an expert trainer. Taking into account the gathered data and ground-truth poses, the proposed pipeline can learn actively from a professional trainer demonstrating an exercise in front of a camera or passively from a recorded video. In our experiment, we used professional fitness exercise videos as the ground truth and measured the performance of five inexperienced participants. The results show positive responses from participants, indicating the feasibility of the proposed approach as well as suggestions for its further improvement.

Keywords: Real-time Pose Tracking · Sustainable Learning · Psycho-motor Skills · Fitness Exercises

1 Introduction

Augmented intelligence (AuI) is a rapidly evolving technology that combines human intelligence with machine intelligence to enhance performance and productivity in various fields, including sports and fitness [2]. In tutoring systems for sport and fitness, augmented intelligence refers to a collaboration between humans and artificial intelligence (AI), where AI assists humans in decision-making and problem-solving [11]. The systems can provide individuals with a highly personalized coaching experience tailored to their needs and goals [4]. By analyzing individuals' performance data, these systems can adjust coaching recommendations to help them improve in areas where they struggle. The use of AuI in tutoring systems [5] holds a lot of potential to improve the effectiveness, safety, and enjoyment of sports and fitness activities. Nevertheless, various

O. Viberg et al. (Eds.): EC-TEL 2023, LNCS 14200, pp. 705–710, 2023.
https://doi.org/10.1007/978-3-031-42682-7_65

sports are primarily done in a do-it-yourself process, which can be unsafe [3]. People watch trainer demonstrations or instructional videos, then perform the exercise while imitating what they have observed. A good plan and guidance are essential to achieve their fitness goals.

In the rest of the paper we first briefly introduce the related work. Then we describe several challenges in fitness training. The core of the paper is the presentation of our experiment and its results, including a short qualitative evaluation. Finally we summarize our findings.

2 Related Work

Early research illustrated the potential of AI techniques in sports, particularly in weight training, to measure the virtual displacement and force determinants while performing various exercises [7]. Li *et al.* introduced spatio-temporal skeleton encoding to recognize and evaluate the gym action in an AI fitness system [6]. Intensive data collection and model training was conducted, but unfortunately, they are unavailable to reproduce. Ueta [10] proposed expensive augmented reality devices and an impractical virtual-real interaction to correct the fitness movement. Conceptual and theoretical models for learning psychomotor skills have emerged from preliminary studies [1] where further work should focus on automatic, individual feedback generation. Multiple methods were investigated to efficiently represent and predict human motion, e.g., a machine learning-supported approach to provide feedback in two example scenarios: running and interacting with a robot. For the first scenario, an assessment was provided of how movements can be compared to show discrepancies between student and expert movement [9]. Some psychomotor tasks require students to perform a specific sequence of poses and movements. A natural teaching scheme for such studies is to match a person's performance with a teacher's demonstration. However, this requires strategies to match the teacher's demonstration of each movement to the person's attempts and to recognize differences between demonstration and attempt. To automatically identify student attempts for poses with only one correct teacher demonstration, the investigated methods included relevance learning, prototype networks, and attentional mechanisms to achieve a robust, few-shot approach that can be generalized to all students. An experiment [8] showed that prototypical networks work best with an attention mechanism.

3 Self-practicing and Feedback in Fitness

Self-practicing of fitness exercises can be challenging for several reasons. First, it may not be easy to maintain proper posture and technique without the guidance of a coach or trainer. Poor posture can lead to injuries and reduced effectiveness of the exercise. Second, staying motivated and tracking progress without external accountability and feedback is also difficult. Third, it is necessary to personalize a workout program to meet individual needs and goals. In the process, a coach or an instructor performs a particular exercise before a trainee.

Then, the participant tries to repeat the movement by imitating what has been observed. Next, by monitoring the trainee's performance, the trainer can provide feedback or perform the exercise again. While having a trainer present during fitness practice can be helpful in terms of guidance, several potential issues can arise. Trainees may become overly reliant on the trainer and need their presence to motivate themselves or maintain a consistent fitness routine. Additionally, hiring a trainer can be expensive, and if the instructor is always present, the cost of their services can add up quickly. If the trainer is always leading the workout, the client may not have the opportunity to try different exercises or workout routines, which can lead to boredom and decreased motivation. It is also essential for clients to perform their workouts and make adjustments based on their individual needs and goals.

4 Experiments

4.1 Fitness Exercises by McFIT GmbH

For our purposes we used the McFIT's YouTube channel for home fitness. The videos are led by experienced fitness trainers who guide viewers through each exercise, providing clear instructions and modifications for different fitness levels. We selected videos corresponding to 15 fitness exercises and analysed them (see Table 1).

4.2 Experiment Setup

Given three key points $u(x_u, y_u), v(x_v, y_v), p(x_p, y_p)$, the joint angle $\theta(u, v, p)$ (in degree) between two rays formed by three mentioned points is calculated as follows: $\theta(u, v, p) = \frac{180(\phi(y_p - y_v, x_p - x_v) - \phi(y_u - y_v, x_u - x_v))}{\pi}$. where the angle $\phi(y, x)$ (in radian) between the ray from the origin to the point (x, y) and the positive x-axis in the Cartesian plane is calculated as follows: $\phi(y, x) = arctan(\frac{y}{x})$, if $x > 0$; $\phi(y, x) = \frac{\pi}{2} - \arctan(\frac{x}{y})$, if $y > 0$; $\phi(y, x) = \arctan(\frac{y}{x}) \pm \pi$, if $x < 0$; $\phi(y, x) = -\frac{\pi}{2} - \arctan(\frac{x}{y})$, if $y < 0$. The setup allowed for effective and efficient data collection and preparation for subsequent analysis using machine learning algorithms. A McFIT studio was chosen as the location to conduct experiments. Five voluntary participants, between the ages of 25 and 30, were asked to mimic the exercise shown to them while receiving real-time feedback and pose tracking through the AI system. The feedback provided by the AI system included information on the correctness of the exercise posture, the positioning of the body and limbs, and the movement range. The results showed that using real-time feedback and pose tracking through the AI system significantly improved exercise mimicry. Participants were able to correct their exercise posture, body and limb positioning, and movement range in response to the feedback provided by the AI system. We decompose our real-time fitness tutoring system into three phases: Keypoints Detection, Pose Tracking, and Output and Feedback, see Algorithm 1.

Algorithm 1. Pipeline for Self-Learning of Fitness Exercises.

Keypoints Detection Phase:

Get input from recorded video or real-time streaming.

Detect $\{x_b, y_b, w_b, h_b, \text{cf}, k_x^0, k_y^0, k_{cf}^0, k_x^1, k_y^1, k_{cf}^1, \ldots, k_x^{16}, k_y^{16}, k_{cf}^{16}\}$ in each frame.

Pose Tracking Phase:

Get predefined keypoints combination and range of joint angles.

Calculate θ and ϕ.

Convert θ to 0-100% range using one-dimensional linear interpolation.

Output and Feedback Phase:

Display the trainee's performance based on a predefined difficulty level.

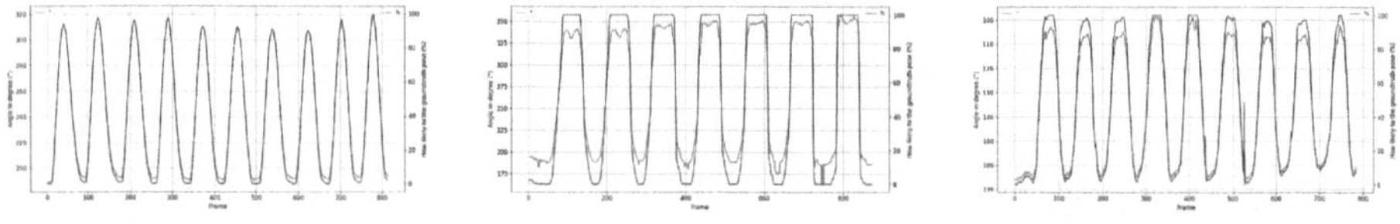

(a) Barbell Shrugs (b) Lateral Pulls (c) Lunges

Fig. 1. Performance tracking of different exercises.

Table 1. Keypoint combination for different sports exercises.

Exercises	Keypoints			
	5 7 9	11 13 15	6 8 10	12 14 16
Barbell Shrugs	[192°,320°]	-	[192°,320°]	-
Bicep Curls	[010°,150°]		[010°,150°]	
Pushups	[210°,280°]		[210°,280°]	
Shoulder Lateral Raise	[171°,194°]		[171°,194°]	
Shoulder Front Raise	[145°,290°]		[145°,290°]	
Shoulder Press	[026°,180°]		[026°,180°]	
Chest Press Rope	[186°,199°]		[186°,199°]	
Upper Chest Press	[177°,285°]		[177°,285°]	
Lateral Pulls	[191°,327°]		[191°,327°]	
Pullups	[142°,321°]		[142°,321°]	
Lunges	-	[142°,321°]	-	[153°,066°]
Squats		[220°,280°]		[220°,280°]
Horizontal Leg Press		[157°,086°]		[157°,086°]
Vertical Leg Press		[252°,170°]		[252°,170°]
Chest Press		[151°,108°]		[151°,108°]

4.3 Experiment Results

First, we propose the ideal range of joint angles in 15 different exercises; see Table 1. Those values are the model's hyperparameters which can be configured by fitness experts, individually adjusting it for each participant. Another vital piece of information is performance tracking, where a trainee can review his execution or later consult feedback from the trainer. Figure 1 shows the measured time series of selected exercises among participants: The visualization of the joint angles, in degree (°), for each repetition and a comparison with the ground-truth pose, in percentage (%). The early performance is characterized by variable displacement fluctuation compared to relatively smooth plots after many executions. Our screenshots of real-time monitoring show two graphical indicators in different contexts (Fig. 2): 1. the percentage bar (on the left) indicating the matching of the executing joint angles with the ground-truth pose, 2. the number (on the right) counting correct movements. Participants observe their performance in real-time on the experiment laptop in the fitness room. We provide the experimental codes at https://github.com/duongtrung/ECTEL2023.

After conducting a month-long series of experiments, we administered a questionnaire to our participants to assess the effectiveness of our proposed system. The questionnaire consisted of three key inquiries: 1. In your opinion, does this pose tracking system, which offers real-time visual feedback, have the potential to be appealing and beneficial for trainees? 2. What do you perceive as the primary advantages of this system? 3. What improvements do you believe are necessary to enhance its performance? Remarkably, all participants responded affirmatively to the first question. Regarding the second question, numerous noteworthy points were raised. Participants highlighted the significance of posturing correction, visual assistance, and instant feedback during workouts. They also emphasized that the system's ability to reduce dependency on personal trainers was an advantage worth noting. Furthermore, participants made several suggestions for improvement, including a more user-friendly interface, voice command functionality, visual workout plans, and performance logging features.

(a) Shoulder Front Raise (b) Squats (c) Leg Press

Fig. 2. Several screenshots of our participants. Image copyright by the authors.

5 Conclusion

The proposed fitness tutoring system suggests an intuitive approach based on computer vision techniques to track the practitioner's pose during fitness exercises and provide instant feedback for improvement, even without a trainer or expert. The three-phase pipeline can actively or passively learn from a professional trainer demonstrating an exercise or a recorded video, respectively, and is powered by the state-of-the-art pose estimation model and human topology-based tracking technique. The demonstration using professional fitness exercise videos as the ground truth showed a positive reaction of participants, indicating the feasibility and potential of the proposed method for similar sport exercises.

Acknowledgment. The authors would like to thank the German Federal Ministry of Education and Research (BMBF) for their kind support within the project *Multimodal Immersive Learning with Artificial Intelligence for Psychomotor Skills* (MILKI-PSY) under the project ID 16DHB4014.

References

1. Di Mitri, D., Schneider, J., Limbu, B., Mat Sanusi, K.A., Klemke, R.: Multimodal learning experience for deliberate practice. In: Giannakos, M., Spikol, D., Di Mitri, D., Sharma, K., Ochoa, X., Hammad, R. (eds) The Multimodal Learning Analytics Handbook. Springer, Cham (2022). https://doi.org/10.1007/978-3-031-08076-0_8
2. Fajrianti, E.D., et al.: Application of augmented intelligence technology with human body tracking for human anatomy education. IJIET: Int. J. Inf. Educ. Technol. **12**(6), 476–484 (2022)
3. Farrokhi, A., Farahbakhsh, R., Rezazadeh, J., Minerva, R.: Application of internet of things and artificial intelligence for smart fitness: a survey. Comput. Netw. **189**, 107859 (2021)
4. Graßmann, C., Schermuly, C.C.: Coaching with artificial intelligence: concepts and capabilities. Hum. Resour. Dev. Rev. **20**(1), 106–126 (2021)
5. Kim, J., Davis, T., Hong, L.: Augmented intelligence: enhancing human decision making. In: Albert, M.V., Lin, L., Spector, M.J., Dunn, L.S. (eds) Bridging Human Intelligence and Artificial Intelligence. Educational Communications and Technology: Issues and Innovations. Springer, Cham (2022). https://doi.org/10.1007/978-3-030-84729-6_10
6. Li, J., Cui, H., Guo, T., Hu, Q., Shen, Y.: Efficient fitness action analysis based on spatio-temporal feature encoding. In: 2020 IEEE International Conference on Multimedia & Expo Workshops (ICMEW), pp. 1–6. IEEE (2020)
7. Novatchkov, H., Baca, A.: Artificial intelligence in sports on the example of weight training. J. Sports Sci. Med. **12**(1), 27 (2013)
8. Paaßen, B., Baumgartner, T., Geisen, M., Riedl, N., Kravčík, M.: Few-shot keypose detection for learning of psychomotor skills. In: Proceedings of the 2nd International Workshop on Multimodal Immersive Learning Systems (MILeS 2022) (2022)
9. Paaßen, B., Kravcık, M.: Teaching psychomotor skills using machine learning for error detection. In: Proceedings of the 1st International Workshop on Multimodal Immersive Learning Systems (MILeS 2021), pp. 8–14 (2021)
10. Ueta, M.: Improving mirror fitness through augmented reality technology. In: 2022 3rd International Conference on Big Data, Artificial Intelligence and Internet of Things Engineering (ICBAIE), pp. 186–194. IEEE (2022)
11. Venkatachalam, P., Ray, S.: How do context-aware artificial intelligence algorithms used in fitness recommender systems? A literature review and research agenda. Int. J. Inf. Manag. Data Insights **2**(2), 100139 (2022)

The HCA Framework - A Storification Model to Support and Facilitate Gamification Design

Laura Ferreira, Carlos Santos, Luís Pedro, and Ana Raquel Carvalho(✉)

Digital Media and Interaction Centre, Department of Communication and Art, University of Aveiro, 3810-193 Aveiro, Portugal
{analaura45,carlossantos,lpedro,raquelcabralc}@ua.pt

Abstract. With the growing popularity of gamification and the variety of scenarios it can be integrated into, the number of amateur gamification designers has also increased. This has been the case of K-12 school teachers, who are incentivized to explore gamification with students, but have to cope with workloads that prevent them from taking the necessary time to experiment with gamification, so that it can be used as a cohesive, captivating, and well-balanced strategy. Empirical evidence of how to make the design of well-balanced gamification strategies achievable to the growing number of amateur gamification designers is still scarce. This study presents the Here Comes the Airplane (HCA) Framework as well as its application to a functional prototype. This framework consists of a storification model that integrates the gamification principles of the Octalysis Framework and is aimed at helping gamification designers reimagine the activity they want to gamify as a narrative. The prototype is expected to validate the framework and its impact on the narrative creation process. This study's validation process focused on the assessment of two central aspects: the theoretical principles underlying the framework and its integration into a prototype. Two focus groups were held with researchers from the fields of digital games, narratives, and web development. The next steps include the broader impact evaluation of the final prototype in Portuguese K-12 schools.

Keywords: Storification model · Gamification · Digital platform · K-12 education · Prototype validation process

1 Introduction

The present study describes the Here Comes the Airplane (HCA) Framework - a storification model for gamification contexts as well as its application to a functional prototype. This framework combines a storification model aimed at helping designers reimagine the activity they want to gamify as a narrative with the gamification principles of Octalysis. The prototype is expected to validate the framework and its impact on the narrative creation process, which will function as a feature of Fora d'aulas, a gamified digital platform, currently under development, to be used in K-12 schools to promote extracurricular projects and its users' sense of community.

O. Viberg et al. (Eds.): EC-TEL 2023, LNCS 14200, pp. 711–717, 2023.
https://doi.org/10.1007/978-3-031-42682-7_66

Within the scope of research-based design, the data presented in this study results from the validation process of both the HCA framework and the functional prototype it was applied to. Based on a K-12 schools use case, the main goal of this study is to provide not only K-12 school teachers, but also gamification designers in general, a theoretical framework that is expected to be a guiding tool to create more cohesive, captivating, and well-balanced gamification strategies.

2 Storification: Enhancing Digital Gamification Experiences

Designing digital gamified solutions strongly relies on aspects like interactivity, real-time decision making, and the multimedia resources chosen to improve users' experience [1, 2]. According to the Mechanics-Dynamics-Aesthetics (MDA) framework [3], designers should focus on aesthetics first since it elicits specific emotional responses in the player. "Deeper game elements" [2, p. 10] such as rules, challenge, reward, and feedback mechanisms, as well as narratives have a vital role for its contribution to the generation of aesthetic components like fantasy, drama, obstacles, and discovery [3]. Even though the narrative is still a rarely considered game element in the design of gamification strategies [2, 4], it can become a powerful game element since storytelling is something that permeates human behaviour, such that even people who have never designed a game have certainly told a story before. However, transforming human experience into storylines requires the application of a narrative organization, which coincides with the concept of storification [5, 6].

When storifying an activity it becomes vital to use a narrative structure that is not only familiar to the target audience of the story but also easily perceived and understood by its designer. Narrative arcs and their features serve different purposes that facilitate their interpretation: Freytag's Piramyd [7] has a well-known concept of tension/time progression and a contained number of acts (five in total); the Hero's Journey's [8] acts have very straightforward names that illustrate the expected content of each act (ex. "Call to Adventure", "Threshold Crossing", etc.); and Story Spine [9] acts have generic names that are both easy to understand and do not influence the content to be written in each act (ex. "Once Upon a Time", "Until one Day", etc.).

The narrative structure simplifies the visualization of key moments where the relationship between the player and the activity will evolve and, consequently, influence the gamification strategy. According to Chou [10, 11] people become involved with a game not as a single event, but as an experience that develops gradually as familiarity with its features and structure is gained. We can look at the different acts of a narrative as the moments where the player/activity relationship evolves and adopt a gamification strategy that resembles the one used by Chou [10] in the Octalysis framework (more specifically Level 2 Octalysis), according to which the author identifies four stages of this relationship and the core drives that should be explored in each stage: Discovery, Onboarding, Scaffolding, and Endgame.

3 The HCA Framework

3.1 Theoretical Model

In the HCA framework, the narrative is the focal part of the design process and is used both as a game element and as a guiding tool for the gamification designer.

In its simplest form, the HCA framework tries to (i) position key moments of the real activity into a five-act narrative arc and (ii) create an imaginary parallel narrative based on the activity's key elements. Theoretically supported by the concept of storification, the first characteristic is meant to aid the visualization of the activity as the narrative that will be experienced by the participants. The five mentioned acts correspond respectively to: (i) Once Upon a Time (ii) Call to Adventure (iii) Journey (iv) Moment of Truth (v) And Ever Since That Day. The used narrative arc was designed to answer the specific needs of the HCA framework and is inspired by other well-established narrative acts, namely Freytag's Pyramid [7], Campbell's Hero's Journey [8], and Kenn Adams' Story Spine [9] as depicted in Fig. 1.

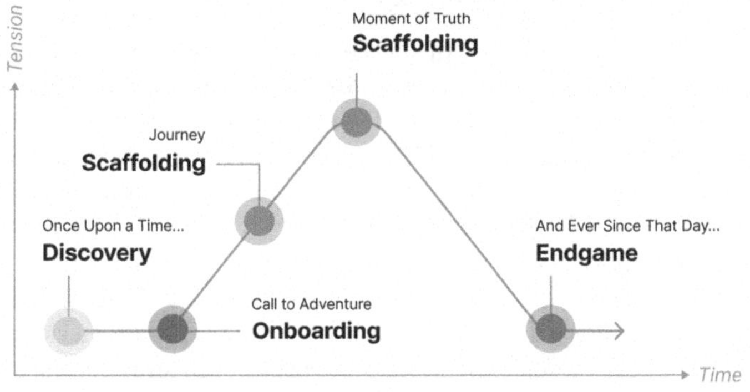

Fig. 1. The HCA framework.

The pin-pointing of the five acts is not only useful for designing the activity's narrative but also to identify its key gamification moments. Inspired by Yukai Chou's Octalysis, more specifically Level 2 Octalysis [10], each of the five acts represent a stage of the end-user's relationship with the activity. Each act should be gamified according to the stages of said relationship. The gamification strategy used during the first act (based on Chou's "Discovery" stage) should incentivize the welcoming of the participant to the activity. The second act (based on Chou's "Onboarding" stage) should teach the rules and dynamics of the activity and introduce the first challenges and tasks. The third act, the longest act of the narrative (based on Chou's "Scaffolding" stage), is where most tasks and challenges will be faced and should also have some short side quests to lighten the main journey. The fourth (based on Chou's "Scaffolding" stage) is the decisive act - it is important to have in mind that even if participants put in the effort, some will not achieve the main goal of the activity, and should still be incentivized to be proud of themselves due to their hard work. The fifth and final act (based on Chou's "Endgame" stage) is supposed to motivate the participant to maintain an active role as an alumnus, mentor, or coordinator.

The second characteristic of the framework is the design of a parallel narrative, setting, and characters. This aspect is mirrored in its name: Here Comes the Airplane framework. Parents of small children, during mealtime, tend to craft stories to get their child to eat. The parallel narrative is the act of pinpointing the key elements of the activity. Since the desired behavior is to make the child open their mouth, there is a process of finding a more appealing narrative where the end goal is shared: "I have a spoonful of food" and "I want to feed it to my child" is transposed to "there is an airplane coming" and "I need a place to land". This process makes it so that the narrative does not stray too far from the real activity, but at the same time provides a more entertaining scenario to fulfill the task at hand.

Joining both characteristics, the resulting product of the HCA framework integrates the structure of the real activity into a narrative arc with a chosen scenario to create a fictional narrative that promotes participants' engagement in the gamified tasks.

3.2 Application to a Functional Prototype

Bearing in mind the target audience of the HCA framework, the need for a friendlier interface to interact with the framework became evident. Therefore, a functional prototype for narrative creation (Fig. 2.) was developed to be later integrated as a feature of the gamified digital platform Fora d'aulas[1]. The prototype developed consists of five broad sections: (i) Onboarding, (ii) Real Activity Characteristics, (iii) Setting and Characters, (iv) Narrative Writing and (v) Badge Drafting.

The Onboarding consists of an initial interaction with a character, "The Guardian of the Narrative", to sensitize the user for the concept of storification. The Section of the Real Activity Characteristics asks the user to define both the tasks of the activity and its main goal. These inputs exist to help the user not to stray too far from the real activity, when entering the Narrative Writing section. The third section, Setting and Characters, is where the user defines the parallel narrative. To aid this decision some premade settings and characters are made available. The decisions made in this section will influence the images that are shown during the Narrative Writing section, with the purpose of inspiring the writing process. The fourth section is where the user will write the narrative according to the HCA framework: the five acts will be presented one by one to the user with some tips and tricks on how each act should be written. To aid this section the prototype also makes four example narratives available that can be used and edited. Badge Drafting is the fifth and final section, since badges are the central reward element of Fora d'aulas. During the writing process the designer can add drafts of the badges to be gained in each narrative act. The drafts allow the user to define properties of the badge without losing focus on the writing process before starting other time-consuming tasks such as badge design. This process is aided by tips that follow Level 2 Octalysis principles.

[1] The working prototype can be consulted here.

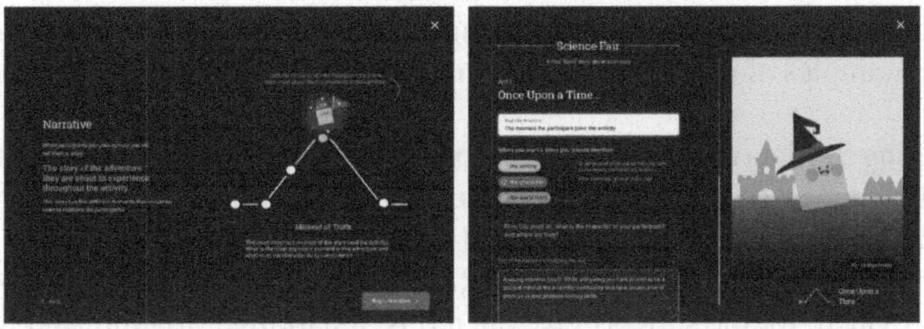

Fig. 2. Screens from the prototype designed to validate the framework.

4 Validation Procedures

The sample for this initial stage of the validation process consisted of two groups of researchers from the fields of digital games, narratives, and web development - the first one including seven higher education teachers and researchers, and the second including six elements of the Research & Development (R&D) team of Fora d'aulas. Two focus group sessions were organized to collect participants' perceptions, which were analyzed through content analysis. The first session, held in February 2023, was aimed at validating the theoretical model of the HCA Framework by collecting participants' perceptions of its utility, comprehensibility, and pertinence. The second focus group session, held in March 2023, was aimed at testing the integration of the HCA storification model into a digital interface prototype for designing narratives (particularly its comprehensibility, users' interaction with the prototype and the narrative creation process) and is going to be part of Fora d'aulas platform.

5 Results

The data collected in the first focus group resulted in a set of codes focusing on (i) the narrative structure; (ii) the terminology used; (iii) properties of the framework (existing ones / others to be considered); and (iv) future prototype functionalities.

Regarding the narrative structure, researchers highlighted the centrality of the narrative conflict and, as a requirement, the flexibility to encapsulate different endings as well as to separate the "scaffolding act" into two distinct moments (one at the beginning of the journey and another at the "Moment of truth"). As for the terminology chosen, researchers stressed the importance of using theory-based terms, able to instill fantasy in the writing process, but being neither too restrictive nor too distant from users with no theoretical background in this field. Properties of the framework to be considered were e.g. the need to convey that the process is more important than the results (hence substituting terms like "Hero" for more neutral ones) and that the narrative should finish in a positive tone. Although converting real activities into a narrative was, according to the researchers, the most challenging feature of the framework, the parallel provided between the real and the fantasy world, along the narrative creation, was its most interesting characteristic. As for future prototype functionalities, researchers highlighted the pertinence of guiding teachers and promoting their creativity, e.g., by means of providing editable examples of narratives, the integration of AI narrative creation mechanisms, etc.

Considering the data collected in the second focus group, the R&D team highlighted aspects of two scopes: (i) the simplicity of the interaction processes (particularly regarding the functionalities and the interface); and (ii) the clarity of the information provided. Regarding the aspects of the first scope, the R&D team stressed the utility of the example narratives provided, for the support given in terms of narrative structure and for unlocking designers' ideas. Browsing through the different acts was a highlight of the interface, despite the reference to the need to keep it simple. As to the clarity of the information provided, the large size of the illustrations was highlighted for their benefits and role in defining the essence of the acts and for their connection to the emotions to be elicited. The segmentation of the narrative into acts was also emphasized for its usefulness in helping users think with more clarity and in fully integrating the activity in the process of narrative creation.

6 Next Steps

Following the positive feedback gathered, the next steps of the project relate to the usability testing of the functional prototype with end users of Fora d'aulas, particularly teachers from a group of partner Portuguese K-12 schools. This stage is expected to precede the software development of the digital solution, which will be followed by its broader impact assessment in K-12 schools.

Acknowledgement. This work is financially supported by Fundação Altice and by national funds through FCT – Foundation for Science and Technology, I.P., under the project UIDB/05460/2020.

References

1. Hajarian, M., Diaz, P.: Effective gamification: a guideline for gamification workshop of WEEF-GEDC 2021 madrid conference. In: Proceedings of 2021 World Engineering Education Forum/Global Engineering Deans Council, WEEF/GEDC 2021, pp. 506–510 (2021)
2. Dichev, C., Dicheva, D.: Gamifying education: what is known, what is believed and what remains uncertain: a critical review. Int. J. Educational Technol. Higher Educ. **14**(1), (2017)
3. Hunicke, R., LeBlanc, M., Zubek, R.: MDA: a formal approach to game design and game research. In: Fu, D., Orkin, J. (Eds.) Proceedings of the Challenges in Game AI Workshop, Nineteenth National Conference on Artificial Intelligence, San Jose, California, p. 4. Menlo Park, CA: AAAI Press (2004)
4. Koivisto, J., Hamari, J.: The rise of motivational information systems: a review of gamification research. Int. J. Inf. Manage. **45**, 191–210 (2019)
5. Akkerman, S., Admiraal, W., Huizenga, J.: Storification in history education: a mobile game in and about medieval Amsterdam. Comput. Educ. **52**(2), 449–459 (2009)
6. Aylett, R.: Emergent narrative, social immersion and "storification". In: Proceedings of the 1st International Workshop on Narrative and Interactive Learning Environments, pp. 35–44 (2000)

7. Freytag, G.: Technique of the Drama: An Exposition of Dramatic Composition and Art . S. Griggs (1895)
8. Campbell, J.: The Hero with a Thousand Faces (1st ed., Vol. 17). Pantheon Books (1949)
9. Adams, K.: How to Improvise a Full-Length Play: The Art of Spontaneous Theater. Allworth Press (2007)
10. Chou, Y.: Gamification Design: 4 Phases of a Player's Journey. https://yukaichou.com/gamification-examples/experience-phases-game/. Accessed 5 Mar 2023
11. Chou, Y.: Actionable Gamification: Beyond Points, Badges, and Leaderboards - Yu-kai Chou (2019th edition). Octalysis Media (2014)

Evaluating Usability and User Feedback in an Immersive Virtual Reality Environment for Computer Science Education

Birte Heinemann(✉) and Ulrik Schroeder

Learning Technologies Research Group, RWTH Aachen University, Aachen, Germany
{heinemann,schroeder}@cs.rwth-aachen.de

Abstract. Virtual reality enables new approaches to teaching various learning content. However, the development of learning environments is complex and there are only a few guidelines that can be used in the development of VR learning environments. This paper addresses this gap and presents the evaluation of a computer science education simulation. The questionnaire of the UXIVE model, combined with feedback analysed with systematic, rule-guided qualitative text analysis, was used to analyse the influence of user experience components. The result is a concept to transfer usability outcomes in a structured way into best practices and conditions for success.

Keywords: Virtual Reality · STEM education · Computer Science Education · UXIVE · Computer Graphics · Text-Sorting-Technique

1 Introduction

Virtual Reality (VR) is one way to deal with learning situations that are too dangerous, expensive, or time-consuming. Additionally, the sensation of presence using VR is an advantage from which all STEM subjects can benefit [7], [8]. Four arguments for using VR in computer science (CS) or especially in computer graphics teaching are that VR could be used for metaphorical representations of abstract concepts, which are beneficial for learning [4]. It can help to accomplish better learning outcomes for mathematical geometry concepts [10] and "embodiment and the subsequent agency associated with manipulating content in 3D" is a strength of VR [7]. Last, VR allows presenting information in context [3].

However, there are also disadvantages and challenges in the use of VR, for which there is research to be found, e.g. cybersickness, and difficulties to compare the effectiveness with other media [2]. Cook et al. argue that standards and best practices are missing [3]. Usability as a challenge is long known and confirmed in newer research, e.g., one obstacle is designing interactions in VR. Pirker et. al list this point in their overview paper, especially if the app is not originally designed for VR and only offers VR as an option [8]. This argument, combined with the

O. Viberg et al. (Eds.): EC-TEL 2023, LNCS 14200, pp. 718–724, 2023.
https://doi.org/10.1007/978-3-031-42682-7_67

increasing criticism that the media comparison studies are not appropriate and missing best practices, leads to the goal of this paper.

After using a VR learning environment from the field of CS, students were asked about their experiences using the User eXperience in Immersive Virtual Environment Model (UXIVE Model) [11]. We analysed qualitative feedback with the text-sorting-technique (TST) [1] to find out which elements and interactions work well and for which usability is improvable.

2 Background and Related Work

VR in CS Education. VR can be used to enhance the learning experience in STEM by providing hands-on, immersive experiences including those that are difficult to replicate in a traditional classroom setting [9]. Topics in CS Education are for example filter rules for firewalls, finite state machines or fundamental programming (Overview: [8]). Pirker et al. describe the challenge of usability, which is a crucial factor for the success of teaching and learning in VR [8].

User Experience in Immersive Virtual Environment (UXIVE). No specialised questionnaire(s) has/have yet become clearly established for Usability/User Experience in VR. The questionnaire used in this study does not only include the aspect of usability but also questions about flow, immersion, skill, emotion, technology adoption, judgement, experience consequence, and presence [11]. UXIVE is a mixture using selected items from appropriate existing questionnaires, which offers the advantage of capturing different concepts without having to schedule longer times and fearing subject fatigue. [11].

For all concepts, there are alternative/full questionnaires. Collecting not only usability but also other concepts, provides opportunities for subsequent studies. For our current research question, we focused on user opinion and usability aspects. The UX scores for the different concepts are generated from 76 items; four open-ended and 73 closed-ended questions using a ten-point Likert scale.

Text-Sorting-Technique. TST is short for text-sorting-technique [1], a method for the inductive evaluation of qualitative text data. In contrast to other methods, TST illustrates a rather pragmatic form of evaluation, which is often sufficient [1]. The TST consists of six steps. First, code the survey form and questions. Secondly, create a digital version of the texts/answers/statements to be evaluated, afterward dissect text passages into sense units and check the link to the question and develop a category system. Lastly, create documentation of the processed text data and a short description of the categories.

3 Object of Investigation

We used a theory-based developed guided tour in virtual reality named RePiX VR. It's designed to educate the rendering pipeline from computer graphics, see

[5]. A robotic virtual avatar leads the tour. After being introduced to the controls and functions in a tutorial the tour starts, followed by nine different steps of a simplified rendering pipeline. Most of the steps contain interactive tasks, while others use animations and pictures, e.g., Fig. 1. For more information, see [6].

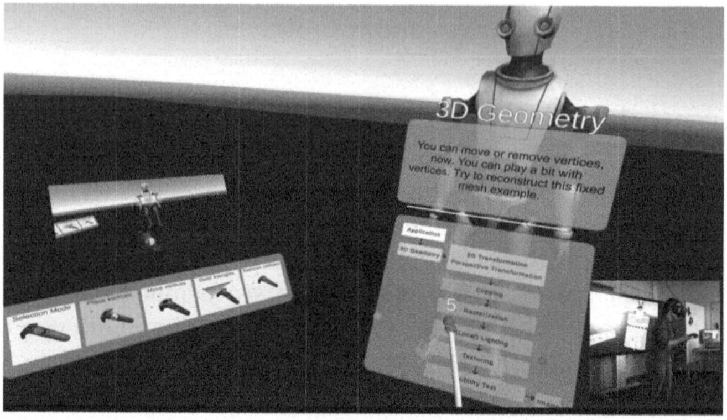

Fig. 1. Interactive task, in which objects with vertices and edges are built.

4 Study and Evaluation

This study is the third (and first larger-scaled) evaluation, results of the first ones see [5,6]. We tested RePiX VR[1] in 2022 with 34 post-graduates (8 female, 26 male). 2/3 were from the University of Dresden in a CS teacher's training program; the others were CS majors at the RWTH Aachen University. In both groups, the application was used at a meta-level (to learn the research methodology of the TEL community and gain experience with VR in education). Thirty students never had contact with VR or under 5 times.

Users had to answer two questionnaires, one before (5 min.) and one after the task (15 min.), in German or English. The first questionnaire contained 12 questions: three demographic items (age, gender, visual aid) and nine items on prior knowledge about familiarity with virtual reality (e.g., "Do you use VR in any form on a regular basis?") and knowledge about computer graphics (e.g., "How are 3D objects constructed?"). The second questionnaire was the UXIVE with two additional questions (suggestions for improvement and other comments). Between the questionnaires, the virtual reality intervention took place. Afterwards, there was a short interview and optionally a discussion about the aspects of the learning experience relevant to the course. Additionally, two persons took notes to identify usability aspects.[2]

[1] RePiX VR is OSS: https://gitlab.com/learntech-rwth/repix-vr/repix-vr-app.

[2] The data, an experimental guide, and TST results are published as supplementary material, see https://publications.rwth-aachen.de/record/960357.

4.1 Results UXIVE

Usability. Across all 33 participants (one drop-out) the value for three items averages at 7.46 (median: 8; 10 points Likert scale). There are some individual answers, where ratings significantly diverged from average: A lower rating in the Usability category is accompanied by overall lower values across the other categories, and the four students with low usability scores also graded other usability aspects lower as well, e.g. the perceived *unnecessary complexity* probably led to perceived inconsistency and reduced ease of use.

Skill. The six items contained statements like "I felt confident moving through the virtual environment with the controllers/headset.", two of which were on a meta-level, like that ability to describe the functions of the controller/headset. This category has been rated with an average score of 7.58 and a median of 8. One person, which also reported struggles with the controls in the Usability category, rated the items in this category exceptionally low as well (avg across both categories of 3.44 with a median of 3). Another participant showed similar struggles with slightly higher values but reported higher confidence regarding their own learning progress and their ability to explain the controls in theory.

Experience Consequence. Eight distinct symptoms, including cybersickness, vertigo, pain in the eyes, or general exhaustion, were queried. In total, seven learners reported uncomfortable feelings, which, however, were verbalized directly during use by only two (who got help to achieve a more comfortable fit). Three of the seven persons also reported difficulties in the other categories.

To investigate dependencies and relations across categories, correlation factors have been calculated. Medium-sized correlations with small effect sizes have been found (confirming the original results, see [11]): *Usability and Skill:* $r(31) = .46$, $p = .020$; *Usability and Experience Consequence:* $r(31) = .51$, $p = .010$; *Skill and Experience Consequence:* $r(31) = .44$, $p = .024$.

4.2 Results TST

Process. The four free-text questions were selected for analysis (positive aspects, negative aspects, suggestions for improvement, any other comments), see supplementary material[3]. The 124 answers were coded and divided into 254 sense units. The category system contained 32 categories, but the assignment showed an imbalance. So they were discussed with two colleagues to compare other approaches. Among other small changes in the allocation of some sense unit statements, we reduced them to 29 categories, e.g. items from the eliminated category "Gamification" could also be assigned to the ideas category. The statistical, quantitative evaluation is not at the centre of the TST method, but the qualitative gain of knowledge, which is why only a few numerical comparisons can be found in the next part, see also [1], and since the data are published, we limit the following description to the most important findings.

[3] https://publications.rwth-aachen.de/record/960357.

Results. Many learners described the interactions as positive (often without providing details), e.g. person 20: "You can <influence> elements yourself and see the effect". Some users proposed suggestions for individual actions, e.g., manipulating the light. Learners wish to interact with the content and named steps critically, which were not interactive. Some *concrete interactions* were criticized, e.g., the interaction with the matrices. The answers show *patterns* combined with the numerical ratings (positive mentions and critical statements). Learners, who stated in the questionnaire that they had had no problems, also noted that it was *easy to interact.* But despite the comparatively good results in the overall numerical data, several learners expressed in the free text responses the wish to get to *know the controller better* to feel more confident in its operation.

Navigation was rated positively overall; learners who used the feature positively rated the ability to view objects from different directions. At the same time, two persons forgot about it and one felt not able to move freely because the cable was disturbing. The *robotic assistant* was seen as helpful, but learners would like more instructions and assistance. The statement that the *amount of text* was exhausting and that the users would therefore have liked a voice for the robot, for example, to read out content to them is also rated as usability.

In the comments about VR in general, many learners indicated that they found the headset uncomfortable or unfamiliar, e.g., "the headset is quite heavy". Disagreements arose regarding the usefulness of VR in education. "I could see the virtual reality experience to be quite helpful in visualizing practical applications of a topic" vs "I could see the virtual reality not to learn theoretical concepts."

5 Future Work, Limitations and Discussion

A key aspect of this study was to investigate (didactic) elements and interactions and their suitability for the intended audience, and to provide an unobstructed learning experience. We have found multiple leverage points for improvements in usability. As VR is still an innovative technology, some of its usual interaction mechanics cannot be considered common knowledge, especially locomotion modalities. Users, specifically novices should be reminded once in a while. Furthermore, the weight of the VR headset can cause an unpleasant experience. Thus, VR learning sessions should be kept short and on point, making use of didactic methodologies like scaffolding the experience and then fading into exploratory interaction, allowing learners to self-regulate. Considering this prototype specifically, there is more work to be done on interactions like the matrices operations. The required precision of interaction is still a challenge for VR.

6 Conclusion

The study dealt with usability in educational VR applications. The TST method was used to evaluate the subjective statements of the test subjects in combination with the results of the UXIVE questionnaire. For further development, the findings have helped educators develop the content and the programmers to better understand the learners and empathize with inexperienced learners.

An important aspect that has become apparent is the navigation, which should be designed as intuitively as possible. The constructivist approach and experiential learning were complimented by the participants of the study. The ability to interact with abstract concepts, such as matrices and see the effects in 3D, is perceived as helpful. But especially for these more mathematical actions, it is particularly important to ensure good usability so that learners can focus on the content rather than on how to use it. A disadvantage of VR headsets is comfort, which is why teaching units should not be designed too long. Further studies should be dedicated to determining the limits.

Acknowledgement. This study would not have been possible without my colleague Sergej Görzen and our students, especially Tobias Möhring. Nadine Bergner & Thiemo Leonhardt - thank you for the opportunity to work with your students during the pandemic.

References

1. Balzer, L., Beywl, W.: evaluiert (E-Book) erweitertes Planungsbuch für Evaluationen im Bildungsbereich. hep verlag, Bern, 2nd edn. (2018)
2. Buchner, J., Kerres, M.: Media comparison studies dominate comparative research on augmented reality in education. Comput. Educ. **195**, 104711 (2023). https://doi.org/10.1016/j.compedu.2022.104711
3. Cook, M., et al.: Challenges and strategies for educational virtual reality. Inf. Technol. Libr. **38**(4), 25–48 (2019)
4. Dengel, A.: Seeking the treasures of theoretical computer science education: towards educational virtual reality for the visualization of finite state machines. In: 2018 IEEE International Conference on Teaching, Assessment, and Learning for Engineering (TALE), pp. 1107–1112 (2018)
5. Heinemann, B., Görzen, S., Schroeder, U.: RePiX VR - learning environment for the rendering pipeline in virtual reality. In: Bourdin, J.J., Paquette, E. (eds.) Eurographics 2022 - Education Papers, pp. 1–8. Reims, France (2022)
6. Heinemann, B., Görzen, S., Schroeder, U.: Teaching the basics of computer graphics in virtual reality. Comput. Graph. **112**, 1–12 (2023)
7. Johnson-Glenberg, M.C., Ly, V., Su, M., Zavala, R.N., Bartolomeo, H., Kalina, E.: Embodied agentic STEM education. In: 2020 6th International Conference of the Immersive Learning Research Network (iLRN), pp. 24–30 (2020)
8. Pirker, J., Dengel, A., Holly, M., Safikhani, S.: Virtual reality in computer science education: a systematic review. In: 26th ACM Symposium on Virtual Reality Software and Technology, pp. 1–8. ACM, Virtual Event Canada (2020)

9. Pirker, J., Holly, M., Almer, H., Gütl, C.: Virtual reality STEM education from a teacher's perspective. In: Proceedings from the Fifth Immersive Learning Research Network Conference (iLRN). Verlag der TU Graz, London (2019)
10. Su, Y.S., Cheng, H.W., Lai, C.F.: Study of virtual reality immersive technology enhanced mathematics geometry learning. Front. Psychol. **13**, 760418 (2022). https://doi.org/10.3389/fpsyg.2022.760418
11. Tcha-Tokey, K., Christmann, O., Loup-Escande, E., Loup, G., Richir, S.: Towards a model of user experience in immersive virtual environments. Adv. Hum. Comput. Interact. **2018**, 7827286 (2018)

Responsive Narrativity in Gamified Situational Judgment Tests: A Dynamic System for Enhanced Soft Skills Development

Jérôme Hernandez(✉), Mathieu Muratet, and Thibault Carron

LIP6, CNRS, Sorbonne Université, Paris, France
{jerome.hernandez,mathieu.muratet,thibault.carron}@lip6.fr

Abstract. The growing recognition of soft skills' importance in organisational contexts has prompted companies to leverage game-based solutions like gamified situational judgement tests. These tests merge the traditional situational judgement test with gamification, forecasting and training employee behaviour. This paper introduces a novel dynamic system for constructing unique and motivating gamified situational judgement tests for assessing and learning soft skills. This system employs adaptable and interactive narratives that respond to player choices, thereby providing individualised and engaging learning experiences. The dynamic, modular approach fosters immersive learning and facilitates soft skills development through context-appropriate, automated scenarios. This research contributes to the advancement of Gamified Situational Judgment Test, paving the way for more effective and immersive soft skills training methodologies.

Keywords: Gamification · Soft Skills · Situational Judgment Test

1 Introduction

In response to the increasing organizational need for effective soft skill development (SSD), interactive narrative games (ING) have emerged as powerful tools, blending gamified situational judgement tests (GSJT) with immersive storytelling [6]. GSJTs capitalize on the proven effectiveness of situational judgement test approaches and role-playing in soft skill training, integrating these methods into a game-based learning environment.

Key to this learning environment is the provision of feedback. Incorporating varied feedback types into GSJTs supports diverse learning preferences, real-time strategy adjustments, and a deeper understanding of consequences [9]. However, for successful integration, feedback must be seamlessly incorporated to maintain the narrative flow and avoid cognitive overload [7].

Another crucial aspect of GSJTs is replayability. Encouraging learners to engage with the game multiple times enhances content retention and motivation,

O. Viberg et al. (Eds.): EC-TEL 2023, LNCS 14200, pp. 725–730, 2023.
https://doi.org/10.1007/978-3-031-42682-7_68

leading to better performance and understanding of the educational content [8]. Replayability can be achieved by implementing strategies such as branching storylines, multiple difficulty levels, and adaptive learning pathways [5].

The design concept of modularity enables the division of a system into independent and rearrangeable components, which can aid in tackling the complexity of developing GSJTs [2]. This approach simplifies the creation and maintenance of intricate game scenarios, promotes customization, and facilitates the integration of diverse components [3,4]. Despite its advantages, the application of modularity to the storytelling aspect of INGs has yet to be extensively researched.

We propose a dynamic modular narrative model to address this gap and enhance the learning experiences offered by GSJTs. The model harnesses the advantages of modularity to generate many unique and engaging learning experiences.

2 Dynamic Narrative Modular System

The model comprises five components: the global game state, narrative module selector, narrative module library, narrative module adaptation mechanism, and narrative feedback system (see Fig. 1).

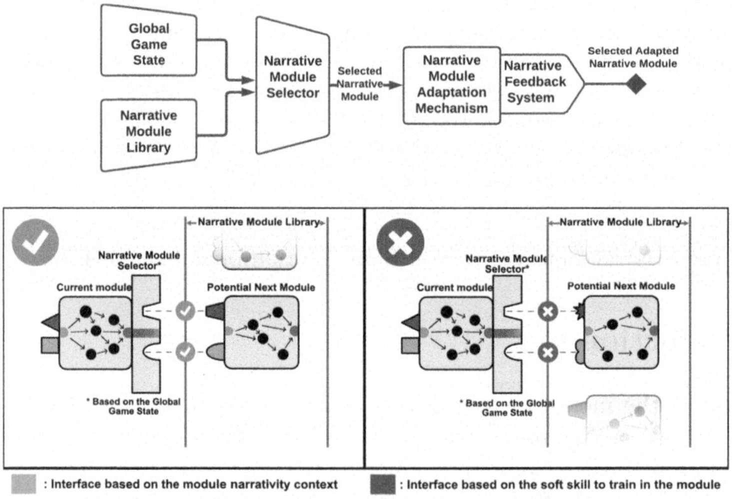

Fig. 1. Dynamic Narrative Modular System

First, the global game state (GGS) comprehensively represents the current game environment essential for effective narrative module selection, adaptation, and player engagement. This state continually updates throughout the game after each player's choice, reflecting the learner's progress and the evolving narrative context. For instance, if a player consistently struggles with communication skills, the GGS will store this information and adjust the learning profile accordingly. It also monitors the game's narrativity, such as the development of a subplot or the impacts of the players on the game world, which may be crucial for the player's SSD. The GGS guides informed decisions and responses in interactive narrative learning games by incorporating learning profiles and narrativity.

In contrast to traditional GSJT approaches, this model employs unique narrative modules as independent units within the broader narrative structure. These modules, found in the narrative module library (NML), combine elements of multi-branching tree storytelling and modular approaches. The library comprises predefined modules tailored for specific soft skill training in different game situations. Each module has conditions, objectives, and interfaces that determine its targeted skill development. This modular design provides multiple narrative paths and various soft skill scenarios and promotes replayability, ensuring sustained player engagement and motivation.

The narrative module selector (NMS) is a critical component that identifies the most suitable narrative module based on the current GGS, the learner's skill development needs, and the narrative context. It utilizes heuristic methods to make informed decisions. For example, in a leadership-focused interactive game, the selector might choose a module featuring those challenges if the learner struggles with decision-making and delegation. The selector considers the narrative state of the game world, facilitating continuity between modules by transitioning to appropriate settings based on the previous module's conclusion.

The narrative module adaptation mechanism (NMAM) and narrative feedback system (NFS) work together to refine the narrative modules and provide feedback based on the GGS. The adaptation mechanism continually adjusts dialogues and narrativity within the modules, ensuring contextual relevance, engagement, and motivation for the learner. For instance, if a player excels in negotiation techniques, the mechanism adapts a negotiation-focused module to present more challenging scenarios, encouraging further skill development. The NFS delivers immediate and delayed narrative feedback based on the GGS, reinforcing the learning experience. After successfully resolving a conflict, immediate feedback may occur through dialogue with virtual characters, while delayed feedback may manifest as a future scenario referencing past actions.

3 Methods and Experimentation

In this research, we introduce a novel method for enhancing the generation of interactive narrative learning games for SSD and implement it through two distinct experimentations.

Experimentation 1 aimed to validate the reliability and effectiveness of the NFS and the NMAM within a narrative interactive learning game with limited modules. The game has been designed to foster and enhance existing soft skills, allowing the system to deliver accurate and relevant feedback for learner growth and development based on their skills. In the experimentation, seventy-six participants were recruited from nine companies. They engaged with six modules from an NML of nine in a game designed to evaluate specific leadership skills. After completing the game, a debriefing session was conducted with a subset of players (27) for reflection and analysis.

Experimentation 2 was focused on generating behavioural profiles for assessment purposes. It implemented a dynamic modular narrative system combining the NMS and GGS. This experimentation aimed to evaluate the efficacy of these components in creating a dynamic and adaptive learning environment tailored to individual learner needs. The game utilized 42 narrative modules in this experimentation to evaluate six soft skills derived from the HEXACO Model [1]. Forty-four participants from five countries first complete the original HEXACO-60 survey test. Afterwards, they were able to play multiple sessions of the game, experiencing unique stories and paths. Each session included at least one soft skill module per soft skill to assess, selected by the narrative module selector. Qualitative insights were gathered through interviews with players and the game creators.

These two experiments aimed to demonstrate the potential of the proposed method in creating engaging and motivating learning experiences that support SSD in various contexts.

4 Results and Discussion

We collected the players' perceptions of the learning experience, engagement, and satisfaction with the two GSJTs through the interviews. In addition, we also performed an internal consistency using Cronbach's alpha analysis for the second experiment that contains enough modules that assess and train the same soft skill. We explore the findings in the following subsection.

4.1 Debriefings Findings and Discussion

The experiments revealed that numerous participants valued the narrative aspects and feedback in training. The impact of their choices on the characters' feelings, emotions, storytelling, and narrativity was especially appreciated. Some participants (7) replayed the game to explore alternative endings, examine the effects of their new knowledge, and appreciate the unique scenarios presented in each session. However, some participants (6) desired to know the potential outcomes without replaying the game.

The narrative also helped participants understand the real-world applications of their acquired skills, providing relevance to the training content. Several participants (23) drew parallels between training situations and their real-life experiences. Overall, participants enjoyed the experiment and recommended such training for practical skill development. However, eight players mentioned that the options needed to reflect their intentions accurately.

The findings suggest that the NMAM and the NFS enhance engagement and motivation. Participants expressed sustained interest in the training and were motivated to explore different choices and outcomes. This curiosity-driven engagement is crucial for improving the learning experience and encouraging the application of new knowledge in the workplace. In summary, the debriefing findings highlight the important role of the narrative feedback mechanism in enhancing participants' learning experiences, engagement, and motivation. However, there is a need to accommodate individual preferences and provide a more flexible and adaptive feedback system that integrates with other model components.

4.2 Internal Consistency Analysis Results and Discussion

Upon assessing the results from the second experiment's players, we observe an internal consistency among items that evaluate identical soft skills. Our experiment's Cronbach's alpha values (see Table 1) range between 0.65 and 0.87 for the six evaluated soft skills. According to academic literature, a Cronbach's alpha value of 0.7 or higher is considered satisfactory for denoting the internal consistency of items, measuring the underlying construct related to soft skills.

Table 1. Means, standard deviations, and internal consistency reliability

Assessment Method	Soft skill	*M*	*SD*	Cronbach's α
GSJT	*1*	3,2	0,37	0,65
GSJT	*2*	3,47	0,5	**0,75**
GSJT	*3*	2,9	0,71	**0,81**
GSJT	*4*	2,95	0,86	**0,87**
GSJT	*5*	3,11	0,6	**0,76**
GSJT	*6*	2,33	0,81	**0,81**

Note. N = 44

The boldface indicates significant internal consistency reliability.

The GSJT soft skills were measured on a scale from 1 to 4.

The outcomes indicate that players can develop soft skills through multiple training sessions with unique combinations of narrative modules. This approach maintains in-game engagement and motivation. Players' expressed enjoyment and preferred this assessment method over traditional ones, especially when faced with repetitive training for different contexts. The participants appreciated the narrative structure and did not perceive disjointed connections between scenarios.

Additionally, following the interviews with the GSJT designers, the modular approach improved productivity without compromising storytelling and coherence, as the model's management of narrative coherence allowed the writers to focus on learning objectives, relieving them of the traditional burden handled by GSJT developers using decision-tree structures.

5 Conclusion

In conclusion, the study's findings support the hypothesis, revealing that the dynamic modular GSJT structure enhances players' learning experiences by integrating engaging narrative elements and tailoring feedback to individual needs. Participants in the experiments reported increased motivation, engagement, and enjoyment while participating in the training sessions, which may lead to better knowledge retention and understanding of the soft skills being taught.

Moreover, the research demonstrates that the dynamic modular approach successfully balances the GSJT production workflow and learning theories. The modular structure allows for the efficient creation of diverse and unique GSJT scenarios without compromising the validity and reliability of the assessments. The approach promotes active learning and encourages participants to apply their new knowledge in their work and real-life situations.

Despite some limitations, this study provides insights into the potential of dynamic modular GSJT structures in enhancing learning experiences and balancing the production workflow with learning theories. Future research should address the limitations by validating the findings with more extensive and diverse datasets and further examining the predictive validity of the approach for training and recruitment purposes. This research contributes to gamified learning and assessment by offering an innovative, engaging, and practical approach to teaching and evaluating soft skills.

References

1. Ashton, M.C., Lee, K.: The HEXACO-60: a short measure of the major dimensions of personality. J. Pers. Assess. **91**(4), 340–345 (2009)
2. Baldwin, C.Y., Clark, K.B.: Design Rules: The Power of Modularity. vol. 1. MIT press, Cambridge (2000)
3. Bellotti, F., Berta, R., De Gloria, A.: Designing effective serious games: opportunities and challenges for research. Int. J. Emerg. Technol. Learn. (iJET) **5**, 22–35 (2010)
4. Gee, J.P.: What video games have to teach us about learning and literacy. Comput. Entertainment (CIE) **1**(1), 20–20 (2003)
5. Göbel, S., Mehm, F., Radke, S., Steinmetz, R.: 80days: adaptive digital storytelling for digital educational games. In: Proceedings of the 2nd International Workshop on Story-Telling and Educational Games (STEG'09). vol. 498 (2009)
6. Hernandez, J., Muratet, M., Pierotti, M., Carron, T.: How to model a visual novel game to train and identify players' soft skills? In: European Conference on Game Based Learning, pp. 322–330 (2021)
7. Nacke, L.E., Drachen, A., Göbel, S.: Methods for evaluating gameplay experience in a serious gaming context. Int. J. Comput. Sci. Sport **9**(2), 1–12 (2010)
8. Salas, E., Tannenbaum, S.I., Kraiger, K., Smith-Jentsch, K.A.: The science of training and development in organizations: what matters in practice. Psychol. Sci. Public Interest **13**(2), 74–101 (2012)
9. Shute, V.J.: Stealth assessment in computer-based games to support learning. Comput. Games Instr. **55**(2), 503–524 (2011)

LA-ReflecT: A Platform Facilitating Micro-learning and Its Multimodal Learning Analytics

Rwitajit Majumdar[1](✉), Prajish Prasad[2], Kapil Kadam[3], Kinnari Gatare[4], and Jayakrishnan Madathil Warriem[5]

[1] Kumamoto University, Kumamoto, Japan
dr.rwito@gmail.com
[2] FLAME University, Pune, India
[3] Kolhapur Institute of Technology, Kolhapur, India
[4] Independent Researcher, Mumbai, India
[5] IIT Madras, Chennai, India

Abstract. The interactive demo highlights LA-ReflecT, an LTI-enabled platform that facilitates the creation of micro-learning activities with multimedia content, and helps track interactions and artefacts created by students within the platform as xAPI logs. The platform facilitates reflection on action in the form of presenting information on a dashboard as a part of the learning activity. LA-ReflecT also enables an app connecting with Bluetooth sensors that stream time series signals. The sensor data from a user is synchronized with their particular activity and can be linked to their learning log. We are doing multiple pilots with research partners in Japan and India. We are open to discussing adaptors who want to potentially pilot LA-ReflecT for creating microlearning material and investigating the potential of the data logged in the platform.

Keywords: LAreflecT · Micro-learning · Multimodal Learning Analytics

1 Microlearning and Multimodal Analytics

Microlearning provides a new teaching paradigm allowing knowledge and information to be divided into small chunks and delivered to the learners. Literature highlights microlearning as an evolving trend and discusses its several proven advantages. Learners can better comprehend and remember information when complex topics are divided into smaller, more accessible bits. Furthermore, microlearning makes it simple to adapt content to the needs of specific learners because it may be presented in various formats, such as videos, quizzes, or interactive simulations [1, 2]. The use of digital technologies and platforms to enhance microlearning experiences is highlighted in the literature and, the significance of mobile devices as a delivery platform and design considerations for mobile-friendly content are discussed. Digital tools can support effective and accessible microlearning experiences. Learning Management Systems (LMS) are leveraged for

O. Viberg et al. (Eds.): EC-TEL 2023, LNCS 14200, pp. 731–735, 2023.
https://doi.org/10.1007/978-3-031-42682-7_69

tracking and delivering microlearning. It examines the role of social media platforms in fostering collaboration and knowledge sharing. The incorporation of gamification, simulations, and multimedia elements is explored to enhance learner engagement and comprehension within the limited time frame of microlearning. [8] On the other hand, multimodal analytics refers to using diverse data sources to understand learner behavior and enhance the efficiency of educational initiatives. Multimodal analytics can further enhance the effectiveness of microlearning by providing insights into learner behavior. Teachers can see potential problem areas and modify their pedagogical approaches by compiling information on how students engage with the material. Due to the incorporation of several data sources and data processing operations, MMLA (Multimodal Learning Analytics) systems are complicated and data-intensive. [3]. The tool presented aims to explore the design of flexible infrastructures that support the entire data value chain, enabling the scalable adoption of MMLA in real scenarios in a sustainable manner. It also seeks to examine the interplay between microlearning and MMLA, understanding how these two concepts can complement each other. The tool delves into the intricacies and nuances of combining microlearning and MMLA, considering how data-driven insights can inform and enhance the microlearning experience.

2 LAreflecT Environment

LAReflect is an LTI-capable authoring platform that users (teachers or researchers) can use to design microlearning activities and connect various sensor data. The technology is based on the Learning Evidence and Analytics Framework [4]. The learning tools are integrated into a central learning management system with LTI protocol, and learner interactions and created artefacts are logged in a learning record store. All the tools are connected by the Learning Tools Interoperability (LTI) protocol, and the learning management system (LMS) does the user management. The common xAPI is used to capture interactions with the tools for the Learning Record Store (LRS). Using the data that has been logged in the LRS, additional data-driven applications can be made and visualized in the learning dashboard. An illustration of the platform's system architecture can be found in Fig. 1. The platform's authoring tool is accessible to users who have the instructor position in the LMS. Once an activity has been created, it must be published for the viewer to display it. An activity attempt interface is present on the viewer. It also records user interaction data, which can be shown in the dashboard later.

2.1 Navigating Through the Interface

Activity Authoring tool: The authoring tool provides the teachers to create activities. Each activity can have multiple tasks. In a task the contents are organized as an element. The activity dashboard has a student-facing and an instructor-facing interface. The teacher creates an activity. The dashboard lets teachers create activities with multimedia content and track learning interactions and artefacts created by their students. Activities can either be for a one-time task (e.g., assignment) or repeated practice (e.g., reading practice). For each activity, the teacher defines the learning objective and sets dependencies of the learning tasks, pre-tasks, or post-tasks with each other.

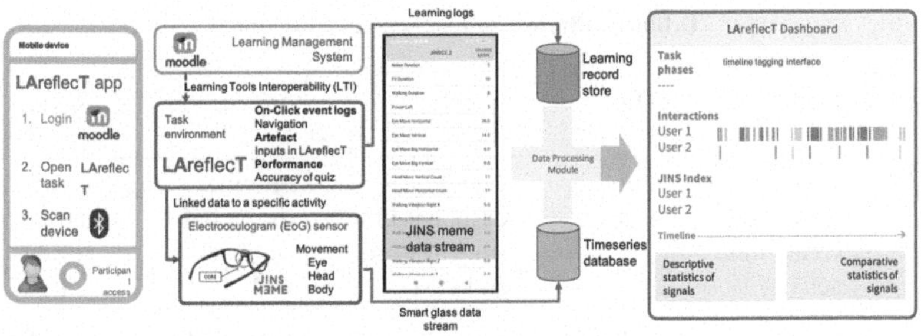

Fig. 1. System Architecture.

Activity Viewer: The viewer enables the user to interact with the elements of the task. Additionally, it keeps track of interactions, artefacts produced, and the time spent on each component (Fig. 2).

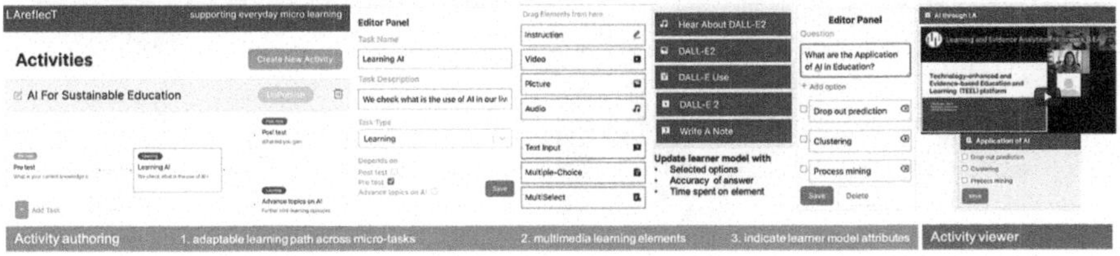

Fig. 2. LAreflecT workflow of activity authoring in the creator and attempting in the viewer [7]

In the student's view of LAreflecT, they enter and get an overview of the activity. Individual learning interactions along with being able to attempt activities. A learning pedagogy based on Deming's Plan-Do-Check-Act (PDCA) cycle is introduced to close the widening gap between traditional teaching methods and the needs of today's college graduates. [5] We introduce a 'review' phase to Deming's Wheel for the workflow of the teacher and the student. The workflow of the teacher and the student highlights a five-phase pedagogy [5] Plan, Do, Check, Act, and Review (see Table 1).

2.2 Example of a Micro-learning Activity

The below example was a short assignment as a part of a Human Interface course for undergraduate students in Japan. The students were asked to create a microlearning activity using LA Reflect tool. The *Activites* denote the created tasks (Figs. 3 and 4).

Table 1. Phases for teachers and students

Activity Phases	Plan	Do	Check	Act	Review
Teacher's task	Collect resources, create mini activity	Publish task	Check dashboard for student's pre and post	Provide formative feedback	Check dashboard and review activity
Student's task	Check activity and pre-surveys	Conduct activity	Check student dashboard Check formative feedback	Go back to activity or conduct second phase of activity	Post-survey Check dashboard and review

Fig. 3. The Micro-learning task with additional reflection scaffolds in the LA-Reflect Platform

Fig. 4. Displays the activity player visible to students

3 Accessing LA-ReflecT for an Interactive Demo and Future Collaboration

To apply for access to a demo for instance and check the system affordances please fill in the request form in the following site: https://sites.google.com/view/la-reflect/tool We are planning the session for demonstrating to teachers, course facilitators and researchers who are interested in adding LAReflect to their LMS. We are doing multiple pilots with research partners in Japan and India. We are open to discussing adaptors who want to potentially pilot LA-ReflecT for creating microlearning material and investigating the potential of the data logged in the platform.

Acknowledgment. This work is partially supported by JSPS KAKENHI Grant-in-Aid for Scientific Research (B) JP22H03902.

References

1. Giurgiu, L.: Microlearning an evolving elearning trend. Scientific Bulletin **22**(1), 18–23 (2017). https://doi.org/10.1515/bsaft-2017-0003
2. Shankar S.K., Prieto L.P., Rodríguez-Triana M.J., Ruiz-Calleja A.: A review of multimodal learning analytics architectures. In: 2018 IEEE 18th International Conference on Advanced Learning Technologies (ICALT), Mumbai, India, pp. 212–214 (2018). https://doi.org/10.1109/ICALT.2018.00057
3. Ogata, H., Majumdar, R., Akçapınar, G., Hasnine, M.N., Flanagan, B.: Beyond learning analytics: framework for technology-enhanced evidence-based education and learning. ICCE 2018 - 26th International Conference Computational Education Work. Proc, pp. 486–489 (2018)
4. Loyd, N., Gholston, S.: Implementation of a plan-do-check-act pedagogy in industrial engineering education. Int. J. Eng. Educ. **32**(3), 1260–1267 (2016)
5. Majumdar, R., et al.: Design of a critical thinking task environment based on ENaCT framework. In: 2021 International Conference on Advanced Learning Technologies (ICALT), pp. 294–296 (2021)
6. Majumdar, R., Ogata, H., Warriem, J.M., Prasad, P.: LA-ReflecT: a platform for data-informed reflections in micro-learning tasks. In: Proceedings of ICCE 2022, pp. 476-480 (2022)
7. Kapp, K.M., Defelice, R.A.: Microlearning: short and sweet. American Society for Training and Development (2019)

Statoodle: A Learning Analytics Tool to Analyze Moodle Students' Actions and Prevent Cheating

Pedro Manuel Moreno-Marcos[1](✉), Jorge Barredo[2], Pedro J. Muñoz-Merino[1], and Carlos Delgado Kloos[1]

[1] Universidad Carlos III de Madrid, Avda. de la Universidad 30, 28911 Leganés, Madrid, Spain
{pemoreno,pedmume,cdk}@it.uc3m.es

[2] IKERLAN Technology Research Center, P°. J. M.ª Arizmendiarrieta 2, 20500 Arrasate-Mondragón, Spain
jbarredo@ikerlan.es

Abstract. In higher education, Learning Management Systems (LMS) are widely used to enable a space where instructors can deliver the materials, propose and collect activities, and interact with students, among other functionalities. These LMSs allow collecting a vast amount of information whose analysis may improve the learning process and can even detect cheating situations. In the literature, there are some plugins to analyze LMS data, but the issue is that plugins need to be installed by the administrators. This demo presents Statoodle, a simple desktop tool aimed to analyze Moodle data based on exported logs, which can be obtained by any instructor. Among its functionalities, it can inspect activity within the exams to determine whether or not there are unauthorized accesses, which is something not often included in other plugins, it can provide detailed PDF reports about the overall performance of the quizzes (using algorithms, such as the Item Response Theory to analyze items' difficulty), Excel reports with indicators about students' activity and overall statistics about the grades. The tool has been tested in two courses, showing potential to detect exam fraud and/or prevent students from cheating when they are alerted that logs will be processed.

Keywords: learning analytics · students' logs · Item Response Theory · cheating detection · Moodle

1 Introduction

Learning Management Systems (LMS) are widely used in higher education institutions as a platform to share materials, submit activities or perform quizzes, and interact with students, and their large amount of information allows the analysis of data to improve learning. One of those LMSs is Moodle, which collects lots of data, although it does not include sophisticated dashboards by default. To visualize that information, several plugins have been proposed [3,8]. For example

O. Viberg et al. (Eds.): EC-TEL 2023, LNCS 14200, pp. 736–741, 2023.
https://doi.org/10.1007/978-3-031-42682-7_70

Moodog, [8] provides several statistics and comparison between students, and reminders about not downloaded materials. However, one issue of these plugins is that they need to be installed in the Moodle platform by the administrators. This underscores the necessity for a tool that can provide analysis based on the logs that instructors can download on their own.

In addition, new learning analytics modules that combine novel indicators and existing ones can improve the learning process in Moodle. For example, in the current Moodle version (4.2), facility index of questions is reported as the percentage of students who answer correctly [4] but there are other more accurate methods, such as the Item Response Theory (IRT) [2], which can better estimate difficulty, and students' skills. Moreover, other indicators, such as the efficiency ([6] can serve to track if students correctly solve exercises in a quick way.

Apart from that, one important issue in online platforms is gaming the system and cheating. For example, there are multiple behaviours such as hint abuse, systematic guessing or copy of hints [5]. Another example is in MOOCs, where there are detectors of students who use multiple accounts to get the correct answers in one account and transfer them to the other [7]. In the academic world, there are also tools to prevent plagiarism comparing texts and even more sophisticated commercial proctoring tools (e.g., SMOWL[1], Proctorio[2]). However, there is a lack of simple tools that process Moodle data to detect accesses of unauthorized materials during the exams and a detector of that can be very beneficial to prevent cheating.

Considering the abovementioned issues, this demo aims to present Statoodle, a tool that uses exported Moodle data to provide instructors both (1) detailed reports and analytics about students' activity in the platform, including multiple indicators and reports about quizzes performance, and (2) logs analysis to detect suspicious activity in quizzes due to the usage of non-unauthorized materials. The latter functionality, while simple, is a contribution respect to other plugins and highlights the importance of cheating detection.

2 Description of the Tool

Statoodle is a tool designed to analyze exported Moodle data and provide reports and processed logs about students' actions. The tool was designed using Python and its graphic user interface library *Tkinter*. After the implementation, library *PyInstaller* was used to convert it to an .exe file. This way, the tool is provided as an executable (with size around 50 MB) and no installation is needed. This also allows using the tool without needing Internet connection and, as it is a desktop tool, personal data are used locally and they are not transferred to any external server, which is positive in terms of data protection regulations. The tool is open source[3] and it could be adapted to other specific contexts.

[1] https://smowl.net/es/.
[2] https://proctorio.com/.
[3] https://github.com/JorgeBarredo14/statoodle.

The main window when opening the tool provides four options to select the file to be processed. Particularly, three files are considered, which can be directly exported from Moodle by the instructors. These files are: (1) quiz report, which can be obtained when students take a Moodle quiz, (2) log report, which contains all clicks in the platform, and (3) grade report, which contains all the grades of the gradebook. The first two options use quizzes reports (one file in the first option and multiple files in the second) and the latter two options use the latter two files mentioned. What follows is a description of the analytics provided in each of the options [1]:

Single Quiz Report Analytics. It generates a PDF report with aggregated information about a quiz (as can be partially seen in Fig. 1). It first contains information about the distribution of overall grades and for each question. Next, it contains the estimation of questions' difficulty using the IRT Rash model (to facilitate model convergence when there are few items), the probability of students answering correctly based on their ability, and the student's efficiency, which is computed as the number of points obtained per unit of time (e.g.,. if a student gets 10 points in 5 min, the efficiency is 2 points/minute). In addition, some figures representing the IRT curves for each question are saved as .png images in case advanced users want to review them.

Multiple Quiz Report Analytics: When selecting several quiz reports, they are first analyzed individually and when this process finishes, another iteration of the loop is executed for calculating a summary report that provides the average values from the previous quiz reports, bringing a general overview of the course results in terms of global students skills and difficulty of each exam [1].

Log Report Analytics: In this option, Moodle logs are processed and an Excel file is generated with many indicators that are calculated for each student. This way, the instructor has the processed information and can use it for evaluation or to better know about student's behaviours and performance. The Excel file contains several sheets that present the following information:

- Student profile: It contains a summary of the students' indicators, including the % of sent tasks, % of answered consults, forum interactions, poll interactions, resources visualizations, visualized modules, % of days of visualized modules, % of done and cheated exams.
- Effort bonification: it highlights students above the mean who have viewed at least 80% of the modules and have taken all the exams without cheating
- Quiz status: it indicates the % of taken exams and the exam where the student may have cheated (see example in Fig. 2). For each exam, the state can be UNOPENED (not taken), ATTEMPT SENT (finished without issues) and CHEATED (where cheating may appear). Cheating is detected when students interact with the materials between the log when quiz is started and the log when the quiz is finished. Moreover, it can also detect when IP address changes during the quiz. While this does not necessarily imply cheating (particularly if IPs are in the same network), it can warn the instructor to further check the situation.

This method of cheating detection may appear basic and limited, as interactions outside the platform are not tracked, although it is a first step for cheating prevention and an analysis of the tool showed it was very powerful. Particularly, the tool was used in a course about Spreadsheets with 20 groups and dozens of cases were detected and verified, which supports its usefulness. In fact, previous manual analyses of logs by the authors raised this concern and need of the tool to ease work.

Nevertheless, it must be noted that cheating status needs to be considered just as a warning (to be later confirmed by instructors) and not something final. In the tests, a couple of false positives were found because Moodle did not correctly registered the log when finishing the quiz, and three cases were identified with changing IPs but no significant changes of network were identified so these changes could be justified with changes in the WiFi access point. Moreover, if the instructor allows the usage of notes, all students will have cheating status without having actually cheated. Therefore, this can be an useful tool but data must be correctly interpreted by instructors.

- Visualized modules: it indicates whether specific modules of the course have been accessed by each student, and the sum and % of visualized modules.
- Course activity: it indicates the number of interactions each day by each student, the average and % of active days.
- Others: there are other sheets to provide details about (1) time devoted in quizzes, (2) number of attempts in quizzes, (3) specific IPs used in the quizzes, (4) sent tasks, (5) answered consults, and (5) number of forum interactions (created threads and messages posted).

<u>Grade Report Analytics:</u> It takes the grades in the gradebook, computes the mean and standard deviations of each item, and the global results, calculates and plots the normal distributions, and export the results to an Excel file.

3 Use Cases

The different visualizations and indicators of Statoodle can be combined to extract conclusions from the learning process in Moodle. For example, students can be firstly checked for cheating, detecting students who frequently cheat and whether this issue could be specific for a few questions or massive. For students who cheat, the rest of parameters and indicators could be useless. Based on the experience, we encourage to carry out this check for every assessment.

Moreover, global student activity can be tracked with the tool, using the number of attempts, the number of interactions, if they perform activities regularly, etc., and some performance indicators and students' efficiency can also be analyzed. In addition, we can know if students engage with all the materials, including the optional ones to know about their interest in them.

Furthermore, the tool can be used to evaluate the suitability of the materials based on their difficulty. For example, if some of the items are found to be quite difficult, instructors may decide to modify the activities, provide further materials, etc. Finally, instructors could use the tool to measure students' engagement and get feedback about their learning process, which may be used to give personalized feedback, adapt the classes or improve class orchestration.

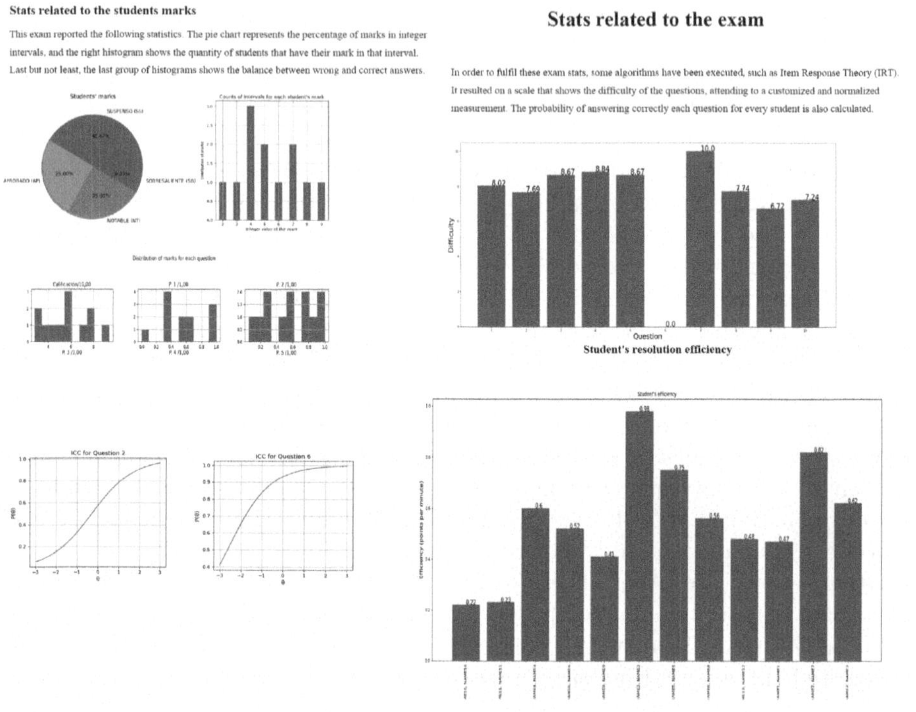

Fig. 1. Part of a sample PDF report of the Single Quiz Report with simulated data and IRT curves. Distribution of grades (top left), questions' difficulty (top right), IRT curves (bottom left) and students' efficiency (bottom right)

	Students	Cuestionario: prueba	Done exams	Percentage of done exams	Cheated exams	Percentage of cheated exams
0	XXXXXX YYYYYYYY ZZZZZZZZ	UNOPENED	0	0	0	0
1	XXXXXX YYYYYYYY ZZZZZZZZ	ATTEMPT SENT	1	100	0	0
2	XXXXXX YYYYYYYY ZZZZZZZZ	ATTEMPT SENT	1	100	0	0
3	XXXXXX YYYYYYYY ZZZZZZZZ	ATTEMPT SENT	1	100	0	0
4	XXXXXX YYYYYYYY ZZZZZZZZ	ATTEMPT SENT	1	100	0	0
5	XXXXXX YYYYYYYY ZZZZZZZZ	CHEATED (Opened resources while answering)	0	0	1	100
6	XXXXXX YYYYYYYY ZZZZZZZZ	ATTEMPT SENT	1	100	0	0

Fig. 2. Example of Quiz status sheet.

4 Conclusions

This work has presented Statoodle, a simple desktop tool to analyze exported data from Moodle. Its two main functionalities allow (1) processing quiz, grades and logs reports to generate aggregated data about the quizzes (using the IRT) and students' indicators, and (2) and examine logs to detect possible cases of cheating. Some of the advantages of this tool respect to other tools are that it does not require installation, and it does not depend on university administrators, it can be executed locally to prevent data protection issues when sharing data, it outperforms the way to measure item's difficulty with respect to the classical methods used in Moodle with the usage of IRT, and it contributes towards cheating detection, which is an issue where more research is needed.

Among the limitations of this work, the cheating algorithm only considered Moodle activity, so only a subset of actions are inspected. Moreover, Moodle logs can also be limited when the platform is used to share materials (e.g., if materials are downloaded and used offline, few records are stored). However, they can be useful and provide meaningful insights to instructors. As further work, it would be relevant to further test the tool and see if more visualizations or indicators can be added. Moreover, this work opens some lines where more research is needed: (1) how to ensure that implemented learning analytics tools can be reached by instructors easily, while complying with data protection regulations, and (2) how to improve cheating detection systems, since computer-based exams are needed in many practical courses (e.g., those about learning a software tool) and there is a loot of room to improve in this area.

Acknowledgement. This work was supported in part by the FEDER/Ministerio de Ciencia, Innovación y Universidades-Agencia Estatal de Investigación, through the H2O Learn Project (grant PID2020-112584RB-C31), and the Madrid Regional Government through the e-Madrid-CM Project (Grant S2018/TCS-4307), which is co-funded by the European Structural Funds (FSE and FEDER).

References

1. Ferreira, Barredo, J.: Implementation of a external learning analytics tool for aula global courses: Master's thesis. Universidad Carlos III de Madrid, Madrid (2022)
2. Corbett, A.T., Anderson, J.R.: Knowledge tracing: modeling the acquisition of procedural knowledge. User Model. User-Adap. Inter. **4**, 253–278 (1994)
3. Foster, H., et al.: Moodlebot: Moodle: Learning analytics (2023). https://docs.moodle.org/33/en/Learning_analytics#Moodle_Plugins
4. Hunt, T., Pratt, J.: Quiz statistics calculation (2023). https://docs.moodle.org/402/en/Quiz_statistics_report
5. Muldner, K., Burleson, W., Van de Sande, B., VanLehn, K.: An analysis of students' gaming behaviors in an intelligent tutoring system: predictors and impacts. User Model. User-Adap. Inter. **21**(1–2), 99–135 (2011)
6. Munoz-Merino, P., Ruiperez-Valiente, J.A., Delgado Kloos, C.: Inferring higher level learning information from low level data for the khan academy platform. In: Proceedings of the Third International Conference on Learning Analytics and Knowledge, pp. 112–116. ACM, New York (2013)
7. Ruiperez-Valiente, J.A., Munoz-Merino, P.J., Alexandron, G., Pritchard, D.E.: Using machine learning to detect 'multiple-account' cheating and analyze the influence of student and problem features. IEEE Trans. Learn. Technol. **12**(1), 112–122 (2017)
8. Zhang, H., Almeroth, K., Knight, A., Bulger, M., Mayer, R.: Moodog: tracking students' online learning activities. In: EdMedia+ Innovate Learning, pp. 4415–4422. Association for the Advancement of Computing in Education (AACE), Waynesville (2007)

An Enrollment Dashboard to Reinforce Decision-Making for Students and Advisors

Noe Rivas[1], Julià Minguillón[1(✉)], and Jonathan Chacón-Pérez[2]

[1] Universitat Oberta de Catalunya, Barcelona, Spain
{seosve,jminguillona}@uoc.edu
[2] Elisava, Barcelona, Spain
jchacon@elisava.net

Abstract. Over the past years, there has been a significant increase in the number of students attending online courses in higher education, in some cases due to the COVID-19 pandemic. Online higher education provides greater flexibility in selecting courses in the preferred order, but it also presents challenges due to the amount of different combinations during the enrollment process. In this paper, we describe a dashboard for supporting enrollment in higher education using a map as a visual metaphor, in order to provide students and their advisors with a clear overview of their situation within the degree, and help them to make better decisions. The enrollment dashboard has been evaluated through an initial series of interviews with advisors, which showed positive results in terms of usability and usefulness. However, several concerns were raised about the parameters used to create the map. These results will be used in future rounds of interviews with students and advisors.

Keywords: Recommendation system · enrollment · online higher education · advisors · data visualization · enrollment dashboard

1 Introduction

Most open universities offer flexible programs that allow students to choose from a wide range of courses according to both the semester organization and their personal interests. Although this can be seen as a convenient and flexible advantage for students, it also allows for inadequate enrollments, as students may find it challenging to sort through an overwhelming amount of information or may even find it insufficient to plan and select courses strategically [11,12]. Some authors have explored the relationship between enrollment patterns and students' performance and dropout rates, since some combinations of courses may lead to failure [13]. Therefore, this hidden knowledge in institutional enrollment data could be utilized to support decision-making during enrollment, enabling students to be aware of their learning process in the forthcoming semester [8]. Data visualization, especially learning dashboards, have been used in educational

O. Viberg et al. (Eds.): EC-TEL 2023, LNCS 14200, pp. 742–747, 2023.
https://doi.org/10.1007/978-3-031-42682-7_71

settings as a way to understand significant amounts of information. However, researchers often encounter difficulties in identifying the appropriate indicators to effectively apply data visualization in students' learning experiences [2,10].

In [6], the authors described the typical uses of recommendation systems in higher education, namely e-learning, classroom activities and course selection. For instance, Karga and Satratzemi [3] designed a system that provides suggestions to enhance the quality of teaching practices and learning designs, while Zhang et al. [14] developed a recommendation system that maps students to supervisors based on quality, relevance, and connectivity criteria. A more specific study [5] compiled various examples of course recommendation systems based on principles and techniques from traditional ones. Nevertheless, although recommendation systems and data visualization are emerging fields of study within technology applied to education, there are only a few examples where both are incorporated into a learning dashboard (see Table 8 in [1]). One of the most remarkable can be found in CourseQ, an interactive course recommendation system [4], which allows courses to be explored using a visual interface, aiming to improve the transparency and user satisfaction of course recommendations. This paper presents a dashboard that enhances enrollment in higher education by providing students and advisors with an overview of their progress, facilitating informed decision-making.

2 Our Proposal

When students have a list of potential courses to enroll into, they often rely on various sources of information to make an informed decision. One such source is their academic advisor, who can provide guidance on which courses are most relevant to the student's academic and career goals. Additionally, students may consult other resources such as online course catalogs, syllabi, and course evaluations to gather information about course content, prerequisites, and workload [removed]. Based on this textual information, which can be very difficult to manage or even hard to find, students typically propose a set of courses to their advisor for validation. Unfortunately, some students do not make a good decision when planning their enrollment. The advisor may provide additional recommendations or suggest alternative courses based on the student's academic history, personal circumstances and goals. This process is an essential component of academic advising, as it helps students make informed decisions about their academic coursework and ensures that they are on track to meet their educational goals, avoiding inadequate course combinations.

Our proposed design is an enrollment dashboard based on a visual metaphor, specifically a map, in which the curriculum is depicted as a set of connected regions that must be visited in a specific order, separating courses that should not be taken at the same time. In order to do so, our dashboard supports the aforementioned enrollment procedure that students employ when making academic decisions. First, a map with the student's academic record is shown. Then, the student selects those courses that should not be recommended, such as validated courses. The student can distort the map according to her preferences,

Fig. 1. Map showing a real student's academic record. Completed courses are highlighted in blue, validated or discarded courses in light blue, failed courses in red, and potential courses to enroll in are displayed in gray. (Color figure online)

giving different weights to enrollment indicators [removed]. Once the map is accepted by the student, the dashboard recommends up to six courses, which can be selected or not by the student. For those courses selected by the student, additional information such as course calendar is shown. To avoid inappropriate enrollments, the map separates away those courses that should not be taken together, using the distance within the map as an abstract concept. This distance is a convex combination of different factors important for students [9], such as popularity, difficulty, prerequisites, and overlaps between course deadlines. The resulting distance matrix is then projected onto a 2D map [7], as shown in Fig. 1.

Once their preferences have been introduced by means of the sliders in Fig. 1, users (students and their advisors) can click on *Recommend courses* and the dashboard will highlight six courses in different shades of green, being the darkest the most recommended course to enroll. Notice that recommended courses are close to those courses that were already taken and passed, as if advancing in the degree was "conquering" new regions (i.e. courses) in the map, avoiding gaps. Then, users can select up to six courses (recommended or not). The selected courses are then marked in blue and additional information is provided, as shown in Fig. 2. Course assignments are displayed on the calendar, indicating the number of activities to be completed and the number of days with overlapping, which can be adjusted with an additional slider. This process can be repeated until the user considers the course selection appropriate.

3 Evaluation

Following the procedures described in some of the papers reviewed in [10], a prototype was initially tested by carrying out a pilot protocol for a single advisor (male, considered an expert advisor), including the following steps. First, the academic records of four different students were sent to the advisor, along

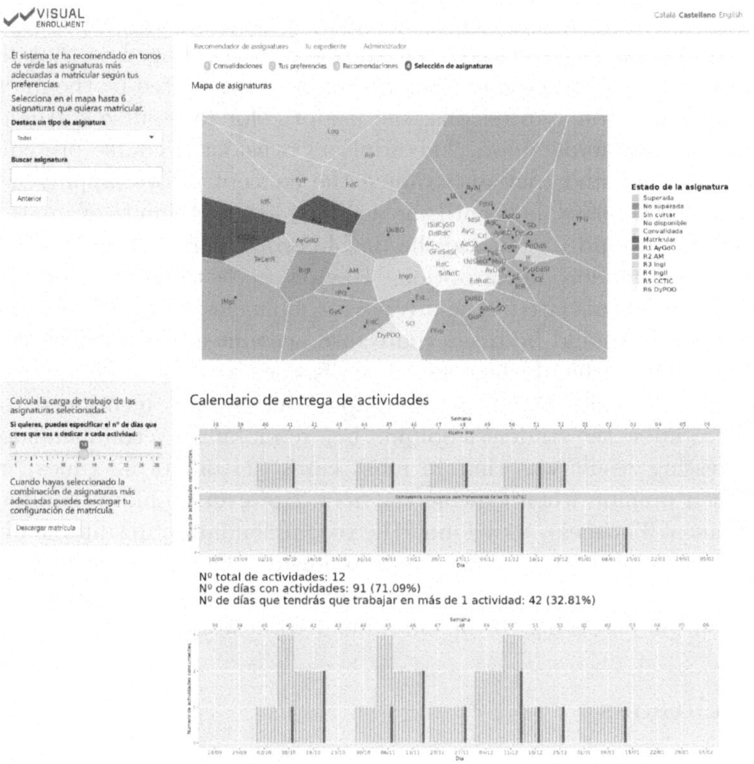

Fig. 2. Result of the selection of two courses (in dark blue) with their associated activity calendars. (Color figure online)

with a brief survey to find out which courses the advisor would recommend and why for each student, as well as the information taken into account when recommending courses. The second step involved conducting an interview, showing the enrollment dashboard to the advisor to gather his opinions on usefulness, effectiveness, usability, and overall understanding of the map metaphor. The advisor was asked about his opinion and whether there had been changes in his recommendation after viewing the dashboard or not.

This initial pilot study brought some interesting insights. Although the advisor had some difficulty in understanding certain aspects, such as the map visualization and the use of sliders, he found the visual recommendation (as shown in Fig. 2) very helpful. The possibility of viewing the student's complete academic record as part of the map depicting the degree was also appreciated. Two important objectives were achieved. First, the enrollment dashboard was able to integrate a significant amount of information that was previously dispersed throughout various information sources or was hard to find. Second, the result of this evaluation allowed us to identify elements to be corrected in a following phase. After making some minor improvements to the dashboard, a second round of interviews was conducted with eight advisors (four males, four females, all of them experienced). The protocol was changed so that the advisors themselves would use the tool instead of being presented by the interviewer. Quoting advisors' first impressions, the use of color for course status and recommendations was understood. The advisors considered course prerequisites a fundamental value, and they also valued the concept of overlapping deadlines. Adjusting the number of days until the deadline helped them to evaluate the real workload. They would like to use the dashboard in a real scenario, as it made them consider other enrollment options. Having access to the student's academic record was very appreciated. The advisors also suggested that the validated or discarded courses should be taken more into account as part of the recommendation. On the other hand, the concept of distance was not understood, and the courses were not easily found on the map. Advisors also mentioned that they would like to know the student's opinion before making a recommendation. The most interesting result was that in most cases (24 out of 32 times), advisors changed their opinion when viewing the map. However, in more than half of the cases (18 out of 32 times), they found the recommendation unsuitable because it did not give enough weight to course prerequisites. On the other hand, in most cases (26 out of 32 times), the deadline calendar was crucial to decide about the recommendation according to the enrollment total workload.

4 Conclusions

It must be stated that the proposed dashboard replicates a particular enrollment system. Therefore, it would not be suitable for other scenarios, with different curricula, enrollment procedures, or data collection methods. However, it should be noted that dashboards must often be adapted to the context for which they were created [10]. The initial pilot study provided valuable insights and identified areas for improvement, as advisors appreciated visual recommendations and suggested improvements regarding course prerequisites and recommendations. In general, the dashboard was well received as a tool to reinforce the current enrollment process. However, some aspects related to its usability and usefulness need to be better explained, such as the concept of distance embedded in the sliders and course prerequisites. For instance, sliders could be eliminated or replaced by values obtained from simulations with real data and the recommendation system could be also adjusted to give more weight to course prerequisites. Finally, a further iteration with students and their advisors will be carried out in order to evaluate the dashboard in a real enrollment scenario.

References

1. Bodily, R., Verbert, K.: Review of research on student-facing learning analytics dashboards and educational recommender systems. IEEE Trans. Learn. Technol. **10**(4), 405–418 (2017). Conference Name: IEEE Transactions on Learning Technologies https://doi.org/10.1109/TLT.2017.2740172

2. Duval, E.: Attention please! learning analytics for visualization and recommendation. In: Proceedings of the 1st International Conference on Learning Analytics and Knowledge, LAK 2011, pp. 9–17. Association for Computing Machinery, New York (2011). https://doi.org/10.1145/2090116.2090118
3. Karga, S., Satratzemi, M.: Using explanations for recommender systems in learning design settings to enhance teachers' acceptance and perceived experience. Educ. Inf. Technol. **24**(5), 2953–2974 (2019). https://doi.org/10.1007/s10639-019-09909-z
4. Ma, B., Lu, M., Taniguchi, Y., Konomi, S.: CourseQ: the impact of visual and interactive course recommendation in university environments. Res. Pract. Technol. Enhanc. Learn. **16**(1), 18 (2021). https://doi.org/10.1186/s41039-021-00167-7
5. Maphosa, M., Doorsamy, W., Paul, B.: A review of recommender systems for choosing elective courses. Int. J.Adv. Comput. Sci. Appl. **11**(9) (2020). https://doi.org/10.14569/IJACSA.2020.0110933
6. Maphosa, V., Maphosa, M.: Fifteen years of recommender systems research in higher education: current trends and future direction. Appl. Artif. Intell. **37**(1), 2175106 (2023). https://doi.org/10.1080/08839514.2023.2175106
7. Minguillón, J., Rivas, N., Chacón, J.: Supporting enrollment in higher education through a visual recommendation system. In: Artificial Intelligence Research and Development: Proceedings of the 23rd International Conference of the Catalan Association for Artificial Intelligence, vol. 339, p. 177. IOS Press (2021). https://doi.org/10.3233/FAIA210131
8. Othman, M.H., Mohamad, N., Barom, M.N.: Students' decision making in class selection and enrolment. Int. J. Educ. Manage. **33**(4), 587–603 (2019). Publisher: Emerald Publishing Limited https://doi.org/10.1108/IJEM-06-2017-0143
9. Rivas, N., Minguillón, J., Chacón, J.: Enrolling habits in higher education. what sources of information do students have and what are missing? In: INTED2021 Proceedings, pp. 4980–4988. 15th Int. Technology, Education and Development Conf, IATED (8–9 March, 2021 2021). https://doi.org/10.21125/inted.2021.1025
10. Schwendimann, B.A., Rodriguez-Triana, M.J., Vozniuk, A., Prieto, L.P., Boroujeni, M.S., Holzer, A., Gillet, D., Dillenbourg, P.: Perceiving learning at a glance: a systematic literature review of learning dashboard research. IEEE Trans. Learn. Technol. **10**(1), 30–41 (2016). https://doi.org/10.1109/TLT.2016.2599522
11. Scott, M., Savage, D.A.: Lemons in the university: asymmetric information, academic shopping and subject selection. High. Educ. Res. Dev. **41**(4), 1247–1261 (2022). https://doi.org/10.1080/07294360.2021.1887094
12. Stevens, M., Harrison, M., Thompson, M.E., Lifschitz, A., Chaturapruek, S.: Choices, identities, paths: Understanding college students' academic decisions (2018). https://doi.org/10.2139/ssrn.3162429
13. Wladis, C., Wladis, K., Hachey, A.C.: The role of enrollment choice in online education: Course selection rationale and course difficulty as factors affecting retention. Online Learn. **18**(3) (2014). https://eric.ed.gov/?id=EJ1043163, publisher: Online Learning Consortium, Inc ERIC Number: EJ1043163
14. Zhang, M., Ma, J., Liu, Z., Sun, J., Silva, T.: A research analytics framework-supported recommendation approach for supervisor selection. Br. J. Edu. Technol. **47**(2), 403–420 (2016). https://doi.org/10.1111/bjet.12244

A Moodle Plugin for Rich xAPI Data Logging

Daniela Rotelli[1](✉), Yves Noël[2], Sébastien Lallé[2], Vanda Luengo[2], and David Pesce[3]

[1] Department of Computer Science,University of Pisa, Pisa, Italy
daniela.rotelli@phd.unipi.it
[2] LIP6, CNRS, Sorbonne University, Paris, France
[3] Exputo Inc., Honeoye Falls, NY, USA

Abstract. The eLearning specification xAPI, which employs a shared format for receiving and transmitting data, is used to collect data about the diverse range of experiences within online learning activities, thereby enabling the exchange of knowledge between multiple systems. This paper presents *Logstore xAPI*, a plugin that emits Moodle events as xAPI statements, allowing a modular, interoperable, performing and secure way of logging user interactions and learning experiences, and send them to a Learning Record Store (LRS) to be stored and further analysed. We describe all phases of mapping Moodle events to statements and storing them in the LRS, along with the issues we encountered and our solutions.

Keywords: xAPI · Moodle · Leaning Analytics · Educational log data

1 Introduction and Related Work

The processing and analysis of educational data have fostered a significant expansion of knowledge discovery approaches and created new opportunities for data-driven support and evaluation of learning practices. To facilitate the dissemination of relevant educational data and their interoperability across learning platforms, standardised data formats have emerged, with xAPI being the most recent and versatile standard [5]. However, the existing LMSs typically use ad-hoc data format that makes it harder to implement, replicate and generalise educational data analysis. Indeed, the migration from ad-hoc data format to the xAPI format remains a time-consuming and challenging task, especially in complex systems such as LMSs where numerous actions and activities are possible.

Moodle is one of the most popular LMS, with over 350 millions unique users as of 2023 (*stats.moodle.org*). Despite the steep learning curve when it comes to the Moodle database [6], Moodle logs have been extensively used in Learning Analytics research. Numerous studies have been conducted on Moodle logs to understand how learners organise their learning time [4], as well as to model their learning [2], academic performances [1], and engagement [8], among other traits. However, to the best of our knowledge, these works did not rely on a

O. Viberg et al. (Eds.): EC-TEL 2023, LNCS 14200, pp. 748–754, 2023.
https://doi.org/10.1007/978-3-031-42682-7_72

standardised data format, and rather directly queried or exported logs from the Moodle's tables, which is a threat to generalisability and privacy. In this paper, we make a further step toward standardisation by proposing *Logstore xAPI*, a plugin to convert Moodle logs into xAPI statements (*shorturl.at/zTV23*).

Logstore xAPI processes and stores the xAPI statements derived from Moodle logs into a Learning Record Store (LRS), where data from other platforms can be integrated as well in the same format, thus maximising interoperability. Logstore xAPI also augments the statements with information about the user roles and course content, which is key for contextualising the data when they were generated. Logstore xAPI provides options to anonymise the logs, and can be used both live and on historical data. While there has been another attempt at xAPI logging for Moodle, TRAX Logs plugin is currently still in the alpha version and the developers advise against using it in production [3]. Moreover, they only supports a few statements, whereas we handle all of the 216 possible student interactions. Furthermore only our plugin can handle historical data, which is key for learning analytics. As a test-bed for testing Logstore xAPI, we have deployed it in a major French university with over 25,000 students, and we report on the plugin's performances and reliability.

2 Moodle Logs

Moodle stores user activity in a relational database (*moodleschema.zoola.io*) When a user access a course, submit an assignment, take a quiz, or read/write posts in a forum, a log of that activity is recorded in the *mdl_logstore_standard_log* table (*logstore* in the following) of Moodle database. Recorded log data can be extracted in two ways, albeit both are specific to Moodle and suffer from important drawbacks.

Database. Stored log data can be extracted by directly querying the *logstore* table that is supplied with 21 fields, among which: *eventname, component, action, target, objecttable, objectid, contextid, contextinstanceid, userid, courseid, relateduserid, timecreated.* Originally, Moodle logs were not intended for data mining, but rather as a necessary part of maintaining the LMS. Therefore, despite being exhaustive, they are unintelligible to humans and lack context. To make them useful for analysis, it is necessary to perform multiple joins with other database tables, which requires in-depth knowledge of the Moodle system.

Log Generation Interface. Logs stored in the *logstore* table can also be extracted via the *log generation interface* [7] and converted into a table with 9 features: *Time, User full name, Affected user, Event context, Component, Event name, Description, Origin, IP address.* Despite being human-readable, this table lacks information about the course and the role assigned to the user in a specific context [7]. In addition, as the number of logs increases, PHP's memory size limit must be enlarged so that the table can be downloaded for analysis.

Importantly, the *logstore* table can be periodically purged. This occurs more frequently on larger Moodle instances and, as a result, direct *logstore* querying could not provide a complete data sample. Moreover, both approaches require admin privileges in Moodle, which is not always possible nor advisable in educational institutions, due to safety and privacy issues. The Logstore xAPI plugin we propose in this work alleviates the aforementioned issues, as it produces rich and comprehensive real-time data in an interoperable format, without needing admin rights, as described next.

3 The Logstore xAPI Plugin

Logstore xAPI retrieves logs from the *logstore* table, stores them in the *mdl_logstore_xapi_log* table (*logstore_xapi* in the following) to produce xAPI statements, and emits them to a Learning Record Store (LRS). The LRS (*shorturl.at/bpFX1*) is the central repository of any xAPI ecosystem, receiving, storing, and providing data on learning experiences, achievements, and performance from a range of systems. To avoid blocking page responses, the plugin operates in the background by default (this can be changed in the settings) via Cron tasks. While this makes the process less real-time, it prevents Moodle's performance from fluctuating based on the performance of the LRS. The endpoint, key/username, and password to the LRS must be specified in the configuration page after installation. The plugin is currently compatible with Moodle versions 3.9 to 4.1.

3.1 Plugin Architecture

The plugin is made up of three parts, an *Expander*, a *Translator*, and an *Emitter* (Fig. 1). Every log entry goes through each of these parts before finally reaching the LRS, as follows.

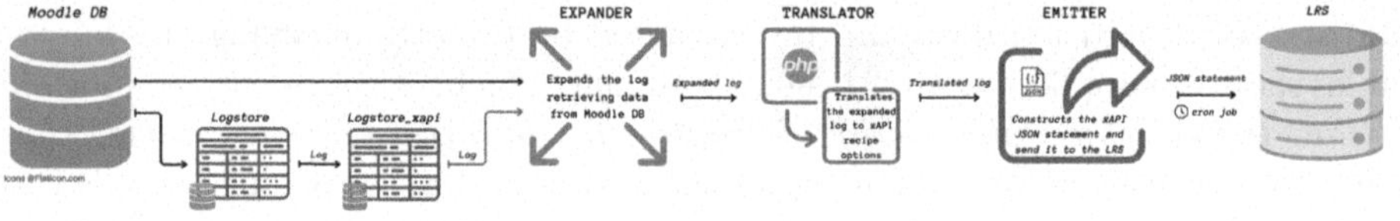

Fig. 1. The plugin architecture.

Expander. The Expander augments the log entry with data from Moodle database and passes them to the Translator. This step is key to retrieve the context related to the log entry. Information about the context is retrieved from both the *logstore* table and all the tables referenced in the event. For example, in Table 1, to retrieve the *actor* whose userid is 24, the plugin queries the *mdl_user* table to retrieve all associated information. The *mdl_forum_discussions* table and the *mdl_course_modules* table (contextinstanceid=62) contain the entirety of the information relevant to the discussion *object* (objectid = 4). The *context* of the discussion is the course and the forum in which the discussion is created. Course information is retrieved from the *mdl_course* table (courseid 38), whereas forum information is retrieved from the *mdl_forum_discussions* table, where objectid=4 corresponds to forumid=3, whose information is retrieved from *mdl_forum* table.

Table 1. Entry example in the *logstore* table.

eventname	target	objecttable	objectid	contextinstanceid	userid	courseid
mod_forum\ discussion_created	discussion	forum_discussions	4	62	24	38

Translator. The Translator converts the expanded logs to xAPI using a set of xAPI "recipes", i.e., standard ways of expressing a particular event. A statement must include at least three properties: an *actor*, a *verb*, and an *object*, along with additional optional properties such as the *id*, *context*, and *timestamp* (*shorturl.at/mzMU9*). It is worth noting that xAPI provides a predefined list of verbs and objects to enforce a shared terminology across learning platforms (*shorturl.at/iluT0*). Our plugin currently implements xAPI recipes for 216 events, thus accounting for all *participating* events (i.e., related to student learning experience) performed in Moodle standard and some external plugins such as BigBlueButton, Questionnaire, and Scheduler (*moodle.org/plugins*).
Emitter. The Emitter constructs the translated event into an xAPI JSON statement and emits it to the LRS. The event is removed from the *logstore_xapi* table once it has been sent. If something goes wrong and the translated event is not sent to the LRS (e.g., because of connection issues), it is moved to the *mdl_logstore_xapi_failed_log* table (*xapi_failed* in the following).

3.2 xAPI Implementation

To transform logs in xAPI statements, information is retrieved from both the *logstore* table and all the tables referenced in the event. For example, in Table 1, to retrieve the *actor* whose userid is 24, we query the *mdl_user* table to retrieve all associated information. The *mdl_forum_discussions* table and the *mdl_course_modules* table (contextinstanceid=62) contain the entirety of the information relevant to the discussion *object* (objectid=4). The *context* of the discussion is the course and the forum in which the discussion is created. Course information is retrieved from the *mdl_course* table (courseid 38), whereas forum information is retrieved from the *mdl_forum_discussions* table, where objectid=4 corresponds to forumid = 3, whose information is retrieved from *mdl_forum* table. The transcription of the statement is accessible on GitHub (*shorturl.at/eoRY1*).

3.3 Historical Events

The plugin is not natively designed to handle historical events that occurred prior to its installation into Moodle. These events can however be copied from the *logstore* table to the *logstore_xapi* table, e.g., via a SQL query. The plugin will then process them whenever the Cron script is executed (Sect. 3). The main challenge with historical events is that part of the information might be missing in the database due to a deleted course, activity, module, or user. Except for the user, Moodle does not keep track of deleted entries. During the development

of the plugin, this caused a number of failures, resulting in the transfer of the events in the *xapi_failed* table. We thus handled these issues as follows.
Deleted Users. When users are deleted in Moodle, they are not erased from the database; instead, the 'deleted' field in the *mdl_user* table changes from 0 to 1. To account for the user deletion, we use the value 'deleted' as their fullname.
Deleted Courses, Modules and Related Activities. Courses and modules can be deleted from Moodle, along with all related data (e.g., grades, groups). However, logs of actions performed by users on deleted courses and modules are still available in the *logstore* table. This means that attempting to retrieve data from the database about that deleted course, module or their related activities to enrich the statements will fail. To avoid losing these events, we add the 'deleted' value to the description of these items in the xAPI statements. We do the same for the deletion of a group, a grade, a forum post reply, or a message.

We wish to emphasise that with the log generation interface (Sect. 2), it is not possible to identify deleted users, but actions performed on deleted modules or courses can be identified looking at the "Event context", which is set to *Other.* These two elements of information are inaccessible in database-extracted logs. Our plugin thus allows retrieving more than the simple interaction.

3.4 Privacy

The data sent to the LRS include information about the users, their profile, and details about completed courses. Therefore, if Moodle and the LRS are not within a private network, a secure connection between them is always advised. To answer the challenge of protecting students' privacy and enhancing reproducibility by permitting data sharing, we introduced the option to pseudonymise user data (i.e., userid, username, email, and user fullname). To enable this option, the user must select to hash data and specify a secret key in the plugin configuration so that data will be hashed with the secret key before being sent to the LRS.

4 Plugin Application

To assess the plugin, we deployed it in the Moodle installation of Sorbonne University, and we report on the plugin's reliability and efficiency. To demonstrate quantifiable elements of what we performed and to evaluate the management of deleted elements, we used historical data (Sect. 3.3).

The *logstore* table contained 89,865,813 entries of the activities performed by 25,386 users over the course of a year. To copy all entries to the *logstore_xapi* table required approximately two days (500,000 every 15 min). To process data and send them to the LRS, the plugin required approximately 6 d (5,000 every 30 s). We did not get any failed logs, which shows in particular that our solutions to handle missing and deleted events (cf. Section 3.3) was suitable. Since the logs are processed every minute via Cron, it can be assumed that even if there was an overload of approximately 500,000 logs in real-time during the day, these would be processed within an hour overnight.

5 Conclusion and Future Work

In this paper, we proposed *Logstore xAPI*, a plugin that converts Moodle logs into xAPI statements to be sent to an LRS, where data from other platforms can be integrated as well in the same format, thus maximising interoperability.

Currently, we have focused on all events relating to student actions (*participating* level - Sect. 3.1), which was a prerequisite for analysing student behaviour. As future work, we intend to include all *teaching* level activities and events that Moodle categorises as *other* level activity, as well as all the statements we were unable to transcribe because either the *verb* or the *object* was absent in the Registry. In an effort to make educational data more accessible and to comply with GDPR, we would like to give the users the option to retrieve only the data that they specifically request. Thus, we intend to include an option to specify which types of data to extract.

In the long run, we aim to support researchers and data scientists in analysing Moodle logs, as well as integrating them with data from other educational systems typically used in conjunction with LMSs, e.g., video platforms, serious games. This is thanks to the standardised, interoperable, and well-documented xAPI data format outputted by Logstore xAPI.

Acknowledgements.. We thank Capsule (*capsule.sorbonne-universite.fr*), the pedagogical innovation center of Sorbonne University, for the data collection. This work has been partially supported by "SoBigData++: European Integrated Infrastructure for Social Mining and Big Data Analytics" and by PNRR - M4C2 - Investimento 1.3, Partenariato Esteso PE00000013 - "FAIR - Future Artificial Intelligence Research" - Spoke 1 "Human-centered AI", funded by the European Commission under the NextGeneration EU programme.

References

1. Ademi, N., Loshkovska, S., Kalajdziski, S.: Prediction of student success through analysis of moodle logs: case study. In: Gievska, S., Madjarov, G. (eds.) ICT Innovations 2019. CCIS, vol. 1110, pp. 27–40. Springer, Cham (2019). https://doi.org/10.1007/978-3-030-33110-8_3
2. Ikawati, Y., Al Rasyid, M.U.H., Winarno, I.: Student behavior analysis to predict learning styles based felder silverman model using ensemble tree method. Int. J. Eng. Technol. (2021)
3. Judel, S., Schnell, E., Schroeder, U.: Performantes xapi logging in moodle. 20. Fachtagung Bildungstechnologien (DELFI) (2022)
4. Maslennikova, A., Rotelli, D., Monreale, A.: Visual analytics for session-based time-windows identification in virtual learning environments. In: 26th IV. IEEE (2022)
5. Nouira, A., Cheniti-Belcadhi, L., Braham, R.: An enhanced xapi data model supporting assessment analytics. Procedia Computer Science (2018)
6. Romero, C., Romero, J.R., Ventura, S.: A survey on pre-processing educational data. In: Peña-Ayala, A. (ed.) Educational Data Mining. SCI, vol. 524, pp. 29–64. Springer, Cham (2014). https://doi.org/10.1007/978-3-319-02738-8_2

7. Rotelli, D., Monreale, A.: Time-on-task estimation by data-driven outlier detection based on learning activities. In: LAK (2022)
8. Rotelli, D., Monreale, A., Guidotti, R.: Uncovering student temporal learning patterns. In: EC-TEL 2022. Springer, Cham (2022). https://doi.org/10.1007/978-3-031-16290-9_25

PEER: Empowering Writing with Large Language Models

Kathrin Seßler(✉), Tao Xiang, Lukas Bogenrieder, and Enkelejda Kasneci

Technical University of Munich, Munich, Germany
kathrin.sessler@tum.de

Abstract. The emerging research area of large language models (LLMs) has far-reaching implications for various aspects of our daily lives. In education, in particular, LLMs hold enormous potential for enabling personalized learning and equal opportunities for all students. In a traditional classroom environment, students often struggle to develop individual writing skills because the workload of the teachers limits their ability to provide detailed feedback on each student's essay. To bridge this gap, we have developed a tool called PEER (Paper Evaluation and Empowerment Resource) which exploits the power of LLMs and provides students with comprehensive and engaging feedback on their essays. Our goal is to motivate each student to enhance their writing skills through positive feedback and specific suggestions for improvement. Since its launch in February 2023, PEER has received high levels of interest and demand, resulting in more than 4000 essays uploaded to the platform to date. Moreover, there has been an overwhelming response from teachers who are interested in the project since it has the potential to alleviate their workload by making the task of grading essays less tedious. By collecting a real-world data set incorporating essays of students and feedback from teachers, we will be able to refine and enhance PEER through model fine-tuning in the next steps. Our goal is to leverage LLMs to enhance personalized learning, reduce teacher workload, and ensure that every student has an equal opportunity to excel in writing. The code is available at https://github.com/Kasneci-Lab/AI-assisted-writing.

Keywords: Large Language Models · Writing · Personalized Education

1 Introduction

The introduction of transformers-based technologies [13] for natural language processing (NLP) has been a breakthrough that pushed the field significantly forward. It enabled the development of pre-trained large language models (LLMs) which can process natural language more effectively and efficiently than previous approaches [1,10]. The most recent models, like ChatGPT [8], have been fine-tuned using reinforcement learning with human feedback [9], enhancing their ability to generate human-like conversations and leading to a wide range of novel

O. Viberg et al. (Eds.): EC-TEL 2023, LNCS 14200, pp. 755–761, 2023.
https://doi.org/10.1007/978-3-031-42682-7_73

applications and use cases in various domains, also in the field of education [5]. Since LLMs are trained to write high quality texts, they can assist users in their writing process [15]. More specifically, LLM-based tools can help improve writing skills already from the very young age up to professional writing.

During their academic years, students are learning various types of essays. However, in the traditional classroom setting, teachers are not able to provide detailed feedback for each student's work due to time constraints and heavy workload. Also, feedback is usually only given once (e.g. in the context of graded homework or assessments) without further possibility to enhance the writing afterwards and receive an updated feedback, impeding a continuous process of improvement.

To tackle this challenge in essay writing education, and hence support both learners and teachers, we have developed an AI-based tutor named PEER, Paper Evaluation and Empowerment Resource. The idea behind PEER is to offer comprehensive textual feedback on the learner's essay, including specific suggestions for improvement, while being always constructive, specific and engaging. This stands in contrast to previous work, where the focus was often on merely grading the essay rather than offering comprehensive feedback [11]. PEER also allows students to make adjustments to their work and receive updated feedback to provide an ongoing process of improvement. From an educator's perspective, PEER provides an initial structure and suggestions for constructive and thorough feedback that can serve as a basis for further enhancements by the teacher. Such AI-assisted feedback can save a lot of time and energy, reducing hence the teacher's workload and offering more space for interaction with the students. Existing work that uses LLMs to improve writing skills often focuses more on general strategies and does not have a concrete focus on the different essay types that are part of the school curriculum with their demands and challenges [12].

The difficulty of this project lies in the limited availability of student's essay data and corresponding feedback of the teachers. Due to privacy reasons, such data is typically not publicly available in vast amounts, making it less likely for large language models to have encountered this type of data during their pre-training phase. However, the use of LLMs eliminates the need for costly hand-crafted features that previously formed the basis of many automated essay scoring systems [4]. PEER explores how the capabilities of LLMs can be leveraged to assist students and teachers in personalizing essay writing education, which involves teaching the model to provide reasonable and helpful feedback tailored to different types of essays.

We argue that by interacting with PEER, a learner can gain the necessary skills to comprehend the essential elements of good essay writing, and thereby enhance their own writing abilities. In order to evaluate the efficacy and implications of PEER, we have initiated collaborations with various German educators, schools, and academic institutions who expressed interest in our endeavor.

While the current version of PEER has been designed specifically to hone writing abilities in the German language and for the German educational system, we envision expanding its applicability to encompass other pedagogical frameworks and languages.

2 PEER

PEER is a user-friendly, web-based tool designed to analyze students' essays and generate comprehensive feedback that includes concrete suggestions and engaging tips to improve writing.

2.1 Pedagogical Background

Providing effective feedback is crucial for enhancing students' learning experience [3], as it can significantly impact their performance and motivation [7]. However, traditional classroom settings often do not allow teachers to provide comprehensive and engaging feedback to each student, hindering the learning process. To address these challenges, PEER adopts two main approaches:

1. **Thorough and Constructive Feedback**: PEER provides detailed and constructive feedback that is always positive, engaging, and helps to motivate students. The feedback highlights the strengths of the students' work and provides suggestions for improvement. PEER also uses a visual indicator (green instead of red color) to represent feedback that is encouraging and supportive.
2. **Continuous Learning Environment**: PEER follows a continuous learning principle that allows students to receive feedback as many times as they require without any fear of being discouraged or judged. This approach fosters a safe and barrier-free learning environment where students can learn at their own pace, and feedback is always readily available.

2.2 Technical Background

Our approach aims to provide students with comprehensive and constructive feedback on their essays. In the absence of a task-specific data set, we achieve this by combining zero-shot learning (inference without prior training only based on semantic information) with Elo ratings (numerical system to compare the relative performance) for different prompts. Through collecting feedback from the users on the quality of the output, we can continuously improve our model.

Zero-Shot Learning. Traditionally, machine learning models have been trained to perform on specific tasks. One significant advantage of LLMs is their versatility [10], including zero-shot learning, which is the ability to follow textual instructions [1]. Finding the optimal instructions already evolved into an own field of research [6,14] and several heuristics can aid in crafting suitable prompts. By providing the right instructions, LLMs can be guided to generate feedback that closely resembles that of a teacher. For example, a possible prompt can look like the following (translated from German into English):

```
The following text is a {article_type} from a student in the
{year}th grade. {extra_infos} The topic is "{title}". Text:
"{essay}". Analyze the text based on the criteria and give feedback
and suggestions for improvement like a teacher.
```

Prompt Elo Rating. Our approach involves systematically identifying the optimal model instructions from a set of prompts through user feedback, utilizing the Elo rating system [2]. When a user requests feedback on an essay, two different responses generated from distinct instructional prompts are presented. Based on the user's preference, the ratings for the corresponding instructional prompts are updated using the Elo system. By incorporating human feedback into the process, our system continuously improves, guided by the success of reinforcement learning with human feedback deployed to fine-tune ChatGPT [9].

Weighted Lottery System. When generating new feedback, the two instructional prompts that wrap the user's essay are selected using a weighted lottery system based on their respective Elo ratings. This ensures that prompts with higher ratings have a greater chance of being chosen from the set, resulting in feedback that is more likely to be of superior quality. At the same time, the use of a random selection process ensures that all prompts are evaluated.

3 Prototype

To make PEER available for all students, we have developed a website and are currently working on an accompanying application, in order to further reduce the barriers to access and ensure widespread availability (Fig. 1).

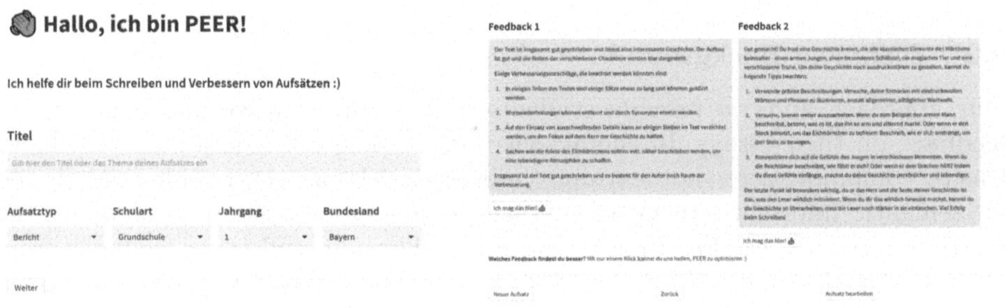

(a) (b)

Fig. 1. (a) The Start Page. In the first step, the topic of the essay and the relevant meta data is entered. (b) The Feedback Page. The user is provided with two feedback texts and can mark the preferred one to improve our model.

In the first step, users can input the topic or title of their essay, along with relevant meta information such as essay type, school year, and school type. Then, they can choose to insert the text manually or upload an image, which is scanned using an OCR and post-processed by GPT-3 [1] to remove any artifacts from the image. Next, PEER evaluates the input and generates two feedback texts. The users are then encouraged to indicate which feedback they find more useful. To facilitate continuous learning and improvement, the users can modify their essay according to the feedback and request new feedback. This process can be repeated as many times as necessary to enhance the writing skills of the users.

4 Preliminary Results

Over 4000 essays have already been uploaded for evaluation, with argumentation being the most frequently requested category. The platform was primarily used by students from middle and upper levels.

Prompt Evaluation. Based on the Elo scores, prompting the model to approach the task as a friendly teacher and providing it with additional information about the specific essay type leads to the best results. It enables the model to focus on the relevant characteristics and use the extra information to improve and adapt its feedback accordingly.

Feedback from Teachers. The quantitative results are complemented by feedback from teachers who assessed the tool from a qualitative perspective. Several teachers reported to us their experiences of trying PEER themselves as well as applying it together with their students in their classrooms. Overall, they acknowledged PEER's usefulness for both students and teachers, highlighting its user-friendliness, respectful tone, and timely feedback that facilitates individualized learning. However, they also identified some areas for improvement. For instance, they noted that the feedback provided by PEER can be too general at times, such as suggesting to "use more adjectives." Additionally, one teacher pointed out that in the German language, both the male and female forms for professions are typically used to be inclusive. Unfortunately, PEER currently does not account for both versions in its output text, and sometimes even marks them as redundant in students' essays. Other criticisms included missing essay types on the start page and sometimes small grammar errors in the generated feedback texts. This initial qualitative assessment and teacher feedback is incorporated in the further development of PEER before a more comprehensive and larger user study is conducted.

5 Conclusion and Future Agenda

Based on the amount of feedback we have received from teachers so far, it is clear that PEER is meeting a need in schools for both learners and teachers. However, our project is still in its early stages and requires further development, model fine-tuning and user evaluations. As our objective is to bring PEER to schools and establish it as a valuable assistant in the process of learning how to write an essay, our concrete current and next steps are as follows:

- Creating a solid data basis consisting of real-world essays and high-quality feedback provided by teachers. This data set will then be used to fine-tune a large language model for our specific domain to improve the performance.

- Conducting a user study at schools to assess the performance of PEER and gather valuable insights into the positive and negative aspects of the tool for both teachers and students.

Given the inherent stochastic nature of the underlying model, it is important to acknowledge that a fully error-free outcome cannot be guaranteed. Consequently, and as for all applications based on large language models, users are advised to carefully evaluate the feedback provided and selectively incorporate only the pertinent critiques. This type of critical thinking is not limited to PEER but should be a fundamental aspect of interacting with any generative AI model.

References

1. Brown, T., et al.: Language models are few-shot learners. In: Advances in Neural Information Processing Systems, vol. 33, pp. 1877–1901 (2020)
2. Elo, A.E.: The Rating of Chessplayers, Past and Present. Arco Pub., New York (1978)
3. Hattie, J., Timperley, H.: The power of feedback. Rev. Educ. Res. **77**(1), 81–112 (2007)
4. Hussein, M.A., Hassan, H., Nassef, M.: Automated language essay scoring systems: a literature review. PeerJ Comput. Sci. **5**, e208 (2019)
5. Kasneci, E., et al.: ChatGPT for good? On opportunities and challenges of large language models for education. Learn. Individ. Diff. **103**, 102274 (2023)
6. Liu, J., Shen, D., Zhang, Y., Dolan, W.B., Carin, L., Chen, W.: What makes good in-context examples for GPT-3? In: Proceedings of Deep Learning Inside Out (DeeLIO 2022): The 3rd Workshop on Knowledge Extraction and Integration for Deep Learning Architectures, pp. 100–114 (2022)
7. Molloy, E.K., Boud, D.: Feedback models for learning, teaching and performance. In: Handbook of Research on Educational Communications and Technology, pp. 413–424 (2014)
8. OpenAI Team: ChatGPT: optimizing language models for dialogue (2022)
9. Ouyang, L., et al.: Training language models to follow instructions with human feedback. In: Advances in Neural Information Processing Systems, vol. 35, pp. 27730–27744 (2022)
10. Radford, A., Wu, J., Child, R., Luan, D., Amodei, D., Sutskever, I., et al.: Language models are unsupervised multitask learners. OpenAI Blog **1**(8), 9 (2019)
11. Ramesh, D., Sanampudi, S.K.: An automated essay scoring systems: a systematic literature review. Artif. Intell. Rev. **55**(3), 2495–2527 (2022)
12. Schick, T., et al.: PEER: a collaborative language model. arXiv preprint arXiv:2208.11663 (2022)
13. Vaswani, A., et al.: Attention is all you need. In: Advances in Neural Information Processing Systems, vol. 30 (2017)
14. Wei, J., et al.: Chain-of-thought prompting elicits reasoning in large language models. In: Advances in Neural Information Processing Systems (2022)
15. Yuan, A., Coenen, A., Reif, E., Ippolito, D.: Wordcraft: story writing with large language models. In: 27th International Conference on Intelligent User Interfaces, pp. 841–852 (2022)

Using Accessible Motion Capture in Educational Games for Sign language Learning

Joshua Leon Tobias[1(✉)] and Daniele Di Mitri[2]

[1] Johann Wolfgang Goethe-Universität Frankfurt, 60629 Frankfurt am Main, Germany
joshua.t@hotmail.de
[2] DIPF — Leibniz Institute for Research and Information in Education, 60323 Frankfurt am Main, Germany
https://www.dipf.de

Abstract. Various studies show that multimodal interaction technologies, especially motion capture in educational environments, can significantly improve and support educational purposes such as language learning. In this paper, we introduce a prototype that implements finger tracking and teaches the user different letters of the German fingerspelling alphabet. Since most options for tracking a user's movements rely on hardware that is not commonly available, a particular focus is laid on the opportunities of new technologies based on computer vision. These achieve accurate tracking with consumer webcams. In this study, the motion capture is based on Google MediaPipe. An evaluation based on user feedback shows that the prototype's capabilities meet the functional requirements. This study corroborates the thesis that new technologies, such as motion-tracking-based software, can make language learning more accessible.

Keywords: multimodality · motion capture · language learning · computer vision

1 Introduction

Multimodal interactions require multiple stimuli to be processed in parallel which can help to understand better and internalize a topic [6]. Among others, this can include the perception of self-movement and body position, also referred to as 'proprioception'. This paper will mostly concentrate on this kinetic context which often goes hand in hand with using motion tracking. Game-based learning has proven itself a valuable tool in teaching as it can provide many advantages over traditional methods of teaching, such as increased motivation [7]. However, motion tracking in educational games is often limited to simply pointing at the screen. The full potential could be used by making the user perform unique gestures. While this usually required expensive hardware, there is an alternative

O. Viberg et al. (Eds.): EC-TEL 2023, LNCS 14200, pp. 762–767, 2023.
https://doi.org/10.1007/978-3-031-42682-7_74

in the form of body pose estimation libraries that are based on computer vision. Among these is MediaPipe by Google, which is a pipeline that can track different features including hands based on webcam input [4]. While there are already applications that use MediaPipe, such as the *Ace ASL* App[1], none of those combine the benefits and the potential of being at the same time educational and game-based.

In light of this rationale, in this study, we formulated the following research question: *Is it possible to use multimodality in a game without additional specialised hardware?* This question was answered by developing a prototype for an educational game that teaches parts of the German fingerspelling alphabet. This subject was chosen because it requires some form of pose estimation to detect the user's gestures and could not be substituted by a pointer. Since MediaPipe was used for the implementation, only a webcam was needed for input. The prototype used a game setting to utilise the benefits of gamification.

2 Background

Game-based learning and gamification enhance the learning process by utilising serious games or elements of games. This can lead to an increase in motivation and effectiveness of learning [7]. Multimodality can also help the learner to understand the given information more efficiently as it offers the brain more options to process the input, which reduces the load on each individual channel and avoids creating a cognitive overload [6]. This can also lead to a higher rate of interaction and engagement [1]. Tsai et al. [8] found that using Kinect by Microsoft with software that uses multimodality enhances learning achievements due to an improvement of bodily-kinesthetic intelligence. This is supported by Granja et al. [3].

The position of hands can be tracked by handheld devices such as smartphones which can be considered accessible by most persons but limit the level of detail of the tracking as no finger movement can be detected. Another option is optical devices such as Kinect. Those can track more details but are less accessible due to their acquisition cost. New machine learning-based solutions in the field of computer vision offer even higher accuracy while reducing costs as they only require a webcam as hardware. This greatly increases the accessibility of motion tracking. One such solution is MediaPipe which can track the positioning of a variety of body parts, including face, head and hands, based on a static image or video stream [4,5].

Fingerspelling is an ideal topic for multimodal learning as it includes a variety of unique gestures. It is important to note that sign languages are independent languages that should not be confused with body language or paralinguistic gestures. Usually, sign alphabets are present in different countries and regions besides sign language. These are used not only by deaf people but also by hearing individuals in loud environments or other occasions where the spoken language is unsuitable. The manual alphabets are, therefore, often more widespread than the corresponding sign language.

[1] https://www.signall.us/ace-asl.

3 Methods

The prototype is implemented as a game where the player is on board a spaceship whose onboard systems malfunction due to an accident. This includes the communication channels to the ship's AI, except for optical input. The user has to help the AI gather enough data for a backup by providing information about the systems using signed letters. The gameplay is presented in different interfaces between which the user can navigate freely. The structure of the screen only changes a little between the different situations and always at least includes the following UI elements: A text field showing the current message of the ship's AI, the currently captured video already annotated by MediaPipe and a progress bar representing the current process. In problem mode, they are presented with letters to reproduce and a timer equating five seconds times the number of letters. Depending on whether the problem was solved in the given time, the progress bar at the top of the screen is increased or decreased by ten per cent points. They can use a horizontal scroll bar to choose a letter for practice in selection mode. In training mode, they are given written feedback as well as an image of the desired gesture overlaid with a skeletal representation of the current positioning of their hand. The joints are coloured red or green to show which parts are not yet positioned correctly (Fig. 1). It is intended that the user is motivated to use the prototype by the game-based setting and the variation in problems.

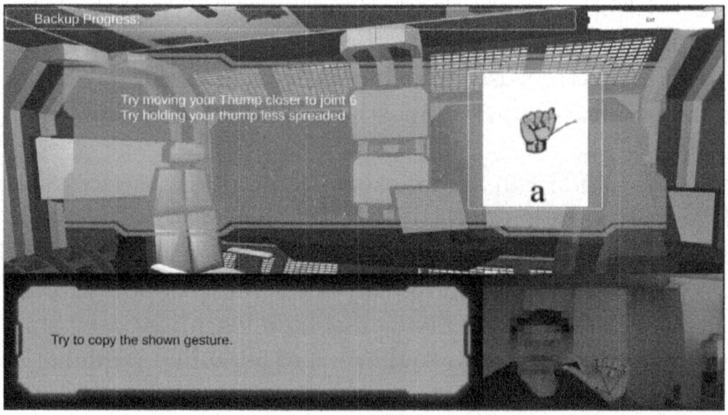

Fig. 1. The training screen in the game shows written and visual feedback as well as the desired posture.

3.1 Implementation

The application was created in C# in the 3D game engine Unity. The motion capture is based on the Python solution of Google MediaPipe. It continuously outputs an annotated stream of a detected hand and the coordinates of its joints according to Fig. 2. The Visual Inspection Tool (VIT) [2] was used to define the required finger positions for each letter.

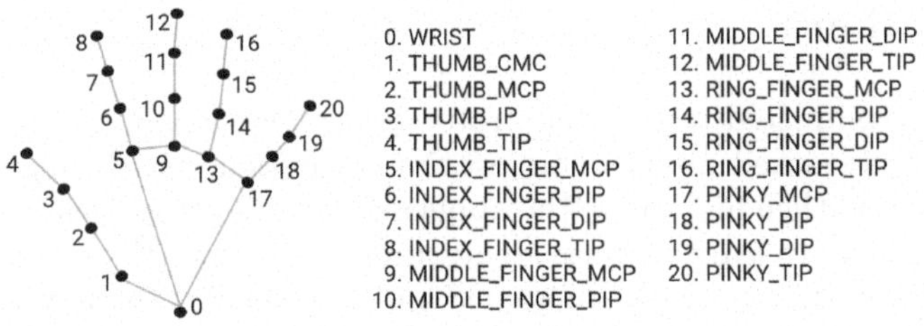

Fig. 2. The 21 joints with their corresponding label (Source: Google MediaPipe)

Based on the provided joint coordinates, less abstract values for describing the finger postures are calculated. These include the straightness of all fingers, the spread and rotation of the thumb and whether the thumb touches certain joints. The conditions for the five letters that are currently available can be seen in Table 1. In this table, the boolean *MustTouch* determines whether the touch condition must be fulfilled or explicitly must not be fulfilled.

Table 1. Conditions (Zero values will be ignored for the respective letter)

Letter	A	B	C	D	E
Index finger	Full	Straight	Half	Straight	Full
Middle finger	Full	Straight	Half	Half	Full
Ring finger	Full	Straight	Half	Half	Full
Little finger	Full	Straight	Half	Half	Full
Straightness	15	0	40	0	100
Rotation	130	0	0	0	80
Spread	180	160	140	0	155
Touches	6	9, 13	8	12,15,19	9,13
MustTouch	True	True	False	True	True

The bend of a finger is determined by calculating the angle between the vectors of the first two joints and the last two joints of the finger. The finger is considered straight if the angle is below 45° or fully bent if it is over 140°. Otherwise, the finger is considered half-bent. The straightness of the thumb is calculated similarly, but the value is returned directly as a float. For the spread of the thumb, the angle between the side of the hand and the vector between joint 2 and 3 of the thumb is calculated. The rotation of the thumb indicates how close the thumb is rotated towards the palm. It is represented by the angle between joint 3 of the thumb and the root of the little finger (joint 17) relative to the axis from the root of the hand (joint 0) to the root of the index finger (joint 5). To determine whether the thumb touches a specific joint, the distance between the tip of the thumb (joint 4) and the other joint relative to the distance between joints 5 and 9 is taken to compensate for the variation in differently-sized hands.

Also, a function is provided to check whether the user shows a requested letter correctly and give feedback if needed. The calculated values of the current finger position need not match the required values exactly. The requirement is fulfilled if they are in a particular range around the target values.

The VIT is used to define the criteria that have to be met for each finger. For this, a screen recording and calculated values for the finger states are exported. In the VIT, each gesture is annotated with the correct values.

4 Evaluation

A survey was conducted to test the prototype's effectiveness and usability. The participants were asked about their previous experience with fingerspelling or sign language and then had to use the application and solve at least ten problems. This requires them to learn and use all gestures. After that, the participants were asked to evaluate the general experience and usability of the application. This includes the accuracy of the tracked hand coordinates as well as the game's ability to recognise the correct gestures based on that information. Another question aimed to find out how many letters the users remembered. All ratings are on a scale with one as the minimum and five as the maximum.

The questionnaire was answered by a total of eleven participants and all but one had no prior experience with fingerspelling. The usability, navigation and user experience were all answered with averages ranging between 3.64 and 3.73. The accuracy with which MediaPipe annotates the hands got an average rating of 3.82 while the interpretation of those annotations regarding gestures was rated with an average of 3.55. The majority of respondents felt motivated to continue learning by the setting and remembered all five gestures.

5 Discussion

The accuracy of the motion capture as well as the ability of the game to recognise gestures achieved satisfying results. While a good performance of hand detection by MediaPipe was anticipated, the recognition of gestures with a wide variety of hand sizes worked better than expected. Even better results might be possible by using machine learning instead of calculating whether certain conditions for the different fingers are met.

The results also support the benefits of motion capture and educational games, as most remembered all five learned gestures after playing the game. Since the answers were given immediately after using the prototype, it only shows the effects on short-term memory. A possible future evaluation could examine how many letters are remembered after certain periods and whether the quota changes with an increased number of letters taught in the game.

Overall, the survey results show that the produced prototype successfully implements webcam-based motion capture that works sufficiently.

6 Conclusions

New computer vision-based approaches show potential to provide the advantages of multimodal learning with high accessibility. The feedback on the prototype showed that it is possible to create an educational game that uses motion capture while only relying on a webcam as input. The software was considered usable and easily accessible to all participants. Therefore, it is shown that developing a functioning software as described in the research question is possible.

The next step would be the implementation of all missing letters. Since the gestures for *J* and *Z* are not static, the application must be able to detect and interpret movements. If that is achieved, it is also possible that the implementation of gestures used in sign language works. Therefore, a future goal would be to create an educational game that teaches fingerspelling and signs for any sign language. Furthermore, various pre-trained models other than MediaPipe implement motion capture based on machine learning, whose performance could also be investigated.

References

1. Wandera, D.B.: Teaching poetry through collaborative art: an analysis of multimodal ensembles for transformative learning. J. Transform. Educ. **14**(4), 305–326 (2016). https://doi.org/10.1177/1541344616650749
2. Di Mitri, D., Schneider, J., Klemke, R., Specht, M., Drachsler, H.: Read between the lines. In: Proceedings of the 9th International Conference on Learning Analytics & Knowledge, pp. 51–60. ACM Other conferences, ACM, New York, NY (2019). https://doi.org/10.1145/3303772.3303776
3. Granja, F.T.M., Escriba, L.R., Lozada, R.M.: Ms-kinect in the development of educational games for preschoolers. Int. J. Learn. Technol. **13**(4), 277 (2018). https://doi.org/10.1504/IJLT.2018.10019949
4. Lugaresi, C., et al.: MediaPipe: a framework for building perception pipelines. https://arxiv.org/pdf/1906.08172
5. Lugaresi, C., et al.: Mediapipe github repository. https://github.com/google/mediapipe
6. Moreno, R., Mayer, R.: Interactive multimodal learning environments. Educ. Psychol. Rev. **19**(3), 309–326 (2007). https://doi.org/10.1007/s10648-007-9047-2
7. Sailer, M., Homner, L.: The gamification of learning: a meta-analysis. Educ. Psychol. Rev. **32**(1), 77–112 (2020). https://doi.org/10.1007/s10648-019-09498-w
8. Tsai, C.H., Kuo, Y.H., Chu, K.C., Yen, J.C.: Development and evaluation of game-based learning system using the microsoft kinect sensor. Int. J. Distrib. Sens. Netw. **11**(7), 498560 (2015). https://doi.org/10.1155/2015/498560

Correction to: What Makes Problem-Solving Practice Effective? Comparing Paper and AI Tutoring

Conrad Borchers, Paulo F. Carvalho, Meng Xia, Pinyang Liu, Kenneth R. Koedinger, and Vincent Aleven

Correction to: Chapter 4 in: O. Viberg et al. (Eds.): *Responsive and Sustainable Educational Futures*, LNCS 14200, https://doi.org/10.1007/978-3-031-42682-7_4

In relation to Section 3.1 and specifically the main effect of condition reported in Table 2, we note a correction to the original analysis. The original version of this paper inadvertently included data from a substantial number of participants who did not fully complete the pre-test and whose responses were treated as incorrect (71% in the tutor and 81% in the paper condition within one of the units). Correcting this oversight by removing relevant incomplete responses changed some of the study's conclusions: We now find a significant difference in learning gains favoring the tutor condition ($M = 0.12$, CI95% = [0.08, 0.16]) over the paper condition ($M = 0.07$, CI95% = [0.03, 0.10]), $F(1, 159) = 5.30$, $p = .023$, $d = 0.22$. This leads us to reject the initial conclusion that both forms of practice are equally effective for learning.

The updated version of this chapter can be found at
https://doi.org/10.1007/978-3-031-42682-7_4

O. Viberg et al. (Eds.): EC-TEL 2023, LNCS 14200, p. C1, 2025.
https://doi.org/10.1007/978-3-031-42682-7_75

Author Index

O. Viberg et al. (Eds.): EC-TEL 2023, LNCS 14200, pp. 769–772, 2023.
https://doi.org/10.1007/978-3-031-42682-7

The manufacturer's authorised representative in the EU is Springer Nature Customer Service Centre GmbH, Europaplatz 3, 69115 Heidelberg, Germany. If you have any concerns regarding our products, please contact ProductSafety@springernature.com

Printed and bound by CPI Group (UK) Ltd, Croydon, CR0 4YY
01/10/2026
02225834-0020